The Roman World from Romulus to Muhammad

This volume provides a detailed examination of nearly 1,400 years of Roman history, from the foundation of the city in the eighth century BC until the evacuation of Roman troops from Alexandria in AD 642 in the face of the Arab conquests.

Drawing on a vast array of ancient texts written in Latin, Greek, Syriac, Armenian, and Arabic, and relying on a host of inscriptions, archaeological data, and the evidence from ancient art, architecture, and coinage, *The Roman World from Romulus to Muhammad* brings to the fore the men and women who chronicled the story of the city and its empire. Richly illustrated with 71 maps and 228 illustrations—including 20 in colour—and featuring a detailed glossary and suggestions for further reading, this volume examines a broad range of topics, including ancient climate change, literature, historiography, slavery, war and conquest, the development of Christianity, the Jewish revolts, and the role of powerful imperial women. The author also considers the development of Islam within a Roman historical context, examines the events that led to the formation of the post-Roman states in Western Europe, and contemplates affairs on the imperial periphery in the Caucasus, Ethiopia, and the Arabian Peninsula.

Emphasising the voices of antiquity throughout, *The Roman World from Romulus to Muhammad* is an invaluable resource for students and scholars interested in the beguiling history of the world's most famous empire.

Greg Fisher is a graduate of the University of Oxford in the United Kingdom, and the author and editor of numerous works on the ancient world, including *Between Empires* (Oxford University Press 2011), *Arabs and Empires Before Islam* (Oxford University Press 2015), *Hannibal and Scipio* (The History Press 2015), and *Rome, Persia, and Arabia* (Routledge 2020).

The Roman World from Romulus to Muhammad

A New History

Greg Fisher

Routledge
Taylor & Francis Group

LONDON AND NEW YORK

First published 2022
by Routledge
2 Park Square, Milton Park, Abingdon, Oxon OX14 4RN

and by Routledge
605 Third Avenue, New York, NY 10158

Routledge is an imprint of the Taylor & Francis Group, an informa business

© 2022 Greg Fisher

British Library Cataloguing-in-Publication Data
A catalogue record for this book is available from the British Library

Library of Congress Cataloging-in-Publication Data
Names: Fisher, Greg, 1976– author.
Title: The Roman world from Romulus to Muhammad : a new history / Greg Fisher.
Description: Abingdon, Oxon; New York: Routledge, 2022. |
Includes bibliographical references and index. |
Identifiers: LCCN 2021010444 (print) | LCCN 2021010445 (ebook) |
ISBN 9780415842860 (hardback) | ISBN 9780415842877 (paperback) |
ISBN 9781003202523 (ebook)
Subjects: LCSH: Rome–Civilization. |
Egypt–History–Greco-Roman period, 332 B.C.-640 A.D.
Classification: LCC DG77 .F745 2022 (print) | LCC DG77 (ebook) | DDC 937–dc23
LC record available at https://lccn.loc.gov/2021010444
LC ebook record available at https://lccn.loc.gov/2021010445

ISBN: 978-0-415-84286-0 (hbk)
ISBN: 978-0-415-84287-7 (pbk)
ISBN: 978-1-003-20252-3 (ebk)

DOI: 10.4324/9781003202523

Typeset in Bembo
by Newgen Publishing UK

For Averil Cameron

Contents

Figures

Maps

Acknowledgements

It gives me great pleasure to dedicate this book to Averil Cameron, who has taught me so much about the Romans and their complex, beguiling world. Averil patiently guided me through my DPhil at Keble College, indulging my interests in anthropology, comparative history, archaeology, and many other tangents along the way. Above all, she taught me to think about antiquity from perspectives that I would never otherwise have considered, and inspired me to keep going when completing a doctoral thesis seemed like an impossible task. It is an enormous privilege to have been her graduate student, and I am honoured by her friendship and her continued support as I tackle new projects.

I am also very grateful to Elizabeth Digeser for her comments on the early chapters of this book, and her encouragement throughout my career.

To guide a book through to publication takes the work of many people. My thanks go to Amy Davis-Poynter and Lizzi Risch at Routledge for all their work, and most of all for their endless patience with my drifting deadlines. I am also very grateful to Susan Jarvis for her meticulous work copy editing the manuscript, and to Ed Robinson and his team at Newgen Publishing for bringing this book smoothly through the production process.

Many of the illustrations in this book have been provided by people I have never met, but who have taken the generous step of licensing their material through Creative Commons. This has made it possible to bring pictures of places and artefacts in a range of countries to the reader—I am grateful to you all.

Once again, my tabby kept me company as this book wound its way to completion, and I will never forget the brightness that Willow brought to the grim days of the coronavirus pandemic.

Finally, I am grateful to my family, who kept me going when I wondered whether I would ever get to the seventh century. I am also eternally thankful to my mother, who patiently read every chapter as it was completed, catching errors and making suggestions. Any errors that remain are, of course, mine alone.

Greg Fisher
Montréal, Canada

Copyright notices

The author acknowledges the kind permission of the copyright holders listed below, and also the generosity of the many individuals who have made their work available under Creative Commons licences. Numerous images are used under the terms of Creative Commons licences 1.0, 2.0, 2.5, 3.0, and 4.0. These are identified in the individual figure captions, and the licences can be found here:

https://creativecommons.org

Also licensed under Creative Commons are several maps that I used to help develop my own. These are:

Licensed under https://creativecommons.org/licenses/by-sa/4.0/deed.en:
https://commons.wikimedia.org/wiki/File:Relief_Map_of_Mediterranean_Sea_hires.png
Licensed under: https://creativecommons.org/licenses/by-sa/3.0/deed.en:
https://en.wikipedia.org/wiki/File:Relief_Map_of_Spain.png
https://en.wikipedia.org/wiki/File:Relief_map_of_Italien_Latium.png
https://commons.wikimedia.org/wiki/File:Relief_map_of_Italien_Kampanien.png
https://commons.wikimedia.org/wiki/File:BLANK_in_Europe_(relief)_(-mini_map).svg
Figure 1.9 courtesy of Beinecke Rare Book and Manuscript Library, Yale University
Figures 10.36, 12.7, and 12.9 courtesy of the Yale University Art Gallery, Dura-Europos Collection
Figures 8.26 and 8.27 courtesy of Philip Wood
Figures 1.2, 1.11, 1.15, 3.1, 3.2, 3.3, 3.4, 3.6, 3.7, 3.8, 3.9, 3.11, 4.1, 4.2, 4.3, 4.4, 5.1, 5.2, 5.3, 5.5, 5.10, 6.4, 6.5, 6.7, 6.8, 6.9, 6.10, 6.11, 6.12, 7.4, 7.6, 7.8, 7.9, 7.10, 7.14, 7.15, 7.16, 7.17, 7.18, 7.19, 7.20, 7.22, 7.23, 7.24, 7.25, 7.26, 7.28, 7.29, 7.30, 7.32, 8.1, 8.2, 8.7, 8.18, 8.19, 8.22, 8.25, 8.28, 8.29, 8.34, 8.37, 9.1, 9.2, 9.6, 9.7, 9.9, 9.10, 9.11, 9.12, 9.13, 9.18, 9.19, 9.20, 9.21, 9.24, 9.25, 9.30, 10.1, 10.2, 10.4, 10.5, 10.7, 10.18, 10.19, 10.20, 10.21, 10.24, 10.25, 10.26, 10.32, 10.33, 10.37, 10.39, 10.40, 10.50, 11.1, 11.3, 11.4, 11.5, 11.6, 11.9, 11.10, 11.20, 11.21, 11.22, 11.23, 11.25, 11.28, 11.29, 11.30, 11.32, 12.1, 12.2, 12.4, 12.15, 12.16, 12.17, 12.18, 12.20, 12.21, 12.31, 12.32, 12.33, 12.35, 12.37, 12.38, 13.1,

13.3, 13.7, 13.10, 13.12, 14.2, 14.4, and 14.14 courtesy of Classical Numismatics Group: www.cngcoins.com

Figures 1.14, 2.4, 6.1, 7.13, 7.31, 9.15, 10.8, 10.47, 10.48, and 12.11:

Google Earth Pro images are used in accordance with the Google Terms of Service and Permissions Policy, provided at: www.google.com/intl/ALL/help/terms_maps and www.google.com/permissions/geoguidelines/attr-guide

Note to the reader

Roman legions are referred to by their number, in Roman numerals, and by their number and name, once legions started to be named after the first century BC. A table of Roman numerals can be found in the Glossary.

I have attempted to avoid excessive italicisation of Latin, Greek, Syriac, and Arabic terms. Words in common use in English, such as consul or dictator, have not been italicised. A complete list of terms with their definitions can be found in the Glossary.

I have kept references to modern sources to a minimum, except where a direct quote is being used; the relevant modern works can be found in the Further Reading section.

Quotations from the ancient written texts and inscriptions are drawn from a diverse collection, and readers can find details of the translations and editions used in the Further Reading section. I have tried as much as possible to use texts available on the internet that are free, open-source, or out of copyright, to facilitate access. Where it has seemed to be helpful to do so, I have also cross-referenced primary sources to the more common source collections for Roman history (where a source is cross-referenced, it is normally the translation in that particular collection that is being used). The collections are identified in the text through the following abbreviations:

AEBI	Fisher G. (ed) *Arabs and Empires Before Islam*. Oxford, 2015
AH	Sherk R.K. *The Roman Empire: Augustus to Hadrian*. Cambridge, 1984
HW	Austin M.M. *The Hellenistic World from Alexander to the Roman Conquest*. Cambridge, 1994
IRB	Maxfield V.A. & Dobson B (eds) *Inscriptions of Roman Britain*, 3rd edn. London, 1995
RA	Campbell B. *The Roman Army, 31 BC–AD 337. A Sourcebook*. New York, 2000
REF1	Dodgeon M.H. & Lieu S.N.C. *The Roman Eastern Frontier and the Persian Wars, AD 226–363. A Documentary History*. New York, 2002
REF2	Greatrex G. & Lieu S.N.C. *The Roman Eastern Frontier and the Persian Wars, Part II: AD 363–630*. New York, 2008
RGE	Sherk R.K. *Rome and the Greek East to the Death of Augustus*. Cambridge, 1984
RIB	https://romaninscriptionsofbritain.org
RLA	Maas M. *Readings in Late Antiquity. A Sourcebook*. New York, 2000

Chapter 1

The origins of Rome

In AD 116, the emperor Trajan stood on the shores of the Persian Gulf after a blistering campaign against Parthia, Rome's ancestral enemy. Trajan's decisive victories brought Assyria and Mesopotamia into the Roman empire; never again would its reach be so extensive. As Trajan stared out over the water, watching ships come and go, his thoughts turned to Alexander the Great. According to the historian Cassius Dio, Trajan envied Alexander for his own conquests, which had taken him as far as Afghanistan and India. At the same time, however, Trajan dared to think that he had surpassed Alexander, and prepared to write letters to the Roman senate reporting his achievements. As the emperor left Iraq to return home to Europe, he paused in Babylon 'because of Alexander, to whose spirit he offered sacrifice in the room where he died' (Cassius Dio, 68.29). Trajan was never to see Rome again. Like his hero Alexander, he died from illness, far from home.

Dio's remembrance of Trajan displays two elements central to understanding Roman history. The first is the ethos of conquest and the militarised nature of political life. Trajan's conquests were as natural to him as they were in earlier times to Julius Caesar, Marius, Scipio Africanus, or any of their ancestors: from its foundation, Rome had been built on violence, and the *fasti triumphales*, the list of victorious Roman magistrates from Romulus to the time of Augustus, was inscribed on marble plaques in the Roman forum, the centre of the city's public life. The second element is the importance of the broader Mediterranean world, including Etruria, Latium, the Greek colonies of Italy, and particularly the Greek east and many of its most celebrated figures. Alexander the Great occupied a special place for Rome's leaders as the pinnacle of human achievement, which explains Trajan's ambivalence: Alexander was someone to admire, but he was also someone to surpass. Trajan was not alone in this, as Augustus would send an expedition to Yemen partly to out-do Alexander's own travels and explorations, while half a millennium after Alexander's death, the emperor Caracalla equipped an entire Roman unit with the weapons and kit of the Macedonian phalanx on his doomed eastern expedition.

Rome's evolution from a small village on the Tiber to one of the most long-lived empires in world history greatly depended on a willingness to conquer and to subjugate neighbours and enemies alike, and a willingness to fight and die for Rome on a horrific scale; the only recent parallel is to be found on the Eastern Front in World War II. The Romans did not agonise over the demise of their foes: for them, their matchless performance in battle was one of the things that made Rome great. Yet their conquests allowed the cultures, religions, political ideas, and other aspects of the Mediterranean world to play a tremendously important role in Rome itself. From its earliest days, Rome

DOI: 10.4324/9781003202523-1

welcomed outsiders and internalised their traditions and beliefs. Rome became an empire and an absolute monarchy only after its reach embraced the Hellenistic kingdoms of the eastern Mediterranean, while Etruscan and Greek religious and political ideas found fertile ground in Rome from its very earliest days. Rome's famous Republican constitution did not survive its bloody dealings with the Greek king Pyrrhus of Epirus and the state of Carthage intact, and eventually the very sort of demagogues that the Romans claimed to despise presided over the destruction of the state that they had laboured so hard to build. Eventually the centre of gravity in the Roman world would shift east, to the new city of Constantinople and the rich and ancient lands of Syria. In modern parlance, the history of Rome is therefore, in more ways than one, a 'global history'—one that can only be understood by thinking about Rome though the lens of the world in which it grew and that it then subsequently conquered. That world was a vast area that stretched from Scotland to Arabia, from Spain to Egypt, and from the Caucasus to the Syrian desert.

Troy and Rome

Rome was born in violence—at least, that is how its later inhabitants chose to remember it. Roman writers created a foundation myth to explain where they and their state had come from. In this myth, Aeneas, a hero from Homer's famous *Iliad* and a relative of king Priam of Troy, crossed the Mediterranean to Rome after the Trojan War with his father Anchises and his son Ascanius (Iulus, in Latin, and hence a fictional ancestor of the Julii family, the clan of Julius Caesar). In some versions of the story, Aeneas fought the king of Latium, Latinus, and after defeating him he married the king's daughter, Lavinia. Founding a city called Lavinium, Aeneas relinquished rule to Ascanius, who in turn founded a city called Alba Longa. The appearance of Latium (the district around Rome) in the earliest mythologies of Roman origins emphasises the importance of Latium to Rome, and the centrality of the relationship between Rome and the Latin communities in Rome's political development (Chapter 2).

Twelve generations later in the story, the reader encounters the tale of the twins Romulus and Remus, of whom Aeneas was a distant ancestor. The twins were the offspring of the war god Mars and Rhea Silvia, a Vestal Virgin—a member of a holy female order tasked with caring for the communal hearth. Rhea Silvia was also the daughter of Numitor, the 12th king of Alba Longa after Ascanius. Numitor himself had been violently deposed by his brother, Amulius, who went on to murder all of Numitor's offspring except for Rhea Silvia. As the Vestals were sworn to chastity, and Amulius had made Rhea Silvia a Vestal to prevent her from having children, the twins were punished by being left out to die near the Tiber river, but as luck would have it, they were saved by a she-wolf and later raised by a shepherd, Faustulus, and his wife, Larentia. As young boys, the twins honed their hunting techniques, growing strong by testing themselves against 'fierce beasts of prey' (Livy, 1.4). Later, both Romulus and Remus decided to found a city close to where they had been abandoned; however, as they were twins, neither could claim seniority over the other. Accordingly, they each took up a position on two of the prominent hills that would later be part of Rome: the Palatine and the Aventine. Despite relying on augury—the observation of birds—to decide who should have precedence, they could not agree on the signs provided by the gods; in the melee that followed, Romulus killed his brother, who had jumped over Rome's walls—representing the city's future sacred boundary, the pomerium—without permission. Romulus gave his name to the new foundation, Rome, serving the city as the first of its seven legendary kings.

This is the story told by Livy in the first book of his monumental history of Rome, written during the tumultuous final century of the Republic. Livy (c. 64 BC–c. AD 12) was a contemporary of both Julius Caesar and Caesar's great-nephew Octavian, the future emperor Augustus. Livy was also a contemporary of the poet Virgil, from whose pen the story of Aeneas would receive its fullest and most patriotic treatment in the *Aeneid*. Livy's history, which also includes a famous moralising treatment of Rome's war with Hannibal (Chapter 4) says a great deal more about the concerns of his own time than it does about Rome's actual foundation, which the Roman historian Marcus Terentius Varro, a contemporary of Caesar, dated to 753 BC.

Sources for Roman history

To get to grips with 'what happened' in ancient Rome, we rely on the five main groups of primary sources—that is, sources produced in or dating from antiquity. The primary sources for the Roman world include:

- written texts—biography and autobiography, histories, poetry, and other literary works
- inscriptions, ranging from texts on monumental buildings to casual graffiti
- papyri and other texts written on perishable materials
- coins
- archaeological evidence, such as structures that have survived from antiquity ('built heritage') and data from excavations carried out on land and at sea; this category includes ancient art and sculpture.

Historical writing in the ancient Mediterranean world, and in the Roman world in particular, was driven by a different set of expectations and ideologies than it is today. In Roman antiquity, history was a literary activity and its purpose was not to record the true outline of events, nor was it intended to offer a dispassionate record. It was, instead, a means of moralising and teaching, and a guide to political behaviour. It focused on individuals and their deeds, and on their character—whether poor or exemplary. It was often deeply religious, concerned with questions of hubris, piety, and proper behaviour that could earn the favour of the gods that made up the Roman pantheon, and that guided the state's leaders in good times and punished them in bad times. It was perfectly reasonable to invent speeches and provide other useful rhetorical flourishes to accentuate the deeds of one family or another, and there was no requirement to provide citations to sources or even say where information had come from. Despite relying heavily on the Greek historian Polybius for his treatment of the war between Rome and Hannibal, for example, Livy barely mentions him.

This is not to say that there was *no* analysis—indeed, the great Greek writer Thucydides, who chronicled the epic fifth-century BC struggle between Athens and Sparta, is generally considered to be the father of 'classicising' history, a style in which an elementary form of evidential analysis can be found and which was the closest thing in antiquity to modern expectations of what historical writing should look like. Classicising histories normally focused on the political life of the state, the careers of great men, wars, and other topics central to the life of the dominant political class. Some of the most famous historians of the Roman era followed this style of writing, including Polybius (third century BC), Tacitus (first century AD), Cassius Dio (second/third centuries AD), Ammianus Marcellinus (fourth century AD), and Procopius (sixth century AD). This genre of writing was particularly long-lived, and the last recognised classicising historian, Theophylact Simocatta, was working in the early seventh century shortly before the armies of Islam conquered much of the eastern Roman empire. The men who wrote these histories were well placed to do so, as they were often members of the government or the military and they had access to documents and eyewitnesses. They attempted to form opinions or judgements based on these sources, all the while adhering to the politically motivated guidelines of their discipline. Polybius, for example, was a politician, and he was deeply interested in issues of causation and political analysis. Tacitus was a magistrate and a provincial governor. Cassius Dio was a senator and active in the Roman civil service; Ammianus was a staff officer to the Roman general Ursicinus and eyewitness to much of which he wrote; and Procopius was the secretary to Belisarius, the most senior Roman general in the east, with access to papers, high-ranking individuals, and the loftiest levels of political power in the Roman state.

Classicising histories can be very useful for certain subjects, but they do not give much attention to social issues, family, issues of gender, the activities of the lower classes, and so on, except when they overlap with the concerns of their authors. Even when they do, the reader often finds clumsy stereotypes: the lower classes are portrayed as an unruly mob while women lack the ability to think rationally, in contrast to aristocratic men. Compounding this general issue is the fact that history writing of any sort was an activity largely confined to aristocratic males; when women appear in the texts, they do so from the viewpoint of men. Within the context of Roman historical writing, this bias further meant that non-Roman voices such as those belonging to the Greeks or Etruscans were often excluded, suppressed, or refracted through the lens of Roman power. Even though Polybius was Greek, for instance, he worked under the tutelage of Scipio Aemilianus, a prominent politician of the day, and his surviving writings very much reflect the influence of Roman political supremacy.

As noted earlier, a great deal of ancient historical writing focused on moralising, didactic tales that could be used to illustrate character flaws, feats of hubris, and acts of valour, and that served as a guide to navigate the needs and shortcomings of the contemporary world. Thucydides justified his history of the Peloponnesian War by explaining that a thorough inquiry had led him to the conclusion that it was the greatest war in human history, and was therefore worthy of a detailed treatment. In contrast, even though he had access to numerous official sources and other works, such as the *Histories* of Polybius, Livy's critical thinking was inconsistent and his project was more concerned with a need to exemplify the lofty principles of Rome's long-ago ancestors in comparison to the vices and lax morals of his own times, advocating traditional Republican values such as piety and austerity as a tonic for a troubled world. The lodestar for Livy's history of Rome did not, therefore, guide him towards a factual history of Roman origins, aided by diligent and critical labour in the city's temple archives. Furthermore, when writers such as Livy recounted stories of Rome's foundation, their tales became fossilised in a sort of literary canon. Impossibly distant for Livy, Rome's origins were even more so for later historians, such as Tacitus and Cassius Dio. Aeneas, Romulus and Remus, the she-wolf, the shepherd, the seven kings—these were parts of an established set of principles of early Roman history that were never subjected to any sort of serious analytical scrutiny. They were also canonised in religious practice, since the Lupercalia festival, held annually on February 15, involved the sacrifice of animals in the cave where the Romans believed Romulus and Remus had been suckled by the she-wolf, and the Romans continued (well into the fourth century AD) to venerate the space where they believed Romulus had built his first home—a mud hut—on the Palatine Hill.

Evidently, one of the main difficulties involved in getting to grips with the early history of Rome is that the first efforts to write about it were made some five centuries after the city's presumed eighth-century BC foundation. The story of Romulus and Remus was first told in Greek by Fabius Pictor, the earliest of Rome's 'annalist' historians—those who chronicled the city's history year by year. The stimulus behind Fabius Pictor's efforts (as it would be for Polybius) was a desire to justify and explain Roman power to the broader Mediterranean world following Rome's victory over Hannibal in the Hannibalic or Second Punic War (218–202 BC), as well as to situate Rome's ascent in the context of prevailing historical and literary trends. It is telling that Pictor composed his work in Greek; only later did Roman historians write in Latin. As a relative newcomer to the ancient arena of Mediterranean politics, Rome required a suitably impressive history to measure up to the older societies in Greece and the eastern Mediterranean. This could be accomplished by giving the city a Greek-style foundation myth, by endowing the city's ancient past with valiant kings and leaders, and by linking the history of Rome with the Trojan War, which ancient writers thought had ended towards the end of the period we know as the twelfth century BC. Rome's foundation myth bookended the four or so centuries between the end of the Trojan War and the eight century with the arrival of Aeneas in Italy from Troy, and the birth of Romulus and Remus. This neatly dispensed with an inconveniently long period of time, and ensured that the city's past would fit into the ancient history of older, more established parts of the Mediterranean world.

The sources used by Fabius Pictor and others to create this early written record remain obscure, but may have included annals kept by Rome's priests, which recorded the names of magistrates and other officials, alongside major events and religious festivals. These records were later used by the emperor Augustus to erect two lists in the forum, the *fasti triumphales* and the *fasti consulares*. The *fasti triumphales* (Figure 1.1) recorded magistrates who had been awarded a triumph, an elaborate celebration for a victorious military campaign; the *fasti consulares* listed the chief magistrates elected annually under the Republic. The *fasti*, engraved on marble tablets, were discovered in the Roman forum in the mid-sixteenth century as material was being quarried for St Peter's Basilica. Rescued by a pair of keen-eyed officials, they were restored by none other than Michelangelo.

While our records of the *fasti* are problematic, given that they are incomplete and in their current form date to a much later period, they remain a vitally important source for the study of Rome. Other sources, including an oral tradition of myths, stories of great families, and songs recording the deeds of warriors and magistrates, may also have played a role. Interestingly, claims of descent from Trojan émigrés proved popular among the fourth-century BC Roman aristocracy and, as far back as the sixth century BC, the cult of Aeneas was being celebrated at Lavinium, south of Rome. In the early third century, a statue of the she-wolf suckling Romulus and Remus was installed on the Palatine Hill, and

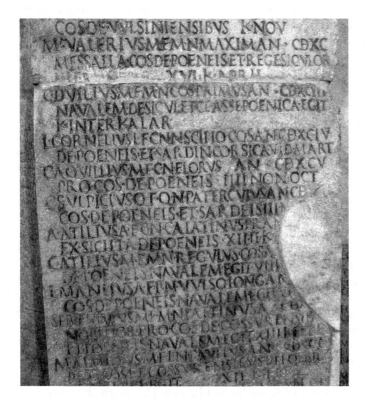

Figure 1.1 A portion of the *fasti triumphales*

Source: Photograph by Rossignol Benoît (CC BY-SA 3.0).

not long afterwards this image began appearing on Roman coins; the subject remained popular well into the imperial period (Figure 1.2).

These vignettes show that by the fourth/third centuries BC, the basic elements of the foundation story were sufficiently current to be worthy of commemoration. The work of Fabius Pictor does not survive, but the stories he reported went on to influence Cicero's *On the Republic* and Livy's own history. The Greek writers Diodorus Siculus and Dionysius of Halicarnassus also report versions of the story related to Aeneas, Romulus and Remus, as well as a further account linked with Evander, an ally of Aeneas who hailed from Greek Arcadia. Cicero, Diodorus, and Dionysius were all writing in the second half of the first century BC.

With all of this in mind, it is no surprise that the stories of early Rome tend to be fantastical in nature and sometimes reflect more contemporary needs to moralise, provide plausible explanations for past events rooted in current preoccupations, and supply a guide for the future. In one example, Livy explained how Romulus built up the population of Rome by inviting the women of neighbouring Sabinum to the city. Believing they were attending a religious festival, the women were seized by force and compelled to accept Roman husbands. This tale not only further illustrates the significance of violent behaviour (and, in this case, gender-based violence) to later Republican-era ideas about

Figure 1.2 Gold aureus of the emperor Hadrian (AD 117–38). The obverse displays the head of the emperor right; the reverse shows the she-wolf suckling Romulus and Remus.

early Rome; it is also of interest because of the way it helps to explain how Rome came to be made up of people from different communities, by reconciling the historical role of Sabines in the early Roman community. Indeed, Sabines appear to have settled early Rome along with Latins, the people of the Latium plain, with the Sabines perhaps providing two of Rome's early kings.

Livy's fantastical tale of Romulus and Remus is similarly violent, and reflects a range of concerns related to the disintegrating Republic. The story of the twins included the curse of unfettered human ambition, which by Livy's day had destroyed the state; acts of savage violence, which from the very early days, through the great victory over Hannibal and then the triumph of Augustus, were believed to have continually renewed and expanded the state; and the primacy of piety, embodied in the decision to settle the dispute via augury and in the violation of the pomerium. The struggle between the twins also reflected the interclass strife that had plagued Rome since its foundation, and that was manifested in a lengthy class struggle in the fifth and fourth centuries. By the first century BC, the struggle had become resuscitated in the guise of the *optimates* (aristocratic conservatives) and the *populares*, led by demagogues. Other aspects of the Republic are visible in the story, such as the description of twins instead of a single undisputed founder, which mimics the collegial magistracies that characterised Rome's post-monarchical Republican government, and the allocation of the prestigious Palatine to Romulus and the Aventine, a stronghold of Rome's urban poor, to Remus. Rome's foundation story is distinctive in its savagery and violence, and explains a great deal about the impact of near-death experiences such as the Hannibalic War on the self-image of the Republic.

There are dozens of historical texts that have survived from Roman antiquity, but the majority have come down to us severely truncated. From Livy's original 142 books— for example, only 35 exist today, while Cassius Dio's history is largely fragmentary and much of it is known from later summarisers, especially Xiphilinus, a monk who lived in the eleventh century. (Note that the numbering of the surviving chapters in the text of Cassius Dio, whether in original survivals or in the text of Xiphilinus, is hopelessly confused. In the references to Dio in this book, I follow the organisation of the Loeb Classical Library text as it is presented online—see Further Reading section). A complete survival, such as the *Wars* of Procopius or Julius Caesar's *Gallic Wars*, is the exception. Some very high-quality works, such as the *History* of Ammianus Marcellinus or the *Histories* of Polybius, have substantial gaps. Historical texts are, however, only a part of the literary output of antiquity. Other types of written sources include correspondence, such as the letters between Trajan and Pliny the Younger, who was serving as the emperor's governor in the province of Bithynia in Asia Minor. Letters like these can provide insight into administrative and lower-level political matters, as well as imperial decision making. Numerous prominent individuals wrote memoirs in antiquity, although the one text that is surely on every historian's wish list—the memoir of Agrippina the Younger, the mother of the emperor Nero—has not survived. There were also numerous biographies written in antiquity, such as the famous *Parallel Lives* by Plutarch, who compared prominent Greeks and Romans in order to provide cautionary tales and celebrate fantastical achievements. Alexander the Great's biography, for example, was paired with that of Julius Caesar, as both men exemplified almost unattainable—but fleeting—human greatness. Several autobiographies, such as the *Res Gestae* of Augustus, also survive, although these must be used carefully due to their self-serving content. While few examples of the *Res Gestae* have come down to us from antiquity, with the best-preserved example found at Ancyra in Turkey, the text was given a modern treatment by Mussolini in 1938. Cast in bronze letters on travertine panels on the Via di Ripetta in Rome, the *Res Gestae* can be admired by visitors to the nearby Mausoleum of Augustus and the Ara Pacis Museum (Figure 1.3).

A substantial corpus of poems and a small number of ancient novels also still exist. Poetry was an important way of conveying ideology, invective, political ideas, or pushing back against government policies. Some of the most famous poems include the *Aeneid* by Virgil, which displays much of the ideology of Augustus; the poetry of Catullus, admired for its elegance and caustic wit, and full of clues to the scandalous goings-on amongst the Roman aristocracy; the poems of Ovid, who was exiled by Augustus for mocking his piety; and many more. Sometimes poems form a valuable historical source where other sources are few or lacking, as in the case of the poems of Claudian, which shed some light on the very difficult period around the turn of the fifth century AD.

After the persecution of Christians ended in the early fourth century AD, new genres of literature emerged. These included works of history skewed towards the affairs of the church and its organisation, as well as the relationships between different religious communities. (Foundation stories in these works naturally veered towards the Creation). There were also chronicles, which followed ecclesiastical and lay events in parallel. Hagiographies (biographies of saints) and texts celebrating martyrs represent another important group of Christian texts. Many of the best-known works of the later Roman empire were written by Christians, such as the *Wars* of Procopius. In this period Greek or Syriac (a dialect of Aramaic) became the preferred vehicles for historical writing, supplanting Latin's dominance in the Republican and early imperial periods.

The written record is supplemented by inscriptions, papyri, coins, and archaeological evidence. Inscriptions include a vast range of texts from those carved on arches or buildings commissioned by the ruling elite, to casual graffiti written on rocks in the desert or the walls of cities such as Pompeii—and everything in between, including writing on altars, milestones, mosaics, plaster, tablets, pieces of broken pottery, and so on. Monumental inscriptions required great skill on the part of the craftsman and were very expensive to

Figure 1.3 Mussolini's edition of the *Res Gestae*, with the Ara Pacis in the background.

Source: Photograph by the author.

produce. They are therefore often associated with grand building projects such as triumphal arches, paid for by the state or local elites and intended to glorify them and their activities. The Arch of Titus in Rome and its accompanying inscriptions, for example, were intended as a testament to Titus's suppression of the Jewish Revolt (AD 66–71); the arch still stands today, close to the Roman forum (Figure 1.4). These texts provide a curated and manicured window onto government policy and the ways in which individual Roman leaders sought to portray themselves and their deeds. Other 'professional' inscriptions include foundation texts recording when structures were erected or repaired (Figure 1.5) or even things as routine as reserved seating at the theatre (Figure 1.6).

Graffiti offers a completely different viewpoint. Often written by commoners looking to record their thoughts, leave messages for one another, mention places or events, or simply doodle to pass the time while engaged in boring jobs such as shepherding, it gives us more of an insight into the daily lives of the population (Figure 1.7). Thousands of examples of graffiti have been found all over the ancient world, notably at Pompeii, where they were preserved by the eruption of Vesuvius, and new texts crop up all the time—especially in places such as the Jordanian and Saudi deserts. Due to its authorship, graffiti provides evidence for a surprising level of literacy in the Roman world, although it may not have been as high as some scholars have argued. Monumental inscriptions, for

Figure 1.4 The Arch of Titus in Rome with its prominent dedicatory inscription. The inscription reads
SENATVS POPVLVSQUE ROMANUS DIVO TITO DIVI VESPASIANI F VESPASIANO
AUGUSTO—'The Senate and the Roman People to divus [divine] Titus, son of divus
Vespasian, Vespasian Augustus'.

Source: Photograph by the author.

example, which tended to follow various formulae or abbreviations to express specific
ideas—SPQR for *senatus populusque Romanus*, 'the senate and the Roman people'—did
not require a high degree of literacy to understand the main message.

Mosaic inscriptions, which became a particularly popular medium to record the dedication of churches as Christianity spread throughout the empire, can help to reveal
the activities of mid-level officials such as priests and local elites in the foundation
of monasteries, churches, and martyria (churches housing the relics of saints). These
unique records were created by arranging the individual tesserae of mosaic floors or
wall decorations to create a written text, and were usually written in Greek, Latin, or
Syriac (Figure 1.8).

The earliest Roman inscription dates from the sixth century BC, but there are few
other surviving examples before the second century BC. Many of the examples from the
late Republic provide information about senatorial decrees, laws, decisions of magistrates,
and so on, illuminating the activities of local and municipal government as well as the
highest official bodies of the state. Of particular interest for social history are the hundreds
of surviving funerary inscriptions, often accompanied by carved images of the dead and
other visual representations, which shed light on funerary customs and religious beliefs,
and which also personalise our understanding of these long-dead individuals. Another category of inscription is that of military diplomas, copies of texts inscribed on metal plaques

Figure 1.5 Latin building inscription from the Roman fort at Qasr Bshir in Jordan, recording its construction between AD 293 and 305.

Source: Photograph by the author.

in Rome recording the discharge of non-Roman troops from the military. Diplomas recorded a cache of information, including the unit, the soldier involved, the benefits he was to be given in retirement, dates, and locations of military units.

Priceless caches of papyri have been discovered in several parts of the Roman world. The bulk have been found in extremely dry locations in Egypt, with other important groups from Petra in Jordan, the abandoned fortress city of Dura-Europos in Syria, and Nessana in Israel. Like the graffiti, these documents can show us what was happening in daily life; many of the papyri record debts owed or paid, deeds of sale, taxation records, information about slaves, marriages, and property transfers, and all manner of other routine activities. Military papyri, such as the famous cache concerning the affairs of Cohors XX Palmyrenorum (20th Palmyrene Cohort) discovered at Dura-Europos, provide an insight into the lives of soldiers, discharges and promotions, and the structure of military administration (Figure 1.9).

As perishable as papyri, and quite rare, are the surviving examples of thin wooden tablets used for writing. The most famous collection of these is the Vindolanda Tablets, found at the Roman fort of Vindolanda south of Hadrian's Wall and dating to the second century AD (Figure 1.10). The Vindolanda Tablets include such touching notes as the letter by Claudia Severa, the wife of a fort commandant, inviting a friend to her birthday party; another text reveals that Roman soldiers wore underwear! Caches of wooden tablets have also been discovered at Pompeii, and between 2010 and 2013 another haul of over four

Figure 1.6 Greek inscription on reserved seating in the North Theatre at Jerash, Jordan. The picture shows the end of the Greek word ΑΦΡΟΔΙΤΗΣ (APHRODITES), with Σ rendered as C and the Τ and Η connected by a ligature. The civic tribes of the city were named for members of the Graeco-Roman pantheon; this row was reserved for members of the city's civic tribe of Aphrodite.

Source: Photograph by the author.

hundred tablets was retrieved from an excavation in London. Known as the Bloomberg Tablets, they record legal affairs and identify a hundred or so different individuals living in Roman Londinium in the first century AD.

Numismatics, the study of coins, is also a vitally important tool for understanding Roman history. The Romans began to mint coins around the fourth century BC, some two centuries after the Greek colonies of southern Italy and Sicily had started to issue their own. As the state expanded, numerous mints were established across the Mediterranean and mints also travelled with Roman armies, minting coins to pay the troops. Roman coins were an effective form of mass media, achieving wide circulation throughout the Mediterranean, the Middle East, and even as far away as India. Roman coins could be used to express ideological, political, and religious ideas, as well as to commemorate important events. The obverse side of ancient coins typically showed the 'heads'—normally depictions of mythological heroes such as Heracles, or gods and goddesses drawn from the Mediterranean pantheon. Later, heads of famous individuals such as Julius Caesar replaced images of gods and heroes. The reverse of the coin could be used to deliver another message—a famous story from the history of the city, colony, or state minting the coin, such as a foundation myth, or an historical event worthy of commemoration. One of the most famous of all

Figure 1.7 Hunting scene accompanied by pre-Islamic graffiti from Wadi Rum, Jordan.

Source: Photograph by the author.

Figure 1.8 Greek inscription in the mosaic pavement of the Church of Bishop Isaiah, at Jerash, dating the church's construction to AD 558/9.

Source: Photograph by the author.

Figure 1.9 P.Dura 82, a 'morning report' on the strength of XX Palmyrenorum

Source: Image courtesy of Beinecke Rare Book and Manuscript Library, Yale University.

Figure 1.10 Vindolanda Tablet #343, recording a letter discussing supplies of food and matériel.

Source: Photograph by Michel Wal (CC BY-SA 3.0).

Roman coins was issued on behalf of Brutus, one of the assassins of Julius Caesar, with the legend 'EID MAR'—that is, the Ides of March, the date of the murder, surmounted by two daggers (see Figure 7.17 in Chapter 7).

The principal Roman coin, in service after the Hannibalic War, was the silver denarius, which retained its prominent role until the political and economic crisis of the third century AD. During the late Republic, silver coinage became ever more politicised, a reflection of the desperate struggles being waged by various factions who used coins to celebrate their family's fortunes, achievements, and divine links. Caesar, for instance, promoted his family's links with Venus and the story of Aeneas (Figure 1.11). Caesar also introduced gold coinage, and the use of gold continued in various forms (as an aureus, then the solidus after the fourth century AD) through to the collapse of the western empire and the Muslim conquests of the seventh century and beyond. Aside from silver and gold, coins in denominations lower than the denarius were minted using bronze. Coins were also made from billon, a base metal alloy with a tiny amount of silver. As Greek coins had done—south Arabian coins have been discovered minted with the head of Athena and the famous owl that instantly identified a coin as Athenian—Roman coins could influence local issues, such as the 'Class B' coins from Sanaa in Yemen featuring the head of the emperor Augustus.

Roman coins are frequently found in archaeological deposits, where they can help to date individual structures, as well as in hoards, buried during times of crisis and never

Figure 1.11 Silver denarius of Julius Caesar, minted in 48/47 BC. Obverse: head of Venus right; reverse: Aeneas with his father, Anchises, on his shoulder.

retrieved by their owners. Several hoards were found at Dura-Europos, with the latest dating from the Persian sack of the city between AD 255 and AD 257. One of the most famous hoards is the Hoxne Hoard, now housed in the British Museum (Chapter 13). Containing nearly 15,000 coins, including 569 gold solidi, the hoard has been dated to the first decade of the fifth century AD, when Britain was under sustained attack by Saxon raiders and was rapidly falling out of Roman control. Another large find in Britain, the Seaton Down Hoard, is held at the Royal Albert Memorial Museum in Exeter. While not as valuable as the Hoxne Hoard in financial terms, it is still enormous: 22,888 coins, weighing in at 68 kilograms (150 pounds). Most date from the reign of Constantine, another violent period in the Roman west, and depict more than 20 members of the imperial household. The precious metal content of Roman coins can also be used to assess economic trends and understand periods of crisis. Just prior to the military crisis of the third century AD, for example, a new coin, the antoninianus, was introduced by Caracalla. It was initially a silver coin worth two denarii, but by the end of the century it was being manufactured from billon, with a minimal silver content. The excessive demands on the Roman treasury exerted by civil and foreign wars are partly to blame for the slow devaluation of this coin type.

The archaeological record, another crucial tool for historians, provides information on buildings and technology, and through associated finds it can illuminate daily life at a particular moment in time. A sunken ship loaded with wine or olive oil amphorae, for instance, can tell us about naval technology and about the type of trade in a given area at a given time, whereas the excavation of a house or a temple might reveal household objects or cult relics. Along with artefacts recovered from excavations, the surviving 'built heritage'—buildings and other structures—can tell us a great deal about ancient life. Because of their contexts, artwork and sculpture also form part of the archaeological record. The so-called Altar of Domitius Ahenobarbus, for instance, discovered in Rome in the seventeenth century (and now divided between the Musée du Louvre, the Glyptothek in Munich, and the Pushkin in Moscow), provides a sculpted bas-relief record of the census and the ritual sacrifice of animals for the *lustrum*, the ritual purification that followed the

Figure 1.12 Plaster cast of part of the carved scroll on Trajan's Column, showing Roman legionnaires in the characteristic *testudo* ('tortoise') formation.

Source: Photograph by Christian Chirita (CC BY-SA 3.0).

census itself. The Altar is also famous for the detailed representation of late second-century BC arms and armour. Another important monument is Trajan's Column, which provides an astonishing visual record of the emperor's campaigns in Dacia (Romania) (Figure 1.12). The arches of Titus, Septimius Severus, Constantine, and other monuments reflect the cultural preoccupations of the time, celebrate victories and the defeat of enemies, and make grand political statements.

While only a few maps have survived from antiquity, one of the most intriguing is the Forma Urbis Romae, also known as the 'Marble Plan'. This was a massive representation of Rome in Proconnesian marble made during the reign of Septimius Severus (AD 193–211), measuring 234 m² (2,580 ft²), of which 1,186 fragments have survived. The Marble Plan was installed vertically on one of the walls of the Templum Pacis (the Temple of Peace, dedicated in AD 75; see Chapter 10). It is an important resource for constructing topographical maps of ancient Rome and for locating structures described by ancient authors, and it informed some of the best-known resources, including Samuel Platner's *A Topographical Dictionary of Ancient Rome* (revised by Thomas Ashby and published in 1929) and the monumental *Lexicon Topographicum Urbis Romae*, edited by Eva Steinby (published in six volumes between 1993 and 2000). Platner's *Topography* remains essential and, together with a digital version of the Marble Plan, it is available online (see Further Reading section).

New archaeological finds are not uncommon, continually updating our understanding of antiquity—even if many areas rich in Roman archaeology, such as Syria, have seen an almost complete cessation of excavation work and the deliberate looting and destruction of archaeological sites on an unimaginable scale (see Figure 12.11 in Chapter 12). One of the problems faced by archaeologists is gaining suitable access to a prospective site. In places that have seen more or less continual habitation, such as London, this can be rather difficult; the Bloomberg Tablets were found only *after* the demolition of an existing building on the site and prior to the next phase of development. In other places, archaeological sites have remained more or less untouched since antiquity. This was true of Dura-Europos in Syria, and many of the desert forts in Jordan (Chapter 12).

Finally, source material produced *outside* the Roman world often contains content relevant to the study of Roman history. These include inscriptions, such as those from the kingdoms of Himyar (Yemen) and Axum (Ethiopia), as well as inscriptions and sculpture from Persia. There are also texts written in Arabic after the Muslim conquests, and Christian Syriac material from the Persian empire. There have also been a range of modern scientific studies of events in antiquity, such as the various visitations of the plague, the eruption of Vesuvius, and the ancient climate, all of which help to shed important light on the Roman world.

With this brief overview of the main sources for Roman history in mind, we shall turn now to see what, beyond the story of Aeneas, Romulus, and Remus, can reliably be said of early Rome and the contexts in which the settlement there developed.

Rome, Italy, and the Mediterranean

In the eighth century BC, Italy was a patchwork of communities, many of which had greater antiquity than Rome. The Italian peninsula protrudes into the Mediterranean Sea about halfway between the Straits of Gibraltar and the Levant, and in antiquity it was connected by a network of maritime trade routes lining the various settlements around its shores. Between and around Rome lay the communities of Etruria (Tuscany) and Latium (Lazio), both of which would play a tremendously important role in Rome's early development from a small village to the master of central Italy (Chapter 2). Colonists from Greece founded settlements in Italy as early as 750, and these eventually spread to encompass much of Sicily and southern and central Italy, including the area around Naples (in Greek, 'Nea Polis', or 'New City'), which became the most densely populated city in Campania. The Greek colonies of Italy and Sicily were so many (22 according to ancient sources) that the Romans took to referring to them as Magna Graecia, or 'Great Greece' (Figure 1.13).

The Levantine Phoenicians were also colonists, although they preferred western Sicily and North Africa, where their most famous settlement, Carthage, a colony of the Phoenician city of Tyre, was established around 800 BC. Carthage, now a UNESCO World Heritage Site close to modern Tunis, prospered through its easy access to trade routes and its excellent harbour facilities (Figure 1.14). Carthaginian traders established outposts among the Etruscans, and close to the Etruscan city of Caere a temple to the near eastern goddess Astarte was dedicated at the turn of the sixth century. Well before the Romans began to expand their horizons beyond Italy, Carthage had become a Mediterranean political and economic heavyweight, with the best equipped and most advanced navy of its time.

Figure 1.13 Italy and surrounding regions in antiquity.

Source: Illustration by the author.

Just as Italy was a patchwork of communities, it was also a geographical patchwork that hindered the easy integration of the various towns and villages. The Apennine mountains run through the peninsula, slowing access from one coast to the other and creating three flat areas: the Po valley in the north, Apulia in the south, and the area around Rome, including the Latium plain, Campania, and Etruria in the centre. The Po valley was partly inhabited by Gauls, who earned notoriety in early Roman history due to their supposed sack of the city in 390 BC, an event that was never truly forgotten (Chapter 2). With characteristic pragmatism, the Romans referred to northern Italy as Cisalpine Gaul, 'Gaul this side of the Alps'.

Greece's Italian colonies evolved into self-governing city states that included both an urban settlement and a zone of villages and agricultural land that supported its inhabitants. These communities also developed forms of sociopolitical organisation that provided

Figure 1.14 Google Earth Pro image of the ancient harbours of Carthage.

Source: Image data © Maxar Technologies and TerraMetrics.

Figure 1.15 Silver nomos from Taras (Tarentum) minted in the mid-fifth century BC. Obverse: a nude Taras rides a dolphin; reverse: a nude youth riding a galloping horse, with ΤΑΡΑΣ inscribed to the right.

leadership for civic, military, and religious matters. Most had foundation myths, of the sort later imitated by the Romans, which explained where their people came from and how their society had evolved. Taras (Tarentum), for example—one of the most important Greek cities of southern Italy and possessing a superb natural harbour—traced its development to an eponymous founder named Taras, who is featured on Tarentum's elegant silver coinage riding a dolphin. Like Romulus and Remus, Taras had divine ancestry: he was the offspring of Poseidon (Neptune) and a sea-nymph named Satyria (Figure 1.15).

The cosmopolitan, international nature of early Italy is also reflected in the fact that the earliest examples of writing found in the peninsula include a graffito in Phoenician Aramaic and an inscription in Greek. Italy, indeed, was a collage of different languages: early inscriptions show that Rome's inhabitants spoke a form of Latin, while Rome's neighbours, the Etruscans, spoke an obscure language that has long defied classification. It was written in an alphabet derived from Greek but, lacking a Rosetta Stone-like set of comparisons to another language, has proven very hard to read. (The bilingual Etruscan/Punic Pyrgi gold tablets provide an exception, but have not allowed for a full understanding of the Etruscan language.) The inhabitants of Latium, the district around Rome, also spoke Latin, and inland the peoples of central Italy spoke languages similar to Latin, including Oscan, which would come to prominence with the rise of the Samnites in the fourth century (Chapter 2). Greek, naturally, was the language of Greece's Italian colonies.

Rome was situated amidst these different communities at the edge of the Latium plain. It sat astride the junction of routes that led from Campania to Etruria and, via the Tiber—the estuary of which was some 24 kilometres (15 miles) distant—was connected with Mediterranean commercial traffic. Immediately to the west of the Capitoline Hill, the Tiber Island slowed the river, providing a suitable offloading point on the opposite bank for loading and unloading river craft, and the island also eased the river's crossing. Another route that lay under the watchful gaze of Rome's easily defended hills was the via Salaria, through which salt was carried inland up the Tiber estuary. This combination of a defensible position, access to and control over important trade routes, and access to the sea seemed almost providential to later writers. Livy, for example, said Rome's location was 'a position singularly adapted by nature for the expansion of a city' (5.54).

There is evidence for settlement on the Capitoline Hill as early as about 1000 BC, and pottery recovered from the same area might indicate an even earlier period of settlement dating as far back as 1700 BC. The valley separating the Capitoline and Palatine hills, a part of which had previously been used as a cemetery, was drained via the *cloaca maxima*, the 'great drain'. (So important was the *cloaca maxima* that the Romans assigned it a goddess, Cloacina—the 'drain goddess'—to ensure its proper functioning.) A large structure, the Regia, was later constructed there as a residence for the king and as a centre of religious practice. This area was paved and later developed into the city's famous forum, the centre of civic and religious life, serving a function similar to the Greek agora. Other important public spaces were Rome's famous Circus Maximus, a grand arena for chariot racing, which was finished by the end of the seventh century; the *forum boarium*, the city's cattle market; and the Temple of Jupiter and Juno on the Capitoline Hill, another important focus for civic and religious activities in the city as early as the mid-eighth century. An early road, the via Sacra, led from one of the city's entrances to the shrines of the Capitoline Hill and the forum itself. By the end of the seventh century, the *comitium*, an open-air place for political assembly, was laid out in the north of the forum, as well as the curia Hostilia, where community elders could gather and offer counsel to the king. There were also other important religious spaces in the forum from a very early date. At the south end, there was space that was sacred to Vesta, while at the north there was the Vulcanal, a sanctuary devoted to Vulcan and thus also, like the shrine of Vesta, concerned with fire. These early structures are illustrated in Figure 1.16, together with the defensive wall thought to date from the mid-sixth century BC.

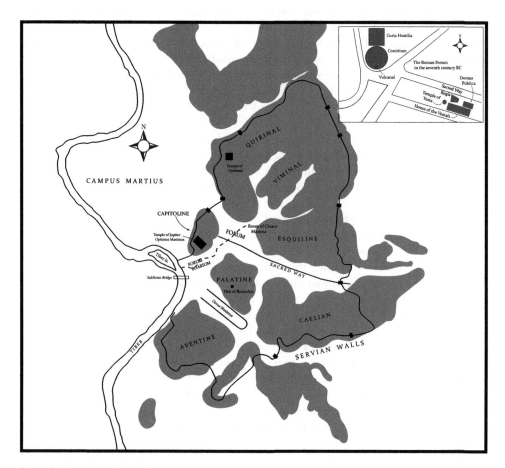

Figure 1.16 Archaic Rome. The inset at the top right shows the installations of the Roman forum in the seventh century BC.

Source: Illustration by the author.

The development of religious sanctuaries, public gathering spaces, and areas such as the *comitium* was indicative of the trend towards urban development that was characteristic not only of early Rome, but also of the communities of Etruria, Latium, and Magna Graecia in the seventh century BC.

Aristocratic male elites dominated this early Roman society as they would throughout the Republic. Who exactly were these elites? Between the eighth and early sixth centuries BC, Greek, Egyptian, and near eastern influences were pervasive throughout Italy and the Mediterranean, leading this era to be called the 'orientalising period'. One of its features was the emergence of a pan-Italian aristocracy whose graves reveal that they possessed significant disposable wealth—enough to bury exotic, high-status goods from across the archaic Mediterranean world with their dead. Deposits of Phoenician and Greek pottery, ivory and silver, and expensive goods from Egypt and the Levant have been found in graves in Latium, Campania, and Etruria, alongside locally produced, high-quality wares such as the distinctive bucchero Etruscan pottery. In Latium, the famous Barberini tomb at Praeneste, excavated in 1855, furnished a trove of luxury goods in the shape of a delicately incised Phoenician silver bowl, gold brooches, ivory, and amber. Etruscan tombs of the period were either hypogea (chambers built under the ground) or tombs built to resemble small houses, and many have provided similar evidence of lavish and wealthy lifestyles. The most elaborate tombs were designed to accommodate several generations of the same family, a fact that highlights the importance of clans made up of families and their dependants.

The importance of a pan-Italian and shared Mediterranean culture is also expressed through architectural design and the spread of religious cults. This is especially noticeable in the construction of temples, financed by the elite as a form of community investment and self-promotion. A statue of the Greek god Apollo, for example, graced the famous Portonaccio Temple at Veii in Etruria, while a mid-sixth century temple in Rome featured statues of Heracles and the patron goddess of Athens, Athena. At Lavinium, a Greek dedication to the Dioscuri (the twins, Castor and Pollux) provides a link with the cities of Tarentum and Locri in southern Italy, where the cult of the Dioscuri was very popular. Foreign influences are also visible in the growth of the cult of Ceres, a goddess popular in Sicily and Magna Graecia, and a version of the ancient Magna Mater, or 'Great Mother', who later became identified with the Roman goddess Demeter; the goddess Diana, imported to Rome from nearby Aricia; Mercury, an interpretation of Hermes; and Liber Pater, who, via an evolution which saw him joined with Dionysus and the Etruscan god Fufluns, emerged as Bacchus, the god of wine. From its beginnings, Roman religious custom, an important aspect of Roman communal identity, was flexible enough to admit newcomers and to find correspondences with other gods, goddesses, and heroes.

The developing Roman community was also flexible in who it accepted, and there appears to have been a certain degree of social mobility among the elites of archaic Italy. One of Rome's kings, Tarquin the Elder, was thought to have come from Etruscan Tarquinii, while the Claudii, an ancient family who would play a key role in the late Republic and early empire, arrived from Sabinum in 504. Rome's later mythologies preserve the memory of this kind of mobility. In one vignette, described by Livy, Romulus opened the sanctuary on the Capitoline Hill to outsiders; among the newcomers were Italian aristocrats whom Romulus enrolled among the Roman elite.

In Rome, the elites headed clans or family groups called *gentes* (sg. *gens*), which each claimed a nominal common ancestor. The *gentes* were not simply the direct relations of the leading male, the patron, but included other branches and dependent clients who relied on the patron for support, and who in turn repaid this gesture through political backing, work, or military service. Despite this broad membership, there was a clear divide between the dependants and the patron, who passed on his aristocratic status to his sons and reinforced it through links to ancient ancestors—either mythological or, in the case of colonies, to the presumed original colonists—and through connections with specific religious cults. The perpetuation of a tightly demarcated aristocratic class, controlling the bulk of the wealth and with a heavily dependent clientele, helps to explain the emergence of the wealthy patrician order in later Roman society and the agitation by others against their privileges (see below and Chapter 2).

Roman *gentes* were eventually identified by their *nomen*, or family name; it was not unusual for some prominent men to have up to four separate names, with the last, the *agnomen*, denoting a special honour. One famous mid-Republican example is Publius Cornelius Scipio 'Africanus', a member of the Scipio branch of the *gens* Cornelia (the Cornelii Scipiones) who took the *agnomen* 'Africanus' after his defeat of Hannibal in 202 BC. Throughout the Republican period, it is possible to trace the continued dominance of these families who, despite reforms that aimed to ensure that power would be shared more evenly between the wealthy aristocrats and other members of the community, continued to dominate certain offices such as senior priesthoods and magistracies. Practices of guest-friendship and intermarriage between aristocratic elites helped to perpetuate the importance of individual families.

The primary basis for aristocratic wealth in an agrarian society was, of course, land, and the long-term control over landed property was one of the ways by which the leaders of the *gentes* maintained their grip. By the eighth century, olives and vines were being cultivated in central Italy, and by the seventh century oil and wine were being exported to the coasts of France and Spain. These developments in agriculture required a workforce to tend to the trees and vines, and to process the raw fruit into a finished product, and this workforce was made up of subordinates who served the needs of the wealthy landowners. Quite often, these subordinates had little choice but to depend on their richer patrons to help them survive droughts, crop failure, and other natural disasters. In entering a dependent relationship, in which they worked for their patron to ensure the survival of their families, the poorer farmers very often fell into crippling levels of debt that kept them subordinate for life and in extreme circumstances might get them killed or sold into slavery (Chapter 2).

Among the numerous external influences on Roman politics, religion, and culture, the Etruscans are of particular interest. They were loosely organised in a network of strong city states, which were the most powerful political and military forces by the turn of the seventh century BC and the only urban civilisation of the time in central Italy. Much of Etruscan history is obscure due to the difficulty of reading the some 13,000 surviving inscriptions, as well as the fact that we are reliant on Greek and Roman texts—the views of 'outsiders', who could be hostile, indifferent, or envious. The Greeks, for example, viewed the Etruscans as devotees of affluent living, a byword in antiquity for indolence and licentiousness; this was more than a little ironic given that the word 'sybarite', referring to a person devoted to luxury, was derived from the city of Sybaris in Magna Graecia!

Etruscan influences on Roman politics, religion, and culture were significant. Etruria's cities were initially ruled by kings, advised by a council of elders. Later, in the fifth century, the monarchy vanished and in its place appeared magistrates serving one-year terms. Etruscan politics also featured the office of dictator (*mastarna*), an emergency position used in times of great crisis, usually following a military catastrophe; the *mastarna* was granted absolute power for a limited period of time. All these features found their way into Roman political life in varying forms, as did symbols of royal power including luxurious purple robes and sceptres, crowns, and eagles. The Etruscans also used the *fasces*, the famous bundle of tied rods with axe heads that represented supreme authority, and that became the symbol of the authority of elected magistrates in the Republic. Etruscan society was highly stratified, featuring a powerful oligarchy of landed wealthy men above a population of rural workers and slaves, while its religious pantheon found easy correspondence with the Olympian gods, headed by Jupiter, that found favour in Rome. The Capitoline Triad, the trio of deities housed in the Temple of Jupiter on the Capitoline

Hill, which was started in the sixth century, corresponded with their Etruscan and Greek counterparts: Jupiter with Greek Zeus and Etruscan Tinia; Juno with Greek Hera and Etruscan Uni; and Minerva with Greek Athena and Etruscan Menrva. The temple itself was distinctively Etruscan in design, with a tripartite arrangement on a raised podium; each member of the triad occupied an individual *cella* (an internal room containing a cult statue or other artefact) within the temple.

Etruscan technology was sophisticated, particularly with regard to sewerage, drainage, and water management. Rome's main sewer, the *cloaca maxima*, was an Etruscan innovation thought to date to the reign of Tarquin the Elder. Interestingly, the Etruscans also seem to have linked their own mythical history to the Trojan War cycle for much the same reason as the Romans would go on to do in their own time: it proved their antiquity to the Greeks with whom they traded and interacted. The famous image of Aeneas carrying his father, Anchises, popular on later Republican Roman coinage (Figure 1.11, above), is also a staple of Etruscan funerary art. Most importantly, perhaps, was the literary heritage of Etruria, for it was from the Etruscan alphabet, derived from the Greeks, that the Latin alphabet was developed; it would be used to record much of Rome's history.

Early Roman political life

The development of Rome's political institutions and sense of community took place in tandem with the increase in urban development characteristic of many Italian settlements in the sixth century BC. Stone walls replaced less-permanent defences, while many of the cities of Magna Graecia adopted the characteristic street layout attributed to the fifth-century BC architect Hippodamos (hence, 'Hippodamian'), based around parallel and intersecting streets. The development of public spaces was an important feature of urban development, and included expensive and time-consuming work on temples, meeting areas (the agora and the forum), and places for civic assembly that contributed to the development of the population's sense of community. The wealth that underwrote such grand projects came from the leading aristocrats in the various communities, as well as from the plunder won in the interminable summer campaigns and skirmishes between neighbours. While the lavishness of grave goods in Etruria was less extravagant in the sixth century than in the seventh, it is to this later period, as well as to the fifth and fourth centuries, that some of the most celebrated Etruscan funerary paintings belong. Instead of commemorating opulence through grave deposits, these paintings celebrate the opulence of the daily life of the Etruscan elite, hinting at a more complex society. Etruscan tombs have become world famous for their haunting images of a vanishing civilisation, earning the Banditaccia Necropolis (Caere) and the Monterozzi Necropolis (Tarquinii) spots on the list of UNESCO World Heritage Sites. One of the most famous works of Etruscan funerary art is the depiction of a woman identified as Velia Velcha, discovered in 1868 in the fourth-century Tomb of Orcus at Tarquinii (Figure 1.17).

The urbanisation of Italian communities and the development of more sophisticated forms of political expression helped ideas of communal membership to evolve. Cities might share various religious rights and festivals, such as the Etruscans; or Rome and the cities of Latium, which participated in the annual Feriae Latinae, devoted to Jupiter Latiaris, the chief deity of the Latins. The Temple of Diana in Rome, dated to the sixth century, was built outside the pomerium and was apparently intended to be shared with the Latins.

Figure 1.17 Head of Velia Velcha, from the Tomb of Orcus.

Source: Photograph by Robin Iversen Rönnlund (CC BY-SA 3.0)

Mutual defence leagues such as the Latin League, the loose federation of Etruscan cities, and the Italiote League, which brought together the cities of Magna Graecia, could also provide a form of overarching political identity or sense of communal membership. Still, local identities remained to the fore, and one was a citizen of Praeneste before Latium, or of Caere before Etruria. The most significant change to this picture would only come with the extension of forms of Roman citizenship throughout central Italy by the third century BC (Chapter 2).

From a very early period, the Romans developed a concept of imperium. This was primarily a form of arbitrary political-religious authority that allowed individuals to exercise absolute control over the city's population, to lead its soldiers in wartime, and to preside over certain religious matters. Imperium had a dual nature that was divided by Rome's sacred boundary, the pomerium. Outside the pomerium, this concept of power was primarily military in nature; inside, it was more concerned with civic and religious matters. Imperium occupied a central place in the later Republican government, and was only conferred on a limited number of specific offices. During Rome's early period, it was the assembly of Rome's adult male fighting population, who bestowed imperium upon the kings. Later, imperium would be conferred at the ballot box as officials were elected by Rome's main political assembly, the *comitia centuriata* (below).

Rome's first known efforts at forming a political constitution were based around three tribes, the Tities, Luceres, and Ramnes. The tribes reflected geographical and/or ethnic divisions within the city. (It has been suggested, for example, that the three corresponded to Sabines, Etruscans, and Latins, respectively.) Each tribe comprised ten *curiae* (sg. *curia*), a sort of sub-grouping which provided the basis for the army and for political expression in an assembly called the *comitia curiata*, which gathered in the *comitium* in the forum to confer imperium or listen to the king's ideas and proposals. Several curial offices are known, namely the *curiones*, *flamines*, and *libones*, all of whom likely served a religious function. Separately, the king was attended by the senate, a group of older men made up of the *patres* or 'fathers', later known as the patricians, who initially assembled in the curia Hostilia. The name *patres* reflects the distinctively hierarchical and patriarchal nature of Roman society and the degree of control wielded in the social sphere by the male family head, the *paterfamilias*. The council itself was the forerunner of the Republican senate, which provided advice and debated matters of policy, but did not engage in making laws.

The early *patres* were probably the men in charge of the individual *gentes* that wielded the most power in the tribal system, and who could act as patrons for their less-wealthy clients. This latter group would, in turn, support the *patres* politically and pledge their fealty, which helped to perpetuate this patriarchal hierarchy: this became institutionalised in Rome as the patron–client relationship and was an important feature of Republican social and political life. In early Rome, the *patres* maintained a tight grip on the city's priesthoods, a role derived from their position as the heads of *gentes* that each had their own family cults. As the *gentes* became politically organised through the *curiae*, these cults then became part of the city's religious life.

As the apex of Rome's political hierarchy, the patricians constantly faced challenges from those *gentes* that were not part of this inner circle, but that might have had as much wealth as the patricians, more influence, or greater ability as military leaders. The non-patricians later became known as the plebeians—a somewhat misleading term, since it implies a lack of wealth or status. In contrast, some plebeian families were as influential or as rich as many patrician families, and patrician families could be less well off than their plebeian counterparts.

The monarchy in Rome certainly existed, even if the historicity of the lists of kings provided by later historians is open to debate. Roman monarchy was not hereditary, nor were the kings particularly powerful. The institution clearly had religious duties: an inscription discovered on a broken piece of pottery in the Regia preserves the word *rex*, 'king', and this term appears on another text known as the Black Stone inscription, belonging to the late sixth century and associated with the Vulcanal. The Black Stone text is fragmentary, and is written using letters that are more closely related to Greek than those used for later Latin texts, reflecting an early stage of the adoption of the alphabet. It is also written using a Greek technique called *boustrophedon*, where the direction of writing alternates between left to right and right to left, mimicking the ploughing of a field by an ox. The inscription, which has proven challenging to translate, appears to refer to a law governing a religious ritual of some sort in which the king is mentioned. Further indications of the religious functions of the early kings are found in the use of the office of *rex sacrorum* ('king of the sacrifices') under the Republic, and by the fact that the chief priest of Rome, the *pontifex maximus*, used the nearby *Domus Publica* as his house. The Regia itself included two shrines: one to Mars, the god of war, and the other to Ops Consiva, associated with prosperity. The Regia may also have expanded later to include the space sacred to Vesta.

Roman writers thought that the sixth king of Rome, Servius Tullius (whose reign was dated by Varro to 578–535 BC) engaged in a series of constitutional reforms that refined the existing system. It is unlikely that the system described by ancient writers sprang fully formed during a particular moment in time; rather, the Servian reforms likely reflect a system developed over a much longer period, perhaps well into the fifth century BC. Nevertheless, the reforms attributed to Servius are significant in that they envisaged a greater role for the citizenry in politics and helped to pave the way for the development of the Republican constitution. The growing participation of the citizen body in governance was characteristic of the period between the seventh and sixth centuries: in Magna Graecia, for instance, magistrates elected by popular assemblies came to wield political authority, while in Latium and Etruria there is evidence for elected officials, even while kings continued to rule in some communities. The close interactions between these different communities have raised the question of whether the Servian reform was a result of an outside influence: Servius Tullius who, along with his predecessor Tarquin the Elder and his successor (and final king) Tarquin the Proud, is often thought to have come from Etruria. The later emperor Claudius, who had a deep scholarly interest in Roman history, referred to Servius as *mastarna*, the Etruscan term for a dictator. During the sixth century, the Etruscans spread their influence southwards as far as Campania, a development reflected in bucchero pottery found in grave deposits and a number of Etruscan inscriptions discovered in the region. As a result, some historians speak of the sixth century as a period of Etruscan rule or heightened Etruscan influence in Rome that helped to transform the architecture, topography, and political map of the city.

It was apparently during the reign of Servius Tullius that the first census was taken, creating a list of adult Roman males—the citizens of Rome—that provided the basis for military service and participation in the city's political life. Another innovation attributed to Servius Tullius was a rethinking of the tribal system, whereby four tribes were created for four distinctive geographical areas in Rome. Ten rural tribes were also created to account for those living around Rome (as Rome expanded there would later be more than 30 rural tribes). From this point, the Latin word *tribus*, which gives us 'tribe', was not used to denote race, ethnicity, or kinship, as it may have done with the original three—the Tities, Luceres, and Ramnes. The Servian urban and rural tribes were instead based squarely on geographical origin and it was these, rather than the three original tribes, that came to be important for defining citizenship, and that formed the basis of military recruitment in times of war via the wealth of the individual tribal members.

The Servian reforms therefore moved the curial system towards a system based on wealth and place of residence, rather than ethnicity, as the key markers of communal membership, obligations, and privilege: in theory, each tribe would provide a cross-section of Roman society, from the wealthiest to the poorest. It is a distinctive feature of Roman citizenship that from a very early time it possessed a legal dimension that was disconnected from racial or ethnic origins. This meant that when it became necessary to do so, expanding the citizen body could be done fairly easily, and conquered and allied peoples could be absorbed into Rome's citizen body by being assigned to a tribe and being enrolled in the census (Chapter 2). While ethnic, group, or family ties—via the *gentes*, the original three tribes, and then the *curiae*—naturally remained relevant, they now became *less* important than wealth and territorial location in determining eligibility for what was arguably the most important function of the census at the time—military service. Prior to the sixth century, wars were fought by the aristocratic elite, who armed their dependants. These militias fought for their clan leaders, rather than for a broader political community. Between the sixth and fifth centuries BC, this situation changed across Italy, as heavy infantry similar to the hoplite phalanx of ancient Greece became the norm across the Graeco-Italian world. The warriors who fought Rome's early battles, and against whom Rome's neighbours fielded their own infantry, had to pay for or otherwise provide their own armour and kit: only much later would the state assume this responsibility, either through paying a stipend or via wholesale reform. Such armour was expensive, consisting of metal helmets and breastplates, as well as large wooden shields, spears, swords, and other equipment.

How could an individual's ability to afford this hoplite panoply be determined accurately? The Servian reforms envisioned five classes of citizen, assessed by wealth measured in the *as*, a specific weight of bronze. These five classes were divided once again into centuries, groups that theoretically comprised 100 men each and whose members—classified by wealth, not location—would be drawn from across the different tribes, cutting through local rivalries and power blocs. This was an important feature of the system and was presumably intended to reduce friction between rival districts in Rome.

The first class was made up of the landed wealthy, who could contribute cavalry and heavy infantry at their own expense, and counted 98 centuries. The next four classes, ranked in decreasing order of wealth, mustered only 92 centuries between them. Those in the fourth class were not expected to provide the same level of heavy equipment as those in the first or second; the fourth, for example, might make up the skirmishers or light infantry who operated in the no-man's land between opposing armies. Together, in times of war, these centuries would make up the *legio*, or legion, the city's army, which would focus on *juniores*, young men who were expected to take their place on the front lines, and *seniores*, veterans who formed a sort of reserve. Those with inadequate wealth, exempted from military service, only counted one century between them. The political clout of the first class group, with 98 centuries, was therefore enough to form a majority in the new *comitia centuriata*, the political manifestation of the Servian reforms and the successor to the *comitia curiata*. Voting in the *comitia centuriata* was collective, in that a majority vote within a century ensured that that century's single vote went towards approval. This was rather different from the 'one man, one vote' system that characterised Athenian democracy. It was therefore often not necessary to count votes beyond the first and second classes, since the first could carry an individual motion by itself. Only men could vote; women and slaves were excluded from the franchise.

An important feature of these reforms was the way political privilege and responsibility were connected directly to the privilege and responsibility of serving in the military. That the lowest rung on the Servian ladder was *denied* the right to serve in the heavy hoplite infantry and similarly *denied* any sort of political clout is worth underlining. Greater wealth resulted in a higher degree of privilege, obligation, and responsibility. The wealthy bore a disproportionate risk in providing for the army and fighting in it, but stood to gain disproportionately in civic life as a result. Since the wealthy were drawn (in theory) from all of Rome's tribes, this created a powerful sense of communal belonging and mutual obligation. The commingling of the political and the military also resulted in a high level of participation in government by Rome's citizens, and a similarly high level of participation of those citizens in the army, for whom service was not only a duty but a right of citizenship and something worth valuing and fighting for. The reforms also help to explain the development of an ethos among Rome's fighting citizens that was grounded in a fierce pride in the state, and that allowed for repeated long, bloody, and costly conflicts to be sustained, often with tremendous casualties: at the battle of Cannae in 216 BC, for example, it is reckoned that some 80,000 Roman soldiers lost their lives. Livy's magisterial treatment of Cannae and the struggle with Hannibal (Chapter 4) is suffused with an overbearing patriotism and self-belief that many of us today would find strange. Nevertheless, Livy's narrative reflects the social and political cohesion that was afforded by the way that Rome's constitution evolved.

It is sometimes pointed out that the move away from the *curiae* and the reworking of Rome's electoral map via the new tribal organisation broke older aristocratic power blocs, suggesting that the reforms were an early response to the imbalance between rich and poor in Roman society and represented a degree of pushback against the traditional power of Rome's leading families. Certainly the Servian system allowed for a deeper participation in government by the citizenry. On the other hand, family ties, perpetuated by friendship, patronage, and marriage, proved central to Republican government right through the civil wars that transformed it (Chapters 6, 7, and 8). Patronage—favours and support dispensed by a wealthy aristocrat to clients, who could be relied on to further the patron's political career or back him in any number of ways—was a particularly powerful phenomenon in Roman society, which placed the family and its *paterfamilias* at the centre of dense political and financial webs. Furthermore, the *comitia centuriata* entrenched the wealthy at the apex of Rome's political structure, underscoring the oligarchic nature of Roman society, which remained a distinctive feature of the Republic—even if the Romans themselves, and outsiders such as Polybius, occasionally thought otherwise.

From a political standpoint, early Rome was not very different from other ancient communities, particularly regarding the high degree of power exercised by the aristocratic oligarchs relative to the *rex*, who could be fairly weak, and the later struggles between the different groups in society that, over time, resulted in the creation of a more egalitarian political structure and the abandonment of monarchy. In Athens, for example, the tyrant Peisistratus (d. 528/7 BC) championed a form of populism that benefited the lower classes, while weakening the power of the Athenian aristocracy. (Tyrants were not necessarily tyrannical in the modern sense, and Peisistratus gained good press from some of his reforms. Yet he had still seized power by force, and this is what made him a tyrant.) After Peisistratus's son Hipparchus was murdered (514) and his other son, Hippias, deposed (c. 509), Athens became a democracy. As part of that process, the politician Cleisthenes created ten *phulai*, tribes that, like those of the Servian reforms, cut through kinship, ethnicity, and family ties, and were instead based on geography. The political life of Athenian citizens henceforth focused on the *demoi*, sub-tribal units that held the promise of greater democratic participation. This is just one example, but the similarities it offers underscore the relevance of the Mediterranean-wide setting to our understanding of early Rome. The city's political institutions did not develop in a uniquely central 'Roman' context.

On the other hand, Rome's political life was not a mere imitation of Greek city-states as exemplified by the settlements on the Greek mainland or in Magna Graecia, and came to possess distinctive features. Furthermore, Rome succeeded in expanding the state in ways that the Greek city-states never achieved. Later thinkers like Cicero saw in the Servian constitution an idealised form of government, mixing monarchy (the king), democracy (the *comitia centuriata*), and aristocracy in the guise of the patricians in the senate. Precisely the same sort of claim was also made by Polybius in his famous exposé of the Republic (Chapter 2). What made Rome really different from the Greek city-states was that it was what scholars have called a 'citizen-state', where membership—that is to say, citizenship—was not defined by ethnicity, ancestry, or a specific culture. It was also not defined by birth to parents who were citizens, a system that constrained franchise to a limited number of individuals, as was the case in many of the Greek city-states. Instead, citizenship was a legal construct that depended on where one lived and how much wealth one possessed, and was further bolstered by a bedrock of shared laws, communal obligations, privileges, rights, duties, and religious beliefs. Newcomers, like the immigrant Etruscans, Sabines, and Latins remembered in Roman histories, could be incorporated into this form of citizenship, swelling the strength of the state. By reforming the curial system, the constitution attributed to Servius Tullius was therefore the first step in creating an elastic form of citizenship that was compatible with future military expansion. It was also a harbinger of further constitutional reform that revolved around the tension between the wealthy and the less wealthy in society, and questions about the broader question of franchise. The logical endpoints of this were a greater participation of the less wealthy in senior magistracies, the extension of citizenship to the communities of Italy in the first century BC after a bloody struggle known as the Social War, and eventually the extension of Roman citizenship to all free adult males in the empire by the emperor Caracalla in AD 211. None of these developments, of course, happened without violence and bloodshed.

By the end of the sixth century BC, Rome's power was growing rapidly. In about 550, the city had been endowed with a defensive wall of the sort that ringed Etruscan cities, encircling an area significantly larger than most other cities in central Italy (indicated on Figure 1.16, above). Assessing the city's size and population presents a difficult challenge, and historians have offered anywhere from 2.5–3 to 4.25 square kilometres (1–1.15 to 1.64 square miles) with a population anywhere in the region of 20,000 to 35,000. It is, however, clear that by the end of the sixth century Rome possessed significant clout in central Italy and especially in Latium: a treaty between Rome and Carthage, preserved by Polybius (3.22) and dated to 507 BC, agreed that the Carthaginians 'shall not harm the communities of Ardea, Antium, Lavinium, Circeii, Tarracina, or any other Latin community subject to Rome', and further respected Rome's primacy in central Italy by stating that 'any Latin communities that are not subject to Rome shall remain inviolate'. At about the same time, the Etruscan city of Caere made a similar agreement with Carthage, recorded on the Pyrgi tablets. These treaties were agreed during a time of great change: just as the Peisistratid tyrants in Athens were thrown out, so the monarchy at Rome did not last. At some point towards the end of the sixth century—remembered by the Romans as 509 BC, the same date as the demise of Hippias in Athens—the monarchy was abolished as Tarquin the Proud was expelled from Rome. According to legend, Tarquin had abused his office and mistreated the senate. Tarquin's son was also implicated (Chapter 2). Roman historians accorded the place of honour in this transition to Lucius Junius Brutus, who led the movement to rid Rome of Tarquin. (Much later, Brutus, one of the assassins of Caesar, would play up his supposed familial connections to this distant freedom fighter.) Another story involved an Etruscan adventurer from Clusium, Lars Porsenna, who would quickly find himself in conflict with Rome. It is unclear whether either of these men had anything to do with ending the monarchy, since the 'expulsion of a tyrant' narrative was a favourite literary theme for ancient historians, and playing up the removal from Rome of an unsavory character might help to obscure episodes of revolutionary violence. Whatever the case, in place of the monarchy, a republican form of government was established that would last, in various forms, until it was ripped asunder by civil war in the first century BC, and then remade by Rome's first emperor, Augustus. It is time now to consider how that government was formed, and how the people of Rome managed the new challenges and obstacles posed by interclass conflict, external wars, and the expansion of their city.

Chapter 2

The early Republic, 509–280 BC

In the sixth book of the *Histories*, Polybius made a famous digression about the Roman constitution. 'There were,' he said, 'three fundamental building blocks' in the Roman government—monarchy, aristocracy, and democracy, appearing respectively in the guise of the consuls, the senate, and the people. 'Each of them was used so equitably and appropriately in the ordering and arrangement of everything,' Polybius continued, 'that even native Romans were hard put to say for sure whether their constitution was essentially aristocratic, democratic, or monarchic.' The key was balance: more than two thousand years before the French and American revolutions ushered in a new era of distinctively anti-monarchical republican government that was built with checks and counterweights between the different offices, the Romans managed to create what was, to Polybius, 'the best system of government'.

The constitutional question was crucial to Polybius, and the world that he inhabited. In the opening of the *Histories* he asked, with disarming candour, whether any reader could possibly be dull enough not to want to learn about the political machinery of the state that had conquered the Mediterranean (1.1). In practice, of course, the Roman government was far from perfect and was quickly corrupted by cliques, business interests, and ambitious politicians. Foreign wars stretched and tested a government intended to manage local interests, and to run a small city. Rome's nascent imperialism hastened the Republic's demise, as the political system failed to contain the internal discord that accompanied the state's meteoric rise to Mediterranean supremacy.

The picture of the government provided by Polybius reflects his impression of it at a specific moment in time: the end of the war with Hannibal (202 BC), where he judged it to be at its zenith. His analysis therefore offers a sort of idealised and fossilised view of the government, something of which Polybius was well aware. Yet for Polybius it was precisely the constitution and its strength that allowed the Romans to recover from the near-total collapse in their fortunes at the beginning of the Hannibalic war, and ultimately prevail over Hannibal and spread Roman power across the eastern Mediterranean. Three centuries of Republican government preceded that momentous event, however, during which time the constitution evolved in the face of the various influences, both internal and external, that were brought to bear upon it. Many of these influences interacted with one another. Warfare against Rome's enemies, for example, disrupted farming, trade, and commerce, and aggravated debts; it also killed many of Rome's citizens, who farmed the land and created a surplus that was ploughed back into the city's infrastructure and funded its wars. Families and their dependants could be brought to the edge of extinction, as was the case with the Fabii in war against the Etruscans in 479. Such situations helped to

DOI: 10.4324/9781003202523-2

trigger demands for political change, particularly the need for a written legal code, and for greater balance in government.

From monarchy to democracy

The story that Roman writers devised to explain the shift from monarchy to republic was yet another violent tale. In this instance, the story revolved around a vicious assault on a Roman noblewoman, Lucretia, by the son of the king known as Tarquin the Proud. (The twisted nature of the story and the discomfort it caused in Roman society is reflected in the later chauvinistic assertion by Valerius Maximus (6.1.1) that, while Lucretia was 'the champion of Roman chastity, by a nasty mistake of Fortune her manly spirit was allotted the body of a woman'). The story is unlikely to be true, but instead it rather handily provided a clear moral rationale for taking the momentous step of removing the king. The monarchy was replaced by an annual magistracy, which eventually became known as the consulship. Rome's unique contribution to the history of government, the consulship, was eventually an annual and collegial office, held by two elected individuals. The *fasti consulares* is one of our best sources for the holders of the consulship, and its annalistic record reflects the fact that, for a long time, the primary means of dating was through reference to the office. Things took place, for instance, 'in the year when x and y were consuls' (Figure 2.1).

The dual consulship was not instituted immediately, however, and it is possible that at first a single elected official occupied the position of head of government. Livy mentions an official known as the praetor maximus, and the praetor is mentioned elsewhere as an early elected office. (These first mentions of a praetor should not be confused with the later Republican praetorship, which only came into being in 366 BC). In addition to the mysterious praetor maximus, there were also a number of consular tribunes, who resembled the later consuls in their level of imperium. This consular tribunate was used repeatedly throughout the fifth and fourth centuries, often in times of crisis when two consuls would not be sufficient to fight multiple wars simultaneously, and only disappeared with the

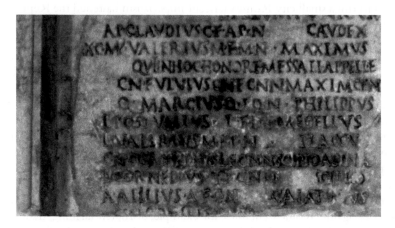

Figure 2.1 Detail of the *fasti consulares*: the top line records the tenure of Appius Claudius Caudex (Chapter 3) as consul in the year 264 BC.

Source: Photograph by José Luiz Bernardes Ribeiro (CC BY-SA 4.0).

Licinian-Sextian laws of 367/66 BC. As much as the Romans might have imagined their *res publica*, 'the public thing', to have sprung fully formed out of the wreckage of the monarchy, the government underwent many changes, and it was only after a century and a half that it began to resemble the system described by Polybius.

The shift from monarchy to a government of magistrates took place in a period of turbulence and uncertainty as new groups challenged the tightly held power of kings and tyrants, demanding greater participation in state governance. Across the Mediterranean world, cities were leaving monarchies and tyrannies behind and, through political turmoil, developing new ways of managing their affairs. As noted in Chapter 1, Athens underwent a momentous change with the removal of the Peisistratids and the transformation of the state towards a democracy. In Italy, conflict in Magna Graecia resulted in constitutional shifts towards annual positions elected by the free male populace. Dictators (magistrates, rather than tyrants) are known from Latium. Internal struggles among the cities of Etruria resulted in the emergence of elected magistrates, known as *zilath*—analogous, perhaps, to the praetor maximus mentioned by Livy. In Campania, Etruscan influence was being challenged by the charismatic tyrant of Cumae, Aristodemos, a holdout among Italy's tyrants of the time. Rome was therefore not unique in suffering from an internal power struggle that resulted in changes to how the government was run.

As the government developed, numerous extraordinary and subordinate magistracies were added over time to manage domestic affairs such as markets, the treasury, the census, and so on, as the need arose. The constitutional arrangement was never formally recorded in writing by the Romans, which helps to account for its malleable nature. On the other hand, there were numerous written laws that governed the rules for different offices and set out their rights and responsibilities. There was also the *mos maiorum*, a phrase that invoked the customs and authority of the elders in society, together with its attendant moral values. To do things according to the *mos maiorum* meant following a tradition of good past practice.

Voting took place in assemblies, and by custom could only take place in Rome. This meant that those from the rural tribes, and later from the growing body of citizenry in Latium and further afield, were placed at a disadvantage. While the *comitia curiata* continued to exist, it ceded its voting power to the *comitia centuriata*, where Rome's adult male citizens elected officials and voted on matters of legislation, war and peace, and all manner of decisions concerning the state. Two new councils were added later on. These were a tribal assembly known as the *comitia tributa* and the *concilium plebis*, or council of the plebs. From about 471 BC, the *concilium plebis* began to vote by tribes, which favoured the large number of rural tribes whose members shouldered the twin pressures of land-related debts and a constant demand for their service as soldiers. It is not entirely clear when the *comitia tributa* was established, but it was certainly working by 367/66 BC, at which time it was given the task of electing the curule aediles. Presiding over these councils was the senate, which usually met in the curia Hostilia or the Temple of Jupiter on the Capitoline Hill, dedicated in 509 and thus providing a symbolic link between Rome's tutelary deity and the new Republic. The senate continued its earlier, pre-Republican role of assembling the city's elder statesmen to provide advice and guidance to the elected magistrates. Over time, the senate's membership came to be drawn from men who had held elected political office. A late fourth-century law ensured that once enrolled in the senate by the censors (below), senators remained there for life. The leading senator, the *princeps senatus*, functioned as a sort of speaker. Contrary to popular belief, the senate did not make law, but it came to possess immense decision-making powers and moral authority as Rome's empire developed, and the determinations it reached were ignored by consuls at their peril.

The system of individual offices, as it was constructed throughout the fifth and fourth centuries BC, built on earlier Italian traditions, such as the position of dictator, as well as Roman innovations, of which the best example is the collegial consulship. Eventually, the Roman system came to look like this:

- *Interrex*   Appointed to provide continuity of government in an extreme emergency; time-limited to five days, during which he would arrange consular elections. Chosen from among the patrician *gentes*.
- Dictator   Appointed by the consuls and the senate during an emergency, such as in the aftermath of a military catastrophe. Assumed the imperium of both consuls, and was attended by 24 lictors, attendants who carried the *fasces* and represented the dictator's imperium. Time-limited to six months, after which consular elections would be held; expected to resign if the emergency ended (e.g. Cincinnatus, below).
- Master of   The dictator's second in command, similarly time-limited to six months.
  cavalry

These three positions were unique in that they were appointed rather than being elected. The dictatorship was a common feature of many of the military crises in which Rome found itself between the fifth century and the end of the third century BC.

The government's main working machinery was the group of unpaid elected positions that, with the exception of the censor, were all limited to a single year in office. The offices outlined here made up what later became known as the *cursus honorum*, the career-track for the ambitiously minded Roman nobleman. Such an individual would begin with the quaestorship or, later, the tribune of the plebs, and aim to be elected consul later in his career.

- Censors   Elected for an 18-month period once every five years to carry out the census, the basis for political and military duties, and to assign individuals to tribes, assess property, family members, etc. Also maintained a roll of 'morally good' senators, and thus became responsible (after the fourth century) for determining membership of the senate; managed Rome's public lands, the *ager publicus*; and purified the state via a ceremony at the close of the census. The two office holders were ex-consuls with an impeccable moral pedigree and considerable experience. The office dates to 443 BC, and carried no imperium.
- Consuls   The two chief magistrates of the Republic, and the pinnacle of political life. Consuls held imperium *domi militiaeque*—literally 'at home and at war', which meant both inside and outside the pomerium. Within the city they presided over civil affairs, while outside they led Rome's armies on campaign. Consuls also retained some of the religious duties of the monarchy and took the auspices—a rite through which consuls looked for divine approval for their office and major actions, such as setting out

to wage war. They were attended by 12 lictors and were elected by the *comitia centuriata*, which they had the right to summon to assembly. The use of the *fasces*, carried by the lictors, together with the purple-hemmed toga worn by consuls, represented continuity with older Etruscan royal paraphernalia.

- Praetors   Initially just one (366 BC), intended to deal with matters of jurisdiction in Rome. Later, a second praetor joined the first (242 BC). The praetorship was greatly expanded in response to the need to manage Rome's growing empire after the end of the Hannibalic War. The praetors' imperium was less than that of the consuls, to whom they were subordinate, and a praetor was allowed only six lictors. Praetors could command armies and represented the consuls when the latter were out of the city. Elected by the *comitia centuriata*.

- Aediles   The aediles managed the games in Rome, as well as the markets and other duties, including weights and measures, and policing. The office dates from 493 BC, but was later expanded in 366 to include two curule (patrician) aediles as colleagues to their plebeian aedile counterparts; the aediles possessed no imperium and were elected by the *comitia tributa/ concilium plebis*. Much of the work carried out by aediles was funded at their own expense, which could benefit a rich family of poor standing looking to increase its political visibility.

- Quaestors   Financial officials who managed the public treasury. In common with the praetors, the quaestorship was expanded as the territory controlled by Rome grew. The quaestors, of whom there were four elected each year, possessed no imperium, and were elected by the *comitia tributa*.

Another office introduced during the Republican period was the tribune of the plebs, which is discussed in more detail below. It occupied a special place in the ascending hierarchy of offices, sitting somewhat to the side and able to throttle any official except for a censor or a dictator. Below the quaestors, a collection of 20 minor offices known as the *vigintivirate* was later instituted, which gave junior politicians a start in government.

Not formally part of the *cursus honorum*, but indivisible from the social and political life of the city, were the various religious offices that existed alongside the religious functions of elected magistrates, forming a bridge between the land of man and the land of the gods. Roman polytheist religion was performative and ritualistic, involving rites such as sacrifices that were intended to regulate the relationship with the gods and earn their favour. The *rex sacrorum* represented a continuity from the Roman monarchy and was responsible for the rites and practices that previously had been performed by the king. A patrician who held the job for life (and who was barred from other public office), the *rex sacrorum* served the god Janus; the nobility of the position ensured that sufficient respect was afforded the gods through being served by a 'member of royalty'. The second most important priest was the *pontifex maximus*, the chief priest, who held an office that was a long-time patrician bastion and jealously guarded. He presided over the college of pontiffs, initially made up of three senior *flamines*, or priests, who served the Capitoline Triad. Patricians initially held a stranglehold on the college of pontiffs as well, but eventually, as it expanded, plebeians came to make up nearly half of their number, contributing junior *flamines* who tended to other gods and goddesses such as Ceres (below). The *flamines* possessed immense authority: they managed the religious calendar, maintained records, including the *fasti*, and carried out important rituals such as burying the dead. Their control over the calendar also meant that it was they who decided on what days certain activities, such as electing officials or carrying out business, were permissible, and they also provided advice and counsel to public officials. Furthermore, since public business was typically conducted in a place that had been prepared by priests or had religious significance—the senate, for example, could only meet in a sacred place—Rome's priests had important political clout.

Also members of the college of pontiffs were the six Vestal Virgins who tended to Rome's communal hearth and carried out ritual functions at festivals. Drawn from patrician families at a very young age and expected to serve with celibacy for a 30-year period, the Vestal Virgins represented one of the rare opportunities for women to hold important positions within the state's hierarchy.

Besides the college of pontiffs, a plethora of other groups and officials existed. The college of augurs assisted elected magistrates in taking the auspices, principally by observing birds or other animals, and conducted rituals that 'inaugurated' important structures such as temples. Auspices determined whether all manner of activities, from going to war to public business, could be carried out, and a poor reading of the auspices could cause even the most carefully managed event to be postponed or cancelled; failure to follow the auspices or correctly read omens could lead to disaster. Another college of priests maintained the *Sibylline Books*, a collection of oracles that arrived in Rome from Cumae, and could be consulted during times of crisis. A fourth, the college of the *fetiales*, conducted rituals concerned with war and peace treaties between Rome and her neighbours. There were also more than 60 *haruspices* who inspected the innards of animals that had been sacrificed, and whose services were used before meetings of the senate and other important events such as elections. The *haruspices*, like the augurs, traced their practices to older, Etruscan religious customs.

The establishment of magistracies in place of a single king benefited the wealthy aristocrats in Roman society by spreading power among a series of offices for which they could compete each year. Similarly, the near-monopoly on the senior priesthoods held by the patrician *gentes* ensured that the important moral authority that such positions carried remained within a tightly circumscribed group. All this helped to perpetuate the oligarchy at the apex of Roman politics, which might otherwise appear to outsiders such as Polybius as a balanced, ideal form of government. Nevertheless, there were checks and balances. Offices were (eventually) collegial, which meant that each consul or junior magistrate had a colleague who could, in theory, rein in wayward behaviour. Typically, each office required the candidate to have held its direct predecessor: one could not be praetor, for example, without having held the office of quaestor. At various times, age requirements were also part of these restrictions, and these rules were aimed to ensure that only the most experienced men could run for the individual offices, and to ensure an equitable sharing of power for Rome's leading families. As with many of the rules governing the Republic, those governing experience and age requirements were quickly broken (Chapters 3 and 4).

Experiments in government

One of the driving forces behind the development of the Roman constitution, and particularly its system of checks and balances, was a class conflict commonly known as 'the struggle of the orders'. It revolved around tension between patrician and plebeian families and competition for the top magistracies, in particular the consulship. Debt, interest rates, and debt repayment were also key concerns. It has long been debated whether the key moments of the struggle remembered by Rome's historians actually happened in the shape that has come down to us in the literary sources, or whether they were adjusted or fabricated in the later historical record to make sense of more contemporary events. For instance, concerns over private ownership of the *ager publicus*, addressed in a law of 367/66 BC, overlap considerably with similar, but far more passionate, debates on the same topic from the 130s BC, which witnessed considerable public violence (Chapter 6). Those arguing that the historical record preserves the memory of actual events point to the fact that issues of land ownership, together with questions of debt, had a long history among the political and class struggles of the ancient Mediterranean, and especially ancient Greece; there is no reason to suppose that these were not significant problems in Italy, which was also an agrarian society. It is therefore reasonable to find legislation and debates in the historical record addressing the serious problems that occurred, especially during difficult economic times or periods of sustained military conflict. In the fifth century, for instance, numerous food shortages caused havoc in Rome, and at certain points a corn dole was instituted, while it was necessary to bring in grain from Latium, Etruria, and even as far afield as Sicily. The people most likely to feel the impact of these issues were, of course, the less well off in society, who worked the land as subsistence farmers. Furthermore, following the establishment of the Servian constitution, land had become intimately linked to the duties and obligations of military service. The rather pragmatic solutions to problems of land and debt that were found during the struggle of the orders reflect the fact that the state needed its farmers to succeed so they could feed the state and defend it in time of war.

Historians have also questioned the rather neat distinction between patricians and plebeians found in ancient sources. Livy, for example, traced the origins of the patrician order back to Romulus, thus providing it with an unassailable level of moral authority. This view of the patricians is more likely to reflect efforts by leading families to hold on to what they saw as their prerogative to wield power in the Republic. Romulus had been king, so his foundation of the patrician order devolved some of that authority onto them. Remus, by contrast, had violated the pomerium, was murdered, and was also associated with the Aventine Hill, which became a centre for plebeian religious activity in the Republic: the implications were clear for all to see. This simplistic notion of two classes in society pitted against each other is belied by the fact that some of the *gentes*, such as the Claudii, possessed both patrician and plebeian branches. The view provided by the struggle of the orders in ancient sources is exaggerated and was largely driven by later political concerns—the first-century BC Republic had sharply split down political lines—but it is also thoroughly believable that some families shut out of the top magistracies and priesthoods by somewhat anachronistic views of patrician privilege would agitate for access to those positions to improve their lot and the lot of their dependants. So, while the struggle of the orders as presented to us by Livy and others does not present an unbiased picture of what happened, it is clear that solutions were found to complex problems through negotiation, dialogue, and occasional violence, and that these managed to shape the development of Rome's constitution.

According to the narrative, in around 495/94 BC the plebeians seceded from the city in protest against what they judged to be an unfair system, rigged for the benefit of the patricians. One of the central issues of this secession was debt, along with the arbitrary nature of judgements against debtors. In extreme situations, a debtor could be killed or sold into slavery if he was unable to repay his patron within a specified timeframe; at the very least, given the astronomical interest rates that were levied, he could be expected to work for the rest of his life for his creditor, never escaping his debt. This cruel situation was known as *nexum*, or debt bondage, and occupied a recurring place in the struggle of the orders before it was finally outlawed at the end of the fourth century BC (a fact that reflects the plentiful supply of slaves through other means, such as conquest). By seceding, the plebeians physically left the city, ceased working on the farms and, most importantly given Rome's conflicts against the Volsci and the Sabines at the time, took no part in Rome's military levy. The complaints of the plebeians were recognised, and some debts were lifted while a new office, the tribune of the plebs (or, more simply, 'plebeian tribune'), was created to provide better representation for the plebeians in government and to protect them against arbitrary judgement. Elected only from among plebeian candidates, there were initially two plebeian tribunes, before another two were added around 470 BC; later, the number grew to ten. The *concilium plebis*, which elected the plebeian tribunes, is thought to date from the post-secession settlement.

While it remained a low-ranking office throughout the Republican period, the plebeian tribune had special powers inside the pomerium. By a law of 449 BC (below), it could veto the decision made by a magistrate, including a consul, if it was felt to be against the interests of the plebeians. The holder of the office was also sacrosanct and inviolate for the duration of his tenure, meaning that he could stand up to an otherwise more powerful magistrate without fear for his safety. This was especially useful when intervening on another's behalf. Plebeian tribunes also possessed the authority to convene the senate, and to submit motions and laws for debate. The secession and the creation of the tribunate were the first hints that a parallel political organisation was emerging, which over time empowered the plebs even as they broke the patrician stranglehold on senior offices. This political correspondence is also visible in the emergence of religious cults specifically linked to plebeians and centred on the Aventine Hill in Rome, which lay outside the pomerium. These cults were of Ceres (goddess of the harvest), Liber (wine), and Libera (also wine, but linked to Demeter, Greek goddess of the harvest). This Aventine triad balanced the Capitoline Triad and its link to the *pontifex maximus*, an office on which the patricians held a firm grip throughout the fifth and fourth centuries BC.

The next major development was the creation of the Twelve Tables, a set of laws that regulated some of the most important concerns of an agricultural society comprising owners, borrowers, and lenders. These laws had been assembled by a group of ten men, the *decemviri*, who appeared in place of the consuls in 451 and 450 BC. Plebeians formed a part of this commission, which was essentially superimposed over the normal workings of government for the two-year period it needed to complete its task. Some of the Twelve Tables addressed ownership of slaves, land, livestock, fruit trees, and so on; other parts set rules for marriage and divorce, the status of women, ownership of property, and the rights of duties of the male head of the household, the *paterfamilias*—the most important individual in the fifth-century Roman social hierarchy. Rudimentary legislation also provided for the settlement of disputes and for the application of the death penalty, and the lot of debtors was improved somewhat. (Interestingly, the Twelve Tables took a dim view of luxurious burials, suggesting that the period was either a time of financial uncertainty, or that a change had taken place in society that frowned upon Sybaritic displays of wealth).

The Twelve Tables represented a momentous event in the development of the state, which now had a written law code that limited arbitrary judgements: henceforth, the citizen body 'owned' the laws, and could consult the written texts themselves on public display in the forum (although today only fragments survive). The need to codify a basic set of laws in order to prevent arbitrary actions by the elite, or to prevent the manipulation of an oral set of laws to the benefit of a particular group, had a lengthy precedent elsewhere in the Mediterranean, notably in archaic Greece. Draco, who gave us 'Draconian' laws, carried out such a task in seventh-century BC Athens, and the Romans thought that a mission had once been sent from Rome to Athens to see what could be learned about the law code of Solon, the famous seventh/sixth-century BC statesman. (This legend may reflect Greek influences on Roman law from the much more accessible cities of Magna Graecia, rather than Athens.) The demand for the Twelve Tables had largely come from the newly formed *concilium plebis*, which represented plebeian interests under the leadership of the plebeian tribunes. Towards the end of their mandate, the *decemviri* tried to usurp political power and keep themselves in office. In response, the plebeians seceded once again, the *decemviri* were forced to step down, and the consulship returned.

After the establishment of the Twelve Tables, a new round of laws were passed in 449 by the consuls for the year, Marcus Horatius Barbatus and Lucius Valerius Potitus. Once again, these further strengthened the position of the plebeians in Roman society. They granted a veto to the plebeian tribune, as noted earlier, and declared the sacrosanctity of the plebeian tribunes: the penalty for attacking one was forfeiture of property to Ceres, Liber, and Libera (the plebeian cults on the Aventine Hill), with the guilty party then given over to Jupiter's wrath. The Valerio-Horatian laws, named for the two consuls, also firmly established the existing right of *provocatio*—the right of appeal—and allowed for plebiscites. These were decisions of the *concilium plebis* and later, under the Hortensian law of 287 BC, they were eventually considered binding on all of Rome's citizenry. Four years after the Valerio-Horatian laws were passed, in 445 BC, another law permitted the intermarriage of plebeians and patricians. One of the consequences of these fifth-century laws was the clear establishment of the sovereignty of the people over the consuls. The later Hortensian law confirmed this by underscoring the importance of the *concilium plebis* (which by then had essentially merged with the *comitia tributa*) as the main decision-making body in the Republic. No law could be passed, and no new positions in the government created, without putting the matter to the people.

Despite these important steps towards a more balanced constitution, which included the election of the first plebeian to the quaestorship in 409 BC, the major prize—the consulship—still largely eluded the plebeians. In many years, only patricians held the consulship, and this pattern of inconsistent access to plebeian candidates continued into the fourth century BC. In the second quarter of the fourth century, however, two plebeian tribunes clung to office—for another rather suspicious ten-year period, according to

Livy—and disrupted the work of the consuls, requiring the senate to activate the emergency office of dictator to restore order. The result of this period of strife was ultimately a triumph for the plebeians, and the so-called Licinian-Sextian laws, named for the two troublesome tribunes, opened up the consulship to the plebeians in 367/66 BC. A later law in 342 BC mandated that one of the two consuls had to be plebeian, and imposed some limits on the system by preventing an individual from holding more than one magistracy at the same time, as well as by banning the tenure of the same office twice in a ten-year period. The Licinian-Sextian laws also formalised the consulship as the highest elected office in Rome (the consular tribunate was henceforth abolished) and instituted the praetorship, to which plebeians gained access nine years later, in 356 BC. In 351 BC, plebeians could run for the censorship and finally, at the turn of the third century BC, plebeians were allowed access to the chief priesthood, the *pontifex maximus*. Plebeians also made up close to half of the college of pontiffs, which was expanded to accommodate its new members.

The Licinian-Sextian laws are usually understood to be a watershed moment in the history of the Republic, because they fixed the quintessential features of the *cursus honorum*: quaestor, aedile, praetor, consul. However, the laws also contained two other elements addressing much more serious problems: debt and land ownership. In the first instance, debts were reduced and action was taken against sky-high interest rates. Creditors would be repaid in instalments rather than in one single sum, the non-payment of which, when demanded, could often force someone into debt bondage. The second question was more complex. In tandem with the struggles within the city, Rome had engaged in a number of conflicts with its neighbours, (examined in the next section). One of the benefits that accrued to Rome was the *ager publicus*, the 'public land' captured after a successful military campaign. The main questions about this land were how it should be used, and by whom. The issue was made all the more urgent in 367 because by then Rome was technically at peace with its Latin neighbours, so there were not many opportunities to add to the *ager publicus*. The solution proposed by the Licinian-Sextian laws was to restrict private ownership of the *ager publicus* to about 130 hectares (330 acres) per farmer, which curbed the apparent tendency of some among Rome's wealthiest to gobble up large tracts to the detriment of subsistence farmers. This would not be the last word on the matter, and it would return to haunt Republican law-makers in the 130s BC.

The changes to Rome's government outlined here took place over a long period of time—almost a century and a half from the date when Roman writers thought the monarchy was abolished. The constitution was a continual work in progress, characterised by a willingness to experiment but also a readiness to respond to and accommodate grievances and complaints. This dialogue between the different groups in Roman society, expressed most of all through the struggle of the orders, was not without violence and heated argument. Nor did it always resolve some of the imbalances in the system: in the 50-year period following the passing of the Licinian-Sextian laws, a small number of people dominated the highest offices of the state despite efforts to limit precisely this taking place.

On the other hand, the continual negotiation between the different members of society resulted in the creation of a government with some remarkable features. The hierarchy of offices provided an outlet for aristocratic ambition, channelling it towards service to the state. It was by vying for the consulship that *gloria*—renown—could be won by courageous and dedicated individuals who exhibited *virtus*, or virtue (see below). Success on the battlefield might earn the victorious Roman consul, dictator, or praetor a triumph, a parade inside the pomerium that enshrined his service for eternity in the *fasti*: indeed, for the fifth and fourth centuries alone, the *fasti* record 51 separate triumphs. Above all, and despite serious problems and differences, political consensus was often found amidst an increasingly broadly based political elite. For Polybius, this was what explained Rome's incredible ability to survive periods of shocking adversity, and to prevail in time of war over the fiercest of opponents.

Rome and her neighbours

Running parallel to and influencing the political developments discussed earlier was regular conflict between Rome and her neighbours. The participation of the plebeians in Rome's military levies made them necessary partners for the patricians; without their manpower contribution, the state could not have survived, which helps to explain how negotiation and compromise resolved the struggle of the orders in favour of the plebeians. Rome's early wars quickly became part of the city's mythology, and are sometimes diffi-cult to date with precision or narrate with confidence. The Romans went to war almost every year, which meant that virtually all of Rome's adult male citizens could be expected to fight at one point or another—a fact that entrenched violence at the heart of Roman identity.

In order to ensure that war was conducted in accordance with the wishes of the gods, the Romans carefully nurtured a concept of the legal and morally just war. The college of the *fetiales* were tasked with demanding restitution from communities that were deemed to have crossed Rome or hurt its interests. If the ritual was followed properly and no res-titution was forthcoming within the 33-day prescribed time period, the Romans could claim—if only to themselves—that the war was a just and fair conflict that had divine support. War could then be declared by a fetial priest hurling a spear into enemy territory. Closely linked to ideas about legal warfare was the concept of *fides*, good faith overseen by the gods, which governed important agreements such as treaties and acted as a guarantor of good behaviour. Later, communities at war with Rome could surrender through a process known as *deditio in fidem*, whereby they placed themselves at the mercy of Rome's good faith. After the Romans violently sacked the towns and villages of the Aequi, for example, a number of neighbouring communities pre-empted a similar result for their own people by petitioning for Roman 'friendship'. *Fides* was also idealised as one of the Republic's defining moral characteristics, alongside *pietas* (piety), *gravitas* (self-discipline and control), and *constantia* (constancy, a sort of tenacity or persistence). Together, these made up what the Romans called *virtus*, or virtue, which could be expressed best through selfless service towards the state and the suppression of personal ambitions. Late Republican writers such as Livy excelled in providing examples of virtuous individuals as lessons for their readers.

Roman writers remembered a series of struggles with Rome's neighbours at the turn of the fifth century BC. In about 505 or 504 BC, there was a conflict with Lars Porsenna and the ousted king Tarquin, which ended in a Roman victory. From this came the famous story of Horatius Cocles, one of many individuals displaying *virtus* who Livy and others plucked from Rome's ancient past for the benefit of their readership. According to legend, Horatius heroically defended the Sublician Bridge over the river Tiber, delaying the advancing forces of Lars Porsenna until the bridge could be brought down. Horatius was from the *gens* Horatii, a family that had earned fame in an even older legend dating to the seventh century. The Horatii had settled a dispute with neighbouring Alba Longa by sending three brothers to fight the same number of kinsmen from Alba Longa, thus sparing Rome an all-out battle; two of the Horatii died, expending their lives to save the population of Rome, while the survivor prevailed over all three from Alba Longa. Both of these stories proved popular in later years, with Horatius receiving an epic treatment in verse by Thomas Babington Macaulay's *Lays of Ancient Rome* (1842). Macaulay captured the heady patriotism that the story of Horatius at the bridge came to hold for later Romans, endowing the noble warrior, who was willing to die to save the city, with a speech that included the famous lines:

> And how can man die better
> Than facing fearful odds
> For the ashes of his fathers
> And the temples of his gods

Such devotion to the *patres* and to *pietas* was *virtus* exemplified. The sacrifices of the Horatii in the conflict with Alba Longa were immortalised by the French master Jacques Louis-David in his famous work *The Oath of the Horatii* (1784, now in the Louvre).

Following their victory over Lars Porsenna, the Romans found themselves in a new conflict with the cities of Latium, which came together in times of military need in an alliance known as the Latin League. Facing a determined onslaught, the Romans appointed a dictator, who Livy says was Aulus Postumius Albus, a scion of one of Rome's leading patrician families. Many of the *gens* Postumia would hold high office in the Republic, and several would lose their lives defending it. Together with his deputy, the master of cavalry, Aulus won a famous triumph at Lake Regillus (a few miles northeast of Frascati) against a combined Latin force led by Rome's ousted king Tarquin, in either 499 or 496 BC. Afterwards, in 484 BC, the Romans dedicated a temple to the Dioscuri—Castor and Pollux, who legend declared had fought on the Roman side; such thanksgiving dedications emerged as a common product of Roman military triumphs. With this show of strength, Rome cemented an alliance, the Cassian Treaty, with the Latin League in 493 BC. This mutual defence pact placed Rome and the Latins as equals with common interests, which meant that troops from the Latin League became involved in Rome's wars. This situation worked to both parties' advantage, strengthening trading ties between the different cities; it was also effective because Rome and the Latins were both threatened by their fierce and warlike neighbours, particularly the Aequi, Hernici, and Volsci (Figure 2.2).

Later, the Cassian Treaty was extended to include the Hernici, who were uncomfortably sandwiched between the Aequi and Volsci in Latium Adiectum ('Adjacent Latium'), the southern, hilly district of Latium bordering on Campania. (The Hernici judged that an alliance with the settlements of Latium Vetus ('Old Latium'), which included Rome and the cities of the Latin League, was preferable to putting themselves at the mercy of either the Volsci or the Aequi.) On the other hand, the Cassian Treaty was somewhat lopsided: the Romans retained half of the plunder and booty that came from a successful campaign, even though much of the army was supplied by the cities of the Latin League.

Not long after the battle at Lake Regillus, the Romans fought the Volsci, generating another of Rome's many heroic legends. In about 490/89 BC, a Roman general named Gaius Marcius had warded off an aggressive sally from the Volscian city of Corioli and

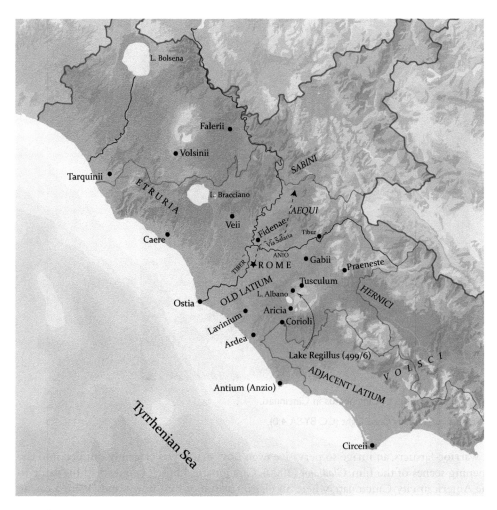

Figure 2.2 Rome and her neighbours in the fifth century BC.

Source: Illustration by the author.

then managed to capture it. For this he gained the epithet Coriolanus—although, after falling out with his patrician brethren in Rome, he then aligned himself with the Volscians. Leading an army against Rome, he agreed not to attack the city after both his mother and wife, in a staunch display of the power of Roman matriarchs, appealed to his better sentiments. The story of Gaius and his career inspired numerous works of art, including Shakespeare's play *Coriolanus* and Beethoven's *Coriolan Overture*. Another famous Roman warrior was Lucius Quinctius Cincinnatus, who in 458 BC was famously plucked from his farm, where he was diligently tilling the land, to save Rome from the depredations of the Aequi. His job done in a little over two weeks, Cincinnatus laid down his army command and went back to his farm, offering an unwavering display of *virtus* for future generations. From this and other stories developed the persistent Roman idea of Romans

Figure 2.3 The statue of Cincinnatus in Cincinnati.

Source: Photograph by Chris Light (CC BY-SA 4.0).

as warrior-farmers, an image so pervasive even now that it was elegantly distilled into the opening scenes of the film *Gladiator* (2000). Cincinnatus himself bequeathed his name to the American city Cincinnati, where an elegant statue of him now stands. With a caring look on his face and deep, intelligent eyes, Cincinnatus returns the fasces and takes up the plough (Figure 2.3).

During the same stretch of time, Aristodemos of Cumae was engaged in a determined attempt to lessen Etruscan influence in Campania, eventually succeeding with a naval victory over the Etruscans in 474 BC. This had been won with the assistance of the Sicilian city of Syracuse, whose tyrant, Hiero I, was flexing his muscles in southern Italy and was keen to prevent any further spread of Etruscan power. In the meantime, relations between Rome and the Etruscan city of Veii deteriorated and the two cities fought a short conflict between 483 and 474. Struggles continued with the Aequi and the Volsci, and the Sabines raided Roman territory successfully in the 460s BC. Tensions between Rome and Veii continued to simmer, particularly over the city of Fidenae, which lay adjacent to the via Salaria. In a short war between 437 and 435 BC, the Romans wrested control over Fidenae; the conflict is notable for the tales woven about the heroics of Aulus Cornelius Cossus, who bested Veii's leader, Lars Tolumnius, in single combat. For his bravery, Cossus earned the *spolia opima*, an honour merited by the man who killed the enemy leader. The weapons and gear of Lars Tolumnius were taken back to Rome and dedicated to Jupiter in thanksgiving for the Roman victory.

Rome's historians assign a somewhat suspicious ten-year period for the third and final war with Veii, which included a lengthy siege (406–396 BC). This dating reveals the pervasive influence that stories of the Trojan War held among the city's literary elite; the war was probably longer than usual, on the other hand, and saw the state establish a stipend (likely funded by war plunder) for its soldiers to cover basic costs. Legend says that the great Roman hero of the war, the dictator Marcus Furius Camillus, achieved victory after calling out Veii's patron goddess Juno–Uni to desert the city, after which it was sacked and the cult statue of Juno taken to Rome to be installed in a purpose-built temple on the Aventine. Shorn of its divine protection, Veii and its territory was annexed by Rome and Camillus was hailed as a new Romulus. Those of its citizens not enrolled in the four new Roman tribes created after the war were enslaved or exiled, and Roman citizens settled in Veii's territory. This combination of added land and additions to the citizen body created a larger pool of military manpower, a process that became something of a self-fulfilling prophecy as Rome's reach expanded. Afterwards, Rome began to capture port cities on the Etruscan coast—but in 390 BC, disaster struck.

The supposed sack of Rome by the Gauls in the early fourth century BC, followed by two subsequent Gallic incursions, made a significant impact on Rome's collective memory and its self-identity. The Gauls, who hailed from northern Italy and the districts beyond the Alps, raided deep into Etruria and Latium in about 390 BC. It is unclear how much damage was actually done to Rome's buildings and infrastructure, since the 'sack' described by later writers has not shown up clearly in the archaeological record. Nevertheless, the Romans remembered a terrible defeat at the river Allia, north-east of Rome, and felt sufficiently threatened to buttress their existing network of defensive walls. Roman historians viewed the Gallic invasion as a near-death experience, and this idea of the past did much to galvanise the Roman people's sense of community, as well as to strengthen Rome's militaristic, aggressive ethos. Livy says that in the aftermath of the catastrophe, the Romans decided to rebuild their shattered city rather than decamp to Veii, which was thought to offer defensive advantages over Rome. The rebuilding is presented as a sort of rebirth—and indeed, in the Roman view of the past, violent setbacks provided opportunities for renewal, most notably under the emperor Augustus (Chapter 8). The Gallic leader Brennus became, like Vercingetorix (Chapter 7), a French national hero. A pre-dreadnought battleship launched in 1896 bore his name; the ship's figurehead, showing a proud and moustachioed Brennus with a winged crown, has been preserved in the Musée Nationale de la Marine in Toulon.

The 390s BC were also a turbulent period in southern Italy, as the tyrant of Syracuse, Dionysius I, launched an ambitious campaign against the Greek cities of Locri and Croton. Dionysius was not the only outsider to covet southern Italian territory, with the Spartan mercenary Cleonymos and Alexander of Epirus (the brother of Olympias, Alexander the Great's mother) fighting hard in the relentless local struggles. In central Italy, the mid-fourth century saw Roman power re-established in the aftermath of the Gallic invasion. Wars were fought with Praeneste and Tibur in Latium, who were eventually beaten and compelled to accept Roman friendship. Several Latin cities broke from Rome and allied themselves with the Volsci, while there were conflicts with the Etruscan cities of Caere and Tarquinii. These recurring bouts of violent conflict may have helped bring about the Licinian-Sextian laws, through worsening the lot of debtors and bringing significant additions to the *ager publicus*; the abolition of the consular tribunate may also be linked in some way to the performance of Rome's armies against her neighbours. The consuls, who in 367/66 BC had replaced the consular tribunes, were soon in action when the Gauls returned in 350/49 BC. Rome was forced to fight alone as the cities of Latium ignored their treaty obligations—perhaps in the hope that the Gauls would help to redress the growing power imbalance between Rome and her neighbours. The clash was of sufficient concern to attract a fleet from Sicily, which apparently stood offshore and waited to see which side emerged victorious. Those wishing for a Roman humiliation were disappointed. If anything, the outcome of this round of conflict with Gallic invaders served to confirm Rome's dramatic emergence as the regional powerbroker in central Italy.

In about 343, the Romans became embroiled in a contest with the Samnites, a hill people who lived in the Apennines east of Campania. The Samnites, who spoke the Oscan language, a relative of Latin, had emerged as a serious foe during the fifth century BC. Their cultural and political life was focused around villages, religious sanctuaries, and hilly redoubts, and they were organised under the authority of an elected official, known as a *meddix*, whose position was analogous to a *zilath* or a consul. The Samnites have left behind fascinating archaeological remains, such as the temple and theatre complex high up in the hills at modern Pietrabbondante (Figure 2.4).

The architecture of the sanctuary at Pietrabbondante is distinctively Greek in inspiration—likely due to the cultural traffic between Samnium and Campania. Indeed, during the fifth century the Samnites expanded their influence south and west into the settlements of Campania, and many of the beautiful funerary frescoes associated with the Samnites were discovered in this region, including at Paestum and Nola (Figure 2.5).

Figure 2.4 Google Earth Pro image of the Samnite archaeological site at Pietrabbondante, Italy.

Source: Image © 2020 Google.

Figure 2.5 Fresco depicting Samnite warriors, from a tomb at Nola in Campania.

Source: Wikimedia Commons/Public Domain.

In 423 BC, the Samnites took control of Capua, the metropolis of Campania that controlled a large territory. Through its port cities, Capua boasted an enviable access to the trade routes of the Mediterranean. Subsequently a number of the Greek colonies in the region fell to the Samnites in isolated bouts of violence, and over time the Etrusco-Campanian nobility was supplanted by an Oscan-speaking elite. Even though there is evidence for the continuity of Greek religious practices and material culture, Etruscan customs that had been common in the sixth century BC disappeared. These demographic changes, accompanied by a noticeable shift in burial practices, did much to change a society dominated by the older, Etrusco-Campanian aristocracy. Before long, Roman and Samnite interests collided, and in 354 BC the two states agreed a treaty, which fixed the boundary between them at the river Liris. Not long afterwards, however, open conflict erupted in the First Samnite War (343–41 BC). The trigger was a request for help from Capua. This forced the Romans to weigh their options carefully, as the treaty with the Samnites was still in force. Desperate, Capua offered itself up through a *deditio in fidem*, which ultimately trumped Rome's other obligations.

After the First Samnite War fizzled out, Rome fought the Latin War (340–38 BC), a far more serious conflict. In an illustration of the shifting alliances of the period, Rome fought its erstwhile allies, the Latin League, with the Samnites as Roman allies and the Gauls and Campanians, who were helping the Latins, as their enemies. In this conflict, the Romans crushed the remaining resistance in Latium and among the Volsci, whose own motives for fighting were, like those of the Latins, driven by concern about Rome's growing power. One of the most famous examples of *virtus* belongs to this period. Livy tells the story of how one of the consuls had his own son, Torquatus, executed for disobeying a prohibition against single combat—despite the fact that Torquatus had been victorious over an immense and powerful Gallic warrior. This parable of duty over personal glory was arrayed alongside the stories of incredible suffering and devotion that emerged from the Samnite Wars and the Gallic invasions, all of which could be used to build Rome's myths and legends, and provide guidance during times of great catastrophe.

The Romans found it difficult to suppress the Samnites, and they never forgot their defeat at the Caudine Forks during the Second Samnite War (327–04 BC), where beaten and demoralised Roman soldiers—including both consuls—were made to march, with backs bent, under a yoke of Samnite spears (Figure 2.6). The humiliation of defeat was long lived; the senate, furious at what had happened, was said to have given the defeated consuls back to the Samnites for punishment. Also well suited to the purposes of writers such as Livy—although for different reasons—was the personal sacrifice of the plebeian Publius Decius Mus at Sentinum (near modern Sassoferrato) in 295 BC during the Third Samnite War. Facing not just the Samnites but also formidable levies of Etruscans, Gauls, and Umbrians, Publius Decius Mus, who had been consul numerous times between 312 and 295 BC, sacrificed himself in order to save the Roman army, repeating the sacrifice of his own father in similar circumstances against the Latins in 340 BC. Livy records that he performed the *devotio*, a religious ritual presided over by the *pontifex maximus* during which Publius exchanged his life for Roman victory. In his final moments, Publius called down curses on the enemy and then charged to his death (Livy, 10.28).

By the time that the Third Samnite War concluded in 291, Rome was in command of vast swathes of central Italy and in a position to force its neighbours into uneven

Figure 2.6 Campania and Samnium in the fourth and third centuries BC.

Source: Illustration by the author.

agreements where Rome decided the terms. Even as Roman armies operated in Samnium, others crushed the Aequi and campaigned against the Umbrians and Etruscan holdouts such as Volsinii (sacked in 265). The later revolt of Falerii in 241 was the last glimmer of Etruscan resistance, and ended with savage Roman retribution and the 'capture' of its tutelary deity, Minerva, and her transportation to Rome. The Etruscans were finally defeated, their vanquished people eventually disappearing into the growing population of the Roman state and many of their aristocrats joining the Roman nobility. It is a noteworthy coincidence that the defeat of the Latins, and the end of individual city states as viable political units, was paralleled in Greece by the victory of Philip II, the father of Alexander the Great, over the various Greek city states led by Athens and Thebes that stood against him on the battlefield at Chaeronea (338 BC).

Master of central Italy

Rome concealed its virtual conquest of the Latins, Samnites, Etruscans, and others through a system of treaties, alliances, and a variable form of citizenship. This flexible and pragmatic approach turned defeated enemies into subordinate allies with limited incentive or means to revolt. The network of allies also provided an important source of manpower. These new alliances were individual and bilateral: all interaction between Rome's new dependents had to go through Rome, which made the future development of a rebellious power bloc unlikely.

After 338 BC, the federation of Latin towns and cities, the Latin League, was disbanded, and many of the Latin cities became Roman satellites, their inhabitants absorbed into Rome's growing community as Roman citizens and their land added to the Roman *ager publicus*. Because Roman citizenship was a legal construct disassociated from ethnic ties or place of birth (Chapter 1), the extension of citizenship was an administrative process that could be provided to just about anyone. It is worth noting that in the fourth century, the extension of citizenship was actually interpreted by many of its recipients as a sort of punishment, because it took away pre-existing political identities and freedom of action. Some, like the Hernici, were unhappy when citizenship was forced upon them. By the time of the Social War in 91/90 BC, Rome's long-suffering allies actively agitated for greater political inclusion, but this was not always the case after the end of the Latin War in 338 BC.

Many of the cities swallowed up by Rome were given the status of a *municipium* (pl. *municipia*); these included most of the Latin cities that previously had been part of the Latin League. Citizens of the *municipia* were granted full Roman citizenship (*civitas optimo iure*); through inclusion in the census, this gave them valuable political rights, such as the right to stand for office and vote in elections in Rome if they lived close enough to make the journey. Full citizenship also carried with it the obligation and duty to serve in the army. The *municipia* surrendered all policy making to the Roman government, even though they were left to run their own local affairs under the guidance of a twin elected magistracy that superficially resembled the consulship. The first of the *municipia*, Tusculum, predated the Latin War. Taken by force in 381 BC, the city's people were enrolled among Rome's tribes; new tribes were added regularly in the fourth century to absorb and register new Roman citizens.

A different type of *municipium* was created for towns and cities further away from Rome. The citizens of these *municipia* were similarly absorbed into Rome's political community, but they were not permitted to vote. These *municipia sine suffragio*, which included Capua, had greater freedom of action but—as Capua itself would find out during the Hannibalic War—could expect swift retaliation if they acted against Roman interests. Those who possessed *civitas sine suffragio*, or 'citizenship without the vote', were still expected to enrol in Roman troop levies and pay taxes. Communities of such semi-citizens could be crafted wherever Rome conquered, providing for an almost limitless expansion of the Roman populace. For many of Rome's new allies, the actual political impact may have been little more than a veneer or the formalisation of an existing state of affairs. By leaving many of the *municipia* under local leadership, the Romans permitted the illusion of self-government and a form of independence.

A third sort of alliance was agreed between Rome and Italian cities on a case-by-case basis. These cities became known as *socii*, or 'allies'. They received Roman protection, and in exchange for providing troops (serving under their own officers), they were given a form of the 'Latin rights'—the right to intermarry and do business with Romans, and the right to move to Rome; these rights dated back to the Cassian Treaty in 493, which had put Rome and the Latin League on an equal footing. *Socii* remained independent and self-governing, as long as their actions and interests aligned with those in Rome. Some of these arrangements could be very advantageous to both parties, since the Romans shared plunder with their allies and did not necessarily impose taxes on them. Following their defeat in the Third Samnite War, the Samnites joined the Roman commonwealth as *socii*.

Alongside the *socii* and these two types of *municipia*, the Romans established colonies. Colonisation went back to the fifth century BC, where Latin colonies had been established after successful campaigns carried out by Romans and the Latin League together. These colonies were made up of inhabitants from Latium, who were granted the Latin rights and provided with land to farm. Eventually the Romans began implanting Roman colonies made up of Roman citizens. Both types of colony—those of citizens with the Latin rights, and those with Roman citizenship—embedded citizens in a newly conquered or restive area, or at locations of strategic value (Figure 2.7).

Colonies exported Roman ideas about government, along with concepts of public space, culture, and so on. For example, when Paestum was re-founded as a Latin colony in 273 BC, its Greek public spaces, including the agora and *ekklesiasterion* used for public assemblies, were razed and replaced by a forum and a Roman-style meeting place. Colonisation thus possessed an inherent aggressive dimension and almost always had a political motive. Not all states accepted the expansionism that such policy represented. It was a Roman colony, Fregellae, founded in Samnite territory in 328, that had helped to trigger the Second Samnite War.

Alongside colonisation came the construction of roads, with one of the most famous—the via Appia—begun in 312 BC as Rome battled the Samnites. The road took its name from Appius Claudius Crassus 'Caecus' ('the blind'), a member of the ancient Claudii family, which traced its origins to archaic Sabinum, and struck out south from Rome towards Capua. More than anything else, Roman roads were intended to facilitate the swift movement of troops, and the via Appia was constructed to improve Rome's chances against her dangerous Samnite enemies. (Some parts of the via Appia survive, as Figure 2.8 shows.) Alongside colonisation, Road building served a political purpose and was also a visible, permanent reminder of Roman power.

Rome's expansion into central Italy had already begun to have an important impact on its social and economic life. As noted earlier, by the turn of the fourth century a stipend was paid to troops on active service, in recognition of the fact that the archaic custom of summer campaigning had given way to the new reality of longer wars in more distant places. Rome's conflicts proved to be very expensive, and to help cover the costs of war it became necessary to levy a property tax and fine defeated enemies an indemnity on the cessation of hostilities. On the other hand, the huge numbers of slaves captured as resistance to Rome collapsed across central Italy helped end the curse of debt bondage—although this only replaced one sort of misery with another.

Slavery had been part of Mediterranean and eastern life for centuries. Chattel slavery, whereby a person became the property of another, denied any and all rights, was a common form of misery from Greece to Babylonia. Alexander's conquests in the fourth century BC helped to spread chattel slavery to places where it had hitherto been rare or unknown, such as Egypt. The Greeks also knew a form of subservience that was neither chattel slavery nor freedom, called helotage (after the Helots of Sparta). Here a second-class population of peasant serfs worked the land for their Spartan overlords; the *laoi* of the Hellenistic east performed a comparable function with similarly circumscribed privileges.

Figure 2.7 The political map of Italy in the early third century BC, showing a representative distribution of Roman and Latin colonies, together with the approximate division of Italy between
municipia, municipia sine suffragio, and *socii.*

Source: Illustration by the author.

Both were controlled rather than enslaved, but they were not truly free. Sacred slaves
could be found attached to the sanctuaries of the east, performing tasks as diverse as sacred
prostitution and caring for cats. Slaves also toiled in royal workshops, making goods for
sale and export. The full spectrum of slavery was an accepted part of Roman life, and had
been since its foundation. The Romans believed, for instance, that the mother of Servius
Tullius had been a slave. More importantly, laws regulating slaveholding appear in the
Twelve Tables, revealing that the institution was of sufficient importance to be included in

Figure 2.8 A stretch of the via Appia in the southern suburbs of modern Rome.

Source: Photograph by the author.

this first rudimentary legal code. What changed in the fifth and fourth centuries BC was the availability of slaves, who were predominantly war captives who became 'things' (*res*, pl. *res*) in Roman law. Slaves provided an abundant, low-cost source of manpower and could be found doing anything from domestic service to heavy physical labour in mines or in the fields. Along with slaves came large additions to the *ager publicus*, either through colonisation or through the acquisition of territory from a vanquished foe, such as Veii, whose territory alone has been reckoned at about 560 square kilometres(216 square miles) even if not all of it ended up in Roman hands. As we have seen, the enlargement of the *ager publicus* informed the Licinian-Sextian laws, and the influx of slaves may be connected with the law of 326 BC that decisively put an end to debt bondage.

Rome's successes on the battlefield, as well as its plucky responses to times of crisis, may also have contributed to the easing of tensions between plebeians and patricians. The struggle of the orders is normally considered to have ended with the passage of the Hortensian law in 287 BC; following the final plebeian secession amidst new concerns over debt, this made the results of plebiscites binding on both plebeians and patricians and thus reinforced the sovereignty of the people. The composition of the Roman aristocracy had changed considerably between 509 and 287 BC: in addition to the larger number of plebeians who had held public office, and who were therefore eligible to be enrolled in the senate, Rome had welcomed elites from the cities of central Italy. The fortunes of individual families can be traced, such as the Claudii from Sabinum, the Furii from Tusculum, the Sempronii from Umbria and the Volumnii from Etruria. These and many others became established in Rome as their home cities lost their independence. A new patrician-plebeian oligarchy, enriched by newcomers, was taking shape at the apex of Roman politics. Membership of this elite group depended on successfully competing to serve the state in any position, but most notably the consulship. Rome was still dominated by the wealthy and their webs of clients, who depended on them for patronage and financial support. Even as the struggle of the orders came to a close, Rome's democratic institutions only thinly concealed the increasingly oligarchic power of the decision-making elite.

Rome's new citizens joined a community that was being profoundly shaped by an ethos of violence and victory. The regular conflicts between Rome and her neighbours, together with the shock of individual events such as the defeat at the Caudine Forks, underwrote a shared identity and solidarity among the Roman people. There was a marked increase in temple construction in the fourth century, a reflection of Rome's successes on the battlefield. These thanksgiving temples provided public, visible commemorations of Roman military might and contributed to the development of an ethos of irresistible victory over Rome's enemies. In turn, these reminders, embedded in the topography of the city, were further renewed and immortalised by yet more conflict and further near-death experiences, most notably against Pyrrhus and Hannibal (Chapters 3 and 4).

There had also been changes to Rome's military organisation. Rome fought against coalitions of enemies and also fought conflicts that overlapped or closely followed one another. This necessitated an expansion of the army, with two legions (of between 4,500 and 6,000 each) assigned to both consuls, giving four in total, for between 18,000 and 24,000 troops on campaign at any given time. The consuls were provided with elected military tribunes as staff officers to help them manage these larger armies. Rome's army represented a significant financial expenditure, especially once the stipend was introduced; it also needed a consistent pool of manpower to be successful. Estimates for Rome's population vary tremendously, but Polybius (2.24) reports the details of the Roman census for 225 BC, just before the Hannibalic War. He cites close to 700,000 adult males (citizens and *socii*) available for service in the infantry, and 70,000 for cavalry. These numbers are sometimes criticised for being too high, but even the lower numbers of about half a million infantry and 50,000 cavalry reveal the incredible depth of Rome's manpower resources. The conquest of central Italy, and the development of the *municipia* and the *socii*, thus brought Rome an almost limitless pool of soldiers to fight the city's wars.

There was another important military development that came about in the fourth century. At the river Allia in 390 BC, a Roman army had been overwhelmed by a mass of Gauls, who charged the Roman line and easily turned its flanks. The Gallic victory exposed a problem with mobility; later, in the Second Samnite War, the Romans had found it hard to manoeuvre over broken, hilly ground, further showing that the army needed to change. Eventually the Romans developed the concept of the maniple, which replaced the hoplite phalanx. (The name comes from the Latin word *manipulus*, or 'handful'.) Roman legions were henceforth arrayed in a series of maniples, about the strength of a modern rifle company at 120 men. Arrayed in a checkerboard pattern with substantial gaps in between, the manipular legion occupied a large space on the battlefield but was far more agile than a single phalanx. Each maniple was made up of four ranks: *velites* or skirmishers, with *hastati*, *principes*, and *triarii* behind. As Livy explains (8.8.9–12), the *hastati* and *principes* could be rotated constantly, giving men engaged in the brutish and physical act of face-to-face combat regular opportunities to rest. Fresh maniples could also be fed into battle through the gaps made by the checkerboard, and tired maniples full of wounded brought to the back of the legionary line. Other structural improvements involved a lightening of the armour worn and the development of a throwing javelin, the *pilum*, which was launched prior to an attack to disrupt the enemy line. Later, a nasty and brutish sword, the *gladius*, became the legionnaire's standard weapon. Despite all these improvements, it would take a war against a highly unconventional foe—Hannibal—for the maniple to realise its true tactical potential (Chapter 3).

Plutarch, writing of the looming war with Pyrrhus (280–75 BC), noted that 'the army of the Romans, as if from a fountain gushing forth indoors, was easily and speedily filled up again' (*Life of Pyrrhus*, 21). Each time Pyrrhus defeated Rome's armies, another was raised to take its place. Rome's conquests in central Italy set the conditions for a sort of self-fulfilling prophecy. It proved difficult to bring the Roman army to a decisive defeat, and more often than not exhausted enemies gave up and surrendered in the face of such a manpower disadvantage. As wars concluded in Rome's favour, more territory, more land, and more manpower were added to the commonwealth. By the third century BC, the Romans had more or less resolved their internal difficulties, and the emergence of a patrician-plebeian aristocracy provided a form of leadership that could be said to at least represent the whole of Rome's population. Finally, as the state expanded, Rome's flexible concept of citizenship made it relatively straightforward to enrol outsiders into the census, and demand their participation in more wars.

By the end of the fourth century BC, Rome had emerged as the undisputed powerbroker in central Italy, a development that made conflict with the cities of Magna Graecia a virtual certainty. Carthage, too, loomed large as a potential adversary; in 348 BC, the Romans had agreed a second treaty with this powerful North African city that defined Rome's trading rights and set out spheres of influence, and the treaty was renewed in 306 BC. Within a generation of the end of the Third Samnite War, Rome's armies were in southern Italy, and not long afterwards they were operating in Sicily and North Africa. Anti-monarchical ideas of republican government collided violently with those of Hellenistic kingship and the political legacies of Alexander the Great, while the wars with Carthage resulted in technical innovations and the establishment of Rome's first overseas province. The bloody third century BC witnessed a series of decisive changes that transformed Rome from an Italian power to a Mediterranean superpower—and altered its society, economy, culture, and government in momentous and unexpected ways.

Chapter 3

'True athletes of warfare'

Rome, Carthage, and Pyrrhus, 280–225 BC

Polybius wrote that the Romans had benefited immensely from the conflicts of the fourth century BC: 'First they became so inured to being hacked to pieces by Gauls that nothing that happened to them or might possibly happen to them could be more terrible than what they had already experienced.' Having teetered on the edge of extermination, they believed, the Romans found the deep well of resilience and courage required to defeat later, far more dangerous opponents. Another benefit to the Romans, Polybius said, was that 'by the time they faced Pyrrhus they had become true athletes of warfare'—near matchless on the battlefield, resilient when defeated, and practically immune to catastrophe (2.20).

The third century BC was dominated by three separate conflicts: two against the Mediterranean heavyweight Carthage, and another against the city of Tarentum and its charismatic champion, Pyrrhus of Epirus. If the fourth century BC cemented Rome's dominance in central Italy, the third established the city's mastery of the Mediterranean. By the end of the third century BC, Rome was fighting in Italy and Sicily, North Africa, Spain, Gaul, and Greece. Powerful kingdoms such as Ptolemaic Egypt and Seleucid Syria were forced to take notice of this seismic shift in Mediterranean politics. In Rome, these conflicts created profound challenges to the Republic's society, culture, and political life that would eventually contribute to the collapse of the state amidst a series of violent civil conflicts and foreign wars.

Given their importance for the development of the Republic, it is useful to treat these three conflicts in some detail. In this chapter, we shall consider the war with Pyrrhus, which was Rome's first conflict with a foreign force, and the war with Carthage, Rome's first war outside Italy. In Chapter 4, we shall consider the second war between Rome and Carthage, conventionally known as the Second Punic War or the Hannibalic War.

Rome, Tarentum, and Pyrrhus, 280–275 BC

King Pyrrhus of Epirus was a product of the political order created in the Greek world after the death of Alexander the Great (323 BC). As Alexander breathed his last in Babylon, a bloody struggle erupted between his leading generals and ambitious pretenders for control of his vast kingdom, which stretched from Greece and Macedonia as far as Iraq, Persia (Iran), and Bactria (Afghanistan). A generation of warfare resulted in Ptolemy victorious in Egypt; Seleucus in Syria, Persia, and Bactria; and Antigonus 'the One-Eyed' initially in much of Asia Minor, and then, via his descendants, in Macedonia. It was not long before

DOI: 10.4324/9781003202523-3

Figure 3.1 Silver tetradrachm of Alexander the Great, minted at Myriandros or Issus in 324/23 BC. Obverse: head of Heracles, right, wearing a lion skin; reverse: Zeus seated on the throne. The Greek legend reads ΒΑΣΙΛΕΩΣ ΑΛΕΞΑΝΔΡΟ (BASILEUS ALEXANDRO[U]), 'of king Alexander'.

all these men crowned themselves kings—but they were kings with a difference. Whereas Alexander had come to the throne of Macedonia, a defined territorial polity, following the death of his father, he had subsequently gone on to conquer Persian-controlled Egypt, after which he became its pharaoh; then, after defeating the Achaemenid Persian monarch Darius III, Alexander took on the mantle of the Persian 'King of Kings'. His kingdom was the land that he had won through conquest, and his royal behaviour was adapted accordingly.

Both the pharaonic and Persian royal institutions were intimately linked to the divine, and it was not long before Alexander began to cultivate the notion that he was descended from both Heracles and Zeus. (Hercules, the famous hero, was known as Heracles to the Greeks.) The link with Zeus was bolstered by a visit early on in his campaign to the important sanctuary of Zeus–Ammon at Siwa in the Egyptian desert. Alexander's complex ancestry also involved descent from the Trojan war hero Achilles, whom he revered greatly; Plutarch wrote that in later years, his family ties to Zeus, Heracles, and Achilles were 'accepted without any question' (*Alexander*, 1), and Alexander's divine parentage was prominently displayed on Hellenistic coinage (Figure 3.1). By the time of Alexander's death, the concept of divinely linked kingship had permeated the Macedonian elite. After his death, Alexander appeared on Hellenistic coinage with clear references to his divine ancestry (Figure 3.2) and personality cults quickly sprang up around Alexander's successors. For example, Seleucus, who took the epithet 'Nicator' ('Victorious') and founded the Seleucid empire in 312 BC, named his royal capital for himself (Seleucia, near modern Baghdad), and built a family dynasty that leaned heavily on its connections with Alexander. Seleucus's descendants developed and nurtured the cult of Seleucus, claiming descent from Zeus and further linking the cult to the god Apollo. Seleucid coinage imitated that of Alexander, providing clear connections to Alexander, Zeus, and Heracles (Figure 3.3).

Seleucus's contemporaries, Antigonus and Ptolemy, followed a similar path. They established absolutist royal lines and personality cults, and nurtured links to Heracles and

Figure 3.2 Silver tetradrachm of Ptolemy I Soter, minted at Alexandria between 306 BC and 300 BC. Obverse: head of the deified Alexander the Great, wearing an elephant's skin and with an aegis around his neck; reverse: Athena Alkidemos with spear and shield, eagle with thunderbolt to the right. The legend reads ΑΛΕΞΑΝΔΡΟ (ALEXANDRO[U]).

Figure 3.3 Silver drachm of Seleucus I Nicator, minted at Seleucia-in-Pieria, 300–281 BC. Obverse: head of Heracles right, wearing lion skin; reverse: Zeus seated on the throne. The legend reads ΒΑΣΙΛΕΩΣ ΣΕΛΕΥΚΟΥ (BASILEUS SELEUKOU, 'of king Seleucus').

Zeus, often via the epithet 'Soter' ('Saviour'), a name freely applied to both divine figures. Other favoured epithets included 'Euergetes' (benefactor) and 'Epiphanes' (god apparent). Greek cities and communities participated in promoting such ideas—indeed, it was the island of Rhodes that gave Ptolemy the moniker 'Soter'. The Hellenistic kings also took on the mantle of the ancient royal traditions in the lands they had inherited: the famous cuneiform inscription of Antiochus I Soter (281-261 BC), from the Temple of Nabu at Borsippa in Iraq, proclaimed him 'Antiochus, the great king, the legitimate king, king of the world, king of Babylon, king of all countries' (Peter Green, *Alexander to Actium*, p. 148). His successor, Antiochus II (261–246 BC) took the unambiguous epithet 'god'. The successors to Alexander in Greece and Macedonia, the Levant, and Egypt were

Figure 3.4 Gold hemistater of Pyrrhus, minted at Tarentum. Obverse: head of Heracles, right; reverse: Taras, holding a trident, driving a *biga*; the legend in the exergues reads TAPANTINΩN (TARANTINWN, 'of the Tarentines').

There was already a Roman army in southern Italy, since Lucius Aemilius Barbula, a member of the patrician *gens* Aemilia and consul for 281 BC, had campaigned against Tarentum and overwintered with his army into 280 BC. The new consuls for 280 BC were Publius Valerius Laevinus, of the patrician *gens* Valeria, and Tiberius Coruncanius, a plebeian (and later, the first plebeian *pontifex maximus*). Laevinus was given command of the army and brought Pyrrhus to battle at Heraclea, not far from Tarentum (Figure 3.5).

Plutarch wrote that, on the eve of battle, Pyrrhus rode close to the Roman camp and admired their order and discipline, and that he was stricken by a bout of nerves; the Romans were not the barbarians he was expecting to fight (*Pyrrhus*, 16). In the end, the battle of Heraclea was a Roman defeat, as the elephants proved too much for Laevinus and caused the Roman cavalry particular problems. The Roman horses, according to Florus, writing in the second century AD, were 'frightened by [the elephants'] huge bulk and ugliness and also by their strange smell and trumpeting', and fled in terror, 'imagining the unfamiliar monsters to be more formidable than they really were' (*Epitome*, 13.18). As the Roman horsemen retired, a charge from Pyrrhus's crack Thessalian cavalry routed the legions and carried the day. Lucretius, in his work *On the Nature of Things* (5.1) and Pliny (*Natural History* 8.6) related that the Romans, seeing elephants for the first time, called the beast the 'Lucanian cow', after the district of Lucania in which the battle of Heraclea took place.

Heraclea cost the Romans dearly, but Pyrrhus also paid a stiff price, despite presenting himself as the victor through ostentatious thanksgiving dedications as far afield as the sanctuary of Athena in Athens. He only had a limited number of troops at his disposal, and his losses were not easily replaced. A very late tradition preserved in the fourth-century AD *Breviarium* of Eutropius recorded that when Pyrrhus viewed the Roman dead, he noted that all of them bore wounds to their front and looked grim, even in death. Shocked, Pyrrhus muttered that 'he might himself have been master of the world, if such soldiers had fallen to his lot' (2.11). Pyrrhus did, however, have one reason to feel confident about the outcome, for it was common in Hellenistic warfare for a defeated side to sue for

Figure 3.5 The Pyrrhic War.

Source: Illustration by the author.

peace. After an abortive march to within a short distance of Rome, Pyrrhus accordingly dispatched his honey-tongued herald, Cineas (a former student of the great Athenian orator Demosthenes), to parlay with the Roman senate. Plutarch (*Pyrrhus*, 18) wrote that many of the senators, in shock over the defeat at Heraclea, were taken in by Cineas's proposals. At this point, legend muddies the tale: hearing this talk of surrender, none other than Appius Claudius Caecus (censor in 312 BC and builder of the via Appia) had himself carried to the senate house—he was too old to walk—and berated his fellow senators for their cowardice, declaring indignantly that he wished he was 'deaf as well as blind, that I might not hear the shameful resolutions and decrees of yours which bring low the glory of Rome' (Plutarch, *Pyrrhus* 19.1). Caecus's attitude presents a fine example of Rome's vaunted 'no surrender' mentality, forged in the third century against Pyrrhus and Carthage and much embellished with excessive *virtus* in the texts of later writers like Plutarch and Livy. A similar story of *virtus* is found in Plutarch's tale of Gaius Fabricius, consul in 282 BC, who was sent as an ambassador to Pyrrhus to negotiate the release of Roman

Figure 3.6 Silver tetradrachm of Pyrrhus, minted at Locri c. 278 BC. Obverse: head of Zeus, with oak wreath; reverse: Dione (goddess of the oracle of Dodona and, with Zeus, mother of Aphrodite) seated on the throne, holding a transverse scepter.The legend reads ΒΑΣΙΛΕΩΣ ΠΥΡΡΟΥ (BASILEUS PYRROU, 'of king Pyrrhus').

captives. Pyrrhus, hearing that Fabricius was poor, offered him a large sum of gold with no conditions attached. Naturally, Fabricius, a paragon of *virtus*, declined. Later, Pyrrhus tried to intimidate Fabricius with one of his elephants. 'Your gold made no impression on me yesterday,' replied Fabricius stoically, 'neither does your beast today' (*Pyrrhus*, 20).

Brave and courageous Fabricius may have been, but the Romans, led by another Publius Decius Mus and his consular colleague, Publius Sulpicius Saverrio, succumbed to the mayhem caused by the elephants at Ausculum in 279 BC. Dionysius of Halicarnassus (22.1) recorded the curious detail that the Romans had come up with a device, covered in burning pitch, that could be used to beat the trunks and faces of the elephants, but it was to no avail. In the end, the legionnaires were overwhelmed by an army that was reinforced by yet more disgruntled former Roman allies, including the Greek cities of Croton and Locri, which went on to mint coins advertising their alliance with Pyrrhus and their opposition to Rome (Figure 3.6).

Again, the battle cost Pyrrhus dearly. By now he had squandered the majority of his original levy, and many of his best generals were dead. Plutarch related the memorable words, uttered by Pyrrhus as he was congratulated for his triumph, 'if we are victorious in one more battle with the Romans, we shall be utterly ruined'—words which have given us the phrase 'Pyrrhic victory' (*Pyrrhus*, 21). Pyrrhus was starkly aware of his disadvantage. The Romans quickly raised another army, even while many of their *socii* continued to defect to Pyrrhus. Worst of all, the Romans refused all talk of surrender or peace and became more determined each time they were beaten. This too is part of the 'no surrender' narrative that was grounded in the very real refusal by the Roman senate to accept defeat. Faced with setbacks, the Romans often started again, raised a new army, and fought on. This would be the pattern with Pyrrhus and with both the third-century wars with Carthage.

In 278 BC, Pyrrhus was offered another job: the city of Syracuse in Sicily was fending off Carthaginian attempts to spread their influence to the east of the island. By chance, Pyrrhus was the erstwhile son-in-law of Agathocles, the tyrant of Syracuse who had died in 289. (He had married Agathocles's daughter, Lanassa, who later left Pyrrhus for

Demetrius 'the Besieger.') It was thus an opportune time to leave Italy and put the conflict with Rome behind him. The throne of Syracuse beckoned, and for the moment Pyrrhus installed his own son on it. While Pyrrhus enjoyed considerably better success against the Carthaginians than he had against Roman legionaries, his absence was bitterly resented by his Italian allies, who suffered from Roman reprisals. A treaty between Rome and Carthage in 279/78 BC, based on their struggle against Pyrrhus, the common enemy, heaped further pressure on the mercenary king. It also led to a famous story repeated by Valerius Maximus (writing in the first century AD) that offers of Carthaginian military help in 279/78 BC were rebuffed, because 'the Roman people undertook only wars that it could fight with its own soldiers' (3.7.10). And so, in 276 BC, amidst desperate appeals from his Italian allies, Pyrrhus sailed back to Italy, staving off a savage mauling by the Carthaginian fleet on the way.

At Maleventum in 275 BC, the Romans finally prevailed. The Roman army was commanded by the plebeian consul Manius Curius Dentatus who, after initially being driven back to his camp, managed to turn Pyrrhus's elephants against him; Florus (13.18) wrote that it was concentrated javelin fire that carried the day. However, a curious story preserved by Aelian, a third-century AD writer from Praeneste, recorded that the elephants at Maleventum were tormented by squealing pigs (*On Animals*, 1.38). It is unclear whether the squealing was the result of a tactic reported by a Macedonian writer, Polyaenus, whose second-century AD work collected the various methods of famous generals. This story is so bizarre that it merits quoting the relevant section (*Stratagems*, 4.6.3): 'At the siege of Megara [266 BC], Antigonus [II Gonatas, the Macedonian king] brought his elephants into the attack; but the Megarians daubed some swine with pitch, set fire to it, and let them loose among the elephants. The pigs grunted and shrieked under the torture of the fire, and sprang forwards as hard as they could among the elephants, who broke their ranks in confusion and fright, and ran off in different directions. From this time onwards, Antigonus ordered the Indians, when they trained up their elephants, to bring up swine among them; so that the elephants might thus become accustomed to the sight of them, and to their noise.'

The convergence of the dates of the conflict between Antigonus and Megara (in central Greece) and the Roman victory at Maleventum, alongside Dionysius's record of the use of burning pitch to torment the elephants at Ausculum in 279 BC, suggest that the Romans may well have achieved victory over Pyrrhus with this method or something like it. Pyrrhus gave up at this point and returned to Greece, where he was killed in bitter street fighting in Argos in 272 BC, apparently by a woman who crushed the base of his neck with a roof tile (*Pyrrhus*, 34). Aelian (7.41) wrote that Pyrrhus's favourite elephant recovered his body and returned it to his friends. Tarentum fell to the Romans in the same year. Dentatus had celebrated a triumph in February of 274; elephants formed part of the procession through the streets of Rome.

The fallout from the Pyrrhic war was considerable. The Romans had faced their first foreign enemy, as well as a disciplined, experienced professional army organised around the Macedonian phalanx, a menacing formation 16 deep, armed with a 5 m (16 ft) infantry pike called a sarissa. The Romans had beaten the phalanx and also overcame the major difficulties posed by the elephants, and they had also managed to deal with the Greek cavalry, which Philip II of Macedon, and then his son, Alexander the Great, had developed into a potent offensive weapon. Prevailing over these considerable obstacles, the Romans

Figure 3.7 Modern electrotype of the silver nomos issue minted at Locri c. 275 BC. Obverse: laureate head of Zeus; reverse: ΠΙΣΤΙΣ (PISTIS), faith, crowning PΩMA (ROMA), the personification of the Roman state.

earned what Plutarch called a 'reputation for invincibility' (*Pyrrhus*, 25). The Romans had also encountered their first Hellenistic warrior king. Contacts with some of the other Hellenistic kingdoms were initiated in the aftermath of the Roman victory: an embassy to Ptolemy II Philadelphus, the king of Egypt (284–46 BC), returned laden with exotic gifts and promises of friendship. Smaller cities followed suit: in 266 BC, for example, the Greek city of Apollonia, across the Strait of Otranto from the heel of Italy, sent an embassy to Rome.

Whether by accident or design, Rome now controlled all of Italy. The Samnites, who had thrown in their lot with Pyrrhus, were crushed, and the other allies of Rome that had rebelled were cowed and humbled by the vicious retribution that continued for nearly a decade after the conclusion of the war. Some wayward allies, such as Locri, minted coins that obsequiously recognised Roman power (Figure 3.7).

Maleventum, renamed Beneventum ('welcome', the prefix *bene–* replacing *male–*, which meant 'ill' or 'bad'), became a Roman colony in 268 BC, and colonies were established elsewhere, including at Paestum in 273 BC (Chapter 2), to reinforce Rome's authority. Before the Pyrrhic war, the cities of Magna Graecia had been the only remaining political entities in Italy that could have stood up to Roman aggression, but they had now been humbled. Neither Tarentum nor any of the other southern Italian cities could hope to play any meaningful role if a situation such as unrest in Sicily required outside intervention. That task would fall to Rome.

War with Carthage, 264–241 BC

As noted in Chapter 1, Carthage had been founded around 800 BC as a Phoenician colony. Its mother city was Tyre, on the Levantine coast, and Carthage's foundation myths gave pride of place to Dido (also known as Elissa), the sister of the Tyrian king Pygmalion. In its earliest centuries Carthage was a monarchy, but in common with the changes experienced across much of the Mediterranean world, the monarchy was eventually abolished. In Carthage, it was replaced by a republican constitution dominated by aristocratic interests.

Annual collegial-elected offices managed the various needs of the city and its dependent communities; the highest elected official was the suffete, broadly analogous to consuls or the Etruscan *zilath* (Chapter 2). A council of elders guided state policy (usually called a 'senate' in ancient sources), while a popular assembly and a court of judges maintained oversight. One major difference within the Carthaginian constitution, however, was that suffetes were solely civic officials and warfare was the preserve of *strategoi* (generals), who stayed in command for as long as was needed. Carthage's tutelary deity, Melqart, imported from Tyre, found an easy equivalence with Heracles; Melqart's consort, Tanit, found an equivalence with Juno (elsewhere in Italy, Juno was also identified with Astarte), and the Levantine deity Baal was equated with Jupiter (Figures 3.8 and 3.9). There was therefore much that Carthage had in common with its peers in Italy and Greece, an important point that is sometimes overlooked due to the way that its most famous son, Hannibal, has often been portrayed (Chapter 4).

On the eve of the First Punic War, Carthage had a considerable stake in western Sicily, a legacy of bitter conflict with the Greeks that went back to the sixth century BC. The city had also colonised parts of Sardinia, Corsica, and the Balaeric Islands, had a presence in southern Spain, and controlled large swathes of territory and a plethora of communities in modern Libya and Tunisia. From its territories, Carthage produced a diversity of important products, from figs, wine, and pomegranates to silver, copper, iron, and tin. As we have seen, Carthage had long made treaties with Rome and other Italian cities, prior to the latter's loss of independence. These close contacts heightened the possibility of a collision with Rome following the war with Pyrrhus. When it came, the First Punic War—like the Pyrrhic conflict—had a local cause.

The spark was an appeal for help from a group calling itself the Mamertines, or 'Men of Mars'. These were mercenaries from Campania who had gone to Sicily to fight for Agathocles, the tyrant of Syracuse. After the death of Agathocles in 289 BC, the Mamertines installed themselves at Messana (modern Messina) on the Sicilian coast. Following the departure of Pyrrhus from Sicily in 276 BC, Hiero II, one of Pyrrhus's confidants, became tyrant of Syracuse and came to the aid of the people victimised by the Mamertines' rule at Messana. Later, Hiero defeated the Mamertines in battle, and the beaten mercenaries appealed to outsiders for help, sending envoys to both Rome *and* Carthage. The proposition was attractive to Carthage, due to its pre-existing interests in Sicily and intermittent conflicts with Syracuse; it was less attractive to the Romans, who were engaged in suppressing the last resistance among their recalcitrant allies after the end of the Pyrrhic war. The Carthaginians responded first, providing a garrison for Messana and throttling Hiero's ambitions. Later, the Romans also responded, and in a classic example of what we would today call 'mission creep', the effort to rescue the Mamertines soon blossomed into outright conflict with Carthage (Figure 3.10).

Why did Rome help the Mamertines? The 'official' explanation was that, as Campanian mercenaries, the Mamertines were allies of Rome, and *fides* demanded that help be provided. This conveniently glossed over the fact that Rome had only recently suppressed a different group of Campanian mercenaries in Rhegium, across the water from Messana. This group had been dispatched there during the Pyrrhic war, but went on to pursue their own agenda in imitation of their successful compatriots at Messana, taking control of the city and conducting a reign of terror. How could Rome rationalise helping one group of Campanians, but at the same time take vengeance on another and pay restitution to their

Figure 3.8 Electrum tridrachm minted at Carthage during the First Punic War. Obverse: head of Tanit left with a wreath of grain, reflecting Carthage's agrarian wealth; reverse: a standing horse.

Figure 3.9 Silver Carthaginian half shekel struck between 220 and 205 BC. Obverse: head of Melqart left with laurel wreath; reverse: elephant.

victims? The Romans besieged Rhegium, killing many of the mercenaries and taking the remainder captive, after which they were paraded and publicly beheaded. In Rome, there was therefore considerable discomfort over the prospect of aid for the Mamertines at Messana, 'because it was glaringly obvious how unjustifiable it would be for them to send help' (Polybius, 1.10). Diodorus Siculus (23.1.4) wrote that the Romans: 'Harping as they did on the word *fides*, certainly ought not to protect assassins who had shown the greatest contempt for good faith; if, on behalf of men so utterly godless, they should enter upon a war of such magnitude, it would be clear to all mankind that they were using pity for the imperilled as a cloak for their own advantage.'

Faced with the prospect of Carthage cementing its influence in eastern Sicily—a virtual certainty given their garrison at Messana, said the policy hawks—the Romans decided to safeguard their interests in southern Italy. They were painfully aware of how easy it was to cross the worryingly short distance from Messana to Rhegium, even if Carthage

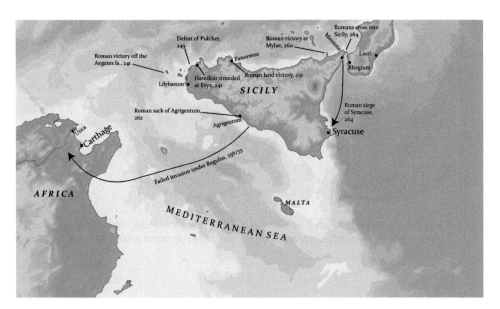

Figure 3.10 The First Punic War.

Source: Illustration by the author.

had displayed no discernable interest in doing so and had, on the other hand, concluded treaties with Rome that were focused on protecting Carthaginian interests in Sicily and Africa. It is noteworthy that the potential threat posed by the ancient and powerful city of Syracuse barely figured in Roman deliberations—a sign, perhaps, that what has come down to us has been heavily distilled through Roman propaganda. Hiero later became a devoted ally of Rome, so he and his formidable opposition may have been whitewashed out of later justifications for the war. Indeed, in 265/64 BC, if there *was* a threat to southern Italy, it was surely from Syracuse, not Carthage. It was Syracuse, after all, that actually had a proven track record of interfering in Magna Graecia from the mid-fourth century BC onwards. On the other hand, a Carthaginian fleet had taken station off Tarentum as the Romans reduced the city in 272 BC, apparently in a show of force. It was an historical inevitability that Rome and Carthage would clash one way or another.

Polybius (1.11) said that the senate held back from providing its moral assent to the operation to rescue the Mamertines, and that the matter was decided by a popular vote in the *comitia centuriata*. The people were swayed by the consuls' promise that there was a prospect of significant plunder. One of the consuls, Appius Claudius, a patrician from the venerable *gens* Claudia who earned the agnomen 'Caudex' ('hunk of wood' or 'block-head'), was entrusted with an army and headed south. The Mamertines evicted a small Carthaginian force that was in Messana (afterwards, the Carthaginian *strategos* was cru-cified by the Carthaginians for cowardice) and prepared to receive their rescuers. After initially being forced back by the Carthaginian navy, the Roman force crossed the strait to find Hiero, who had made an expedient alliance with the Carthaginians, blockading the city. This was the first time a Roman army had left Italy to wage war. Caudex duly defeated Hiero outside Messana, then went on to lay siege to Syracuse. Roman spirits soared, even as the Carthaginian commander, Hanno, urged Caudex against escalation.

This had all taken place in 264 BC. Caudex had achieved the mission with which he had been entrusted and this should have been the end of it. But the following year saw new consuls elected, and both were sent to Sicily with a full levy. This intimidating show of force convinced Syracuse to switch sides, and many of the smaller communities allied to Carthage followed suit. The three-way challenge between Rome, Carthage, and Syracuse and her allies had thus lost a key contestant—Syracuse—which had acted as both a buffer between Rome and Carthage and a distraction from expanding the scope of the war. Even as Hiero dropped out of the contest, the Carthaginians belatedly dispatched a force to help him, an act that only served to arouse Roman anger and identify Carthage as the key enemy. Faced with a rampant Roman army on their turf, the Carthaginians hired mercenaries from Greece, Libya, and Numidia to bolster their forces and prepared for a war. A straightforward mission conceived to assist those under *fides* to Rome had spun quickly out of control. In 262 BC, two consuls were again sent to Sicily and dramatically escalated the conflict by sacking Agrigentum (Agrigento). Shocked, some of Rome's new Sicilian allies rejoined their alliance with Carthage, but in Rome, there was elation at the ease of the Roman victory. Polybius wrote that the Romans 'were no longer satisfied' with their rescue of the Mamertines, but now saw that they could run the Carthaginians out of Sicily and take it for themselves (1.20).

The Romans faced a significant problem. They did not possess a sizeable naval force, and in 264 BC, Caudex had been forced to rely on the Tarentine fleet and ships from Locri and Naples to get his troops across to Messana. Since the Carthaginian navy was the lynchpin for the successful defence of Carthaginian Sicily, and the essential factor for supplying Carthaginian troops there, the Romans needed to find a way to address their disadvantage. Similarly, the Carthaginians needed to find a way to surmount Roman superiority on land: whichever side managed to achieve their respective aim first would be victorious, in much the same way that the Peloponnesian War had pitted Athens, a naval power, against Sparta, a land power. Polybius described a rapid ship-building program that followed the fortuitous capture of a Carthaginian quinquereme, a formidable decked warship with a crew of several hundred—the capital ship of its day. It is difficult to know how much is bluster, playing up Roman ingenuity in the face of a much more experienced Carthaginian naval tradition; Polybius related how Roman soldiers were taught to row on land, then practised hard at sea along the coast of Italy (1.21). Rome's Italian allies, however, possessed considerable experience with shipbuilding, and in 338 BC, when the Romans captured Volscian Antium, they had commandeered much of its substantial fleet for their own purposes. According to Livy (8.41), some of the Volscian ships had been burned, with their prows saved and used to decorate a raised platform in the forum known as the rostra, thus bringing a maritime flavour to Rome's most important public space. In 311 BC, a collegial command, the *duoviri navales*, had been instituted to manage Rome's growing fleet, and it was a Roman naval force that had been implicated in the beginnings of the Pyrrhic war when parts of it were sunk by the Tarentines. Moreover, Rome's Sicilian ally, Syracuse, was a naval power in its own right and the quinquereme had been invented there. The Romans were not, therefore, complete newcomers to the sea. What they needed was a modernisation program and a wholesale expansion of the pool of trained sailors to match and surpass what Carthage possessed.

In 260 BC, the remodelled Roman fleet put to sea under the command of Gnaeus Cornelius Scipio, one of the many patricians of the *gens* Cornelia to hold the consulship. Things got off to a bad start, however, when the Romans panicked in the face of a small Carthaginian force. The crews abandoned their vessels, leaving Scipio to be captured; for this he earned the epithet Asina, or 'ass'. Nevertheless, the Romans quickly gained experience at sea and came up with an unique technological innovation known as the *corvus*, or 'crow'. This was an ingenious attempt to turn a naval battle as much as possible into a land battle. The *corvus* was an 11 metre (36 feet) boarding ramp with a sharp spike, located in the prow of a vessel. The contraption could be swivelled around in order to drop over the bow or to port or starboard, depending on the situation. When an enemy ship was rammed, the ramp would drop, the spike gripping the enemy's deck; heavily armed marines could then board the opposing ship and capture it. The invention of the *corvus* reflected the determination of the Romans to make up for their lack of skill at sea.

The *fasti triumphales* records that in 260 BC, Gaius Duilius—a *novus homo*, or 'new man', someone who was the first in their family to hold a major political office—made up for Scipio's poor performance, capturing the Carthaginian flagship and a sizeable part of Carthage's fleet at the battle of Mylae, not far from Messana. For this he earned a triumph, and in celebration he dedicated two columns near the rostra, adorned with the prows of Carthaginian warships, which were still standing in Pliny the Elder's day. (Numerous Roman sources report that one of the honours given to Duilius was the peculiar right to be accompanied by a flautist as he came back home after dinner each night.) The Romans followed up the success at Mylae by inflicting a humiliating defeat on a Carthaginian fleet at anchor off Sardinia. The beaten *strategos*, Hannibal—who had presided over the debacle at Mylae—was crucified for his incompetence. (This Hannibal is not to be confused with the far more famous Hannibal in Chapter 4).

Roman confidence was sharply undermined by an ambitious infantry expedition in 256 BC, which landed in Africa in order to lay siege to Carthage. Polybius (1.25) wrote that the fleet comprised 330 ships—if true, this represented a staggering effort on the part of the Romans, especially given the need to constantly refit damaged vessels and build replacements for warships lost in storms or to enemy action. Marcus Atilius Regulus, consul for the second time in 256 BC and from a mixed patrician/plebeian family, initially gained the upper hand against Carthage and managed to stir a revolt among the indigenous Numidians that threatened the city. As his consulship was drawing to a close, Regulus tried to make peace with Carthage so he could gain the glory for the successful conclusion of the war. The terms he offered were, however, outrageous, and rejected with 'considerable bravery' by the Carthaginian senate (Polybius, 1.31). Not long afterwards, Regulus was captured by a talented Spartan mercenary, Xanthippus, who inflicted a crushing defeat on him and handed him over to the Carthaginians.

The humiliating story of Regulus was turned into yet another stirring example of *virtus*, and almost everything about him quickly passed into legend. Both Carthage and Rome were tiring of the war, and in what is most likely a purely fictional episode, Regulus was sent to Rome to try to persuade the senate to make peace. He had given his parole to his Carthaginian captors and undertaken to return to Carthage, no matter the outcome of his mission. After arriving in Rome, rather than push for peace, he persuaded the senate to continue the war and disavow all talk of surrender. His job done, he returned to Carthage where he died in what the Romans thought were gruesome circumstances. Appian, for example, recorded that he was sealed up inside a sort of iron maiden (*Punic Wars*, 4), while Cicero claimed that Regulus had his eyelids peeled off so he could not sleep (*Against Piso*, 19). Later Christian writers delighted in narrating the horrendous deaths of pagans like Regulus. Augustine wrote in the fifth century AD: 'They shut him up in a narrow box, in which finely sharpened nails were fixed all round about him, so that he could not lean upon any part of it without intense pain; and so they killed him by depriving him of sleep' (*City of God*, 15)

The most sober-minded of the historians, Polybius, made no mention of any of this. Instead, he poured scorn on Regulus for his hubris and insolence, and for the arrogant way in which he tried to make peace with Carthage. He was also surely aware that Regulus's wife, Marcia, had gained a macabre reputation for torturing Carthaginian captives. In spite of this, or perhaps because of it, Regulus was turned into a hero by the Augustan-era poet Horace, who entitled one of his famous odes (3.5) 'No Surrender', and in which he wrote that Regulus 'spurned the foul disgrace of peace'. Xanthippus was deemed to have done his job so well that the Carthaginian senate sent him home in a ship whose commander, according to Appian, was instructed to throw him overboard lest it get out that Xanthippus, not a Carthaginian general, had been the instrument of Regulus's defeat (*Punic Wars*, 4).

In 255 BC, the Romans succeeded in retrieving some of the survivors of Regulus's doomed expedition, only for the bulk of the force to founder in a storm. Polybius wrote that only 80 of 364 ships survived, and pointedly noted that the Roman commanders had been warned by local pilots that the stretch of sea through which they were about to travel was exceedingly dangerous at that time of year (1.37). The ineptitude displayed by these commanders (both of whom were awarded triumphs) was matched by the impiety of Publius Claudius Pulcher, consul in 249 BC. Prior to engaging with a Carthaginian fleet off the Sicilian coast, Pulcher took the auspices, which in this case involved feeding the sacred chickens on board his flagship. A story much-repeated by Roman writers related that when they would not eat, he dumped them over the side, saying, 'Let them drink!' Pulcher lost the fleet action and was later successfully tried for his sacrilegious behaviour. In spite of such horrendous losses and hopeless leadership, however, the Romans managed to keep building new fleets and thus sustained the war effort for 15 years after the death of Regulus. Nevertheless, the war drained the resources of both Rome and Carthage and devastated the countryside—especially in Sicily, which bore the brunt of the fighting. The Roman census for 247 BC hints at the extent of naval losses, in particular: whereas in 252 BC the census recorded 297,797 adult males, for 247 BC the census recorded only 241,712—a loss of 56,085, or nearly 19 per cent.

In 254 BC, the important city of Panormus (Palermo) was captured, a severe blow to Carthaginian fortunes. In 251 BC, the plebeian consul Lucius Caecilius Metellus defeated a large Carthaginian army outside the walls of Panormus, successfully turning the Carthaginian war elephants against their own troops and triggering a rout. Metellus was awarded a triumph for his action, with 120 captured elephants paraded through the streets of Rome. Meanwhile, Hamilcar—the father of the great Carthaginian warrior, Hannibal (Chapter 4)—held out for as long as possible in his stronghold at Mt Eryx. In 241 BC, however, the decisive Roman naval victory that was needed to knock Carthage out of the war finally took place. The Carthaginian *strategos* Hanno took a large fleet laden with grain and other supplies intended for Hamilcar, but his attempts to sail to Sicily undetected failed. The plebeian *novus homo* and consul Gaius Lutatius Catulus launched a surprise attack while the enemy vessels were still heavily laden with supplies, and off the western Sicilian coast, in the battle of the Aegates Islands in 241 BC, Catulus inflicted a crushing defeat. Bereft, exhausted, and facing starvation, Hamilcar was forced to surrender. Hanno was crucified in Carthage and the war came to a close. Between 2016 and 2019, archaeologists from the Egadi Islands Project discovered a bevy of rams, helmets, amphorae, and other equipment on the sea floor, believed to be the detritus of this final Roman victory.

Unlike Regulus, Catulus demonstrated good judgement and offered reasonable terms to Hamilcar. Both sides wanted the war to be over. By this treaty, the Carthaginians would leave Sicily, which would become Roman; they would refrain from attacking Syracuse; prisoners would be returned; and over a 20-year period, Carthage would pay a war indemnity of 2,200 talents of silver (representing 57,200 kilograms (125,400 pounds); an Attic talent was 26 kilograms (57 pounds). The Carthaginians agreed to these terms, but the treaty encountered resistance in Rome. Instead, stiffer conditions were exacted: 3,300 talents (85,800 kilograms, or 188,100 pounds) would have to be repaid in only ten years, and the Romans would also take control of the various islands dotted between Sicily and Italy. Carthage itself was left to its own devices, however, and there would be no Roman garrisons in Africa or any form of control exerted over Carthaginian policy.

After the war, Carthage became mired in a savage conflict against its Greek, Spanish, and Gallic mercenaries, many of whom had gone unpaid, and with whom much of the local Numidian population sided. Rebel coinage of the period can be identified in the surviving examples, often overstruck on Carthaginian coins, bearing the Greek legend ΛΙΒΥΩΝ, 'of the Libyans' (Figure 3.11). This war dragged on for three years; mercenary revolts also took place in Sardinia and Corsica. Using these rebellions to claim a treaty violation, the Romans annexed both islands and levied an additional fine in 238/37 BC.

The First Punic War was Rome's first overseas conflict, and as a generational war it gave the Romans a long and useful experience of keeping armies and navies at readiness or in the field for extended periods of time. The war confirmed Rome's arrival as a major naval

Figure 3.11 Bi-metallic shekel, uncertain North African mint. Obverse: head of Heracles with lion skin; reverse: lion standing to the right, with Punic 'M' above and Greek ΛΙΒΥΩΝ (LIBYWN) beneath.

power, and delivered its first overseas territories: Sicily, Sardinia, and Corsica. In 227 BC, the praetorship was formally expanded, with one praetor each sent to safeguard Rome's interests in Sicily and Sardinia, in addition to the two normally elected to serve in Rome. Even though the result of the war was arguably the acquisition of what amounted to 'imperial' territory, as an imperial venture the war does not seem to hold up: it is difficult to see it as a planned and deliberate effort to obtain territory or to humble Carthage. From the Roman perspective (expressed by Polybius, who was most likely relying on Fabius Pictor), the initial brief was defensively minded, to curb the possibility that Carthage might gain control of all of Sicily and thus threaten Italy. Even though this view plays too greatly into the Romans' need to justify their conflicts, once a Roman army was in Sicily, it was not much of a step for ambition and greed to overcome rational thinking, a situation for which Polybius also allows. The way the conflict unfolded was rather haphazard, as if both sides were working out their intentions in response to the latest mishap, victory or defeat, or violent storm.

What the war *did* do, Polybius thought (1.63), was to go a long way to create the necessary circumstances for the great drama of the third century: the struggle for supremacy between Hannibal and the Romans, which handed the Romans further overseas territory, strengthened their already considerable reputation for martial skill, and set the foundations for future Roman conquests in the Hellenistic world. Even though the Romans would frame the Hannibalic War as a defensive enterprise, many of the conflicts that followed in Macedonia and Syria were predatory in nature and unnecessarily violent, as was the destruction of Carthage in 146 BC (Chapter 5). Polybius clearly thought that the experience fighting Pyrrhus and then Carthage gave the Romans the daring and confidence 'with which they set out to make themselves rulers and masters of the whole world' (1.63). On the Carthaginian side, there was bitterness and resentment at the way Carthage had been treated after the war, and particularly towards 'the Truceless War', the name Polybius gave to the mercenary revolt. A clique in the Carthaginian government, the Barcid clan, led by Hamilcar, struck out in the 230s BC for Spain to rebuild Carthaginian fortunes and prepare for a new war with Rome. Even if imperial ambition did not lie at its heart, the First Punic War was nonetheless a harbinger of things to come.

Chapter 4

'The empire of the world'

Rome, Greece, Macedonia, and Hannibal, 241–200 BC

> I am about to write the story of the most memorable war of any ever fought—the war that the Carthaginians, under the leadership of Hannibal, waged against Rome.
>
> —Livy, 21.1

Thus began Livy's treatment of the war between Rome and Hannibal, consciously imitating the way Thucydides had started his own epic recounting of the Peloponnesian War between Athens and Sparta. For Polybius, the war and its outcome were no less monumental. At stake for Carthage was 'their own safety and the dominion of Africa', but for the Romans, it was 'the empire of the world' (15.9). This was written with the benefit of hindsight, when the Romans had decisively conquered Macedonia, beaten the Seleucid king Antiochus III 'the Great', and reduced large portions of Greece to vassalage (Chapter 5). For much of the war, however, it was not Carthage but Rome that struggled for 'safety and dominion'. That Rome did not collapse was due to its alliances, the moral tenacity of its people and the senate, the brilliance of numerous Roman commanders, and the tensile strength of the plebeian-patrician oligarchy that guided matters of policy and military leadership.

Between the wars, 241–220 BC

During the Pyrrhic Wars and the First Punic War, the Romans began to mint coins in a manner similar to their Greek neighbours. Early Roman coins were based on Greek standards, such as the drachm, a silver coin weighing 4.3 grams (0.15 ounces). The stimulus for developing a monetary policy was the surge in demand for funds needed to pay for the war effort, which proved so intense that the Roman fleet raised to fight the final, decisive action in 241 BC was privately funded, the money to be repaid later out of plunder and the war indemnity levied against Carthage. This private initiative reveals the extent of the financial strain caused by sustained warfare. That strain also spawned the emergence of a merchant class, the *publicani*, to whom the state contracted important war work such as naval construction; eventually, the *publicani* came to contract all manner of duties from tax collection to public works. As Roman coinage developed, the artisans who designed the dies took full advantage of the inherent propaganda value of mass-minted coinage. Early issues were proclaimed to be coins 'of the Romans' (Figure 4.1), showing Mars, the god of war. Another (Figure 4.2) celebrated the myth of Romulus and Remus, while yet another (Figure 4.3) featured the prow of a fighting vessel, signifying Rome's arrival on the Mediterranean scene as a naval power.

DOI: 10.4324/9781003202523-4

Figure 4.1 Silver didrachm minted in Rome during the First Punic War. Obverse: diademed head of Hercules; reverse: the she-wolf and the twins, Romulus and Remus, with ROMAN[ORUM] in the exergue.

Figure 4.2 Silver drachm, probably minted at Metapontum. Obverse: head of Mars left, with a Corinthian helmet; reverse: horse's head right with 'ROMANO[RUM]', 'of the Romans', very faint; a stalk of grain to the left of the horse.

In the aftermath of the First Punic War, the Roman army campaigned against the Gauls in the Po valley, as well as against Illyrian pirates operating in the Adriatic. This conflict, the First Illyrian War, had begun after the murder of the Epirote queen created chaos on Macedonia's western borders, just as the Macedonian king Demetrius II (239-229 BC) was staving off an invasion to his north. Demetrius invited the Illyrians to intervene, which they did with gusto by land and by sea. The threat from piracy was so great that Roman commercial traffic was interrupted, Rome's friends such as Apollonia threatened, and a military intervention proved necessary. After witnessing the professionalism and speed with which the Romans dealt with the Illyrians, several Balkan communities, including Apollonia, Epidamnus, and Corcyra, placed themselves under Rome's protection via the procedure of *deditio in fidem*; the *fasti triumphales* records a triumph for Gnaeus Fulvius Centumalus, plebeian consul in 229 BC, for a naval victory over the Illyrian pirates. The

Figure 4.3 Bronze semis, minted in Luceria between 211 and 208 BC. Obverse: laureate head of Saturn right; reverse: prow of a warship with ROMA below.

campaign had been launched, in part, from Brundisium (Brindisi), the port city on the Italian side of the Adriatic that had been founded as a Latin colony in the early to mid-third century BC; the war came to an end in 228 BC when Teuta, the charismatic widow of the Illyrian leader Agron, agreed to an indemnity and a peace treaty. In the aftermath, Roman embassies were sent to the Achaean and Aetolian Leagues (below), as well as to Athens and Corinth, where the envoys arrived in time for the occasion of the Isthmian Games in 228 BC, where Greeks from all over the Hellenic world were gathered for this famous festival.

A Second Illyrian War soon followed, spurred by dynastic developments in Macedonia as the expansionist Antigonus III Doson (229–221 BC) threw his weight behind Teuta's successor, Demetrius of Pharos (the Adriatic island of Hvar). Demetrius tested the limits of Rome's patience, and in 219 BC the consuls Lucius Aemilius Paullus and Marcus Livius Salinator—both of whom would play prominent roles in the war with Hannibal—fought vigorously against him. These Illyrian campaigns were Rome's first forays eastwards, and set up a clash between the kingdom of Macedonia and the Republic that would be realised as the third century came to a close.

Meanwhile, a group of Gauls whom the Romans called the Boii attacked the Roman colony of Ariminum (Rimini) in 238 BC, and in 228 BC an unsettling prophecy foretelling the demise of Rome at the hands of the Gauls induced the Romans to make a rare human sacrifice: two Gauls and two Greeks were buried alive to ward off the ill omens. This incident shows how deeply entrenched the fear of the Gauls still was, over a century and a half after the presumed sack of Rome. The Romans weathered the Gallic invasion that followed and achieved a famous victory over their nemesis at Telamon (Tuscan Talamone) in 225 BC; the movement of Roman troops northwards was facilitated by the construction of the via Aurelia, which had begun in 241 BC. Polybius (2.28) recorded that at Telamon one of the consuls, Gaius Atilius Regulus (son of Marcus Atilius Regulus, Chapter 3) was slain in the fray and beheaded. The Romans soon gained the upper hand, however, assisted by the fact that the front ranks of the Gauls were fighting naked and thus susceptible to the slingshots and javelins of the *velites* (skirmishers). Polybius also remarked on

Figure 4.4 Silver quarter shekel, minted in Punic Spain. Obverse: laureate male head, left, with club behind; reverse: elephant.

the effectiveness of the Roman weapons, noting that they used 'swords [that] were made for both cutting and thrusting', a reference to the Roman *gladius*, a brutishly effective and terrifying weapon that could dismember an enemy just as easily as it might cut his throat (2.30).

The First Illyrian War and the campaigns in the Po valley secured Roman ascendancy in these areas. This was timely, since a new threat was rapidly emerging in Spain. The Carthaginian Barcid family, led by Hamilcar Barca, who had surrendered at Mt Eryx in 241, had struck out for Spain not long after the conclusion of the Truceless War in order to revive Carthaginian fortunes. In a surviving fragment of Cassius Dio, it was claimed that the Spanish project was against the advice of the Carthaginian senate (12.17), but this was more in tune with later Carthaginian efforts to disown Hannibal than the realities of the time. Spain was a good prospect, as it was rich in manpower and raw materials—particularly silver. Surviving examples of Punic Spanish silver coinage from the Barcid era provide elegant portraits (Figure 4.4).

Hamilcar earned high praise in antiquity, with Polybius stating that it was he 'to whom the palm must be given for both his daring and genius' in the First Punic War (1.62). Hamilcar's son, Hannibal, had been born a little earlier, in about 247/46 BC, and accompanied his father to Spain; several Spanish coin types are suspected to bear Hannibal's portrait, but it is not known for certain what he looked like. Cassius Dio (frag. 48) said that the Romans sent an embassy to Hamilcar in 231 BC to find out what he was up to. A mischievous Hamilcar replied that he was hard at work raising money to pay off the indemnity imposed by the treaty that had ended the First Punic War. Hamilcar died in 229/28 BC, and was succeeded by Hannibal's brother-in-law, a man known as Hasdrubal 'the fair'. Polybius, our main source for these events, was scathing about Hasdrubal, writing that Hasdrubal possessed a 'self-seeking ambition and lust for power' (3.8). Much of Polybius's account drew on the work of Fabius Pictor, who was very much a senatorial apologist for Rome and its actions. The Roman view was that Hamilcar's general hatred of the Romans—an understandable outcome of the First Punic War—combined with Hasdrubal's own character to create a potent and heady mix that guided the impressionable young Hannibal in a singular direction. In a surviving fragment of book 9, Polybius was more blunt in his assessment, remarking that 'of all that befell both nations, Romans and Carthaginians, the cause was one man and one mind—Hannibal' (9.22).

In 226/25 BC, not long before the battle of Telamon, the Romans arranged a treaty with Hasdrubal that laid out respective spheres of influence. This treaty should be seen in the context of the long tradition of treaty-making between Rome and Carthage that stretched back to the sixth century BC, as well as in the context of Rome's preoccupations with the Gallic menace much closer to home. Under this new agreement, the Carthaginians would not venture north of the river Ebro, which ran roughly parallel with the Pyrenees before emptying into the Mediterranean. The area north of the Ebro was of interest to Massilia (Marseille), a friend of Rome, which had colonies between it and the Ebro and was also a regional economic rival to the Barcids. Massilia was not shy about alerting the Romans to what was happening in the south, and later its worried bulletins would fall on fertile ground in Rome. It is generally agreed that the treaty implied that the Romans would not go *south* of the river Ebro, although this was never clearly stated. Was this agreement an attempt to delay the inevitable? Polybius seemed to think so, suggesting (2.13) that the Romans had suddenly realised how successful the Barcids had been, creating alliances with Spanish chieftains and amassing a considerable war chest. Roman concerns over the looming showdown with the Gauls made it desirable to stall Hasdrubal for the time being, and between 226 and 221 BC, the treaty sustained a period of phony war. In 221 BC, Hasdrubal died and Hannibal, who Polybius wrote 'made no secret of his intention to make war on the Romans' (2.36), took command of the Carthaginians in Spain.

The outbreak of war, 219–218 BC

Like the Pyrrhic War and the First Punic War, the conflict that became known as the Second Punic War, or the Hannibalic War, had local origins. The sticking points were the treaty of 226 BC and a city south of the river Ebro called Saguntum (Sagunto). Campaigning south of the Ebro, Hannibal began reducing cities close to Saguntum, which sent an appeal to Rome for help. Further noises were also made by Massilia, which counted Saguntum as a friend. This placed Rome in a quandary because Saguntum was an ally of Rome and under its *fides*. Nobody is quite sure when Saguntum entered into this arrangement, and its very existence seems rather convenient given the city's role in starting the war. It was also an impractical agreement: how, precisely, was Rome supposed to respond effectively to an appeal for help from its ally, which lay some 1,600 kilometres (990 miles) distant? It has even been suggested that the 'friendship' was established with the express intention of letting the city fall, in order to justify a war to seize Barcid Spain, with all its riches, snuffing out the Carthaginian revival in the process.

The Romans responded to Saguntum's pleas for help not with an army, but by sending an embassy to Hannibal, asking him to leave Saguntum alone. Hannibal responded that Saguntum was a menace to his own interests, and it seems likely that the city had indeed been campaigning against its neighbours. Under the treaty of 226 BC, Hannibal was thus fully justified in his actions. Faced with this impasse, the ambassadors went on to Carthage to try to find a resolution. Meanwhile, Hannibal followed up on his words by laying siege to Saguntum in 219 BC, and Rome's ambassadors were rebuffed in Carthage. The Romans, notably, did exactly nothing to help Saguntum during the eight months of the siege, although they did have the excuse of the conflict in Illyria at the time. With nobody coming to its aid, Saguntum eventually capitulated. Livy (21.14) wrote that the city's leading citizens threw themselves into a fire rather than be captured. Only now did the Romans act, sending a new embassy to Carthage to demand Hannibal's surrender, with the alternative being war. Backed into a corner, the Carthaginian senators took the only realistic choice available to them and hostilities quickly followed.

How had this come to pass? It was widely believed in antiquity that Hannibal nursed a burning hatred of Rome inherited from his father, Hamilcar. The most famous of the stories reported that Hamilcar had made a young Hannibal swear during a religious sacrifice to Baal that he would always be Rome's enemy (Polybius, 3.11–12). The Romans, however, had acted in bad faith by taking Sardinia and Corsica, and had unnecessarily punished Carthage with additional indemnities at the end of the Truceless War. Polybius pointed fingers at both sides. He wrote that, 'Relations between the Carthaginians and Romans were marked by mutual distrust and tension [and] it was clear to anyone with an open mind that before long they would be at war' (2.36). It was a combination of interwar resentment, ambition, bad behaviour on both sides, and a general unwillingness to stop the slow march to war that brought Rome and Carthage into this second conflict. When Saguntum emerged as the flashpoint, it is probable that the word 'Messana' would not have been far from Hannibal's lips as he contemplated the likely course of Roman action.

Hannibal was a complex figure who has both benefited from and been demonised by stories of the Hannibalic War and his starring role within it. For modern audiences, his image has been shaped by colonialism: the Italian film *Scipione l'africano* (1937; dir. Carmine Gallone) was bankrolled by Mussolini and its production was deeply intertwined with Fascist Italy's ambitions for conquest in Africa, including the region where the ruins of ancient Carthage lie. More recently, Hannibal has received a certain sort of attention in the documentary *Battles BC* (The History Channel), where he is portrayed in less than flattering terms as a brute who grunts his way through legions of Roman soldiers. While Roman consuls appear dressed in spotless white togas, Hannibal takes to the field of battle half dressed, wielding strange, exotic weapons, and lusting for Roman blood. Neither of these two ideas of Hannibal is accurate, and even the more balanced treatment given by the BBC's *Hannibal* (2006) reflects modern expectations of what barbaric enemies of Rome should look and act like.

Hannibal was already a legend by the second century BC, leading Polybius to complain that 'it is no easy thing to state the truth about him' (9.22). Nevertheless, some aspects of his character and temperament can be teased from the ancient sources. Cornelius Nepos (c. 110–24 BC), who wrote a biography of Hannibal, reported that he was fluent in Greek and had received a classical education (*Hannibal*, 13), and Cassius Dio added the comment that he was well-versed in how to take the auspices (13.54). It was believed that Hannibal had access to Pyrrhus's memoirs and familiarised himself with Roman tactics and the pitfalls of fighting in Italy. This educational background is very much in line with Hannibal's skilful interpretation of the Heracles legend and his manipulation of Greek propaganda (below). Like other leading Greek figures of his day, such as Pyrrhus, Hannibal's power was shaped more by battlefield success and the support of the army than any official position he held. Even though Hannibal operated with the consent of the Carthaginian senate, the bond between the commander and his troops was extraordinary, and very much in line with Hellenistic expectations of military command that had been fashioned by

Alexander the Great. This was clearly recognised in antiquity. Diodorus Siculus, writing in the first century BC, penned a glowing assessment of Hannibal, rating him 'first among all Carthaginians in strategic skill and in the magnitude of his achievements' (29.19).

Like Pyrrhus, Hannibal needed to remain victorious in order to maintain his primacy—and, remarkably, he achieved this, losing only one battle: to Scipio at Zama in 202 BC. Also putting him squarely in the Hellenistic camp was the fact that, like Alexander, Hannibal was accompanied by Greek savants and writers who chronicled his exploits. Their work is only known from excerpts and discussions in later writers; unflatteringly, Polybius derided them as 'the common gossip of the barber's shop' (3.20). Other attributes attached to Hannibal in antiquity—and borne out by the events that followed—included a mastery of tactics and battlefield deception (Livy, 21.4); an affinity for flexible thinking (Nepos, *Hannibal* 1, 4–5); and pragmatism in command (Polybius, 3.48). Cassius Dio said he was honourable, shared the dangers with his men, and always put them first (13.54). His negative traits were few, but included a weakness for cash (Polybius, 9.25).

In 219 BC, Hannibal set off on his celebrated invasion of Italy. This involved an epic journey over the Alps that has rightfully become memorialised for the endurance of his soldiers and Hannibal's determination to see it through. Before he left, he set in train a complex propaganda campaign that began at the Temple of Melqart in Gades (Cadiz). As noted earlier, Melqart's Greek equivalent was Heracles, the tales of whose mythical exploits were popular across the Mediterranean basin from Carthage to Seleucid Syria and Ptolemaic Egypt. Everyone knew the story of Heracles driving the oxen of Geryon out of Spain, all the way to Greece on a land route that passed through southern Gaul and over the Alps into Italy. During this epic voyage, Heracles had encountered Cacus, a giant who happened to live on the Aventine Hill in Rome. Tempted by this passing herd of oxen, Cacus prepared to steal the beasts, but was slain by Heracles in the process. The parallels could not have been clearer. Hannibal's route (Figure 4.5) clearly mimicked the Heraclean way. Here was a latter-day Heracles, destined to rid the Italians and the Greeks of the overbearing Roman giant.

This was extremely clever on Hannibal's part. Pyrrhus had styled himself as a liberator, and had prominently displayed the head of Heracles on his coinage. Alexander had likewise set out on his expedition to 'free the Greeks' suffering under Persian domination in Asia Minor; as we saw earlier, he also claimed strong ties to Heracles. Hannibal's links to this heroic past and his understanding of the Greek world show that, far from being a brutish thug, he was a member of the pan-Mediterranean Hellenistic aristocracy, squarely in the mould of the successors to Alexander (Chapter 3). Would Hannibal's propaganda find fertile ground in Italy? The history of the wars with Pyrrhus and Carthage suggests that Hannibal was well aware of the tenuous grip Rome had on its allies, especially in places such as Samnium and Tarentum; in Samnium, as in Magna Graecia, it just so happened that the cult of Heracles was particularly popular. Hannibal could also reasonably expect that the Greek colonists in Sicily—who had recently come under Roman domination—might also yearn to be free of the Roman yoke. Pyrrhus had rallied the Sicilians against their Carthaginian overlords by invoking the deeds of Heracles—and, indeed, Hiero's successor in Syracuse, Hieronymus, would quickly go over to Hannibal when the time came.

Despite a number of strenuous efforts, including an intrepid on-the-ground attempt by Polybius, it has proven impossible to locate the exact route that Hannibal took over the Alps. He was, however, meticulous in his preparations, hiring guides and storing food. The

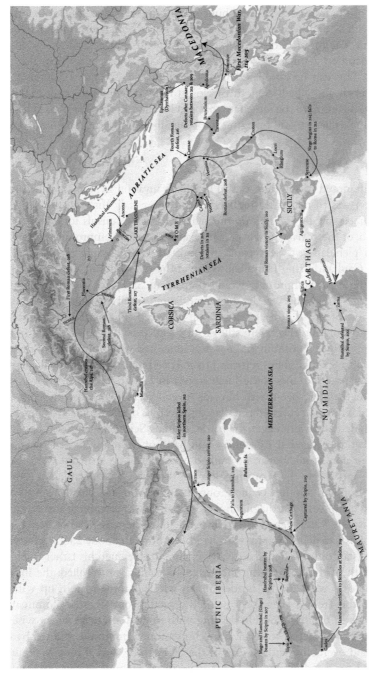

Figure 4.5 The main events of the Hannibalic War. The solid line shows Hannibal's journey from Spain to Italy, and then to Africa; the dotted line approximates the campaigns of the younger Scipio in Spain.

Source: Illustration by the author.

crossing seems to have taken about five months, and was finished by the early autumn of 218 BC. Ravines, snow, ice, and all manner of natural obstacles wrought havoc on his army, and parts of the trail needed to be built up to support the weight of the elephants. The numbers with which he started are unknown, but a dedication from the Temple of Hera (Juno/Tanit) Lacinia at Croton—which local legend asserted had been constructed by Heracles—recorded a force of 20,000 foot and 6,000 horse surviving the crossing (Polybius, 3.56). This can be compared with the census of 225 BC (Chapter 2), giving a combined Roman and allied strength of close to 700,000 infantry and 70,000 horse. Would Hannibal succumb to the same fate that had befallen Pyrrhus, or would he succeed in breaking Rome's alliances and bringing the Roman senate to the bargaining table?

Annihilation, 218–216 BC

The Romans attempted to interfere with Hannibal's invasion as soon as it became clear that his intention was to march through Gaul and enter Italy through the Alps, a route that was made necessary by Rome's dominance at sea. The consuls for 218 BC, Publius Cornelius Scipio, of the patrician *gens* Cornelia, and Tiberius Sempronius Longus, of the mixed patrician/plebeian *gens* Sempronia, formulated the following plan: Scipio would cross by ship to Gaul and bring Hannibal to bay at the river Rhône, thus preventing him from reaching the Alps; Sempronius would prepare in Sicily for an invasion of Africa to knock Carthage out of the war. In the event, Scipio narrowly missed Hannibal, who effected a crossing of the Rhône by using rafts covered in grass and mud to deceive the elephants into thinking they were still on dry land (Polybius, 3.62). Scipio's brother, Gnaeus Cornelius Scipio (consul in 222 BC) was entrusted with command of the consul's army and sent on to Spain. Publius returned to Italy to prepare for Hannibal's arrival.

Before long, the two sides met at the Ticinus river in 218 BC. Hannibal's troops were his experienced elite: they had been with him for several years of combat in Spain and had been well trained. They had endured the shared privations of the Alpine crossing, had faith in their commander, and were eager for battle. Publius Scipio, in contrast, had a citizen levy that had been put together in a hurry and had not been granted adequate time to get to know their commander or to be trained effectively. The Romans were also operating in a restive area where the Roman colony of Placentia (Piacenza) had recently been attacked by the Boii and another Gallic group that the Romans called the Insubres. The result of this first clash was a Carthaginian victory. Scipio was wounded, and was confined to bed rest in his tent. Later legend asserted that Scipio's life was saved by his young son, also named Publius Cornelius Scipio, who had been born in about 236 BC. Serving as a military tribune (staff officer), he led a cavalry charge that rescued his father (Livy, 21.46).

In the aftermath of the clash at the Ticinus, Sempronius was recalled; the invasion of Africa would have to wait, and he headed north with his force to join up with Scipio at a position on the Trebbia river. Livy painted a picture of a Roman command riven with indecision, with the two consuls clashing with one another: the older, wiser patrician, Scipio, urged caution; the younger, more impetuous Sempronius, tainted by his plebeian ancestry and overcome with visions of the glory to be won if only *he* could defeat Hannibal, argued for rapid action. In Livy's magisterial account of the war, consuls are often portrayed as opposing couplets, with a tension between experience and youth, patrician and plebeian, duty and personal glory. It is quite possible that, in some of these cases, such clashes between consuls did take place; after all, this was exactly the reason why the constitution provided for a collegial magistracy—to check unwieldy ambition. On the other hand, the outcomes can be so clumsily contrived—arrogance and impiety lead irrevocably to disaster, prudence to success—as to tax even the most trusting reader. They also belie Hannibal's remarkable ability to read his opponents. He knew the consuls would alternate command, and given the choice of Scipio or Sempronius, with spies in the Roman camp reporting the mettle of each, Hannibal waited for Sempronius to take command of the army.

Hannibal prepared carefully. He was well aware that he was at a numerical disadvantage, so he depended on using his enemies' strengths and weaknesses against them through his mastery of battlefield deception. He knew that the Roman maniple was extremely strong in the advance, but that it had a limited ability to manoeuvre on the battlefield. He therefore assigned his brother Mago to a concealed position on the flank of where he judged the Romans would make their attack. He then tempted Sempronius to battle by launching a surprise raid on the Roman camp. Hannibal's troops were fed, warm, and rested; the Romans, in contrast, were rudely summoned from their tents and formed up for battle on a cold December morning. The Trebbia river lay between them and the Carthaginians, which meant that they were forced to cross through the freezing water in the face of driving sleet.

The Roman advance was aggressive, and the leading maniples broke the Carthaginian line. The Roman cavalry, however, was spooked by the smell of the Carthaginian war elephants and fled the battlefield. At this point, Mago sprung his trap, attacking the flanks of the Roman formation. Even as the victorious Roman centre continued straight ahead, the bulk of the Roman army was penned against the frigid Trebbia and massacred on its banks and in the shallows. The victory was total, even if both consuls managed to flee the battlefield. Hannibal took hundreds of prisoners, but after interrogating each one he allowed the Italians to go free, while he kept the Romans in chains. Here was his propaganda at work: his quarrel was with Rome, not with the oppressed peoples of Italy.

The Romans dealt with this setback in the way that they had addressed those against Pyrrhus. They elected new consuls and levied new armies. The consuls for 217 BC were Gnaeus Servilius Geminus, of the patrician *gens* Servilia, and Gaius Flaminius, of the plebeian *gens* Flaminia, who had begun his career in 232 as a plebeian tribune. Livy portrayed Flaminius as a hothead, reflecting a later tradition that sought to cast his tribunate as anti-senatorial and populist, mired in a controversial law that aimed to settle Roman citizens on land captured from the Gauls. Livy also cast doubt on Flaminius' future, dramatizing his tenure as consul as a time when he was 'at war not only with the senate, but with the gods' (21.62). A sacrifice duly went horribly wrong when the animal escaped, drenching onlookers with blood. 'Most people', wrote Livy, 'took the incident as an omen of coming disaster' (21.63). Flaminius was very much cast in the same mould as Sempronius: impatient, arrogant, and lacking the *virtus* that Livy felt should be displayed by a Roman consul. As Flaminius and his army sheltered behind the walls of Arretium in Etruria, Hannibal approached north-central Italy via a treacherous route through the swamps of the river Arno, where he and many of his men became ill. His efforts were rewarded however as he pushed Flaminius past his breaking point and drew him into a hasty action. As at the Trebbia, Hannibal knew which consul he preferred to fight. Flaminius was rash and impetuous; 'all his officers', wrote Livy, 'urged a policy of caution', but the consul ignored them. They begged him to wait for Servilius to arrive from Ariminum with his army, but Flaminius was determined to stop Hannibal. His next move, however, portended his doom, when his horse tripped and threw him to the ground (Livy, 22.4). Despite these grim omens, Flaminius ordered his force out of Arretium and in pursuit of the Carthaginian army. Once again Hannibal prepared carefully, luring Flaminius into a narrow defile along the edges of Lake Trasimene. The Roman army marched into this killing ground without any scouts and in marching order, their weapons slung, ill-prepared for battle. In Livy's dramatic retelling of events, a thick fog arose from the lake, obscuring the foothills and higher ground which kept the Roman column on a single track as they pursued what they thought was Hannibal's main force. That was a lure, however: it was merely Hannibal's rearguard, whose lights flickered dimly to Flaminius' front. At Hannibal's order, the trap was sprung and Flaminius was attacked from three sides by Hannibal's crack Numidian cavalry and his Carthaginian and Spanish soldiers. 'Taken by surprise', recalled Polybius, the Romans perished 'while they were still trying to decide what to do'. Those who sought to escape into the lake either drowned or were bludgeoned to death in the shallows (3.84). Lake Trasimene became a byword for defeat and calamity in antiquity; not only was the army lost, but the consul commanding it was killed as well. The humiliation was oppressive and Rome was cast into a deep and hopeless gloom. A small number of troops escaped, but they were quickly run to ground and surrendered. Servilius, hearing of the disaster, sent a column to help, but this, too, was captured. Hannibal, ever gracious in victory, searched for the body of his slain adversary in order to afford it the proper burial rites, but he was unsuccessful. He had better luck once again with his captives: the Italians were freed, the Romans consigned to chains.

In the aftermath of this disaster the Romans appointed a dictator, Quintus Fabius Maximus, from the illustrious *gens* Fabia. Fabius became famous as the *cunctator*, or 'delayer', an uncomplimentary epithet he earned through the wise tactic of refusing battle with Hannibal unless he was absolutely sure of victory. Instead, he preferred to attack Hannibal's supply lines and wear him down through harassment. Fabius also bade the Romans look to the *Sibylline Books* for help and guidance, which resulted in the dedication of a temple to Venus Erycina, a cult derived from Eryx in Sicily and explicitly associated with Roman victory over Carthage. Fabius' kinsman, the historian Fabius Pictor, was dispatched to Delphi to consult the famous oracle there, returning with directions that a measure of Roman plunder be dedicated to Apollo. The involvement of the Delphic oracle was a shrewd way of reminding Rome's allies that she had a stake in Greek affairs and had the favour of the gods. Not long afterwards, the Romans once again sacrificed two Gauls and two Greeks, buried in the *forum boarium* while still drawing breath. Not satisfied with these measures, the senate called up slaves and young boys to fight.

As much as Scipio Africanus (below), Fabius saved the state. But in Rome, Fabius had his critics. These appeared in Livy in the guise of young, impious men who were willing to go against the *mos maiorum* to seek personal glory instead of selflessly doing their duty. Polybius thought that the strategy taken by Fabius was the right one, saying that he decided Rome should look to its strengths, 'an inexhaustible supply of provisions, and plenty of men' (3.89). Hannibal did his best to undermine Fabius, whom he greatly admired as a capable tactician. For instance, he plundered the countryside around the dictator's estates, but ostentatiously left Fabius' own property alone, encouraging whispered rumours that Hannibal and Fabius were in league together. One night, when Fabius thought he had his man, Hannibal drove cattle with torches attached to their horns in one direction while he retired in the other, fooling Fabius into pursuing the wrong target. In the end, Fabius' enemies succeeded in winning concessions, and a politician named Minucius was appointed to the unprecedented office of co-dictator.

Eventually, Fabius stepped down after the six-month period of the dictatorship was up and new consuls were elected. These were Lucius Aemilius Paullus from the venerable patrician *gens* Aemilia, who had been consul in 219 BC, and a man whom Livy derided for his populist demagoguery, Gaius Terentius Varro, from the plebeian *gens* Terentia, the son of a butcher who had led the opposition to Fabius and agitated for Minucius to be appointed as co-dictator. Livy contemptuously wrote that Varro had made his name through 'impassioned speeches on behalf of the underdog and against the privileges of the dominant class' (22.25). There was no future for him in Livy's telling of the story: under his consulship, statues wept blood, cold springs turned hot, and all the omens pointed towards further gloom. In the senate, Livy placed an impassioned speech into the mouth of Quintus Fabius Maximus, who characterised the state as staggering along on 'one sound leg'—Aemilius Paullus—and on 'one lame one'—Varro (22.39). 'The wishes of Varro,' Fabius warned, 'will play straight into the hands of Hannibal' (22.40).

The elder statesman Fabius was, of course, right. The two armies prepared to meet each other in the summer heat at Cannae in Apulia, in 216 BC. Hannibal planned carefully for the contest, placing his faith once again in the maniple's aggressive forward movement. The new Roman levy was massive, an instrument forged to end the war. As the anxious troops fidgeted, awaiting battle, Livy portrayed Aemilius Paullus and Varro sparring like gladiators in the arena. Hannibal's spies kept him informed of the tensions between the two consuls, and on a day when he knew Varro had command, he offered battle. Hannibal arranged his troops in a convex bow, with his weakest solders in the bulge that faced the Roman legions. The temptation was too great, and Varro ordered the maniples forward. As they cut deep into the Carthaginian army, the bow gave way, creating a concave shape. According to Appian, a vicious wind had also whipped up the dry, dusty earth, making it hard to see what was happening (*Hannibalic War*, 18–26). Anticipating an easy victory, Varro ordered the Roman army even further into the trap, which had now became a deep U-shaped formation with the wings made up of Hannibal's experienced veteran infantry. In the meantime, the inferior Roman horsemen had been driven from the field, and the Numidian cavalry returned to seal the trap. The infantry in the 'U' turned inwards, and the killing began.

It is thought that some 80,000 Roman soldiers lost their lives on this hot, bloody afternoon. Aemilius Paullus was one of them; so were some 80 or so senators, men who fought as commoners in the ranks of the legions. Varro fled, and later turned up in Rome. Somehow he avoided prosecution for his incompetence and, amazingly, retained his army command into the year 215 BC. Most of the small number of survivors escaped to nearby Canusium, from where many were organised into punishment battalions and sent to Sicily. One of the officers who evaded this fate was Scipio, the son of Publius Cornelius Scipio (consul in 218 BC), who was vividly portrayed by Livy rallying his dejected companions by pledging to Jupiter that he would not rest until Hannibal was beaten (22.53). The disaster at Cannae assumed such a legendary status that Ammianus Marcellinus, writing of a similar catastrophe at Adrianople in AD 378 (Chapter 13), lamented that 'in the annals there is no record of such a massacre, other than the one at Cannae' (31.13). Livy wrote that the

Roman soldiers sold their lives dearly, recording with unbridled patriotic fervour the case of a Roman soldier who had died biting his enemy when he could no longer lift his sword (22.52). No amount of patriotism could obscure the fact that by the traditions and expectations of Hellenistic warfare, Cannae signalled the total defeat of Rome. Hannibal, like Pyrrhus before him, had every reason to expect the city to sue for peace.

Total war

Elated with his victory, Hannibal sent his brother Mago to Carthage to obtain reinforcements. Only a token force was provided in response, far short of what Hannibal actually needed; he would have to intensify his efforts in Italy. A later tradition that worked its way into Livy alleged that one of Hannibal's associates, Marhabal, urged his general to march on Rome (22.51) to end any further thought of resistance. Yet capturing Rome was not required to knock Rome out of the war. For Hannibal to succeed where Pyrrhus had failed, he knew he had to convince a sufficient number of Rome's allies to break their agreements with Rome and instead bring their military levies over to Hannibal's side, making good his own manpower shortages and leaving Rome bereft of support. Surely Cannae, the third stunning defeat of the invincible Romans in three short years, would provide ample incentive? Some of Rome's alliances *were*, after all, showing signs of falling apart. Tarentum, many of the Samnite settlements, and numerous cities in Magna Graecia eventually chose Hannibal over Rome. Hannibal worked hard to support these defections, and not long after the battle of Cannae he won a diplomatic coup in Campania when Capua defected. Resentment against Roman domination, the lure of Hannibal's promises that Campanians would be exempt from military duty and the pledge that Capua itself was to be the metropolis of Italy after Rome's final defeat played a significant role in the Capuan decision to back Carthage over Rome. There was even the possibility that Capua's territory could be enlarged at Rome's expense, and a group of jubilant Capuan citizens celebrated by murdering some visiting Roman military officers in the public bath-house; Capuan coins were also minted that imitated Carthaginian coins with the head of Tanit (such as Figure 3.8 in Chapter 3). Meanwhile, Hannibal tried his luck at negotiation, sending his envoy Carthalo to Rome, but he was dismissed without an audience. Rome would fight on with everything it had. Hannibal was ultimately frustrated in Italy and Sicily, largely because the Romans, contrary to all reasonable expectations and the customs of war, failed to recognise that they were beaten. Instead, they engaged in a form of total war, mobilising as many troops as they could from all parts of society, keeping successful generals in the field, importing food from Egypt and Sicily to make up for the loss of farmers, land, and the harvest in Italy, and pledging their entire financial reserves to victory.

Hannibal wintered his army at Capua in 216/15 BC, and Roman writers later thought that the supposed lax discipline of the Carthaginian soldiers as they gave themselves over to Capua's brothels and its taverns took the edge off their fighting prowess. Hannibal meanwhile heard the unwelcome news that the Scipio brothers, Publius and Gnaeus, had checked his own brother, Hasdrubal, in northern Spain. Balancing this was the more welcome development that the tyrant of Syracuse, Hieronymus, had offered his services to Hannibal after the death of Hiero II in 215 BC. In 215 BC, Hannibal also made a treaty with the king of Macedon, Philip V, who provided naval support and contingents of troops, hoping in return to be rid of Rome's nascent presence on his borders in Illyria and win back some of Rome's allies, like Corcyra and Apollonia, which had put themselves under Rome's protection during the Illyrian wars. When the Romans found out about this agreement, they initiated a campaign in Greece to keep Philip occupied and to prevent him from honouring his treaty commitments. It is astonishing to think that even as the Romans grappled with the aftermath of the terrible defeat at Cannae, they were able to support operations in a wholly separate theatre, even if they did so with substantial support from Philip's enemies, including Pergamum and the Aetolian League (a central Greek confederation of city-states historically opposed to Macedonian power). This conflict, the First Macedonian War, began in 214 BC and would sputter to a close in 205 BC.

Marcus Claudius Marcellus (from the *gens* Claudia, and consul in 215 BC), who had won the *spolia opima* fighting the Gauls, steadily chipped away at Hannibal's position in Italy. Later, Marcellus dealt a further blow through his leadership of the dramatic siege of Syracuse in 212 BC, which has become famous for the 'super weapons' of the mathematician Archimedes. These included the so-called 'death ray', a system of mirrors to magnify the sun and set Roman ships on fire, as well as the 'claw of Archimedes', a device that could lift Roman ships out of the water and capsize or drop them. (An enterprising class at MIT tested the former, proving that it was feasible, while Discovery Channel's series *Superweapons of the Ancient World* achieved success with its model of the claw.) As well as relating the more fantastical machinery, Plutarch reported conventional weapons such as trebuchets and ballistae, which fired heavy metal bolts at the attacking Romans (*Marcellus*, 15). Even the skill of Archimedes was not enough to save the city, however, and nor could he save himself. Marcellus gave orders that the mathematician be spared, but he was killed by a legionnaire in the sack that followed.

By 212/11 BC, the Romans had an astonishing 25 legions on operations—just four years after the calamity at Cannae. A year later, the Romans were strong enough to turn their attention to Capua, laying siege to their recalcitrant ally with a vengeance. Desperate to help the Capuans, Hannibal marched for Rome, and made it as far as the Temple of Hercules (the Roman name for Heracles) on the city's outskirts. Pausing at this auspicious spot, Hannibal was unable to either lift the siege of Capua or prevent a Roman army marching out from the other side of the city for duties in Spain. Capua was taken and its population enslaved or killed, an event that sent shockwaves through Hannibal's Italian allies. With the fall of Capua, Livy noted approvingly that 'the enemy were forced to acknowledge what power the Romans possessed to exact punishment from faithless allies, and how helpless Hannibal was to defend those whom he had taken under his protection' (26.16). Roman actions soon proved the truth of this statement. Tarentum was recaptured by Fabius Maximus in 209 BC, and even though Hannibal managed to kill Marcellus in battle at Venusia in 208 BC, he must have realised that his days in Italy were numbered.

Spain

The stunning Roman revival from a point of near-annihilation in 216 BC to retaking Capua and Tarentum between 211 BC and 209 BC suggests that the outcome of the war was decided primarily in Italy. This is misleading: the outcome of the war was instead largely determined hundreds of kilometres away in Spain. It was there that the only meaningful supply of manpower available to Hannibal was systematically reduced, and it was there that a new type of commander arose who had the tactical brilliance to defeat his opponent. To understand the importance of the war in Spain, we must turn back the clock several years.

In 211 BC, Publius Cornelius Scipio (consul 218 BC) and his brother Gnaeus (consul 222 BC) were killed in two separate engagements within a short time of one another. This left the Roman army in Spain stranded, and also left the young Publius Cornelius Scipio (henceforth, 'Scipio'), who had saved his father at the Ticinus (219 BC), as the head of the family. Little is known of his early career. At some point he married into the *gens* Aemilia, a long-time ally of the *gens* Cornelia; his father-in-law was Lucius Aemilius Paullus, killed at Cannae. In 212 BC, Scipio was elected curule aedile, even though he was too young for the position. Ominously, Livy reported that his election occurred because of the 'will of the people', cast in opposition to the *mos maiorum* and making Scipio something of a populist. This paradox was never fully resolved by Livy, who was forced to accept that his great hero was not cut from the stern patrician mould of an Aemilius Paullus or a Fabius Maximus. Following the deaths of Scipio's father and uncle a year later (211 BC), there was a brief interlude in Spain where a number of officers sought to rally the troops. Eventually the senate determined that a more senior official was needed, and proposed an election for the Spanish command that would carry the rank of proconsul. The prefix 'pro-' affixed to Roman magistracies, such as proconsul or propraetor, was used to denote an individual with the imperium of the office but who had not been elected to the formal office itself. This was the practice of prorogation, which saw the imperium of a consul or praetor extended past the end-date of their magistracy if required. A prorogued consul was thus a proconsul, a praetor a propraetor. Numerous consuls and praetors were prorogued during the war due to the need to keep experienced men in command of the armies. As the need for qualified individuals expanded even further, men could be appointed specifically as proconsuls or propraetors even if they had not held rank in the previous year.

Scipio was too young to be proconsul; he was perhaps 24 at the time, well under the traditional age limit of about 42. Nevertheless, he was elected as the only plausible contender, a man from an illustrious family that had bled and died for Rome in Spain. Scipio's ineligibility was fudged by making him a private citizen with imperium, and after a year in office he would then be prorogued as a proconsul. Scipio's candidacy was also made attractive by a Hannibal-like ability to judge people and to shape their temperament to his own advantage. This ability was aided by the fact that from an early age Scipio made it a point to nurture the image that he possessed a special relationship with the gods. He would, Livy said, spend time by himself in the Temple of Jupiter on the Capitoline Hill, and would only go about his business after he had communed with Rome's most important deity (26.19). The general opinion among the ancient writers who chronicled Scipio's career was that he did this for political reasons, and that by saying nothing but allowing his actions to be observed, he deliberately allowed people to spread certain favourable rumours about him. By behaving in this way, however, Scipio was acting more like a Hellenistic dynast than a Roman consul. Everyone knew the stories of Alexander's career and his links to the divine; here was a young Roman politician tapping into this rich Mediterranean heritage. It was a worrying omen for the institutional corporation that was the Republic, and threatened to transfer a focus on selfless duty and *virtus* to something altogether different—the terrible spectre of the powerful individual. After his appointment, Scipio travelled to Spain, and in 210 BC called his army together on the river Ebro. He addressed his soldiers publicly, appealing to their years of service with his father and his uncle, and doing nothing to suppress a rumour that he was divinely appointed to bring an end to the long conflict. By presenting himself in this way, and in particular by casting himself as the latest in a family marque that had led Rome's armies for close to a decade, he was once again behaving in a manner that owed more to Hellenistic ideas about military kingship than Roman ideas of the consulship.

Scipio knew that there were three Carthaginian armies in Spain. In order to starve Hannibal in Italy and to compel him to face Scipio at a time and place of his choosing, these three would have to be destroyed. First, though, Scipio decided on a surprise strike against the enemy's stronghold, the city of New Carthage (Cartagena, a foundation of Hasdrubal 'the fair' in 229 BC) on the eastern coast. The city occupied a highly defensible position, as it was situated on a promontory to which access was provided only by a slender isthmus. To the west and south was a lagoon. Scipio and his lieutenant Laelius struck south with the army; after reaching the vicinity of New Carthage, Scipio learned from local fisherman that the lagoon could be forded under certain tidal conditions. Distracting the defenders with a showy and costly attack over the isthmus, the Romans crossed the lagoon under the right conditions and scaled the walls. New Carthage was theirs, and Scipio did nothing to distract from the rampant rumours that Neptune had revealed to him how to conquer the city in a dream.

The capture of New Carthage was a stunning success for Scipio, and did much for his popularity among the troops. The plunder, too, was immense, and included a valuable human cargo: a bevy of Spanish hostages, kept by the Carthaginians to guarantee their Spanish alliances. In one famous story, Scipio brought together a sobbing young woman with her fiancé, sending the pair on their way to get married, an act of calculated generosity that was much admired by the Spanish population. There were further human dividends, for over the winter of 209/08 BC, a wave of Spanish defections bolstered Scipio's position. Three Spanish noblemen, Edeco, Mandonius, and Indibilis, together with their powerful levies, threw in their lot with the Roman proconsul. With this added manpower, Scipio determined to attack Hasdrubal, but he made it clear that he intended to fight a different war from that of his father and uncle. He trained his troops to form maniples into larger units called cohorts (about the size of an infantry battalion, at 600 men or so) and then back into maniples at short notice. He taught an elasticity on the battlefield that gave maniples and cohorts the ability to move and flank in a way that undid older Roman tactical ideas of the aggressive advance of the maniples—which, of course, had been their undoing at the Trebbia (218 BC) and Cannae (216 BC).

In 208 BC, Scipio set his army loose on Hasdrubal, who was bivouacked at Baecula, near Córdoba. Scipio found Hasdrubal at the top of a hill fenced with steep slopes and a river to the rear. Distracting the Carthaginians with a frontal attack that held them in place, he sent two groups of cohorts from his rear ranks around either side of the hill, with one led by himself and the other by Laelius. With Hasdrubal still focused on the feint, the cohorts climbed the sides of the hill and assaulted the enemy flanks, setting them to flight in short order. Hasdrubal escaped, but Scipio captured the grandson of Masinissa, one of Hannibal's Numidian allies and a feared cavalry commander. Scipio showed clemency to the prisoners, but most especially to this young man, for whom he provided an armed escort with orders to bring him home safely to his grandfather.

In desperation, the three Carthaginian commanders—Hasdrubal, Hannibal's brother; Mago, Hannibal's other brother; and Hasdrubal, son of Gisgo—realised that a collapse in

Spain would mean the end of the war. Hasdrubal immediately raised a new army and set out for Italy. Crossing the Alps, he sent messengers to his brother to meet in Umbria, but these were intercepted by the Romans, who formulated a plan to counter this new threat. One consul, the plebeian Marcus Livius Salinator, was given the job of defeating Hasdrubal, while his colleague, Gaius Claudius Nero, a patrician consul from the *gens* Claudia—who had cut his teeth as propraetor during the Capuan revolt in 211 BC and then briefly led the Roman forces in Spain—shadowed Hannibal in the south. Tiring of this duty, however, and seized by a spontaneity not normally shown by Roman commanders, Nero arranged matters so that it appeared to Hannibal as if he were still in camp, and took a picked force north on a rapid march to join his consular colleague. On arrival at the river Metaurus in northern Italy, a similar deception was likewise used to mislead Hasdrubal and make him think that only a single force was in camp. On the march, people streamed from their homes, feeding the troops and urging them on. The Roman soldiers 'were marching everywhere between lines of men and women who had poured out from the farms on every side', wrote Livy, 'amidst their vows and prayers and words of praise' (27.45). Appian called the battle that followed 'compensation for the disaster of Cannae' (*Hannibalic War*, 53). Overwhelmed by the Roman force opposing him, Hasdrubal charged a Roman cohort, only to be dragged down and killed. Hannibal's lifeline was gone, and Nero sent Hasdrubal's severed head to his brother.

Back in Spain, a sign of the changing political temperament came with the unexpected acclamation of Scipio as a *rex*—king—by the Spanish troops. Scipio balked at this, and insisted that if they were going to call him anything, it should be *imperator*, a word that at this juncture did not have the lofty connotations of adoration and hero-worship that it later acquired. During Scipio's time, it merely meant 'commander' and, as he explained to the forlorn Spaniards, his Roman troops had started to call him this in any case. Nevertheless, this was the first recorded use of *imperator* and it was an undeniable reflection of the growing personal links between Scipio and his soldiers, which would eventually have the senate concerned about the nature of Scipio's ambition.

In 207/06 BC, Mago and Hasdrubal, son of Gisgo, gathered a sizeable force at Ilipa, near Seville. Here, Scipio displayed the magnitude of his talent; it was certainly one of the most sophisticated Roman victories of all time, although it rarely receives the recognition it deserves. Scipio toyed with Hasdrubal, son of Gisgo, who was in command, by repeatedly drawing up his own force and then retiring without offering battle. Each day Scipio placed his legionnaires in the centre and his weak Spanish troops on the wings. Hasdrubal responded in kind, drawing up his battle-hardened Libyans in the centre and his Spaniards on the wings. This went on for a number of days. Then, one morning, with his troops fed and rested, Scipio reversed the formation and sent skirmishers into action against the enemy. Lulled into complacency, Hasdrubal and his troops stumbled from their tents with their best troops in the centre and the Spanish on the flanks, just as before. The Roman advance was faster in the wings than in the centre, with the developing attack resembling the horns of a bull. Facing the Libyans in the distance was the forehead of the bull, a slow-moving mass of Spanish; facing Hasdrubal's Spanish on either side, though, and growing closer by the minute, were the horns of the bull—the Roman legionnaires. Hasdrubal could do nothing, for if he rushed his Libyans forward to reduce the Spanish line to his front, his attack would be crushed from the flanks. If he sent his Libyans to reinforce his weak Spanish on the flanks, he would be cut to pieces by the Spanish opposite him. With one bold stroke, Scipio had taken Hasdrubal's most experienced troops out of the fight. This remarkable formation broke with decades of Roman tactics and has rightly been titled a 'Cannae in reverse' (the phrase of historian Richard Gabriel), for Scipio swallowed the Carthaginian formation, setting Hasdrubal and Mago to flight. With this remarkable victory, Scipio destroyed Carthage's fortunes in Spain. Not long afterwards, Masinissa defected to Scipio, bringing his experienced and valuable cavalry. Diodorus (29.20) praised Scipio for his Spanish campaign, remarking that by 'artful planning, without battle [with Hannibal] or risk', he had given Hannibal no choice but to leave Italy and retire to Africa. Italy would henceforth be spared further devastation. Before he left Spain, however, Scipio fell gravely ill, and for a while it was feared that he would die. Almost as if in response, a terrible rebellion broke out, involving Mandonius, Indibilis, and a number of Roman troops. It was a nasty coda to a victorious campaign that had been masterminded by a truly brilliant tactician, who had bent years of Roman military dogma to ensure victory.

In 206/05 BC, Scipio returned to Rome, formally gave up his imperium, and turned over all of the plunder he had amassed in six years of fighting. Scipio did not receive a triumph for his success in Spain, as he had not been elected consul. Elaborate preparations were made for the final push against Carthage, and the Romans ensured that they sought the approval of the gods for ending the war. A further consultation of the *Sibylline Books* resulted in the cult of Magna Mater being transported to Rome from her ally, Pergamum, in the shape of a black meteorite. At about the same time, a delegation was sent to Delphi to dedicate the share of plunder earlier vowed to Apollo.

Scipio immediately ran for the consulship, and was duly elected in 205 BC. He pushed for an African campaign and got his way, although the senate's commission to him was rather opaque: he was to prepare an army in Sicily, and fight in Africa if it was determined to be in Rome's interest. (His colleague was Publius Licinius Crassus, a plebeian who was also *pontifex maximus*, and thus not permitted to depart from Italy, which left the senate little choice.) In the meantime, Mago tried to foment a rebellion in northern Italy, but achieved little and died of wounds two years later, in 203 BC. Sicily swelled with Roman troops, and Laelius sailed for Africa with the vanguard. Keen to follow, Scipio was waylaid by an intensive investigation prompted by a growing clique in the senate that was suspicious of his motives and wary of his ambition. He was accused, among other things, of 'going Greek', exercising in the gymnasium and generally acting in ways that conservative senators thought to be unbecoming for a Roman consul. Scipio narrowly survived his inquisition, but this would not be the end of the matter—even if there were still strong voices who thought that, for Scipio, 'the army was his work; the gymnasium was his relaxation' (Valerius Maximus, 3.6.1). In 204 BC, the main Roman force established itself at the *castra Cornelia* (the 'Cornelian camp'), and after an abortive siege of the city of Utica, near Carthage, Scipio finally got his campaign moving with a dramatic night action that mauled Carthaginian confidence and put Hasdrubal, son of Gisgo, on the run. Recovering his nerve some time later on, Hasdrubal, together with the Numidian prince Syphax, raised a new army and met Scipio at an unknown location that ancient writers called 'the Great Plains'. The result was a Carthaginian slaughter, achieved by Scipio wheeling his rear ranks out on each side as he done at Baecula, and flanking his opponents.

The war was rapidly drawing to a close. Syphax fell into Laelius's hands, and Carthage sued for peace. Hannibal and his clan, the Barcids, were blamed for all that had gone wrong in the war; the Carthaginian senate professed that it had never wanted conflict. This was patently not true, as Carthaginian representatives, *synedroi*, had accompanied Hannibal on campaign and taken the customary oaths for the treaty agreed with Philip V of Macedon. There was real fear in Carthage, however; Livy wrote that the Carthaginian senate said of Scipio that 'they dreaded him as though he had been destined from his birth to be their ruin' (30.28). Scipio agreed to terms, levying an indemnity, decreeing the virtual destruction of the remnants of the Carthaginian navy, and deciding that all of Carthage's territory outside Africa would be given to Rome—including Spain. According to the ancient sources, which seemed to favour the more triumphant ending of a violent showdown between Scipio and Hannibal, the peace was never ratified. Instead, Carthage violated the truce when Hasdrubal captured some Roman transports that had foundered on the beaches near the city. Learning of this, Scipio sent heralds to ask for them back, but on their return the envoys were attacked by a Carthaginian vessel, breaking the sacred laws that ensured the safety of heralds and ambassadors. The Romans could thus claim that *fides* had been broken on the Carthaginian side, and that they were left with little choice but to finish off their old enemy. On the other hand, Polybius (15.1–2) suggested that this was a deliberate Carthaginian provocation by a clique angry with the peace treaty and determined to make one final gamble for victory.

After the drama of the war and the tactical brilliance displayed by both Hannibal and Scipio throughout, the showdown at Zama (202 BC) was something of an anticlimax. Scipio had the advantage of Masinissa and his own cavalry, who he had trained to play a fuller and more decisive role than they had been used to performing in the past. In rather contrived scenes, the ancient sources recalled a meeting between Hannibal and Scipio before the battle, where Hannibal asked for peace; predictably, Scipio turned him down. In the melee that followed, both sides tried to outflank the other, but without success. A brilliant cavalry charge by Laelius and Masinissa drove the Carthaginian horse from the field, even as Roman soldiers, including the punishment battalions, the survivors of Cannae, struggled amidst a battlefield slick with blood and the mangled bodies of dead men and animals. With his cavalry gone, and his elephants wasted on the open formation of Scipio's maniples, which allowed the beasts harmlessly through to the Roman rear, Hannibal was beaten and fled the battlefield. Scipio returned triumphantly to Rome, taking the agnomen 'Africanus' and paying a huge bonus to his troops out of the plunder seized on campaign. The Hannibalic War was over.

Rome, 202–200 BC

In his 1959 novel *Starship Troopers*, Robert Heinlein created a stark dichotomy between 'citizens' and 'civilians'. The former earned the franchise through loyal service to the state; the latter shirked their duties and forever remained cut off from the sombre obligations and responsibilities of citizenship. Heinlein was writing amidst the memory of World War II, a period of total war that created tensions between those prepared to do their duty and others focused on personal liberties and self-interest. Heinlein wrote that 'the basis of all morality is duty' (p. 151) and, describing a period of turmoil wrought by those who had 'lost track of their duties', Heinlein commented that 'no nation, so constituted'—that is, around the individual—'can endure' (p. 152). In today's highly individualistic world, where a premium is placed on individual rights and freedoms, the willingness of Romans to die in vast numbers for their city over a prolonged period of time is so abstract as to be almost incomprehensible. Yet it was the Romans' concept of duty and their deeply moral understanding of what citizenship demanded of them that sustained the war effort. An indication of the savage toll that the war took is provided by the census figures: if they are correct, in 234 BC a total of 270,713 adult male Roman citizens were registered, but in 209 BC there were a mere 134,108—a devastating loss of 136,605 Roman citizens, or close to 50 per cent. Not all of these will have been combat losses, but even if the numbers are not accurate to the last individual, a disparity of anything remotely close to this degree is shocking. For any state of any size to lose a substantial portion of its population and recover sufficiently to bring a successful conclusion to a prolonged war is nothing short of astounding.

After Zama, Carthage surrendered and agreed to a peace deal that resembled the earlier agreement made in 203 BC. This time, however, the Carthaginian navy was burned offshore, in full view of the senate and the city's population. A hefty fine was levied, and Roman deserters were publicly beheaded. Masinissa became a Roman friend, and because of this Carthage was forced into a dependent relationship with both Masinissa, its neighbour, and the Romans. Polybius regarded the Hannibalic War as a turning point in Mediterranean history. He wrote: 'Before this time, things happened in the world pretty much in a sporadic fashion, because every incident was specific, from start to finish, to the part of the world where it happened. But ever since then history has resembled a body, in the sense that incidents in Italy and Libya and Asia and Greece are all interconnected, and everything tends towards a single outcome.' More than anything, Polybius understood that the defeat of Carthage led inevitably to the Roman conquest of Greece, and then, in turn, to Asia (1.3).

That this was to be the outcome of the war was uncertain—even right to the end. There was a sizeable clique in the senate that looked at Scipio with suspicion. Some, such as the venerable Fabius Maximus, were firmly against an invasion of Africa; they wanted Hannibal defeated in Italy and for that to be the end of it. Such an outcome would have left Carthage more or less intact and independent, even though it would also have left Carthage as a potential rival in the future. The loudest voice in favour of laying siege to Carthage was Scipio, who argued vociferously that it was time for Libya to feel the devastation suffered by Italy. The two sides represented two separate visions of Rome's future. Fabius Maximus presented the insular case, focusing on Italy and Sicily, and leaving Carthage and the Greek world to their own devices. Scipio's vision, on the other hand, would enfeeble Carthage, resulting in Rome's unrivalled supremacy in the western Mediterranean and guaranteeing further collisions with Macedonia, and almost certainly Seleucid Syria and Ptolemaic Egypt. For the isolationists, Scipio's promotion of the African war also raised questions about his motives. How much, people wondered, had his successes in Spain gone to his head? What of this business with the Spanish calling him *rex*? Would defeating Hannibal only add further to an already inflated sense of self-importance? Did Jupiter *really* talk to him on the Capitoline? And what of Neptune, and New Carthage? The danger Scipio presented to the Roman constitution was recognised in antiquity: 'because of his great achievements,' wrote Diodorus, 'Scipio wielded more influence than seemed compatible with the dignity of the state' (29.21). He had held imperium in one guise or another for close to a decade; the donative he paid to his adoring soldiers only stoked these concerns further, raising the dread spectre of an absolutist general with a de facto private army. This was the paradox that Livy found impossible to reconcile. By the end of the war, the only person capable of defeating Hannibal was someone who looked more like him than Livy was willing to admit.

The isolationists lost, and Scipio went to Africa. Rome emerged from the Hannibalic War with an unparalleled position of dominance in the western Mediterranean. Having set the precedent of interfering in Greek affairs in the First and Second Illyrian Wars, and then in the First Macedonian War, the Romans would soon find themselves embroiled in the simmering cauldron of Greek inter-city rivalries. The Aetolian League, a Roman friend during the war, was a rival not only to Philip V of Macedon but also to the Achaean League, a powerful federation of occasionally pro-Macedonian Peloponnesian city states. Philip had other enemies, including the powerful city-state of Pergamum, ruled by the staunchly pro-Roman Attalus I (241–197 BC) and his successor Eumenes II (197–159 BC), as well as the island of Rhodes, whose friendship with Rome had begun with a Rhodian embassy in 305 BC. Antiochus III 'the Great', the Seleucid ruler of Syria (222–187 BC), had designs on Greece, and both he and Philip V coveted the Levantine territories of Ptolemaic Egypt. The question Fabius Maximus should have asked was not whether Scipio should go to Africa; rather, it was whether, after the end of the Hannibalic War, there was any realistic prospect that Rome would be able to stay out of Greek affairs.

Chapter 5

'Against our own Roman gods'

Rome and the Greek east, 200–146 BC

The Roman senate emerged from the Hannibalic War with immense confidence and authority. More than any other part of the Roman government, the senate had provided the moral leadership required to sustain the effort against Hannibal. As a result, the senate now came to play a far more central role in Roman political life than it had previously enjoyed. The senate prorogued magistrates beyond their year in office, and set the tasks for newly elected consuls and praetors; it also defined the geographical territories, the *provinciae*, in which they would serve. The senate arranged for military levies and their provisions, listened to foreign embassies, and appointed Roman envoys to carry their messages of support or threats of action to distant lands. Senators listened to recommendations from returning consuls and praetors concerning their military deeds, and ratified or amended peace treaties. While still advisory, a senatorial decree, a *senatus consultum*, carried significant weight. Embassies arrived regularly at the doors of the senate, looking to establish diplomatic or economic ties, or asking for the intervention of Rome's powerful armed forces in local conflicts. More often than not, these requests were honoured, enhancing Rome's reputation in the process. And as victorious generals and armies trudged home, they returned with all manner of plunder, as well as political and cultural ideas from the lands in which they fought.

Conservative politicians and later Roman writers such as Livy liked to lay some of the blame for what they saw as the political decline of the state on the various foreign influences that trickled into Rome. For Livy, it had all started in Sicily during the Hannibalic War. After the capture of Syracuse, the victorious general, Marcellus, had sent back to Rome much of the city's artwork and cultural heritage. Agreeing that Marcellus had every right to do so, Livy nonetheless thought that this act opened the floodgates for all manner of 'Greek art' to pollute Rome, tarnishing the *mos maiorum* and turning the people 'against our own Roman gods' (25.40). Polybius took a similarly dim view of Rome's sack of Syracuse, saying that the Romans should have decorated their city 'not with [stolen] paintings and reliefs, but with dignity and magnanimity' (9.10). The sack of Tarentum at the end of the Hannibalic War had also resulted in an influx of Greek art northwards to Rome, but in reality the Romans had been exposed to foreign art and ideas long before the third century BC, due to their interactions with their neighbours (Chapter 1). Nevertheless, conquests and overseas wars had a greater impact on Rome in the second century BC, as the senate's gaze became fixed on the political dramas and interstate rivalries in Greece, the Aegean, and Asia Minor. Warfare had always provided Roman magistrates with the opportunity for self-enrichment, glory, and dispensing patronage to

DOI: 10.4324/9781003202523-5

their clients, but Rome's wars now had a far more significant impact on the behaviour of Roman aristocrats, and on the way the Roman senate chose to exercise its power.

Rome and Greece, Greece and Rome

The first piece of Roman literature was written by Livius Andronicus, a Greek from Magna Graecia who came to Rome as a slave following his capture on the battlefield. He worked first as a tutor, and then in 240 BC he created a Latin version of the Odyssey called the *Odusia*, tapping into Rome's long association with the myths and legends about the Trojan War and bringing a version of Homeric epic to a Roman audience. Not long afterwards, Naevius, from Campania, wrote the Latin epic *Bellum Poenicum* ('The Punic War') to celebrate Rome's victory over Carthage in 241 BC. Naevius began his work with stories of Aeneas and his travels in the Mediterranean, borrowing from Homer. Both writers thus leaned heavily on Greece's justly celebrated literary traditions and cultural heritage, and their work represented a form of cultural assimilation that had a weighty impact on Roman culture and the development of Roman identities. Ennius, a Calabrian born just after Livius Andronicus finished the *Odusia*, provided a further version of this cultural fusion with his Latin *Annales*, an epic treatment of Roman history that drew inspiration for its title from the temple records kept in Rome. Ennius set himself a formidable challenge by choosing to write the *Annales* in dactylic hexameter, the meter used for the Greek *Iliad* and the *Odyssey*—but in a version adapted to the Latin language. By doing so, Ennius set the stage for the later use of the meter by Virgil and Ovid. The *Annales* proved very popular, and it was Rome's 'national' epic for two centuries until political circumstances changed and it was dethroned by Virgil's *Aeneid*. Like the *Odusia* and the *Bellum Poenicum*, the *Annales* was deeply influenced by Homeric epic: indeed, Ennius told the reader that Homer himself had been reborn within him! It is noteworthy that in these works the inconveniently long centuries between the Trojan War (twelfth century BC) and the foundation of Rome (eighth century BC) have almost completely vanished. At the same time, the links between Greek and Roman mythical history became ever more closely intertwined through a profusion of creative storytelling that gave Aeneas an Arcadian background. Far from distancing the Romans from the Greeks, works such as the *Odusia* and the *Annales* brought them closer together.

These poetic and literary efforts were matched by the earliest historical writing in Rome. Fabius Pictor wrote his history in Greek sometime between 215 and 200 BC, as the Hannibalic War was coming to a close. Pictor created a Roman history for a Greek audience, using Greek historiographical models that stretched back to Thucydides. As Ennius struggled to make Greek dactylic hexameter work in Latin, so Fabius Pictor attempted to cast the history of Rome within a scheme of historical writing that was fundamentally Greek. Fabius entrenched the Roman foundation myths that linked the city's past with Aeneas; he also gave the quintessential Greek hero Heracles an association with Italy, and asserted that the alphabet was introduced to Italy by Evander, who also hailed from Arcadia (Chapter 1).

With its rich tapestry of history, culture, and myth, Greece was central to Rome's developing identity. Later, after the sack of Corinth in 146 BC and the sack of Athens in 86 BC, Greek sculpture poured into Rome, making a significant impact on the development of Roman art. Rome's history with the Greek mainland and the islands was an old one: the Romans had made a dedication in the shrine of Massilia at Delphi in 394 BC, in celebration of their defeat of Etruscan Veii, and at their darkest hour during the Hannibalic War, it was to the oracle at Delphi that the Romans looked for divine guidance. In 228 BC, Roman athletes were permitted the honour of competing at the Isthmian Games. Other foreign influences abounded in Rome, in the shape of Juno, the *Sibylline Books*, and the cult of Magna Mater. In 293 BC, the Greek god of healing, Asclepius, was 'imported' to Rome from Epidaurus after the city suffered from an outbreak of the plague; a temple was duly built on the Tiber Island. In spite of these links, or perhaps because of them, the Romans freely denigrated the Greeks, along with Gauls, Syrians, Sardinians, and many others. They reserved their worst scorn for the Egyptians, whose 'exotic' customs made them particularly worthy of contempt.

This nativist celebration of diversity at home sits uncomfortably alongside public attacks on Greeks and others in the Mediterranean. Nobody captures this paradox better than Cato the Elder (234-149 BC), a *novus homo* who was very much in the isolationist camp towards the end of the Hannibalic War. Cato argued against the expansion of the war into Africa, and was sent to Sicily as quaestor in 204 BC to keep an eye on Scipio. Cato thought poorly of Scipio, and considered him to be a corrupting influence on the 'native simplicity' of the Roman troops (Plutarch, *Cato the Elder*, 3.6). Later, on campaign in Greece in the 190s BC, Cato visited Athens and, according to one version of events, made a speech in Greek celebrating Athenian culture and the beauty of the city. Plutarch says, however, that this was a lie, and that Cato addressed the Athenians using an interpreter, even though he was perfectly capable of speaking Greek. This was because 'he always clung to his native ways, and mocked those who were lost in admiration of anything that was Greek'. As for the assembled Athenians, they were, Plutarch wrote, 'astonished at the speed and pungency of his discourse' (*Cato the Elder*, 12.4-5). Cato set great stock in his understanding of Republican *virtus*: when king Eumenes II of Pergamum was in Rome on an embassy, for instance, Cato revealed his anti-monarchical bona fides by noting sourly that 'the animal known as king is by nature carnivorous' (*Cato the Elder*, 8.8). He reinforced his thoughts with his austere piety, making it a point to rise well before dawn and doing nothing for himself until he had finished with his public service, carried out—of course—for the good of the state and its citizens. According to Plutarch, he was 'addicted from the very first to labour with his own hands, a temperate mode of life, and military duties' (*Cato the Elder*, 1.3). He associated himself with the great heroes of the Roman state, such as Manius, the consul who had beaten Pyrrhus in 275 BC and was living out his retirement on a turnip farm like a latter day Cincinnatus. Returning from the warfront in 204 BC, Cato met Ennius and brought him to Rome from Sardinia to teach his children Greek.

Cato, a skilled and highly educated orator, possessed a sharp and wicked wit that he freely unleashed on anyone he thought deserved it. To one Aulus Postumius Albinus, a self-proclaimed Hellenophile who had written a history in Greek and apologised to his readers for his poor command of the language, Cato responded that 'to undertake of his own accord and under no compulsion to write a history, and then beg to be pardoned for his barbarisms, was obviously ludicrous' (Polybius, 39.1). Cato was also a capable writer, and composed a Roman history in Latin (now lost) entitled the *Origines*. In some ways, it was the Latin companion to the Greek history of Fabius Pictor. Even though the *Origines* was a 'nationalist', conservative work, paying due homage to the state and the successes it achieved through its virtuous statesmen and generals, it also further entrenched Rome's

Greek past. The *Origines* followed the tale of Aeneas and Lavinia, the foundation of Alba Longa, and many of the elements familiar to the diverse tellings of the Roman foundation myths. The Arcadian hero, Evander, also made an appearance, and Cato proposed that Evander had introduced a specific Greek dialect—Latin!—that was taken up and spoken by Romulus.

The sharpest contradiction between Cato's different thoughts about the Greeks is found in his assertion that the Romans had distant links to the Spartans, via an eponymous ancestor of the Sabines called Sabus. The Spartans had a reputation in antiquity for their ascetic and militaristic character, living a tough, harsh life and performing magnificently in battle. Whether Cato saw something of himself in the Spartans is debatable. He did, however, live on an estate in Sabinum, fought in many of Rome's wars, including at Thermopylae—where Leonidas and the Spartan 300 had made their epic stand, back in the distant past—and he liked to think that he had a Leonidas-esque toughness and regard for his duty as a soldier and public servant. For Cato, this Spartan lineage, intertwined with Roman *virtus* somewhere deep in the mists of antiquity, helped to engender a similar hardiness and rigor in the Roman spirit. Much later, Valerius Maximus likewise imagined that the Spartans and the Romans of preceding generations shared much in common (2.6.1).

This cultural-ideological tug of war played out in oratorical flourishes in Rome and before the senate, in poetry and in written histories, and later at festivals and on Roman coinage. Its occasional Hellenophobic bluster concealed the ongoing centrality of the Greek world to Roman ideas about their origins and about their place in the Mediterranean, as well as the importance of the ongoing dialogue between Mediterranean elites speaking either Latin or Greek. It was simply not possible for Romans to think about their own history without thinking about Greek history in the process. This is why Cato could denigrate the Greeks in one moment, but give them a starring role in his *Origines* in the next. It also explains how, when Cato was censor in 184 BC, he spent a staggering amount of public money endowing the Basilica Porcia, which gave a Greek architectural term—*basilica*—to a commercial building intended for Romans. Equally important was the plethora of other foreign influences that came to populate Roman religious life, culture, and eventually politics. Rome's elastic notions of citizenship, based around service to the Republic and subordination to the state's objectives, eased the assimilation of conquered cultures and their ideas into the state, and ultimately ensured that the development of Roman ideas about identity became fully grounded in ideas about membership of the wider Mediterranean world.

Rome and Macedonia

Macedonia had become the most important power in the Greek world under the leadership of king Philip II (359-336 BC), the father of Alexander the Great. Philip revolutionised the Macedonian army by introducing the 5 metre (16 feet) sarissa, which allowed his soldiers to spend less on costly hoplite armour. This made many more men than before eligible for military service, and at the same time Philip paid close attention to the development of cavalry as an offensive weapon on the battlefield. In a short period of time, Philip broke the coalition of Greek city-states opposing Macedonian expansion. Athens lost its struggle for influence in the northern Aegean, and at Chaeronea in 338 BC, Philip defeated the last organised resistance; the decisive moment during the battle came when a young Alexander crushed the elite Theban Sacred Band. Afterwards, most of the various Greek city states found themselves forced to join the League of Corinth, which supplied levies for Philip's upcoming war with Persia. Philip was assassinated in 336 BC, and his Persian campaign was carried out by Alexander with the support of Greek auxiliaries. Greek animosity towards the Macedonians continued to simmer, however, and thousands of Greek mercenaries fought for the Persian king Darius III. On Alexander's death, an anti-Macedonian revolt known as the Lamian War broke out in Greece, led by Athens. It was eventually suppressed by Antipater, an aristocrat who had remained behind in Macedonia when Alexander left. The Athenian democracy was abolished, and Demosthenes, the famous orator who had railed against Philip II with his 'Philippics', committed suicide.

Macedonia was subsequently ruled by a number of different monarchs, including Pyrrhus of Epirus (Chapter 3). Macedonian kings managed to keep a firm grip on Greece despite occasional periods of chaos caused by the succession wars, which spread to encompass Greece and Macedonia after the death of the venerable Antipater in 319 BC. Periodically, one or another of the successors would attempt to 'free the Greeks', a common rallying cry in the ancient Mediterranean for all sorts of military expeditions and ill-starred political projects. As a result, pro- and anti-Macedonian oligarchic factions in Greece were alternately supported and deposed, and from time to time pliant aristocrats were appointed by Macedonian kings to control restless communities such as Athens. Further disruption was caused by a series of Gallic invasions deep into Greece and Macedonia, one of which reached as far as the sanctuary at Delphi. Within this fractured landscape, the Aetolian League (Chapter 4) retained a fierce independence. Further resistance to Macedonia came with the Chremonidean War (267-261 BC), named for the Athenian general who, in vain, built an anti-Macedonian coalition of Athens, Sparta, and Ptolemy II Philadelphus, king of Egypt. During the same period, the Achaean League, centred on Corinth, emerged as an additional rival to Macedonian authority and to the surviving power blocs in Greece. The Leagues were federations with a central administration that handled affairs of interest to their members, such as financial matters, diplomacy, justice, and military expeditions, while inhabitants of the member cities remained citizens of those communities (Figures 5.1 and 5.2).

The Achaean League's most famous son was the historian Polybius, whose father Lycortas was on several occasions the League's *strategos*, its military commander. A particularly talented Achaean *strategos* was Aratus, who helped to make the League one of Greece's most formidable political blocs. Briefly, the Aetolians and Achaeans entered an alliance to counter the Macedonian king Demetrius II (239-229 BC), the father of Philip V. Later, under its charismatic king Cleomenes, Sparta clashed with the Achaean League amidst widespread social unrest that was reflected in calls for land redistribution and debt relief. (Cleomenes was also trying to restore Sparta's ancient reputation for martial vigour, with a social revolution that would bring back the lost world of the semi-mythical Lycurgus, who gave Sparta its fearsome educational system, the *agoge*.) Despite being bankrolled for a time by Ptolemy III Euergetes (246-222 BC), Cleomenes was defeated at Sellasia in 222 BC, and Demetrius II's half-cousin and successor, Antigonus III Doson (229-221 BC) captured Sparta, extending Macedonian influence deep into the Peloponnese. The fact that Antigonus had been drawn into the war by the hitherto anti-Macedonian Achaean League only serves to illustrate the bewildering complexity of

Figure 5.1 Silver stater of the Aetolian League, 250–225 BC. Obverse: laureate head of Apollo right; reverse: Aitolos (mythical hero) standing left, right foot on rock, with spear and sword.

Figure 5.2 Silver hemidrachm of the Achaean League. Obverse: laureate head of Zeus right; reverse: AX (Achaea) monogram, with part of goat within a wreath.

intra-Greek rivalries and the fluidity of political alliances. Adding to the general air of political uncertainty was the new, destabilising influence created uncomfortably close to Macedonia by Rome's Illyrian wars, which had eventually concluded largely to the benefit of the Aetolian League.

Philip V came to the Macedonian throne in 221 BC (Figure 5.3) He played up his tenuous links to Alexander, and for a period he was so popular that 'he was the darling of the whole of Greece' (Polybius, 7.11). The king inherited a fractured world (Figure 5.4). For the splintered Greek cities and leagues, Macedonia had come to play the role of the regional strongman, much as Rome had been doing in Italy. With the defeat of the Spartan Cleomenes in 222 BC, the Macedonian–Achaean alliance was formalised in the shape of the so-called Hellenic League (not to be confused with the League of Corinth, mentioned earlier, which was also sometimes called the Hellenic League). Philip assumed leadership of this new coalition, and was quickly drawn into the Social

Figure 5.3 Silver didrachm of Philip V, minted at Pella or Amphipolis. Obverse: diademed head, right; reverse: club within an oak-wreath, trident to the left. The legend reads ΒΑΣΙΛΕΩΣ ΠΙΛΙΠΠΟΥ, 'of king Philip'.

War (220–217 BC), which pitted the Hellenic League against the Aetolians and Sparta. Meanwhile, Demetrius of Pharos, who had fled to Philip following the end of the Second Illyrian War in 219 BC, urged Philip in the aftermath of the Roman defeat at Lake Trasimene (217 BC) to exploit Rome's weak position before the battered legions could recover their strength. Demetrius's efforts reflected a widespread unease about Rome's growing power, and another who raised the alarm was Agelaus of Naupactus, who spoke up during the negotiations that ended the Social War. Agelaus said somewhat unrealistically, 'Greeks should never go to war against one another.' Referring to the struggle between Hannibal and the Romans, Agelaus nevertheless advised that 'under the current circumstances, [the Greeks] should cooperate and take precautions, in view of the massive armies to the west and the major war that was being fought there'. The Greeks feared Carthage as well as Rome, and Agelaus declared that 'people who even now paid little attention to world affairs could not be blind to the fact that whether the Carthaginians or the Romans won the war, it was inconceivable that the victors would rest content with the rulership of Italy and Sicily' (Polybius, 5.104).

Philip was also concerned about Roman encroachment, so the advice of both Agelaus and Demetrius of Pharos fell on receptive ears. Agelaus urged Philip to watch Italy carefully: 'if he contained himself and waited his turn, he could make a bid, when the time was right, for worldwide dominion' (Polybius, 5.104). Philip's decision to ally himself with Hannibal is perfectly understandable under the circumstances, as Rome really did appear to be on the edge of a humiliating and total defeat after Lake Trasimene, and even more so after the calamity at Cannae. Philip probably thought a treaty with Carthage might just help 'the clouds now gathering in the west' to blow well away from Greece, allowing Macedonia to maintain its position of pre-eminence there (Polybius, 5.104). Of course, as noted in Chapter 4, the Romans found out about the treaty between Philip and Hannibal, resulting in the outbreak of the First Macedonian War in 214 BC. Rome found willing allies in the Aetolian League and king Attalus I Soter of Pergamum (241–197 BC), both of whom were suspicious of Philip's motives in Greece. Rome's treaty with the Aetolian League is of particular interest because it specified that any land or cities captured would

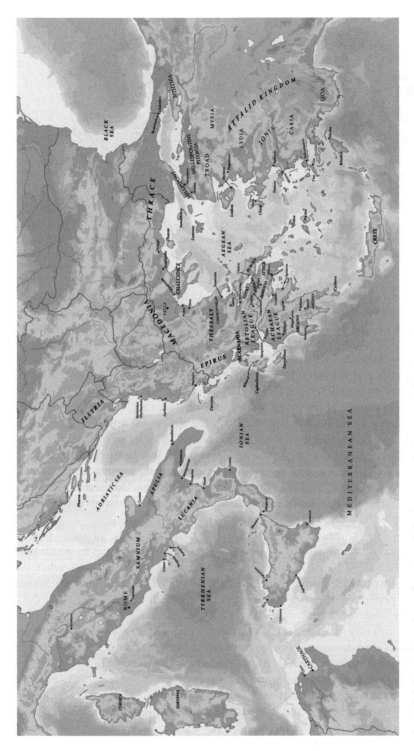

Figure 5.4 Rome, Macedonia, Greece, and the Aegean at the beginning of the second century BC.

Source: Illustration by the author.

go not to Rome, but to the League (*RGE* §2). There was no vision for parts of Greece or Macedonia to come under Roman rule, and Rome could profit from the war while rewarding its allies with territory.

In 205 BC, the various parties agreed an end to the First Macedonian War with the Peace of Phoenice, but the conflict had already pulled the Romans inextricably into the tangled web of competing interests in Greece. After the battle of Zama in 202 BC, a Macedonian embassy was sent to settle matters with the Romans. Livy reported that when questioned about Macedonian involvement in the Hannibalic War, the envoys 'gave unsatisfactory and evasive replies'. The Roman senate grew frustrated by their obstinacy, and delivered a stark ultimatum: the envoys, Livy wrote, 'were told that their king was looking for war, and if he went on as he was doing, he would very soon find it' (30.42).

The dust had barely settled at Zama before Roman troops were ordered across the Adriatic. Philip had spent 202 and 201 BC consolidating his position in the Aegean Sea, conducting raids against his Egyptian and Rhodian enemies. He made a miscalculation by enslaving the inhabitants of Chios, which brought a raft of negative publicity, and his navy soon succumbed to defeat at the hands of a combined force from Pergamum, Byzantium, and Rhodes. Undeterred, he attacked Pergamum and captured Ptolemaic Samos. It was widely believed at the time that Philip had made a secret agreement with Antiochus III to carve up Ptolemaic Egypt and its bevy of possessions in Syria and the Aegean: Egypt was in the grip of violence and instability after the death of Ptolemy IV Philopator in 204 BC, and the eight-year-old Ptolemy V Epiphanes was under the avaricious guidance of a minister, Agathocles, who had murdered Ptolemy IV's sister and was overseeing Egypt's descent into anarchy.

Antiochus had recently returned from an epic journey through the eastern fringes of his vast empire, which were falling out of royal control. Travelling as far as India, he challenged even his staunchest opponents, the Parthians, who had detached the Seleucid satrapy of Parthia in the mid-third century and, under Arsaces I (247-217 BC) pursued an independent policy. Antiochus made terms with Arsaces II (217-191 BC) and several other local rulers, and after four years away returned to accolades of 'Antiochus the Great' (Figure 5.5). Despite the fanfare and the inevitable comparison with the (far more) epic journey conducted by Alexander the Great, Antiochus had not accomplished much on his campaigns, so an agreement with Philip to enlarge Seleucid territory in the west—if it existed—was both timely and welcome. Before long, Antiochus opened hostilities with the fifth of the six 'Syrian Wars', all of which were conflicts between the Seleucids and the Ptolemies over where the Syrian frontier between their kingdoms should lie. The Fifth Syrian War took place between 202 and 195 BC, and Antiochus won a key victory in 200 BC. Meanwhile, Philip's campaigns in the Aegean and along the coast of Asia Minor worked to the benefit of Antiochus, who was no friend to either Rhodes or Pergamum.

Philip had clearly ignored the advice of Agelaus of Naupactus, who had urged him to hold off on his quarrels with the Greeks: 'all the games we now play with each other, our truces and wars' (Polybius, 5.104). By the end of 201 BC, Attalus and the Rhodians had endured as much as they could from Philip, who, despite periodic setbacks, had built up a large and powerful naval fleet. A joint embassy was dispatched to Rome with a detailed brief of what was happening in the Aegean and Asia Minor. The Romans responded by giving the rank of propraetor to the patrician Marcus Valerius Laevinus, who had fought

Figure 5.5 Gold octodrachm of Antiochus III 'the Great'. This massive coin, weighing 34 g, dates to 211/10 BC. Obverse: diademed head of the king; reverse: Apollo with bow and arrow. The legend reads ΒΑΣΙΛΕΩΣ ΑΝΤΙΟΧΟΥ, 'of king Antiochus'.

in the First Macedonian War and was familiar with the different parties, and sent him off to investigate. At the same time, Athens went to war with the Acarnanian League, a federation of communities on the Ionian coast of Greece. Philip dispatched troops to assist the Acarnanians, subsequent to which Attalus convinced the Athenians to open hostilities with Macedonia.

Laevinus, meanwhile, met with a Roman ambassador returning from Egypt, the patrician Marcus Aemilius Lepidus, who had been sent to Alexandria to announce Rome's victory over Hannibal to Ptolemy V and to confirm the friendship between Rome and Egypt. Laevinus and Lepidus discussed the situation and sent reports back to the Roman senate, after which an ultimatum was delivered to Philip's general, Nicanor, near Athens. Philip paid no heed to the Roman warnings and continued to ravage territory throughout the eastern Mediterranean and Aegean, 'as though none of these countries concerned the Romans' (Appian, *Macedonian Affairs*, fr.) In 200 BC, Philip began a siege of Abydus, strategically located on the Hellespont in the northwest of Asia Minor—trying, as Polybius wrote, 'to cut off the resources and stepping-stones of the Romans in those parts' (16.29). Hearing about the terrible plight of the people of Abydus, and spurred on by Attalus, Lepidus went to Abydus to confront Philip in person. He delivered the message that the senate had adopted a *senatus consultum*, asking him to leave Ptolemy's territory alone—Egypt was, after all, a Roman friend—and to cease from making war on the Greeks, some of whom were also Roman friends. Philip was also to pay damages to Rhodes and Pergamum. Polybius wrote that Philip was taken aback by the confident and stern manner in which he was addressed, a reflection of his manifest failure to appreciate the strength of the state that lay behind it. Yet Philip was simply acting in the way that Macedonian monarchs had been acting for nearly a century and a half—that they, descending in a long line from Philip II and Alexander, were the ones to decide the destiny of Greece and its squabbling city states. Philip demurred in the face of these warnings and Abydus fell, with the mass suicide of its population. The Second Macedonian War was now inevitable.

The consuls for 200 BC were the patrician Publius Sulpicius Galba, who had directed operations in Greece during the First Macedonian War, and the plebeian Gaius Aurelius

Cotta. After drawing lots, Galba was assigned Macedonia and put the matter of war with Philip to the people. Livy wrote that the Romans were so fed up with war that Galba lost the vote when it was first mooted, but the senate told Galba to try again, and at the same time censured the people in Rome 'for their want of spirit' (31.6). It is telling that when the war was finally approved, Cotta was retained in Italy and an army raised for his use, as many of Rome's allies were still seen as untrustworthy following the long war with Hannibal. Galba's fleet crossed the Adriatic from Brundisium, making landfall close to Rome's ally Apollonia. Athens remained under siege despite Roman attempts to lift it, and Philip tried unsuccessfully to repair his deteriorating relationship with the Achaean League. Instead, the persistent gossip that Philip had issued an order to assassinate Philopoemen, the venerable *strategos* of the League, slowly pushed Achaean opinion towards Rome. As winter approached, Philip laid waste to large parts of Attica, then settled down to prepare for a direct confrontation with the Romans. Livy reported that Philip, who had yet to fight the Romans himself, attempted to steel his population for the upcoming struggle. He did so by publicly burying some horsemen who had been killed in a skirmish with Roman forces. However, as Livy noted, 'nothing is so uncertain or so unpredictable as the mental reaction of a crowd'. He continued by noting that the people were used to seeing injuries resulting from arrows and javelins; but 'when they had seen bodies chopped to pieces by the Spanish sword, arms torn away, shoulders and all, or heads separated from bodies, with the necks completely severed, or vitals laid open, and the other fearful wounds, realized in a general panic with what weapons and what men they had to fight' (31.34). The 'Spanish sword' is a reference to the Roman *gladius Hispaniensis*, which had come to Italy via Spanish contacts and the Roman campaigns in Spain, and had acquired a fearsome reputation.

Between 199 and 198 BC, Roman naval forces, together with those of Pergamum and Rhodes, waged a successful campaign to capture Macedonian naval bases throughout the Aegean. Galba, meanwhile, was unable to bring about a decisive clash with Philip, and in 198 BC the Macedonian command passed to the patrician Titus Quinctius Flamininus, who had served in the Hannibalic War as a military tribune under Marcellus. Despite the fact that he was too young and had not held the office of praetor, Flamininus was elected as consul in the face of complaints by the plebeian tribunes that too many were trying their hand at the consulship without serving in the lower ranks of the *cursus honorum*. The senate, probably with the memory of Scipio Africanus in mind, decided that if the people wanted Flamininus, then they could elect him—although they did subsequently increase the number of praetors to six, to take into account the Spanish provinces (below), and enforced the requirement that the praetorship must be held before applying for the consulship. Arriving in Macedonia in the spring of 198 BC with his brother Lucius and an army that included many of Scipio's seasoned veterans, Flamininus offered Philip terms: the war could end, he said, but Philip had to give up the cities that he had captured and make reparations to those he had harmed. The peace offer also required Philip to give up cities that his predecessors had taken, which he had inherited when he became king. This was too much for the proud monarch, and he stormed out of the meeting.

In the meantime, the Aetolian League, scenting plunder, had joined the war against Philip. After watching events carefully, the Achaean League finally abandoned its three-decade alliance with Macedonia and followed suit. Tellingly, the debates over the Achaean League's involvement had been attended by ambassadors from Rome, Pergamum, Rhodes, and Athens. A second attempt at making peace took place as winter approached at the end

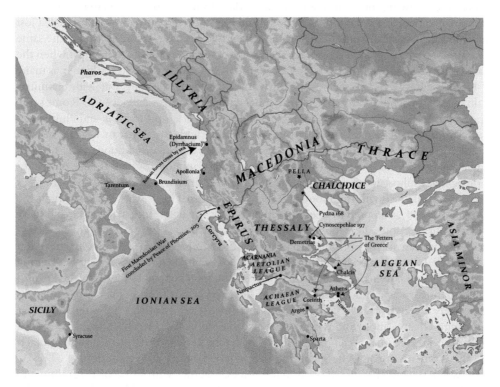

Figure 5.6 Rome's Macedonian wars, 202–168 BC.

Source: Illustration by the author.

of 198 BC. The Roman demands were similar to their previous requests, but now included the restoration of Ptolemaic property to Ptolemy V, Rome's Egyptian ally. Flamininus also gave the podium to the roster of Roman allies, who had a long history of enmity with Macedon and an even longer list of demands. Most contentious—and practically impossible for Philip to accept—was the requirement that the Macedonians evacuate their garrisons in Greece, particularly the cities of Corinth (with its dominant citadel, the Acrocorinth), Piraeus, Chalcis, and Demetrias, most of which had been under tight Macedonian control since the days of Alexander (Figure 5.6). These cities, known as the 'fetters of Greece' (Polybius, 18.11), controlled access to the Peloponnese, Attica, Euboea, and Thessaly respectively, and directly threatened the independence of groups such as the Achaean and Aetolian Leagues. Philip was stung by these demands, and asked Flamininus indignantly whether 'he thought it fair that he should renounce all claim to the cities that he had captured himself and held by the rights of war, and even to those that he had inherited from his ancestors' (Livy, 32.34).

According to Polybius, this second round of negotiations was a ruse on the part of Flamininus. He agreed to Philip's request to send an embassy to the Roman senate, to settle those parts of the dispute that were still hotly debated by the various parties. Flamininus gave him a two-month time limit, which coincided with the next round of consular elections in Rome. In Italy there was unrest in the north among the Gauls, and it seemed likely that at least one consul, or even both, would need to remain in Italy to address this problem. This would likely leave Flamininus to be prorogued, and when the winter was over he would be able to bring Philip to battle and force peace upon him. Once it became clear that *both* consuls would be in Italy, the envoys of Rome's Greek allies, who had also gone to the senate to plead their side, denounced Philip in the strongest possible terms and the political allies of Flamininus in Rome also made their own case known. There was, therefore, no real prospect of peace. Flamininus, who spoke Greek, had presented himself as a philhellene and a liberator who would free the Greeks from the Macedonian yoke, and sure enough, Polybius wrote that the Greek envoys 'entreated the senate neither to cheat the Greeks out of their hope of liberty, nor to deprive themselves of the noblest title to fame'—fame that could only come from toppling Philip and freeing the Greeks (18.11).

Philip's embassy was given little chance in Rome, and Flamininus was prorogued as a proconsul. Both sides prepared for war, and the Roman force was swelled by troops from the Boeotian League, which had been pressured to join the coalition. The two armies met at Cynoscephalae in Thessaly; this engagement would prove to be the crucial test of the Roman maniple (Figure 5.6, above). Flamininus found the contest uneven until a tribune took 20 maniples around the rear of the enemy formation. The Macedonian phalanx was not designed to respond to such an approach, and a rout ensued. The flexibility of the maniples, a product of Scipio's training programme in the Hannibalic War, signalled the demise of the phalanx—a formation that had dominated Mediterranean warfare for almost 140 years.

Polybius thought the other reason for the Macedonian defeat was that the phalanx was suited only to very specific battlefield conditions, 'level and clear ground with no obstacles such as ditches, clefts, clumps of trees, ridges, and water courses' (18.31). Cynoscephalae was a battle of rough, broken ridges, and was not Philip's preferred setting to confront Flamininus. Polybius also noted that the phalanx infantry were useful only as entire units, whereas the manipular army was flexible and could be grouped into larger units or divided to work in small groups. This, too, was the legacy of Scipio.

Philip fled the battlefield of Cynoscephalae, and was forced to accept peace on Roman terms. Elsewhere in the Aegean and in Greece, Macedonian forces were beaten by Rome's allies in numerous smaller actions. At the peace conference, the Aetolians demanded nothing less than Philip's execution or exile. The reply of Flamininus to this extreme position is illuminating: he calmly pointed out to the enraged Aetolian envoys that at no point earlier had the Romans called for Macedonia to be destroyed, or for its king to be put to death. On the contrary, Flamininus said, one only had to look at the peace agreed with Carthage to see the generosity of Rome's spirit and the magnanimity with which it treated its vanquished foes. Carthage was still intact, and Hannibal was a free man. Flamininus also pointed out that it was in everyone's best interests for Macedonia to continue to exist. For if it was destroyed, he alleged, 'Thracians, Illyrians, Gauls, savage and barbarous tribes, would pour into Macedonia and then into Greece' (Livy, 33.12). In the end, Flamininus got his way and Philip was fined an indemnity, had to surrender his Greek possessions and most of his fleet, return prisoners, and make other reparations. He also suffered dramatic cuts to his army and could not make war outside Macedonia without Roman permission.

The Aetolians now viewed Flamininus with distrust, and suspected that the Romans would not be content with this settlement of affairs but would, in some form, take over

Macedonia's role as their overlord. They were right to be suspicious, for the final terms of the peace, delivered by a commission of ten men carrying the orders of the senate, were somewhat opaque. The Aetolians complained that the terms were 'an arrangement of words and not an arrangement of things': Philip would hand over to Rome 'the cities in which he had garrisons', a clear reference to the 'fetters of Greece', but it was not clear what would happen to these cities later (Polybius, 18.45). Would Roman troops be garrisoned in place of Macedonians? Flamininus tried to allay Greek concerns, giving Corinth to the Achaean League, but he kept Demetrias, Chalcis, and Piraeus in Roman hands, officially out of concern that Antiochus III might take advantage of Philip's defeat and invade Greece.

At the Isthmian Games, held in Corinth in 196 BC, Flamininus proclaimed the freedom of the Greeks. The decree was so unexpected that a roar of approval drowned out the herald, who was forced to repeat the announcement several times. Plutarch wrote with great flourish that the cheering could be heard at sea, while birds flying overhead dropped stunned to the ground (*Flamininus*, 10). In 194 BC, Flamininus celebrated an extraordinary three-day triumph in Rome, and paid a large donative to his victorious troops. Crucially, the *senatus consultum* that was the official declaration of Greek freedom was universal in scope, and therefore included the Greeks of Asia Minor, whom the Seleucid monarch Antiochus III claimed for himself. New conflicts lay ahead.

Rome, the Aetolians, and Antiochus

Flamininus remained in Greece after the peace settlement was concluded, acting as a de facto governor for Greek affairs. Since all the Greeks were now 'free', old power blocs had been weakened and Flamininus would keep a paternalistic eye on his new clients. In 195 BC, a new conflict emerged over Sparta's occupation of Argos. After Argos seceded from the Achaean League during the Second Macedonian War (it had joined the League earlier, in 229 BC), Sparta had received the city from Philip in exchange for Spartan support. Just before the war ended, however, Sparta turned its back on Philip and went over to the Romans, but had kept Argos, enraging Philip in the process. The Romans allowed this state of affairs to stand after the war was over. Now, however, king Nabis of Sparta—whom Plutarch called a 'most pernicious and lawless tyrant' (*Flamininus*, 13)—was arousing suspicion with his policies and reforms, which included a strengthening of the Spartan army. The Achaeans, in particular, felt threatened by Sparta, and they also wanted Argos back. In Corinth, Flamininus convened a meeting of Rome's allies, at which the Aetolian representatives made their own displeasure over the state of events in Greece abundantly clear. Their envoy, Alexander, accused Flamininus of hypocrisy: there were still garrisons at Chalcis and Demetrias despite Rome's proclamations of Greek liberty, and it seemed clear that the dispute over Nabis and Argos would provide further excuses to entrench the occupation of Greece by Roman forces. Alexander told Flamininus that he and his troops should go home and leave Nabis to the Aetolian League. This triggered an angry rebuttal from the Achaean envoys and a desperate plea for action against Sparta. Eventually, another coalition of Rome and her Greek allies was created. Flamininus was armed with a *senatus consultum* to settle things according to his best judgement, but Sparta refused to hand Argos over and was subjected to a determined siege. After several days, realising that his position was hopeless, Nabis surrendered. The chief beneficiary of this conflict, the Laconian War, was the Achaean League, to which Argos was returned. Many of the communities in Laconia that had come under Spartan rule were also transferred to the Achaeans, who repaid Roman help by freeing over a thousand Roman slaves, former troops who had ended up in Greece after being captured and sold by the Carthaginians in the Hannibalic War. Like Philip, Nabis remained on his throne; he agreed to curb his reformist behaviour and to remove Spartan garrisons elsewhere. Flamininus, attending the Nemean Games close to Argos, celebrated the newfound freedom of the Argives by public proclamation, exactly as he had done in 196 BC at the Isthmian Games. Once again, a squabble between competing interests in Greece that really had nothing to do with Rome had been settled by appealing to Rome, even if the results were somewhat inconclusive: while the Achaean League was strengthened by the war, Nabis and Sparta were left intact as a counterbalance. The Aetolians were still unhappy, not only with the continued Roman presence in Greece but with the failure of the Romans to remove Nabis. Later, after Nabis was murdered (below), Philopoemen took advantage of the turmoil to force Sparta into the membership of the Achaean League, cementing the League's dominance in southern Greece.

As all of this had been happening, the Romans had been negotiating with the Seleucid monarch, Antiochus III. Shortly before his death in 197 BC, Attalus I of Pergamum complained to Rome that Antiochus was on his borders, and by 196 BC other pleas for assistance were coming in from communities in Asia Minor, threatened by the military campaigns that Antiochus was conducting in the area. One remarkable plea, directed to Flamininus's brother, Lucius, via the city of Massilia, came from the community of Lampsacus on the Hellespont and urged intervention on the basis that both they and the Romans were 'kinsmen' (*HW* §155). A separate embassy was sent by Ptolemy V and reported that parts of Syria and Cilicia, in the south of Asia Minor, had been wrested from Egyptian control. There had been a flurry of diplomatic contacts between Flamininus and other Roman envoys and Antiochus, but now, as part of a general effort to contain Antiochus, the patrician Lucius Cornelius Lentulus was dispatched with a number of other experienced Roman envoys to persuade the king to relinquish his control of Ptolemaic possessions in the region. Antiochus was also required to give up the territories previously occupied by Philip. These Antiochus had rather opportunistically poached in the aftermath of the Second Macedonian War, shifting the balance of power in the Aegean to his favour. The Romans were also aware that some of Antiochus's activity was taking place on the European side of the Hellespont, where he was rebuilding the city of Lysimacheia, ostensibly as a residence for his son. The Romans had no issue with the Asian empire of Antiochus, but they saw his activities in Europe and the Aegean differently, so Lentulus directly accused Antiochus of trying to cause problems with the Roman senate. Antiochus replied indignantly that Rome had no right to question his activities, and that they should not bother themselves about his affairs, 'for he himself did not in the least go out of his way to concern himself with the affairs of Italy' (Polybius, 18.51). The king's reasoning was perfectly understandable when considered alongside the approach taken some time earlier by Philip V; he too was taken aback at the haughtiness of Roman demands that he give up his position of dominance in Greece. Just as the Macedonians had a long history of controlling Greece, so the Seleucids did in Asia Minor, the European Hellespont, and the Levant. In the view of Antiochus, it simply was not the business of the Romans to send embassies with such ridiculous questions and concerns. After all, the European territory of Thrace where the forces of Antiochus were operating had once belonged to Lysimachus, one of the successors whom Seleucus himself had bested in battle. Antiochus was the great-great-grandson of Seleucus, and this was Seleucid spear-won territory. Antiochus was well within his rights to recover such territories by force. In the world view of Hellenistic monarchs, it is hard to disagree with the claim made by Antiochus that 'he had a better title to the sovereignty of this place than anyone else' (Polybius, 18.51). As a final snub to Lentulus, Antiochus decided to refer some of the disputes that he had with Ptolemy to Rhodes, rather than the Roman senate, for arbitration.

One factor playing into Roman suspicions about Antiochus had its origins thousands of kilometres away to the west. After the battle of Zama in 202 BC, Hannibal had been elected suffete in Carthage, turning his formidable talents to reforming the city's battered finances. A clique in the Carthaginian aristocracy, however, wanted nothing more than to see the back of him, and sent messengers to Rome claiming that he was plotting against the senate. Hannibal was forced to flee even as Scipio Africanus came to his defence, but he had few options. Ptolemy V was still very young and under the wing of the Romans; Philip V had recently been beaten by them. The squabbling leagues and cities of Greece were also unattractive, so Hannibal presented himself to Antiochus, who he met at Ephesus, and offered his services.

At some point around this time—according to legend, at any rate—it was thought that Hannibal met with Scipio Africanus (also in Ephesus, but on a different occasion than Antiochus) where Scipio was part of a Roman embassy. It is tempting to imagine the two old soldiers splitting a flask of wine and reminiscing about the war—and indeed, the romanticised story that emerged from this meeting was one of Scipio asking Hannibal whom he thought to be the greatest general in history. Livy, who (along with Appian) reported the story, stated that Hannibal rated Alexander the Great in first place, followed by Pyrrhus. And third, prompted Scipio? 'Myself,' Hannibal replied. At this, Scipio wondered aloud what the response would have been if Hannibal, and not Scipio, had been victorious at Zama. 'In that case,' said Hannibal, 'I should say that I surpassed Alexander and Pyrrhus, and all other commanders in the world' (Livy, 35.14). Scipio was delighted with the compliment.

Antiochus strengthened his position by marrying his daughter, Cleopatra, to Ptolemy V, and perhaps returned some Syrian territory to him in the process. He also attempted to marry another daughter to Eumenes II, who came to the throne of Pergamum in 197 BC. He hoped that Eumenes would accept, as this would help to weaken the alliance between Rome, Pergamum, and Rhodes that threatened him considerably. Wise to the ruse, however, and determined instead to strengthen his ties with Rome, Eumenes refused the offer. Shortly afterwards, Antiochus crossed the Hellespont with a large army, and 'freed the Greeks' he found there. An embassy sent to the Romans announced that Antiochus had no hostile intentions, but his envoys also firmly rejected Rome's moral authority to decide the fate of areas that had historically been under Seleucid control. In particular, Antiochus was troubled by the way the Romans talked to him. 'Yours are not the exhortations of friends,' he said through his envoy, 'but resemble orders given by victors to the vanquished' (Appian, *Syrian Wars*, 2.6). The Roman senate sent a sharp rejoinder, reminding the king that there could only be friendship with Rome if Antiochus left the Greeks of Greece and Asia Minor alone. At some point, as part of a secret mission to Antiochus, Flamininus had floated exactly this idea at a more informal level, but nothing had come of it. In public,

Flamininus loudly reassured the Greeks that Rome would free them once more if necessary. Both Rome and Antiochus were rapidly heading for an armed clash, and there was
little appetite on either side to stop it.

The Aetolians, meanwhile, had given up on Rome and were openly agitating for
Antiochus to intervene directly in Greece. Rumours abounded that Demetrias was about
to be given back to Philip. Worse, other rumours were abroad that the Romans had acted
too leniently towards Philip's son, Demetrius, who had been taken to Italy as a hostage
to guarantee Macedonia's observance of the treaty that ended the Second Macedonian
War. Thoas, a former Aetolian *strategos*, was given a speech by Livy in which he argued the
merits of a Seleucid invasion, whereby Antiochus could take command of the League's
forces and 'restore the fortunes of Greece, such as they are' (Livy, 35.32). Others, though,
were not so eager. If the rumours about Demetrias *were* true, then it was better to have
Philip back than a king about whom many knew little. None other than Flamininus then
arrived on the scene and pleaded with the Aetolians not to 'create a world-wide disturbance and utterly ruin Greece' by starting a war between Antiochus and the Romans (Livy,
35.33). Flamininus's efforts were not rewarded, and the Aetolians invited Antiochus to free
the Greeks from the Romans; the Aetolian *strategos* Democritus followed up this warlike
talk by saying that he would speak with Flamininus when he was on the banks of the Tiber
with the army of the Aetolian League.

According to Appian, Thoas had made extravagant promises about the popularity of
Antiochus in Greece and about the military support that Antiochus could expect to
receive. The Aetolians had seized Demetrias in 192 BC, and were on a war footing when
Antiochus hurriedly arrived in Greece with a small force of only 10,000 soldiers and a
handful of elephants, the best he could do at such short notice. (In the same year, the
Aetolians had managed to win over Nabis of Sparta, only to arrange his murder, after
which Sparta was poached by the Achaean League.) Antiochus enjoyed some early success,
surprising a Roman force at Delium and killing several soldiers, but the promised support
failed to materialise. In light of this, Hannibal advised Antiochus to change his strategy
and invade Italy, but Antiochus was not convinced. The Romans responded to the deaths
of their troops with fury, declaring war on Antiochus and raising an army to cross the
Adriatic. They also stationed a large force at Tarentum, clearly aware of the threat of a sea-
borne invasion. Antiochus found that the Greeks were not that happy to see him after all,
and those he 'freed' had to be liberated against their will. The Achaean League and Philip
joined the Roman side, and as Antiochus sent desperate messages to his armies in Syria to
join the fray, he fortified the pass at Thermopylae where the Spartan king Leonidas and
the 300 warriors had held up the Persian invasion of Greece some three centuries earlier
(Figure 5.7).

Antiochus was undone by Cato the Elder, serving under the command of the plebeian
consul, Manius Acilius Glabrio. Cato rediscovered the track that the Persian troops of
Xerxes had used long ago to outflank the Spartans in the night. Cato, who Plutarch wrote
was 'very pompous in his account of this exploit', intrepidly battled his way through the
undergrowth in the dark, up and down ravines and mountainsides, and led his picked force
into position just before dawn (*Cato the Elder*, 14). As the sun came up, Cato surprised
the Aetolians beneath him while Glabrio attacked Antiochus from the front. Afterwards
(perhaps simply to get rid of him), Glabrio sent Cato to Rome to announce the Roman
victory.

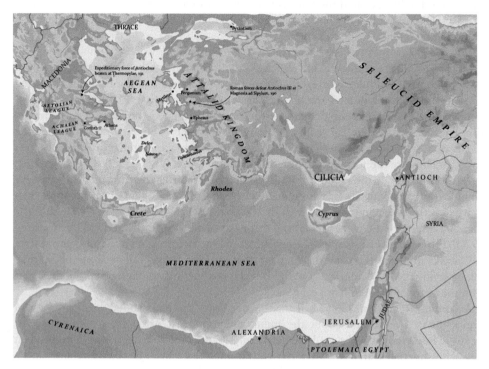

Figure 5.7 The eastern Mediterranean during the wars between Rome and Antiochus.

Source: Illustration by the author.

The Romans were relieved: Antiochus had a daunting reputation as a warrior, but now they had him on the run and could turn their full attention to the wayward Aetolian League in a short conflict known as the Aetolian War (191–89 BC). Glabrio laid siege to Heraclea in central Greece, and the city's subsequent capture cast gloom over the Aetolian leadership. Even as they sent messages to Antiochus begging him to return, the patrician Lucius Valerius Flaccus arranged a peace with the Aetolians, who agreed to put themselves under the *fides* of Rome. This agreement, however, was soon broken, because, as Polybius (20.9–10) wrote, the Aetolians did not understand that by taking this course of action, they were essentially surrendering. It would not be the last time a conquered people made this mistake. When the Aetolians realised what they had done, and when encouraging news arrived from Asia that Antiochus was promising further aid, the war resumed. At the same time, the senate and senior Roman oligarchs had come to the decision that the threat to the stability of Greece and the Aegean posed by Antiochus could not be settled simply by giving the king a bloody nose at Thermopylae. Aetolian resistance crumbled as the main Roman force, raised to give the Romans satisfaction against Antiochus, arrived in Greece and Roman forces laid siege to the Aetolian centre of Naupactus. At this point, the consular year changed, and Lucius Cornelius Scipio, consul for 190 BC, took over from Glabrio. Lucius had little military experience, but was accompanied by his brother, Scipio Africanus; Scipio's old friend Laelius was the other consul, and had promoted

Lucius' candidacy for the war. As one of his last acts before assuming the consulship, Lucius arranged a lengthy truce with the Aetolians. The League was later reduced to the status of *socii*, its powerful position in Greece and its control of the Delphic Amphictyony—which looked after the sanctuaries of Delphi—utterly destroyed by its reckless involvement with Antiochus.

As affairs with the Aetolians were settled, a Roman fleet, supported by a flotilla from Pergamum and Rhodes, defeated the large navy of Antiochus near Myonnesus. Hannibal, present at an earlier naval defeat, had fled to Pamphylia (a district in southern Asia Minor), where he was being kept under a tight blockade by a Rhodian force. The Scipio brothers had been moving quickly, keen to cross the Hellespont and defeat Antiochus before Lucius's consulship expired at the end of the year. Appian reported that Philip provided valuable support to the Romans during this phase of the war, for which he achieved the return of his son, Demetrius (*Syrian Wars*, 5.23); Polybius added that the Romans also cancelled the balance of the indemnity owed after the end of the Second Macedonian War (21.3). The Romans found the Hellespont unguarded, and quickly crossed at Lysimacheia: this was the first Roman army to cross from Europe to Asia. A terrified Antiochus sent envoys to the Scipios asking for terms, but was rebuffed. Africanus himself became ill, and when Antiochus realised that he faced the inexperienced Lucius and also that he was not going to receive favourable terms, he reached the conclusion that it was worth gambling everything in battle.

The result was the famous Roman victory at Magnesia ad Sipylum, northeast of modern Izmir. Lucius was aided by the valiant leadership of king Eumenes of Pergamum, who distinguished himself, according to Appian (*Syrian Wars*, 6.34). Eumenes was no doubt eager to see the power of Roman arms harnessed to batter his old enemy Antiochus; the key moment came, as at Cynoscephalae, when the phalanx was flanked and broke under relentless pressure. The Romans were triumphant, not having expected such an easy victory. Now, Appian wrote, they 'were in high spirits and considered no tasks too hard for them'. They were all the more elated to have prevailed over 'the renowned Macedonian phalanx, and the king himself, ruler of this vast empire and surnamed the Great—all in a single day. It became a common saying among them: "there was a king—Antiochus the Great!"' (*Syrian Wars*, 7.37).

After the battle, Scipio Africanus, who had by this time recovered his health, recounted the Roman view of Antiochus's crimes as the Romans deliberated over the terms of the peace treaty. Antiochus, Scipio said, had acted with avarice and greed, despite the fact that he possessed a large empire in which the Romans had no interest. His worst crimes were robbing the Greeks of their freedom under the guise of bringing liberty—a rather rich irony coming from a Roman statesman—and rejecting peace with Rome even after the Roman army had made the effort of coming all the way to Asia. In the end, Antiochus retained much of his kingdom, but was forced to surrender his European possessions and much of Asia Minor, and pay a large fine on top of reimbursing the Romans for their costs in waging the war. All his elephants were surrendered and his fleet was pared down to a shadow of its former self. Antiochus had to accept this peace without treachery, Scipio warned—another rich irony, given the conduct of Flamininus during the peace negotiations with Philip V in 198/97 BC. Even as the patrician consul Gnaeus Manlius Vulso (189 BC) campaigned against the Galatians, a group of Gauls living in Asia Minor, officially in response to the assistance they had given to Antiochus but also as a brazen opportunity to plunder, the Treaty of Apamea was agreed in 188 BC. This was the conclusive peace between Antiochus and Rome, and it delivered a windfall of territory to Rhodes and Pergamum. The commercial links between these two states and Roman traders made them valuable allies, and they had also backed Rome without complaint during the war. Rome's armies departed from Asia, leaving the Aegean and large swathes of Asia Minor under the safe control of their allies. Manlius was given a triumph for the Galatian War. Lucius Cornelius Scipio took the title 'Asiaticus' and, according to the *fasti triumphales*, was awarded a triumph in 189 BC for his victory over Antiochus; the Seleucid monarch ended his days in violence in 187 BC, when he was murdered while plundering a temple in Elam.

Masters of the Mediterranean

Roman pre-eminence was now undisputed, and Rome's politicians richly rewarded their allies by allowing them parcels of territory and shares of the plunder taken from the vanquished. For themselves they kept money, furniture, clothing, and fabrics, alongside which Livy (39.6.7) unsympathetically listed slaves destined to toil in the homes of Rome's elite. The works of the Roman playwright Plautus, who died a few years after Magnesia, also provide a callous reflection of the centrality of human chattel to Roman society through his repeated use of slave characters. The human cost of Rome's victories extended well beyond the dead littering the battlefields of the eastern Mediterranean.

Envoys flocked to Rome. There were embassies from Antiochus, Rhodes, Pergamum, and the various independent communities in Asia Minor who the Romans had 'freed' from Antiochus in the war. Some of the embassies cravenly sought further favours from Rome: Eumenes II of Pergamum, in particular, made a saccharine speech before the senate in which he declared himself the most faithful of Rome's allies, pointing to the alliance not only between Rome and himself, but between Attalus, his father, and Rome's elder statesmen and ancestors. He begged the Romans to occupy the Asian side of the Hellespont, but knowing full well that they would not, he suggested that nobody other than himself deserved Rome's generosity. Not to be outdone, the Rhodian ambassadors fawned over the newfound liberty of the Greeks, both in Greece and in Asia Minor. Referring to the Second Macedonian War, they gushed that the Romans 'went to war with Philip and made every sacrifice for the sake of the liberty of Greece. For such was your purpose and this alone—absolutely nothing else—was the prize won by that war' (Polybius, 21.23). In the end, Eumenes got his territory, giving the lie of Rome's love of liberty, since some of the cities now given to Pergamum had only recently been 'freed' by the Romans. Eumenes took the epithet 'Soter', and it was during this time that work began on Pergamum's famous Great Altar, now in the Pergamon Museum in Berlin. Further proof of Rome's grip on local affairs is found in the ten-man commission dispatched to Asia to hear grievances between different communities. Previously the arbiters of these everyday neighbourly disagreements had been Rhodes, Antiochus, Pergamum, or other regional powers. Now the Romans had made it their business to be the sole arbitrator of the Mediterranean's problems.

Was this imperial behaviour? If the acquisition of territory is considered, then the answer is no. On the other hand, the Romans had reduced the status of dozens of communities to one of dependence, adapting the basic social–political contract of the Roman patron–client relationship to the international, diplomatic sphere. The failure of the Aetolians to understand what was meant by placing themselves under the *fides* of Rome, versus Rome's expectations of them, is a case in point. Perhaps the most important architect of this process was Flamininus, a committed patrician whose political world was one of patrons and clients. His actions following the victory over Philip in 197 BC are revealing, for he stayed in Greece, managing Greek affairs as a kind of *paterfamilias* and acting as a node through which grievances, arbitrations, and pleas for help could be channelled. There was no real effort on the part of the Romans to govern Greece or Macedonia, even while the balance of power clearly lay with the Roman senate. Cities and leagues continued to govern themselves, but under the paternalistic umbrella of the senate's *gravitas* and Flamininus's keen eye. This meant that Roman figures on the ground, such as Flamininus, unhindered by a cumbersome provincial bureaucracy, had tremendous opportunities for patronage; often a *senatus consultum* dealing with a problem would give considerable leeway to Roman commanders in the field, who were, for all practical considerations, normally physically remote from effective senatorial oversight anyway.

With Philip and Antiochus humbled by the power of Roman arms, the Aetolians reduced to near servitude, and Achaea, Rhodes, and Pergamum firmly dependent on Roman patronage, the traditional roles of the Hellenistic monarchs and the Greek leagues were therefore utterly taken over by the Roman senate and by individual Romans who appeared in endless embassies, commissions, and fact-finding missions. Such individuals now began to behave in interesting ways. After 'freeing the Greeks', Flamininus minted a gold stater with his portrait in the Hellenistic fashion—a stunning leap forward from the more symbolic coinage featuring gods and goddesses, prows of ships, or allegorical representations of the Roman state. This was unambiguously a coin *of* Flamininus: his name appeared next to Nike, the winged goddess of victory, on the reverse (Figure 5.8).

In a dedication made by Flamininus at Delphi, the general referred to himself as the 'son of Aeneas'—one of the earliest public declarations of a link between a Roman oligarch and

Figure 5.8 Illustration of the gold stater coinage of Flamininus, minted at Chalcis in 196 BC. On the obverse, head of Flamininus, right; on the reverse, Nike (Victory) standing left, holding wreath in one hand and palm-branch in the other. The legend reads T. QUINCTI.

Source: Illustration by the author.

a mythical or divine figure. In Rome, a bronze statue of Flamininus with an accompanying Greek inscription was erected by grateful Greeks. In Greece itself, Argos made Flamininus president of the Nemean Games, and he was accorded a series of other honours. In Chalcis, for example, a statue was dedicated to 'Heracles and Titus' [Flamininus], and a sanctuary of Apollo was also dedicated in the name of Titus (see *RGE* §6a–g). Flamininus was even given quasi-divine honours, with a priesthood in his name still active in Plutarch's day, and his name appeared in a hymn dedicated to Zeus and Apollo, calling him 'Titus our saviour!' (*Flamininus*, 16.3). The Greek word for saviour, *soter*, was noted in Chapter 3, and it was the chosen epithet of numerous Hellenistic kings, including some who were alive at the same time as Flamininus. It is clear that Flamininus was heavily influenced by the heady aromas of the Greek east, and at some level was seeking to set himself as the equal of a Hellenistic dynast. Aemilius Paullus, while not behaving quite as ostentatiously as Flamininus, would pursue a similar direction by having a statue of himself erected at Delphi (below).

Not everyone approved of what was happening with Flamininus, or indeed with other factions in the senate. One of the loudest voices was Cato the Elder, who had been elected consul in 195 BC alongside his patron Lucius Valerius Flaccus. Cato balloted for the province of Nearer Spain (Hispania Citerior), the coastal strip of Spain between the Pyrenees and New Carthage, below which the southern coastal areas were named Hispania Ulterior—'Further Spain' (Figure 5.9).

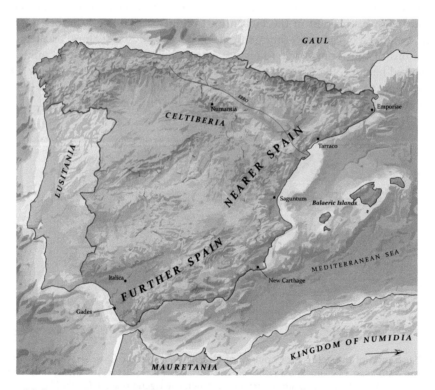

Figure 5.9 Spain at the end of the third century BC.

Source: Illustration by the author.

Just before he took up his post, Cato opposed the repealing of an unpopular piece of legislation in Rome, called the Oppian Law. This was an austerity law passed out of necessity after the Roman defeat at Cannae, limiting the amount of gold that women could own and placing further restrictions on dress and what was seen to be 'extravagant'. By this point, Cato was increasingly at loggerheads with Scipio Africanus, and his opposition to the Oppian Law was thought by some to be an attack on Scipio's wife, Aemilia, who had a penchant for dressing in style. In the end, Cato failed and left to take up his consulship. Spain had remained restive following the conclusion of the Hannibalic War, and Rome's continued military occupation there was not universally approved. Cato set himself the task of bringing his province under control, which he did through savage pacification actions. He also brought the silver and iron mines back into productivity, which benefited the Roman public purse. Livy remarked that Cato dismissed the *publicani* assigned to the army, who had been hired to keep the Roman troops provisioned, and told them take their stores back to Italy. 'War feeds itself,' he is thought to have said, as he proceeded to sack the Spanish countryside, killing adult males and stealing the food for his soldiers. For this, Cato was later awarded a triumph in Rome (Livy, 34.9).

Scipio Africanus had been censor in 199 BC and was elected consul in 194 BC. The following year, Titus Quinctius Flamininus, as censor, made him the *princeps senatus*, the elder statesman of the senate. Then, as we have seen, Scipio accompanied his brother Lucius for most of the campaign against Antiochus. After this war, Cato's anger with the Scipios increased, and he took particular aim at Lucius, boasting that his own victory at Thermopylae was far greater than that of Lucius at Magnesia. In either 188 or 187 BC, Lucius was accused of skimming off the indemnity levied on Antiochus; vast fortunes were being made in Rome's overseas wars, which makes the charges at least somewhat believable. (Lucius claimed that the money in question was booty and did not require formal accounting, a statement that gives us an insight into the myriad opportunities for corruption). Scipio Africanus intervened, however, dramatically ripping up the account books in the senate, and Lucius was saved from a serious penalty when a powerful patron also took his side. But Cato and his faction were not satisfied, and soon Africanus was accused of the same sort of crime, and others even raised the old canard of Scipio's 'phil-hellenic' ways back in Sicily during the final stages of the Hannibalic War. Before long, Scipio Africanus had been pushed out of Rome's political life. He retired to his farm at Liternum, where he became ill and died in relative obscurity.

It was perhaps inevitable that Cato, who saw himself as a bastion of Roman morality, would became censor. This he achieved in 184 BC, with Valerius Flaccus as his colleague. One of his first acts was to expel Flamininus's brother, Lucius Quinctius Flamininus, from the senate, supposedly for his poor behaviour but really as a way to hurt Cato's rivals. Cato applied such single-minded dedication to his job that Plutarch reported he expelled another senator for the crime of embracing his wife in public—Cato himself only embraced his wife when he heard thunder (*Cato the Elder*, 17)! Cato took particular aim at the wealthy and those who expended money purely for self-gratification; he also exacted punishing taxes and he ordered that pipes siphoning the public water from Rome's aqueducts into people's homes be destroyed. Meanwhile, he spent vast sums of public money on temples and other civic buildings, which Titus Flamininus managed to curtail. This struggle over the use of money in public life reflects the increasingly ostentatious behaviour of Roman elites (below).

There were rising divisions and factionalism within the senate between those who took an arch-conservative view about morality, such as Cato—men who saw Greek influences as pollution, and despised public honours like statues—and those, such as Flamininus, who saw nothing wrong with statues, coins bearing their likeness, honours, appearing in hymns, and long careers overseas. This emergent rift in Roman political life was made worse by each war, as the eminence of the state and its leading figures increased in proportion to the amount of wealth and influence won abroad. Flamininus's three-day triumph had all the hallmarks of a Hellenistic-style festival, and exposed ordinary Romans to unimaginable levels of wealth and ceremony of the sort that they imagined would never have been endorsed by the selfless heroes of Republican Rome, such as Cincinnatus.

Hannibal, Rome, and Perseus

After the war with Antiochus, Hannibal had little choice but to flee. He may have gone to either Armenia or Crete, or perhaps both, but later he appeared with king Prusias I of Bithynia (a northern district of Asia Minor), who was in conflict with the Pergamene king Eumenes II at the time. In his biography of Hannibal, Cornelius Nepos revealed that the old general could still outfox his opponents; outnumbered in a naval battle, he evened the odds by catapulting earthenware jars full of poisonous snakes at the Pergamene fleet (*Hannibal*, 10). Two pieces of correspondence attributed to Hannibal, one directed towards the Rhodians and another to the Athenians, warned presciently about the risks of accepting Roman friendship. Despite all this, he did not represent any sort of threat to Rome, and Plutarch wrote that 'all ignored him on account of his weakness and old age, regarding him as a castaway of Fortune' (*Flamininus*, 20). An ageing Titus Quinctius Flamininus, however, after seeing him in the court of Prusias, determined that Hannibal should be captured, and after Flamininus recruited Prusias to his scheme, Hannibal committed suicide rather than be paraded through the streets of Rome.

Throughout the 180s and early 170s BC, the Romans routinely interfered in quarrels between cities and leagues in Greece, despite having positioned themselves at the Isthmian Games as the benefactors of the Greeks. They also chose to ignore violations of their own proclamations. In 188 BC, the Achaean *strategos* Philopoemen—architect of the League's policy of cooperating with Rome, but at a certain distance—was still nurturing a grudge against Sparta and its indifferent membership of the League. He took reprisals against Sparta, wrecking the lingering effects of Nabis' revolutionary program by restoring Spartan exiles. This had been done even though envoys from the Achaean League and Sparta had been invited to Rome for arbitration. The senate made some uncomfortable noises, but took no action. In 183 BC, Philopoemen was captured by his enemies and compelled to take hemlock, after which the pro-Roman voices in the Achaean League became stronger and the League's attitude towards Rome changed considerably. Philopoemen's replacement and the representative of this faction, the sycophantic flatterer of the senate, Callicrates, headed an embassy to Rome in 180 BC, where he urged the senate to support those—like him—who would do whatever the Romans wanted.

In 179 BC, Philip V of Macedon died; he was succeeded not by the former hostage Demetrius, but by the latter's warlike brother Perseus. In his final years, Philip had fallen out with the senate after numerous decisions concerning territorial awards were made against him, and at a conference held to discuss the various complaints made by his neighbours,

Philip grew angry and remarked that 'the sun of all his days had not yet gone down' (Livy, 39.26). The Romans interpreted this as a threat, and Demetrius was later murdered on Philip's orders. One rumour popular in antiquity was that the ailing king had arranged this so Perseus could finish what he could not. Another story pinned the blame on the discovery of forged correspondence between Demetrius and Flamininus, which Demetrius had concealed and not passed on to his father. Ordering Demetrius's murder, the old king later died of a broken heart after realising he had been duped by Perseus. Both of these stories reflect a climate of mutual suspicion between Rome and Philip. Whatever the precise case, Demetrius was dead and Perseus was king, and many preferred the simplicity of rumour over the inconvenience of fact.

Demetrius was a known quantity in Rome, and had proven popular during his time as a hostage; it was even rumoured that Flamininus had told the young Macedonian that he would succeed Philip. Inevitably, there was suspicion of Perseus and his motives in Rome, and Roman discomfort with Philip in the final years of his rule was easily transferred to Perseus. Despite the fact that Perseus sent an embassy to Rome seeking senatorial permission to take the Macedonian throne, whispers of war were already afoot, and soon complaints about Perseus were landing in front of the senate. In 172 BC, Eumenes travelled to Rome in person to make his case. Eumenes was very much the architect of the coming war between Rome and Perseus: in secret hearings, he breathlessly reported Macedonian rearmament and accused Perseus of being behind an attempt on his life at Delphi. (The 'attempt' was an entirely coincidental shower of rocks from an unstable cliff-face, but Eumenes was quite convincing.) Shortly afterwards, a Roman envoy named Gaius Valerius returned from Greece and supported Eumenes's claims, while the apparent perpetrator of the assassination attempt, a Cretan named Evander, materialised at the Macedonian court at Pella. A fragmentary inscription addressed to the Delphic Amphictyony (*HW* §76), preserving a Roman manifesto of sorts, accused Perseus of hiding exiles, corrupting Greek politicians, and even (based on one particular restoration of the text) plotting to eliminate the senate—something Livy suggested was to be carried out using an untraceable poison. Perseus also engaged in a series of marriage alliances that were rather common behaviour between Hellenistic dynasts, but that alarmed the Romans: he married the daughter of Seleucus IV, Laodice, and his own half-sister married Prusias II of Bithynia, son of Prusias I, who had sheltered Hannibal. The Rhodians inserted themselves uncomfortably into this drama by conveying Laodice across the Aegean with much pomp and ceremony, an act they would come to regret. Later, Perseus was also accused of establishing links with Carthage. Perseus had thus strayed outside of Macedonia and straight into Rome's Mediterranean and Aegean spheres of influence, an act incompatible with his position as a client and a dependant of Rome. Worse, Perseus did things that could only anger oligarchic plutocrats and aristocratic conservatives, such as cancelling debts and trying to better the lives of the lower classes. Eumenes dressed all these things up as crimes, but the real 'crimes' of Perseus were that he was daring to act as if Roman authority in Greece were something that could be managed—and he had made an enemy out of the cavilling Eumenes, one of Rome's most important clients. The Romans were perfectly happy to listen to even the wildest claims made by Eumenes, and shamefully stalled Perseus's envoys in Rome until the invasion army had set off.

This was the Third Macedonian War, and it would be the final contest between the two states. Perseus raised a huge army, including many mercenaries (Figure 5.10). Quickly

Figure 5.10 Silver drachm of the type used at Rhodes, minted in Thessaly and intended to pay Cretan mercenaries in Macedonian service.

winning a cavalry victory over the Romans, Perseus found himself awash with offers of support from disaffected Greek cities that were delighted, as Polybius says, at the luck of the underdog (27.9).

In the end, the support did not matter. Perseus was crushed at Pydna in 168 BC by Lucius Aemilius Paullus, son of the consul of 216 BC (Chapter 4) and a general with ample experience of warfare fighting the Gauls in northern Italy. Perseus massed his phalanx together in a very tight formation, and its charge was so terrifying that it momentarily unnerved Aemilius Paullus. Eventually, as at Cynoscephalae, the Romans were able to turn the flank of the phalanx and penetrate its dense formation, killing from the sides and the rear where the phalanx had little protection. Perseus and his sons were captured, and along with tons of plunder, slaves, artwork, and expensive fabrics, they were paraded through the streets of Rome in Paullus's triumph; Perseus later starved himself to death in 165 or 162 BC. Plutarch remarked that the amount of plunder was so great that no special taxes or tributes were levied for the next 125 years (*Aemilius Paullus*, 38), although it is sometimes argued that this gigantic influx to the treasury was instead the result of an annual tribute levied on Macedonia in perpetuity. Before he came home, Paullus visited Delphi, where he appropriated a half-built pillar that was intended to act as the base for a statue of Perseus. Paullus ordered that a statue of himself should adorn the structure instead, with a Latin inscription arrogantly declaring that he had taken the pillar from the Macedonian king (*RGE* §24). Later, a sculpted representation of the battle of Pydna was dedicated to the consul at Delphi (Figure 5.11), its centrepiece an unbridled and unsaddled horse whose flight from their lines the Romans thought had started the engagement.

Paullus also took terrible revenge on the communities that had supported Perseus, selling 150,000 Epirotes into slavery and, on the orders of the senate, allowing Roman troops to sack their towns and cities. This retribution was out of all proportion to the causes and nature of the war. He also deported or killed large numbers of senior Achaeans and Aetolians. Among the Achaean hostages taken to Rome was the historian Polybius, whose political faction within the League had aroused irritation in Rome by its attempts to maintain a form of Achaean sovereignty and which, for a time, looked set to join

Figure 5.11 Illustration of a carved marble frieze from Delphi depicting the battle of Pydna.

Source: Illustration by the author.

Perseus. This time, there could be no independence for Macedonia, which was divided into four, its entire court with its scribes and bureaucrats and the royal library transported to Rome. Harsh laws were applied to prevent any kind of restoration of the kingdom, and the Romans also punished Rhodes, which had overstepped its position as Rome's client by carrying Laodice to Macedonia, and by offering to arbitrate between the senate and Perseus. Arbitration and mediation in Greek affairs were Rome's business, and like so many others in the Hellenistic world, Rhodes did not always understand what it meant to be Rome's 'friend'. Now the Rhodians lost control of Caria and Lycia, which they had received after the war with Antiochus. Rhodes, which benefited financially from its position on key shipping lanes, was further harmed when Rome gave control of Delos to Athens and made it a free port, even if ruining Rhodes financially was not what Rome initially had in mind. Delos quickly became a nexus for the booming Mediterranean slave trade, further enriching Roman and Italian traders, *negotiares*, in the process. The so-called 'Agora of the Italians' on Delos, a massive structure from the second-century BC covering 6,000 square metres (65,000 square feet) stands in mute testament to the volume of the Delian slave trade.

The Achaean League and the end of Carthage

As the Third Macedonian War was drawing to a close, the Sixth Syrian War (170-68 BC) had broken out between Antiochus IV Epiphanes (175-64 BC) and the teenage king Ptolemy VI Philometor, who had come to the Egyptian throne in 180 BC. The Romans were unsympathetic towards the rising popularity and success enjoyed by Antiochus, and after Pydna the senate felt it was time to send Gaius Popillius Laenus on a diplomatic mission to the king in Alexandria and remind him of the realities of Mediterranean politics. Popillius handed over a letter from the senate and demanded that Antiochus read it, after which the king asked for time to consult with his advisers. On this, Popillius, who was holding a vine rod, 'drew a circle around Antiochus and told him he must remain inside the circle until he gave his decision about the contents of the letter'. Taken aback, Antiochus recognised the veiled threat behind Popillius's actions, and gave in (Polybius, 29.27). No doubt Magnesia and the fate of his father, Antiochus III, were at the forefront of his mind. Not long after this fateful meeting, a frustrated and angry Antiochus ordered his troops to sack Jerusalem, killing some 80,000 people over a bloody three-day period and looting the Temple, before returning to Antioch with some 1,800 talents' worth of plunder. The resulting Maccabaean Revolt led to a treaty between Judaea and Rome (161 BC), although Rome did nothing when Demetrius I Soter crushed the rebellion, killing Judas Maccabaeus in the process.

A brief glimmer of hope flickered in Macedonia in 148 BC when a man named Andriscus, who portrayed himself as a son of Perseus, staged an uprising. He sought help from Syria, and it was reported that he had made an alliance with Carthage, but this seems unlikely. Like other individuals whom the Romans deemed dangerous, he promoted the interests of the lower classes and acted against the interests of the plutocratic elite. In the end, his revolt only invited further military intervention and suffering, although he scored a notable success when he met and killed in battle the praetor Publius Iuventius Thalna. Later, after suffering defeat (ironically, at Pydna) at the hands of the plebeian praetor Quintus Caecilius Metellus 'Macedonicus', Macedonia, along with Illyria, became a Roman province in 146 BC. Unlike previous occasions, this time Metellus did not evacuate his army. Conquest was followed by the construction of the via Egnatia, a road that linked Epidamnus/Dyrrachium (Albanian Durrës) with Thessalonike and eventually Byzantium, cutting east through Macedonia and Thrace. In Rome, Metellus celebrated his victory with the construction of a portico, the Porticus Metelli, along with temples to Jupiter and Juno. The portico was an architectural feature inspired by Greek models, designed to surround temples dedicated in the aftermath of military victories.

After the Third Macedonian War, friendly relations with the Achaean League had been maintained through the obsequious Callicrates, who had arranged the deportation of Polybius and the other hostages. After some wrangling and intervention by Scipio Aemilianus (below), the small number of surviving deportees were eventually returned to Achaea in 150 BC. Callicrates died in the same year, and was succeeded as the League's representative by Diaeus, who was more Philopoemen than Callicrates. Indeed, to Rome's displeasure, the League began charting its own course once again, this time warring with Sparta, a city for which Diaeus had little more than contempt. A Roman embassy sent to intimidate the League's politicians by announcing that Sparta, Corinth, and Argos would be separated from the League ended in failure, and the next year was marked by procrastination, endless embassies, and stalling from both sides. Diaeus and his faction pursued economic reforms, which increasingly hurt Rome's position in Greece. Final attempts at diplomacy in front of the League's assembled members were met with hoots of derision, and the Roman envoys were chased out of the hall; Rome declared war on its erstwhile ally in 146 BC. Polybius was an eyewitness to the unfolding catastrophe, and he began his 38th book by lamenting that it contained 'the completion of the disaster of Greece' (38.1). He had intended Perseus's defeat at Pydna in 168 BC to be the end of his *Histories*, but the passage of contemporary events led him to return to tell the rest of the story. Polybius could do nothing about the relentless march of Rome's armies, and his work often seems to be an attempt to come to terms with this impotence, in part by blaming the various factions within Achaean politics for dragging the League into a war it could not win.

The Achaeans suffered several defeats at Roman hands. The bellicose *strategos* Critolaus, part of the faction led by Diaeus, succumbed to Caecilius Metellus near the storied battlefield of Thermopylae. In desperation, 12,000 slaves were freed and enrolled into the League's forces, but it was to no avail. Corinth surrendered to the plebeian *novus homo* consul Lucius Mummius, with terrible consequences. Under orders from the senate, Mummius let his troops loose on the city, with the result that vast numbers of slaves—mostly women and children—were taken and sold. The majority of the adult male population was murdered. Polybius was there, and although he recorded what he saw in his *Histories*, the relevant parts of book 39 have not survived, and it fell to Strabo, writing some 150 years later and with access to the full text, to tell us what happened. He wrote that Polybius saw artworks and religious objects looted, and soldiers 'playing dice' on famous paintings (Strabo, 6.6.28). Strabo noted afterwards that Mummius—no art collector—had simply allowed his troops to take whatever they wanted. The first-century BC historian Velleius Paterculus said derisively of Mummius that as he was arranging for 'the transportation to Italy of pictures and statues by the hands of the greatest artists, he gave instructions that the contractors should be warned that if they lost them, they would have to replace them by new ones' (1.13). Only a few items were spared, including statues of Philopoemen, who was still well regarded in Rome. In the aftermath, Mummius, who took the agnomen 'Achaicus', dissolved the Achaean League, as well as the other remaining leagues that had clung on to a precarious political freedom in the face of the Roman onslaught. Democratic government was replaced by Roman-style oligarchy, and city walls across Greece were demolished and military matériel confiscated. It was the end of Greek independence; southern Greece came under the authority of the new Roman governor of Macedonia, and Corinth would lie in ruins until it was rebuilt on the orders of Julius Caesar in 44 BC. In Rome, the Temple of Hercules Victor in the *forum boarium*, built in Greek marble and in imitation of an old Greek design encircled by a Corinthian colonnade, was probably dedicated by Mummius in honour of his victory.

At virtually the same time as the Achaeans fought their uneven contest, the Romans also took decisive action against Carthage. An elderly Masinissa was at war with the Carthaginians, and to try to settle their differences, the senate dispatched a commission that included Cato the Elder. According to Plutarch, Cato was incensed and infuriated when he found that life had returned to normal at Carthage and that the city was prospering. Cato returned home, where he began to harangue the senate about the danger Carthage posed to Rome. In reality, of course, there was no danger, but Cato had taken it upon himself to be a judge of morality, and the prosperity of a vanquished enemy was morally unacceptable and an offence to Roman power. He had previously railed against the young Romans who had 'gone Greek' after Pydna, spending money on prostitutes instead of getting back to work on the farm. This was no different. With great drama, he withdrew a plump fig from the folds of his toga, then revealed where he had got it from. Cato famously ended all of his speeches from this point with the Latin phrase *delenda est Carthago*, meaning 'Carthage must be destroyed'. Not everyone agreed with Cato, but his argument that 'external threats to [Roman] sovereignty ought to be done away with altogether' found an appreciative audience among senators more inclined to intervention and war than towards following the insular path that Quintus Fabius Maximus had once advocated in the long-distant past (Plutarch, *Cato the Elder*, 27).

Cato died before the outcome of his senatorial bluster could be realised. The war began badly in 149 BC, but later, with some historical irony, the Romans entrusted the campaign to Scipio Aemilianus, the grandson of Lucius Aemilius Paullus (consul in 216 BC), who had been adopted into the Cornelii Scipiones by the son of Scipio Africanus; Scipio Aemilianus was therefore Scipio Africanus's adoptive grandson. Controversially, and despite senatorial attempts to curb the practice, Aemilianus was yet another ambitious Roman politician who was elected to the consulship (in 147 BC), despite never holding the praetorship or even being old enough to be consul. Both the senate and the consuls still in office tried to block his appointment, but such were his pedigree and popularity with the people that his opponents were forced to back down. His candidacy was also helped by a plebeian tribune who threatened to veto consular business if he was not permitted to stand; later, Scipio was given the Carthaginian campaign by popular vote, instead of following past practice and balloting for his province.

Polybius, who had spent 17 years in Rome and become close to Scipio Aemilianus—the two had befriended one another over a good book—subsequently accompanied his patron on campaign to Africa and was an eyewitness to much of what went on. Unfortunately, like those dealing with Corinth, the parts of his *Histories* dealing with the Carthaginian war only exist in fragments. The prosecution of the final year of the conflict was characteristically savage, and included bitter street fighting in Carthage. Envoys sent to Rome, begging for mercy, were ordered to return to Carthage and to tell their fellow citizens that the senate had determined to destroy their city. Some hid in Italy, says Diodorus, while the rest, 'electing to return, made their way back, their fatal mission completed' (32.6). Scipio called out Carthaginian Tanit in the same way that Furius Camillus had called out Juno-Uni from Veii two and a half centuries earlier. Only a small number of Carthaginians survived the onslaught to be sold into slavery, after which the city was sacked, razed, and destroyed. Masinissa kept his kingdom, and the Romans annexed the best of Carthaginian land as the new province of Africa. Polybius described an emotional and dramatic scene, as he and Scipio Aemilianus watched the city burn (38.22). Quoting the *Iliad*'s prophecy of the destruction of Troy and the death of king Priam, Scipio expressed the fear that Rome would suffer in the same way. Such was the destiny of powerful cities and their empires.

'They confirmed their power by terrorism'

Carthage suffered a worse fate than either Macedonia or Greece, and was regarded by historians in antiquity to have barely merited the calamity that the Romans visited upon its people. Commenting on the destruction of Carthage and events in Macedonia, Diodorus Siculus observed that up to this point, while the Romans won their empire through violence on the battlefield, they had nevertheless gained a reputation for clemency and treated their beaten adversaries fairly—often far better than the traditions and customs of warfare of the ancient Mediterranean dictated. In this, Diodorus was correct, insofar as those who placed themselves under the *fides* of Rome and knew what this meant gained protection. They also participated in Rome's wars, which was exacting and dangerous but at least gave them a share of the profits. At some point in the third and second centuries BC, however, a decisive shift occurred in Roman thinking, particularly among Rome's ambi-tious and competitive aristocrats, and there was a corresponding shift in Roman behaviour. Triumphs became so regular that many were disputed or denied by a wary senate and *comitia centuriata*. (This did not always work: Appius Claudius Pulcher, denied a triumph in 143 BC, held it anyway.) The payment of cash bonuses to troops also assumed an alarming regularity, creating politically lucrative bonds between commanders and their levies. Ever more lavish public games were held in Rome, paid for by foreign wars: after the defeat of Antiochus III, for example, Lucius Scipio bankrolled a ten-day extravaganza that did much to bolster his political profile—and his electability—among the people. There were other ways to advertise: victory arches had been constructed in Rome as early as the beginning of the third century BC, and in 190 BC, Scipio Africanus commissioned an arch in front of the Capitoline Hill, decorated with glitzy statues. Funerals and tombs also provided an outlet for elite competition. The famous Tomb of the Scipios, for example, discovered along the route of the via Appia in the eighteenth century, contained 30 niches for members of this illustrious family (although Africanus was interred at Liternum) and the poet Ennius was reportedly buried there. Lawsuits alleging misdeeds were also a useful way to self-advertise and knock down political opponents: Cato, for example, was tried and acquitted 44 times. Outright bribery with donatives made by patrons to their clientele became common. Fortunes were made by *publicani* following Roman armies of conquest and picking up contracts from the censors for weapons manufacture, roads, bridges, mine operations, ship building, tax collection, and every conceivable need. Corruption also followed these armies, and financial misconduct by provincial governors became apparent as early as 171 BC in Hispania. The expansion of the praetorship to manage the new provinces—but without expanding the consulship—only increased aristocratic competi-tion for the consulship and made corruption more likely. The huge influx of cash, from tribute, slaves, war plunder, and indemnities, and the irrepressible lure of more of it, was the culprit in many of these situations.

As a result, Rome's politicians were no longer content with intervening in disputes, normally after being invited to do so, but started to act in a predatory and exploitative manner. They took advantage of defeated peoples, turning them into tributary clients who answered to Rome and its diktats. Macedonia's silver mines, for example, which had closed in 167 BC after the defeat of Perseus, reopened a decade later, coinciding with a surge in minting of silver coins in Rome. Diodorus recognised this rapacious nature, noting that 'once [the Romans] held sway over virtually the whole inhabited world, they confirmed their power by terrorism and by the destruction of the most eminent cities' (32.4). Polybius, who was often more circumspect about passing judgement on Rome due to his position as the client of Scipio Aemilianus, nevertheless 'reported' Greek opinions on Rome's behaviour, allowing him to put in the mouths of others things that he may have been privately thinking to himself. He acknowledged that 'some Greeks' thought that the Romans had acted in a 'wise and statesmanlike' way by cutting off opposition, real or imagined, before it could harm the state. On the other hand, Polybius continued, others believed that the principles that had once guided Rome, and that had made the city and her people worthy of admiration, had been forgotten and replaced by the 'lust for domination' that had, in more ancient times, dragged Athens and Sparta to their ruin. By 'utterly exterminating the kingdom of Macedonia', he wrote, the Romans had given early notice of their change in policy 'and they had now completely revealed it by their decision concerning Carthage'. This is Polybius at his most unforgiving. He finished his thoughts by saying that 'the Carthaginians had been guilty of no immediate offence to Rome, but the Romans had treated them with irremediable severity, although they had accepted all their conditions and consented to obey all their orders' (36.5-6). Velleius Paterculus made a similar comment, remarking that the city was destroyed 'because the Romans were ready to believe any rumour concerning the Carthaginians' (1.12). There could be no sound justification for what happened in Macedonia, Achaea, or North Africa.

It is hard to locate when the shift towards more violent and rapacious behaviour took place. Indeed, it is worth noting that even in the face of possible war with Antiochus III in 194 BC, the Romans recalled Flamininus from Greece and evacuated the Roman garrisons there, even though the faction of Scipio Africanus, consul for that year, was arguing for vigilance. The senate may have been seeking to establish a moral high ground for the looming showdown with Antiochus, but whatever precisely it was thinking then, the truth stands that none of these *later* wars—the attack on Corinth, the sack of Carthage, the end of the Macedonian monarchy—can possibly be thought of as defensive campaigns in the way that characterised ancient assessments of the causes behind the First Punic War or the First Macedonian War. Instead, between the turn of the second century and 146 BC, there were unmistakeable signs that Rome's attitudes were hardening and governed ever more by self-interest. The arrogance of Popillius before Antiochus III was matched by that of Gnaeus Octavius, who was part of a three-man commission dispatched to see whether the Treaty of Apamea was being followed to the letter. Finding that Antiochus IV had been building up the Seleucid fleet and amassing war elephants, he acted on senatorial orders to hamstring the elephants and burn the fleet, 'and by every means to cripple the royal power' (Polybius, 31.2). In 171 BC, despite being allied to Rome, Chalcis was plundered by the praetor Gaius Lucretius, its population sold into slavery. Closer to home, Popillius's kinsman, Marcus Popillius Laenas, consul in 173 BC, conducted an illegal war against the Ligurians in northern Italy. Disregarding their *deditio in fidem*, he sold the survivors into slavery. That Roman officials—whether acting on senatorial orders or not—felt they had the moral authority to act as they saw fit says a lot about Rome's idea of its place in the world, and particularly in the Hellenistic world, a space governed by much older ideas of political authority. Another indication of a shift in Roman attitudes is the greater attention paid to self-serving politicians such as Eumenes and Callicrates, with a correspondingly decreased interest in acting as a *neutral* arbiter in Greece's many disputes—even if Rome demanded that all those disputes be referred to Roman arbitration.

Nathan Rosenstein has aptly called the crucial period of Roman expansion and dominance discussed in this chapter (and in parts of the previous two) 'the imperial Republic'. This might appear to be a contradiction if one is looking for a date or key event when the Roman state ceased to be a republic and the empire came into being. Yet the development of what we call the 'Roman empire' was a complex process that took place over many centuries, and could be argued to have its roots far back in early Italian colonisation and wars against the Samnites, the Etruscans, and the peoples of Magna Graecia. It also depends on what definition is used to describe imperial behaviour: the Romans sent out colonies from an early date, as did the Greeks; they fought interminable wars against their neighbours; they intervened increasingly in matters that had nothing to do with them, and at certain points they seemed almost to be looking for excuses to send armies into the field in order to generate opportunities for glory and plunder, which included inflicting incalculable misery through murder and the acquisition of slaves. In 172 BC, the consuls asked for Macedonia to be assigned to one of them as their province, a ridiculous and war-mongering request given that Macedonia was still a Roman friend, and in 171 BC, the plebeian consul Gaius Cassius Longinus was so irritated at receiving Italy and not Macedonia that, on his own initiative, he set off for Macedonia anyway. Recalled by the senate, Longinus pillaged the communities he passed through, selling their terrified people into slavery.

With this sort of behaviour in mind, Peter Green has characterised third-century Rome as 'imperial despite itself' (*Alexander to Actium*, p. 217), reflecting the almost haphazard way in which responses to requests for help underpinned exploits that turned out, during and after the fact, to be imperial in nature. Rome's empire was, in the third and second centuries, typified above all by the way it exercised power: the Romans subordinated once-powerful states such as Macedonia within the vertical relationship of patron and client, with correspondingly narrow definitions of what each party's rights, duties, and responsibilities were. By 146 BC, much of the Greek world existed to serve Rome's interests, whether this be supplying silver for Roman coinage, paying an annual tribute, or providing men and matériel for Roman wars.

In Rome, worries about philhellenism and extravagant living would persist, but would be supplanted by even graver threats that eventually brought about the transformation of the state into an absolute monarchy (Chapters 6 and 7). These emerging threats were recognised quite early on: during the early second century, the senate cracked down on election rules in an attempt to curb ambition, setting minimum ages for the positions of aedile, praetor, and consul, then banning the holding of second consulships by 152 BC. There were no dictators appointed until the time of Sulla (Chapter 6), and the earlier expansion of the praetorship had lessened the need for prorogation. The senate also tried to limit the amount of money that could be spent on public games, recognising their inherent value as political propaganda, and came up with all sorts of decrees, including one stating that no more than 45 kilograms (100 pounds) weight of silverware could be used at a banquet. Meanwhile, diligent censors cracked down on questions of morality, punishing the over-indulgent—including one man who ate so much that he was unable to mount his horse—or those who mistreated their clients. Nevertheless, Rome's politicians would no longer be content with the mere rewards of service and duty. Once toppling wealthy foreign kingdoms became routine, and vast fortunes and *gloria* had been won by young men eager for war, the Roman constitution would struggle to restrain the ambitions of the political class. It would not be the Greeks who turned the people 'against our own Roman gods', but the Romans themselves.

Chapter 6

The collapse of public order, 140–63 BC

In 134 BC, Scipio Aemilianus was elected consul for the second time and dispatched to the distant edges of Nearer Spain, where the Romans had been locked in a struggle with the city of Numantia for almost 20 years. Spain was crucial for Rome, as its silver mines provided one-fifth of the city's annual revenue. Even though Scipio Africanus had settled veterans at the colony of Italica in the south of the Iberian Peninsula, and subsequent colonisation efforts continued to strengthen Rome's grip in the region, Roman armies struggled through a long conflict against the Lusitanian and Celtiberian peoples that was marred by massacres, double-dealing, and broken promises. In Further Spain, the Lusitanians conducted a spirited guerilla war under their talented and visionary leader, Viriathus, who kept the Roman armies at bay for eight long years before he was betrayed and murdered. Meanwhile, the war against the Celtiberian stronghold of Numantia in the Douro valley had been marked by staggering degrees of military incompetence on the part of successive Roman commanders until Scipio, who was elected to bring the war to an end, conducted a determined and sophisticated siege that included a complete circumvallation of the doomed city. Appian reported that a system of ditches, palisades, a substantial stone wall punctuated by towers, and a blockade of the river Douro using logs studded with spear blades and knives, completely cut Numantia off from assistance and supplies (*Spanish Wars*, 90–1). Archaeological work at the site, located in northern Spain close to the town of Garray, has identified remnants of this complex effort. Rome's well-deserved reputation for savagery in victory was widely known, and the population of Numantia chose mass suicide over the less appealing alternatives. Scipio returned to Rome in triumph, taking the agnomen 'Numantinus' (Figure 6.1).

Scipio's second consulship came in the face of stiff conservative opposition and determined efforts to crack down on irregularities in the *cursus honorum*. The seeds of this senatorial discomfort had been laid a generation earlier when Marcus Claudius Marcellus, grandson of the Marcellus killed in battle with Hannibal at Venusia in 208 BC, had held the consulship for the third time. An unsettled senate made efforts to regulate office holding, but when the time came it could do nothing to rein in Scipio's popularity. He had earned widespread admiration by volunteering to go to Spain as a military tribune in 151 BC, breaking a recruitment crisis that had seen the plebeian tribunes throw the consuls-elect into prison until they had come up with better terms of service for their soldiers. On campaign, Scipio distinguished himself with conspicuous bravery, winning the *corona muralis*, the mural crown, for being first over the enemy's defensive walls. In 142 BC he had held

DOI: 10.4324/9781003202523-6

Figure 6.1 Google Earth Pro image of the ruins of the city of Numantia, surmounting an imposing hill to the south of the Spanish town of Garray.

Source: Image © 2020 CNES/Airbus © 2020 Google.

the censorship, angering many conservatives during his election campaign by spending his time in the forum in the company of freedmen (freed slaves) and the poor and destitute. By the time that he announced his candidacy to end the Numantine War, there was little his opponents could do to stop him winning at the ballot box. Scipio's career, built very much on running against conservative tradition, reflected the growing tussle between populists and conservatives. The former mobilised the will of the people—often through the plebeian tribunate—and the latter, falling back on the *mos maiorum*, sought to strengthen the position of the senatorial aristocracy and tried to regulate the tenure of the senior elected offices like the consulship. In the period between 140 BC and 63 BC, this struggle was played out in numerous ways. Ambitious legislative agendas sought to address structural issues in the Roman state, both perceived and real. Overseas campaigns against a succession of enemies provided opportunities for rival politicians to win *gloria* and fill the state treasury—and their own pockets. At home, battles were waged over whether senators should be tried in the increasingly common corruption cases by their peers or by Rome's emerging middle class, the equestrians. The struggle led to shocking levels of public violence in Rome, civil war between Romans and between Romans and Italians, and the perversion of the constitutional framework to suit the needs of powerful individuals. At the centre of this political unravelling lay the unwavering importance of family and family connections, which heightened intracommunal hostility and created fleeting and tenuous alliances between friends and rivals.

The Gracchi: land reform and public violence in Rome

A few years before Scipio's decisive siege against the Numantines, a trapped Roman army had been spared after a deal was brokered by the plebeian quaestor Tiberius Sempronius Gracchus. The army was allowed to depart, although it was looted and humiliated in the process. When the senate found out about the peace terms, its members were so enraged that they ordered the hapless consul, the patrician Caius Hostilius Mancinus—'not bad as a man, but most unfortunate of the Romans as a general'—to be delivered by the fetial priests to the Numantines naked and in fetters; the Numantines, unimpressed, sent him away (Plutarch, *Tiberius Gracchus*, 6-7). One of the loudest voices arguing against making peace with Numantia was Scipio Aemilianus, who was on the hunt for military glory. Scipio was Tiberius's brother-in-law, as he had married Tiberius's sister, Sempronia. Tiberius' mother Cornelia was the daughter of Scipio Africanus and Aemilia, who was herself the daughter of Lucius Aemilius Paullus (consul 216 BC). Tiberius added further to his illustrious pedigree by marrying Claudia, the daughter of Appius Claudius Pulcher, consul in 143 BC, censor in 136 BC, *princeps senatus*, and scion of the patrician Claudii family. Despite the close links between Scipio Aemilianus and Tiberius Gracchus—or perhaps because of such intimacy, and the lofty social station of each—the two were bitter rivals.

In 134 BC, Tiberius was elected as plebeian tribune, and proposed a law that sought to limit the amount of the *ager publicus* that could be farmed by a single individual. In doing so, Tiberius revisited one of the main issues addressed by the Licinian-Sextian laws (Chapter 2), and sought to build on the numerous attempts made after the Hannibalic War to deal with land ownership. According to Plutarch, Tiberius argued that the poor were progressively being driven from the land by the rich, who resorted to fraud and threats to consolidate large parts of the *ager publicus* under their control. Plutarch's account of the issue is romanticised, casting the land question as a moral one that threatened one of the fundamental pillars of Roman society. Driving the peasants from the land, and replacing them with slaves and large estates, wrecked the moral compact of citizenship that demanded military duty for the state in return for a say in government and a share of the spoils. From this perspective, a peasant working the land was a voter and a legionnaire, but a slave was just a slave, and his (or her) contribution to the state would always be less than that of a free man. Slavery and the use of slaves to work the land predated Tiberius Gracchus, but in 133 BC the vast numbers of available slaves, the destruction wrought by war, and the skyrocketing wealth of the elites gave his argument new impetus. That wealth was on clear display in Rome's endless construction projects, and particularly in the lavish villas being built in Rome and in Campania—as Velleius Paterculus noted, 'private luxury followed public extravagance' (2.1). In Rome, the best addresses were those adjacent to the forum, the Capitoline Hill, and the Palatine Hill, but the most famous surviving examples of these homes of the Roman 1 per cent are at Pompeii, preserved by the eruption of Vesuvius in AD 79. Many of these opulent dwellings were influenced by Greek architectural styles, which provided for a careful delineation between public and private space. The villas included places for peaceful seclusion, such as colonnaded gardens, and were decorated with beautiful paintings; these included the First Pompeian Style, with painted stucco used to imitate the look of expensive marble, and the Second Pompeian Style, popular in the first century BC, which portrayed scenes from Greek mythology and other 'eastern' themes. The artworks and sculptures that adorned these houses were either looted during wartime or purchased on the burgeoning international art market, financed by the deep purses of the Roman elite. One avid collector would be the famous lawyer and orator Cicero, who relied on his equestrian friend and publisher Titus Pomponius Atticus, based in Athens, to act as his broker. As the taste for foreign art spread, more affordable Roman copies of Greek art became available on the local market. A particularly popular architectural feature was the peristyle, a square or rectangular colonnade that might enclose a pleasing feature such as a fountain or a garden, and Cicero would later imagine Scipio Aemilianus and his entourage philosophising within a peristyle at his estate in the Alban Hills. One of the best examples of the sophisticated artistic tastes of the ultra-rich is the famous mosaic from the House of the Faun, depicting Alexander the Great in battle with the Persian king Darius III (Figure 6.2). The House of the Faun was a colossal residence bigger than most royal courts, and featured two separate peristyles, two atria (entrance rooms), and more than seven bedrooms.

Plutarch says Tiberius was educated by a Stoic philosopher from Cumae named Blossius, and there is indeed something of the philosophical in the way Tiberius framed his position. Rome was losing its soul, and only by reconnecting the peasants with the land could this situation be wrestled back from the precipice (*Tiberius Gracchus*, 8-9). The situation may not have been as dire as Tiberius suggested, but soldiers were indeed periodically gone from home on long, multi-year campaigns, many of which yielded questionable results for the rank-and-file legionnaire. The damage done to Italian agriculture during the Hannibalic War, and the depopulation caused by colonisation, death, deportation, and exile, along with a trend towards urbanisation as the Italian population sought the safety of the cities, favoured the growth of large farms run by the wealthy at the expense of smallholders. The large-scale land confiscations from disaffected allies during and after the Hannibalic War had added considerably to the *ager publicus*, and for those enriched by the gold and silver that flowed from Carthage, Greece, and Macedonia, land provided an attractive investment and avoided the prohibition on senators engaging in business activities. Cato the Elder's treatise *On Agriculture*, which celebrated the link between farming and soldiering, provided reams of advice on how to deploy the vast fortunes being made and described the sort of large plantations, mostly based on slave labour, that would offer a steady income. Such plantations were not staffed uniquely by only a single gender; indeed, it has been argued that entire slave families, including children, were crucial for agricultural output and the management of large estates. A later work of the same title by the scholar Marcus Terentius Varro (Chapters 1 and 7) referred to slaves as the 'articulate' amongst the tools available to the farmer (1.17.1)—the others being the 'inarticulate' animals and the 'mute' wooden and metal tools for tilling the soil, revealing the appalling pragmatism with which the Romans viewed their slaves. Such a viewpoint would have made sense to Cato, who advised landowners not to by shy about getting rid of sick or old slaves. (Not to be outdone, Columella, writing about agricultural estates in the first century AD, advised keeping slaves chained in underground prisons when not at work.) Appian said slave labour had replaced free labour on estates, and he explained how landowners easily absorbed vacant land or the plots of the poor (*Civil Wars*, 1.7). From the perspective of the free Roman, however, in such a scenario where something as essential to life as arable land could be portrayed as the preserve of the super-wealthy, it is easy to see how Tiberius could argue that the benefits of empire should be enjoyed by all citizens, not just the wealthy. 'The men who fight and die for Italy enjoy the common air and light,'

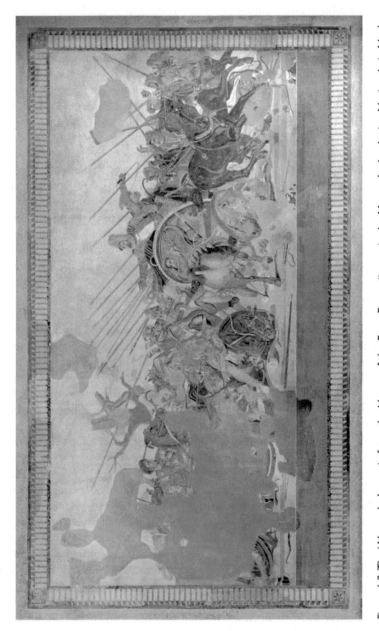

Figure 6.2 The 'Alexander' mosaic from the House of the Faun, Pompeii, now in the Museo Archeologico Nazionale in Naples.

Source: Photograph by Berthold Werner (CC BY-SA 3.0).

he said in a speech imagined by Plutarch, but 'houseless and homeless they wander about with their wives and children' (*Tiberius Gracchus*, 9).

The accuracy of this picture has been hotly debated for many years. An examination of census figures and estimates of the vast numbers of slaves working in Italy once suggested that there *was* indeed a significant decline in the free rural population, accompanied by a correspondingly large increase in the slave population. Modern scholarship, however, no longer accepts that this was the case. There is scant archaeological evidence supporting it, for one thing, and it has also been argued that there may have been a form of 'census evasion' to avoid military service on unpopular campaigns, concealing the actual number of citizens living in Italy. Tiberius Gracchus may also have based his reading of the situation on only a small part of Italy where farmers had indeed been pushed out by powerful land-owners, or he may have misread the situation completely and not realised that competition for land was a result of an increase in both the slave *and* the free population of rural Italy. Nathan Rosenstein, for example, has argued that there was something of a 'baby boom' in the aftermath of the Hannibalic War, creating a growth in the population that in turn helped to create a land crisis. Roman men, he argues, married some 13 years after their first eligibility for military service at age 17, and to much younger women; men over 30 were thus less likely to be recruited or, if they were, less likely to serve in the front-line *hastati* or *principes*. In this view, husbands were not being wrenched from young families, leaving wives alone to fend off avaricious land speculators. The problem instead was that there simply was not *enough* land to go around, a crisis made worse by a suspension in overseas colonisation, which meant that there was nowhere for the excess population to go except to flood into Rome, swelling the ranks of the urban poor. Tiberius Gracchus probably therefore based his proposals on a fundamental misunderstanding of the situation, but his argument, based as it was on romanticised ideas about Roman morality and the ancient compact between the soldier and the soil, resonated with his audience. Tiberius's proposals to solve the crisis would only make it worse—and his behaviour would irritate conservatives in the senate.

The amount that Tiberius set as the maximum for one individual was approximately 122 hectares (300 acres). The *ager publicus* should be surveyed, he proposed, to determine how much excess was available, and then this excess land could be parcelled in 8 hectare (20 acre) tracts and given to the Roman poor, who would farm it. Private land would not be affected by this proposal, but those in the senate who controlled parts of the *ager publicus* were unlikely to favour the legislation. Tiberius Gracchus has gone down in history as a revolutionary, but his approach was essentially a conservative one: he was adopting a rather Catonian position, trying to strengthen the basis of army recruitment and attempting to put people back on the land. (He was also largely unconcerned with improving the lot of slaves; on the contrary, he depended on slaves and freedmen to protect him as his pos-ition in Rome deteriorated later on.) Tiberius had the backing of his father-in-law and *princeps senatus*, Appius Claudius Pulcher, and one of the consuls, the patrician Publius Mucius Scaevola, an accomplished lawyer. (Scaevola's plebeian consular colleague Lucius Calpurnius Piso opposed Tiberius, but was engaged in battling the Sicilian slave revolt—see below). Nevertheless, Tiberius made the fateful decision to propose the bill to the people rather than the senate. This was his right as a plebeian tribune, but some thought it clashed with the *mos maiorum*. A fellow plebeian tribune, Marcus Octavius, duly opposed the law; Appian remarked that he had been 'induced' by the wealthy landowners to do so at any cost (*Civil Wars*, 1.12).The two tribunes then duelled in front of the senate. Octavius continued to use his tribunician veto, which eventually prompted an exasperated Tiberius to submit a bill that would remove Octavius. Pausing dramatically as the votes were cast, Tiberius begged his colleague to withdraw his opposition before a majority was reached. Octavius refused, and the voting reached its inevitable conclusion.

With Octavius gone, Tiberius's land law passed, and a group of three men—a triumvirate, made up of Appius Claudius Pulcher, Tiberius, and his brother, Gaius—was established to organise the land survey and to enact the provisions of the bill. The senate signalled its displeasure by withholding funding for the triumvirate to carry out their work. Starved of cash, the triumvirs could do little but fume with anger, but then a Pergamene envoy arrived in Rome with the stunning news that king Attalus III of Pergamum, who died in 133 BC, had bequeathed his kingdom to the Roman state. Attalus had adroitly judged the political realities of the times and was also seeking to stave off the ambitions of his half-brother, Aristonicus (see below). Without seeking senatorial permission, Tiberius set before the people a motion to accept this inheritance and use Pergamum's vast wealth to cover the missing funding. This was a further worrying development for conservative Romans, because it had been firmly established during the third and early second centuries that foreign policy was the preserve of the senate, which received and dispatched embassies and provided written advice, the *senatus consultum*, to guide magistrates operating overseas. Given the amount of land and money involved, a mere plebeian tribune had no right to blunder into matters that clearly belonged to the senate. It was becoming clear that Tiberius was increasingly at war with the senate and its conservative membership by insisting that the people, not the senate, could—and should—make decisions on matters of grave importance.

Unsettling questions were now being asked of Tiberius, and he fuelled them by running once more for the plebeian tribunate. Nobody had held sequential tribunates in living memory, and unease rippled through Rome. Rumours about Tiberius abounded, including one that Eudemus, the Pergamene envoy, had given Tiberius a royal diadem and a purple cloak. Senior senators reminded Tiberius of his father's tenure of the censorship, during which he had been such a strict disciplinarian that 'the citizens put out their lights, for fear they might be thought to be indulging immoderately in entertainments and drinking bouts'. In contrast, they sneered, Tiberius went on his way around town surrounded by the uncouth and rowdy urban poor (Plutarch, *Tiberius Gracchus*, 14). Tiberius fared poorly in the elections and withdrew to the Capitoline Hill with a group of his closest friends and allies. The situation quickly degenerated, and Publius Cornelius Scipio Nasica, who was the *pontifex maximus* and the cousin of Scipio Aemilianus, overrode Scaevola's reluctance to deal with Tiberius and set off with an armed mob to do so himself. Tiberius and his followers were bludgeoned to death and their bodies dumped into the Tiber. Later, senatorial investigations led to extensive reprisals against his surviving supporters and added many more lives to the tally. Blossius narrowly escaped with his life after intense questioning by Scipio Nasica, and fled to Pergamum.

The Romans had just witnessed the stunning travesty of the murder of a plebeian tribune by none other than the state's chief priest. It was also the first time since the foundation of the Republic that violence had been used in Rome to settle a political quarrel, and it acted as a precursor of the savage political violence that would soon grip the city, culminating in the murder of Julius Caesar in 44 BC. Some in the senate realised with horror what had just happened, and before long Scipio Nasica was sent away 'on an embassy' to Pergamum. When Scipio Aemilianus found out about the death of Tiberius, he was on campaign against Numantia. Plutarch relates that he uttered a line from the *Odyssey*, grimly stating 'so perish all others who on such wickedness venture' (*Tiberius Gracchus*, 21 & *Odyssey*, 1.47).

As this drama came to its denouement in Rome, a rebellion had begun in Pergamum under the leadership of a man named Aristonicus, who said that he was the son of Eumenes II and the brother of Attalus III. He pledged a utopian society where the lot of slaves and peasants would be drastically improved. Advised by the newly arrived philosopher Blossius, and taking the royal name Eumenes III, Aristonicus called his new community 'the City of the Sun'. An army was duly sent out under Publius Licinius Crassus Dives Mucianus, consul for 131 BC and the father-in-law of Tiberius's brother, Gaius Gracchus. Crassus led the campaign against Aristonicus even though he was *pontifex maximus* (Scipio Nasica had died in mysterious circumstances in 132 BC), and technically not allowed to leave Italy. Crassus quickly fell afoul of his opponents and lost both his life and his head on the battlefield. Later, however, Aristonicus, with an army of slaves, landless peasants, and disaffected Macedonians, was brought to bay by the determined Marcus Perperna (consul 130 BC). The hapless king was captured and brought to Rome, where he was later murdered in Rome's state prison, the Tullianum. Pergamum was divided up, with the wealthiest part becoming the Roman province of Asia in 129 BC and other parcels given to king Ariarathes VI of Cappadocia and Mithridates V of Pontus (the father of Mithridates VI—see below). In the same year, Scipio Aemilianus was found dead at his home shortly before he was due to give a major speech concerning the position of Rome's Italian and Latin allies. Allegations of foul play emerged immediately; one report said that Scipio had 'marks as though of strangulation upon his throat' (Velleius Paterculus, 2.4). Fingers were pointed squarely at Cornelia, others at his wife Sempronia, with whom the union had been less than happy (Appian, *Civil Wars*, 1.20).

Six years later, in 123 BC, Tiberius's brother, Gaius Gracchus, was elected as plebeian tribune. In the interim, the land commission had done its work, and much of the land law had been addressed by a succession of triumvirs; boundary stones recording their efforts have been discovered in Italy. Now, Gaius proposed an entirely new legislative agenda intended to deal with some of the consequences of his brother's own legislation. There had been unrest among many of Rome's Italian allies at what would happen to portions of the *ager publicus* in their territory, and tensions between Romans, Italians, and Latins had seen a plebeian tribune pass a law in 126 BC expelling all non-citizens from Rome. Gaius, who had administrative experience as a quaestor in Sardinia, tackled this problem by carving out large tracts of land in allied territory, which he placed off-limits for allocation. With his political allies, Gaius also proposed new colonies to shift the urban poor away from the city and onto large landholdings in Italy and overseas. This was only partially successful because it relied on the willingness of people to leave Rome for an uncertain future as subsistence farmers.

Numerous aspects of Gaius's populist agenda worried Rome's oligarchs. Frequently invoking the memory of his murdered brother, he proposed that the state should stockpile grain, and make it available to the poor at a low rate to deal with the unpredictable swings in the grain price. Furthermore, management of the storage of this vital resource would pass from the hands of wealthy families in Rome and be administered instead by the government. He also proposed that military service should be shortened and that the state should provide equipment to soldiers, relieving them of the obligation to purchase their own gear. This essentially 'social' program stood to benefit all parts of society, including the rich, who would hardly benefit from a restive population of the urban poor. Nevertheless, it attracted criticism: Gaius, the rumours went, was a popularity-seeking revolutionary, and even worse than his brother. Senators were also worried by Gaius's attempt to take capital cases out of senatorial purview and place them under the authority of the people. Another proposal that authorised severe consequences for any magistrate who had sanctioned a capital sentence—and who had done so in the wake of an investigation that had *not* been permitted by popular vote—also angered the senate, since it was a naked attack on the senators who had presided over the investigation and murder of Tiberius's supporters. Senators were also excluded from certain courts, and in others their monopoly over acting as jurors in criminal cases was pared back in favour of equestrians—wealthy men who were not members of the senate, but whose membership in the 'equestrian order' similarly required a wealth and property qualification. Worse, the consular provinces would be decided before elections took place, a clear attempt to tackle the problem of consuls angling for specific places to wage war for the purpose of *gloria* and personal enrichment. Funding for Gaius's proposals, particularly the purchase and stockpiling of grain, was met by tax collection in the territory of Pergamum—a bounty that Peter Green has called 'one of the biggest gold mines in all Roman history' (*Alexander to Actium*, p. 531). Equestrian *publicani* were able to bid every five years for the Asian tax contract, pledging a fixed amount that was paid up front by the winning bidder. This auction was managed by the censors, and while the arrangement provided a foreseeable revenue for the state, it encouraged extortion in the actual collection of the tax: the *publicani* made profits when they extracted more than they had to pay under the contract. Gaius also terminated a privilege held by the triumvirs to adjudicate in disputes that had arisen because of their own actions. While some saw him as a dangerous radical, Gaius was also determined to use the framework of Roman law to bring about a more transparent government that was accountable to the people, and served more than just the interests of its senior members.

Gaius's legal agenda was met by a range of emotions from withering scorn to unbridled enthusiasm. He was re-elected as plebeian tribune in 122—even though he did not put forward his name as a candidate—and was joined by a former member of the triumvirate established to carry out Tiberius's land laws, the plebeian and former consul Marcus Fulvius Flaccus. Through his political ally Marcus Acilius Glabrio, Gaius put forward further legislation that prevented magistrates from being adjudged for extortion and corruption by a senatorial jury, replacing senators with equestrians. (This could, however, be easily manipulated. In 92 BC, Publius Rutilius Rufus—who Velleius Paterculus (2.13) called without hyperbole 'one of the best men not only of his age, but of all time'—would attempt to reign in the avarice of the *publicani* in Asia. He was tried and convicted for extortion by an all-equestrian jury with deep ties to the tax collection racket.) It is sometimes thought that Gaius also proposed the extension of Roman citizenship to Latins and Italians who did not possess it, a recognition that Rome's allies were dissatisfied with the virtual fossilisation of their status stretching back to the fifth and fourth centuries BC, and chafing under Rome's increasingly imperial demands—but this may be part of the disinformation campaign waged against him by his enemies. Gaius eventually managed to persuade some 6,000 colonists to leave Rome for North Africa, where they would be settled in a new colony called Iunonia, which one of Gaius's allies, Rubrius, had pushed to be built on the site of the destroyed city of Carthage. Ironically, it was this venture out of all those the two Gracchi brothers had proposed that was the most likely to 'solve' the land crisis in Italy. Gaius himself left Italy to oversee the establishment of this colony, and his absence gave his enemies in Rome, led by the senate's man among the plebeian tribunes, Marcus Livius Drusus, time to organise their resistance. Lurid pictures were painted of Rome's sacred institutions swollen by the influx of new citizens, and Gaius was attacked for daring to think that Roman citizenship was something that could be extended to outsiders. Allies in the senate now turned against Gaius, and when he returned from Africa, he faced far stronger political headwinds than before.

In 121 BC, as in 133/32 BC, these disagreements soon degenerated into violence. Gaius failed to win a third tribunate, and as he and his supporters gathered on the Capitoline Hill, a consular lictor was killed in a scuffle. This affront could not pass unpunished, and soon afterwards the senate passed what has become known as 'the ultimate decree', the *senatus consultum ultimum*. This literally ordered the consul to 'see to it that the state should suffer no harm' (*consul videret ne quid respublica detrimenti caperet*, known from Cicero's *Against Catiline*, 1.2.4) and was a mandate to do whatever was necessary to restore order. The plebeian Lucius Opimius, the sole consul in Rome—his colleague was on campaign in Gaul—ordered the senators, together with the equestrians, to move in on Gaius and his allies, who had decamped to the Aventine Hill. The result was another slaughter. Gaius died during the assault, his head affixed to a javelin and taken to Opimius, his body dumped into the Tiber. Afterwards, Opimius used the senatorial decree to have Flaccus executed, and for months afterwards hundreds of members of the Gracchan faction were rounded up and put to death. The 'legalised murder' of Gaius and his followers had been carried out not at the instigation of the people, but by a clique in the senate who resented his agenda and his popularity. Opimius was widely hated for his role in this affair, and after he had ostentatiously restored the Temple of Concord, a local wit scathingly carved under the restoration inscription 'a work of mad discord produces a temple of Concord' (Plutarch, *Gaius Gracchus*, 17). The bloodguilt of the senatorial mob was expiated by a *lustrum*, the ritual purification of the city that normally followed the completion of a census. Later, in 111 BC, a land law was passed that allowed land allocated by the triumvirs to be sold, essentially undoing much of what the Gracchi had tried to achieve.

Gaius and his brother had transformed the plebeian tribunate into a powerful office that possessed almost as much potential to destabilise the state as it did to strengthen it. Velleius Paterculus blamed Tiberius for bringing the Roman state 'into a position of critical and extreme danger' with his actions towards Octavius, and even accused him of seeking the plebeian tribunate as a way to avoid being prosecuted for his role in the botched peace with Numantia. He said of Gaius that 'he left nothing undisturbed, nothing untouched, nothing unmolested' and deplored his 'mistaken ambition' (2.2 & 2.6–7). Nevertheless, the two brothers were widely commemorated in antiquity and were heroes to the populist faction that was emerging in Roman political life. The Gracchi remained prominent in much later times of political turmoil—a French revolutionary, François-Noël Babeuf (1760–97), even called himself 'Gracchus Babeuf'—and the brothers were a favourite topic for French artists. Among the various depictions is a famous marble sculpture at the Musée d'Orsay in Paris by Jules Cavalier depicting Cornelia and her two young sons (1861), as well as a bronze funerary monument completed by Jean-Baptiste Guillaume (1848-53). Cornelia herself was a remarkable woman and bore her husband 12 children, of whom only three survived childhood. After she was widowed, Ptolemy VIII reportedly sought her hand in marriage and offered her the Egyptian crown; fiercely independent, highly educated, and a sponsor of philosophers and writers, she declined (Plutarch, *Tiberius Gracchus*, 1). Some of Cornelia's correspondence is purported to survive in the work of Cornelius Nepos. In one letter, she advised against the taking of revenge, while in another, addressed to Gaius, she berated him for causing her excessive maternal anxiety and bringing the Republic to the edge of ruin. Cornelia was no less attractive a focus for artists than her famous children, and depictions of her refusing the Egyptian crown, looking after her children, or holding court at home were popular during the Romantic period.

Unrest in Rome was mirrored by conflict and turmoil in Sicily. In 135 BC, the slaves there revolted against widespread poor treatment under the leadership of Eunus, a Syrian from Apamea. Eunus claimed to receive visions from the goddess Atargatis and claimed he could tell the future; he also had a reputation as a skilled magician, and these qualities made his leadership attractive for a population existing in terrible and grim conditions. In Sicily, the Roman conquest had opened up the island's fertile land to the rich, and the growth of large estates populated by an abundant supply of slave labour had greatly harmed the position of peasant farmers. Slavery is the great stain on human existence: slaves were often kept in appalling conditions, and even though some—such as Tiro, the secretary of Cicero—enjoyed a favourable working environment, Romans had numerous ways for freeing slaves (manumission), and freedmen could attain citizenship and positions of prominence in business and society, for the vast majority who were sold into slavery—often at the whim of a victorious consul or praetor—it was a life devoid of hope, family, and future. Both male and female slaves were subject to sexual violence, exploitation, and random punishment, and had no recourse whatsoever against it. While slaves may not always have been shackled on the job or dispatched to the proverbial salt mines, they were often branded or wore collars that made any thought of escape into a normal life virtually unthinkable.

In Sicily, Eunus gathered a group of several hundred slaves, and captured the city of Enna and killed most of its inhabitants. Eunus then proclaimed himself 'king Antiochus', and other groups of slaves joined his cause and swelled his ranks, including some 5,000 under a man named Cleon. Peasants and subsistence farmers, trodden over by the rich only slightly less than the slaves, made common cause with Eunus and his allies. The Sicilian cities fell rapidly, including Agrigentum and Messana, and a succession of Roman forces sent to deal with Eunus were beaten off. It was not until 132 BC that the revolt was suppressed, with Cleon killed fighting and some 20,000 slaves crucified by the consul Publius Rupilius. Eunus was captured and thrown into prison, where he died, 'consumed by lice' (Diodorus Siculus, 34.23). Further revolts took place on the island of Delos in 134 BC, and there were two others in Sicily in 104/03 BC and in Campania. Elsewhere, at Dyme in Greece, reports of a mob burning debt records and turfing out the government in favour of a democracy resulted in a Roman military expedition sent to enforce the rights of the senate's preferred oligarchs.

The slave revolt of 135 BC prompted the senate to send a ten-man commission to Sicily, overseen by Rupilius, to examine the government of the island. A similar process was enacted in Asia after the defeat of Aristonicus. The results of these efforts reveal a certain degree of unimaginative pragmatism. In Asia, the Romans decided to pursue a policy of continuity, keeping the laws and decrees of Pergamum set out under its Attalid kings, but now enforced by a Roman governor (*RGE* §40). In order to facilitate commerce and the movement of Roman troops, and ease tax collection, Manius Aquilius (consul 129 BC, succeeding Marcus Perperna) improved the existing road network. During this time, work on the via Egnatia (Chapter 5) continued, with the aim of extending its reach to Asia, and not long afterwards the via Domitia (named for one of the consuls of 122 BC) was begun, linking Arles with the Roman colony of Narbo Martius (Narbonne), and onwards to Nearer Spain. The region of southern Gaul became the Roman province of Transalpine Gaul in 121 BC (Figure 6.3). Further colonies were founded on Majorca.

The dominant characteristics of early Roman provincial administration were the establishment of communication routes and, in some places, colonisation, together with the collection of taxes. As noted earlier, in Asia the *publicani* bid on five-year contracts, while quaestors collected a tax from the allied Spanish communities to cover the cost of the Roman occupation. Tax collection in Sicily followed the precedents set by Hiero II of Syracuse (270-215 BC, Chapter 4). The individual provinces were under the control of governors who could be either of consular or praetorian rank; under them served quaestors and junior officials. Over time, the business of governing became more complex, as the letters between Pliny the Younger and the emperor Trajan so elegantly show (Chapter 10). In the second and first centuries BC, on the other hand, governorship of a place such as Nearer Spain or Further Spain might be taken up as much by travelling to the province and then campaigning there as by attention to sewers, public buildings, and legal disputes.

Marius, Jugurtha, and Caecilius Metellus

The Numidian king Masinissa lived until the age of 90. In 118 BC, his son and successor Micipsa died, and in his will he imprudently envisaged a joint rule between his sons, Hiempsal and Adherbal, together with Jugurtha, his nephew. The result of this unhappy triumvirate was the immediate murder of Hiempsal and the expulsion of Adherbal. Jugurtha, who had fought alongside Scipio Aemilianus at Numantia, set about making Numidia his own. Opimius, the former consul who had earned notoriety for his violent suppression of Gaius Gracchus and his faction, was sent by the senate to find a more equitable solution. Opimius, Plutarch says, 'could not keep his hands from fraud', and there were persistent rumours that he had been bribed by Jugurtha to recommend that the senate rule in his favour (*Gaius Gracchus*, 18). Sure enough, there was a generous settlement, essentially giving Jugurtha licence to raise an army and remove Adherbal once and for all. As Jugurtha set to this task, and bribes flowed from his pockets, his allies in the senate deflected repeated calls for a new inquiry to be mounted. 'At Rome,' wrote Sallust, 'anything could be bought' (*War with Jugurtha*, 8). Adherbal finally surrendered his stronghold at Cirta (Constantine, in eastern Algeria), and he and his defenders, including many Italian businessmen and colonists, were put to death. With this, Jugurtha showed that the Romans did not possess a monopoly on needless violence.

In Rome, the senate dithered, its pro- and anti-Jugurtha factions duelling and achieving little. Eventually Jugurtha was summoned to Rome to explain his actions, but there he used his apparently bottomless pockets to bribe more key individuals. Living in Rome, however, was another relative of the royal family, Massiva, who soon became the preferred candidate to replace Jugurtha; yet before long Massiva turned up dead, and fingers were

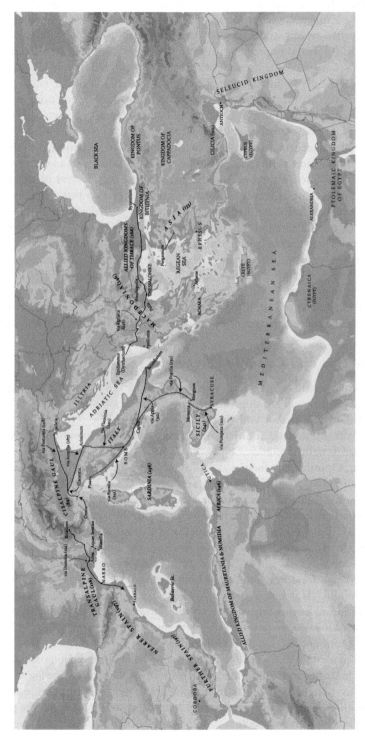

Figure 6.3 The major Roman roads at the end of the second century BC, indicated by black lines with their names and construction dates. Routes are approximate. Roman provinces are indicated in bold italics with the date of their acquisition.

Source: Illustration by the author.

pointed firmly at Jugurtha, who quickly left Italy. In Rome, the patrician consul Spurius Postumius Albinus, who had championed Massiva's candidacy, gathered an invasion army and set off to Numidia to resolve the situation by force. Albinus achieved little before his year was up, and Jugurtha continued to bribe and suborn Roman officials. There seemed to be no end to the corruption, and eventually public fury in Rome resulted in Albinus, Opimius, and several others being tried and convicted of corruption.

One of the two consuls for 109 BC was the wealthy plebeian Quintus Caecilius Metellus. He was an experienced magistrate, having moved smoothly through the *cursus honorum* from the quaestorship in 126 BC to the praetorship in 115 BC, followed by a stint as the governor of Sicily in 114 BC. He enjoyed more success in Africa than any of his predecessors, but Jugurtha remained at large. At this point, sensing the need to call in new blood, Metellus brought in the remarkable Gaius Marius. This man, a disciple of the Caecilii Metelli, was from an obscure equestrian background. Plutarch thought Marius to be something of an arrogant Hellenophobe, saying that he 'never used the Greek language for any matter of real importance, thinking it ridiculous to study a literature the teachers of which were the subject of another people' (*Marius*, 2). Whatever his thoughts about the Greeks, however, Marius was experienced: he had fought at Numantia with Scipio Aemilianus, who acknowledged his skill and suggested that he might be the next great Roman general (*Marius*, 3). He had served as military tribune, quaestor (120s BC) and plebeian tribune (119 BC), held the praetorship in 115 BC and was sent as propraetor to the governorship of Further Spain in 114 BC. Marius could not escape his non-senatorial background, however, and Metellus, while allowing for his brilliance, was determined to keep him firmly in his place. So when Marius expressed an interest in running for the consulship (108 BC), Metellus was shocked, and indicated that he should wait until his own son—at that point still a young man—had held it first. Marius was 50 and would be dead before the young Metellus was eligible. Marius ran anyway, and won as a *novus homo*: his candidacy was supported by the equestrian *publicani* and spurred on by his defamatory comments about Metellus, who was thought to be needlessly dragging out the conflict. He also made a dramatic promise to the people that 'he would either kill Jugurtha or take him alive' (*Marius*, 8).

Metellus was confirmed in command of the Roman army in Africa as proconsul for 107 BC, with Marius elected consul alongside the plebeian Lucius Cassius Longinus. As Metellus was remaining in his Numidian command, the senate had already chosen different provinces for the two consuls. Longinus was sent to Gaul. Marius yearned for Numidia, and in Rome a plebeian tribune persuaded the people to strip Metellus of his commission and give it to Marius instead. Metellus was furious, and now Marius, 'contrary to law and custom', opened the recruitment of his army to anyone who put his name forward. The property requirements were jettisoned, and the urban poor of Rome flocked to serve under the famous general (*Marius*, 9). Once in Africa, Marius made short work of Jugurtha, who fled to his father-in-law, Bocchus of Mauretania. Under immense pressure from the Romans, Bocchus handed the fugitive king over to the patrician Lucius Cornelius Sulla, who was serving as Marius's quaestor. Marius was elected consul again in 104 BC, another break with 'law and custom', but by now he had made powerful enemies. Not only were the Caecilii Metelli angry with the way their protégé had treated their senior statesman, but Marius also fell out with Sulla, who was busy boasting that he, not Marius, had brought the Jugurthine War to a close. Sulla was so sure of his own success that he

Figure 6.4 Silver denarius minted at Rome by Faustus Cornelius Sulla in 56 BC. Obverse: diademed bust of Diana, right, with FAVSTVS; reverse: Sulla wearing a toga. On the left is Bocchus of Mauretania, and on the right is Jugurtha, kneeling with his hands tied behind his back. The legend FELIX appears to the right.

had a signet ring made, with a tawdry scene showing Bocchus handing over Jugurtha: 'by constantly using this ring,' Plutarch wrote, 'Sulla provoked Marius, who was an ambitious man, loath to share his glory with another' (*Marius*, 10). The story of Jugurtha's surrender stuck in Roman folklore, and Sulla's son, Faustus, later minted coinage in his father's name in 56 BC depicting the scene (Figure 6.4). Jugurtha was later paraded through Rome in Marius's triumph, before being starved to death in prison.

Jugurtha was quickly forgotten due to a rapidly emerging security crisis in the west. In 106 BC, Cassius Longinus was killed near Bordeaux, fighting a coalition of Helvetii and a group of Germanic peoples from Jutland whom the Romans called the Cimbri, Ambrones, and Teutones. In 105 BC, Quintus Servilius Caepio, appointed as proconsul in Cisalpine Gaul, faced another powerful Germanic army at Arausio on the river Rhône. Caepio apparently refused to cooperate with the consul Gnaeus Mallius Maximus, a *novus homo* who Caepio, a staunch patrician from the ancient *gens* Servilia, regarded with disdain. Caepio himself was not above suspicion in his conduct and behaviour: on campaign he was reported to have found some of the gold and silver looted from Delphi by the Gauls in 279 BC, and had it shipped to Rome. The robbers who pounced on the shipment while it was in transit, stealing some 15,000 talents of gold and silver, were apparently hired by Caepio himself. Caepio subsequently led his army without Maximus in support, with the result that both armies, containing some 60,000–80,000 men, were lost in one of Rome's worst military defeats. Both Maximus and Caepio were driven into exile by furious tribunes.

Against the backdrop of this unfolding disaster, a sense of panic and the historical fear of the Gauls (Chapter 2) gripped Rome. The degree to which the senate and the people were willing to abandon past practice is found in the unprecedented election of Marius to the consulship every year between 104 and 100 BC—seven consulships in all, in 107, 104, 103, 102, 101, 100, and 86 BC. The people's faith in Marius was well placed, as he checked the Germanic advance near modern Aix-en-Provence in 102 BC. Marius' consular colleague and political ally, the plebeian Quintus Lutatius Catulus, did not have as much success, but in 101 BC, both men faced the Germans in the Po Valley in Cisalpine Gaul. They were victorious at Vercellae (modern Vercelli), and both men celebrated a triumph. Like Sulla, however, Catulus became a bitter rival to Marius and resented his success, flamboyantly dedicating a temple to the goddess Fortuna in the Campus Martius, the ruins of which stand today in Rome's Largo Argentina, in commemoration of *his* victory. (Like the Temple of Hercules Victor (Chapter 5), this was a Greek structure, built in the round with an encircling colonnade, although it used local travertine and tufa instead of marble.) Problems were brewing elsewhere, too: when facing the Cimbri in 103 BC, Marius had tried to levy troops from Rome's ally Nicomedes III of Bithynia (127–94 BC), to which the king replied that Roman *publicani* had sold many Bithynian men into slavery to raise money for Asia's massive tax bill, and he had few to offer to fight alongside Rome's legionnaires.

In Rome, the struggle between senatorial and popular authority continued. Before his exile, Caepio attempted to return senators to the board of jurors hearing cases of corruption and extortion. This bill died with his departure, and subsequently the position of the equestrians was strengthened with the establishment of a new court designed to try those accused of treason. This was the work of the plebeian tribune Lucius Appuleius Saturninus. This man was a Gracchan in his unbridled belief in the power of the tribunate, and he was also an ally of Marius, having earlier looked after Marius's veterans with land allotments in Africa. Another tribune, Gaius Servilius Glaucia, who memorably appeared in Cicero's *On Oratory* as 'the turd of the senate' (3.164) and in his *Brutus* as 'the most abandoned wretch that ever existed' (224), was likewise in the Marian camp. In 102 BC, Metellus held the censorship and tried in vain to have both Saturninus and Glaucia removed from the senatorial roll. Later, in 100 BC, Saturninus, once again a tribune, proposed a bill that would provide further for Marius's veterans by settling them in colonies over a wide area from Gaul to Macedonia. The bill also gave Marius the right to grant Roman citizenship to a limited number of the colonists, and gave preference to Italians, many of whom had fought for Marius. The bill aroused senatorial anger, and an armed intervention briefly interrupted proceedings. Claims that thunder had been heard were even deployed to bar voting for religious reasons. When the bill finally passed, it included a rider that demanded that the senate and the elected magistrates swear to abide by its provisions on pain of exile. Metellus refused to take the oath and was exiled. For Marius, the position of the senate was paramount, despite his populist leanings—so he took the oath.

Glaucia now had his eyes set firmly on the consulship, but Marius declared his candidacy illegal: there had not been a sufficient amount of time since he had been praetor. The elections were delayed when one of Glaucia's rivals was murdered, apparently at the instigation of Saturninus, and then Saturninus stepped in to help his friend by holding an opposing assembly on the Capitoline Hill. For a second time in a generation, the senate resorted to the *senatus consultum ultimum*, but this posed a problem. The chief target of this decision was Saturninus, who was plebeian tribune for the third time and protected by his office. Marius tried to diffuse the situation by offering Saturninus safe passage—the man had, after all, looked after his veterans—only for the unfortunate tribune and his allies to be strung up by a mob in the senate house. Glaucia fared little better, and after being run to ground, he too was murdered. Appian regarded the murder of these two politicians as another in an unhappy sequence of events that followed the murders of Tiberius and

Gaius Gracchus, and that set the Republic on course for its eventual destruction (*Civil Wars*, 1.33).

Marius now found himself in an impossible situation. As a populist, he had presided over the unlawful killing of a plebeian tribune and his followers; as a consul and a senator, he had directed the exile of Quintus Caecilius Metellus, his former patron and a senior statesman from one of Rome's most celebrated families. Marooned as he was between these two political realities, he could only watch in despair at the rising levels of faction-alism poisoning Roman politics. One clique was the *optimates*, the 'best'—the senatorial nobility, conservative custodians of the *mos maiorum*. The other was the *populares*, those who courted the favour of the people for their own ends, often by using the plebeian trib-unate. These were not political parties in the modern sense, and most of the *populares* and the *optimates* were rich men from a wealthy senatorial or equestrian background. There was also a certain fluidity between these different positions: as the careers of Pompey, Caesar, and others show, it was possible to be associated with the *populares* and the *optimates* at different times (see below and Chapter 7). These factions had been developing for some time, but they were brought into sharp relief by military incompetence, security problems, and a willingness to break the rules, both written and unwritten, that governed Roman political life. Faced with the anger of the people over the deaths of Saturninus and Glaucia, and with Metellus restored to Rome in 98 BC, Marius fled.

The Social War

Whether or not Gaius Gracchus had indeed mooted the idea of extending citizenship to the Italian and Latin allies, these communities had been largely left behind in terms of their political rights, despite supplying disproportionately large numbers of troops for Rome's wars and receiving paltry compensation for their efforts. The Italians were also barred from competing for lucrative opportunities, such as the tax contract for Asia. Tentative efforts at improving the lot of the allies began in earnest as the second century BC gave way to the first. In 97 BC, the two censors, allies of Marius and sympathetic to the contributions and sacrifice of the Italian allies, began to enrol Italians into Rome's tribes. Attempts to repeal this process were met with understandable disappointment and anger, and in 91 BC the plebeian tribune Marcus Livius Drusus (son of the Drusus who had championed the cause of the senate against Gaius Gracchus) proposed a widespread grant of citizenship to the Latins and Italians. He also put forward an enlargement of the senate through the enrolment of equestrians, many of whom were drawn from Italian elites, and at the same time he tacked on a proviso that juries would be drawn from this new, larger senate. This was, in essence, an effort to undo the gains made by the equestrians, particularly in the composition of juries. The proletariat also stood to lose out under this law, which would dramatically increase the number of Roman citizens, so Drusus proposed that the large parcels of *ager publicus* that had not been swallowed up as private property by the land law of 111 BC (above) would be used to assuage their concerns. Drusus took it upon himself to adjudicate decisions over land. Much of this legislative package was in the process of being passed when Drusus was fatally stabbed by a 'shoemaker's knife' outside his house (Appian, *Civil Wars*, 1.36). Velleius Paterculus reported that as he expired, he gazed at the crowd that had gathered to watch him die and muttered, 'Will my country ever have a citizen like me?' (2.14). Marius, still very influential and now back in Rome after several years in self-imposed exile in the eastern Mediterranean, urged that those parts of the bill that had become law be repealed immediately.

The outcome of this dramatic *volte-face* in Rome in 91 BC was a widespread rebellion of Roman allies, the *socii*—hence the name given to the conflict, the Social War. While many accounts of the war focus on the desire for citizenship as a motivating factor, it is also possible that this latest development in Rome was the proverbial last straw and that many communities were thoroughly sick of Roman duplicity. Indeed, only a generation earlier, in 125 BC, the colony of Fregellae had revolted, with typically brutal consequences over-seen by Lucius Opimius: there was clearly sufficient resentment against Roman hegemony in Italy, even at this late date, for such a hopeless course of action as armed revolt to be contemplated. It was probably a combination of factors, all linked in some way by a simmering bitterness towards Rome, which propelled many allied communities into a particularly bitter struggle. The Social War was characterised by a level of savagery peculiar to civil conflicts, with numerous cities—most famously Ausculum—almost completely eradicated. The rebel communities, which included large numbers of cities in Samnium, Campania, and the south, seceded, minting their own coinage and offering the first real alternative to Roman power in Italy for centuries. Their capital was Corfinium in central Italy, pointedly renamed 'Italica' (Figure 6.5).

Two consuls were killed during the war, and shock and concern in Rome saw the pro-posal of a law in 90 BC that would give citizenship to any allies who stopped fighting, and in 89 and 88 BC numerous other concessions were made that ended up with almost every free person south of the Po a Roman citizen. While the Italians lost the military con-flict at the hands of experienced generals such as Marius, Sulla, and the talented Gnaeus Pompeius Strabo, they had gained recognition by the Roman senate of their contribu-tion to the Roman commonwealth. The result was the *de facto* unification of Italy under Roman control, with the allies and Latins becoming *municipia populi Romani* (*municipia* of the Roman people). The Latin language spread throughout Italy at the expense of other languages such as Umbrian, Oscan, and Etruscan, and this was accompanied by the

Figure 6.5 Silver denarius struck in 89 BC at Corfinium, during the Social War. Obverse: laureate head of Italia right; reverse: Italia, sitting on shields, with sword and sceptre. Victory stands behind, crowning Italia with a wreath.

development of an Italian urban culture that more closely resembled fashions in Rome, and that became the focus for urban political life. Pompeii, for instance, acquired a public bath-house, a temple of Jupiter, and a senate house modelled on the curia Hostilia in Rome alongside its older, Greek-style theatres. It was also endowed with a stone amphi-theatre with the characteristic oval shape, which could be used for gladiatorial fights. Rome's erstwhile allies were enrolled as citizens, initially in a small number of tribes who could only vote after the other 35 had cast their ballots—a measure to limit their political weight in elections. The Social War also had an important impact on the army, as the allied and Latin contingents vanished. Theoretically, all troop levies raised in Italy south of the Po were now drawn from Roman citizens.

Mithridates, Marius, Sulla, and the march on Rome

Far away from Rome, the Black Sea kingdom of Pontus, benefiting from the steady decline in Seleucid power set in train by the Treaty of Apamea (188 BC, see Chapter 5) and accelerated by the establishment of the province of Asia, had become a regional power under its remarkable king, Mithridates VI Eupator (120-63 BC). Mithridates—'in strategy a general, in bodily prowess a soldier, in hatred to the Romans a Hannibal'—began his career at the age of 12 when he was made regent with his mother after his father was assassinated (Velleius Paterculus, 2.18). After spending seven years in exile, he then had his brother and mother murdered, after which he married—and then executed—his sister, Laodice, whose erstwhile husband was the king of Cappadocia. After establishing his reign in this way, he set about enlarging Pontic power at the expense of Bithynia and Cappadocia, and extended his influence as far as the Crimea (Figure 6.6).

This behaviour had not gone unnoticed in Rome, and Sulla, while propraetor of Cilicia in southern Asia Minor, had restored the balance of power between Mithridates and his neighbours. Later, however, both Nicomedes IV of Bithynia (94–74 BC) and the Cappadocian ruler Ariobarzanes I (95–63 BC) were ousted, and the inevitable Roman commission was sent to the region to resolve the crisis. The commission demanded an indemnity from Mithridates, who already had a dim view of the Romans since parts of Pontus had been taken by Rome in the late 130s BC even though his father, Mithridates V, had supplied troops for the fight against Aristonicus. The leader of the Roman commission was a former consul named Aquillius, who had fought with Marius against the Germans, crushed the slave revolt in Sicily in 104/03 BC, and was then narrowly acquitted of a corruption charge in 98 BC. Aquillius dealt with Mithridates' polite refusal to pay up by encouraging Nicomedes and Ariobarzanes to invade Pontus (89 BC). Marius was thought to have once told Mithridates either 'to be stronger than Rome, or do her bidding without a word' (Plutarch, *Marius*, 31), and now the enraged king made his choice, declaring war. The resulting Mithridatic War and its numerous sideshows provided an almost limitless number of opportunities for ambitious Romans to cement their personal *gloria*, enrich themselves and their clients, and add further territory to the Roman state. The war also ran in parallel to periods of shocking violence in Rome and a breakdown in law and order across the Mediterranean.

Mithridates moved fast, seizing most of Asia Minor. The governor of Asia, Lucius Cassius, fled; Aquillius was captured, and paid for his arrogance with the symbolically anti-Roman fate of having molten gold poured into his throat (Appian, *Mithridatic Wars*,

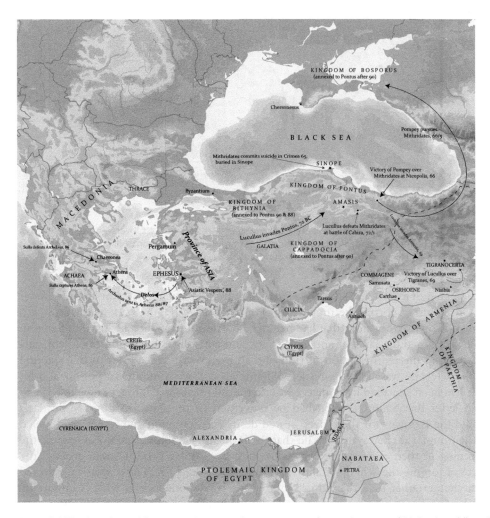

Figure 6.6 The kingdom of Pontus and surrounding territories during the time of Mithridates VI, with some of the major events of the Mithridatic War. The dotted line represents the territory of the kingdom of Tigranes in c. 69 BC.

Source: Illustration by the author.

21). In 88 BC, Mithridates further punished the Romans for the extortion and greed of the *publicani* by carrying out what became known as the 'Asiatic Vespers': the whole-sale murder of some 80,000 Romans and Italians in Asia, including many *publicani* and *negotiares*. Mithridates urged the Greeks of Asia Minor to kill the hated Romans, which they did with alacrity and relish. In Ephesus, Romans who had sought sanctuary in the Temple of Artemis were dragged into the streets and murdered, while along the coast Italian women and children were butchered in the Mediterranean surf. Mithridates worked hard to portray himself as a liberator both to Greeks and to those who had historical ties to ancient Persia. He claimed descent from the founder of the Persian

Figure 6.7 Gold stater of Mithridates VI Eupator, minted at Istros 88–86 BC. Obverse: diademed head of the deified Alexander right, with horns of Ammon; reverse: Athena Nicephorus seated, left arm on shield with spear in background.

Achaemenid dynasty, Cyrus the Great, as well as from Seleucus I Nicator and Alexander the Great, whose portrait he imitated on Pontic coinage (Figure 6.7). Mithridates also claimed to own an old cloak that had belonged to Alexander, which he loved to flaunt in public. He raised the familiar anti-plutocratic and anti-oligarchic promises of debt cancellation and the redistribution of land, and allowed myths and stories to swirl around his character: he was able to wrestle wild animals and was immune to poison, and his birth had been signalled by comets and other astral phenomena. In an embellished and florid letter that Sallust fancied had been written to the Parthian king, Mithridates blamed the Romans for their 'deep-seated desire for dominion and riches', and reeled off their numerous betrayals. He said that the Romans 'have possessed nothing since the beginning of their existence except what they have stolen', and he even accused the senate of forging the will of Attalus III (Sallust, *Histories*, 4.67). The sentiment reflected in the letter, rather than the authenticity of the correspondence, is what is important. For the first time since the mid-second century BC, the Mediterranean was offered an alternative vision of leadership that might free its oppressed peoples from the greed and violence of Roman rule.

Backed by widespread anger at Roman behaviour, the king embarked on a quest to build an Aegean superpower. He found support in Greece almost immediately: in Athens, a popular revolt had overthrown the pro-Roman government of a local business tycoon, who had shut down many of the city's institutions, including the universities and the gymnasia. Mithridates offered his support, pledging to protect Athenian democracy and returning the Athenian envoy home loaded with gifts. The surviving representatives of the Athenian *ancien régime* were lynched or exiled, and the new populist leader, Aristion, prepared for the arrival of the certain Roman punitive expedition. Mithridates' general Archelaus captured Delos, purging some 20,000 Italian *negotiares* in the process. The Romans gave the leadership of the war to Lucius Cornelius Sulla, who had served as quaestor to Marius (above) and was a member of the *optimates*. Before he could take command, however, political drama in Rome intervened.

Sulla had reinforced his position by marrying Caecilia Metella, the niece of Marius's former patron Metellus and daughter of the current *pontifex maximus*, another of the Caecilii Metelli. For this, 'many verses were sung in ridicule of him by the common people', who thought Caecilia to be too good for him (Plutarch, *Sulla*, 6). Sulla had other powerful political allies: his daughter was married to the son of Quintus Pompeius Rufus, an influential former plebeian tribune (99 BC) who had engineered the recall of Metellus from exile, and Sulla was also associated with Marius's former colleague and rival Quintus Lutatius Catulus. Sulla was elected consul in 88 BC with Pompeius Rufus as armed gangs patrolled the streets of Rome, warning off rival candidates. In this nervous atmosphere, the plebeian tribune Publius Sulpicius Rufus tried to adjust the grants of Roman citizenship given to the Latins and Italians, enacted in the aftermath of the Social War. Sulpicius Rufus, who had renounced his patrician status to run for the tribunate, was firmly in the populist camp, carrying around with him 600 equestrians whom Plutarch says he called his 'anti-senate' (*Marius*, 35). Sulpicius Rufus proposed that the Italians be enrolled evenly across the 35 Roman tribes, rather than as a bloc in a newly created tribal group, thus giving them greater political clout than previously envisioned—but this was blocked in the senate and aroused anger among the people. Sulla, who had been favourable to Sulpicius Rufus earlier, now opposed him and was forced to shelter with Marius, who used his authority to urge the law to be passed; after agreeing under pressure to support the law, Sulla was allowed to leave Rome, and set about preparing for the war with Mithridates. Sulpicius Rufus, however, angered by Sulla's attitude, proposed a bill that would strip Sulla of command and give it to Marius. The bill duly passed, and Marius dispatched two military tribunes to Nola, where Sulla's army was mopping up the last resistance at the end of the Social War. Marius was in his seventies and a private citizen, whereas Sulla was the elected consul. It was quite clear who the law favoured, but Marius was determined.

In desperate straits, Sulla appealed to his soldiers on the pretext that if Marius took command, he would lead others, and not them, to plunder the riches of the east. In response, his troops set upon the two tribunes and murdered them. The majority of Sulla's officers, horrified, left him; undeterred, Sulla gathered his army and set out for Rome. The news of the approaching force was met with panic and disbelief: aside from the sacred and carefully regulated occasion of the triumph, a Roman army was *never* allowed across the pomerium. Sulla carried on in the face of desperate senatorial appeals for him to stop, and Marius and Sulpicius Rufus tried in vain to defend the city. A savage battle was waged just inside the Esquiline Gate, 'the first regularly fought in Rome with bugle and standards in full military fashion' (Appian, *Civil Wars*, 1.58). Afterwards, triumphant and in control, Sulla addressed the people, explaining in an aggrieved fashion that the city had been overrun by demagogues and he had done what he did 'as a matter of necessity' (Appian, *Civil Wars*, 1.59). He attempted to neuter populism by declaring that no legislation should be put to a public vote unless the senate had granted its approval. This was intended to avoid any return to the chaos of the Gracchan years and their aftermath, and sought to entrench the power of the *nobiles*—those aristocrats who had held the consulship—over others who Sulla adjudged to be second-rate senators with only a quaestorship or a praetorship to their name. Finally, Sulla had the senate declare his political rivals public enemies. Sulpicius Rufus was murdered, and Marius fled to Africa where he sought protection among his loyal veterans of the Jugurthine War, living 'in a hut amid the ruins of Carthage' (Velleius Paterculus, 2.19). Sulla's consular colleague Pompeius Rufus, who had been briefly stripped of his consulship by Sulpicius Rufus, and was now reinstated, left Rome to take command of the other consular army. On the way, he was murdered by troops loyal to the previous year's consul, his cousin Gnaeus Pompeius Strabo, who had refused to disband his force and kept it in readiness at Picenum. Strabo, as Sulla would do later, was funding a private army from war profits; he had quietly kept the loot taken in the Social War during the sack of Ausculum.

Writing about Sulla's march on Rome, Appian commented that even during the worst episodes of the struggle of the orders, the Romans had resolved their internal conflicts through consensus and dialogue. Now, for the first time in Roman history, a Roman army had taken control of the city and its public institutions by force. 'To such extremity of evil,' he wrote, 'had the recklessness of party strife progressed' (*Civil Wars*, 1.1–2 & 1.58). Sulla's hatred of Marius was deep seated, stretching back to the Jugurthine War, and Marius's distaste towards his rival was made worse when Bocchus, who had surrendered Jugurtha to Sulla, later set up a gaudy statue in Rome showing the exact moment of the surrender ceremony—in which Marius was nowhere to be seen.

The two consuls for 87 BC were Lucius Cornelius Cinna, from the same illustrious *gens* Cornelia as Sulla—but Sulla's enemy—and the plebeian Gnaeus Octavius. There was immediate discord between the two consuls, and Cinna, vainly taking up the Sulpician proposal concerning the enrolment of the Italians and Latins among the tribes, fled Rome as armed thugs, spurred on by Sulla's ally Octavius, roamed the streets. Octavius replaced Cinna with Lucius Cornelius Merula, the high priest of Jupiter. Cinna, meanwhile, found succor with a legion stationed at Nola, and quickly raised additional legions from the Samnites, which he used to besiege Rome. Cinna welcomed Marius, who had returned from Africa, and Marius called his Italian veterans back to active service. The senate tried to recruit Gnaeus Pompeius Strabo to their cause, but through the intermediary of Quintus Caecilius Metellus Pius (the son of Metellus, the former patron of Marius), he had been treating with Cinna to try and engineer another consulship in Rome. At the head of some ten legions, Cinna was reinstated by the senate as consul and Merula prudently agreed to retire. Opposition to Cinna and Marius evaporated when Pompeius Strabo was killed by a lightning bolt outside the walls of Rome, and his body was ripped from its funeral cortège and desecrated. Meanwhile, Octavius, whose safety Marius and Cinna had guaranteed, was murdered, his severed head nailed to the rostra in the forum. This, Appian said, was 'the first head of a consul that was exposed in this way' (*Civil Wars*, 1.71).

More severed heads piled up in the forum as Cinna and Marius presided over a reign of terror, taking revenge on their former allies and friends who had turned against them. Catulus committed suicide rather than be executed; Merula too, even though he had done little wrong, followed suit. In a dramatic reversal of recent events, Sulla was now declared a public enemy; his house was burned to the ground, and Cinna and Marius were declared consuls in a rigged election with no opposition. Shortly afterwards, Marius died, his seventh and final consulship completed by Lucius Valerius Flaccus, a staunch ally of the Marian faction. Cinna subsequently maintained his grip on the consulship, with the plebeian Gnaeus Papirius Carbo, another Marian supporter, as his colleague. Some genuine changes were effected during this time, including re-standardising the coinage, which had become fraudulently debased by the dishonest officials appointed to oversee the mint, and recognising the position of the equestrians in the census of 86 BC. In the end, Plutarch's verdict on Marius is telling: most of the Roman people, he wrote were moved to pity at the sight of his greed and ambition, because, even though he had risen from poverty to the greatest wealth and from obscurity to the highest place, he knew not how to set bounds to his good fortune, and was not content to be admired and enjoy quietly what he had.

(*Marius*, 34)

Velleius Paterculus noted that Marius was 'as excellent a general as he was an evil influence in time of peace, a man of unbounded ambition, insatiable, without self-control' (2.11). Marius also raised eyebrows in Rome by flaunting his mystical links with a prophetess from distant Syria and by cultivating a connection with Dionysus/Bacchus, related in various legends to great eastern conquerors such as Alexander the Great. Marius did little to put down rumours that he was 'the third founder of Rome', following Romulus and Marcus Furius Camillus, the conqueror of Veii. People believed that divine, prophetic assent followed Marius and his troops, in the shape of two vultures with bronze neck-rings (Plutarch, *Marius*, 27 & 17). Marius's confidence in his own magnificence also led him to commit terrible blunders, such as wearing his triumphal robes into a meeting of the senate. His wealth was excessive even by the standards of the Roman elite, and he owned a luxury residence at an exclusive address: on the promontory at Misenum, looking out over the bay of Baiae.

The more positive legacy usually attributed to Marius is his reform of the Roman army on the back of the military disasters at the end of the second century BC. The Romans excelled at warfare, and through their rigid discipline and training were more 'professional' and better adapted to the demands of constant warfare than many of their adversaries. There were, however, few elements that we might think of as necessary for a professional army: there was no such thing as a general staff or staff college in Rome, for instance, which would have provided a way for strategic and tactical experience to be passed effectively from one generation of centurions and tribunes to the next. Marius did not entirely solve these problems, nor did the reforms popularly linked with his career necessarily belong wholly to him or even happen while he was alive. Yet it was under his guidance that the army began to make the transition from a force raised for specific campaigns to one that was closer to our understanding of a professional standing army. The first element of this was, as noted earlier, opening recruitment to the poorest in Rome, and thus breaking the link between property and service. This may have been intended by Marius as a one-time solution to a recruitment problem, but it set the tone for the future. Army service could now therefore be a career choice, rather than primarily a moral duty bound up with ideas about citizenship. Legions were reorganised, moving away from the maniple to armies of ten cohorts, each made up of six centuries. The cohort was about 480-500 men, roughly the same strength as a modern infantry battalion; like their manipular predecessors, cohorts could be detached from the main army or joined with others as the situation warranted. This structure predated Marius—Scipio Africanus had pioneered its use in Spain—but it now became standard throughout the army. The old four-line distinction of *velites*, *hastati*, *principes*, and *triarii* (Chapter 2) was progressively absorbed into a formation organised around cohorts. Each cohort contained three units of *hastati*, *principes*, and *triarii*, with five centurions: the *primus pilus*, or 'first spear', followed by *princeps prior*, *hastatus prior*, *princeps posterior*, and *hastatus posterior*. The old legionary terminology thus became part of the way that cohorts were organised, and this persisted well into the time of the empire (30 BC

Figure 6.8 Silver denarius minted in 82 BC. Obverse: Winged bust of victory; reverse: eagle between two individual standards. The standard on the left is marked 'H' for *hastati* and that on the right 'P' for *principes*.

and afterwards). The cohorts, like the old legions, also remained in an open, checkerboard formation. It also seems that the *velites* were done away with completely, with the role of cavalry and additional light-armed troops given to auxiliary soldiers levied from Rome's foreign allies. (Latin and Italian allied horsemen are not known after the war with Jugurtha.) Infantry legions were now numbered, even if the numbering system used in the Republic has proven difficult to comprehend. Eventually the famous eagle standards, which had existed for generations alongside other mythical and real animals such as the wolf, the minotaur, and the boar, became *the* legionary standard. At the same time, individual lines, the *hastati* and *principes*, kept individual standards (Figure 6.8).

Later on, legions also came to acquire names and emblems (Chapter 8). The combination of voluntary service, unit names and designations, and insignia helped to instil a fierce pride in individual units and a competitive rivalry with other units in the army. Training was carried out all year round, including specialised training given by professional gladiators, and soldiers signed up for extended periods rather than individual campaigns. Another major change that occurred during this transition that had its roots in older proposals was that the state, not the soldier, finally assumed the role of providing the necessary equipment and weapons that were manufactured in state *fabricae* (factories). This allowed for a greater standardisation of equipment and ensured all soldiers in the legion were armed in the same manner. Part of this equipment included adjustments to a heavier *pilum* (javelin), with a head that bent or snapped off on impact. The missile could not be thrown back, and when embedded in a shield, it rendered the shield useless. There was now so much equipment to be carried that soldiers called themselves, with pride, 'Marius's mules'.

These changes to the army also helped to ensure the development of specific professional classes. Centurions, the backbone of Rome's officer corps, might serve in the same legion for many years. The compact between soldier and the state, which had been shifting since the days of Scipio Africanus, had decisively changed. On retirement, soldiers and their officers could expect a plot of land and a bonus, and as this tended to come increasingly from their generals, the loyalty of soldiers was transferred accordingly. Finally, the Roman army gained a well-deserved reputation for its engineering excellence and skill at siegecraft. This is clearly visible in Scipio's siege of Numantia, and later in Sulla's ruthless siege of Athens in 86 BC.

Sulla, Mithridates, and the Great Proscription

In the interim, Sulla had rallied veterans of the legions that had fought under his command in the Social War, and had crossed over to Greece in the spring of 87 BC. Sulla appeared barely inconvenienced by the fact that he had been declared a public enemy, and was equally indifferent to the fact that Lucius Valerius Flaccus (consul in 86 BC, replacing Marius) had brought a consular army to Asia to fight Mithridates. Instead, Sulla carried on with what was now essentially his own private army, and Valerius Flaccus was soon murdered by one of his lieutenants, the Marian ally Gaius Flavius Fimbria, who scented the opportunity to win *gloria* for himself.

Sulla, funded by loot plundered from the sacred treasuries of Greece, laid siege to Athens, which had emerged as the centre of anti-Roman resistance in Achaea. Roman artillery bombarded the city, and the population within starved, resorting to eating boiled leather and even each other. Almost a year later, Sulla's army finally broke through the Athenian defences and sacked the city, murdering the survivors of the siege, destroying the city's most famous buildings, looting it of its artwork and cultural treasures, and burning the port of Piraeus. The Roman sack even despoiled the Stoa of Zeus Eleutherios, where the Athenian dead of its many wars were commemorated. Much of the loot went to adorn public buildings in Rome, while some of the rest ended up in the luxury villas of the elite in Campania. According to Appian, Sulla also made off with a personal fortune of a talent of gold and some ten talents of silver from the Athenian treasury (*Mithridatic Wars*, 39). He also had the library of Aristotle and his disciple Theophrastus sent to Rome, and installed marble columns from the Temple of Olympian Zeus on the Capitoline Hill. The transplantation of this new wave of Greek art and culture further intermingled Greek and Roman history, and the accompanying emigration to Rome of highly educated refugees such as Philo of Larissa, the director of Plato's Academy, provided experienced tutors for aspiring intellectuals such as Cicero. Coins minted in Athens at the time featured the owl of Athena, long the hallmark of Athenian coinage (Figure 6.9).

After destroying the forces of Mithridates' general, Archelaus, then compelling Fimbria to commit suicide, Sulla—whose eyes were firmly fixed on his wilting fortunes in Rome—made peace with Mithridates in 85 BC. The Pontic king retained his kingdom and his

Figure 6.9 Silver drachm minted in Athens under Roman occupation, 86–84 BC. Obverse: head of Athena Parthenos right, with Pegasus in flight; reverse: owl standing on amphora.

title, and agreed to a friendship with Rome, while Sulla absorbed the additional Roman forces in Asia under his command. On the cities of Asia, which had supported Mithridates instead of their Roman overlords, Sulla levied a massive fine of 20,000 talents, a sum so vast that many communities were driven into crippling levels of debt. The rapacious *publicani* were only too happy to loan the money required to the destitute cities at usurious rates of interest. It is important to note that Sulla did all of this as a private citizen with a private army, essentially subverting the tax collection of a province to his own benefit: this huge amount of money would keep his army going for many years and ensured that Sulla stayed in power, especially since he allowed his troops generous leeway to loot and extort the local population. The peace with Mithridates caused panic in Rome, and both Cinna and Carbo desperately raised troops to stave off Sulla's imminent return. Cinna, however, was murdered by his legionnaires and Carbo struggled to replace him. It is telling that Cinna was killed because the campaign he had in mind was one in which the soldiers were unlikely to have any serious opportunities for plunder.

Sulla wrote letters to the senate, and in the same hurt tone he had used earlier to justify marching on Rome with an army, he enumerated his valiant deeds in the service of the state and asked how there could be any justification for being declared a public enemy. Chillingly, he announced that he would soon arrive in Rome and dispense justice upon those who had betrayed him. In 83 BC, Sulla returned to Italian soil, landing at Brundisium with his army. He quickly defeated Caius Norbanus, the *novus homo* Marian sent by the senate to fight him, and subsequently the army of the second consul, Lucius Cornelius Scipio (great-grandson of Scipio Asiaticus) went over to Sulla. Gnaeus Pompeius, son of Pompeius Strabo—and better known to history as Pompey—raised an army from his father's retired veterans at Picenum on his own initiative and at his own expense, and set his troops at Sulla's disposal. Before long, Sulla's camp was brimming with Roman oligarchs looking to ingratiate themselves with the clear winner of this round of the civil war. Quintus Caecilius Metellus Pius was one of them, as was Marcus Licinius Crassus, son of a consul and shortly to become infamous in his own right. Sulla quickly quashed senatorial resistance in the guise of Marius's son, also named Marius, who was consul in 82 BC with Carbo. The battles were marked by wide-scale desertions from one side to the other and characterised by extreme savagery. After a narrow victory outside Rome's Colline Gate, where Sulla overcame a determined attack by a Samnite army, the younger Marius committed suicide. His head, sent to Sulla, found its way to the forum, where Sulla gazed at it contemptuously, paraphrasing Aristophanes's *The Knights* with derision: 'first learn to row,' he smirked, 'before you try to steer' (Appian, *Civil Wars*, 1.94). Carbo was captured later and executed by Pompey, who scolded him at length before cutting off his head. (For this and other crimes, Pompey earned the nickname *adulescentulus carnifex*, 'The Teenage Butcher'.) Praeneste, which had sheltered Marius, was subjected to a prolonged siege with a complete circumvallation of the city. It eventually capitulated and was sacked, with much of its population murdered. As Sulla picked off the opposition, a military mint travelling with his army produced coins in 82 BC celebrating his triumphant return (Figure 6.10).

The legally appointed officials of the government and the legally levied armies were no more. Sulla and his private army now controlled Rome, and he took terrible revenge even as he told the people 'to cheer up, as the troubles would soon be over'; he used the same wounded sense of justice as before to defend his actions (Appian, *Civil Wars*, 1.89). Prisoners taken in the various battles and skirmishes were murdered *en masse* in public,

Figure 6.10 Silver denarius of Sulla, 82 BC. Obverse: helmeted head of Roma right; reverse: Sulla driving a triumphal chariot (quadriga). Victory flies above the scene and L. SVLLA is below in the exergue.

including four legions given safe conduct and 6,000 Samnites who were slaughtered while Sulla addressed the senate nearby; this, in conjunction with the Social War, marked the end of the Samnites as a distinctive people in Italy. The ashes of the deceased Marius were exhumed and thrown out into the river Anio like common rubbish. Marius's nephew, Marius Gratidianus, who was also Cicero's cousin, was viciously put to death by a man named Sergius Catilina, better known as Catiline (Chapter 7). He reportedly gouged out Gratidianus's eyes and broke every bone in his body, a lesson in cruelty so shocking to onlookers that they fainted on the spot (Seneca, *On Anger*, 3.18 & Valerius Maximus, 9.2). Sulla was only getting started: 'doctoring one evil with another', he drew up a list of political wrongdoers and posted a bounty for each, publishing the list in the forum (Appian, *Civil Wars*, 1.3). This was the Great Proscription of 82 BC, which ruined hundreds of senators and thousands of equestrians. A small fortune was paid for each murder, and the male offspring of these unfortunates were forever barred from election to a public office. Spies were everywhere, hunting for the bounty to be made for each man delivered to his death. One of those proscribed was the former consul Lucius Cornelius Scipio, who fled to Massilia and later died there in obscurity. Any conceivable offence against Sulla was punished, including 'hospitality, private friendship, the borrowing or lending of money' (Appian, *Civil Wars*, 1.96), while many 'were killed to gratify private hatreds, although they had no relations with Sulla' (Plutarch, *Sulla*, 31). Rebellious towns and communities were burned, colonised by Sulla's veterans, or had their defences torn down. Dispossessed people were turfed out and made homeless in their own land. All regular government business ground to a halt. 'There was no longer any occasion for laws, or elections, or for casting lots', wrote Appian, 'because everybody was shivering with fear and in hiding' (*Civil Wars*, 1.97). Meanwhile, as Pompey ran the surviving Marians to ground in Africa, Sulla— mindful of the rapidly growing importance of the relationship between commander and soldiers—generously rewarded his troops with land taken from his political enemies. Most radical of all, Sulla was named to the dictatorship, the first for over a century. He held the position well beyond the customary six-month limit. He cloaked this corruption of the constitution by directing an *interrex* to appoint a suitable individual to the dictatorship, strongly hinting that he was the best qualified candidate. During his dictatorship, Sulla embarked on a program to restore the balance of power in favour of the *optimates* and the senate, at the expense of the people. Anyone in any doubt of where power lay in Rome had only to gaze at the sizeable equestrian statue of Sulla in the forum, close to where the severed heads were displayed; such was Sulla's authority that the Olympic Games were not celebrated in 80 BC because the athletes were summoned to Rome to cheer up an exhausted and terrified people. He made his power felt even further afield, by setting his own appointee on the Egyptian throne; after three weeks, however, the unfortunate man was lynched by a mob in Alexandria. The conspirators, noted Appian, 'were still without fear of foreigners', a situation that would soon change (*Civil Wars*, 1.102).

Sulla's reforms legalised the proscriptions and gave him power of life and death over the citizens of Rome. He decreed that the plebeian tribunes could no longer propose legislation, a serious curb to the principle of popular power that had been triumphed by Tiberius Gracchus, and the tribunate was turned into a political cul-de-sac. Once it was held, the incumbent was banned from standing for any other public office. The senate regained control over jury selection—another blow to the gains won by the equestrians over the past half-century; at the same time, the senate was restocked and enlarged by large numbers of wealthy equestrians-turned-senators, who owed their good fortune—and even their continued ability to draw breath—to Sulla. Sulla strengthened the *cursus honorum* by enforcing the traditional route of quaestor, praetor, and consul, instilling age limits and mandating a ten-year period between each consulship. He also passed legislation that conferred senatorial membership on any politician who had been quaestor: one had to start at the correct place on the *cursus*, in other words, to gain membership of the elite senatorial group, rather than be installed in the senate on the whim of the censors or through tenure of the wrong office at the wrong time. The praetorship was expanded, creating a pool of experienced bureaucrats that could be dispatched overseas as provincial governors after their year in office was completed. In an attempt to ensure that nobody else would do what he had done, he dusted off an earlier law dealing with governors taking armies beyond the borders of their provinces, making it an offence under the laws governing *maiestas*, treason, to do so. Finally, Sulla also commissioned numerous construction projects to repair some of the extensive damage done to Rome during the civil war. These included the structure known as the Tabularium on the Capitoline Hill (perhaps a records office), the remnants of which still stand in the Roman forum, and the rebuilt curia Hostilia, damaged during the civil war and now enlarged to accommodate the increased membership of the senate.

Sulla's legacy is a complicated one. For some—especially those exiled by Marius— Sulla was the saviour of the Republic, a man who restored the traditional position of the senate at the heart of Roman government. Yet for others he was a tyrant who abused his authority and further entrenched the yawning fracture in Roman politics, who had filled the rebuilt senate with people who owed everything to him, who essentially became his clients. Appian said that Sulla behaved as a king, ruling not by consent or through election but by force and terror (*Civil Wars*, 1.98). Valerius Maximus opened his chapter on cruelty with an account of Sulla's savagery, declaring that 'while he was on the path to victory, he acted like Scipio to the Roman people, but once he had acquired it, he acted like Hannibal' (9.2). On the evidence of later events, his contemporaries clearly grasped how normalising such shocking behaviour would affect the conduct of Roman politicians in the future. Sulla also freed 10,000 slaves of those whom he had proscribed and gave them Roman citizenship. All took the Cornelian name, so in this way Sulla became a super-patron of this group, which was completely dependent on his goodwill. In a similar vein, he forced men to divorce their wives so he could create political alliances with his growing web of clients: Pompey, for example, had to divorce his wife to marry a step-daughter of Sulla, Aemilia, who soon died in childbirth. When Sulla's own wife, Caecilia Metella, was on her deathbed, Sulla divorced her and refused to be by her side.

Further indications of the shifts taking place in Roman political life were to be found in Sulla's open associations with Venus and Apollo, which were reinforced by his epithet 'Felix'—'lucky' or 'fortunate', implying divine assent for his actions. Parthian holy men were reported to have told him that 'his fame would be worthy of a god' (Velleius Paterculus, 2.24). Sulla dedicated rich gifts taken from the spoils of his wars at the Temple of Venus, and Appian thought that the senate itself had given Sulla the surname 'Eupaphroditus', Greek for 'beloved by Aphrodite' (*Civil Wars*, 1.97). The cultivation of divine links was decidedly Hellenistic in nature, and aligned Sulla more with eastern ideas of rule than Republican concepts of collegial political authority. It can be argued, of course, that Sulla was merely following trends in aristocratic behaviour that had begun with Scipio Africanus, Flamininus, and others; Marius had also possessed his own share of mysterious and divine connections. Pompey was also on the lookout for ways to build his own brand, and he too looked to eastern models, taking the agnomen 'Magnus', 'the great', in clear imitation of Alexander. He then haughtily demanded a triumph after finishing off the remnants of Carbo's army in Africa. Sulla opposed the idea, reminding Pompey that a century and a half earlier, Scipio Africanus had not taken a triumph for his glittering campaigns in Spain because he was merely a private citizen with imperium. Pompey, Sulla went on, not only held no office but was also too young ('had scarcely grown a beard'). Pompey's response to this admonishment was to bid Sulla to remember 'that more worshipped the rising than the setting sun'. Sulla backed down, but Pompey botched his celebration; bringing an impractical four-elephant chariot from Africa, he found it would not fit through the gates of Rome (Plutarch, *Pompey*, 14).

Sulla liked to regard himself as accessible, and after laying down his dictatorship and serving as consul in 80 BC, he would wander around the forum, amenable to political discussions. Of course, after his actions, one can imagine that such discussions stayed well away from dangerous territory; he had once killed a loyal supporter in public after he refused to renounce his intention to run for the consulship in opposition to Sulla's decrees. The restored Republic was not the same as the *ancien régime*. Having retired and returned political power 'to the very people over whom he had tyrannised', Sulla died in 78 BC, and Pompey quickly seized the advantage provided by his funeral to build up his own political status (Appian, *Civil Wars*, 1.103). Plutarch wrote that Pompey was offended at being excluded from Sulla's will, but he kept the body safe from Marcus Aemilius Lepidus, a member of the *populares* who had been elected consul in 78 BC at Pompey's own instigation (Sulla's anger at Pompey for arranging this populist coup was precisely the reason he had written Pompey out of his will.) The funeral was a glitzy affair, with a large statue of Sulla 'moulded out of costly frankincense and cinnamon' (Plutarch, *Sulla*, 38). Sulla was buried in the Campus Martius in Rome; his tomb was still there in the early third century AD, when the emperor Caracalla restored it.

After Sulla: Mithridates and Lucullus

The decade following Sulla's death saw Rome riven by fratricidal strife and a resurgence of the war with Mithridates. The two consuls for 78 BC, Marcus Aemilius Lepidus and Quintus Lutatius Catulus (son of the Catulus, who was earlier Marius's rival—see above) duelled over Sulla's legacy. Lepidus emerged as a champion for the rights of dispossessed landowners, even though his fortune had been earned by buying up proscribed property at a deep discount and through plundering Sicily as its governor, for which was he was prosecuted and acquitted. Lepidus made impassioned speeches condemning Sulla, deriding him as a 'caricature of Romulus' who had systematically robbed the people of Italy, and defended his own wealth by saying that if he had done what was right, he would be dead (Sallust, *Histories*, 1.48). With further political opportunism, Lepidus joined a revolt against Sullan settlers in Etruria. Catulus, on the other hand, was presented by a craven and terrified senate with the *senatus consultum ultimum* to defend Rome. Pompey sided with the senate, and together with Catulus and Metellus Pius he crushed Lepidus's allies in northern Italy; Lepidus himself fled to Sardinia, where he subsequently died. Afterwards, Pompey refused to disband his troops. A showdown with the senate was avoided as he was given a hurried grant of proconsular imperium: a rebellion of Lusitanians and disaffected Romans led by a talented and proscribed Marian, the equestrian Quintus Sertorius, and the proscribed Marian ally Marcus Perperna was causing chaos in Nearer Spain. Moving from northern Italy, Pompey, continuing to operate as a private citizen with imperium and holding no other formal office, worked hard with Metellus to check Sertorius, but his patience ran thin at the shortage of support from the senate. Pompey wrote angry letters in 75 BC, self-servingly blaming the *patres* for exposing him to so much war at such a young age, and seeking their approval for acting with restraint and not 'adding to my popularity' (Sallust, *Histories*, 2.82).

In the east, Mithridates was in a good position. There was chaos in Rome and the peace with Sulla (85 BC) had never been confirmed. Sulla, who had forced it on him, was dead. In the intervening years, Mithridates had strengthened his position in Cappadocia and had begun, once again, to engage in anti-Roman measures that included freeing slaves and allying himself with local pirates. In 75 BC, Mithridates and Sertorius joined forces. The Pontic king gave his Roman ally a substantial fleet and several talents to fund his war, and Sertorius recognised the right of Mithridates to rule much of Asia Minor and sent him advisers to train his army in a bid to improve their odds of success against Rome's legions. (This began a process of military imitation by other kingdoms and states in the Mediterranean—consider, for instance, the legions of king Deiotarus, fighting for Caesar in 47 BC—see Chapter 7). In 74 BC, Nicomedes IV of Bithynia died and, like Attalus III, left his kingdom to the Romans. Mithridates was deeply threatened by this development and, once again condemning Roman greed, went on the offensive, invading Bithynia and driving the new Roman governor from office. In Rome, the senate was sufficiently concerned about these developments to send both consuls for 74 BC, Lucius Licinius Lucullus and Marcus Aurelius Cotta, to the eastern Mediterranean. Lucullus hailed from a large plebeian family, the *gens* Licinia, a distant member of which had helped to propose the Licinian-Sextian laws back in the fourth century BC. Lucullus's half-uncle was Metellus, the former patron of Marius; he was also closely linked with Sulla, by whose side at Nola he had stayed when the rest of Sulla's officers deserted him, and it was to Lucullus that Sulla dedicated his memoirs and to whom he entrusted the guardianship of his son.

Figure 6.11 Silver tetradrachm of Tigranes II 'the Great' minted at Tigranocerta between 80 BC and 68 BC. Obverse: diademed and draped bust right; reverse: the Tyche (fortune) of Antioch seated on a rock holding a laurel branch. Below, the god of the river Orontes (the river running through Antioch) swimming.

While Cotta floundered at sea, losing a large part of his fleet, Lucullus mounted a vigorous campaign that chased Mithridates out of Bithynia and into Pontus itself, capturing key cities along the way. Mithridates fled to Armenia, which had—under the energetic leadership of its king, Tigranes, who had married Cleopatra, the daughter of Mithridates— rapidly emerged as a mini-empire that included large parts of Syria and the intervening districts of Osrhoene, Adiabene, and Atropatene (Figure 6.11). Roman troops pressed on and sacked the Armenian capital Tigranocerta in 69 BC, forcing Mithridates to flee once again, and a victorious Lucullus paid his men a hefty bonus from the mountains of loot they had plundered in the course of their successful campaign.

With Asia now firmly under Roman control, Lucullus, with admirable pragmatism, sought to address the problems that had caused such virulent anti-Roman sentiment to be kindled in the region. The Greek cities in Asia were reeling under Sulla's indemnity, which, with unchecked interest, had grown six-fold from the original 20,000 talents. Lucullus ensured that interest rates were lowered and took measures to reduce the total amount owed. This won him many friends in Asia, but he made powerful enemies among the equestrian *publicani* and their political allies in Rome. These businessmen had grown so bold that some years earlier, as the war with Mithridates was getting underway, they had organised the public lynching of a praetor who had tried to address problems of debt and interest rates. Lucullus was eventually undone by political manoeuvrings in Rome and he was deposed from his army command, which was eventually transferred to Pompey. That Pompey could engineer such a dramatic shift had much to do with one of the most famous events in Roman history: the revolt led by Spartacus, which Appian called 'the gladiatorial war' (*Civil Wars*, 1.111).

At the beginning of the Spartacan Revolt in 73 BC, Pompey was still in Spain, fighting the combined forces of Sertorius and Perperna. The two rebels eventually fell out, and Perperna murdered his colleague at an alcohol-fuelled banquet before succumbing to defeat late in 72 BC, after which he was put to death by Pompey. Meanwhile, Spartacus, who hailed from Thrace and had served in the Roman army, had become enslaved and was trained as a gladiator at Capua. With a small force and assisted by one of his close allies, Crixus, Spartacus broke out of the gladiatorial school and holed up near Vesuvius. The two men soon gathered a mob of close to 70,000 slaves, gladiators, the dispossessed, and the proscribed, but split up over disagreements about their next course of action. Some wanted to pillage, but Spartacus had loftier goals and made his way north to Cisalpine Gaul. While Crixus was defeated and killed by a Roman army in 72 BC, Spartacus was remarkably successful and, supplied by the same pirates who were helping Mithridates, he and his largely professional gladiatorial force beat several Roman armies arrayed against him. Spartacus gained a reputation for bloody behaviour; he reportedly sacrificed captured Roman troops 'to the shade of Crixus' (Appian, *Civil Wars*, 1.117).

Eventually, out of desperation, the senate gave the Sullan ally Marcus Licinius Crassus the task of ending the revolt. Crassus was one of the richest Romans of his time and supplemented the senatorial army with several additional legions that he raised and paid himself. Reversing the tide of woeful Roman defeats, Crassus drove Spartacus across southern Italy and later massacred his army. Spartacus died on the battlefield, and Crassus followed up his victory by crucifying thousands of captives along the length of the via Appia from Rome to Capua. This was not the end of the story, since a band of survivors, fleeing north, ran straight into Pompey and his army on their return from the campaign against Sertorius. Pompey would later boast that while Crassus had only been of slight service in the war, it was *he* that had given the greatest exertion by destroying the sur-viving members of the revolt. Marching towards Rome with his army, Pompey generated considerable suspicion, but he announced grandly that he would disband his force—when he was awarded a triumph. A cowed senate agreed, demoting the triumph that was to be awarded to Crassus to an ovation, a second-tier celebration. Pompey was 'elected' consul for 70 BC, even though he was too young and had not held the praetorship. With Crassus as his colleague, he set about dismantling the last of Sulla's reforms, restoring the power of the plebeian tribunate in the process and rebalancing juries between senators and equestrians. Throughout this remarkable period, Pompey managed to champion the causes of both the *optimates* and the *populares*. At the end of 70 BC, both he and Crassus stepped down, but nobody expected them to be out of the public eye for too long.

Caesar, Pompey—and Mithridates

One of the most influential figures in world history, Gaius Julius Caesar, was born in about 100 BC. The patrician *gens* Julia claimed descent from Ascanius (Chapter 1), but the family's influence in the first century BC largely came through an association with Marius, who had married Caesar's paternal aunt, Julia. The Marian association ensured that Caesar's father, when praetor, received the plum position of the governorship of Asia. At age 16, Caesar became the head of the family, and in 84 BC, when Rome was under the grip of Marius and Cinna, he married Cinna's daughter, Cornelia, and was nominated to the chief priesthood of Jupiter. When Sulla took control of Rome, these connections proved unsavoury; Sulla considered putting Caesar to death and demanded that he divorce Cornelia. Refusing, Caesar went into hiding until his mother, who had connections to Sulla's allies, managed to defuse the situation. By this point, Caesar had lost the priesthood and left Rome to join the fight against Mithridates. He served with distinction during the war; he was first over the wall at Mytilene in 81 BC, and he won the *corona civica*, the civic crown, awarded to a Roman who saved the life of another. After Sulla's death, Caesar returned to Rome and lived in a slum, having lost his property and his inheritance to Sulla's vengeful proscriptions. He was appointed to the college of pontiffs in 74 BC, and for a time he also tried his luck as a lawyer, developing a reputation for the skill of his oratory. Encouraged by this new venture, he decided to study rhetoric in Rhodes with the famous teacher Apollonius Molon, who also taught Cicero. There is some confusion in the ancient sources over the exact chronology of events, but either on the way there or on the way back across the Aegean, Caesar was captured by pirates.

Caesar's captivity proved to be a life-changing experience. According to Plutarch, the pirates set his ransom at 20 talents, but Caesar 'laughed at them for not knowing who their captive was, and of his own accord agreed to give them fifty'. When he slept, he ordered his captors to keep quiet; he worked out with the pirates, practised his speeches on them, and threatened to find them after his ransom was paid and have them executed. The pirates scoffed at this and thought that these were the nervous jokes of a young and inexperienced man (*Julius Caesar*, 2). Later, after he was freed, Caesar hunted down the pirates and, when they were thrown into jail in Pergamum, he personally ensured that they were executed—just as he had said he would. Afterwards, Caesar raised a force and set it at the disposal of Lucullus, who was busy fighting Mithridates. Following this second stint in the Mithridatic War, Caesar returned to Rome and was elected as a military tribune in 71 BC. In 69 BC, Caesar was quaestor, and in that year both his wife, Cornelia, and his aunt, Julia, died and Caesar used the funerals as a political opportunity to rehabilitate Cinna and Marius. He impressed the people with his funeral oration for Julia, during which he claimed descent from Venus; he also incorporated images of Marius in the funeral procession. Later, however, he married Pompeia, the granddaughter of Sulla, and was admitted to the senate. Like Pompey, Caesar adroitly manipulated the shifting alliances and fluid politics of the time, able to cast himself as a friend to both *optimates* and *populares*, depending on the advantages that each gave to him.

As Caesar's own experience demonstrated, there was a problem with piracy in the eastern Mediterranean and the Aegean. This was part of the fallout from the ongoing war with Mithridates and the spillover of Rome's factional strife into that conflict. Piracy eventually proved so damaging that the supply of Egyptian grain, needed for the realisation of the Gracchan-era proposal to provide grain at a subsidised rate (eventually enacted in 73 BC), was being interrupted. To some extent, the piracy crisis was also Rome's fault: in earlier times the highly effective navies of Rhodes, Macedonia, and the Seleucids had patrolled the seas, but now all were either subordinated to Roman interests or had vanished completely. The pirates willingly stepped into this power vacuum, which was made worse as civil war in Rome diverted senatorial attention. It has also been suggested that slave-dealing *negotiares* working out of Delos made pacts with the pirates, who would snatch their human prey and deliver them to Delos for sale at preferred rates. Not content with merely raiding passing ships, pirates were also known to attack cities and towns, and rob temples, treasuries, and shrines. Appian wrote that pirates 'had castles and towers and desert islands and retreats everywhere' and controlled 'the whole Mediterranean to the Pillars of Hercules', routinely defeating praetors sent out against them (*Mithridatic Wars*, 92–3); according to Cassius Dio, they had even dared to raid the Roman port of Ostia (36.22).

Eventually, in Rome, the plebeian tribune Aulus Gabinius called for something to be done: a man was needed, he said, an ex-consul who could be appointed for three years to bring the pirates under control. He would be invested with proconsular imperium and given command of an army and a substantial navy. This was not the first time such a plan had been mooted; it had been tried before in 102 and 74 BC. But now all heads turned to Pompey, the man who had ended Sertorius, Perperna, and Spartacus. He was called out of semi-retirement and dispatched to the east. Not everyone was happy with the extraordinary amount of power being invested in a single individual: Quintus Lutatius Catulus, who had been consul with Lepidus in 78 BC, regarded Pompey as 'too great for a free republic' (Velleius Paterculus, 2.32). Nevertheless, Pompey was given lavish resources, including some 500 warships, 24 propraetors, and over 100,000 troops; he also levied additional troops from the various cities and kingdoms of Asia Minor. He proved so efficient that the pirates were defeated in less than two months, leaving Pompey with an additional 34 months in his commission. Setting his sights on ending the Mithridatic War, he encountered resistance in the senate, which supported its commander on the ground, Lucullus. Yet, hoping to curry favour with the people, both Caesar and Cicero supported Pompey, and his fame, earned on the battlefield, drew the right kind of attention in Rome. In 66 BC, Pompey was given command in Asia, and he unceremoniously relieved Lucullus of his command and took over most of his troops. For Lucullus, who Plutarch praised for his restraint and self-control, this was too much: he angrily commented that Pompey was 'like a lazy carrion bird', always finishing what other people had started and taking credit for the success of his rivals. 'For it was in this way that he had appropriated to himself the victories over Sertorius, Lepidus, and the followers of Spartacus, although they had actually been won by Metellus, Catulus, and Crassus.' The two were on the point of coming to blows until their friends intervened (Plutarch, *Pompey*, 31). Lucullus surrendered to the inevitable and returned to Rome, carrying with him the looted libraries of Pontus. Mithridates was not cowed by the change in command and refused to surrender to Pompey, doggedly declaring that he could not give in to 'the cupidity of the Romans' (Appian, *Mithridatic Wars*, 98). Yet Pompey pursued his enemy ruthlessly, pushing Mithridates out of Cappadocia and then his own kingdom until, in 63 BC, Mithridates chose to die by the hand of a bodyguard rather than be captured and paraded in Rome; he met his end at Panticapaeum in the eastern Crimea. Tigranes had surrendered some years earlier, paying Pompey a monumental 6,000 talents on top of a handsome bonus for the Roman troops. The treasury of Mithridates, overflowing with loot, came into Pompey's hands. Like his predecessors, Pompey also returned with cultural artefacts (Mithridates's medical library) and highly educated captives who would involuntarily enrich Rome's academic scene.

Lucullus was prosecuted in Rome by his enemies, including his brother-in-law, the unpleasant Publius Clodius Pulcher (Chapter 7), who accused him of fraud and needlessly prolonging the war. He managed to ward off this clumsy attempt to destroy his legacy and celebrated an elaborate triumph featuring a 1.8 metre (6 feet) gold statue of Mithridates. Lucullus used the wealth taken during the war on various projects in Rome, including a vast public library and a lavish park known as the 'Gardens of Lucullus', the site of which is close to the present-day Spanish Steps and the Villa Borghese. Lucullus was a follower of Epicureanism, a philosophy that emphasised enjoying life's pleasures, and after his retirement Lucullus tended to his luxury estate with its fantastical waterworks, 'thereby escaping the unhappy lot of Marius', and made a positive contribution to the people of Italy by introducing from Asia the *prunus lucullus*, the cherry tree (Plutarch, *Lucullus*, 38). Although he made a few additional political forays before he died, Lucullus was a rarity in Roman politics: he was satisfied with what he had achieved.

The defeat of Rome's wily Pontic adversary, on the other hand, did not stop Pompey or curb his ambition, although it did occasion a grand public festival of thanksgiving in Rome. With the Seleucid kingdom a shadow of its former self, with Tigranes and Mithridates defeated, and with Egypt cowed by Roman friendship, Pompey saw nothing but disorder and chaos in the Middle East. He used the opportunity to wade into the morass of city-states, princes and tyrants, petty kingdoms, and warring neighbours, and in 63 BC created the Roman province of Syria out of the power vacuum left by the collapse of Rome's rivals. The Seleucid monarchy was abolished, despite the fact that only a few years earlier Lucullus had confirmed Antiochus XIII on his throne; no doubt the establishment of a more direct form of Roman rule in its place was considered the best option to maintain security in the region. The only other state with the ability to intervene was Parthia, which had steadily enlarged itself at the expense of the Seleucid dynasty. In 141 BC, in Babylon, the Parthian king Mithridates I had taken the old Persian title 'King of Kings', and Parthian power became established at the capital city of Ctesiphon, built on the opposite side of the river Tigris from the older foundation of Seleucia (Figure 6.12). Parthian territory encompassed much of modern Iraq, Iran, and Afghanistan, and the kingdom's influence was felt among a network of client states in the Caucasus and the northern part of the Fertile Crescent.

In 96 BC, Sulla had made the first diplomatic contact with the Parthians, confirming Rome's friendship. With a brief exception in 66 BC, the Parthians had declined to join the Mithridatic War, despite repeated requests from both sides to do so. As that war ended, therefore, they had no moral stake in shaping the future of the lands that now fell under Roman control, so it was Pompey and the Romans, not Parthia and its kings, that became the most influential power broker in Syria, Asia Minor, Egypt, and the Levant. Pompey may also have felt that Syria was Roman by right, as Tigranes, who had most recently

Figure 6.12 Silver tetradrachm of Mithridates I of Parthia, struck at Seleucia in 141 BC. Obverse: diademed bust of the king, right; reverse: Heracles standing with club in his left arm. The legend reads ΒΑΣΙΛΕΩΣ ΜΕΓΑΛΟΥ ΑΡΣΑΚΟΥ ΦΙΛΕΛΛΗΝΟΣ, 'of the great king of Arsaces [eponymous founder of the Parthian Arsacid dynasty], friend to the Greeks'. Note the similarity with the coinage of Alexander the Great and his successors (Chapters 3 and 5).

controlled it, had been beaten by the Romans (Appian, *Mithridatic Wars*, 106). Ironically, this was the same argument that Hellenistic kings since Philip V and Antiochus III had used to justify their own policies of expansion and consolidation that had so irritated the Roman senate.

Pompey's approach to the problem of governance was pragmatic. Even though the Seleucid monarchy was abolished, most of the region's kings and rulers were confirmed in their positions as friends of the Republic, but beholden to Roman commands, subject to tribute, and under the overall control of a Roman provincial governor. Pontus was joined with Bithynia as a Roman province. Judaea became a Roman friend under a pliable member of the ruling Hasmonean dynasty after a brief siege of Jerusalem in 63 BC, and the northern kingdom of Commagene likewise fell under Roman patronage; its king during this period, Antiochus I (69–31 BC), called himself *philoromaios*, 'friend of the Romans'. Tigranes was rewarded for his submission and left in control of a truncated Armenia. In Egypt, Ptolemy Apion, dying without an heir in 96 BC, had left the kingdom and the adjoining district of Cyrenaica to the Republic. After initially refusing this bequest, the senate later accepted it, annexing Crete at the same time. Ptolemies remained on the Egyptian throne, but they did so under increasing levels of Roman oversight.

The de facto boundary of the new Roman province of Syria and the dependent kingdoms around it was the Euphrates river; on the other side lay the Parthian kingdom. Pompey's associate Afranius campaigned vigorously throughout the Levant, cowing bandits, restoring law and order, and settling disputes through judicial commissions and boards of inquest. Cilicia, which had been provincialized during the war against Mithridates and the pirates, and through which roads had been built to facilitate the movement of Roman armies, was enlarged (Figure 6.13). Throughout the eastern Mediterranean, Pompey and his associates distributed money, most notably in Athens, where a gift of 50 talents helped to pay for restoration work in the battered city.

This eastern settlement is remarkable in that, without senatorial instructions, Pompey decided to create policy on his own initiative and only later present it to the senate for official approval. This can be contrasted with the approach of Lucullus who, before he was stripped of command, had requested a ten-man commission to be sent to him to make the necessary arrangements in Asia Minor. It could be argued that Pompey was merely following the precedent of men such as Flamininus and Sulla; it could also be argued that it was hardly efficient to wait months for a message to be sent to Rome, considered, and for a *senatus consultum* or commission to reach him. Like Flamininus, Pompey also became a super-patron of the communities with which he had treated and, like Flamininus, Pompey became a celebrity. On the island of Delos, he was venerated as a saviour and a cult in his honour was set up. Athens, too, gave him divine honours (see *RGE* §75a–e). The magnitude of Pompey's achievement was so much greater than anything realised to date by a single man, and inevitably aroused tremendous worry in Rome over his next move—how would such a man, with such a success, behave when he came home? On returning to Brundisium after a long victory lap through the Aegean in 62/61 BC, however, Pompey dismissed his legions after paying them a colossal donative of 16,000 talents. He was no less generous to the Roman state, filling the treasury with gold, silver, and other loot, and he rewarded his loyal client Afranius, who later became consul in 60 BC amid well-founded allegations that Pompey had bought the election. In his triumph, Pompey rode 'in a chariot studded with gems, wearing, it was said, a cloak of Alexander the Great' (although

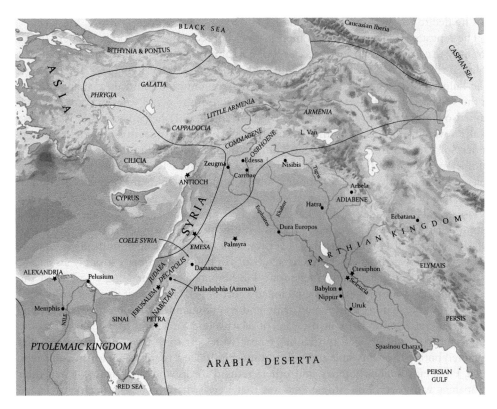

Figure 6.13 Pompey's eastern settlement of 63 BC. Names in *italics* are client kingdoms of the Roman state; names in Roman (normal) type are Roman provinces.

Source: Illustration by the author.

Appian sensibly added 'if anyone can believe that'). The image, rather than the substance, was what mattered (*Mithridatic Wars*, 117). Pompey also paraded nearly 13 talents' worth of silver coin, as well as a 3.6 metre (12 feet) gold statue of Mithridates, outdoing Lucullus by some distance. Pompey's eastern campaigns had brought him unimaginable prestige and wealth. Caesar, Crassus, and their rivals could hardly have missed the hint.

A failing state

Lawsuits had always been a way for Roman politicians to strive against one another: they provided a means through which political battles could be fought and ambitions safely channelled. As the empire expanded, they also provided the only practical means for governors and others in senior posts to be held to account for crimes such as extortion and corruption. One of the most famous cases was Cicero's prosecution of Verres, who had bribed his way to the praetorship in 74 BC and subsequently been appointed governor of Sicily. There, he robbed temples, levied sky-high taxes, slept with other men's wives, extorted money and art, and executed Roman citizens without trial. Despite desperate attempts to have the trial delayed, Verres was subjected to such a damning attack in court that he fled to Massilia, where he died in 43 BC.

The repeated emphasis on the composition of courts in the period covered here shows not only that there was an increased level of corruption warranting investigation, but that political rivalries, for which trials provided an outlet, were intensifying at a dizzying rate. The failure of the empire's administrators to make significant constitutional adjustments in the wake of territorial growth, and the expansion of the dense webs of patronage that fanned out from Rome and across the Mediterranean, only helped to ensure that these rivalries would continue to simmer. While there were some 20 quaestors and eight praetors under Sulla, for instance, there were still only two annual consulships, along with a limited number of provincial governorship positions, available to a Roman elite that had been enlarged significantly through conquest and assimilation. Given this degree of political inertia, it is perhaps unsurprising that dialogue and consensus were abandoned in favour of violence. The episodes of the Gracchi and the actions of Marius and Sulla normalised extraordinary levels of violence as a means to solve political disputes, and the quasi-royal rule of Sulla tilted Rome towards a reversion to a monarchy tinged with divine associations. It is noteworthy that several characteristics of political authority strongly associated with kingship, and particularly Hellenistic kingship, became increasingly visible in the second and first centuries BC. These included a sort of personality cult that was manifested in the tight connections between an army and its commander; the link between a commander and a deity or hero, in the case of Marius and Sulla, and later Caesar; and the importance of military victory granting 'spear-won' territory as an affirmative act that sustained both personality cult and political success. Indeed, there were clear reasons why Sulla, Pompeius Strabo, Pompey, and others refused to disband their armies when their campaigns were over. The simple fact was that it was their armies, rather than elected office, that gave them power and authority. The Roman consulship was starting to look a little bit like Hellenistic *basileia*.

With a few high-profile exceptions, such as Sulla, few of the main players had any real ideological program or political vision for Rome and its problems. Despite his angry whinging to the senate, Pompey was in it to win primacy against his peers and bask in public admiration. In the Roman city-state of 500 BC, this may not have been a problem, but in a world empire of the first century BC, it most certainly was. The great strength of the Roman Republic that had fought Pyrrhus and Hannibal had been the unity of purpose sustained by a plebeian-patrician nobility that governed through consensus and dialogue. That unity was now riven by corruption, greed, unimaginable wealth, and poisonous ambition that was thinly disguised through legislative agendas and spiteful court cases, and that routinely exploded into shocking violence: as Sallust wrote with a jaded spirit, 'avarice destroyed honour, integrity, and all other noble qualities', and a lust for power 'drove many men to become false, and to have one thought locked in the breast, another ready on the tongue' (*Catiline Conspiracy*, 10). A stiff breeze was blowing from the east as Crassus, Pompey, Caesar, and Cicero digested the fallout of Pompey's vast achievement. Writing to Pompey in the summer of 62 BC, Cicero told him that his 'new friends'—an allusion to Caesar and his entourage—were 'prostrated with disappointment at the collapse of their high hopes' (*To Friends*, 5.7). Caesar had wanted Pompey to fail, or at least to have achieved a far more modest success. The worst was yet to come.

Chapter 7

Coup, 63–30 BC

The 33-year period between the victory of Pompey over Mithridates, and that of Octavian over Antony, is one of the most important epochs in both world and Roman history. It was during this timespan that the practice of extrajudicial political murder claimed the life of the de facto head of state and *pontifex maximus*, Julius Caesar; that the authority of the senate and the people of Rome was decisively subverted to individual ambition; and that the last remnants of Republican consensus-driven government finally surrendered to the rule of one individual. The Republic did not, however, 'fall'—there is no one single incident that can be identified as a definitive catalyst for such an event, nor is it realistic to expect that kind of event to have occurred in the first place. Rather, the state was slowly transformed through a long process that stretched back to the Gracchi and further into the third century BC, with the clashes between Rome and Pyrrhus, and then between Rome and Carthage. In the previous chapters, we have seen how the constraints on Roman aristocrats were loosened by the acquisition of an empire, leading to unprecedented opportunities for self-enrichment and the normalisation of individualistic behaviour increasingly freed from accountability and oversight. The progressive division of the elite against itself—a result of this growing individualism—was most prominent in the cleavage between the *optimates* and the *populares*, and between those who sought to restore the state, such as Sulla, and those who viewed the state primarily as a vehicle for winning glory, such as Pompey. Events such as the proscriptions, the Social War, and socio-economic phenomena such as debt, famine, and the pressures exerted by constant warfare only further undermined senatorial consensus, divided the elite against itself, and prevented any serious attempt to address the problems that plagued the Republic. The labyrinthine connections between leading families that produced fleeting alliances and lethal levels of competition played a more important role than ever before. Between 63 and 30 BC, this long process reached its denouement, as the inequalities in wealth and political power reached new heights and each new crisis was met with further division instead of consensus.

The Catiline conspiracy

In 63 BC, the wealthy equestrian Cicero ran for the consulship and was elected as a *novus homo*—the first for over a generation—alongside Gaius Antonius Hybrida, uncle of the famous politician and general Marc Antony. As consul, Cicero championed the cause of the senate and the *nobiles*, blocking legislation that would have transferred private plots of land to Pompey's returning veterans. In the face of Cicero's posturing, Catiline

DOI: 10.4324/9781003202523-7

(Chapter 6), who had stood for the consulship in 63 BC and lost to Cicero, ran again for the consulship of 62 BC, promising to relieve the debts of both the very poor and those who had nearly been ruined by the costs of running for (and holding) public office. Even the moderately well-off were feeling the pinch, and such was the odour of malcontent that in 64 BC, the senate had disbanded the *collegia*, associations in Rome that brought together tradespeople, religious cults, and so on, and which had become implicated in the episodic public violence plaguing the city. Catiline's message resonated with many, but he lost once again, leaving him fuming with resentment at Cicero and the establishment, and determined to do something about it.

While he had failed at the consulship and had only narrowly avoided being convicted for corruption after a stint as governor of Africa, Catiline's anti-establishment position was more successful. This was not simply because of the perennial popularity of relieving people of their debts: there were also many who had been viciously impoverished by Sulla's proscriptions, Marius's vengeful actions, and conflicts such as the Social War. The families of the proscribed saw in Catiline a way to square their differences with the *optimates*, while some of Sulla's veterans, settled on the property of others, had fallen on bad times as retaliation was taken against them after Sulla's death. A proposed land law moved by the plebeian tribune Publius Servilius Rullus sought to alleviate some of this agony, but was effectively killed off by Cicero, who was worried about the amount of power and money the ten-man commission envisioned by the bill would wield. In the meantime a former army officer, Manlius, emerged as Catiline's ally and set about raising an army in Etruria. News of these developments soon reached Cicero, who also discovered that Catiline had arranged for a man to assassinate him; others were assigned to stage an uprising in the city. Meanwhile, one of Catiline's allies, the disgraced Publius Cornelius Lentulus Sura, had tried to rouse the Allobroges of Transalpine Gaul to the cause, only for an Allobrogian delegation to report on this matter to the senate. Lentulus was outed and he and four others were quickly arrested.

After avoiding the attempt on his life on November 6, Cicero had convened the senate and begun delivering his famous speeches attacking Catiline. In early December, the news about the Allobroges broke. The senate instructed Cicero that the *senatus consultum ultimum* was at his disposal, and as he continued to berate Catiline in public, the fate of Lentulus and his co-conspirators hung in the balance. The senate deliberated over how to proceed. Some, including Julius Caesar, who had been elected praetor for the following year, argued that the imprisoned men should remain under lock and key. There was no reason to kill them, as some were advocating, especially since Roman law provided for a trial prior to the administration of capital punishment. Invoking the Macedonian wars and the conflicts with Carthage, the historian Sallust imagined Caesar reminding the senate that even when faced with far more serious challenges, the Romans acted with temperance and restraint; addressing his fellow oligarchs, Caesar urged them not to let the evident guilt of the conspirators 'have more weight with you than your own dignity' (*Catiline Conspiracy*, 51.7). After finishing his impassioned plea for clemency, Caesar was followed by Marcus Porcius Cato (Cato 'the Younger'), an unwavering conservative in the mould of his great-grandfather Cato the Elder. Cato the Younger had distinguished himself as a soldier in the Spartacan war and spent much of his career fighting corruption, but he irritated many of his fellow senators with his uptight moralising tendencies. Cicero, for instance, privately remarked in a letter to his friend Atticus that 'although [Cato] has the best intentions and the highest degree of loyalty, he does harm to the Republic because he declaims his opinions as if he lived in Plato's republic [*politeia*] rather than in the dregs of Romulus' (*To Atticus*, 1.2). Cato was also a devotee of Stoic philosophy, a movement that had become popular in first-century Rome. Stoicism's focus on service for the public good, generosity, and persistence in the face of adversity aligned with the way Rome's *optimates* politicians thought about themselves and their *virtus*. Stoicism also allowed unpopular questions about Rome's overseas conduct to be avoided: through the pro-Roman writings of Posidonius of Apamea, Roman imperialism was portrayed as a civilising force that brought a public good to the less fortunate peoples of the Mediterranean.

Cato's shaming of his fellow senators thus took a predictable approach:

> In the name of the immortal gods, I call upon you, who have always valued your houses, villas, statues, and paintings more highly than your country; if you wish to retain the treasures to which you cling … if you even wish to provide peace for the enjoyment of your pleasure, wake up at last and lay hold of the reins of state.
>
> (Sallust, *Catiline Conspiracy*, 52.5)

Cato dismissed Caesar's comparison of past wars with the current crisis, and laid the blame for the current emergency firmly on the degradation of the senate's moral authority, which had become corrupted by 'private interests'; the senators, he said, had become 'slaves to pleasure in [their] homes and to money and influence' (*Catiline Conspiracy*, 52.23). He finished with a thundering enumeration of examples of Roman *virtus*, going back as far as Torquatus (Chapter 2), then demanded the execution of Lentulus and his co-conspirators. Towards the end of the deliberations, the sombre mood was lightened somewhat when a messenger entered the senate meeting and delivered a note to Caesar. Cato, who had begun to suspect Caesar of involvement in the plot, demanded that the note be read out loud to the senate. Caesar obliged; according to Plutarch, it was a steamy *billet-doux* from Cato's half-sister Servilia, with whom Caesar was having an affair (*Cato the Younger*, 24).

The argument of Cato carried the day. Lentulus was strangled to death in the Tullianum on Cicero's orders, and the other four—one of whom had been tasked with the murder of Cicero—met the same fate. Catiline, whom Lentulus had implicated, had already fled the city in November and reached Manlius and his army north of Rome. Eventually Catiline was run down by Gaius Antonius in the cold winter of 62 BC, although Antonius elected not to fight Catiline personally and handed over command of the army to his deputy, the competent Marcus Petreius, who had over 30 years' experience in the legions and epitomised the growing professionalism of the Roman officer corps. Catiline's resistance earned Sallust's grudging respect: 'when the battle was ended,' he wrote, 'it became evident what boldness and resolution had pervaded Catiline's army. For almost every man covered with his body, when life was gone, the position which he had taken when alive.' Sallust saved his greatest admiration for Catiline, who 'was found far in advance of his men … showing in his face the indomitable spirit which had animated him when alive' (*Catiline Conspiracy*, 61.2–5).

Catiline's populist platform, his recourse to violence when political options failed, and his eventual death in a civil conflict were not particularly exceptional in the context of late Republican political life. Indeed, Cassius Dio remarked that Catiline 'gained a greater name than his deeds deserved, owing to the reputation of Cicero and the speeches he delivered against him' (37.42). Cicero's decision to sanction the death of Lentulus and his co-conspirators without affording them a trial, however, has long been a subject of criticism, because only a few years earlier, Cicero had prosecuted Verres for his actions in Sicily, making a great deal of the execution of Roman citizens without trial under Verres's governorship. Now Cicero had presided over exactly the same violation of Roman law. While some in the senate could point to the *senatus consultum ultimum* as justification for Cicero's actions, the need to kill Lentulus and the others was dubious, since they had already been captured and given up the conspiracy and its ringleader. Cicero's hypocrisy was, however, also as unexceptional as Catiline's violent conspiracy. The worst excesses of the Gracchan era, the proscriptions of Sulla, the actions of Marius, Cinna, and their allies, not to mention Pompey's own viciousness—all had normalised jettisoning the legal framework that sought to protect Roman citizens from their magistrates. Indeed, in his attack on Catiline, Cicero looked directly to the past for guidance, noting with approval the murder of Tiberius Gracchus by Scipio Nasica. In parts of the speech that followed, Cicero brought up Opimius, Gaius Gracchus, and Fulvius Flaccus, as well as the plebeian tribune Saturninus. There is little in Cicero's speeches to suggest that he viewed it as particularly scandalous to have the conspirators murdered. Perhaps the reason why the Catiline conspiracy continues to arouse controversy and debate is that the senate actually deliberated about whether or not they should kill Lentulus, rather than simply killing—as Sulla, Marius, and others had done before them. Cicero became a national hero for his murderous actions, and was fêted as *parens patriae*, 'father of the country'. In a letter written in January 62 BC, he pompously referred to himself as 'the preserver of the senate from massacre, of Rome from arson, of Italy from war' (*To Friends*, 2).

The First Triumvirate

In 63 BC, Julius Caesar had unexpectedly been elected *pontifex maximus* over the candidacy of Quintus Lutatius Catulus (consul in 78 BC). Caesar was 'perfectly ready to serve and flatter everybody,' wrote Cassius Dio, 'and shrank from no speech or action in order to get possession of the objects for which he strove' (37.37). Indeed, he had grown bolder in the way he presented himself to the public, setting up images of Marius one night, for example, on the Capitoline Hill. These, revealed in the light of the rising sun, drew scorn from Catulus and the senate, and accusations that Caesar was seeking to take over the government. The rising star of Roman politics also possessed a caustic wit. When one of his rivals was showing off facial scars that he claimed had been earned fighting with Caesar, the latter replied, 'You should never look back, when you are running away' (Quintilian, *Education of the Orator*, 6.3.75).

The following year, Caesar was praetor; he was then sent to Further Spain as its propraetorian governor. Suetonius (AD 69–122), biographer of Rome's emperors and leading men, wrote that while he was in Gades, Caesar fell under the spell of a statue of Alexander the Great in the temple where Hannibal had sacrificed before setting out on his epic journey to Italy. 'He heaved a sigh,' wrote Suetonius, 'as if out of impatience with his own incapacity in having as yet done nothing noteworthy at a time of life when Alexander had already brought the world to his feet.' Not long afterwards, however, he received a divine summons in his dreams that 'he was destined to rule the world' (*Julius Caesar*, 7). This was good news, since Caesar was heavily in debt after his spending spree to fund the public games while curule aedile, not to mention the equally massive amount he had spent bribing his way to the chief priesthood. Marcus Licinius Crassus was his main creditor, and he struggled to keep the others at bay while he campaigned in Spain; Plutarch reckoned his personal debt at a colossal 830 talents. Plutarch did note that Caesar's financial position improved measurably in the aftermath of his murderous campaigns against the Lusitanians, which had also made his soldiers wealthy. They saluted him as *imperator* in return (*Julius Caesar*, 11–12).

Caesar was not only in Spain admiring Alexander; he was also escaping a difficult domestic situation at home. In 62/61 BC, Rome had been rocked by a scandal involving Caesar's wife Pompeia, the granddaughter of Sulla, and Publius Clodius Pulcher. Clodius, who had been elected to the quaestorship, had slipped disguised as a flute player into the annual celebration of the Bona Dea ('the good goddess', associated with fertility), an all-female gathering from which men were barred. The celebration was held at the Regia, the seat of the *pontifex maximus*, and was thus under the guidance of Pompeia along with the Vestal Virgins. Clodius was apparently intent on seducing Pompeia—who was 'not unwilling', according to Plutarch (*Julius Caesar*, 9). When Caesar found out that Clodius had been caught in a place where his mere presence was enough to turn Rome's aristocracy on its head, he promptly divorced his wife.

The scandal also offered some tantalising legal opportunities. Lucullus seized the chance to gain revenge on Clodius for prosecuting him after his return from Asia, and duly accused him of incest with his sister, Clodia Pulchra—the wife of the future consul Quintus Caecilius Metellus Celer and granddaughter of Appius Claudius Pulcher, the father-in-law of Tiberius Gracchus. Lucullus rounded up witnesses ranging from slaves to Caesar's mother, Aurelia, who gave lurid testimony. Also at loggerheads with Clodius was Cicero, because Terentia, Cicero's wealthy wife, suspected that Clodia was secretly coveting her husband. During Clodius's trial, Cicero testified against him, declaring Clodius a liar when he avowed under oath that he had not been in Rome on the night of the Bona Dea festival. (This was clearly untrue, as he had been caught red-handed in the Regia.) Clodius was nevertheless acquitted. The jury, 'in order that they might neither risk their lives with the populace by condemning him, nor get a bad name among the nobility by acquitting him', scratched their ballots and there was no verdict (Plutarch, *Caesar*, 10). Clodius walked free. In a letter to Atticus, Cicero alleged that the jury had been bought. Some of its members, he said, were even provided with upper-class courtesans to sway their reluctant minds (*To Atticus*, 1.16).

As the dust from this scandal settled, Caesar returned in 60 BC to Rome, which was under the consulships of Pompey's loyal associate Afranius and the patrician Quintus Caecilius Metellus Celer. Caesar was determined to stand for the consulship, but he faced a dilemma. He was in the running for a triumph, which meant that he had to remain outside the city; however, to stand for office, he had to be *inside* the pomerium, which meant giving up the imperium that a triumphant general was required to possess. He could have one, but not the other: the triumph was close to assured, given the acclamations of his troops, but the consulship was a risky gamble. He tried to stand in absentia, but Cato the Younger, who was emerging as a stubborn guardian of the senatorial *mos maiorum*, insisted on the correct procedure. He judged that Caesar would take the triumph, but Caesar surprised everybody by opting to run for the consulship instead. In Rome, Caesar found a disgruntled Pompey, who was still waiting for his eastern conquests to be ratified by the senate and land granted for the settlement of his veterans. Pompey also wanted the consulship but, like Caesar, was opposed by Cato. Lucullus, Crassus, and Metellus Celer also voiced their concerns, and Pompey had learned that his name and reputation were less effective than when he had his legions backing his demands. Lucullus was particularly obstructive, insisting on a line-by-line examination of Pompey's eastern arrangements, while Metellus Celer had turned against Pompey when the latter divorced Celer's half-sister, Mucia Tertia. Pompey was also getting inadequate help from his protégé, Afranius. While a good general, Afranius 'understood how to dance better than to transact any business' (Cassius Dio, 37.49).

Caesar also discovered that Marcus Licinius Crassus was facing his own difficulties. Crassus was the patron of the *publicani* who held the current tax contract for Asia; they had not been able to extort as much as they had hoped, and their profits were imperilled. Unsurprisingly, the *optimates*, led by Cato and Metellus Celer, were fending off attempts to renegotiate their contract. Caesar immediately recognised that he, Pompey, and Crassus could help one another, and Caesar himself could benefit politically if he could bring about the reconciliation of Pompey with Crassus; the pair still harboured grudges against one another from the days of the Spartacan Revolt. 'He would master others at once through their friendship,' wrote Cassius Dio of Caesar's approach to Pompey and Crassus, 'and a little later master them through each other' (37.56). Plutarch considered that Caesar won Pompey and Crassus over by reminding them that if they failed, Cicero, Cato, and others would take their place (*Crassus*, 14).

The result of all these maneouvrings was that Caesar was elected as consul in 59 BC with the conservative Marcus Calpurnius Bibulus, Cato's son-in-law, as his colleague. Bibulus had bribed his way with the connivance of Cato and the senate, who wanted a moderating influence to keep an eye on Caesar. For his part, Caesar adopted a populist approach with a proposed land law that benefited Pompey and his veterans, as well as legislation that favoured Crassus and his *publicani*. Caesar's agrarian bill received only a tepid response in the senate, however, and was vigorously opposed by Cato. Bibulus took to announcing signs of divine displeasure whenever Caesar sought to move the matter forwards, in an attempt to cancel any and all public business. Eventually, a frustrated Caesar appeared before the *comitia tributa* with his new allies, Pompey even declaring armed support for Caesar if the need arose. Bibulus was smeared with human excrement and prevented from delivering his divine prognostications. 'The nobility were distressed,' wrote Plutarch, 'but the populace were delighted' (*Julius Caesar*, 14). Caesar's agrarian law benefiting war veterans was finally passed, and he even insisted, in a Marian throwback, that the senators should swear an oath to obey it. After this, Bibulus stayed home, although he and several plebeian tribunes continued to issue proclamations of heavenly disapproval, providing a conservative narrative that undercut the legality of Caesar's consulship. Local wits in Rome joked that this was not the consulship of Caesar and Bibulus, but 'the consulship of Julius and Caesar' (Suetonius, *Julius Caesar*, 20). Meanwhile, Caesar's subsequent legislation bypassed the senate entirely, supporting the insolvent *publicani* and confirming Pompey's arrangements in the east.

Cicero had watched as the association between Caesar, Pompey, and Crassus coalesced into what became known as 'the First Triumvirate'. Cicero had been asked to join, but decided against it; he was also suspected by some of being behind a fantastical plot to have both Pompey and Caesar killed, but the proof died with the would-be assassin in the

Tullianum (another Roman citizen, killed without trial). Cato had also been approached by Pompey, who sought to bind him to Pompey's favour through a marriage alliance, but Cato saw through the ruse and spurned the offer. Instead, Pompey cemented his pact with Caesar by marrying Julia, Caesar's daughter by Cornelia. The union was reportedly a happy one, with the much older Pompey devoted to his young wife. Further support for Caesar and his allies emerged in the unlikely shape of Clodius, who managed his transfer from patrician to plebeian blood with the help of Pompey (as augur) and Caesar (as *pontifex maximus*) after Cicero attacked the triumvirate in a speech. With his new status, Clodius immediately ran for the plebeian tribunate and was elected in 58 BC. He pursued a legal agenda that appealed to the people, who would now receive a free grant of grain every month and have their *collegia* restored.

Clodius's main target was Cicero: he deviously proposed a law that would exile a magistrate who had ordered a citizen executed without a trial, a clear reference to the controversial outcome of the Catiline conspiracy. Clodius also disliked Cato the Younger, who looked askance at the tribune's escapades. Cato was removed from Rome when Clodius arranged for him to be sent to Cyprus, which was in the process of being annexed to the new Roman province of Cilicia as a way to fund the free grain allotments. With Caesar's approval, Clodius then banished Cicero, allowing his house on the Palatine to be looted and destroyed. Ever the opportunist, he replaced it with a shrine to Libertas—freedom. Cicero fled Rome for Sicily and then Macedonia, fearing for his life. He had emerged as one of the main critics of the triumvirate, and had written to Atticus in July 59 BC, describing it as a regime that was 'the most infamous, disgraceful, and uniformly odious to all sorts and classes and ages of men that ever was' (*To Atticus*, 2.19).

Through his plebeian tribune ally Publius Vatinius, Caesar had already been named to a five-year governorship in Cisalpine Gaul and Illyria, places that were 'the most likely to enrich him and furnish suitable material for triumphs' (Suetonius, *Julius Caesar*, 22). The lengthy governorship would also shield him from his political enemies, who were drawing up lawsuits with which to attack him for his behaviour during his consulship. When the governor of Transalpine Gaul died, Pompey, together with Caesar's new father-in-law, Lucius Calpurnius Piso Caesoninus (Caesar had married Calpurnia after divorcing Pompeia), persuaded the people to add that province to his command. In 58 BC, Piso was elected consul alongside Gabinius, who had earlier endorsed Pompey for the anti-piracy operation (Chapter 6). Caesar quickly left Rome to address the growing threat posed by the Helvetii, groups of whom were moving towards the valley of the river Rhône and seeking land on which to settle under their leader, Orgetorix. To some, this migration conjured unpleasant and fearful memories of the Cimbri and Teutones during the time of Marius, not to mention the long-ago invasions of Italy by the Gauls; Caesar was more than ready to capitalise on these anxieties and saw an opportunity to put his army to work. His force was a large one, made up of a number of legions including VII, VIII, IX, and X, as well as the newly raised XI and XII. Without seeking permission, he took his troops out of Transalpine Gaul, violating the law against this very thing resuscitated by Sulla, and with an extremely capable set of subordinate legates commanding the legions on the battlefield, won a decisive victory over the Helvetii at Bibracte (Figure 7.1).

Caesar's own account of his campaigns, the *Commentaries* (known more commonly as the *Gallic Wars*), is a remarkable survival from antiquity. The war diaries or memoirs of Pyrrhus and other generals have, in contrast, been lost; we are fortunate to have all eight chapters

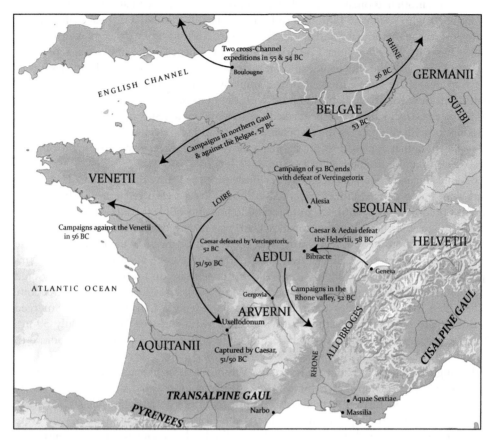

Figure 7.1 Caesar's Gallic Wars, 58–50 BC.

Source: Illustration by the author.

of the *Gallic Wars*, written in the aftermath of each campaigning season, although the final chapter was completed by Aulus Hirtius, one of Caesar's senior commanders. Caesar's work is also one of the first full texts encountered by students of Latin. This is because—despite his disconcerting habit of referring to himself in the third person—he wrote in a manner that was 'plain, correct, and graceful' (Cicero, *Brutus*, 262). Like Sulla's memoirs, Caesar's text was intended as a form of propaganda, highlighting his achievements and those of his men, and largely suppressed the shocking levels of violence, rape, and pillage, and the wanton and merciless destruction of entire communities. We read in the second chapter, for instance, of the fearsome reputation of the Helvetii and their immense prestige, forged in the cauldron of battle, that required a swift and violent response. How much of a threat the Helvetii actually posed is debatable, but Caesar portrayed the situation as an emergency that compelled him to march from Rome to Geneva at breakneck speed, desperately raising levies along the way (the XI and XII, above) to forestall the imminent collapse of civilisation.

The 'barbarians' were also not as barbaric as Caesar would like his readers to believe. Many of the tribal groups living in Gaul were known to the Romans as neighbours, trading partners, and allies. The territory of the Allobroges straddled the north-eastern boundaries of Transalpine Gaul. Both the Aedui and the Arverni, whose territory lay adjacent to Transalpine Gaul, were friendly to Rome, and Ariovistus, king of the Suebi, was also on friendly terms with the Roman senate. None of this mattered. 'He did not let slip any pretext for war,' wrote Suetonius, 'however unjust and dangerous it might be, picking quarrels with allied, as well as with hostile and barbarous nations' (*Caesar*, 24). Delegations from the Aedui soon called on Caesar to help stave off Ariovistus, with dramatic doom-laden prophecies of a Germanic takeover in eastern Gaul. The delegates declared Ariovistus to be 'an arrogant and cruel tyrant'; they could not, they said, deal with him any longer. According to Caesar, the delegates lay prostrate and crying on the ground, begging him for help. Presented with such a request, the rest followed a predictable and violent pattern. Ariovistus, summoned to a conference with Caesar, made a reply that Caesar chose to interpret as arrogant, thereby providing a pretext for war on the spurious basis that the king had 'insulted all the Romans' (Cassius Dio, 38.34). The result was yet another victory for Caesar, who was rapidly making his mark as a general whose astute mastery of battlefield tactics, along with a facility for elaborate engineering and fortification works, were proving to be the decisive factors. He was no less shrewd in his management of plunder, carefully hoarding it and distributing it to his men as rewards for gallantry and bravery.

While Caesar was fighting in Gaul, the famous poet Catullus (c. 85–54 BC) had joined those taking aim at his excesses, particularly his sexual escapades. Catullus was a member of the so-called 'New Poets', aristocratic intellectuals influenced by Greek Lyric poetry. (This group included a female poet, Cornificia, but her work has not survived). In one memorable poem (57), Catullus labelled Caesar and Mumurra, his chief engineer, 'A peerless pair of brazen buggers, each as voraciously adulterous as the other.' Caesar was also widely believed to have had an affair with king Nicomedes IV of Bithynia, something that he denied repeatedly until his death. Catullus was hardly free from scandal: he was the lover for a time of Clodia Pulchra, the 'Lesbia' who appears in so many of his poems—some tender and loving, others that shock, viciously and pornographically dragging the reader through their horrific breakup.

With Catullus skewering Caesar in verse, Clodius was taking aim at Pompey. Temporarily removing himself from public view for his own safety, Pompey responded through two friendly plebeian tribunes, Titus Annius Milo and Publius Sestius, who recruited a private army through the *collegia* to battle Clodius and the urban poor who had flocked to his standard. As these two proxy forces battled for control of the streets of Rome, and Clodius ran for the aedileship in order to hold an elected office and thus avoid being prosecuted, Pompey proposed a bill that would lift Cicero's exile and bring him home. Despite determined opposition from Clodius, the bill passed. A grateful Cicero, returning after 18 months, persuaded the senate to reward Pompey with what he thought would be an easy way to enhance his reputation—the management of the city's grain supply, the beneficiaries of whom were overwhelmingly those who otherwise supported Clodius. The job came with a level of imperium equal to that of Caesar in Gaul. Plutarch suggested cynically that there was no need for any 'management' of the grain supply. Instead, he hinted that an artificial shortage had been created in order to benefit Pompey (*Pompey*, 49).

In 56 BC, as Caesar's armies notched up success after success in Gaul—and the senate granted 15 days of thanksgiving for his victories—Pompey was coming under increasing pressure. The two consuls for that year were Gnaeus Cornelius Lentulus Marcellinus, grandson of Scipio Nasica, and Lucius Marcius Philippus, whose stepson (born in 63 BC) was Octavius, the future emperor Augustus. Neither of the consuls was well disposed towards the triumvirate and pursued legislation that sought to curb its powers. Clodius had succeeded in obtaining the aedileship and, without a shred of irony, pursued Milo in the courts for keeping an armed gang. A distraction emerged when, after an affair with Catullus's friend Marcus Caelius Rufus, Clodia Pulchra prosecuted Caelius, alleging that he had tried to poison her. The trial was sensational: Caelius was defended by Cicero and acquitted, which only intensified Cicero's rivalry with Clodius. Meanwhile, Clodius himself was berating Pompey on a near daily basis. One of his favourite tricks was to pause while making a speech and call out, 'Who was it that did or said so-and so?'—to which the rousing answer from his supporters was always 'Pompey!' (Cassius Dio, 39.19). Pompey had also been harmed by the arrival in Italy of the unsavory Ptolemy XII Auletes ('flute player', but also known to Egyptians as 'the bastard'), who had arrived with a young Cleopatra in tow seeking the restitution of his kingdom, which he had lost to his eldest daughter Berenice in a civil dispute. Pompey was receptive to Ptolemy's concerns, but the senate, after consulting the *Sibylline Books*, was not swayed by his requests; in the end, Ptolemy spent three years exiled in Rome before bribing Gabinius with the colossal sum of 10,000 talents to invade Egypt on his behalf.

Another obstacle to the triumvirate was materialising in the shape of Lucius Domitius Ahenobarbus, who was campaigning for the consulship on the platform of recalling Caesar from Gaul. While Pompey and Caesar might stand to gain from each other's weakness, and Cicero appeared to be playing both sides against the middle, the parties agreed to meet in 56 BC at Luca and Ravenna in Cisalpine Gaul. Crassus was of particular concern to Caesar, as he had become close to Pompey and both men were openly vying for the consulship. Appius Claudius Pulcher, the senior member of the Claudii Pulchri, agreed to rein in his brother, Clodius, who now threw his weight behind Pompey. Cicero was also neutered by this set of meetings, becoming Caesar's leading champion. Cato, who was best positioned to attack the triumvirs, was away in Cyprus. The most important outcome of these meetings, however, was the arrangement benefiting the triumvirs themselves. In a violent election campaign that intimidated Ahenobarbus, Pompey and Crassus ran virtually unopposed and became the consuls for 55 BC. Each of the triumvirs was also 'granted' a five-year proconsular command, which would begin in 54 BC. Caesar, who scented further opportunities for glory and personal enrichment in Gaul, took an extension to his existing extraordinary governorship, although the law granting him an extra five years was so opaquely worded that it was never clear whether Caesar's command would end in 50 or 49 BC. Pompey received Spain, and Crassus, who wanted a military triumph that would surpass anything that Pompey or Caesar could achieve, decided on Syria, his eyes set firmly on the Parthian kingdom. He was well aware that despite his fantastic wealth, he had yet to earn a major triumph; Syria would, he hoped, change all that. Pompey opted to remain in Rome and sent subordinates to Spain in his place. In the city, he oversaw the completion of his immense theatre complex, which was finished in 55 BC. It had been inspired, Plutarch wrote, by a visit to Mytilene after his victory over Mithridates. At its opening, Pompey—who always had a flair for violence, the more cruel and exotic

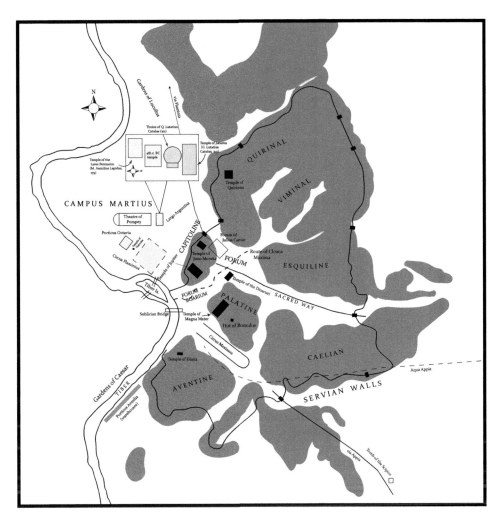

Figure 7.2 Rome's topography and principal architectural features in the mid-first century BC.

Source: Illustration by the author.

the better—held extravagant games that included 'combats of wild beasts in which five hundred lions were killed, and above all, an elephant fight, a most terrifying spectacle' (*Pompey*, 52). He also installed a gigantic nude statue of himself within the theatre. Caesar, too, was making his mark in Rome with a new forum that began construction in 54 BC. It included a Temple of Venus Genetrix ('Ancestor'), publicly endorsing Caesar's claims to divine descent (Figure 7.2).

As Crassus departed for the east, encouraged by letters and reinforcements from Caesar and dreaming of an easy victory, the consular elections for 54 BC resulted in the appointment of Appius Claudius Pulcher and Lucius Domitius Ahenobarbus. The former defended the triumvirs, while the latter, along with Cato the Younger who was now

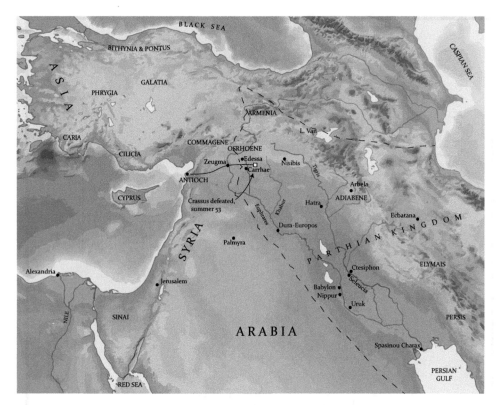

Figure 7.3 The Parthian campaign of Crassus, 54–53 BC. The dotted lines represent the approximate limits of the Parthian kingdom.

Source: Illustration by the author.

back in Rome as praetor, attacked them. Crassus meanwhile crossed the Euphrates with a colossal army of seven legions, some raised at his own expense, with which he was determined to sack the Parthian capital at Seleucia-Ctesiphon. A low-level conflict had been simmering with the Parthians under Gabinius, who had blundered into a Parthian succession dispute, but this was now far more serious and, in fact, an unprovoked act of war: Cassius Dio remarked that Crassus 'had no complaint to bring against [the Parthians] nor had the war been assigned to him; but he heard that they were exceedingly wealthy and expected that Orodes [II, king 57–37 BC] would be easy to capture, because he was but newly established' (40.12). Crassus wintered in Syria as he waited for reinforcements and his son to join him from Gaul. In the spring, a message arrived from Orodes in which he revealed that he knew full well that Crassus had come for personal gain and under no sanction from the senate. Crassus contemptuously replied that he would give Orodes his answer in Seleucia, the part of Seleucia-Ctesiphon that lay on the right bank of the river Tigris in Iraq (Figure 7.3).

The Parthians dispatched their capable general Surena to meet Crassus at Carrhae (Harran, in Turkey), in 53 BC. The Roman march had been long and difficult. Crassus was led by his guide, Ariamnes, through the desert wastes of Mesopotamia, while Ariamnes tormented the Roman troops by reminding them of troughs awash with Campanian wines and bottomless fountains in the shade of broad, cool trees. Ariamnes was on the Parthian payroll and he was guiding Crassus to his doom. Crassus pressed on despite unfavourable auspices and disquiet voiced by his quaestor, Gaius Cassius Longinus, one of Caesar's future assassins. The climactic engagement at Carrhae has become famous for the skill of the Parthian mounted archers, whose 'Parthian shot'—firing rapidly backwards while riding away—caused grievous casualties amongst the Roman infantry. Crassus's son, Publius, who had fought with Caesar in Gaul, was killed early in the battle. Charges from armoured cavalry known as cataphracts further weakened Roman resistance. Surena offered peace terms, and Crassus, 'at the extremity of fear', agreed to meet with him, but he was killed in a scuffle that followed. Lurid reports that found their way into the text of Cassius Dio alleged that the Parthians poured molten gold into Crassus's mouth, mocking his wealth (40.26). A large part of the Roman army escaped to Syria under the command of Cassius, who then staved off a Parthian incursion led by an enraged Orodes. Despite this minor success, Carrhae was a humiliating defeat for Rome, with numerous legionary standards captured and thousands of prisoners deported to Alexandria Margiana (Merv, in Turkmenistan). None would return from their captivity. Surena, meanwhile, sent Crassus's severed head to Orodes, who was in Armenia; later, Surena fell out with the king and was murdered. Like the Spartan mercenary Xanthippus (Chapter 3), he had become too successful for his own good. Crassus was survived by his wife, Caecilia Metella, whose imposing tomb still stands just south of Rome on the via Appia.

Crassus's defeat was mirrored in reverse by the extraordinarily violent and self-serving campaigns of Caesar in Gaul. Caesar had been busy, responding to numerous requests for help from beleaguered Gallic chieftains, righting various things he deemed to be wrong, and punishing human-sacrificing vagabonds. He also raised new legions, the XIII and XIV, giving him an almost unmatched superiority on the battlefield. Caesar and his troops committed horrific war crimes in Gaul, such as the massacre of women and children in 55 BC that he describes in gory detail in Chapter IV of the *Gallic Wars*. Some one million inhabitants of Gaul are thought to have been murdered and another million sold into slavery—all on the altar of Caesar's untrammelled ambition. In the same year, Caesar crossed the Rhine in yet another blatantly self-serving expedition, which nevertheless became famous for the engineering proficiency displayed by his men in bridging the river. He then followed up his suppression of the people of Armorica (Brittany) by staging a cross-Channel assault from Portius Itius (Boulogne) that landed in southern Britain. Part of the rationale for the British expeditions, besides glory and plunder, was that during his Gallic campaigns, Caesar had defeated the Belgic tribe of the Atrebates, whose territory lay in the region of Portus Itius. Caesar appointed a certain Commius as their king, and invited him to join his expedition in order to ease negotiations with the British tribes, many of which had close associations with those in Gaul: there was a group of Atrebates, for instance, in southern Britain. In 55 BC, Commius assisted Caesar with a small military detachment, but failed to win over the British tribes. Commius had better luck in 54 BC, when Caesar returned to Britain with a fleet of 800 ships. With Commius's diplomatic assistance, Caesar accepted the surrender of a coalition of tribes under the British king Cassivellaunus, and the British communities provided political hostages and agreed to pay tribute to Rome. These cross-Channel raids naturally provided propaganda coups for

Caesar, who had surpassed anything Pompey or Crassus had achieved by traversing the 'Ocean', as the Channel was known, quite literally breaking new ground in the process. 'The formerly unknown had become certain,' gushed Cassius Dio, 'and the previously unheard-of accessible' (39.53). Plutarch was no less fulsome: Britain was a *terra incognita*, a land that for some in Rome 'never had existed and did not then exist', a place of exotic fancy into which Caesar 'carried the Roman supremacy' (*Caesar*, 23). It would be nearly a century, however, before the emperor Claudius, in search of a military victory to offset his bookish, scholarly character, invaded Britain and permanently added it to the Roman empire.

Caesar was now a rich man—the debt problems that had plagued him in Spain and in Rome were decisively solved. His soldiers, too, had been made rich beyond their dreams and idolised him. He sent plunder back to Rome regularly, where it found its way into the pockets of aediles, quaestors, consuls, senators, private citizens—all a growing clientele of Rome's man of the moment. A gambler, Caesar nearly lost it all in 54 BC when a revolt erupted in northern Gaul under the leadership of a man named Ambiorix. After the destruction of one of his legions, XIV, Cicero's brother, Quintus, in command of a Roman force in what is now modern Belgium, was saved at the eleventh hour by a desperate rescue mission. The XIV legion was replaced with a new levy, confusingly given the same number; Caesar then borrowed another legion, I, from Pompey, and levied two more, XV and VI, to bring Caesar's army up to 11 legions—over 50,000 men at full strength. A more serious rebellion took place in 52 BC under the leadership of Vercingetorix, king of the Arverni. Vercingetorix proved to be the most capable of Caesar's opponents, burning fields and destroying stores, and inflicting a stinging defeat on him at Gergovia. This battle showed that Caesar could indeed be beaten, and it is sometimes thought that only good fortune spared him from the catastrophe that had befallen Crassus in the east. Certainly Gergovia, which cost Caesar 46 centurions alone, emboldened the Aedui, who abrogated their alliance with the Romans; Commius, Caesar's erstwhile ally, also defected. In September of 52 BC, Caesar laid siege to Vercingetorix at Alesia in eastern Gaul. Caesar constructed a complete circumvallation, studded with watchtowers and military camps. As a Gallic relief force approached, intending to relieve the besieged defenders of Alesia, Caesar built a further line of obstacles and fortifications consisting of water-filled trenches, iron caltrops, and punji traps comprising ditches covered in grass and branches, beneath which lay fire-hardened, sharpened wooden stakes. Finally, he constructed another set of walls behind which he and his troops could shelter if they came under siege. Legionary artillery in the shape of *ballistae*, stone-throwing catapults, and scorpions, which fired large metal arrows, gave Caesar considerable firepower. This engineering excellence was a continuation of the pioneering efforts of Scipio Aemilianus and Sulla, and it proved to be decisive in the Roman victory; even when the Gallic relief force arrived, they could do little to wear down the Romans, and Vercingetorix gave himself up (Figure 7.4). In a glittering triumph, that was superbly recreated in HBO's series *Rome*, Vercingetorix was paraded in front of a victorious Caesar, his men, and the people of Rome, before being murdered in the Tullianum. Vercingetorix has long been remembered as a Gallic hero, and is today commemorated by a massive statue at the site of Alesia (Figure 7.5).

At its height, Caesar's army comprised 12 legions. While he recruited in his province, as was his right as a proconsul, he freely recruited non-citizens from north of the Po. The non-citizen force raised in Transalpine Gaul in 52 BC became the famous V Alaudae, or

Figure 7.4 Silver denarius minted at Rome in 48 BC by the moneyer Lucius Hostilius Saserna. Obverse: a long-haired Gallic captive, sometimes thought to be an idealised representation of Vercingetorix; reverse: two Gallic warriors driving a chariot of the sort described by Caesar in his *Gallic Wars*.

'Larks', whose name referred to the bird's crest that topped their helmet, a native Gallic custom. Some of the legions were paid for and equipped by the state, while the rest Caesar funded from plunder, booty, and his own deep pockets. Other non-citizens played valuable roles in Caesar's army, including Gallic and Germanic horseman. In the Gallic campaigns, Caesar 'had practised his troops and increased his fame' (Plutarch, *Caesar*, 28). Crassus was dead. It was only a matter of time before Pompey and Caesar came to blows.

Civil war

In Rome, Julia had tragically died in childbirth in 54 BC; the child also died, and both Pompey and Caesar were consumed with grief. The city was in a state of electoral chaos, with rampant bribery and corruption causing repeated delays to the election calendar. The death of Crassus was also a destabilising influence, because it meant that the trium-virate was now down to two men: it was essential for Caesar and Pompey to maintain cordial relations. Caesar therefore proposed that Pompey marry his great-niece, Octavia the Younger, the sister of Octavius and wife, at the time, of Gaius Claudius Marcellus, a distant descendant of Marcus Claudius Marcellus, the conqueror of Syracuse during the Hannibalic War. Caesar also suggested that he would divorce his wife, Calpurnia, and marry Pompey's daughter, Pompeia, who was married at the time to Faustus Sulla, the only son of the famous dictator. This complex proposal fell apart. Instead, Pompey focused on the situation in Rome. The elections of 52 BC were, like those of 53 BC, delayed. The roster made grim reading: Milo, Pompey's enforcer, fancied a chance at the consulship. The choice of the *optimates*, Milo was supported by the Cato the Younger and the ever-opportunistic Cicero, although another blue-blooded candidate emerged in the shape of Quintus Caecilius Metellus Pius Scipio Nasica (henceforth 'Metellus Scipio'). This man, born Publius Cornelius Scipio, had been adopted into the Caecilii Metelli through Metellus Pius, the son of the former patron of Marius. Also on the roster was Clodius,

Figure 7.5 The statue of Vercingetorix at Alesia, modern Alise-Sainte-Reine. The statue was commissioned by Napoleon III and designed by Millet Aimé; it was constructed in 1865.

Source: Photograph by Myrabella (CC BY-SA 4.0).

running for praetor. Milo resurrected his gang of thugs and sparred with Clodius, and Rome again descended into violence, which culminated in the murder of Clodius on the via Appia in January 52 BC.

Clodius' supporters seized his body and set the senate house on fire, a fitting funeral pyre for their beloved champion. In desperation, the senate mooted a proposal to appoint Pompey as dictator, but the recent memory of Sulla made such a move unsavoury and nothing came of it. Instead, Cato persuaded the senate to install Pompey as a solitary consul—what he considered to be 'a more legal monarchy' than a Sullan dictatorship, although later Metellus Scipio joined him (Plutarch, *Julius Caesar*, 28). Many of the malefactors, including Milo and numerous supporters of Clodius, were tried and convicted. Abandoned by Pompey, Milo was exiled to Massilia, an increasingly popular choice for Rome's unwanted. Having spurned Caesar's offer of Octavia the Younger, Pompey now married Cornelia Metella, the daughter of Metellus Scipio and former wife of Crassus's son Publius, who had been killed fighting at Carrhae. The consular elections were quiet in 51 BC, to the relief of all: Cato ran, but lost to Marcus Claudius Marcellus, a fervent opponent of Caesar. (Marcus Claudius Marcellus was the cousin of Gaius Claudius Marcellus, the husband of Caesar's great-niece Octavia, mentioned earlier; Gaius would be consul in 50 BC). Marcus Marcellus attacked Caesar, and despite resistance from his consular colleague Servius Sulpicius Rufus, he managed to pass a motion that the fate of the Gallic provinces—and thus Caesar's command—would be addressed a year later, in 50 BC. Cicero, meanwhile, had left the cauldron of Roman politics to govern Cilicia, which he did with self-restraint and admirable transparency. He could hardly have done it otherwise, given his prosecution of Verres and his public stance on corruption. In the summer of 50 BC, he returned to Rome, happy to be shorn of the burden of governing, about which he had complained bitterly in his letters to Atticus.

The consuls for 50 BC were Lucius Aemilius Lepidus Paullus, who had been thoroughly bribed with 15,000 talents by Caesar, and Gaius Claudius Marcellus, the husband of Caesar's great-niece, Octavia, and cousin of Marcus Claudius Marcellus (consul in 51 BC). Cato and Gaius Marcellus sought to end Caesar's extraordinary proconsular command and bring him back to Rome to face prosecution. In public, Pompey still supported Caesar: he amended a law requiring candidates for office to be present in Rome, allowing Caesar to stand for the consulship in absentia, thus keeping Caesar in his command outside the pomerium and invested with the proconsular imperium that would shield him from prosecution. In private, however, Pompey was become more closely identified with Caesar's enemies in the senate, who scented victory now that Caesar 'had no longer any plausible excuse for not disbanding his troops and returning to private life' (Cassius Dio, 44). Caesar, like Sulla and Marius before him, knew that his power increasingly rested on his army, and he was as determined to keep his army as his enemies were to take it away from him and force him into private life, where he could impeached. Cato, said Suetonius, was to be first in an exceedingly long line of people eager for a legal reckoning with Caesar (*Julius Caesar*, 30).

On January 1, 49 BC, Caesar's friend Scribonius Curio—whom Caesar had reportedly freed from crushing personal debts—read a letter from Caesar suggesting that both he and Pompey lay down their imperium. With neither willing to take the first move, the senate debated the issue and agreed that Caesar should step down. A motion that Pompey should follow suit failed to reach an agreement, but it was clear that the choice was soon going to be war between Caesar and Pompey if peace could not be reached. Cato continued to rail against Caesar in the senate, fully aware of the danger he posed. 'Assailing Caesar's plans from the outset and revealing clearly to all his purpose,' wrote Plutarch, 'he declared that it was not the sons of Germans or Celts whom they must fear, but Caesar himself'; later, Cato warned that Caesar would give up diplomacy and resort to war, 'using the forces which he got by deceiving and cheating the state' (*Cato the Younger*, 51). In late December, Cicero had written to Atticus, relating a long afternoon that he had spent talking with Pompey. 'The answer to your question about whether there is any hope of a pacification,' he wrote, 'is that there isn't even the desire for one' (*To Atticus*, 7.8).

Cicero and Cato were both proved right. A young plebeian tribune named Marc Antony, Caesar's relative, ally, and future lover of Cleopatra, vetoed a senatorial proposal put forward by Metellus Scipio that would have declared Caesar a public enemy. Antony—whose grandfather had been murdered by Marius—was also in Caesar's pocket, having run up an astonishing 250 talents' worth of debt through his drunken gambling with Curio. Antony was despised by Pompey, who derided him as a 'feckless nobody' (Cicero, *To Atticus*, 7.8). Further attempts at compromise were made, and Caesar softened his demands. He would be happy, he said through his tribunes, with just two legions and Cisalpine Gaul to be left with him, while he ran for the consulship. Pompey refused, well aware of the danger posed by Caesar's army. The two consuls for 49 BC, Lucius Cornelius Lentulus Crus and Gaius Claudius Marcellus (the brother of Marcus Claudius Marcellus, consul in 51 BC, not to be confused with the consul of 50 BC), invoked the *senatus consultum ultimum*. With this development, Antony and Curio left Rome on January 7, fearing for their safety as it became clear that civil war could not be avoided. Caesar and one of his legions, XIII, crossed the river Rubicon on January 10, which marked the boundary of the province of Cisalpine Gaul. By doing so, he violated Sulla's law on treason, temporarily ceding the moral advantage to those who supported Pompey. Caesar, fully aware of what he was doing, may indeed have muttered the three words that have gone down in history as the mark of an irrevocable act: *alea iacta est*—'the die is cast' (Plutarch, *Caesar*, 32). 'Even yet we may draw back,' Suetonius had Caesar gravely state, 'but once across this bridge, and the whole issue is with the sword' (*Caesar*, 31).

The sense of drama provided by Plutarch and Suetonius is completely missing from Caesar's own account, the *Civil War*. Like his account of the Gallic campaigns, this text—begun by Caesar, but completed by others—very much related his own perspective and was intended as justification for his actions. Here Pompey is the primary cause of the war because he 'was reluctant to let anyone stand on the same pinnacle of prestige as himself' (*Civil War*, 1.5). This may have been true, but more incisively, Caesar recorded a speech that he made to his troops, attacking Pompey for his 'jealous belittling of his merits'. Caesar carried on by reminding his legionnaires of their nine years of service together, their shared privations and glittering successes that had done so much to benefit the Roman state. 'Now,' he finished, 'I ask you to defend my reputation and standing against the assaults of my enemies' (1.7). From Caesar's perspective, he was not rebelling against the Republic, nor did he have any interest in destroying it. Pompey and his allies had attacked his *virtus* and his dignity as a man who had enriched the state, extended its boundaries, and showered himself and his troops with *gloria*. Caesar's troops were more than willing to follow him; he could represent as well as any other the claim to defend the Republic. Besides, he had doubled their pay, and they would surely triumph under the leadership of their talented and beloved general. Despite the self-serving nature of the *Civil War*, it is here that we find the most compelling reasons for Caesar's actions. He had reached the pinnacle of Roman political life, only to be attacked by jealous enemies. If the situation were reversed, he must have reasoned, Pompey would surely have followed the same course of action.

Given the disposition of the two men and their associates—one on the outside with an army raised in the provinces, the other in Rome with the backing of the consuls—it was inevitable that Pompey would resemble the senate's champion. In reality, there was no truly pro- or anti-senatorial side. There were now only Pompeians and Caesarians, although even this demarcation was artificial since both Pompey and Caesar strived for the same supremacy. Pompey had already decided not to contest the issue in Italy and left Rome immediately, embarking his troops at Brundisium and crossing the Adriatic to Greece, where he intended to raise an army to fight Caesar. Meanwhile he placed his faith in his Spanish army, which would either buy him time or destroy Caesar while he prepared. Cicero had also left Rome, writing tenderly to his family and advising them to stick close to Publius Cornelius Dolabella, who had married Cicero's daughter Tullia in 50 BC. Cicero continued to exchange letters with Pompey, who he ostensibly supported in recognition of Pompey's role in ending his exile. One letter from Pompey written in February of 49 BC urged Cicero to join him, and asserted the legality and the righteousness of his cause: the senate and both consuls were on his side, he claimed, and Cicero could play a role in saving the Republic now as he had once before from Catiline. Meanwhile, Cicero wrote repeatedly to Atticus, asking his advice on what to do. It was clear to Cicero that duty demanded he remain with Pompey, rather than with Caesar, whose offers of friendship were fickle at best. On the other hand, it was equally clear to Cicero that Pompey was the principal architect of Caesar's position. He had presided over 'his building up and aggrandizing and arming Caesar against the state, his backing the violent and unconstitutional passage of Caesar's laws, his addition of Transalpine Gaul to Caesar's command, his marriage to Caesar's daughter, his appearance as augur at Clodius's adoption, his greater concern for my restoration than for the prevention of my banishment, his prolongation of Caesar's tenure, his consistent support during Caesar's absence' (*To Atticus*, 8.3). Just a few days later, Cicero fumed again to Atticus that 'Pompey cherished Caesar, suddenly became afraid of him, refused all peace terms, failed to prepare for war, evacuated Rome, culpably lost Picenum, got himself tied up in Apulia, and then went off to Greece without getting in touch with us or letting us know anything about his unprecedented plan on which so much depended' (*To Atticus*, 8.8).

Cicero's mind was finally made up by Caesar, who moved quickly: at Corfinium, Pompey's associate, Lucius Domitius Ahenobarbus, was forced to surrender his three legions to Caesar. Instead of massacring the soldiers or taking revenge, as Sulla might have done, Caesar treated them with *clementia*—clemency. Caesar now behaved in almost the opposite way to that which everyone expected and in the process created a powerful propaganda victory. Not long afterwards, a copy of a letter written by Caesar to Gaius Oppius and Cornelius Balbus, friends of Atticus and Cicero and confidants of Caesar, was forwarded to Cicero. In the letter, Caesar declared his willingness to reconcile with Pompey, his determination to avoid the precedent set by Sulla, and his intention to follow 'a new kind of conquest, to make mercy and generosity our shield' (*To Atticus*, 9.7C).

Cicero tried to position himself as a mediator between Caesar and Pompey, but the gulf between the two was already too great. In April of 49 BC, Caesar wrote to Cicero, warning him to stay out of the looming conflict, but in June Cicero left Italy and joined Pompey and his allies Metellus Scipio and Cato the Younger at Dyrrachium (Epidamnus) in Illyria. Pompey resisted Caesar's peace overtures, pointing out that Caesar was legally in the wrong for leaving his province under arms, while Pompey had the support of the consuls. As Pompey raised an army across the Adriatic, Caesar executed a lightning campaign directed against Petreius and Afranius, in command of Pompey's armies in Spain. On the way, he had besieged Massilia, which had revolted against him under the leadership of Ahenobarbus, who he had released after the debacle at Corfinium. (Ahenobarbus escaped and joined Pompey in the east). Afterwards, at Ilerda, Caesar defeated his opponents and absorbed the beaten legionnaires into his army by offering clemency and forgiveness.

Figure 7.6 Silver denarius of Caesar from a mint travelling with his army in the summer of 49 BC. Obverse: elephant trampling a serpent; reverse: symbols of the priesthood.

Petreius and Afranius fled to Pompey in the east. The scholar Terentius Varro, who had sided with Pompey, joined Caesar. Minting coins on the move to pay his soldiers (Figure 7.6), Caesar returned unopposed to Rome and was appointed dictator with Marc Antony as his master of horse. One of his first actions was to give citizenship to the people living north of the Po—a district from which many of his soldiers had been recruited.

Through the dictatorship, Caesar arranged his election to the consulship of 48 BC alongside his friend and client Publius Servilius Vatia Isauricus. In the same year, Caesar was beaten by Pompey at Dyrrachium, only to win a crushing victory at Pharsalus in Thessaly in the late summer in which Antony distinguished himself (Figure 7.7). Pompey did not need to fight, but was pushed into premature action by his associates, who had been complaining that he was needlessly prolonging the conflict.

Pompey's army fell apart under Caesar's assault and he was forced to flee to Pelusium in Egypt, where he hoped to find help from Ptolemy XIII, the son of Pompey's some-time friend Ptolemy XII. A civil war was developing between Cleopatra and Ptolemy XIII, however, and the king's advisers considered Pompey to be too much of a liability. Instead, they preferred to ingratiate themselves with Caesar. As he landed, Pompey was murdered in the surf by one of his former soldiers. 'Do I not know you, comrade?' Pompey asked, before turning his head and submitting to the inevitable (Appian, *Civil Wars*, 2.84). His wife Cornelia looked on, horrified. Lentulus Crus, the consul for 49 BC who had fought with Pompey at Pharsalus, was taken captive not long afterwards and perished, forgotten, in an Egyptian prison. The beaten troops from Pharsalus were offered *clementia* and absorbed into four legions, perhaps XXXIV, XXXV, XXXVI, and XXXVII. Afterwards, while settling the conflict between Cleopatra and Ptolemy XIII, Caesar famously fell in love with Cleopatra, who bore him a son, Caesarion—'little Caesar'—in June 47 BC.

Pompey's head was cut off and sent to Caesar, while his body was recovered and returned to Italy for burial by Cornelia. (There was also a tomb of Pompey at Pelusium in Egypt, which became something of a tourist attraction in later years.) Caesar was pained by Pompey's end, and he tracked down the assassins and later had them executed. Caesar was even more pained by his victory at Pharsalus. Gaius Asinius Pollio, art-collector, historian,

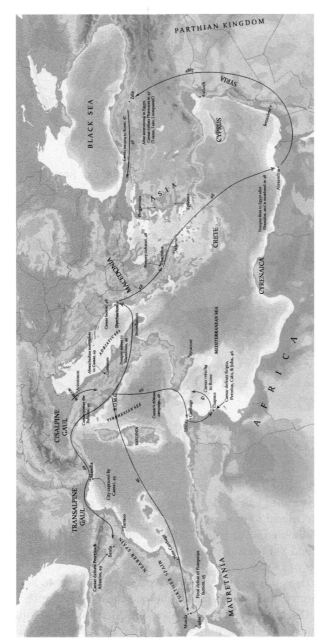

Figure 7.7 The conflict between Caesar and Pompey, 49–45 BC.

Source: Illustration by the author.

Figure 7.8 Silver denarius minted at Utica in **46** BC. Obverse: bust of Roma right, M. CATO PRO
PR[aetor]; reverse: Victory seated.

Figure 7.9 Silver denarius from a military mint travelling with Scipio. Obverse: head of Jupiter, with Q
METEL PIVS; reverse: elephant with SCIPIO above and IMP[erator] below.

and later patron of the poet Virgil, was with Caesar in the aftermath of his triumph: 'they
would have it so,' he recalled Caesar muttering in sadness, a reference to the fact that his
enemies were so determined to prosecute him in the Roman courts that they had forced
him to resolve their dispute on the battlefield (Suetonius, *Caesar*, 30). There is something
of Sulla's aggrieved and sad tone, deployed in the aftermath of his march on Rome, in
Pollio's remembrance of Caesar.

After Pharsalus, Cicero was reconciled with Caesar and he spent 46 BC in quiet study,
working on his famous books on oratory, *Brutus* and the *Orator*. The Pompeian faction
showed some life in the same year, and both Cato and Metellus Scipio fought a vigorous
propaganda campaign against Caesar, portraying themselves as true to Rome and her gods,
as their coinage illustrates (Figures 7.8 and 7.9). Their efforts were for nought, however,
as a sizeable Pompeian army was beaten at Thapsus in 46 BC. V Alaudae proudly earned
an elephant as its legionary emblem for its deeds during the battle. Juba I, the Numidian

king, was killed by Petreius, who then killed himself, while Afranius and Faustus Sulla were run to ground and murdered. Cato the Younger and Metellus Scipio also committed suicide; Scipio's dignity in death was praised later by the philosopher Seneca, while Plutarch recorded that Caesar expressed sadness that he had not been able to save Cato's life (*Apophthegmata Romana, Caesar*, 13).

An opportunistic revolt by a son of Mithridates VI, Pharnaces, was also quickly suppressed, and the lands of the east, which had close connections to Pompey, were forced to recognise their new master. In Spain, Pompey's sons, Gnaeus and Sextus, along with Caesar's former senior legate Labienus, who had deserted him, fought a stubborn insurrection. At Munda in 45 BC, Caesar, with his equestrian great-nephew Octavius along for some on-the-job education, beat the coalition arrayed against him, with both Labienus and Gnaeus killed fighting. The Pompeian army included *legiones vernaculae*, locally raised units made up of Spanish troops and Roman veterans settled in Spain. On the Caesarian side once again, the veteran force of V Alaudae, together with men of VI and X called out of retirement, fought for their beloved general. The war was over, but Caesar's problems were only just beginning.

Dictator for life

During the war, Caesar had paid his troops with gold, silver, and coins looted from the state treasury, held within the Temple of Saturn in the Roman forum. This had ensured the continued loyalty of his soldiers and allowed him to push the firm propaganda message of irresistible and inevitable victory, supported by the favour of Venus (Figure 7.10). Now he celebrated four separate triumphs, featuring yet more loot and exotic features such as lamp-bearing elephants, used to illuminate a night-time parade.

Having conquered fellow citizens, Caesar carefully staged his triumphs as victories over foreign enemies such as Juba and Pharnaces, but tacky paintings of members of the Pompeian faction killing themselves went down poorly with the assembled masses. The triumph for the Spanish war caused particular disgust: the dead were brothers, husbands, fathers, and uncles of many in Rome. Caesar then paid a huge donative not only to

Figure 7.10 Silver denarius of Caesar from a military mint in Spain, 46/45 BC. Obverse: head of Venus, with Cupid behind; reverse: victory trophy with shield between seated captives, and CAESAR in the exergue.

his soldiers, but also to the citizens of Rome, bestowing upon them a rent holiday, oil, corn, and free communal banquets. It was in his triumph for the victory over Pharnaces that an inscription appeared featuring the immortal words *veni, vidi, vici*, 'I came, I saw, I conquered', an allusion to the ease and speed of the campaign. (The conflict with Pharnaces was also notable for the participation, on the Roman side, of units raised by the Galatian king Deiotarus, trained and equipped in the legionary fashion; later, their veterans became XXII Deiotariana). Extravagant games were held, including one where the Campus Martius was flooded for a mock naval battle. There were also gladiatorial shows and lion hunts. All of this further won the people over to Caesar and laid the foundation for what came next.

Between 49 and 46 BC, Caesar had held the dictatorship on numerous occasions. In 46 BC he was consul and was also named to a ten-year dictatorship, but in 44 BC, after a stint as consul, Caesar was made dictator for life, finally demolishing Cicero's hopes that he would protect and respect the Republican constitution and work within its increasingly feeble laws. Plutarch wrote that the people accepted this, 'regarding the monarchy'—for what else was a lifetime dictatorship?—'as a respite from the evils of the civil wars' (*Caesar*, 57). A cowed senate called him *imperator, pater patriae*, and *liberator*, and vowed him a temple to Libertas. Some of Caesar's actions were decidedly authoritarian, such as choosing candidates for appointment to public office rather than using the electoral process. Caesar also governed without much thought of the senate, relying on trusted advisers such as Hirtius, Balbus, and Oppius. With no sense of shame for his own scandals, Caesar became the protector of public morality, cracking down on adultery and bringing in sumptuary laws that banned extravagant displays of luxury.

Yet Caesar also showed clemency to his enemies, pardoning Marcus Marcellus and ordering Pompey's statues to be restored in Rome. He engaged in some genuinely beneficial reforms, adjusting the calendar by making one year 365 days instead of 355, adding an extra day in February every fourth year. This gave us the Julian Calendar and leap years, and with some later tweaking by Pope Gregory XIII in 1582, the system has remained in use up to the present day. The reforms were necessary because the calendar had fallen badly out of sync with the seasons, creating all sorts of problems for farmers and priests, and for the timing of important events such as harvest festivals. Caesar also addressed the numerous problems plaguing Italy—many of which were the results of the civil war or had been aggravated by it. Debts were reduced, limits were imposed on governors, a new census was taken, and land was parcelled out for his veterans. New colonies were founded, many bearing Caesar's name; the city of Fréjus in southern France, for example, was founded as Forum Julii between 49 and 43 BC. Lugdunum (Lyon), Colonia Julia Viennensium (Vienne), Nemausus (Nîmes), Arelate/Colonia Sextanorum (Arles), and Hispalis (Seville) were also established as colonies. Veterans of one of Caesar's legions, X, were settled at Narbo, while those of VI were settled at Arelate/Colonia Sextanorum in 45 BC, an event commemorated in the modern city (Figure 7.11). The census ensured that the grain dole could be reorganised and become more efficient—only 150,000 were eligible, instead of the previous figure of over twice that many. While this saved money, Caesar was concerned about the population size and brought in measures to encourage larger families.

Caesar also took steps to repair the infrastructure in Rome and provide the city with the sorts of institutions that a world capital should possesses; a 'great' Rome would also

Figure 7.11 Modern relief on a wall adjacent to the Hôtel Jules César in Arles, the work of the Marseilles-born sculptor Etienne Bentz (1868–1942). The relief celebrates the city's links with Caesar's VI. The Latin *sta viator* commands the traveller to stop and admire.

Source: Photograph by the author.

reflect and magnify *his* own greatness. Inspired by the library he had seen in Alexandria (and perhaps wracked with guilt over his role in partially burning it), Caesar decided to install a new public library in Rome, which Terentius Varro was chosen to run. A new senate house, the curia Julia, was started to replace that which had gone up in flames after the murder of Clodius, and the new forum was dedicated in 46 BC. Numerous projects such as the Basilica Julia and a temple dedicated to *clementia* were either on the drawing board or begun before Caesar's assassination (Figures 7.12 and 7.13).

Away from Italy, Corinth and Carthage, which had lain in ruins since their destruction in 146 BC, were to be rebuilt and settled by 80,000 colonists. Caesar gave further recognition to the growing importance of the provinces—many of his troops had, after all, been recruited in Gaul, and Pompey's soldiers had likewise been drafted outside of Italy. The senate was enlarged to 900 members, with many of the newcomers drawn from the provinces and including retired centurions and even sons of slaves; citizenship was extended to leading provincials from Gaul and Spain. The quaestorship was doubled from 20 to 40 annually, and the praetorship from eight to 16. The abusive tax collection system for Asia was ended, with taxes henceforth to be collected by the Asian communities themselves. Rome's coinage was given a facelift under the guidance of Aulus Hirtius, who introduced the gold aureus (Figures 7.14 and 7.15), setting a new standard for international trade and

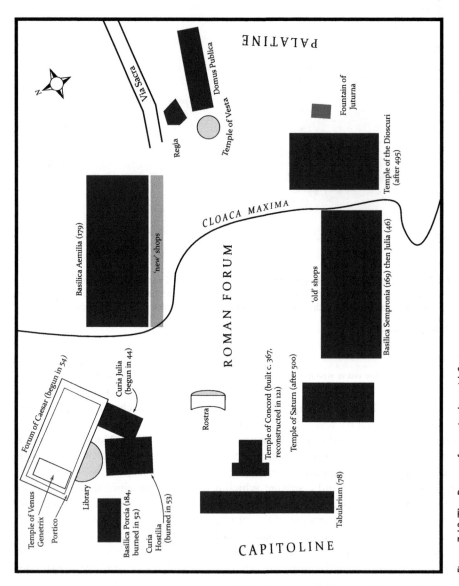

Figure 7.12 The Roman forum in the mid-first century BC.

Source: Illustration by the author.

Figure 7.13 Google Earth Pro image of the Roman forum as it appears today. Clearly visible are (1) the Curia Julia (now a church), (2) Caesar's forum, (3) the Temple of Venus, and the remains of (4) the Basilica Julia and (5) the Basilica Aemilia. Also visible are (6) the Temple of Saturn, (7) the tent structure covering the remains of the Vulcanal, with the location of the rostra just below and to the left, (8) the Regia, (9) the Temple of the Dioscuri, (10) the Temple of Vesta, and (11) the Temple of Julius Caesar erected by Octavian after Caesar's assassination.

Source: Image © 2020 Google.

Figure 7.14 Gold aureus minted at Rome in 46 BC. Obverse: veiled head of Pietas/Vesta right, with COS TER celebrating the third consulship of Caesar; reverse: the insignia used by the pontifices and augurs. Minted by Aulus Hirtius, praetor.

Figure 7.15 Gold aureus minted at Rome in 45 BC. Obverse: draped Victory with CAES DIC TER, celebrating his dictatorship; reverse: a *praefericulum*, a metal container used by augurs and priests. Minted by Lucius Munatius Plancus, as urban prefect.

reflecting the wealth of the state and the greatness of the city of Rome. (Such is the prestige of the gold aureus coinage that even today it remains one of the benchmarks in coin collections, with well-struck specimens routinely selling for five- and six-digit sums.)

Caesar was given tribunician power by the senate, and he was also taking divine honours and a cult dedicated to him was taking shape before he died. There was a precedent of sorts for this in the behaviour of Flamininus and Sulla. Divine honours and associations with the pantheon were, however, one thing; steps veering towards deification were something else. The senate decided that Caesar's image, bearing the inscription 'to the unconquered god', would be installed in Rome at the Temple of Quirinus, the deified Romulus. Antony was named as the priest who would in the future be responsible for worship of the deified Julius, yet ruler worship was an eastern innovation and had no basis in the Republic, so this caused considerable disquiet. Caesar's vicelike grip on the dictatorship also continued to rankle: even Sulla had resigned his position and retired to his villa. Caesar instead concentrated power around him, taking the consulship in tandem with the dictatorship. In the senate he was 'granted' the honour of sitting before the consuls (on a custom-made golden chair, no less) and having the first say on matters under debate. The month of July (Julius) was named for him, and the senate allowed him to wear the garb of the old kings of Rome. In the new Temple of Venus, Caesar erected a golden statue of the goddess that resembled Cleopatra, who had come to live in Rome in the autumn of 46 BC. In December of that year, Cicero had dinner with Caesar, but it was a tense affair and he remarked that Caesar was 'not the sort of guest to whom you would say "do please come again on your way back"' (*To Atticus*, 13.52). Later, Caesar began to mint coins that featured his image in place of gods and goddesses, which further unsettled many (Figure 7.16), and he continued to use coinage to celebrate his family's descent from Aeneas.

A conspiracy against Caesar was being steeped in the houses of key senators, and Cicero was slowly drifting towards their cause. Cicero had written a panegyric of Cato in which he praised the dead senator's *virtus* and held him up as an example of what it *truly* meant to be a Roman. The text is lost, as is Caesar's reprisal, a tract known as the 'Anti-Cato', but this response did little to improve Caesar's image. In February 44 BC, Marc Antony

Figure 7.16 Silver denarius of Caesar minted in February/March 44 BC. Obverse: bust of Caesar, draped as the *pontifex maximus*, with his name to the right; to the left, DICT PERPETVO (dictator for life); reverse: Victory.

offered Caesar a royal diadem at the Lupercalia festival, which Caesar rejected when the assembled crowd made signs of their displeasure. Antony's bizarre actions were interpreted by some at the time as a testing of the waters, to see whether the public would accept him as their king. Too early, perhaps; it has also sometimes been thought that some of Caesar's royal pretensions were deliberately instigated by others in order to make the case against him more palatable. Worries that Caesar was intending to stay in power indefinitely, however, were only further entrenched with preparations for an ambitious campaign against the Parthians that would perpetuate the current political situation in Rome. Caesar could be expected to be absent for many years, fossilising his fellow senators and magistrates in their subservience: who would dare oppose Caesar on his return?

Caesar, who had been drawn towards the east by dreams of Alexander, by his love for Cleopatra, and by his need to quash Pompey's memory in the provinces, was at the precipice overlooking one possible terminus of the political trajectory that began when Roman warriors and politicians first encountered Hellenistic kings and the regal cultures of the east. Even Caesar's calendar improvements were informed by Alexandrian science. If kingship was bad, divine kingship—an eastern invention—was even less acceptable to Roman opinion. Cleopatra's presence in Rome also proved offensive to conservative sensibilities. Cicero, for one, detested her, as he freely admitted to Atticus. A return to collegial government was never in the offing; only something that resembled a monarchy would do. 'What he felt,' wrote Plutarch of Caesar, 'was nothing else than emulation of himself, as if he had been another man, and a sort of rivalry between what he had done and what he purposed to do' (*Caesar*, 58). Nothing would ever be enough to satisfy Caesar's ambition.

Shortly before he was due to leave for Parthia, Caesar attended a meeting of the senate in the Theatre of Pompey, which had an annex purposely designed for such gatherings. His ally Marc Antony was detained at the entrance; inside, 60 conspirators awaited, led by Marcus Brutus and his brother-in-law, Gaius Cassius Longinus. Brutus was the son of Caesar's paramour Servilia, and there were wild rumours in antiquity that Brutus was actually Caesar's son. Both Brutus and Cassius had fought Caesar in the civil war, and both had been pardoned by him; Brutus, who claimed descent from the Brutus who had ousted the final king of Rome, had recently signalled his anti-Caesarian credentials by marrying Cato's daughter, Porcia, the widow of Caesar's foe Bibulus (consul in 59 BC). Caesar was apparently aware of the threat Brutus posed, but did little about it. Another conspirator was Gaius Trebonius, one of Caesar's lieutenants in the Gallic wars and holder of the consulship in 45 BC. Caesar was stabbed repeatedly and collapsed next to a bust of Pompey. Inevitably, the general whose life had ended in misery on an Egyptian beach seemed almost to be 'presiding over this vengeance upon his enemy' (Plutarch, *Julius Caesar*, 66). Nobody seemed the least concerned that a group of senators had just murdered the *pontifex maximus*. Three weeks after Caesar's murder on the Ides of March, Cicero, who was close to Brutus but did not, in the end, take part in the plot, wrote approvingly to Atticus: 'Come one, come all, the Ides of March are a consolation. Our heroes most splendidly and gloriously achieved everything that lay in their power' (*To Atticus*, 14.4).

Libertas

Why was Caesar murdered? Appian wrote that Pompey's considerable authority 'had an almost democratic appearance' when set against that of Caesar (*Civil Wars*, 86). Caesar was a king in all but name, and there were certainly those who wanted him dead because of it—purists and ideologues who resented his royal pretensions, his quasi-divine status, and his polluted eastern affectations. But there were more squalid reasons for Caesar's assassination. 'A baleful frenzy,' wrote Cassius Dio, 'fell upon certain men through jealousy of his advancement' (44.1). Caesar had offended members of the senate by refusing to rise in their presence when they came to him at the Temple of Venus, an act that was not soon forgotten, and his later excuse that he was suffering from diarrhoea drew hoots of derision. Many of his friends were appalled at his policy of *clementia*, which gave favour to former enemies and sometimes actively rewarded what was perceived to be treasonous behaviour. Greed, avarice, and corrupt self-interest were qualities in abundance among Rome's leading politicians, and for many of them Caesar's policies did not provide sufficient rewards for the hardships they had endured by supporting him. His imminent departure for an indefinite campaign in Parthia pushed them to action. Caesar's government—a one-man show supported by a council of friends and advisers, similar to that which had coalesced around Alexander the Great, and later Marius and Sulla—left few opportunities for self-enrichment, *gloria*, or plain corruption outside the coveted inner circle.

In the aftermath of Caesar's murder, his assassins cried 'libertas!' in the streets and celebrated their actions on late Republican coinage that, following Caesar, increasingly featured images of living men and women alongside deities such as Libertas herself (Figures 7.17 and 7.18). The problems began almost immediately. Caesar's killers were in hiding and the city was tense. When he was killed, Caesar had been consul and dictator, with Marcus Aemilius Lepidus, son of the consul for 78 BC, as his master of horse. Publius Cornelius Dolabella reminded the senate that Caesar had promised him the consulship when he left for his Parthian expedition, and seized the office by pandering to the assassins. Nevertheless, it was Marc Antony who moved most quickly. On the night of the murder, Antony robbed Caesar's widow, Calpurnia, of both 4,000 talents of cash and Caesar's confidential papers, and also stole 700,000 sesterces of money Caesar had left in the Temple of Ops on the Capitoline Hill. Along with Lepidus, who quickly seized the office of *pontifex maximus*, Antony soon brokered a deal with Brutus and Cassius that was agreed at a meeting of the senate on March 17: the primary assassins were granted suitable positions in Crete and Bithynia away from Italy, in a hopeful but doomed attempt to ensure that it remained business as usual in Rome. Trebonius, who had detained Antony outside the senate, had already left Rome for the proconsular governorship of Asia. In Athens, Brutus and Cassius were honoured as latter-day incarnations of Harmodius and Aristogeiton, the famous lovers who had murdered one of the Peisistratid tyrants in 514 BC (Chapter 1). Cleopatra and her entourage also left Rome. Antony was clearly positioning himself to take control, but he was undone when Caesar's will was made public. It declared Octavius, his equestrian 19-year-old great-nephew, to be his heir, and the will made him Caesar's adopted son. Octavius—who took the name Gaius Julius Caesar, but who is better known as Octavian—returned to Italy from Apollonia, where he had been awaiting Caesar for the start of the planned Parthian expedition. Antony was also included in Caesar's will, but stood to inherit only a fraction of what was due to Octavian. At Caesar's funeral on March 19, a dangerous rift opened up between the two.

The funeral was a deeply political occasion. The dictator's will had left a large amount of cash for each free man in Rome, and generously allocated some of his private property for

Figure 7.17 Silver denarius of Brutus minted in autumn 42 BC by a travelling military mint. Obverse: Brutus, bare-headed, with BRVT and IMP; reverse: the commemoration of Caesar's murder, two daggers and a cap representing liberty. This issue is always in high demand; this particular coin sold at auction for US$300,000.

Figure 7.18 Silver denarius of Cassius from a military mint in Asia Minor. Obverse: diademed head of Libertas, the deified personification of liberty; reverse: the name of the minting authority, P. Cornelius LENTVLVS SPINT (Lentulus Spinther).

public use. Antony whipped up the febrile crowd with his eulogy, and the people gathering around the cortège set fire to Caesar's corpse, throwing on benches, clothes, wood, and anything else that would burn. Thus energised, the multitude besieged the houses of the assassins, most of whom had already fled. Antony, with the help of Caesar's confidential papers, tried to have pending decisions accepted as decrees, essentially appropriating Caesar's legislative agenda as his own. He also tried to block Octavian's adoption, but when Antony proved unable to furnish the funds necessary to pay Caesar's largesse to the public, Octavian met the cost from his own pocket, a fact the people never forgot. Octavian also found that his adoptive father's council, including Balbus and Oppius, welcomed him and had little trouble with his appointment as Caesar's successor. He further solidified his position by erecting a statue of Caesar in the Temple of Venus, days after a comet had been

Figure 7.19 Silver denarius minted by the emperor Augustus (Octavian) after 28 BC. The reverse illustrates the comet with the legend DIVVS IVLIV (DIVUS IULIUS, 'divine Julius').

seen in the sky, which was widely taken to be a sign of the dictator's passage into deified immortality; later, this image appeared on Roman coinage (Figure 7.19).

After his consulship in 44 BC, Antony was given the province of Macedonia to govern as proconsul, but he wanted Cisalpine Gaul instead. This province, under the control of Decimus Brutus, a cousin of the assassin Brutus, was transferred to Antony in mid-43 BC via a law that would give him a five-year command redolent of the arrangements made under the First Triumvirate. Antony recalled four legions from Macedonia (II, IIII, XXXV, and the unnumbered Martia) to strengthen his position in Italy. On arrival, two of these Macedonian legions (IIII and Martia) defected to Octavian, who used the strength of the Caesarian name and his deep pockets to purchase their loyalty. Octavian raised further troops from veterans in Campania (VII and VIII), who had been settled there by Caesar. He minted coins displaying both his and Caesar's images to strengthen his association with the slain dictator and, by a sleight of hand, he even managed to purloin the elephants intended for Antony's army. Across the Alps lay additional legions—Lepidus was still in Gaul, despite having been assigned the governorship of Nearer Spain, while the mysterious Lucius Munatius Plancus was governor of Gallia Comata, the vast district added to the empire by Caesar's Gallic wars. Neither of the two seemed particularly interested in becoming involved, especially as Octavian, made propraetor and granted imperium by the senate at Cicero's instigation, was dispatched northwards with the two consuls for 43 BC, Gaius Vibius Pansa and Caesar's old comrade-in-arms Aulus Hirtius. Decimus Brutus had refused to give up Cisalpine Gaul, and Antony laid siege to him at Mutina (modern Modena). Octavian, with Hirtius and Pansa in tow, fought two battles against Antony, who had been declared a public enemy at the urging of Cicero. The experienced troops fought each other in silence, noted Appian, since they knew each other's tactics and could only win through sheer perseverance (*Civil Wars*, 3.68).

In the interim, faultlines were forming as the senate reverted to craven self-interest by acquiescing to the illegal seizure of seven legions and Macedonia by Brutus, the assassin, and of ten legions and Syria by Cassius; in Macedonia, Brutus had also put its governor, a brother of Antony, to death. Sextus Pompey, the sole surviving son of Pompey who had come through Caesar's vengeful Spanish war unscathed, was also waiting in the wings

Figure 7.20 Gold aureus of Sextus Pompey minted in Sicily in 42 BC. Obverse: bare head of Sextus Pompey; reverse: Pompey the Great (left) and Gnaeus Pompey (right).

with seven legions, and the senate sent out feelers to determine where his loyalties lay (Figure 7.20). Eventually, the senate granted Sextus the title of *praefectus classis et orae maritimae*, 'commander-in-chief of the fleet and of the shores of the sea'.

Very quickly, therefore, the situation had descended into turmoil. Caesar's Pompeian assassins were aligned with the senate, but the senate was also aligned with its propraetorian champion—the adopted son of the murdered Caesar, who was quickly beginning to resemble a *new* Caesar. With Octavian were the consuls Hirtius and Pansa, one of whom was very close to Caesar and both of whom died on the Mutina campaign in rather murky circumstances. 'The circumstances of Pansa's death, in particular, were so mysterious,' wrote Suetonius (*Augustus*, 11), 'that the physician Glyco was imprisoned on the charge of having applied poison to his wound.' Antony, a confidant of Caesar, was now opposed to both the senate and Octavian. Legions of doubtful loyalty were in Gaul, Macedonia, and Syria, and legions or veterans loyal to Caesar could be found everywhere: V Alaudae was with Antony, and Lepidus called the retired soldiers of VI (in Arelate) and X (at Narbo) once more back to the ranks. Large parts of the armies in the field had been bought. Octavian paid regular bonuses to each man under arms, and promised still more if they won, and was increasingly subverting the apparatus of the state for his own use. Cicero wrote to Plancus on March 20, 43 BC, begging him to align himself 'with the cause of Roman freedom and senatorial authority', and expressing doubts about the reliability of Lepidus (*To Friends*, 10.6). For Cicero, 'Roman freedom and senatorial authority' were identified with the Pompeians—the faction that killed Caesar and now opposed Antony and, very soon, Octavian.

Cicero had emerged from his semi-retirement to become one of the loudest voices against Antony and was now the *princeps senatus*. In a letter to Cassius in the spring of 43 BC, he declared that 'the only refuge left for honest citizens is with you and Brutus' (*To Friends*, 12.6). A short time earlier, in September 44 BC, Cicero had begun to write invectives against Antony, which he called 'The Philippics' in imitation of the attacks on Philip II of Macedon written by the great Athenian orator, Demosthenes (384–322 BC). In the Philippics, Cicero attacked Antony's wanton and licentious character and his lax morals: 'You were an augur, yet you never took the auspices,' he wrote. 'You were a consul, yet you blocked the legal right of other officials to exercise the veto … You are a drink-sodden, sex-ridden wreck' (*Second Philippic*). There would be over a dozen Philippics in all, delivered by pamphlet and as speeches in the senate. In a letter to Gaius Trebonius written on February 2, 43 BC, Cicero also expressed disappointment at the survival of the 'pestilential character', Antony, whom the assassins had considered killing on the Ides of March, but whom they thought could instead be turned to their cause.

About Octavian, Cicero initially felt positive: in the same letter to Trebonius, he called him 'an excellent boy' for whom he had 'high hopes for the future' (*To Friends*, 10.28). In several of the Philippics, Cicero even promoted the idea of an alliance between Octavian and the senate. It seemed that Cicero thought he could control Octavian, who was young and inexperienced; soon, however, Octavian—who had no interest in restoring the senatorial Republic and who 'abandoned the cause of the *nobiles* without hesitation'—caused consternation in Rome (Suetonius, *Augustus*, 12). With Hirtius and Pansa dead, Octavian took control of their senatorial troops and set off after Antony. Decimus Brutus, who Octavian had been sent to save from Antony's siege, sought an audience with Octavian, but this was refused; his army defected and Decimus Brutus was later murdered on Antony's orders. Eventually, Octavian caught up with Antony, who had since joined forces with Plancus and Lepidus. Instead of fighting, however, the men listened to their troops, who urged them to reconcile with one another and go after Brutus and Cassius; Lepidus, Antony, and Octavian agreed to join forces. Still only 19, Octavian extracted the remainder of Pansa's consulship for 43 BC from a reluctant senate and stole from the treasury to pay his legionnaires. Octavian's consular colleague Quintus Pedius, a nephew of Caesar who completed Hirtius's term, arranged for a show trial of Caesar's assassins to take place in absentia. All were found guilty by the *lex Pedia*. With these stunning developments, the Second Triumvirate was born, and *libertas*—if indeed it had ever existed—vanished forever.

The Second Triumvirate, 43–36 BC

Octavian gave up his extorted consulship, which was completed by the Caesarian ally Publius Ventidius Bassus. (This was a remarkable turnaround for Ventidius, who had been paraded as a captive by Pompeius Strabo during the Social War in 89 BC.) The now familiar five-year terms were resurrected, and the three men took over the management of the state with geographical regions designated for each: Cisalpine Gaul and Gallia Comata for Antony; Transalpine Gaul and Spain for Lepidus; and Africa, Sardinia, Corsica, and Sicily for Octavian (Figure 7.21). Unlike the First Triumvirate, this new agreement was made legal through the passage of the *lex Titia*, drawn up by the plebeian tribune Publius Titius in November of 43 BC. The law formally invested the three men with extraordinary powers. Business could be carried out without the senate, magistrates appointed, and the triumvirs were given absolute judicial control. The soldiers were won over with promises of land and loot. The triumvirs took the title *tresviri rei publicae constituendae*, 'three men for the restoration of the Republic', and the institution was commemorated on Roman coinage (Figure 7.22).

The arrangement was solidified when Antony, who was married to Fulvia—the widow of both Clodius and then Curio—offered the hand of Fulvia's daughter Clodia to Octavian. (This Clodia should not be confused with Clodia Pulchra, the wife of Quintus Caecilius Metellus Celer, consul in 60 BC.) The triumvirate granted Caesar unprecedented honours

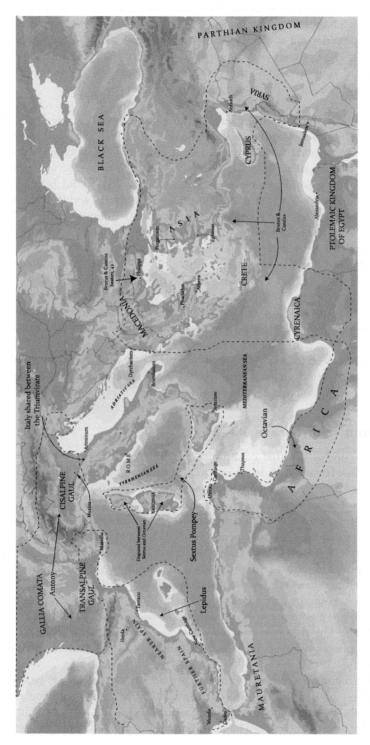

Figure 7.21 The Second Triumvirate, 43 BC. Illustration by the author.

Figure 7.22 Bronze coin of the Second Triumvirate minted in 40/39 BC. Obverse: Octavian, Antony, and Lepidus; reverse: statue of Artemis.

in death as a way to conceal their coup. Caesar's birthday was to be celebrated publicly each year, while the day on which he was murdered was declared void for public business. The curia Julia was to be completed, and all of Caesar's laws and pronouncements were to be upheld. Having established their political position as the guardians of Caesar's legacy, the triumvirs carried out a program that would have horrified the murdered dictator and his penchant for *clementia*.

On November 23, 43 BC, the three men compiled a large number of names for proscription in order to fund their massive army. The proscriptions may have come at a particularly bad time for Rome's farmers: new research has suggested that a volcanic eruption in the Aleutian Islands in the same year worsened climactic conditions in Europe, dropping the temperature and severely stunting the harvest, and it is very likely that such conditions would have made social unrest in Italy worse. One of the first names on the proscription list was Cicero, whom Antony despised not only for the Philippics but also because Antony's stepfather was Lentulus Sura, who had been murdered on Cicero's orders in 63 BC. When Cicero found out that he was on the list, he had already become disillusioned with Octavian and had determined to throw in his lot with Brutus in Macedonia. He had not gone far, however, when his assassins found him. Antony had demanded Cicero's head and his hands, wanting to nail them to the rostra and thus exhibit his vengeance over the 'the hands with which he wrote the Philippics' (Plutarch, *Cicero*, 48). 'When Cicero was beheaded,' wrote Velleius Paterculus, 'the voice of the people was severed' (2.63). In death, Cicero's head was mutilated by Fulvia, who pulled out the tongue and stabbed it with hairpins. Cicero's brother Quintus, who had fought for Caesar in Gaul, also perished as hundreds were hunted down and murdered, their property and wealth flowing to the triumvirs. Antony, who 'killed savagely and mercilessly' (Cassius Dio, 47.8), even proscribed his own uncle, Plancus his brother, and Lepidus his own brother, while an aristocrat seen crying at the show-trial of Brutus and Cassius was also put on the list. Slaves sold out their owners, lured by the promise of freedom and wealth; others impersonated their owners and died while they escaped, demonstrations of servile loyalty that were praised by Valerius Maximus (e.g. 6.8.6). Plebeian tribunes were not spared; the rostra filled up with heads and bodies clogged the Tiber. Fulvia actively drew up lists of

Figure 7.23 Silver denarius of Octavian minted in Italy in 32 or 31 BC. Obverse: head of Octavian; reverse: Apollo playing the lyre. The legend reads CAESAR DIVI F[ilius], 'son of the divine Caesar'.

her own enemies for Antony to proscribe. Sextus Pompey, recently courted by the senate, was now proscribed, but remained at large, financing his exploits through piracy and rescuing people desperate to get out of Italy. Antony aroused public anger by openly living in Pompey's house, which he had purchased at a knock-down rate. Meanwhile in January of 42 BC, Caesar was officially proclaimed a god, and Octavian took to proclaiming his divine parentage on his coinage (Figure 7.23). The proscriptions filled the triumvirate's coffers and allowed them to make vast grants of cash and land to their troops. Funds were also raised by taxing rich women—although the levy was reduced by the fiery public oratory of Hortensia, the daughter of a contemporary of Cicero—and appropriating the territory of rich cities in Italy.

After a few false starts, Antony and Octavian crossed the Adriatic, eluding Sextus Pompey's fleet, although the triumvirate's naval forces suffered at the hands of Gnaeus Domitius Ahenobarbus (son of Lucius, consul in 54 BC), who had been forced from Rome by the *lex Pedia*. (Lepidus, as *pontifex maximus*, remained in Rome as consul for 42 BC with Plancus as his colleague.) At Philippi in the autumn of 42 BC, Antony beat Cassius, who subsequently died by his own hand. Octavian, who had few instincts as a general, missed the action due to illness. His part of the army was beaten and he was forced to make his escape from camp. Antony's aggressive tactics proved decisive in a second battle in which Brutus was beaten; he too chose suicide over the grisly alternatives, although in a show of *nobilitas*, Antony recovered Brutus's body, cremated it, and sent the ashes to Servilia. The great Roman historian Tacitus (AD 56–120) wrote sparingly of Philippi's aftermath by noting that 'after the slaughter of Brutus and Cassius, there were no more Republican armies' (*Annals*, 1.2). The surviving aristocrats fled to Sextus Pompey in Sicily, while an amnesty to the legionnaires defeated at Philippi resulted in large-scale defections to the triumvirate, sufficient to fill a score of new legions. Two praetorian cohorts— bodyguards—were raised from the victorious veterans and divided between Antony and Octavian. The campaign had not all gone the triumvirate's way: two legions, including the Martia, were lost at sea. As a final coda to Philippi, Brutus's widow, Porcia, took her own

Figure 7.24 Silver denarius minted at Ephesus in 41 BC. Obverse: head of Marc Antony; reverse: head of Octavian.

life in uncertain circumstances. The rumour in antiquity was that she swallowed hot coals, a grisly method popularised by Shakespeare's play *Julius Caesar*.

After Philippi, a sort of settlement emerged in which Octavian slowly became dominant in the west and Antony in the east. Coins were minted bearing both of their portraits (Figure 7.24). Octavian took control over a large swathe of territory stretching from Africa to Sicily and Sardinia. Antony, meanwhile, remained in the eastern Mediterranean, a region that would emerge as his power base over the following decade and where he would spend increasing amounts of time with Cleopatra, whom he first met fighting with Gabinius on behalf of Ptolemy XII and whom he now met again in Cilicia after the Philippi campaign. With him he counted some of Caesar's old units, including V Alaudae, as well as VI, which had gained the name Ferrata, 'ironclad'. Lepidus, who was suspected of collusion with Sextus Pompey, was being progressively squeezed out and was also scorned by Fulvia for his idleness. The biggest problem facing Octavian was what to do with his share of the veterans of Philippi, who either needed to be paid off or settled. The latter was more straightforward and could be financed by further proscriptions and property confiscations. This proved extremely unpopular with the people of Italy, who were already suffering from war fatigue and a famine made worse by Sextus Pompey, who was interrupting the supply of grain coming from Sicily. Soldiers had priority for food, and the civilian population was beginning to starve. Octavian persevered regardless, settling troops in new colonies at Capua, Beneventum, Venusia, and many more towns in Italy.

The result of this chaotic situation was a new civil war, pitting Octavian against Antony's brother, Lucius Antonius, who was consul for 41 BC and a self-declared Republican champion of the people being dispossessed by Octavian. The war was notable for the emergence of a young equestrian named Marcus Vipsanius Agrippa, who had been born in obscurity. Agrippa had been with Octavian when Caesar died, had returned with him to Italy, and had now taken over military duties for his friend. Lucius Antonius was taken under siege at Perusia in Umbria. There he was bottled up with Antony's wife, Fulvia, a woman whom Plutarch memorably wrote had 'no mind for spinning or house-keeping, who did not condescend to control a private citizen, but wished to lead a leader, and command a commander' (*Antony*, 10). Octavian had already divorced Fulvia's daughter, Clodia, in irritation at his mother-in-law's overbearing character, and now Fulvia's presence at Perusia fuelled rumours that Antony himself was helping his brother, although he always denied it and remained absent and inaccessible throughout; in the end, Lucius was undone because Plancus and Publius Ventidius Bassus, in whom he had placed his hopes, failed to come quickly to his aid. The conflict is also notable for the discovery by archaeologists of inscribed sling bolts, used by skirmishers on both sides. (This was the ancient version of writing messages on bombs: 'Berlin or bust'.) The lead bolts, about 4 centimetres (1.5 inches) long, were made on site with the texts and images created by a mould. Catalogued in volume 11 of the *Corpus of Latin Inscriptions*, they include such gems as:

> Greetings, Octavius. You suck (6721.9). (The Latin verb *felas* used here implies a sexual act, while the name 'Octavius' is a deliberate denial of his inheritance from Caesar).
> I'm heading for Octavian's butt (6721.7).
> Sit broadly on this, Octavian (6721.11, accompanied by a drawing of a phallus).
> Spread your butt, bald Lucius Antonius and Fulvia (6721.14).

During the Perusia campaign, Octavian also composed a viciously pornographic poem about Antony and Fulvia, which was preserved by the poet Martial (c. AD 38–104) in his *Epigrams*; Lucius struck back with lurid claims that Octavian had pimped himself to Aulus Hirtius in Spain, and that he used heated nutshells to wax his legs. Other, less rude inscriptions from Perusian sling bolts record the participation of individual soldiers and their units: one, for instance, was engraved by Titus Etrius, *primus pilus* of IIII, a legion originally raised by Caesar in 48 BC (6721.18); another (6721.27) logs the presence of XI, another unit initially recruited by Caesar in Gaul (58 BC), which had now been brought out of retirement to fight for Octavian.

The Perusia campaign ended in 40 BC with a truce, whereby Lucius and Fulvia, along with Plancus, who had belatedly supported them, were allowed to depart. Fulvia died near Corinth, while Octavian opportunistically took control of Antony's Gallic territories when the incumbent governor died in office. Earlier, he had reinforced his credentials by murdering the governing magistrates and the leading senators of Perusia at an altar to the deified Julius. According to Suetonius, he met 'all attempts to beg for pardon or to make excuses with the one reply: "You must die"' (*Augustus*, 15). In the interim, Asinius Pollio, who had cautiously backed Antony from the beginning, had raised seven legions, which he set at Antony's disposal. Asinius Pollio had also won over Gnaeus Domitius Ahenobarbus, providing Antony with a significant naval resource. Ahenobarbus was a talented commander and celebrated his achievements on his coinage (Figure 7.25).

Brought to the edge of war by these developments, Octavian and Antony—who had also made moves to attach Sextus Pompey to his cause—were reconciled in 40 BC following an abortive siege of Brundisium by Antony. A new division of territory and resources was made between them, and Antony married Octavian's sister, Octavia the Younger, whose husband had recently died (Figure 7.26). Through the intercession of his shadowy equestrian friend Maecenas, Octavian then married Scribonia, a relative of Sextus Pompey's

Figure 7.25 Silver denarius of Gnaeus Domitius Ahenobarbus from an uncertain mint c. 41/40 BC. Obverse: bare head of Ahenobarbus; reverse: naval prow with a military trophy. CN.DOMITIVS.IMP[erator] below.

Figure 7.26 Silver cistophorus of Antony, minted at Ephesus in 39 BC to celebrate his marriage to Octavia. Obverse: head of Antony; reverse: draped head of Octavia. The Latin legend commemorates the triumvirate and Antony's title of *imperator*.

wife, in an effort to lessen the threat posed by Sextus Pompey. By this new arrangement, the so-called Treaty of Brundisium, Octavian was given Illyria and confirmed in control of the Spanish and Gallic provinces, while Antony gained Macedonia, Epirus, Asia, Syria, Cyprus, and Cyrenaica. Despite the fact that Italy 'belonged' to them both, Antony's prolonged absence from the West inevitably left Octavian in control of Italy, a fact that gave him a tremendous moral advantage. Lepidus continued to be marginalised, and was granted only a token amount of territory in Africa. Cavalry, infantry legions, and the sparse naval resources were carefully divided between the two senior triumvirs to ensure some form of stability (Figure 7.27). The consuls and praetors for 40 BC were dismissed, and new officials appointed—all without an election.

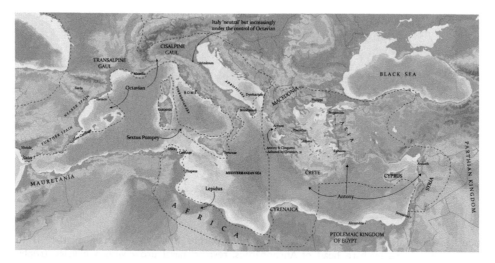

Figure 7.27 The Mediterranean following the Treaty of Brundisium in 40 BC.

Source: Illustration by the author.

The following year, 39 BC, a new round of negotiations was opened up between Sextus Pompey and the triumvirs. Pompey had proven difficult to control and possessed a stranglehold over Italy's coastal waters, and he was able to interrupt grain shipments to Rome at will. This, in turn, caused riots and unrest. In exchange for ending his piratical actions and allowing commercial activity to restart, Sextus Pompey was accorded the governorship of Sicily, Corsica, and Sardinia—places he already controlled—and he was also given territory in southern Greece. He was further bribed with an unrealised promise of the consulship. This arrangement, in which Pompey's ex-wife Mucia played a significant role, was known as the Pact of Misenum, and it also allowed for many of the proscribed to return to Italy. The deal was concluded on board Sextus Pompey's flagship, but it quickly broke down when Antony failed to deliver on his part of the bargain. He wantonly plundered the cities of Achaea in order to leave Sextus with a weakened power base. To the Athenians, Antony declared himself a new Dionysus, and when the city's rulers jokingly offered him Athena's hand in marriage, he agreed—extracting a massive dowry in the process. Coins minted at the time show Antony wearing a crown of ivy, one of the symbols of Dionysus; earlier in his life, he had sought to portray himself as Hercules.

Against Sextus Pompey, Octavian suffered numerous reverses, underscoring his weakness in naval resources. In the east, a Parthian army led by Quintus Labienus, the son of Caesar's former lieutenant, and Pacorus, son of king Orodes II, launched an opportunistic attack into Roman Syria. Distracted by Cleopatra and events at Perusia—Cassius Dio wrote with hyperbole that Antony 'was so under the sway of his passion and of his drunkenness that he gave not a thought either to his allies or his enemies' (48.27)—Antony initially chose to manage the war through his client Herod of Judaea and the capable soldier Publius Ventidius Bassus, who won a series of victories in which Labienus was put on the run (and later captured) and Pacorus killed. Not long afterwards, Antony arrived on the scene and, riven with jealousy, stripped Ventidius of command and shipped him back to Rome, where he allowed him to celebrate a triumph—the first Roman to celebrate a victory over the Parthians. Antony took over the conduct of the Parthian war, but achieved little. Then one of Sextus Pompey's senior staff delivered himself and his forces to Octavian, who had caused great offense to Sextus Pompey himself when he divorced Scribonia on the day that she gave birth to their daughter, Julia.

The five-year terms of the triumvirs expired in 38 BC, but were renewed for another five in the summer of 37 BC by the Treaty of Tarentum, brokered once again by Maecenas with the assistance of Octavia, who had emerged as a vital diplomatic link between her husband and her brother. Antony delivered naval reinforcements to Octavian, who promised legions that were never sent. Octavian persevered against Sextus Pompey, but it took until 36 BC to overcome the threat. Victory was achieved through the diligence of Agrippa, who held the consulship in 37 BC alongside the grandson of Antony's uncle Hybrida (consul 63 BC). Agrippa oversaw a naval construction program, the recruitment of thousands of sailors, and a training regime that filled Italy's lakes with ships and their crews. In the meantime, Octavian had married Livia, whose husband (an opponent of Octavian from the *gens* Claudia) had been forced by Octavian to divorce her despite the fact that she was pregnant. Quite aside from the question of morality, this was technically not legal, but Rome's submissive priests decided to make an exception for Octavian and allowed the marriage to go ahead. (The union joined together the *gens* Julia and the *gens* Claudia, from which Livia hailed: their adoptive, dynastic offspring (there were no natural children) would be known as the Julio-Claudians, the dynasty that ruled the empire in the first century AD—see Chapters 8 and 9.) While Antony provided some support against Sextus, and Lepidus scored some successes in Sicily, much of the war was conducted by Agrippa, who proved as capable at sea as he had been on land. Sextus Pompey was beaten at Naulochus off the north-eastern Sicilian coast, and later died in 35 BC at the hands of one of Antony's assassins (Figure 7.28).

After the campaign was over, Octavian rode into the camp of Lepidus and convinced his army to defect. Lepidus was forced into retirement at Circei, although he remained *pontifex maximus* until his peaceful death in 12 BC. Octavian was now in possession of a massive force: some 45 legions of infantry, over 20,000 horse, and a fleet of 600 ships. Octavian was granted golden statues in Rome and given the sacrosanctity of a plebeian tribune by a grateful senate. In the same way that the removal of Crassus brought Pompey and Caesar to blows, now the disappearance of Lepidus made a showdown between Antony and Octavian inevitable.

The final break, 36–31 BC

In the five-year period between the defeat of Sextus Pompey and the battle of Actium in 31 BC, a rift opened between Antony and Octavian that completed the long and violent process that the historian Ronald Syme famously called the 'Roman Revolution'—a reversion to monarchy. Antony's behaviour was viewed with increasing concern in Rome, where Octavian conducted a masterful propaganda campaign centred on traditional Roman values that utterly destroyed Antony's image, credibility, and reputation.

Plutarch's biography of Antony is every bit as lurid as James Purefoy's brilliant portrayal in HBO's *Rome*. Much of this distasteful picture is the result of Octavian's propaganda: in

Figure 7.28 Gold aureus of Octavian minted in Italy 30/29 BC and commemorating the defeat of Sextus Pompey. Obverse: bust of Diana; reverse: IMP.CAESAR on a frieze surmounting a temple containing military trophies.

control, and in Rome, Octavian could say whatever he pleased about Antony, and he found that the people were ready to believe even the most outlandish allegations. Plutarch wrote that Antony was 'swashbuckling and boastful, full of empty exultation and distorted ambition', and detailed his sexual exploits and poor conduct at some length (*Antony*, 2). Antony surrounded himself with exotic luxury, flute-players, dancing girls, and all the trappings of the 'decadent' east. Everyone was certain that he really *had* entered Ephesus surrounded by revellers, who hailed him as Dionysus; in the evenings, addled with drink, he really *did* harangue the people of Alexandria from the street, sometimes in the nude. Octavian also controlled the propaganda message about Cleopatra, who was turned into a menace to men, and a cunning and treacherous woman who used all sorts of exotic means to un-man Antony and overwhelm his ability to behave rationally. 'So swiftly was Antony transformed,' wrote Appian, 'and this passion was the beginning and the end of the evils that afterwards befell him' (*Civil Wars*, 5.9). Antony of course was perfectly capable of rational thought, and had many practical reasons to systematically exploit a relationship with Cleopatra. If a bid for world empire was to be made, it might as well be made from the historic store of wealth and power that was Egypt. Cleopatra also had *her* own reasons to attach herself to Antony. Ptolemaic Egypt's old possessions overseas, Cyprus, Coele ('Hollow') Syria, and Cyrenaica, were now under Roman rule. Antony offered *her* the chance for world empire, and she was the last Hellenistic dynast cast in the old and individualistic mould of Alexander and his successors.

In Octavia, however, Cleopatra found her foil, and Antony helped to bolster the public image of his wife even as he carried on his affair with Cleopatra. The marriage between Antony and Octavia collapsed when she arrived in Athens with fresh troops and supplies in 35 BC, hoping to meet him there. What she discovered were letters telling her to stay away, after which she returned to Italy with a wounded but unyielding pride. The true picture of either Antony and Cleopatra is exceedingly difficult to recover from the sources; the vastness of the events in which they took part ensured that they quickly passed into legend—star-crossed lovers who destroyed one another in a desperate and hopeless cause. Cleopatra has suffered the most as a result, and the misinformation campaign pursued by

Octavian obscures the fact that she had command of nine different languages, and was an accomplished businesswoman and powerful queen in her own right. As for Antony, some of his last acts proved beyond doubt that he had a better grasp of traditional Roman *virtus* than Octavian. When his friend, the consul Gnaeus Domitius Ahenobarbus, defected prior to the Actium campaign (below), he sent his belongings to him without any ill-will.

As Octavia exemplified all the idealised qualities of a dutiful Roman wife—she continued to live in Antony's home in Rome and raised their children, along with those of Fulvia—Octavian portrayed himself as the only one capable of guarding the people's interests, liberty, and safety. There was a semblance of truth to his propaganda, as he had ended proscriptions and confiscations in Italy, and his defeat of Sextus Pompey stopped the piratical behaviour that had caused shortages of grain in Rome. He had also waged a number of minor campaigns in Central Europe that provided his soldiers with an opportunity for enrichment and for himself to claim victory. Through Agrippa and his allies, the city of Rome had undergone repairs to its public buildings and water supply, barbers were hired by the state to dispense free haircuts, and distributions of olive oil, salt, and other necessities were made. Extravagant public shows were provided free of charge, along with banquets and supplies of free clothing. Agrippa took the junior post of aedile in 33 BC (he had been consul in 37 BC) in a dramatic show of leadership by example, and cleaned out the *cloaca maxima*; he even sailed through it to ensure that everything was in order! Octavian's marriage to Livia, although it began with a scandal, had been approved by the priests in Rome and Livia herself was originally from an ancient plebeian family of great standing. Octavian's reinvented monogamy and his sister's praiseworthy qualities only highlighted Antony's scandalous escapades. Antony, marooned in the east, had no opportunity to control the message that was delivered by Octavian to the people of Rome and Italy—and, inevitably, long-distance attempts to sling the mud back in the other direction by pointing out Octavian's hypocrisy and his own sexual escapades invariably failed.

Antony's missteps delivered precious propaganda opportunities to Octavian. He made a terrible gaff in 37/36 BC when he declared Cleopatra to be queen of Egypt and 'returned' Cyprus and Coele Syria to her control. This was, essentially, a restoration of the Ptolemaic kingdom to its third-century BC height. Following a disaster-prone war begun in 36 BC with the fratricidal Parthian king Phraates IV (37–2 BC), during which thousands of Roman troops died from disease, and after snubbing Octavia in 35 BC, Antony captured his erstwhile ally Artavasdes II, the king of Armenia. Coin issues of the late 30s BC by Antony, minted to pay his troops, projected an image of military might that celebrated the link between himself and the soldiers, even while his campaign floundered. Millions of these denarii were minted, and they form an important record of Antony's forces. Of particular note are the coins that refer to the *cohors speculatorum*, a select force serving Antony himself (Figure 7.29).

Returning to Alexandria, Antony celebrated what looked suspiciously like a triumph— a uniquely Roman tradition, his enemies pointed out, which took place not in Rome but in Egypt, and where Antony dedicated the spoils not to Capitoline Jupiter but to Cleopatra herself. Antony had wasted 'the honourable solemn rites of his native country upon the Egyptians', wrote Plutarch, 'for Cleopatra's sake' (*Antony*, 50). The failure of the Parthian war also caused some of Antony's allies, such as Plancus—'pathologically treacherous' (Velleius Paterculus, 2.83)—to defect to Octavian. Other Antonian partisans, such as Statilius Taurus, who would command the infantry for Octavian at Actium (below), also deserted. The pseudo-triumph had taken place in 34 BC, and in the same year Antony

Figure 7.29 Silver denarius minted in 32/31 BC. The galley on the obverse refers to Antony's reliance on sea power in the eastern Mediterranean. Note [CO]HORTIS SPECVLATORVUM on the reverse.

and Cleopatra, dressed as Osiris (Dionysus) and Isis (Venus), held a grand ceremony at the Gymnasium in Alexandria. Caesarion was installed as joint-ruler of Egypt alongside Cleopatra and named 'King of Kings', an echo of the old Persian royal title used since the sixth century BC and the antithesis of Republican ideals. One of the children of Antony and Cleopatra, Alexander, had even been named for the great conqueror Alexander the Great. He was introduced to the crowd in Alexandria in Persian dress, and declared ruler of a vast area in the Middle East—much of it actually outside Roman or Egyptian control. Another of their children, Ptolemy, appeared in the attire of a Hellenistic king and was appointed ruler of Syria and swathes of Asia Minor. The couple also had a daughter named Cleopatra Selene, and Antony gave her Cyrenaica and Crete to rule. This was all known as 'The Donations of Alexandria', and its exaggerated retelling by Octavian aroused considerable anger in Rome. Antony was giving away many territories that properly belonged to the Roman people and appeared to be setting himself up as an Egyptian dynast. Caesarion had taken an Egyptian name, becoming Ptolemy XV Philopator Philometor Caesar: would Antony, too, become a pharaoh? It was also clear that Cleopatra would be by his side for the foreseeable future; she was already appearing on Antony's coinage (Figure 7.30), and was using Egypt's wealth to pay Roman troops and line the pockets of Roman generals.

Octavian's successful propaganda campaign against Antony and the firm grip he held on the narrative is made clear by the fact that Appian ended his chronicle of the Roman civil wars with the death of Sextus Pompey. The final struggle between Octavian and Antony he consigned to a book, no longer extant, known as the *Egyptian Wars*. This division reflected the official line that Octavian was battling a foreign enemy—Cleopatra—and not a fellow Roman citizen in a fratricidal struggle for world supremacy. Octavian did his best to turn Rome's anger on Cleopatra when he eventually declared war by, acting as a fetial priest, symbolically hurling a spear outside the Temple of Bellona in Rome.

Lepidus was already gone, but the legal basis for the Second Triumvirate remained in place until the end of 33 BC. In 32 BC, Octavian and his bodyguard broke into a meeting of the senate that was taking place outside the pomerium. In front of the consuls, Gnaeus Domitius Ahenobarbus and Gaius Sosius, both of whom were partisans of Antony, Octavian

Figure 7.30 Silver tetradrachm of Antony and Cleopatra minted at Antioch between 36 and 34 BC. Obverse: Cleopatra with necklace and earrings and the Greek legend ΒΑΣΑΛΙϹϹΑ Κ[ΛΕΟΠΑ]ΤΡΑ ΘΕΑ ΝΕΩΤΕΡΑ, translated variously as 'Queen Cleopatra the younger goddess' or 'Queen Cleopatra Thea, junior'. Reverse: head of Antony, with the Greek legend ΑΝΤΩΝΙΟϹ ΑΥΤΟΚΡΑΤΩΡ ΤΡΙΤΟΝ ΤΡΙΩΝ ΑΝΔΡΩΝ, 'Antonius Autokrator [*Imperator*] Third Man'—that is, triumvir.

declared himself the sole head of state. Not long afterwards, he illegally retrieved Antony's will from the Vestal Virgins. Octavian had been briefed on the will by Plancus and knew that it contained provisions for Antony's burial in Alexandria instead of Rome. It also declared that Caesarion was the rightful heir of Julius Caesar, a vicious snub to Octavian and a clear attempt to commandeer the Caesarian agenda, and he used this information to further stress Antony's unsuitability as a Roman leader. Ignoring the fact that similar rumours had circulated about Julius Caesar, Octavian now circulated gossip that Antony intended to name Alexandria as the capital of the empire, and to place Cleopatra in charge of Rome. In response, Antony divorced Octavia and married Cleopatra—a marriage illegal under Roman law, as Cleopatra was not a Roman citizen—and this was the final break between the two men. Ahenobarbus, Sosius, and a sizeable contingent of the senate fled to Antony. (Ahenobarbus, finding Cleopatra unmanageable, later defected to Octavian.) As in the earlier civil war, where there had been Pompeians and Caesarians, now there were supporters of Octavian and supporters of Antony. Furthermore, as it had with Pompey and Caesar, and then with the Second Triumvirate against Caesar's assassins, the struggle for supreme power between a tiny number of ambitious individuals consumed the entire Mediterranean world. Octavian cemented his position as the champion of Italy by having all Roman citizens swear an oath of loyalty to him, and to him alone.

Actium

The anticlimactic denouement took place off the promontory of Actium in 31 BC (Figure 7.31). Antony had consolidated his position in Greece with the apparent intention of invading Italy across the Adriatic, a tactic that had proven successful for Sulla but fatal to Pompey and his faction. Octavian's forces—under the command of competent subordinates like Agrippa and Statilius Taurus—prevailed in an early infantry battle. When the two sides began their naval engagement, Cleopatra's squadron set sail for Alexandria.

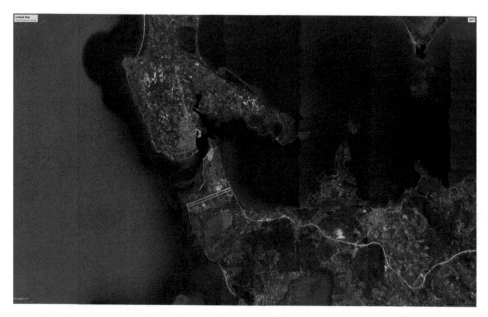

Figure 7.31 Google Earth Pro image of the Actium promontory (marked by the airstrip running west–east) and the Gulf of Ambracia, to the right of the image. The naval battle took place just to the west of the promontory itself.

Source: Image © 2020 TerraMetrics. Data from SIO, NOAA, US Navy, NGA, GEBCO.

Seeing his bride depart, Antony followed suit and resistance to Octavian collapsed. There have been numerous attempts to locate the remnants of the battle, but despite an optimistic announcement in 1980 that shipwrecks were found off the promontory, neither the heavy bronze rams nor the ships themselves have turned up. In 1994, however, stone catapult balls consistent with what is known about first-century BC naval warfare were located on the sea floor by a joint team from the University of South Florida and the Greek Ministry of Culture; on land, investigation of the Actium victory monument has offered intriguing clues for the monumental size of the vessels deployed by Antony and Cleopatra (Chapter 8).

It took a year for the victory to be realised, following defections from Antony's remaining forces to Octavian, and after the suicide of both Antony and Cleopatra and the execution of Caesarion and Antony, Antony's eldest son by Fulvia. Afterwards, the capture of Egypt was publicly celebrated (Figure 7.32) and its immense wealth came into Octavian's hands; henceforth, it would be a province that belonged to him, and him alone.

The Second Triumvirate was over. His enemies eliminated, Octavian was master of the Mediterranean world. It had been an astonishing 14 years: Syme judged that 'on no rational forecast of events would [Caesar's] adopted son have succeeded in playing off the Republican cause against the Caesarian leaders, survived the war of Perusia, and lived to prevail over Antonius' (*Roman Revolution*, p. 114). Now Octavian would have to devise a way to prevent himself from suffering the fate of Pompey, Caesar, and Antony: one of the most ambitious and successful political programs in world history was about to be unveiled.

Figure 7.32 Silver denarius of Octavian minted in 28 BC. Obverse: head of Octavian; reverse: a crocodile with the legend AEGYPTO CAPTA.

Chapter 8

Monarchy and empire

Augustus, 30 BC–AD 14

The careers of the warlords of the late Republic starkly revealed the limitations of political power. At one end of the spectrum, Sulla had tried to defend the Republic's institutions and the traditional position of the senatorial oligarchy. At the other, Caesar had attempted to rule without senatorial participation and, through a lifetime dictatorship tinged with divinity, flirted with a form of autocratic rule that was more at home in the Hellenistic east. After Actium, Octavian proved that he was the only person with a credible alternative to these failed, polarising opposites. He realised that the Republic could not be restored; nor could he follow Caesar's example. Furthermore, he could not ignore the role of the army, which had proven so important for his meteoric ascent to the apex of political life.

Octavian's solution to these problems was his lasting achievement. With greater success than any of his predecessors, he resolved the problems that plagued Roman life by artfully combining absolute power with the traditions of the senatorial Republic, governing from behind the scenes while allowing the people the illusion that the Republic had been restored. Over the subsequent decades the idea of the *res publica* was quietly and carefully overlaid by that of the *patria*, the fatherland, a construct in which all Romans could unite in pride at their achievements under the benevolence of their *paterfamilias*, Octavian. By gradually fusing the patriotic idea of a fatherland with his own role in society, Octavian, who took the name Augustus in 27 BC, overcame the factional strife that had plagued the Republic. He correctly judged that the exhausted Roman people would rally behind a man who upheld the *mos maiorum*; that they would overlook his own part in the deaths of thousands; and that they would not protest his accumulation of power as long as it was steeped in the traditional political language of the Republic: consul, tribune, imperium. Much of Roman tradition was strengthened, including the centrality of family values, the primacy of Latin, the construction of public buildings, and the endurance of religious practices. To many, it probably did not seem that too much *had* changed: senators still debated in the senate, the *concilium plebis* passed legislation, consuls were elected by the *comitia centuriata*, and one leading man who had triumphed in battle looked more powerful than his peers. The one change that *was* evident, however, was by far the most important. For the first time since the murder of Tiberius Gracchus, Octavian delivered an era of peace, and in exchange his opinion was accorded greater weight than that of anyone else; and by identifying himself as the individual who broke the toxic cycle of constant warfare, Augustus inspired personal loyalty on a level that the senatorial Republic had never managed to achieve. His soft-power approach was alternately developed, undermined, and squandered by his successors, Tiberius (AD 14–37), Caligula (AD 37–41),

DOI: 10.4324/9781003202523-8

Claudius (AD 41–54), and Nero (AD 54–68)—the Julio-Claudian dynasty, whose careers are discussed in Chapter 9.

After Actium

Following the suicides of Antony and Cleopatra and the capitulation of Egypt, Octavian paused in Alexandria to admire the sarcophagus of Alexander the Great, who had been buried there by Ptolemy I shortly after his death in 323 BC. (According to Cassius Dio (51.16), Octavian was unable to resist the temptation to open the sarcophagus and touch the body, and in the process accidentally broke off the conqueror's desiccated nose.) Afterwards, Octavian returned to Italy in 29 BC and celebrated an elaborate triumph. An assassination attempt by the son of the triumvir Lepidus was quashed by Maecenas—'a man who was literally sleepless when occasion demanded, and quick to foresee what was to be done and skilful in doing it' (Velleius Paterculus, 2.88).

An urgent question for Octavian was the basis of his authority: the triumvirate had ended in 33 BC. One triumvir was in forced retirement, while the other was dead. All of Italy had sworn an oath to Octavian in 32 BC, but this was not a secure basis for his power. In 31 BC, he had started holding the consulship, but this was also unlikely to prove suitable in the long term. In 28 BC, Agrippa joined him in the consulship, and then in 27 BC, Octavian called a meeting of the senate and staged a symbolic power transfer by announcing that he was returning control to Rome's traditional ruling mechanisms: the senate and the Roman people. While this may have appeared a somewhat risky gamble, he had in fact judged the mood perfectly, allowing him to 'have his sovereignty voluntarily confirmed by the people, so as to avoid the appearance of having forced them against his will' (Cassius Dio, 53.2). Many of Octavian's supporters in the senate had already been read into his intentions, and the senators clamoured for him to remain on as consul. Acquiescing to their 'demands', he also 'agreed' to manage those parts of the empire which were considered to be at risk, including Egypt, Spain, Gaul, and several others that now became 'imperial' provinces, administered by men of his own choosing and in which the bulk of the army was garrisoned (see Figure 8.35, below). Cassius Dio wrote: 'His professed motive in this was that the senate might fearlessly enjoy the finest portion of the empire, while he himself had the hardships and the dangers; but his real purpose was that by this arrangement the senators would be unarmed and unprepared for battle, while he alone had arms and maintained soldiers' (53.12).

A grateful senate gave Octavian the name 'Augustus' at the urging of the ever devious Lucius Munatius Plancus; the month of August (so named during a calendar revision by Augustus himself) bears this new name, which was laden with all sorts of religious ideas perfectly in tune with Octavian's status as the self-declared son of a god and self-professed saviour of Rome. Ideas mooted that he be called Romulus were discarded for their connotations of royalty, and it was felt that 'Augustus' was both innovative and 'more honourable' (Suetonius, *Augustus*, 7). Laurels were placed on the doors of his house; a golden shield, the *clipeus votivus*, was made for him, inscribed with the Republican and Caesarian values of *virtus, pietas, clementia*, and *iustitia*, and placed in the curia Julia—an ancient marble copy exists today in the Musée d'Arles in Provence. A statue of Nike (Victory) was also installed in the curia Julia, where it remained for 400 years before its removal in controversial circumstances (Chapter 13). Augustus was also awarded the *corona civica*, the 'civic crown'—given to a citizen who saved the life of another, and awarded without irony for all the lives he had 'saved' by ending the civil wars. Contemporary coinage of Augustus celebrating this event bore the legend *ob civis servatos*, 'for having saved the citizens'.

This arrangement became known as the First Settlement, and it *legally* established imperial rule in Rome while allowing the senate and the people the pretence that everyday business would carry on as before, but in a new, peaceful world. The First Settlement was celebrated on coins with the legend *leges et iura P[opulo] R[omano] restituit*: 'I restored the laws and justice to the Roman people', often with an image of Augustus on the obverse seated on a curule chair—the type of seat used by consuls at meetings of the senate. At the same time as Augustus was flamboyantly 'returning' power to the state, he had many of the garish silver statues that had been made of him destroyed, and granted Agrippa, his colleague in the consulship, the right to the same number of fasces.

Writing with the benefit of hindsight and after experiencing the dreadful rule of Domitian (AD 81–96), the historian Tacitus (who somewhat misleadingly claimed to be able to write 'without indignation or partisanship') condemned these developments. 'Giving out that he was a consul,' he wrote, 'Augustus won over the soldiers with gifts, the populace with cheap corn, and all men with the sweets of repose … he was wholly unopposed, for the boldest spirits had fallen in battle or in the proscription.' Everyone else, Tacitus concluded, 'preferred the safety of the present to the dangerous past'. It was clear to Tacitus that the Augustan government was little more than a 'personal régime', and his assessment was a direct rebuttal of the version of history provided by the ideologically charged *Res Gestae* of Augustus, inscribed throughout the empire on Augustus's death (below). Yet it is important to place Tacitus's assessment in context. At the time of Augustus's ascendancy, there had been so many irregularities in government over the preceding century that the promise of *any* sort of peaceful normalcy that allowed the senate to meet, elections to be held, governors to be appointed, and care and attention to be paid to Rome and its battered population was liable to be seized with open arms—even if the person providing this peaceful normalcy was responsible for misery and murder on a massive scale. With the return of elections came the illusion that political consensus—the ancient bedrock of the Republic and the source of its cohesion and success—had also returned. This view was strengthened by the fact that Augustus was careful to listen to the senate and to allow its members to regain much of the prestige and position in society that they had once held. He did not dare to wear a crown, like Caesar, nor did he take a perpetual dictatorship. The title attached to him, *princeps*, 'leading man' (leading to the term 'principate' being used for the period of Roman history governed by Augustus and his successors), alludes to his soft-power approach that integrated his own authority with that of the senate. While Caesar had bullied the senate and ostentatiously flaunted his lofty position, Augustus used his *auctoritas*—his authority, buttressed by his wealth, his legions, and his political clout—to provide advice to senators and guide their policy. There was no office of *princeps*, nor did Augustus take any novel office that had no precedent in the Republic. His was an entirely new and even refreshing approach. For a time, it worked, even though the 'free and fair' consular elections tended to provide Augustus with willing colleagues: Agrippa in 28 and 27 BC, Statilius Taurus in 26 BC, the old Caesarian Junius Silanus in 25 BC, Norbanus Flaccus, scion of a loyal Caesarian family, in 24 BC. Augustus was also given a ten-year command over a number of provinces that happened to contain the bulk of the Roman legions, including Gaul, Syria, Spain, Egypt, and Cyprus.

The First Settlement was given a ten-year lifespan, but a foiled assassination plot and growing aristocratic discontent caused by his repeated tenure of the consulship convinced Augustus that a more permanent arrangement was required. Before he could do anything, however, he fell seriously ill in 23 BC and came close to death. Fearing the worst and in order to prepare for the future, he transferred his official documents to Gnaeus Calpurnius Piso, his consular colleague and an unwavering Republican who had backed the *optimates*, opposed Caesar, and fought against Octavian in the civil wars. Agrippa was given his signet ring. There was no successor designate, nor any attempt to create an hereditary monarchy. Had Augustus died, Piso would have been left as the surviving consul. Augustus's actions here are thus often taken to be traditional rather than radical, and show his understanding of the delicacy of his position.

After he recovered, Augustus resigned the consulship in 23 BC and replaced this position with the power of two offices that he did *not* hold. First, he was given a proconsular *maius* imperium ('greater' imperium) by the senate, a recognition of his leading status in Roman society. The *maius* imperium, the precedent for which was Pompey's extraordinary grant of authority (Chapter 6), provided a legal way for Augustus to administer the imperial provinces of the Mediterranean and to maintain control over the legions. Second, he took the powers of a plebeian tribune, permitting him to call the senate and—if the need ever arose, which it never did—to use the tribunician veto. Holding tribunician power also allowed Augustus to enhance one of the benchmarks of his propaganda campaign: that he was the protector of the people of Rome, a man who freed them from Egyptian tyranny and the threat of the dysfunctional and unnatural union of Antony and Cleopatra. This novel constitutional development became known as the Second Settlement (Figure 8.1).

By holding power without office he was now well outside the traditional framework of annual and collegial offices, but the Second Settlement was still framed in ways that were easy to understand, and 'in most ways he comported himself towards the Romans as if they were free citizens' (Cassius Dio, 53.33). Later, the senate allowed Augustus the consular fasces and the right to sit between the consuls—another example of power without office.

Figure 8.1 Bronze dupondius celebrating Augustus's tribunician power. Obverse: the legend AVGVSTVS TRIBVNIC POTEST (*tribunicia potestas*) within a laurel wreath; reverse: the name of the moneyer (Censorinus) and the abbreviation S C (*senatus consulto*), the senatorial guarantee of the coin's value.

It is something of a paradox that late Republican history was littered with violence and discord linked with plebeian tribunes, and the repeated and damaging tenure of the office of the tribunate and the abuse of its authority, yet the tribunician power became such a cornerstone of imperial power that it was never again possessed by anyone outside the imperial inner circle. Indeed, it became so central to his authority that Augustus dated the years of his rule according to its tenure. Much later, in 2 BC, Augustus was awarded the title of *pater patriae*, and on coins he became *parens*, a *paterfamilias* and father figure to the Roman people, who inhabited a new *patria*. Contemporaries recognised the importance of fatherly guidance. The poet Ovid explicitly referred to Augustus as 'Father of the world' (*Fasti*, 2.130), while in a particularly sycophantic part of his *Geography*, Strabo understood that only the firm hand of a father could carry out the 'formidable task' of governing the Roman empire (6.4). Paternal rule brought stability and freed everyone from what Strabo called the 'drunken violence' of people such as Antony (17.11).

The development of Augustus's political authority in this way was not intended for wholesale public consumption. Those parts of it that were—*maius* imperium, tribunician power, the consulship, and eventually, after the death of Lepidus, the office of *pontifex maximus*—were traditional and easy to understand. By holding these offices or being granted extraofficial powers, Augustus performed the traditional roles of a Republican oligarch, while simultaneously diluting any lingering chance of the dwindling numbers of the *nobiles* regaining power. The people did not need to know, nor could they probably detect, the concentration of authority that the consecutive settlements gave to Augustus. Those senators who understood what was taking place either accepted the inevitable in exchange for peace and their own prosperity, or joined the small number of unsuccessful murder plots. When discord arose, it provoked anxiety among the people: despite the rules surrounding the *cursus honorum*, for example, an ambitious politician named Egnatius Rufus sought the consulship immediately on the back of his praetorship. The spectre of Cicero's 'dregs of Romulus' bared its ugly teeth, and after some prevarication Egnatius was arrested, tried, and put to death.

For the people, Augustus provided a remarkable 'information' campaign that we would now think of as an elaborate and well-crafted propaganda operation. It emphasised the return of peace and irresistible victory over the enemies of Rome, and it was accompanied by handouts of money, food, and clothes, and the cancellation of debts. 'Agriculture returned to the fields,' wrote Velleius Paterculus, 'respect to religion, to mankind freedom from anxiety … old laws were usefully amended, new laws passed for the general good' (2.89). Augustus's clever political messaging to the people also underscored the celebration of traditional Roman values and a renewed connection to Roman gods, and in this it was the evolution of the campaign he had used to destroy Antony. This campaign was managed in ways that were accessible and easy to understand: through the ostentatious commemoration of the Actium campaign; through features of Rome's built landscape and that of the provinces; through visual art, literature, inscriptions, and legislation; and by means of mass gatherings and religious celebrations.

The Actium memorials

Close to the site of Actium, Augustus constructed a new city, Nikopolis ('city of victory'), populated by Greeks drawn from the surrounding area. A special emphasis was placed on the link between Augustus and Apollo: the god was seen as the opposite of the 'despotic' Dionysus, favoured by Antony, and it was common knowledge in Rome that Apollo had saved the Julian ancestor Aeneas at Troy in the mythical past. Stories repeated by Suetonius crafted myths of a divine conception for Augustus, with Octavian's mother Atia seduced by a snake while she was attending to the rites of Apollo. Such lore recalled the myths surrounding the conception of Alexander the Great, via a serpent or even a thunderbolt, a representation of Zeus (Suetonius, *Augustus*, 94 & Plutarch, *Alexander*, 2).

North of Nikopolis, Augustus dedicated a temenos (a sacred area) to Apollo made up of a stadium, gymnasium, and theatre. The temenos was linked with a reimagined Panhellenic festival, the Actian Games. Augustus set this gathering on the same level as the Olympics and the famed Isthmian Games, and it was to be celebrated every four years as a recurring reminder of his victory. Further reinforcement of the message was the inception of a new era that dated from the battle itself in 31 BC. Known as the Actian era, it was used to date various coinage issues and inscriptions throughout the eastern Mediterranean. On the southern side of the strait leading into the Gulf of Ambracia, Augustus refurbished the Temple of Apollo Aktios, an ancient foundation from the fifth century BC and the former site of the Actian Games; he also bestowed upon it ten captured enemy vessels that were docked nearby and could be admired by curious visitors. (The remains of the temple, partly submerged, were discovered in 2009.) The association between victory, Apollo, and Augustus was thus reinforced on multiple levels at Actium as well as on coinage circulating in the Roman world (Figure 8.2), and at Nikopolis this association was also cemented in a way that merged the Augustan triumph with the built heritage, customs, and religious practices of Greece.

North of Nikopolis and close to the site of his old military camp, Augustus built a memorial dedicated to Mars and Neptune on a hill commanding magnificent views out over the Ionian Sea (Figures 8.3 and 8.4). The monument was a victory trophy of the sort common in the Greek world, displaying the captured weapons, arms, armour, and equipment of a vanquished foe. The structure was designed as a podium with 35 sockets,

Figure 8.2 Silver denarius minted in 29 BC celebrating the Actium victory. Obverse: Octavian with the laurels of Apollo; reverse: column with six rams of galleys and two anchors, with Octavian standing.

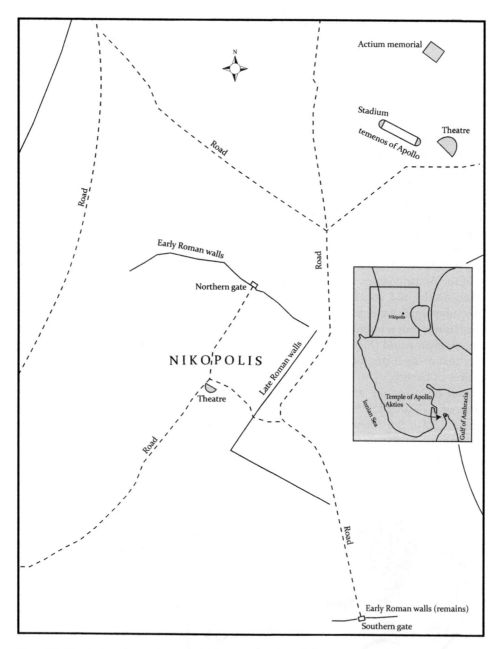

Figure 8.3 The Actium memorials, showing features visible today.

Source: Illustration by the author.

Figure 8.4 The remains of Augustus's Actium monument. In the foreground lie the remains of its dedicatory inscription, while immediately behind can be seen the sockets into which the rams of captured ships were slotted.

Source: Photograph by Vassiliki Feidopoulou (CC BY-SA 4.0).

into which the bronze rams of Antony's captured ships could be mounted. The podium itself was complemented by a tripartite stoa, and terracotta fragments found throughout the area have revealed depictions of legendary scenes connected with Rome's foundation myths, such as the twins and the she-wolf, asserting the greatness of Rome's past and symbolically linking Rome's (re)birth with Augustus.

The monument lay undisturbed for centuries; despite being mentioned by numerous ancient writers, it was only rediscovered in 1913. Its original appearance and the precise function of the sockets remained elusive until the fortuitous discovery of a Hellenistic-era ship's ram off the coast of Haifa in 1980. Weighing close to half a ton, its internal structure offered a close match to the intricately carved sockets on the Actium trophy and revealed that the captured rams were intended to be slotted into the sockets much like a plug into a light switch. Each socket was made-to-measure for individual rams, and this has allowed archaeologists to reconstruct the long-vanished rams using 3D laser scanning technology. Some of the rams were colossal—one was nearly 2 metres (6.5 feet) wide—and ancient visitors to the memorial would have marvelled at the greatness of the fleet overwhelmed by Octavian's forces. A lengthy Latin inscription at the memorial further stressed the nature of Octavian's victory, as a just war fought for the Republic against a dangerous and implacable foe (*RGE* §92). An idea of what the monument might have looked like in antiquity has been created by the Institute for the Visualisation of History (see Further Reading section).

Rome

Rome had suffered greatly throughout the civil wars, and Augustus was now presented with an unparalleled opportunity to remake the city in his image and communicate his vision to the Roman people through built heritage, art, and statuary. His projects, many of which were in the works as he solidified his position in Rome before the Actium campaign, also provided long-term employment for the city's growing population, and allowed them to participate in his political ascendance.

Julius Caesar first grasped the need to develop Rome after being awed by the magnificence of Alexandria. In the Mediterranean, Rome still paled behind Athens, Pergamum, and the lost glories of places that the Romans had destroyed, such as Corinth and Carthage. This situation changed dramatically under Augustus, who oversaw a building programme that both dazzled and instructed. The centrality of the Augustan building program to Roman public life is reflected by the fact that the architect Vitruvius—a major influence on Renaissance thinkers, including Michelangelo—dedicated his magisterial *Ten Books on Architecture* to Augustus shortly before his death around 15 BC. In a similar vein, Strabo would come to regard Rome as 'a spectacle that one can hardly draw away from' and summed up his enumeration of its wonders with a pithy—'such is Rome' (*Geography*, 5.3.8). Augustan development was fundamentally conservative, in that it sought to build a *Roman* city of Rome, rather than simply imitate the grandeur of Alexandria or Athens. As such, foreign influences were suppressed unless they served an ideological purpose, such as the obelisk adjacent to the Ara Pacis (below). Elaborate public gardens, a staple of places like Alexandria, were turned into Roman parks through the patronage of men such as the Epicurean Maecenas, who constructed the lavish Gardens of Maecenas on the Esquiline. One notable exception

Figure 8.5 The Pantheon in Rome. The inscription reads 'Agrippa, son of Lucius, made [this] when he was consul for the third time' [27 BC].

Source: Photograph by the author.

to this conservatism was the striking pyramidal tomb of C. Cestius, completed in 12 BC; however, its effect was not to 'Egyptianise' Rome, but instead to recall Octavian's triumph over Cleopatra.

Many of these public works were carried out by Agrippa, whose name can still be read on the architrave of Rome's iconic Pantheon (temple to 'all the gods'), which was later expanded and rebuilt by Hadrian (Figure 8.5). In a striking example of historical continuity, the Pantheon now houses the tomb of king Victor Emmanuelle II (d. 1878), the *pater patriae* of a united Italy. Agrippa also began the Diribitorium, a vast building in the Campus Martius used for counting ballots during elections. Completed in 7 BC by Augustus, its roof was the widest in Rome for the following two centuries. In tandem with this project, Agrippa finished the Saepta Julia, one of the many architectural fancies of Julius Caesar, in 26 BC. The Saepta lay adjacent to the Diribitorium and was used for casting votes as well as for gladiatorial games.

Agrippa's sister, Vipsania Polla, dedicated the Porticus Vipsania in the Campus Agrippae, part of the Campus Martius, which became a public park. In a clear indication of Rome's supremacy in the empire, a marble map of the world adorned the Porticus Vipsania. Other elaborate projects were the work of Caesar's associates, including Plancus (repairs to the Temple of Saturn), Statilius Taurus (an amphitheatre in the Campus Martius), Pollio (building works at the Atrium of Libertas and a public library), and Lucius Cornificius, an associate of Agrippa (renovations to the Temple of Diana on the Aventine). Augustus's

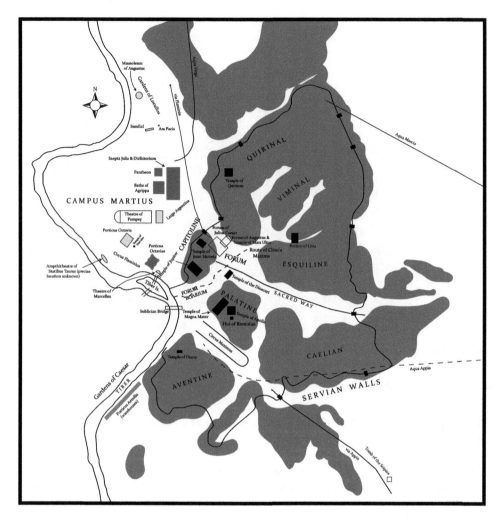

Figure 8.6 Augustan Rome.

Source: Illustration by the author.

stepfather, Lucius Marcius Philippus, restored the second-century Temple of Hercules and the Muses, surrounding it with the Porticus Philippi (Figure 8.6).

Augustus was the first to exploit the marble quarries at Carrara, leading to Suetonius's famous aphorism that the *princeps* had discovered Rome 'built of brick and left it in marble' (*Augustus*, 31). With this expensive and elegant new material, he built a new forum, the centrepiece of which was the massive Temple of Mars Ultor, Mars 'the avenger', which he had vowed after Brutus and Cassius were vanquished in 42 BC. The remains of the forum and the ruins of the temple still stand today; numerous Augustan coin issues included portraits of the temple, emphasising the link between Augustus and the god of war (Figure 8.7).

Figure 8.7 Silver denarius minted in Spain in 19 or 18 BC. The reverse shows the Temple of Mars Ultor in Rome.

The temple, built in the traditional manner with its roots in Etruscan-era temple design, was completed in 2 BC. Like the Actium monuments, the forum and the temple provided a visual reinforcement of Augustus's victory—and, through statues of Venus and Julius Caesar and a building inscription proclaiming Augustus's ancestry, demonstrated continuity with the past and proof of his filial loyalty to his adoptive father. Mars was the consort of Venus in Roman mythology, and thus the new temple also offered a fitting counterpoint to the Temple of Venus Genetrix in the nearby forum of Julius Caesar (Figure 8.8). Further emphasising the mythological strands that connected Augustan Rome with the distant past were statues of Aeneas and Romulus in the *exedrae*, the semi-circular features that lay to each side of the temple precinct. Augustus also planned to include statues of famous Romans and his own family, with inscriptions detailing their role in Roman history. Like Virgil's *Aeneid* (below) and the *fasti triumphales* and *fasti consulares* (Chapter 1), erected in the forum by Augustus, the forum and the Temple of Mars represented an essentially patriotic project that united the people in a single *patria*, infused with a common, glorious, and very *Roman* history. In the forum, Augustus also erected a bronze milestone, symbolically marking Rome as the centre of a world empire, and a similar function was performed by the Porticus ad Nationes, featuring the nations of the world represented by statues.

Another visual reminder of the Augustan triumph was the anti-Dionysian (and thus *contra* Antony) Temple of Apollo next to his own residence on the Palatine, vowed during the defeat of Sextus Pompey in 36 BC, and dedicated in 28 BC along with a lavishly appointed library. Just before ground was broken in 36 BC, a massive lightning bolt had hit the site, which had originally been earmarked for Octavian's private residence. Consulting the *haruspices*, Octavian was informed that the portent signalled the interest and favour of Apollo—thus beginning the long and important association between the man and the god.

In gratitude for escaping death from a (different) lightning bolt, Augustus also vowed a marble Temple to Jupiter the Thunderer, completed in 22 BC. Moreover, he built or completed other structures linked with Julius Caesar and his own broader family. For Caesar, Augustus finished the Basilica Julia, the forum of Caesar, and the partly-built curia Julia, together with a Temple of the Divine Julius—located on the site of Caesar's funeral pyre in the forum—that was vowed after Philippi and dedicated in 29 BC. (Later, and

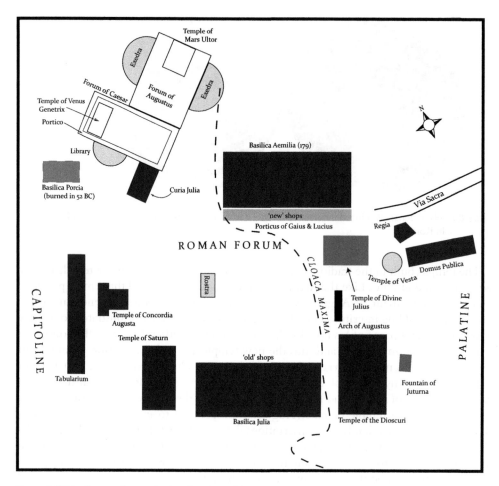

Figure 8.8 The Roman forum during the time of Augustus.

Source: Illustration by the author.

directly in line with the Temple of the Divine Julius, the Temple of Concordia Augusta
(celebrating peace and harmony and a refurbishment of the existing Temple of Concord)
was completed in AD 10.) For his sister, Octavia, he constructed the Porticus Octaviae
(not to be confused with the Porticus Octavia, dedicated in 168 BC), a colonnaded edifice
that included a library, meeting room, and two temples; it may also have included statues
of famous women, a mirror to the display of famous Roman men in the Augustan forum.
Augustus also completed the Theatre of Marcellus, named for Augustus's nephew and son-
in-law Marcus Claudius Marcellus (son of Octavia and Gaius Claudius Marcellus, consul
in 50 BC). Work on the structure had begun shortly before Caesar's assassination, and it was
finally completed in 13 BC. In 17 BC, the partly finished theatre was used for the Secular
Games, a festival that marked the end of one *saeculum*—a period of 110 years—and the
start of another. The festival had ancient origins, and had last been celebrated in the second

Figure 8.9 The Mausoleum of Augustus, prior to restoration.

Source: Photograph by the author.

century. As part of his message of renewal and rebirth, Augustus revived the Games to celebrate the start of a new era for the Roman people, simultaneously anchoring that new era in the misty traditions of Rome's timeless past—a message that was hammered home by the near-contemporary restoration of the Temple of Quirinus, the deified Romulus, in 16 BC. In tandem with the Secular Games, Augustus also resurrected the equally ancient Lupercalia, which had fallen out of favour after the death of Julius Caesar.

Two important buildings in the Campus Martius formed a vital part of Augustus's message to the people. The first was his Mausoleum on the via Flaminia, intended for himself and members of his family. This structure was probably begun prior to the Actium campaign to show that Octavian intended to be buried in Rome: he was the leader for everyone, a man who cherished and valued the Italian past in contrast to the eastern ambitions of Antony—especially Antony's desire to be buried in Egypt (Figure 8.9). It is sometimes suggested that the Mausoleum drew its inspiration from Etruscan models, but it has also been pointed out that other influences were to be found in the tombs of Trojan nobles, the tomb of Mausolus of Caria (the very first 'Mausoleum'), and even the tomb of Alexander the Great. Strabo recorded that the tomb was surmounted by a bronze statue of Augustus (perhaps rendered as a 'new' Alexander) and had dense tree plantings that reached the summit (*Geography*, 5.3.8). In 2017, a €6 million renovation project got underway to give this important monument a much-needed facelift—the first restoration since the time of Mussolini—and the Mausoleum reopened to the public in March 2021.

Figure 8.10 Relief panel from the Ara Pacis showing a garland of fruits and vegetables with a *patera* above.

Source: Photograph by the author.

The second structure was the Ara Pacis—the Altar of Peace—which further communicated to the Roman people that they were living in a new era of peace and plenty, secured by the return of piety and traditional values and the end of war. The Ara Pacis was begun in 13 BC and consecrated on Livia's birthday four years later. Built from Carrara marble, it was erected in the Campus Martius close to the Mausoleum, and took the form of a raised altar surrounded by an enclosure wall.

The panels of the Ara Pacis are rich with Augustan political and religious ideology. Many feature images of plenty, such as garlanded fruits and vegetables from all four seasons, together with *paterae*, shallow bowls used for preparing sacrificial libations (Figure 8.10). Relief carvings of swans, the symbol of Apollo, are repeated multiple times on the lower panels covering the exterior of the enclosure wall, above which other reliefs display the goddess of Peace with children, animals, and fruit (Figure 8.11). The allegorical image of Peace is particularly laden with imagery: a water jar at the bottom of the relief indicates an abundance of life-giving water, while the ocean waves to the right illustrate the limitless geographical reach of the new Augustan era—the *imperium sine fine*, 'empire without end', a grant from Jupiter immortalised by Virgil's *Aeneid* (1.279). A prominent swan of Apollo appears to the left, with smaller swans repeated at the top of the lower frieze.

Figure 8.11 The goddess of peace on the exterior of the Ara Pacis.

Source: Photograph by the author.

Another heavily charged relief is that showing a sacrifice being carried out by a figure identified as either Aeneas or Numa Pompilius, the legendary king of Rome who succeeded Romulus (Figure 8.12). At the top left is a shrine in which are installed the *lares* and *penates*, the household gods. Interpretations favouring Aeneas fit the genealogy claimed by Julius Caesar and Augustus, while whether one chooses Aeneas or Numa, the scene affirms the importance of piety in Roman society.

A badly damaged part of the altar is thought to show Mars with Romulus, Remus, and the she-wolf, while another poorly preserved panel displays Dea Roma, the deified persona of Rome (Figure 8.13). Dozens of figures run in a frieze on the north and south sides of the altar; they include priests, lictors, senators, and members of the imperial circle, reinforcing the unity of the empire and its people under the leadership of Augustus. The appearance of children in this frieze, as well as elsewhere on the altar, signals the transmission of the Augustan peace to the next generation. The portraits of the imperial family have proven difficult to identify with certainty, but it is believed that Augustus, Agrippa, Livia, the future emperor Tiberius, and possibly Augustus's grandson Gaius Caesar are depicted on the south frieze (Figure 8.14).

Figure 8.12 Aeneas or Numa Pompilius making a sacrifice on the exterior of the Ara Pacis.

Source: Photograph by the author.

This complex interplay of ideas and images confirms the new era as one of peace and prosperity, as well as one in which the people are partners in government with Augustus. The message was further reinforced by the installation of a monumental sundial nearby. Using an obelisk removed from Heliopolis in Egypt, the installation was arranged so that on Augustus's birthday, the sun—a representation of Apollo—would shine through the main doorway of the Ara Pacis. The pairing of an Egyptian obelisk with the Ara Pacis also reinforced the subjugation of Antony and Cleopatra, explicitly tying the Egyptian victory to the new era of peace.

The Ara Pacis eventually fell into disrepair and disappeared under feet of alluvial silt deposited by the nearby river Tiber. It remained buried until the mid-sixteenth century, when fragments of its exquisitely carved panels started to appear on the art market. Later, the ideological power of the Ara Pacis, so potent during the Augustan era, was revived during the time of Mussolini when the entire structure was excavated and placed on display, becoming one of the highlights of Hitler's tour of Rome in 1938. During the same year, and on a wall adjacent to the Ara Pacis museum and the Mausoleum, the *Res Gestae* of Augustus was inscribed in large bronze letters. Mussolini saw himself as a new Augustus, and on Augustus's birthday in 1937, he had held the *Mostra augustea della romanità*, a celebration of 'Augustan Romanness' that retrospectively portrayed ancient

Figure 8.13 Dea Roma on the Ara Pacis.

Source: Photograph by the author.

Rome as a militarised Fascist state. Close to the Ara Pacis and the Mausoleum of Augustus lay the Istituto Nazionale Fascista della Previdenza Sociale, featuring two striking images of winged victories holding the fasces, and a Latin 'Res Gestae' inscription honouring Mussolini. In 2006, the Ara Pacis was once again placed on display—this time in a new museum (Figure 8.15) that replaced the older Fascist pavilion, demolished in 2000.

The messages and achievements of the Augustan era were also proclaimed through statuary, sculpture, and portable artwork such as vases and cups. Several of these items are among the most famous artworks of the ancient world: the silver Boscoreale Cups, for example, are part of a hoard of precious objects stashed during the eruption of Vesuvius in AD 79; they feature representations of the Augustan theme of irresistible victory. On one, Augustus holds a globe while Venus presents him with a winged Nike, or Victory; Mars stands to his left, further reinforcing the link between the *gens* Julia and the god of war.

Statues produced during the Augustan period were laden with symbolism, and through a conservative blend of classical styles set the tone for the idealised representation of the human form. Numerous statues portrayed the ageless *princeps* as a priest, placing emphasis not only on the importance of piety but also showing Augustus leading by example, as he became *pontifex maximus* when Lepidus died in 12 BC. Other statues evoked the legendary Alexander the Great or the god Apollo, especially through the insouciant lock of hair that

Figure 8.14 Figures in the upper south frieze on the exterior of the Ara Pacis. The fragmentary figure on the left is thought to be Augustus, followed by attendants; to the right, the veiled figure is Agrippa, with Livia and a child (Gaius Caesar?) between them. Note the swans of Apollo at the top of the lower frieze.

Source: Photograph by the author.

characterised statues of Alexander and that had earlier been revived by representations of Pompey. Statues were also produced showing Augustus with the *corona civica* and intricate cameos of both Augustus and Livia showed idealised portraits of the imperial couple. Portraits of Livia (Figure 8.16) show her characteristic stylised bouffant hairstyle and reveal a woman of great strength and determination whom Tacitus called 'the feminine bully' (*Annals*, 1.3) and 'a curse to the realm' (1.10).

It is noteworthy that *public* statues of women in Rome were the exception; only one, of Cornelia, the mother of Tiberius and Gaius Gracchus, is known from the Republican period. After the Second Triumvirate, however, as Roman women such as Octavia began to appear on Roman coinage, public statues of imperial women such as Livia and Octavia slowly began to appear in Rome. The numerous statues of both male and female members of the Julio-Claudian family carefully resembled one another, creating a fiction of a family dynasty unified by blood, rather than through adoption and political match-making.

Many of the Augustan-era statues show the deep debt owed by Roman art to Greek convention. This is found in the imitation of statues of Alexander or the translation of the

Figure 8.15 The *Res Gestae* and Ara Pacis museum, with the Ara Pacis visible behind the glass to the right.

Source: Photograph by the author.

ageless perfection of classical Greek statuary to Roman artwork. The famous Prima Porta statue of Augustus also uses the classical pose of *contrapposto*, where the weight is mostly placed on one foot; yet if the Prima Porta is Greek in style, it is thoroughly Roman and Augustan in its messaging. The centre of the intricately carved breastplate shows the diplomatic triumph achieved by Augustus in 20 BC (below), with a Parthian soldier returning the legionary standards captured from Crassus and Antony to Dea Roma. Peace with Parthia translates into peace for the whole world, indicated by the sky god above and Mother Earth below, holding a cornucopia. At the bottom left is the figure of Apollo, with Diana to the right. The message, complemented by numerous coinage issues, is once again laid bare for all to understand: an era of peace, the gift of Augustus (Figure 8.17, Figure 8.18, and Figure 8.19).

The Prima Porta statue was discovered in 1867 at the Villa of Livia in the northern suburbs of Rome, a house famous for its sumptuous wall paintings carried out in the Second Pompeian Style. Now in the Palazza Massimo alla Terme in Rome, the paintings depict trees heavy with fruit—yet more allegorical images of prosperity and peace. Livia's lesser-known house on the Palatine was similarly well appointed with Second Pompeian Style paintings illustrating scenes from Graeco-Roman mythology and images of luscious landscapes. Augustus's own surprisingly modest house can also be seen in modern Rome: it

Figure 8.16 Detail of a statue of Livia from the Museo della civiltà Romana; modern plaster cast of a first-century BC original found at Paestum.

Source: Photograph by Olga Lyubimova (CC BY-SA 4.0).

Figure 8.17 Detail of the breastplate of the Prima Porta statue of Augustus.

Source: Photograph by Sailko (CC BY-SA 3.0).

Figure 8.18 Silver denarius minted at Tarraco in 19 BC. Obverse: bare head of Augustus; reverse: Shield inscribed with CL V (*clipeus votivus*, worn and not very visible) with SPQR around, and legionary standard (left) and eagle (right). The Latin legend SIGNIS RECEPTIS means 'standards recovered'.

Figure 8.19 Silver denarius minted in Rome. Obverse: head of Honos (honour); reverse: a kneeling Parthian returns captured Roman standards.

too was decorated in the same style. Many of the frescoes feature theatrical backgrounds, props, and masks, which fit the Augustan emphasis on public spectacle.

This feast of built heritage and the visual arts was complemented by a panoply of public games and festivals in Rome, all of which centred around Augustus, his achievements, and those of his family. (Outside Rome there were festivals such as the Actian Games in Greece, and in Naples, a Greek festival called the *Sebasta*—'Augusta', the feminine Greek parallel to Augustus—was held every four years from AD 2.) The familiar themes were once again irresistible victory, peace, and divine favour, and together these events relentlessly underlined the greatness of the city, the empire, and the man himself. Other festivals included the *ludi* (games) *Victoriae Caesaris*, games dedicated to Julius Caesar, held annually in tandem with the festival honoring Venus; a festival celebrating the naval defeat of Sextus

Pompey; and another commemorating the historic grant of Octavian's imperium in 43 BC prior to the Mutina campaign. The *Augustalia* was added in 19 BC, and the dedication of the Temple of Mars Ultor in 2 BC occasioned yet another annual festival. Just as important for political messaging were the theatrical displays that often formed part of the *ludi*—the Secular Games, for example, offered spectators a week's worth of Latin and Greek plays, which could be used to stress key themes such as piety and reverence. Favourites included works by antiquarians such as Ennius and Naevius (Chapter 5) as well as more recent playwrights such as Plautus and Terence; Augustus also commissioned special works such as the *Thyestes* by Lucius Varius Rufus, performed for the occasion of Octavian's triumph in 29 BC. By the turn of the century, Rome was littered with new and restored theatres, including those of Marcellus, Pompey, and Balbus, with the latter built in 13 BC. A theatrical law carefully regulated seating at events by social class, creating stratified examples of the Roman people in miniature—and all under the benevolent tutelage of the *princeps*.

One of the keys to the success of this relentless message of peace and plenty was that Augustus accompanied it with a well-designed plan to look after the people of Rome and repair Italy's ageing infrastructure. Throughout the peninsula, roads underwent extensive repairs, easing the movement of people and their goods to market. A new postal system, the *cursus publicus*, improved administration and communication. New aqueducts brought fresh water into Rome and officials drawn from the senate were appointed to manage the water supply. Problems with Rome's debased and unreliable wartime coinage were solved through the standardisation of weights and measures, particularly the gold aureus and the silver denarius, at near proof and 98 per cent proof respectively. After several reforms concerning the supply of grain, Augustus centralised this crucial public service under the control of an equestrian manager. With Egypt securely under Roman control, there need not be any further grain shortages for either the free dole or rations purchased on the open market. Rome was divided into 14 new districts in 7 BC, in an effort to ease municipal management, and the ancient office of urban prefect, the city administrator, was reconstituted; freedmen filled many of the new positions. In the city, Augustus also took measures to end the climate of violence that had become the city's unenviable hallmark through much of the first century BC. This was achieved with the creation of the urban cohorts, a rudimentary police force commanded by a senator, which was buttressed from time to time by the Praetorian Guard. The Guard itself was a force of political soldiers paid as much as twice (and later as much as three times) more than legionnaires to guard the emperor, with a shorter term of service (nominally 16 years), and which was under a double equestrian leadership. The Guard was an extension of the Republican-era practice of allowing a consul or praetor on campaign a bodyguard called the *cohors praetoria*; two *cohortes praetoriae* had been maintained by Antony and Octavian during the Second Triumvirate (Chapter 7). The Praetorian Guard was supplemented by a picked force of German troops, often freedmen, a custom that also had its roots in the civil wars. Later, Augustus established the *vigiles*, who kept watch for and tackled fires; these, too, were under the control of an equestrian. Tighter building regulations helped to ensure a higher quality of construction, which reduced the incidence of serious fire. A plentiful supply of grain, checks on public violence, and the promise of protection from natural and human-made disasters all helped to reinforce Augustan propaganda, and periodic cash handouts meant that for the first time in living memory the people of Rome were at last receiving some of the benefits of Roman imperialism.

The provinces

During the reign of Augustus, a great deal of attention was paid to the provinces. This was an extension of Caesar's own policies, as well as a reflection of the growing importance of the Italian and provincial elites whose families were *not* part of the old Roman aristocracy that had ruled the Republic. It was these 'outsiders' who had fought for Caesar in Gaul, fought for Caesar against Pompey, and later formed the basis of support for Octavian: men like Agrippa, from rural Italy and from a poor family, and Maecenas, a wealthy equestrian who claimed ancient Etruscan roots. The old families of the *nobiles* had suffered grievously during the civil wars and were now being eased out by new Italian and provincial blood. There had also been a significant diaspora of Romans into the provinces, often veteran soldiers who married and lived out their retirement far from the city. Their families were raised along the coasts of Gaul, Spain, and Africa, their children educated through Latin literature, their meals resembling those consumed in Italy. The new nation crafted by Augustus deliberately included the provinces, particularly in the western parts of the empire where the ancient imprint of the Hellenistic and Semitic worlds was light or completely absent.

The provinces were important for other reasons. Polybius had recognised in the second century BC that the emergence of Rome in the Mediterranean had triggered a seismic shift in 'world' politics, and his *History* was an attempt to explain Rome's *global* ascendance to the Greek-speaking audience of the world once conquered by Alexander. The Roman empire in the first century BC was in the process of surpassing that of Alexander—if not in territory, for the Romans would never truly conquer Persia, but in its universal outlook. The Roman state was the *oikumene*, a Greek term meaning the whole populated world. The term also had connotations of a world commonwealth, a single state under the guidance of a single ruler. More than ever before, the Mediterranean had become politically unified under Augustus, and this message was reinforced in particular through the work of poets like Virgil (below). This concept made the provinces crucial elements of the *oikumene* and necessary beneficiaries of the attention of Augustus.

Much of the effort made by Augustus and his circle to acknowledge the role played by provincials—and to instil Roman conventions away from Rome—can be seen in the plethora of UNESCO World Heritage Sites in southern France, a region that was heavily colonised in the years following Caesar's victory over Pompey (Figure 8.20). While the longest surviving stretch of aqueduct (85 kilometres, or 53 miles) in France is found south-west of Lyon, the most famous survival of hydraulic architecture is undoubtedly the Pont du Gard, begun by Agrippa in about 19 BC and widely recognised as a masterpiece of Roman engineering (Figure 8.21). Carrying water for nearly 50 kilometres (31 miles), it supplied the city of Nemausus (Nîmes) with a supply of fresh water. Nemausus was the Celtic name for the local god of water, and numerous Roman urban and religious sites grew up around Celtic water shrines. The Roman site of Glanum (Saint-Rémy-de-Provence), for instance, took its name from Celtic religion (the god Glanis) and became home to a famous sanctuary dedicated to healing. The colony at Nemausus featured an Augustan-era Nymphaeum and a Temple of Diana, centred around the ancient healing spring. The attention paid to Nemausus is also evident in the exceptional Maison Carrée, one of the best-preserved Roman buildings in the world. A traditional structure that paid homage to Etruscan temple models, it was dedicated to Gaius and Lucius Caesar, the grandsons of Augustus. The importance of Nemausus was also celebrated on Augustan coinage,

Figure 8.20 Southern France in the Augustan period. Square markers indicate Roman colonies.

Source: Illustration by the author.

Figure 8.21 Detail of the Pont du Gard, near Nîmes.

Source: Photograph by the author.

Figure 8.22 Bronze as minted at Nemausus between AD 10 and AD 14. Obverse: Agrippa (left) and Augustus (right); reverse: COL NEM with chained crocodile and palm frond.

as veterans from the Actium and Egyptian campaigns were settled there. One famous issue displays the heads of Agrippa and Augustus, along with a crocodile, symbolising the connections between Nemausus and Egypt (Figure 8.22).

From the Caesarian colony of Lugdunum (Lyon), Agrippa constructed a road network that spread south, west, and north as far as the Roman military camp and future colony of Colonia Claudia Ara Agrippinensium (Cologne) and Bononia (Boulogne). One branch of the via Agrippa led southwards to the UNESCO World Heritage Site of Arelate/Colonia Sextanorum. Many of Arles' most famous monuments, such as its impressive amphitheatre, date to the decades following the death of Augustus, but can also be viewed as a continuation of Augustan provincial policy. Forum Julii (Fréjus) was chosen for the settlement of veterans and was subject to intensive development during the Augustan period, including an aqueduct (Figure 8.23) and an amphitheatre still in use today.

Another well-known Augustan site located along the via Agrippa (and included on the UNESCO list) is Arausio (Orange), with its famous triumphal arch and theatre. The city was colonised as Colonia Julia Firma Secundanorum Arausio, intended for the settlement of veterans who had fought for Octavian in II Gallica. The arch commemorating the legion probably dates to the reign of Augustus's successor, Tiberius, but the theatre was begun before the death of the *princeps* in AD 14. Like Arelate, Arausio's well-appointed public buildings were a result of continued and careful attention.

Perhaps the most famous of the Augustan-era monuments in Provence is the enormous Trophée des Alpes at La Turbie. Constructed on the summit of an imposing hill in 6 BC to commemorate the subjugation of the Alpine tribes, the monument was surmounted by a gigantic statue of the *princeps*. The gold-lettered inscription and the statue have long since vanished, but the first-century AD polymath Pliny the Elder copied the text in his *Natural History*, listing the 45 tribes that 'were reduced to subjection by the Roman people' (3.24)—a euphemism that obscures the savage treatment of the local population. At nearby Vienne, a foundation of Julius Caesar placed in the territory of the Allobroges, a Temple of Augustus and Livia has survived over the centuries and rivals the Maison Carrée in its elegance and state of preservation (Figure 8.24).

Figure 8.23 Remains of the aqueduct in the suburbs of Fréjus.

Source: Photograph by the author.

Figure 8.24 The Temple of Augustus and Livia at Vienne in southern France.

Source: Photograph by Troyseffigy (CC BY-SA 3.0).

Gaul was the main beneficiary of Augustan provincial construction activities, but other areas also received the attention of the *princeps*. Modern Mérida in Lusitania began as Augusta Merita, founded in 25 BC to settle military veterans from the Cantabrian War (below). The city's remains today include a well-preserved aqueduct, a reservoir, and a theatre built by Agrippa in 18 BC.Veterans from the war were also settled at Caesareaugusta (modern Zaragoza). Such expensive Augustan building projects served as a constant reminder of the links between Rome and the provinces, and most of all they underscored the bonds of loyalty between the population of these numerous colonies, many made up of retired soldiers, and Augustus and his father, Julius Caesar.

Provincial elites, including non-Roman clients and friends of Rome, played a leading role in provincial urban development. King Herod the Great, for instance, had pledged his loyalty to Octavian in the immediate aftermath of the battle of Actium in 30 BC and was on particularly friendly terms with Agrippa; he was also a Roman citizen, his citizenship earned through his father Antipater, a confidant and supporter of Julius Caesar. Herod named one of his palaces the 'Agrippaeum' and founded a city that he named Sebaste ('Augusta'). Its centrepiece was the Sebasteion, a gigantic 25 metre (82 feet) tall shrine dedicated to Rome and Augustus. Herod was a prolific builder: in addition to lengthy renovations to the Temple in Jerusalem (the Second Temple), he also constructed the city of Caesarea Maritima on the coast, named for Augustus and home to an expensive gold-roofed shrine to Rome and Augustus. (The city's well-appointed harbour was built with the help of Roman engineers, who had long perfected the art of setting concrete under-water.) Both Caesarea Maritima and Sebaste were built according to the well-established city plans of the Hellenistic world, but featured Roman amenities such as aqueducts, colonnaded streets, a forum, and Roman theatres. Herod also dedicated yet another shrine to Rome and Augustus at nearby Panias (Caesarea Philippi), and during his reign he built the famous fortresses of Masada and Machaerus (Chapter 9).

In Africa, the king Juba II of Mauretania, who had fought for Octavian and married Cleopatra Selene, the daughter of Antony and Cleopatra, refounded the coastal port city of Iol as Iol Caesarea and hired Italian masons to recreate some of the awe-inspiring archi-tecture of Rome. Such installations provided conspicuous links between these subordinate provincial allies and the family of Caesar, offering avenues for their deep political and cul-tural integration into the rungs of Roman high society. Juba, for example, gained Roman citizenship, became a patron of Greek and Latin literature, and was well regarded by Pliny the Elder. Mauretanian royal coinage reflected the distinctive influence of contemporary Roman issues (Figure 8.25).

With citizenship and integration into Roman society came expectations for dress, lan-guage, epicurean choices, and manners, which helped to extend Roman culture throughout the Mediterranean provinces. Military service alongside Roman legions provided one avenue for political and cultural exchange, while education served another. Juba II's son, Ptolemy, was dispatched to Rome to be tutored; there he came under the wing of Antonia the Younger, the daughter of Antony and Octavia. Cleopatra Selene had likewise enjoyed a lengthy sojourn in Rome, where she was raised by Octavia alongside Antony's many children. A striking feature of this sort of provincial interplay was the continuation of native traditions in the provinces, even as those traditions were artfully blended with new political expectations. The mausoleum in which Juba and Cleopatra were buried, for example, is a circular stone tumulus distinctive to the Berber people of the region, a

Figure 8.25 Silver denarius of Juba II, minted at Caesarea. Obverse: diademed head of Juba with Latin legend REX JVBA; the reverse records the name of his queen, ΚΛΕΟΠΑΤΡΑ, in Greek.

style best represented by the pre-Roman Medracen at Batna in Algeria. The mausoleum occupies an imposing position overlooking the main route between Iol Caesarea and the Punic trading post of Tipasa (modern Tipaza). At the same time, however, the tomb of Juba and Cleopatra bears more than a passing resemblance to the Mausoleum of Augustus, their patron in Rome (Figures 8.26 and 8.27).

Even as they continued local traditions, provincial elites thus helped to reinforce the position of Caesar and Augustus in the provinces; and by behaving as middlemen between the *princeps* and the provinces—lesser *principes* in the image of their patron, able to mediate the grandeur of Rome for a population remote from Italy—they also emphasised the relationship between the fatherly Augustus and the provincial population of the empire. This relationship was further reinforced by periodic grants of Roman citizenship, as recipients often took the name 'Julius' in homage to their benefactor.

In line with the religious program of Augustus (below), the *princeps* also paid due attention to numerous sacred sites in Italy. The important sanctuary of Diana Tifatina in Campania received imperial support, while several Roman colonies were founded at the sites of shrines in Etruria and Umbria. By endowing these places with the legal rights of Roman (rather than Latin) colonies, Augustus incorporated them into Roman religious practice and further emphasised the unification of Italy that had begun with the Social War, and that had been dramatically strengthened by the oath of 32 BC. This focus on Italy could also be portrayed as a stark contrast to the 'despotic orientalism' of Antony, as displayed in Augustan propaganda. In the east, Augustus restored the property of those temples in the province of Asia that had been stolen by Antony, a fact that he mentioned prominently in the *Res Gestae* (below) and that was also recorded by Strabo (e.g. *Geography*, 14.1.14).

Augustan ideology

Augustus recognised the importance of the senate to the stability of his rule, but he could not allow it to revert to the position of dominance it had once held during the heyday

Figure 8.26 The tomb of Juba II and Cleopatra Selene.

Source: Photograph by Philip Wood.

of the Republic. With Agrippa's help, he approached this problem by making the senate a select group of the very rich: a new level of wealth was established and 400 senators were cut from the rolls between 29 and 18 BC. Senators could no longer leave Italy without prior authorisation, a rule that allowed Augustus to monitor their activities. Whereas there had once been as many as 40 quaestors, that number reverted to 20 and the quaestorship was reasserted as the requirement for senatorial membership. The praetorship was reduced to ten. The consulship was amended so that four served each year: two 'ordinary' consuls for the first six months and two 'suffect' consuls for the following six. Careful to maintain the impression that he was following the *mos maiorum*, Augustus allowed senators to advise him on policy, as they had once advised the Republican consuls. He also took the position of *princeps senatus* for himself, by which he could influence the senate and, acting in accordance with the censorship, determine its membership. Augustus understood the importance of allowing elections to continue: the Roman oligarchy must still be allowed to compete for office. In reality, of course, the old routes to *gloria*—military conquest, and the acquisition of wealth for the individual or for the state—were now determined by Augustus, who kept tight control over senior political and military appointments even as he courteously attended senatorial meetings and encouraged polite debate. A senatorial advisory council was formed to provide assistance to the princeps and draft legislation, and

Figure 8.27 The Medracen.

Source: Photograph by Philip Wood.

the *comitia tributa* and *comitia centuriata* still voted on business. Much of that business was naturally decided by Augustus.

As part of his policy towards the provinces—particularly those in the west—Augustus fostered the entry of small groups of provincial elites into the senate. Augustus took a special interest in the equestrians, channelling their talents into reserved positions in the army and navy, and assigning them as procurators to manage the bulging portfolio of imperial land and property; they were also explicitly mentioned in the *Res Gestae* (below). The equestrian order had played a particularly prominent role in the armies that fought the civil wars, and Octavian had originally been born as an equestrian before his adoption by Julius Caesar transferred him to patrician status. Now the equestrian order was monitored with the same diligence applied to the senate, and its membership reviewed annually. In this way Augustus undermined and de-politicised the *nobiles* even as they were allowed to continue to run for public office. Equestrian procurators took on increasingly complex responsibilities, including tax collection and provincial government, as well as the management of Augustus's voluminous correspondence and the drafting of laws. As noted above, the important offices of the *vigiles*, the grain supply, and the Praetorian Guard were all under the command of equestrians hand-picked by Augustus. Augustus banned senatorial travel to Egypt without his express permission, and all the senior positions there were held by equestrians, including the commander of the Egyptian garrison, the *praefectus Aegypti* (prefect of Egypt).

Slaves and freedmen continued to play an important role in Augustan Rome, managing the daily work of such crucial tasks as the grain supply, water management, and the imperial mint. As the careers of people like the remarkable Narcissus or Antonia Caenis would show (Chapter 9), freed slaves could attain positions of exceptional importance through their access to the highest levels of Roman government. On the other hand, the misery of slavery still continued unabated and Augustus did little to change this fact, beyond allowing freed slaves to attain a form of citizenship under the *lex Junia Norbana* (17 BC), or full citizenship through marriage and child rearing (the *lex Aelia Sentia* of AD 3 or 4). Aggressive campaigns in Spain and elsewhere ensured a plentiful supply of slaves for Roman markets. In short, the 'opportunities' for slaves only materialised if they were fortunate enough to be freed. Under Augustus, however, the practice of manumission was more closely regulated, further discouraging the practice (the *lex Aelia Sentia*, and the *lex Fufia Canina* in 2 BC).

These policies towards senators, equestrians, and slaves were not simply motivated by political requirements; they were also part of a broader effort at social engineering. In 19 BC, the senate appointed Augustus to oversee the laws and customs of the state. A return to the *mos maiorum* was key if Roman society was to last, and for Augustus this meant a decisive end to the corruption that had been a defining feature of the old Republic— government service was now actual service, and not an opportunity for extortion, graft, and self-enrichment. This was a conservative approach of which Sallust and Cato the Elder would have approved, and that would put an end to corruption and bribery, which Tacitus identified as the key reason for the failure of Republican government in the provinces (*Annals*, 1). Grain-hoarding was seriously punished and citizenship was restricted. Displays of luxury were frowned upon—Augustus wore simple clothes, disliked palaces, and his own house was conspicuously modest when set against the later monstrosity of Nero's *Domus Aurea* (Chapter 9). Augustus also interpreted the senate's commission as an invitation to legislate in domestic matters. Despite his own scandalous past—and that of his adoptive father, Caesar—Augustus promoted the institution of child-bearing monogamous marriage as the foundation of the Roman people. Adultery was severely punished in the courts, and *pudicitia*, a female counterpart to *virtus* represented through faithful marriage, was highlighted as a desirable and necessary quality of Roman women. In this, Augustus besought women to believe like one Claudia, whose funeral inscription (dating from c. 120 BC) recorded that:

> Her wedded lord she loved with all her heart
> She bore two sons, and one of them she left
> On earth, the other in the earth she laid.

Her speech was pleasing and her bearing gracious.
She kept house; span her wool. I have said. Farewell.
(*Oxford Book of Classical Verse*, §232)

At the Secular Games in 17 BC, Augustus presided over choirs of children whose living parents looked on as witnesses, while 110 *married* women—one for each year of the *saeculum*—were also in attendance. (Unmarried men and women could only attend the festival if they were accompanied by an elderly chaperone.) The Augustan approach contained both incentives and punishments for couples. Men received benefits commensurate with the number of children that they raised, such as the right to stand for office earlier than usual. Men who failed to have children and adults who remained single faced censure, including the denial of their inheritance. Augustus was also concerned about the *right* kind of people procreating—so aristocrats were forbidden from relations with the lower classes. (Despite the popularity of the theatre, many types of stage performers, considered to be at the bottom of society, were not only barred from citizenship but also from marrying senators; Suetonius (*Augustus*, 45) describes the drastic penalties meted out to various actors for their 'lawlessness'.) These new rules were unequal and oppressive, particularly towards women, who could now be divorced *and* sued for adultery, while men could still get away with the same offence. The Augustan focus on *pudicitia* also pushed women (and especially elite women) towards a narrowly closeted set of social expectations.

Augustus's family policies went hand in hand with his religious programme, which also sought to strengthen what he regarded as traditional Roman values and which were designed to appeal to a fundamentally conservative audience. These values had been 'lost' over the past century, most of all because of Antony and his dreadful behaviour, and so were now 'restored' to the people by Augustus. In Rome, this restoration took shape in the scores of temples built or repaired, including the Temple of Mars Ultor, the Temple of the Divine Julius, and the Temple of Apollo on the Palatine. Piety itself was also restored so the Roman people would have the correct relationship with their gods. This meant the proper performance of religious ritual, and due attention paid to those officials who carried out religious duties on behalf of the state. Augustus led by example, holding multiple priesthoods, scrupulously following the auspices, and assuming the office of *pontifex maximus* in 12 BC. Having sidelined Lepidus in this role for more than two decades, Augustus now performed his duties with conspicuous care, appointing a new chief priest of Jupiter; after burning Greek and Latin prophecies he considered heretical, he then transferred the *Sibylline Books* to the Temple of Apollo on the Palatine, seizing control of this important state resource. Augustus carefully regulated elections for the priesthoods, dividing them between equestrians and senators and promoting his own candidates. He harkened back to the mists of 'old Rome' with his restoration of the Lupercalia and the Secular Games, along with his even earlier spear-throwing declaration of war on Cleopatra, which signalled the revival of the fetial priests (Chapter 7). Augustus also reinvented the ancient *sodales Titii*, an obscure cult with links to Romulus. Augustus's family members took part in these performative displays, with Livia and Octavia granted sacrosanctity—a right otherwise given only to male magistrates and guaranteed by the gods—and freedom from guardianship—a right normally only given to the Vestal Virgins. Octavia and Livia were allowed statues, and in 7 BC Augustus followed the earlier dedication of the Porticus

Figure 8.28 Bronze as minted at Lugdunum (Lyon), probably between 10 and 7 BC. The reverse shows the Altar of Lugdunum with the Latin legend ROM ET AVG—Rome and Augustus.

Octaviae with that of the Porticus Liviae to his wife. The wife and sister of the *princeps* thus both achieved a public role unmatched by any other woman in Rome.

While Augustus decisively rejected efforts to grant him divine status while he was alive, there was already precedence for an imperial cult in the shape of honours accorded to Julius Caesar. Augustus therefore permitted reverence for a cult of 'Rome and Augustus', which was celebrated in the provinces in a range of different forms (Figure 8.28), and where 'Rome' was often represented through the militarised goddess of Dea Roma. Provincial elites could hold the priesthood of Rome and Augustus, an increasingly important position that tied them and their communities, including the *curiae*, the bodies of wealthy officials who managed local affairs, to the Roman government. Inscriptions from Vienne, for example, refer to *flamines* appointed by the town council to attend to the imperial cult.

Throughout the empire, altars appeared dedicated to Rome and Augustus: at Tarraco in 26 or 25 BC, and at Augusta Merita in 15 BC. After 9 BC, an altar to Augustus was established at the future site of Cologne, known at the time as Oppidum Ubiorum. In Egypt, Augustus had already been recognised as the new pharaoh, and by 26 BC at Mytilene, an altar dedicated to Augustus himself was established. Further indications of the cult are found in the reorganisation of the calendar used in Asia, which from 9 BC reckoned time from the birth of Octavian. In Rome itself, the cult was implicit in Augustus's tenure of the office of *pontifex maximus*, his seizure of the *Sibylline Books*, the naming of the month Augustus, and his control of the religious calendar as exemplified, for instance, by the revival of the Secular Games. Furthermore, as the *paterfamilias* of the Roman people, the Augustan household gods—the *lares Augusti*—were publicly worshipped. The importance of the *lares* was further emphasised by the restoration of the Compitalia, an annual festival dedicated to the *lares* that had fallen into neglect during the civil wars. At the Compitalia, families adorned the *lares Augusti* with images of their family members—as well as 'balls' representing their slaves.

Augustan family values and the morality of the new order were reinforced by the literary stars of the day, who came under the patronage of Augustus and his circle. Many of

Latin literature's biggest names started their careers less than enthusiastic about Octavian, and found it difficult to create a heroic narrative for the uninspiring Actium campaign. Horace (65–8 BC), for instance, was the equestrian son of a freedman from Venusia who had fought on the losing side at Philippi, and did not always find it easy to accommodate his lyric poetry to life under Augustus. His *Odes* and *Epodes* were dedicated to Maecenas, a prominent patron of the arts and occasional poet himself, about whom Horace gushed that he was 'born of monarch ancestors / the shield at once and glory of my life' (*Odes*, 1.1–2). Horace drew on the rich heritage of Greek lyric poetry, particularly the famous seventh-century BC poet Archilochus of Paros, whose self-effacing poem about throwing away his shield during a battle in Thrace—an act distinctly frowned upon in the face of the enemy—was echoed by Horace's admission of ditching his own to run for his life at Philippi (*Odes*, 2.7). Horace eventually paid due homage to Actium and Octavian's victory over Sextus Pompey (*Epodes*, 9) and celebrated the patriotic *virtus* of Regulus during the First Punic War (*Odes*, 3.5). The political ambivalence characteristic of some of his poetry is reflected by cautious praise for Cleopatra's dignity in death (*Odes*, 1.37), but elsewhere Horace was more 'on programme', lauding the role of Augustan women, including Octavia, Livia, young mothers, and married women in an idealised Roman society. In the *Secular Hymn* that he composed for the Secular Games in 17 BC, Horace extolled the new era of peace and plenty, and also called directly on Apollo and Diana to protect young mothers and appealed for the new marriage laws to bear fruit.

By writing in this way, Horace reflected not only the renewed emphasis on marriage in Rome, but also highlighted the crucial role played by aristocratic women in the imperial family. Julius Caesar had come to power largely through the women around him: Julia, his aunt, whose funeral he had used for political gain; Caesar's first wife, Cornelia, the daughter of Cinna; his second, Pompeia, the granddaughter of Sulla; and his third, Calpurnia, the daughter of his loyal friend Calpurnius Piso (consul in 58 BC). Caesar's much-loved daughter Julia had provided a stable link between himself and Pompey, and her funeral in 54 BC had turned into a public spectacle; her ashes were buried on the Campus Martius, a rare honour. Augustus was no less reliant on aristocratic women. He owed his adoption to his grandmother Julia, who was Caesar's older sister; he owed much of his success during the civil wars to the loyalty and the shrewd diplomacy of his sister, Octavia; and he benefited from the sharp political abilities of his third wife, Livia, who was his adviser and confidante. Augustus's only living child, Julia, the daughter of Scribonia, he heartlessly manipulated through marriage for his own purposes as he sought to find a means for his political arrangements to continue after his death. The importance of these aristocratic women is also reflected in the honours they were granted. After Augustus died, Livia was accorded a lictor, in tune with her status as a Vestal-like figure (although Tacitus (*Annals*, 1.14) says that Tiberius rescinded this honour); when Octavia died in 11 BC, she received the full honours of a state funeral, as had Augustus's mother, Atia, in 43 BC. Many of the imperial women also became prominent patrons in Rome. Octavia became the patron of Vitruvius, both she and Livia provided banquets for Roman women, and Antonia the Younger befriended foreign dignitaries. Roman women were still barred from office, but through Augustus's legislation and through the women around him, Augustus highlighted their central role in his version of the ideal state as wives, mothers, and daughters. Despite their evident importance, however, it is noteworthy that none of the women on whom the *princeps* relied appeared in the *Res Gestae*, and nor did Livia earn the right to

Figure 8.29 Bronze diobol minted in Alexandria between AD 1 and AD 5. The obverse shows the head of Livia.

appear on Augustan coinage minted in Rome, although she did appear on coins minted in Egypt (Figure 8.29).

Horace's equestrian contemporary Propertius (c. 50–15 BC) also lauded the Augustan achievement in his *Elegies*—one of his poems (2.31) was entirely dedicated to the Temple of Apollo on the Palatine—and in addition he wrote tender love poetry directed at his pseudonymic paramour Cynthia. Propertius thrived under the patronage of Maecenas, who he called 'the hope and envy of our youth' (2.1), and provided fine examples of upstanding Roman matrons (4.11). Yet he too could stray off message. Hailing from Perusia, he still felt sufficiently bitter to direct a snide comment at Octavian for ending the life of one of his friends in Etruria (1.21), and preferred partying and drinking to more serious pursuits such as praising Augustus. Other poetic contemporaries included the equestrian Cornelius Gallus, the first prefect of Egypt (70–26 BC), who composed love elegies that influenced Ovid. A fragment of papyrus with several lines of his poetry was found at Qasr Ibrim between the First and Second Cataracts in Egypt in the late 1970s—a remarkable survival from antiquity. Tibullus (c. 55–19 BC) suffered during the proscriptions, but came under the patronage of the wealthy Messalla Corvinus (64 BC– AD 8), who had been educated at Athens alongside Horace and Cicero. Tibullus wrote elegies, some of which were addressed to his own paramour, Delia, and one of which offered a Sibylline prophecy about the career of Aeneas that tied in neatly with the plot of Virgil's *Aeneid* (below). Another offered a beguiling vision of peace and plenty, represented by ears of corn, women's breasts, and a cornucopia of apples. The surviving corpus of Tibullus contains six poems believed to have been composed by the only known female poet of the Augustan era, Messalla Corvinus' niece, Sulpicia (c. 50 BC–?). The poems are addressed to her lover, Cerinthus, and match the tenderness, ardour, and power of those written by Catullus and Ovid:

> Stay spirit, take this glad incense, and favour my prayers:
> if only he's inflamed when he thinks of me.
> But if even now he sighs deeply for another,

then leave your faithless altar, sacred one.
And don't you be unjust, Venus, let us both serve you,
equally as slaves, or lighten my chains.

(Sulpicia = Tibullus, 3.4)

Messalla Corvinus also patronised Ovid (43–17 BC), whose prolific output included the *Metamorphoses*, steeped in Graeco-Roman mythology, the *Fasti*, which addressed the Roman religious calendar, and the *Ars Amatoria*, the famous *Art of Love*. The three books of the *Ars Amatoria* offered disarmingly candid advice for meeting, wooing, and keeping a mate. Ovid irritated Augustus, however, and was exiled to the distant edges of the Black Sea, where he subsequently died. It has never been truly clear why Augustus banished one of Rome's most brilliant poets, but in the *Ars Amatoria* (1.724–7), Ovid had suggested that the imperial events cherished by Augustus as ways to communicate his politico-religious ideology were, in fact, good places to flirt with young women—something that was decidedly *off* message. Ovid was also close to Augustus's daughter Julia, who fell out of favour and was later exiled; this may have spurred Augustus to banish him. In December 2017, politicians in Rome formally rescinded the exile—2,009 years after the fact!

The most important of the era's poets was Virgil (70–19 BC), whose *Aeneid* became the nationalist epic of the Augustan age and remains an undisputed classic of world literature. Virgil, whose patron was the old Caesarian Gaius Asinius Pollio (Chapter 7), had started off in the late 40s BC alluding to the misery caused by the proscriptions and the civil wars in his Hellenistic-style *Eclogues*, which were published around 38/7 BC. The most famous of the *Eclogues*, the fourth, took place during a 'glorious age' under the reign of Apollo and prophesied the birth of a boy who would free the earth and bring peace; this message was later appropriated by Christians, who imagined that it referred to Jesus. The later *Georgics* reveal a shift in orientation, praising Octavian and holding him aloft alongside Scipio, Camillus, and Marius (2.1.67–9). The nearly 10,000-word *Aeneid* was, however, Virgil's crowning achievement. Written in dactylic hexameter, it drew heavily on the poetic voice of Homer through its appropriation of the *Iliad* and the *Odyssey*, the universal and archetypal stories of the ancient Mediterranean world. Strabo regarded Homer as having surpassed everyone 'in his acquaintance with all that pertains to public life' (*Geography*, 1.2), and Virgil's appropriation of the Homeric tradition allowed him to create a universal epic that followed the marathon journey made by Aeneas from Troy to Italy, and which then realised the subsequent foundation of Rome. The *Aeneid* was unfinished on Virgil's death, and Virgil apparently wanted the manuscript to be burned—fortunately, it came under the editorial guidance of the playwright Lucius Varus Rufus, who completed it. An awestruck Propertius (2.34) famously claimed that the *Aeneid* was better than the *Iliad*.

Throughout the *Aeneid*, Virgil reworked the foundation myths discussed in Chapter 1, glorifying Rome's past and further legitimising the Augustan regime. In book 6, for example, Augustus appears as the 'son of a god, who will again establish a golden age in Latium'. The *princeps* is also tied to the theme of irresistible victory. The Romans are a chosen people, and under Augustus's guidance the empire will inevitably spread to cover all the lands on earth—the *imperium sine fine* (6.788 & 1.279). Virgil's treatment of his subject matter wove the histories of Greece and Rome more tightly than before, drawing on the rich tapestry of his forbears, including Naevius and Ennius, the latter of whom had pioneered the use of dactylic hexameter in Latin (Chapter 5). Among the nationalist fervor of the *Aeneid*, Virgil explicitly stated Rome's manifest destiny to rule the world and create a universal commonwealth, the *oikumene*. Following a long enumeration of Rome's great military heroes paraded before Aeneas, his father Anchises reminds him—and the reader—of Rome's sacred mission:

> Remember, Roman, it is for you to rule the nations with your power,
> (that will be your skill), to crown peace with law,
> to spare the conquered, and subdue the proud.
>
> (6.851–3)

The vision of patriotism that Virgil offered was communal—it was about the greatness of Rome, not the greatness of powerful men. Indeed, earlier in book 6, Caesar and Pompey were criticised for their actions, which were cast as rebellious and bordering on treason. Greeks, Romans, Trojans, and others are instead joined together in the communal *patria*: Aeneas is given an Italian relative (Dardanus) and encounters the Arcadian Evander at the future site of Rome. The diversity of cultures included in the poem also strengthens the universality of Virgil's vision, and the epic journey undertaken by Aeneas draws the reader through the *oikumene*, covering the Greek-speaking east, Punic Carthage, and the different districts of Italy.

The Actium campaign also occupies a special position in the *Aeneid*—here, in book 8 (671–92) of the famous translation by John Dryden, Poet Laureate of England in 1668:

> Betwixt the quarters flow a golden sea;
> But foaming surges there in silver play.
> The dancing dolphins with their tails divide
> The glitt'ring waves, and cut the precious tide.
> Amid the main, two mighty fleets engage
> Their brazen beaks, oppos'd with equal rage.
> Actium surveys the well-disputed prize;
> Leucate's wat'ry plain with foamy billows fried.
> Young Caesar, on the stern, in armor bright,
> Here leads the Romans and their gods to fight:
> His beamy temples shoot their flames afar,
> And o'er his head is hung the Julian star.
> Agrippa seconds him, with prosp'rous gales,
> And, with propitious gods, his foes assails:
> A naval crown, that binds his manly brows,
> The happy fortune of the fight foreshows.
> Range'd on the line oppos'd, Antonius brings
> Barbarian aids, and troops of Eastern kings;
> Th' Arabians near, and Bactrians from afar,
> Of tongues discordant, and a mingled war:
> And, rich in gaudy robes, amidst the strife,
> His ill fate follows him—th' Egyptian wife.

The text pours scorn on Antony and Cleopatra, emphasising their barbarism through the inclusion of exotic Arabians and Bactrians, and 'tongues discordant'. In contrast, Caesar (that is, Augustus) fights with the Roman people and with the support of the Roman gods, with the 'Julian star'—the comet, symbolising the deification of Julius Caesar—watching over benevolently. All of nature, too, fights on Octavian's side, including the dolphins and the waves of the sea. The link between Caesar and Octavian is also an invocation of filial *pietas*, a central characteristic of Aeneas himself, who carried his father Anchises to safety from Troy. In the poem, Dido of Carthage—cast very much as a pious, hardworking, and virtuous Roman matron—occupies a prominent role, and in book 4, after Aeneas leaves her to continue his journey, she prophesies a future vengeance to be wrought on Rome from Carthage. This is sometimes taken to be a reference to Hannibal, but curiously there would indeed be a much later vengeance from Carthage, under the Vandal king Gaiseric in the fifth century AD (Chapter 13).

Virgil remains the most famous writer of the Augustan age, but there was also a renaissance of historical writing that produced some tremendously important texts. Velleius Paterculus (19 BC–AD 31, quoted numerous times in this and the preceding chapters) was an equestrian from Campania who flourished under the guidance of both Augustus and his successor, Tiberius. Livy (59 BC–AD 17), who we have also met at some length, hailed from Padua and likewise came under the patronage of Augustus. Livy's magisterial work proved central to the way the collective memory of the Hannibalic War was forged, and in its criticism of impiety and arrogance it was closely aligned with Augustan values (Chapter 4). His books dealing with the crucial second and first centuries BC have been lost, but the surviving summaries reveal a reverence for Caesar and a particularly jaded view of Tiberius Gracchus. In this, Livy was very much in tune with Appian, and promoted the Augustan view of political stability. In Livy's text it is not a coincidence that men like Varro, the villain of Cannae, looked rather much like unfettered plebeian tribunes in their eagerness to court the favour of the people and undermine the *mos maiorum*.

A number of important texts written in Latin have not survived: Gaius Asinius Pollio, the Caesarian eyewitness to and participant in much of the drama of the era (75 BC–AD 4), wrote a history of the civil wars to which Horace referred (*Odes*, 2.1) and which proved an important source for Cassius Dio, Plutarch, Velleius Paterculus, and Appian. Messalla Corvinus also composed a lost history of the period, while Aulus Crematius Cordus wrote a decidedly Republican history of Augustus and the civil wars, in which he praised Brutus and Cassius, referring to Cassius as 'the last of the Romans'. He later committed suicide under a new and more repressive political regime (AD 25) and the majority of the copies of his work were burned (Tacitus, *Annals*, 4.34). A similar fate met the historian Titus Labienus, who harboured Pompeian sympathies, as well as the orator Cassius Severus. In Gaul, Pompeius Trogus (50 BC–AD 25) wrote a 44-book work called the *Philippic Histories*, much of which was focused on the career of Alexander the Great and the fortunes of his successors; a small and important part of the work recounts the early history of Parthia and its Arsacid dynasty. The work is lost, but an epitome (an abridgment or digest) of Pompeius's work was composed by a later writer named Justin, and is part of the canon of sources for Alexander's life.

Alongside these Latin works were several important texts written in Greek. The most notable is the *Geography* of Strabo, which drew on the immense wealth of Hellenistic sources for the inhabited world, but clearly situated Rome at the centre of the new *oikumene.* In this approach, it matched the vision of Virgil and continued the universalism (or 'globalism') begun by Polybius. Similarly sweeping is the *Library of History* by Diodorus Siculus, written between 60 and 30 BC; it followed a thread that began in the depths of Rome's mythical past, concluding with the career of Julius Caesar. Another important figure was Dionysius of Halicarnassus (c. 60–7 BC), who was born in western Anatolia before moving to Rome to study literature. There he composed a history heavily laden with Rome's mythological past, and in the process he further entrenched Rome's Greek origins and Rome's role as the leader of the world. Nicolaus of Damascus (b. c. 64 BC), a Jewish historian close to Herod the Great, wrote a biography of Augustus in Greek, of which substantial fragments remain. One of the most interesting Greek survivals is a poem written sometime after the fact to celebrate Octavian's arrival in Alexandria in 30 BC, which was most probably intended to be inscribed on the base of a statue of Apollo. The poem is known from a manuscript in the British Museum—a fortuitous survival as part of an archive compiled by a man in antiquity who had a fascination for odd poetry! Laden with references to divine parentage, liberation, and the glory of Augustus, it is fulsome about Actium in a way that many of the Latin poets found hard to achieve.

Finally, an event took place during the reign of Augustus that was to have a transformative impact on the politics, literature, society, and religious culture of the Roman empire: the birth of Jesus. In AD 6, Augustus ordered the propraetorian legate of Syria, Publius Sulpicius Quirinius, to carry out a census in Judaea. ('Propraetorian legate' was the title given to a governor appointed by Augustus to an imperial province such as Syria: see further below on the administrative terminology of the Augustan era). The census was necessary because the monarchy had been dissolved following the crises that took place after the death of Herod the Great in 4 BC, and because the tax obligations of the region had subsequently come under Roman control. This census, one of the earliest carried out in the provinces, is connected to the birth of Jesus in the Bible (Luke 2.2, who correctly names the legate) but it has also been argued that Jesus was born sometime earlier, prior to Herod's death, which would square the discrepancy found in Matthew (2.1). Whichever date is to be preferred, Jesus was born into a kingdom with a diversity of religious beliefs. There were polytheists in the Herodian cities of Sebaste, Caesarea Philippi, and Caesarea Maritima. There were Samaritans, whose religion was derived from Judaism but was viewed with disdain by the Hasmoneans, who had ruled an independent Judaea and conquered much of the surrounding countryside, including Idumaea and Galilee prior to Pompey's arrival in 63 BC. Among the Jews were Pharisees, Sadducees, and Essenes, variously at odds with Herod, and often the Romans. Rome itself was home to one of the largest Jewish communities outside Judaea, but the position of the Jews vis-à-vis the Romans, and especially the imperial cult of Rome and Augustus, played a complex role in the relationship between the Jews and the Roman authorities. We shall return to this thorny problem in Chapter 9.

Army and empire

The relationship with the army was tremendously important to Octavian. Those in the army were his clients; he was their patron. Nobody else could impinge on this relationship, so events such as triumphs now became the prerogative of the *princeps* and his family alone. Octavian also took care to provide for his troops in recognition of their loyalty.

At the conclusion of the Actium campaign, he faced an overwhelming task: the need to provide land to about 150,000 veterans. He was keenly aware of the political hazards this entailed. The army could quickly undermine his position if he lost the loyalty of the troops, so through the wealth of Egypt he financed a costly settlement scheme, and retired soldiers were given plots of land and a cash pension to support them. Purchasing land was also a symbolic step back from the older unpopular practices of land confiscation and proscription, and reinforced the new peaceful approach of the *princeps*. This large demobilisation reduced the number of legions to 26, comprising those raised either by himself or Caesar, as well as those that previously had served with Lepidus and Antony. Well aware of the importance of the navy, Octavian kept a standing force split between Ravenna and Misenum, each under the command of an equestrian *praefectus classis*. There were also subsidiary dock facilities at places such as Forum Julii in Gaul.

Later, Augustus amended the terms of service enjoyed by the army by instituting the *aerarium militare*, a military pension fund that paid out 13 or 14 years' wages if a soldier completed his enlistment terms (up to 25 years) and survived long enough to retire. Gradually the cash payment (funded in part by taxes on inheritance) replaced land, which was becoming scarce. These changes completed the long transition from a militia recruited on the basis of property to a professional military that became a deliberate career choice, although special levies could and were demanded in extremis, such as after revolts or military disasters. Extraordinary levies are known to have existed from the time of the revolt in Pannonia (AD 6) and the defeat of Varus (AD 9, see below).

Between Caesar's campaigns in Gaul and the aftermath of the civil wars, the legions began to acquire distinctive unit titles that reflected customs, places of service, and battle honours, and helped to identify individual legions and build camaraderie. I Germanica, for instance, which had been raised either by Caesar or Pansa and came into Octavian's control, acquired its name from service along the Rhine. IIII Macedonica, raised by Caesar, fought for Antony before going over to Octavian; its name honoured its Macedonian service. Other names could be more allusive, such as V Alaudae, which we met in Chapter 7. Numerous legions acquired the title of Augusta, for their recruitment or renewal, and other Augustan characteristics are found in legionary emblems of Capricorn, Augustus's favourite sign of the zodiac, Taurus (the bull), associated with Venus and therefore Julius Caesar, or titles such as Apollinaris, referring to the link between Augustus and Apollo. Sometimes the exact origin of a specific title, or even its meaning, is not entirely clear: there has been some controversy over how and when precisely XX Valeria Victrix, 'valiant and victorious', acquired its name. During the civil wars, both Octavian and Antony possessed legions with identical numbers—V Alaudae with Antony, V Macedonica with Octavian. The incorporation of Antony's legions meant that this dual numbering system persisted, leaving names to distinguish between individual units. The name Gemina, 'twin', often reflects the amalgamation of two units. A distinctive feature of the army under the principate was the preservation of the post-Actium structure, with numbered and named legions that filled vacancies with new recruits; this perpetuated unit identities, further professionalised the force, and ended the practice of releasing time-served legions *en masse*.

The standing legionary force that garrisoned the empire was complemented by a force of provincially recruited auxiliaries, comprising cavalry, archers, skirmishers, and other specialised troops who swore an oath to the *princeps*. The recruitment of non-Roman provincials into the army helped to disseminate Roman culture, religious beliefs, and political ideas among communities of non-Romans. This phenomenon has become known as 'Romanisation'; we shall consider it in greater detail in Chapter 11. Service in the auxiliaries also came to confer citizenship on the successful completion of the required period of service. Grants of citizenship were to some extent an extension of Republican recruitment practices: Julius Caesar had recruited an entire legion from southern Gaul, for example, all of whom received citizenship on their discharge. While non-Romans were Romanised through military service, legionnaires were 'provincialised' through serving for extended periods of service hundreds of miles from Italy. Banned from marriage, Roman soldiers inevitably formed relationships with members of the communities in which they were stationed, and thus citizen soldiers put down roots far from Italy—especially if, on retirement, they chose to settle close to their final posting. Over the centuries, armies of distinctive provincial character emerged: the armies of the Rhine, of the Danube, of Syria, and later of Britain. Certain groups of auxiliaries gained a reputation for excellence, such as archers from Syria or cavalry from Central Europe. The Germanic people of the Batavi, who became clients of Rome during the bloody wars at the turn of the millennium, were recruited in vast numbers for the auxiliaries and formed their own distinct Batavian units; in recognition of their role, they were free from taxes and tribute. More than ever before, the legions and their auxiliaries became important vehicles for the dissemination of Roman culture into the provinces as well as an institution in which virtually any freeborn male from anywhere in the empire, or along its fringes, could serve. In Italy, conversely, fewer men served in the army than in the Republican period, creating a widening rift between professional soldiers and demilitarised citizens.

To address the likelihood that ambitious officers would become mutineers, Augustus significantly raised the pay of centurions. This increased the gulf between centurions and their men—potential troops in a mutiny—and closed the gap between the emperor and the army's leadership. It also helped to further professionalise the officer corps. Augustus personally appointed the senior leadership of the legions, and ordered officers and men alike to swear a personal oath of loyalty to him alone as their patron. This was a mirror of the pre-Actium oath of 32 BC, as well as the natural extension of the close links between *imperator* and soldiers that stretched back to the third century BC; the legionary name Augusta cemented this relationship.

The cost of maintaining Rome's army and navy was a colossal 40–50 per cent of the state's gross national product (GNP). Some of this amount went towards the production of arms and armour, including the new 'Mainz' type swords that had replaced the older *gladius Hispaniensis*. The Mainz swords were shorter than their predecessors, but still included a viciously sharp point designed to kill through stabbing. During the Augustan period, Roman armour also underwent changes—examples of the famous *lorica segmentata*, made up of overlapping iron plates and probably related to Hellenistic cavalry armour encountered in the east, were found at Kalkriese (below), alongside examples of chain mail, the *lorica hamata*, which had been in use since the third century BC. Items continue to emerge from the earth at Kalkriese: in the autumn of 2020, archaeologists discovered a complete cuirass that had once belonged to a Roman legionnaire.

Between 29 and 19 BC, Roman legions battled to complete the conquest of Spain in a bloody struggle known as the Cantabrian War. For a brief period, Augustus personally took part in this conflict, which eventually brought the northern districts of Asturias, Cantabria, and what is now Léon under Roman control. According to Cassius Dio, Augustus planned

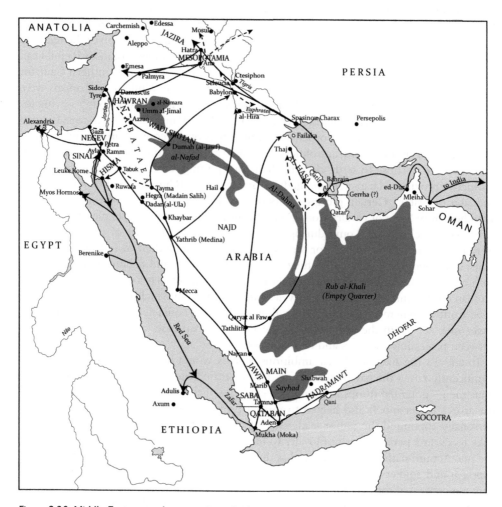

Figure 8.30 Middle Eastern trade routes in antiquity.

Source: Illustration by Aaron Styba with amendments by the author.

an invasion of Britain, but was forestalled by unrest in Gaul (53.22). In North Africa, there were skirmishes with inhabitants of the steppe, the Garamantes, and the Gaetuli. Two military conflicts during this period, however, are of particular importance. The first was the ambitious expedition to South Arabia carried out by Aelius Gallus, the prefect of Egypt; the second was the disaster in Germany.

The background to the Arabian campaign was complex. An intricate network of ancient trade routes criss-crossed the Middle East, bringing valuable spices from the kingdoms of South Arabia to Mediterranean markets via Gaza in Palestine and through the Nabataean city of Petra in the south of modern Jordan (Figure 8.30). Strabo is our main source for much of this, and he was able to draw on a rich well of information from explorers and writers. As far back as the rule of the Persian king Darius I

(522–486 BC), an explorer named Skylax of Caryanda had attempted a circumnavigation of the Arabian Peninsula. Later, Alexander the Great set in train a similarly bold mission, with two prongs departing simultaneously from the head of the Red Sea and the Persian Gulf. Ptolemy II Philadelphus (285/84–247/46 BC) sent out an explorer named Ariston, who wrote an account of his adventures that was used by Agatharchides of Cnidus (c. 200–131 BC), one of Strabo's main sources. Another learned antiquary was Eratosthenes of Cyrene (c. 285–194 BC), the chief librarian at Alexandria; he penned a three-volume work called the *Geographica* that also found its way into Strabo's hands. Through the work of Strabo and also of his near-contemporary Diodorus Siculus, the Romans were therefore well informed about the geography of the Arabian Peninsula and of the wealth of cities such as Petra and the emporium of Gerrha on the Persian Gulf.

Just as Julius Caesar had campaigned over the Ocean and into Britain, so Arabia proved too much of a lure for Augustus. The possible financial windfall of interfering in the luxury spice trade was great, and here was an opportunity to out-do Alexander himself and deliver a message to Parthia about Roman strength. Wild stories about Arabia and its exotic landscape and fauna also proved a tempting lure. There were 'rock-crystals', wrote Diodorus, 'composed of pure water which has been hardened ... by the influence of divine fire'—not to mention the 'struthcameli', a bizarre animal 'like a newly born camel' but with heads that 'bristle with fine hair' and a 'beak which is very short and contracted to a fine point'. In case this was not enough, Diodorus pointed out the existence of gold nuggets 'about the size of chestnuts' that could be extracted from the ground with little effort (2.50–1).

The expedition of Aelius Gallus, who had succeeded Cornelius Gallus as the prefect of Egypt, got underway in 25 BC, and travelled down the west coast of Arabia (Figure 8.31). The troops were likely drawn from the garrison of Egypt, III Cyrenaica, XXII Deiotariana, and perhaps XII Fulminata. The mission was prone to misadventure from the very beginning. The guide hired by Gallus was Nabataean, and as he dragged the Romans southwards through the dry and desolate desert, some began to suspect that he was more than aware of the Roman threat to Nabataea's prime position on the incense route and determined to scupper the expedition. In the *Res Gestae*, Augustus claimed that 'very large forces of the enemy were cut to pieces in battle' (§26), but there appears to have been little action despite the capture of Baraqish (Yathil) and Najran in 24 BC; the penetration of Roman forces to this point is confirmed by the bilingual Greek/Latin inscription of one P. Cornelius, *eques* ('cavalryman'), discovered at Baraqish. There are also two South Arabian texts that mention the Romans—one from the Great Temple in the city of Marib and another from Tamna. Not long after reaching the south, Gallus and his forces returned to Alexandria.

Ancient assessments of the Gallus expedition vary from the pessimistic (Strabo) to the flattering (Pliny the Elder). Modern assessments have been just as divided, but it now appears that Gallus was more successful than it appears. Embassies from the important South Arabian kingdoms of Himyar and Saba were sent to Rome. According to Strabo (basing his account on that of Nicolaus of Damascus), an embassy from India later sought an audience with Augustus. Strabo's derivative version is steeped in Orientalising fancy: 'the gifts carried to Caesar [Augustus] were presented by eight naked servants, who were clad only in loin cloths besprinkled with sweet-smelling odours'. Among the gifts was a giant 'river-tortoise three cubits in length [54 inches, or nearly 1.4 metres!] and a partridge

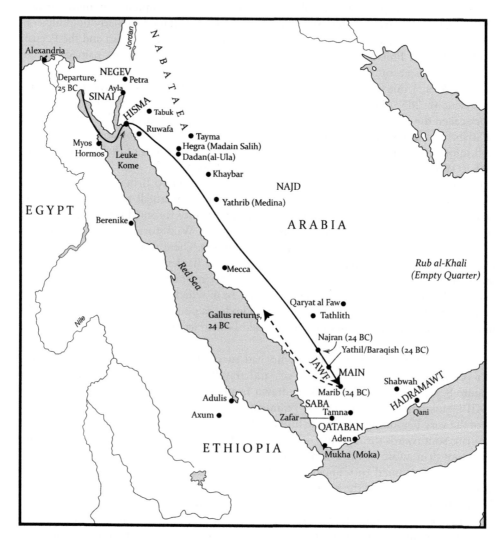

Figure 8.31 The expedition of Aelius Gallus, 25/24 BC.

Source: Illustration by the author.

larger than a vulture' (*Geography*, 15.1.73). In the preceding centuries, coins had been minted in South Arabia that imitated Athenian coinage, and now a series of coins (known as the 'Class B' coins) was minted in South Arabia that displayed the head of Augustus. The Gallus expedition may have accomplished little from a military standpoint and even less from a financial one, but it had resulted in diplomatic recognition for Rome from an array of wealthy and distant lands.

At the opposite end of the empire, numerous campaigns were waged throughout Western and Central Europe, notably in the Cantabrian War and in the series of military expeditions between 25 and 14 BC that subdued the Alps; these campaigns brought

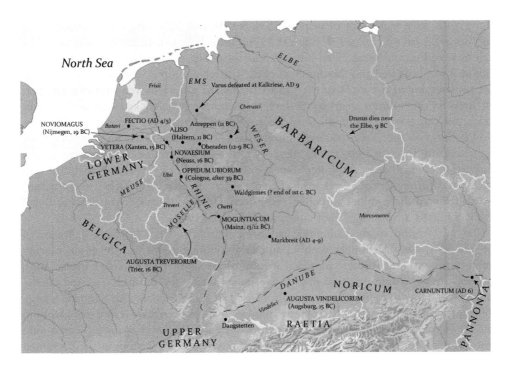

Figure 8.32 Northern Europe at the end of the reign of Augustus. The dashed line represents the *de facto* limits of Roman authority along the Rhine and Danube (Ister) rivers. The map includes major Roman military installations (VETERA) along with their modern names and dates of foundation; modern names for other installations (Dangstetten); Roman provinces (BELGICA); and major tribal groupings (*Marcomanni*).

Source: Illustration by the author.

Raetia and Noricum into the empire. Agrippa and a young Tiberius also campaigned in the Balkans, fighting the Pannonians, Dacians, and Dalmatians along the Danube basin. In AD 6, a rebellion arose in Dalmatia and Pannonia as well as in adjacent Bohemia, and a year later Velleius Paterculus recorded a colossal punitive army of ten legions, 70 cohorts of auxiliaries, 14 troops of cavalry, and a substantial levy of veterans massed on the Save river in Dalmatia to punish the rebels (2.113). The main drama, however, was in the north, in the conflict memorialised by the Netflix drama *Barbarians*. East of the Rhine in Germany, in the vast area known as 'Barbaricum', Roman rule had never been securely established despite a series of highly aggressive campaigns led by Tiberius and his brother Drusus, which had attempted to push the frontier to the river Elbe (Figure 8.32). Velleius Paterculus, who served as an equestrian prefect and then legionary commander in Germany and on campaign in Illyricum, wrote that under Roman arms, 'all of the flower of the [German] youth, infinite in number though they were, huge of stature and protected by the ground they held, surrendered their arms' (2.106). This was, however, far too optimistic.

In AD 9, the Roman general Publius Quinctilius Varus came to grief in Germany. Varus had been propraetorian legate in Syria and had also served as the governor of Africa; he was a close friend of Agrippa and was married to Augustus's great-niece Claudia Pulchra. Along with three legions of infantry—XVII, XVIII, and XIX—he was ensnared in an ambush as his troops trudged through the Teutoburg Forest in northern Germany. The legions were lost, and Varus killed himself; this was not at all *imperium sine fine*. In Rome, Augustus was horrified and the numbers of the shattered legions were retired. Gauls and Germans serving in the ranks of the Praetorian Guard were removed from the city and sent away for other duties, so great was the fear of a rebellion. A shocked Velleius Paterculus wrote that this was the worst calamity for the Roman army since the defeat of Crassus (2.119). Six years later, a Roman expedition under Drusus's son Germanicus reached 'the dismal tract, hideous to sight and to memory'. All over the ground lay 'bleaching bones, scattered or in little heaps … splintered spears and limbs of horses'. Worse were the 'human skulls nailed prominently to tree trunks' and the 'savage altars at which [the Germans] had slaughtered the tribunes and chief centurions' (Tacitus, *Annals*, 1.61). The chastened Romans buried the bones of their comrades and withdrew.

The mastermind of the slaughter had been one Arminius ('Hermann'), leader of the Cherusci, who had fought with an auxiliary contingent allied to the Roman army before turning on his former comrades. Arminius was admired by Tacitus (*Annals*, 2.88), and became something of a folk hero in Germany during the Romantic period. As the Germans sought to 'rediscover' their nationalist past in the nineteenth century, a large military statue of Arminius, the Hermannsdenkmall, was erected close to Detmold and his victory proved an irresistible topic for German Romantic painters. For a long time, the location of the Roman defeat was unknown, but excavations at the presumed site of the battle at Kalkriese (near Venne in northern Germany) began in 1988 after the discovery of some artefacts by a retired British army officer. In 1990, archaeologists found the remains of a collapsed rampart covering Augustan-era coinage and Roman equipment. Subsequent investigations uncovered burial pits containing disjointed animal and human remains (almost all of the human remains were of males between the ages of 25 and 45), the analysis of which suggests that they had lain unburied on the surface for a number of years before being interred. Work at the site has also uncovered delicately wrought belt buckles, a silver ceremonial mask, and the remains of shields, swords, daggers, javelins, and many other parts of military matériel, including bronze surgical equipment. There are other famous legacies of the Varian catastrophe: one of the best-known Roman military tombstones, that of Marcus Caelius, a senior officer with XVIII, was discovered in Xanten (Roman Vetera) in 1620 (Figure 8.33).

Despite the fact that the Arabian expedition yielded questionable results, and that the defeat of Varus was an unmitigated catastrophe, Augustus died with the frontiers of the empire well established along the geographical demarcation lines of the Rhine, Danube, and Euphrates rivers, the north African steppe, and the Nile up to Qasr Ibrim in the region known as the Dodekaschoenus, which remained under Roman control for two centuries. The push into upper Egypt and Sudan, which brought Roman troops to Qasr Ibrim, had been undertaken by Gaius Petronius, prefect of Egypt between 25 BC and 21 BC, and brought the Romans into conflict with the kingdom of Meroe; later efforts to explore even further south during the reign of Nero would be stymied by the tough terrain. In the east, many of the client kingdoms that dated from Pompey's settlement in 63 BC were still under Roman guidance, with the notable exception of Judaea. King Herod the Great had died in 4 BC, and divided his kingdom between his sons Philip the Tetrarch, Herod

Figure 8.33 The tombstone of Marcus Caelius. The epitaph records that Caelius OCCIDIT BELLO
          VARIANO—'died in the Varian war'.

Source: Photograph by Agnete/Public Domain via Wikimedia Commons.

Antipater (Herod Antipas), and Herod Archelaus. After the central provinces of Samaria,
Idumaea (Edom) and Judaea fell into mismanagement under Archelaus, and following
vociferous complaints from delegations of Jews and Samaritans, Augustus brought Judaea
into the Roman administration in AD 6. This was the first time a 'subordinate' province
had been created—through an equestrian prefect at Caesarea, Judaea came under the
propraetorian legate of Syria. Archelaus himself was exiled to Vienne, where he died.

The gravest threat in the east was posed by the Parthians, but through diplomatic means
Augustus obtained some degree of satisfaction for the defeats of Crassus and Antony and
avoided armed conflict. Augustus even travelled to the east in person, although in the end
it was Tiberius, his eventual successor, who retrieved the lost Roman standards. Tiberius
also gained a concession from the Parthians that the strategically important region of
Armenia should have its ruler appointed by the Romans. In the meantime, a substantial
garrison remained in Syria, initially made up of III Gallica (Antioch), VI Ferrata (Laodicea),
and X Fretensis (Cyrrhus). XII Fulminata was likely added later, based at Raphaneae.
Augustus may also have intended to influence the course of Parthian politics by his 'gift'
of an Italian slave girl named Musa, who was sent to Phraates IV. Musa quickly became a

Figure 8.34 Silver drachm of Phraates V and Musa, minted at Ecbatana. Obverse: bust of Phraates V; reverse: Musa.

favourite of the Parthian king and persuaded him to send his four children from his first marriage to Rome. This was done either to privilege her own offspring or to keep the succession free of bloodshed; in the *Res Gestae* § 29, Augustus obliquely mentioned the arrival of these hostages and two of them are known from funerary inscriptions discovered in Rome. Musa, who appears in very few sources (perhaps the longest description of her career is from Josephus, *Jewish Antiquities*, 18.2), became the queen of Parthia (Figure 8.34) and in 2 BC, she arranged for Phraates IV to be murdered in favour of her son, Phraates V (r. 2 BC–AD 4). Musa later married her son, but both were unseated by a coup led by Parthian nobles revolted at such open displays of incest and parricide, and they fled to Rome. The diplomatic mission of Gaius Caesar to the Euphrates (below) should be understood in the context of these developments.

One of the most important decisions taken by Augustus was to divide the Roman empire into senatorial and imperial provinces. The former would be governed by representatives of the senate and the Roman people, while the latter—containing most of the garrisons and armies on campaign—were governed by appointees of Augustus himself. A small number of important or wealthy provinces, including Africa (grain) and Macedonia (with a large garrison), were made available to the senate to govern. As the imperial provinces essentially formed an 'imperial fisc', Augustus sent equestrian procurators to these territories to manage their financial affairs and the revenue raised from the estates there. The administrators of the imperial provinces held the rank of propraetor, and were formally known as *legati Augusti pro praetore*, 'propraetorian legates of Augustus'; they were normally of senatorial rank, having held the praetorship, and represented the *princeps*, who could clearly not personally govern each of 'his' provinces. Such legates were governors and legionary commanders; they wore a military uniform and bore arms, and had the right to carry out capital punishment. Later, the office of legate was stratified to recognise senior legates (governors) and the office of *legatus Augusti legionis*, regimental officers who previously had held office in Rome, appointed to command individual legions. Alongside them served military tribunes, up-and-coming equestrians dispatched to learn their trade with the legions in the reserved occupations of cohort tribune, cavalry commander, and legionary tribune. A new office that reflected the growth of a standing army was that of

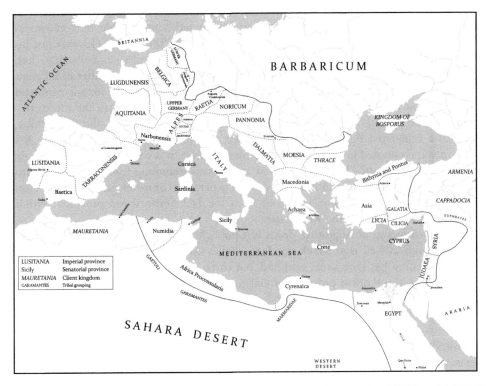

Figure 8.35 The Roman empire at the death of Augustus in AD 14. (Note that UPPER and LOWER GERMANY are properly military districts, not provinces).

Source: Illustration by the author.

praefectus castrorum, camp prefect, a kind of very senior quartermaster who took care of camp construction, training in camp, discipline, and equipment. In many cases (at least at this early stage), the propraetorian legates, their military underlings, and the procurators represented the only Roman bureaucratic presence in the imperial provinces, with governance left to loyal clients such as Herod the Great.

The senatorial provinces were governed by proconsuls, whose service requirement was the praetorship. Senatorial proconsuls were carefully demilitarised: 'they were to carry no sword at their belt nor wear military uniform' (Cassius Dio, 53.13). By being given essentially bureaucratic tasks both at home and abroad, the proconsuls and senators more generally were also depoliticised (vis-à-vis their role during the Republic) and transformed into an organisational arm of Augustan government. Senatorial prestige was maintained through high-value reserved occupations such as the governorship of Asia. Procurators also served in the senatorial provinces alongside quaestors, a nod to the administrative traditions of the Republic. In this way, Augustus combined both traditional and innovative methods of government: he gave just enough to the senate, but also aimed to forestall any future coup attempts by ambitious aristocrats and kept a tight rein on the army (Figure 8.35).

The *Res Gestae* of Augustus

Shortly before his death in AD 14, Augustus composed a remarkable text known as the *Res Gestae*—literally 'the things having been done', or 'the deeds'. This was not his autobiography—that had already been written, but was incomplete and was later lost. The *Res Gestae* was, instead, an ideological statement that drew on a number of different influences. In part, it was a Roman funerary inscription, enumerating his successes and endeavours, but one that was distinctively written in the first rather than the more conventional third person. The near-contemporary epitaph of Cornelius Gallus from Philae, home of a celebrated Egyptian temple complex, is often cited as a model for the *Res Gestae*: it was composed in Latin, Greek, and hieroglyphics, was written in the first person, and was full of majestic claims of conquest and success stemming from a campaign into Nubia. Augustus's text was also influenced by first-person Roman elegies and it has even been suggested that epigraphic traditions from the Hellenistic world provided further inspiration for the form of the *Res Gestae*.

The official record of Augustus's deeds was publicly inscribed on bronze slabs outside his Mausoleum, as well as in Greek and Latin copies throughout the empire. The version erected in Rome has long since vanished, but three examples survived from Turkey, in what was then the Roman province of Galatia. At Colonia Caesarea Antiochia, the old Seleucid city of Pisidian Antioch refounded by military veterans in 25 BC, the *Res Gestae* was displayed in Latin on an archway that formed part of a temple complex. The archway was decorated with features recalling those on the Ara Pacis—fruit and garlands—as well as images of naval victory that evoked the Actium campaign. A Greek version of the *Res Gestae* was put up at nearby Apollonia (not to be confused with Apollonia on the Adriatic coast), surmounted by statues of imperial worthies, including Augustus, Tiberius, and Germanicus. The best-preserved version, however, is found in the Greek and Latin texts discovered at the Temple of Rome and Augustus at Ankara, a city founded by Augustus in 25 BC. The texts were accompanied by images of peace and abundance similar to those found on the Ara Pacis.

The Latin text of the *Res Gestae* employs a distinct sense of nationalist identity represented by its avoidance of foreign words—even those in Greek, a language long familiar to Romans. The Greek text is a *version* of the Latin text, rather than a direct translation, but both texts emphasise the same themes transmitted by Augustan art, built heritage, and public works, and meticulously conceal the nature of the *princeps'* power and his own vicious actions. The enemies of Augustus, for instance, are the enemies of the Republic, and are never named in the text: the Mutina campaign was waged against 'the tyranny of a faction' (§1, Figure 8.36). The Philippi campaign was fought against common criminals, 'those who slew my father' (§2). Misdirection, dissembling, and outright lies are frequent. The extorted consulship held by Octavian after Mutina was the result of a peaceful election (§2). Octavian defeated Brutus and Cassius 'twice' when they 'waged war upon the Republic'—no mention is made of Antony's victory or Octavian's own defeat (§2). Antony himself appears only as 'my antagonist in the war' (§24) and Sextus Pompey is a 'pirate' (§25). The oath that Octavian forced Italy to swear to him was voluntary; likewise, the Italian people 'demanded me as leader in the war in which I was victorious at Actium' (§25). The latter is particularly misleading given the large number of senators and magistrates who took Antony's side and fought against Octavian. Octavian claims that he

Figure 8.36 The opening chapters of the *Res Gestae* erected by Mussolini. In the second line can be read 'A DOMINATIONE FACTIONIS'—'by the tyranny of a faction'.

Source: Photograph by the author.

forgave his enemies (§3), another point that fails to stand up to scrutiny in the light of the Perusian massacre.

The text is careful to portray the actions of Octavian/Augustus as a peaceful acquiescence to the demands of the senate and the people, and ostentatiously shows how he refused extraordinary honours. He rejected the dictatorship, demanded by the people in 22 BC during a famine, which they attributed to his absence from government. Suetonius says that on his refusal he 'threw off his toga from his shoulders and with bare breast begged them not to insist' (*Augustus*, 52). He also rejected the position of consul for life, and wrote in the *Res Gestae* that 'I refused to accept any power offered to me which was contrary to the traditions of our ancestors' (§6). When he did carry out actions that 'the senate wished', he did so through his tribunician power (§6). Nor did he take the position of *pontifex maximus* from Lepidus. Only 'when he at last was dead who, taking advantage of a time of civil disturbance, had seized it for himself' did he accept the people's desperate pleas for him to assume the chief priesthood. People came to Italy to 'elect' him in greater numbers than had ever before been seen in Rome (§10).

Augustus's love for the people and his generosity to them are mentioned frequently: mass donations were made and taxes paid from his own pocket (§15–18). Long sections enumerate in monotonous detail the public works carried out under his tenure (§19–21). Gladiatorial festivals, athletic contests, and games bearing his name were frequently bestowed upon the people (§22–3). These included the Secular Games and a naval battle that involved 'thirty beaked ships' (§23). That love was, of course, graciously returned and the senate and the people set up vows for his health, games and other celebrations, and religious honours such as altars dedicated to Fortuna Redux ('Fortune Returned'), at which celebrations of his birth took place every four years. Statues of Augustus were erected all over the empire (§24) and many of the provinces spontaneously took the personal oath of loyalty that the people of Italy had been compelled to take prior to the Actium campaign (§25). Of course, these things could only take place in a climate of peace: the Ara Pacis, 'voted in honour of my return [from Spain]' is mentioned in §12, while in §13, Augustus boasts that the doors of the Temple of Janus—opened while the state was at war—were closed for only the third time since the foundation of Rome. (A famous earlier closing took place in 235 BC, after the conclusion of the First Punic War.) No less important were his diplomatic and military conquests: the frightened Parthians were 'compelled to restore to me the spoils and standards of three Roman armies', while Roman troops campaigned in Spain, Germany, Arabia, and Ethiopia, with rather more success than actually occurred, as we have seen (§26). The image of irresistible world conquest aligns closely with the ideas expressed through the *Aeneid*, while mentions of both India and Gades provide a clear link with the world-beating deeds of Alexander the Great. Throughout the *Res Gestae*, much is also made of Augustus's service in the religious life of the state, itself a benefit and a model to the people.

Perhaps the most important part of the *Res Gestae* is §34, the penultimate paragraph of the text. It explains how 'When I had extinguished the flames of civil war'—a war he had played a considerable role in starting—'after receiving by universal consent the absolute control of affairs, I transferred the republic from my own control to the will of the senate and the Roman people'. This is a masterpiece of misdirection; there was no universal consent, or at least none that was given willingly, and the transfer of power that marked the First Settlement was a cold political calculation. 'By decree of the senate,' the text continues, he was given the name Augustus, and the other honours such as the *corona civica* and the *clipeus votivus*. In §35 Augustus states that the award of the title *pater patriae* was given by *senatus et equester ordo populusque Romanus universus*, a subtle adjustment to the traditional Senatus Populusque Romanus (SPQR) formula that recognised the position of the equestrians and underscored the unity of the Roman people as a 'universal people' or a people of 'togetherness'.

The *Res Gestae* is a tour de force of propaganda that provided the Roman people with a victorious narrative of national unity against 'factions' and 'antagonists', as well as an equally false image of the peaceful partnership between the senate and the people, and a man who took only the powers that were given to him by the government. Like all great lies, it contains strands of truth—no more so than in the majestic final sentence of §34. 'After that time,' wrote Augustus of the First Settlement, 'I took precedence of all in rank, but of power I possessed no more than those who were my colleagues in any magistracy.' Later, the famous jurist Ulpian (c. AD 170–228) proved the lie with the legal formula *princeps legibus solutus est* (*Digest*, 1.3.31). 'The *princeps* is released from the laws.'

After Augustus

Much of what Augustus achieved was done through loyal associates, especially Agrippa and Maecenas, as well as members of his own family (Figure 8.37). This is unsurprising, since the tightly meshed Roman aristocracy had always operated in this way and both patronage and family connections were essential for success in life, as we have seen (Chapters 5, 6, and 7). With the career of Augustus, however, it proved more important than ever to exploit these connections to plan for the time after his death: he had laboured too hard to leave his succession to chance. It is therefore rather odd that his efforts to plan for the future were haphazard at best, to the point that some modern scholars have even suggested that there was *no* plan for the succession. This was because none of the elected offices was heritable, nor was it immediately clear how powers-without-offices—the *maius* imperium and the tribunician power—could be transmitted from one generation to the next. These were things that belonged to Augustus, and to nobody else. There was also the recent spectre of Hellenistic royalty in the shape of Julius Caesar, as well as Antony and Cleopatra. Neither of these would find favour among the Roman people and even less so among the aristocracy. Instead of imagining the problem as one of a 'successor', therefore, it is perhaps best to think of the question facing Augustus being about which part of his social network could best be relied on to maintain the stability and direction of the state after he died.

In 23 BC, as Augustus lay sick and close to death, it was Calpurnius Piso, not any blood or adoptive relative, who would have assumed control of the state. Suetonius even suggested that it was Augustus's intention that the Republic be restored if he died (*Augustus*, 28). It is also sometimes wondered why Augustus's nephew Marcellus was not 'marked' at this point as a favourable candidate to continue Augustus's work, had he died in 23 BC. Marcellus had been born to Octavia in the year of the Philippi campaign and had clearly been identified as a favourite: he had been aedile, held a senior municipal position in Rome, and had been given the right to stand for the consulship a decade early. Yet he lacked the experience of someone like Agrippa or Maecenas and, as it turned out, he died in the same year that Augustus recovered from his illness, becoming the first occupant of the Mausoleum.

Figure 8.37 Silver denarius of Augustus, minted in Rome in 13 BC. Obverse: bare head of Augustus; reverse, bare head of Agrippa.

If anyone could continue the stability created by Augustus, it was surely Agrippa, who had already joined the imperial family through his marriage to Claudia Marcella, the eldest daughter of Octavia and the sister of the young Marcellus. In 21 BC, Julia, the daughter of Augustus and Scribonia—and widow of the recently deceased Marcellus—married Agrippa (who divorced Claudia Marcella), thus further entrenching Agrippa's position at the side of the *princeps*. In 18 BC, Agrippa was allowed the *maius* imperium and the tribunician power hitherto held only by Augustus and, like his patron, began to reckon time from the year that this grant was made. Agrippa and Julia had two sons, Gaius (20 BC) and Lucius (17 BC), whom the equestrians addressed as the *principes iuventutis*, 'princes/ leaders of youth', a title that had the connotation of 'crown prince'. The two boys were honoured with a porticus on the Basilica Aemilia and were swiftly adopted by Augustus, but only five years later Agrippa, who had been busy stamping out revolts and waging war on behalf of the *princeps*, died suddenly in Campania. Augustus delivered the eulogy (*RGE* §99), and Agrippa's remains joined those of Marcellus in the Mausoleum. Cassius Dio heaped praise on Agrippa, calling him 'the noblest of the men of the day', one whose loyalty to his patron was unswerving (54.29). In his will, he left baths and gardens to the people of Rome, and the estates that he left for Augustus also ended up in public hands.

Gaius and Lucius were too young to offer the advice and stability that only their father could provide, but there was another experienced man to whom Augustus turned—albeit reluctantly, according to Cassius Dio (54.31). This was Tiberius, the son of Livia and her first husband, Tiberius Claudius Nero (d. 33 BC). Through his father, Tiberius was from the ancient *gens* Claudia, which traced its ancestry back to ancient Sabinum and counted many illustrious Romans among its numbers, including Appius Claudius Caecus (censor 312 BC), Appius Claudius Caudex (consul 264 BC), and Tiberius Claudius Nero, who defeated Hasdrubal at the Metaurus River (consul 207 BC). More nefarious members of the *gens* Claudia included the dreadful plebeian tribune Clodius. Tiberius, born like Marcellus in 42 BC, had fought as a military tribune in the Cantabrian War, and was later entrusted with the important tasks of recovering the Roman standards from Parthia and managing the succession in Armenia. He moved quickly through the *cursus honorum*, achieving the consulship in 13 BC and fighting with distinction in Raetia and Pannonia. (His brother Drusus also earned a reputation as a military commander, campaigning aggressively along the Rhine frontier; in 15 BC he had been *legatus Augusti pro praetore* in Gaul, four years later he was elected praetor in Rome and then consul in 9 BC, before dying in a riding accident the same year. The Drususstein in modern Mainz was erected by legionnaires to commemorate his death.) After the death of Agrippa in 12 BC, Tiberius married Julia, who was beginning to resent her father's political match-making. Tiberius was compelled to divorce his beloved wife, Vipsania Agrippina, the daughter of Agrippa and granddaughter of Cicero's friend Atticus—something Tiberius, too, resented. He may have found solace fighting in central Europe and on the Rhine between 11 BC and 8 BC, before taking up the consulship once again in 7 BC, the year after Maecenas died. In his final years, Maecenas had fallen out with his old friend Augustus—perhaps over a plot involving Licinius Varro Murena, the adopted brother of Maecenas's wife, Terentia.

In 6 BC, Tiberius was granted tribunician power—but then mysteriously vanished from the picture, exiling himself to Rhodes for a period of self-reflection, sulking, or anger. The reasons for this act have never really been clear. There had been problems with Julia, whose anger at her constrained life was being purged in a series of very public affairs. According to Cassius Dio, there were similar problems with Gaius and Lucius, who were hardly models of Augustan morality either (55.9). Tiberius may also have been worried about a rivalry developing between himself and Gaius and Lucius—especially given his dislike of Julia, their mother—and thus he removed himself to avoid interfering in their careers. This was the opinion of Suetonius (*Tiberius*, 11) and of Velleius Paterculus (2.99). In Rome, the response of the *princeps* to this crisis was to advance the careers of his grandsons: after exiling Julia to Pandateria (modern Ventotene) for her transgressions of his moralising laws, which included a public affair with Iullus Antonius, the son of Antony and Fulvia, he then refused the request of Tiberius to return to Rome in 1 BC, just as his tribunician power was due to expire.

Soon afterwards, both Gaius and Lucius perished: Lucius died of illness at Massilia in AD 2, while Gaius died of wounds received in the east in AD 4. His death followed a successful diplomatic meeting with the Parthian king at the Euphrates, witnessed by Velleius Paterculus, who was a military tribune at the time, and a brief campaign in Armenia. (A surviving fragmentary inscription from the Mausoleum of Augustus records the interment of Gaius's remains.) The unexpected deaths of Lucius and Gaius raised suspicions, and fingers were pointed at Livia, whose son Tiberius now possessed the best opportunity to take over from an increasingly frail Augustus—but nothing was ever proven (Tacitus, *Annals*, 1). In the year that Lucius died, Tiberius finally returned to Rome; while Gaius still lived, he had remained a private citizen, but with Gaius dead, Tiberius was adopted by Augustus along with Agrippa Postumus, born to Agrippa and Julia after the former's death in 12 BC. Tiberius himself adopted Germanicus, his popular nephew. Agrippa, who 'spent most of his time fishing', soon fell afoul of Augustus and was exiled to the island of Tremirus in AD 6, followed by his sister Julia the Younger two years later (Cassius Dio, 55.32). Tacitus saw in this the work of Livia, who 'had the aged Augustus firmly under her control' (*Annals*, 1.1). All eyes were now on Tiberius. In AD 12 he was granted a triumph, and in AD 13 he received a further grant of the *maius* imperium. It was clear that he would succeed Augustus.

Augustus died after a brief illness one year later at his Campanian villa, a few days short of the astonishing age of 76. To this day, he remains a paradox, a man worthy of both revulsion and respect. On the one hand, Augustus created an era of peace that was without precedence in the ancient Mediterranean—the *pax Romana*. (He had help with this from nature, since between c. 100 BC and AD 200, the Mediterranean climate enjoyed an era of stability with warm temperatures that favoured agricultural production and community prosperity.) On the other hand, the end of the civil wars and the resulting *pax Romana* followed a generation of death and suffering on a shocking scale—one of whose principal architects was Augustus. He was controlling, devious, and manipulative, particularly towards women. The peace that he built was created through misery, and not just of free-born soldiers and civilians, for it was also built on the misery of slaves who continued to be exploited and mistreated: the most famous Augustan representation of this phenomenon is found on the Gemma Augustea, the engraved cameo fashioned from Arabian onyx showing a triumphant Augustus in the upper register and, in the lower register, dejected and bound captives in the process of being tied to a war trophy. The ease with which this sort of juxtaposition is understood by the modern eye underscores the way in which the Romans made slavery seem normal, to the point that this fact would be used, much later on, to justify more recent forms of forced servitude.

Apologists for Augustus point out that he attended to Rome's problems in a systematic fashion that could not help but highlight the incompetence of his predecessors. Cassius Dio, no stranger to civil war and savagery after witnessing the career of Septimius Severus (Chapter 11), excused the unrestrained savagery of the *princeps*, stating, 'I may state that he put an end to all the factional discord, transferred the government in a way to give it the greatest power, and vastly strengthened it.' For Cassius Dio, the ends justified the means. The Romans were 'subjects of royalty, yet not slaves, and citizens of a democracy, yet without discord' (56.43). Seneca, who was a contemporary of Caligula and tutor to the unpredictable Nero (Chapter 9), and equally familiar with bloodshed, noted that while Augustus had perpetrated 'the holocaust of Perusia and the proscriptions', he was a ruler who only displayed cruelty when it was necessary (*On Clemency*, 1.11).

At the death of Augustus, Tiberius already held powers-without-office. He immediately exercised his tribunician power by calling the senate and used his *maius* imperium to take command of the army. Tiberius had succeeded Augustus, but he had never been named as successor—merely the adopted son and beneficiary of Augustus's will. Right to the end of his life, Augustus had judged the political game perfectly. He could not be accused of royal, dynastic pretensions—on the basis of his will and his pronouncements, he had none. Romans had been adopting children to continue the family business for hundreds of years, and this was no different. It was the crucial innovations of the Augustan period, however— the grant of tribunician power and *maius* imperium—that created the means for imperial power to be transmitted between the two generations. Both were framed in Republican terms, although they presented a distinct departure from precedent. Both had been part of Rome's political landscape since the Second Settlement; people had been born under the Second Settlement and died before AD 14, and some had only known a state governed by a man wielding this untouchable twin authority. Indeed, 'Actium,' wrote Tacitus, 'had been won before the younger men were born' (*Annals*, 1.1) It was now left to be seen whether Tiberius could live up to expectations.

Chapter 9

From stability to chaos, AD 14–74

In stark contrast to the austere persona he offered while alive, the funeral of Augustus was glitzy and lavish. A wax model of the *princeps* led effigies of ancestors and famous Romans stretching all the way back to Romulus. Images of the conquered nations followed, after which Tiberius delivered the eulogy. Earlier, Augustus's will had been read to Tiberius by his son, Drusus the Younger: the document advised against freeing slaves and enrolling new citizens, and Augustus also advised Tiberius to be content with the size of the empire. There were grand displays of generosity—a large cash payment for the praetorian guardsmen, a smaller one for the legionnaires, and money for all of Rome's citizens. Augustus's *Res Gestae* was included in the will, with the instructions that it be inscribed on bronze doors outside his Mausoleum. Livia was adopted into the *gens* Julia and granted the title of Julia Augusta. In a final sign of pique towards his daughter, Julia, Augustus barred her from interment in the Mausoleum and ordered that his granddaughter should share the same fate. In death, Augustus was deified by the senate.

The death of Augustus created an unusual power struggle between Tiberius and the senate. While the senate sought to continue Augustan policy, Tiberius was reluctant to step into the position vacated by his adoptive father and needed careful persuasion, even as he strove for a measure of continuity (Figure 9.1). Tiberius's reign was important—his was the first effort to confront the legacy of Augustus and to decide whether the state would or could stay on the course that Augustus had set, and it was for this reason that Tacitus began his *Annals* with the transfer of the imperial throne to Tiberius. While Germanicus was alive, and before Tiberius turned on Germanicus's widow Agrippina the Elder, it appeared as if the stability of the Augustan age could be maintained. Yet the rule of the four Julio-Claudian emperors who followed Augustus proved to be cruel and uninspiring, and laid bare the problems of concentrating such vast amounts of power in a single individual. The principal sources for much of the period, Tacitus, Suetonius, and Cassius Dio, are conservative and pessimistic, and particularly hostile to Caligula and Nero. These writers are sometimes thought to overstate the power of the individual in shaping the course of events. Yet this was also a time when the historical means of political oversight, the senate, had been successfully neutered. Conversely, imperial decision-making in Rome by emperors and their cliques could have far-reaching consequences. Nero's desire for cash, for example, played a role in triggering both the rebellion of Boudicca in AD 61 and the Jewish Revolt in AD 66. It is noteworthy that only a small number of individuals wielded effective power: the emperors and their courtiers, professional officeholders such as the praetorian prefect, provincial procurators and legates,

DOI: 10.4324/9781003202523-9

Figure 9.1 Silver denarius minted at Lugdunum on the accession of Tiberius. Obverse: laureate head of Augustus, listing Tiberius' titles; reverse: Tiberius, bare-headed.

and the small but important number of freedmen under imperial patronage. When opposition emerged, it did so in the shape of conspiracies, often led by survivors of the Roman *nobiles*, who resented the subversion of traditional status markers such as class and family by wealth and proximity to the emperor. Opposition also emerged through rival power blocs in the palace, represented by the praetorian prefect or royal women, notably Agrippina the Younger, often with equestrian and senatorial support. But the conspiracies usually failed and rivals too often exploited particular situations to suit their own ends. Remarkably, and despite these institutional and individual failings, the principate survived.

Tiberius, Germanicus, Agrippina—and Sejanus, AD 14–37

Mutiny

Tiberius's principal concerns in AD 14 were familiar: the army and the senate. On the death of Augustus, there was a serious and widespread mutiny of troops on the Rhine and Danube frontiers, with calls for improved enlistment terms and better pay. The double pay of the Praetorian Guard, viewed by frontier troops as an easy billet, was a particular source of resentment. The legionnaires also seemed apprehensive about the future and about what role the popular Germanicus might play in it. Whatever its precise causes, the army mutiny came at a very delicate time for the Roman state. It is tempting, in retrospect, to dismiss the threat that it posed. Yet the sheer number of legions involved, and the sensitivity of their deployment along the Rhine and Danube, threatened to wreck the precious stability that Augustus had so carefully built.

The revolt among the Pannonian legions at Emona (Ljubljana) came first, and was particularly worrisome because these units were less than a week's march from northern Italy. It was temporarily brought under control by the propraetorian legate Junius Blaesus who, after narrowly avoiding death, gave in to the mutineers' demands that his own son, a tribune, be dispatched to Rome to plead their case. The trouble was not over, however, and the troops quickly turned on the camp prefect and some of the more overt disciplinarians among the centurions and tribunes—including one whom the soldiers called 'Fetch Another', for his habit of calling for a new cane each time one broke over a legionnaire's back (Tacitus, *Annals*, 1.23). Tiberius was alarmed when he found out about the mutiny and sent his son, Drusus the Younger, to deal with the Pannonian troops. A strong contingent of the Praetorian Guard under the praetorian prefect Aelius Sejanus travelled with him to guard Drusus' safety and intimidate the legionnaires. Drusus read a letter from Tiberius addressed to the troops of VIII Augusta, IX Hispana, and XV Apollinaris, in which Tiberius appealed to their better side, recalled his own service in Pannonia with VIII Augusta and XV Apollinaris, and directed Drusus to attend to any grievances that could be addressed immediately. The rest, he wrote, appealing to a vanishing sense of tradition, would be referred to the senate. Tiberius's diplomacy, and the good sense and stern hand of Drusus, who had the ringleaders of the mutiny executed while promising clemency for the great majority of the troops, won the day.

The Germanic legions, under the overall command of Germanicus, who was absent in Gaul, presented a different problem. The troops were split between Upper Germany and Lower Germany, military districts that only acquired imperial provincial status between AD 85 and 90 (Chapter 10). Four legions in Lower Germany under the command of Germanicus's subordinate, the propraetorian legate Aulus Caecina—I Germanica, V Alaudae, XX Valeria Victrix, and XXI Rapax—turned on their officers, beating the centurions to death and dumping their bodies into the Rhine. The concerns of these troops were broadly the same as those of their colleagues in Pannonia, but the legions of Lower Germany were bolder in their mutiny and there was a greater number of vociferous agitators. Hurrying from Gaul, probably to Novaesium (Neuss), Germanicus met the troops—many of the same soldiers he had personally led into battle—and tried to bring the situation under control by appealing to the link between the men and the imperial family, pointing out that Tiberius himself had served with I Germanica and XX Valeria Victrix. Tacitus provided a vivid (if somewhat overblown) portrait of the physical cost paid by the legionnaires and the human effort required to serve in the legions. The mutineers in both Pannonia and the two Germanies complained that even when they were discharged, they were kept on as reserves and forced to work. Furthermore, wrote Tacitus, 'suppose that a man survived this multitude of hazards: he was dragged once more to the ends of the earth to receive under the name of a 'farm' some swampy morass or barren mountain-side'. The retirement benefits, the soldiers complained, were simply not worth the effort required to receive them (*Annals*, 1.17). The soldiers were also worn out from 'the miserly rate of pay, and the severity of the work—parapet-making, entrenching, and the collection of forage, building material, and fuel … along with the other camp drudgeries'. The duration of service was onerous, and barred men from a normal family life and often any hope of seeing home again. Troops who had survived 30 years or more showed Germanicus their scars, their wasted bodies, their toothless gums, and begged to be released from service (*Annals*, 1.35). Germanicus partly acceded to their demands for early discharge and increased pay, desperate to prevent a fatal weakness from spreading along the frontier. As tensions calmed, Caecina, with V Alaudae and XXI Rapax, set out for Vetera (Xanten) for winter quarters. Germanicus took I Germanica and XX Valeria Victrix to his own headquarters at Oppidum Ubiorum (Cologne). Afterwards, Germanicus set out for Upper Germany and the legionary base of Moguntiacum (Mainz), where with only minor resistance he convinced the soldiers of the propraetorian legate Gaius Silius, II Augusta, XIII Gemina,

XIV Gemina, and XVI Gallica, to swear an oath of loyalty to Tiberius. Returning to Vetera, Germanicus discovered that the mutinous spirits of Caecina's legions had not been quelled as he had thought, and soon the camp was riven with violence. A dreadful purge followed, the ferocious butchery of which was witnessed by Agrippina the Elder and her young son, Gaius (better known as Caligula, 'little boots', after the military shoes, *caligae*, that he was accustomed to wear in camp). Meanwhile, Caecina was quickly losing control of V Alaudae and XXI Rapax; spurred on by a letter from Germanicus that reached him at Vetera, he liquidated the ringleaders, saving his own life in the process.

Later, Germanicus led a punitive raid against the Germanic tribes that restored some of the army's morale. It was not long after this that Germanicus and Caecina came across the battlefield where Varus and his legions had been lost, and the Romans buried their dead (Chapter 8). They were also able to retrieve some of the standards lost during the disaster (Figure 9.2). During this campaign, Agrippina the Elder managed to save the Rhine bridge at Vetera from destruction as a rumour arose that the legions had been defeated and a vengeful Germanic horde was flooding straight for the camp. She was, Tacitus wrote, 'a great-hearted woman who assumed the duties of a general' (*Annals*, 1.69). Her daughter and namesake, born in AD 15 at Oppidum Ubiorum, became the equally formidable Agrippina the Younger. In the same year, Caecina and Gaius Silius were granted 'triumphal distinctions' for their part in the campaign that followed the suppression of the mutinies. In reality, this amounted to little more than the opportunity to wear the garb of a triumphant general; the actual triumph, a relic of the Republic, now belonged to the imperial family. After being fêted, Silius was dispatched to Gaul to suppress a revolt of two of the Gallic elite, Sacrovir and Florus, who had emerged as champions of those downtrodden by heavy taxation and even heavier debt—problems that plagued the empire throughout the first century.

In AD 16, Germanicus set about looking for a decisive set-piece battle away from the forests, marshes, and bogs where the Germans held the advantage. On level ground, he

Figure 9.2 Bronze dupondius minted at Rome under Caligula between AD 37 and AD 41. Obverse: GERMANICVS CAESAR with triumphal quadriga; reverse: Germanicus standing left, SIGNIS RECEP / DEVICTIS GERM—'the standards recovered from the vanquished Germans'.

reasoned, he would crush the Germans and punish Varus's conqueror Arminius, who was still at large. Caecina and Silius constructed a fleet that could ferry troops and supplies down the network of rivers in Germany. Eventually, the Germans were brought to battle, and Tacitus provided a haunting image of 'eight eagles seen aiming for, and entering, the glades'; Germanicus urged his troops forward to 'follow the birds of Rome, the guardian spirits of the legions!' (*Annals*, 2.17). The result was a decisive victory at Idastaviso on the Weser River—Tacitus wrote that 'the enemy were slaughtered from the fifth hour of daylight to nightfall', and the spoils included fetters with which the Germans had hoped to lead away their Roman prisoners (*Annals*, 2.18). Arminius escaped, yet he was murdered not long afterwards by relatives envious of his success. Tacitus spoke approvingly of Arminius, calling him 'the liberator of Germany' (*Annals*, 2.88).

Germanicus also suspected that *his* relatives were jealous of his success when pleas for one final year of campaigning in Germany were denied. On the other hand, Tiberius perhaps judged—no doubt correctly—that further fighting in Germany served little purpose. Tiberius did allow Germanicus a triumph, which took place in late May of AD 17. On parade was Arminius's wife, Thusnelda, and her infant son. Like Arminius, Thusnelda was reinvented much later on by German nationalists and became a favourite topic for German artists (Figure 9.3).

Figure 9.3 Karl Theodor von Piloty, *Thusnelda at the Triumphal Entry of Germanicus into Rome* (1875).

Source: Image courtesy of metmuseum.org (CC0-1.0 Universal).

Germanicus in the east

After denying Germanicus a final year in Germany, Tiberius took the opportunity to send him far away to the east, where the fallout from the Parthian succession crisis that had taken place during the reign of Augustus continued to simmer. Following the flight of Musa and Phraates V, there was a brief period where an obscure individual named Orodes III occupied the throne. In AD 6, Vonones, the eldest son of Phraates IV, was sent from Rome to assume the crown in Ctesiphon. Only four years later, however, Vonones was unseated by his nephew, Artabanus II. Vonones fled to Armenia, where he crowned himself king. A furious Artabanus subsequently tried to remove Vonones and install his own son on the Armenian throne, but this act was regarded as a violation of the Roman right to crown the king of Armenia. To solve this problem, Germanicus was granted *maius imperium*, marking him as a firm favourite to succeed as emperor in place of the young son of Tiberius, Drusus the Younger. On a tour of the east with Agrippina the Elder, Germanicus visited Nikopolis to pay his respects to Augustus, his great-uncle, as well as his grandfather, Antony, and to visit the commemorative sites there, pondering 'the whole great picture of disaster and triumph' that lay spread out below him as he stood at the Actium monument (Tacitus, *Annals*, 2.53). Germanicus even competed in the 199th Olympiad in AD 17, and won a prize with a four-horse chariot. His pleasant journey via Athens, Troy, and the sanctuary of Apollo at Colophon was soon soured by the newly appointed propraetorian legate of Syria, Gnaeus Calpurnius Piso, and his wife, Munatia Plancina. Piso was the son of Augustus's staunchly Republican consular colleague in 23 BC and a relative of Julius Caesar's wife, Calpurnia, while Plancina was the granddaughter of Lucius Munatius Plancus (Chapter 8). The official reason for Piso's appointment was to avoid a conflict of interest between Germanicus and the outgoing propraetorian legate, Creticus Silanus, whose daughter was due to marry into Germanicus's family.

Both Piso and Plancina inveighed against Germanicus and Agrippina and sought to undermine their popularity with the soldiers garrisoned in Syria. Piso further undermined Germanicus by supporting Vonones. Tacitus saw the hand of Tiberius in this, noting that 'a whispered rumour was gaining ground that these doings were not unacceptable to the emperor' (*Annals*, 2.55). Nevertheless, Germanicus resolved the situation in Armenia by installing the son of the client king of Pontus under the royal name of Artaxias III, a choice acceptable to both Artabanus and the Armenian people. In neighbouring Commagene, king Antiochus III had died in AD 17, and Germanicus oversaw the absorption of this territory into the province of Syria. (Cappadocia likewise became a Roman province under a procurator in the same year, when its king was deposed by Tiberius.)

Germanicus also held an audience with the Nabataean client king Aretas IV, and there were dealings with the important caravan city of Palmyra in the Syrian desert. Creticus Silanus had fixed the boundary between Palmyra and the Roman client kingdom of Emesa (Homs) during his tenure as propraetorian legate of Syria; this is known from an inscribed Latin boundary marker from the time of the emperor Hadrian (AD 117–38) discovered at Khirbet al-Bilaas, between Palmyra and the Emesene city of Epiphania (Hama). From Palmyra itself, a text in Palmyrene, a dialect of Aramaic, records that one Alexandros was sent by Germanicus to establish friendly relations with the semi-independent Parthian neighbor of Mesene (Characene) at the head of the Persian Gulf, which had important trading links with Palmyra and was a trans-shipment point for luxury products sold in the Roman empire. The famous Greek-Palmyrene bilingual Tariff

Figure 9.4 The Temple of Bel at Palmyra, viewed from the Palmyrene oasis. The central structure surrounded by the colonnade is the *cella*. Along with a substantial part of the surrounding installations, the *cella* was destroyed by Daesh/ISIS terrorists in August 2015.

Source: Photograph by the author.

Inscription (AD 137), which records the taxes levied on goods passing through the city, also mentions Germanicus. Finally, Germanicus is also mentioned on an inscription found in the *cella* of the Temple of Bel, the most important place of worship at Palmyra; the *cella* was constructed between AD 19 and AD 32, and the Latin inscription, written on a statue base and dedicated by the commander of X Fretensis, Minucius Rufus, reveals that it was intended for images of Germanicus, Drusus the Younger, and Tiberius (Figure 9.4). The epigraphic evidence from Palmyra is some of the earliest evidence for Roman interest in the city, and particularly in regulating its role in local and regional economies, even though the Palmyrenes maintained a prized independence between Rome and Parthia (Figure 9.5).

In AD 18, Germanicus and Agrippina welcomed another daughter, Julia Livilla, born on the island of Lesbos. In AD 19, Germanicus engaged in some light tourism in Egypt, visiting the pyramids, 'reared mountain high by the wealth of kings among wind-swept and all but-impassable sands', according to Tacitus's romantic account (*Annals*, 2.61). Germanicus went to Egypt without permission and, thus breaking the rules set by Augustus, earned a harsh censure from Tiberius. Germanicus received a rousing welcome in Alexandria

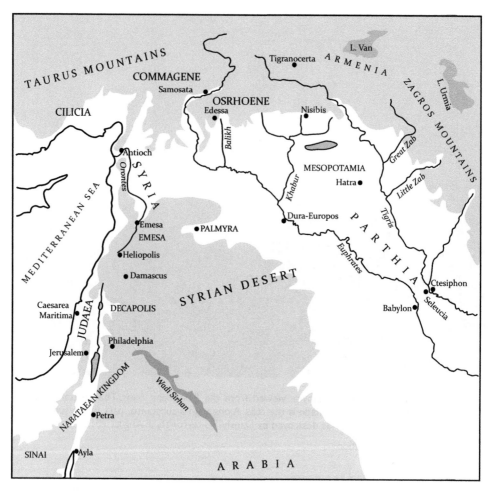

Figure 9.5 Palmyra and the Middle East in the first century AD.

Source: Illustration by the author.

but subsequently discovered that Piso and Plancina had continued to work against him. Not long afterwards, he returned to Syria and became sickly. From his bed in Antioch, he stripped Piso of his governorship. In October AD 19, Germanicus died; with him passed many of the prospects that Augustus would have held for Tiberius and the stability of his rule. Germanicus was sorely missed in death: he became so popular, in fact, that he was freely compared with Alexander the Great. Tacitus idealised Germanicus's Alexander-esque journey through eastern lands, his tragic death in mysterious circumstances, his young age—33, practically the same as Alexander—and the promise of glorious and fair imperial rule that died with him in Antioch, a latter-day Babylon. In his *Natural History*, Pliny fancifully connected Augustus, Alexander, and Germanicus for their love of horses—Alexander's mount, Bucephalus, was granted a city on his death and Augustus raised a sepulchre for his horse, about whom Germanicus wrote a touching poem (8.64). Tacitus enthused that 'foreign nations and princes felt the pang' caused by Germanicus's death (*Annals*, 2.72) and as the news reached Rome, the city fell into a paroxysm of mourning, quickly followed by a near-excessive bout of ostentatious commemoration with arches, inscriptions, and honours, including new voting centuries named for Germanicus. (New centuries had been named for Gaius and Lucius Caesar, and would similarly be named for Drusus the Younger on his death in AD 23, reflecting changes to the composition of the *comitia centuriata* in the early imperial period.) The honours voted to Germanicus are known not only from Tacitus but also from the *Tabula Siarensis*, an inscribed bronze copy of the *senatus consultum* on the issue from AD 19 found in southern Spain, as well as the *Tabula Hebana*, an inscribed bronze tablet found in Italy. Germanicus's ashes joined those of Augustus in the Mausoleum; he left not only a soaring posthumous reputation, but also a Latin translation of the Greek poet Aratus's *Phaionomena*, which dealt with astral bodies, weather, and the constellations. Germanicus's version, the *Aratea*, remained popular well into the Middle Ages.

The trial of Piso

Prior to his death, Germanicus had come to believe that Piso had poisoned him, and a rumour quickly emerged that Piso had done so at the behest of Tiberius. Tacitus gave some credence to the existence of some kind of plot, referring to 'a document seen more than once in Piso's hands' that allegedly implicated Tiberius (*Annals*, 3.16), and the emperor was criticised for showing insufficient grief at the funeral. Suetonius claimed that early in Tiberius's tenure, the legions called on Germanicus to usurp the imperial throne, sowing discord between uncle and nephew (*Tiberius*, 25). Piso provided a straightforward scapegoat for this thorny dilemma, and he was swiftly brought to trial on charges of sedition for attempting to win favour with the troops, a prerogative that belonged to the emperor alone. He died—or was silenced—before a verdict could be returned. Nevertheless, Piso was posthumously found guilty and suffered a *damnatio memoriae*, the most crushing punishment the state could inflict. His name was removed from inscriptions and any portraits of him were destroyed—his very memory was consigned to the underworld. Plancina was accused of 'blasphemous rites and sacrifices', but was close to Livia and through her 'private intercessions' was acquitted, although she later committed suicide in AD 33, four years after Livia's death (Tacitus, *Annals*, 3.13–15).

A record of the *senatus consultum* concerning Piso was inscribed on bronze tablets and distributed throughout the empire. Numerous copies in varying states of preservation were discovered in the old Roman province of Baetica in the 1980s, and have aroused scholarly interest ever since. The text presents a snapshot of a real crisis—the death of a much-loved heir apparent, the possible involvement of the emperor and his mother, the unhappy relationship between emperor and senate—and the way it was handled. The senate stripped Piso of his Roman character, declaring him an enemy, and closed ranks around Tiberius and Livia. The portrait of Piso is damning. He was outside the law, killing Romans without trial, damaging the discipline of the army, taking it upon himself to meddle in foreign policy, and ignoring the *maius* imperium of Germanicus. Worse, by corrupting the army, Piso had raised the spectre of civil war, a terrible prospect that 'had long since been laid to rest by the divine will of the deified Augustus and the virtues of Tiberius Caesar Augustus'

(*SCPP*, l. 46–7). Livia shines in the text as a beacon of Roman matronhood, her devotion to her deified husband and living son manifest and apparent.

Tiberius in Rome

In Rome, Tiberius was greatly impaired by his earlier, lengthy absences in Rhodes and on campaign for Augustus, finding the senate house and the degree of respectful conviviality required for debate and the taking of advice difficult to manage. He also appeared prone to fits of jealousy, and was annoyed by the popularity of Germanicus and the people's love for Agrippina the Elder. Cassius Dio delighted in the apocryphal story of 'one of the largest porticos in Rome' that had started to fall down, until 'it was set upright in a remarkable way by an architect whose name nobody knows' (58.21). Tiberius was so jealous of the man's success that he forbade his name to be recorded! He was kinder to Valerius Maximus, whose epic collection of Roman miscellany was dedicated to the emperor. Tiberius governed awkwardly through the consuls, 'as though the old Republic were in being', and called together the first meeting between himself and the senate using the tribunician power provided to him by Augustus (Tacitus, *Annals*, 1.7). He held the consulship himself on three occasions, in AD 18, 21, and 31, with Germanicus, Drusus the Younger, and the praetorian prefect Sejanus as his respective colleagues. He tinkered little with the government built by Augustus, with the exception of changes to elections (below) and his practice of keeping provincial governors in office after their terms were complete. (One, in Moesia, served a for a quarter of a century.) Suetonius considered Tiberius to have used the consuls and the senate to allow 'a semblance of free government', referring business to them, rising to greet the consuls, and providing other traditional flatteries (*Tiberius*, 30–1). In comparison with Augustus, he was frugal, with few building projects beyond the Temple of the Deified Augustus, about which Velleius Paterculus could barely restrain himself: 'With what pious munificence, exceeding human belief, does he now rear the temple to his deified father!' (2.130). When natural disaster struck, Tiberius was more forthcoming, providing low-interest loans or free grants to repair the damage. Tiberius's timidity is also reflected in his resistance to senatorial attempts to give him the title of *pater patriae* and his refusal to accept a whole range of honours, including the title *imperator*. He also had something of a puritanical streak, getting rid of actors from Italy in AD 23 and curbing the wildly popular gladiatorial shows; this forced people to host shows in secret or in poorly constructed arenas, leading to a calamity at Fidenae when an amphitheatre collapsed, killing hundreds. Overall, he earned the ire of many, including an anonymous satirist who lampooned his snobbery and his poor relationship with his mother, Livia. Suetonius wrote that Tiberius resented Livia's overbearing manner and her desire to share in ruling the principate, and Tiberius consequently 'shunned' her at every opportunity (*Tiberius*, 50). In contrast to his clear discomfort when dealing with Rome's aristocrats and members of his own family, Tiberius was much firmer with the Praetorian Guard, for whom, under the direction of Sejanus, he constructed a new, large base on the outskirts of Rome.

The presence of some 9,000 soldiers so close to the seat of government directly undermined the delicate balance between emperor and senate—even if Tiberius gave greater leeway to the senate by allowing it to elect magistrates. Later, he also allowed senators to address claims for arbitration made by communities in the senatorial provinces.

Tacitus wrote that Tiberius found the senators so sycophantic that he referred to them as 'men ready for slavery' (*Annals*, 3.65), and he became increasingly suspicious of the senate's activities and began to imagine all sorts of plots against him. An early inclination of Tiberius's problematic character was gruesomely displayed by the murder of Agrippa Postumus, quietly dispatched in AD 14 not long after Augustus died. Tacitus characterised this act as the 'opening crime of the new principate', and squarely implicated Livia (*Annals*, 1.6). Instead of the senators, Tiberius took advice from an equestrian confidant, Gaius Sallustius Crispus, the great-nephew of the historian Sallust, who was involved in the murder of Agrippa Postumus and counselled Tiberius not to include the senate when it came to making decisions. For the senate's part, its members suspected that Tiberius did not quite understand the position he held, and mocked him for it. When asked by Asinius Gallus—the son of Virgil's patron Gaius Asinius Pollo and the new husband of Tiberius's much-loved ex-wife, Vipsania—which department of government he would like to manage, Tiberius stammered his way through the response. Gallus used the occasion to imply that Tiberius could not grasp 'that the body politic was a single organism needing to be governed by a single intelligence', and was thus unfit for duty (Tacitus, *Annals*, 1.12). It was also said of Tiberius that 'others were slow in doing what they promised, but that he was slow to promise what he was doing'—in other words, his reluctance was a fiction to conceal his concentration of power (Suetonius, *Tiberius*, 24).

Because Tiberius often said one thing and meant another, he assumed that others did too, which created a climate of mistrust. 'He certainly gave people a vast amount of trouble,' wrote Cassius Dio, 'whether they opposed what he said or agreed with him.' Dio pointed out for the benefit of his readers that everyone who held a consulship with Tiberius went on to suffer 'violent and miserable deaths' (58.1 & 58.20). Much of this mistrust and trouble manifested itself in paranoia and trials for *maiestas*, treason. Treasonable activities were not confined to assassination plots or other seditious acts, and came to encompass defamation and even adultery involving any member of the imperial family. Aristocrats eager to destroy their enemies pounced gleefully on this new opportunity, which promised all the long-vanished rewards of the spiteful lawsuits of the Republic. One of the earliest trials was of Marcus Libo Drusus, the great-nephew of Scribonia, Octavian's second wife. His enemies maneouvred him into an untenable position, where he was accused of consorting with astrologers, raising 'spirits by incantations', and coveting extreme wealth. Eventually, he was accused of conspiring against Tiberius and committed suicide (Tacitus, *Annals*, 2.28). There were many others: one Falanius, for instance, an equestrian, was prosecuted for selling a garden together with its statue of Augustus; another equestrian, Rubrius, was pursued through the courts for perjury, a 'violation of the deity of Augustus' (*Annals*, 1.73). Before long, men began to turn on one another—one magistrate accused another of compiling 'sinister anecdotes' about Tiberius (*Annals*, 1.74). Even aristocratic women were not spared, with a niece of Octavia, Appuleia Varilla, accused of insulting Augustus, Tiberius, and Livia. Informers were everywhere, and were rewarded for their gossip: it was in this terrible climate that the pro-Republican historian Aulus Crematius Cordus (Chapter 8) was prosecuted by agents of the praetorian prefect Sejanus. During his trial, Cordus pointed out that Livy had been so generous to Pompey in his work that Augustus playfully called him 'the Pompeian', but allowed him his freedom of speech, and further pointed out that Augustus himself had read Cordus's own history and was not offended. But times had changed. Cordus starved himself to death, and much of his work was destroyed, which Tacitus reckoned to be 'an act of despotism' (*Annals*, 4.34–5 & Cassius Dio, 57.24).

Both Tacitus (*Annals*, 6.51) and Cassius Dio (57.13 & 58.19) reckoned that the death of Germanicus had marked a turning point in Tiberius's comportment, and contributed markedly to the climate of suspicion and terror in Rome. Signs of derision and unhappiness were everywhere. When Junia, sister of Brutus and wife of Cassius, died in AD 22 at the astonishing age of 97, her funeral was an extravagant aristocratic affair that involved almost all the survivors of Rome's once-great noble families. She snubbed Tiberius in her will, which he was forced by her illustrious family pedigree to accept. In her funeral procession, the wax effigies of 'twenty great houses preceded her to the tomb', wrote Tacitus. 'But Brutus and Cassius shone brighter than all by the very fact that their portraits were unseen' (*Annals*, 3.76).

Sejanus

Further worsening this delicate situation was the fact that the dual leadership structure of the Praetorian Guard was subverted by Sejanus, who assumed sole leadership after his father, the other co-holder of the prefecture, was sent to Egypt. In control of such an important resource, Sejanus's ambition soon gained the better of him. Too close to the action to have a dangerous opinion, and one of Sejanus's disciples, Velleius Paterculus lauded the praetorian prefect as the 'incomparable associate in all the burdens of the principate' (2.127). With the benefit of some historiographical distance, Tacitus despised Sejanus, vilifying his character in the *Annals*—alleging, for instance, that he 'disposed of his virtue for a price' to the famous Roman gourmand, Apicius (4.2). Tiberius was soon wholly in Sejanus's confidence and referred to him as 'the partner of his toils', allowing him to hold the praetorship even though he was an equestrian and not a member of the senatorial class (Tacitus, *Annals*, 4.2). When the Theatre of Pompey was repaired following a fire, a statue of Sejanus was installed there with the tacit approval of the emperor.

Powerful men stood in Sejanus's way. Chief among these was Drusus the Younger who, in AD 21, had been appointed consul with Tiberius as his colleague, although the weary emperor retired to Campania for nearly two years. In AD 22, Drusus received the tribunician power, marking him as Tiberius's favourite. In the same year, Livia became ill and nearly died; a grateful senate minted coins in her honour on her recovery (Figure 9.6). According to Tacitus, Sejanus seduced Livilla, the wife of Drusus (Livilla was also the sister of Germanicus and the granddaughter of Octavia and Antony—see Figure 9.7). For his part, Drusus hated Sejanus, and he was openly angry at the fact that Tiberius showed Sejanus such favour while he, Tiberius's son, was alive. In AD 23, Drusus died in mysterious circumstances. A slow-acting poison administered with the connivance of Livilla was the probable culprit. A tearful Tiberius presided over the funeral, and Drusus was accorded the same honours that had been given to Germanicus after his death.

With Germanicus and now Drusus the Younger dead, the two most likely heirs to the principate had vanished. Tiberius grasped for alternatives (Figure 9.8). Drusus had welcomed twin sons, Germanicus Gemellus and Tiberius Gemellus, in AD 19. Being only four years old in AD 23, however, they were hardly suitable, and Germanicus Gemellus died in the same year. Tiberius's other options were the children of Germanicus and

Figure 9.6 Bronze sestertius minted in year 24 of Tiberius's tribunician power (AD 22/23). Obverse: the mule-drawn cart is a *carpentum*, a form of transport granted to Roman matrons, similar to that known from coinage honouring Agrippina (Figure 9.9); reverse: S.C. guaranteeing the coin's value, and the official titles of Tiberius.

Figure 9.7 Bronze dupondius minted in Rome by Drusus the Younger. The portrait on the obverse of Pietas is thought to be a rare image of Livilla.

Agrippina the Elder: Nero Julius Caesar (b. c. AD 6), Drusus Julius Caesar Germanicus (b. AD 8), and Gaius (Caligula, b. AD 12), who was favoured by a growing faction in the senate.

Nero and Drusus were both duly adopted in AD 23, and this event may have occasioned the commission of the Great Cameo of France, a spectacular sardonyx relief illustrating the members of the imperial family dating from the early first century and now in the Bibliothèque Nationale in Paris; the Cameo is one of the first instances where both deified and living members of the imperial family are portrayed together. Even as the young boys joined the imperial family, however, a schism was growing between Tiberius, and Agrippina the Elder and her supporters in the senate. Sejanus sensed an opportunity to further his ambition and strove to widen this division, fabricating lawsuits against the surviving friends and associates of Germanicus and Agrippina. Germanicus's old comrade-in-arms, Gaius Silius, was targeted, as was his wife, Sosia Galla, who was close to Agrippina.

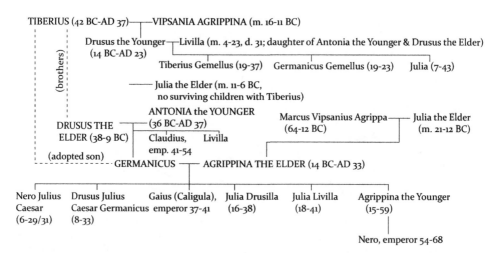

Figure 9.8 Schematic of the family tree of Tiberius and his relationship with the family of Germanicus and Agrippina the Elder.

Source: Illustration by the author.

Silius committed suicide and Sosia Galla was driven into exile; their estate was confiscated. In AD 26, Claudia Pulchra, the granddaughter of Octavia, great-niece of Augustus, former wife of Publius Quinctilius Varus (Chapter 8) and Agrippina's second cousin, was put on trial. The charges were stiff: adultery, too much knowledge of dangerous poisons, and a plot to get rid of Tiberius. Agrippina became angry and rebuked Tiberius for sacrificing to the deified Augustus one moment and persecuting members of his family the next. Tiberius was unmoved, and Claudia met her fate.

Sejanus acquired even greater influence when Tiberius abruptly retired to his estate of Villa Jovis on the island of Capri in AD 27, never to return. The reasons for his actions are as murky as those for his earlier departure to Rhodes during the reign of Augustus. Tacitus, admitting that he did not know the precise cause, nevertheless cited annoyance with Livia, vanity (he had an 'ulcerous face generally variegated with plasters'), a desire to tame his cruelty, and irritation with Sejanus (*Annals*, 4.57). Cassius Dio wrote that Tiberius was desperate to get away from Livia (57.12). Suetonius credited his longing to satisfy his vices in a salacious and vicious passage of character assassination. These included a love for wine (for which he had earned the moniker 'Biberius') and cravings for sex that were satisfied by 'experts in deviant intercourse' selected to copulate 'before him in triple unions to excite his flagging passions'. Suetonius's allegations fuel the stereotype of the licentious despot. 'Once, at a sacrifice, attracted by the acolyte's beauty, he lost control of himself,' he wrote. 'Hardly waiting for the ceremony to end, he rushed him off and debauched him and his brother, the flute-player, too; and subsequently, when they complained, he had their legs broken' (*Tiberius*, 42–5). Sensationally, Suetonius wrote that 'at Capri they still point out the scene of his executions, from which he used to order that those who had been condemned after long and exquisite tortures be cast headlong into the sea before his eyes' (*Tiberius*, 62). Much of what was written about Tiberius in this vein is likely to be false. But Tiberius's absence from Rome gave Sejanus total control over what information reached him and what was concealed, as well as a stranglehold over appointments and other political matters in the capital. Sejanus's star was rising; the only setback that he experienced was Tiberius's denial of his application to marry Livilla, which would have made him a member of the imperial family.

While on Capri, and being drip-fed choice morsels of gossip by Sejanus, Tiberius continued his machinations against the family of Germanicus. His target was Nero Julius Caesar, who had married Julia, the daughter of Drusus the Younger and Livilla. Having long held Livilla's confidence, Sejanus sedulously used her to extract every piece of information, gossip, and slander he could about Julia's marriage in order to build a dossier that might implicate Nero. In AD 29, the imperial mood hardened even further when Livia died at the age of 86. Tiberius chose not to attend his mother's funeral, prevented her deification, and ignored her will; her eulogy was read by Gaius (Caligula), one of his first important public engagements. The death of Livia seems to have freed Tiberius's hand for what Tacitus saw as the final phase of his reign, in which he 'plunged impartially into crime and ignominy' (*Annals*, 6.51). He began by intensifying his attacks on Agrippina the Elder and Nero. A 'letter' of doubtful authenticity materialised in Rome, condemning mother and son. After some prevarication, Nero was declared an enemy of the state, and died in exile sometime between AD 29 and 31. His brother, Drusus Julius Caesar Germanicus, fared little better, dying in prison on the Palatine in AD 33. 'Drusus was so tortured by hunger,' wrote Suetonius, 'that he tried to eat the stuffing of his mattress' (*Tiberius*, 54). After a beating that robbed her of the sight in one eye, Agrippina was exiled to the island of Pandateria, where her mother, Julia the Elder, had been banished (Chapter 8); Agrippina died there in AD 33. The young Gaius, held as a virtual hostage on Capri, watched dispassionately as Tiberius destroyed his mother and his brothers. In the same year, Asinius Gallus died after being arrested in AD 30. Tiberius accused him of an affair with Agrippina and, like Piso, Gallus suffered a *damnatio memoriae*.

Sejanus himself was finally undone in AD 31, after Antonia the Younger (the younger daughter of Antony and Octavia) learned from Apicata, Sejanus's estranged wife, of a plot against Tiberius. She was able to send two of her freed slaves, the remarkable Antonia Caenis (who would become the long-term partner of the emperor Vespasian) and Antonius Pallas (who went on to serve Claudius and Nero), to Capri to inform Tiberius of the looming danger. The senate condemned Sejanus to death; according to Cassius Dio, his corpse was 'abused' for three days before being dumped into the Tiber. His children by Apicata were also murdered—Tacitus added the gruesome detail that since Roman custom prohibited carrying out a capital punishment on a virgin, the executioner savagely raped Sejanus's daughter Iunilla before she was strangled, her body dumped like common rubbish onto the *Scalae Gemoniae*, the steps leading past the prison (*Annals*, 5.9). Apicata, overcome with grief, and having written to Tiberius confirming her husband's treachery, took her own life. It is thought that Velleius Paterculus, who was close to Sejanus, also perished in the purges. Livilla paid heavily for her part in the supposed conspiracy; shut up in her house by her mother, Antonia the Younger, she died of starvation in AD 31.

Tiberius was now grasping for a successor. He passed over Germanicus's brother Claudius, who was 46, because he considered him to be mentally unstable, and chose instead to elevate Gaius (Caligula) and Tiberius Gemellus. Tiberius eventually died in the old house of Lucullus at Misenum in AD 37, close to 78 years of age, and Gaius (henceforth Caligula) and Tiberius Gemellus succeeded to the principate. Rumours that Tiberius was murdered were rife in antiquity. According to Tacitus, Macro, the ex-commander of the *vigiles* in Rome and now praetorian prefect, had Tiberius suffocated with a pillow (*Annals*, 6.50). This seems unlikely, as does Suetonius's suggestion that Caligula poisoned him (*Tiberius*, 73). In any case, wrote Suetonius, 'the people were so glad of his death that at the first news of it some ran about shouting' (*Tiberius*, 75). They could not possibly have known, of course, the horrors that were to come.

Caligula and Claudius, AD 37–54

The early rule of Caligula

The sections of Tacitus's text dealing with Caligula are lost, leaving us to rely on the biography of Suetonius and the text of Cassius Dio, along with the comments of two contemporaries: Philo of Alexandria, a Jewish philosopher living in Egypt (c. 20 BC–AD 50) who took part in a diplomatic mission to Rome in AD 40, and the Stoic philosopher Seneca (c. 4 BC–AD 65). One of the best-known thinkers from antiquity, Seneca was born into an equestrian family in Córdoba and came to Rome with his family as a young boy; he also spent several years in Egypt, where his uncle Gaius Galerius was prefect during the reign of Tiberius. Seneca was a prolific writer, leaving a large corpus of plays and essays, as well as letters that he wrote to his friend Lucilius, a procurator in Sicily. In one of his letters (86), Seneca praised Scipio Africanus for his sense of moderation and admired the simplicity of his lifestyle, which he contemplated while relaxing at Scipio's former country estate. A clash between Seneca and the extravagance of the Julio-Claudians was inevitable.

Caligula had grown up among soldiers, and because of this—as well as because of his father, Germanicus—he was particularly popular among the army. 'He fulfilled the highest hopes of the Roman people,' wrote Suetonius colourfully of his accession in AD 37, 'or I may say of all mankind' (*Caligula*, 13). Caligula had been sequestered to some extent, living with Antonia the Younger, his paternal grandmother, and two client princes—Herod Agrippa I of Judaea and Ptolemy, the son of Juba II and Cleopatra Selene. In AD 31, Caligula was appointed as pontiff and in AD 33, he held the quaestorship in an honorary capacity. In the same year, he married Junia Claudilla, daughter of the former consul Marcus Junius Silanus (AD 15), only to lose her in childbirth. Caligula then suborned Ennia Naevia, the wife of the praetorian prefect, Macro. Despite this, the beginning of Caligula's rule was almost auspicious: the memories of Agrippina, Nero, and Drusus were restored, their ashes reinterred in the Mausoleum of Augustus (Figures 9.9 and 9.10), and their correspondence burned in public to deny any lingering informers the opportunity for gossip and slander.

Caligula gave the title of Augusta to his grandmother, Antonia, and also gave her the prestigious position as the priest of Augustus. Caligula's sisters were accorded all the honours and rights of the Vestal Virgins. Public works were once again underway in Rome, with the Temple of Augustus completed, along with the construction of the Vatican Circus and the aqueducts of the Aqua Anio Novus and the Aqua Claudia (the impressive remains of which can be seen in the Parco degli Acquedotti in southern Rome). The Vatican Circus

Figure 9.9 Bronze sestertius struck during the reign of Caligula to commemorate the return of Agrippina's ashes. Obverse: portrait of Agrippina; reverse: the legend *memoriae Agrippinae*, 'to the memory of Agrippina'. Note the *carpentum*, similar to Figure 9.6.

Figure 9.10 Bronze dupondius minted in AD 40 or 41, commemorating Nero and Drusus Caesar, the brothers of Caligula.

was adorned by an Egyptian obelisk brought to Rome from Alexandria; it now stands in St Peter's Square.

Caligula had been under virtual house arrest on Capri between AD 31 and AD 37, so he was unfamiliar with Rome's leading senators and equestrians. Because or in spite of this, he made overtures to the senate in an attempt to undo the climate of suspicion and paranoia. He ended trials for *maiestas* and opened the imperial accounts to inspection. Cash was given to the people, and banquets held for the senatorial and equestrian orders. Men whose work had suffered under Tiberius, such as Cassius Severus, Titus Labienus, and Aulus Crematius Cordus, had their memories rehabilitated and the surviving copies of their work collected for preservation. Caligula held the consulship for several months each year in a nod to tradition, and in AD 37 he appointed as his consular colleague his uncle, Claudius, who would eventually succeed him.

'So much for Caligula as emperor'

Suetonius wrote, 'So much for Caligula as emperor', adding that 'we must now tell of his career as a monster' (*Caligula*, 22). Less than a year into his rule, Caligula's attitude changed. He suffered a serious illness at around this time, with Philo commenting that afterwards that he began to indulge in 'everything that tends to destroy both body and soul' (*Embassy to Gaius*, 14). On the other hand, Suetonius noted that Caligula had been sickly as a child and painted an unflattering physical portrait of him that suggests a life of ill-health (*Caligula*, 14 & 50). A great deal of effort has been made by modern historians to go beyond the generalised description of 'madness' favoured by ancient writers, in order to understand what afflicted Caligula, and whether the illness that he suffered in AD 37 was the cause of the change in his behaviour. Some of the possibilities that have been suggested include epilepsy, hyperthyroidism, alcoholism, chronic insomnia, childhood emotional trauma, psychopathy, or an attachment disorder. His sequestered teenage years with Herod Agrippa and Ptolemy have also been identified as problematic; from them, some argue, he developed ideas of kingship that were incompatible with the principate. It is also thought that he was simply ill-prepared to assume the almost limitless amount of power that the post-Augustan senate allowed him; indeed, one of the remarkable differences between the succession from Augustus to Tiberius, and then from Tiberius to Caligula, is the almost complete dearth of serious preparation. Whatever his faults, Tiberius had been trained meticulously by Augustus, and Germanicus and Drusus the Younger were likewise 'career men', rather than princes hurried forward, like Caligula, when other prospective successors died. This lack of training, combined with the traumas of his upbringing—the loss of his father, the awful treatment of his mother and siblings, and his confinement on Capri with an unpredictable Tiberius—likely contributed to his increasingly cruel, erratic, and auto-cratic behaviour.

This conduct was quickly exhibited when Tiberius Gemellus, who Tiberius had designated his co-heir, was ordered to commit suicide. The death of the praetorian pre-fect Macro soon followed, and Macro's wife—who had been Caligula's lover—was forced to kill herself. Others fell, including Marcus Junius Silanus (the father of his first wife, Junia Claudilla), who was murdered—the first of many from the ancient patrician house of the Junii Silanii to meet their demise under the Julio-Claudians. It has been pointed out that Macro and Silanus were father figures to Caligula, with Silanus in particular continuing to show him fatherly devotion even after Junia's death; the removal of these father figures may have worsened Caligula's mental state by eliminating any remaining fatherly restraints on his behaviour. Caligula's sisters also felt the brunt of his anger, with Agrippina the Younger and Julia Livilla exiled, although he deified his third sister, Livia Drusilla, who died in AD 38. (She was the first woman in Rome to receive this honour and became known as 'Panthea', 'of all gods'.) Livia Drusilla's husband, Marcus Aemilius Lepidus, a distant relative of the triumvir, was less fortunate; he was accused of adultery and executed. Gaetulicus, one of the few associates of Sejanus who had escaped the earlier purges by building a military fiefdom with his father-in-law in the two Germanies, was also killed after being implicated in a 'conspiracy'. Caligula's hitherto pleasant interactions with the senate were replaced by dictatorial behaviour, the restoration of treason trials, and the scornful treatment of senators, who were forced to run alongside his chariot or, in some cases, beaten in public (Seneca, *On Anger*, 3.18). If the fantastical stories told by our sources are to be believed, Caligula also carried out bizarre actions such as having his horse, Incitatus, given a marble stall and ivory feeding trough and a legion of slaves to attend to his equine needs. During a public spectacle of a fight between men and wild animals, noting that there was an insufficient number of condemned criminals on hand, Caligula had some of the spectators thrown into the arena to be eaten.

Caligula performed as a singer, dancer, and gladiator, amusing the people but horrifying the senate. He also dressed up as Alexander the Great, and ordered a massive gold statue of himself to be erected and a temple to his 'godhead' established. Philo recorded that he dressed up as Castor and Pollux and began to liken himself to Hercules and Bacchus. Via a metaphor of a shepherd and his flock, Philo also suggested that Caligula believed that as the shepherd of the human race, he was 'not merely human' (*Embassy to Gaius*, 76). Caligula cancelled the Actian Games and slandered the memory of Augustus by saying that his own mother, Agrippina the Elder, had been born of incest between Augustus and his daughter, Julia the Elder. Having honoured her earlier, Caligula now scorned his grandmother, Antonia the Younger, leading to her death by suicide or murder in AD 37. He was widely suspected of incest, and Suetonius also accused him of being an inveterate thief of others' wives (*Caligula*, 25). His late rule took on an anti-intellectual flavour, and Caligula railed against Virgil ('a man of no literary talent'), Livy, and Homer (*Caligula*, 34). A profligate spender, he freely ignored the food requirements of the urban population of Rome, and Seneca charged him with bringing the Roman people to the edge of famine (*On the Shortness of Life*, 18.5). Treason charges were rampant, and any charge could be made to stick—even one based on the papers that Caligula had so publicly burned. 'Others owed their ruin to the emperor's illness of the preceding year and to the death of his sister Drusilla,' wrote Cassius Dio, 'since, among other things, anyone who had … even bathed during those days incurred punishment' (59.10).

Caligula's foreign policy was equally erratic. Greatly offending the people of Judaea, he tried to have statues of himself placed in the Temple in Jerusalem, although Herod the Great's grandson, Herod Agrippa I, was able to talk him out of it. Caligula also faced problems with the Jewish population of Alexandria, when the prefect of Egypt, Flaccus, sparred with Herod Agrippa during an unannounced visit to the city. Riots erupted as Flaccus tried to rescind the rights of Alexandrian Jews, including their Alexandrian citizenship. (Alexandria was *in* Egypt but was constitutionally separate: it was thus possible to be an Alexandrian citizen.) These are the two issues that led Philo of Alexandria to pen the *Embassy to Gaius* as well *Against Flaccus*, a tract denouncing the prefect, who was later recalled by Caligula and executed. Mauretania, too, was thrown into chaos. During the reign of Tiberius, a minor revolt had taken place there under the leadership of a Berber, Tacfarinas, who had—like Arminius—once served as an auxiliary in the Roman army. Large numbers of Mauretanians joined the revolt, which began in AD 15 or 16 and simmered for nearly a decade until it was put down in AD 24. Like the Jugurthine War, this new African conflict required repeated efforts by successive proconsuls, and many of Rome's most brilliant military minds came up empty. Ptolemy, the son of Juba II of Mauretania, who had succeeded to the throne in AD 23, supported the Romans during the revolt. But when Caligula subsequently invited him to Rome for an audience in AD 40, he was executed, ostensibly for the grandeur of his robes, bringing the Ptolemaic dynasty to an abrupt end. (A desire for Mauretania's wealth was a more likely cause.) In Commagene, the monarchy was restored in the shape of Antiochus IV, only for the king to be summarily deposed afterwards. In neighbouring Parthia and Armenia, the situation also remained volatile, especially as Caligula seemed disinterested in maintaining Roman influence in Armenia. Shortly before the death of Tiberius, the Parthian monarch, Artabanus II, had made yet another attempt to place his son on the Armenian throne. A faction of Parthian nobles hostile to Artabanus requested Roman intervention, and a Roman expeditionary force under Lucius Vitellius, propraetorian legate of Syria in AD 35 and father of the future emperor Vitellius (see below), provided the grandson of Phraates IV, Tiridates III, who had been living in Rome as a hostage and now assumed the Parthian throne. Tiridates's appointment led to Artabanus's flight into self-imposed exile, but when Tiridates proved unable to hold his gains, Artabanus returned. A subsequent rebellion deposed the hapless Artabanus once more, and following one final restoration, he died, leaving Parthia to the uncertain rule of his son, Vardanes I.

It is naturally difficult to know how much of what Suetonius and others reported of Caligula is true, and how much was invented later on. Did he really 'wallow' in a bath of gold coins, 'for a long time with his whole body?' Did he *really* command his troops to 'gather shells' from the Gallic beaches 'and fill their helmets and the folds of their gowns' with them as he called off an abortive invasion of Britain? (Suetonius, *Caligula*, 42 & 46). On the other hand, the contemporary witnesses to Caligula's behaviour, Seneca and Philo, recorded abundant examples of his cruelty, licentiousness, and criminality. Philo held little back, calling him 'a common pest and murderer' (*Embassy to Gaius*, 89). Caligula also emptied the treasury, exhausting the reserves that Tiberius had carefully built up. Finally, a tribune in the Praetorian Guard, Cassius Chaerea, who had cut his teeth in the legionary mutiny in AD 14, delivered his verdict on Caligula's premiership by murdering him in an underground passage in AD 41. The conspiracy also included Julius Callistus, a prominent freedman who would go on to serve Claudius. Caligula was the first, but by no means the last, to be killed by those sworn to protect the emperor, and in death the senate decided that Caligula should suffer a *damnatio memoriae*.

Caligula was married four times: to Junia Claudilla (AD 37), Livia Orestilla (AD 37/38), Lollia Paulina (AD 38) and, finally, Milonia Caesonia (AD 39/40, see Figure 9.11), who he exhibited to his soldiers in the nude, according to Suetonius (*Caligula*, 25). Junia had

Figure 9.11 Bronze as minted at New Carthage during the reign of Caligula. The reverse shows the portrait of Milonia Caesonia.

died in childbirth, while Livia was banished for 'adultery' with her husband, Piso (not the legate of Syria, but of the anti-Nero Pisonian conspiracy, below), from whom Caligula had shamelessly stolen her. Caesonia and her daughter, Julia, were both murdered along with Caligula in AD 41; with characteristic savagery, Julia was murdered by a soldier who smashed her head against a brick wall. One of the oddest vestiges of Caligula's reign was his two 'pleasure barges', which were raised from Lake Nemi near Rome by Mussolini as part of his reimagining of the Roman empire; their remains were destroyed in 1944 by Nazi forces as they retreated from Italy.

Claudius

Caligula's successor was Claudius, the younger brother of Germanicus. Claudius is well known from Robert Graves' books *I, Claudius* (1934) and *Claudius the God* (1935). Claudius shared Tiberius's love of alcohol and a weakness for lustful encounters—both of which, said Cassius Dio, were used by his enemies to manipulate him. Seneca, Cassius Dio, and Suetonius recorded a range of mental and physical infirmities, including involuntary movements of the head, problems walking, and difficulties with his speech. Suetonius also stated that his own mother, Antonia the Younger, called him 'a monster of a man' (*Claudius*, 3). As with Caligula, there have been numerous modern efforts to identify what disease, if any, afflicted Claudius. While Robert Graves thought that he had suffered from polio as a child, it has also been suggested that he was afflicted by cerebral palsy or even Tourette's syndrome. Nevertheless, despite the problems that plagued Claudius's daily life, he was able to manage the strain of running the empire with greater success than Tiberius, Caligula, or his later successor, Nero, and it was under Claudius's guidance that freedmen emerged as managers of an effective bureaucratic administration close to the emperor. In addition to Narcissus, Antonius Pallas, and Callistus (below), Claudius employed freedmen in various positions, including as the procurator of Ostia, the director of a library in Rome, and the procurator of inheritance tax in Achaea. Claudius also sponsored legislation that protected slaves from abandonment while ill, and further protected them from arbitrary killing. Claudius's intelligence was clear in antiquity: one of his teachers had been Livy, who encouraged him to write, and Claudius became a prodigious scholar, although none of his works has survived. He was the author of an Etruscan history as well as a book of Carthaginian history. A keen gambler, he wrote the *De arte alae*, 'On the art of dice-playing'. Claudius also penned a history of Caesar and the civil wars, but struggled with political interference from his mother, who disliked his refusal to whitewash the past. Claudius was fluent in Greek, proposed reforms to the alphabet, and created an Etruscan dictionary.

Caligula's dreadful rule triggered fleeting senatorial discussions about restoring the Republic, but they quickly ended when the Praetorian Guard accepted a handsome donative from Claudius and gave in to the people's 'demand' that Claudius assume leadership of the principate. Claudius was 'the first of the Caesars', wrote Suetonius, 'who resorted to bribery to secure the fidelity of the troops' (*Claudius*, 10). This was a payment in advance, a purchase of good behaviour, and was commemorated on coinage of the time (Figure 9.12).

Despite this inauspicious beginning, Claudius took a respectful attitude towards the senate: he avoided taking conspicuous honours, and even asked the permission of the consuls

Figure 9.12 Gold aureus minted by Claudius on his accession to the imperial throne. The reverse shows the camp of the Praetorian Guard, with the legend IMPER RECEPT, 'the emperor welcomed'.

to hold events at his home. He also allowed the senate to once again elect magistrates, an honour that had been suspended by Caligula. Claudius gave games, including the Secular Games in AD 47 to celebrate the 800th anniversary of the foundation of Rome. He distributed largesse, and performed the acts expected of the emperor: during his reign, the Aqua Claudia, begun by Caligula, was finished, and Portus, a deep harbour capable of handling large transports, was developed close to Ostia to resolve difficulties involved with the importation of grain. The banishment of his nieces, Agrippina the Younger and Julia Livilla, was lifted, and they returned to Rome along with many others exiled by Caligula. Nevertheless, the circumstances of Claudius's accession created friction, as did those of his upbringing, where he had been sequestered with freedmen, women, and slaves, leading to awkwardness and unfamiliarity when dealing with senators. According to Suetonius, Claudius could also be heavy-handed and irritable, especially in court cases. In these, he meddled with areas that the senate regarded as its own territory. Even when he revived the long-lost office of censor (AD 47/48), his conduct was 'variable' and 'inconsistent' (*Claudius*, 15–16).

Claudius and the provinces

Claudius was born in Lugdunum, and was thus the first man born in the provinces to achieve imperial leadership. He took a provincial view to governance, and it was at his instigation that Roman citizen elites from Gaul were admitted to the senate. Members of the Aedui, long-time friends of Rome, were the first to be welcomed. He faced resistance from the senate, but Claudius could plausibly claim 'outsider' status with his distant Sabine ancestors from the *gens* Claudia, and he used the history of his family and of the other great *gentes* of Rome to persuade sceptical senators that the Romans had always welcomed 'true excellence, let it be found where it will' (Tacitus, *Annals*, 11.24). In both Tacitus's record of his speech and the inscribed speech itself (the source for Tacitus's summary), Claudius shrewdly pointed out that both Sparta and Athens had failed, in part, because they had not bothered to incorporate the leading men of their conquered peoples into their government—a situation that bred resentment. Many in the senate, already suspicious of the growing power of Claudius's freedmen, grasped that fresh Gallic senatorial blood meant a new faction of clients that would support Claudius, but the emperor won the argument. Claudius, as well as Tacitus, clearly grasped the importance of providing representation for the provincial elites and making 'Roman' a broad category to which anyone, in theory, could belong. This was the natural continuation of Rome's early growth, its acceptance of other peoples, cultures, and their gods; in time, it would become one of the empire's great strengths. An analysis of legionary membership suggests that the army, too, was becoming provincialised by recruiting more from outside Italy. While the proportion of Italians in the Augustan army is thought to have been about 65 per cent, this number had dropped to under 50 per cent by the death of Nero (Keppie, *Roman Army*, p. 180). Italians still made up most of the forces stationed in Rome, the urban cohorts and the Praetorian Guard.

Claudius briefly restored the independence of Judaea (below) and returned Antiochus IV of Commagene to his kingdom. Sophene, a small kingdom that lay between Osrhoene and Armenia east of the Euphrates, came under Roman clientship. Claudius also cleaned up the mess created by Caligula in Mauretania, annexing the kingdom as the two provinces of Mauretania Tingitana and Mauretania Caesariensis in AD 42. Thrace became a province four years later, and there were extensive expeditions into Germany in AD 47, during which the final legionary eagle from the defeat of Varus was recovered. In Germany, the talented general Gnaeus Domitius Corbulo achieved so much that Claudius recalled him out of concern for the warrior's soaring popularity with the troops. 'How happy were those who led our armies in olden times,' wrote Cassius Dio, imagining Corbulo—who he thought was fine imperial material—lamenting his misfortune and the meddling of the emperor (61.30). Along the border with Parthia and Armenia, there were still periods of instability. Orodes, the brother of Vardanes I of Parthia, was opportunistically removed from the Armenian throne by Claudius in AD 42, while Vardanes was locked in a civil war with another of his brothers. A newcomer was placed on the Armenian throne, but problems here would continue well into the time of Nero.

The invasion of Britain

The most famous provincial foray of the Claudian period was, however, the conquest and annexation of lowland Britain. Following the successful expeditions of Caesar, British kings had sent embassies and gifts to Augustus, and Italian wine amphorae found their way into the tombs of the British elite in the south and east of the island. Despite these friendly relations, by the mid-first century there were several reasons for imperial authorities to consider an invasion. The first was Claudius's desire to achieve a military triumph that would offset his scholarly character, and win some of the glory and affection that had accrued to his brother Germanicus. The other was the over-ripe political situation in Britain. Verica, the son of Commius, the king of the British branch of the Atrebates who had first assisted Caesar and then defected to Vercingetorix (Chapter 7), had succeeded his two elder brothers as head of the Atrebates. On his coins, Verica called himself *rex*, king, a common Latin term for client kings friendly to the Roman state used well into late antiquity (Figure 9.13).

Figure 9.13 Gold stater of Verica minted at Calleva (Silchester). Obverse: COM F [son of Commius]; reverse: horseman throwing spear with VIR above and REX below.

In AD 43, Verica fled to Claudius. His departure was related to the relentless expansion of the Catuvellauni, whose king, Cunobelin, had first captured Camulodunum (Colchester), swallowing the Trinovantes and making the settlement his capital, and had then taken Calleva (Silchester), the centre of the Atrebates. Cunobelin's neighbours, the Iceni, Dobunni, Regnenses, Durotiges, and others, looked on nervously. While Cunobelin was alive, the Romans seemed content not to intervene, but on his death in AD 40/41, his kingdom was thrown into disorder under the rule of his impetuous and aggressive sons Caratacus and Togodumnus. Verica's pleas for help thus fell on willing ears in Rome (Figure 9.14).

The invasion was entrusted to Aulus Plautius, suffect consul in AD 29 and the former propraetorian legate of Pannonia. His force was made up of II Augusta, IX Hispana, XIV Gemina, and XX Valeria Victrix, and a strong contingent of auxiliaries. II Augusta and XIV Gemina were drawn from Upper Germany, XX Valeria Victrix from Lower Germany, and IX Hispana from Pannonia. (II Augusta was under the command of the future emperor Vespasian, while his son and heir Titus also fought in Britain.) Parts of VIII Augusta were also involved; the epitaph of one Gaius Gavius Silvanus, *primus pilus* within the legion, records that he was 'decorated by the deified Claudius in the Britannic War' (*CIL* 5.7003 = *AH* §49A). Claudius dispatched his capable freedman Narcissus to join the army at Bononia (Boulogne), where he calmed the fears of the nervous legionnaires as Plautius urged them to board the transports for the rough Channel crossing. A Latin inscription discovered at Boulogne in the eighteenth century records another freedman serving as master of one of the invasion vessels (*CIL* 13.3542 = *IRB* §7). The troops landed at Richborough in Kent, and quickly prevailed over Caratacus and Togodumnus. The British forces fell back to the river Medway, where they were defeated once again. At the river Thames, Togodumnus was beaten and killed, and Caratacus fled west. By the autumn of AD 43, Claudius, after a long voyage from Ostia via Massilia and through Gaul, arrived

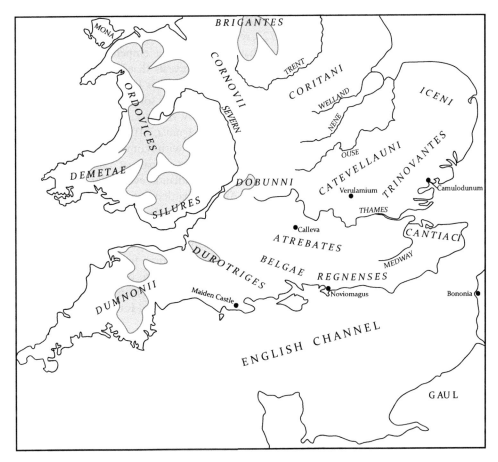

Figure 9.14 The political map of southern Britain on the eve of the Roman invasion in AD 43.

Source: Illustration by the author.

in Britain with a contingent of war elephants, after which the defeated Britons were compelled to accept a Roman garrison at Camulodunum. The victorious troops saluted Claudius as *imperator*, and the emperor returned to Rome in triumph. Far from Britain, at Aphrodisias in south-western Turkey, Claudius's victory was also celebrated on one of the reliefs on the famous Sebasteion, a temple built between c. AD 20 and AD 60, dedicated to the Julio-Claudian line.

As with many ambitious military projects—for example, the 'reconquest' of the Mediterranean empire by Justinian (Chapter 14)—insufficient thought had been given to what a post-invasion Britain should look like. The province thus evolved in fits and starts, and periodically erupted into violent rebellion. Initially, the Romans installed client kings and queens who were persuaded to cooperate, such as Cogidubnus (also known as Cogidumnus or Togidubnus), who took over Verica's old kingdom, and Prasutagas of the Iceni in East Anglia. Cartimandua, the formidable queen of the Brigantes in the north, was well outside the initial territory of the new province, but chose a policy of cooperation.

Cogidubnus had probably spent time in Rome as a hostage and enjoyed an education at the imperial court. A temple inscription (*RIB* §91), dedicated to Neptune and Minerva, which was discovered at Chichester in 1723, recorded Cogidubnus as 'Tiberius Claudius Cogidubnus', a distinctive naming form that honoured the emperor Claudius, who awarded him Roman citizenship. The inscription also reveals that he was granted the title of *rex magnus Britanniae*. This title, known from several other Latin inscriptions and a number of Greek texts (e.g. βασιλεύς μέγας, 'great king'), was sometimes given to client kings who ruled over multiple regions. In his biography of his father-in-law, Agricola, Tacitus referred to Cogidubnus as 'a most faithful ally' (*Agricola*, 14).

Even as numerous chieftains and kings made their peace with Rome, fighting continued in Britain. IX Hispana was sent to the north, and made its base at Lindum (Lincoln, later a colony), while XIV Gemina struck out for the Midlands, eventually establishing a base at Viroconium (Wroxeter). Vespasian and II Augusta battled their way across southern Britain, leaving XX Valeria Victrix in garrison at Camulodunum. Four years after the initial invasion, the Romans controlled much of southern England. The Roman fort at Hod Hill in Dorset, set within a pre-existing Iron Age earthwork (Figure 9.15) is associated with Vespasian's push into the south-west; bolts fired by Roman field artillery (*ballistae*) were found there, and at nearby Maiden Castle further evidence of heavy fighting was discovered, including a *ballista* bolt buried in the spinal column of one of the defenders. Another site associated with the first years of the Roman invasion is the earliest phase of Fishbourne Palace in Chichester.

Figure 9.15 Google Earth Pro image of Hod Hill, near Blandford Forum in Dorset. The Roman fort can be seen in the top left of the Iron Age defensive circuit.

Source: Image © 2020 Google.

By the mid-AD 50s, II Augusta had established a base at Isca (Exeter) and it or its successors and auxiliaries constructed smaller satellite fortifications in the surrounding area, including at Tiverton, Wiveliscombe, Bury Barton, Cullompton, Okehampton, and as far west as Nanstallon in Cornwall: all were built at strategic locations such as river fords and hills, close to hill forts, or sited on lines of communication. The sites in Cornwall appear to have been established specifically to protect (and exploit) nearby silver and tin mining operations. Marching camps associated with the early fighting in the west have also been discovered, primarily through aerial photography and sometimes in close proximity to British hill defences. These first-century sites in the remote corner of western Britain offer a useful example of the determination and professional effort with which the Roman army invaded and occupied a specific region, and set about imposing itself on the local population (Figure 9.16). This pattern of occupation through small forts and static legionary bases was repeated throughout the conquered regions of lowland Britain and would be a feature of the later phases of Roman conquest in the north (Chapter 10).

Military colonies were also founded to settle veterans. The best known colony of this early period was Colonia Victricensis at Camulodunum, established after XX Valeria Victrix was sent west to join the tough fight along the Welsh Marches. Together with various subsidiary routes, a Roman road, the Fosse Way (Figure 9.17), cut diagonally between the lowlands and the uplands across the island, linking Isca with Lindum, and passing through or close to Aquae Sulis (Bath), Corinium (Cirencester), and Lindinis (Ilchester).

Aulus Plautius, the first propraetorian legate of the imperial province of Britannia, was awarded an ovation for his work and was relieved by Publius Ostorius Scapula in AD 47. Scapula faced determined resistance among the Silures and Ordovices in Wales, led by Caratacus and supported by the Druid priests whose religious centre was on the island of Mona (Anglesey). The Druids baffled the Romans and their political role in the resistance to Roman arms was deeply hated; this combination of political and religious ideologies would also be a feature of the Jewish Revolt (see below). Despite Caratacus's anti-Roman bona fides, he signalled his Mediterranean credentials on his contemporary coin issues that featured the head of Hercules and a rather Roman eagle (Figure 9.18).

After leaving to suppress a revolt by the Iceni in East Anglia, who resented a newly imposed effort to restrict arms ownership, Scapula returned to the Welsh Marches. Fighting a coalition that now included disaffected members of the Brigantes, he eventually overcame Caratacus in AD 51/52, and the British king fled to Cartimandua. Realising that she had little to gain by protecting him, Cartimandua handed the fugitive over to Scapula, and Caratacus lived out the rest of his life in Rome after impressing the senate with his rhetoric. Later, he became a Welsh folk hero, appearing in important medieval literary works such as the *Mabinogion* and the Welsh Triads. Claudius celebrated his victory with coin issues (Figure 9.19) and a triumphal arch in Rome. The remains of the dedicatory inscription that once graced the arch, celebrating victory over 11 British kings, are now in the Capitoline Museums (*ILS* 216).

At first, the Roman approach to governing Britannia was based on holding the lowland zone behind the Fosse Way through a mixture of military installations and client kings; intimidation and good diplomacy would secure the friendship of those beyond the frontier to the north and west. In the lowlands, self-government under Roman supervision was extended to the province through the emergence of urban centres, the *civitates*. In contrast to the eastern provinces, many of which had ancient traditions of government

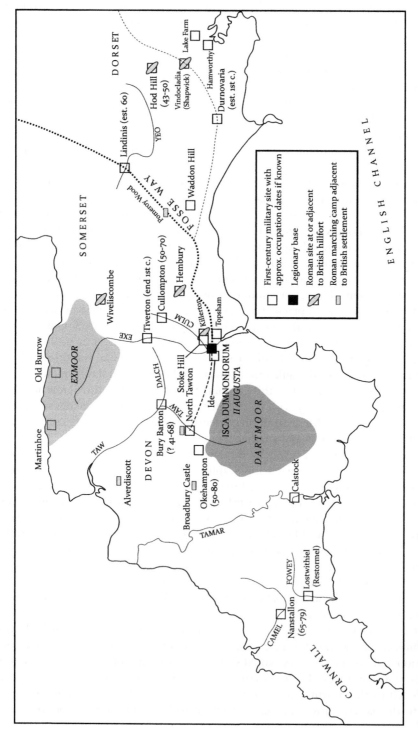

Figure 9.16 First-century Roman military installations in south-west Britain.

Source: Illustration by the author.

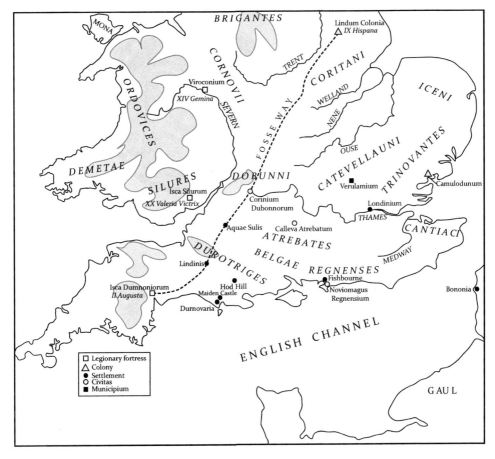

Figure 9.17 The military occupation of Britain towards the end of the Julio-Claudian period.

Source: Illustration by the author.

based on urban centres, there was no pattern of widespread urbanisation in Britain—nor, indeed, had there been in Gaul or Spain. The foundation of self-governing urban communities, organised around Roman architectural features such as the forum, the meeting house, temples, the law courts, the baths, amphitheatres, and the theatre, was a distinctive feature of Roman provincial government in the west, even if it developed at a rather uneven rate in the different provinces. Writers such as Strabo recognised the potential of such settlements to transmit Roman culture and political ideas (e.g. *Geography*, 4.1.5, 3.2.15), and Tacitus recorded that Agricola promoted urban building and renewal as a way to turn people from war to more peaceful pursuits (*Agricola*, 21). In Britain, the *civitates* became nodes of administration—places where taxes could be delivered to the imperial procurator or senatorial quaestor, and suits adjudicated in the courts. Within these communities, local elites served as decurions (municipal magistrates), assisted by a senate-like council. While freedmen could find opportunities in municipal governments or within

Figure 9.18 Silver coin of Caratacus, minted between AD 43 and AD 51.

Figure 9.19 Silver denarius minted in Lugdunum (Lyon) in AD 49/50, celebrating the conquest of Britain. Note the triumphal arch on the reverse with the legend DE BRITANN, 'over the Britons'

the priesthoods of the imperial cult, it was the wealthy elites who had the most to gain by assimilating to Roman cultural, educational, and political expectations, and it was these elites who governed on behalf of Rome. The *civitates* administered large tracts of the countryside, the farming of which supported the urban settlement and paid the necessary taxes. In Britannia, many of these *civitates* developed close to or at sites that had previously been centres of tribal activity, and in this way tribal identities were 'mapped' onto these new urban foundations: Chichester, for instance, was Noviomagus Regnensium, the 'New City' of the Regnenses; Exeter was Isca Dumnoniorum, Isca of the Dumnonii; Silchester was Calleva Atrebatum—Calleva of the Atrebates. The incorporation of tribal identities into the new urban culture of Britannia was another facet of the provincialisation of the empire—the successful incorporation of conquered peoples into government and Roman cultural activities.

These tribal *civitates stipendiariae*, 'tax-paying cities', were initially made up of *peregrini*, non-citizens. As such, they were separate in status from several other important settlements in Britain that emerged with the Roman invasion. The first was the capital of the province, Londinium, founded towards the end of the 40s, and becoming a *municipium* with the Latin rights towards the end of the century. Some of the recently discovered Bloomberg Tablets (Chapter 1) date from London's very first phase of development and reflect a thriving business life in the new capital. Verulamium (St Albans), built on a pre-Roman settlement of the same name, was also a *municipium* with the Latin rights. There were numerous military colonies, such as Lindum Colonia (founded in the 80s) and Camulodunum (founded in AD 49), which became the centre of the imperial cult in Britain. Despite the success of the British conquest, and the steady development of an effective means of administration, resistance to the Romans remained, as the bloody revolt of Boudicca would show (see below).

Conspiracies and plots

Despite his numerous successes, Claudius faced several plots against his life. One originated in 42 with the legate of Dalmatia—a member of the *nobiles*—and had some support from the army, amidst a mistaken belief that the death of Claudius would restore the Republic. At the last moment, however, the troops withdrew their support. For their betrayal of their legate, the two legions involved, VII Paterna and XI, were handsomely rewarded by Claudius for their 'loyalty' and took the name Claudia Pia Fidelis—'Claudius's Loyal and Faithful'. One of the factors that contributed to such plots was Claudius's erratic family life. When he was a young man, Claudius was engaged to Aemilia Lepida, the daughter of Julia the Younger, but when Julia was exiled by Augustus, the betrothal was broken off. Claudius's eventual first marriage was to Plautia Urgulanilla, and the couple had a boy, named Drusus, who died in a bizarre suffocation accident involving a pear and in which the hand of Sejanus was alleged. Claudius later divorced Plautia on suspicion of adultery. His second wife was Aelia Paetina, who was close to Sejanus; this too ended in divorce, although there was a child, Claudia Antonia. It is Claudius's third wife and second cousin, Valeria Messalina, who is most notorious. The two married in AD 38 or 39 and two children were born, named Claudia Octavia (henceforth Octavia) and Germanicus (later changed to Britannicus, following the success in Britain).

Messalina colluded with Narcissus in the climate of fear that followed the failed Dalmatian army plot to rid themselves of their enemies. Messalina accused Julia Livilla (the sister of Caligula) of adultery with Seneca, who was exiled; Julia was executed. Another Julia, the daughter of Drusus the Younger and Livilla, also perished at Messalina's instigation. Informers wrought vengeance on the senatorial and equestrian classes in a collective expurgation reminiscent of the worst excesses of Tiberius. Appius Junius Silanus, another unlucky member of the Junii Silanii, had the misfortune to marry Messalina's mother, Domitia Lepida, and was executed in AD 41. Marcus Vinicius, who had been on Claudius's staff in Britain in AD 43, and to whom Velleius Paterculus dedicated his history, was murdered in AD 46. 'Excellence,' wrote Cassius Dio, 'no longer meant anything else but dying nobly' (60.16).

Messalina was unpopular—particularly with Agrippina the Younger, whose lost memoirs (below) may have fuelled much of Messalina's negative press—and acquired a lurid reputation in antiquity for her sexual prowess. Many of the stories are of doubtful veracity. Pliny the Elder noted, for instance, that she outdid a prostitute hired specifically for the purpose, obtaining 25 orgasms in 24 hours (*Natural History*, 10.83). The satirist Juvenal, a contemporary of Tacitus, accused her of working as a prostitute, after which she would be 'A disgusting creature with filthy face, soiled by the lamp's / Black, taking her brothel-stench back to the emperor's bed' (*Satires*, 6.131–2). (It is from Juvenal, *Satires* 10.80–1, that we have the famous aphorism 'bread and circuses': it appears in a passage lamenting the powerlessness of the population of Rome, who have given themselves over to these two delights.) Messalina's greatest notoriety, however, was earned through her tryst with Gaius Silius, son of the former propraetorian legate of Upper Germany and now consul-designate. Tacitus scorned their affair, lamenting that it brought a premature end to the life of the 'most handsome of Roman youths'. Messalina destroyed Silius's marriage, while Silius, fearing that he would be killed if he refused Messalina, 'consoled himself by closing his eyes to the future and enjoying the present' (*Annals*, 11.12). Not long afterwards, Silius became 'convinced that the antidote to impending danger was actual danger' (*Annals*, 11.26), and placed all of his cards on the table. He was keen to adopt Britannicus and fancied that he could safely occupy the apex of Roman politics as Messalina's consort. The two 'married' in AD 48, while Claudius was in Ostia checking on the grain supply. 'If you don't choose to obey,' wrote Juvenal of Silius's dilemma, 'you'll be dead before evening / If you commit the sin, there'll be the briefest delay before / What's known to Rome, and the mob, reaches Caesar's ear' (*Satires*, 10.338–40).

Even with the 'marriage' between Messalina and Silius, Claudius was unwilling or unable to see the political threat represented by Silius. One group that *did* see what was happening—and whose members saw opportunities of their own—was the coterie of freedmen on whom Claudius depended to run the government—Narcissus, now his chief of staff; Antonius Pallas, the freedman of Antonia the Younger, who had become a financial official in the palace; and Callistus, who had taken part in the conspiracy against Caligula and who, in the office of *a libellis*, administered the petitions sent to Claudius. (Such petitions were an important part of the emperor's day-to-day administration, and could be requests from clients for assistance or privileges, letters from city councils seeking the remittance of taxes, or pleas for help.) It was Narcissus who, in the end, arranged for two of Claudius's favourite concubines to tell all to Claudius. Narcissus himself elected to stay at arm's length and claim ignorance. Claudius finally realised the political threat that Messalina and Silius posed, and moved on them while they celebrated the year's vintage with unbridled Bacchanalian excess; Narcissus temporarily seized control of the Praetorian Guard, whose prefect, Geta, was of doubtful loyalty. Eventually brought before the troops, Messalina and Silius were condemned. After a wine-drenched supper, Claudius appeared to change his mind, but Narcissus hastened the executions. A bloody purge followed that also claimed the life of Mnester, a celebrated pantomime actor who had been a favourite of Caligula.

Agrippina Augusta

Claudius's final marriage, arranged at the instigation of Antonius Pallas, was to his niece, Agrippina the Younger—daughter of Germanicus and Agrippina the Elder. When she was a teenager, Agrippina had married Gnaeus Domitius Ahenobarbus, the son of Antonia the

Elder, the oldest of the two daughters of Antony and Octavia; he was also the grandson of the famous admiral of the same name (Chapter 7). Gnaeus Domitius had held the consulship for the full year in AD 32. In 37, he and Agrippina welcomed their son, Lucius Domitius Ahenobarbus, better known to history as the future emperor Nero. On the accession of Claudius, when Agrippina was recalled from exile, Lucius, whose inheritance from his father (d. AD 41) had been stolen by Caligula, found himself a newly enriched young man at the heart of Roman high society. He was scorned by Messalina, but managed to survive attempts to kill him. Agrippina had meanwhile remarried to a relative of Sallust, who became Lucius's devoted stepfather, but she poisoned him in AD 47. For the following two years, she diligently eliminated her rivals, including Lollia Paulina, the ex-wife of Caligula, who she drove to exile and then suicide, and even her own cousin, Lucius Junius Silanus Torquatus, who had become engaged to Claudius's daughter, Octavia. Silanus dramatically killed himself on the day that Agrippina married Claudius in AD 49. So that she may appear less cruel, suggested Tacitus, Agrippina persuaded Claudius to end Seneca's exile. She then became so central to developments in the palace that the disappearance of her memoirs, the existence of which is known only from Tacitus (*Annals*, 4.53) and Pliny the Elder (*Natural History*, 7.46), is an incalculable loss for historians. Composed between AD 54 and 59, it is sometimes thought, as noted earlier, that they contained the salacious gossip and stuff of character assassination that proved such a boon to writers such as Juvenal.

As empress, Agrippina became the most powerful woman in the empire. She ruthlessly promoted her son and continued to remove threats and rivals, including Domitia Lepida, the mother of Messalina. She used Antonius Pallas (Callistus was dead and she viewed Narcissus with disdain) with great efficiency, and carefully stage-managed her public appearances and those of her son. She was awarded the title of Augusta in AD 50 (a title that was never given to Messalina) and soon afterwards Oppidum Ubiorum, her birthplace, was refounded as Colonia Claudia Ara Agrippinensium in her honour. She was granted the right to ride in a *carpentum* (see Figure 9.6 above); and she appeared on coins with Claudius (Figure 9.20), and later with Nero, something that Livia had never achieved during the reign of Augustus. Agrippina possessed two lictors, one more than had been granted to Livia, and she listened to senatorial debates, albeit from behind a screen.

Figure 9.20 Gold aureus minted at Lugdunum in AD 51. Obverse: laureate head of Claudius; reverse: bust of Agrippina the Younger, with legend AGRIPPINΛE AVGVSTΛE.

Figure 9.21 Silver denarius minted in AD 51. Obverse: Bare headed bust of Nero; reverse: shield and spear with legend EQVESTER ORDO PRINCIPI IVVENT.

Agrippina also engineered a change in the leadership of the Praetorian Guard, removing Geta and his colleague and installing Sextus Afranius Burrus, a former procurator who had served Livia. Along with the rehabilitated Seneca, Agrippina intended that Burrus would play a key role as an adviser to her son, Lucius. Like Seneca, Burrus was a provincial equestrian, and his elevation to the prefecture was a further reflection of the growing presence of wealthy provincials in government.

Claudius subsequently adopted Lucius, who took the name Nero Claudius Caesar Drusus Germanicus (henceforth, Nero). Britannicus's tutor was murdered on a pretext, and Britannicus himself was pushed to the side. Agrippina 'did him all the harm she could' and put out that he was 'insane and an epileptic' (Cassius Dio, 61.32–33). Nero was hailed as *princeps iuventutis* by the equestrians, and coins were minted to celebrate the event (Figure 9.21). Octavia married Nero in the summer of AD 53, causing her to be adopted by another family in order to avoid a brother–sister union—something that not even the Julio-Claudians could contemplate.

By AD 54, Claudius had come to regret his marriage to Agrippina and the virtual disappearance of his son, Britannicus, whom Narcissus was trying desperately to safeguard from Agrippina. In the same year, Claudius died at the age of 64. Cassius Dio wrote that Agrippina fed Claudius a suspicious dish of mushrooms and was the chief architect of his demise. She covered up her crime by plying her husband with a vast quantity of wine, so that his retirement from dinner, paralysed by poison, could be explained by his drunkenness. Narcissus had been sent to Campania to get him out of the way, and he was now tracked down and was either murdered or committed suicide 'beside the tomb of Messalina', a satisfying (if unlikely) example of historical payback that delighted Cassius Dio (61.34). Suetonius reported a similar story of the emperor's death, but added the gruesome detail that a second dose of the poison was administered to Claudius rectally by a syringe (*Claudius*, 44). None of these stories should be taken too seriously.

Given the bloody and manipulative character of the later part of her career, it would be tempting to understand Agrippina the Younger as yet another conniving, cruel member of the Julio-Claudian family, but this would be unfair. Agrippina had received horrendous treatment from Caligula, and in her banishment she must have expected the executioner daily. She had also seen palace conspiracy and intrigue consume her father, her mother, and all five of her siblings. Yet she was also heir to the model of strong female power represented by both her mother and by Livia. She enjoyed substantial popularity, a by-product of the fame of her father Germanicus, and when her second husband died in AD 47, she combined that fame with the wealth of his estate. When she returned from exile and married Claudius, she did so in the full knowledge of what was required to thrive in a brutal system. It was necessary to eradicate rivals, to attach herself to competent, loyal, and politically bland people such as Antonius Pallas and Burrus, and to promote Nero's candidacy ruthlessly, to acquire his protection and favour as a male heir to Claudius. In this extremely risky game, Agrippina the Younger emerged victorious. She had, however, made one fatal error: she underestimated her own son.

Descent into anarchy: the 'sun king' Nero, AD 54–68

In death, Claudius was deified. 'Agrippina and Nero pretended to grieve for the man whom they had killed,' wrote Cassius Dio, continuing his tirade against the new emperor and his mother, 'and elevated to heaven him whom they had carried out on a litter.' Nero 'declared mushrooms to be the food of the gods', Dio continued, since they had sent Claudius to the deified afterlife (61.35). Seneca, still nursing a grudge for his long exile, lampooned Claudius in his *Apocolocyntosis*, usually translated as 'Gourdification' or 'Pumpkinification'. The title was a play on apotheosis, the ritualistic process by which emperors were deified: the body or a wax effigy of the body was burned on a pyre, an eagle sent off into the sky, and the ashes placed in the tomb. In the *Apocolocyntosis,* Claudius pleaded with a senate of the Olympian gods for his deification, only to be undone by Augustus. 'Is it for this,' he said, indicating Claudius with contempt, 'that I have made peace by land and sea?' (11). After providing a lengthy list of Claudius' many misdeeds, Augustus persuaded the senate to banish Claudius to Hades, where his gambling vice was to be punished by condemning him in a Sysiphean manner 'to rattle dice forever in a box with no bottom' (19). Things went from bad to worse: 'all of a sudden,' Seneca wrote with evident glee, 'who should turn up but Caligula!' (19). In the text, praise is lavished on Nero, Seneca's ward; the new emperor is radiant and glittering, an eternal Apollo for the new age.

The early years of Nero

Nero became emperor at the age of 17 and, following the precedent of Claudius, paid a large donative to the Praetorian Guard. Burrus and Seneca (who was suffect consul in AD 55, and wrote the influential tract *On Clemency* in the same year) kept a watchful eye over their charge and also attempted to rein in Agrippina, who was continuing to purge her rivals. Marcus Junius Silanus (brother of her earlier victim Lucius Junius Silanus Torquatus), consul in AD 46, ex-governor of Asia, and a distant relative of Augustus, was the first of her casualties under the new order. Despite Agrippina's murderous ways, things began well enough for Nero. With Seneca penning his speeches, Nero grandly declared that he would 'rule according to the principles of Augustus' and behave in a moderate and balanced fashion (Suetonius, *Nero*, 10). The historian Aurelius Victor (c. AD 320–90) looked favourably on the first years of Nero's rule and remarked that Trajan (r. AD 98–117), who was widely admired by later historians, thought Nero to be 'outstanding' during this early time (*On the Caesars*, 5). Others close to Nero exercised influences ranging from the positive to the craven. Petronius, a man who 'idled into fame', was a competent governor of Bithynia and suffect consul. He later became Nero's 'Arbiter of Elegance', a sort of sartorial adviser, and one of Nero's closest confidants (Tacitus, *Annals*, 16.18). Petronius is thought to be the author of the *Satyrica*, with its famous section, the 'dinner of Trimalchio', providing a sensational account of excessive banqueting. (Later, the character of Trimalchio proved an important influence for F. Scott Fitzgerald's *The Great Gatsby*.)

It did not take long for things to go wrong, although with the sources it is often hard to separate fact from venom. Echoing the anti-Neronian stance of the later Flavian emperors Vespasian and Titus, Pliny the Elder—whose patron was Titus—bluntly called Nero 'the enemy of the human race' (7.6). Beneath the party line, however, there were numerous problems. Antonius Pallas was fired from imperial service in AD 55, and later poisoned. Britannicus was murdered in the same year at a dinner party, and Agrippina's influence rapidly waned. Nero's detractors claimed that he was disinterested in government and much more taken by shows and acting, pursuits that were deemed to be beneath the dignity of the principate but that reflected his commitment to philhellenism, a product of his upbringing and education that imbued him with the history and culture of the Hellenistic east. This eastern background also lay behind Nero's cultivation of Apollo and his links to solar worship, deepening an association that stretched back to Caesar and Augustus and that, in time, would inform the monotheism of the emperor Constantine (Chapter 12). Apollo had also appeared in Virgil's fourth *Eclogue*, where he presided over a gilded age, and Nero's Apollonian persona, similarly ushering in an era of peace and prosperity, was expressed on imperial coinage through a radiate crown that resembled the rays of the sun. Nero was a keen poet, although little has survived; Seneca (*Natural Questions*, 1.5) recorded a Catullus-esque snippet: 'The neck of Venus' dove glitters as the bird tosses its head.' In AD 60, Nero held the unabashedly Greek Neronia, the first instalment of a planned quinquennial games featuring music, riding, and gymnastics. He appeared on stage in Naples, and hired a mob of equestrians to cheer for him when he sang. Such activities delighted the people of Rome, but horrified conservative elements among the senatorial and equestrian classes, which viewed the concept of *otium*, 'leisure'—an idea that combined sophisticated Hellenistic indulgence with artistic pursuits—as something that should remain private. Nero earned senatorial opprobrium by moving *otium* into the public sphere, but his love of *otium* was influential: Nero's late portraits, with their luxurious facial hair, would go on to inspire another famous philhellene, the emperor Hadrian. Tied to this pursuit of *otium* was Nero's desire for the favour of the people, which he cultivated through his activities. Indeed, he was sensitive to the opinions of others and could be jealous of their success. In one fit of irritation, for example, he banned the poet Lucan from public performances. Lucan was the author of the *Pharsalia*, an epic poem about the civil war between Caesar and Pompey, and had won a prize at the first Neronia.

The murder of Agrippina

In AD 59, in what was perhaps the most elaborate (and unlikely) assassination plot of antiquity, Nero tried to murder his mother with a boat that had a specially weighted roof. The device was the suggestion of Nero's freedman and former tutor, Anicetus, who had ascended to command the fleet at Misenum. While cruising in the bay of Baiae on her way to meet Nero for a 'reconciliation', the boat's roof was intentionally collapsed by the crew, crushing one of Agrippina's attendants. Agrippina herself survived and was able to escape over the side. With her was her maidservant Acerronia, who called out for help; the assassins, mistaking her for Agrippina in the darkness, battered her to death as she floundered in the water. Agrippina was taken to shore by fishermen, but when Nero found out that she had survived, he summoned Seneca and Burrus, hoping that the Praetorian Guard would quietly murder her. Burrus refused; the soldiers would never harm a daughter of Germanicus, and so it was left to Anicetus to finish the job. Cassius Dio, who is extremely hostile to Nero, wrote that Agrippina instructed Anicetus to stab her womb, since it had brought forth Nero into the world (62.13).

Privately, Nero was wracked with guilt, and complained of being haunted by his mother; he hired priests to bring her 'shade' back from the underworld so he could apologise (Suetonius, *Nero*, 34). In public, however, he blamed her for an insurrection against the imperial throne and charged her with all manner of offences. Without Agrippina's restraining influence, Nero spent excessively until the treasury was empty, devaluing the silver denarius and gold aureus coinage and raising taxes to compensate, causing economic misery for thousands. He then moved against others who he viewed as a threat. After several affairs, most prominently with Poppaea Sabina, a wealthy and ambitious woman from Pompeii who quickly became pregnant, Nero divorced Octavia after trying and failing to strangle her. He persuaded Anicetus to confess to 'adultery' with Octavia—the alternative for Anicetus if he refused was death—and gave him a wealthy retirement in Sardinia in compensation. Poppaea's husband, the future emperor Otho, was bought off with the position of propraetorian legate of Lusitania. Octavia was exiled to Pandateria, where she was later steamed to death in a hot bath-house, and her head was severed and sent to Rome so Poppaea could view it. Octavia was young and popular, and her death was met with profound sadness and shock; the melancholy of the final months of her life was captured in the play *Octavia,* once attributed to the pen of Seneca, who was in fact dead by the time it was composed. In the meantime, said Suetonius, Nero slept with one of the Vestal Virgins, suborned boys and women, and even had a boy castrated to play the part of his 'wife' (*Nero*, 28). Like the wildest stories about Caligula, these are probably exaggerations.

Nero's cruelty was nevertheless excessive, even by the standards set by his predecessors. He was widely believed to have killed Poppaea by kicking her in the stomach while she was pregnant, causing a fatal miscarriage. His third wife was Statilia Messalina (a relative of Ovid's patron Messalla Corvinus), whose husband Nero ordered to commit suicide so that she would be free to marry. Nero ordered Claudius's daughter Claudia Antonia to marry him in AD 66, but she refused. Her first husband, descended from Pompey, had been murdered by Claudius; her second, a distant relative of Sulla, by Nero. The emperor arranged Claudia's execution on the grounds that she was fomenting revolt. Nero compounded this crime by personally raping one of his enemies, Aulus Plautius (a possible relative of the first legate of Britannia), suspecting him of adultery with his mother Agrippina.

The remaining moderating influences on Nero were now removed. Burrus was poisoned with a counterfeit throat balm in AD 62 and replaced at the head of the Praetorian Guard with Ofonius Tigellinus, a cruel sycophant who had once been banished from Rome and later raised horses for the races. Tigellinus undermined his co-prefect and used corrupt factions in the senate to influence Nero. With Burrus gone, Nero turned on Seneca, who sought to escape by petitioning his erstwhile charge for an early retirement. Nero refused, and Seneca was then implicated in the failed Pisonian conspiracy, a broad and complex plot that reflected the widespread anger at Nero's excesses. Piso, from the ancient plebeian *gens* Calpurnia and grandson of the man who antagonised Germanicus, planned to have himself elevated by the Praetorian Guard—although there also appears to have been a substantial desire among the plotters to be rid of the principate altogether. Dozens of Romans fell victim to Nero's rage when the plot was discovered by his freedman Eupaphroditus. Among those ordered to commit suicide were Seneca and Lucan; Piso, who was also forced to kill himself, became the subject of an anonymous panegyric. 'If my prayers have reached your heart,' reads part of the final verse, 'then you, Piso, shall one day be chanted in polished verse, to be enshrined in memory as my Maecenas' (*In Praise of Piso*, l. 246–9). Piso was quickly forgotten, however, as the killings continued. Nero brought to trial Thrasea Paetus, a Stoic philosopher and senator who openly admired Cato the Younger and who made no secret of the fact that he was appalled by Nero's arbitrary rule. Paetus was condemned, and a number of his friends were exiled. Not even Petronius was spared. Isolated and attacked by Nero and Tigellinus, he took his own life in AD 65. The climate of mistrust and suspicion also claimed the life of Decimus Junius Silanus Torquatus—yet another member of the Junii Silanii.

In AD 64, Rome had been engulfed by a vast blaze that damaged or destroyed large areas of the city. Despite a quick humanitarian response from Nero that gave succor to the many thousands of homeless in Rome and a well-thought restoration and fireproofing program, rumours persisted that Nero, Tigellinus, or one of his acolytes had started the fire, because a large chunk of prime real estate between the Palatine and the Esquiline was appropriated in the aftermath for Nero's lavish *Domus Aurea*, 'Golden House'. This monument to extravagant *otium* was strongly influenced by Hellenistic models and included parks with wild animals, a vast pond to mimic the ocean, and, according to Suetonius's ornate description, 'pipes for sprinkling guests with perfume' (*Nero*, 31). Part of the project included a massive gold-leafed nude statue of Nero in the guise of Apollo, which may have been as high as 35 metres (115 feet). (The remains of the *Domus Aurea* were first discovered during the Renaissance, and Raphael and Michelangelo marvelled at the artwork concealed within; in 2018/19, workers uncovered yet another part of the palace, decorated with a sphinx, centaurs, and panthers.) The structure was so hated that in his later redevelopment of Rome, Vespasian built the Flavian Amphitheatre—Rome's famous Colosseum—directly over it.

Nero openly blamed Christians for the fire. The growing Christian community in Rome was poorly understood; Suetonius called them 'a class of men given to a new and mischievous superstition' (*Nero*, 16). The Christian historian Eusebius of Caesarea (AD 265–339) wrote that Pontius Pilate had sent reports to Tiberius about the purported resurrection of Jesus and his transformation into a god, which a bemused senate rejected since it alone possessed the prerogative of deification (*Ecclesiastical History*, 2.2). Tiberius was also approached by the king of Edessa, Abgar V, who had reportedly engaged in correspondence with Jesus; the legend of Abgar and Jesus would later form the first part of the fifth-century Syriac *Teaching of Addai*, an important, if heavily embellished, account of the conversion of Edessa to Christianity and the basis of Edessa's claim to divine protection. A much-discussed passage from Acts (18.2) reported that Claudius exiled the 'Jewish' community from Rome, an event that Suetonius said had come about because of 'Chrestus'

(*Claudius*, 25). Cassius Dio, however, clearly stated that Claudius did not banish the Jews (60.6), and Claudius also passed legislation supporting Alexandrian Jews in the aftermath of riots in Alexandria, providing a contradiction that has led to suggestions that the 'Jews' exiled by Claudius were in fact Christians. The early picture is thus rather muddled. To the extent that they could even tell the difference between Christians and Jews at this point in time, many Romans would likely have found them to be an odd people—monotheists who rejected the imperial cult and revered the Jewish Old Testament. In such a climate, persecution followed, and in lurid testimony Tacitus wrote that Nero burned Christians at night to illuminate the grounds of the *Domus Aurea*. Such savage treatment earned sympathy from the people of Rome, however, many of them homeless and ruined by the fire of AD 64 (*Annals*, 15.44). One of the Christians to perish at Nero's hands during this purge was believed to be Paul, who Eusebius said was beheaded in Rome (*Ecclesiastical History*, 2.25); Peter, likewise, was believed to have met his death at the same time (*Apocryphal Acts of Peter = Vercelli Acts*, 37).

From Britain to the Sudan

Nero's foreign policy has traditionally been viewed as unsuccessful, but this is largely a result of the negative views provide by writers such as Tacitus and Cassius Dio. In fact, Nero achieved success in Armenia and the Caucasus through diplomacy and force of arms, suppressed a violent revolt in Britain, and sent soldiers to discover the sources of the Nile.

In Armenia, another dispute had flared up on Nero's accession as the Parthian king Vologases I (r. AD 51–78) sought to place his own brother Tiridates on the Armenian throne. Corbulo was dispatched to the east to address this problem, but once there he found the legions ill-disciplined. Through tough training and sharing their privations, he managed to restore their confidence (Tacitus, *Annals*, 13.35). Vologases was soon distracted by the revolt of his own son and a rebellion in Hyrcania, south-east of the Caspian Sea; this ceded the advantage to Corbulo, whose forces captured Armenia and installed Tigranes VI, a relative of Herod the Great and a member of the royal family of Cappadocia who had spent time in Rome. Tigranes quickly precipitated a new conflict with Parthia, however, and disaster followed at Rhandeia in AD 62 as an over-extended Roman army of IV Scythica and XII Fulminata under Caesennius Paetus (consul in AD 61) was beaten and forced to accept terms. Later, Corbulo was given a proconsular command similar to that wielded by Pompey (Chapter 6) and, through careful diplomacy, Corbulo and Tiridates met at Rhandeia and a peace deal was arranged. The Romans agreed to allow Tiridates the Armenian throne, as long as Vologases agreed that Tiridates be crowned in Rome by Nero. Tiridates, who was much admired by Cassius Dio and made a strong impression on his nine-month journey, visited Rome in AD 66 and was crowned Tiridates I of Armenia. The glittering ceremony took place on a 'Golden Day', a festival infused with light. The city celebrated and Nero closed the doors of the Temple of Janus, indicating that the world was at peace; a bedazzled Tiridates renamed his capital Artaxata 'Neronia'. While Tacitus may not have wanted to give Nero the credit, the crisis over the Armenian throne had been settled and peace with Parthia largely preserved. It has been suggested in consequence that what Gaul was to Caesar and Britain was to Claudius, so Armenia was Nero's most significant foreign policy triumph. Nero, like Claudius, was celebrated on the Sebasteion at Aphrodisias. In one relief, he stands, nude, the personification of a victorious Hellenised king, taking an Armenian captive; in another, the goddess of peace, styled after Agrippina the Younger, awards Nero the imperial crown.

Rome's concurrent diplomatic efforts in the areas around the Black Sea can be placed in the context of this struggle for influence in Armenia. In AD 61, the propraetorian legate of Moesia, Plautius Aelianus, had campaigned both in Moesia and also into the Crimea as far as Chersonesus (Sevastopol) in aid of Rome's ally, the kingdom of Bosporus. Roman troops had been stationed at Panticapaeum in the eastern Crimea since the time of Claudius, and it is possible that plans were underway to annex Bosporus to Moesia, where Aelianus was hard at work cowing Rome's enemies, as his funeral inscription indicates (*CIL* 14.3608). Later, in AD 64, Nero persuaded king Polemo II of Pontus to abdicate, and the eastern districts of Pontus (Pontus Polemonaicus) that were not part of the senatorial province of Bithynia and Pontus were annexed, along with the neighbouring kingdom of Colchis. Beyond Colchis lay the client kingdom of Iberia, a Roman ally that contributed troops for Corbulo's wars. These developments in the Caucasus gave Rome better management of key supply routes for its eastern legions, as well as control of territory adjacent to Armenia. Polemo's Black Sea fleet, under Roman command, was now renamed the *classis Pontica*; soldiers from I Italica, V Macedonica, and XI Claudia would leave military graffiti and inscriptions in the Crimea reflecting Rome's commitment to the region. Nero also seems to have nurtured plans for an Alexander-esque trip beyond Iberia to the Caspian Gates. This pass, the modern Darial Gorge, was also known in antiquity as the Gate of Alexander; it gave access into modern North Ossetia and Ingushetia (Figure 9.22). Behind the grandeur of this project lay a desire to safeguard this difficult region from the Sarmatian Alans, a warlike people who lived on the northern side of the Caucasus Mountains and who frequently raided into Parthia, Armenia, and the Caucasian kingdoms being absorbed by Rome. Nero even imagined a special legion for the expedition, I Italica, made up of all-Italian recruits over 6 feet (1.8 metres) tall, which he called his 'phalanx of Alexander'. Nero died, however, before any of this could be fully realised.

In Britain, there was a revolt of the Iceni and their allies in AD 61, led by the famous British queen Boudicca, whose nineteenth-century bronze statue showing her fighting from a chariot alongside her daughters graces Westminster Bridge in London. On his accession, Nero had decided that a fresh effort should be made to subdue Wales, and after his choice for legate died in office in AD 57/58, the campaign was entrusted to Suetonius Paulinus, who had been consul (perhaps in AD 43) and won fame campaigning for Claudius in Mauretania. Paulinus and his troops had reached the Druidic centre of Mona when news arrived that Prasutagas of the Iceni had died. Prasutagas had no male heir, and had left his kingdom jointly to his daughters and to Nero. The Romans had already showed their intention of allowing client kingships to 'die out', with their people and territory absorbed directly into the province. Through his split legacy, Prasutagas was attempting to find a way for his people's semi-independence to be continued, but a procurator dispatched by Nero quickly arrived to take control of the affairs and wealth of the Iceni. Anxiety amongst the Iceni turned to anger in the face of the arrogance and cruelty of the Romans. After protesting, Boudicca, the widow of Prasutagas, was whipped and her daughters raped.

There were other grievances that helped to push the Iceni and their allies to revolt. Despite the involvement of British elites in the imperial cult at Camulodunum, the Roman

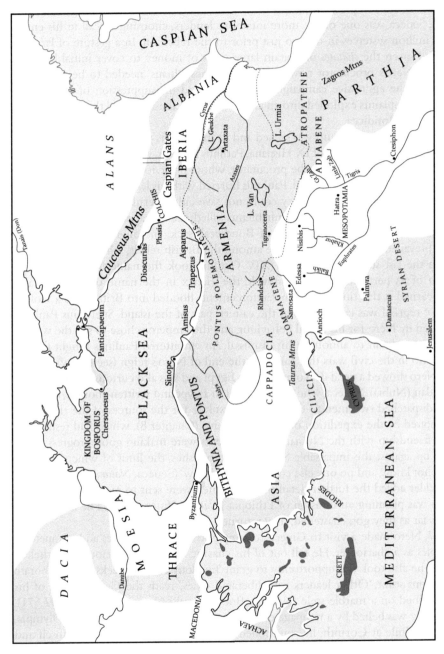

Figure 9.22 The Black Sea, Armenia, and Parthia during the reign of Nero. The dotted line indicates the approximate boundary of the kingdom of Armenia.

Source: Illustration by the author.

colonists had long irritated the Trinovantes, in whose historical territory the colony lay, and mercenary rates of interest charged by money lenders for provincial construction projects such as the Temple of Claudius only made matters worse. According to Cassius Dio (62.2), Seneca was one of the more infamous lenders, choosing to call in his entire loan of 40 million sesterces in one go just prior to the rebellion. In a gesture of largesse, Claudius had given the *civitates* of Britain large sums of money to cover initial building expenses, but Nero's procurator now decided that these 'loans' needed to be paid back. Together with the aggressive campaigns of Paulinus and his suppression of the Druids, these various complaints exploded into an armed revolt by the Iceni and their allies, under the leadership of Boudicca.

The colony at Camulodunum was sacked and its inhabitants put to the sword. Rushing to provide assistance, the legate of IX Hispana, Petillius Cerialis, was ambushed on the road and forced to retreat. Meanwhile, the procurator, whose behaviour had caused such great offence among the Iceni, fled to Gaul. Paulinus hurried with his legions XX Valeria Victrix and XIV Gemina from Wales, but they could not save either Verulamium or Londinium, both of which were pillaged and their inhabitants killed; the archaeological record at both sites preserves evidence of the ferocity of Boudicca's sack. In tough fighting, Paulinus eventually prevailed, with huge loss of life among the British rebels, while Boudicca herself died in the last stand of the Iceni. (XIV Gemina took the name Martia Victrix in recognition of its performance in the revolt; the Victrix in the name of XX may also have been earned at this time.) Roman reinforcements flooded into Britain and a violent campaign of reprisal was carried out in the eastern part of the island. Suetonius Paulinus was later fired by Nero for his brutal behaviour, and the emperor chose to salt the wound by sending a freedman to announce his dismissal. An embittered Paulinus fought for the emperor Otho in the civil wars that followed the end of Nero's reign (see below).

Finally, Nero showed a great deal of interest in Egypt and was also curious about Ethiopia and the Sudan (Nubia). Seneca, who had travelled in Egypt and written about it, recorded that Nero dispatched two men to the Sudan to explore for the sources of the river Nile, perhaps inspired by the expedition of Gaius Petronius (Chapter 8), which had resulted in a treaty of friendship with the Nubians. Nero's agents were making good progress when they came up against the impassable Sudd—'huge marshes, the limit of which even the natives did not know, and no one else could hope to know' (Seneca, *Natural Questions*, 6.8). Pliny the Elder added the further detail that these men were sent to reconnoitre the area since Nero was planning an invasion of Ethiopia (*Natural History*, 6.35). The Sudd, however, was as far as they got; chastened, they returned to Egypt.

In AD 67, Nero made a visit to Greece to sample its cultural treasures and compete in the Olympics as a charioteer. He fell out of his chariot, but was 'victorious' nonetheless. At Corinth, he also took the opportunity to grant 'freedom' to the Greeks in an elaborate public relations stunt. 'Other leaders have liberated cities,' reads the Greek record of his speech, inscribed on a marble stele found in Boeotia, 'only Nero a province' (*AH* §71). (His generosity was belied by a rampage of statue-stealing carried out at Athens, Olympia, and Delphi.) While at Corinth, he summoned Corbulo to meet with both himself and Tigellinus. Corbulo's success had made him a political liability, and Nero ordered him and two other top legates to commit suicide. Soon afterwards, a provincial insurrection began in Gaul under the leadership of the propraetorian legate of Gallia Lugdunensis, Gaius Julius Vindex, who was from an ancient Aquitanian family and was one of the beneficiaries of

Claudius's policy of opening senatorial membership to the Gallic elite. He found support from a fellow legate, Servius Sulpicius Galba, in nearby Hispania Tarraconensis. Galba appeared to be the next name on Nero's suicide list and Vindex proclaimed him emperor. Vindex was then defeated by the legate of Upper Germany, Verginius Rufus, who was subsequently proclaimed emperor by his troops; he declined, deferring to the senate instead. Recovering its nerve after years of near servitude, the senate then declared for Galba and announced that Nero was a public enemy. Tigellinus made himself scarce as the people turned against Nero in an outpouring of hatred that included a harsh critique of his artistic talent. On June 9, AD 68, the Julio-Claudian experiment in imperial government reached its bloody denouement when Nero killed himself with the help of his freedman Epaphroditus. He was nearly 32 and, like Caligula, suffered a *damnatio memoriae*, but this did not stop persistent rumours that he was still alive and in hiding in Parthia. Those who believed the legends about Nero's death found occasional succour in a series of counterfeit Nero-pretenders that emerged from time to time in the east. 'Even now everyone desires him to be alive,' wrote Dio Chrysostom (AD 40–115), referring to sightings of Nero during the reign of Domitian, 'and the majority of people think he really is, even though in some way he died not once but often, along with those who have been convinced that he is still alive' (*On Beauty*, 10). It would be for the Jews, and then the Christians, to transform this legend into something truly memorable. In the meantime, Nero was in fact dead. He had no heir, and with a ferocious revolt getting underway in Judaea and a new European civil war, the Roman world was plunged into chaos.

Romans, Jews, and civil war, AD 68–74

The Jewish Revolt (AD 66–74) was an immensely important event in Jewish history. It resulted in the destruction of the Second Temple in Jerusalem, the imposition of permanent, direct Roman rule with a legionary garrison, and a new diaspora. It was caused by the intersection of a number of aggravating factors: the system of clientship used in Judaea; mistrust, confusion, and ideological differences between Romans and Jews, and between gentiles and Jews; divisions in Jewish society; and the insulting behaviour of Roman officials. The revolt manifested as a civil war between different Jewish factions, combined with a war against the Romans, who were also involved in their own devastating civil conflict.

Herod the Great, who ruled Judaea for the Romans between 37 BC and 4 BC, was viewed by many in the region as an outsider. He was the son of Antipater, who was from Idumaea, south of the Dead Sea. The Idumaeans were themselves seen as outsiders to the Hasmoneans, who had ruled Judea after gaining independence from the Seleucids. Antipater, Herod, and their family were thus outsiders on two different levels—as Idumaeans, and then again as Roman clients. Herod acknowledged his dependence on Rome through his loyalty to Augustus, his friendship with Agrippa, and his diligence in temple-building. Herod and his family further signalled their loyalties by giving their cities Roman-inspired names such as Tiberias, Neronias (a renamed Caesarea Philippi), Livias, Iulias, and Autocratoris. Neither Herod's marriage to a Hasmonean, Mariamne, nor the extravagant and costly renovations to the Second Temple in Jerusalem carried out under his guidance could hide his ties with Rome, and he earned a degree of public scorn: a contemporary Hebrew prophecy recorded in a Greek document, for instance, referred to Herod as the 'insolent king', 'bold and shameless' (*The Assumption of Moses*, 6). Herod and his successors sent their children to be educated in Rome, and some of the royal women married into Roman families. Herod also showed deference to the imperial cult and was an open admirer of Hellenism: he sponsored the Olympics in 16 BC and offered Greek athletic games in Jerusalem. Resistance to Hellenism ran deep among conservative Jews, which caused tension between Jewish conservatives and Jewish Hellenisers, Jews, and Romans, and also between Jews and the gentile inhabitants of cities such as Caesarea Maritima and Sebaste. A passage in the Jerusalem Talmud, for instance, recorded a ban on teaching male children Greek, for fear that this would detract from reading the Torah (Jerusalem Talmud Sotah 9:14, 24c).

As noted in Chapter 8, following Herod's death Judaea briefly became part of the provincial structure of Syria. Between AD 41 and AD 44, Herod's grandson Herod Agrippa I was returned to the kingdom by Claudius. Agrippa was a friend to both Caligula and Claudius, and took credit for persuading Caligula to abandon his idea of placing a statue of himself in Jerusalem. In Judaea, Agrippa pursued a policy of cautious semi-independence that played well with Jewish nationalists. The Jewish historian Joseph ben Matthias, a Hasmonean aristocrat better known to us as Josephus, admired Agrippa's attention to Jewish law and tradition. At the same time, however, Agrippa engaged with the sort of Hellenised pagan pursuits favoured by his grandfather, and he set up statues of his children and built Roman bath-houses. On Agrippa's death, Judaea was re-annexed (this time under a procurator, rather than a prefect). Agrippa's son, Herod Agrippa II, was also an enthusiastic client of the Romans and was later rewarded with control over several of the districts surrounding Judaea (Figure 9.23). Later, Agrippa II provided troop levies to support the legions, fought against the Jewish rebels, and opened his doors to both Vespasian and Titus during the Jewish Revolt. Furthermore, just as client kings such as Herod, Agrippa I, and Agrippa II were viewed by some parts of the population as complicit with the Roman occupation, so the high priests in Jerusalem, appointed by the Roman administrators or by Roman client kings, aroused suspicion for their corruption and perceived slavish obedience to Roman orders.

From the arrival of Roman forces in Judaea during the time of Pompey, the Romans generally accepted the Jewish sacred texts and respected the rules concerning ritual purity, food, and so on—which, among other things, made it difficult for Jews to be recruited into the army where these rules would be near impossible to follow. In an acknowledgement of Jewish monotheism, the imperial cult was altered, becoming a sacrifice for the health of the emperor. Philo of Alexandria praised Augustus in particular for respecting Jewish traditional laws (*Embassy to Gaius*, 153–58 & 311–13). The Roman authorities also accepted the role of the Sanhedrin (the council of Jewish elders) as a legal authority for the Jews in Judaea, and protected the Temple, forbidding Romans to set foot inside it. The problem, however, was that Mosaic Law was a basis for both religious *and* political life. This overt politicisation of religion posed an ideological problem for Roman administrators appointed to Judaea, whose ultimate political authority was the emperor, and Roman ideas about Jews illustrated the sort of hostile ideological resentments that emerged as a result. In his lost work *On Superstition*, discussed by Augustine (AD 354–430), Seneca lamented that 'the customs of that most accursed nation' had spread throughout the empire and referred to the sabbath as a way for the Jews to 'lose through idleness about the seventh part of their life' (*City of God*, 6.11). Cassius Dio expressed astonishment that the Jews 'do

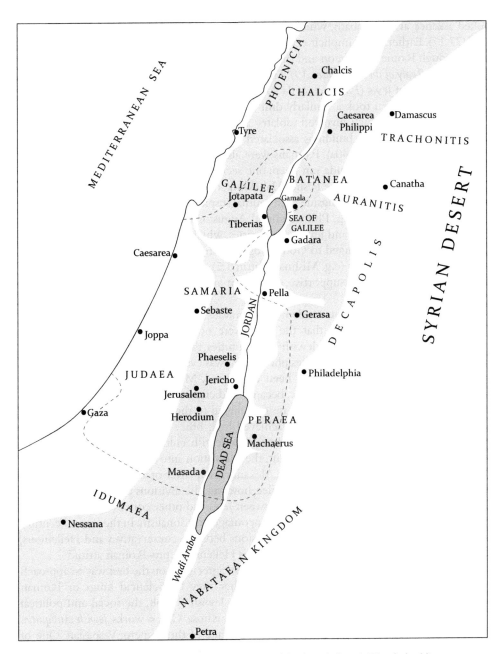

Figure 9.23 The Roman province of Judaea on the eve of the Jewish Revolt. The dashed line represents
the approximate provincial boundary.

Source: Illustration by the author.

not honour any of the other gods, but show extreme reverence for a single one' and also looked askance at the sabbath, which he placed 'among their many other most peculiar rites' (77.17). Earlier, in an implicit criticism of foreign religions, Cicero had declared that it was through Rome's pantheon and the piety of individual Romans that the empire was built (*On the Reply of the Haruspices*, 19). The first-century orator Quintilian also harboured pejorative views of Jews (*Education of the Orator*, 3.7.21).

Jewish sources often took a similarly dim view of the Romans, prohibiting attendance at public spectacles (which involved idolatry and bloodshed) and forbidding Jewish participation in constructing buildings associated with the Roman legal system (Jerusalem Talmud, Avodah Zarah 1:7 40a). Romans were also loathed for their arrogance (e.g. Sifre Numbers 131), and this attitude ran deep: one second-century BC text (preserved in the Dead Sea Scrolls, see below), the Pesher Habakkuk, referred to the *kittim*—the Romans— as a violent and evil power. Alongside such mutual suspicion, however, there were examples of respect and understanding. Philo admired Augustus for ushering in an era of peace (*Embassy to Gaius*, 143–47), and Jewish authorities, which distinguished between practical matters and those that belonged to God, recognised the validity of many legal documents produced by Roman courts (e.g. Mishnah Gittin 1:5). As noted above, Claudius, who was close to the Herodians, was supportive of Judaism and was particularly favourable to the Jews of Alexandria.

One important factor that tended to aggravate periods of tension and inflame misunderstanding was the fact that the Jews were not a homogenous group. Outside Judaea, the diaspora had created Jewish communities throughout the Mediterranean in places like Alexandria, Rome, and Ctesiphon; there was even a Jewish community in Ostia, where a first-century synagogue has been discovered. Many of these Jews spoke Latin and Greek, served in local government, became soldiers, welcomed pagans ('God-fearers') into the synagogue, and variously gave up or adhered to their ancestral laws and customs. Some, like Tiberius Alexander (below), achieved high office under the Romans. Despite intercommunal tensions, especially in Alexandria, Jewish culture thrived in the cities of the ancient Mediterranean: the Septuagint, the translation into Greek of books from the Old Testament, had been accomplished in Alexandria a quarter of a millennium before the Jewish Revolt. In Judaea, Samaria, and Galilee, however, the divisions between conservative and Hellenising elements in society, and between Jews and other communities such as the Samaritans, provoked sharper responses and encouraged factionalism. In the second century BC, the Maccabaean Revolt had revealed tensions between conservatives and Hellenisers, and Herod also faced armed insurrections for his Hellenising, pro-Roman attitude.

Among the Judaean Jews, there was no consistent agreement on the best way to approach the relationship with powerful outsiders, whether they be Seleucid kings or Roman prefects. For the period immediately prior to the Jewish Revolt, the social and political details of Jewish society are provided by Josephus, whose Greek works *Jewish Antiquities* and *The Jewish War* were written under the patronage of the emperor Vespasian. One of Josephus's aims was to mediate the continuous, national history of the Jewish people and the suffering of the Jews during the Jewish Revolt to a Mediterranean audience. (The Aramaic version, intended for Jews across the Middle East, had been composed earlier.) Josephus also sought to pin the blame for the revolt on extremist elements, an apologetic and pro-Roman approach that has earned him fierce criticism. Josephus explained to his readers that in Judaea there were different 'philosophical sects' based on different approaches to Jewish law, religion, and customs. The different positions adopted by these sects affected the prospects of cooperation with outsiders like the Romans. The Sadducees were open to cooperation, under the right circumstances; the Pharisees were reserved; and the Essenes were vehemently opposed (*Jewish War*, 2.8). The Essenes have been linked with the desolate settlement at Qumran on the western side of the Dead Sea, and the caches of priceless documents found in the caves nearby—the Dead Sea Scrolls.

One of the most hated aspects of Roman rule was taxation. In AD 6, a revolt against taxation began when Quirinius announced the census, a task that had the support of the high priest in Jerusalem. The leader of this rebellion was Judas of Galilee, and Josephus identified his insurrection with a more extremist 'fourth philosophy' (*Jewish Antiquities*, 18.1). Judas is often connected with the Zealots, a militant group whom Josephus covered in books four and five of the *Jewish Wars*. The Zealots (named for their 'zeal' for God) followed a similar theology to the Pharisees, but called for violence to solve political problems. It is not clear whether the Zealots emerged as a distinct political force in the decades before the Jewish Revolt or during the war itself, where they are often to be found in the thick of the fighting. It is also unclear what relationship the Zealots had with the violent Sicarii (below). Nevertheless, Judas's politics and those of his followers were nationalist, religious, and profoundly anti-Roman. These attitudes were collectively stoked by end-time and Messianic prophecies, stemming from the Babylonian exile and its aftermath, which increased Jewish fervour for a decisive conflict as well as Roman concerns about subversive political activity. Belief in end-time apocalyptic prophecies was widespread, and written texts had long been prophesising the imminence of a new covenant with God, focused on Jerusalem. In a section of text related to the vision of the 'star in the east' (Matthew 2.1), the book of Numbers declared that a Messianic 'star of Jacob' would return to free the Jewish people (24.17). This prophecy was widely known: it was quoted in the War Scroll, one of the Dead Sea Scrolls, and discussed by Philo of Alexandria. In his *Histories*, a chronicle of the period between AD 68 and AD 96 that was composed before the *Annals*, Tacitus reported a version of the prophecy, noting that 'this was the time when the east should grow strong and that men starting from Judaea should possess the world' (*Histories*, 5.13). *Sibylline Oracle* 3 (not to be confused with the *Sibylline Books*, kept in Rome), which was probably composed in Alexandria, foretold repayment many times over for Rome's greed. It also contained a powerful prophecy about the arrival of a messianic figure, stating that 'a holy prince shall come to wield the sceptre over all the world / unto all ages of hurrying time' (*Sibylline Oracle* 3.49–50). Later, the oracle prophesises the divine judgement of God, which will come from the sky in a 'fiery cataract', all as part of an 'inexorable wrath on Latin men' (3.51). This section of the oracle is believed to have been composed very close to the beginning of the revolt in AD 66. Elsewhere, psalm 17 of the *Psalms of Solomon* prophesied the liberation of Jerusalem from its ungodly overlords, while the War Scroll from Qumran, which used the term *kittim* to describe the Romans, characterised the coming end-time war as a struggle between light, under the archangel Michael, and darkness, led by the satanic Belial and a bevy of gentiles and wayward Jews. End-time was, for many, imminent. Roman rule would soon come to a dramatic and violent end, and the lost utopian vision of an independent Judaea, centred on Jerusalem, would be realised. In AD 66, a comet shaped like a sword—possibly Halley's Comet—appeared over Jerusalem (Josephus, *Jewish War*, 6.5 & Cassius Dio, 66.1). It was taken as a favourable omen and found an easy concordance in contemporary prophecies.

The death of Agrippa I and the return of Judaea to provincial rule in AD 44 brought gloom to Jerusalem. Taxes remained high, and petitions to lower them were made in vain. The tax system was also complicated, with some taxes collected by Roman officials and others collected by tax farmers who resembled the Republican *publicani*. The degree of resentment that taxes continued to provoke can be measured by Talmudic sources giving permission for Jews to lie to Roman tax collectors; the tax was viewed as unlawful and its collectors were little more than bandits (e.g. Jerusalem Talmud Nedarim 3.4, 38a). The heavy taxation rate joined with famine, over-population, and the consolidation of landholdings to cause ongoing social unrest, which triggered a rise in violence and law-lessness. The poor had little to show for the taxes that they paid, and while debt-bondage had long been abolished in the Roman world, a form of it existed in Judaea. Roman administrators worsened this volatile situation. Pontius Pilate (prefect from AD 26 to 36/37) had triggered unrest due to plans to tax the Temple, by bringing troops and images of the emperor into Jerusalem, and by minting coinage in Caesarea Maritima with images of the *lituus*, a wand used by Roman augurs. At the midpoint of the first century, riots in Jerusalem killed thousands, and an emergent hardline group known as the Sicarii ('dagger men') murdered Romans and Jews alike, hoping to foment open war and fulfil the end-time prophecies. Roman officials suppressed unrest with the troops under their command in Judaea, who were often raised from the gentiles of Caesarea Maritima and Sebaste, and who were not always respectful towards their Jewish neighbours.

Against this backdrop of tactless administration, social unrest, and variances among Jewish society, a succession of visionary voices emerged whose teachings offered an escape from the misery. Most met violent ends: John the Baptist was executed around AD 30, Jesus in 33, Theudas in 45. There were many others, including one known only as the 'Egyptian Jew', who rallied the masses to the Mount of Olives to watch Jerusalem's walls come down. As these prophetic voices preached in Jerusalem, Roman officials continued to mete out violence. In AD 51/52, the procurator Ventidius Cumanus suppressed unrest between Galilean Jews and Samaritans, but his actions were seen as extreme even by Roman standards and he was sent into exile by Claudius. The freedman Antonius Felix, brother of Antonius Pallas, was procurator between AD 52 and AD 60. Felix gained a repu-tation as an enthusiastic crucifier; his actions included the suppression of the throngs that flocked to hear the Egyptian Jew and, during his tenure, the Sicarii murdered the high priest Jonathan, ostensibly on Felix's orders. It was to Felix that Paul defended himself after falling afoul of the Sanhedrin and the high priest (Acts 23–25), after which Paul was imprisoned at Caesarea Maritima until he was placed on trial by Felix's successor, Festus (AD 60–62). Under Festus, Albinus (62–64), and Florus (64–66), the relationship between the Jews and the Roman authorities soured even further, and Nero inflamed the situation by barring Jews from Caesarea Maritima amidst soaring tensions between gentiles and Jews in the city.

When Florus imposed a 17-talent indemnity on the Temple to meet Nero's demand for cash, riots broke out in Jerusalem. In Caesarea Maritima, frustration and anger between Jews and gentiles produced a massacre, and violence spread to the cities of the Decapolis. The Romans carried out a savage crackdown in Jerusalem with widespread crucifixion; in an act calculated to degrade and cause further anger, Florus ordered the cowed popu-lace to host a banquet for his murderous troops, who had arrived from Caesarea. The rioters barricaded themselves inside the Temple and Florus left Jerusalem, while an effort

Figure 9.24 Silver half shekel minted in Jerusalem, in year 2 (AD 67/68). The Hebrew legend reads 'Jerusalem the holy'.

by Agrippa II to calm tensions failed. The Roman garrison at the fortress of Masada was murdered and, Josephus said, sacrifices for the health of the emperor abruptly ceased on the orders of Eleazar, son of the high priest Ananias (*Jewish War*, 2.17). This, together with the dispatch of Jewish aristocrats to organise anti-Roman forces in the field, signalled that the elites in Jerusalem had given up on cooperation with Rome. Nevertheless, the divisions within Jewish society ensured that the rebellion would have an essentially fractured character: there was no Boudicca or Tacfarinas around whom resistance would be anchored.

In the summer of AD 66, Ananias was murdered by the Sicarii, the debt records were tossed into a bonfire, the royal palaces in Jerusalem were set ablaze, and the small Roman garrison there was put to the sword. Coins were minted from a notional 'year zero' with nationalist and religious mottos (Figure 9.24). The propraetorian legate of Syria, Cestius Gallus, hurried to Judaea with XII Fulminata, supported by strong allied contingents from Commagene and Emesa. Agrippa II threw in his lot with the Romans and raised several thousand royal troops. Even with such a large force, Gallus failed to capture the Temple. He then suffered horrendous casualties, and lost his legionary eagle at the hands of an expert ambush by the Zealots. By the end of the year, the revolt had become well organised under a council of elected generals, one of whom was Josephus. In Rome, Nero decided to recall Vespasian from retirement, and placed under his command V Macedonica, X Fretensis, and XV Apollinaris, together with 23 cohorts of auxiliaries and six cavalry *alae*, supported by levies from Commagene, Emesa, Nabataea, and Judaea. At the head of this vengeful army—which contained Jewish soldiers and their king, Agrippa, who was wounded during the fighting—Vespasian and his son, Titus, made steady progress throughout AD 67. Galilee capitulated and Josephus, who was a senior commander there, was taken captive. He was later set free when he remarked that Vespasian would go on to fulfil the Messianic prophecies that had circulated prior to the war by ascending to the imperial throne. (Eusebius (*Ecclesiastical History*, 2.8) poured scorn on this, pointing out that Vespasian merely ruled the Roman empire, whereas Christ's message reached to the ends of the earth.) Cassius Dio remarked that it was Josephus who was able to make sense of the various 'portents' that foretold Vespasian's future (65.1).

As the war continued, Vespasian reduced the areas around Jerusalem one by one, leaving the defenders in the Temple isolated—but then other matters intervened. In the summer of AD 68, Vespasian was informed of Nero's suicide and the senate's choice of Galba as his replacement. The new emperor was from the ancient patrician *gens* Sulpicia and, with decades of service, was old enough to remember the death of Augustus. However, problems were quick to appear. 'Galba,' wrote Tacitus, 'was weak and old' (*Histories*, 1.6). The praetorian prefect Nymphidius Sabinus, the grandson of Callistus, staged an opportunistic revolt, which Galba crushed, but the new emperor's relationship with the soldiers soured fast. Galba had refused to pay the expected donative to the Praetorian Guard and then compounded this error by punishing the troops who had fought against Vindex, murdering thousands of them as he made his way into Rome, and dismissing the Germanic imperial bodyguard, contributing to a revolt of Batavian troops. His vindictive policies also included honouring the cowardly and broadly despised Tigellinus. Even as Galba carried on in this way, he minted coins proclaiming the return of *libertas* in a conscious echo of earlier freedom fighters (Figure 9.25). Other coins of Galba included those proclaiming the unity of Spain and Gaul, while still others used the freedom cap and daggers of Brutus (Figure 7.17) and legends of 'restoration', similar to coins minted by Augustus (Chapter 8).

Titus was en route to Rome to seek instructions from Galba when the legions in Upper Germany declared that they would champion the choice of the senate and the people for a new emperor—just as long as it was not Galba. This evaporation of support reflected deep discontent among the army, a sentiment made worse by a change in command that deprived Upper Germany of the competent and popular Verginius Rufus. On January 2, AD 69, all eight of the legions stationed in Upper and Lower Germany declared Aulus Vitellius emperor. Vitellius was the propraetorian legate of Lower Germany, and the son of Lucius Vitellius (governor of Syria in AD 35). The legions in Britain followed, and Titus aborted his journey to Rome and returned to his father in Judaea. In the face of this shift in his fortunes, Galba desperately tried to shore up his position in Rome. He took the practical and conservative step of naming a successor, but his choice snubbed Otho, the ex-husband of Nero's paramour Poppaea Sabina, who had been with him since the beginning

Figure 9.25 Bronze sestertius minted in Rome. Obverse: head of Galba; reverse: *libertas* standing with the legend *libertas publica*, 'freedom of the people'.

of the rebellion. In a remarkably short time, Galba had become irredeemably unpopular with every sector of Roman society that mattered—the people, for suspending games and festivals; the senate, for his over-reliance on a personal council of three men, including a freedman-turned-equestrian, and his plans to limit senatorial offices; and the troops, for his heavy-handed discipline and for failing to compensate them for their efforts. His slight to Otho was the last straw. Otho bribed the Praetorian Guard, and both Galba and his designated successor were murdered in the forum on January 15. A grateful senate soon conferred tribunician power and the title of Augustus on Otho, but a new round of civil war began between Otho and Vitellius, in which Suetonius's father fought for Otho as an equestrian tribune with XIV Gemina. The conflict was waged principally in northern Italy, devastating the countryside and killing thousands. Vitellius's troops, many of whom were raised along the Rhine and appeared alien to the inhabitants of Italy, sacked, raped, and stole with impunity.

After an engagement near Cremona in which his troops were defeated, Otho committed suicide in March AD 69. He earned praise for taking his own life to spare the blood of his men, although it would not be the end of the war. 'He looked with horror on a contest which would cost great bloodshed,' wrote the poet Martial, 'and with resolute hand plunged the sword into his breast / Grant that Cato, in life, was even greater than Caesar; was he greater in death than Otho?' (*Epigrams*, 6.32). A jubilant Vitellius made for Rome, ruining the communities through which he marched. On his arrival, he replaced the Praetorian Guard with his own loyal troops and moved into the hated *Domus Aurea*. Coins minted under his leadership also proclaimed *libertas*, but his coup was not widely accepted. On July 1, AD 69, Vespasian was proclaimed emperor by Tiberius Alexander, an Alexandrian Jew and nephew of Philo of Alexandria. Alexander was the prefect of Egypt and had, a year earlier and in very different political circumstances, appeared on an inscription at the Kharga Oasis referring to Galba as a saviour of 'the whole race of men' (*AH* §80). Now Alexander's support joined that of Vespasian's troops and the client kings of Commagene and Emesa. Legions that had been loyal to Otho and his dignified memory threw their lot in with Vespasian as their best opportunity for revenge. Rumour, prophecy, and gossip promoted Vespasian's candidacy—'chance occurrences which, amid the general credulity, were regarded as omens' (Tacitus, *Histories*, 2.1). These 'omens' included such gossip-worthy events as a statue on Tiber Island turning to point to the east. Operations in Judaea were suspended as Vespasian departed for Egypt, securing possession of Alexandria and its grain supply; a damaged Greek papyrus fragment found in Egypt recorded Vespasian's arrival in the city in almost Messianic terms as 'the one saviour' (*AH* §81). The war itself was left to Gaius Licinius Mucianus, the propraetorian legate of Syria who had served for many years under Corbulo, and who played an important role in promoting Vespasian's candidacy; now he made for Italy with VI Ferrata and scores of auxiliaries. The Pannonian legions also declared for Vespasian, and Antonius Primus, the commander of VII (later VII Gemina), battled his way from Pannonia into northern Italy, where he won a famous victory near Cremona close to the spot where Otho's troops had been beaten by the Vitellians the year before. Finally, Rome came under siege, and in heavy fighting the Temple of Jupiter Optimus Maximus was destroyed. Vitellius was killed shortly before the end of December AD 69; Flavius Sabinus, the urban prefect and Vespasian's brother, also fell in the battle for Rome. It would be another 12 months before Vespasian himself reached the city, where he found that his younger son, Domitian, had survived after going into hiding.

Figure 9.26 The Herodian fortress of Machaerus.

Source: Photograph by the author.

While this drama was unfolding in Europe, Jerusalem had fallen into a terrible state, facing a three-way civil war between leaders with drastically different visions for the future, as well as a looming resumption of the war with Rome and her allies. The food supply was vanishing quickly—Josephus said that a measure of wheat cost an entire talent and people were reduced to eating animal dung (*Jewish War*, 5.13). When the war in the west was over, Titus restarted operations in AD 70 with V Macedonica, X Fretensis, a reconstituted XII Fulminata, and XV Apollinaris, together with elements of III Cyrenaica and XXII Deiotariana from Egypt, auxiliary cohorts and *alae*, and royal levies from Rome's clients—a colossal force. After a five-month siege and abortive negotiations where Josephus acted as a mediator, Roman troops finally captured the Antonia Fortress adjacent to the Temple and then broke through into the Temple itself, which was destroyed at the end of August. The Sicarii still held out at strongpoints dating from the time of Herod the Great: Herodium, on the west side of the Dead Sea; Machaerus, on the east side (where John the Baptist was reputedly executed); and the famous fortress of Masada. These were imposing and formidable obstacles (Figure 9.26), but at Herodium and Machaerus the Sicarii surrendered as the Romans began siege preparations; remnants of their efforts can still be seen at Machaerus (Figure 9.27).

It took a further three years for the Sicarii on Masada to be reduced. The siege was an expert demonstration of Roman engineering: an entire circumvallation was constructed around the fortress, with an assault ramp built to allow legionnaires to break in over its

Figure 9.27 Roman siegeworks at Machaerus. The incomplete assault ramp, with the outline of the small construction camp and the Dead Sea behind, viewed from the fortress citadel.

Source: Photograph by the author.

walls. The remains of the wall, eight Roman camps, and the ramp itself are still there, as mute testament to Roman skill (Figure 9.28). In AD 73 or 74 the fortress fell, but the defenders committed mass suicide rather than be taken prisoner. A Roman garrison temporarily took their place. Archaeologists working at Masada in the 1960s found destruction layers of ash throughout the site, accompanied by the remains of burned food, coins, and clothing. They also found round, heavy stone slugs of the sort fired by Roman artillery, fragments of scrolls containing verses from the Old Testament, and scrolls that featured the same sorts of tracts as those discovered at Qumran. One of the most dramatic discoveries was a mass of disarticulated skeletons in one of the caves nearby; another was a papyrus fragment quoting lines from the *Aeneid*—a literary interloper in a savagely conquered landscape.

The afterlife of the Jewish Revolt

The Jewish Revolt was commemorated on two arches in Rome, both erected in AD 81. One was built at the eastern end of the Circus Maximus and included a Latin inscription that lauded Titus's feats: 'he tamed the race of the Jews and destroyed the city of Jerusalem, a thing either sought in vain by all commanders, kings, and races before him, or never attempted' (*ILS* 264 = *AH* §83C). (The claims are misleading, as Pompey had captured Jerusalem earlier, in 63 BC). The second arch is the better known Arch of Titus, erected

Figure 9.28 Camp 'F' at Masada.

Source: Photograph by Carole Raddato (CC BY-SA 2.0).

Figure 9.29 Interior panel of the Arch of Titus in Rome, commemorating the Jewish Revolt.

Source: Photograph by Dnalor 01 (CC BY-3.0).

close to the forum. The most famous of its panels shows Roman troops with the Menorah, the silver trumpets, the Table of Shewbread, and other sacred objects from the Temple (Figure 9.29). A study of this panel carried out by Yale University's Arch of Titus Project has determined that the Menorah was originally painted with yellow ochre to mimic its golden appearance. Not depicted on the arch, but believed to also have been looted, was what Josephus called 'the Jewish law'—the Torah scroll (*Jewish War*, 7.5). All these objects were paraded through Rome in triumph in AD 71, an event during which Simon bar Giora, the Zealot who had helped bring Cestius Gallus to ruin and then led one of the factions in Jerusalem, was publicly executed. The Temple objects were later installed in Vespasian's Templum Pacis (Chapter 10), but according to the late antique historian Procopius (c. AD 500–70), these objects subsequently found their way into the possession of Gaiseric, the Vandal king, who looted them from Rome in the fifth century AD (*Wars*, 4.9, and Chapter 13). The Menorah was eventually returned to Constantinople and then Jerusalem in the sixth century, only to be looted once more at the beginning of the seventh, this time by a victorious Persian army; neither it nor the rest of the Temple treasure has ever been seen since.

In the aftermath of the Jewish Revolt, Judaea became an imperial province and was garrisoned by X Fretensis in Jerusalem and a strong force of auxiliary cavalry and infantry.

Figure 9.30 Silver denarius of Vespasian struck in Rome in AD 70. The reverse shows a Jewish captive and a trophy, with IUDAEA in the exergue.

(Several small areas remained under the control of Agrippa II, but were later annexed in the 90s.) Judaea's second propraetorian legate, Lucilius Bassus, reduced Herodium and Machaerus; its third, Flavius Silva, was responsible for the successful siege of Masada. Mountains of loot refilled the empty Roman treasury, funding the construction of the Flavian Amphitheatre in Rome and other public buildings (Chapter 10). Refugees left Judaea in large numbers to join diaspora settlements across the Mediterranean world. The Sanhedrin was abolished, and the tax formerly paid by Jews for the upkeep of the Temple now went to Jupiter, a painful and regular reminder of the crushing Roman triumph. The Temple remained in ruins; the Western Wall in modern Jerusalem, one of the retaining walls from the time of Herod, represents its surviving remnant. Even as coins were triumphantly minted proclaiming the submission of Judaea (Figure 9.30), these acts of vengeance sowed the seeds of the next revolt.

Titus was naturally loathed in later Jewish writings. In one fifth-century AD exegesis, God punished Titus for his violation of the Temple by sending a mosquito that 'entered his nose and gnawed its way up until it reached his brain' (Leviticus Rabbah 22:3). Nero had a more important afterlife in Jewish literature, however, even though his role in the revolt was minimal. While Josephus steered clear of the sensational stories that surrounded Nero and his demise, the emperor appeared in dramatic end-time contexts in three (or perhaps four) of the *Sibylline Oracles* that developed the legendary ideas about Nero's flight to the east. In *Sibylline Oracle* 4, a (Syrian?) Jewish text that dates to the period after the Revolt, Nero appears as a matricidal figure who will return from the east and wreak destruction on Rome. In so doing, he will also 'burn down Solyma's temple with fire, and therewith slay many men, and shall waste the great land of the Jews' (4.25–7). In *Sibylline Oracle* 5, similarly written after the destruction of the Temple, Nero is easily recognised through his love of athletics, singing, and charioteering. 'Even when he disappears, he shall be malignant,' the oracle proclaims. 'Then he shall return, making himself equal to God, but God shall convince him that he is not' (5.33–4). Nero's actions against Jerusalem will invite a ferocious response, as a 'king sent from God' will destroy him (5.108). In *Sibylline Oracle* 8, composed before AD 300, Nero's return will result not only in the destruction of the Jews but also the Roman empire itself. Another possible mention of Nero is found in *Sibylline Oracle* 3, which refers to Beliar coming 'from the stock of Sebaste' (3.63). This could be seen as a reference to Beliar (Belial) coming from Samaria, but some have supposed that 'Sebaste' is a reference to the line of Augustus. In the text, Beliar raises the dead, performs miracles, and deceives Jews into believing him, only for all to be destroyed in an apocalyptic furnace—'fiery energy [that] comes through the swelling surge to earth' (3.72).

Together, these views of Nero as a legendary evil-doer with a distinctly satanic bent became transmitted to Christian writers, who already detested Nero for the deaths of Paul and Peter and the purge of AD 64, and he developed into the apocalyptic figure of the Antichrist: an enemy of God, whose sporadic and prophetic reappearances created a figure of timeless hatred and impiety. In the Apocalypse of John (Revelation), usually dated to the end of the first century, whose author was a Jewish-leaning Christian, Nero appears as a correspondingly timeless figure of terror—the beast, whose fatal head wounds have been healed, allowing him to return from the dead (13.3). The famous mark of the beast, 666 (13.18), is derived from the rendering of Nero's name and title from Greek into Hebrew via the assignation of mathematical numbers to specific letters of the alphabet, an approach known as gematria that was also used in the *Sibylline Oracles*. Augustus, for instance, is referred to as 'first' and Caligula as 'three' from the position of α (A) and γ (G, for Gaius) in the Greek alphabet, while 'seventy' refers to Vespasian, whose name begins with o (O) in Greek (e.g. *Sibylline Oracle* 5.15, 5.24, 5.37). A third- or fourth-century manuscript from Oxyrhynchus in Egypt gives Nero the value of 616, but this is also achieved by rendering Nero's name into Hebrew in a slightly different way. Later (Apocalypse, 17), the text foretells the return of the beast who will destroy Babylon, a name used for Rome in the *Sibylline Oracles* (e.g. *Sibylline Oracle* 5.143). It has also been argued that, via Nero, the 'beast' could stand for any Roman emperor. The literature that grew up around and after the Jewish Revolt thus helped, through the elaboration of legends about Nero's survival in the *Sibylline Oracles*, to create one of Christianity's most powerful and detested figures.

Chapter 10

Consolidating the principate, AD 72–138

In the *Histories*, Tacitus noted that the secret of empire was out: an emperor could be created anywhere, not just in Rome (1.4). Vespasian, from an equestrian family in northern Italy, had been made in the provinces, as had Galba and Vitellius. Key to kingmaking was the army, as all three men had been elevated by the provincial legions; Plutarch noted that the soldiers were able to usher emperors in and out, 'as if in a play' (*Galba*, 1). The civil wars thus created a problematic tension between the heavily armed provincial periphery and the harsh realities of politics in Rome, and Vespasian faced an immediate need to heal the divisions caused by the civil war and to institutionalise his own authority. He addressed the disunity in Roman society by following the Augustan precedent of concealing a civil war with a foreign conflict, making the Jewish Revolt a centrepiece of his political ideology: his triumph was over the Jews, not different Roman factions. Vespasian also promoted a vision of renewal and common purpose that was deeply anchored in Roman tradition. To buttress his rule, forestall the creation of further harmful divisions, and resolve the political uncertainties of the Julio-Claudian dynasty, he used a combination of political precedent and shrewd innovation. The Flavian dynasty—Vespasian and his two sons, Titus and Domitian—healed the schisms in Rome and laid the foundations for the apex of the *pax Romana* (Figure 10.1). Under Domitian's successors, Nerva (96–98), Trajan (98–117), and Hadrian (117–38), the empire reached its geographical zenith, secured by the power of Roman arms, and produced a period of unparalleled military triumph and consolidation in the provinces.

The Flavians: Vespasian (AD 69–79), Titus (AD 79–81), and Domitian (AD 81–96)

Rome

In Rome, Vespasian celebrated a month-long triumph for ending the Jewish Revolt. As Augustus had framed his civil war with Antony as a foreign campaign against Cleopatra and her barbarous horde, now Vespasian could mask the recent violence that had plagued Italy with a crushing victory in a remote war in a far-flung province. Vespasian also benefited from the neat coincidence that precisely 100 years had elapsed between the battle of Actium and the defeat of Vitellius; like Augustus, Vespasian positioned himself as a bringer of peace, declaring the freedom of the people on early coin issues that showed Libertas wielding the *vindicta*, the rod used to manumit slaves (Figure 10.2).

DOI: 10.4324/9781003202523-10

Figure 10.1 A rare triple portrait of Vespasian (obverse) with Titus and Domitian (reverse), struck at Ephesus in AD 71.

Figure 10.2 Bronze sestertius of Vespasian, minted in Rome in AD 71. The reverse declares LIBERTAS PVBLICA; note the *vindicta* in the goddess's left hand.

Vespasian also began a building program to restore Rome's battered architectural treasures and 'return' Rome's public space to its people. The Temple of Jupiter Optimus Maximus, which had suffered grievously in the civil war, was carefully restored. North of the Basilica Aemilia on part of the *Domus Aurea*, and opposite the Forum of Augustus, Vespasian ordered the construction of the Templum Pacis—the Temple of Peace, a complex including gardens, a Library of Peace, and a shrine dedicated to the goddess Pax. The very name and message of the structure evoked those of the Ara Pacis of Augustus; the massive Templum Pacis, however, exceeded its predecessor in size by over ten times, with Josephus remarking that it 'was beyond all human expectation' (*Jewish War*, 7.5). The Templum Pacis was dedicated in AD 75, and displayed the spoils of the Jewish Revolt as well as precious artworks from throughout the Mediterranean world, including many 'restored' to the people from the *Domus Aurea* (Figure 10.3).

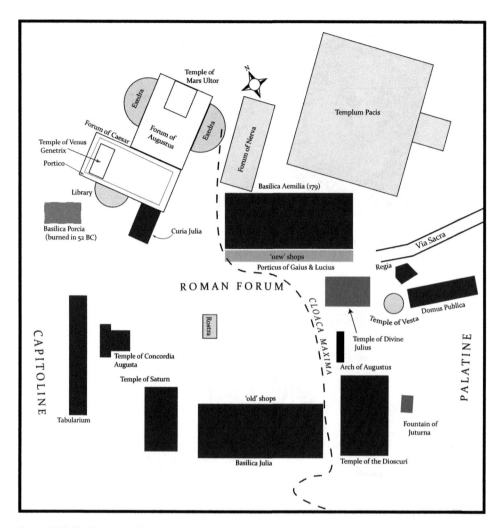

Figure 10.3 The Temple of Peace within the Roman forum.

Source: Illustration by the author.

The rest of the *Domus Aurea* was demolished, creating the Baths of Titus and making space for the massive Flavian Amphitheatre—Rome's famous Colosseum, which derived its name from the colossal statue of Nero, refashioned by Vespasian as a statue of the sun god, Sol. As its dedicatory inscription reveals, the amphitheatre was financed with the plunder from Judaea (*ex manubis*: *CIL* 6.40454a). The partially built Temple of Claudius on the Caelian Hill, begun by Agrippina the Younger, was also restored and completed. With these expensive and grandiose architectural projects, and through his policy of returning land to its proper owners, Vespasian 're-founded' Rome and portrayed himself as a purveyor of peace and plenty after a time of violent, foreign conflict (Figures 10.4 and 10.5).

Figure 10.4 Bronze sestertius minted in Rome in AD 71. Obverse: laureate head of Vespasian; reverse: the goddess of peace with olive branch and cornucopia, with PAX AVGVSTI.

Figure 10.5 Bronze sestertius minted in Rome in AD 77/78. Obverse: laureate head of Vespasian right; reverse: Annona, the personified goddess of the corn allotment, enthroned with ears of corn, and legend ANNONA AVGVSTI.

Later, Vespasian was viewed so positively that admirers and new citizens took the name Flavius in honour of his dynasty.

Like Augustus, Vespasian had come to power in an illegal coup, and the political basis of his rule required urgent attention. The evidence for his approach is the *lex de imperio Vespasiani*, an inscribed bronze tablet discovered in the fourteenth century that outlined the powers of the new emperor and his position in Roman political life. The text, which is incomplete, is dated to January AD 70, prior to Vespasian's arrival in Rome. Numerous clauses in the text appealed to tradition and past precedent in determining Vespasian's powers, noting, for instance, that 'he shall be permitted to make … a treaty with whom he wishes, just as permission was given to the deified Augustus, / to Tiberius Iulius Caesar Augustus' (*AH* §82, l. 1–2). Past precedent only included emperors of whom Vespasian approved, however; Caligula, Nero, Galba, Otho, and Vitellius were omitted, and Claudius was pointedly not referred to as 'deified'. Elsewhere in the text, Vespasian's powers clearly departed from precedent, such as in the clause determining that 'in accordance with his wish or authority or order or command', a meeting of the senate might take place and his decisions would be 'held in accordance with law' (l.7–9). The text also stated that he could do as he pleased, so long as it was 'in accordance with the advantage of the Republic and with the majesty of things divine' (l.17–19 & l. 25)—a magnificently vague proviso. The text further legalised all his prior actions as if they had been carried out by the 'order of the People or the Plebs' (l. 34). Vespasian was effectively placed outside the law, and by explicitly connecting the emperor's decisions with 'things divine', developed Augustus' own connections with divinity and anticipated Trajan's more direct links with Jupiter (below). The *lex de imperio* further allowed Vespasian to assume all the imperial powers at once, in contrast to the way the powers of Augustus had gradually evolved, and the text also established a new form of the imperial title. As Imperator Caesar Vespasianus Augustus, Vespasian acknowledged the divine lineage of Augustus and Julius Caesar, while the emphasis on the title 'Imperator' reflected the importance of the army in bringing him to power. 'Imperator' now became the official first name of the emperor, and indicated his office and his superior position vis-à-vis the senate. To bolster his authority, either Vespasian or his sons enlarged the Praetorian Guard by endowing it with a cavalry arm, the *equites singulares Augusti*. With a strength of between 500 and 1,000, the *equites* were raised from Germanic tribesmen and were garrisoned in a camp on the Lateran.

Despite the expansion of powers reflected in the *lex de imperio Vespasiani*, the emperor's relations with the senate and the equestrians generally reflected a concern for past practice and a desire to address the recent wayward conduct of Roman emperors and senators that demanded an urgent recalibration of public morals and political leadership. For instance, Suetonius Paulinus—who Tacitus regarded as the best general of his day and who had backed Otho in the civil wars—admitted to Vitellius following his defeat that he had intentionally worn out his troops with a long march, and then mixed up the cumbersome baggage with the legions to undermine their ability to fight Vitellius effectively (*Histories*, 2.60). That generals behaved in such a shameful way was the fault of their rulers, Tacitus suggested, so Vespasian and Titus set out to provide a more positive example. Aurelius Victor wrote that Vespasian was 'honourable in all respects', and that he 'restored a world long debilitated and exhausted' (*On the Caesars*, 9). Vespasian and Titus also returned some of the nobility to Rome's upper classes by removing the influence of freedmen in government, and by improving access to magistracies. Vespasian held the censorship with Titus in AD 73, resulting in the reestablishment of the senatorial roll, and re-emphasising the correct hierarchy of Roman political society. In tandem with the reconstitution of the senate, Vespasian also used his imperial prerogatives outlined in the *lex de imperio Vespasiani* to elevate talented men to patrician status, allowing them access to specific magistracies and positions. As Claudius had encouraged the arrival of new blood from Gaul, Vespasian brought in men from both Gaul and Spain. One of those ennobled through this process was Marcus Ulpius Traianus, born in the Roman colony of Italica in Spain. Traianus was the former legate of X Fretensis and had fought under Vespasian in Judaea; he was also the father of the future emperor, Trajan. Vespasian favoured intellectuals, and gave special dispensations to teachers and doctors, freeing them from billeting soldiers, as a marble inscription from Pergamum shows (*AH* §84). In Rome, he funded a chair each in Greek and Latin rhetoric. Vespasian's administration benefited from the skill and experience of the freedwoman Antonia Caenis (Chapter 9), who became his partner after his wife died. Cassius Dio noted that Antonia had a photographic memory, but accused her—like Vespasian—of an unseemly love of money (66.14).

The provinces

In the provinces, the Latin rights were granted wholesale to Spanish communities, and the suppression of rebellions and improvements in defences (below) brought periods of calm after the civil war, fostering tighter economic and cultural links with Rome and blurring the distinction between Italian Romans and 'provincial' Romans. Several of the era's most famous Roman literary voices had provincial origins: Martial (Hispania Tarraconensis), Plutarch (Greece), Quintilian (Hispania Tarraconensis), and Suetonius (Numidia)— as did some of their successors during the time of Trajan and Hadrian, such as Appian (Alexandria), the geographer Pausanias (Lydia) and Apuleius, the author of the raucous Latin novel addressing the cult of Isis, *The Golden Ass* (Numidia). Tacitus may also have had provincial origins, although his precise place of birth is disputed. However, the interweaving of Roman and provincial, and of Roman and foreign, is best seen in the changing nature of the army during the Flavian period.

The civil wars had reflected the increasingly provincial character of the Roman armies, with the legions of Vitellius viewed as virtual outsiders in Italy. Vespasian's eastern troops likewise found Italy foreign, and in the prelude to the decisive battle near Cremona, the soldiers of one of the eastern legions greeted the sunrise, a local custom in Syria; after their victory, the troops sacked Cremona as if it were an enemy city, raping and murdering its inhabitants. The emergence of provincial blocs presented a distinct political threat that had also manifested itself in the rebellion in AD 69 of Batavian auxiliaries from the Rhineland, led by Gaius Julius Civilis, a Batavian Roman citizen. Civilis, who Tacitus described as 'a Sertorius or a Hannibal', was promoted by a prophetess named Veleda and enjoyed substantial early success, beating a Roman army that was then penned up at Vetera (*Histories*, 4.13). The rebellion spread westwards: secessionists clamoured for an 'empire of the Gauls' as another citizen auxiliary, Julius Classicus, joined the revolt, and Veleda's prophetic visions declared the imminent collapse of Rome. The war eventually petered out in the aftermath of Vespasian's triumph over Vitellius, and Civilis was beaten at Augusta Treverorum and subsequently vanished into the vastness of Germany. In the aftermath of Civilis's revolt, Roman policy was adjusted and auxiliary soldiers were recruited in one part of the empire, but dispatched for service and discharge in another, to counter the creation of dangerous provincial power blocs.

This 'internationalisation' of the auxiliary troops is particularly visible in the military discharge certificates, known as diplomas. Diplomas were issued to all branches of military service except the legions, and they recorded discharges and grants of benefits, such as the right to marry or grants of citizenship. Each diploma issued was a notarised extract of a legal document deposited in Rome, and normally belonged to a single recipient. Since the diplomas recorded details of the various units being discharged—the broader document from which the diploma was taken—they provide a wealth of information about recruitment and garrisons. One diploma for auxiliary troops, for instance, dating to AD 88, dealt with three cavalry *alae* and 17 cohorts of infantry. It shows that the troops, serving in Syria, had been recruited from as far afield as Pannonia, Gaul, Judaea, and Numidia. Another from Pannonia (dated to AD 100), recorded a similar mass discharge and documented soldiers from Thrace, Spain, Antioch, and Britain, with some already Roman citizens and others receiving citizenship for their service (*RA* §324). A diploma dated to AD 122, recording a citizenship grant to a soldier from a Raetian cohort, provides an even more diverse viewpoint. The document lists 13 cavalry *alae* and 37 infantry cohorts; between them, these units were recruited from Spain, Gaul, the Danube, Germany, Syria, Africa, and the Balkans (*AE* 2008: 800). This impression of an international army is also illustrated by the *Expedition Against the Alans*, written by Arrian, the propraetorian legate of Cappadocia in AD 135 and the author of a well-regarded biography of Alexander the Great. Arrian listed troops from Raetia commanded by a Corinthian, men from Cyrenaica from the Bosporus, bowmen from Arabia, troops from Trapezus, and many more (*AH* §155a). The auxiliary army of the Flavian era was rapidly becoming dependent on provincial recruitment, and by the time of Trajan and Hadrian, even a citizen legionnaire was four to five times more likely to have joined the army from the western provinces in particular than from Italy.

In the provinces, a key strategic concern for Vespasian and his sons was the region called the Agri Decumates, the difficult angle between the Rhine and the Danube. This angle was pinched off during the Flavian period, improving troop movements and regional security, and the renewed emphasis on Germany stimulated Tacitus to pen the *Germania*, an ethnographic study of the German tribes and their customs. The military districts of Upper and Lower Germany were formally established as imperial provinces, and wooden forts at places such as Vetera were replaced with permanent stone structures. The permanent garrison of so many troops along the frontier stimulated the rise of settlements (*vici*) adjacent to fortress walls, and also had a material effect on the economies of Gaul and Britain, whose markets played a key role in supplying the legions.

In Britannia, the Romans campaigned westwards and northwards under Agricola, the father-in-law of Tacitus, who later penned his biography. Agricola was another provincial, born at Forum Julii in Gallia Narbonensis. Agricola had been a military tribune under Suetonius Paulinus, and briefly commanded XX Valeria Victrix; he was also one of the many promising young men who Vespasian admitted to patrician status. Following a consulship in AD 77, Vespasian sent Agricola to govern Britannia between c. AD 78 and 84. Agricola had a large force at his disposal: in addition to XX Valeria Victrix, he had IX Hispana, quartered at Eboracum (York), II Adiutrix Pia Fidelis (Lindum Colonia), and II Augusta, recently transferred from Isca Dumnoniorum (Exeter) to Isca Silurum (Caerleon in Wales). Agricola scored early successes in Wales, capturing Anglesey as his dismounted auxiliary cavalry swam with their horses across the Menai Strait. These men were probably Batavians, who excelled at swimming in armour; later, they would show off their skills to Hadrian (below). In AD 79, Agricola began his first of six campaigns into northern England and Scotland against the warlike Caledonii, building roads and establishing military bases and depots along the way. One of the most important was Trimontium (Newstead), southeast of Edinburgh (Figure 10.6).

After a stinging setback, Agricola fought a decisive battle at Mons Graupius, the location of which has long since been lost to legend. Tacitus placed a speech in the mouth of the Caledonian war leader Calgacus, which castigated the Romans for their greed, savagery, and avarice, demonstrating a penetrating awareness of the predatory side of Roman imperialism (*Agricola*, 30). Agricola's campaigns were celebrated by Titus (Figure 10.7), and

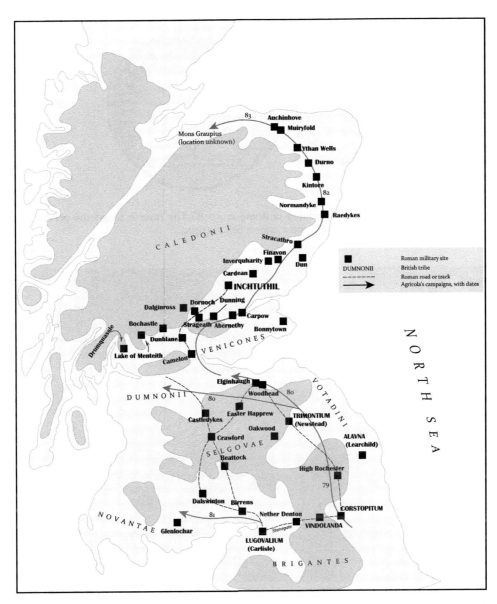

Figure 10.6 The campaigns of Agricola in Scotland; note the emphasis on military installations at the edge of or below 300 metres (1000 feet) altitude, marked by the darker shaded areas.

Source: Illustration by the author, after Frere 1987.

have left some intriguing archaeological evidence for the way Roman military installations were constructed for specific campaigns and then demolished.

The legionary fortress at Inchtuthil, for instance, was entirely dismantled once the campaigns were over. The Romans were so thorough that metal nails removed during

Figure 10.7 Silver denarius of Titus, minted in Rome in AD 80. The reverse shows the personified Britannia in mourning (left) and a captive Briton (right).

Figure 10.8 Google Earth Pro image of Inchtuthil Roman fort. The main installation lies in the centre of the photograph; to the bottom left, disturbances in the fields reveal the outline of labour camps constructed to protect the troops while the main fort was built.

Source: Image © 2020 Google.

the dismantling of the fortress were buried deep in the ground to stop their reuse by the region's inhabitants—875,400 of them, weighing 7 tons (6,350 kilograms, or 14,000 pounds) were recovered by archaeologists in the 1960s. The fort was so completely demolished that today it exists only as faint cropmarks in the soil (Figure 10.8).

While the Roman army withdrew from northern Scotland, northern England and much of southern Scotland were incorporated into the province of Britannia. To consolidate Rome's hold on lowland Scotland, Trimontium was enlarged and new forts were built nearby. A military road, the Stanegate, linked Corstopitum (Corbridge) in the east to Luguvalium (Carlisle) in the west. On the Stanegate lay the turf and timber fort of Vindolanda, garrisoned by two auxiliary units, the Cohors I Tungrorum and Cohors IX Batavorum. These double-strength 1,000-man 'milliary' infantry cohorts had been raised from Gallia Belgica and Batavia, and excavations at Vindolanda have uncovered hundreds of well-preserved wooden writing tablets associated with these two units—the Vindolanda Tablets. The collection, dating from AD 90 to 105, includes reports on military activities, accounting ledgers, and the largest single corpus of Latin letters found to date. There are requests for beer, quotes from the *Aeneid*, letters written by a military surveyor, demands for warm clothing, and the famous birthday invitation from Claudia Severa (Chapter 1).

In the aftermath of the Jewish Revolt, the eastern provinces also required attention. In AD 72, the kingdom of Commagene was forcibly incorporated into the province of Syria by Caesennius Paetus, Syria's propraetorian legate, on the specious pretext that its king was conspiring with the Parthians. Further adjustments saw Lesser Armenia added to Cappadocia and Galatia. Hitherto under the control of a procurator, the new imperial province of Cappadocia now came under the control of a propraetorian legate with XVI Flavia Firma and XII Fulminata for its garrison at Satala (Sadak) and Melitene (Malatya). The reorganisation of Cappadocia and the annexation of Commagene made good strategic sense: control of Cappadocia eased supply concerns for Roman forces operating in the Black Sea region and Armenia, while Commagene straddled the Euphrates and controlled numerous military supply and trade routes. VI Ferrata and part of III Gallica were duly stationed at Samosata, the principal city of Commagene, to keep a watchful eye on the frontier, while IV Scythica was stationed at Zeugma, a key crossing of the Euphrates where a road from Antioch led eastwards into the Parthian client kingdom of Osrhoene. The Pannonian diploma from AD 100, mentioned above, included a unit called the Second Flavian Commagenians; given that auxiliaries generally served 25 years, this unit must have been recruited in about AD 75, shortly after Commagene was annexed.

In the south, the kingdom of Emesa was added to Syria between AD 72 and 78. This kingdom had long been in the safe hands of loyal kings with long and stable reigns, Iamblichos II (20 BC–AD 14), Sampsigeramos II (AD 14–48), and Gaius Julius Sohaemus (AD 54–73). Sohaemus had also ruled Sophene for a time after AD 54. There were strong commercial ties between Emesa and Rome's ally Palmyra, reflected by the acclamation of Sampsigeramos II as 'great king' on a mutilated Palmyrene Aramaic inscription from the Temple of Bel at Palmyra. Emesene kings were also valuable allies of Rome: Sohaemus had provided forces to Caesennius Paetus for the annexation of Commagene, and he had also supported Roman forces during the Jewish Revolt. Sohaemus was himself acclaimed as 'great king' on an inscription from Heliopolis (Baalbek), as the patron of the Roman colony at Berytus (Beirut). The close involvement of the Emesene royal family in Roman affairs, and their financial ties to Palmyra, likely accelerated Emesa's annexation into Syria. In Judaea, Agrippa II died at some point during the 90s, and his remaining territory was annexed along with the small kingdom of Chalcis. Finally, the province of Cilicia was reorganised with territory taken from Commagene, and became an imperial province

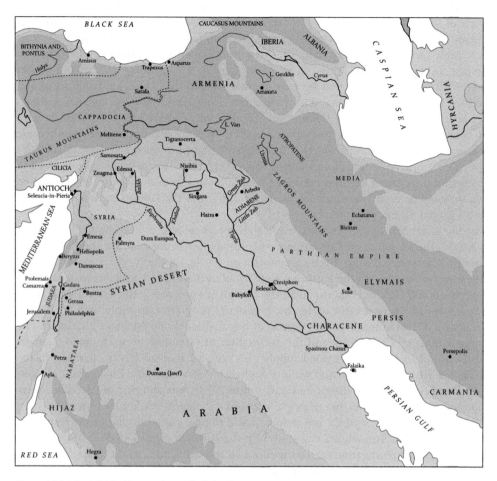

Figure 10.9 The Middle East at the end of the first century AD.

Source: Illustration by the author.

under a propraetorian legate. These developments effectively ended the client system created by Pompey, pushing Roman territory to the Euphrates. Only the Nabataean kingdom and Palmyra retained a sense of semi-independence (Figure 10.9).

Along with Berytus, Ptolemais and Caesarea Maritima also became colonies, the latter explicitly honoured for its connection to Vespasian as Colonia Prima Flavia Augusta Caesarea. In Greece, Corinth also honoured the emperor, who had provided succor after an earthquake; in AD 77, it was renamed Colonia Julia Flavia Augusta Corinthiensis. Vespasian strengthened Roman defences across the eastern provinces, and improved communication networks. A milestone set up by Marcus Ulpius Traianus in AD 75, while he was propraetorian legate of Syria, recorded the work of four separate legions on canal works and bridges near Antioch to improve river access to the city (*AH* §85a); as part of these works, Vespasian also expanded Antioch's port, Seleucia-in-Pieria, establishing the *classis Syriaca*, a Roman naval squadron. To the north, a Latin inscription on a still-extant bridge over the Cendere Çayı river in southeastern Turkey recorded its construction under Vespasian, part of the road network that was expanded in tandem with the acquisition of Commagene. Another road milestone set up by Traianus in AD 75 was discovered northeast of Palmyra, and is sometimes thought to have stood on a road leading to the Roman fort at Sura on the Euphrates. Yet another milestone was found at the intersection of the principal routes between Apamea, Palmyra, and Emesa. All these artefacts reflect a concerted effort to improve the road network in the eastern provinces.

Flavian religious policy reflected the emperors' provincial outlook. Egyptian cults, shunned as too exotic by the Julio-Claudians, were accorded a prominent place in Rome. Isis was given particular emphasis, as the goddess was believed to have protected Domitian from Vitellius during the civil wars; before celebrating their triumph over the Jews, both Vespasian and Titus slept in the Temple of Isis in Rome. Coins minted in Egypt displayed Vespasian on the obverse and Isis on the reverse, explicitly linking the Egyptian goddess with the god-to-be. The relaxation of concerns over Egyptian cults was accompanied by a strengthening of the imperial cult in the provinces: new chief priests were selected in several western provinces to serve alongside the provincial government, shifting the focus for the cult from the municipal to the provincial level. A new college of priests, the *sodales Flaviales*, was created, and Domitian later built a temple to the Flavians (the Temple of Vespasian and Titus). This renewed emphasis on the imperial cult ran in parallel to the more authoritarian style of rule expressed in the *lex de imperio Vespasiani*. Another important religious development in the Flavian period was the arrival of the cult of Mithras from Persia. Mithraism was a mystery cult involving tauroctony (bull sacrifice) and clandestine meetings in subterranean crypts. It quickly became popular with the army, and its sanctuaries have been found in military sites across the empire from Housesteads on Hadrian's Wall to Dura-Europos in eastern Syria.

The eruption of Vesuvius (AD 79)

One of the most famous events that took place during the Flavian era was the eruption of Vesuvius in the late summer of AD 79. Pliny the Younger's account of it is the first known eyewitness description of a volcanic event, and the aftermath of the eruption was dramatically revealed later on by the spectacular rediscovery of Pompeii in the late sixteenth century and its subsequent excavation, together with the discovery of the nearby towns of Oplontis and Herculaneum, found in the seventeenth and eighteenth centuries respectively.

Pliny, the nephew of Pliny the Elder, and a student of the famous rhetor Quintilian, recounted the eruption of Vesuvius in two letters to his friend, Tacitus. Pliny witnessed the eruption from Misenum, 32 kilometres (20 miles) from Vesuvius, and in the first letter he described how a vast plume appeared above the volcano from which ash and pumice fell in a steady torrent (*Letters*, 6.16). While Pliny the Younger remained in Misenum, his uncle, who was commander of the fleet at Misenum, set off across the Bay of Naples in a galley to take a closer look; receiving a plea for help from a friend, he diverted and put in at Stabiae, where he remained overnight. The following morning, 'flames and [a] smell of sulphur' triggered panic of 'the approaching fire', and the people of Stabiae fled in terror. Pliny the Elder was unable to escape, and perished—probably through suffocation (Figure 10.10).

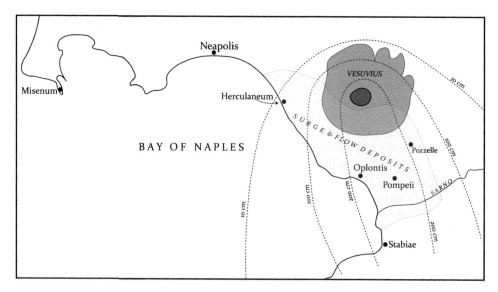

Figure 10.10 The eruption of Vesuvius. The dashed line represents the accumulation of pumice and ash.

Source: Illustration by the author, after Sigurdsson et al. 1982.

In the second letter, written many years later (*Letters*, 6.20), Pliny described his youthful cool in reading Livy while ground tremors unsettled those around him. He was not worried, he said, because earthquakes were common in the area; a major earthquake in AD 62 had demolished large parts of Pompeii and repairs were still going on in AD 79 (Tacitus, *Annals*, 15.22). The next morning, however, Pliny had awakened to the danger, and he and his mother decided to leave Misenum. On the road, Pliny felt further tremors and saw the sea withdraw—the prelude to a small tsunami. At about the same time as the earthquakes, Pliny saw 'a black and dreadful cloud, broken with rapid, zigzag flashes', which was riven by 'variously shaped masses of flame' and studded with lightning. This cloud sank to ground level, obscuring Capri and bringing darkness to Misenum. Ashes continued to fall, and, soon afterwards Pliny saw the terrifying spectacle of a 'dense black cloud', apparently the same cloud as before, moving rapidly, 'spreading over the earth like a flood'. The 'black and dreadful cloud' was a *nuée ardente*, a combination of fast-moving gassy ground surges and slower and denser pyroclastic currents. The surges, containing an explosive discharge of superheated toxic gas and volcanic matter (tephra), are known from modern eruptions to be capable of speeds of up to 725 kilometres per hour (450 miles per hour), turning even small rocks and other debris within into lethal missiles and either cooking or asphyxiating their victims. In 1902, the combination of surge and the denser pyroclastic current killed 28,000 people living adjacent to Mt Pelée on Martinique in just a few minutes.

Pliny's detailed observations of a two-stage volcanic event are remarkable for their clarity, and have been confirmed by numerous analyses of the stratigraphic evidence left by the eruption. Following a small event that deposited ash onto the slopes of the volcano, there was an initial major eruption that begun at about 1.00 pm. This was described to Tacitus as a cloud towering into the sky, which modern models suggest reached an altitude of 33 kilometres (20 miles). Still known today as a Plinian eruption, this tall pumice and ash column produced deposits that were carried as far as the Ionian Sea, and Cassius Dio remarked that 'dust' from the eruption fell as far away as Syria and darkened the sky in Rome (66.22). Tree-ring data from Austria reveals a period of cooling temperatures between c. AD 75 and AD 93, the latter part of which may be related to the volcanic ejecta obscuring some of the sunlight reaching the Earth. At Pompeii, the fall of ash and pumice was heavy, collapsing buildings and burying people alive. One study has estimated the rate of fall at 15 centimetres (6 inches) per hour. By the next morning, as much as 3 metres (10 feet) of white and grey pumice and ash had buried the city: large amounts of this fall layer were found in Pompeii's *impluvia*, hollow openings in Roman houses that allowed rainwater to be collected.

The second part of the eruption consisted of several devastating surges and pyroclastic currents that Pliny saw as dark clouds and 'sheets of fire'. In several areas near Pompeii, such as the Pozzelle quarry, the pyroclastic currents have left deposits that include chunks of lava up to 3 metres (10 feet) thick. At Pompeii, the ground surges and the pyroclastic flows would have reached the city in about five minutes, dooming those who had not already fled. The sixth and largest surge, which Pliny saw as the 'black and dreadful cloud' that occurred at daybreak and sank to ground level, and that he then saw racing towards him and his mother as they fled from Misenum, proved devastating at Pompeii, destroying buildings and leaving a deposit of 1.8 metres (6 feet), littered with building fragments.

The burial of the UNESCO-listed Campanian settlements below Vesuvius allowed for a remarkable degree of preservation. Herculaneum was buried under a staggering 23 metres (75 feet) of surge and pyroclastic current deposits that instantly carbonised wood and, with temperatures in excess of 400–500°C (750–930°F), immolated 340 people and at least one horse sheltering in stone boathouses on the beach (Figure 10.11). At Pompeii, the pyroclastic current deposits are shallower, but are still nearly 2 metres (6.5 feet) deep in places, lie over nearly 3 metres (10 feet) of pumice, and were subsequently covered in nearly 1 metre (3.3 feet) of ash. Pompeii's

Figure 10.11 The Herculaneum boathouses with skeletons found *in situ*.

Source: Photograph by Norbert Nagel (CC BY-SA 3.0).

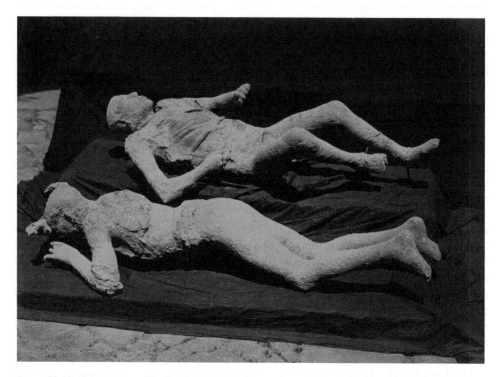

Figure 10.12 Plaster casts of bodies from Pompeii.

Source: Photograph by Giorgio Sommer; image provided by the Metropolitan Museum of Art (CC BY1.0).

grisly secrets were revealed in the 1860s when Giuseppe Fiorelli developed a way to create plaster casts of the bodies of people and animals whose form, outlines, and terrified expressions in death were delicately preserved above the initial pumice and ash layer in the fine-grained surge deposits (Figure 10.12). The ruins of Pompeii have also preserved wheel ruts in streets, scandalous graffiti in brothels, and breathtaking mosaics, frescoes, and artworks (Figure 10.13), many belonging to the Fourth (and final) Pompeian Style. At Oplontis, the so-called Villa of Poppaea (Oplontis Villa A) is thought to have belonged to Nero's wife, Poppaea Sabina, on the basis of a potsherd recording one of her freedmen.

Titus and Domitian

Titus became emperor in AD 79, following the death of Vespasian. He had been carefully prepared by his father: in AD 69 he was named *princeps iuventutis* as well as Caesar, a term that had come to denote a favoured successor. He enjoyed sole command of the Praetorian Guard from AD 71 (a constitutional oddity on two counts as he was a senator, not an equestrian, and the Guard was usually under a dual command), and he had been consul with his father seven times. He was granted *maius* imperium and the tribunician

Figure 10.13 Fresco from Pompeii, thought to represent Terentius Neo, a baker, and his wife.

Source: Photograph by Carole Raddato (CC BY SA 2.0).

powers. As emperor, Titus organised a quick relief effort to aid the stricken communities of Campania, and a year later he also attended swiftly to the aftermath of a catastrophic fire in Rome. Ever one for hyperbole, Suetonius regarded Titus as 'the delight and darling of the human race' (*Titus*, 1). During the Jewish Revolt, Titus had fallen in love with Agrippa II's sister, Berenice, and she had since joined him in Rome; yet Titus had little opportunity to enjoy her companionship or establish his rule. He died in AD 81, and was succeeded by his brother, Domitian. The Praetorian Guard received a handsome bonus, and the change in rulership was accepted by the senate and the people. In contrast to Titus, Domitian was inexperienced in both civilian and military matters, although he had been named Caesar and *princeps iuventutis* in AD 70. Vespasian was sufficiently concerned about Domitian's abilities that when the latter held the praetorship, Mucianus, Vespasian's lieutenant during the civil wars, was given the task of watching over him. Domitian held the consulship six times, but five of those were as suffect consul. Cassius Dio reported that Domitian was so jealous of the favour shown to Titus that he banned castration: Titus had a weakness for eunuchs (67.2).

Whereas Titus had refused to hear the hated *maiestas* trials and rid Rome of informers, Domitian took to them with alacrity. The Stoic philosopher Epictetus, one of Domitian's victims, noted in his *Discourses* (preserved by his pupil Arrian) that people were sent out specifically to entrap men with loose talk. 'A soldier sits by you in civilian clothes,' he related, 'and begins to speak ill of the emperor.' But this is a ruse, for when 'you are led to speak your own mind', you are 'arrested and imprisoned' (4.13.5). Tacitus, too, complained about informers (*Agricola*, 2). Juvenal addressed the issue with a fanciful story of a giant Atlantic turbot that spooked the fishermen: 'Who'd dare sell or buy such a thing when even the beaches / Were covered with spies?' (*Satires*, 4.47–48). On Domitian's watch, Vestal Virgins were buried alive; he impregnated his own niece; he clashed with the Stoics; and relations with the senate soured rapidly. Vespasian's rule had indicated a hardening of the imperial position, and he had famously told the senate that 'either his sons would succeed him or he would have no successor' (Suetonius, *Vespasian*, 25), but Domitian fractured the delicate balance between emperor and senate by declaring that he would be called 'Lord and god'. Eastern ideas, including the kissing of feet—a form of ritual obeisance known as proskynesis that had helped to splinter the relationship between Alexander the Great and his conservative Macedonian companions, centuries before—found their way into the Roman court. Domitian's lodgings also assumed an unseemly grandeur; Martial compared them to the pyramids and the ancient monuments of Memphis (*Epigrams*, 8.36). Domitian declared himself perpetual censor in AD 84, and insulted the senate by wearing triumphal robes to its meetings. Even though Tacitus acknowledged Domitian's patronage, which led to a suffect consulship in AD 97, it was this return to authoritarianism that so horrified him and contributed to his pessimistic and conservative outlook. This viewpoint tainted his assessment of Augustus and the Julio-Claudian emperors in the *Annals*, and in the *Agricola*, the opening chapters are a thinly veiled attack on Domitian's tyranny and his persecution of the Stoics. Tacitus also had a personal grudge against Domitian, since it was alleged that the emperor played a hand in Agricola's premature death at the age of 54; Cassius Dio was certain that Domitian had murdered him (66.20). Agricola had been a beacon of hope: 'Even under bad emperors', wrote Tacitus, 'men can be great' (*Agricola*, 42).

The overwhelmingly negative portraits of Domitian reflect not only actual instances of bad behaviour, but also a long tenure on the throne that presented ample opportunities for his biographers to search for and identify all sorts of failings in his early days. Suetonius, for instance, declared that Domitian spent his younger years 'in great poverty and infamy'; he spent a great deal of time alone, 'doing nothing but catching flies and stabbing them with a keenly-sharpened stylus' (*Domitian*, 1 & 3). Juvenal caustically referred to Domitian as 'that last of the Flavians mangling a dying world' (*Satires*, 4.38). There were also sycophantic poems of praise and reverence, including some of the verses by the acclaimed poet Statius (AD 45–96), one of which included a lengthy encomium on the equestrian statue of Domitian in the forum: 'What ponderous mass is that, magnified to twice the size by the giant / surmounting figure, stands as if with the Roman forum in its clasp? / Has the work dropped down completely from the sky?' (*Silvae*, 1).

Despite his negative portraits, Domitian, like his authoritarian predecessor Nero, was well liked by the Roman people, for whom he celebrated the Secular Games and threw lavish festivals; he also expanded the chariot races, creating two new teams, although they did not last. Domitian completed the Flavian Amphitheatre (and its attendant gladiatorial school), the Flavian Palace on the Palatine (the *Domus Augustana*), as well as the Temple of Vespasian and Titus. The Stadium of Domitian, built in the Campus Martius, now lies under the Piazza Navona, whose oval form traces that of the structure beneath (Figure 10.14).

Infrastructure in Italy also received imperial attention. In AD 95, work began on the via Domitiana, a route that improved transportation access to the base of the fleet at Misenum. Domitian also curried favour with the soldiers, raising their pay by 35 per cent. This was a wildly popular move since the extent to which soldiers could be impoverished by their jobs is laid bare by a Latin papyrus dated to AD 81, the very beginning of Domitian's reign. From the 247 ½ drachmas paid to a legionnaire, only 25 ½ were left after deductions for hay, food, boots and leggings, for the Saturnalia celebration 'in camp', and for clothing (*AH* §94). Domitian also won over the troops by leading campaigns against the Chatti in Germany (for which he took the title *Germanicus*) and against the Dacian king, Diurpaneus (later known as Decebalus, see below). The Dacian campaign, however, was of questionable success. The Dacians beheaded the governor of Moesia and destroyed the force under his command; in AD 86, the praetorian prefect Cornelius Fuscus lost his life and many of his troops, including most (if not all) of V Alaudae, on an ill-fated punitive expedition. In AD 88, the Romans finally inflicted a severe defeat on the Dacians at Tapae, but elements from nine legions were required to overcome the enemy. Moesia was divided into Upper and Lower Moesia, and six legions were assigned to this troubled region. Further efforts in Dacia ended in a negotiated peace that was more favourable to the Dacians than the Romans, and drew scorn from Domitian's detractors. During Domitian's reign, Roman troops also reached the Caspian Sea, where an officer from XII Fulminata left an inscription dedicated to Domitian at Gobustan, 70 kilometres (43 miles) from modern Baku in Azerbaijan—the most easterly Latin inscription ever found (Figure 10.15). Earlier, in AD 75, an inscription had recorded Roman involvement in fort repairs close to modern Tbilisi, in Georgia (*CIL* 3.6052). Ongoing conflicts in central Europe continued to inflict further pain, however: in 92, XXI Rapax—founded by Augustus—was annihilated in Pannonia.

With an attention to detail that bordered on obsession, Domitian oversaw a more efficient bureaucracy and significantly increased the silver content of the denarius, bolstering confidence in Roman coinage. Numerous inscriptions found in Italy and Spain attest to the effort that he made towards settling financial and land disputes fairly (e.g. *AH* §92 & §96), while others display concern for the wellbeing of provincial citizens, such as the letter to the people of Pisidian Antioch that accompanied the provision of relief during a famine in AD 91 or 92 (*AH* §107). Eventually, however, those closest to him tired of his behaviour, as a power struggle resulted in punitive actions against Stoics, Jews, and Christians, and a reign of terror that claimed the life of Nero's freedman, Epaphroditus, on the ludicrous charge that he had not made a sufficiently adequate effort to save Nero's life.

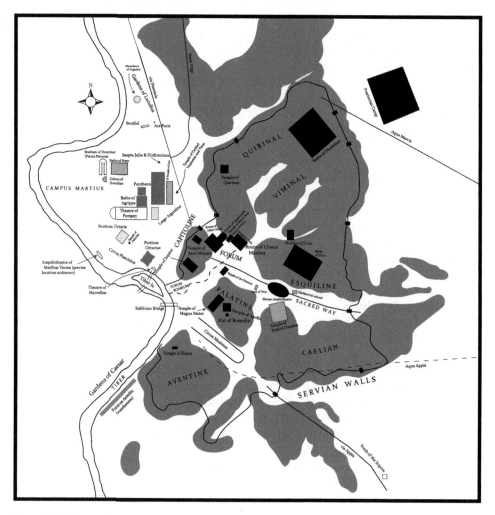

Figure 10.14 Rome during the Flavian period.

Source: Illustration by the author.

The persecution of Jews left an impression on Suetonius, who recalled a 90-year-old man being forced to bare himself before a procurator and a 'very crowded court' to see whether or not he was circumcised (*Domitian*, 12.2). Domitian had suppressed a revolt by the Chatti and the propraetorian legate of Upper Germany in AD 89/90, but in a conspiracy involving Domitia, his wife, and the Praetorian Guard, he was murdered in AD 96 and suffered a *damnatio memoriae*. The Cancelleria Reliefs, two marble panels found in an ancient rubbish pit in Rome in 1937 and 1939, reflect the effacement of Domitian's memory: Domitian's face in Frieze A was recarved to resemble Nerva—one of the conspirators, who had been chosen in advance as Domitian's successor.

Figure 10.15 The Latin inscription of XII Fulminata at Gobustan, Azerbaijan.

Source: Photograph by Grandmaster (CC BY-SA 3.0).

International trade, imperial ideology, and the Templum Pacis

The movement of goods sustained the prosperity of the empire: much of this trade was internal, transferring agricultural products and necessities such as pottery or worked metal to local markets throughout the Mediterranean. Large ports such as Carthage, Alexandria, Seleucia-in-Pieria, and Ostia shipped and received goods across the Mediterranean by boat, while rivers and canals allowed inland access to trading centres such as London and centres of consumption such as the legionary bases on the Rhine and the Danube. The grain shipments that supported the *annona* in Rome, drawn principally from Egypt and Africa, represented one of the largest movements of commodities in the ancient Mediterranean. Certain regions gained a reputation for the excellence of their products, such as wine from Italy or olive oil from the Levant (Figure 10.16).

The movement of goods can be measured through textual sources as well as by archaeological deposits, such as pottery. Ceramics were used for all kinds of purposes: fine red-slipped *terra sigillata* wares such as African Red Slip adorned dining tables; coarsely made cooking pans, jars, and mortars performed vital functions in the kitchen; and distinctive oblong amphorae were used to transport a wide variety of products, including

Figure 10.16 Mediterranean trade routes during the Roman era, together with some of the most widely traded goods.

Source: Illustration by the author.

wine, garum (fish sauce), nuts, olives, fruit, and olive oil. The distribution of coarsewares and finewares can reflect the export or import of these goods themselves, and amphorae—which often appear whole or in pieces in shipwrecks, or in gigantic rubbish dumbs such as the 35 metre (114 feet) high Monte Testaccio in Rome—are also a useful indication of the movement of the goods that they contained. Furthermore, since the design of finewares, coarsewares, and amphorae, and the materials used to make them, varied across different regions, trade routes can be reconstructed by tracking their movements. Complementing the routes that criss-crossed the Mediterranean was a web of external trade routes that linked Rome to the Indian Ocean and China. During the Flavian period, these external routes became more active than ever before. A consideration of these routes, and the way Vespasian exploited exotic products, provides an insight into Rome's position in global commercial and political networks outside the Mediterranean; it also offers an interesting way to consider Flavian political ideology.

The Roman empire was part of an ancient extensive 'globalised' trade network that linked it to India, Sri Lanka, China, Parthia, and Arabia. Commercial trade was closely intertwined with imperial power, via the acquisition of knowledge through expeditions and travelling merchants, and through control over valuable resources. This intersection was not new: Persian kings, Alexander the Great, the Ptolemies, Augustus, and even Nero, via his ill-fated Sudan expedition, had all sought control over natural resources and the wealth they offered, often resorting to commercially driven armed conflict in the process. Through eastern trade networks, Roman merchants, seamen, and travellers came into contact with old and rich civilisations. The Chinese, for instance, had diplomatic relations with Parthia, and became aware of the Roman empire, which Chinese texts call 'Da Qin'—'Greater China', a sort of Western counterweight to China—in the first century AD. Early Chinese sources looked favourably on the Romans as commercial partners, with the *Hou Hanshu* (the history of the Later Han dynasty, covering the period from AD 25 to 221) noting approvingly that the Romans only had a single price—that is, they were honest brokers (*Hou Hanshu*, §12). While one source suggests that Chinese ambassadors reached Augustus in tandem with the Indian embassy reported by Strabo (see Chapter 8), the first documented effort was made in AD 97 by the Chinese general Ban Chao, although his ambassador, Gan Ying, only got as far as Characene before his efforts were undone by the Parthians: their own diplomats spun the tale that the journey across the Persian Gulf might take up to three years, with death a constant peril from homesickness and sadness. The Parthians, of course, had any number of reasons to prevent Rome and China from establishing direct diplomatic and commercial ties, and later gifted the Chinese emperor wild animals from Characene in gratitude for his ambassador's lack of perseverance. Long-distance trade, and particularly the trade in rare and expensive goods, possessed an inevitable political dimension and was an important facet of imperial competition.

Following the victory over Antony and the acquisition of Egypt, the established routes from Egypt to the east came under Roman control. Roman maritime trade with India expanded rapidly, and Roman merchants entered a broader world that had long existed without them. The interconnectedness and antiquity of this world is illustrated by the *Thirteenth Rock Edict* of the ruler of the Indian Mauryan empire, Ashoka (268–232 BC). This text, inscribed in Greek and Aramaic at Alexandria-in-Arachosia (Kandahar), recorded embassies sent to the Hellenistic successors of Alexander the Great in 250 BC. Nevertheless, the Romans proved quick to adapt to the requirements of their new trading partners, and by the first century AD, Roman commercial exchange with eastern markets reached its peak via routes through the Red Sea, along the coast of Arabia, and across the Indian Ocean. Indeed, Strabo mentioned that while exploring Egypt with his friend Aelius Gallus in 26 BC, he had learned that 120 cargo ships left from the Red Sea port of Myos Hormos (Quseir al-Qadim) each year, bound for India, as against only a few under the Ptolemies (*Geography*, 2.5). Diplomatic contacts followed, including an embassy that reached Claudius from Sri Lanka and another from India sent to Trajan (Cassius Dio, 68.15).

The evidence for much of this comes from Pliny the Elder's encyclopaedic *Natural History*. Pliny took great interest in trade routes, in the origins of various spices and luxury goods, and in botany and the use of plants as a means to express political power. He recorded that frankincense, lemons, and cassia were already being grown experimentally in Italy as a way both to subvert their expensive importation and to display the wealth of their owners (*Natural History*, 12.7, 31, & 43). Roman artefacts, including worked metal and glass, Red Sea pearls, sculptures, imperial gold coins—particularly of the Julio-Claudian dynasty, but some as late as the sixth century—and amphorae containing all manner of goods, were sold across the Indian subcontinent. Examples of these items have been discovered throughout the region, from the port of Barbarikon in northern India to Limyrike (Malabar) in the south, and many examples of Roman coinage have come from interior and eastern central India. Elegant Roman glasswares of Egyptian origin of a first- or second-century date were found as part of a spectacular hoard of art at Bagram (Alexandria-in-the-Caucasus), and Roman worked metal, pottery, Campanian olive oil amphorae, gold, and glass have turned up on the eastern coast of India at Arikamedu. One of the most striking items found in India, in Tamilnadu, was a seated figure holding a thunderbolt, with ROMAE inscribed across the base of the statuette. Items from as far away as Vietnam, transhipped through Indian ports such as the great emporium of Muziris on the Limyrike, have turned up at the port of Berenike in Egypt, one of the main shipment points into the empire for Indian Ocean trade. Finds at Berenike also included pepper, sandalwood, coconut, and onyx, while archaeologists at Myos Hormos discovered pepper, coconut, amethyst, and rice. The vitality of these cultural and economic exchanges is further illustrated by the Peutinger Table—a medieval copy of a fourth-century Roman map, preserving a first-century view of the world—which located a Temple of Augustus at Muziris. Furthermore, one of the items recovered from Pompeii was the so-called Pompeii Lakshimi, a small Indian ivory figurine that may have come from eastern Afghanistan.

A number of Roman shipwrecks, including the first- or second-century vessel sunk off Abu Fendera, south of Berenike, and the first-century wreck at Fury Shoals, north of Berenike, have preserved stoppered amphorae containing wine and olive oil. These goods and other precious substances such as malabathrum (an aromatic plant similar to cinnamon), beryl, ivory, and topaz were exported and imported through the Red Sea and the Persian Gulf, via the oasis emporium of Palmyra, Omana (Ed-Dur in the United Arab Emirates) and the Parthian client of Characene. Inscriptions from Palmyra written by traders who plied the route from Palmyra to Characene reveal the close involvement of Palmyrene family firms with the maritime routes that led to India, facilitated by trading colonies of Palmyrenes or the appointment of Palmyrene officials at strategic points in the Parthian empire, such as Babylon, Vologesias (near Ctesiphon), and Tylos (Bahrain). A text from the Temple of Bel at Palmyra records a dedication made by the Palmyrene merchants resident at Seleucia (AD 19), while another (between AD 50 and 71) was made by the Palmyrene mercantile community at Spasinou Charax, the principal city of Characene. A text from Koptos, the inland customs clearing house that linked Myos Hormos and Berenike with Alexandria, recorded the 'Palmyrene Red Sea Ship Owners'. Ships sailed east with the monsoon in the summer, and returned west during the winter months (Figure 10.17).

A number of textual sources describe these ancient long-distance trade routes, popularly known as the 'Silk Roads'. This term was invented in the nineteenth century and is somewhat misleading, because silk was not consistently the main luxury product in demand in the Roman empire. Furthermore, the majority of long-distance trade during this period between east and west was moved by river and sea, not by land, and trade between Rome and China was carried out via intermediaries in Central Asia and India. One of the most important sources for Roman trade with the east is an anonymous first-century handbook of maritime navigation, the *Periplus of the Erythrean Sea* (the Red Sea and the Indian Ocean). The *Periplus*, written by a Graeco-Egyptian sailor, detailed the ports between the Red Sea and India, and the goods favoured by each. It offers a wide array of information about the movement of goods and intercultural exchange, recording the presence of coins in the market of Barygaza (Bharuch, in western India) 'engraved with inscriptions in Greek letters', and included the earliest reference to China ('Thinae') in classical sources, describing the passage of 'raw silk and silk yarn and silk cloth' from Bactria and onwards via the Ganges and the Indian Ocean (§47 & §64). Examples of Chinese silk have been found at Palmyra, and silk was processed and rewoven in the Roman empire before being exported back for sale in eastern markets. The roughly contemporary *Parthian Stations* of Isidore of Charax (Spasinou Charax) provided instructions for the long overland journey from Zeugma on the Euphrates to Arachosia, the area of southeastern Afghanistan that bordered the river Indus.

One of the most intriguing pieces of literary evidence for Rome's eastern trade is the double-sided second-century Muziris Papyrus from Egypt. It recorded, on one side, a contract between a merchant and a financier for a commercial trip from Muziris to Alexandria, detailing the payment arrangements for the Roman import duty—a painful 25 per cent, levied at Koptos. (The 25 per cent tax, known as the *tetarte*, was also levied at Antioch, Alexandria, Palmyra, and the eastern Red Sea port of Leuke Kome; the Koptos Tariff, dating from AD 90, yields further details on duties levied for goods and services between Koptos and the coastal ports). On the other side of the Muziris Papyrus were details of a ship called the *Hermapollon*, and its cargo—167 elephant tusks, spikenard (an aromatic), and a number of unspecified items. The papyrus related the generous loan terms that were afforded to the merchant, whose specialised sailing skills and knowledge of foreign markets made him a highly prized commodity in himself.

Other important Egyptian sources for long-distance trade include the Berenike ostraca and the Nicanor Archive. The Berenike ostraca, a collection of inscribed potsherds, include *laissez-passer* from customs agents in Koptos allowing merchants to move their goods through the customs barrier at Berenike. They provide a particularly valuable insight into outbound traffic, much of which was wine from Italy and southern Greece destined for export. The ostraca in the Nicanor Archive comprise receipts for the transportation, by camel, of goods between Koptos and Berenike and Myos Hormos. Koptos lay

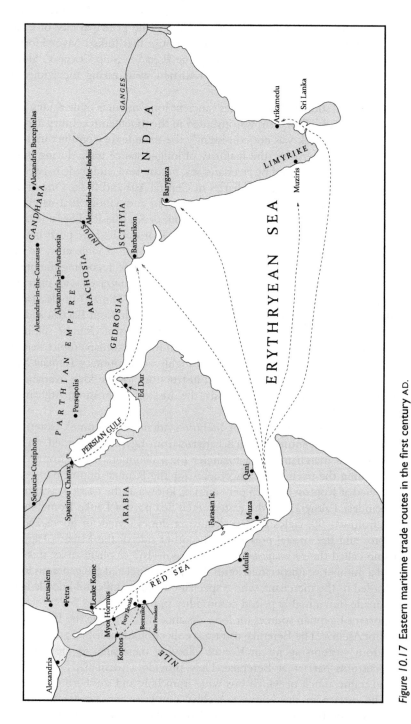

Figure 10.17 Eastern maritime trade routes in the first century AD.

Source: Illustration by the author.

174 kilometres (108 miles) from Myos Hormos and 392 kilometres (244 miles) from Berenike; the routes were studded by caravanserai (*praesidia*) and wells where travellers could rest in safety and draw water. The archive, covering the business run by Nicanor, his brothers, and his sons, dates from between 18 BC and AD 62, and includes references to the sorts of goods moving between the ports and Koptos: these included grain, wine, wood, barley, anise, and *pharmaka*, medicinal ingredients and chemicals for dyeing.

A range of evidence shows a certain degree of effort on the part of imperial authorities to safeguard the Red Sea trade routes. The ostraca, for instance, mention Roman naval officers—a *trierarchos* (trireme commander) and a *tesserarius liburnae* (commander of a galley)—as well as details of grain shipments destined for Roman military garrisons, all reflecting a Roman military commitment in the Red Sea. Other indications of military activity include an inscription from Koptos recording the construction of a bridge by troops of III Cyrenaica during the reign of Domitian (*CIL* 3.13580), the existence of a *praesidium* at Koptos with a cavalry *ala*, and a papyrus from Myos Hormos that mentioned a soldier serving on board a vessel named the *Hippocampus* ('Seahorse'). Elsewhere, a cache of inscribed amphorae dumped at Krokodilo, on the road between Myos Hormos and Koptos, has furnished evidence for running skirmishes between Roman troops and *barbaroi* in the desert in the early second century AD. Finally, an inscription from the Farasan Islands near the southern end of the Red Sea has revealed the presence of a unit from II Traiana Fortis, a legion raised by Trajan, dated to between AD 143 and AD 144; the same inscription also mentioned a prefect of the local port. Another text from the Farasan Islands, badly mutilated, recorded the abbreviations PR PR, *pro praetore*, suggesting the presence of a propraetorian legate in the region. This individual was connected with the VI FERR (possibly VI Ferrata) mentioned on the stone.

Outside the empire, Tamil sources from India recorded Roman ships unloading wine, gold, and fine pottery, and returning west, their holds filled with pepper. First-century Chinese sources, aware of the importance of Petra on international trade routes, also talked of the wealth of Syria and the abundance of gold and other precious items that were in demand for eastern markets. The outflows of Roman money were so immense that imperial coins influenced the designs of those in the Kushan empire, which arose after AD 30 in Gandhara, the old territory of the Indo-Greek Bactrian kingdom. Issues of Kujula Kadphises, the first of the Kushan rulers (c. AD 30–80), featured an obverse displaying a bust of Augustus and a senatorial curule chair on the reverse (Figure 10.18), while Huvishka, who ruled the Kushan empire between AD 150 and 180, produced gold coinage that resembled the aureus coins of Marcus Aurelius.

The cultural exchange facilitated by Roman trade with the east can also be measured through contemporary Kushan sculpture. Gandharan Buddhas bear a curious resemblance to Roman imperial portraiture, particularly of the second century. Narrative sculptures such as Trajan's Column (see below) are also believed to have influenced the reliefs that decorated contemporary Buddhist stupas. Some of the 20,000 sculptures recovered from Hadda (Tepe Shotor), south of Jalalabad, feature Mediterranean themes, such as the Trojan horse and Heracles, or depict Graeco-Roman wine amphorae.

Not everyone approved of the trade arriving from eastern markets. In Rome, Seneca bemoaned the perverting effects of luxurious items on the Roman upper class (*On the Happy Life*, 20), while Tiberius lamented the drain on Roman capital (Tacitus, *Annals*, 3.53). Both comments reflected contemporary concerns over a perceived trade deficit

Figure 10.18 Copper coin of Kujula Kadphises, minted in Taxila (Pakistan) between AD 50 and AD 90. Obverse: laureate head of Augustus; reverse: Kujula on a curule chair.

with the east, as well as the money to be earned through eastern trade. An indication of the fabulous sums at stake is provided by the Muziris Papyrus: the cargo of the *Hermapollon* was valued, *after* the import duty, at nearly seven million Athenian drachmas—many times the minimum wealth requirement to belong to the Roman senatorial order and nearly 1 per cent of the province of Egypt's annual GNP at the time. While most cargoes were sold on from Koptos through Alexandria, the archive of one Apollonios (AD 115/17) recorded his agent purchasing expensive purple dyes and military equipment in the markets at Koptos, along with spices and silver-chased household goods that had been imported from the east.

In Rome, the vitality of the Indian Ocean trade found political expression in the Templum Pacis. Little of the structure survives today, and what is known about its layout stems from its inclusion on the later third-century Marble Plan. One of the Plan's fragments shows rectangular structures that have been interpreted as the gardens that adorned the Templum Pacis complex, and it has been argued that these gardens were a 'colonial' project, whereby the exotic flora of the east were brought to Rome to be grown and exhibited as a statement of imperial power and ideology. Gardens have long been used to demonstrate imperial might: Kew Gardens in London, for instance, with its exotic botanical collections gathered from the colonies, proved the wealth and the long reach of the British Empire to the British public. In Flavian Rome, a spice market was constructed adjacent to the Templum Pacis, where indulgent items such as pepper could be purchased. The market allowed for the regulation of prices and taxation—Vespasian was extremely conscious of revenue sources, raising taxes throughout the empire and even taxing urinals. The market thus provided a final way for the emperor to control the sale and distribution of luxury products to Rome's wealthy citizens. This was particularly important for pepper: Pliny complained about its taste, but noted that it suffered from poor imitations and was easily cut with lesser substances ('Alexandrian mustard'!), ripping off the consumer and the imperial coffers in the process (*Natural History*, 12.14). Vespasian also dedicated 'chaplets of cinnamon in embossed gold' in the Templum Pacis, and Pliny noted that Vespasian was the first to make such an exotic and expensive offering (*Natural History*, 12.42). Together with the spice market, the Templum Pacis, which harkened back to the

Ara Pacis and its extensive use of botanical imagery to underscore a new era of peace, prosperity, and wealth, served to underscore Rome's mastery over the empire and control of both natural resources and the exotic miscellany of goods from the east.

Apex of empire

Nerva (AD 96–98) and Trajan (AD 98–117)

Nerva's brief tenure of the imperial throne was unexceptional. He had served as consul in AD 71 and AD 90, and was an elder statesman who had helped unmask the perpetrators of the Pisonian conspiracy during the reign of Nero. On his accession, Nerva paid a donative to the Praetorian Guard and gave money to the citizens of Rome. Coins minted during his brief tenure featured reassuring slogans such as LIBERTAS PVBLICA and AEQVITAS AVGVSTI, with the latter celebrating a return of justice and equality. *Maiestas* trials ended, and there was a purge of slaves and freedmen. Cassius Dio also suggested that a measure of religious freedom returned, remarking that it was forbidden to accuse anyone of practising Judaism (67.1), and Nerva also relaxed the collection of the Jewish tax (Figure 10.19).

Nerva consulted a council of advisors before making decisions, and he spent vast amounts of money on restoring unfairly confiscated property. The imperial finances were strained, but funds were replenished by melting down gold and silver statues of Domitian. One of the few building projects carried out by Nerva was the completion of the Forum of Domitian, subsequently known as the Forum of Nerva, positioned between the Templum Pacis and the Forum of Augustus. In Rome, Nerva appointed Julius Frontinus to oversee the water supply; Frontinus, famous for his work on military tactics, the *Stratagems*, also wrote the well-regarded treatise *On Aqueducts*.

In AD 97, Nerva faced a plot among the Praetorian Guard. The plot fizzled out, but Nerva reacted by adopting Trajan, an experienced and popular soldier. Trajan was the son of the well-liked Marcus Ulpius Traianus, Vespasian's old comrade in arms, who had served

Figure 10.19 Bronze sestertius minted in Rome in AD 96. The reverse shows a palm tree and the legend FISCI IVDAICI CALVMNIA SVBLATA. The meaning of this legend, literally 'deception over the Jewish tax has been abolished', reflects Nerva's policy of only assessing the tax on those who declared *themselves* to be Jews, and not those denounced by others.

as propraetorian legate of Syria between AD 74 and 77, and then as proconsul of Asia from AD 79 to 80. Trajan himself was born in Italica in 53. His mother was Marcia, Titus's sister-in-law, and Trajan would be the first emperor born and raised in the provinces—another reflection of the growing integration of provincials into Roman political life. Trajan's career amply prepared him for imperial duties: he had spent ten years as a military tribune under his father; he had commanded X Fretensis; and he subsequently commanded VII Gemina in Hispania Tarraconensis. In AD 91, he held the ordinary consulship, and in 97 he was appointed propraetorian legate of Upper Germany. There, his young great-nephew Hadrian, who had become his ward, joined him and served as a military tribune in XXII Primigenia. Trajan's wealth of military experience, his provincial origins, and his senatorial connections through his father made him acceptable to the senate, the people, the provinces, and the Praetorian Guard.

On Nerva's death in AD 98, Trajan had already been designated Caesar by the senate and granted tribunician power and proconsular imperium, yet he remained absent from Rome for nearly nine months on a military inspection tour in Pannonia and Moesia. The degree to which the various stakeholders in Rome consented to his succession is reflected by the peace in the city during this period. Trajan was quick to demand the retirement of the troublesome praetorian prefect who had challenged Nerva, but there were no pretenders in Trajan's absence, nor was there significant agitation from senators or equestrians. When he finally came to Rome in AD 99 for his *adventus*—the solemn ritual of an emperor entering the city—he caused a stir with his humility, approaching the city on foot and in civilian clothes. Able to charm civilians and senators, he was also popular with his troops. During the later invasion of Parthia, he joined the legionnaires for a dip in the Euphrates, and marched beside them as they trudged across Mesopotamia.

Trajan in government

Trajan came to Rome with his wife, Plotina, a woman greatly admired by Cassius Dio and who became the Augusta in AD 105. Trajan's sister, Marciana, also occupied a prominent place in society, and was granted the title of Augusta at about the same time—the first sibling of an emperor to receive this honour; in death, Marciana was deified (Figure 10.20).

Trajan held the consulship in AD 98, 100, and 101, and used his time in Rome to develop and fund public welfare schemes, including the *alimenta*, a scheme (possibly begun by Nerva) that benefited children through a modest monthly stipend. The *alimenta* was a popular subject for contemporary sculpture, and was illustrated on the Plutei of Trajan, carved reliefs that once stood in the Roman forum. In one relief, Trajan sits in the forum, accompanied by the personification of Italia carrying a baby. The welfare program was also illustrated on the Arch of Beneventum (see below).

Trajan was courteous to the senate and encouraged new blood from the provinces, and he also increased the number of equestrian procurators in government. His generosity to the people was underscored by periodic grants of cash (in AD 99, 102, and 107), and by a release from an unpopular tax that was traditionally levied on the accession of a new emperor. Trajan expanded public grain distributions, supporting the bakers' guild, and provided free games, funded by the loot taken from the wars that he later fought in Dacia and Parthia. In one series of games, 10,000 gladiators battled each other in a festival lasting for 127 days. Trajan also renovated the Circus Maximus, which had been badly

Figure 10.20 Silver denarius minted in Rome in AD 114, after the death of Trajan's sister, Marciana. The obverse contains a detailed portrait of Marciana with the title DIVA AVGVSTA MARCIANA. The eagle on the reverse signifies her apotheosis with the legend CONSECRATIO, 'deification'.

damaged by fire during the reign of Domitian, and he began detailed renovations of the Pantheon. In response to the various issues plaguing Italian and provincial communities, Trajan appointed curators, officials who were able to cut through financial red tape at the municipal level. In Italy, he also carried out renovation works at Portus, near Ostia, to improve the movement of grain shipments from Egypt and Africa. The striking hexagonal 'Lake of Trajan' adjacent to Rome's Fiumicino Airport dates from this period.

An important measure of Trajan's interest in governance is provided by his correspondence with Pliny the Younger. Pliny had served as the curator of the 'banks of the Tiber' and was suffect consul in AD 100, before being dispatched by Trajan to govern Bithynia and Pontus as propraetorian legate in 109. Trajan and Pliny had a good relationship, and even before he became governor, Pliny was already exchanging frequent letters with the emperor. In one despatch, for instance, Pliny asked Trajan to allow a friend of his to join the senatorial order (*Letters*, 10.4), while in another, he asked for Roman citizenship for a doctor who had saved him from a serious malady, a request that Trajan quickly granted (10.5 & 10.6). On occasion, Trajan was less forthcoming: once in office, Pliny wrote asking for land surveyors; find your own, the emperor replied (10.18). The correspondence is wide ranging and at times staggeringly banal, but it reveals an efficient, friendly, and responsive emperor interested in the minutiae of correct provincial governance. Trajan approved the construction of a new public bath-house (10.24), corresponded with Pliny over corruption amongst building contractors in Nicomedia (10.38), discussed moving a temple of Magna Mater (10.50), and addressed the validity of permits for the *cursus publicus*, the imperial postal and courier system (10.45). Legal precedent dating as far back as Pompey caused Pliny problems (10.80 & 10.114), as did the thorny task of draining a lake. 'I can see, my dear Pliny,' wrote the emperor, 'that you are applying all your energy and intelligence to your lake' (10.61).

In stark contrast to the letters of Cicero, Pliny's correspondence shows the extent to which the power balance had shifted in Roman politics. Cicero saw himself as a participant in government, capable of influencing policy; Pliny instead addressed Trajan as *dominus*, lord, and there is no doubt that decision making lay with the emperor. While Trajan was occasionally irritable at being asked this or that, he also clearly understood his own role, and he was also the first emperor to employ 'correctors', another reflection of his intense managerial style. These were intrusive officials with imperium who he appointed to regulate and oversee matters in the eastern provinces. Another reflection of his approach is found in his suspicion of associations—which, he thought, could quickly become subversive: in one letter, for instance, he denied Pliny's request for a company of firemen in Nicomedia. 'If people assemble for a common purpose,' Trajan wrote, 'they soon turn into a political club' (*Letters*, 10.33–34). Trajan's sense of public duty evidently impressed Pliny, who continuously strived to find equitable solutions to problems that respected local customs and past precedent. He was also keenly aware of Rome's privileged place in the world. In a letter to a friend who was shortly to leave for his post as corrector in Achaea, Pliny urged him to show deference to Greek culture and customs, and to understand that much of what was great in Rome had come from Greece (*Letters*, 8.24). Pliny left his hometown of Como a public bath and funds for its upkeep when he died, apparently in office, in c. 113. The accompanying inscription recorded a long life in government service (*AH* §200).

Much of Pliny's writings appear rather obsequious to a modern audience. His *Panegyric in Praise of Trajan*, penned in AD 100 to thank the emperor for his suffect consulship, took a particularly sycophantic tone: 'You have heard us curse a wicked prince,' Pliny read to the senate, 'now hear us praise a good one.' Yet Pliny regarded Trajan as a law-abiding emperor who listened to his counsellors and the senate, and he was not alone in holding such a positive opinion. Tacitus also thought highly of both Nerva and Trajan, noting that 'Nerva harmonised the old discord between autocracy and freedom', while 'day by day Trajan is enhancing the happiness of our times' (*Agricola*, 3). Dio Chrysostom's Stoically influenced *Discourses on Royalty* addressed Trajan as the 'most noble prince', and conceived of the emperor as a man who ruled with the consent of the gods. He was, Dio Chrysostom continued, 'kindlier to his subjects than a loving father' (*Third Discourse*, 5). Later authorities such as Cassius Dio and Aurelius Victor thought Trajan one of the best emperors in Roman history. 'It would be difficult to find a more distinguished man than he whether in civil or in military affairs,' Aurelius Victor claimed in the fourth century; the emperor was 'fair, merciful, extremely patient, and loyal to his friends' (*On the Caesars*, 13). Centuries later, Machiavelli provided a similarly positive view of Trajan, ranking him favourably alongside Titus, Nerva, Hadrian, Antoninus Pius, and Marcus Aurelius (*Discourses on Livy*, 1.10).

The type of ruler portrayed by Pliny and Dio Chrysostom represented the development, in the post-Flavian era, of the Augustan model: the *paterfamilias* of the Roman people, ruling through a concord with the divine and providing ample examples of *virtus* and *pietas*. Trajan was later known as *optimus princeps*, 'the best *princeps*', a Jupiter-esque legend that soon appeared on Trajanic coinage following his victory in Dacia (Figure 10.21). The implicit connection between Jupiter and Trajan was expressed on the Arch of Trajan at Beneventum, dedicated in AD 114, where the emperor appeared in the presence of Jupiter Feretrius. Images of Jupiter and other gods appeared frequently on Trajan's coinage. This so-called Jovian style of rule identified the emperor with the Capitoline Triad more closely than ever before, a development that inevitably strengthened the imperial cult and the authority of the emperor.

Figure 10.21 Gold aureus minted in Rome in AD 107. Note the reverse with the legend SPQR OPTIMO PRINCIPI.

One of the most important exchanges of letters between Pliny and Trajan concerned the growing visibility of Christians in the Roman commonwealth. Pliny was not sure what to make of them, except that if they were non-citizens and confirmed three times that they were Christians, he would have them executed for 'their stubbornness and unshakeable obstinacy'. When Roman citizens were encountered professing the faith, Pliny opted to send them to Rome for trial, while Christians who recanted were encouraged to make offerings to a statue of Trajan in the courthouse; if they passed the test, they lived. Pliny was especially confused when he found that Christians took oaths 'not for any criminal purpose, but to abstain from theft, robbery, and adultery'. Like Trajan's suspicions about the firemen of Nicomedia, however, these oaths and the shared purpose of the Christians he interviewed seemed to Pliny too much like dissident political activity. After torturing two deaconesses for good measure, Pliny concluded that Christianity was nothing but 'a degenerate sort of cult'. Eventually, Pliny involved Trajan because of the sheer numbers of people ending up on trial after being denounced, and because of his concerns to restore the correct relationship with the gods: there was plenty of sacrificial meat on sale, he said, but it was hard to find people to use it (*Letters*, 10.96). In reply, however, Trajan urged moderation. The emperor forbade Pliny from engaging in any kind of persecution; furthermore, he declared that anonymous accusations were not to stand. Such accusations recalled the climate of terror surrounding *maiestas* trials, and this, Trajan wrote, would be 'quite out of keeping with the spirit of our age' (10.97).

In the provinces, Trajan founded colonies, including Colonia Marciana Ulpia Traiana Thamugadi (Timgad, in Algeria), named for his sister. The key military base of Vetera received colonial status in AD 98/99, when it was renamed Colonia Ulpia Traiana. Trajan lavished attention on his native Spain; the imposing bridge over the Tagus river at Alcántara, today heavily restored, was originally built in AD 105. In Egypt, the emperor enlarged an existing canal to create a link between the Red Sea and the Nile. The canal met the Nile at Babylon (not to be confused with Mesopotamian Babylon), where the imposing ruins of the Trajanic-era fortress of Babylon still stand in Old Cairo. Another important monument in Egypt linked with Trajan is at the Dendera Temple complex, north of Luxor. A small

Figure 10.22 The emperor Trajan at Dendera.

Source: Photograph by Aidan McRae Thomson (CC BY-2.0).

mammisi (chapel) there features reliefs of Trajan, depicted as the pharaoh, sacrificing to the Egyptian deities Hathor and Ra, the sun god (Figure 10.22). A number of Roman emperors were commemorated in this way, stretching back to Augustus. The Temple of Isis at Philae had also received benefactions from Augustus, Tiberius, Claudius, and Nero, and at Philae a temple known as Trajan's Kiosk (or simply the 'Roman Kiosk') features a relief of Trajan in the interior.

Trajan's Dacian wars

Two wars were fought with the Dacian king, Decebalus, in AD 101–02 and 105–06. The wars were motivated by a traditional concern for *gloria* on the part of the emperor, as well as by the lingering concern over the Dacian threat to Moesia that had arisen during the reign of Domitian. Trajan cancelled the unfavourable treaty made by Domitian, under which Decebalus received a subsidy; war soon followed. The preparations for the first campaign included the challenging engineering task of constructing a road projecting out over the river in the region of the Iron Gates, a gorge on the Danube. Troops from IV Flavia and VII Claudia Pia Fidelis proudly recorded their participation on a Latin inscription found in a cave nearby (*AH* §112b), and an inscription known as the

Figure 10.23 The Tabula Traiana in 1930.

Source: Anonymous photograph for the Museum of Science and Technology in Belgrade (CC BY-SA 3.0).

Tabula Traiana recorded that Trajan 'cut down mountains, erected the projecting arms, and constructed this road' (*AH* §112a; Figure 10.23). Fighting in the tough terrain was accomplished with the assistance of surveyors, and a remarkable record preserves the account of one Balbus, who was called upon to calculate the width of rivers and the height of mountains that Trajan wished to capture, and to lay out plans for camps and fortresses on the march (*AH* §113).

During the first conflict, Decebalus was cowed and accepted a new alliance with the Romans. Consolidating his early victory, Trajan ordered a stone bridge constructed over the river, east of the Iron Gates, spanning a distance of over 1 kilometre (0.6 miles), guarded by a fortress at nearby Drobeta. The task was carried out by Trajan's talented architect, Apollodorus of Damascus. By AD 105, relations with an increasingly bellicose Decebalus had broken down, and a new conflict began. In heavy fighting involving the newly raised XXX Ulpia as well as II Adiutrix and IV Flavia Felix, Trajan eventually defeated the Dacian army outside the walls of Sarmizegetusa. Decebalus was run to ground by Roman horsemen, and he committed suicide. The Latin inscription of a cavalry trooper found at Philippi, Tiberius Claudius Maximus, proudly recorded how he took the king's head to the emperor (*AH* §117). Trajan took the title DACICVS in celebration of his victory (Figure 10.24). Trajan set up a trophy at Municipium Tropaeum Tropaensium (Adamclisi, in south-eastern Romania), where veterans of the war were settled. Dedicated to Mars Ultor, the trophy stood on top of a nine-stepped platform and was decorated with images of victorious Roman soldiers (Figure 10.25).

Figure 10.24 Bronze sestertius minted in Rome in AD 109/10. The dejected figure on the reverse is a Dacian, adjacent to a trophy.

Aside from the military victory, and the peace and security it brought to the Danube frontier, reinforced by the establishment of colonies in Moesia, Trajan's conquest provided an astonishing windfall for the Roman treasury. Dacia was rich in gold, and this production could now be diverted to Rome under the watchful eye of an imperial procurator; Illyrian miners were brought into Dacia to tap the rich veins at Alburnus Maior, leaving their thoughts, letters, and prayers on the dozens of wax tablets found there. XIII Gemina and IV Flavia Felix were garrisoned in the new Roman imperial province of Dacia, and I Adiutrix joined them for a while before being returned to Brigetio (Hungarian Komárom) in Upper Pannonia, the western part of Pannonia that had been carved off in AD 103. II Adiutrix was dispatched to Aquincum (Budapest) in Lower Pannonia, where it remained for centuries. Dacia's capital became the new colony of Colonia Ulpia Traiana Dacica Augusta Sarmizegetusa. Over 100,000 slaves were sent to Rome, where they were put to work on Trajan's ambitious building projects. Largely designed by Apollodorus, these included the massive Forum of Trajan, with its Greek and Roman libraries, a triumphal arch, an equestrian statue of Trajan, the Baths of Trajan, the Basilica Ulpia, and Trajan's Market. Some of these elements may have been embellished by Hadrian after Trajan's unexpected death, and it has been argued that the most famous commemorative monument, Trajan's Column, only received its famous carved relief sculptures recording the Dacian wars at Hadrian's later instigation. The record was created in ascending spiral bands 1–1.2 metres (3–4 feet) high around the 38 metre (125 feet) structure. Trajan's Column was featured on contemporary coinage (Figure 10.26) and was popularly believed to have held Trajan's ashes on his death. It became a tourist attraction almost immediately, thanks to its internal staircase and fenced viewing platform at the summit that afforded visitors scenic views of Trajan's reimagined Rome. In the sixteenth century, Pope Sixtus V erected a statue of St Peter at the Column's summit. This ongoing religious use, like that of the Pantheon (below), ensured the Column's survival; with the exception of the remains of the market and the Basilica, the monuments created with Dacia's conquered wealth have largely disappeared (Figure 10.27).

Figure 10.25 One of the metopes from the trophy at Adamclisi, showing a Roman legionnaire and a Dacian armed with the fearsome hooked falx.

Source: Photograph by Carole Raddato (CC BY-SA 2.0).

The images on Trajan's Column depicted Roman troops on the march, in action, crossing rivers, and building camps. Trajan is featured over 50 times—addressing the soldiers, speaking with embassies, dealing with prisoners—and the death of Decebalus was vividly portrayed. The Column was an important piece of military propaganda celebrating Trajan's *virtus* and the strength of Roman arms, and provided a visual companion to the emperor's

Figure 10.26 Silver denarius struck in Rome in AD 113/14, illustrating Trajan's Column on the reverse.

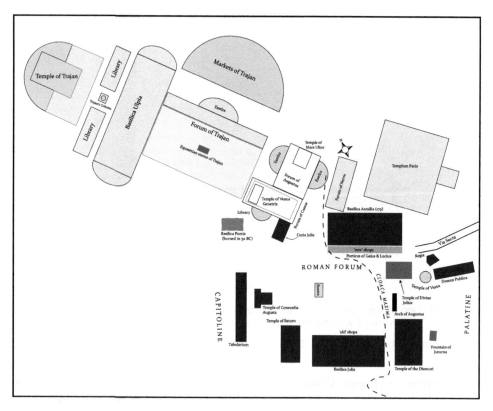

Figure 10.27 The imperial forum during the reign of Trajan.

Source: Illustration by the author.

Figure 10.28 Detail of the eastern side of Trajan's Column. On the left of the top panel, legionnaires
   attack using the *testudo* formation, revealing oblong shields and segmented armour; in the
   two panels below, a fortification is built; at the bottom, Trajan addresses his troops.

Source: Photograph by Matthias Kabel (CC BY-SA 3.0).

lost account of the wars, the *Dacica*. The Column also provides a glimpse of contemporary
equipment: troops are shown with the characteristic oblong shields and the *lorica segmentata*,
and military standards are also represented in meticulous detail (Figure 10.28).

At least one of Trajan's inner circle of counselors, Licinius Sura, a Spaniard and
former governor of Lower Germany, was depicted in the reliefs, and it is thought
that one of the bearded men appearing in Trajan's company is Hadrian. Trajan's close
friends also included Cornelius Palma (below) and Lusius Quietus. Quietus is particularly interesting: a Berber from North Africa, he had been made an equestrian under
Domitian and a senator under Trajan. He earned a prominent position as a commander
of Berber cavalry during the Dacian war (Figure 10.29) and went on to play a key role
in Trajan's war against Parthia.

Figure 10.29 Berber cavalry on Trajan's Column.

Source: Photograph by Matthias Kabel (CC BY-SA 3.0).

The annexation of Nabataea

In AD 106, Cornelius Palma, the propraetorian legate of Syria, oversaw the annexation of the Nabataean kingdom, which became the imperial province of Arabia under a propraetorian legate. By AD 107, Claudius Severus had been appointed as the first governor and by 127 a census had been taken. From its prime position on the trade routes that led into the Arabian Peninsula, Nabataea was wealthy, and the kingdom had profited from the stable rule of its kings Aretas IV (9 BC–AD 41), Malichos II (AD 41–70), and Rabbel II (AD 70–106). The kingdom stretched from Bosra (Bostra) in the north to the less well-known settlement at Hegra (modern Madain Salih, near al-Ula), which was positioned close to a key pass through the mountains of the Hijaz. The buildings of both cities illustrate the ways in which the architectural Hellenistic lingua franca had permeated the kingdom. At Petra, this is particularly visible in the famous structures of al-Khazneh ('The Treasury') and al-Dayr ('The Monastery') (Figures 10.30 and 10.31). Petra remained important well into late antiquity, and one legate of Arabia, Sextius Florentinus, was sufficiently enamoured of the city to make it his final resting place.

The policy decisions that led to the annexation are not well understood. Trajan nurtured an ambition to campaign in the east, so the annexation may have been tied to security concerns. It could also have been motivated by economic considerations, given Petra's links to international trade routes. Whatever the case, the annexation was largely bloodless. Whereas Caesennius Paetus had invaded Commagene on a pretext, there is little evidence of fighting between Roman and Nabataean forces, and coinage displayed the legend ARABIA ADQVISITA—Arabia 'acquired' (Figure 10.32).

The province of Arabia incorporated the Decapolis cities of Philadelphia (Amman) and Gerasa (Jerash). A military road, the via Nova Traiana—'Trajan's New Road'—linked the port of Ayla (Aqaba) to Nova Traiana Bostra, following a Nabataean caravan route; the road eased the movement of troops and was also designed for the *cursus publicus*. III Cyrenaica was garrisoned at Bostra in a camp whose outline is still visible on aerial photographs. Bostra's Nabataean features, such as the tetrapylon, built from the black basalt of the region,

Figure 10.30 Al-Khazneh at Petra.

Source: Photograph by the author.

were retained, but elsewhere in the city its layout was partially redeveloped and adorned with marble structures typically found in Hellenistic cities: a hippodrome, baths, a massive and well-preserved theatre, and a nymphaeum, an architectural feature sacred to water nymphs. The establishment of the via Nova was marked by milestones, many of which have been discovered (e.g. *AH* §124), and precipitated yet another commemorative coin

Figure 10.31 Al-Dayr at Petra.

Source: Photograph by the author.

Figure 10.32 Silver denarius minted at Rome in AD 112 or 113. The reverse features the personification of Arabia, standing, holding a branch and cinnamon, with a camel to the left; the legend reads ARAB ADQ.

issue, although it is possible that these coins celebrate an offshoot of the via Appia, also known as the via Traiana (Figure 10.33).

The development of the via Nova encouraged changes in urban planning throughout the former kingdom. Both Petra (which vied with Bostra for pre-eminence in Arabia) and Philadelphia underwent significant changes; modern Amman is still graced with a

Figure 10.33 Silver denarius minted in Rome in AD 113/14; the reverse shows the personification of the via Traiana, with a wheel balanced on her right knee.

magnificent theatre, forum, and odeon, and the road that runs past these monuments is built over the old east–west Roman decumanus.

The Nabataean army was incorporated as auxiliaries, but they continued to use Nabataean terms for 'cavalry trooper' and 'centurion' in their new role. A diploma from AD 139 recorded the discharge of soldiers from cohorts of 'Petraeans', and another from 156 recorded the 'Cohors Ulpia Petraeorum'. Troops from III Cyrenaica also found their way to the south. Excavations at Hegra have uncovered an inscription that recorded later work on the city's walls with the assistance of two centurions from the legion. A Roman centurion named Flavius Dionysius left an inscription at Dumata (Jawf) in Saudi Arabia, and military graffiti in the desert near Hegra recorded the presence of a North African auxiliary cavalry unit. Throughout the province, the via Nova was progressively supplemented by forts, watchtowers, and subsidiary roads (Figure 10.34).

A glimpse of the transition to Roman rule in Arabia from the perspective of one of its inhabitants is provided by the Babatha Archive, a group of documents found in the Cave of Letters in Nahal Hever (Wadi al-Khabat) near Ein Gedi in the Judaean desert. The documents, written in Greek and Aramaic, belonged to a woman named Babatha from Mahoza on the south-eastern end of the Dead Sea, and covered the period between AD 94 and 132. The documents recorded, for instance, the assessment of Babatha's property in the census of Arabia in AD 127, her water usage rights, land ownership, and civil litigation with a Roman woman named Julia Crispina. The legal texts, in particular, show how cases were heard by the propraetorian legate at various centres, such as Petra or Rabbath-Moab, which represented an assize 'circuit', the *conventus*, where the governor travelled throughout the province to specific places to settle legal cases. The papyri also discussed the role of Roman military officers in providing low interest loans, and described speculation on the prices of crops. One of the last documents is a Greek marriage contract dated both by the consular year in Rome as well as by the number of years that had elapsed since the annexation of Arabia, a way of reckoning time known as the 'era of Bostra'. The final letter placed Babatha in the midst of the Bar Kochba war (see below), and close to the letters a large number of skeletons was found. Above the Cave of Letters archaeologists

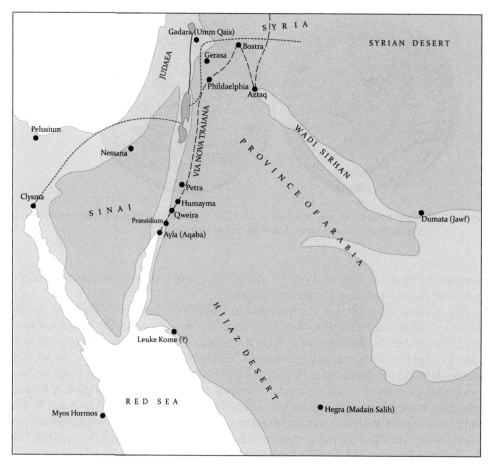

Figure 10.34 The Roman province of Arabia in the first century AD.

Source: Illustration by the author.

discovered a Roman military installation capable of holding between 80 and 100 troops; it is thus presumed that Babatha, and those with her, were besieged and killed in the war.

Another ground-level perspective of daily life in the new province and its adjacent territory is provided by the thousands of examples of desert graffiti, largely written between the first century BC and the fourth century AD, in a region stretching from southern Syria into northern Saudi Arabia. These texts were written in Greek, Latin, and Safaitic, a dialect of Ancient North Arabian. Many of these texts are personal, while some have political content and many demonstrate awareness of various towns, forts, and individuals. One Greek inscription from northern Jordan, for instance, was written by a certain Abchoros (a barber) and Diomedes (a musician), grumbling about being pressed into military service and sent to guard a remote position in the middle of nowhere. The text begins with a gloomy 'life is worth nothing' (*AEBI* §7.22). Numerous texts refer to *qsr*, 'Caesar' and *rm*, 'Rome' and one text mentions Germanicus. Others refer to the deaths of individuals such as Agrippa II or to local military successes and failures. The texts illustrate the degree to which members of the settled communities, such as Abchoros and Diomedes, ended up doing various jobs in the desert. The texts also mention officials, *strategoi*, Roman officers coordinating with troops raised from nomadic communities. As such, these graffiti offer a valuable correction to the ancient ethnographic stereotype of barbarous nomads and civilised settlers—a favourite subject of Greek and Roman writers from Aristotle onwards.

Trajan in the east

In AD 110, the Parthian king Pacorus II died. He was succeeded by his son, Vologases III (AD 110–47), but an ongoing insurrection led by a pretender, Osroes I, caused instability in the western part of the Parthian empire. Osroes appointed his own candidate, Parthamasires, to the Armenian throne, violating the long-standing arrangements between Rome and Parthia, and Trajan responded with an invasion of Armenia and then the Parthian empire: he was the first emperor to campaign in the east since the time of Augustus (Figure 10.35).

The possible motives for the war have long been debated. There may have been a desire to strengthen Rome's friendship with Palmyra, which would help to gain better control over the trade routes that moved goods through the Persian Gulf. Marcus Cornelius Fronto, an aristocrat from Cirta in Numidia who educated the future emperors Marcus Aurelius and Lucius Verus, noted that Trajan restructured customs collection for horse and camel traffic along the Euphrates and Tigris rivers in the aftermath of the conflict (*Principia Historiae*, 17.4). Certainly the invasion led to good relations between Trajan and the king of Characene, a key trading partner of Palmyra, and Palmyra itself had undergone important political developments at the end of the first century. The city had acquired a Hellenistic government made up of a 'council' (Palmyrene Aramaic BWL, from the Greek *boule*) and 'assembly' (DMS, from *demos*), and the city was shortly to undergo a period of extensive monumental construction funded by its immense wealth. Palmyra also played an important strategic role, as its troops safeguarded the movement of caravan traffic. By Trajan's time, Palmyrene units were stationed on the Euphrates downriver from Dura-Europos at the islands of Anatha, Telbis, and Bijan, and a unit of Palmyrene auxiliary cavalry, the Ala I Ulpia Dromedarium Palmyrenorum, is thought to have taken part in Trajan's expedition. Trajan's desire for *gloria* should also not be discounted. No Roman leader, as yet, had met the Parthians in battle on their territory and won a truly resounding victory. Such a conquest would realise Trajan's desire to match the exploits of his hero, Alexander the Great.

In AD 113, Trajan, with Hadrian in tow, led his troops into Armenia from Satala and Melitene, his northern flank secured by the friendly kings of Bosporus and Caucasian Iberia. In Armenia, he removed and executed Parthamasires. Trajan's army for the multi-year campaign was colossal, and consisted of II Traiana Fortis (raised specifically for the expedition), III Cyrenaica, VI Ferrata, X Fretensis, XII Fulminata, XVI Flavia Firma, and XV Apollinaris, together with auxiliaries and cavalry. Personnel from some European units, such as I Adiutrix from Brigetio in Pannonia, and XI Claudia from Durostorum (Silistra) in Lower Moesia, were also attested to have taken part in the campaign, as were naval officers from the fleets at Misenum and Ravenna, who left graffiti at Seleucia-in-Pieria.

Armenia was quickly subjugated, and much of its territory became a new Roman province in AD 114, managed by the legate of Cappadocia. Elated by his victory, Trajan pressed

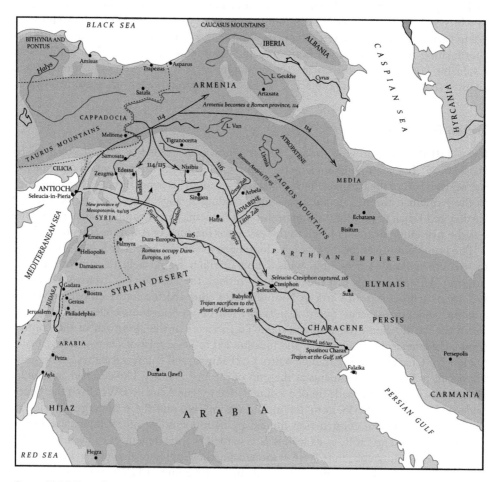

Figure 10.35 Trajan's eastern campaigns.

Source: Illustration by the author.

on. The king of Parthia's client Osrhoene, Abgar VII (AD 109–116) succumbed to the inevitable, and during this phase of the campaign the important cities of Nisibis and Singara also fell to the Romans. A remarkable Greek funerary inscription from Nisibis of a prince from Caucasian Iberia, fighting 'as a companion to the leader of the Italians', recorded the presence of Roman clients in Trajan's entourage (*AH* §131). With the fall of Osrhoene and Nisibis, Mesopotamia became a province in AD 115; the personification of Mesopotamia, knee bent in surrender, was portrayed on the Arch of Beneventum. Trajan was saluted *imperator*, and in AD 115, Roman forces pushed over the Tigris into Adiabene, which may have become the ephemeral province of Assyria, reported by Festus (*Breviarium*, 20). After spending winter in quarters in Antioch, in AD 116 Trajan divided his forces, with one arm heading down the Euphrates and another following the Tigris. The Euphrates force captured the Parthian fortress of Dura-Europos, where a triumphal arch honouring Trajan

Figure 10.36 The triumphal arch of Trajan at Dura-Europos.

Source: Excavation photograph 1933/34 (Dura-g101-b~1). Yale University Art Gallery, Dura-Europos Collection.

was erected by III Cyrenaica some distance outside the city's walls, probably at the location of a clash between Roman and Parthian troops. Simon James has identified the remains of three Roman camps west and north-west of Dura, at least one of which likely dates to the time of Trajan and the easternmost of which was apparently reused by the Persians in the 250s. The Romans did not stay at Dura, however, and after they left, an annoyed citizen wrote down his angry thoughts on a stone tablet: the Romans had taken away the doors from a shrine, which he was forced to replace at his own expense (*AH* §137). This tablet and the remains of the arch were discovered in the 1930s (Figure 10.36, and see the brief discussion of Dura in Chapter 12).

In AD 116, after Characene declared its friendship with the Romans, Trajan moved down the Tigris with a fleet and became the first Roman emperor to capture the Parthian capital of Seleucia-Ctesiphon. The Parthians were beaten, Osroes was on the run, and Trajan, who took the title *Parthicus Maximus*, was jubilant (Figure 10.37). Roman legions were stationed at Singara and possibly at Rhesaina (Ras al-Ain in northeastern Syria). It is even thought that a Roman unit was briefly based near modern Mosul, which may have been the site known as *Ad Flumen Tigrem* on the Peutinger Table; however, the evidence for this, a stone bearing the image of an eagle and the Latin legend *oc[c]uli legionum*, 'the eyes of the legions', has long since vanished. A more reliable piece of evidence is a Trajanic milestone discovered in the pass at Karsi, which provided access from Nisibis across Jabal

Figure 10.37 Gold aureus minted in Rome in AD 116 on the occasion of Trajan's victory; the obverse demonstrates Trajan's new titles, DAC[ICVS] and PARTHIC[V]S; the reverse shows the familiar image of a beaten captive, with PARTHIACAPTA in the exergue.

Sinjar to Singara, on the south side of the mountain, instituting a Roman presence at this key location that would last until the fourth century. Trajan sent a victory dispatch to the senate, a record of which was recorded in the calendar from Ostia known as the *fasti Ostienses* (*AH* §133).

It was at this point that Cassius Dio imagined Trajan staring out across the Persian Gulf, watching trading vessels leave for India, and imagining himself as a new Alexander (Chapter 1). He left a statue of himself at the head of the Gulf, according to the sixth-century historian Jordanes (*Romana*, 268); Jordanes' near-contemporary, John of Ephesus, recorded that during the reign of the Persian king Khusrau I (AD 531–79), the Persians toppled the statue in a fit of anger (*Ecclesiastical History*, 6.23). Not long afterwards, Trajan visited the ruins of Babylon. 'He had gone there because its fame,' wrote Cassius Dio, 'though he saw nothing but mounds of stones and ruins to justify this'. Trajan paused long enough to visit the room where Alexander was thought to have died, and there he made a sacrifice to the spirit of the dead conqueror (68.30).

The reality of Trajan's campaigns was less inspiring. While Trajan successfully recruited allies on the march, he was spurned by others. Sporaces, the phylarch ('chief') of Anthemusia (Batnae/Sarug), and Mannus, a phylarch of Singara, both rejected Trajan's overtures. Following the capture of Seleucia-Ctesiphon, Edessa and Nisibis joined a revolt led by Sanatruces, the nephew of Osroes, and the Parthian client of Hatra followed. Trajan's capable general, Lusius Quietus, suppressed the rebellion in Mesopotamia, while Trajan defeated Sanatruces and installed an obedient client, Parthamaspates, on the Parthian throne. Hatra proved a far tougher prospect. The city lay beyond the edge of the steppe lands in Mesopotamia, over 100 kilometres (62 miles) from modern Mosul. Hatra had emerged as a desert settlement around an important shrine to the sun god Maren (Shamash), and developed a cosmopolitan character reflected in the multiplicity of shrines and temples there and in its extensive links with trade routes connecting the city to Palmyra, Hit, Singara, Nisibis, Seleucia-Ctesiphon, and Characene. Trajan attempted to besiege the city, but found that there was little water, food, or fodder for his animals. The heat proved stupefying to the legionnaires, who were tormented by swarms of flies. Trajan narrowly

Figure 10.38 The cardo at Apamea.

Source: Photograph by the author.

avoided serious injury when he rode too close to the skilled Hatrene archers manning the walls and was recognised. Realising the futility of further action, he abandoned Hatra and moved on.

Other problems plagued Trajan on campaign. In December AD 115, as the army was regrouping at Antioch and preparing for the approaching campaigning season, a catastrophic earthquake hit the city. Trajan and Hadrian survived unscathed, but many others were less fortunate. The earthquake also flattened nearby Apamea, but the city was rebuilt, largely through local philanthropy. The result was Apamea's spectacular 2 kilometre (1.2 miles) colonnaded north–south cardo, one of the most stunning architectural survivals from antiquity (Figure 10.38). As rebuilding progressed throughout the second century, the city was provided with a nymphaeum, the largest theatre ever constructed in the Roman empire, and the elaborate Temple of Zeus Belos. Unfortunately, like many other Syrian sites, Apamea has practically been obliterated by looting during the Syrian civil war.

In AD 115, further calamity struck in the shape of a widespread Jewish rebellion known as the Diaspora Revolt. Like the revolt of AD 66, this event was foreshadowed by apocalyptic and prophetical texts; in addition to *Sibylline Oracle* 4 (Chapter 9), a text known as the *Greek Apocalypse of Baruch* was circulating before AD 115. The revolt was also, once again, characterised by vicious internecine violence between Jews and their Greek neighbours: Jews in Cyrenaica, Cyprus, and Egypt joined the revolt, with Cyrenaican Jews attacking settlements in the Egyptian countryside and burning pagan temples. The Roman response on Cyprus is known from a sole inscription commemorating a tribune of VII Claudia Pia Fidelis, who took part in it (*AE* 1992: 1689), while a text from AD 117 recorded a senior officer of III Cyrenaica, deputed by Trajan to colonise Cyrene with 3,000 military veterans in the aftermath of the revolt (*SEG* 17.584). Serious repair work was needed after the war was over: a milestone commemorated road repairs for a route from Cyrene that had been 'thrown up and destroyed' during the war (*AE* 1951: 208) and both the Temple of Hecate and the Basilica at Cyrene needed to be rebuilt after being set ablaze (*AE* 1929: 9 & *AE* 1974.672). In Egypt, a papyrus from Hermopolis recorded terrified villagers taking up arms to defend themselves against 'unholy Jews' (a term used pejoratively by several different sources) and waiting in desperation for a Roman legion to arrive (*AH* §129e). Their calls for help were eventually answered with the transfer of III Cyrenaica from Bostra to Alexandria. The repression in Alexandria was particularly brutal: the synagogue was destroyed and the Jewish population killed. Later Jewish sources blamed 'Trajan the wicked' for the slaughter of Alexandrian Jewry (Jerusalem Talmud Sukkah 5:1, 55b). The revolt eventually spread as far as Mesopotamia, until it was quashed by Lusius Quietus in AD 117.

On the Danube, disturbances in Moesia and Dacia necessitated a transfer of men and troops from Syria after Trajan's friend and veteran military commander, Quadratus Bassus, died campaigning against the Sarmatians, including the fearsome Roxolani. Bassus was replaced in Dacia by Hadrian's friend, Quintus Marcius Turbo, while Hadrian became legate in Syria and Lusius Quietus legate in Judaea. In the aftermath of the Diaspora Revolt, despite little unrest existing in Judaea, Quietus increased the military garrison of his province by temporarily posting II Traiana Fortis there and adding VI Ferrata, which moved to a semi-permanent home at Caparcotna in Galilee. Peace had returned, and leaving Hadrian at Antioch, Trajan set off for home. He died suddenly in Cilicia on the journey, at the age of 64.

Retrenchment: Hadrian, AD 117–38

'Hadrian,' wrote Cassius Dio, 'was a pleasant man to meet and he possessed a certain charm.' Dio praised the emperor, noting his preference for dignity over flattery, the care he took in the management of affairs, and his restraint from warfare (69.3 & 69.5–6). The poet Annius Florus had a different opinion, being on the receiving end of Hadrian's caustic wit. Remarking one day in verse that 'I don't want to be a Caesar / Stroll about among the Britons / Lurk about among the ... / And endure Scythian winters', Hadrian responded in kind. 'I don't want to be a Florus / Stroll about among the taverns / Lurk about among the cook shops / And endure the round fat insects'. This witty repartee was reported by the *Historia Augusta* (*Hadrian*, 16). The *Historia* (henceforth *HA*) is a series of Latin biographies dating to the fourth century, whose multiple authorship and sources have long aroused controversy. Hadrian did show genuine compassion on occasion, however, and, like Trajan, cared particularly for the provinces. When the Nile flood failed to reach expectations in AD 136, he temporarily cancelled taxes in Egypt (*AH* §156).

Figure 10.39 Gold aureus featuring images of Hadrian (obverse) and the divine Trajan (reverse), minted in Rome in AD 117.

Hadrian was born in either Italica or Rome in AD 76, to an émigré Italian family with roots in Italica. His career was rich in military and administrative experience: in AD 95 he served as a military tribune with II Adiutrix, then in 96 with V Macedonica. As noted earlier, he was with Trajan in Upper Germany in 97 as a tribune with XXII Primigenia. In AD 100 he was married to Vibia Sabina, the daughter of Trajan's niece, and he continued to serve with Trajan, first as his quaestor in 101 and then in command of I Minervia in Dacia (105/06). In 108, he was the propraetorian legate of Lower Pannonia and suffect consul, in 112, he served in Athens and, following the Parthian war, he was appointed propraetorian legate of Syria in 117. Hadrian was a firm favourite, but he was only adopted after Trajan died; in antiquity, it was suspected that Plotina had secured his candidacy. A second key individual in the succession was Publius Acilius Attianus, another member of the Italica aristocracy who had been appointed alongside Trajan as Hadrian's co-guardian, and who then became Trajan's praetorian prefect.

Hadrian remained in the east while Trajan's ashes returned from Antioch to Rome with Plotina, and after appointing a replacement to govern Syria, he returned to Europe, where he minted coinage commemorating his accession and Trajan's divinity (Figure 10.39). Early in Hadrian's reign, four prominent men were executed, including Lusius Quietus and Cornelius Palma. The four had all held the consulship and were executed without trial, even though the senate had begun proceedings against them for treason. Even before these extra-judicial killings, relations with the senate were problematic. Hadrian's early acts had included pulling out of much of Rome's hard-won territory in the east and in eastern Europe (below). This was a slight to Trajan that could not be offset by Hadrian's prompt deification of his predecessor, and his refusal of a Parthian triumph and the title of *pater patriae*. Hadrian redressed some of the damage by embarking on a program of largesse, boosting the *alimenta*, a program in which Sabina was also involved, remitting the imperial accession tax, cancelling debts, and providing cash to senators and the people of Rome. In AD 119, the biographer Suetonius joined Hadrian's government as his *ab epistulis* to manage his Latin correspondence. Later, Attianus—who Hadrian publicly blamed for the deaths of Cornelius Palma and his colleagues—was forced out as praetorian prefect; he was replaced by Quintus Marcius Turbo, who had gained equestrian status after discharge through a policy that promoted former centurions as a reward for honourable service.

In Rome, Hadrian applied his legalistic mind to the institutions of the principate. He increased the number of curators to assist municipal governments, and he strengthened the informal council of friends who advised the emperor, bringing in legal experts for the first time and making the council a formal part of government. New positions were created for equestrians, such as a legal official who looked after taxation matters. He also created a board of four judges, the *quattuorviri consulares*, to manage Italy's division into four separate provinces. (This move was brief, as Hadrian's successor, Antoninus Pius, rescinded it.) Most importantly, Hadrian organised an updated set of legal procedures relating to the praetorship. The *Edict of the Praetor* was codified by Salvius Julianus, a legal expert, and brought permanency to a field of Roman law that had been open to modification and interpretation by individual praetors and jurists. The *Edict* covered questions of citizenship, slavery, clothing, and military matters. It is often pointed out that Hadrian sought additional protections for slaves—making it mandatory to obtain legal permission before putting a slave to death, for instance—yet it would be erroneous to see the lot of slaves improving in any meaningful way. There is plentiful epigraphic evidence for the widespread continuation of the practice during this period and the misery it caused (see *AH* §178a–j & 179).

Hadrian was an unabashed Hellenophile and had earned the disparaging Catonian nickname *Graeculus*, 'little Greek', for his love of Greece. He enjoyed engaging in pursuits popular in Greece, such as the hunt, although Hadrian also used the hunt to display his *virtus*. He also enjoyed people declaiming about his marital exploits: a poem written by Pankrates, *The Lion Hunt*, celebrated a heroic hunting expedition against a 'manslaying lion' in the Libyan desert while Hadrian was visiting Egypt. Hadrian was also an intellectual, and he later dedicated the Athenaeum in Rome, a place for scholars and poets to meet and recite their work. He fancied himself an architect, designing a Temple of Venus and Roma to be built out of expensive Proconnesian marble adjacent to the Colosseum. The temple was dedicated in 135, but Apollodorus of Damascus reportedly disliked the temple and mocked it; he was driven out of Rome and executed (Cassius Dio, 69.4). Hadrian's other building projects included a basilica dedicated to the deified Plotina after her death in 123 (at Nemausus), a Temple of Trajan in Rome (125), and a restored Basilica of Neptune, also in Rome. Hadrian also completed the lengthy overhaul of the Pantheon begun by Trajan. The columns of the Pantheon's portico were quarried in single blocks (rather than being assembled from individual drums) from Aswan and the remote Mons Claudianus quarry in Egypt, and transported to Rome by sea—with each column likely weighing as much as 80 tons (72,574 kilograms or 160,000 pounds), this was an expensive and challenging endeavour. (Those for the Temple of Trajan were some 20 tons (18,143 kilograms or 40,000 pounds) heavier.) The Pantheon as it stands now, including the inscription honouring Agrippa, is very much a second-century structure; it owes its survival to its later reuse as a church. Remarkably, the Pantheon's unreinforced concrete dome, cleverly lightened through coffering of the interior, remains one of the largest ever built. The Pantheon's monumental portico faced the Mausoleum of Augustus on the same axis, and inside the visitor would have found images of the gods and the emperors of Rome. In a clear imitation of the Augustan Mausoleum—which, Cassius Dio mentioned (69.23), was 'full'—Hadrian built himself an ornate circular Mausoleum, now the Castel Sant'Angelo, connected to the Campus Martius by a bridge. As the Mausoleum of Augustus had become the family tomb of the Julio-Claudians, so now Hadrian's Mausoleum received the ashes of the imperial families down to the early third century.

Hadrian's best known building effort was his elaborate villa complex at Tibur (Tivoli). With this project, he followed the efforts of his predecessor, Trajan, who had constructed a number of villas in the countryside, but Hadrian's effort was on a much grander scale. Taking nearly 20 years to build, Hadrian's residence featured 900 public and private rooms spread out over 40 hectares (100 acres)—a city in miniature, with staff residences, elaborate dining rooms, meeting areas, gardens, and features of Graeco-Roman urban life such as baths and a nymphaeum. The complex was linked by road to Rome, 30 kilometres (18.5 miles) away to the west. The architecture of the villa structures was designed to impress: one of the most famous elements was the Canal, a water feature lined with statues that ended with an outdoor dining room, the Scenic Tricinlinum, located within an open, half-domed awning. Another feature, the Maritime Theatre, was a private suite surrounded by a colonnade and moat. Sculpture and artwork abounded, including copies of famous Greek works such as the Caryatids from the Erechtheion in Athens and statues depicting mythical beasts from Egypt. Different parts of the complex were named for specific places in the empire that held significance for Hadrian. These included Canopus in Egypt, close to where his youthful lover, Antinous, drowned in the Nile in strange circumstances that resembled the legendary death of Osiris. Antinous was further commemorated with a shrine, the Antinoeion, bordered by palm trees evoking a bucolic Egyptian landscape. The villa also featured sophisticated mosaics and waves of opus sectile, a method of decoration involving materials such as marble or porphyry recessed into pavements or walls to form attractive patterns.

Hadrian's travels

In an era of small government before the enormous bureaucratisation of the imperial administration that took place in the fourth century, Trajan had showed his protégé that it was not necessary to rule from Rome. Hadrian travelled extensively, and on his travels 'he personally viewed and investigated absolutely everything' (Cassius Dio, 69.9). He spent 121 in Germany, 122 in Britain, and 123 in Spain. He was in Anatolia and Greece in 124, after which he spent several years in Italy. On the move again in 128, he set off for North Africa, and from there he travelled to Syria and Judaea, and thence to Egypt, where he restored a funerary monument commemorating Pompey. By 135 he was back in Rome, where he died in 138.

Hadrian's voyages throughout the empire were marked by cultural events and by honours granted to cities and communities that were of special interest to him, and coin issues celebrated his journeys (Figure 10.40). His visits also provided provincials from all over the Mediterranean world, in particular the Greek eastern provinces, the rare opportunity to see an emperor in the flesh. They also allowed community worthies to meet him, as well as to petition him and his officials (who travelled with him) on all kinds of civic and legal issues. Hadrian's visits coincided with a flurry of dedicatory and building activity at places across the empire, as well as the induction of Greek elites into Hadrian's inner circle and thence into government careers. For instance, Herodes Atticus, a sophist (itinerant teacher) from Athens whose father was a friend of Hadrian, was granted access to the senatorial order and made one of Hadrian's *amici*, his council of friends. Hadrian

Figure 10.40 Commemorative gold aureus from the so-called 'travel series'. The reverse shows Egypt personified.

showed favour to individual settlements through grants of municipal or colonial status, so the important legionary base of Carnuntum in Upper Pannonia became a municipium, as did Augusta Vindelicorum in Raetia, while at Italica in Spain—which he refused to visit— a temple dedicated to Trajan together with new baths and an amphitheatre—still standing, and one of the biggest in the ancient Mediterranean—were constructed. In Africa, Utica became a colony and Carthage received an upgrade to its aging water supply infrastructure. In Asia, Hadrian heaped attention on Cyzicus on the Sea of Marmara, which he honoured as a *neokoros*—a provincial centre for the imperial cult. Pergamum and Smyrna, which already held this honour, received it again—a rare mark of prestige. The famous Library of Celsus in Ephesus, a combination of mausoleum and library, was dedicated to Hadrian towards the end of his reign (Ephesus, too, would be honoured with a double grant of *neokoros*). Gerasa, which had already honoured Trajan with regular games (*SEG* 7.825), erected an enormous arch to commemorate Hadrian's visit, and around this period its famous oval plaza was built (Figure 10.41), together with the hippodrome, an additional theatre, and the massive Sanctuary of Artemis. The provision of extra performance space at Gerasa reflected the ongoing importance of performances to Graeco-Roman city life. Through prayer and ritual that preceded performances, and via the public display of images of the imperial family, theatrical shows and events at the hippodrome also reinforced the imperial cult.

Several cities, such as Petra and Palmyra, took the epithet 'Hadriana/e' in Hadrian's honour. The earliest parts of Palmyra's Great Colonnade date to this period (Figure 10.42). Another structure dating from this period was the Temple of Baalshamin. Destroyed by ISIS in 2015, the temple was classical in design, with a pronaos decorated with Corinthian capitals (Figure 10.43). A dedication inscription from the Temple of Baalshamin provides a glimpse into the cosmopolitan nature of second-century Palmyra. Dating to AD 131, the Greek and Palmyrene text records that Male, son of Yarhai, dedicated the monument when 'the god Hadrian' visited the city. In the Palmyrene text, Male identified himself as a GRMTWS—a literal translation of the Greek word for secretary, *grammateus* (*CIS* 2.3959). Palmyra's famous Tariff Inscription, a Greek/Palmyrene

Figure 10.41 The oval plaza and cardo at Jerash (ancient Gerasa).

Source: Photograph by the author.

bilingual dating to 137, recorded Hadrian's visit to 'Hadriana Palmyra and the Wells of Aelius Caesar', and detailed import duties on all manner of goods being sold on to Roman markets by Palmyrene merchants (*AH* §158).

Hadrian admired Egypt and its religious cults, and he instituted a new one to commemorate his deceased lover, Antinous, earning ire from Roman conservatives who viewed his romantic love affair with the youth as a little 'too Greek'. The Pincio Obelisk, standing on the Pincian Hill in north-eastern Rome, features a hieroglyphic inscription that commemorated the cult of Antinous, which had been assimilated with Osiris as Osirantinous. Coins were minted for Antinous, and a frenzy of sculptural and artistic activity commemorated the youth (see below, Figures 10.52 and 10.53). Hadrian also founded a new city, Antinoopolis, connected by the new via Hadriana to Berenike, and inaugurated a festival, the Antinoeia. An inscription from the via Hadriana reassured travellers that the 'wells are always full', and that the route was studded with military garrisons and secure *praesidia* along the way (*AH* §157). Antinoopolis flourished, and its cemeteries later furnished many of the Fayum mummy portraits, exquisitely painted representations of the dead Graeco-Egyptian elite that were placed over their faces in burial. The images replicated contemporary imperial fashions and hairstyles, such as the tightly coiffed hair of the empress Sabina. Undimmed by time and preserved by the dry desert climate, the portraits remain hauntingly lifelike (Figure 10.44).

Figure 10.42 The Great Colonnade of Palmyra at sunset.

Source: Photograph by the author.

Figure 10.43 The pronaos of the Temple of Baalshamin at Palmyra.

Source: Photograph by the author.

While in Egypt in AD 130, Sabina joined the hundreds who had already left their mark on the side of the Colossi of Memnon at Luxor, twin statues of Amenhotep III, a pharaoh of Egypt's Eighteenth Dynasty. The statues were a famous ancient tourist attraction, as they 'sang' at sunrise as the heat warmed the stone. In Greek, Sabina scratched into the stone, 'Sabina Augusta / wife of the emperor Caesar / Hadrian / heard Memnon twice during the first hour' (Figure 10.45). In all, eight messages were left by Hadrian's entourage, including several poems by Julia Balbilla, an aristocratic woman from the old Commagenian royal family.

One of Hadrian's favourite city stops was in Athens; the city's citizens honoured him with the appointment of archon, or chief magistrate. Hadrian's love of Greece inspired Pausanias, from Lydia in Asia Minor, to write his epic *Description of Greece* in the 120s. In Athens, Hadrian was inducted into the Eleusinian Mysteries; he also bestowed a triumphal arch upon the city and set about finishing the Olympeion, a vast temple complex dedicated to Olympian Zeus that had been started in the sixth century BC. His travels in Greece included a stint as master of the Dionysiac Games, as well as visits to Nikopolis,

Figure 10.44 Funerary portrait from Fayum of a young boy.

Source: Photograph by Anagoria (CC BY-SA 3.0).

the Caesarian colony at Corinth, and the oracle at Delphi. He showed a deep concern for Greece's legendary heroes, 'restoring' the tombs of Ajax, the famous Athenian Alcibiades, and the Theban hero Epaminondas, who had earned immortal fame for defeating the Spartan army at Leuktra in 371 BC. Back in Athens once again in AD 132, Hadrian

Figure 10.45 Graffiti on the Colossi of Memnon, with Sabina's text indicated.

Source: Photograph by Carole Raddato (CC BY-SA 2.0).

dedicated the Olympeion and inaugurated the Attic Panhellenion, an association of cities based in Athens that drew representatives from across the Greek world. On the inscription inaugurating the Olympeion, Hadrian declared himself to be a new founder of Athens—upstaging its legendary hero, Theseus.

In the provinces, Hadrian adopted a conservative and introspective policy that preferred diplomacy to war. He had pulled the Roman army out of Armenia, Mesopotamia, and Assyria on his accession, with Armenia returning to the arrangements made during the reign of Nero. Parthamaspates was unceremoniously shifted to the throne of Osrhoene, which had since become a Roman client, leaving Parthia to Vologases and his rivals. In Europe, Hadrian faced immediate problems stemming from the death of Quadratus Bassus, but these were settled through the legateship of Turbo and by negotiations with Rasparaganus, the king of the Roxolani. The king was awarded Roman citizenship and took the name Publius Aelius Rasparaganus; fragments of his funerary inscription, written in Latin, were later discovered at Pula in Croatia. Hadrian shrewdly attended to Rome's clients, recognising their importance. A Latin inscription from Panticapaeum, dated to 133, records the gratitude of the Bosporan king Rhoimetalkes for 'being enrolled among the friends' of Rome (*AH* §154c).

Hadrian reduced the size of Lower Moesia, giving back some of the land taken from the Roxolani but leaving V Macedonica at Troesmis (Iglita), located on an imposing plateau overlooking the Danube. Between 120 and 123, he divided Dacia into three sections: Upper Dacia, Lower Dacia, and Dacia Porolissensis (Figure 10.46), and partially dismantled Trajan's bridge to provide an additional measure of protection.

On the Danube, Hadrian drilled his troops, including a unit of Batavian auxiliaries, who particularly impressed him when they swam the broad river in full armour (Cassius Dio, 69.9). A now-vanished inscription from 121 by a man calling himself 'first in bravery among one thousand Batavians' (i.e. among a milliary cohort) also recorded this athletic feat (*AH* §145). Hadrian's concern for the army and the defence of the empire was also expressed in a series of inscriptions from Lambaesis in Numidia, the base of III Augusta. Hadrian gave five speeches to the troops in 128, which they later proudly inscribed at their camp: the text recorded praise lavished by Hadrian on cavalry *alae* from Commagene and Pannonia, noting their skill at arms and the fluency of their riding. Hadrian praised their legate, the ease with which they accomplished physically draining construction tasks, and the maintenance of their equipment and animals (*AH* §148). Part of the troops' excellence was based in their discipline, a key preoccupation for Hadrian as he toured military units, encouraged their training, and shared their privations, even eating 'bacon, cheese, and vinegar' with the legionnaires (*HA Hadrian*, 10). The goddess Disciplina acquired a cult in the second century, and coins from the period featured a reverse with Hadrian leading troops with their standards, accompanied by the legend DISCIPLINA AVG; Arrian, in his *Taktika*, also praised Hadrian's training regimen and elevated it as a standard that Hadrian's successors aspired to reach.

One of Hadrian's most famous legacies is a series of fixed barriers in Europe and Africa. There were barriers in eastern Pontus, as well as on the Rhine and Danube; there, the barrier took the form of a wooden fence studded with watchtowers; 550 kilometres (340 miles) of this network is now a UNESCO World Heritage Site. Another was Hadrian's Wall in Britain, also a UNESCO World Heritage Site, and the third was a series of barriers in North Africa. The purpose of these barriers has aroused considerable debate. Linked with static fortifications such as legionary bases, they clearly performed a military purpose, but their primary function was never to permanently separate Roman territory from foreign lands; instead, they were designed to control the movement of people. This function is particularly visible in the third group of barriers, the *clausurae* in Africa. These comprised combinations of stone walls, ditches, and embankments, probably begun in 122. Four separate lines of the *clausurae* have been identified; they typically were built at the intersection of the steppe and desert in southern Algeria and Tunisia, lying across transhumance corridors and limiting traffic to individual passes or roads (Figure 10.47). The *clausurae* walls were no higher than 3 metres (10 feet) and no large garrisons were stationed along their lengths. For the tax-conscious Romans, the *clausurae* offered a means to encourage people to move between monitored points where they and their goods could be monitored and taxed.

The most famous of Hadrian's barrier projects was Hadrian's Wall, built by troops from II Augusta, VI Victrix (transferred from Vetera), and XX Valeria Victrix. Aside from its function as a control barrier, designed to funnel people and goods to heavily fortified passages where they could be controlled and inspected, Hadrian's Wall was an imposing piece of military engineering and the project has been linked to unrest in Britain between

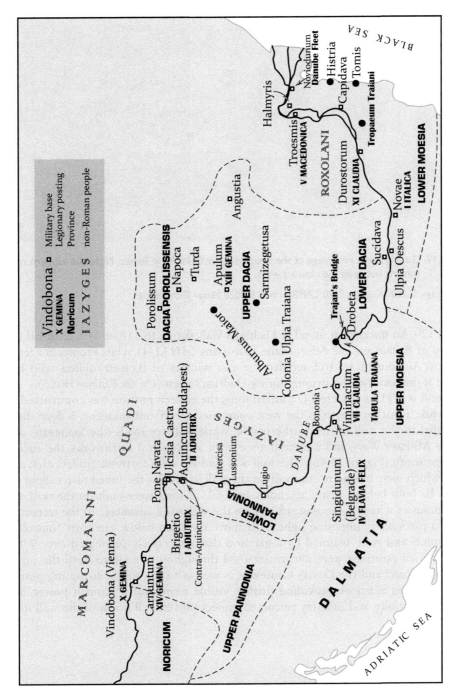

Figure 10.46 The frontiers of Moesia, Pannonia, and Dacia during the reign of Hadrian, with known legionary deployments.

Source: Illustration by the author.

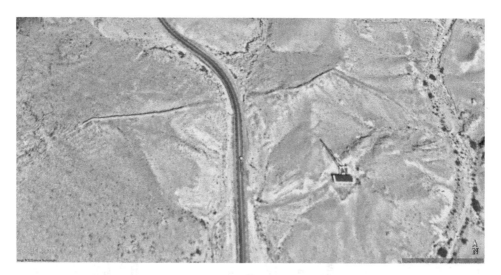

Figure 10.47 Google Earth Pro image of the *clausura* at Bir Oum Ali in Tunisia. Note the modern road running between the *clausura* walls.

Source: Image © 2020 Google, 2020 CNES/Airbus, & 2020 Maxar Technologies.

117 and 120. An inscription found at Hadrian's Wall, dating to 118 or 119, recorded the 'recovery' of Britain and the defeat of the 'barbarians' (*AH* §141), while Fronto, in a letter to Marcus Aurelius in AD 162, recalled the vast number of Roman soldiers who had perished at the hands of the Britons during Hadrian's reign (*On the Parthian War*, 3).

The wall was 118 kilometres (73 miles) long; the eastern portion was constructed of stone, while a smaller length in the west comprised a turf embankment. A deep ditch ran parallel to the wall on its northern side, while military roads (the Stanegate, and later the Military Way), and a cleared zone with a ditch and earthworks, the *vallum*, ran to the south (Figure 10.48). The wall was studded with fortresses, milecastles, and turrets, which were moved north to sit on the wall itself after the initial plan calling for them to be built behind it was amended. In total, 12 forts were built on the wall, the most famous of which is Housesteads, where the wall took advantage of the terrain to provide a particularly imposing sight, high above the plain below. The forts controlled access points and were manned by a garrison that collectively numbered over 9,000 men. Fortified positions were also maintained throughout a zone to both the north along Dere Street and the Devil's Causeway, as well as to the south, disrupting potential anti-Roman alliances, providing further visible examples of Roman power, and allowing for cavalry and infantry patrols to project power well north of the wall itself (Figure 10.49).

The Bar Kochba revolt

The last great Jewish revolt took place during the reign of the man remembered by Talmudic sources as 'Hadrian the wicked' (Jerusalem Talmud Peah 7:1, 20a). The revolt

Figure 10.48 Google Earth Pro image of Hadrian's Wall near Cawfields, just west of Housesteads. The wall runs along the craggy ground from the quarry at left, diagonally out of the frame at the upper right; the vallum is clearly visible behind it, as are numerous marks in the earth outlining temporary structures.

Source: © 2020 Infoterra Ltd and Bluesky.

was caused by pent-up resentment following the suppression of the rebellions in AD 66 and 115, combined with Hadrian's Hellenising tendencies, which led him to declare Jerusalem a Roman colony under the name Aelia Capitolina, with a Temple of Jupiter as its centrepiece. Hadrian may also have banned circumcision, but there is some confusion in the sources over whether the edict dates to his reign or that of his successor, Antoninus Pius. The colonisation of Jerusalem may have been acceptable to some, but it also caused fear and hatred among others, especially coming so soon after the destructive end of the Diaspora Revolt.

During the construction of the Temple of Jupiter, the Tomb of Solomon collapsed and anger towards the Romans swelled rapidly. Resistance crystallised around a man named Simeon bar Kasivah, who took the name 'Bar Kochba', 'son of the star', in reference to the prophecy from Numbers (Chapter 9). On his coinage, Bar Kochba depicted the star and also referred to himself as 'prince of Israel', a distinctly Messianic term also known from the texts from Qumran. The coins also illustrated the Ark of the Covenant and the Temple, reflecting Bar Kochba's aims in the war to drive the Romans from Judaea and restore Jerusalem as a Jewish city (Figure 10.50).

In the years before the revolt there had, once again, been an increase in end-time anxieties. The fifth book of the *Sibylline Oracles* is dated to Hadrian's reign, while the *Apocalypse of Baruch* (also known as *2 Baruch*) was circulating in Judaea during the time of Trajan, providing visions of suffering and Messianic triumph. *4 Ezra* (the *Jewish Apocalypse of Ezra*), composed around the turn of the second century, described an apocalyptic vision

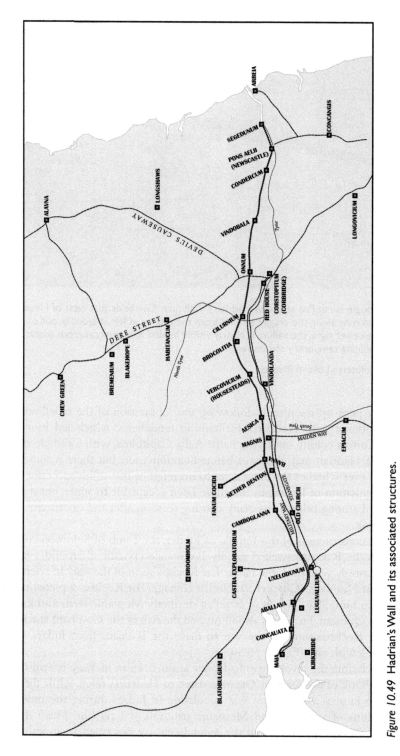

Figure 10.49 Hadrian's Wall and its associated structures.

Source: Illustration by the author.

Figure 10.50 Silver tetradrachm minted in Jerusalem. Obverse: The Temple with star above; reverse: the Hebrew legend reads 'Year 2 of the freedom of Israel'.

of a Messiah who burned up his enemies with flaming breath. Many years later, the Roman theologian Jerome (AD 347–420) alleged that Bar Kochba fraudulently performed 'miracles', using a burning straw in his mouth to 'give the impression that he was spewing out flames' (*Against Rufinus*, 3.31). Bar Kochba was duly declared to be the Messiah by Rabbi Akiva (Jerusalem Talmud Ta'anit 4:6, 68d), a respected scholar and the chief religious authority in Judaea, and the region collapsed into violence.

Hadrian brought Sextus Julius Severus, who had just been appointed as propraetorian legate in Britannia, across the breadth of the Roman world to suppress the rebels. The war was fought in small guerilla actions, largely in the countryside, and the fighting was savage. The Roman army was mauled by Bar Kochba and it was clear that there was to be no victory in Judaea; there could only be an end to the war. XXII Deiotariana was destroyed in heavy fighting, and conscription was briefly introduced to stem the horrific losses among the Roman infantry. As the legionnaires rooted out pockets of resistance, people—apparently including Babatha and her family—fled into hiding with their relatives and precious documents. The remains of these individuals and their possessions were later found in the Cave of Letters and similar archaeological sites around Ein Gedi. In nearby Nahal Darga (Wadi Murabba'at), caves were found in 1951 that contained Trajanic-era coins and Roman weapons. Discoveries in this bleak landscape included four letters authored by Bar Kochba himself.

By 135, Hadrian was in Judaea and the rebels were penned in at Betar, where they were starved to death by a vengeful and determined Roman siege cordon; aerial archaeology of the site has outlined a typically thorough effort, including a circumvallation and at least six individual installations, and in the nineteenth century a hill near Betar was still called 'the place from which the king bombarded the Jews'. Afterwards, Roman troops systematically repressed the last embers of the revolt, killing wantonly and selling thousands into slavery; one of the casualties was Rabbi Akiva. Later Jewish sources, including those openly hostile to Bar Kochba for the failed revolt, claimed dreadful atrocities: children burned alive in Torah scrolls amidst killing so dreadful that a horse 'sank in blood up to its nose'; so much blood was spilled, it was asserted, that the vineyards of Judaea bloomed for seven full years without fertiliser (Jerusalem Talmud Ta'anit 4:6, 69a & Babylonian Talmud Gittin 58a). Betar became known in Arabic as Khirbet al-Yahud, 'the ruin of the Jews', and its dead were left to rot unburied in the sun—one text alleged that Hadrian created a macabre fence of unburied bodies (Jerusalem Talmud Ta'anit 4:6, 69a). Bodies were also abandoned in the natural and human-made caves of the Judaean Desert. One, the Cave of Horror in Nahal Hever (close to the Cave of Letters and similarly surmounted by a Roman siege camp), contained 40 skeletons from the war that were found in 1961. Across Judea, synagogues were burned and replaced with temples. X Fretensis, which was based in Jerusalem, carried out some of this building work and left tiles stamped with the legionary title and its mascot, the pig, the depiction of which was a deliberate provocation. As a final insult, the name of Judaea was erased: henceforth the province became known as Syria Palaestina, and Jews were forbidden to enter Aelia Capitolina.

Julius Severus and the legate of Arabia, Haterius Nepos (another favourite promoted by Hadrian) were granted the *ornamenta triumphalia*. Nepos was also awarded a suffect consulship in 134, and Hadrian was hailed as *imperator* by the army. A lost inscription from Puteoli recorded the *primus pilus* of II Traiana receiving the *corona aurea*, the golden crown for courage, during 'the Jewish war' (*CIL* 10.3733), and in 1977 a large bronze statue of Hadrian was discovered at Tel Shalem in Israel, where units of VI Ferrata were stationed during the conflict. A year later, fragments of a triumphal arch inscription were found nearby; a proposed restoration of the text dates the arch to 136 in commemoration of the end of the Bar Kochba war. In Rome, a base for a statue of Hadrian commemorated his deliverance of 'Syria Palaestina from the enemy' (*CIL* 6.974).

One intriguing aspect of the war's aftermath was an acceleration of the growing divergence of Christianity from Judaism. Ever since the death of Christ, the Septuagint had provided a common Greek Bible for both Christians and Jews; Christians as yet had no text that was specific to Christianity. As noted in Chapter 9, Judaism fostered gentile participation as 'God-fearers', with no demand to convert or abandon pagan beliefs. In the second century, however, as Trajan and Hadrian pursued punitive measures against the Jews, Christianity developed from its messianic and apocalyptic Jewish roots into a society that accepted gentiles, just as Judaism had done—but with the proviso that baptism required the abandonment of prior faiths. Within this demanding context—and even as gentile Christians carried on going to the synagogue for years to come—a vigorous debate began among early Christian leaders regarding how Christianity should be understood in the context of Judaism, and what attitude Christians should take to Roman authorities. The debate proceeded in a variety of different directions.

The *Letter of Ignatius* (the *Letter to the Romans*), for instance, was written either during the time of Hadrian or Antoninus Pius. Ignatius was the bishop of Antioch, and penned seven letters with his thoughts on false prophets and his desire for martyrdom while on his way to be executed in Rome. Another tack was taken by the *Epistle of Barnabas*. Attributed to a friend of Paul, it was probably written in Alexandria between 70 and 135; it discussed the Old Testament texts in an anti-Jewish critique that sought to claim the Old Testament and the covenant of God for Christians, contrasting the spirituality of Christians with the materialism of Jews, who it claimed were overly focused on the Temple. The *Epistle* had a strong end-time tone and anticipated an imminent final judgement. Another anti-Jewish position was taken by a man named Marcion, who lived in the mid-second century. He arrived at the idea of rejecting the Old Testament and producing a collection of religious texts that were particular to Christianity—the New Testament. As part of this endeavour, Marcion penned the lost *Antitheses*, an attempt to compare Jewish and Christian texts. Marcion's work was accompanied by that of Valentinus (active in the 130s) and Justin Martyr (in the 150s). Justin, from the Roman colony of Neapolis (Nablus) in Syria Palaestina, attempted with his *Dialogue with Trypho* to refute criticisms levied by Trypho, a Jew, against Christianity; like the *Epistle of Barnabas*, it is an anti-Jewish text that sought to enhance Christianity's claims to Jewish scripture.

Justin's *Dialogue* was also an 'apologetic' text, belonging to a genre designed to justify Christianity in the face of censure from imperial authorities or other bodies. An early apologetic effort had been made by Quadratus of Athens, who directed an apology to Hadrian (quoted in Eusebius, *Ecclesiastical History*, 4.3.1–2). Justin Martyr also appealed to Roman authorities with his *First Apology*, an attempt to rationalise Christianity and to gain protection for Christians from arbitrary punishment based on denunciations and the name 'Christian' alone, reflecting continued anxieties over the legal approaches to Christians discussed by Trajan and Pliny the Younger. Justin's approach was notable for the way he interweaved Greek philosophical tradition with emergent Christianity, claiming that Greek thinkers had provided the necessary preparation for the correct 'philosophy'—Christianity—to flourish. Despite Justin's assurance that Christians would 'render therefore to Caesar that which is Caesar's … acknowledging you as kings and rulers of men' (*First Apology*, 17), Roman authorities still viewed Christians with suspicion. This situation continued even though Hadrian had provided sound advice on dealing with Christians to the proconsul of Asia in 122/23, the written text of which Justin appended to his *First Apology* to strengthen his argument. Hadrian asserted that Christians should only be punished if they were found to have broken Roman laws during a proper trial, and that judges and procurators should not give in to 'mere entreaties and outcries' (*AH* §146). Like Trajan, Hadrian would not accept denunciations. These texts show that even as Christianity developed distinctly from Judaism, its apologists were seeking to find a modus vivendi with the empire, and many went out of their way to underscore their political loyalties. Justin overplayed his hand, however, when he warned Antoninus Pius that he would 'not escape the coming judgement of God' (*First Apology*, 68). He was later tried and beheaded during the reign of Marcus Aurelius.

Hadrian and his family

Wearing a beard became popular in Hadrian's time, and many of the surviving portraits show a bearded emperor. The beard would eventually become something of a political choice: the emperor Julian (AD 360–63) was a fierce defender of his philosopher's beard, which brought him into conflict with the people of Antioch. The reasons for Hadrian's fashion choice have been long debated, and range from an admiration of Greek culture (and Greek philosophy) to a desire to project a more robust and masculine image. The *Historia Augusta*, however, alleged that it was simply to cover up unsightly blemishes (*HA Hadrian*, 26). Hadrian's bearded face stood in stark contrast to portraits of the clean-shaven Trajan.

Hadrian's wife, Sabina, received numerous portraits that reflect the coolness and intelligence seen in statues of Livia. In a relief created to celebrate her apotheosis, Hadrian looks on as she rises heavenward with the assistance of a winged female figure (Figure 10.51).

Figure 10.51 The apotheosis of Sabina, from the Arco di Portogallo in Rome, dating to AD 136–38.

Source: Photograph by Carole Raddato (CC BY-SA 2.0).

Figure 10.52 Antinous as Silvanus, AD 130–38.

Source: Photograph by Carole Raddato (CC BY-SA 2.0).

Another figure who received great attention from artisans of the period was Antinous, Hadrian's lover. His image is one of idealised classical purity: on one relief, as the god Silvanus, Antinous is suspended in a pastoral paradise, ready to prune a vine and accompanied by a dog (Figure 10.52). Reflecting the assimilated nature of his cult, Antinous was also depicted, again in an idealised fashion, as the Egyptian deity Osiris (Figure 10.53).

Hadrian's relationship with Sabina was often strained, and in 122 he dismissed the historian Suetonius and the praetorian prefect Septicius Clarus from government service for acting improperly with her; a romantic tryst was suspected. Nevertheless, Sabina was celebrated as a virtuous example of *pietas* and *pudicitia*, and she was widely commemorated

Figure 10.53 Antinous as Osiris, from Hadrian's Villa at Tivoli.

Source: Photograph by Marie-Lan Nguyen (CC BY-SA 2.5).

on Roman coins. Sabina died in 136/7, with rumours that she had been poisoned or had taken her own life. Her marriage to Hadrian had produced no children, but the emperor prepared carefully for the future. He initially adopted Lucius Ceionnius Commodus, 'although this man frequently vomited blood', whom he renamed Aelius Caesar (Cassius Dio, 69.17). Aelius, a relative of one of the four men killed in the first year of Hadrian's reign, soon died, and in 138 Hadrian adopted a man who would take the imperial name Antoninus Pius. Antoninus also had no children, so he adopted two others. The first was Marcus Annius Verus, better known as Marcus Aurelius, drawn from the same Baetican aristocracy that had supplied Trajan and Hadrian. The second was the son of Aelius Caesar, who would take the name Lucius Verus. Hadrian's decisions hurt some who possessed imperial ambitions: his long-time friend and brother-in-law, Lucius Julius Servianus, felt particularly left out when his grandson, Pedanius Fuscus, was excluded. A possible coup attempt led to Fuscus's execution in 137, while, at the age of 91, Servianus was forced to kill himself. Despite these difficulties, Hadrian's adoption strategy purchased a period of royal stability that would last until the death of Marcus Aurelius. Hadrian died in the summer of 138, broken by illness. Studies of the earlobes on his statues have since suggested that he suffered from coronary heart disease; he was 62.

Chapter 11

Decay, 138–235

> Our history now descends from a kingdom of gold to one of iron and rust.
>
> Cassius Dio, 71.35

In the film *Gladiator* (2000), a deranged Commodus murders his father, presides over a reign of terror in Rome, then succumbs to the army hero Maximus during a gladiatorial contest in the arena. Commodus's gladiatorial bent was not entirely fictional: in common with Caligula, Titus, Hadrian, and several others, Commodus underwent instruction from gladiators to sharpen his sword skills. Later, he competed in the arena, albeit in situations where the odds of him losing were slight. *Gladiator* also captured a more sombre reality of the period, in its dark portrayal of a drained and sickly Marcus Aurelius watching his exhausted soldiers struggle in the forests of Europe against a vicious hoard of Germanic warriors. Marcus Aurelius, whose collection of personal Stoic reflections, the *Meditations*, still appears on bestseller lists, spent almost his entire career fighting along the Danube. When his wars were over, they were commemorated on a monument that superficially resembled Trajan's Column. Yet, whereas the images of Trajan's war reflected strength, courage, and a clean, precise victory over a beaten foe, the shocking reliefs on the Column of Marcus Aurelius tell a very different story. Theirs are images of death, pain, and suffering, of victories purchased at too steep a cost against a determined enemy. And even as Roman armies once again routed the old foe in Parthia and pillaged Seleucia-Ctesiphon, they did so only to carry a devastating plague back to Europe. Eventually the triumphal era of Trajan became just a memory, as—once more—the Roman world collapsed into chaos. The *pax Romana* was over.

From Antoninus to Commodus

Antoninus Pius

Antoninus, whose epithet 'Pius' was earned for pushing Hadrian's deification through a reluctant senate, was born in Latium in 86, the son of a consul from Nemausus. His family benefited from Flavian patronage. His grandfather, Gnaeus Arrius Antonius, was highly regarded by Pliny the Younger, who once cooed that his letters were filled 'with sweetness culled from flowers' (*Letters*, 4.3). At some point after 110, Antoninus Pius married Faustina, the daughter of Marcus Annius Verus, a relative of Sabina and ordinary consul in 121 and 126. Faustina died prematurely in 140 and, like Marciana and Plotina, she was subsequently deified (Figure 11.1). Under Hadrian, Antoninus followed a traditional

DOI: 10.4324/9781003202523-11

Figure 11.1 Gold aureus struck in Rome after 141, commemorating the deification of Faustina. The reverse shows the goddess Ceres.

career track, and held the ordinary consulship in 120. He served as one of Hadrian's four *quattuorviri consulares*, then spent 135/36 as proconsul of Asia; like his predecessors, he was a highly experienced administrator.

The reign of Antoninus was calm, without any significant crises. Despite his lack of military experience, both the Praetorian Guard and the army accepted the new emperor, and his consular background ensured acceptance by the senate. Minor conflicts fought by subordinates were waged in Dacia, Upper Germany, Mauretania, and the east. A brief war was prosecuted in Britannia by the African native Quintus Lollius Urbicus, where Roman control was briefly extended into southern Scotland and a turf barrier, the Antonine Wall, erected (Figure 11.2). Punctuated by forts every 3 kilometres (1.8 miles), the wall was accompanied by a deep ditch and equipped, like its southern counterpart, with a military road running directly behind it; units stationed along its frigid length included a cohort of archers raised at Epiphania (Hama, in Syria). In 143, a century after the initial invasion of Britain, a commemorative coin issue was struck and Antoninus was acclaimed *imperator*.

During this time, Trimontium was rebuilt in stone, but Rome's presence was cut back by the end of the 150s when the Antonine Wall was abandoned. The reasons for the withdrawal are not clear, but Marcus Aurelius sent a new legate to Britannia in 161, and it is possible that under his guidance, with problems brewing in the Levant, a retrenchment along Hadrian's Wall seemed advisable. As with sites such as Inchtuthil (Chapter 10), many of the installations constructed during this period, such as the auxiliary fort at Drumlanrig, which lay in the swathe of land between Hadrian's Wall and the Antonine Wall, were carefully dismantled. While little remains of the wall today, numerous inscriptions have survived recording building work carried out by units of the British garrison; many are now in the Hunterian Museum in Glasgow.

Antoninus never left Italy and ruled largely through delegation. In 148, he presided over celebrations for the 900th anniversary of the foundation of Rome, and throughout his reign he carefully hoarded cash, leaving an enormous surplus on his death. During his reign and that of his successors, provincials continued to reach the highest rungs of

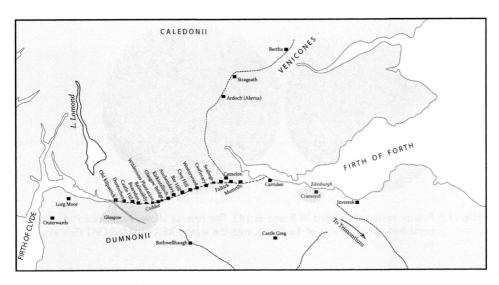

Figure 11.2 The Antonine Wall.

Source: Illustration by the author.

Roman office, with Greek-speaking elites in particular inspired to pursue careers in service in the aftermath of Hadrian's eastern travels. Notable provincial officials of the time included Cassius Dio from Bithynia, Marcus Cornelius Fronto from Numidia, and the Athenian sophist Herodes Atticus. Both Fronto and Herodes taught Marcus Aurelius and Lucius Verus, while Fronto was suffect consul in 142 and Herodes held the ordinary consulship in 143. Another important sophist of the time was Publius Aelius Aristides, from Mysia in Asia Minor. Aristides, whose name shows that he received citizenship during the reign of Hadrian, was the author of *The Roman Oration*, a panegyrical text that expressed a deep admiration for Roman culture and Rome's achievement of the *pax Romana*. One of the foci of the *Oration* was Roman citizenship, portrayed as a benefit that effaced the differences between Italian Romans and provincial Romans, and provided a way for the Greek-speaking elite of the east to become full partners in the Roman commonwealth. The influence of sophists in Rome reflected the growing acceptance of Greek culture in the western part of the empire, and the vigour of the cultural movement known as the Second Sophistic. This movement was based on oratorical skill and a command of Attic Greek, and a cultivation of the high culture of classical Athens; it is instructive that Marcus Aurelius wrote the *Meditations* in Greek, while Dio composed his history in Attic Greek following a Thucydidean style. The lives of the great sophists were chronicled by the Athenian Philostratus (c. 170–244), who was close to the emperor Septimius Severus, and his wife, Julia Domna.

Antoninus followed many of the policies of his predecessors, continuing the *alimenta*, exempting intellectuals from various types of public service, and commissioning numerous infrastructure projects, including a Temple of Hadrian. Antoninus sought to protect slaves from arbitrary punishment and allowed a judicial hearing if a slave experienced undue cruelty, starvation, or persistent abuse. The emperor was popular in Rome, and his

Figure 11.3 Bronze sestertius minted in Rome in 143. The reverse shows Antoninus Pius offering a royal diadem to the king of the Quadi, with the legend REX QVADIS DATVS: 'a king given to the Quadi'.

biography in the *Historia Augusta* verges on the panegyrical, recording donatives to troops and the people as well as assistance to impoverished children. For the provinces, Antoninus remitted taxes for earthquake-stricken areas and maintained good relations with Rome's clients in the Caucasus. Antoninus's status was sufficiently high that the Quadi, a Germanic people in Barbaricum who would soon become a dangerous enemy to Marcus Aurelius, asked the emperor to choose their king (Figure 11.3).

Antoninus, Marcus Aurelius, and Lucius Verus

Recreating a narrative of Marcus Aurelius' career is a challenge. While Cassius Dio covered his life in books 70 and 71, this part of the text is known only from the eleventh-century epitome of Xiphilinus and fragments of Cassius Dio preserved in the later *Suda*. There is also the biography of the emperor in the *Historia Augusta*, forming part of the *vitae* between Hadrian and Caracalla that were derived from the lost, but factually reliable, *Life of the Caesars* by the historian, soldier, and bureaucrat Marius Maximus. Complementing the meagre textual record are archaeological sources, numismatics, epigraphy, and monuments such as the Column of Marcus Aurelius.

In 139, Antoninus Pius took the title *pater patriae* and his daughter, also named Faustina, married Marcus Aurelius. The couple would have an astonishing 14 children together, but only four survived their childhood. In 140, Marcus Aurelius was *princeps iuventutis* and ordinary consul with Antoninus Pius. Together with Lucius Verus, he was honoured with a rare dynastic coin issue (Figure 11.4). Seven years later, Marcus Aurelius was given tribunician power and Faustina was honoured as Augusta. In 161, Lucius Verus was engaged to Marcus's daughter Lucilla and promoted to Augustus, providing the principate with its first collegial rulership, although Marcus Aurelius remained the senior partner with the indivisible office of *pontifex maximus*. The *concordia augustorum*—harmony between the two emperors—was commemorated on a coin issue of 161 (Figure 11.5), while both men, and Faustina, appeared on a separate issue in the same year (Figure 11.6).

Figure 11.4 Gold aureus minted in Rome in 140 by Antoninus Pius; the type is exceptionally rare and indicates Antoninus, together with Marcus Aurelius and Lucius Verus in a quadriga on the reverse.

Figure 11.5 Gold aureus struck in Rome in 161. The reverse shows Marcus Aurelius and Lucius Verus each clasping the hand of the other.

Antoninus died near Rome in 161 after ruling for a longer period than anyone since Augustus. Marcus Aurelius deified his adoptive father, who he praised with evident affection in the *Meditations*. Marcus noted that he was courteous in debate and listened to proposals, that he had no favourites, and that he paid close attention to the health of the government and the treasury. Furthermore, he did not hurry business or indulge in unseemly luxury. Marcus also wrote that he had learned from Antoninus the importance of limiting flattery at court and maintaining a certain distance from the people (1.16). 'Do everything as a disciple of Antoninus,' he wrote later, 'pray imitate these good qualities of his, that you may have the satisfaction of them at your last hour as he had' (6.30). These comments flatter Antoninus, but they also say a great deal about Marcus and his philosophy as emperor. Deeply influenced by Stoicism, to which he had devoted himself since his teenage years,

Figure 11.6 Bronze medallion struck in 161. Obverse: Marcus Aurelius (facing right) and Lucius Verus (facing left); reverse: Faustina as Salus, the personification of health, with *patera* and serpent.

Marcus was a humble intellectual who understood that to be emperor was to follow a precious duty where his conscience would guide his acts and decisions. Keenly aware of his role in the world, he wrote that 'reason and social principles are suited to my nature, and Rome is my town and country; but consider me a man in general, and I belong to the corporation of the world' (6.44). Machiavelli praised Marcus Aurelius, noting that, along with Trajan, he was 'protected by [his] own good conduct' (*Discourses on Livy*, 1.10). Even when Marcus became emperor, he continued his philosophical training, becoming a student of Plutarch's nephew Sextus and attending lectures given by leading Stoics (Cassius Dio, 70.1 & *HA Marcus*, 3). According to Philostratus, Marcus, on the way to a lecture one day, remarked to Lucius, a philosopher friend of Herodes Atticus, that 'it is a good thing even for one who is growing old to acquire knowledge; I am going to Sextus the philosopher to learn what I do not yet know'. An exasperated Lucius threw up his hands and declared amazement that the ageing emperor was still going to school, while Alexander the Great had burned out and died at 33 (*Lives of the Sophists*, 557). Marcus also sought the guidance of Fronto, whom he addressed affectionately as *magister meo*, 'my teacher', and he would send him drafts of speeches for correction. In turn, Fronto encouraged his former student in his new duties by pointing to his careful education. 'Philosophy will tell you what to say', he wrote, 'eloquence how to say it' (*On Eloquence*, 1.18, AD 162).

Marcus insisted that the wishes of Hadrian be followed, so Lucius Verus remained as co-emperor. The two paid the expected donative to the Praetorian Guard, and erected a column for Antoninus Pius and Faustina. Only the base of the column has survived; part of its relief depicts the apotheosis of the emperor and the empress (Figure 11.7). After the mourning period for Antoninus Pius was over, Marcus 'abandoned himself to philosophy' (*HA Marcus*, 8). He had little time to do so, however; a devastating flood of the Tiber required his urgent attention, then from the east came the rumblings of war.

The Parthian War

Antoninus Pius had long-running concerns about Parthia, and as early as 138 had ordered Neratius Proculus, legate of XVI Flavia Firma, to move troops from his base at Samosata

Figure 11.7 The apotheosis of Antoninus Pius and Faustina from the Column of Antoninus Pius.

Source: Photograph by Lalupa (CC BY-SA 3.0).

eastward in a show of strength. On his deathbed, Antoninus complained about 'certain kings with whom he was angry', presumably referring to Vologases IV, king of Parthia since 147 (*HA Antoninus Pius*, 12). Vologases had spent his early career restoring royal authority in several districts that had declared for Rome during Trajan's invasion. These included Characene, which had managed a precarious semi-independence since the departure of Roman troops in 117, as well as Armenia, where the reigning monarch, Sohaemus, was deposed in favour of Vologases's son, Pacorus. Roman efforts to forestall this aggression failed. Sedatius Severianus, the propraetorian legate of Cappadocia, lost his life and a legion—perhaps IX Hispana, which abruptly vanished from the sources in the late second century—at Elegeia in Armenia. According to the satirist Lucian, Severianus had fallen under the spell of a charlatan named Alexander, who had urged him to invade Armenia with the seductive prophecy that, 'Under your charging spear shall fall Armenians and Parthians / Then you shall fare to Rome and the glorious waters of the Tiber / Wearing upon your brow the chaplet studded with sunbeams' (*Alexander*, 27). The propraetorian legate of Syria, Lucius Attidius Cornelianus, fared little better, and was beaten by a strong Parthian foray across the Euphrates.

In the aftermath of the disaster at Elegeia, a flurry of provincial appointments installed capable men in the empire's vulnerable spots. Statius Priscus was transferred from the legateship of Britannia to replace Severianus in Cappadocia, and Marcus Annius Libo, a cousin of the emperor, was sent to Syria. Fronto's son-in-law Aufidius Victorinus became propraetorian legate in Upper Germany, and a veteran hand was installed in Upper Pannonia. Together, these men faced the formidable task of preventing opportunistic raids when I Minervia (Bonna), II Adiutrix (Aquincum), and V Macedonica (Troesmis), as well as X Gemina (Vindobona), were sent to the east to bolster Roman forces. The eastern campaign was given to Lucius Verus, but Marcus was sufficiently concerned about the abilities of his adoptive brother that he urged Fronto to write to him and provide counsel. Marcus also sent Furius Victorinus, one of the praetorian prefects, and a coterie of ex-legates to advise Lucius. The campaign proceeded slowly, however, and Lucius's role in it was minimalised by excessive tarrying on the journey. A lethargic, Nero-esque excursion was made through Greece, and winter was spent enjoying the pleasures of Athens, where he was initiated into the Eleusinian Mysteries and whiled away the days with Herodes Atticus. Once in Antioch, Lucius Verus was more often to be found sunning himself at nearby Daphne with his mistress Panthea or hunting in the Syrian forests than planning strategy with his officers. The *Historia Augusta* scorned Verus, accusing him of succumbing to vanity by focusing on his blond highlights, created with gold dust (*HA Lucius Verus*, 10). Marcus Annius Libo fell out with Lucius and died in mysterious circumstances, but Statius Priscus was able to stabilise the northern frontier with Armenia and then invade Armenia itself. Priscus was doing everything that Lucius should have been doing; he captured Artaxata in 163 and established a new capital, Kainopolis, to replace it. Lucius took the title *Armeniacus*, despite having made virtually no contribution to the successful campaign, while Gnaeus Julius Verus, the son of Hadrian's general Sextus Julius Severus, replaced Libo as the legate of Syria.

These events had dominated the period between 161 and 164, at the end of which Lucius had married Lucilla, who was only 14, at Ephesus. While the Romans were pre-occupied with Armenia and preparing for a general offensive, the Parthians had invaded Osrhoene and captured Edessa, putting its pro-Roman king Manu VIII to flight. In 163/64, Roman troops fought their way down the Euphrates from Zeugma, beating a Parthian army near Carchemish, then crossed over to the left bank at Nicephorium (Callinicum, modern Raqqa) after defeating a Parthian army at Sura. At much the same time, legionnaires under the talented Marcus Claudius Fronto (not to be confused with the emperor's tutor) crossed into Osrhoene and captured Anthemusia, near Edessa. In the same year, Sohaemus was reinstalled on the Armenian throne at Kainopolis, and Marcus Aurelius accepted the title *Armeniacus*. In 165, Manu was reinstalled at Edessa, and thanked his benefactors with a coin issue that referred to him as *philoromaios*, 'friend of the Romans'. Roman troops pressed eastwards, capturing Nisibis and forcing the Parthian commanding general to make a daring escape by swimming the Tigris. Meanwhile, the Syrian native Avidius Cassius, an equestrian who had been promoted to the senatorial order, took III Gallica to Dura-Europos on the Euphrates and then, towards the end of the year, captured Seleucia-Ctesiphon and sacked the palace of Vologases at Ctesiphon. Lucius took the title *Parthicus Maximus* and wrote excitedly to his former teacher Fronto, who had been given the task of chronicling the war. He pompously stated that 'it is essential to make quite clear the great superiority of the Parthians before my arrival, so that the magnitude of my achievements may be manifest'. In case Fronto was in any doubt about how this should be done, Lucius provided him with the lofty example of Thucydides.

'My achievements, whatever their character, are no greater, of course, than they actually are,' wrote Lucius in 165, 'but they can be made to seem as great as you would have them seem.'

Meanwhile, Cassius continued his campaign, pressing across the Tigris into Media, adding *Medicus* to the imperial title. Marcus Aurelius was so impressed with Cassius that he awarded him a suffect consulship (held in absentia) and then the propraetorian legateship of Syria (Figure 11.8). In Rome, Marcus and Lucius celebrated a triumph in October 166—the first since the posthumous event for Trajan in 118—and took the title *pater patriae*. Marcus's son Commodus became Caesar along with his brother Annius Verus, but Annius died three years later, in 169, from a failed operation to remove a tumour.

Years before, in 151, Vologases had defeated the king of Characene, plundering the statue of Heracles that guarded the Characenian royal family and installing it in the Temple

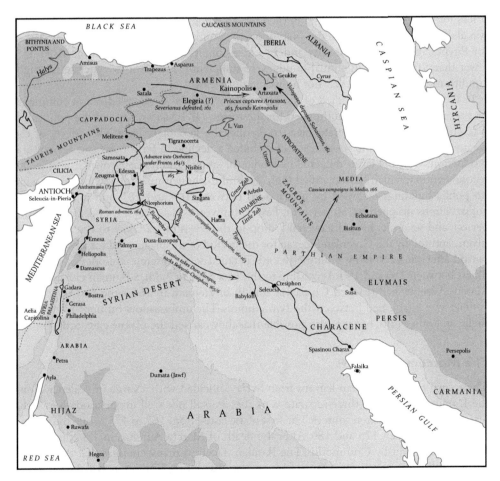

Figure 11.8 The Parthian wars of Marcus Aurelius and Lucius Verus; note that the precise locations of Elegeia and Anthemusia are unknown.

Source: Illustration by the author.

of Apollo at Seleucia. This building, along with the rest of the city, had been burned by Cassius's troops during their triumphant campaign. When the European legions returned to their bases and the eastern legions to their quarters, they carried with them a deadly illness that became known as the Antonine Plague. A later tradition, based on the story that 'a pestilential vapour arose in a temple of Apollo from a golden casket which a soldier had accidentally cut open', asserted that the plague was Apollo's vengeance for the desecration of Seleucia and his shrine there (*HA Lucius Verus*, 8.1). It has never been entirely clear what the disease actually was, although one account described a weeping rash and ulcerated eyes, which has suggested to some that it was variola major (smallpox). The emergence of the plague had coincided with a period of extensive warfare with large-scale movements of troops and civilians, and it spread quickly with dire results. Marcus provided special dispensation in 174/75 that relaxed office-holding rules in Athens, due to the deaths of many eligible office holders, while evidence from Egypt reveals a sharp decrease in registered taxpayers—as much as 93 per cent, at one village in the Nile Delta—and prices for Egyptian wheat doubled in the years to come. The uptick in the price of wheat was also a result of a change in the Nile flood, the annual appearance of which was crucial for Egypt's agricultural prosperity and, by extension, its ability to feed Rome. After 155, fewer than 10 per cent of annual floods were sufficiently abundant to generate the right conditions, a situation that was not remedied until 299.

In Rome, many senators died of the plague, as evidenced by the plethora of commemorative statues that Marcus authorised for the forum (*HA Marcus*, 13) and the population was ordered to make desperate pleas to Apollo, the god of healing. The effects of the plague went well beyond mortality, and included a decline in farm rents and agricultural production, with the latter reflected by studies of animal and human bones from the late second century, which have revealed high levels of malnourishment. In Rome, there were no public buildings recorded by inscriptions between 166 and 181, and in Italy public constructions dropped by 50 per cent. Fewer shipwrecks have been found dating to this period, and scientists have discovered a drop in the levels of lead, key to the smelting of silver, captured by the Greenland icecap for the period of the plague and for a considerable period afterwards. Notably, Chinese records detailed seven discrete episodes of epidemic illness between 160 and 190. According to the *Hou Hanshu* (§88), a Roman embassy from Marcus Aurelius had reached China via Tonkin in Vietnam in 166—the first time direct contact was established between the two empires. The ambassadors brought ivory, turtle shells, and other gifts, but it is also possible that they carried the plague eastwards.

The Marcomannic Wars

The return of the European legions from Syria coincided with a surge in violence along the Danube. This led to three separate wars that are still not well understood, due to the scarcity of reliable written sources. The first phase lasted from 167 to 175, while the second was fought between 178 and 180. After the death of Marcus Aurelius in 180, there was a third phase fought by Commodus. The Romans faced so many enemies that the *Historia Augusta* called the conflict 'the War of Many Nations', listing 17 discrete tribal groups that 'banded together against us' (*HA Marcus*, 22). The principal enemies were the Marcomanni ('inhabitants of the marches') and the Quadi, who shared a common Germanic linguistic and cultural background. The other major group of enemies was the Sarmatians, including the Roxolani and the Iazyges, whose origins lay in Iran and who spoke an Indo-European language.

In 167, Iallius Bassus, who had fought alongside Lucius Verus in Parthia, faced an invasion of tribal groups into Upper Pannonia, which the Romans called the Langobardi (Lombards) and the Obii. The raids were caused by large-scale movements of people hundreds of miles from the Danube that placed pressure on the Germanic and Sarmatian tribes in the frontier districts of Barbaricum adjacent to Roman territory. The instability that these population movements caused appears fleetingly in the written sources: in the preface to his history of Rome's overseas wars, for example, Appian reported an increase in foreign envoys at court during the reign of Antoninus Pius, while the *Historia Augusta* mentioned 'other tribes, who had been driven on by the more distant barbarians and retreated before them' causing problems on the frontier (*HA Marcus*, 14.1). In Pannonia, Bassus and his cavalry commander, Macrinius Vindex, were able to suppress the Lombards and the Obii; meanwhile, a union of tribes represented by Ballomarius, the king of the Marcommani, opened negotiations with the Romans. In 168, Marcus Aurelius and Lucius Verus travelled to the front through northern Italy, using the colony of Aquileia as a forward base. There they found that the Quadi wanted the Romans to bestow a king upon them once more, and for a while there was a temporary peace. The disturbances had, however, made the emperors realise how vulnerable northern Italy had become, and an emergency force, the *praetentura Italiae et Alpium*, was created under the leadership of Antistius Adventus, who had commanded II Adiutrix during the Parthian war. At the same time, the emperors raised two new legions, II Italica and III Italica, to replenish losses from both the Parthian war and the plague, which was ravaging Rome. On the way back to the capital in January 169, Lucius suffered a stroke and died; he was hurriedly deified and his ashes placed in the Mausoleum of Hadrian. His widow, Lucilla, only 19, was remarried with unseemly haste to an equestrian from Antioch, Tiberius Claudius Pompeianus, who had become the legate of Lower Pannonia in 167.

In 169, Marcus faced a severe financial and recruitment crisis caused by the plague and ongoing unrest along the frontier. The strain was so great that no military diplomas were issued between 167 and 178, and Marcus resorted to selling off imperial property in the Forum of Trajan and raising military units from trained gladiators and slaves. Elements of the eastern army were also transferred west, principally from XV Apollinaris and XII Fulminata. In a further sign of desperation, Marcus consulted Alexander, the oracle derided by Lucian. Alexander's prophetic snake, Glycon, recommended that the emperor cast two lions ('a pair of Cybele's faithful attendants / Beasts that dwell on the mountains') into the Danube, but the hapless beasts swam across and were bludgeoned to death by the enemy waiting on the other side (Lucian, *Alexander*, 48). This ill omen was a portent of things to come, for in 170 the Danube frontier collapsed and Italy was invaded by the Quadi and Marcomanni. Raiders from the borders of the kingdom of Bosporus, the Costoboci, penetrated through Moesia and Macedonia as far as Attica in Greece, where they sacked the sanctuary at Eleusis. The Costoboci were eventually driven out by an equestrian procurator, Julius Julianus. In Italy, the invasion was reversed in 170 by Helvius Pertinax, the son of a freedman who had recently been promoted to the senate, together with Pompeianus, who had become Pertinax's patron. The fighting was savage and consumed some of the empire's top people: the general Marcus Claudius Fronto, who had been placed in command of a unified Dacia ('Tres Daciae') and Upper Moesia, was killed fighting there, and Marcus Aurelius and his army were briefly stranded in enemy territory on the left bank of the Danube, dependent on emergency supplies ferried by river craft. An inscription from Diana Veteranorum in Numidia dedicated to Marcus Valerius Maximianus, an equestrian from the colony of Poetovio (Ptuj in Slovenia), records how he was tasked to ferry cavalry and troops with the Danube fleet to keep the armies supplied in Pannonia and prevent a total catastrophe (*AE* 1956 = *RA* §114).

In 171, Marcus crushed the Marcommani and Quadi on the Danube and then welcomed ambassadors from the Quadi at Carnuntum. The Quadi accepted peace terms, which included settlement of surrendered tribesmen, *dediticii*, inside the empire, and the Marcomanni were left isolated. In 172, Marcus campaigned across the Danube from Pannonia, concentrating all his strength against the Marcomanni. Macrinius Vindex, who was now the praetorian prefect, was killed in heavy fighting, but the Marcommani were finally defeated amidst a series of 'miraculous' events that saved the Roman army. One, the 'rain miracle', took the form of a sudden downpour that rescued the legionnaires from their terrible thirst; another, the 'lightning miracle', materialised as a hail of lightning bolts that electrocuted the Germans. The emperor took the title *Germanicus* in recognition of his triumph and was acclaimed *imperator* for the seventh time. Lucilla, together with her brother Commodus, had by now joined their father on the Danube, and Faustina took the title *mater castrorum*, mother of the camps, a rare honour among the troops and a reflection of the tight bond between Marcus and his legionnaires (Cassius Dio, 71.10). Subsequently, Marcus campaigned against the Quadi, who had broken the peace treaty in 173, and then from Sirmium he fought against the Iazyges in 174, including a memorable battle waged on the frozen surface of the Danube (Cassius Dio, 71.7). The raids of the Iazyges had proven devastating to the civilian population—Marcus ransomed 100,000 of them, taken prisoner during the wars (Cassius Dio, 71.16).

The revolt of Avidius Cassius

Even as calm was returning to the Danube frontier, unrest had arisen among 'Bucoli' (herdsmen and country workers) in Egypt, and the Parthians took the opportunity to overturn the arrangements in Armenia, deposing Sohaemus. Preoccupied with the Marcomannic War, Marcus gave Avidius Cassius an extraordinary command with the task of restoring peace in the east. The Bucoli revolt was put down, but in 175 Cassius proclaimed himself emperor. It is often thought that Cassius had heard that Marcus had died, or that Faustina, worried during a period when Marcus was taken ill that the unstable Commodus would succeed before he was ready, encouraged Cassius to seize the throne to preserve her husband's achievements. Whatever the case, when Cassius found out that Marcus Aurelius was very much alive, he was left with little choice but to continue his revolt. Cassius's friends were dumbfounded. Herodes Atticus wrote to him with one simple line: 'Herodes to Cassius. You have gone mad' (Philostratus, *Lives of the Sophists*, 563). Cassius did have several advantages: he possessed royal family links to Augustus, Herod, and Antiochus IV of Commagene, and he was also popular with the troops. As he prepared for war with Cassius, Marcus found that he had the support of the propraetorian legate Martius Verus in Cappadocia, and he further countered Cassius's coup by presenting his son, Commodus, to the army. Commodus was only 13, but he nevertheless received the traditional mark of manhood, the *toga virilis*, and was designated *princeps iuventutis*. Marcus

Figure 11.9 Gold aureus minted in 175, showing a youthful Commodus on the obverse, with the title PRINC IVVENT (*princeps iuventutis*) on the reverse with an image of Commodus being presented to the army as the heir apparent.

also sent a loyalist to secure Rome against any move by disaffected senators, but he was spared the need to fight when a centurion murdered Cassius. Martius Verus then destroyed all of Cassius's correspondence, preventing any further fallout.

Even though the revolt had fizzled out, Marcus Aurelius decided to make a tour of the eastern provinces with Commodus and Faustina; on the way, the Augusta died in Cappadocia. Before leaving the Danube in 175, Marcus took the title *Sarmaticus* and demanded a levy from the Iazyges in return for peace. He also raised units from the Marcomanni, Quadi, and Naristae, entrusting these forces to Marcus Valerius Maximianus, who had been decorated by the emperor for his valour and promoted to procurator. After raising two auxiliary cohorts in Syria for service on the Danube, Marcus and Commodus returned to Europe in 175/76. On the way they, like Hadrian, were inducted into the Eleusinian Mysteries, and in Athens the emperor founded chairs in Platonic, Peripatetic, Epicurean, and Stoic philosophy. In Rome, debts were cancelled and a donative of eight gold aurei given to each citizen (Cassius Dio, 71.31). In 176, Commodus was consul—at the age of 15—and took the *maius* proconsular imperium and the tribunician power, and in 177 he was made Augustus, joining his father in collegial imperial rule as Lucius Verus had done earlier. Both Commodus and his sister Lucilla were widely commemorated on contemporary coinage (Figures 11.9 and 11.10).

The Danube—again

The years 177/78 were a time of high anxiety as the fragile peace on the Danube frontier disintegrated. These anxieties produced dreadful civic violence, because reverses on the battlefield, coups against the emperor, and the suffering caused by the plague could all be blamed on a misaligned relationship with the gods—and for Roman conservatives, Christians were the most visible and cancerous cause of this broken relationship. In 177, the Christians at Lugdunum were purged in one of the most ferocious persecutions of the early church. The excuse was a legal ruling by the emperor demanding that people should not incite superstition. Christians were already considered suspect and subversive,

Figure 11.10 Gold aureus minted in 161/62, with the portrait of Lucilla on the obverse and PIETAS on the reverse.

and the people of Lugdunum took it upon themselves, with the collusion of the provincial governor, to prosecute this new ruling to its furthest extent. Eusebius provided a searing account in his *Ecclesiastical History*: Christians, accused of eating children, were tortured to death; the nonagenarian bishop of Lugdunum, 'strengthened by spiritual zeal through his earnest desire for martyrdom', died in prison; the Christian dead were burned and their remains dumped into the Rhône, effacing them from the earth (5.1). At around the same time, Christians were also attacked by the Greek philosopher Celsus, who branded them as turncoat, separatist Jews who deserved the harsh treatment that Roman law handed to them.

In 178, Commodus was married to Crispina, the daughter of Marcus's friend Bruttius Praesens. The wedding offered a bright moment in a gloomy period, and donatives were made to the people of Rome in celebration. Commodus, as co-emperor, then accompanied Marcus, Bruttius, the council of advisers, and the new praetorian prefect, Taruttienus Paternus, to the Danube, following the traditional fetial ceremony whereby Marcus threw a spear symbolically into enemy territory (Cassius Dio, 71.33). Inscriptions show that Marcus Aurelius and Commodus suspended use of their titles *Germanicus* and *Sarmaticus* on the outbreak of this new campaign, which was chiefly directed into the territory of the Quadi. In 179/80, some 20,000 Roman troops were campaigning far north of the Danube, disrupting crops and livestock and curbing the movement of people. There appear to have been plans to bring the territory of the Quadi and others into the empire to create provinces of Marcomannia and Sarmatia, either in 175—interrupted by the rebellion of Cassius—or later (*HA Marcus*, 24 (AD 175) & 27). Recent discoveries of Roman camps far north of the Danube indicate that this was a distinct possibility, but before the campaign could be completed, Marcus Aurelius died in 180 at either Vindobona or Sirmium. While it is unlikely that he was murdered by Commodus, as *Gladiator* depicts, it is quite possible that the emperor was killed by the plague.

Archaeological research has helped to make up for the lack of literary evidence for the Marcommanic Wars (Figure 11.11). Regensburg-Kumpfmühl (the predecessor to Castra Regina), Sorviodurum (Straubing), and Augusta Vindelicorum (Augsburg) all feature

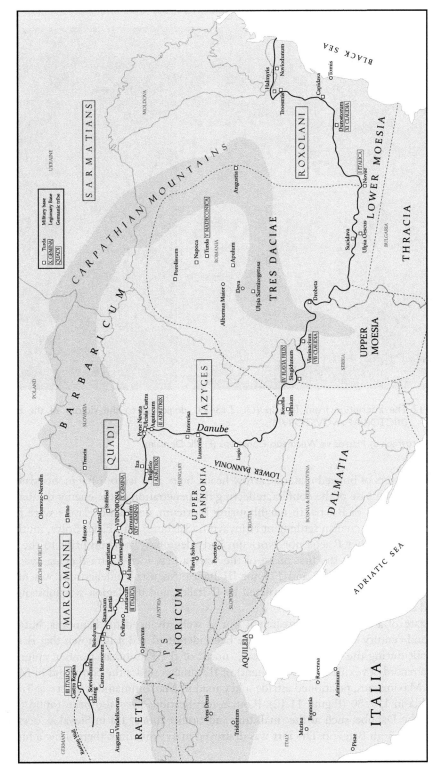

Figure 11.11 The Danube frontier during the Marcommanic Wars overlaid on modern political boundaries, with sites discussed in the text.

Source: Illustration by the author.

Figure 11.12 The inscription from Trencín (*CIL* 3.13439), dedicated to the victory of the *augusti* (VICTORIAE AVGVSTORVM).

Source: Photograph by Matros via Wikimedia Commons (Public Domain).

destruction layers of burned material, arrow heads, bolts, and armour fragments, dated by coins to the first phase of the conflict, reflecting the penetration of the enemy through the Danubian defences of Raetia. In neighbouring Noricum, destruction layers were found at Lentia (Linz), the civilian settlement at Juvavum (Salzburg), and Flavia Solva, southwest of Vindobona. Neither Raetia nor Noricum had a legionary garrison prior to the wars, and towards the end of the first phase of the wars, a new fort, Castra Regina, was built at Regensburg between 172 and 179 for III Italica. Augusta Vindelicorum was further protected by a defensive wall, constructed by II Italica, and this legion was subsequently stationed at Lauriacum (Ens-Lorch).

The state of archaeological research is not as well advanced for Pannonia, but mid/late-second century destruction layers have been identified and it is known that Brigetio was rebuilt during the wars. Furthermore, north of the Pannonian frontier, epigraphic evidence records a vexillation (detachment) of II Adiutrix under the command of Marcus Valerius Maximianus, positioned astride a key road in Marcommanic territory at Trencín in Slovakia in 179/80 (Figure 11.12). Roman fortifications have also been found to the north of the Danube, such as the small turf-and-timber fort at Iza in Slovakia, occupied by I Adiutrix from Brigetio. The fort was destroyed in 179/80: finds there show a hurried evacuation, with deposits of nails from military *caligae*, coins, weapons, and a destruction layer of burned timber and parts of bows. Numerous marching camps have also been found dating to the wars, including Brno in South Moravia and even as far north as Olomouc-Neredín, in the region bordering southwestern Poland. Other temporary installations include Stillfried and Musov, occupied by elements of X Gemina between 172 and 180. In some places, such as Bernhardstal, Germanic settlements were destroyed and then replaced with Roman military structures, reflecting a hostile and deliberate policy of subjugation. Finally, a stark indication of the state of affairs north of the Danube is the dearth of deposits of Roman coinage and terra sigillata. According to Cassius Dio (71.11), envoys from the Quadi had tried to negotiate access to Roman markets, but this was denied; Dio also reported the creation of a buffer zone along the Danube between Roman positions and the Marcomanni, and the establishment of a trading schedule that would regulate their movement (71.15). The lack of ceramics and coins is a reflection of this policy of denial and control.

The Column of Marcus Aurelius

Of the various pictorial representations of Marcus Aurelius and his time—his numerous coin issues or the famous equestrian statue now in the Capitoline Museums—the Column of Marcus Aurelius demands our attention. This monument to his European wars was built at some point prior to 193 out of Carrara marble and installed on the via Flaminia, the road by which the emperor left Rome for the Danube. It was clearly modelled on Trajan's Column, containing an internal staircase and decorated by an ascending spiral frieze, large parts of which, especially at the beginning, were copied or derived from the images of Dacia made by Trajan's artists. The sculpted reliefs show the same meticulous attention to detail (Figure 11.13).

The later Column differs from the Trajanic monument in the scale of its frieze, which did not taper, and in its more robust construction: it is a larger, heavier structure than its predecessor. The Column was badly damaged in the Middle Ages, but was carefully restored between 1588 and 1599, where new images were carved to replace those parts of the frieze that had been lost beyond repair. What has remained has troubled scholars ever since: it has proven difficult to match even obvious scenes, such as the rain miracle, with the historical record, and events appear to be chronologically displaced from what is known through the evidence from coins, epigraphy, and the textual sources. The equipment of the soldiers has also aroused interest, with many wearing chain mail instead of the *lorica segmentata* and using oval shields instead of the characteristically rectangular *scuta* of Trajan's time. Other developments are visible in the images, such as the preference for beards in imitation of imperial grooming habits, and the lengthening of Roman swords, which could be used to cut and slash more effectively than their shorter predecessors. Roman troops on the Column wear their swords on a baldric over the shoulder, and are dressed in trousers—a Germanic style better adapted to fighting in the frigid winters of central Europe.

The most intriguing aspect of the Column's depictions is the disturbing style in which the reliefs were carved and the high proportion of violent images. The smooth, classical lines that presented Trajan's victories have been replaced by harsh diagonal lines that slash across individual scenes, and the viewer is assaulted by images of horror and anguish

Figure 11.13 Roman legionnaires on the Column of Marcus Aurelius in Rome.

Source: Photograph by Barosaurus Lentus (CC BY 3.0).

reflecting the desperate fighting that took place (Figure 11.14). This jarring disjunction is further highlighted by the column erected not long before for Antoninus Pius. Opposite the depiction of his apotheosis (Figure 11.7, above), the other side provides an image of a military review. It is sculpted neatly, with straight vertical and horizontal lines—the very essence of order.

In the images on the Column of Marcus Aurelius shown in Figure 11.14, the terror of unarmed Germanic captives being put to the sword is unmistakeable in their tormented expressions, and the slashing of swords and the thrusting of javelins have an almost visceral effect on the viewer. In the panel immediately above the doomed captives, contrasting diagonal lines, represented by the weapons of the infantry, create a similar sense of unease and disquiet. On the Column, there are also scenes of wanton violence directed at civilians: women and children are terrorised by legionnaires burning their villages (Figure 11.15) and women are executed in cold blood (Figure 11.16). In these scenes, the unarmed captives are portrayed with greater sympathy than their captors, who belong to a more vile and base world. Even in scenes of triumph, there is a feeling of unease, as in the wraithlike depiction of the rain god (Figure 11.17).

It has been suggested that the wars of Marcus Aurelius were simply more violent than those of Trajan, or that the Germans were singled out for particularly savage treatment in response to the violence in Italy. Cassius Dio (71.11) noted that some of the Germanic

Figure 11.14 Images from the Column of Marcus Aurelius.

Source: Photograph by Matthias Kabel (CC BY-SA 3.0).

tribesmen initially settled in Italy had then gone on to seize Ravenna, prompting Marcus to put an end to settlement so close to Rome. Dio also wrote that the emperor was angry with the Quadi in particular, who had agreed an armistice with the Romans and then broken it (71.13). They had taken in fugitives from the Marcomanni; they had fought alongside the Iazyges, despite being at peace with Rome; and they had not returned Roman prisoners. All of this merited savage treatment. As for the Iazyges, when they finally surrendered, the emperor still wanted to 'exterminate them utterly' (71.16). Dio attributed a personal level of anger and calculated severity to Marcus Aurelius, and images from the Column support this appraisal: in one, for instance, the emperor contemplates a doomed prisoner; in another, he accepts the severed heads of Germanic captives while another miserable prisoner, hands behind his back and held by a legionnaire, awaits his brutal fate. The war was violent because it was a war of retribution, and its savagery finds a parallel in the vicious suppression of Boudicca and the three Jewish revolts. It is noteworthy that the

Figure 11.15 Roman troops burning German villages.

Source: Photograph by Matthias Kabel (CC BY-SA 3.0).

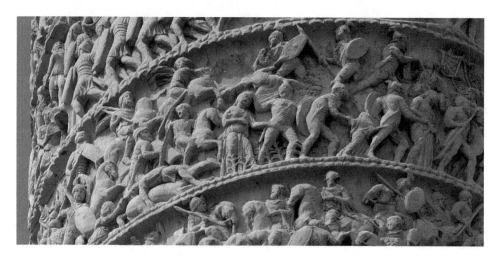

Figure 11.16 Roman soldiers executing a female captive.

Source: Photograph by Matthias Kabel (CC BY-SA 3.0).

violent images from the Column are paralleled by the near contemporary Sarcophagus of Portonaccio, which is thought to have been intended for a senior officer who had fought on the Danube. Dating from between 180 and 190, the carved reliefs feature the same slashing, diagonal lines and jumbled bodies, and reflect the chaotic way in which the war was remembered (Figure 11.18).

Figure 11.17 The 'rain miracle', showing the rain god delivering Roman troops from their thirst.

Source: Photograph by Barosaurus Lentus (CC BY-SA 3.0).

The emperor and his empire

Despite incessant war and the ravages of the plague, the period between 161 and 180 was also a time of institutional continuity. That the empire was able to function despite the recurring crises on its borders was a reflection of the endurance of Augustan institutions, and the actions of conscientious emperors—particularly the Flavians and then Trajan, Hadrian, and Antoninus Pius—who had paid attention to governance and improved on what Augustus had created. It was also, of course, a reflection of the character of Marcus Aurelius and his approach to government. Aurelius Victor praised Marcus, calling him a man of 'wisdom, gentleness, integrity, and learning' (*On the Caesars*, 16). Following his Stoic beliefs, the emperor 'refrained from all offences and did nothing amiss, whether voluntarily or involuntarily', wrote Cassius Dio, noting further that 'he was a good man and devoid of all pretence', who maintained the security of the empire 'amid unusual and extraordinary difficulties' (71.34–5).

The demands of constant campaigning meant that Marcus Aurelius, like Hadrian, conducted affairs on the move. This was still possible in the late second century, since many of the key posts, held by equestrians, were able to operate away from the capital. These included, for instance, the men who responded to petitions (*a libellis*), those who handled Latin correspondence (*ab epistulis*), and those who looked after the imperial fisc. Under Marcus Aurelius, a manager for Greek correspondence (a second *ab epistulis*) was added to this group. The emperor's council of advisers, the most important group of

Figure 11.18 Detail from the Sarcophagus of Portonaccio.

Source: Photograph by Jean-Pol Grandmont (CC BY 4.0).

men in the empire aside from the senate, also travelled with him; by necessity, these men needed to be in close proximity to the emperor and so the Roman government was, as Herodian noted (1.6.5), wherever the emperor was at any given time: Carnuntum, Sirmium, or Vindobona. Warfare and the plague created numerous vacancies in high positions, but these were usually filled through direct promotions: Pertinax, for instance, had been recognised for his abilities, and from lowly origins he was soon propraetorian legate of Dacia. Like Hadrian, Marcus spent a good deal of time on legal matters, for which he relied on Quintus Cervidius Scaevola, a leading jurist of the day and member of his council of advisers. Cassius Dio remarked that even while he was at the front, Marcus gave full attention to judicial problems, even holding court at night (71.6), while the *Historia Augusta* noted that Marcus allowed 230 days *per year* to be court days (*HA Marcus*, 10); even before he became emperor, Marcus complained to Fronto that while the latter was able to pass time relaxing with the works of Cato the Elder, *he* was obliged to listen to lawyers all night long! The legal issues of the day concerned the manumission of slaves, the question of guardians for children, for which Marcus created a praetorship to administer wards and guardians, and the composition of municipal government. Like Trajan and Hadrian, Marcus looked askance at false testimony and denunciation. On slavery, Marcus was keen to give slaves the benefit of the doubt, and created ways for their freedom to be attained. The emperor also addressed municipal affairs through the continued provision of curators, by replacing Hadrian's four consular divisions of Italy with praetorial

Figure 11.19 Inscription III from Ruwafa. In the middle line can be read the Greek word POBAΘOY—
Robathou, the Greek name for the place called Rbtw (Ruwafa) in the Nabataean text in
Inscription IV.

Source: Photograph by the author.

divisions managed by *iuridici*, judges, and by requiring senators to direct a portion of their income towards Italian, rather than provincial, investments. One of the cases that Marcus was forced to adjudicate included complaints made against his former teacher, Herodes Atticus. An influential man in Athenian society, Herodes frequently aroused irritation, and managed to fall out with Cornelius Fronto, local enemies, and two influential brothers, Sextus Quintilius Condianus and Quintilius Valerius Maximus, who were in Achaea as plenipotentiary governors.

Numerous inscriptions illustrate the way imperial affairs continued to function despite the strain of constant war. One of the most intriguing examples was discovered at Ruwafa, at the southern extremities of the province of Arabia. The five inscriptions, written in Nabataean Aramaic and Greek, belonged to a small temple established in a semi-verdant valley now located in north-western Saudi Arabia. The inscriptions are in the National Museum of Riyadh, save for one that is lost and another that still lies in the sand close to the ruins of the temple (Figure 11.19). Aside from a spring and a flurry of petroglyphs on nearby rocks, there is little else nearby, and it is the last place one would expect to find formal inscriptions recognising the authority of the Roman empire.

The inscriptions record that the temple was constructed during the reigns of Marcus Aurelius and Lucius Verus by Thamud, an Arab tribe known from a number of sources from the eighth century BC onwards. The most detailed recent assessment of the inscriptions

(*AEBI* §1.18–22) suggests that the *ethnos* of Thamud mentioned in the Greek text was an auxiliary military unit, raised locally and allied with the Romans. The construction and dedication of the temple took some amount of time: in one section of the inscriptions the emperors are named along with their title of *Armeniaci*, and the propraetorian legate of Arabia, Antistius Adventus, is also named; in another section, a second propraetorian legate is named (Claudius Modestus) and the emperors are also called *Parthici Maximi*, which places the text after 165 and before Lucius Verus died in 169. The significance of the Ruwafa inscriptions lies in the link between two separate Roman governors, both emperors, and an allied auxiliary unit in this very remote area, along with the explicit acknowledgment of imperial suzerainty. That distant Arabia still received attention, even while war raged elsewhere in the empire, reveals the political strength of the empire as well as the importance of local representatives—in this case, two different propraetorian legates—in executing imperial policy.

Almost at the opposite end of the empire, an equally fascinating inscription was discovered at Banasa in Morocco. In a response to a legal petition, Marcus Aurelius and Lucius Verus granted citizenship to a certain Julianus, chief of the Zegrenses tribe in Mauretania, together with his family. The text was proudly inscribed on a bronze tablet, the *tabula Banasitana*. Its lengthy record includes a notarised extract from a legal document in Rome that continuously recorded citizenship grants from the time of Augustus, and names twelve members of the advisory council of Marcus Aurelius. The *tabula* documents a particular type of citizenship grant that could only be given personally by an individual emperor. In this case, citizenship was awarded for Julianus's loyalty, and it was expressly indicated in the text that the grant of citizenship might have the effect of persuading others, potentially less loyal to Rome, to see the advantages to be gained by cooperation. Despite the gulf that separates the *tabula* from the Ruwafa inscriptions, the context is remarkably similar. Julianus is recorded on the *tabula* as 'one of the leading men of his people', and in Africa, the Romans preferred to use such local elites as middlemen to preserve peace and good relations with those who lived at the steppe and desert fringes, for whom direct control by Roman officers or governors was neither desirable nor especially feasible. In southern Arabia, it similarly made far more sense to co-opt local tribesmen to police the difficult desert areas with which they were familiar, and retain the garrison of Arabia at Bostra—nearly 1,000 kilometres (620 miles) distant. In many of these sorts of cases the Romans allowed the use of prestigious titles such as *dux* (war leader) or *rex* (king), and also provided subsidies, technical and military advisers, and other forms of material support. After the third century, distinctive *reges* or *mlk* (Aramaic/Arabic for 'king') emerged at the edges of Roman territory as a result of this process of contact, support, and cooperation.

Aside from political and institutional continuity, the Antonine era was also a time of great cultural creativity that has left us with some of the most important works from antiquity. A flurry of Greek novels, including the *Babylonian Tale* by Iamblichus, *Leucippe and Clitophon* by Achilles Tatius, *Daphnis and Chloe* by Longus, and the *Ethiopian Tale* by Heliodorus, formed part of the surge in Greek writing that took place during the Second Sophistic. Another prominent writer was Lucian, who recorded the prophesies of the snake, Glycon. Hailing from Samosata, Lucian wrote some of the most memorable and satirical Greek prose of antiquity. In *How To Write History*, he skewered historians who engaged in ridiculous flattery or outright invention, mocking the appearance of fabulous and instantaneous Thucydidean accounts of the Parthian war such as the one that claimed that Cassius and III Gallica had crossed the Indus like Alexander the Great and his Macedonians (31). Lucian's *True Story* is a raucous journey through the impossible— 'Once upon a time, setting out from the Pillars of Hercules and heading for the western ocean with a fair wind, I went a-voyaging …' (6). Lucian's Atticising tendencies, typical of the Second Sophistic, were reflected in Latin by Cornelius Fronto, whose lengthy correspondence with Marcus Aurelius reveals a near pedantic obsession with the correct use of the Latin language, a total absence of Virgilian influence, and a delight in turns of phrase and rhetorical devices. Like their Greek counterparts, Latinists of the period gazed fondly backwards to an imagined morally and linguistically pure pre-imperial past. Fronto was among them, as was Aulus Gellius, author of the Latin *Attic Nights*. In a letter to Lucius Verus in 163, Fronto described Augustus as 'master of but the dying elegance of his times', and deplored the state of the language from Tiberius onwards. Other letters from Fronto to his correspondents fixated on the nobleness of great Roman Republicans, men and women alike. Such antiquarian views had also been favoured by Hadrian, who preferred Cato the Elder and Ennius but considered Virgil decidedly *passé*. Similarly, when Marcus wrote to Fronto asking for reading material, he sought not Virgil, but Cato the Elder and Sallust. Within this blossoming of literary culture, the most important historical voices of the time were Arrian and Appian, both of whom wrote in Greek. Appian also exchanged correspondence with Fronto and, as we have already seen, his history is an invaluable source for the Republican period. Arrian, propraetorian legate of Cappadocia under Hadrian and collector of the *Discourses* of Epictetus, was so deeply enmeshed in the Athenian past that he imagined himself as a new Xenophon: he even called his history of Alexander the Great the *Anabasis*, in imitation of Xenophon's famous account of his epic journey home following the death of the Persian king Cyrus the Great in battle in 401 BC. The *Stratagems* of Polyaenus, who we met in Chapter 3, can also be mentioned here. Polyaenus, a rhetor from Macedonia, dedicated his Greek work to Marcus Aurelius and Lucius Verus; he imagined that his encyclopedic collection of military anecdotes might assist them in the war against the Parthians.

The most famous of the era's Greek works is, however, the *Meditations*: its 12 books offer the emperor's reflections on what he learned from his teachers, his thoughts about the passage of time, and how an emperor should act. The *Meditations* were influenced by the principles of Stoicism and the *Discourses* of Epictetus, a copy of which had been given to Marcus by one of his teachers (1.7). The exploration of how Stoic axioms could be applied to his own unique situation, and how they could help a man become the master of his own self, recurs frequently in Marcus' text. Marcus explained, for instance, that a man would achieve a positive existence by adhering to the axiom 'that nothing is for a man's good save what makes him just, temperate, manly, and free' (8.1). An important influence on the *Meditations* and Marcus' political philosophy was the idea inherent in the Second Sophistic that the *oikumene* was, above all, a commonwealth. Its collection of different peoples, united by citizenship, were best ruled by a 'good king'—Marcus, guided by Stoicism and a deep sense of duty, was that king and his role was to preserve order and peace in the empire. In just two instances (books 1 & 3) the text ends with a location: 'Written in the territory of the Quadi, near the river Granua'—the Hron, in Slovakia—and the laconic 'Written in Carnuntum.' It has proven difficult, however, to match these books to specific moments during the Marcommanic Wars, but it has been argued that books 2 and 3 were written before Marcus Aurelius transferred his base of operations to Sirmium to fight the Iazyges.

The late second century was also a time of great interest in medical knowledge. No doubt this was due, in part, to the plague, but many of the literary personalities of the era also discussed their maladies in rather candid ways. Marcus Aurelius was often sickly, and he and Fronto exchanged frequent letters about their bodily aches and pains. In 163, for instance, Fronto wrote to Marcus about how he was 'seized with pain in all my limbs, but especially in my neck and groin', and as late as 166, Fronto was complaining about his ill health to Lucius Verus, although his pain was tempered by Verus's 'great glory.' The Roman elite had access to good medical care in the shape of Galen, who was born in Pergamum in 129 and lived an extraordinary life until the age of 87. He studied with the best teachers throughout the Mediterranean, and learned his early trade tending to wounded gladiators. By the mid-160s he had acquired sufficient fame to be called on to look after Marcus Aurelius and Lucius Verus at Aquileia, and also tended to Commodus, who shared his father's ill-health. Galen put great store in Hippocrates, Plato, and Aristotle, entwining philosophy and medical knowledge, and he developed an understanding of anatomy and physiology that would be unequalled for over a millennium. Galen was a prolific writer, and his texts were translated into Latin, Armenian, Hebrew, Syriac, and Arabic. The exact number of his works has never been truly established, but a ninth-century Arabic translator in Baghdad could count 50 (!) manuscripts alone that *he* knew of, but which had not been listed by Galen in the list of works that he made, *On His Own Books*. Galen's medical advances were complemented by the Alexandrian Claudius Ptolemy, whose Greek *Geography*, translated into Latin and Arabic and illustrated with maps of the world, remains one of the great scientific works of antiquity.

Commodus

History has not been kind to Commodus. The *Historia Augusta* characterised his many deficiencies as a man and a leader: 'Not only was he wont to drink until dawn and squander the resources of the Roman empire', it related, 'in the evening he would ramble through taverns and brothels.' He was bloodthirsty, installed criminals as legates, and engaged in immoral pursuits that included 'rioting in the palace amid banquets and baths along with 300 concubines' (*HA Commodus*, 3 & 5). Aurelius Victor thought that he was 'quite detestable', and his rule created 'a burden on successive generations' (*On the Caesars*, 17). Opinions differed about his appearance: Marius Maximus wrote that 'he had such a conspicuous growth on his groin that the people of Rome could see the swelling through his silken robes', a reference to a probable hernia (*HA Commodus*, 13), while Herodian purred breathlessly that 'his commanding eyes flashed like lightning; his hair, naturally blond and curly, gleamed in the sunlight as if it were on fire' (1.7).

In a more balanced assessment, Cassius Dio ascribed Commodus' dreadful rule to his cowardice and the ease with which he was manipulated by others. 'This, I think', he wrote, 'Marcus clearly perceived beforehand' (72.1), and Marcus is thus often criticised for breaking with the successful adoption policy initiated by Nerva. On the other hand, Marcus ensured that Commodus was surrounded by capable people whom he trusted, and certainly Commodus' rule started well enough: against the advice of Pompeianus, the war with the Marcommani and Quadi was ended with a treaty that funnelled thousands of men into auxiliary regiments, extracted a grain tribute, forced a political alignment with Roman policy, barred settlement along the left bank of the Danube, and severely limited rights of assembly (Cassius Dio, 72.2). While this was viewed by some as an unmanly retrench-ment, peace returned to the Danube frontier for the first time in a generation, and further drains on Rome's military resources, battered from the plague and combat losses, were avoided. After returning to Rome, however, the first signs of trouble were quickly evident. Commodus celebrated a triumph in the autumn of 180 with his hated Nicomedian cham-berlain Saoterus, a freedman and 'his partner in depravity' (*HA Commodus*, 3). Cassius Dio, who was in Rome at the time, was deeply unimpressed by Commodus' first appearance as emperor, noting that he addressed the senate with 'a lot of trivialities' (72.4).

Only two years later, Commodus faced a coup organised by his sister, Lucilla, whose plot included Marcus Ummidius Quadratus Annianus, whom she had taken as her lover in pro-test at her forced marriage to Pompeianus. Quadratus was the nephew of Marcus Aurelius, and another of the plotters was Pompeianus's own nephew. This dynastic ménage-á-trois was doomed to fail from the start, and when the assassin unwisely paused in front of Commodus, knife in hand, to offer some dramatic words prior to his heroic deed, he was killed by Commodus's bodyguard. Quadratus was executed, and Lucilla was banished to Capri. The praetorian prefect Tigidius Perennis used the opportunity to initiate a wider purge, targeting prominent men and members of Commodus's inner circle. The victims included Taruttienus Paternus, Perennis's colleague in the prefecture, who had executed Saoterus in the aftermath of the failed conspiracy in which he was, himself, probably involved. Perennis took particular aim at powerful senators, and Pertinax, propraetorian legate of Syria, was stripped of his office and sent into forced retirement. Septimius Severus, legate of IV Scythica, was similarly relieved of his command and retired to Athens. By the mid-point of the decade, virtually all of the men appointed by Marcus Aurelius to advise and protect Commodus were dead, banished, or in hiding. These included Cornelius Fronto's son-in-law, Aufidius Victorinus, who had taken his own life, and Pompeianus, who had left Rome, blaming bad eyesight and a need to convalesce. While the character of the general Maximus in *Gladiator* is fictional, the manner of his fall from grace was entirely consistent with the brutal realities of the time.

Together with Cleander, a Phrygian freedman of Marcus Aurelius, Perennis took over much of the daily work of running the empire. Cleander became the imperial cham-berlain, a position from which he enjoyed unprecedented access to Commodus. A very capable administrator, Perennis nevertheless created friction with the senate, whose class-conscious members resented taking orders from an equestrian and a freedman, and disliked Perennis's policy of appointing equestrians as legionary prefects in place of senat-orial legates. While Rome teetered on the edge of constitutional chaos, a revolt in Britain breached the Antonine Wall and caused severe damage before it was repressed by Ulpius Marcellus, but his martinet behaviour led to a mutiny. In 185, an angry delegation of some 1,500 troops from the British garrison arrived in Rome to petition the emperor. Their grievances included the poor treatment received from Ulpius Marcellus, the lack of donatives from the stingy Perennis, and the equestrian rank of many of their new commanders. Perennis, who was suspected of plotting a coup, was stripped of his pos-ition and, with his family, was 'delivered up to the soldiers to be torn to pieces'. This was done with the full connivance of Cleander, who not only used the opportunity to gain control of the government, but also profited from selling coveted positions within it (*HA Commodus*, 6; Herodian, 1.8). With the hated Perennis gone, both Pertinax and Severus returned to the imperial fold under Cleander's patronage—Pertinax was sent to Britain as its propraetorian legate, where he suppressed another rebellion, while Severus became the propraetorian legate of Gallia Lugdunensis. After a stint in charge of the *alimenta*, Pertinax then received the coveted proconsular post of governor of Africa, a conservative bastion of the senate. That Africa was given to the son of a freedman sowed further disquiet among the senate and further hatred towards Cleander, who had spent the previous three years quietly eliminating his rivals and ensconcing himself as *a pugione*, 'dagger bearer', a supreme position with two praetorian prefects serving beneath him. Pertinax followed his stint in Africa by becoming the urban prefect of Rome, his presence in the city a stinging reminder to the senators of their progressive disenfranchisement. Remarkably, the government continued to function despite the many headwinds, but there were troubling signs of what was to come. In 187, Cleander suppressed an incipient revolt by Lucius Antistius Burrus, who had held the ordinary consulship with Commodus in 180. Burrus had tried to enlist Pertinax, but judging that the coup would fail, Pertinax divulged the plot and Burrus and his fellow conspirators were murdered. Commodus's long-suffering wife, Crispina, was caught up in the purge and banished to Capri, where she was later murdered. As Rome simmered with plots and purges, unrest and banditry in Upper Germany left VII Augusta under siege; on the Rhine, a legionnaire named Maternus deserted, taking many of his fellow soldiers with him. The civil war that followed, the Deserters' War, spread quickly and was accompanied by jail breaks, robbery, and armed assaults on towns and villages. Maternus evaded the general sent to quash him, Pescennius Niger, and set himself up in Italy as a new Spartacus, making it as far as Rome before he was betrayed by one of his inner circle. The Deserters' War, along with the revolts in Britain, exposed a worrying lack of discipline in the army.

In 190, Cleander sold an astonishing 25 consulships, but fell victim to Papirius Dionysius, an unscrupulous equestrian who was prefect of the *annona*, the grain supply. With the collusion of Pertinax, the urban prefect, and Julius Julianus, the praetorian prefect, and with the prompting of Cleander's many enemies in the senate, Papirius created an artificial grain shortage in order to sow chaos in Rome. Before long, the urban poor had flocked to riot in the streets; at the Circus Maximus, a group of chanting children were used to stir the anger of the crowd to denounce Cleander as the culprit for their hunger. Large-scale chanting in public venues had become a legitimate way for the people to communicate their anger and needs to the palace, and, finally spurred to action, Commodus recovered his nerve and ordered Cleander's execution. Cleander's erstwhile allies—men like Pertinax, who had returned from exile through his graces—watched impassively. Cleander's murder spurred another expiatory orgy of killing, in which the praetorian prefects turned on each other; both perished. In the aftermath Commodus came out of political hiding, proclaimed a Golden Age of Commodus, and began to style himself as a second Hadrian—he even persuaded the Athenians to give him Athenian citizenship. Commodus's newfound energy took alarming turns as he openly declared himself to be Hercules and ordered dozens of statues of himself, dressed as the great hero, set up around Rome—and it was now that he ventured into the arena to fight as a gladiator. If the *Historia Augusta* is correct, he took part in over 1,000 individual matches (*HA Commodus*, 12), but always stacked the odds in his favour by fighting opponents with leaden swords. Aurelius Victor wrote that Commodus shied away from fighting a gladiator named Scaeva hand-to-hand, with just one sword between them, fearful that he might lose his sword and be killed—exactly, of course, what happens at the end of *Gladiator* (*On the Caesars*, 17). Worst of all, Commodus charged his own treasury a million sesterces *per show*. This, together with his other excesses, undid all of the prudent fiscal governance of Marcus Aurelius.

It was not only because gladiators were slaves that the senate was angered by Commodus' foray into the arena. Senators were also forced to watch Commodus's exploits. Cassius Dio noted that after killing an ostrich, Commodus decapitated it and waved it in front of the senators' faces, implying that he intended to decapitate the senate as well. Dio wrote that he would have been summarily executed for laughing, 'if I had not chewed on some laurel leaves, which I got from my garland' (72.21). Dio also recorded the chants that the assembled senators were forced to shout with all their strength: 'You are the lord and you are first, of all men most fortunate. You are the victor, and you shall be the victor, everlasting, Amazonian' (73.20). While he may have attempted to become a new Hadrian, Commodus was behaving rather more like a new Nero. The senators were appalled, but their hatred of the emperor only invited more show trials and executions. Cassius Dio reported the startling tale, for instance, of Sextus Quintilius Condianus. This man was the son of one of the Quintilii brothers (the enemies of Herodes Atticus), both of whom Commodus had already killed and whose property he had confiscated. The young Condianus, finding himself on the execution list, faked his own death by falling off a horse, all the while vomiting animal blood that he had held in his mouth. Afterwards, he arranged for a ram to be cremated inside his own coffin. He then tried his hardest to disappear, without much luck (72.6). This example would have to do, wrote Dio, for 'it should render my narrative very tedious were I to give a detailed report of all the persons put to death by Commodus' (72.7).

Commodus eventually perished in a palace coup hatched by the praetorian prefect Aemilius Laetus together with the chamberlain, Eclectus, and Marcia, a Christian freedwoman who was the former lover of Quadratus and now both the wife of Eclectus and concubine of Commodus. Laetus, from Thaenae in Africa, maintained tight control of imperial appointments and carefully placed loyalists in key positions. He sent his fellow African Septimius Severus to become the propraetorian legate of Upper Pannonia (three legions) and Severus's brother Septimius Geta to Lower Moesia (two legions). Clodius Albinus, another African (from Hadrumetum), who had commanded a legion in Dacia in the previous decade, assumed the legateship of Britannia with its strong garrison. The intention of the plot was to replace Commodus with the venerable Pertinax, and the conspiracy took shape as Rome descended into farce. In 192, the city was renamed *colonia Commodiana*, and the emperor, who had renamed himself Lucius Aelius Aurelius Commodus and declared himself a god, took extravagant titles including *Amazonius*, *Gladiatorius*, *Effeminatus*, *Hercules Romanus* (a title that appeared on coinage), *Pacator Orbis* ('pacifier of the world'), and *Exsuperatorius* ('the supreme one'). Above all, he was particularly fond of his likeness to Hercules and apparently used to have Marcia dress up as an Amazon for him (Figure 11.20), while the famous bust of Commodus in the Capitoline Museums depicts the emperor as Hercules, with its base offering a portrayal of an idealised Amazonian woman.

Commodus also ordered that the legions should take the title *Commodiana*, and he continued to channel Nero, placing the likeness of his own head on top of the Colossus and adding a club so it resembled Hercules. He had August renamed 'Commodus' and September 'Hercules'. Amazingly, these were not purely ephemeral fancies, but were actually used: an altar found at the Palmyrene Gate at Dura-Europos was dedicated to

Figure 11.20 Bronze medallion of Commodus, minted in the final year of his reign. Obverse: head of Commodus over that of Marcia (?), portrayed as an Amazon; reverse: Hercules naked on the left, with Commodus as a priest on the right.

Commodus, *Pacator Orbis* and *Hercules Romanus*. The dedicant was an officer in an auxiliary cohort, II Ulpia Commodiana, and he recorded the date of his inscription to the 17th of the new Commodian month Pius—the anniversary of the imperial reign (March 17).

In Rome, natural disasters struck, including a return of the Antonine Plague and a fire that burned Vespasian's Templum Pacis to the ground; repairing the damage, Commodus took the title '*Conditor*', or 'founder'. Finally, getting wind that she and the two new consuls were due to be murdered in a New Year's Day gladiatorial procession, Marcia, together with Laetus and Eclectus, decided that their plan to kill Commodus could wait no longer. Commodus was poisoned on New Year's Eve, but the dose was not sufficient and his personal trainer, Narcissus, strangled him to death in his bathtub. It soon became clear that knowledge of the plot was widespread. Pertinax was in the camp of the Praetorian Guard when the emperor was killed, while Pompeianus had returned to Rome from self-imposed exile, his vision miraculously restored. On New Year's Day, 193, Pertinax was presented to the troops as their new emperor, and the senate joyfully overcame their dislike of his humble origins, preferring a *novus homo* emperor to their tortured relationship with Commodus. Pertinax honoured the dead emperor, interring him in the Mausoleum of Hadrian, and appealed for calm in Rome. The Praetorian Guard were bought, as was the custom, but Commodus had spent so deeply that the treasury was empty, even after a dramatic devaluation of the silver denarius coinage and an outrageous head tax on the senate. Like Marcus Aurelius, Pertinax was reduced to selling the imperial silverware to purchase peace; as it turned out, he did not have nearly enough to ensure that it would last.

Civil war

Pertinax, Didius Julianus, and Septimius Severus

Pertinax faced problems almost immediately over the size of the donative that he was prepared to pay to the Praetorian Guard. Aurelius Victor squarely blamed the troops, 'to whom nothing seemed sufficient even though the world was already exhausted and ruined'

(*On the Caesars*, 18). Machiavelli, in a later assessment, broadly agreed: the troops had been so thoroughly corrupted by Commodus that any attempt to act sternly with them was liable to cause a violent backlash, even if the intentions were honest (*The Prince*, 19). Pertinax did, however, manage to raise a great deal of money by selling imperial property, and made good nine years' worth of unpaid *alimenta*. He was keenly aware of the financial state of the empire, and had come to the conclusion that the troops could wait while he attended to more pressing problems, including increasing the percentage of silver in the denarius coinage. Before long, though, a direct challenge came from the Praetorian Guard, which promoted one of the ordinary consuls for 193, Quintus Pompeius Sosius Falco, to replace Pertinax. The insurrection fizzled out, but another quickly followed. Laetus stood by and let his guardsman run amok, and by the afternoon of March 28, 193, Eclectus had been murdered trying to protect the emperor. Pertinax was then decapitated. Pertinax had the support of the senate and some support amongst the people, but these meant little without the support of the troops.

The Praetorian Guard seemed momentarily unsure of how to act and nobody came forward to take Pertinax's place. Finally, a group of guardsmen accosted Didius Julianus, who was 60 years old and had enjoyed a long career in government service. A relative of the jurist Salvius Julianus (Chapter 10), Didius Julianus had benefited from the patronage of Marcus Aurelius. He was suffect consul with Pertinax in 175 and had served as propraetorian legate in difficult areas such as Lower Germany; he had also commanded XXII Primigenia. This mixed senatorial and military background theoretically made him acceptable to the Guard, the army, and the senate. However, a standoff took place at the praetorian camp when it emerged that a rival faction supported Pertinax's father-in-law Flavius Sulpicianus, who was the urban prefect. According to a later story, the Guard agreed a compromise: they would sell the throne to the highest bidder. Didius Julianus— 'always eager for revolution'—emerged with the best offer, or simply made the *only* other offer, but while the senate cautiously accepted his candidacy, the people of Rome emerged in large numbers, chanting for Pescennius Niger, the propraetorian legate of Syria, to save them from Julianus. Cassius Dio, who was in Rome at the time, expressed his fear of Julianus, and when the new emperor addressed the senate, 'he reminded us [the senators] of our knowledge of the kind of man he was, in consequence of which we both feared and hated him' (Cassius Dio, 73.11–12). While Julianus had purchased the support of the Praetorian Guard, his popularity with the senate was wavering and he was clearly not welcomed by the people, who continued to chant in the Circus Maximus and riot in the streets.

Before Niger could move, however, Septimius Severus took action. Severus was from the Punic city of Leptis (or Lepcis) Magna in Tripolitania, now a UNESCO World Heritage Site in Libya. The geographical location of Leptis, sitting on the coast astride a trade route that led via Malta to Sicily and southern Italy, had long favoured communication with Rome, and the city and its hinterland became a major producer of olive oil for Italian markets. Many of the city's inhabitants were Roman citizens who fostered a particular devotion to the imperial cult and, under Vespasian, Leptis was raised to the status of a *municipium* with the Latin rights. In the early second century, Leptis produced its first equestrians, including the grandfather of Septimius Severus, and the city was granted the rank of colony in 112 under the name Ulpia Traiana Fidelis, a move that gave citizenship to all of its inhabitants. Severus's family was wealthy and well educated; his grandfather had been a pupil of Quintilian in Rome, and two members of the family served as consuls. Severus himself was born in 146, and enjoyed the patronage of Marcus Aurelius, who allowed him to enter the senatorial order. After serving as a junior magistrate, Severus was quaestor in Rome in 169 and in Sardinia the following year. A stint assisting a family member who was serving as proconsul of Africa followed, and he was later sent to Hispania Tarraconensis as a praetor. Afterwards, he was appointed as the legionary legate of IV Scythica, a position from which he was dismissed by Perennis a few years later.

The career of Septimius Severus to this point is striking in its banality and would fit the description of hundreds of senators throughout the imperial period: an array of government positions, a military command, and then perhaps a prosperous retirement. But while he was stationed in Syria under the command of the legate Pertinax, who had become his friend, Severus had a life-changing experience. Even though the kingdom of Emesa had long since lost its independence, the city remained important as a node that linked western Syria to Palmyra, and it also contained an important shrine to the god Elagabal. The god's cult relic was a betyl, an aniconic holy image which, in this case, took the form of a black meteorite. The cult itself was long assimilated to the worship of the sun god, Sol (Helios), which meant that it could be translated from its Semitic roots to a broader Mediterranean audience. The priests of the cult were members of the old Emesene royal family—as we saw in Chapter 10, these were close allies of Rome and had held Roman citizenship for some time. While he was at Emesa, Severus befriended the priest of Elagabal, Julius Bassianus, who introduced him to his two daughters, Julia Domna and Julia Maesa. When Severus's first wife died in 186 or 187, Severus, who was back in public life serving in the quiet backwater of Gallia Lugdunensis, rekindled his acquaintance with Bassianus and, in 187, he married Julia Domna. Two boys were born to the couple in 188 and 190, and Severus became one of Cleander's 25 consuls in 190. In 191, as noted above, Laetus sent Severus to Upper Pannonia, where he had three legions at his disposal.

In 193, Severus not only had a significant military command, he was also closer to Italy than Pescennius Niger. In early April, 193, the troops of XIV Gemina at Carnuntum proclaimed Severus emperor on the promise that he would exact vengeance for the death of Pertinax, whose memory loomed large in central Europe due to his loyalty to Marcus Aurelius during the Marcomannic Wars. The acclamation by XIV Gemina was taken up by the other 15 legions serving on the Rhine–Danube frontier. Severus underscored his new loyalties by proclaiming himself Imperator Caesar Lucius Septimius Severus Pertinax Augustus, but declared that he would await a formal ratification of his title by the senate. This was, in part, to respect the tattered remnants of Augustan tradition, but also because there was a third challenger waiting in the wings—Clodius Albinus, the legate of Britannia, to whom Severus now offered the junior position of Caesar. Knowing that Severus would need to fight Niger, who had proclaimed himself emperor from Antioch with the support of ten legions, and given his remote station, Albinus accepted and settled down with his own three legions to await the outcome of events in Europe and Syria.

Niger had a strong position, commanding all of the eastern armies and controlling the Egyptian granaries. In the west, in addition to the core of the Rhine-Danube legions, Severus also had the support of his brother Septimius Geta, legate in Lower Moesia and subsequently of Tres Daciae, as well as the backing of the commander of III Augusta at Lambaesis. Severus moved rapidly into Italy, seizing the important bases of Aquileia and then Ravenna. As Severus approached Rome itself, Didius Julianus fortified the palace

Figure 11.21 Legionary issue gold aureus struck in Rome in 193. Obverse: head of Severus with IMP CAE L SEV PERT AVG; reverse: legionary eagle with two standards, honouring XIV [XIIII] Gemina.

and initiated a purge in which Laetus and Marcia perished. He then panicked, sending an embassy to Severus from the senate, but the embassy joined Severus and marched with him to Rome. Julianus was deserted by everyone that mattered, including the old survivor Pompeianus, and from his position outside Rome, Severus ordered the praetorian prefect Veturius Macrinus to deliver the murderers of Pertinax. The Guard defected, and Severus appointed Macrinus to serve alongside his own man, Flavius Juvenalis. Macrinus was the sole element of continuity, however, since one of Severus's first acts while still outside the city was to dismiss the guardsmen, strip them of their rank and weapons, and banish them from Rome. A new guard, twice as large as its predecessor and made up of Severus's Danubian legionnaires, was created in their stead, and augmented by an increase in the size of the *vigiles* and the urban cohorts. Meanwhile, the prefect of the *vigiles*, an African native named Fulvius Plautianus, had signalled his loyalty to Severus by taking the children of Niger hostage. Under a rule made by Commodus, governors had to leave their children in Rome while abroad in their provinces to guarantee good behaviour. Severus had managed to have his spirited away to safety, but his enemies were not so fortunate. An intimidated senate ordered the execution of Julianus and accepted Severus as emperor; he then performed his *adventus* into Rome, making a profound impact on Cassius Dio. Severus subsequently organised an equally important display—the apotheosis of Pertinax.

Severus had been made emperor by the army: he now paid them a donative to retain their loyalty, honouring individual legions on a new series of coins known as the legionary issue (Figures 11.21 and 11.22). As with Octavian's declaration that he was avenging Julius Caesar, Severus's 'vengeance' for Pertinax was a political fiction which the senate, far less powerful than that which had faced Octavian, was forced to accept. It was also obliged to admit new provincial blood, for Severus took the opportunity to elevate Julius Avitius Alexianus, a relative of Julia Domna, along with several others whom he wished to reward. Albinus was to share the ordinary consulship with Severus, in absentia, for 194—another political fiction. Before long, Severus set off to deal with Niger, raising three new legions, I, II, and III Parthica, as he went. Then, after Niger began his own move on Rome by

Figure 11.22 Legionary issue gold aureus struck in Rome in 193. Obverse: head of Severus with IMP CAE L SEV PERT AVG; reverse: legionary eagle with two standards, honouring XXII Primigenia.

ousting a Severan ally from the city of Byzantium, Severus persuaded the senate to declare Niger a public enemy.

Severan propaganda would claim otherwise, but Niger's forces fought bravely against the experienced European legions that made up the core of Severus's army. Niger's advance towards Rome was slowed, however, by the Baetican native and former propraetorian legate of Upper Moesia, Lucius Fabius Cilo, at Perinthus in Thrace, while the historian Marius Maximus laid siege to Niger's headquarters at Byzantium. Meanwhile, Claudius Candidus crossed over to Asia and defeated Niger at Nicaea, and in the aftermath of this failure Niger's allies began to desert him. Egypt declared for Severus, and in 194 at Issus—a famous battlefield where Alexander had beaten the Persians in 333 BC—the proconsul of Africa, Cornelius Anullinus, with timely assistance from his cavalry commander, Valerius Valerianus, defeated Niger and his army. Historical accounts produced at the time claimed the providential intervention of a heavy thunderstorm, but this was part of Severan propaganda which emphasised divine favour and also sought to bolster a fictional relationship between the Severan dynasty and Marcus Aurelius, in this case by recalling the rain miracle.

In the aftermath of the Issus campaign Niger fled, but he was run to ground, his head cut off and sent to Severus. All of the east except for Byzantium had now fallen, and accompanied by the Augusta Julia Domna, Severus engaged in a savage punitive campaign against the cities and districts that had supported his rival. He knew that some had done so on their own account, while others had done so at the instigation of the new Parthian king, Vologases V, who sought to profit from the Roman civil war, and so the war was both one of revenge against wayward Roman cities and one of conquest to punish Vologases. Antioch was stripped of its leading position and demoted to the status of a village, losing its Olympic Games in the process. Nisibis was conquered and became a Roman colony under an equestrian prefect, and Adiabene and its principal city of Arbela (Erbil in Kurdistan) were captured. Osrhoene was annexed in 195, although its king, Abgar VIII, kept the throne; in gratitude, he called himself Lucius Aelius Septimius Abgar on his coinage. Abgar was also patron to the Christian philosopher Bardaisan and was reportedly converted by him, strengthening Edessa's claim as an ancient centre of Christian learning. Victorious in this punitive conflict that became known as the First Parthian War, Severus took the titles *Parthicus Arabicus* and *Parthicus Adiabenicus* in 195, but Cassius Dio was less impressed, lamenting the cost of maintaining these new conquests which hardly seemed worth the effort and would only drag the Romans into other people's wars (75.3).

The showdown with Albinus

The cities of the east were cowed and Niger was dead. After giving Julia Domna the title of *mater castrorum* and thus associating her with Faustina, Severus arranged for himself to be retroactively adopted by the deified Marcus Aurelius. He now also openly supported the memory of Commodus, deliberately wore an 'Antonine' beard, and proclaimed his devotion to Hercules (Figure 11.23). Severus's son Bassianus was promoted to Caesar and took the royal name Marcus Aurelius Antoninus, although he is better known to history as Caracalla. The new *princeps iuventutis* was acclaimed by the troops at Viminacium, and Severus placed loyalists in key positions throughout central and eastern Europe. Albinus drew the inevitable conclusions from this development, and after evading assassins dispatched by Severus and fending off a skilful propaganda campaign that spread scurrilous rumours about Albinus's ambitions and his supposed role in murdering Pertinax, he crossed the English Channel with his army. Severus prepared to leave for the west with his troops, and the senate sided with their champion; there was little choice, as Rome was in the grip of Cornelius Anullinus, whom Severus had appointed as the urban prefect.

Albinus now proclaimed himself Augustus and made Lugdunum his headquarters. In 197, after a stint in Rome where he made himself visible and performed some of the expected administrative and judicial duties of a sitting emperor, Severus marched his army to Gaul and brought Albinus to battle in mid-February. The result was a slaughter that brought Severus perilously close to disaster, as his front ranks were drawn in by a

Figure 11.23 Bronze medallion minted at Pergamum. Obverse: Septimius Severus and Julia Domna; reverse: Hercules and the Cerynean Hind. The Greek legend ΠΕΡΓΑΜΩΝ ΝΕΟΚΟΡΩΝ refers to the city's prestigious status of *neokoros*.

false retreat and succumbed to a series of bloody punji traps. Eventually a timely cavalry charge by Julius Laetus (no relation to the former praetorian prefect) eventually produced an unexpected victory. The aftermath particularly horrified Cassius Dio, who wrote that he could not accept the version of events that he had read in Severus's autobiography (which has not survived). Dio wrote instead that after Severus gazed at Albinus's head, 'feasting his eyes on it to the full', he abused it with foul language and ordered Albinus' body to be discarded in the Rhône. 'This action,' wrote Dio, 'showed clearly that he possessed none of the qualities of a good ruler' (75.7). The *Historia Augusta* sensationally recorded that Severus rode over the headless torso with his horse (*HA Septimius Severus*, 11). Less sensational, but more brutal, was the sack of Lugdunum that followed—yet another example of provincial armies from other parts of the empire taking vengeance on a beaten Roman city.

Vologases V had opportunistically invaded Syria in 196 and the eastern provinces demanded his attention, but Severus decided to return directly to Rome with the new praetorian prefect Fulvius Plautianus, sending Julius Laetus on ahead to the east in his stead. With his Roman enemies eliminated, Severus revealed his true character to the senate. 'He caused us especial dismay,' Cassius Dio wrote, 'by constantly styling himself the son of Marcus and the brother of Commodus and by bestowing divine honours on the latter, whom but recently he had been abusing.' The climate worsened as Severus 'praised the severity and cruelty of Sulla, Marius, and Augustus as the safer course, and deprecated the mildness of Pompey and Caesar' (75.7). For Cassius Dio, Severus was a brute, an uncouth thug who was little better than Commodus. His worst fears were to be realised: after Lugdunum, a broad round of proscriptions decimated the Gallic and Spanish elites and caused misery in Africa as the supporters of Albinus were punished. Cassius Dio's mood was not improved when Severus appointed equestrian prefects (instead of senatorial legates) for the new Parthica legions, stationed II Parthica at Alba, just outside Rome, and then followed the proscriptions with a purge of the senate. Severus also took the sides of slaves over their masters, peasants over landowners, and followed other anti-senatorial policies that included granting Commodus his apotheosis—a prerogative that historically belonged to the senate.

Severus the military emperor

In 197, a restless Severus left for the east to join Julius Laetus for the Second Parthian War. The situation concerning Parthia was complex. The empire was characterised by Cornelius Fronto as the only force 'of all mankind' that the Romans should never underestimate (*Principia Historiae*, 7), but the campaigns of Trajan and Marcus Aurelius had set the precedent that Seleucia-Ctesiphon lay within reach of Roman arms, and could and should be conquered. The Roman army had also developed an expertise in siege-craft, was proficient at bridging rivers with pontoons, had found ways to neutralise Parthia's excellent horsemen, and had also developed the tactic of using the Euphrates and Tigris valleys as invasion routes—all of which led to a great degree of success. Roman strength in the second and early third centuries stood in stark contrast to Parthian weakness, reflected by the secession of the satrapies of Bactria and Hyrcania. To Parthia's east, the Kushan empire presented a growing threat that had triggered a brief conflict. The victories of Trajan, and particularly the sack of Seleucia-Ctesiphon by the troops of Avidius

Cassius, had done immense damage to royal prestige, and the plague, experienced by the Parthians as an illness that emanated west from the Kushan empire, had not left the kingdom untouched.

The long rule of Vologases IV had come to a close in 191, and he was succeeded by Vologases V, who made a political calculation on the most likely victor in the civil wars and offered Niger his support, knowing that Niger had also petitioned the kings of Armenia and Hatra. When Severus and his troops abruptly left the eastern theatre in 196 to confront Albinus, Vologases was presented with a favourable opportunity to restore some of the monarchy's prestige. There is some confusion in the sources over the course of events, with the *Historia Augusta* suggesting a Parthian invasion across the Euphrates into Syria, and Herodian arguing that the target of the expedition was Armenia. Narses, the pro-Roman king of Adiabene, was drowned in the Great Zab river, and Parthian forces laid siege to Laetus and his army at Nisibis, but a rebellion in Persis caused a fatal distraction and Vologases was forced to break off his operations, leaving only a token force behind.

Severus's second eastern campaign began in 197, and the course of events reveals a concerted effort to evoke the memories of Trajan, Hadrian, and Marcus Aurelius. The first target for Severus was Armenia, as it had been for Trajan; the next phase of his campaign included a division of forces, as it had for Trajan. Severus led the main effort down the Euphrates, and although Babylon and Seleucia had been evacuated, in 198 he reached Ctesiphon, where Vologases awaited him outside the city's walls. Severus defeated the Parthian king and a brutal sack followed, with over 100,000 of the city's inhabitants sold on the slave market. In a further effort to link his achievements to those of Trajan, Severus, who had once again established the eastern frontier of the Roman empire at the Tigris, took the title *Parthicus Maximus* on the date of Ctesiphon's capture, which happened to be January 28—the centenary of Trajan's imperial accession. The next target was Hatra: the city had contributed archers to Niger's army, Trajan had failed there, and the city occupied an important location on the routes that linked Seleucia-Ctesiphon with Nisibis and Singara, both in Roman hands and part of the new province of Mesopotamia that Severus, in a further imitation of Trajan, created from the conquests east of the Euphrates. In addition to the natural obstacles posed by its desert location, in the eighty years since Trajan's abortive siege, Hatra had undergone a monumental building campaign that included a major upgrade to the city's fortifications, raising its walls to a height of 10m (30ft). In recognition of the city's new importance for the protection of Parthia in the aftermath of the campaigns of Trajan and Lucius Verus, Hatrene rulers had—with Parthian permission—begun to call themselves in Aramaic *mlk*, 'king', instead of their previous title, *mry*, 'lord'. Hatra had become a prestige target, a place of value to the Parthians as well as to his own obsession with Trajan, that Severus simply had to capture.

During Severus's first attempt in 198/99, the Hatrene defenders destroyed his siege engines and he suffered stiff losses. The failed siege was also marred by the ugly denunciation and murder of Julius Laetus, who had supported Severus throughout; Cassius Dio blamed the incident on Severus's jealousy of his popular subordinate (75.10). For his second attempt in 199/200, Severus had made thorough preparations that included hoarding food and rebuilding his siege equipment. Yet his siege engines were once again destroyed, his men suffered from the Hatrene cavalry, and flammable naphtha was poured onto the attackers as they tried to breach the walls. According to Herodian, the Hatrenes also possessed another nasty weapon—clay pots filled with poisonous insects that were catapulted at the Roman troops (3.9). Severus did achieve a small breach in the wall, but as his army was poised to exploit it, he recalled the troops to give the Hatrene king an opportunity to beg for terms. Nobody came to see him, however, and Cassius Dio wrote that when he angrily ordered an assault, some of his troops mutinied. When a contingent was finally persuaded to go into action, the legionnaires found that the wall had been repaired, and thus Severus failed once again (75.11). It has been suggested that the mutiny took place not because the troops were called back when they could have effected entry into the city and sacked it, but because the death of Julius Laetus had left an open wound and they wished to punish Severus. The other element that stands out in the accounts of the second siege is that it lasted only 20 days. When this is considered in the light of the three years eventually required to reduce Niger's base at Byzantium, or the long sieges of Jerusalem and Masada, it is clear that a difficult target like Hatra was unlikely to give in after just three weeks.

Severus installed an equestrian prefect to govern Mesopotamia—a further slight to the senate—and stationed I Parthica at Singara and III Parthica at Nisibis. These two cities, along with Rhesaina, were made colonies. He also reorganised Syria, dividing it between Coele Syria and Syria Phoenice, which included the 'Punic' Syria of Julia Domna's family. Coele Syria stretched eastwards to Dura-Europos, skirting Palmyra, which had hosted a Roman unit, Ala I Herculiana Thracum, since 167 (Figure 11.24). Legions were based at Samosata (XVI Flavia Firma) and Zeugma (IV Scythica) in Coele Syria, and Raphaneae (III Gallica) in Syria Phoenice. The division of Syria, and, later, Britannia, was intended to break up regions with particularly large garrisons and to forestall the ability of future pretenders to amass a significant army of the sort enjoyed by Niger, Albinus, and indeed Severus himself.

Beginning in the Severan period and continuing throughout the third century, the army was particularly active in the two Syrias and Arabia. The evidence comes from inscriptions: troops from III Cyrenaica, based in Bostra, were at the city in 216 completing its amphitheatre, and left an inscription in the Azraq oasis dating to 200/02 commemorating the construction of *Castellum Novum Severianum* (Qasr al-Uweinid)—the earliest Latin building inscription from the province. An inscription from 213/14 records the construction by four separate units of a new fort at Qasr al-Hallabat, near Amman, and Severan milestones have been found north of Azraq on the so-called via Severiana, constructed to improve the movement of troops. Downriver from Dura-Europos at Kifrin, a Severan-era military installation was constructed and legionnaires from III Cyrenaica left their graffiti at the wells of al-Namara in Syria.

In 199, Severus journeyed to Egypt, recalling Hadrian's own travels there, and took in the obligatory tourist stops at the tomb of Pompey at Pelusium, the tomb of Alexander the Great, the Pyramids, Luxor, Thebes, Philae, and the Colossi of Memnon. Before he left in 200, the city of Alexandria was rewarded for its timely defection during the civil war with the grant of self-government via a *boule*. In 202, Severus and Caracalla, in Antioch (whose colonial status was quietly restored), held the ordinary consulship in absentia, an indication that Rome as a physical location was increasingly irrelevant to governance. A coin issue was minted celebrating the imperial family, with the clear intention of furthering Severus's dynastic ambitions for his two sons (Figure 11.25).

Meanwhile, Severus richly rewarded his friends: Lucius Fabius Cilo, for example, became so wealthy that his house was transformed into a must-visit location for the Roman elite. Severus also populated his government with favourites from his

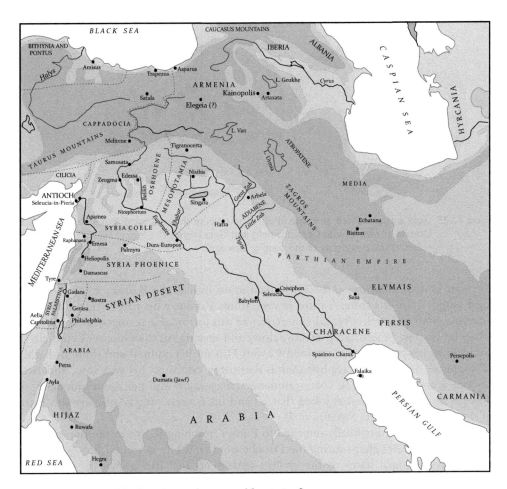

Figure 11.24 The Middle East during the reign of Septimius Severus.

Source: Illustration by the author.

native Africa, as well as from Egypt, whose elites were finally allowed to enter the senate. In so doing, Severus accelerated the provincialisation (or 'internationalisation') of the senate that had begun with Augustus and Claudius. In addition to Africans and Egyptians, Severus's Syrian connections through his wife also ensured a flow of Syrian elites into Roman government. His Syrian brother-in-law was admitted to the senate, while the Syrian (or African) Aemilius Papinianus (Papinian) become one of Severus's secretaries for petitions (*a libellis*). The equestrian Domitius Ulpianus (Ulpian) joined Severus's government from Tyre, which had been promoted to colonial status along with Heliopolis (Baalbek). Ulpian, like Papinian, worked in the chancery, and both men were celebrated jurists whose work would go on to make up a significant portion of the *Digest*, the famous law code compiled in the sixth century. Papinian wrote the mammoth *Problems* (37 books) and *Ordered Opinions* (19 books);

Figure 11.25 Gold aureus minted at Rome in 202. The reverse shows a remarkable portrait of Julia Domna, at centre, with Caracalla (left) and Geta (right). The legend FELICITAS SAECVLI refers to the prosperity of the coming 'new age'.

the later Law of Citations (AD 426) looked upon him as the Roman world's leading legal authority of his time. A third lawyer, Julius Paulus, who had been a student of Scaevola, Marcus Aurelius's legal expert, joined this formidable team, assisting Papinian when he became praetorian prefect (below) and serving on the emperor's council. In addition to lawyers, Severus retained Cassius Dio on his council and thought highly of sophists—an Egyptian sophist, Aelius Antipater, educated his two sons, and later became secretary for Greek correspondence (*ab epistulis*) and penned a biography of Severus himself. Philostratus joked that he and his friends called Antipater the 'tutor of the gods' (*Lives of the Sophists*, 607).

Severus and his court finally returned to Europe, reaching Rome in the late spring or early summer of 202 after touring the Danube frontier. While in central Europe, Severus had granted colonial status to the civilian settlements that had grown up around the legionary forts at Aquincum and Carnuntum. In Rome, a large gold donative was paid to the Praetorian Guard. Its Sejanus-esque prefect, Fulvius Plautianus—in sole command, having murdered his co-prefect—was elevated to honorary senatorial rank and joined the imperial family when his daughter, Fulvia, married Caracalla in a glitzy ceremony attended by Cassius Dio, who mysteriously reported on the strange 'live meat' that was served at the banquet (77.1). Severus did not stay long in Rome, and after celebrating the marriage and presiding over the elaborate and expensive games that followed, he once again followed Hadrian's example and set off for Africa. Both his native Leptis Magna and Carthage were given the Latin rights, which exempted them from taxation, and Leptis was adorned with a nymphaeum, a basilica, a new forum, and its famous quadrifrons (tetrapylon) archway (Figure 11.26). In return for this lavish support, the merchants of Leptis agreed to provide free olive oil to the city of Rome, with the supply to be managed by a procurator. An additional procuratorial position was also created to administer imperial estates in Tripolitania. During Severus's time, or shortly afterwards, Numidia was carved off from Africa Proconsularis, and became its own province.

Like Hadrian, Severus stopped off at Lambaesis to visit the loyal III Augusta. In 197, Anicius Faustus had assumed command of this legion, and under his leadership the troops

Figure 11.26 The quadrifrons arch at Leptis Magna.

Photograph by Davie Gunn (Wikimedia Commons/Public Domain).

had set about improving Roman fortifications in Tripolitania along what the *Antonine Itinerary* (a catalogue of roads and distances dating to the reign of Caracalla) called the *limes Tripolitanae*—the Tripolitanian frontier. New installations were constructed at Ghadames, Si Aioun, Bu Njem, and a particularly large fort at Gheriat el-Garbia, the latter two by III Augusta. A number of other sites were occupied, leading to a doubling of the military

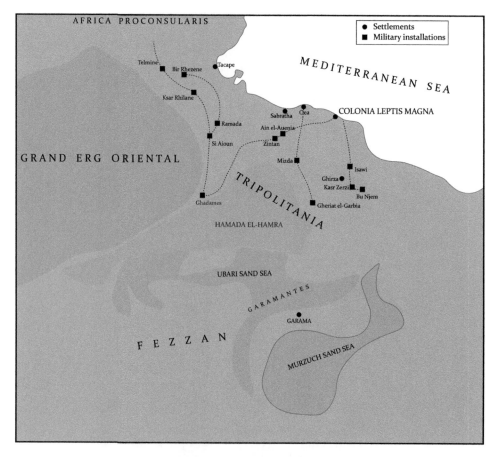

Figure 11.27 The *limes Tripolitanae* during the time of Septimius Severus.

Source: Illustration by the author.

garrison along the region's major communication routes. These developments were in response to a growing problem with the Garamantes, an important tribal confederation that occupied Garama and several other oases in the Fezzan. The Garamantes had been known to the Romans since the Republic and had fought alongside Juba I against Julius Caesar; numerous conflicts had followed since. In common with other peoples at the edges of the empire, such as the Marcomanni and the Quadi, there was extensive contact via trade, and fine glass and pottery imported from Rome have been found at Garama, while Garamantian tombs reflect a blend of Roman and Punic styles. Nevertheless, the Garamantes conducted dangerous raids into Roman territory and Severus campaigned against them, perhaps in early 203, and further forward installations were added (Figure 11.27). These were never intended to prevent interactions between Garamantians and the inhabitants of the coastal cities and villages; the two populations, like nomads and settlers in the Middle East, were not separate and each served a purpose for the other—Garamantians worked the olive harvest, for instance, and sold or bartered their goods in local markets. Nevertheless, closer supervision and control of access to markets was desirable to keep the peace.

Severus was back in Rome in 203, with Plautianus and Geta serving as ordinary consuls. The emperor commissioned the vast triumphal arch that still stands in the Roman forum; its anti-senatorial message is neatly encapsulated by its imposing position, blocking the track between the senate house and the rostra. The arch's panels portray fighting at Nisibis, the sack of Ctesiphon, and the siege of Hatra, along with depictions of beaten Parthian soldiers and other captives. In a clear echo of Augustan propaganda, the arch's dedicatory inscription records that Severus restored the Republic. In Rome, Severus also restored the Templum Pacis and had the Marble Plan installed on one of its walls, while a second inscription was added to the Pantheon, recording its restoration in 201/02. Another important monument was the Septizodium, which provided entry to the imperial palace from the southeastern side of the Palatine. Oriented towards Africa, it showed the seven planets known to the Romans grouped around Severus, who was portrayed as the sun. The Septizodium reflected Severus's domineering style of rule, as well as his fervent belief in astrology. In the palace, his horoscope was painted onto the ceiling above his tribunal, and, like Vespasian and Augustus before him, he had advertised the divine favours that he had enjoyed via his horoscope. Julia Domna's horoscope, that foretold she would marry a king, was also used to justify his position. In a manner that recalled Josephus' flattery of Vespasian, Cassius Dio had 'written and published a little book about the dreams and portents' that foretold the rule of Severus, and the emperor courteously wrote a 'long and complimentary' letter to the historian in return (72.23).

The main event in 204 was the Secular Games, which once again were used to under-score the beginning of a new era of peace and prosperity for the Roman people—and to conceal the ugly truth about the basis of Severan power. Hymns were sung to Hercules, beloved of Commodus, and to Bacchus, the patron deity of Leptis Magna. The autocratic nature of the emperor was, however once again starkly revealed with the sudden demise of Plautianus, who was murdered in front of Severus and Caracalla in the midst of pleading that he was not, in fact, planning a coup. His property was seized and the unfortunate Fulvia, whom Caracalla loathed, was exiled to Lipara, never to return; a vicious purge followed in which Severus's enemies in the senate were rounded up and disappeared. Plautianus, who had commanded the Guard alone, was replaced by Papinian and Quintus Maecius Laetus. Another sign of simmering discontent was the career of Bulla Felix, an Italian brigand who was 'never seen when seen, never found when found, never caught when caught' (Cassius Dio, 76.10). This Robin Hood figure was eventually apprehended, but brigandage and robbery at the heart of the empire continued. Cassius Dio considered Italian brigandage to be on the rise because the youth of Italy could no longer serve in the Praetorian Guard, and had little future beyond robbery or fighting in the arena (74.2).

In the final years of his life, Severus became concerned about his two sons, who quarrelled constantly. In response to persistent trouble in Britannia, the consequence of Albinus having drained the province of much of its garrison for the civil wars, Severus set off with both sons and Papinian for a sustained campaign against the Caledonians and a group called the Maeatae (wholly unknown outside the text of Cassius Dio), north of Hadrian's Wall, which had been undergoing extensive repairs since 205. The construction of a permanent legionary base at Carpow on the river Tay, intended for VI Victrix, reflected Severus's apparent intention to finalise the conquest of Scotland.

The campaign also involved rebuilding work at important sites such as Trimontium, and Severan marching camps have been identified along a lowland trajectory very similar to that followed by Agricola (Figure 10.6). Geta remained at Eboracum, leaving Severus and Caracalla to take the title *Britannicus* in celebration of their victory, and not long afterwards Britannia was divided into lower and upper provinces. Even as he celebrated his victory, however, Severus fell ill, and in 210, he promoted Geta to the rank of Augustus. He finally died on February 4, 211 at the age of 65. His oft-quoted final words urged his sons not to argue, to make the soldiers rich, and not care too deeply about anything else; it was a fitting encomium for a military emperor who had come to power in a bloody coup. The *Historia Augusta* noted that in death he was confident, because, like Antoninus Pius, he was leaving the state with two co-Augusti (*HA Septimius Severus*, 20).

Severus had dominated the senate: its vacillations during the civil wars had rendered it politically obsolete, and Severus had preferred to promote equestrians to major commands, such as the legates of the three Parthica legions and the 50 new procuratorial positions that he created. He was the dominant force, an absolutist monarch appointed, like Trajan, by Jupiter, a fact he freely advertised (Figure 11.28). Severus was also backed by the provincial armies, which achieved a hitherto unrivalled importance in imperial politics that exceeded even their role in the civil war of 68/69. The troops received large bonuses, improved rates of general pay (increased by as much as 100 per cent, according to some estimates), and better conditions, including improved promotion prospects and the right to marry legally. Cassius Dio was keenly aware of the army's changing importance, blaming Severus for causing unrest in Rome by billeting so many troops, and by relying on the army rather than his 'associates in government' (Cassius Dio, 74.2). Whereas Trajan and Marcus Aurelius had been military emperors out of necessity, but had ruled as much as they could as civilians, Severus unashamedly ruled as a military emperor.

The Severan reforms had not only dramatically enlarged the Praetorian Guard, which was recruited from the provinces, not from Italy, but had also positioned a reserve army—II Parthica—close to Rome, where it could be used to browbeat the senate, fight future usurpations, or forestall a repeat of the incursions into Italy that had taken place during

Figure 11.28 Gold aureus minted at Rome in 194. The reverse shows Jupiter handing a globe to Severus, symbolising his divine right to rule.

the Marcommanic Wars. The recruitment of the new Parthica legions complemented the pre-existing policy of recruiting regiments known as *numeri*. These were drafted from foreigners, since the progressive spread of Roman culture and shifts in recruitment patterns meant that by the early third century most auxiliaries, as well as the legions, were made up of Roman citizens. *Numeri* are known, for example, at Palmyra, where Numerus Vocontiorum was swapped with Ala I Herculiana Thracum, transferred to Koptos on the Nile in 185. It was also becoming the norm for legions to be broken up into vexillations, which could be joined with other vexillations for specific campaigns or stationed away from the main legionary bases in individual forts. The cache of 146 ostraca found at Bu Njem, for instance, dating from 253 to 259, show that the fort housed a vexillation from III Augusta together with an unnamed *numerus* of cavalry. At Dura-Europos, there is evidence for subunits of XVI Flavia Firma and IV Scythica, and an auxiliary unit from Palmyra, Cohors XX Palmyrenorum, was based there. The army of the early third century was also much larger than its predecessors: Simon James has estimated that as many as 450,000 men may have been under arms during this period—a significant increase from the Augustan era (*Rome and the Sword*, p. 182).

'Romanisation'

Changes within the army and the appearance of emperors with distinctive provincial origins emphasise the importance of a process normally known as 'Romanisation', briefly mentioned in Chapter 8. Romanisation refers, in the most general terms, to the spread of Roman cultural, political, and religious ideas as well as language, material culture, art, cuisine, dress, architecture—even beards—leading to the emergence of what might be considered a 'common culture' across the empire. Romanisation has long resisted a narrow definition, and one problem with the term is that the adoption of a certain culinary habit or dressing in a toga did not necessarily 'make' somebody Roman. Romanisation was, rather, a dialogue between the dominant political and cultural fashions of the time and the people who came into contact with them. It could therefore take many forms: the movement of provincial elites into government, and the development of a Mediterranean urban culture in places like Britain, for instance, were facets of Romanisation, as were syncretic practices of native deities being assimilated to the Roman pantheon and vice versa. The spread of a culture that was perceived as offering tangible benefits naturally facilitated Romanisation. Learning Latin, winning the patronage of important Romans, and adopting certain cultural practices improved the chance of joining the Roman elite. Once within the equestrian or senatorial orders, there was a range of opportunities to participate in the political culture of the empire that were not available to average citizens. We have seen, for instance, how Hellenising emperors facilitated the entry of Greek-speaking elites into the senate. Imperial patronage was a crucial vehicle for Romanisation.

Romanisation as a process was uneven, and the degree to which anyone was actually 'Roman', outside of the legal definition, was very much a matter of self-perception, snobbery, or elitism. Roman culture itself was also constantly changing, because of the very outside influences that had been so important to Roman identity from the city's earliest days. Marcus Aurelius's decision to compose the *Meditations* in Greek, and for it to become a seminal *Roman* text, offers a useful example of how imperial identity was itself shaped and developed by external factors. Viewed from another perspective, frontier legions, for instance, had much greater contact with non-Roman peoples and their members may have never even been to Italy or seen the great monuments of the city of Rome. Their world might be framed instead by punitive expeditions across the Danube or the Euphrates, marriage to local women, or trading with Germans, Garamantians, or Parthians, while their experience of urban centres was of settlements that had developed alongside or because of the presence of the army, places like Vindobona, Sirmium, or the military camp within Dura-Europos. Their experiences of other Roman cities may have come, as we have seen, from sacking them and murdering their inhabitants. Veterans of military units often settled not in Rome or in Italy but in their province of discharge. A papyrus from Dura-Europos, for instance, describes the sale of a vineyard and orchard to a veteran of Cohors III Augusta Thracum, who chose to live out his retirement not in Thrace (assuming he had even been recruited there) but tending to fruit in a sleepy village on the Khabur river in eastern Syria (*P. Dura* 26). Provincial recruits could also find themselves in Rome, where they caused unease: Cassius Dio deplored the Severan policy of recruiting the Praetorian Guard from the Danube, since it brought the 'wrong sort' of Romans to Rome (74.2). Military technology was particularly receptive to foreign influences, and after adoption, such advances could be claimed as 'Roman'. Roman sword designs of the late second century, for instance, show a clear resemblance to those used by the Roxolani and Iazyges; other trans-Danubian influences included dragon-headed standards of the sort depicted on a tombstone from Deva (Chester) in Britannia, and the development of armoured horsemen. Even trousers had a non-Roman provenance.

As we have already seen (Chapter 10), even as early as the wars of 68/69 Roman legions from Syria and the Rhine were seen as foreign in Italy, and they themselves treated many of the Italian communities as conquered foreign lands, ripe for pillage and plunder. Cassius Dio, who represented a conservative, urban viewpoint, observed that the Severan army was 'most savage in appearance, most terrifying in speech, and most boorish in conversation' (74.2). At the same time, soldiers fought for the emperor and belonged to a proud warrior tradition that celebrated the great heroes of the past, including recent soldier-emperors such as Trajan. The internationalised frontier 'Romanness' of the army, therefore, was not necessarily the same sort of comprehensive culture represented by the cities of the empire, nor was it the culture of the villages, the nomads, the steppe, the mountains, or the deserts. Neither did the cities necessarily share the same culture: there were many differences between 'Roman' Alexandria, 'Roman' Damascus, and 'Roman' London. Regional differences also became increasingly noticeable by the third century, due to an economic decline in Italy as staple products such as wine, olive oil, and ceramics were increasingly imported from provincial suppliers like Leptis Magna. Conversely, the eastern provinces benefited from the continuity of Hellenistic city-based rule that the Romans did little to alter, the efflorescence of an international literary culture, part of the Second Sophistic, and from sustained imperial attention that underwrote the growth of metropoli such as Palmyra, Apamea, and Antioch. Romanisation is best thought of, therefore, as a developing process that moved at a different rate, and took different shapes, throughout the empire. What all shared, however, was the imperial cult, citizenship after 212 (below) and, by the fourth century, a new cultural glue: Christianity, which would become an exceptionally strong marker of what it meant 'to be Roman' in late antiquity.

From Caracalla to Severus Alexander

Julia Domna had spent much of her time as empress cultivating a literary circle that included Ulpian, Papinian, and Philostratus. In the second decade of the third century, Ulpian was at his most creative, compiling 81 books on the *Edict of the Praetor*, 51 books on Roman civil law, and a text dealing with the duties of proconsular governors. Meanwhile, following Severus's death, Julia Domna accompanied the emperor's ashes to Rome, after Caracalla—a nickname given by the soldiers, from a type of cloak that he wore—had negotiated an end to the war in Britain. Caracalla and Geta continued to quarrel, however, and in late February 212, Caracalla engineered the murder of his younger sibling by the Praetorian Guard on the pretext that the bookish and quiet Geta had been plotting against him (*HA Caracalla*, 2). While the Guard accepted this fiction, II Parthica initially refused and required careful persuasion.

Cassius Dio wrote that after Caracalla's later death in 218, he had a vision of the Roman army arrayed in battle order with Septimius Severus addressing them from a tribunal. 'Come here, Dio,' Severus said to the senator in his dream, 'that you may both learn accurately and write an account of all that is said and done' (79.10). Yet history has been barely kinder to the sick and violent Caracalla than it was to Commodus. Geta's murder was followed by a violent purge and a round of proscriptions targeting anyone Geta had favoured, including the son of Claudius Pompeianus—a man who also had the distinction of being the grandson of Marcus Aurelius. One of Caracalla's victims was the praetorian prefect Quintus Maecius Laetus, whom he ordered to commit suicide, another was Lucius Fabius Cilo, while the jurist and praetorian prefect Papinian, who was close to Geta, was also murdered. Papinian's death greatly vexed Marius Maximus, who remarked via the *Historia Augusta* that Papinian had refused to cover up Caracalla's murder of his brother. 'It is not so easy to defend fratricide,' the *Historia Augusta* imagined Papinian saying to the emperor, 'as to commit it' (*HA Caracalla*, 8). Nor was Papinian dispatched cleanly: after his death, Caracalla punished the assassin for 'using an axe instead of a sword' (Cassius Dio, 78.3). Geta himself suffered a *damnatio memoriae*: the famous painted panel known as the Severan Tondo, a remarkably vivid portrait of the imperial family, had Geta's image scrubbed out in antiquity. The *damnatio* was so widespread that as far away as northern Britain, Geta's name was chiselled from military inscriptions.

The devaluation of the denarius (down to 51 per cent silver instead of 90 per cent under Trajan), the increased expenditure on the army (whose wages were increased once more), and the construction of public buildings such as the Baths of Caracalla, necessitated a concomitant devaluation of the gold aureus together with the introduction of a new silver coin worth two denarii, the antoninianus. At the same time, Caracalla declared the 'Antonine Constitution', which granted citizenship to all of the free inhabitants of the empire while permitting new citizens to retain their ancestral customs. When set against the very tightly held sort of citizenship that characterised the early Republic (Chapters 2–5), the apparent egalitarianism of the universal grant of citizenship provided by Caracalla appears to be liberal and progressive. On the other hand, Caracalla had recently increased inheritance tax from 5 per cent to 10 per cent, and these new citizens would now be liable to pay both it and the tax on manumitting slaves. Citizenship was also of dubious value in an increasingly cosmopolitan world where Roman law had adapted to provide similar protections to non-citizens in the empire, and where class distinctions—wealth, status, and access to patronage—arguably counted for more than whether one was a citizen or not.

Nevertheless, a measure of the impact of the unifying undercurrents that resulted from the Constitution can be seen in a significant increase in people taking the name 'Aurelius' upon becoming Roman citizens, in honour of Caracalla and his family.

Like his father, Caracalla was not content to remain in Rome. In 213, he fought a group of Germanic tribes whom Roman sources called the Alamanni. This Germanic name meant 'All Men' and lives on in the French words for German and Germany, Allemagne and Allemand. It has always been unclear, however, whether this was a generic designation for the group as a whole, or the name of only a few core groupings, and it has also been suggested that Xiphilinus retroactively inserted a reference to the Alamanni into the text of Casssius Dio much later on. After the campaign, which had drawn in units from as far away as Egypt, Caracalla celebrated victory with the title of *Germanicus Maximus*. His major campaign, however, was a do-over of the feats of Alexander the Great. He equipped 16,000 Roman troops as a phalanx with Macedonian arms—undoing the advances made by military technology by some five hundred years—and followed the route taken by Alexander to invade Persia. With him were elements of II Parthica from Alba, whose legionnaires left a series of their gravestones, dated to between 215 and 252, at Apamea in Syria. After sacrificing to Achilles at Troy, Caracalla reached Antioch. There he found envoys from the new Parthian king Artabanus IV (who had come to the throne in 213 amidst yet another Parthian civil war), asking him for peace and decidedly unreceptive to his suggestion that he should marry into the Arsacid royal family. This did not improve Caracalla's mood, and while he was subsequently in Egypt, he ordered a massacre of the people of Alexandria after the initially friendly crowd jeered at him for his uncouth manner of speech, for murdering his brother, and for his pretentiousness. He then left for Mesopotamia, visiting the battlefield at Gaugamela where Alexander had beaten Darius III in 331 BC. In Syria once again in 216, Caracalla honoured Emesa and Palmyra with promotions to colonial status with the Latin rights. Palmyra's Hellenistic *boule* was replaced by a new constitution with collegial, annual magistrates, and its garrison was bolstered with the auxiliary unit Cohors I Flavia Chalcidenorum. Edessa, too, became a Roman colony in the province of Osrhoene, after Caracalla deposed its king in 212 or 213; the Osrhoenian city of Carrhae was also made a Roman colony, and Caracalla tarried there, visiting its religious sanctuaries. War had begun against the Parthians, with the Romans pillaging the royal tombs of Adiabene at Arbela, when Caracalla was murdered near Carrhae while he was in a bush attending to the call of nature. The murderer was quickly cut down, and so it was not immediately discovered that it was the praetorian prefect, Marcus Opellius Macrinus, who had given the assassination order. He was now pragmatically declared emperor by the legionnaires. In death, Caracalla, who had told the senate that Alexander had come alive in his own person, finally got close to his hero—one of Macrinus's first acts was to deify him as Caracalla 'the Great'.

Macrinus was a Berber from Caesarea in Mauretania, and had worked as a lawyer for the former praetorian prefect Plautianus. As an equestrian, Macrinus was the first man from outside the senatorial class to ascend to the purple, and, as has often been noted, this should have marked a decisive turning point in Roman history. However, his rule lasted for only a year and was an unqualified disaster, and in any case, there were far more surprises to come in the third century (see below and Chapter 12). Macrinus was more bureaucrat than warrior, and mismanaged relations with the troops; he also failed with the senate, whose members were appalled when a semi-illiterate soldier of fortune, a friend of Macrinus, was made urban prefect in Rome; he failed again with Artabanus IV, who defeated him at Nisibis in 217; and above all, he proved unable to handle the remaining members of the Severan family, despite taking the Severan name and calling his son Antoninus. The troops were especially distraught at Caracalla's demise, and after peace was purchased with the Parthians at an astronomical price and Macrinus fraudulently called himself *Parthicus Maximus*, the pay of new recruits was reset to its pre-Caracalla rates. Before long, the unease of the soldiers spread to the people of Rome, who once again took to the Circus Maximus to chant against the emperor. Meanwhile, Julia Domna died at Antioch, reputedly after starving herself following the loss of her husband and both of her children—but her sister, Julia Maesa, was more than ready to step into her place.

Maesa's daughters, Julia Soaemias and Julia Mamaea, each had a son. Varius Avitus Bassianus was born in 203 or 204 to Soaemias and her husband, who had served Septimius Severus as an equestrian procurator and later finished his career as a senator. The second son was Gessius Alexianus, born to Julia Mamaea in 205. The elder child, Bassianus, was the priest of Elagabal in 217. Julia Maesa looked askance at Macrinus, who was a product of the equestrian bureaucracy and whom, she thought, had no place as emperor; that prerogative belonged to someone chosen from the imperial court. As the Oracle of Bel at Apamea prognosticated on the looming dismal fate of Macrinus, the troops of III Gallica, who were quartered not far to the north-west of Emesa at Raphaneae and who were frequent visitors to the shrine of Elagabal, reacted favourably to the rumour that Bassianus was the bastard son of Caracalla, and the priest was quickly declared emperor. II Parthica, quartered at Apamea, moved immediately to quash the rebellion under the leadership of the praetorian prefect Ulpius Julianus, but the assault faltered as the new emperor was displayed to the troops. Julianus perished in the fighting, and after Macrinus was presented with his severed head he left Apamea for Antioch, while Bassianus took the royal name Marcus Aurelius Antoninus. A rebel army commanded by one of Julia Maesa's freedmen, Gannys, and Publius Valerius Comazon, a one-time common soldier who was now prefect of III Gallica, forced a showdown with Macrinus. In the aftermath, Macrinus and his young son were killed and there was a purge of provincial governors and the equestrian bureaucracy. The legionnaires, in a febrile state after the demise of Caracalla and Macrinus and the failed war with the Parthians, were restrained from sacking Antioch only by a timely donative. The Severan family, in its Syrian guise, now returned to the imperial throne. One of the few survivors of the period was Marius Maximus, who was urban prefect in Rome and a pragmatic supporter of the Severan dynasty.

The new emperor is known to history not as Aurelius Antoninus, but as Elagabalus; some ancient writers called him Heliogabalus, because of the assimilation of Elagabal with Sol/Helios. The young man had no political or military experience, but having come to power in a coup, and following the widespread purge, his family minted a military coin series with the hopeful legend CONCORDIA MILITVM, anticipating the peaceful acquiescence of the rest of the army. Meanwhile, Elagabalus's actions as the cult priest of Elagabal upset Roman conservatives such as Cassius Dio. In an elaborate procession that took an entire year, Elagabalus made his way to Rome with the large black betyl that was the cult object of his faith. (Figure 11.29). Once in Rome, the betyl 'married' Vesta, Athena, and then Astarte/Juno Caelestis, the Carthaginian veneration of Juno; Caelestis also appeared on the reverse of coins minted for the Augusta, Julia Soaemias. Elagabal was then installed in a custom-built temple, the Elagabalium, and inside, Elagabalus subordinated the Roman

Figure 11.29 Silver denarius minted in Antioch in 218/19. Obverse: Elagabalus; reverse: quadriga bearing the cult stone of Elagabal.

pantheon, including Jupiter and the Vestal flame, to Elagabal. Herodian (5.6) described a bizarre parody of a Roman triumph, in which the betyl 'drove' the triumphal chariot with Elagabalus running backwards before it. At the head of the procession, as symbolic captives, were images of the Roman gods, who were led in submission not to the Temple of Jupiter, but to the Elagabalium. It was this, Cassius Dio wrote, that caused offence, rather than the introduction of a new deity—something which the Romans had long accepted (79.11). Despite what conservative commentators scorned as sacrilegious behaviour, however, Elagabalus was merely making real in Rome what many also accepted, which was that many gods could exist in the presence of a higher god, a concept known as henotheism. For the Romans, however, the subjugation of Jupiter to a foreign meteorite was just too much to accept.

Elagabalus was only 15, and his mother, Julia Soaemias, and his grandmother, Julia Maesa, governed on his behalf. In an attempt to provide a dynastic succession, Elagabalus adopted his younger cousin in 221, and in 222 both held the ordinary consulship. Some normal governance continued: Elagabalus honoured cities close to his family, such as Sidon, which was made a colony, as was Petra, which was also known as *Metropolis Arabiae*—the metropolis of Arabia. It seems that the legal expert Julius Paulus had been made praetorian prefect in 219, as his daughter was one of the four wives taken, and then divorced, by Elagabalus; the emperor's later marriages involved a relative of Marcus Aurelius and, shockingly to Roman sensibility, a Vestal Virgin. There was, however, to be no real stability in Rome, as the tension between 'Elagabalus as emperor' and 'Elagabalus as high priest of a foreign cult' resisted all attempts at resolution. The praetorians and the army despised this unsoldierly emperor, and the senate, whose members had imagined that things could not get worse after Caracalla and Macrinus, were horrified at what had now been visited upon them. Elagabalus was prone to appointing favourites like Comazon to key positions, usurping the prerogatives of senators and scandalising Cassius Dio and his colleagues. Others were equally disgusted with Elagabalus's behaviour, and the *Historia Augusta* opened his biography by lamenting that it was ever written in the first place. The stories are so ridiculously salacious, however, that it is difficult to know what is real and what has been invented. For instance, Aurelius Victor related that the emperor 'searched the whole world for the lewdest men so that he might watch them or participate in their practice of filthy obscenities' (*On the Caesars*, 23). Cassius Dio, who called Elagabalus 'the false Antoninus', wrote that the emperor brought a man named Aurelius Zoticus to the palace in order to corrupt him. He had been picked, Dio wrote, because 'he greatly surpassed all others in the size of his private parts' (79.16). Marius Maximus, who wrote his biographies during the later reign of Severus Alexander once a semblance of sanity had returned, scorned Elagabalus for his uncontrolled lust, and an Egyptian papyrus refers to the emperor as 'Antoninus the pervert' (*P. Oxy* 3298i.2). The issue was not so much that Elagabalus had an eccentric sex life, but rather that it got in the way of governance and that people like Aurelius Zoticus, a mere commoner known as 'Cook', possessed an unnatural amount of influence over him; for the same reason, Saoterus had been hated during the reign of Commodus. Julia Maesa finally appeared to have sensed that the only way for she and her family to retain power was for Elagabalus to be removed, and when it became clear that Elagabalus was plotting against his designated successor, Julia Maesa arranged for her grandson and her daughter to be purged in a palace conspiracy that also claimed both praetorian prefects and the urban prefect. Dumped into the Tiber, Elagabalus earned the epithet 'Tiberinus'. One of the few survivors was Comazon, who became urban prefect in the aftermath.

The final Severan incumbent on the throne was the young Gessius Alexianus, who took the name Severus Alexander (also known, confusingly, as Alexander Severus). The royal women still maintained a firm grip on governance, however, appearing frequently on imperial coinage as the Augustae (Figure 11.30). After Julia Maesa died between 224 and 226, Julia Mamaea became the de facto head of state, ruling on behalf of her teenage son. Ulpian was appointed praetorian prefect, but he was unable to control an increasingly ill-disciplined Praetorian Guard whose troops openly clashed with the people of Rome. The twelfth-century imperial secretary Zonaras, whose ambitious universal history covered the period from the Christian Creation to AD 1118, recorded that the people managed to defeat the Praetorian Guard in a pitched battle and only gave in when the troops began to set fire to their homes (12.15). The praetorians had also denounced Cassius Dio, complaining about his strict discipline while he was propraetorian legate in Upper

Figure 11.30 Silver denarius minted in Rome in 218 or 220. Obverse: bust of Julia Maesa, Augusta, one of the most powerful women in Roman imperial history. Reverse: Pudicitia, seated.

Pannonia, but when Ulpian failed to deliver Dio to them, and on the urging of an imperial freedman, Ulpian was killed in front of Julia Mamaea and the emperor in 223.

Severus Alexander continued some of the policies of his namesake, furthering the opportunities available to equestrians that included allowing praetorian prefects to enter the senate on retirement, and sending more equestrians to govern as propraetorian legates in imperial provinces. In a conservative retrenchment of sorts, Elagabal was returned to Emesa and Roman cults were restored to their traditional place. A gold coin issue was struck that portrayed the emperor as the new Romulus, and Severus Alexander enjoyed cordial relations with the senate, whose prerogatives were partially restored. The conventional career of Cassius Dio, proconsul of Africa, propraetorian legate of Dalmatia and then Upper Pannonia, and ordinary consul in 229, reflected Julia Mamaea's efforts to undo the earlier use of such positions as rewards for political cronyism—although continued sour relations with the Praetorian Guard led to Dio holding his consulship in absentia, on the advice of the emperor. Cassius Dio's writings also reflect the party line under Mamaea's government. Together with the opinion of Marius Maximus (ordinary consul in 223), the universally scathing view of the excesses of Elagabalus provided by Dio was clearly shared by the contemporary Roman elite and could be used to portray the reign of Severus Alexander as one of restorative stability and calm. Another important reaction to the Roman experience of Elagabal was a return to the cult of the deified emperors, as well as an effort to welcome all religions; Christian writers, including Origen (185/6–254/5) and Hippolytus (c. 170–c. 236) flourished during this period. Hippolytus penned the enormous *Against all Heresy* in which religious belief classified as *haeresis*—a Greek term that came to mean 'the wrong choice'—was shown to stem from outside influences, rather than from scripture. Mystery cults, philosophy, magic, and astrology were all culprits, and those proclaiming ideas based on these sources were not 'really Christians' at all. Hippolytus's claims fell flat in part, however, since he revealed in his arguments his very dependence on Plato for his understanding of the four Gospels.

Origen was born in Alexandria and visited Julia Mamaea in Antioch in 232/33, at her invitation, to discuss his faith. He was an ascetic, depriving himself of worldly pleasures as a form of martyrdom, and went to the extreme length of castrating himself in a drastic interpretation of Matthew 19.12. Narrowly surviving Caracalla's Alexandrian massacres, he found his way to Caesarea where he completed the *Hexapla*, a six-columned version of the Old Testament combining the Hebrew text, the Greek transliteration of the Hebrew text, three Greek translations of the Hebrew bible, and the Septuagint—an enormous piece of scholarship. Origen is particularly interesting because his ascetic lifestyle, which had long been practised by Greek philosophers, was emerging as an important aspect of early Christianity. For Christians, choosing an ascetic life meant retreating from the world of polytheism and rejecting some of what it meant to be a member of the Roman commonwealth. The retreat could be spiritual, physical, geographical, or a combination of all three, and such practices eventually led to the spread of ascetic and monastic traditions, particularly in the deserts of the east in late antiquity (Chapter 13).

Another key Christian figure of the period was Tertullian (c. 155–240). Born in Carthage, Tertullian wrote numerous texts in Latin, including an *Apology* and the *Against the Jews*. The latter text, like some of the works of his predecessors (Chapter 10), was a fictional dialogue between a Jew and a Christian intended to show the superiority of Christian thought. One of the most fascinating individuals of this period was the mysterious Elchasai, known from a man named Alcibiades of Apamea who had translated an obscure Persian text from Syriac into Greek, which thus made it more accessible in the Roman empire. The *Book of Elchasai* was a prophetic text recording Elchasai's revelation, experienced in the shape of a gargantuan angel during the time of the Diaspora Revolt. The gist of his movement was to establish a purist, Jewish Christianity that would cleanse second-century Christianity of its philosophical contamination. Just as the work of Hippolytus reflected the ongoing dialogue between philosophy and religion that was a feature of some of the apologetic works discussed in Chapter 10, so the Elchasite revelation similarly reflected the continued tensions between traditionalists and innovators in early Christian thought.

Revolt in Persia, murder on the Rhine

While the drama of Caracalla, Elagabalus, and the powerful Syrian royal women played out in the Roman empire, dramatic changes were afoot in Persia. The Parthian kings had long faced endemic instability and frequent revolts, but a particularly potent challenge to the throne was launched from Istakhr in Persis during the reign of Septimius Severus by Pabag, priest of the Zoroastrian goddess Anahita and descendant of a certain Sasan (hence, 'Sasanid' or 'Sasanian'). Repeated Roman invasions had hamstrung the ability of the Arsacid kings to respond effectively to revolts, but in this case the rebellion was also very dynamic, infused from the very beginning by strong religious fervour. The new dynasty of 'Sasanian' kings emerged with a man named Ardashir, Pabag's second son (the first had died in mysterious circumstances sometime after 208). In 224, Ardashir defeated and killed the Parthian king, Artabanus IV, and refounded the battered city of Seleucia as Veh Ardashir (known as Coche in Syriac). After his victory had been secured with the capture and execution of the last Arsacid aristocratic holdouts, Ardashir was crowned *shahanshah*, 'King of Kings'—the ancient royal title of the Achaemenid Persian empire. The historian Agathias (c. 532–80) wrote that this event took place in year 538 of the Seleucid era, that is, between October 1, 226 and September 30, 227. Ardashir campaigned vigorously to secure his authority. Both the ninth-century *Tarikh* of al-Tabari and an eleventh-century Arabic source, the anonymous *Nihayat al-Irab fi-ahbar al-Furs wa'l'Arab*, recorded an ambitious eastern campaign that took Ardashir as far as Merv (Alexandria Margiana / Antiochia in Margiana), modern Mary in Turkmenistan.

Cassius Dio wrote that the civil war in Persia and the emergence of a new royal dynasty 'inspired a genuine fear' for everyone—'not merely the people of Rome, but the rest of mankind as well' (80.3). This was apparently because the Romans believed that Ardashir intended to reconquer the territory of the old Achaemenid empire, which included swathes of real estate that now formed the eastern provinces of the Roman empire. Dio's statement is normally seen as an exaggeration in modern scholarship. However, even though at no point before the seventh century did the Sasanian kings actually attempt a large-scale offensive against Rome's eastern provinces with the intention of occupying territory (Chapter 14), an important factor that tied the Sasanian kings to the memory of the Achaemenids was the strong connection between 'church' and state, where royal rule was explicitly connected to the ancient religion of Zoroastrianism. One of the most important older exponents of this connection was Darius I (522–486 BC), whose Old Persian inscription at Behistun in western Iran established Darius as the viceroy of the supreme Zoroastrian god, Ahuramazda, represented by the winged *genius* above the tableau

Figure 11.31 Firuzabad 2 relief, depicting the investiture of Ardashir (right), receiving the royal diadem from Ahuramazda (left).

Source: Photograph by Milad Vandaee (CC BY-SA 3.0).

accompanying the text. Seven centuries later, Ahuramazda would again be represented alongside a Persian monarch, but this time in human form: in a relief at the UNESCO World Heritage Site of Firuzabad, for example, Ardashir is shown receiving the royal diadem, the cydaris, from Ahuramazda (Figure 11.31). Another famous portrait of this ceremony was sculpted at Naqsh-i-Rustam, the ancient Achaemenid necropolis near Persepolis. Ardashir's coinage further cemented the association between royal power and Ahuramazda by displaying a Zoroastrian fire altar on the reverse (Figure 11.32). From the second phase of Ardashir's coinage, the title 'King of Kings' changed to 'King of Kings of the Iranians', and by the third phase, dated to between 233 and 240, a new legend was added that declared the king's 'lineage from the gods'.

The appearance of 'Iran' on royal coins was paralleled by that of *Iranshahr* on Sasanian royal inscriptions. *Iranshahr* was a place inhabited by Iranians and was also a concept within the Avesta, the holy text of Zoroastrianism. *Iranshahr* existed as one part of a dualism, opposed by *an-Iran*. This was a zone where people could be conquered by the Sasanian monarchs, who conceived of themselves as offering a militant universal monarchy, and Sasanian royal reliefs promoted the power of the monarchy with themes of irresistible victory and the violent conquest of their enemies. These ideas were most potently expressed

Figure 11.32 Silver drachm of Ardashir I, from the third phase (233–40). Obverse: bust of Ardashir; reverse: diademed fire altar.

by Ardashir's son, Shapur I (Chapter 12), and Rome was a particular target for Sasanian militarism: in Sasanian cosmology, the Romans possessed a distant link to the Sasanian kings, but through bad behaviour—specifically, dishonesty and treachery—they had wandered from the true path. This, again, was a dualistic idea characteristic of Zoroastrian thinking; at Behistun, for example, Darius had proclaimed victory over those who had 'lied' by rebelling against him. For the Sasanians, the theme of dishonest and untrustworthy Roman emperors would be used to justify acts of war, and from the outset, the Sasanian kings proved themselves to be aggressive and capable adversaries. They possessed a logistical and organisational ability that far exceeded that of their predecessors, they were experts at siege warfare, and they fielded a new sort of cataphract in battle—heavily armoured cavalry that proved devastatingly effective. Furthermore, while Roman monarchs repeatedly grappled with devalued coinage, the principal issue of the Sasanian kings, the silver drachm, maintained a silver content in excess of 95% for most of late antiquity. Over time, a complex relationship of cooperation and hostility developed between Roman emperors and Sasanian kings: Khusrau II (590/91–628), writing a letter to his counterpart Maurice (582–602), would refer to the respective empires as 'two eyes' through which 'the disobedient and bellicose tribes are winnowed, and man's course is continually regulated and guided' (Theophylact Simocatta, 4.11).

For now, Severus Alexander faced the immediate threat posed by the defeat of the Parthians and the emergence of Ardashir—although his campaign was unencumbered by his wife, Orbiana, whom Julia Mamaea had banished to Libya in a fit of jealousy in 227. In 230, Ardashir invaded the Roman province of Mesopotamia and also moved against Hatra, whose rulers were still loyal to the Arsacids. In response, Severus Alexander assembled a massive invasion army at Antioch, transferring additional troops from the Rhine–Danube frontier, but discipline continued to be a problem; II Traiana Fortis, for instance, staged a brief mutiny in the face of a new and dangerous war. Embassies were rebuffed on both sides, including one where Severus Alexander failed to intimidate Ardashir by referring to the Roman victories of yesteryear (Herodian, 6.23). Eventually, and clearly borrowing from the successful campaigns of Trajan, Lucius Verus, and Septimius Severus, the Romans divided their forces to attack simultaneously with a column directed through Armenia, a second column towards the place where the Tigris and Euphrates almost meet, and a third, central arm commanded by Severus Alexander that was aimed at Mesopotamia. An inscription from Palmyra records a visit by Severus in the course of this campaign, while a marriage contract found at Dura-Europos, dated to 232, refers to a site on the Khabur river where an auxiliary cohort bearing the epithet Severiana Alexandriana was spending its time in winter quarters. Severus thus appeared to have set out from Antioch via Palmyra and Dura-Europos, and then possibly progressed up the Khabur river and towards the Tigris into Mesopotamia. The emperor later claimed victory, and in 232 a road was built from Carrhae to the Roman frontier outpost at Singara, which suggests that the Mesopotamian portion of the campaign had been at least partly successful. Some Roman accounts, however, were less certain: Herodian (6.5–6) wrote that the column led by the emperor stalled for lack of water and food and because the troops were suffering from the heat. Herodian also talked of a terrible defeat at the hands of Persian cataphracts and archers, apparently referring to the third, southern column that had advanced unsupported due to the emperor's failure to move his men far enough into Mesopotamia. 'The Romans suffered a staggering disaster', Herodian wrote, adding that 'it is not easy to recall another like it, one in which a great army was destroyed, an army inferior in strength and determination to none of the armies of old' (6.5). Severus Alexander's grand expedition was, if anything, a draw—although it was a draw that had also clearly exhausted Ardashir for the time being. However, the removal of so many soldiers from Europe only encouraged Rome's enemies amongst the Alamanni, who crossed the Danube and forced the emperor to make preparations for his return to Europe that included raising large numbers of auxiliaries from Osrhoene, Armenia, and 'Parthian deserters' (Herodian, 6.7). Administrative business saw Petra raised to the rank of *metrocolonia*, an honour that was only granted to Emesa and Palmyra, but after a brief period in Rome in 233, where he celebrated a triumph, Alexander prepared to open an offensive from Moguntiacum (Mainz) in 234. Yet he faced disquiet and unease amongst his European troops, who had returned from the Persian war to find their homes and bases under siege. In an army mutiny led by an equestrian from Thrace named Maximinus, whom Zonaras (12.15) asserted had once been a sheep herder, Julia Mamaea and Severus Alexander were murdered in their quarters. With this, the Severan dynasty ended—and the Roman empire was plunged into a new crisis.

Chapter 12

The empire transformed, 235–337

In the 49-year period between 235 and 284, 18 emperors assumed the imperial throne. Nearly all had come to power through the assassination of their predecessors, only to be slain in turn. The murderous banality of the period was aptly summarised by Eutropius: 'Aemilianus came from an extremely insignificant family,' he wrote of a pretender who seized the throne in 253, 'his reign was even more insignificant, and he was slain in the third month' (*Breviarium*, 9.6). This bloody half-century stretch is also one of the murkiest periods in Roman history. Herodian's text ends with the year 238, and historians are dependent on the increasingly unhinged later *vitae* in the *Historia Augusta*, as well as *Sibylline Oracle* 13, written in Syria during the third century. An important contemporary viewpoint is provided by the work of two Greek historians, Dexippus and Philostratus (perhaps a descendant of the biographer Philostratus—see Chapter 11). Although their work only survives in fragments, both were important sources for parts of the *Historia Augusta* and a series of later historians including Jordanes and Zosimus (sixth century), and Zonaras (twelfth century). The excavations at Dura-Europos recovered large numbers of papyri, and these, together with other papyri from elsewhere in Mesopotamia and the epigraphic and archaeological records, complement the literary sources. On the Persian side, sources are limited to rock reliefs and monuments, as well as the autobiographical inscription of Ardashir's son, Shapur I, supplemented by later material written in Arabic or Persian after the Arab invasions of the seventh century.

For the period between 284 and 337—very much the start of what has become known as 'late antiquity'—the sources are more numerous, but present a variety of problems. Several texts from the collection of praise tracts known as the *Latin Panegyrics* are addressed to Constantine; written in the florid style of Pliny's address to Trajan, which is the first text included in the collection, the panegyrics are a mixture of flattery, lies, and censorship. Christian texts become more numerous following the conversion of Constantine, with both Lactantius (first quarter of the fourth century) and Eusebius of Caesarea (first half of the fourth century) penning important works, including a biography of Constantine himself. A key source for understanding the transformation of government in the later period is the document known as the *Notitia Dignitatum* (*ND*), the 'Register of Dignitaries'. Preserved in four copies of an illustrated medieval manuscript, the *ND* is divided between east (*ND Or.*) and west (*ND Oc.*). The text gives a sense of the military and civilian offices of the empire for the late fourth century in the east, and for the early fifth century in the west. While the western half appears to have undergone numerous revisions, it is generally accepted that the list for the east preserves the general disposition of the army units made by Diocletian prior to 305.

DOI: 10.4324/9781003202523-12

Traditionally, the mid- and late-third century period has been framed as one of intense, sustained crisis. Yet it is common today for historians to challenge long-held ideas about decline and change that run deep in Roman historiography. On the face of it, the third century appears at first to be a good candidate for the catastrophists. For much of this time the Roman empire was consumed by incessant war, political instability, spiritual problems, secessionist movements, serious financial issues, plague, and some of the worst failures of Roman arms: these included the death and disappearance of the emperor Decius in a Bulgarian swamp in 251, the loss of Dura-Europos in 255/57, and the capture of the emperor Valerian and his army at Edessa in 260. Along the Rhine and Danube, Rome's neighbours repeatedly took advantage of civil strife to raid deep into imperial territory, and after the mid-third century, those neighbours began to coalesce into more powerful groups—the Alamanni, Goths, and Franks. The crisis was particularly serious between c. 250 and 270, when the empire's population was culled by a vicious hemorrhagic fever known as the Plague of Cyprian. The plague may well have been related to changes in the Nile flood, and recent work on ancient climatic patterns has also identified several volcanic events between 235 and 285 whose ejecta shrouded sunlight and brought on cooler conditions. The shift to a drier and cooler climate was also recorded in the Greenland Ice Sheet, and reflected by the advance, at the time, of the Great Aletsch glacier in the Swiss Alps. In tandem with the heavy military casualties and deaths from the plague, such conditions would have further affected agricultural production and the ability of the state to sustain itself. On the other hand, it can be noted that some of the sociopolitical phenomena evident during the period, such as the decline of senatorial influence, the growth of the equestrians, an increase in bureaucratic complexity, and the declining relevance of Rome to the empire as a whole, all offer continuities from earlier periods.

In the fourth century, Constantine brought to fruition some of the administrative, political, and military reforms instituted by his predecessors Gallienus and Diocletian. These resulted in a divergence between field armies and garrison armies, as well as the development of a late antique Roman aristocracy defined by service to the emperor. Constantine's famous conversion to Christianity linked Christianity and Christians to imperial favour, and contributed to a significant change in imperial religious culture and political ideology. With Constantine, the Roman empire became the standard bearer for a universal monotheism, and 'Jovian' ideas about imperial rule were translated for the new era. No longer Jupiter's viceroy, Constantine and his successors became God's rulers on earth—rulers for all Christians, whether or not they lived in the empire. This viewpoint created a tight bond between church and state, involved the emperor in the faith of his subjects more than ever before, and resulted in armed conflict with Rome's neighbours.

The senate vs. the army

The *Historia Augusta* cast Maximinus, the assassin of Severus Alexander, as a brute thug who came from barbarous parents; as a young man, he impressed Septimius Severus with a display of visceral strength and was recruited into the army (*HA The Two Maximini*, 2–3). This scornful account reflects the deep prejudice among senators towards emperors who muscled their way upwards from the ranks, and tension between the senate and the army characterised the brief reign of Maximinus. The new emperor promised a massive pay rise for the legions, but he paid for it largely through cutting the grain subsidy to the people and curbing financial support for the imperial cult, in which many senators participated. Maximinus further annoyed the senate with a prolonged absence from Rome, fighting the Alamanni and Sarmatians. He was popular among the troops, however, for daring feats of courage that he performed in the front lines of the legions (Herodian, 7.2).

Meanwhile, in Africa Proconsularis—a region with substantial pockets of conservative, senatorial sensibilities—an imperial procurator was lynched by an angry mob at Thysdrus in 238. The assassins then proclaimed the provincial proconsul, an elderly senator named Gordian, as emperor. Gordian was an unexceptional man—but he was a senator, so he became a magnet for senatorial anger towards Maximinus. Gordian's son was proclaimed co-emperor but, in a bizarre twist, the senate then formed a committee of 20 men, ostensibly to deal with Maximinus. As the senate undermined him from Rome, Gordian must have realised that his situation was shaky: he had been proclaimed in a province that had no military garrison, and when the staunchly loyal III Augusta was dispatched by the legate of Numidia to quash the rebellion, both Gordian and his son perished. Afterwards, the senate declared two of their own as co-emperors: Balbinus, an old patrician from Baetica who had been ordinary consul with Caracalla in 213; and Pupienus, an experienced military commander who had held the ordinary consulship in 234. The two men loathed one another, but concealed their mutual hatred with an optimistic coin issue (Figure 12.1).

In Rome, resistance to Balbinus and Pupienus emerged in the shape of Gordian loyalists who rioted in the streets. The urban prefect and one of the praetorian prefects were murdered in the bedlam that ensued, and the mob declared for a surviving family member, Gordian's 13-year-old grandson—another Gordian—and the senate gave in to pressure and awarded him the title of Caesar. Maximinus launched an invasion of Italy, but he stalled at Aquileia, which had become an important and heavily fortified military hub since the Marcomannic Wars. As the campaign faltered, Maximinus and his young son were lynched by the troops, and his head was sent to Rome (Herodian, 8.6). This left the choice for emperor between the senate's champions and the choice of the people; the praetorians split the difference by killing Pupienus and Balbinus and declaring the young Gordian emperor, as Gordian III. The senate had lost one of its final opportunities to play

Figure 12.1 Silver antoninianus minted in Rome in 238. Obverse: radiate bust of Balbinus; reverse: FIDES MVTVA AVGG (mutual faith/trust of the Augusti) with clasped hands.

a meaningful role in Roman politics, and once again the empire was to be ruled by a gang of equestrians and military officials.

War with Persia

As civil war raged in Europe, in the east, Ardashir had set about consolidating his authority amidst the wreckage of the Arsacid empire. An early target was Armenia, where Parthian nobles determined to resist Ardashir had found support from Roman authorities across the Euphrates. Cassius Dio (80.3) and Agathangelos (*History of the Armenians*, 1.18–23) described how a desperate coalition of the surviving sons of Artabanus, exiled Medians, and an anti-Sasanian resistance movement beat off the Sasanian king. Ardashir had better fortune at Hatra, whose final king, Sanatruq II, had positioned himself as a Roman ally. In c. 235, Sanatruq welcomed Cohors IX Maurorum Gordiana, detached from I Parthica, to the city. One of its tribunes left an inscription in Temple IX at Hatra dedicated to the city's chief deity Shamash, who was assimilated in the Roman pantheon to Sol Invictus, the Unconquered Sun (*AE* 1958: 239). Such a small force was of little use to Sanatruq if the Persians arrived in force, and in 240, Ardashir and his son Shapur began a determined siege of Hatra that finally broke through the city's strong defences. Hatra was sacked and abandoned at some point during 240 or 241. The siege represented a colossal effort, and the remains of the Sasanian circumvallation are still visible on satellite photographs, while traces of a large camp and contravallation have been located in the plain to the east of the city. Ardashir also campaigned in the Persian Gulf, strengthening royal control over Bahrain. The ninth-century Persian Muslim writer Hamza al-Isfahani preserved the folk memory of a savage campaign, writing that the walls of the city of Batan Ardashir on Bahrain were built alternately with bricks and the corpses of its disloyal inhabitants (*Tarikh*, p. 48). Other writers suggested that the Sasanian conquests in the Persian Gulf extended as far as Oman (Mazun) and al-Yamama in Arabia, although the archaeological evidence for such expansion is inconsistent. In 240/41, Ardashir died, and the throne passed to his aggressive and talented son, Shapur I.

In the meantime, Gordian III had come under the guidance of the praetorian prefect Furius Sabinius Timesitheus, who strengthened his credentials by betrothing his young daughter Tranquillina to Gordian in 241. There was continued pressure from Ardashir and Shapur in Mesopotamia as the Persians probed Roman defences up and down the Euphrates. A graffito from Dura-Europos, dated to April 30, 239, recorded the time when 'the Persians descended upon us' (*SEG* 7.743b) and, despite the confusion in Roman sources over the precise chronology, it appears that at some point prior to 241, Shapur had not only attacked Dura but had also succeeded in capturing Carrhae together with Singara and Nisibis, where mint activity was disrupted. After installing Julius Priscus as the second praetorian prefect in Rome, Timesitheus and Gordian departed for the east in 242 to counter Shapur's aggressive actions in Mesopotamia. Their campaign began with an elaborate ceremony honouring Minerva, conjuring the celebrated role of Pallas Athena in the Greek victory over the Achaemenid Persian king Xerxes in the early fifth century BC, and the doors of the Temple of Janus were solemnly opened as the emperor and his army set out. Gordian crossed the Euphrates at Zeugma in 243, and won an initial victory over Shapur at Rhesaina; a spectacular medallion issue commemorated the victory (Figure 12.2).

Figure 12.2 Bimetallic medallion minted in Rome in 243/44. The reverse shows Gordian (r) and Timesitheus (l) addressing the troops.

In the aftermath, the Roman mints at Nisibis and Singara resumed striking coins, suggesting that Gordian's victory had managed to drive the Persians from Mesopotamia—but the optimistic mood was soured when Timesitheus died in suspicious circumstances. Priscus's brother, Philip, succeeded with unseemly haste to the praetorian prefecture, and the *Historia Augusta* suggested that a potent laxative administered by Philip himself had been used to do away with Timesitheus (*HA The Three Gordians*, 27–29). Gordian then took his army down the Khabur river in 244, and fought a battle with Shapur at Mishik near modern Fallujah. During this confrontation, or shortly afterwards, he died—either of wounds received in battle or, as numerous Roman sources insinuated, at Philip's hand, since Philip soon became emperor. Shapur celebrated victory over both Gordian and Philip in his autobiographical inscription, the *SKZ*, a triumphant piece of Sasanian propaganda comprising Middle Persian, Parthian, and Greek inscriptions written around the base of a rectangular tower at Naqsh-i-Rustam known as the Kaba of Zoroaster. Shapur further commemorated his victories at the city of Bishapur, founded after his later victory at Edessa in 260. There, along with a colossal statue of the king, a series of rock reliefs depicted his various triumphs; relief 2 shows Shapur mounted, his horse trampling Gordian, while a chastened Philip, down on one knee, begs Shapur for mercy.

Shapur claimed victory over Philip because, after Gordian's demise, Philip was forced to purchase peace from the Sasanian king and made unpopular concessions regarding Persian influence in Armenia. Despite his humiliation, Philip grandiosely took the titles *Persicus Maximus* and *Parthicus* and returned to Rome. He appointed his brother-in-law to a broad military command in Moesia, and left Julius Priscus as prefect of Mesopotamia. Priscus also had a plenipotentiary position in Syria under the title of *corrector orientis*, 'corrector of the east'. Priscus's tenure oversaw the monumentalisation of Shahba, south of Damascus, which was Philip's birthplace and which was renamed Philippopolis in his honour. Priscus's tenure as *corrector* brought anxiety, however: *Sibylline Oracle* 13 prophesied a doom-laden future for Philippopolis because Priscus was so cruel and despotic (90–1). Indeed, he angered so many that he suffered a *damnatio memoriae* at Palmyra, where his name was erased from one of the inscriptions on the Great Colonnade (Figure 12.3).

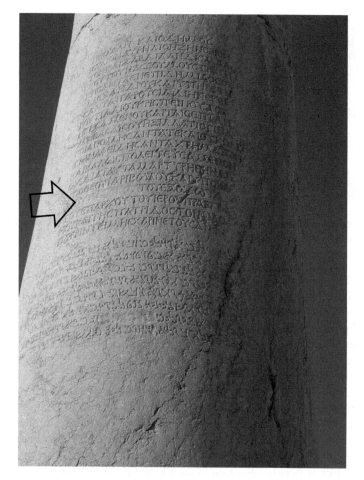

Figure 12.3 Bilingual Greek and Palmyrene inscription from the Great Colonnade at Palmyra, with Priscus's name chiselled from the text, marked by an arrow.

Source: Photograph by the author.

Philip's wife Marcia Otacilia Severa became the Augusta and *mater castrorum*, a clear imitation of Faustina and Julia Domna and an effort to secure the relationship between the imperial family and the army. The senate deified Gordian and provided him with an elaborate funeral, and assented to Philip's decision to elevate his young son to the title of Caesar.

In 246/47, unrest on the Danube forced Philip to fight the Carpi, a tribal group living in the region east of Dacia. Their first raids came in the late 230s and were sufficiently violent that the mint at Olbia, in the old Bosporan kingdom, permanently ceased production. The likely cause of this instability was the growing power of a group of people known in modern scholarship as the Goths. Contemporaries such as Dexippus referred to them in an antiquarian fashion as Scythians, and located them in a region between Romania and the Ukraine. Understanding the early history of the Goths has proven to be highly problematic. The first attempts at writing a unified history of the Gothic people were made in the sixth century by Cassiodorus, a senior palace official living in Ostrogothic-dominated Italy, and Jordanes, a Roman of Gothic ancestry living in Constantinople. Both men created accounts of the Goths that gave them a pre-Roman, continuous history, and (in the case of Cassiodorus) that integrated them within Roman historiography. Jordanes also claimed that the Goths' original home was in Scandinavia, which they had left on a long migration that brought them to the frontiers of the Roman empire. As noted in Chapter 11, during the Marcommanic Wars there were dimly understood reports of movements of people, reported by Appian and the *Historia Augusta*, that were causing difficulties for the peoples along the Danube. These may well reflect movements of Goths or others, but modern historians are sceptical about the length and nature of any Gothic migration. There is similar scepticism about the existence of a uniquely 'Gothic' culture in the archaeological record, represented by the material culture known as the Černjachov (or Sîntana-de-Mureş) culture, unearthed in numerous excavations across eastern Europe between the Donets river and the Carpathian mountains. These concerns relate to the fact that Goths, as well as numerous other non-Roman European peoples, were swept up in the nationalist currents of the Romantic period and the early twentieth century. Because of the discovery that the Gothic language was related to Germanic languages, the migration myth of the Goths reported by Jordanes, taking them from the Baltic, through Poland, and into the Ukraine, was eagerly seized upon to support Nazi racial ideology and Hitler's exterminationist policies of *Lebensraum* in eastern Europe.

What archaeological deposits *have* been able to show is that north of the third-century Rhine–Danube frontier, communities were becoming stratified into hierarchies surmounted by chieftains, whose dwellings occupied central places in villages that were both growing in size and showing a greater capacity for storing and redistributing moveable wealth. These developments were the results of prolonged contact with Rome: of the inflow of Roman subsidies in cash and in kind, trans-frontier military recruitment, the influence of Roman hierarchical models of rulership, and the rising opportunities in the Roman military for talented commanders. This process led to the development of powerful groups such as the Alamanni, Goths, and Franks, all of whom appear in Roman sources during the third century. Indeed, Jordanes thought that by the mid-third century the Goths had reached a position of regional power that was sufficient to place unbearable pressure on their neighbours, and allowed them to demand tribute from the Quadi, Marcomanni, and another Germanic group, the Vandals, who appear to be related to a group known as the Astingi encountered by the Romans during the reign of Marcus Aurelius (*Getica*, 16). Zosimus reported that the 'Scythians' were so strong that they 'collected into one body out of every nation and country within their territory' (*New History*, 1.20).

After suppressing the Carpi, Philip hopefully celebrated the dawn of a new Roman millennium in 248, 1,000 years from the foundation of the city in 753 BC; the event was commemorated by the Secular Games, despite the fact that they were 60 years early. The festival could not, however, conceal the deep woes afflicting the empire. The silver content of the antoniniani had dropped precipitately from the time of Gordian III, and Philip was forced to slash government expenses. In the same year, a revolt emerged in Cappadocia and Syria under a usurper named Jotapianus, apparently out of frustration with Julius Priscus's draconian policies. Another rebellion arose on the Danube, where the legate of Upper Moesia, Pacatianus, was proclaimed emperor at Viminacium in a senatorial backlash against Philip's equestrian roots. Pacatianus was murdered by his troops, but the soldiers then turned to the senator sent to put down the rebellion, Decius, and proclaimed him emperor instead. Taking over the mint at Viminacium, Decius minted coins as Traianus Decius, exploiting the Danubian connection to Trajan as well as his namesake's illustrious fighting record. In 249, Decius invaded Italy and Philip was murdered at Verona. The Praetorian Guard, who had Philip's 11-year-old son in their care, killed him when they found out the result of the contest, and Julius Priscus disappeared from the historical record. Across the Mediterranean, stonemasons got to work chiselling Priscus's and Philip's names from imperial inscriptions as both suffered a *damnatio memoriae*.

Decius sought to present a strong example of continuity. He had deliberately taken Trajan's name, used the personification of Dacia on the reverse of his antoniniani, and the author of *Sibylline Oracle* 13 (110) called him '300', the numerical value of the Greek letter τ. In Rome, Decius took the titles *pontifex maximus* and *pater patriae*, and embarked on a building campaign. He also minted an astonishing series of antoniniani, honouring the great deified emperors of the past (Figure 12.4). Decius picked the best and most respected emperors, beginning with Augustus and ending with Severus Alexander, but deliberately skipped Pertinax and all three Gordians. In a further attempt to make his rule consistent with Roman tradition—but probably also in response to the arrival of a new plague (see below)—Decius tried to reset the relationship with the gods, crucial to the wellbeing of the empire. Decius's preferred vehicle for this was an empire-wide sacrifice. Every citizen was required to sacrifice before a magistrate, who would then provide a *libellus*, a receipt acknowledging that the deed had been carried out correctly. This massive undertaking was achieved by the use of the taxation and census apparatus, and was a testament to the professional expertise of an increasingly bureaucratic government; but its smooth operation was undermined by resistance from Christians. Even if Decius intended otherwise—and the edict was worded opaquely enough, requiring only a sacrifice to 'ancestral gods'—Christians understood his demand as a punitive gesture. Some Christians risked making the sacrifice, for which they were scorned as *libelli* by their peers, but many more chose to die in the vicious persecution that followed.

Figure 12.4 Silver antoninianus minted in Rome in 251. Consecration issue honouring Augustus.

Plague

According to Eusebius, the philosopher Porphyry connected the failure of Christians to sacrifice with a new and devastating pandemic that emerged in Alexandria in 249 (*Preparation for the Gospel*, 5.1). The mysterious illness spread quickly throughout the Mediterranean, reaching Rome and Carthage in 251 and lingering for over 20 years. This disease typically receives far less attention than the Antonine Plague (Chapter 11) or the Justinianic Plague (Chapter 14), but it was arguably the most catastrophic event of the third century. It contributed to some of the period's worst disasters, and had important consequences for the economy. The disease became known as the Plague of Cyprian, after the bishop of Carthage who described its effects in a letter, written in 252, to fortify the spirits of local Christians. Cyprian recorded a terrible and bloody purging of the bowels, bleeding eyes, pain in the throat, vomiting, thirst, and high fever (*On Mortality*, 14). Cyprian's biographer Pontius described a quick-moving illness that killed so many that it undermined the functioning of civil society (*Life of Cyprian*, 9). Another witness, Dionysius, a bishop living in Alexandria, wrote a letter to a fellow Egyptian bishop in 249 that was copied by Eusebius; it recorded a widespread illness that killed the old and the young indiscriminately (Eusebius, *Ecclesiastical History*, 7.21). In 250, Dionysius wrote another letter that described the great mortality of those who looked after the sick, and painted a lurid portrait of the unburied bodies piling up in the streets (Eusebius, *Ecclesiastical History*, 7.22). Later writers, drawing on the lost accounts of Philostratus and Dexippus, noted that the plague was deadly to animals and stripped villages of their livestock, and it was the worst epidemic that anyone could remember (Orosius, *History Against the Pagans*, 7.27 & Zosimus, *New History*, 1.26). Zosimus also recorded the dire impact of the plague on the empire's ability to field healthy and effective armies (*New History*, 1.36–46); indeed, the illness is thought to have hampered the Roman army at Edessa in 260, and it killed the emperor Claudius II in 270. Studies of the textual sources have suggested that the plague was a viral hemorrhagic fever similar to Ebola, and it may have arisen from a rapid rise in the population of rodents, the viral reservoir, following a heavy flood of the Nile that had broken a period of extreme drought (Eusebius, *Ecclesiastical History*, 7.21). Coins minted by a succession of emperors from Trebonianus Gallus to Valerian featured a reverse with the legend APOLL SALVTARI, optimistically evoking Apollo 'the healer', but for a generation of Romans already living through difficult times, the plague proved devastating.

Decius and the Goths

As the plague burned through communities from Alexandria to Rome, Decius made continued orders to sacrifice. He was then faced with an insurrection among the Carpi and their allies among the Goths, whose subsidies had been terminated by an angry Philip before his death. In the spring of 250, there was an invasion of Goths, Carpi, and others under two leaders, Cniva and Ostrogotha. The Carpi invaded Dacia, while the Gothic force divided: one group, under Cniva, cut through the Roman defences at Oescus and menaced Novae before laying siege to Nikopolis ad-Istrum. The other, after an abortive attempt on Marcianople, laid siege to the city of Philippopolis (Plovdiv) in Thrace, later capturing it. Decius arrived in the region with his army soon afterwards and defeated the Carpi in Dacia, but after rejoining the main Gothic force, Cniva inflicted a stinging defeat on him at Beroea (Ulpia Augusta Traiana). A chastened Decius regrouped at Novae with the propraetorian legate of Lower Moesia, Trebonianus Gallus. After passing the winter, the Goths set off to recross the Danube, laden with plunder and prisoners. Decius successfully intercepted Cniva and Ostrogotha at Abrittus (Razgrad) in the summer of 251, but after cutting down the front ranks of the enemy, Decius, his son, and thousands of Roman legionnaires were killed after they became mired in a swamp (Figure 12.5). In the aftermath of their victory, the Goths plundered the Roman treasury, creating instant wealth; gold aurei of Decius have turned up in graves north of the Danube in the Ukraine, while some gold coins minted by the Goths imitate Roman types but feature a distinctive reverse with a galloping rider throwing a javelin. As the Goths left Roman territory with the promise that their subsidies would be renewed, Trebonianus Gallus seized the throne.

Decius (Gordian III notwithstanding) became the first Roman emperor to be killed in battle, and he left a mixed legacy. He was 'a man learned in all the arts and virtues', wrote the anonymous author of the *Epitome De Caesaribus*, 'quiet and courteous at home, in arms most ready' (29). In his polemical tract *On the Deaths of the Persecutors*, however, Lactantius cast Decius as 'an accursed wild beast' who got what he deserved for his treatment of Christians. A different legacy of Decius and the Gothic war is to be found in the way that the conflict illustrates the problems inherent in getting to grips with Gothic history. For a long time, chapters 16–18 of Jordanes' *Getica* were the main source for Decius's conflict with the Goths. Little was known from any contemporary source until a chance discovery at the Austrian National Library in Vienna turned up a palimpsest that had been added to a manuscript of church laws called *Codex Vindobonensis Hist. gr.* 73. The palimpsest overwrote an earlier text that preserved what is generally accepted to be parts of the *Scythica* of Dexippus. The short fragment, set in between the defeats at Beroea and Abrittus, confirmed the identities of the Gothic leaders as Cniva and Ostrogotha, proving that Ostrogotha was not, as had been suspected for centuries, a fictional individual, and finally established the long-suspected credibility of Jordanes's version of events.

Crisis

In Rome, Trebonianus Gallus deified Decius and appointed both his son, Volusianus, and Decius's son, Hostilianus, as Caesars; according to Zosimus, Hostilianus soon succumbed to the plague (*New History*, 1.25.2). The author of *Sibylline Oracle* 13 had a poor view of the imperial family, charitably referring to Gallus and Volusianus as 'destructive Ares with his bastard son' (103–4). Meanwhile, Syria and Mesopotamia were in an uneasy state of equilibrium. At Dura-Europos, which was the military and administrative hub of the Middle Euphrates region known as Parapotamia, there was a strong garrison made up of legionary vexillations and Cohors XX Palmyrenorum. This unit, destined to become the empire's best known auxiliary cohort as a result of the finds later unearthed at Dura, was most likely raised in c. 176 from a contingent of Palmyrene archers who had been at the city since 169. The priceless cache of papyri from Dura, and the cache of documents known as the Euphrates Papyri, have allowed historians to reconstruct the network of ancillary fortifications strung along the Euphrates and Khabur rivers. The troops stationed on this lonely southeastern wedge of the Roman frontier performed a range of peacetime functions, from assisting in tax collection to preserving order and assisting visiting dignitaries. *P. Dura* 60B, for instance, a letter written in 208 by the historian

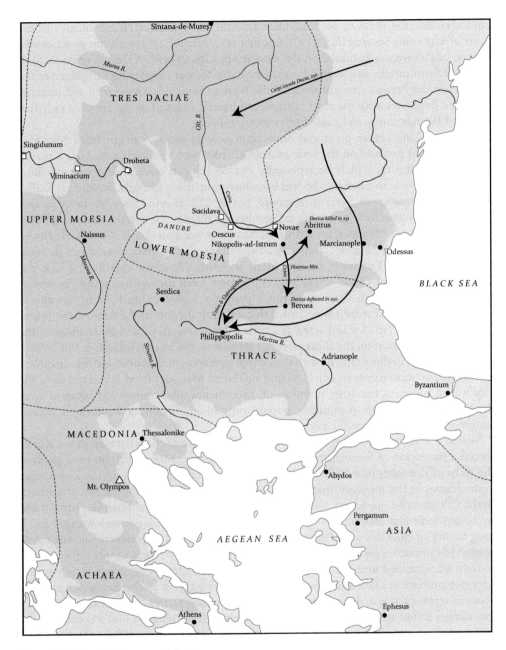

Figure 12.5 The Gothic wars of Decius.

Source: Illustration by the author.

and propraetorian legate Marius Maximus to military commanders at stations along the Euphrates, directed them to accommodate a Parthian ambassador on his journey to the court of Septimius Severus (*RA* §190). Another text, *PEuphr.* 14, reveals the presence of a *numerus* of Palmyrenes stationed on the road at Appadana, north of Dura (Figure 12.6). It was these fortifications that would bear the brunt of Shapur's aggressive campaigns of the 250s, when the Persian emperor reversed the Roman tactic of moving men and matériel down the Euphrates with the river current, and instead attacked *up* the river—a ploy that surprised Roman forces and caused several major defeats.

It was not long before provincial discontent arose in Syria. A man named Mariades, evicted from his position on the *boule* of Antioch, recruited a private army. After a period of brigandage during which he repeatedly evaded Roman soldiers sent to catch him, Mariades went over to Shapur, who had been busy fomenting intrigue in Armenia. Gallus despatched Volusianus to Syria in response, but in 252 Shapur, with Mariades in tow, surprised the Roman force gathering at Barbalissos, a Roman stronghold on the Euphrates only 150 kilometres (93 miles) from Antioch. Shapur boasted on the *SKZ* that he destroyed an army of 60,000 there and 'conquered' a large number of military installations in Syria, from Anatha on the Euphrates as far as Satala and Antioch, whose capture and sack was 'predicted' by *Sibylline Oracle* 13 (125–8). A fragment from the tenth-century *Excerpta de Sententiis*, originally from the sixth-century pen of a high-ranking Roman bureaucrat, Peter the Patrician (Chapter 14), recorded that a significant part of the Antiochene population welcomed Mariades and acted as a fifth column that facilitated the capture of the city. Following so soon on the short career of Jotapianus, the loss of Antioch in this fashion illustrated public disillusionment with the central government in Rome and foreshadowed the breakaway movements to come. Shapur beheaded Mariades for this betrayal once the city was in his grasp, but large numbers of Antiochenes who resisted the invasion were deported to Persia. Mass, involuntary population transfers became a depressingly regular feature of conflict between the two empires.

Shapur was accompanied on the campaign by Kerdir, the Zoroastrian high priest. Kerdir served a succession of Sasanian monarchs, and on his own Middle Persian inscription at the Kaba of Zoroaster (the *KKZ*), he boasted that he established magi for the Zoroastrian communities in the territory that he and Shapur passed through during the invasion of Syria, Cilicia, and Cappadocia. There is no need to believe all the boastful claims made by both Kerdir and Shapur, but Roman territory *did* incorporate kingdoms that had a long history of close ties with Persia, such as Commagene and Cappadocia, and the thinly manned fortifications on the Euphrates known from the papyri were simply not equipped to resist a determined invasion. The Sasanians were also masters of siegecraft, as they would later demonstrate at Dura-Europos, and their aggressive thrust *up* the Euphrates and into Roman territory was a distinct departure from Parthian tactics. The cluster of military gravestones found at Apamea, dating to 252, are thought to reflect a major conflict in the area, and the list of cities captured by Shapur in the *SKZ* finds parallels in the Euphrates and Dura papyri. The Roman defeat was also suitably momentous to spur the author of *Sibylline Oracle* 13 (120–24) to recast Mariades as a new Nero, coming from the east to wreck Rome's fortunes all over again. Another indication that the invasion had major ramifications was the interruption of imperial coinage minted at Antioch. Later, the only resistance offered to the Persians when they returned in 253 came from an Emesene, Uranius Antonius, who, calling on Elagabal, turned the invaders back (*Sibylline Oracle* 13,

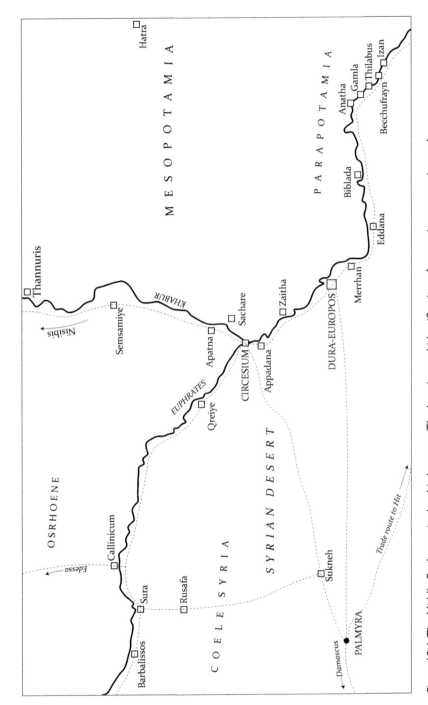

Figure 12.6 The Middle Euphrates in the third century. The location and identification of some sites are conjectural.

Source: Illustration by the author.

147–54). Uranius, like Jotapianus before him, usurped the royal prerogative of minting coins in his image in order to bolster his acceptability to the local population. Mariades, Jotapianus, and Uranius also demonstrated the existence of paramilitary forces that were available when the legions failed or were absent. Why had Shapur invaded? In the *SKZ*, he claimed that 'Caesar lied again [and] did harm to Armenia', a phrase that reflects the essential struggle between truth/lies and light/dark in the Zoroastrian faith, together with the idea of the Roman monarchy as a 'lapsed' entity.

In 252, Gallus also had problems on the Danube. A seaborn force of Goths and their allies raided the coastline of Asia Minor, reaching as far as Ephesus where they burned the sanctuary of Artemis. The raids revealed the impotence of the old *classis Pontica* (Chapter 9)—if, indeed, it still existed. In 253, a conflict erupted in Lower Moesia, and the man who suppressed it, Aemilianus, was proclaimed emperor. Defeating and killing Gallus at Interamna in Italy, Aemilianus, who Zonaras characterised as 'ignoble and grovelling' (12.22), soon found himself in trouble: the man who Gallus had frantically ordered to come to his aid, Publius Licinius Valerianus, defeated and killed Aemilianus at Spoletium. Valerian, a senator who had served as ordinary consul in 238, appointed his son Gallienus as co-emperor and his grandson as *princeps iuventutis* and Caesar; Gallienus's wife, Salonina, became Augusta and *mater castrorum*. Valerian's imperial career during this period is obscure, but epigraphic evidence places him in the east in 255 and then on the Danube and Rhine frontiers shortly afterwards, fighting the Goths. He held the ordinary consulship in 254, 255, and 257, and in 257 he issued an edict that targeted Christians, banning church assemblies and ordering priests and bishops to sacrifice. As with Decius, the edict was motivated by concerns over the proper relationship between the Romans and their gods and the need to regain divine favour. It was rigidly enforced by Valerian, even when an irritated senate attempted to guide him to greater clemency; one of its victims was Cyprian, the bishop of Carthage. Problems continued, however: another naval raid by the Goths hit Asia Minor, capturing Trapezus (Trebizond) in 256. After Gallienus suppressed the rebellion of Ingenuus in Illyria, which was notable for the large numbers of civilians and city-dwellers who fought in its ranks, and III Augusta put down a revolt in Numidia, Shapur invaded Mesopotamia, determined to strike deep into Commagene and Cappadocia.

On his way up the Euphrates, Shapur captured Dura-Europos at some point between 255 and 257 (Figure 12.7). The capture of Dura brought a permanent end to the Roman military presence on the Middle Euphrates. Dura's Roman defenders had tried to forestall the siege by constructing an anti-siege rampart both within the walls, and in a glacis thrown up on the dusty plain to the west. The rampart created exceptionally dry conditions, preserving papyri, textiles, and wall paintings that would otherwise not have survived (Figure 12.8).

Among the finds at what proved to be one of the most sensational archaeological discoveries of the twentieth century was one of the oldest synagogues in the world, whose lifelike and vibrant paintings, now in the National Museum in Damascus, provided further evidence of disobedience towards the second commandment and its prohibition of creating 'graven images'. Excavations also uncovered a Christian church, a Mithraeum, and numerous temples. A mass of papyri discovered in the Temple of Azzanathkona, a deity imported from nearby Anatha, detailed the roster and activities of XX Palmyrenorum. (Figure 1.9 in Chapter 1 is one of these documents, a so-called 'morning report' that recorded the daily strength of the cohort.) A famous wall painting discovered in Dura's

Figure 12.7 Aerial photograph of Dura-Europos. View from the east, with the Euphrates in the foreground.

Source: Photograph Yale-2183. Yale University Art Gallery, Dura-Europos Collection.

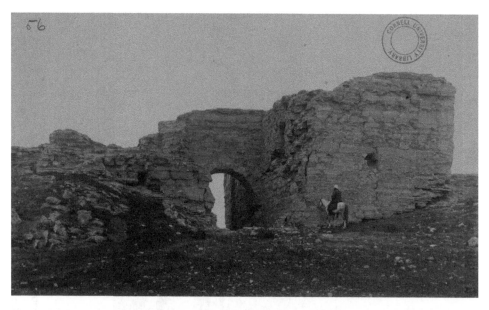

Figure 12.8 The main entrance to Dura-Europos, the Palmyrene Gate, from the interior of the city. The horse and rider are on top of the anti-siege rampart; the height of the city walls, not much higher than the rampart, can be seen either side of the gate. Photograph by John Henry Haynes.

Source: Image from Photographs of Asia Minor, #4776. Division of Rare and Manuscript Collections, Cornell University Library.

Temple of Bel depicted its tribune, Julius Terentius, performing a sacrifice with his troops for three Palmyrene deities on the left, and below them, the *tyche* of Palmyra and the *tyche* of Dura (Figure 12.9). Terentius was killed in action in 239, perhaps in the Persian attack mentioned earlier, and his wife left a touching funerary inscription for him, found nearly 17 centuries later: 'brave in campaigns, mighty in wars, dead … Aurelia Arria buried this her beloved husband, whom may the divine spirits receive and the light earth conceal' (*AE* 1948: 124). The siegeworks also preserved bodies, Persian mines under the walls (Figure 12.10), and a siege ramp in the south-west part of the city, along with a range of military equipment that included painted shields and armoured trappers for Roman cavalry.

The work at Dura advanced our knowledge of many aspects of a poorly understood period in Roman history, and provided a picture of a remarkably cosmopolitan community with a cultural and religious life that fused classical, Hellenistic, and eastern styles. It also furnished a great deal of information about a city that had a segregated military quarter within the walls, reserved for the Roman army. Sadly, in common with other sites of great scientific and cultural significance such as Hatra, Palmyra, and Apamea, Dura was heavily looted in the Syrian Civil War; today, the site is pockmarked with deep pits, the result of a devastating campaign of looting organised by Daesh/ISIS terrorists (Figure 12.11).

Figure 12.9 Terentius performing a sacrifice. Paint on plaster. Courtesy of Yale University Art Gallery, Dura-Europos Collection

Figure 12.10 The partially collapsed Tower 19 at Dura-Europos. A Persian sap ran under the wall
here; excavated in the 1930s, it yielded the skeletons of dead Roman and Persian troops,
together with equipment and their final pay.

Source: Photograph by the author.

Among all of the calamities of the third century, Valerian's defeat at Edessa in 260, as
he attempted to stem Shapur's aggression, ranks among the most dreadful. According to
Zosimus, the Roman troops were suffering from the plague (*New History*, 1.35–6). With
large numbers of his troops unable to fight, Valerian, whom the *Epitome De Caesaribus*
regarded as 'stupid and extremely indolent' (32), sought to negotiate an end to the war,
but Shapur knew about the plague and turned Valerian's desperation into an opportunity
(Peter the Patrician, frag. 9). Valerian, his praetorian prefect, and numerous senators were
taken prisoner, his sick and weary soldiers surrendered, and all were deported to Persia,
never to return: 'And the men who [were] from the land of the Romans, from not-Iran
[an-Iran], were led back as spoils into Iran, into Persis, Parthia, Khuzestan, Asurestan, and
the other lands … [and] there they were settled' (*SKZ* §30). Zonaras wrote that Shapur
drove captured civilians before him like livestock, allowing only the most basic essentials
of life to sustain them on their march eastwards into eternal captivity (12.23).

Lactantius gleefully linked Valerian's grim end to his unwise persecution of Christians. It
was Lactantius, too, who reported the lurid (if unverifiable) story that Shapur used Valerian
as a mounting block for his horse, and later had the emperor flayed, his skin dyed bright

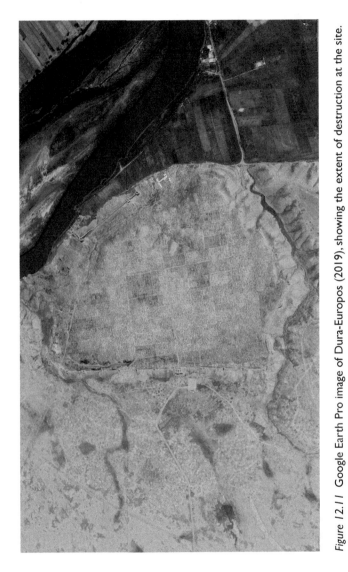

Figure 12.11 Google Earth Pro image of Dura-Europos (2019), showing the extent of destruction at the site.

Source: Image © 2020 Google © 2020 CNES/Airbus.

Figure 12.12 Relief of Shapur at Naqsh-i-Rustam. Shapur, mounted, holds Valerian's hand in acknowledgment of his surrender. The kneeling figure is usually identified as Philip.

Source: Photograph by Sahand Ace (CC BY-SA 3.0).

red and exhibited to Roman ambassadors on their visits to Ctesiphon (*On the Deaths of the Persecutors*, 5). Roman prisoners were set to work on various building projects; the ruins of the dam near Shushtar in Iran are still known today as Band-e Kaisar—'the dam of Caesar'. Roman prisoners probably worked on the city of Bishapur, with its Hellenistic grid-shaped city plan, multi-panelled reliefs portraying Shapur's victories redolent of Trajan's column, probably carved by Roman craftsmen, and an inscribed Corinthian victory column at the intersection of the cardo and decumanus that resembled that at Apamea. Shapur also founded a city that he called Veh-Antioch-Shapur, 'Better-than-Antioch-Shapur', and celebrated his defeat of Valerian with what is certainly the most famous of the numerous Sasanian reliefs, at Naqsh-i-Rustam (Figure 12.12), as well as on an exquisite sardonyx cameo held in the Cabinet des Médailles in Paris (Figure 12.13). Impressive as these monuments are, and as traumatising as Shapur's victories were for the Romans, they conceal the fact that during Shapur's reign, the Persians spent even more time consolidating royal rule in the eastern marches of their vast empire than they did fighting Roman armies. It was under Shapur's rule, for instance, that Persian authority was extended far to the east, encompassing Bactria and the remnants of the Kushan empire in Gandhara. While the Romans floundered from one disaster to the next, the Sasanian empire was establishing a far stronger position.

In the aftermath of the catastrophe at Edessa, the Palmyrene nobleman Udaynath, known in Roman sources via his Romanised name Septimius Odaenathus, together with

Figure 12.13 Sardonyx cameo of Valerian (left) and Shapur (right). Shapur holds his opponent's hand, accepting his surrender.

Source: Photograph by Marie-Lan Nguyen (CC BY 2.5).

Valerian's equestrian logistics expert Macrianus and the praetorian prefect Callistus (also known as Ballista) joined forces. Shapur's troops had almost reached Pompeiopolis on the southern coast of the Black Sea when Callistus, who had scraped together a small fleet and a desperate band of stragglers, defeated the advance elements of the Persian force and plundered its treasury. Odaenathus delivered a second blow when he ambushed the Persian army as it crossed the Euphrates on its way home (Zonaras, 12.23). Macrianus, who was lame and disinterested in seizing the throne, appointed his young sons, Macrianus and Quietus, as emperors. Leaving Quietus in Syria, the two Macriani set off for Pannonia, where they were killed in battle. In the meantime, Gallienus, who made no attempt to rescue his father from captivity, campaigned on the Rhine from Colonia Agrippinensium and faced raids into Italy by the Alamanni and Juthungi. The propraetorian legate of Lower Germany, Postumus, defeated the Juthungi and rescued thousands of Italian captives; then, after a scuffle at Colonia Agrippinensium in which a praetorian prefect was lynched and Gallienus's son Saloninus murdered, Postumus was proclaimed emperor.

Secession

In the late 250s, the unity of the empire had started to crack under the accumulated strain of a generation of war and plague. In a lengthy passage, Aurelius Victor adopted a Tacitean sense of gloom: offices were debased, everyone was a criminal, leadership was conspicuous by its absence (*On the Caesars*, 33). Signs of trouble were everywhere, not least in the money supply. The denarius and sestertius had ceased being minted in the 250s, with their metal directed towards the antoniniani. The gold aureus was losing some of its purity, and hoarding became common. Aurelius Victor blamed Gallienus, whom he accused of having an affair with a Germanic princess and behaving so poorly that he 'shipwrecked the Roman state', but the uncertainties of the time were hardly the fault of a single individual and, as suggested earlier, may also have been related to changes in climate (*On the Caesars*, 33).

In 256, Gallienus fought the Franks, a Germanic group made up of several smaller groups whom the Romans had already encountered, including the Salii, Bructeri, Batavians, and Chatti. The Franks managed to capture Vetera and many of the fortifications constructed along the Rhine under the principate were temporarily or permanently abandoned; the Romans also withdrew from the Agri Decumates, leaving the land to the Alamanni. In Raetia, destruction layers at important centres such as Augusta Vindelicorum have been dated to the early 260s, and Gallienus pulled back to the south, creating a new frontier in Raetia on the Rhine. In Greece, a Gothic invasion in 261–63 plundered shrines in Attica, but was driven off by the Roman proconsular governor of Achaea and a hastily raised local militia; in the aftermath the Athenians rebuilt their city walls. Astonishingly, the city had lain undefended since the time of Sulla, but its security could no longer be guaranteed by a sorely overstretched Roman army.

This dire security situation was one reason for the elevation of Postumus, who took the tribunician power and the titles of consul, *pater patriae*, *felix invictus Augustus*, and *pontifex maximus*, and installed himself at Colonia Agrippinensium as the leader of the 'Gallic empire'. Minting coins at Augusta Treverorum that proclaimed him to be *restitutor Galliarum*, 'the restorer of the Gauls', he was able to bring a measure of stability to the situation along the Rhine. Postumus was content to rule the provinces stretching from Spain to Britain as an emperor with elected consuls, and never directly challenged the authority of Gallienus, who could do little about him in any case (Figure 12.14).

In the east, following the defeat of the Macriani and faced with further challenges from Quietus, Callistus, and Shapur, Gallienus similarly accepted the ascendancy of the Palmyrene Septimius Odaenathus and granted him *imperium totius orientis* (*HA Gallienus*, 10.1). In 261, Callistus and Quietus were killed at Emesa, and Odaenathus drove the Persians deep into their own territory and campaigned as far as Ctesiphon (Eutropius, *Breviarium*, 9.10). Odaenathus was also on hand when the Goths invaded Asia Minor, and in 252 he recaptured Nisibis and Carrhae, which had fallen under Persian control. Gallienus took the title *Persicus Maximus* in recognition of the success won by his de facto eastern subordinate.

Odaenathus had been awarded consular status in 258 and recognised as a senator, and after his victories in 263 he took the title 'restorer of the whole east' on the basis of a Palmyrene inscription (*CIS* 2.3946). He also took the title 'King of Kings' as the leader of Palmyra, but this strayed into uncertain political territory as it linked monarchy with military victory—a prerogative that belonged to Gallienus. Like Postumus, Odaenathus did not directly challenge imperial authority, but when he declared his son 'King of Kings' and held a celebration to commemorate the event in Antioch, he inevitably raised suspicions in Rome. According to Peter the Patrician (frag. 10), Odaenathus also attempted to reach a separate treaty with Shapur, behaviour that would most certainly have been perceived as highly questionable. The author of *Sibylline Oracle* 13 (170–71) portrayed Odaenathus

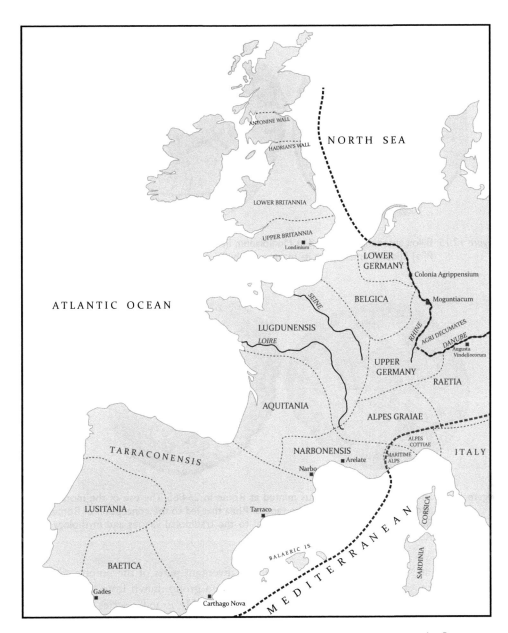

Figure 12.14 The Gallic empire. The heavy dashed line indicates its greatest extent, under Postumus.

Source: Illustration by the author.

as a great man destined to rule the Romans—a contemporary view of Roman rule likely held by many Syrians, who were content to have a vigorous and local military champion instead of the uncertainties of fallible Roman legions, ephemeral emperors, and assassins' daggers.

Figure 12.15 Billon antoninianus minted at Mediolanum in 260/61. The reverse honours VII Claudia as P[ia] F[idelis], and depicts its mascot, the bull.

Figure 12.16 Silver denarius of Gallienus minted at Rome in 264/65. The use of the motif of Mars and Rhea Silvia, alluding to the rape of Rhea that led to the conception of Romulus and Remus, represents a powerful appeal to the traditional virtues and mythology of the Roman state.

Stranded at Mediolanum between these two divergent parts of the empire, Gallienus sought to strengthen the army, which was a fractured group drawn from the Praetorian Guard and vexillations of at least 17 different legions. He issued a series of coins celebrating the faith of the Roman people in the army, as well as issues that honoured individual legions (Figure 12.15), and he also engaged in broad reforms that gave promotion prospects to even the lowliest soldiers, boosting morale.

Gallienus fortified his personal guardians, promoting links to Hercules, Jupiter, Apollo, Diana, and Sol Invictus, with the latter assimilated to the worship of Jupiter Heliopolitanus at Baalbek, Elagabal at Emesa, and Malakbel at Palmyra. The emperor's links with Sol were further represented through his use of the radiate crown, as in Figure 12.15. Gallienus also boasted of his status as a warrior and linked his rule to Rome's mythical origins: a very rare coin issue of 264/65 portrayed the emperor in an archaising style with a Corinthian helmet and featured Mars and Rhea Silvia on the reverse (Figure 12.16).

Gallienus is also credited with creating a mobile cavalry force, which he based at Mediolanum. Heavy cavalry had been part of the army since the time of Hadrian, and distinct cavalry corps serving with the army are known from the war between Severus and Niger, when the cavalry came under the command of an equestrian with the title of *praepositus*. In the wars of the third century, cavalry assumed greater importance: an inscription from Bostra, for example, recorded the constitution of *alae novae firmae miliariae catafractariae Philippianae*—the New Milliary Philippian Cataphracts, a double-strength cohort of armoured cavalry (*IGLS* 9090, c. 244–49). Under Gallienus, the cavalry was brought together for the first time under a single commander who reported directly to the emperor: the first incumbent was Aureolus, who had defeated and killed the Macriani. A distinctive feature of the individual units of *equites* was the epithet *promoti*, 'promoted', denoting their elite status and transfer from their legionary commands to an exclusive mobile force.

Another important innovation under Gallienus (and Valerian) was the appearance of a college of officers, the protectorate, with the rank of 'protector' (L. *protector/protectores*). *Protectores* were originally individual soldiers from the *equites singulares Augusti*, attached to provincial governors and praetorian prefects. Later, centurions and tribunes who had served with the emperor in the field were granted the title, and the protectorate developed into a field officer corps that moved picked individuals into senior commands. The *protectores* formed the basis of Gallienus's response to the loss of so many senior generals and soldiers in the defeat of his father at Edessa, the loss of Decius and his army, Shapur's invasions in the early 250s, and the secession of the Gallic empire. On appointment as *protectores*, men gained equestrian status, and numerous equestrian *protectores* became legionary prefects. In the process, the military became thoroughly equestrianised. Senators disappeared from the hitherto senatorial offices of military tribune and legionary legate, and instead the epigraphic sources record equestrians holding the positions of tribune, *praepositus*, prefect of *alae*, and legionary prefect.

In 267, Odaenathus and his son were murdered at Emesa by a faction at court, and power was seized by his widow, Julia Aurelia Zenobia (later Septimia Zenobia), who ruled through her second son, Septimius Vaballathus. Meanwhile, Gallienus faced a major incursion of the Germanic Heruli that he deflected with some difficulty, but was then faced with a mutiny by Aureolus, his cavalry commander. Returning to Italy, Gallienus was murdered by his officers; Aureolus, who had declared himself Augustus, was murdered in turn and replaced by a man named Marcus Aurelius Claudius. Claudius (II) was an equestrian from the Balkans—a product, ironically, of Gallienus's promotion of the *protectores*. His elevation marked the start of a prolonged line of Balkan men from obscure backgrounds who assumed the imperial throne. Claudius's name showed that his family had gained citizenship under the Antonine Constitution of Caracalla, as had his praetorian prefect, Aurelius Heraclianus. These equestrian interlopers were the *novi homines* of the new order: military men, recently enfranchised, whose education had been received on the front lines of Rome's brutal wars in company with the emperor, rather than in the refined setting of a sophist's classroom.

In the west, Postumus was murdered in a civil conflict with a pretender who had declared himself emperor in Upper Germany; it is telling that Postumus was killed as he tried to prevent his troops from sacking Moguntiacum, yet another reflection of the growing rift between the 'Roman' cities of the empire and the 'Roman' troops ostensibly raised to protect them. Claudius was forced to leave the Gallic empire to its warring factions because of an invasion by the Goths, which he checked at Naissus in Moesia (Serbian Niš) in 269, earning him the title *Gothicus Maximus*. Soon there was a dangerous rift with Zenobia in Syria, who was minting coins issued in the name of Vaballathus and Odaenathus, and being advised by the Emesene philosopher and long-time resident of Athens, Cassius Longinus. Like the coins of Uranius Antonius and Jotapianus, those of Vaballathus were intended for a local audience and not as a challenge to Roman authority—but Claudius took a different view. His disapproval turned to anger when a powerful Palmyrene army under Septimius Zabbai and Septimius Zabda invaded the province of Arabia in mid-270, defeating the propraetorian legate of Arabia on the way: an inscription from the Temple of Jupiter Ammon at Bostra, the base of III Cyrenaica, recorded its reconstruction after being destroyed *a Palmyrenis hostibus*, 'by Palmyrene enemies' (*IGLS* 13.1, 9107). This incursion was followed up by an invasion of Egypt in which the prefect of Egypt, Tenagino Probus, was soundly defeated, and the province and its all-important grain supply came under Palmyrene control. Despite this aggressive act, coins minted afterwards by Vaballathus, under Zenobia's tutelage, clearly indicated that he viewed himself to be subordinate to the authorities in Rome.

Despite the resistance in Arabia and Egypt, Zenobia found no shortage of Roman officials willing to collaborate as Palmyra's army romped to victory. There was likely a remnant of loyalty amongst the provincial garrisons for Odaenathus, who had once been their commander, and for the inhabitants of Rome's battered eastern provinces, the Palmyrenes had seen off the immediate threat of Shapur and his army and restored an element of calm to the region. Zenobia and her son now provided a different vision for the future, reflected in heady, nativist ideas of restoration: links were promoted between Zenobia and both Cleopatra and the famous Emesene Julia Domna, and a spiritual drift towards the east was revealed by the welcome given to emissaries of the prophet Mani from Persia (below). It has even been claimed that Zenobia herself accepted the Manichaean faith. Reflecting a hostile senatorial, Roman view, the *Historia Augusta* covered Zenobia in a notorious section called 'The Thirty Tyrants'; it is shamelessly chauvinistic, reporting caustically that Zenobia ruled 'longer than could be endured from one of the female sex' (30.1–3).

After defeating the Alamanni and claiming the title *Germanicus Maximus* in 269, Claudius II died of the plague at Sirmium in 270. An attempt by his brother to seize the throne was quickly undone by Marcus Aurelius Aurelianus, another Balkan military man who had served under Gallienus and whose family had been enfranchised by Caracalla. Aurelianus, known to us as Aurelian, had served as the cavalry commander for Claudius, and he now faced an immediate threat from raids by the Juthungi and the Vandals. Unrest in Rome followed as the mint workers rebelled, and Aurelian, having suppressed a fresh round of invasions from the Juthungi and Alamanni in northern Italy and realising the parlous state of Rome's defences, fortified the city with a massive wall, much of which still stands. Aurelian (or perhaps Diocletian) may also have been responsible for constructing some of the defensive line controlling access to north-eastern Italy in the area bordering modern Slovenia, known as the *Claustra Alpium Iuliarum*. In Rome, Aurelian dealt a further blow to senatorial prestige by removing the prerogative of minting bronze coins that the senate had held for centuries, and openly favoured the people, handing out donatives and

Figure 12.17 Gold aureus of Aurelian (obverse) and Vaballathus (reverse) minted in Antioch in 270/
72. Vaballathus's titles are recorded as V C R IM D R: *vir clarissimus rex imperator dux
Romanorum*, while Aurelian is identified as AVG—Augustus. This rare coin sold at auction
for $250,000.

burning debt records. The *alimenta*, instituted by Trajan and Hadrian, was cancelled, and a
reform of the *annona* for the people of Rome was carried out, providing wine, salt, pork, oil,
and bread instead of grain, all at a subsidised rate. An attempt either to improve the financial situation in the empire or, as has been argued, to promote coinage bearing Aurelian's
portrait and remove those of his predecessors from use, is reflected in the issuance of a new
silver coin with 5 per cent purity. The coins bore the distinctive stamp 'XX' (KA in Greek),
reflecting the silver to copper ratio of 1:20. Aurelian also created a new pure aureus, but
this coin was not properly tariffed to the silver coinage, which had been the case in the
past—1 gold aureus was worth 25 silver denarii, no matter how much the metal content
fluctuated. As a result, the lower denominations became worthless overnight as nobody
had any confidence that they could be exchanged for Aurelian's new gold coins. The consequence was the collapse of credit and lending, rampant inflation and financial misery,
and eventually a transition from an economy based on silver to one based on gold. The
disappearance at around this time of a great deal of coinage minted by cities in the Greek
east, with a long history of doing so, was probably related to Aurelian's reforms.

Aurelian then set off for the east to deal with Zenobia and Vaballathus. The Palmyrene
prince had been declared Caesar to Aurelian's Augustus; a milestone inscribed in Palmyrene
shows that Vaballathus had taken the title of '*epanorthotes* [=*corrector*] of the whole east',
while Latin milestones along the via Nova Traiana record the titles of *rex*, *dux Romanorum*,
imperator, and consul. It is not clear which of these, if any, had come from Gallienus. In
Antioch, the mint under Palmyrene control had struck coins with Aurelian on the obverse
and Vaballathus on the reverse, with the titles *vir clarissimus* (identifying his senatorial status),
rex, *imperator*, and *dux Romanorum* (Figure 12.17).

On the march through eastern Europe, Aurelian defeated a Gothic army and took the
decision to abandon the Dacian provinces, relocating some of their population south of
the Danube in a new Dacia. The existing Danube fortresses at places such as Drobeta and
Oescus were strengthened as part of a new line of defence. Aurelian then crossed into Asia,
where mysterious oracles began to make favourable pronouncements about his impending

Figure 12.18 Billon antoninianus of Zenobia, minted in Antioch, spring 272. Obverse: draped bust of Zenobia, with legend S ZENOBIA AVG; reverse: Juno with *patera* and peacock, with legend IVNO REGINA.

victory over Zenobia. The queen, meanwhile, had taken the title Augusta (Figure 12.18); a Latin milestone in Arabia records that Vaballathus had begun to claim the title *pius felix Augustus*, along with a string of epithets celebrating victory over the Persians.

A twin-pronged campaign liberated Egypt, in the south, while Aurelian's northern attack defeated Zenobia's army, commanded by Septimius Zabdas, at Immae near Antioch in 272; the Palmyrenes' main asset, their heavily armoured cavalry known as *clibinarii* ('ovens'), were drawn into an ambush and neutralised. After this setback, Zenobia was beaten a second time at Emesa; she was then captured after attempting to flee to the Persians. Appearing in Aurelian's triumph, she lived out her retirement in Rome, married to a Roman senator; it is unclear what happened to Vaballathus, who disappears from the sources (Figure 12.19).

In 272, the Romans received the welcome news that Shapur had died, and Aurelian returned to Europe, where he suppressed a revolt by the Carpi and took the title *Carpicus Maximus*. In 273, however, he was forced to return to the east due to unrest in Alexandria that was almost certainly linked to a fresh Palmyrene revolt, in which an obscure member of the royal family was placed on the Palmyrene throne. A military milestone recorded the presence of large numbers of Danubian troops in the east, drawn from XI Claudia, VII Claudia, I Italica, IV Flavia, and a new levy, I Illyricorum, who were consolidating Roman control over the commercially and strategically important road network from the Azraq oasis to Dumata (Jawf) while campaigning with the emperor (Kennedy, *Roman Army*, p. 60). After a failed attempt to win the prefect of Mesopotamia over to their cause, the Palmyrene rebels were beaten and the city sacked; one of those executed in the aftermath was the philosopher Longinus. A victorious Aurelian proclaimed himself *restitutor orientis*, and with the east finally quiet, he turned to the west in 274 to deal with the Gallic empire, which was foundering under a succession of raids by Franks and Alamanni that plagued the coastal communities and penetrated as deep as the Loire valley. Close to 250 coin hoards from this period have been found in Gaul, cached in the ground for safekeeping and never recovered—a striking reflection of the instability along the Rhine.

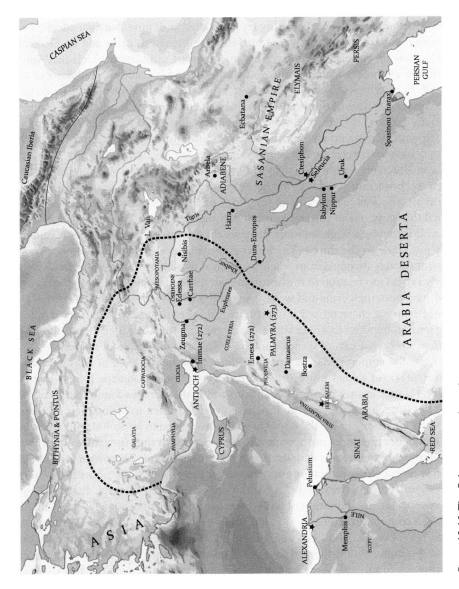

Figure 12.19 The Palmyrene empire at its greatest extent.

Source: Illustration by the author.

Aurelian succeeded in bringing the Gallic empire back under central government control after its leader, Tetricus, negotiated safe passage for himself in return for abandoning his army.

The *Historia Augusta* attributed Aurelian's victory over Zenobia to divine intervention, linked particularly to Emesa and its cult. In triumph, the emperor publicly proclaimed his link with Sol Invictus, who became *dominus imperi Romani*, 'lord of the Roman empire', and portrayed himself as the god's earthly representative; in Rome, Aurelian adorned Sol's temple with the spoils of the Palmyrene war, and the shrine was dedicated on December 25. The legends on Aurelian's coins celebrating imperial unification proclaimed him as *deus Aurelianus et dominus*, 'Aurelian the god and lord', and he later claimed descent from Sol himself. Further links to Sol Invictus were proclaimed by use of the radiate or 'solar' crown, a common feature of third century coinage of emperors such as Balbinus, Gallienus, Aurelian, and Probus, and which had also been favoured by Nero (Chapter 9). This monotheistic self-aggrandisement, accompanied by traditions inspired by eastern royalty, such as wearing a diadem and requiring obeisance, blurred the already murky line between earthly existence and heavenly divinity. Via the promotion of Sol Invictus, it was also important in creating a receptive audience for Constantine's later promotion of Christianity.

Despite his manifest successes in ending both of the secessionist movements that had threatened the unity of the empire, Aurelian was murdered by a conspiracy of his closest officials near Byzantium while en route to attack the Persians, whose new king, Bahram II, had only just come to the throne. There was considerable anger among the troops, and a replacement suitably divorced from recent events had to be summoned from Italy. This was the elderly Tacitus (no relation to the historian), but his tenure was brief. In the decade that followed, numerous men came and went, vying either for the purple or for the sort of local secessionist fiefdom characterised by Postumus, and the major common thread was the ongoing tension between those seeking to unite the empire, like Aurelian, and those who sought to protect what part of it they could in collaboration with local interests.

In 277/78, the emperor Marcus Aurelius Probus, another devotee of Sol Invictus and one of the coterie of soldier-emperors who had served under Gallienus, fought along the Rhine and Danube against groups of Alamanni and Franks. Probus found that local communities in Gaul, wary of relying on imperial forces, had taken to hiring their invaders to protect them, and after gaining the upper hand Probus agreed to settle 400,000 newcomers across a number of provinces and accepted 16,000 recruits for the army: these are likely the men who made up the *cohortes* and *alae* that appear in the *Notitia Dignitatum* with the epithet 'Alamannorum' and 'Juthungorum'. A revolt in Egypt, led by the nomadic Blemmyes from the desert in league with villagers of the upper Egyptian Thebaid, attacked Koptos on the Nile in a further indication of local disenchantment with central government. After celebrating a triumph in Rome in 281, and being hailed as *restitutor Raetiae*—'the restorer of Raetia'—Probus was murdered at Sirmium in 282, and Carus, one of the praetorian prefects and—unusually for the period—not from the Balkans, declared himself emperor. Carus campaigned successfully against the Sasanians, penetrating deep towards Ctesiphon and taking the title *Parthicus Maximus*, but was killed in mysterious circumstances in 283; some reports alleged that he had been struck by lightning (Festus, *Breviarium*, 24 & *Epitome De Caesaribus*, 38). Carus left two sons: Carinus ('little Carus') and Numerian, who had accompanied him to the east. Numerian was murdered by his father-in-law and praetorian prefect Aper, but a man named Diocles, serving as a *protector Augusti*, was proclaimed emperor at Nicomedia and murdered Aper in turn after invoking the wrath of Sol Invictus upon his enemies. Following a campaign against Carinus, during which the hapless emperor was murdered by his troops, Diocles, who became Gaius Aurelius Valerius Diocletianus—Diocletian—emerged victorious as sole emperor in 285.

Diocletian and the Tetrarchy: a return to stability

Diocletian was from Salonae in Dalmatia, and may have been the son of a freedman. Following his proclamation in 284, he held the suffect consulship with the senator Lucius Caesonius Bassus—a conciliatory signal to the conservatives in Rome. He also granted the title of Caesar to his friend Marcus Aurelius Maximianus. The son of a tradesman from Sirmium, Maximian—as he is usually known—had proven a capable general. By the end of the year, Diocletian was campaigning against the Sarmatians on the Danube, who were under pressure from the Goths to their east, and Maximian had been dispatched to Gaul to suppress a rebellion of the Bacaudae. This conflict was another secessionist movement; its leader, Amandus, declared himself emperor and minted coins to pay his troops. The following year, on April 1, 286, Diocletian promoted Maximian to Augustus. The relationship between the two emperors was depicted as a senior–junior partnership: Diocletian took on the aura of Jupiter (Figure 12.20) while Maximian (Figure 12.21) styled himself as Hercules ('Herculius' in Maximian's official title). These associations were prominently displayed on coins by both emperors individually and in issues where they appeared together, surmounted by Victory. In Rome, porticoes on the Theatre of Pompey were renamed as the *porta Iovia* and the *porta Herculia*.

In 289/90, Diocletian was at Palmyra, campaigning in the desert, but Maximian was facing a challenge in Gaul in the shape of Carausius. This man was a senior officer who, like Maximian, had risen through the military from humble provincial origins; he had been set the task of keeping the English Channel free from Frankish and Saxon pirates. Carausius declared himself emperor in 286, and for a time controlled the Channel and northern Gaul. He minted a striking series of coins in which he cast Diocletian and Maximian as his brothers in an optimistic attempt at gaining their support. Defeating Carausius required a naval victory, which Maximian could not achieve, and in the winter of 290/91, Maximian and Diocletian, together with much of the senate, met at Mediolanum to plan for the following years. By 293, the two Augusti had decided to expand the government: Constantius, an Illyrian who was a former bodyguard to Aurelian and now praetorian prefect to Maximian, was appointed Caesar. Constantius married Maximian's stepdaughter, Theodora, divorcing Helena, the mother of the future emperor Constantine. In the east, Maximianus Galerius, a former shepherd from Dacia and also an ex-imperial bodyguard, became Caesar and married Diocletian's daughter, Valeria. Both Constantius and Galerius took Diocletian's family name, Valerius, as Maximian had also done earlier. None of these four men came from senatorial families, but all had attained high positions in the meritocratic proving ground of the mid-third century army and had served in close proximity to their imperial predecessors.

This rule of four has become known as the Tetrarchy. It promised stability: two senior Augusti and two Caesars would, in theory, have sufficient flexibility to manage the many demands of the empire, restore the integrity of the frontiers, and put an end to secession and invasion. The overarching message of imperial unity was proclaimed on the bronze

Figure 12.20 Gold aureus of Diocletian, minted at Cyzicus between 284 and 286. Obverse: Diocletian draped and cuirassed with legend IMP C C VAL DIOLETIANVS P F AUG/ reverse: Jupiter standing, holding a globe on which Victory perches. The legend reads IOVI CONSERVATORI ORBIS.

Figure 12.21 Gold aureus of Maximian, minted in Rome between 293 and 294. Obverse: Laureate head of the emperor right; reverse: Hercules with legend HERCVLI DEBELLAT, 'Hercules conquers'.

follis coinage, featuring four strikingly similar imperial portraits. The same type of homogenisation is also displayed by the famous Tetrarchic statues looted from Constantinople in 1204, and that are now incorporated into St Mark's Basilica in Venice. The concept of the Tetrarchy was innovative, but it also drew on the experiences of the Antonine era and the collegial rules of Philip and Valerian. The demands of office kept all four men on the move, and it is significant that their travelling courts rarely visited Rome; instead, they were most often to be found in the military capitals of the empire. The residences of the Tetrarchs included locations such as Augusta Treverorum, Nicomedia, and Sirmium, sited close to the main pressure points where Franks, Goths, or Persians were likely to attack. The residences themselves were massive and designed to impress. Within, the emperors received their subjects not with the humility of a Trajan or an Antoninus Pius, but with a ceremonial protocol that distinctively separated the Tetrarchs from the mere humans they ruled. Rome was not wholly ignored by the Tetrarchs, but building projects in the city depended on individual rulers. Maximian's son Maxentius, for instance, created a new circus complex south of the city opposite the Mausoleum of Caecilia Metella on the via Appia, and began the massive Basilica Nova in central Rome, later completed by Constantine. Maximian completed a giant set of bath-houses known as the Baths of Diocletian, part of which is now the Museo Nazionale Romano and another part the church of Santa Maria degli Angeli. The curia in the Roman forum, which had been badly damaged by a fire, was also repaired, and the so-called Five-Columns Monument, built as an extension of the rostra, displayed porphyry statues of Jupiter and the four rulers, reinforcing the divinely sanctioned harmony of the Tetrarchy.

In 293, Constantius, based at Augusta Treverorum, drove Carausius from Bononia (Boulogne) and settled his Germanic allies, the Frisii and Chamavi, on imperial soil. Carausius was murdered by his finance minister, Allectus, who continued to defy imperial authorities; three years later, Constantius and his praetorian prefect Asclepiodotus invaded Britannia, and Allectus was defeated and killed. Later, Constantius minted a commemorative medallion at Augusta Treverorum proclaiming himself to be the *redditor lucis aeternae*—the one who returned eternal light to Britannia. Constantius further cemented his reputation by destroying a large Alamanni force at Langres, west of Strasbourg, in 302, while Maximian had helped to restore his reputation with a successful campaign in Africa. Before 307, Galerius won a victory over the Carpi, and in the aftermath large numbers of Carpi were settled in northern Pannonia. Once again, the wars with the Carpi were a result of Gothic pressure, in particular from a group of Goths that *Latin Panegyric* 11 called the Tervingi. More will be said about the Tervingi below and in Chapter 13.

War with Persia

In the east, Shapur's successors Hormizd I (270–71), Bahram I (271–74), and Bahram II (274–93) presided over a strengthening of Kerdir's position at court and persecutions of religious minorities. During the reign of Bahram II, Kerdir's persecutions targeted the prophet Mani, who had been born into a Syriac-speaking family near Ctesiphon in 216. Mani's father was a member of the mysterious Elchasite community (Chapter 11), who had turned their backs on the 'Hellenised' form of Christianity that, uncoupled from Judaism, was becoming canonised by the Gospels. Mani was soon estranged from the Elchasites and left for Gandhara, where he was introduced to Buddhism. He later returned to Persia and became a member of Shapur's court, and while he was determined never to travel to the Roman empire—although it was rumoured that he had accompanied Shapur on the Barbalissos campaign—his missionaries were sent westwards and were welcomed by Zenobia at Palmyra. Mani's religion was Gnostic, redemptive, and universal in conception, and was deeply influenced by Christianity. It embraced figures such as Jesus, Adam and Eve, Zarathustra, Mithras, and Buddha; it also included dualistic elements of Zoroastrianism such as the struggle between Light (Ahura Mazda) and Darkness (Ahriman), as well as the correction of 'errors', and it incorporated apocalyptic expectations of a day of judgement when Light would triumph. This pluralism was one of its main selling points, and Manichaean literature was produced in a diverse array of languages that included Coptic, Sogdian, Syriac, Chinese, and Middle Persian. Another attraction of Manichaean missionaries was their perceived ability to heal, and healing miracles impressed at the court of Zenobia; one of Mani's disciples also preached at Edessa. Shapur's death deprived Mani of his most important patron, however, and he perished in 276. Many of the survivors of Kerdir's persecution of the Manichaeans fled west, where they were subjected to further persecution by Diocletian.

In 287, Diocletian had scored a diplomatic success when a part of Armenia, under Sasanian control following the victories of Shapur I, was returned to the Roman sphere of influence and the Romans installed a client king, Tiridates III. At the same time, parts of northern Mesopotamia also reverted to Roman control and the fortress of Circesium was strengthened. In 293, however, Bahram II died, and a struggle erupted for the throne between Narseh, the youngest son of Shapur I, and the young Bahram III and Vahunam, his regent. Narseh emerged victorious, and recorded his campaign at Paikuli in Kurdistan, on a lengthy Middle Persian inscription that performed the same sort of legitimisation purpose as the *Res Gestae* of Augustus. He then turned his attention to Armenia, invading in 296 and ousting Tiridates III. Following engagements at Carrhae and Callinicum, Narseh was pushed back into Mesopotamia. Galerius spearheaded the Roman response, but he suffered an embarrassing defeat that delivered much of Mesopotamia to Narseh, and he then endured an even more embarrassing public audience with Diocletian, who forced his browbeaten subordinate to run in front of his chariot while he berated him for his failures (Eutropius, *Breviarium*, 9.24). In the aftermath, as Diocletian suppressed revolts in Egypt that were triggered by the introduction of a new census scheme (below), Galerius transferred forces from Moesia and made a second attempt in 298: this time, Narseh was ejected from Armenia, and Galerius captured Narseh's wife and family, who were put away in political exile at Daphne. The victory was an enormous coup for the Romans. Galerius took the titles *Armenicus Maximus*, *Medicus Maximus*, and *Persicus Maximus*, and celebrated his success on a triumphal arch— not in Rome, but in the Tetrarchic city of Thessalonike, as part of the palace complex that he built there (Figure 12.22).

In defeat, Narseh received the Roman envoy, Sicorius Probus, who agreed to return the king's family in return for a distinctly unfavourable treaty, known as the Peace of Nisibis (299). The treaty terms were recorded by Peter the Patrician (frag. 14), and under the arrangement, Rome gained numerous Armenian satrapies that provided a dense buffer protecting western Armenia. The eastern boundary of the Roman protectorate in Armenia was pushed to the edge of Atropatene, and the Tigris became the demarcation line between Roman and Persian territory. The Romans won the right to name the king of Caucasian Iberia, and Nisibis, which was heavily fortified, became the only place where Roman and Persian traders could do business with each other. This was a boon both to Roman customs officials and Diocletian's ongoing concerns about spies masquerading as merchants. By identifying Nisibis as the main trading centre for Roman and Persian merchants, the treaty also recognised the decline of the Euphrates as a medium for exchange, a consequence of the destruction of Palmyra and the loss of Dura-Europos (Figure 12.23). For Narseh, the Peace of Nisibis was a disaster; for successive Sasanian monarchs, it became a humiliation that was never forgotten. Nevertheless, the Persians did eventually redress the balance, in 363 (Chapter 13).

Figure 12.22 Galerius (mounted, beneath the eagle) victorious over Narseh (mounted, opposite Galerius) on the Arch of Galerius at Thessalonike.

Source: Photograph by J. Matthew Harrington (CC BY-SA 2.5).

Diocletian's reforms

Diocletian's lasting achievement was to break the toxic cycle of imperial usurpation and assassination, and he brought peace and a measure of unity to the Roman frontiers for the first time in a generation. These achievements were the result not only of decisive leadership, but also of a series of military and administrative reforms. The evidence for these reforms is found in a somewhat fossilised format in the *Notitia Dignitatum* (*ND*), as well as from legal codes, inscriptions, literary sources, and a document known as the *Verona List*, a seventh-century manuscript that preserves a list of the provinces in the mid-fourth century. Since Constantine also engaged in a series of reforms (below), and because the evidence is so varied, it is not always clear whether individual changes should be attributed to the reign of one or the other, and in numerous cases the reforms of both men were carried out on the back of pre-existing trends, such as the move towards the mobile cavalry army attributed to Gallienus.

Military reforms

The concept of the field army had taken form in the third century, as vexillations of larger units increasingly remained in the field rather than returning to their bases. This practice created a divergence between prestigious units that served with the emperor on campaign,

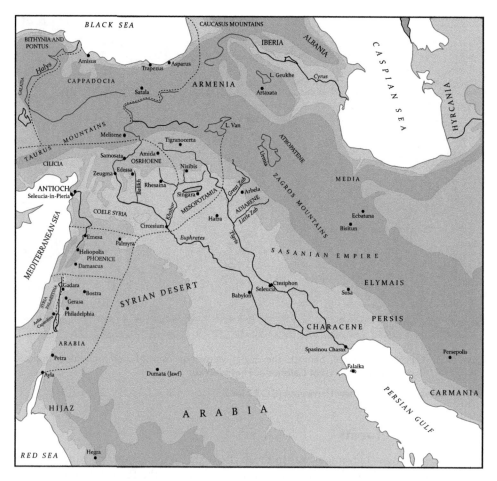

Figure 12.23 The Middle East following the Peace of Nisibis in 299, prior to Diocletian's provincial reorganisation.

Source: Illustration by the author.

and those units that remained in garrison. The practice of awarding the title of *protector* to troops and officers in the field army had sharpened this division. Eventually the field army became known as the *comitatus* (pl. *comitatenses*; Gr. *stratopedon*), a term that meant 'posse' or 'war band'. It had been used as early as the Severan period, when it appeared on the gravestone of a soldier from XXX Ulpia Victrix as *sacer comitatus*, 'the sacred war band'. In the later empire, *comitatus* came to refer to a mobile force based around cavalry and elite infantry formations: these included Diocletian's six new legions of *Ioviani* and *Herculiani*; the *lanciarii*, select infantry who used the light throwing spear known as the *lancea*; and *promoti* cavalry. It is not clear whether Diocletian's *comitatus* was a large force or simply comprised his immediate entourage and personal guards, and funerary inscriptions from his reign recording soldiers who served with the *comitatus* leave us none the wiser (e.g. *RA* §385 & §386). In the west, Maximian took a slightly different approach by raising *auxilia palatina*, units of elite infantry, either through the promotion of existing units such as the long-standing Batavian cohorts, or via targeted recruitment along the Rhine. Cavalry units were promoted with the designation as *Illyriciani*. The Praetorian Guard was maintained throughout the Tetrarchic period, supplemented by the Flavian-era *equites singulares Augusti*, the Guard's cavalry arm. Given the plethora of new units, their size during this period has long remained a matter of debate. Some historians have suggested that Diocletian's new legions may have only been about 1,000 men strong; cavalry *alae* may have been as small as 120 and auxiliary cohorts as few as 160 members. These numbers stem partly from the smaller surface area occupied by later Roman fortresses, but it was already common practice to divide legions into vexillations, stationed at different fortifications. The overall size of the late Roman army is thus also unclear, but estimates have ranged from 435,000 (John Lydus, *On the Months*, 1.27) to over 600,000 based on the *ND*, and as high as 645,000 (Agathias, *Histories*, 6.13).

A feature of the Tetrarchic period and the reign of Constantine was an increase in the settlement of non-Romans in the empire and their recruitment into the army. Both settlement and recruitment resulted from war, pressures on the frontier, or intertribal disputes that prompted individual groups to seek refuge in the empire. Maximian's victories over Frankish warbands in 288/89, for example, resulted in the so-called *laeti* being settled in the *civitates* of Gaul in return for military service. Another category of non-Roman recruits, the *gentiles*, served with Diocletian's bodyguard. A further categorisation of non-Roman troops was *foederati* (from the Latin term *foedus*, 'treaty'; Gr. *hypospondoi*), referring to allied contingents who served under their own leaders. These included the Frankish mercenaries, for instance, who fought for Carausius and Constantius. *Foederati* were typically drawn from Germanic tribesmen and, beginning in the fourth century, desert Arabs the Romans called *scenitae*, 'tent-dwellers.' Recruitment from beyond the frontiers also resulted in non-Romans, particularly Franks and Alamanni, achieving high military rank within the regular army—an important facet of the late Roman military that became particularly noticeable in fifth-century western Europe (Chapter 13).

A slew of defensive construction is traditionally associated with Diocletian's reign. Some of this work may have continued projects begun by his predecessors—the so-called Saxon Shore fortifications in southern and eastern Britannia, for example, or the strengthening of certain positions along the Rhine and Danube. Fortifications in the eastern provinces present a similar problem: the sixth-century Antiochene writer John Malalas reported that Diocletian built forts from 'Egypt' (the Gulf of Aqaba) as far as the Persian frontier, yet many of the points on what milestones called the *Strata Diocletiana*, a military road and zone of control continuing the via Nova Traiana from the Dead Sea to the Euphrates, actually predated Diocletian. Nevertheless, it was during his reign that positions along the *Strata* and along the Euphrates received new or upgraded defences, creating a system of strongpoints, watchtowers, and fortlets at regular intervals. These included the heavily fortified hilltop bastion of Dibsi Faraj, west of Barbalissos, and the fortress at Callinicum, both on the Euphrates invasion route used by Shapur I. A number of the structures on the *Strata* can be identified by inscriptions, textual sources, and information from the *ND*. Sura, located at a key point on the Euphrates invasion route used by Shapur, became the home of XVI Flavia Firma and a fortified civilian settlement, known as a *vicus* (*ND*

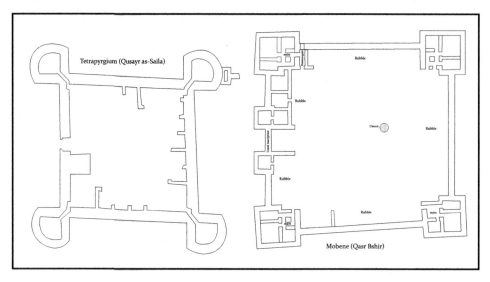

Figure 12.24 Ground plans of Tetrapyrgium (Qusair as-Saila) in central Syria and Mobene (Qasr Bshir) in central Jordan. Note the fan-shaped towers at Tetrapyrgium vs. square towers at Bashir, but the broadly similar arrangement of rooms (now poorly preserved, and at Bshir, mostly rubble) interpreted as either living quarters, storerooms, or mangers/stables for cavalry horses.

Source: Illustration by the author after Sack and Parker.

Or. 65.14). Between Sura and Rusafa stood the fortlet of Tetrapyrgium, whose name is a Greek translation of a distinctive type of late Roman military structure, the *quadriburgium*, a four-towered square or trapezoid fort (Figure 12.24). Rusafa was garrisoned by a locally raised cavalry detachment, the *equites promoti indigenae* (*ND Or.* 65.13), with III Scythica based at Oresa further south (65.9). On the Khabur river where it met the Euphrates, Circesium, which became the lynchpin of the Roman defence on the Euphrates following the loss of Dura-Europos, was garrisoned by IV Parthica (67.11). Palmyra was garrisoned by I Illyricorum (63.14), stationed in a military quarter of the city divided from the civilian housing by a wall, as had also been the case at Dura-Europos. A lintel inscription on the shrine where the military standards were kept was dedicated to 'the restorers of the world and propagators of the human race', Maximian and Diocletian, marking the construction of the camp (*CIL* 3.6661). In c. 300 at the Azraq oasis in north-eastern Jordan, an altar was dedicated to Jupiter Sol Invictus invoking the victory of the Tetrarchs, the *imperatorum duorum et Caesaraum duorum / Ioviorum et Herculiorum* (Figure 12.25). One of the best-known structures belonging to this period is the remarkably well-preserved fort of the *quadriburgium* type known as Qasr Bshir in central Jordan (Figure 12.26); the inscription recording its construction by Aurelius Asclepiades, the governor of Arabia, is still—exceptionally—in situ (Figure 1.5 in Chapter 1). Another well preserved military site dating to this period is the nearby fortress of Da'ajaniya, apparently intended for a unit of c. 500 men, including a contingent of mounted troopers. The fort, which was associated

Figure 12.25 The Tetrarchic inscription from Azraq.

Source: Photograph by the author.

with a large reservoir nearby, was built from the striking black basalt common to the area (Figure 12.27).

A distinctive feature of later Roman fortress design is the appearance of fan- or U-shaped projecting towers, a departure from the characteristic playing card-shaped forts of the principate. Along the Danube, fan-shaped corner towers provided better coverage of the defensive walls; in numerous fortresses that were rebuilt or repaired, doorways were blocked up or covered by the construction of towers, leaving just a single entryway. Forts with U-shaped and fan-shaped towers are also known from the well-preserved ruins of Lejjun and Udruh in Jordan, which are similar in design to contemporary examples from Egypt (Figure 12.28). Lejjun was built around 300 and appears to have been intended for one of the smaller legions of the later empire, the newly raised IV Martia (*ND Or.* 61.10). Thanks to a chance discovery of an inscription during conservation work in 2005, Udruh is now known to have housed VI Ferrata, which had been transferred from Caparcotna in Galilee; it was previously thought that the legion had perhaps been annihilated with the defeat of Valerian. The Udruh inscription is dedicated to the Tetrarchs, establishing a date between 293 and 305, and reflects Diocletian's policy of moving units from rear areas closer to the military frontier at installations such as Circesium and Palmyra (Figure 12.29).

Figure 12.26 The Roman fort of Qasr Bshir in central Jordan.
Source: Photograph by the author.

Figure 12.27 The Roman fort of Da'ajaniya in central Jordan.
Source: Photograph by the author.

Figure 12.28 The Roman fortress at Udruh, with the foundations of its distinctive U-shaped towers.

Source: Photograph by the author.

Social, political, and administrative changes

There had long been an informal, if ill-defined, distinction between citizens known as *honestiores* and *humiliores*. These terms denoted upper and lower classes, with the primary benefit for the *honestiores* being more lenient penalties in civil and criminal cases. In the mid-third century, however, these two divisions were gradually effaced by changes to both the equestrian and senatorial orders. In the imperial provinces, propraetorian legates of senatorial rank were increasingly replaced by equestrian governors. Legionary legates, likewise, were increasingly equestrian prefects. Despite Aurelius Victor's complaints that Gallienus had prohibited senators from serving in senior military commands, the preference for equestrians from the protectorate was not a deliberate anti-senatorial policy (*On the Caesars*, 33). Instead, as noted earlier, it reflected a pragmatic response to the loss of so many qualified men in the wars of the third century, and it is also noteworthy that as Gallienus sought to restock the army with competent commanders, he overlooked equestrians who were following the more bureaucratic procuratorial career path; these men tended to end up as provincial governors. Proconsular provinces for senators, such as Africa Proconsularis, Achaea, and Asia, were still available and carried immense prestige, but some 37 individual posts were slowly removed from the senatorial career track.

As the equestrian order grew in importance, it had acquired a tripartite distinction in the second and third centuries between men who were classed as *eminentissimus, perfectissimus,* and *egregius*. Praetorian prefects and prefects of the *vigiles* and the *annona* held the first

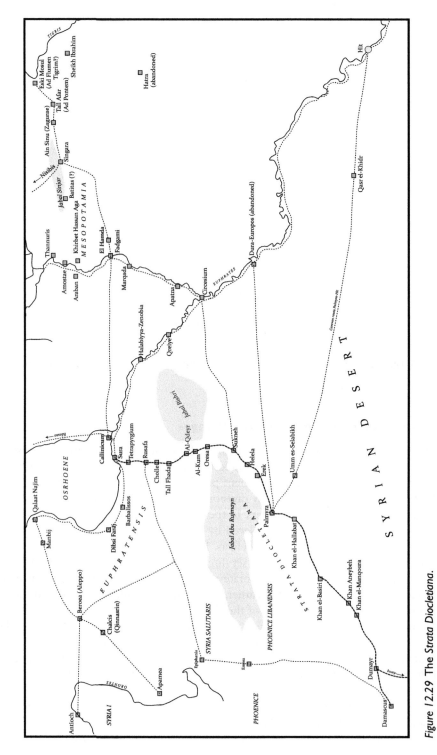

Figure 12.29 The *Strata Diocletiana.*

Source: Illustration by the author.

category; prefects of Egypt, imperial procurators, legionary prefects, and provincial governors the second; and other equestrians, the last. Men striving for status needed to be appointed to specific positions within the imperial hierarchy, as rank came with office or imperial patronage, not necessarily birth or property. This also meant that it was not necessary to be an equestrian to be a prefect, but being a prefect could *create* an equestrian: status came with the job. Senators similarly found that the senatorial status conferred by the rank of *vir clarissimus* came with imperial patronage or specific offices. Because rank depended on office or patronage, there was some degree of crossover between equestrian and senatorial ranks, whereby office holders of specific positions might be appointed from one order or the other. The favour of the emperor became increasingly important in a society that was becoming increasingly conscious of status and class, especially in cases where rank was sought without office: honorary ranks could be given as a mark of esteem or friendship.

The administration of the empire also underwent a process of transformation as peace was restored. In common with the earlier restorations of Augustus and Vespasian, changes in government were accompanied by changes in the way that people and their offices were named. As men who wished to honour Vespasian had taken the name Flavius, in the late third century courtiers would take the name Valerius, in homage to Diocletian. (Later, Flavius would return to favour, this time in honour of the dynasty of Constantine.) In government, the longstanding imperial council of advisers was transformed into the *consistorium*, named for the Latin verb *consisto*, 'to stand', since only the emperor was permitted to be seated. Diocletian and Maximian are also credited with the enlargement of the *scrinia*, the bureaucratic offices of the empire. The secretaries for letters (*ab epistulis*) and petitions (*a libellis*) became the offices of the *magister epistularum* (dealing with petitions from cities in the empire, in Latin and Greek) and *magister libellorum* (dealing with judicial inquiries and rescripts). A third senior post, the *magister memoriae*, drafted memoranda and correspondence, and dealt with foreign powers; one of the earliest holders of this post was Sicorius Probus, who had treated with Narseh after his defeat. All three *magistri* had substantial staffs, and office holders could progress to senior positions such as the praetorian prefecture or provincial governorships. Financial matters were managed by the *res summa* (public money) and the *res privata* (for imperial holdings), run by *magistri* or officials known as *rationales*, who steadily replaced procurators. These developments were the start of a dramatic intensification of central government, staffed, in the main, by equestrians, and one of the main tasks of this rebranded civil service was to take a firm grasp on the law. This was accomplished through the collation of rescripts, laws, and memoranda into codes, known as *codices* (sg. *codex*). Under the Tetrarchs, two important *codices* were assembled, the *Codex Gregorianus* and the *Codex Hermogenianus*. These Latin texts were respectively compiled by Gregorius, who was probably *magister libellorum* in 291, and by Hermogenianus, *magister libellorum* in 295. Notably, the imperial civil service was rebranded as the *militia*, and its members wore military dress, despite holding primarily civilian functions. This fashion choice reflected the increasing militarisation of the Roman elite, a product of the wars of the third century and an imitation of the military styles exhibited by soldier-emperors like Diocletian. Masculine *virtus* was expressed through success in battle, government service, clothing, and participation in militarised sporting events such as the hunt.

A detailed reorganisation of the provinces also took place at the end of the third century. Mindful of the extraordinary commands held by men like Julius Priscus and Odaenathus,

Diocletian continued a practice of subdividing provinces that had begun with Gordian III, dramatically increasing the numbers of provincial governors but, at the same time, curbing their ability to act independently of the emperors. By the early fourth century, there were nearly 100 provinces, and all but Achaea, Asia and Africa Proconsularis (which remained as senatorial proconsular appointments) and Italy (managed by senatorial correctors) were governed by officers known as *praesides* (sg. *praeses*, Gr. *hegemon*). The use of the term *praeses* had existed since the mid-third century in the guise of equestrians appointed as *agentes vice praesidis*, acting 'on behalf' of provincial governors, but now came into common usage. In the late third and early fourth centuries, *praesides* were variously equestrians with the rank of *egregius* or *perfectissimus*, or sometimes senatorial *clarissimi*. Either Diocletian or Constantine grouped this effusion of governors and provinces into 12 dioceses, each run by an equestrian deputy with the title of *vice agens praefectorum praetorio*, 'deputy for the praetorian prefects', an office that later became known as a *vicarius* or vicar. Military authority was removed from the *praesides*, who became civilian officials only, and equestrian *duces* (sg. *dux*, 'duke') commanded provincial garrisons. A snapshot of how this system was developing during the Tetrarchic period is provided by the inscription of VI Ferrata from Udruh, mentioned earlier. After the dedication to Diocletian and his colleagues, it lists a *dux*, Aurelius Heraclides, who is ranked as an equestrian *vir perfectissimus*; a provincial governor, the *praeses* Aelius Flavianus, ranked as a senatorial *vir clarissimus*, and the legionary prefect, an equestrian named Aurelius Mucianus.

At some point after Diocletian's retirement in 305, dioceses were eventually grouped into four prefectures. Each prefecture was nominally under the control of a praetorian prefect who, unlike his underlings, did possess military authority—for now—but aside from the period of factional strife between 305 and 313 (below), where each of the various contestants for the throne had their own praetorian prefect, the number of prefects in office at any given time is unclear. While Diocletian and his government sought to break up potential power blocs and centralise authority, the system of government that he and his colleagues developed resulted in the formation of four mini-empires, each with a functioning court, tax system, and army. The prefectures went through various changes and developments—Illyricum, for example, was alternately part of the prefecture of Italy and Africa, and only later became a stand-alone prefecture (Figure 12.30).

Cities, taxes, and persecution

The growth in government posts created by the Tetrarchy had the consequence of diverting municipal elites away from looking after their cities, which had been a key way for elites of the first and second centuries to celebrate their status. Decurions, men who served in the *curiae* of individual cities (and thus also known as *curiales*) increasingly sought government service to win exemptions from the onerous burdens, financial and otherwise, that cities demanded of them, such as the time-consuming task of collecting taxes from peasants. The rampant inflation of the third century had also made curial work less attractive: much of the funding for the activities of *curiales* was generated from rents and taxes, but this was now received as virtually worthless coin. As a result, the role of the city as a self-governing administrative entity declined, even as cities were under tremendous pressure from raids, the plague, and the financial worries of the period; even as early as 270, many cities that had long-functioning mints had also ceased to strike coinage. A further

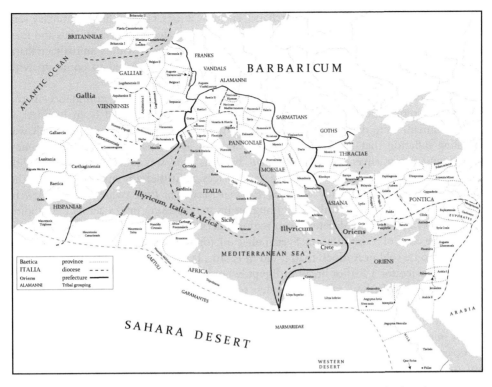

Figure 12.30 The provinces, dioceses, and prefectures of the Roman empire in the fourth century.

Source: Illustration by the author.

change took place after Constantine's adoption of Christianity (below), as the rhythms of city life, grounded in a diversity of pagan festivals and the largesse of the city elites, slowly changed into a more uniform Christian culture explicitly tied to the emperor and his faith. The dedication of churches and shrines replaced that of basilicas and public baths, and the celebration of Christian festivals gradually replaced the myriad of polytheistic events that had preceded them.

One of the key Tetrarchic innovations concerned the census, which was reorganised to take place every five years. Grouped into three iterations, the census created a 15-year taxation 'indiction cycle', the calculation of which became an important way to gauge time in the empire (e.g. 'this building was erected by so-and-so in the second indiction'). Taxation was reimagined in a particularly intricate way that calculated the *iugum*, a measurement of land productivity that varied depending on the crop and the soil in which it was grown, and the *caput*, a measurement of human productivity. At the same time, town and village boundaries were calculated and recorded on inscribed boundary stones, many of which have happened to turn up in rural Syria. The census was intrusive in its minutiae; it even assessed different kinds of livestock on individual farms to determine taxation rates. 'Every spot of ground was measured,' complained Lactantius, 'vines and fruit-trees numbered, lists taken of animals of every kind' (*On the Deaths of the Persecutors*, 23). In addition to the annual *iugum* and *caput* tax, there were others that included the expected donative on the accession of an emperor, taxes on merchants, customs duties, taxes in lieu of military service, and so on. Individual cities and towns were also expected to house officials and feed the army when it passed through, baking bread and biscuits or providing animals; civilians could also be dragooned into public construction projects or forced to come up with money for road repairs.

Much Roman tax was being collected in kind, due to a lack of confidence in the imperial currency. During the late third century, precious coins had been hoarded as the antoniniani were devalued and scorned for their lower silver content; the result was spiralling inflation that demanded economic reform. Diocletian revalued the currency, introducing a pure silver coin, the *argenteus*, but this issue was soon contaminated with billon and triggered another steep increase in prices. A further attempt to deal with the economy then failed miserably with the *Edict on Maximum Prices*, which became law in 301. The intention was to curb price gouging by standardising prices across the empire, but the *Edict* ignored the differences in regional economies and mangled the way that it assessed the costs of transportation: Syrian olive oil, for instance, required lower transportation costs to be sold in Antioch than it did in Rome. It was also no good setting the same maximum price for a loaf of bread in Egypt, where grain was plentiful, as the maximum price in northern Britain, where it was less so. The *Edict* also failed to take into account the fact that the imperial court was an economy all unto itself, capable of causing serious economic disruption whenever it arrived in town. The *Edict* was quietly repealed or no longer imposed in c. 302.

A particularly punitive aspect of Diocletian's restoration and desire for civic conformity was the persecution of Christians and Manichaeans that he ordered in 303. Lactantius called Diocletian an 'author of ill, and deviser of misery' (*On the Deaths of the Persecutors*, 7), and Manichaeans, who Diocletian called 'utterly worthless people', were punished with particular severity. The persecution was enthusiastically supported by Galerius, but it is noteworthy that Constantius, whose son, Constantine, was already slated for high office, did little; and after Constantine came to power in 306 (below), the persecutions ended in the west. In the east, however, Maximinus Daia, appointed Caesar after 305, adopted a Decian census-based sacrifice policy and deliberately contaminated public spaces with sacrificial libations, denying those spaces to Christians. His persecution was particularly vicious in Palestine and, in common with previous periods of civil strife in the region, had the result of driving Christians and Jews further apart.

Abdication

In 303, Diocletian was in Rome to celebrate the 20th anniversary of his rule with Maximian. Central government, he had decided, would determine the succession, but it is not clear whether the plan that unfolded had been in the works for some time or if it was a reaction to his growing illness and old age. Nevertheless, the plan was for Diocletian and Maximian to retire, and for them to be replaced by Galerius and Constantius respectively. Maximian's son, Maxentius, expected to be appointed Caesar, together with Constantine, the oldest son of Constantius. However, the arrangement had no provision for jealousy, nor for the machinations of Galerius: instead of Constantine and Maxentius, a military commander and friend of Galerius named Severus, and Maximinus Daia, Galerius's nephew, were appointed to the rank of Caesar. This left Constantine and Maxentius empty handed, and both Constantius and Maximian fuming with anger. On May 1, 305, Diocletian and Maximian stood down, becoming the only emperors in Roman history to relinquish power voluntarily; Diocletian retired to his palace at Salonae near Split, where he settled into a retirement growing cabbages—a vegetable highly prized by the Romans.

Constantine

The collapse of the Tetrarchy

Flavius Valerius Constantinus was born to a household of middling means at Naissus in c. 272. As a young man, Constantine spent a considerable amount of time at Nicomedia with Diocletian, where he encountered Lactantius, who had been appointed professor of Latin rhetoric, and may have met the Neoplatonist philosopher Porphyry. At the time of Diocletian's abdication, Constantine was under virtual house arrest in the court of Galerius, towards whom Constantius harboured considerable resentment. Galerius was working on his massive retirement/palace complex named Romulania at Gamzigrad in Serbia, when he finally relented to Constantius's requests that Constantine be returned to him. Later Constantinian propaganda told a hair-raising story of Constantine's race across Europe, with agents of Galerius hot in pursuit; the reality was probably a less eventful journey as Constantine returned to Britannia. After a campaign into the north of the island, he was by his father's side when he died at Eboracum in 306. There, Constantine was promptly declared emperor by the army and by an Alamannic king, Crocus, who was campaigning with the Romans. Constantine refused the title of Augustus from his troops, but accepted that of Caesar, then he returned to Europe and installed himself at Augusta Treverorum. Maxentius, meanwhile, was declared emperor in Rome, which was seething at Galerius's decision to end Italy's exemption from taxes, which it had enjoyed since 167 BC. Maximian, who had accepted Diocletian's abdication plan with some reluctance, eagerly returned from his brief retirement as *bis* Augustus—emperor for the second time—to help his son. It was painfully clear to everyone, not least of all Diocletian, that Diocletian had been the glue that had held the Tetrarchy together.

Maxentius played to the needs of the Roman people with a public program that refurbished temples and portrayed himself as the defender of their heritage—he even went so far as to name his own son Romulus, and identified his own cause with the goddess Roma. A seething Galerius dispatched Severus to regain control, but he was arrested by the army as he neared Ravenna, taken to Rome, and later murdered. In the meantime, Constantine agreed to marry Maximian's daughter, Fausta, who was still a child, and Maximian agreed that Constantine could use the title Augustus. Maximian's rapprochement with Constantine took place as a dangerous gulf was opening between himself and his son, Maxentius. *Latin Panegyric* 7, delivered on the occasion of Constantine's marriage to Fausta in 307, cast Constantine as a dutiful son and studiously ignored Maxentius; the following year, Maximian attempted to strip Maxentius of his title, only to be chased out of Italy by his son's troops. In the same year, Galerius reached the limit of his patience and laid siege to Rome. It is telling that he was reportedly astonished at its size—he had never visited the old imperial capital before. The siege stalled in front of Aurelian's massive walls, and as Galerius felt the loyalty of his army slipping from his grip, he was forced to retire to the Balkans. Constantine, meanwhile, was active on the Rhine, slaughtering the Frankish

Figure 12.31   Gold solidus minted in 301–13.The reverse shows a disconsolate Francia with the legend
GAVDIVM ROMANORVM—'the joy of the Romans'.

Bructeri in 306/07 and bridging the river at Colonia Agrippinensium in 308, opposite
which the fortification of Deutz was constructed in Germanic territory. Another bridgehead, Mainz Kastell, was constructed opposite Moguntiacum. During these campaigns,
Constantine captured two Frankish kings, and, after showing them off in triumph, allowed
them to be ripped to pieces by animals in the arena at Augusta Treverorum (Eutropius,
Breviarium, 10.3). At Augusta, he also constructed the massive Aula Palatina (Basilica of
Constantine), which, reused as a church, has survived to this day despite being seriously
damaged in World War II. Constantine's victories occasioned a triumphant coin issue with
a weeping Francia (Figure 12.31).

Diocletian had likely watched the disintegration of the Tetrarchy in horror, and his
mood was surely not improved when, in Africa, Domitius Alexander declared himself
emperor in 308 and used his stranglehold on the grain supply to engineer a famine in
Rome. Diocletian had held the consulship with Galerius in 308 in an attempt to prop up
his old colleague's authority, and in November 308 he convened a meeting at Carnuntum
attended by Galerius and Maximian. Diocletian demanded that Maximian retire for good,
and told Galerius to choose a new Caesar to replace Severus. Galerius's choice was another
soldier from the Balkans, Licinius, but instead of appointing him as Caesar, he upended
Diocletian's last attempt to save the Tetrarchy by awarding Licinius the title of Augustus,
implicitly demoting Constantine to Caesar in the process. Galerius, who was suffering
badly from bowel cancer, died with 'his genitals consumed' in 311; Diocletian also passed
away, his retirement in ruins (*Epitome De Caesaribus*, 40). Maximian had also ignored
Diocletian's wishes, launching an abortive coup against his son-in-law Constantine from
Augustodunum (Autun). Following a period of house arrest, Maximian was forced to
commit suicide after a 'plot' was discovered. Since this meant that Hercules, Maximian's
semi-divine persona, was now 'dead', Constantine proclaimed the divinity of his father
and then organised a retrospective adoption into the family of Claudius II—a move that
was even more audacious than the Antonine adoption of Septimius Severus. Claudius was
chosen because he was the only emperor of recent memory whose reputation had been
enhanced in death; he had also not been murdered, killed in battle, or taken prisoner. The
anonymous author of *Latin Panegyric* 7 thus set stylus to parchment and wrote studiously

about this distant ancestor of Constantine 'of whom most people are still unaware'. This piece of barefaced propaganda was vigorously promoted. Constantine's nephew, the emperor Julian (360–63), wrote in his satirical *Caesares* that the gods gazed in wonder at Claudius and, 'admiring his greatness of soul, granted the empire to his descendants' (313), while Zonaras falsely reported that Constantine's father, Constantius, was the grandson of Claudius (12.26).

In 312, Constantine set about unseating Maxentius, who was still bottled up behind Aurelian's impregnable walls in Rome. Needing an ally in the coming war, Constantine arranged for his half-sister Constantia to marry Licinius; this act was welcomed by Licinius, who was himself threatened by an alliance between Maxentius and Maximinus Daia, who had declared himself Augustus in 310. Constantine moved rapidly through Italy, offering clemency to those who surrendered and keeping the murderous instincts of his troops in check. By the autumn of 312, he had defeated Maxentius's garrisons in the north. At the end of October, Maxentius, who *Latin Panegyric* 12 ridiculed as the 'false Romulus', elected to force a decisive engagement with Constantine rather than remain safely behind Rome's massive walls. His decision was spurred by riots and unrest stemming from the famine caused by Domitius Alexander, and he had also consulted the *Sibylline Books* which prophesied that 'whoever designed any harm to the Romans would die a miserable death' (Zosimus, *New History*, 2.16). Spurred on by these considerations, Maxentius marched up the via Flaminia to Saxa Rubra, about 14 kilometres (9 miles) from the city, where he was defeated by Constantine's experienced troops. Fleeing in the mêlée that followed, Maxentius was drowned in the Tiber. Constantine retrieved Maxentius' corpse and stuck his head on a pike, portraying himself as a liberator who had saved Rome from a despotic tyrant.

Maximinus Daia perished soon afterwards, following an equally decisive clash with Licinius at Adrianople in Thrace. Licinius, who had professed a link with the emperor Philip to counter Constantine's links to Claudius II, won his victory after he had a dream in which he saw the *summus deus*, the 'Highest God', and ordered his troops to pray before battle (Lactantius, *On the Deaths of the Persecutors*, 46). Licinius followed up his victory by purging Valeria, Diocletian's daughter and the widow of Galerius, and Diocletian's widow, Prisca, along with the children of Maximinus, Severus, and Galerius. In fewer than six months Constantine and Licinius had dismantled the remnants of the Tetrarchy. Later, by relying on family members in their own succession plans, Constantine and Licinius ruined Diocletian's dream of a stable succession and the hope of a college of emperors chosen for their ability, and not their blood.

Constantine and Christianity

Latin Panegyric 7 related that on his return to Augusta Treverorum in 310, after Maximian's rebellion, Constantine stopped at the Temple of Apollo at Grand in the Vosges. There, the panegyrist wrote, Constantine had a solar vision of Apollo accompanied by the goddess Nike, and laurel wreaths with an X within each one; together, the vision promised thirty years (XXX) of rule. One of Constantine's coin issues contains a striking image that might indicate the sort of vision that he experienced (Figure 12.32). Sulla, Caesar, and Augustus had divine guardians, Nero had identified himself with the sun, and in more recent memory, Gallienus, Aurelian, and Probus had hitched their

Figure 12.32 Bronze follis of Constantine minted in 319. The diagram on the reverse is ostensibly a military camp, with Apollo standing above.

Figure 12.33 Bronze follis minted at Augusta Treverorum in 308/09. The reverse shows a radiate bust of Sol, with the legend SOLI INVICTO COMITI, 'to the *comes* Sol Invictus'. The title of *comes* was used extensively by Constantine, and is discussed further below.

fortunes to Sol Invictus and Diocletian his own fortune to Jupiter. Even before this extraordinary vision, Constantine had moved firmly away from the Tetrarchic duo of Jupiter/Hercules and publicly declared his link with Sol Invictus, whose cult was also closely linked with Apollo and the military cult of Mithras; on his coinage, Constantine declared his relationship with Sol Invictus as one of companionship, through the Latin title *comes* (Figure 12.33).

Following this vision, and before the final conflict with Maxentius, Constantine reportedly had a dream in which he was instructed to paint a certain design on the shields of his troops. The earliest version of this story is from the pen of Lactantius, whom Constantine had employed since 309/10 as tutor for his son, Crispus. Lactantius (*On the Deaths of the Persecutors*, 44) reported that this design featured the superimposed Greek letters X and P, the first two letters of ΧΡΙΣΤΟΣ (Christos), also known as the chi-rho—a symbol that was not in widespread use at the time:

Constantine's biographer Eusebius reported his own version of the story, written in c. 335–39. Constantine first had a daytime vision of 'a cross-shaped trophy formed by light' and then Christ appeared to him in a dream, instructing Constantine to bear the *labarum*, a cross-shaped standard surmounted by the chi-rho, into battle (*Life of Constantine*, 1.28–31). Eusebius framed the vision in terms of Constantine's need for divine assistance for his war against Maxentius, and vaguely referred to the 'one Supreme God' who had also been the 'God of his father', a reference to Constantius (1.27). At some point between Constantine's solar vision in Gaul and his self-styled deliverance of the Romans from Maxentius, the story became Christianised as Constantine moved ever further from the Jupiter/Hercules conservatism of Diocletian and the Tetrarchy.

Few personal religious experiences in world history have aroused greater controversy or proven more difficult to disentangle. Constantine's eventual decision to ally himself with the emperor's Christians and their God legitimised Christianity. Through his actions as emperor, Constantine endowed the church with immense political clout, changing the course of world history. Edward Gibbon, writing in the eighteenth century, viewed Constantine as a flawed and vain individual who only later began to believe the story that he had invented to explain his success. Other assessments have cast him as an opportunist, an outright charlatan, or simply a creature of his time—intensely superstitious and governed by a world that was profoundly suffused with all sorts of divine powers. For some, the overarching question has long been about the legitimacy of Constantine's conversion. Did he *really* become a Christian? Constantine retained the title of *pontifex maximus*, the imperial cult continued to be celebrated, and he permitted provincial communities to erect temples in his honour; but he sometimes derided Rome's traditional cults as 'temples of lies' (Eusebius, *Life of Constantine*, 2.56). The famous medallion minted at Ticinum after Constantine's capture of Rome displayed the emperor with a chi-rho on his helmet, but holding a shield bearing the she-wolf that had suckled Romulus and Remus in Rome's mythological past. An important element in Christianity's broad success was that being Christian did *not* mean eliminating Rome's history or the achievements it had won under the guidance of the Capitoline Triad of Jupiter, Juno, and Minerva. A classical education was still important, but knowledge of the classics and Latin and Greek could now be put to a different use—as Augustine and a plethora of other Christian writers would demonstrate.

One of the problems with framing Constantine's conversion in terms of personal belief is that it imposes modern expectations on a question that would be unfathomable under the best of circumstances. Such a question also ignores the spiritual currents of the time. Christian communities were rather varied: as Constantine would soon discover with the Donatist controversy (below), there were highly dogmatic Christians who adhered to strict rules, yet there were also Christians whose understanding of their faith was compatible with other ideas in their contemporary world. One of those ideas was the trend towards philosophical monotheism that was underway in pagan communities with whom Christian communities intermingled. Philosophical monotheism is found most prominently in the cult of Sol Invictus, but also, for instance, in the worship of *lh* ('god'), known from pre-Islamic Ancient North Arabian inscriptions. Solar worship and Christianity already shared some common ideas: the passage of the sun evoked death (sunset) and resurrection (sunrise), and Christians prayed to the east, towards the sunrise. In 324, Constantine decided that a weekly day of rest would take place on 'Sun-day', and he also ordered his troops to pray to the sun (Eusebius, *Life of Constantine*, 4.19–20). The philosophical meanderings of the Neoplatonists, who had been favourites of Gallienus and who Constantine may have encountered at Nicomedia, also played a role in the drift towards philosophical monotheism. Plotinus, who had been present on Gordian III's doomed Persian expedition and who had taught Porphyry, advanced a philosophical theory of a single force that he called the One. The Neoplatonists spent time praying and deliberating, and practised theurgy—rituals to summon divinities. Neoplatonism also had a distinctive revelatory streak, via the *Chaldaean Oracles*, revelations derived from Plato's soul. There was also an ancient cult known as Theos Hypsistos, 'the Highest God', which had been worshipped since the Hellenistic era. This cult, like that of Sol Invictus, involved praying towards the sunrise. Eusebius captured these fertile cross-pollinations when he wrote that 'as the sun, when he rises upon the earth, liberally imparts his rays of light to all, so did Constantine, proceeding at early dawn from the imperial palace ... impart the rays of his own beneficence to all who came into his presence' (*Life of Constantine*, 1.43). By spreading his magnanimity in such a way, Constantine was continuing one of the most important and traditional functions of a Roman emperor: to mediate between heaven and earth, to regulate the relationship with the gods, and to impose unity on the empire; he was now doing it as the representative of the Christian God, rather than Sol, Jupiter, or Apollo. It is thus important to note that Constantine's conversion was not exceptional in terms of the world that he inhabited, and nor did not take place in isolation—Licinius had prayed to the *summus deus* and Constantine's adoption of Christianity was closely followed by the conversion of the kingdom of Axum to Christianity, and the adoption of a form of Judaism in the south Arabian kingdom of Himyar, events that promoted political unity under the protection of a monotheistic faith. The Zoroastrian establishment in Persia had also proven to be a potent tool for projecting imperial power, a fact that Constantine would certainly have appreciated. What *was* exceptional about Constantine's conversion was what he did with it after defeating Maxentius. The rapid growth of Christianity in the ancient Mediterranean, and its dominance in the Middle Ages, were direct consequences of the Roman emperor choosing to support the faith.

Constantine's actions following his victory over Maxentius threw the weight of the empire behind Christianity. Constantine destroyed the barracks of the *equites singulares Augusti*, who had fought for his rival, and built the massive Basilica Salvatoris, now St John in Lateran. According to the *Liber Pontificalis*, a set of papal biographies that began with St Peter, Constantine adorned the Basilica Salvatoris with bejewelled, silver statues of Christ and the apostles (34.9). Constantine also built the Church of St Peter, centred around Peter's tomb, which ancient writers located on the right bank of the Tiber where the Vatican and St Peter's Basilica are located today (Figure 12.34). Constantine also

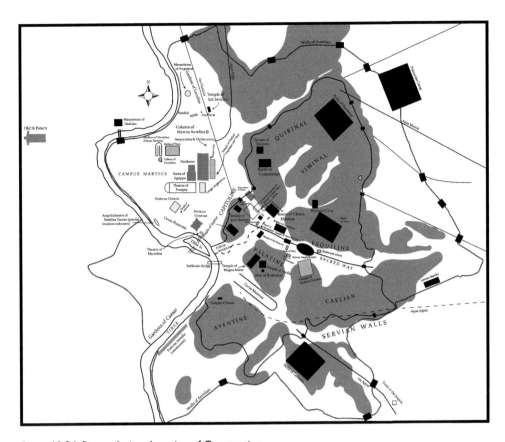

Figure 12.34 Rome during the reign of Constantine.

Source: Illustration by the author.

enacted a number of laws that granted favours and privileges to Christians, notably in in Africa Proconsularis, where the Tetrarchic persecutions had been particularly severe. These measures returned confiscated property and provided exemptions and incentives for priests and bishops; later, priests and clergy received even more favourable treatment, including exemption from Roman laws on childbearing (thus protecting celibacy as an individual choice) and exemption from municipal obligations.

In 313, while he was in Nicomedia after defeating Maximinus, Licinius had published a letter addressed to the eastern provinces that he said represented the upshot of meetings with Constantine in 312/13. The letter followed a deathbed edict of Galerius, promoting the freedom of religion (Lactantius, *On the Deaths of the Persecutors*, 34) and Maximinus's own decision to cease persecution in his final moments (Eusebius, *Ecclesiastical History*, 9.10). In the letter, Licinius and Constantine claimed that they were under the protection of the entity to which they vaguely referred as *summus deus*, 'the Highest God'. This letter has become known as the *Edict of Milan*, erroneously dated to 312 (not 313), and attributed wholly to Constantine (and not Licinius). A Latin version of the text was preserved by

Lactantius. 'It was proper,' it declared, 'that Christians and all others should have liberty to follow that mode of religion which to each of them appeared best.' By choosing Christianity, or 'whatever other religion his mind directed him', the letter went on, the worshipper would ensure that the 'Supreme Divinity, to whose worship we freely devote ourselves, might continue to vouchsafe His favour and beneficence to us' (*On the Deaths of the Persecutors*, 48). The *Edict* thus mediated between polytheistic and monotheistic beliefs, and it left ample room for a range of interpretations. The aim of the letter was also very traditional: to restore, via imperial intercession, the balance between worship and divine favour.

Constantine and Licinius

The peace between Constantine and Licinius proved to be illusory. In an obscure incident, Constantine sent his brother-in-law and unwitting *agent provocateur*, Bassianus, to Licinius, with the 'expectation' that Licinius would accept his promotion to Caesar. Instead, Bassianus turned on Constantine and Licinius began to destroy statues of Constantine in Emona. In 316, Constantine moved his army into Pannonia, and in a momentous clash at Cibalae (Vinkovci in Croatia), he destroyed two-thirds of Licinius's army. Retreating to Sirmium, Licinius picked up his wife, Constantia, and his treasury, and took sanctuary at Adrianople. Constantine caught up with Licinius and beat him a second time, but he had advanced too far, and he lost control over his supply lines. The two settled their differences at the bargaining table, although to Constantine's advantage: his sons, Crispus (17) and Constantine II (a mere seven months old) were appointed as Caesars, while Licinius's own son, Licinius—20 months old—was likewise elevated. Constantine celebrated the event on a dynastic issue (Figure 12.35).

Constantine followed his campaigns against Licinius with a devastating war against the Sarmatians on the Danube in 322. Licinius, meanwhile, had inexplicably started to persecute Christians by banning them from public service and preventing them from gathering together in synods. In 323, Constantine crushed the Sarmatians, taking the title *Sarmaticus*, but pursued them into territory that Licinius regarded as his own; a second

Figure 12.35 Silver medallion minted at Sirmium in 320, commemorating the elevation of Crispus and Constantine II, on the reverse

round of war broke out that was notable for the large contingents of Franks and Goths fighting, respectively, for Constantine and Licinius. Calling Crispus back from Gaul, where he had built a reputation for himself campaigning across the Rhine, Constantine brought Licinius to battle once again at Adrianople. Licinius fled with the remains of his army to Byzantium, where his admiral, Amandus, fought two engagements against Constantine's fleet, commanded by Crispus. After an overwhelming victory in which Amandus lost all but four of his 300 ships, Licinius fled to Chalcedon, but there he was defeated once again. Licinius was penned within the walls of Nicomedia, but Constantine, persuaded by Constantia, allowed him a safe retirement in return for his surrender; in 325/26, however, Licinius and his son were quietly dispatched in a manner eerily reminiscent of the way that Constantine had rid himself of Maximian. After his victory, Constantine delivered his two-hour *Oration to the Assembly of the Saints*, a tract that obscured his less palatable associations with persecutors such as Diocletian and Maximian, and outlined his belief in a supreme deity that had chosen Constantine to protect the faithful and set the world in order.

Constantinople and Helena

In 324, Constantine founded a new imperial residence bearing his name: Constantinople. The city was established at the site of Byzantium, which offered numerous advantages. It was easily defensible, it controlled a key crossing between Europe and Asia, and it sat astride an important maritime communication route. In the city, he began construction on a massive imperial palace, linked by a passageway to a royal box (the *kathisma*) overlooking a huge hippodrome. The palace faced an open campus, the Augustaion, which lay adjacent to a large bath complex. Two churches, Holy Peace and Holy Apostles, were built along with several martyria, shrines for the relics of saints and martyrs. Holy Apostles was also intended to be Constantine's mausoleum, and was adorned with relics that purportedly belonged to Andrew and Luke. As it stands now, Constantinople's most famous church, Holy Wisdom (Hagia Sophia), is largely the work of Justinian (Chapter 14), but its original version was begun during Constantine's reign.

Constantinople's foundation was laden with pagan imagery. The centrepiece of the city's circular forum was a tall porphyry column surmounted by a statue of Constantine grasping a globe, and showing the emperor crowned with the rays of the sun. The city had a Trojan foundation myth, since the base of the column was rumoured to hold the image of Pallas Athena, carried by Aeneas from Troy to Rome, where it had been kept in the Temple of Vesta from time immemorial. This connection distinguished Constantinople from Tetrarchic capitals such as Nicomedia, and neatly sidestepped the recent history of Licinius and the Tetrarchy by appealing to the sacred memory of Aeneas himself. A column dedicated to Claudius II, one of the oldest monuments in the city, likewise erased Licinius from history and celebrated Constantine's 'real' ancestor. This antiquarian zeal was further expressed by the so-called Serpent Column in the hippodrome, the remainder of the famous Greek trophy set up to commemorate the victory over Xerxes in 479 BC (Figure 12.36). Constantine consecrated numerous temples for traditional religions, including shrines to the Capitoline Triad, Cybele, and Tyche (the goddess Fortuna). The city was dedicated in a pluralistic religious ceremony in 330 attended by Sopater, a Neoplatonist who enjoyed Constantine's patronage. In time, Constantinople would become the most important city in the Roman empire, and even in the fourth century it was cast as a 'New Rome'—much

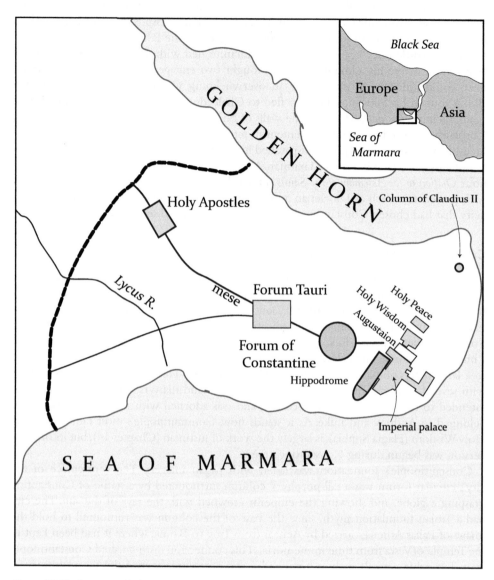

Figure 12.36 Constantinople in the fourth century.

Source: Illustration by the author.

to the irritation of Rome's inhabitants, who had to content themselves with the construction of the Baths of Constantine in the imperial city.

Constantinople was governed by a new council, made up of people who were willing to move from elsewhere, and the city's population was drawn in by various incentives such as a generous grain allowance. Later, the council became a senate, with 300 members who held the rank of *clarissimus*. An *annona* was set up on the model used in Rome,

Figure 12.37 Bronze follis minted at Heraclea in 327/29, commemorating Constantius II as Caesar.

and accounted for a great deal of maritime traffic between Alexandria and the new city. Constantine then granted the title of Augusta to his wife, Fausta, and his mother, Helena, and set about elevating his numerous children. In 324, Constantius II became a Caesar (Figure 12.37) and Constantia, who had been cleansed of her links with Licinius after a suitable time in exile, was rehabilitated. Constantia remained with Constantine and was featured on his coins, identified with the Christian virtue of *pietas*.

Helena soon became the most important Roman royal woman since Julia Maesa and Julia Domna: the city of Helenopolis on the Asian side of the Sea of Marmara was founded in her honour, and in 327 she embarked on a journey throughout Palestine to highlight its sacred sites. Among her efforts were the identification of a cave as the birthplace of Jesus and the 'rediscovery' of the True Cross at the Holy Sepulchre. Helena's travels encouraged Christian pilgrimage and made Jerusalem the most important spiritual focus for Romans, redirecting them away from old, traditional sites such as the temples of Rome.

Constantine the arbiter

Constantine's choice of the Christian faith and his desire to bring order and unity to the world quickly drew him into arbitration between different Christian communities. After his defeat of Maxentius, Constantine became involved in a nasty schism brewing among Christians in Africa. The problem concerned *traditores*, 'traitors', Christian clergy who had handed over sacred texts and holy materials to Roman officials during the Tetrarchic persecutions, and were thus seen to have stained their office and their faith. Were acts and decrees of such *traditores* still valid? A fringe group named 'Donatists' for their bishop, Donatus, did not believe so, and urged that all the polluted sacraments be repeated by properly qualified clergy. A schism emerged between the Donatists and the rest of the African clergy, and the Donatists took their cause to Rome. Constantine could look to Aurelian for precedent, since he had also been called upon to intervene in a Christian dispute; he had chosen to refer it to Christian authorities, agreeing to follow their recommendation. Constantine duly instructed the bishop of Rome, Militiades, to convene a court that was also attended by several Gallic clergy. Militiades bungled the hearing, however, and this time Constantine intervened personally, assembling a council of western provincial bishops at Arelate (Arles) in 314. This time, the emperor himself would attend and influence the outcome, an approach that signalled in no uncertain terms that the unity and peace of the church were matters of imperial interest. The Council of Arles eventually decided that the Donatist case had no merits, but when the inflexible Donatists refused to abide by the settlement, Constantine left them to God's judgement, revealing his frustration with Christians who were unwilling to compromise with imperial expectations—but also his lack of interest in any further persecution.

Shortly afterwards, Constantine was drawn into another argument—this time among the Christian communities in the east. The question was a fundamental one of orthodoxy vs. heresy, and was important since only through following 'the right road' (orthodoxy) and avoiding the 'wrong choice' (heresy) could the Christian promise of the afterlife be assured. Christianity's religious vision was, however, so novel and different from traditional religions that disputes continually arose about what was correct and what was heretical. In 324, the main issue was with an Alexandrian priest, Arius, who had spent a good deal of time pondering the Trinity, and in particular the position of Jesus with regard to the Father. Arius had decided that there was surely some point in time at which Christ did not exist, because there could not be a Son without a Father, and the Father naturally came first. To Arius's enemies, this line of thinking turned the Son into an ordinary mortal and contradicted his status as the Son of God, hindering his capacity to grant the afterlife to the faithful. As Arius's views spread in popularity and the arguments between Arius and his detractors (including his bishop) became more vicious, Constantine intervened.

Constantine's first attempt was to mediate between Arius and his bishop, Alexander, who was his chief opponent. Eusebius preserved a copy of the letter that Constantine wrote to them both, in which he stated that it was normal for men to have divergences of opinion, but that these were better off kept to oneself and not aired in public (*Life of Constantine*, 2.71). When this effort failed, Constantine convened a council of bishops to decide Arius's fate. The Council of Nicaea in 325 was attended by bishops from the eastern provinces and beyond, including those from Caucasian Lazica, Armenia, and Persia; only a few journeyed from the west to take part, but the Council's pronouncements would become a touchstone for Christian orthodoxy. The creed that Constantine helped to develop 'solved' the Arian controversy with the muddy pronouncement that Father and Son were 'of the same substance'. Almost everyone at the council agreed, with the exception of Arius and two others, who were dispatched into exile. An important aspect of the Council of Arles and the Council of Nicaea was that they yoked the effective, local organisational networks of bishops and their subordinates to the needs of the emperor. In the process, bishops became favourites, political actors, and patrons of their own, and came to form an organisational alternative to existing political bodies such as the senate and the *consistorium*.

Constantine's government

Constantine generally continued the trend towards centralised government favoured by Diocletian, but made numerous adjustments and additions to the structure outlined earlier:

- *comes* (Gr. *komes*): The title of *comes*, meaning 'imperial companion', had been introduced after the defeat of Maxentius in 312. *Comites* (pl.) ranked between *duces* and prefects and could be drawn from equestrians, senators, or those from outside the two orders, such as non-Roman allies. Known formally as *comes domini nostri Constantini invicti et perpetui Augusti*—an unambiguous phrase meaning 'companion of our lord Constantine, undefeated and perpetual Augustus'—the *comites* were of senatorial rank and stratified into three grades in the 330s as the number of holders expanded. *Comites* held important military positions as *comes rei militaris* ('military count') as well as specific geographical positions such as *comes litoris saxonici per Britanniam*, 'count of the Saxon shore'—the military commander protecting southern and eastern Britannia. *Comites* also occupied the highest command grades in the field armies and played a role in the imperial bodyguard.

- *patricius* (Gr. *patrikios*): Constantine reintroduced the rank of patrician, which had fallen into disuse. It could be awarded by the emperor as a sign of imperial favour, or earned through holding a specific office.

- *Praetorian prefects*: Additional prefects were added, and five are known from an inscription dated to 332, but their precise geographical responsibilities, if they existed, remain unclear. Praetorian prefects were eventually stripped of their last remaining vestiges of military authority and became civilian administrators managing army pay, tax collection, and logistics. They were increasingly drawn from the senatorial order or from equestrians who were promoted to senatorial status on appointment (below).

- *Equestrians and senators*: The hierarchical divisions among equestrians and senators introduced earlier had produced a sort of office inflation. Constantine abolished the equestrian rank of *egregius* and divided the *perfectissimi* into three grades. Equestrians holding high office as praetorian prefects, vicars, or prefect of the *annona* at Rome became senatorial *clarissimi*, so the highest equestrian rank of *eminentissimus* was eventually abolished after 325. Numerous provincial governorships, such as Coele Syria or Byzacena, were reserved for *clarissimi*, and equestrians appointed to these positions were promoted to senatorial rank. Within the senatorial order, further divisions emerged between those who had held a prestigious post, such as the consulship, and others who merely served in the senate. Notably, those who had held high office or ranked among the top-ranked senators could not pass their status on: their sons would 'reset' to the lowest senatorial rank of *clarissimus*, and if they wanted a higher status, they had to earn it through imperial patronage or office-holding. Constantine also increased the numbers of senators, who later came to total 2,000. The ancient quaestorship became a junior office suitable for the sons of senators, while the position of praetor was demoted to the management of games and festivals. These changes would lead to the eventual disappearance of the equestrian order and the emergence of a new, highly stratified aristocracy closely identified with the emperor and his patronage, and whose members increasingly chose to identify themselves as Christians (Chapters 13 and 14).

- *The army*: Constantine formalised the Tetrarchic organisation of the army, dividing it between a field army, the *comitatus*, and a garrison army, the *limitanei*. A law of 325 (*RA* §394) records the different categories among the army: the *comitatenses*, the *protectores*, the *alae* and cohorts, and the *ripenses*, the 'border troops'. The *ripenses* included the old legions and the auxiliary *alae*, and cohorts that were stationed in forts along the frontiers, along with the *cunei equitum*, mounted 'wedges', found principally on the Danube. In the later empire, the *ripenses* became known as *limitanei* from the Latin word *limes*, 'frontier'. Constantine inherited numerous military formations from his predecessors, recorded in the *ND*, and a number of legions were renamed 'Flavia' for Constantine's family name, Flavius, removing their prior associations with Constantine's enemies. Members of the *comitatus* were increasingly drawn from European tribesmen, particularly Goths, Franks, and Alamanni, and received preferential pay and shorter enlistment periods. A number of laws dated to the early fourth century show that troops who were medically or honourably discharged received exemptions for themselves and their families from taxes, as well as from compulsory municipal and public service.

Either during Constantine's reign or during those of his successors, commanders of the *comitatenses* were eventually divided between a *magister peditum*, a 'general of infantry', and a *magister equitum*, 'a general of cavalry', both of whom were *clarissimi* with the rank of *comes*. The senior commander of the army was the *magister militum*: the eastern portion of the *ND* records five of these commanders, with two ranked *praesentalis*, 'in the emperor's presence'—that is, the army serving with the emperor—and three for distinct commands: *magister militum per Orientem*, serving in the east, whose base was often Antioch; *per Illyricum*, for Illyria; and *per Thracias*, for Thrace. (Occasionally, a *magister militum* appears as *magister utriusque militiae*, the commander of both services—the infantry and the cavalry). In the west, the structure was somewhat different, with a *magister peditum* in Italy, a *magister equitum* in Gaul, and four *comites* for Africa, Tingitana, Britannia, and Hispania; there was also a *comes* for Illyricum when the latter was part of the prefecture of Italy and Africa. The *limitanei* came under the authority of the *duces* assigned to each province. Diocletian and Constantine also maintained a transport fleet, divided between Ravenna, Constantinople, and bases along the Rhine, whose primary purpose was to move troops and supplies to where they were needed.

The *ND* records all the army units in existence when the document was created, with some later additions and corrections in the case of the western portion. Some units clearly belong to the period after Constantine's death, but it is noteworthy that the structure of the older army of the principate, divided between numbered legions raised from citizens, auxiliary cohorts, and cavalry *alae*, was replaced by a very different image. Some units provide a continuity from earlier periods, such as III Gallica or VII Gemina, but many clearly were new: Prima Flavia Constantina, for instance, or the Balistarii seniores—both within the *comitatus*—as well as legions with the epithet Armeniaca. Cavalry units dominate the *comitatus*, including armoured cavalry listed as *cataphractarii* or *clibinarii* (the difference between the two may have been Sarmatian influence on the former and Persian on the latter), reflecting the vital importance of armoured horsemen on the battlefield. Some of the units drawn from the *limitanei* became 'pseudocomitatenses', transferred on a long-term basis to the *comitatus*. Other entries in the *ND* reflect a continued reliance on non-Roman troops—for instance:

- *ND Oc.* 9.8: *Celtae seniores* amongst the *auxilia palatina* of the western *comitatus*
- *ND Or.* 12.35: *Tervingi* listed among the *auxilia palatina* of the eastern *comitatus*, presumably recruited from or linked with Gothic Tervingi

- *ND Or.* 52.5: *equites Saraceni Thamudeni,* presumed to be cavalry recruited from Thamud, the tribe known from the Ruwafa inscriptions and serving under the *comes limitis Aegypti,* 'the count of the Egyptian frontier'
- *ND Or.* 63.11: *equites Saraceni indigenae,* cavalry raised from Arabs of the desert as part of the *limitanei* under the *dux Foenicis,* the commander of the *limitanei* in Phoenicia
- *ND Or.* 65.18: *cohors prima Gotthorum,* 'first cohort of Goths' with the *limitanei* serving under the *dux Syriae et Eufratensis Syriae,* the 'duke of Syria and Euphratensis'
- *ND Or.* 63.21: *ala prima Saxonum,* 'first cavalry wing of Saxons', with the *limitanei* under the *dux Foenicis.*

It is also possible to see where the Romans have apparently absorbed the units of defeated enemies: under the heading for the *magister militum per Orientem,* a unit is listed as *cuneus equitum secundorum clibanariorum Palmirenorum,* presumably Palmyra's *clibinarii* now in Roman service.

Ostensibly because they had supported Maxentius, but also in a further indication of Rome's irrelevance to the day-to-day running of the empire, Constantine disbanded the Praetorian Guard and its cavalry unit. A new imperial bodyguard was created, known as the *scholae palatinae,* divided into five separate units. The *scholae* were supplemented by *candidati,* an elite core group of bodyguards, and the *protectores domestici* under the command of the *comes domesticorum.* The *scholae* attracted Germanic recruits, and Franks, Goths, and others were able to reach high military office within its ranks; like the old Praetorian Guard, the troops of the *scholae* were considered to be elite, and fought in Rome's wars until the fifth century, when emperors generally stopped commanding troops in the field.

With regard to central government, as recently as the time of Diocletian, the praetorian prefect acted almost as a deputy emperor. Under Constantine, the prefect's authority was circumscribed by the creation of a quaestor *sacri palatii,* an imperial quaestor, whose office drafted laws and spoke on behalf of the emperor, and by the creation of the *magister officiorum,* a 'master of offices', who became the most senior official in the palace. Peter the Patrician, who was *magister officiorum* for close to 30 years in the sixth century, penned a history of the office and recorded its first incumbent in 323/24. The *magister officiorum* managed the three *scrinia* established in the third century. These were the *scrinium memoriae* (*magister memoriae*), the *scrinium epistularum* (*magister epistularum*), and the *scrinium libellorum* (*magister libellorum*). The *magister officiorum* commanded the *scholae palatinae* as well as the *schola* of the *agentes in rebus,* an important palatine office that was part spy service and part trusted imperial courier, able to safely deliver messages quickly and accurately. The *agentes* replaced an earlier office known as the *frumentarii,* 'those concerned with the grain supply', whose work provisioning the empire had placed them in an excellent position to gather news and report on provincial gossip. The *agentes in rebus* also worked as chiefs-of-staff for the praetorian prefects and numerous other officials. Finally, the *magister officiorum* supervised numerous smaller offices such as translators, those who looked after the arrangements of audiences with the emperor, imperial arms factories, and door men. A great deal of power was concentrated in the office of *magister officiorum,* and this is reflected in the promotion of the office holder from tribune to *comes* at some point between 324 and 346.

The power of the *magister officiorum* was offset by the creation of a second bureaucratic office, run by the *primicerius notariorum.* This official managed a team of *notarii,* who maintained the *ND* and wrote letters of appointment. There were also additional high-ranking *comites*, including the *comes sacrarum largitionum*, managing the *res summa* (now the *sacrae largitiones*), and the *comes rei privatae*, managing the *res privata*, with both replacing the financial *magistri* of earlier years. The *comes sacrarum largitionum* supervised mints and mines, tax collection, military pay, and customs collection, while the *comes rei privatae* managed imperial estates and the revenues that they earned. The hierarchical nature of the government in which these officials worked is neatly illustrated by the section of the *ND Or.* listing those who worked under the *comes sacrarum largitionum*: there were 12 distinct offices ranging from procurators to *magistri*, and 13 senior clerks dealing with everything from 'the sacred wardrobe' to the shipment of gold. These palatine *comites*, together with the *magister officiorum* and the imperial quaestor, made up the core of Constantine's *consistorium*. In order to prevent centralisation of too much power in individual offices, there was also a certain degree of overlap: for instance, both the *magister officiorum* and the praetorian prefects shared control over the factories that made weapons for the troops.

The development of Constantinian government clearly shared a relationship with the reforms of Diocletian. It also maintained an element of traditionalism by reserving a small number of prestigious offices for senators. These were the urban prefects of Rome and Constantinople, together with the proconsular governorships of Achaea, Africa Proconsularis, and Asia. Yet Constantine's government was also innovative. The structure of the palace was reorganised, and the praetorian prefects were transformed into civilian officials. Attracting talent into the administration, and rewarding it with exemptions from the numerous service and taxation burdens imposed on lesser folk, also helped to co-opt elites who had worked for Constantine's rivals and thus to unify the empire around the emperor and a cadre of powerful, high-ranking palace bureaucrats, many of whom reported directly to the emperor. That, along with Constantine's intervention in religious disputes, firmly cemented the concept of powerful bureaucratic government at the heart of the empire, headed by an omnipotent emperor.

Gold, society, and taxes

Constantine's reorganisation of the government had inevitable consequences for Roman society. At the top were men and their families, demarcated by their various ranks, holders of offices wielding great power and privilege and exempt from numerous civic obligations. Below this lofty perch was a cascading hierarchy of diminishing power and privilege and increasingly onerous obligations. Those at the very bottom, including free peasants in the countryside, slaves, and tribesmen beyond the Rhine and Danube, were treated with extreme severity. Legal protections for slaves had hardly moved over the past hundred years, and slaves were routinely tortured or killed by their masters without penalty. Constantine made it possible to free slaves in churches, and bishops became eligible to grant freedom to slaves. These developments allowed an element of Roman civil law to be managed, in part, by church authorities. Yet if there were any expectations that slaves would gain the support of the church for moral or humanitarian reasons, these were to be dashed; church authorities not only retained slaves for use on their estates, but also enjoined slaves to obey their owners. Basil of Caesarea, a bishop writing in the late fourth century, went so far as to say that 'it is better for a man who lacks intelligence and self-control to become another's possession' (*On the Holy Spirit*, 20).

It is something of a paradox that, despite the unremitting warfare of the period that routinely delivered thousands of prisoners, slaves no longer formed the backbone of the agrarian workforce, and the supply of slave labour actually fell. Many of the burdens previously borne by slaves were thus devolved onto the peasants, who became known as the *coloni* (sg. *colonus*). The impetus for this was the tax reform of Diocletian, which had so carefully measured and assessed everyone and everything in the empire down to its smallest component. The tax law favoured keeping people in their place, and thus helped to create a workforce where agricultural workers, bakers, weavers, dyers, and so on became moored to their professions. Even soldiers were not immune: a law of 319 dealt with the sons of veterans who sought to avoid military service by self-mutilation; Constantine decreed that their punishment would be to carry out the municipal burdens of decurions (*RA* §390). A law of 319 bound *coloni* to their employment, and another of 332 mandated enslavement for *coloni* who tried to leave. The lines between slaves and *coloni* were murky at best, and if land was sold from one owner to another, its *coloni* came with it.

These class distinctions were entrenched further when Constantine introduced a new gold coin, the solidus, in 309. The new coin was slightly lighter than the aureus (struck at 72: Roman pound, making each coin c. 4.51 grams, or 0.159 ounces), but the fact that its weight and purity remained stable for centuries to come makes its appearance once of the most important fiscal developments of late antiquity. New sources of gold for the solidi came not only from the eastern mines, hitherto controlled by Licinius, but also from the treasure stored in pagan sanctuaries. Silver coinage was diminished, and until the early fifth century copper or bronze coins were minted indifferently. Over time, the solidus became the standard Roman currency and the benchmark for payments of debts and obligations. Since it had become increasingly common for the palatine bureaucracy and high-ranking members of Roman society to be paid in gold—but not those below them—the introduction of the solidus also reinforced the rigid social hierarchies of late antiquity. Others who came to differentiate their status based on gold included the soldiers of the *comitatus*, whose grain and equipment supports, the *annona*, also came to be paid partly in gold. Furthermore, since taxes were increasingly collected in the form of gold coin, those occupying the lowest rungs of society without easy access to gold were forced to find more wealthy individuals to pay their taxes for them, which created a new cycle of oppressive debts as they struggled to repay their middlemen. New taxes, payable in gold, were instituted: these included the *chrysargyron*, a broadly detested tax imposed on merchants. Exemptions to the *chrysargyron* became as keenly sought after as exemptions from the burdens that came with municipal service, and eventually several sectors of society, including bishops and peasant producers, gained relief. The *caput* tax of Diocletian's reforms was slowly abandoned to fall back on a taxation system based on land (*iugum*), not human productivity, but tax burdens, along with outright confiscations, remained excessive.

Criticism of taxes and the enrichment of those who had gold versus those who did not was rife in antiquity. The anonymous author of the late fourth-century military treatise, *De Rebus Bellicis* (*On Military Matters*), wrote like a latter-day Cato the Elder of the dire impact of so much pagan wealth emerging into the money supply. The well-connected political elite engaged in extravagant displays of wealth, while the poor were driven further into financial misery (2.1–2). Zosimus dedicated a section of his history to railing against Constantine's taxes ('nor did he spare the poorest prostitute') and wrote of the *chrysargyron* that 'mothers were even forced to part with their children, and fathers to prostitute their daughters, for money to satisfy the collectors of this exaction' (*New History*, 2.56–7). Zosimus, who was a pagan, also decried Constantine for enriching churches and bishops at the expense of pagan temples, and for making recklessly extravagant gifts to the troops and to his political allies. It took time for the new economy, based on gold, to stabilise: in c. 300, a pound of gold was valued at about 40 talents, but inflation was so rampant that the exchange rate had risen to 648,000 talents 50 years later, and to just shy of a million talents by the 360s.

Constantine and art

The best-known monument from Constantine's era is the massive triumphal arch close to the Flavian Amphitheatre, modelled on that of Septimius Severus. Started during the final years of Maxentius and completed by the senate in 315, it freely plundered the decorative art of Constantine's predecessors, including statues of beaten Dacians from the Forum of Trajan and sculpted tondos and panels produced for Hadrian and Marcus Aurelius. The images of the emperor going about his formal business on the arch are firmly anchored in traditional practice: the emperor and his army, the emperor making the *adventus* into Rome in triumph, the emperor making a speech. An image of Victory accompanies Constantine into battle, while images of the sun rising and the moon setting add further layers of meaning consistent with Constantine's beliefs. The links created with Trajan and Marcus Aurelius, and the appeal to traditionalism both reflected Constantine's attempt to portray himself as the natural successor to Rome's most illustrious leaders. Notably, the only nod to Christianity on the arch is the depiction of the sun and the opaque wording of the dedicatory inscription, recording that Constantine's victory over Maxentius was *instinctu divinitatis*—'inspired by a divinity'. An equally ambiguous image of Constantine was found on his later coinage, in issues that resembled the portraits of Hellenistic dynasts but which could be interpreted by Christians in their own way. There, the laurel wreath replaced with a diadem, the emperor's face was turned upwards in an ethereal posture of eternal prayer (Figure 12.38).

Figure 12.38 Gold aureus of Constantine minted at Nicomedia in 326. On the obverse, Constantine's heavenward gaze; on the reverse, the legend CONSTANTINVS AVG with wreaths and star.

Constantine's adoption of Christianity helped to spur the development of Christian art. The discovery of Dura-Europos showed that decorated churches existed in the third century, but imperial support for Christianity triggered an outpouring of church building, ornamented sarcophagi, and painted catacombs. Consistent with Constantine's own ambiguities, however, artists experimented with a blend of traditional mythological iconography and Christian symbolism. Images of vine pruning and winemaking, for instance, as seen earlier on the sculpture of Antinous (Figure 10.52), followed traditional styles, but were now also relevant for a Christian audience. On the massive porphyry sarcophagus of Constantine's daughter, Constantina, cupids tend to the grapes and animals and garlands complement the bucolic scenes. The imagery would not have been out of place on Augustan art, but here, it has been reimagined for a new era.

Constantine and the empire's neighbours

Constantine's foreign policy was informed by his emulation of his forebears, who included Trajan, Augustus, and even Alexander the Great, whose coins influenced some of Constantine's own issues. Constantine was an aggressive emperor, but also one whose mission was to unify a broken world. Because Christianity is a universal religion, Constantine's faith underpinned both missions. 'You are bishops whose jurisdiction is within the church,' Eusebius recorded him saying to a group of assembled clergy, 'I also am a bishop, ordained by God to look after whatever is outside the church' (*Life of Constantine*, 4.24).

In Europe, Constantine pursued a belligerent policy that was waged in part through the leadership of his children—Crispus, Constantine II, and Constantius II. As noted earlier, he had bridged the Rhine at Colonia Agrippinensium and constructed a stronghold on its right bank. He also built a stone bridge across the Danube from Oescus to Sucidava in 328, and heavily fortified the opposite bank at Constantiana Daphne. A network of earthworks 700 kilometres (435 miles) long was built eastwards from Aquincum, along the line of the Carpathians, turning south to Viminacium. This network, known as the Devil's Dyke (Csörsz-árok) is attributed to either Diocletian or Constantine, and served to demarcate the territory of the Sarmatians (who had become Roman clients) from the Goths. Another earthwork, the Brazda lui Novac de Nord, running north of and parallel to the Danube, is also sometimes attributed to Constantine. As part of this process of consolidation, the Danube bend—where the river turns sharply south just before Budapest—became more heavily garrisoned than ever before; many of the new fortifications were the small *quadriburgia*. This infrastructure was crucial to the ongoing wars with the Sarmatians and the Goths: by the 320s, the Goths had become so powerful that the left bank of the eastern Danube was known as the *ripa Gothica*, the 'Gothic bank', and the Romans had begun to call the land beyond it Gothia. The aggressive development of fortifications in and adjacent to Gothia reflected concerns about Gothic support for Constantine's enemy Licinius, as well as the growth in power of the Tervingi.

A new Gothic war was not long in coming. Their defences breached by the Tervingi, the Sarmatians appealed for help, and Constantine won a victory in the Sarmatian lands between the Danube and the Devil's Dyke. Constantine II then won an important victory over the Goths in 332 with a brutal war of starvation, after which, in the triumphalist phrase of Eusebius, 'the Goths finally learned to serve the Romans' (*Life of Constantine*, 4.5). The treaty between Constantine and the Tervingian chief Ariaric established the Tervingi on the left bank of the Lower Danube and tasked them with maintaining peace and providing thousands of young Goths for the Roman army (Jordanes, *Getica* 112 & 145). In 334, further disturbances on the Danube saw large numbers of Sarmatians, who had been attacked by their own slaves, settled along the Danube and their men enrolled into the Roman army. In the aftermath of these wars, Constantine took the titles *Sarmaticus Maximus* and *Dacicus Maximus*, although the old territory of Dacia remained abandoned. An important consequence of these conflicts was the spread of Christianity into Gothia. After the defeat of the Goths in 332, the Arian bishop Eusebius of Nicomedia consecrated a man named Ulfila (or Ulfilas) to minister to the Christians living in Gothia. Later, in 347/48, Ulfila and his flock were driven into Moesia during a persecution initiated by Gothic leaders, but during this time, the resourceful Ulfila developed an alphabet to render the Gothic language, which he then used to create a Gothic version of the Bible.

In the east, Constantine faced a world that had undergone rapid change in the late third and early fourth centuries. Yasirum Yuhanim (c. 265–87) and his son Shammar Yuharish (c. 286–311), monarchs of the south Arabian kingdom of Himyar, had overwhelmed their Sabaean neighbours between 275 and 300 and then conquered Hadramawt on the southern edge of the Arabian Peninsula. The disparate kingdoms of South Arabia were thus united into the single kingdom of Himyar, a unification accompanied by the adoption of a single dating system, the Himyarite era, a common language, Sabaic, and a formulaic royal title: 'kings of Saba, of dhu-Raydan, [Himyar], of Hadramawt, and of Yamnat [the South]'. During his reign, Shammar sent two embassies to Persia that were recorded on inscriptions at the Great Temple at Marib, dedicated to the Sabaean god Almaqah. These missions may have been connected to the accession of Shapur II in 309, or his subsequent raids into the Arabian Peninsula. Shammar sent an embassy to the Romans, also recorded at the Great Temple, but few details of it are known. Under one of Shammar's successors, Tharan Yuhanim (c. 324–c. 75), Himyarite armies, drawn from the communes, the settled tribes of South Arabia, conquered the barren lands of Arabia Deserta; the dhu-Yazan, princes of the communes in the Hadramawt, led most of the 12 campaigns into Arabia Deserta and recorded them on a monumental inscription at Abadan, near Aden, dated to 360 (*AEBI* §3.8).

As Himyarite armies pushed northwards, king Ezana of Axum (Ethiopia) adopted Christianity in c. 330 and began minting coins based on the Roman aureus with a cross on the reverse. In his royal titles, Ezana claimed suzerainty over Saba and Himyar, and Axum and Himyar frequently found themselves at odds with one another. Across the Red Sea, the Himyarite kings also broke decisively with polytheism—but instead of adopting Christianity, they developed a form of Judaism that has become known as 'Judeo-Monotheism'. Inspiration for this shift may have come from the Jewish diaspora; inscriptions from the Hijaz dated to 203 and 356 reveal the presence of Jews at Tayma and Hegra, respectively, and Jews are also known from Safaitic inscriptions found in northern Arabia. For the Axumites, adopting Christianity gave them a valuable alliance with the Romans; for the Himyarite kings, Judeo-Monotheism, which developed over the course of the fourth century, provided an avenue for the unification of their kingdom, but avoided an overt identification with Roman political interests. Himyarite inscriptions are noteworthy for the opaque language used to describe their monotheist deity, which is known variously as 'Lord of the Heaven', 'God', or 'Merciful', terms that recall Constantine's

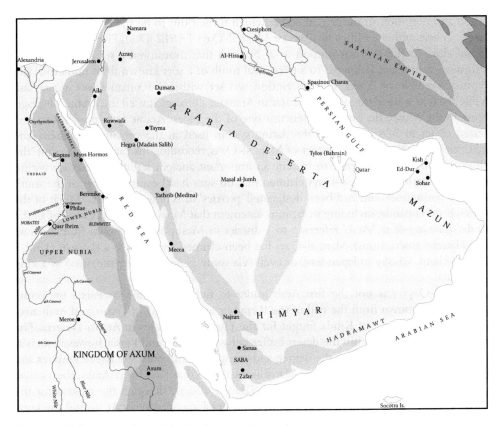

Figure 12.39 Axum and the Arabian Peninsula in the fourth century.

Source: Illustration by the author.

summus deus or Theos Hypsistos. The developments in Axum and Arabia are important because they created a third nexus of politico-religious power and a source of regional conflict, infused with religious overtones, that would increasingly intrude on Roman and Persian interests and provide an opportunity for Romano-Persian imperial competition outside the normal venues of Syria and Mesopotamia (Figure 12.39).

One of Shammar's Persian embassies was sent to 'the land of Tanukh', a reference to al-Hira, near Najaf in southern Iraq, which had emerged as an Arab principality in the third century. Al-Hira was under the control of a family known variously as the Lakhmids (referring to a group or confederation) or the Nasrids (the family dynasty, after a supposed eponymous ancestor, Nasr), who remained in alliance with the Sasanian monarchy until c. 602, and who enjoyed a vivid afterlife in Muslim Arabic and Persian literary sources. In contemporary sources, they are first attested on the Paikuli inscription in the guise of 'Amru king of the Lahmids' (§92 = *AEBI* p. 61), but they are virtually unknown to Roman writers before the fifth century. The advent of the Nasrid kings, and their alliance with the Sasanian monarchs, can be understood as a consequence of the collapse of Hatra and Palmyra as dominant forces in the arid lands between Rome and Persia. The Romans, too, were courting Arab leaders: In 1901, the explorers René Dussaud and Frédéric Macler found an inscription in the Syrian desert which turned out to be the epitaph of an Arab leader known either as Imru al-Qays or Mara al-Qays (*AEBI* §7.3). The inscription was found close to the Roman outpost at al-Namara that monitored a series of wells and irrigation works, and belonged to a pyramidal tomb of a sort known from numerous late Roman examples in Syria. The inscription was set within a Roman *tabula ansata*, and while the text was written in the Nabataean Aramaic alphabet, it used the Arabic language. Now in the Musée du Louvre, it remains one of the oldest Arabic texts ever discovered. Dated either to 328 or 332 by the dating system used in the province of Arabia, the text celebrates the illustrious career of Mara al-Qays, recording his campaigns against 'the city of Shammar', a reference to Najran, an important ancient settlement that lay within Himyarite territory. Mara al-Qays claimed that his sons had become leaders of the south Arabian communes, and had been designated 'proxies' of Rome and Persia. Much of the inscription is opaque, including its famous statement that Mara al-Qays was 'king of all the Arabs' (or king of *rb*, 'Arab' referring to a district in Mesopotamia known from Edessan and Hatrene inscriptions). Mara al-Qays has been claimed variously as a Roman client, a Persian client, wholly independent, or even (via some genealogical gymnastics) as a king of al-Hira.

Mara al-Qays was not the first Arab leader to fight for Rome or Persia (or both); examples are known from the end of the Republic and the wars of Trajan, and Arab auxiliaries from the tribe of Kinda fought for the Himyarite armies in Arabia Deserta. The removal of the states within the desert buffer between Rome and Persia, however, such as Hatra and Palmyra, increased the degree and complexity of contact between empires and the Arabs of the desert. Ammianus Marcellinus wrote that the desert Arabs, the *scenitae*, were in the late fourth century known as Saracens (22.5), although the reasons for the name change are unclear and have aroused considerable controversy. At around the same time, the desert Arabs became known in Syriac as *tayyaye*. The Saracens were no more a monolithic ethnic or cultural group than Goths, Alamanni, or Franks, but like their western counterparts, they came to play an important role as militia and participants in various levels of Roman government, particularly in the sixth century (Chapter 14). In the fourth century, they were, as Ammianus put it, 'good neither as friends nor enemies', although this was a comment appended to his notorious and lurid description of their uncivilised ways (14.4). The Romans did find Saracen raiding difficult and unpredictable, however; towards the end of Constantine's reign, the Roman fort at the Azraq oasis received another round of repairs, and an inscription found to its west, dated to 334, records the construction of a reservoir due to men among the Roman foraging parties finding themselves *insidiados a Saracenos perisse*—'ambushed [and] killed by Saracens'.

In the north, Armenia remained a febrile problem for Roman and Persian monarchs. The Armenians had adopted Christianity by 314, but had long been exposed to the development of Syriac Christianity in neighbouring Osrhoene. Greek-speaking priests were brought to Armenia by Gregory the Illuminator, who was responsible for baptising Tiridates III (the same king caught up in the wars between Narseh and Galerius), but Greek rituals of worship were accepted unevenly in Armenia, parts of which historically enjoyed closer relations with Mesopotamia and Persia. In neighbouring Iberia (whose king, following the Peace of Nisibis, received his crown from Rome), the monarchy became Christian between 324 and 337. Notably, both Armenia and Iberia sought military and political alliances with Rome on the basis of a shared faith, highlighting the latent potential for conflict in the universalising nature of Christianity.

Before his death, Constantine, like a latter-day Abgar V, flush from his encounter with Jesus (Chapter 9), wrote a letter to 'my brother' Shapur II in which he expounded on his understanding of Christianity as a universal religion and his role as God's viceroy on earth. The letter sought tolerance for Christians in Persia (who were under suspicion due to the alignment of imperial power and Christianity in the Roman empire); Constantine also cast Valerian as a wicked man who met a just end after God gave up on him at Edessa in 260. The text, preserved by Eusebius, is intriguing: it invoked a 'divine faith' cast in terms of 'light' and 'truth', concepts compatible with a Zoroastrian worldview (*Life of Constantine*, 4.8–13). The letter inferred that a Christian path was available to Shapur, should he choose to seek it, but such hopes only stoked Persian suspicion of Constantine's motives and highlighted the political importance of Persian Christian communities to Roman policy.

Constantine was also no less affected by the legacy of Alexander the Great than Trajan or Caracalla. An embassy from India had paid its respects to Constantine in his earlier years, and in Eusebius's telling of the story the emperor imagined that his realm extended 'even to the Indian Ocean', just like that of Alexander (*Life of Constantine*, 4.50). Julian wrote scathingly that Constantine thought himself *superior* to Alexander (*Caesares*, 329); and indeed, the emperor's thoughts were very much on eastern conquest. A coin issue of 325 portrayed Constantine as Jupiter, holding a globe with the eternal symbol of rebirth, the phoenix. Waiting to take the orb was Crispus, portrayed as Dionysus, the conqueror of the east, but one year later Crispus had been executed on Constantine's orders, along with Fausta, for reasons that are not well understood (Zosimus, *New History*, 2.51). Constantine's cruelty, so at odds with the Christian faith, remained one of his legacies: in the *Caesares*, Julian introduced Jesus to a meeting of Roman gods and emperors that also included Alexander the Great, who had been invited as a special guest. Jesus offered holy baptism to any who had committed a crime, and a second baptism if the crimes were committed again. 'To him, Constantine came gladly,' Julian wrote (336).

In 330, Tiridates III of Armenia died. This presented a precious opportunity to Shapur, who was persecuting Christians in Persia, and in 334 he duly placed his brother on the Armenian throne. In response, Constantine appointed his nephew Dalmatius to a plenipotentiary command in Thrace, and Dalmatius's brother, Hannibalianus, was appointed as king of Armenia with the grandiose sounding title 'King of Kings and of the Pontic Peoples', which has led some to think that Constantine intended to overthrow Shapur II and annex Persia to the Roman empire. Constantine then sent his son Constantius II eastwards, where he set about fortifying the city of Amida (modern Diyarbakir) with walls and artillery. Deciding at the last minute that he would also travel to the coming war, complete with a mobile church tent, Constantine set off, but fell ill at Nicomedia. Shortly before his death, he was baptised by the Arian bishop Eusebius of Nicomedia. The empire passed to Constantius II, and to his brothers Constantine II and the very young Constans, but Hannibalianus and Dalmatius had both been raised to the rank of Caesar, creating an unwieldy college of five. Constantius II buried his father in the Church of the Holy Apostles, alongside Luke, Andrew, and numerous other holy dignitaries, and in Rome,

Constantine was deified by the senate. Afterwards, Hannibalianus and Dalmatius together with almost all of their living relatives were murdered. Constantine's half-brother, Julius Constantius, was one of the victims, leaving only his young children Constantius Gallus and the future emperor Julian alive. Other victims included Ablabius, Constantine's former praetorian prefect of Oriens, and many of his associates. The three sons of Constantine and Fausta—Constantius II, Constantine II, and Constans—were proclaimed Augusti and inherited their father's empire. Further civil war surely would not be long in coming.

Chapter 13

Division and collapse, 337–493

You are here justly censured, O Fortune of the Roman world! That, when storms shattered our country, you did snatch the helm from the hands of an experienced steersman and entrust it to an untried youth.

Ammianus Marcellinus, 25.9, on the death of Julian (AD 363)

The end of the late fourth century, and much of the fifth, was a period of ferment: divisions and violence between Christians, between Christians and pagans, and between Jews and Christians; unstable leadership; military calamities; and the rise of powerful bishops, warlords, and cliques whose concerns and interests frequently diverged sharply from those of the empire and its inhabitants. Factionalism at court wrecked promising careers and child emperors were manipulated by powerful advisers. In the face of persistent invasions, particularly in the west and in the Balkans, the disintegration of the western provinces of the empire accelerated as the landowners who made up the principal tax base were killed, dropped out of imperial control, or chose to cooperate with their invaders. These invaders were principally Franks, Goths, Alamanni, Suebi, Vandals, and Huns. Contrary to long-held beliefs, they did not arrive in 'barbarian waves', nor did they necessarily nurture a desire to destroy the empire. Neither did the western empire 'fall' at any particular moment; in common with the transition from Republic to Empire (Chapters 7–8), the western empire underwent a violent transition—this time, into a number of smaller kingdoms and principalities, as the ability of the Roman court at Ravenna to provide effective and stable leadership collapsed and control over the populations of Gaul, Spain, Britannia, Africa, and eventually Italy passed into new hands.

The distinctive way in which the relationship between imperial authorities and barbarian leaders developed is a key feature of the period. (For the sake of consistency, the term 'barbarian' is used here in a neutral sense to describe non-Roman groups encountered on the Rhine and Danube.) The leaders of groups such as the Goths, which had largely been created by Roman frontier politics, framed their own ideas about authority in the language of Roman power. This meant that many of the period's most important non-Roman figures initially sought recognition from Roman authorities, often through the office of *magister militum*. (The only exception to this rule was Attila, who never sought Roman rank or position.) When Alaric sacked Rome in 410, it was more out of frustration for his failure to win the acknowledgement he desired from the emperor Honorius than from a desire to destroy the city. On the other hand, the barbarian invasions did tremendous damage to Rome's agricultural tax base, and disasters such as Julian's invasion of Persia (363) and the calamites at Mursa (351), Adrianople (378), and the Frigidus (394)

DOI: 10.4324/9781003202523-13

caused severe difficulties for the army. The loss of tax revenue and destruction of property that resulted from the invasions of Gaul, Spain, and the African provinces also destroyed the ability of the western empire to fund and defend itself.

One of the most important historical sources for the late fourth century is the Latin *Res Gestae* of Ammianus Marcellinus, who was born in Antioch in c. 330. Ammianus was a pagan and served as a *protector domesticus* from 350; he joined the staff of the *magister equitum* Ursicinus, with whom he saw service across the empire from Gaul to Mesopotamia. The *Res Gestae* covered the period from Nerva to Valens (d. 378), but only books 14 to 31 have survived. Their contents are suffused by a dark pessimism that reflected Ammianus's own experiences under the austere Christian leadership of Constantius II, and then on campaign with Julian; his view of his times was also deeply coloured by the Roman defeat at Adrianople. Other important sources include Zosimus, whose *New History* depended in part on the work of several Greek classicising authors whose histories now exist only as fragments: Eunapius, Olympiodorus, Priscus, and Malchus. (Here I follow the numbering of these fragments according to Blockley – see Further Reading section). Eunapius also wrote a volume of sophist biographies, following the work of Philostratus (Chapter 11) and, together with the works of the pagan orator Libanius, Eunapius's work represented a last call for a vanishing, pagan philosophical world in the face of Christianity's relentless advance. A testament to Christianity's ascent is the fact that many of the period's most important writers were Christian; these included numerous ecclesiastical historians, whose work combined political history with a narrative following church events. The fourth and fifth centuries also saw an efflorescence of hagiographies written in Latin, Greek, and Syriac. The acts of the various Roman church councils, written in Greek before being translated into Latin and Syriac, and the acts of the Persian church, the Syriac *Synodicon Orientale*, reflect the changing nature of Christian thought and politics, and the growing political role of bishops (in the west) and patriarchs (in the east, at Alexandria, Constantinople, and Antioch).

Constantius II: church and state

The death of Constantine brought immediate rancour, division, and mutual suspicion. The empire was split between Constantius II, Constans, and Constantine II, who met in Pannonia in September to settle their differences. Their rivalries soon led to bloodshed: in 340, Constantine II and Constans came to blows at Aquileia, where Constantine II was killed. Constans, only 17, now ruled over a vast area from Britannia to Moesia. There was also a poisonous rift within the church. Alexander—the patriarch of Alexandria who had opposed Arius—had been succeeded by a man named Athanasius. A difficult personality, Athanasius was repeatedly exiled throughout his career; he had been banished before the death of Constantine, and when he returned afterwards he became mired in turbulent accusations of magic and misconduct. Constantius harboured anti-Nicene sentiments and took a firm approach to ecclesiastical politics; he deposed Athanasius, who fled to Rome, where he had support from its Nicene bishop. Constantius also removed the Nicene patriarch of Constantinople, Paul, and banished him to Pontus, replacing him with the Arian Eusebius of Nicomedia. There was thus a growing division between eastern, pro-Arian patriarchs, who had the ear of Constantius, and western, pro-Nicene bishops. This gulf widened when Eusebius of Nicomedia died in 341. His replacement, Macedonicus, clashed with Paul, and in the febrile atmosphere Constantius's *magister equitum* was killed by protestors and Paul fled to join Athanasius. The matter was so divisive that for a moment it seemed likely that Constans, who favoured Paul and Athanasius, would go to war with his brother. In the end, facing an opportunistic Persian siege of Nisibis (Shapur II's first attempt on the city), intrigue over the Armenian throne, and Persian attempts to capture Singara, Constantius backed down.

Constantius remained profoundly worried about the state of affairs in the east and the fate of Christians in Persia. He sought to shore up his periphery by sending Theophilus 'the Indian' as an emissary to Himyar, where he tried, unsuccessfully, to persuade the Himyarite kings to convert to Christianity. In 340, Shapur II doubled the tax assessment for Persian Christians, and when Simeon, the bishop of Ctesiphon, refused, he was put to death amidst a savage persecution. It was clear that war was coming: Constantius continued to fortify Amida, he increased the numbers of cataphracts in the eastern *comitatus*, and he bolstered the infantry with thousands of Goths. Julian wrote approvingly of Constantius and gave a striking image of Roman cataphracts, whose armour included 'a metal mask which makes its wearer look like a glittering statue' (*Orations*, 1, 37C = *REF1* §7.2.3). Constantius also won praise from the author of the *Itinerary of Alexander*, who compared the emperor's impending campaign against the Persians to the victorious efforts of Alexander the Great and Trajan (*Itinerary of Alexander*, 1 = *REF1* §7.3.1). In 346, Shapur made a second attempt to capture Nisibis, but failed to take the city. He did manage to capture thousands of prisoners, however; they were later ransomed by Babu, the city's bishop, with money raised from his congregation—an indication of the growing participation of Christian bishops in interstate politics and warfare. In either 344 or 348, the eastern *comitatus* fought a pitched battle at Singara, part of which was fought at night. Both sides emerged bruised and battered from what ended up as a narrow Roman defeat. In 350, Shapur launched his third attempt on Nisibis, diverting the waters of the river Mygdonius (the modern Jaghjagh) to undermine the walls, and using elephants to cow and intimidate the defenders. After four months of resolute resistance, the city's garrison, its clergy, and its citizens fought Shapur off. The Persian army was suffering from disease, and Shapur was also mindful of the pressure being exerted by the Chionites, a Hunnic people who were harassing Persia's unstable north-eastern frontier. The resolute defiance of Nisibis was eulogised by Ephrem the Syrian (c. 306–73), a native of the city who attributed its continued preservation to divine favour. 'Nisibis is planted by the waters, waters secret and open,' wrote Ephrem lovingly in his Syriac *Songs of Nisibis*. 'Living streams are within her; a noble river without her / The river without deceived her; the fountain [holy baptism] within has preserved her' (13.18 = *REF1* §7.5.5).

In 350, Constantius faced a coup in Gaul launched by a *comes* named Magnentius, who had been born to Frankish parents beyond the Rhine. His troops made quick work of Constans, killing him at a city named for Constans's stepmother Helena, and then Magnentius invaded Italy. There Magnentius and his troops killed Constantine's nephew Nepotianus, who harboured royal pretensions of his own. In Illyricum, the *magister peditum* who had served Constans, Vetranio, was proclaimed emperor, an act that appears to have been encouraged by Constantius's sister, Constantina. At the end of December 350, Constantius met Vetranio at Naissus, and after Vetranio agreed to step down, he was allowed to live out his years in exile. 'An utter illiterate and quite dull-witted,' wrote Aurelius Victor scathingly of Vetranio, 'and consequently the worst choice because of his rustic stupidity' (*On the Caesars*, 41). In 351, with Magnentius still at large, Constantius appointed his cousin Constantius Gallus as Caesar and dispatched him to Antioch to watch the eastern frontier. Constantius and Magnentius subsequently met at Mursa, not far from Cibalae, where Constantine and Licinius had clashed in 316. The battle was notorious in antiquity for its dreadful body count—24,000 of Magnentius's 36,000 alone, according to Zonaras (13.8)—but Magnentius survived and was able to retire to Italy with the survivors. On the heels of his victory Constantius called the Council of Sirmium, which promulgated his pro-Arian, anti-Nicene Christianity. The close link between the victory at Mursa and the Council of Sirmium reveals the extent to which Constantius's vision of the empire was tied to his understanding of the Christian faith, as well as his desire to centralise control over religious orthodoxy and maintain divine favour. In 352 and 353, Constantius defeated Magnentius twice more, and Magnentius and his brother Decentius committed suicide. One of the men decorated in the aftermath of Constantius's victory was Silvanus, a Frankish officer who had served under Magnentius, but who had defected during the Mursa campaign. Silvanus's father, Bonitus, had served Constantine I as *magister militum* in the conflict with Licinius in 324, and both men—and, indeed, Magnentius himself—reflect the way in which talented Germanic warriors were being promoted to senior military commands in the late Roman army.

In the meantime, not content with the subordinate role that Constantius clearly envisaged for him, Gallus proceeded to sabotage himself in Antioch. He fell out with his praetorian prefect, Thalassius, and when Gallus tried to have the *boule* of Antioch put to the sword, his *comes orientis*, Honoratus, refused to carry out the order. Thalassius subsequently died, and his replacement delivered a summons for Gallus to attend an audience with his senior partner in Italy. Gallus took offence at being ordered about by Constantius, and his body-guard executed the new praetorian prefect and the imperial quaestor who accompanied him. Gallus eventually agreed to meet Constantius in 354, but when he reached Histria in Moesia II, he was arrested by his former guard commander, Barbatio. He was then taken to Pola, near Aquileia, where he was subjected to intensive questioning by Constantius's palatine chamberlain, the powerful eunuch Eusebius, together with his *notarius*, Pentadius. Eunuchs and *notarii* were regularly entrusted with delicate assignments and, through their privileged access to the emperor, achieved significant influence. Having ascertained that Gallus had no excuses for his poor behaviour, they reported their findings to Constantius and Gallus was executed. Nor was Gallus the only problem: Constantius was having diffi-culty persuading the western bishops to accept his vision of the Christian faith announced at the Council of Sirmium. Athanasius was condemned at a new gathering of bishops in Mediolanum in 355, and the bishop of Rome, Liberius, was driven into exile after an uncomfortable interview with the eunuch Eusebius. Silvanus also fell from grace, due to a series of forged letters that portrayed him as seditious and disloyal. When Frankish officers in the *scholae palatinae* defended him, they too were targeted. Silvanus eventually declared himself emperor, but after he took refuge in a church, he was killed on Easter Sunday in 355 by Ursicinus, the *magister equitum* of Oriens, who had been entrusted to the task by the emperor.

Constantius and Julian

After defeating Magnentius, Constantius realised that he needed to appoint a new junior partner to stabilise the Rhine frontier. The candidate closest to his own blood was Julian, the half-brother of Gallus and nephew of Constantine I. Julian had been educated by a eunuch named Mardonius, who taught him Homer, and the pagan Antiochene sophist Libanius; he had also been inducted into the Eleusinian Mysteries, like Hadrian and Marcus Aurelius before him. Julian was profoundly influenced by his non-Christian teachers, especially a stint spent learning philosophy in Pergamum from Aedesius, whose own teacher had been the Neoplatonist philosopher Iamblichus. Aedesius introduced Julian to Maximus of Ephesus, a Neoplatonist who was a key influence on Julian's eventual decision to abandon Christianity. Under the authoritarian rule of Constantius, Julian maintained a veneer of support for Christianity, and only later did he openly espouse his pagan beliefs and his reverence for the great pagan emperors of the past; for this, he would earn the scornful epithet 'the apostate' from hostile Christian writers.

After a period of house arrest in Nicomedia, then a more pleasant interlude in Athens, Julian was elevated to the rank of Caesar in 355 and married Constantius's sister, Helena. The former *comes orientis* Honoratus was promoted to praetorian prefect and accompanied Julian to Gaul, where Julian was constrained by a rulebook provided by Constantius that even restricted his diet: pheasants and udders were off the menu, but at least Constantius's wife, Eusebia, allowed Julian a copy of Caesar's *Gallic Wars* to give him some background (Ammianus, 16.5 & Julian, *Letters*, 26, 414c). The following year, Julian campaigned against the Alamanni and the Franks in company with Ursicinus and the historian Ammianus, who was a member of Ursicinus's staff. The campaigns of 356 regained Colonia Agrippinensium, which had been captured by the Alamanni in 355. In 357, Julian and his new *magister militum* Severus set off up the Rhine, while Barbatio took a large army into Barbaricum from Raetia. Barbatio was defeated but, left to face the full strength of the Alamanni under their king Chnodomarius, Julian won a famous victory at Strasbourg despite being heavily outnumbered. In the aftermath of their unexpected victory, his giddy troops tried to elevate him to Augustus, but he refused. Yet by 358 Julian was writing letters to his philosopher friends in Pergamum, describing prophetic visions that marked him out for greater glory.

In the interim, Constantius had visited Rome in 357, where he celebrated a triumph for Julian's victories. He again signalled his intentions towards imposing religious unity in the empire when he controversially removed the statue of Nike from the senate house. This had been within the senate house since the third century BC, and Augustus had embellished it following the Actium campaign to create what was known as the Altar of Victory. Constantius's haughty behaviour caused irritation: 'he desired to display an inordinately long procession, banners stiff with gold work, and the splendour of his retinue,' wrote Ammianus scathingly, 'to a populace living in perfect peace and neither expecting nor desiring to see this or anything like it' (16.10). Constantius also became embroiled in another church controversy, with western and eastern bishops unable to find a compromise between those supporting the Nicene Creed in the west and those who had supported the creed developed by the Council of Sirmium. Tensions ran high; Hilary of Poitiers, a bitter critic of Constantius, regarded the emperor as the Antichrist. Eventually, a settlement was found that became known as the Homoean Creed, and duly announced at another council, this time at Constantinople in 360.

In 357, peace negotiations had been opened with the Persians (without Constantius's immediate knowledge) by the praetorian prefect of Oriens, Strategius Musonianus. Together with Cassianus, the *dux Mesopotamiae*, Strategius made contact with Tamshapur, one of Shapur's governors, suggesting that Shapur agree to terms with Constantius so the Persians could bring all of their strength to bear against the Chionites. The desire behind this was not to avoid a war with Persia, but rather to avoid the Romans having to face a two-front conflict, since Constantius was campaigning on the Danube in tandem with Julian's efforts in Gaul. As it turned out, however, Tamshapur had a good source of information in the shape of one Antoninus, who was a *protector* in the office of Cassianus. He had kept careful notes about which units had been withdrawn to serve with Constantius in Illyricum, and was feeding this information to Tamshapur, to whom he subsequently defected in 358. The Roman 'peace offer' was thus immediately rumbled, and when Shapur—who had defeated the Chionites—opened negotiations with Constantius through an envoy, he demanded that Armenia and Mesopotamia be returned or face a fresh invasion.

Constantius stalled for time by dispatching two embassies to Shapur, one of which was made up of envoys whose low rank was calculated to cause offence, while the other was a thinly disguised spy mission. He had also decided that Ursicinus, who had been returned to service in the east, would be recalled to Europe to replace Barbatio, who had been executed following a conspiracy. Ursicinus's subordinate, Sabinianus, was promoted to the position of *magister equitum per Orientem*. Despite these preparations, however, Constantius had remained in Illyricum dealing with quarrelsome bishops rather than moving his *comitatus* eastwards, and he had also misread Shapur's intentions. Constantius expected that Shapur would once again waste his energies around Nisibis or make for the crossing at Zeugma and invade Syria; however, the Persian king, who was aware that Ursicinus had been summoned to Constantius's court in Illyricum and that Sabinianus was not well regarded, decided to bypass Singara and Nisibis, and lay siege to Amida. Having been turned into a bastion by Constantius, Amida was a prestige target, and its capture would leave Armenia and Cappadocia critically vulnerable.

As Shapur marched out of Persia with a large army bolstered by the recently cowed Chionites and a levy from Caucasian Albania, Ursicinus received instructions to return to the east and serve as *magister peditum* under Sabinianus, and Ammianus, on his staff, returned with him. On the march to Nisibis, Ammianus saw the campfires of the enemy and narrowly avoided being taken captive by the Persian vanguard; after being separated from Ursicinus, Ammianus then retired to Amida, where once again roving cavalry patrols came close to capturing him. Shapur may eventually have planned to bypass Amida, but the son of the king of the Chionites was shot and killed by a ballista from the city's walls and Shapur was obliged to avenge him. From within Amida's formidable defences and in the company of seven legions, Ammianus described the Roman scorpions hurling heavy stones at the Persian attackers, smashing heads and sowing chaos in the Persian lines. He also described the efforts of Roman medics to save soldiers who had been shot with arrows and whose limbs had been mangled by Persian artillery (19.2). The contest proved to be uneven. As the siege progressed, the Persians built a siege ramp of the sort used to capture Dura-Europos, although on a far larger scale, and after Sabinianus forbade Ursicinus to bring reinforcements, Amida was stormed amidst an indiscriminate slaughter of soldiers and civilians alike. Ammianus himself escaped through a postern gate in the walls as darkness fell over the smoking city, and he eventually made his way to safety in Antioch. The brutal sack of Amida continued as he fled, and the Persians tortured and executed the city's commandant and his entire command staff (Ammianus, 19.1–9).

After the loss of Amida, Constantius, in desperate need of troops, sent a *notarius* to Julian, instructing him to send reinforcements eastwards. Wintering at Lutetia Parisii (Paris), Julian had successfully sown discord amongst his troops, who were unhappy at the prospect of an eastern war far from their families. The result was a coup veiled as a spontaneous mutiny, and Julian was proclaimed Augustus in a Germanic ceremony in which he was raised aloft on a shield. As he awaited Julian's reply, Constantius faced a fresh Persian campaign that delivered further blows to his position. Singara was captured along with its garrison of I Parthica and I Flavia Constantina (although I Parthica, perhaps reconstituted, later appeared at Constantina (Tella/Viranşehir in Osrhoene) in the fifth century). Cassius Dio had long ago displayed scepticism about the value of the northern Mesopotamian salient of Singara and its satellite fortresses (75.3), and Ammianus wrote that Singara was always difficult to hold due to the lack of water. Despite its value as an advanced base to give early warning of a Persian attack, 'this was a detriment to the Roman cause, since the place was several times taken with the loss of its defenders' (20.6). The Romans also lost the fortress of Bezabde (Bet Zabdai) and the smaller fort of Phoenicia, both of which occupied a strategic position on the Upper Tigris shortly before the river turned to follow a more southerly route. A strong garrison of three legions defended Bezabde—II Flavia, II Armeniaca, and II Parthica—but they were unable to withstand the Persian siege. Once again, the Roman ballistae and scorpions hurled arrows, rocks, and flaming missiles set ablaze with pitch, but the Persians breached the walls and a terrible slaughter ensued (Ammianus, 20.7). A desperate Roman attempt to regain Bezabde was unsuccessful, and the Syriac *Acts of the Martyrs of Bezabde* recorded the suffering of its largely Christian population at Persian hands. In the aftermath of these disasters, Ursicinus was fired and Ammianus subsequently found himself without a job. Meanwhile as Constantius's misfortunes continued to mount, and following the failure of Julian's eunuch Eutherius to convince Constantius of his right to rule, Julian openly took the title of Augustus and defiantly celebrated the fifth anniversary of his 'rule' at Vienne. With civil war looming and the conflict with the Persians looking grim, Constantius died in Cilicia, in November 361, on his way to contest the empire with Julian.

Julian, who was now sole emperor, arrived in Constantinople in December 361 and remained there for the winter. His official persona, as reflected in his own writings, the *Orations* of Libanius, and the history of Ammianus, was a *primus inter pares* warrior- and philosopher-king. Ammianus compared Julian favourably to Trajan (24.3) and Alexander the Great (21.8), as well as to Titus, Antoninus Pius, and Marcus Aurelius (16.1), while the church historian Socrates Scholasticus (b. 380) thought Julian believed he was a reincarnation of Alexander himself (*Ecclesiastical History*, 3.21). Julian was a devout ascetic who refrained from over-indulgence and sex, leading his troops in person and sharing their privations. 'He was a man truly to be numbered with the heroic spirits,' wrote Ammianus—who was also never afraid to criticise him for his defects—'distinguished for his illustrious deeds and his inborn majesty' (25.4). At Strasbourg, Julian 'was courageous in the face of the greatest dangers', and once he had captured Chnodomarius he treated him with chivalry and allowed him to live out his days in Rome (16.12). Julian's coinage depicted him with a beard that would have satisfied the great philosophers and Roman emperors like Hadrian and Marcus Aurelius (Figure 13.1)—and, indeed, the shades of the Second Sophistic permeated Libanius's speeches to his philosopher-king: in one address to Julian, for instance, Libanius celebrated the return of 'reverence for the practice of eloquence' (*Orations*, 13.1).

In the same speech, Libanius emphasised Julian's credentials as the warrior who had crushed the Alamanni, and highlighted the role of Athena, 'your comrade in counsel and

Figure 13.1 Gold solidus struck in Antioch in 362/63. Obverse: bearded bust of Julian; reverse: Roman soldier, with the legend VIRTVUS EXERCITVS ROMANORVUM, 'virtue of the army of the Romans'.

partner in action', in bringing about his victory in explicit opposition to Christ (13.28). Once Constantius was dead, Julian openly promoted the traditional gods and his own piety towards them. He wrote in a letter to Maximus of Ephesus in 363 that the gods 'command me to purify everything that I can, and I obey them with zeal' (*Letters*, 26, 451a–d). The intensity of his piety made Julian a prodigious sacrificer of animals, even in periods of shortage. Julian's piety and his devotion to Mithras made the troops feel that the Roman army was invincible: when the Goths threatened, Julian mocked them, saying that 'he was looking for a better enemy' (Ammianus, 22.7). The Persians had been placed on notice. 'This is my prayer,' wrote Libanius, 'that our army may feast in Susa with Persians waiting upon them' (*Orations*, 12.100).

Arriving in Constantinople, Julian's immediate preoccupation was a vicious purge of Constantius's officials and confidants in retaliation for the death of his father and Gallus, his half-brother, as well as from his desire to cut what he saw as waste in government. A series of show trials resulted in the banishment or execution of numerous high-ranking members of the palatine bureaucracy, including the malicious *agens in rebus* Paul 'the Chain', who was burned at the stake; others, thought Ammianus, deserved a better fate and he criticised Julian for his severity (22.3). Some of Julian's behaviour, indeed, left his contemporaries bewildered: he levied a penalty of ten pounds of gold on himself for illegally freeing several slaves, and moved with distinctly non-regal haste across the floor of the senate to greet his mentor, Maximus of Ephesus. When Julian moved on to Antioch, he caused offence by taking only a passing interest in the chariot races, which occupied a near-sacrosanct place in Antiochene society. He also forced many of those who had earned exemptions from curial duties back onto municipal councils. Julian's most contentious conduct, however, was his attempt to restore traditional religions to the place they had occupied in Roman society prior to Constantine. He would not prevent Christians from worshipping their God, and in his attempt to move the remains of a martyr named Babylas, whose powers were interfering with the ability of a local oracle to make pronouncements, he revealed his understanding and acceptance of Christianity, but he was determined to pull Christianity back from its lofty place in Roman society. Julian thus restored the

Altar of Victory to the senate house in Rome, and on February 4, 362, he issued an edict of toleration. This time, however, the freedom of worship primarily benefited pagans, rather than Christians. Some of the perks that Constantine had allowed for the clergy and churches were cancelled, the Second Temple was to be rebuilt to prove that Jesus had 'lied' in his prediction of its destruction (only for the restoration to be halted by mysterious natural disasters), and Julian decreed that only pagans could teach literature and rhetoric, to avoid polluting these important subjects with Christian ideas. Julian was inconsistent in his pronouncements and contributed to a climate of fear, especially in Alexandria, where his former Christian tutor, George of Cappadocia, had been lynched in the street. Failing to censure his murderers, he gave the impression that killing Christians for their impiety was acceptable behaviour. His official belief in freedom of worship was also contradicted by his refusal to help the people of Nisibis when it was menaced in 362, and his threat to confiscate funds from the churches in Edessa. Both cities were centres for Syriac Christianity, and his refusals were couched in intimidating language that specifically targeted Christians. In this strange environment, Athanasius was restored to Alexandria, but when Julian found that the patriarch was actively working against him, he drove him into exile once again.

In the spring of 362, Julian left Constantinople for Antioch, from where he would lead the campaign against the Persians. His intention, revealed in a letter written by Libanius, appeared to be to replace Shapur II with his brother-in-law, Hormisdas, who had fled to Constantine in 323 (*Letters*, 1402). Ammianus wrote that Julian was also inspired by dreams of the glory that would come with the name *Parthicus* after a victorious campaign in Persia (22.12). Julian's stay in Antioch was unhappy: the arrival of his *comitatus* increased financial hardship in a city that was already suffering from food shortages, and his active promotion of pagan rites won him few friends. The emperor was subjected to rhythmic chanting by the Antiochene populace that called on God to destroy 'His enemies'—a thinly veiled reference to the emperor and his entourage. Worse was to come when the Antiochenes publicly ridiculed Julian's beard. The emperor dealt with this by penning a satirical pamphlet, the *Misopogon*—'the Beard-Hater', which he arranged to be posted on the Tetrapylon of the Elephants in the city. While it poked fun at himself, it also contained a threatening undertone towards Antioch and its population, and he declared his intention for Tarsus, not Antioch, to be his principal residence in the east following his campaign in Persia.

Julian rebuffed peace offers from Shapur and left for the war at the head of an army of some 65,000 men, accompanied by a riverine fleet carrying supplies, baggage, and equipment. The main effort was directed towards Ctesiphon, while a diversionary column was sent with his relative, Procopius, through Armenia. Moving down the Euphrates, Ammianus recorded passing Dura-Europos, where the army feasted on deer hunted in its deserted streets (24.1). Libanius thought the campaign began well enough: he wrote that Julian was running rampant across Persia, sacking towns and taking so many prisoners that they were overwhelming the Romans' ability to deal with them (*Letters*, 1367). The truth was less promising. As Julian pressed towards his goal, he found the Persian commanders flooding the land around the Nahrmalcha, the ancient canal that linked the Euphrates and Tigris rivers. The emperor also suffered from a monumental failure of intelligence. When Julian reached Ctesiphon at the end of May, he found both it and Coche (Veh Ardashir) heavily defended, and his own siege equipment was inadequate to capture either. 'From this point,' wrote Gregory of Nazianzus, the future patriarch of Constantinople and a fierce opponent of Julian, 'like sand slipping from beneath the feet, or a great storm bursting upon a ship, things began to go black for him' (*Orations*, 5.10). Julian abandoned the siege, and since he knew that the strong current of the Euphrates and Tigris rivers would make returning to the north by ship all but impossible, he burned his fleet and all of the army's baggage. Julian was also unable to return on foot via the Euphrates because of the heavy flooding along the Nahrmalcha, so he was forced to take a more perilous route alongside the Tigris, hoping to reach the safety of Nisibis. Shapur harassed the Roman army as it struggled northwards, picking away at the rear guard, and it was in one of these engagements that Julian was killed near Samarra on June 26, 363. Christian writers cheered the death of their hated emperor: Ephrem the Syrian penned one of the more memorable celebrations with his responsorial Syriac *Hymn Against Julian*, inviting his congregation to chant responses that included 'Blessed be he who blotted him out' (2.15) and 'Praise to him who clothed his corpse in shame' (3.1).

The Roman army was leaderless, riven by factions who distrusted each other and stranded in enemy territory. After some debate and the refusal of the praetorian prefect, Salutius, to accept the position of emperor, Jovian was appointed as Julian's successor. Born in 331, Jovian was the 'untried youth' scorned by Ammianus at the head of this chapter (25.9). He had served as a *protector domesticus*; now, placed in an impossible situation, far from home and running out of food, Jovian won safe passage from Shapur, but at the cost of Singara, Nisibis, and several Armenian border districts that were ceded to the Persians. Nisibis itself was completely evacuated, and in yet another large-scale, involuntary, and catastrophic population transfer, its inhabitants went into exile at Amida. In addition to these losses, Jovian's peace, agreed for 30 years, also surrendered the network of fortifications between Singara and Bezabde that, like the Euphrates defences south of Dura-Europos, had proven inadequate to resist a determined invasion. The frontier between Rome and Persia thus reverted to the Euphrates and the Khabur rivers, where it remained until the final Romano-Persian conflict of the seventh century (Figure 13.2).

Ammianus (25.7) and others (e.g. Zosimus, *New History*, 3.33) scorned Jovian's weakness in making this arrangement with Shapur. The loss of Nisibis was certainly a dreadful blow, since it deprived the Romans of the ability to move quickly against Adiabene and Assyria, and removed the customs monopoly that the Romans had enjoyed. It also gave the Persians a ready-fortified strategic perch overlooking Mesopotamia, and made their interference in Armenia both more feasible and more likely. John Chrysostom, a former student of Libanius and patriarch of Constantinople from 398 to 403, was livid with rage over the loss of 'the most secure of all our fortresses, which acted as an unbreachable circuit wall to our empire' (*Homily on St Babylas against Julian and the pagans*, 124 = *REF1* Ch. 9B). For Ephrem, the loss of his home city was a terrible blow, and accounted for much of his anger towards Julian. Ammianus was present when Nisibis was handed over to the Persians, and he wrote bitterly of the anger and sorrow amongst the population and their disbelief at what Jovian had done. 'When all were commanded to leave their homes at once,' he wrote, 'with tears and outstretched hands they begged that they might not be compelled to depart ... lamentation and grief filled the city, and in all parts no sound save universal wailing was to be heard' (25.8). The peace agreement, however, lasted for a surprisingly long time, and it was not until the reign of Anastasius (Chapter 14) that serious and prolonged hostilities returned to the eastern theatre. Jovian also sought to bring peace to the church, inviting Athanasius into his entourage and promoting the Nicene Creed. Jovian did not live long enough to see the benefits of his policies, however: he suffocated

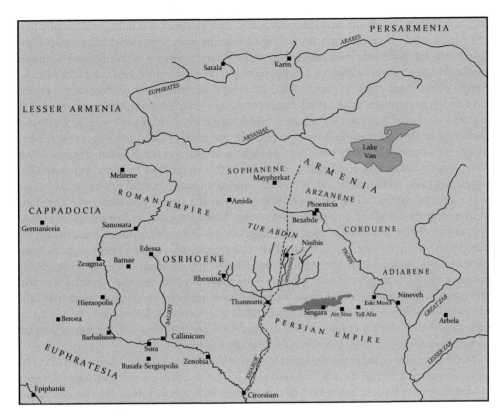

Figure 13.2 Mesopotamia and Osrhoene in the peace settlement of 363. The dashed line represents the new border between Rome and Persia.

Source: Illustration by the author.

to death in an overheated room at Dadastana in Bithynia in the early winter of 364. Julian's funeral took place at Tarsus. A furious and grief-stricken Libanius delivered the funeral oration, railing against Constantius for Julian's failure.

Valentinian I and Valens

On Jovian's death, Salutius was again offered the imperial throne, and again he rejected it. Jovian was instead replaced by Valentinian, a middle-aged *protector* and veteran of Julian's Gallic wars from Cibalae who was serving with the *scholae palatinae*. Ammianus thought poorly of him, remarking that he kept 'two savage, man-eating she-bears, one called Goldflake and the other Innocence' (29.3). In a feisty meeting of the *consistorium*, Valentinian chose as a partner his younger brother, Valens, about whom Ammianus harboured similarly negative views—a man of 'monstrous savagery', he thought (29.1). Afterwards, there was a purge of Julian's associates. Maximus of Ephesus was exiled (and later executed by Valens), and soldiers were sent to seize Procopius. The empire was divided, with Valens appointed to the eastern prefecture of Oriens and Valentinian the west, including the prefectures of

Gallia and Italy, Africa, and Illyricum. (The organisation of the united prefecture of Italy, Africa, and Illyricum frequently changed, and at various times was Italy alone, or just Italy and Africa, while Illyricum was from time to time its own prefecture). Valentinian I and Valens also integrated the various civilian and military positions and ranks into a unified whole, ending the segregation of specific posts reserved for equestrians which had been a feature of the third century. This had the effect of diminishing the prestige of the equestrian order: exemptions from curial duties previously given to *perfectissimi* were now only given to senatorial *clarissimi*, for instance, and high-ranking *perfectissimi* such as *duces* were promoted to the status of *clarissimus*. In general, the positions and privileges that used to be given to equestrians were now only given to senators, and the Roman aristocracy was once again a senatorial body that performed both civilian and military functions. The equestrian ranks still existed, and in 384 the emperor Gratian would subdivide them into seven separate grades, while some positions, such as the *praeses* of Mauretania Tingitana, remained in the hands of equestrian *perfectissimi*; however, status and privilege were now the near-exclusive purview of men of senatorial rank. These changes also resulted in the subdivision of the senatorial order into three classes: *clarissimi* (sg. *clarissimus*) at the bottom; *spectabiles* (sg. *spectabilis*) in the middle; and *illustres* (sg. *illustris*) at the very top. Rank inflation meant that most senior officials—the *magister officiorum*, the imperial quaestor, numerous *comites*, prefects and some *magistri*—were elevated to the top senatorial rank of *illustris*. When Ausonius, Gratian's tutor, made a speech to celebrate his consulship, he presented the equestrian order as a relic of a previous era (*Gratian*, 3). The patronage of the emperor—always crucial—was now all that really mattered.

There were also changes for the church, despite Valentinian's studied disinterest in ecclesiastical matters. Liberius died in 366, and riots in Rome between the factions of different candidates vying for the bishopric killed hundreds. In Mediolanum, a Nicene newcomer named Ambrose became bishop after his unpopular predecessor died in 374. As the son of the praetorian prefect to Constantine II, Ambrose had come to his position via a circuitous route that included a stint as the consular official in charge of the northern Italian province of Aemilia and Liguria. He had the backing of his former superior, the praetorian prefect for Italy, Africa, and Illyricum, Petronius Probus, who was a friend of the eventual victor for the bishopric in Rome, Damasus. Once in office, Ambrose worked to influence other important sees such as Sirmium, where he ensured that a Nicene bishop was selected, while in Mediolanum, he began work on the church known today as the Basilica of Sant'Ambrogio. In the east, Valens's policies towards Christianity differed from those of his brother, for the bishops and patriarchs in the east still maintained the Homoean creed developed under Constantius. Valens's detractors belittled him as an 'Arian', particularly as his dislike of certain Nicene bishops grew under the influence of Eudoxius, the patriarch of Constantinople. Valens also earned the ire of Nicene Christians when he intervened in the succession dispute that followed the death of Athanasius in 373, deposing the choice made by Alexandrian partisans of Athanasius and installing the Homoean Lucius instead.

The growth of asceticism

Athanasius was the author of a hagiography of Antony, the very first *vita* of a Christian holy man. Antony was an ascetic, indeed one of the earliest Christian ascetics to withdraw from society to pursue a life of contemplation and prayer. From his position in the desert,

Antony grew close to God, battling demons and acquiring expertise at healing. The fourth, fifth, and sixth centuries witnessed an explosion of ascetic and monastic activity, principally in the deserts of Egypt and the Levant close to major population centres. Monasticism involved both men and women living in large, organised communities such as the White Monastery in Egypt (whose abbot, Shenute, viciously condemned the continued practice of pagan sacrifice), in communities known as *lauras*, or even individually in cities or in the countryside. Asceticism developed as an important choice for elite women, because it subverted the traditional Roman expectations of gender roles and provided an alternative of sorts, reflected in the way celibacy and chastity, often punished by earlier Roman law, were eventually protected by it (e.g. *Theodosian Code*, 8.16.1). For instance, Pulcheria, the sister of Theodosius II (408–50) and wife of the emperor Marcian (450–57), chose chastity and persuaded her sisters to do the same. Pulcheria also emerged as a patron of Christian buildings and holy sites, providing a way for imperial women to exercise political influence. Melania the Younger, who was an important influence on Theodosius's wife Eudocia (below) and a friend of Augustine, retired to the desert after family tragedy left her childless; a representative of the late antique mass-landowning and slave-owning senatorial aristocracy, she sold her land and her slaves and gave away her vast fortune, reflecting the church's growing interest in philanthropy. Another important female pilgrim was Egeria, who travelled to Palestine in 381–84. The participation of women in late antique Christianity was also bolstered by the development of the cult of the Virgin, which celebrated Mary's purity. This became particularly important given the pejorative viewpoint held by some Christian hardliners, such as Ambrose, that women were tainted through their association with Eve (*Commentary on Paul's First Letter to the Corinthians*, 148 = *RLA*, p. 228).

Asceticism could be practised with excessive zeal, and ascetics known as *boskoi* lived in the countryside like wild animals, surviving on what little food and shelter nature provided. Asceticism was not a Christian innovation—the self-imposed deprivation practised by Christian ascetics echoed that of their pagan, philosophical counterparts, such as Porphyry, who followed a vegetarian diet and abstained from sex. Influenced by the Neoplatonists, Julian had also followed a restrictive lifestyle, Constantius II was 'master of his eating habits, of every passion and all his desires' (Aurelius Victor, *On the Caesars*, 42), and Manichaeism also had an important ascetic component. A favourite topic of Christian hagiographies was, nevertheless, the struggle to maintain the ascetic regime. In his hagiography of St Malchus, for instance, Jerome wrote about his capture by Arab raiders (suitably savage, the better to highlight Malchus's purity) on the road to Beroea (Aleppo), after which Malchus was consigned to herd sheep in the company of a mysterious female companion, parachuted into the story to set Malchus a spiritual challenge (*Life of Malchus*, 4–5 = *AEBI* §6.3). Some monks and ascetics achieved international celebrity status for their self-discipline and miraculous connections to God. Constantine, Constans, and Constantius II all corresponded with Antony, but the most famous ascetic of all was Symeon the Stylite (d. 459), who took up residence at the top of a pillar in northern Syria; crowds flocked to see him from all over the ancient world. When he died, 'the Antiochenes chanted and demanded the body of the righteous man', and his body was borne in state through the streets of Antioch in the presence of the *magister militum per Orientem* (*Easter Chronicle*, p. 593).

Theodoret, the bishop of Cyrrhus (423–57), was the author of one of the numerous hagiographies of Symeon and remarked on his ability to convert entire crowds and heal

Figure 13.3 Clay token from the shrine of Symeon the Stylite.

the sick. The Syriac hagiography of Symeon described a visit to the saint by Naaman, a Nasrid Arab in Persian service. Worried that his men would defect if they spent too much time with the saint, Naaman forbade them to do so, but Symeon entered Naaman's dreams that night and delivered a dreadful beating, after which, confined to his bed, Naaman changed his mind and became an enthusiastic supporter (*Syriac Life of Symeon*, 67 = *AEBI* §6.11). Elsewhere, St Thekla's shrine at Seleucia also became a major attraction, and received imperial attention when it was refurbished by the emperor Zeno (474–91). Celebrity status of the sort enjoyed by Symeon invited mass pilgrimage, leading to the growth of reception centres adjacent to major pilgrimage sites to feed and house pilgrims and provide medical care. Such centres also churned out relics and keepsakes, such as clay discs featuring images of Symeon the Stylite the Younger, the sixth-century namesake of Symeon the Stylite (Figure 13.3).

Monks and ascetics could become influential political actors, and also emerged as important agents of Christianisation for peripheral communities such as the Arabs of the desert. Sozomen (d. 448) told the story of an Arab chieftain named Zokomos, for instance, who converted to Christianity when 'a certain monk of great celebrity' cured his wife's infertility. Zokomos and his people signed on as military allies fighting for Rome in the aftermath of this medical miracle (*Ecclesiastical History*, 6.38 = *AEBI* §6.2). Another story involved one Aspebetus, an Arab *émigré* from the Persian empire encountered by St Euthymius in the Palestinian desert in c. 420. Aspebetus's son Terebon was grievously ill, and Persian magi had failed to cure him. Eventually Aspebetus gained an audience with Euthymius. The holy man healed Terebon, offered Aspebetus and his people catechism for 40 days and nights, and, after baptising them, freed them from their 'older' identities and brought them into the civilised, Roman *oikumene*. He laid out a church, a bakery, and other accoutrements that the Romans associated with settled life. The story is laden with rhetoric, all the more to show the power of the Christian God, but Aspebetus—who became Peter on conversion—appears as a signatory at the Council of Ephesus in 431, as bishop of the *Parembole*, the 'encampments' (Cyril of Scythopolis, *Life of St Euthymius*, 10 & 15 = *AEBI* §6.13 & §6.14).

The church complex that grew up around the pillar of Symeon the Stylite lay within an extensive zone of rural settlement that prospered in the fifth and sixth centuries,

Figure 13.4 Christian sarcophagi in the fields of Serjilla in north-western Syria.

Source: Photograph by the author.

underwritten by the stability of the eastern empire. Over 700 abandoned villages date from this period, the so-called 'Dead Cities' scattered throughout the Belus massif in north-western Syria. Nestled today among olive groves and surrounded by fields and orchards, these villages benefited from a renaissance in agricultural trade that linked them to markets throughout Egypt and the Levant. The wide distribution of Late Roman type I amphorae, many of which were manufactured around Antioch and have turned up in Gaul, Africa, Italy, and across the eastern Mediterranean, is likely connected with trade in Syrian olive oil and wine; within many of the ancient Syrian villages lie the remains of the infrastructure for olive oil manufacture and for pressing fruit and grapes. Ancient terraced fields for crops and mangers for livestock point to a diversity of agricultural produce, the surplus of which would have also found a ready market in the nearby cities of Antioch, Beroea, and Apamea. The villages are also notable for their strong Christian character, with over 1,200 churches, as well as monasteries and Christian cemeteries (Figures 13.4 and 13.5).

The road to Adrianople

After a serious illness in 367, Valentinian appointed his son Gratian as Augustus towards the end of the summer. Britannia came under serious attack from a force of Picts and

Figure 13.5 The village of al-Bara, surrounded by olive groves. The village includes a late Roman pyramidal tomb and the remains of a church (left).

Source: Photograph by the author.

Scotti that bypassed Hadrian's Wall, which was only thinly garrisoned and seems to have been abandoned not long afterwards. The *dux Britanniarum* and the *comes litoris saxonici*, the *comes* who commanded the shore-based units that defended Britannia against raids from the North Sea and English Channel, were both killed. The raids were suppressed by a *comes rei militaris* named Theodosius, who was later sent to Africa as a newly minted *magister equitum* to deal with a dispute between Romanus, the *comes Africae*, and a Romano-Berber noble named Firmus. Theodosius was obliged to take troops from the Danube on his campaign, and Valentinian was busy on the Rhine in 366/67 campaigning against the Alamanni, after which he took the title *Alamannicus Maximus*. In the aftermath of this campaign, Valentinian began the last major renovation of the Rhine frontier, following the policy of establishing fortifications on the right bank, in enemy territory, and also made some changes on the Danube, where he conducted a similar repair and upgrade of the defensive network and moved the base of the riverine fleet to Vindobona. When the Quadi became restive in 374, Valentinian made peace with the Alamannic king, Macrianus, and transferred troops and equipment to eastern Europe in preparation for a long campaign. The Quadi responded by sending a delegation to Brigetio in 375; while they treated with Valentinian and his *consistorium*, the emperor, who was prone to violent rages, lost his temper with the Quadi envoys and suffered either a stroke or a cerebral hemorrhage, dying on November 17. Valentinian followed Jovian to be buried in the Church of the Holy Apostles, and Valentinian's *magister militum praesentalis*, a Frank named Merobaudes, acclaimed Gratian's half-brother, the four-year-old Valentinian, as Valentinian II. Incredibly, this decision was taken without consulting Valens, an act that would likely have been regarded as treasonous in an earlier era, but which was symbolic of the diverging fortunes of east and west. Merobaudes took the opportunity of the transition of power to settle an old score with Theodosius, who had fallen out with Merobaudes' patron Romanus, the *comes Africae*; a fast messenger reached Carthage with the order to execute Theodosius, whose son would, however, shortly become emperor (below). Gratian remained in Augusta Treverorum, from where Merobaudes kept watch on the Franks and Alamanni. Gratian elevated his friend and tutor, Ausonius, who was imperial quaestor in 375 and ordinary consul in 379.

While Valentinian, Theodosius, and Gratian had campaigned across a broad front between Britannia and Africa, Valens was facing unrest on the Danube. Wintering in Constantinople in 364/65 (where he ordered the construction of an aqueduct, much of which remains to its full height), Valens received reports about unrest among the Goths on the Danube and prepared his army to march westwards. His plans were delayed by a determined usurpation effort by Julian's relative, Procopius, who was portraying himself as a member of the Constantinian dynasty and a legitimate successor to Julian. Procopius was popular with the troops, and he quickly established himself in Thrace and suborned the eastern units that Valens had sent on ahead to reinforce the Lower Danube. Through his connection to Julian and Constantine, Procopius appealed to the Goths, reminding them that they could be called to fight for him under the treaty of 332. The Goths complied, and raised a force that they sent on to Procopius.

Procopius faced the army of the newly promoted *magister militum per Illyricum*, advancing from the west, and Valens, who was now moving quickly to intercept him. In the ensuing conflict, Valens defeated Procopius, cut off his head, and sent it to Valentinian; he then took revenge on the Gothic troops who had been on their way to join Procopius, disarming them and banishing them to Asia Minor. Valens followed this with a war of punishment against the Tervingi and their king, Athanaric, for supporting Procopius. He crossed the Danube in 367 at Constantiana Daphne via a pontoon bridge (suggesting that the Constantinian bridge at Sucidava was no longer maintained), and the emperor and his troops burned and sacked Gothic settlements, establishing numerous *quadriburgia* in hostile territory. After a Danube flood prevented operations in 368, Valens returned in 369, crossing the Danube at Noviodunum, pillaging and burning, then defeating Athanaric and the Tervingi on the battlefield. Valens spent the winter of 369/70 at Marcianople, and Athanaric, whose people were facing starvation and whose crucial commercial ties with the Romans had been suspended, asked for terms. According to Zosimus, Athanaric agreed that the Goths would not cross the Danube or molest Roman forces or fortifications (*New History*, 4.11). The treaty of 369 made a clear division between the Tervingi and the Romans: subsidies ended, commercial activity was heavily restricted, lines of communication were limited, and no demands for Gothic troops were made. There would nonetheless be contact between Romans and Goths, however, since Greek/Gothic translators were still being paid—but the inclusion of the Goths in Roman affairs envisioned by the treaty of 332 had come to an end. In the period following the peace agreement, Athanaric became suspicious of those Gothic Christians who had remained in Gothia, identifying them as a potential fifth column. Socrates Scholasticus suggested that Valens was taking advantage of the peace treaty to send missionaries across the Danube, which cannot have pleased Athanaric and surely further raised his suspicions (*Ecclesiastical History*, 4.33–4). The persecution that followed created a number of Gothic martyrs, the most famous of whom was St Saba, whose relics were eventually retrieved by the *dux Scythiae*, Soranus, and sent to a shrine in Cappadocia.

With peace on the Danube, Valens was free to respond to events in the east. Shapur II had taken the Roman client-king Arsaces (Arshak) III of Armenia prisoner in 368 and deposed the Roman client-king of Iberia, Sauromaces, replacing him with his own man, Aspacures. Arsaces was blinded, chained, and imprisoned in a sinister Persian fortress known as the Castle of Oblivion, where he later died (Ammianus, 27.12). His son, Pap, had taken refuge with the Romans, and the Armenians wanted him back; after some dithering, Pap was provocatively crowned in 370 by the *magister peditum praesentalis* Arinethaeus. Roman forces then returned Sauromaces to a portion of his former territory in Iberia. Roman and Persian forces came to open blows at Vagabanta in 371, but otherwise Shapur concentrated on corrupting Pap, who was murdered in 374/75 with Roman connivance and replaced by another Roman choice, Varazdat. A flurry of embassies in 376 and 377 attempted to clarify the status of Armenia and establish Persian control over Iberia, while Varazdat was driven out in 377 by Manuel Mamikonean, who was emerging as the power behind the Armenian throne. A new war was not far off when events on the Danube changed the complexion of the situation in the Caucasus.

The European Huns emerged into Roman historical consciousness at some point in the 370s, after they began to move westwards from the vast Inner Asian steppe northeast of the Caspian Sea. The Huns were nomadic pastoralists and dependent on good conditions to feed their animals and themselves; it is often thought that their migration was triggered by a change in climate that caused a 40-year drought between 338 and 377. The Huns comprised several distinct groups, including those who appeared in fourth-century Chinese sources; the Chionite and Kidarite Huns encountered by the Persians in central Asia in the fourth and fifth centuries; the Hephthalite (or 'White') Huns, who seized Sogdia after the mid-fifth century and killed the Sasanian king Peroz in 484; and the European Huns who tormented Goths, the Sarmatian Alans, and Romans. The Hunnic menace in the east caused Persian authorities to construct a fortification system east of the Caspian Sea, known as the Gorgan Wall (nearly 200 kilometres (124 miles) long), and the shorter Tammisheh Wall. None of these constituent groups of Huns was necessarily a homogenous community, ethnic or otherwise, and like the Quadi, Sarmatians, Goths, and others, there was frequent infighting and division. The European Huns encountered by the Romans included members of other communities that they had incorporated as they moved westward, and Peter Heather has suggested that Attila's Hunnic empire eventually contained Goths, Sarmatians, Alans, Sciri, Suebi, Rugi, and Gepids (*Age of Attila*, p. 221). It is likely that Roman deserters also found a place amongst the Huns, as the fragments of Olympiodorus suggest (= Photius, *Bibliotheca*, 80).

Ammianus wrote that the arrival of the Huns in western Eurasia exerted tremendous pressure on Rome's neighbours amongst the Goths and the Alans. At some point in the mid-fourth century, the Huns, who excelled at horse archery, clashed violently with their westward neighbours: Ammianus outlined in a compressed account how the Huns crushed

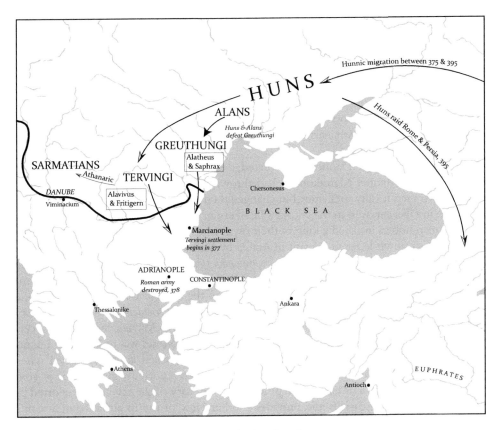

Figure 13.6 The situation in eastern Europe in the late fourth century.

Source: Illustration by the author.

the Alans and then absorbed the survivors, before meting out a similar fate to a Gothic group known as the Greuthungi. Despite the heroic exploits of the Greuthungi king, Ermanaric, the Huns and their new Alan allies destroyed the Greuthungi, whose survivors rallied around two leaders named Alatheus and Saphrax and withdrew to the Dniester river where they encountered the Tervingi and Athanaric (Ammianus, 31.3). Under Hunnic attack, Athanaric and the Tervingi retreated to the river Olt, and the Greuthungi disappeared from the historical sources until 377 (Figure 13.6).

In 376, a group of Tervingi led by two men, Alavivus and Fritigern, reached the Danube and Roman territory. Socrates Scholasticus alleged that Fritigern had become a Christian and fallen out with Athanaric, which might explain the latter's absence (*Ecclesiastical History*, 4.33–4). Fritigern requested permission to settle in Roman territory, and negotiations followed during which he pledged to abide by the requirements made in 369 that the Goths live peacefully. He also agreed to a new request to provide men to serve with the Roman army. For Valens, this new supply of manpower made it possible to embark on a decisive confrontation to solve the Armenian and Iberian issues, so the Tervingi's request was granted, along with the stipulation that those who were not already Christian convert to Valens's own brand of anti-Nicene, Homoean Christianity. Everything went wrong, however: there were too many Tervingi refugees for the Romans to accommodate safely, and Roman officials—principally the *comes rei militaris* Lupicinus and the *dux* Maximus—took advantage of their plight, starving and extorting them, and selling their children as slaves. As the Tervingi endured this criminal abuse, the Greuthungi under Alatheus and Saphrax arrived in 377, also asking for permission to cross the Danube. In desperation, Athanaric arrived with his own group of Tervingi shortly afterwards. Alatheus and Saphrax were refused permission; Athanaric read the situation and withdrew from the Danube into the Transylvanian Alps.

As the situation on the Danube deteriorated, there was grim news for Valens in the east. As noted above, Manuel Mamikonean had thrown out Varazdat in 377. The Armenians then pledged their loyalty to Shapur, but changed their mind when Shapur sent his general, Surena, to install a garrison in the country. The Persian force was annihilated on arrival and the Armenian nobles installed a king of their own, who would cling on for the next seven years. Valens meanwhile faced a revolt in Arabia by Mavia, an Arab queen whose husband had made a treaty with Valens to supply *hypospondoi* (*foederati*) to the Roman army. When Mavia's husband died, the treaty lapsed; Mavia launched a rebellion, 'by no means a contemptible one, although conducted by a woman', in the acerbic words of Sozomen, and Mavia inflicted a stinging defeat on the *magister militum per Orientem* (*Ecclesiastical History*, 6.38 = *AEBI* §1.26). Peace was won only through acceding to Mavia's demand that a certain Moses be consecrated to minister to her people. When Moses was ordained by Lucius, the Homoean patriarch of Alexandria, the rebellion intensified and only ended when Moses received a Nicene ordination; Mavia's daughter also reportedly married the *magister equitum praesentalis* Victor as part of the peace deal. The story of the revolt was reported by several ecclesiastical historians and provides another view of the importance of a shared faith in strengthening political ties and military cooperation. Mavia sent Arab warriors to Thrace; they later played a part in defending Constantinople from the Goths.

Lupicinus began to settle the Tervingi around Marcianople in the spring of 377, but as this was underway, Alatheus and Saphrax boldly crossed the Danube and camped on the right bank. Lupicinus invited Fritigern and Alavivus to a banquet at Marcianople, but while they were feasting together riots broke out between Goths and Romans in the city's streets. Fritigern was able to extricate himself, but Alavivus was never heard from again. Perceiving the 'banquet' (whether rightly or wrongly) as yet another Roman display of perfidy, Fritigern gathered the Tervingi, rejected the treaty arrangements of 376, and travelled northwards to the province of Scythia. The revolt spread and Lupicinus was badly beaten near Marcianople, losing his standard and most of his junior officers. Equipping themselves from the slaughtered Roman army, the Goths rampaged southwards to Adrianople, attracting the miserable and the opportunistic, other Goths, escaped slaves, *coloni*, and anyone with a grudge against Roman authority. Gothic units wintering at Adrianople, set upon by angry residents and members of the city *curia*, threw in their lot with the rebels, plundering the imperial arms factory in the city as they left. In the same year, Valens finally appreciated the rapidly deteriorating security situation and dispatched two trusted generals, Profuturus and Traianus, to Thrace. Gratian, also apprised of the revolt, sent his *comes domesticorum*, a Frank named Richomer, to offer assistance. The rebellion was an eastern matter, and Valentinian and Valens had set the precedent that intrusion from one sphere to another was best avoided, but Gratian was clearly worried that the revolt would destabilise the entire Danube frontier and affect the provinces bordering the western half of the empire. In 377, Richomer, Profuturus, and Traianus fought the Goths to a standstill at Ad Salices, but Profuturus lost his life in the battle. The Goths under Fritigern wintered in the fastness of the Haemus Mountains, where they were blockaded by Traianus and the recently arrived *magister equitum*, Saturninus. Starvation had worked against the Goths numerous times in the past, but Fritigern was able to break free of the trap and subsequently caused so much damage to Moesia and Scythia that Valens slashed their provincial tax bills (*Theodosian Code*, 7.6.3). Gratian's officers had better luck: Frigeridus, who had accompanied Richomer in 377 before falling ill, cordoned off the main routes leading westwards from Thrace, and Gratian, together with Richomer, gathered a large part of the western *comitatus* to come to Valens' aid. By the summer of 378 Valens was on his way to Adrianople, where Sebastianus, a retired *magister militum* who had campaigned against the Alamanni with Valentinian, had gathered the eastern *comitatus*.

Gratian's bid to help his uncle was delayed by an opportunistic Alamannic attack that forced him and his *comites* Mallobaudes and Nannienus to pause and fight the Alamanni and their king, Priarius, and then campaign across the Rhine to compel their submission. In the meantime, Roman scouts reported to Valens that the Goths numbered fewer than 10,000—a significant intelligence failure. After Valens joined Sebastianus at Adrianople, Richomer arrived with the western vanguard, bearing a dispatch from Gratian urging Valens to wait until the armies were combined. Valens, however, was jealous of Gratian's recent victory over the Alamanni and the *consistorium*'s debates proved inconclusive. Ammianus wrote that Sebastianus, who had won some small victories over foraging parties, pushed for immediate action, while Victor, the *magister equitum*, tried to convince his fellow officers to persuade Valens to wait (31.12). Zosimus, relying on the work of Eunapius, claimed that it was Sebastianus who urged caution (*New History*, 4.23). Fritigern was also jittery. Alatheus and Saphrax had not appeared, despite the numerous messages that had been sent requesting that they join him. Fritigern was also aware of the size of Valens's army and of the imminent arrival of the western *comitatus*, so he sent an embassy with a Christian priest asking for peace. In the end, however, Valens decided on action: on August 9, 378, he marched from Adrianople and brought the Goths to battle. Once again, Fritigern sent envoys to ask for terms, but this time, Ammianus wrote, it was a ruse, designed to wear out the tired and hungry Romans in the hot sun and torment them with thirst, worsened by the fires that the Gothic troops had set on the battlefield (31.12). Whether or not Fritigern then asked for terms is unclear, although Ammianus thought so, but the battle was soon joined by two units of the *scholae palatinae*, then the Greuthungi under Alatheus and Saphrax, together with a group of Alans, arrived on the scene and sowed confusion in the Roman lines. The Roman left wing was cut off and annihilated, and the remaining Roman infantry was crowded together 'so tightly that hardly anyone could pull out his sword or draw back his arm', leaving no way to defend against 'the arrows whirling death from every side' (Ammianus, 31.13). Valens was killed in the confusion along with the units of the *scholae palatinae*, and his body was never found—a fate, Eunapius claimed, that had been foretold by Maximus of Ephesus (*Lives of the Sophists*, 7.6). The dead also included Traianus, Sebastianus, and the son of Ammianus's old commander, Ursicinus. Richomer, Victor, and Saturninus fled as the remaining Roman troops were butchered. 'It is certain,' wrote Ammianus, 'that barely a third of our army escaped' (31.13).

Contemporaries immediately recognised that Adrianople marked the beginning of an extraordinarily difficult period for the Romans, and the tussle over who was actually to blame for the catastrophe played out in the histories of the period, reflected, for instance, in the different accounts of the advice given by Sebastianus in the *consistorium*. Ambrose cast the defeat in end-time, apocalyptic terms in 378/79 and again in 388 (*On Faith*, 1.137–8 & *Commentary on the Gospel according to Luke*, 10.10). Vegetius, whose *On Military Matters* was addressed to Valens's successor, Theodosius, implicitly criticised Valens's tactics in his recommendation that the army should remedy the sorts of errors that led to severe defeats. These included marching too great a distance on the day of battle, failing to gather adequate intelligence, and fighting an engagement when there were other, less risky options such as raiding or waiting for reinforcements (3.11, 3.9, 3.3). Another point that Vegetius made was that the army should cease its reliance on barbarian recruits, and instead fill its ranks with local men, another implicit criticism of Valens's recruiting policies (1 & 2). Libanius, however, rejected the charge that the army of 378 was somehow unfit for purpose. 'Let there be no talk of cowardice, weakness, or lack of training,' he wrote, 'the morale of the soldiers and their officers was like that of their ancestors, and they were inferior to them neither in skill nor training' (*Orations*, 24.5). The prevailing reaction, though, was angst-ridden gloom. Jerome terminated his *Chronicle* with a pessimistic report of the 'lamentable war in Thrace, in which the Roman legions, lacking the protection of horse, were surrounded by the Goths and slaughtered to extinction' (s.a. 378). The orator Themistius later wrote despondently of the 'Iliad of disasters' through which 'Thrace was overrun, Illyricum was overrun, armies vanished entirely, like shadows' (*Orations*, 16.206d). Ambrose and Gregory of Nazianzus sought a divine explanation, and blamed the Homoean assault on the Trinity (*On Faith*, 2.139 & *Orations*, 33.2), while Eunapius attributed the disaster to the perilous state of the empire. 'Strife, when it has grown,' he wrote at the time of the defeat, 'brings forth war and murder, and the children of murder are ruin and the destruction of the human race' (Blockley fr. 39.9).

Theodosius I

In the aftermath of Valens's catastrophic defeat, Gratian took in the survivors at Sirmium. The exuberant Goths besieged first Adrianople and then Constantinople itself, but without success; such was the disarray that the defence of the city was organised by Dominica, Valens's widow. The *magister militum* Julius, worried that the revolt would spread within the army, organised the wholesale massacre of Goths in Roman units (Zosimus, *New History*, 4.26). Gratian returned to Gaul to forestall what he imagined was an imminent Alamannic attack, and he chose Theodosius, son of the Theodosius executed in 375, to succeed in the east. Theodosius had previously served as *dux Moesiae* and was promoted to Augustus in January, 379. Theodosius based himself at Thessalonike; prior to his arrival, the bishop Ascholius, lacking troops to defend the city, was forced to resort to fervent prayer instead. Theodosius attempted to raise a new army with which to suppress Fritigern and the Goths, but the sheer devastation across the region from the Adriatic to the Black Sea sorely hampered both recruitment and tax collection—the tax bill for the provinces of Thrace was repeatedly remitted, so utterly broken was their ability to pay. Laws from the time also show attempts to relieve people of their debts and, in a striking reflection of the impact of such massive casualties, legislation to stop people from digging up their neighbours' properties in search of buried treasure (*Theodosian Code*, 4.20.1 & 10.18.2). Evidence from the *Notitia Dignitatum*, which records an unusually high number of *pseudocomitatenses* for the *magister militum per Illyricum*, suggests that some of the losses were made good by promoting units of the frontier army to the *comitatus*. Gratian also took the step of granting control of some western dioceses to Theodosius, in order to provide him with an additional pool of potential recruits. Themistius galvanised Theodosius with a stirring oration in early 379, threatening the Goths with the prospect of spear, sword, and helmet (*Orations*, 14.181c), but early attempts at dealing with the Goths failed. The emperor endured a humiliating defeat in Macedonia in 380, after which the Goths levied a tribute on the communities of Macedonia and Thessaly and accepted thousands of Roman deserters.

Better fortunes followed in 381, when the Frankish generals Bauto and Arbogast managed to evict the Goths from Macedonia, penning them into Thrace. Athanaric was welcomed to Constantinople with a lavish public spectacle in 381, which allowed Themistius to advance the fiction that the Goths had surrendered (*Orations*, 15.190c–d). In the aftermath, Theodosius made a treaty with the Tervingi in 382 which would have far-reaching consequences. No surviving ancient source records the terms of the treaty, but it is thought that the Tervingi were permitted to settle in Thrace, and were obliged to provide troops to serve under their own officers as part of the Roman army. The Tervingi did not become citizens, nor did they have the right to marry a Roman citizen (although both rights were granted to some of their leaders), but they would be maintained with subsidies paid by the government in Constantinople. The treaty helped to conciliate landowners who had been bearing the brunt of an old Diocletianic scheme where cash could be paid for exemptions from military service. By the time of Theodosius, this *aurum tironicum*, which allowed landowners to keep tenants on their land rather than provide them to the army, had become excessive, rising above 50 gold solidi per exemption. The mass of new recruits provided by the Gothic settlement eased the pressure on landowners and alleviated recruitment difficulties for the army. Themistius thought that the deal was a good one, and lauded Theodosius for keeping the fields sown and Thrace full of hard-working farmers, instead of dead Goths (*Orations*, 16.211a–b). Yet the effect of the treaty of 382 was to create a semi-independent power bloc within the empire. This was a new development: it differed from the previous imperial policy of recruiting troops into the army while their communities remained *outside* the empire. Theodosius attempted to mitigate some of the likely pitfalls by making himself and his *consistorium* available to the Tervingi leaders, and by identifying his interests and those of the empire with their own. Fritigern, Alatheus, and Saphrax vanish from the sources after this point; but their victory at Adrianople in 378, and the settlement that followed in 382, profoundly altered the trajectory of the Goths within the Roman empire and led eventually to the Gothic sack of Rome in 410.

A year after the Gothic settlement was agreed, another security issue appeared with the coup launched by the *comes Britanniarum*, Magnus Maximus, who declared himself Augustus in the summer of 383 while Gratian was preparing to campaign against the Alamanni. Gratian's effort to forestall his usurpation failed when his army defected to Maximus, and Gratian was killed at Lugdunum less than two months after the revolt began. The western provinces declared for Maximus, who proclaimed himself 'restorer of the Republic' (Figure 13.7). In 384, Theodosius accepted Maximus as co-Augustus with Valentinian II;

Figure 13.7 Gold solidus minted at Augusta Treverorum in 383/84. The reverse shows Maximus in military costume with the legend RESTITVTOR REI PVBLICAE.

further coins of Maximus depicted himself and Theodosius together, encompassed by the goddess Victory, while others featured the legend CONCORDIA AVGGGG—referring to four Augusti: Theodosius, Theodosius's son, Arcadius, Valentinian II, and Maximus. This *concordia* soon proved ephemeral, as Maximus left his headquarters at Augusta Treverorum and moved over the Alps with his army, capturing Italy. Valentinian II, only 12, absconded with his mother Justina to Thessalonike. Maximus's aggression steeled Theodosius, who declared his loyalties by marrying Valentinian's sister, Galla. With thousands of Goths at his disposal, Theodosius raised a massive army supplemented by levies from Iberia and Armenia, and from among the Alans, under the command of Richomer and Arbogast. Maximus opened his offensive in the spring of 388, striking into Pannonia while his subordinates carried out an amphibious landing in Sicily and struck eastwards from Africa. Defeated everywhere across this broad front, however, Maximus was pushed back to Aquileia; he fell into Theodosius's hands, and he and his son were executed in the summer of 388. Valentinian II was restored to his throne, and Symmachus, a staunch senatorial opponent of Valentinian (below) who had vocally supported Maximus as he approached Italy, took sanctuary in a church. After delivering an effusive apology to Theodosius in Rome, his life was spared and he held the ordinary consulship in 391. While in Rome, Theodosius also presented his second son Honorius to the senate, and received an exceptionally long-winded and saccharine panegyric from Ausonius's friend Pacatus, who received the governorship of Africa Proconsularis as a reward. The rebellion of Maximus all but sealed the fate of the British provinces, which had been drained of much of their garrison. Gildas, a moralising British Christian writer living at the end of the fifth century or at the beginning of the sixth, rejoiced when Maximus 'had his evil head cut off' (*The Ruin of Britain*, 13); 'Britain was despoiled of her whole army' by Maximus, he lamented, 'her military resources, her governors, brutal as they were, and her sturdy youth, who had followed in the tyrant's footsteps, never to return home' (*The Ruin of Britain*, 14).

The conflict between Theodosius and Maximus ran in parallel to tensions between Nicene and non-Nicene Christians. In 378, Gratian had declared a policy of religious toleration which benefited the Homoeans, although he pointedly excluded Manichaeans and a group known as Eunomians, named for Eunomius of Cyzicus, a bishop known for his fervent anti-Nicene opinions. In the same year, however, and at Gratian's request, Ambrose wrote his treatise *On the Faith*, in which he painted all anti-Nicene Christians, whatever their actual persuasion, as Eunomians—effectively banning anti-Nicene Christianity under the terms of Gratian's own edict and making an enemy out of Justina, the Homoean mother of Valentinian II and step-mother of Gratian. In the east, Theodosius was also influenced by a strongly Nicene bishop, Ascholius, and in February 380, Theodosius issued an edict confirming Nicene Christianity as imperial orthodoxy. 'We command that those following this rule will embrace the name of Catholic Christians,' went the ruling, 'judging that the rest, being mad and insane, follow the infamy of heretical doctrine' (*Theodosian Code*, 16.1.2). Following this edict, Ascholius baptised Theodosius as a Nicene Christian—a further powerful statement on imperially sanctioned orthodoxy. Another edict followed in January 381 at the Council of Constantinople, asserting the views of Athanasius and the primacy of Nicene Christianity by declaring that 'the undivided substance of the Holy Trinity thrives with uncorrupted faith' (*Theodosian Code*, 16.5.6). The Nicene-Constantinople Creed came to be the creed adopted in much of eastern and western liturgy. Bishops who failed to change their views were banished, including Demophilus, the patriarch of Constantinople, who was replaced by Gregory of Nazianzus; the political climate was so dreadful, however, that Gregory soon retired, exhausted from endless bickering. He recorded his impressions of his fellow clergy in a withering section of his memoir, *Concerning His Own Life*. 'They were like a swarm of wasps,' he wrote, 'suddenly darting up in one's face' (1680 = *RLA* p. 120). The Council of Constantinople also established the authority of the city's patriarch as second only to the bishop of Rome (eventually, 'the pope'), and underlined the ruling that only Nicene clergy would be permitted to minister to congregations. In Constantinople, Theodosius reinforced the city's growing importance to imperial affairs by opening a new forum in 393, dedicating the Church of St John Prodromos on the via Egnatia in the district known as the Hebdomon, west of the city, and the Golden Gate—the official entrance for the emperor—was built either at this time or later, during the wall-building program begun by Theodosius II. In 393, Theodosius I proclaimed his young son Arcadius Augustus, reasserting the primacy of dynastic succession.

Two years before his death, Gratian had removed the Altar of Victory from the senate house once again, ended state financial support for pagan priesthoods, and given up the office of *pontifex maximus*. These decisions caused offence, and Symmachus, who had been proconsul of Africa (373) and became urban prefect of Rome in 383, petitioned for the Altar to be returned. 'If a long period gives authority to religious customs,' wrote Symmachus in a passionate letter to Valentinian II following Gratian's death, 'we ought to keep faith with so many centuries' (*Relations*, 3.8). With less rhetorical skill, but greater ardour, Ambrose opposed Symmachus's entreaties with an opinionated argument for the irrelevance of polytheist belief. 'If the old rites pleased,' he contended, 'why did Rome take up foreign ones?' (*Letters*, 18.30). Christianity was, he pleaded, the only true faith—and besides, why did the senate house need an altar? Other temples were available in Rome. Symmachus lost the argument; he perhaps failed to appreciate the streak of religious extremism taking hold in Roman ecclesiastical politics, and it is also noteworthy that by this point the Secular Games had also been abandoned. The Vestal Virgins were abolished not long after the controversy over the Altar of Victory, and the sacred fire of Vesta was extinguished in 394, according to Prudentius (*On the Crowns of the Martyrs*, 2.517–28 = *RLA* p. 105). This didn't stop others from railing against Christianity. In an address written for Theodosius, Libanius took aim at the violence done by monks, 'that black-robed tribe' who, while boring people with excessive hymns, 'hasten to attack the temples with sticks and stones and bars' (*Orations*, 30.8).

Ambrose's triumph over the Altar of Victory was tempered by Valentinian's reversion to tolerance in January 386. Valentinian and his mother, Justina, remained sympathetic to Homoean Christians, and the imperial court appropriated the basilica of San Lorenzo in which anti-Nicene Homoean Christians could celebrate the upcoming Easter holiday. Ambrose responded by filling the basilica with partisans who resisted the armed siege that an angry Valentinian ordered. The emperor was eventually forced to concede the point when the besiegers joined the congregation. With this victory and his miraculous 'discovery' of the relics of two fictional martyrs, which were then installed in San Lorenzo, the feisty bishop proved that he had become a potent political force in his own right. Theodosius would himself receive the full force of Ambrose's authority when, after ordering a public massacre in Thessalonike in 390 over the murder of Botheric, his *magister militum per Illyricum*, Ambrose subsequently refused to grant the emperor communion until he had fully repented for his actions. 'You are a man, and temptation has come upon you,' wrote Ambrose in his forthright letter to Theodosius; 'conquer it' (*Letters*, 51.11 = *RLA* p. 113). Ambrose also brought Augustine under his influence when he arrived in Mediolanum from Africa in 384. Augustine had received a philosophical education and was a devotee of Plato's *Phaedrus* and *Timaeus*, as well as Virgil's *Aeneid*; he also had a son, Adeodotus, a rough Greek translation of the Phoenician name that meant 'gift of Baal'. When he was 20, Augustine embraced Manichaeism, which he followed for a decade, but his fortunes changed when he came to the attention of Symmachus, who suggested that he could fill a vacant position in Mediolanum teaching rhetoric. Ambrose made a deep impression on Augustine and, in 386, Augustine achieved the conversion about which he wrote so powerfully in the *Confessions*. In 387, he was baptised by Ambrose himself.

In the east, Shapur II died in 379, and following the brief tenure of Ardashir II, Shapur III came to the throne in 383. There were further problems in Armenia, but in 387 negotiations between Theodosius and Shapur III resulted in the informal division of Armenia between Roman and Persian spheres of influence, recognising the desire of some parts of the Armenian nobility to align with Persia and others with Rome; the eastern part of the country subsequently became known to the Romans as Persarmenia. Arsaces IV remained on the throne in Roman Armenia, while the Persian nominee Khusrau III ruled in Persarmenia. When Arsaces died suddenly not long afterwards, however, the Romans abolished the Arsacid monarchy in their zone of influence and appointed an Armenian prince to serve as a *comes Armeniae* in an honorary capacity while Roman forces stationed at Karin maintained Roman control.

Theodosius celebrated the unity of the imperial household and the empire on the base of the Obelisk of Theodosius. This monument had once graced the fifteenth-century BC Temple of Amun at Thebes, and was transferred from Alexandria to Constantinople by Constantius II to celebrate the twentieth anniversary of his rule (Figure 13.8). The Latin inscription on its base records that the obelisk was erected once the 'tyrants were overcome'—a reference to the revolt of Maximus. A second obelisk (the 'Lateran Obelisk') was

Figure 13.8 Sculpted relief on the base of the Obelisk of Theodosius, now in the Hippodrome in Istanbul.
The members of the imperial family are depicted, seated in the *kathisma* at centre: from
left to right, Honorius, Arcadius, Theodosius, and Valentinian II. Defeated barbarians kneel
in supplication and the imperial family is flanked by senators.

Source: Photograph by the author.

sent to Rome. Originally installed in the Circus Maximus by Constantius II, it now stands
adjacent to the Lateran Basilica.

The final years of Theodosius's rule were marked by internal problems. Christian
activists, emboldened by decades of imperial support, began vandalising the famed Temple
of Zeus Belos at Apamea and destroyed a synagogue at Callinicum. The latter caused a
spat between Theodosius and Ambrose, and in a candid letter that showed Ambrose's contempt for Jewish 'unbelievers' and his belief in the superiority of the Christian church, he
forced the emperor to reconsider his position (*Letters*, 40). In 391, the ancient Serapeum in
Alexandria was destroyed by a mob urged on by the patriarch of Alexandria, Theophilus,
who deepened the wound by marching through the streets with the sacred items stolen
from the shrine and then built a church over the Serapeum's ruins. Elsewhere in the
empire, temples were razed and churches built in their place, such as at Gaza (Mark the
Deacon, *Life of Porphyry*, 75–6 = *RLA* p. 181). Christian intolerance was on display everywhere, extending to sacred groves of trees being razed in Lycia (*The Life of St Nicholas of
Sion*, 16 & 18 = *RLA* p. 182). In 392, Theodosius provided further imperial sanction for

anti-pagan behaviour when he issued an empire-wide ban on pagan sacrifice and ordered the temples closed.

In the west, Theodosius had entrusted Valentinian II to Arbogast, the *magister militum per Gallias*. After a difficult attempt to deal with Frankish raiding along the Rhine in 391, Arbogast fought the Bructeri and destroyed their settlements in a savage winter campaign. In 392, Valentinian attempted to establish his authority over Arbogast, but this brought the two to blows despite efforts by Ambrose to mediate. After Arbogast openly defied a direct order, declaring that Valentinian lacked *any* authority over him because he had been appointed by Theodosius, Valentinian took his own life at Vienne. Arbogast was now in a very difficult position, because Theodosius's younger son, Honorius, was the likely western successor and Valentinian's sister, Galla, was still married to Theodosius; he must have reasoned, therefore, that a conflict with Theodosius was inevitable. In late August 392, Arbogast proclaimed a member of the palatine bureaucracy named Eugenius as Augustus. Theodosius responded by declaring Honorius Augustus in spring 393, and left Constantinople just over a year later at the head of an eastern *comitatus* bolstered, again, by a substantial levy of Goths, Iberians, and Alans. Among his senior officers was his *magister utriusque militiae* Stilicho, a half-Roman, half-Vandal who had married his niece Serena. Theodosius and Eugenius met in early September 394 at the river Frigidus, near Aquileia. Over a two-day battle, Eugenius, Arbogast, and the western *comitatus* were beaten, but the Gothic contingent in Theodosius's army resented the calamitous casualties they were forced to bear when they were deliberately placed in the front ranks to absorb the worst of the enemy attack (Zosimus, *New History*, 4.58). In the same year, Theodosius fell ill: he left the ten-year-old Honorius as Augustus in the west, with Stilicho as his guardian. He may also have intended to appoint Stilicho as the guardian to the 17-year-old Arcadius, but the praetorian prefect of Oriens, Rufinus, soon took that role upon himself. In January 395, Theodosius died of heart failure at Mediolanum. He was, as it would turn out, the final ruler of a united Roman empire.

Stilicho and Alaric

The Goths settled on the right bank of the Danube in 382 and those recruited to die at the Frigidus had given a great deal of their youth—but they had little to show for it. According to Zosimus, one of their leaders, Alaric, had hoped to be given a high army command in return for his loyalty (*New History*, 5.5). When this failed to materialise, Alaric turned to raiding in Thrace and Macedonia. In the midst of this, Theodosius's body was accompanied to Constantinople by Stilicho and elements of the western and eastern *comitatenses*; Stilicho handed over the eastern *comitatus*, which was led by the Gothic *comes rei militaris* Gainas, and retired to Ravenna. When Gainas reached Constantinople, he murdered Rufinus in front of the emperor Arcadius; it was never entirely clear whether Gainas was acting on Stilicho's orders or had taken matters into his own hands. Amidst a general purge, the eunuch Eutropius, who held the key position as the *praepositus* in charge of the sacred bedchamber, emerged as the most influential courtier in the palace. He ensured that Arcadius married Aelia Eudoxia, the daughter of Bauto, one of Eutropius's allies. Between 395 and 398, and unusually for a palatine eunuch, Eutropius established a new set of credentials as a capable general, fending off predatory raids from the Huns moving through the Caspian Gates and into the Caucasus. Numerous Syriac, Latin, and

Greek sources reported the raids, which reached as far as Edessa and Ctesiphon (see *REF2*, pp. 17–19). Eutropius impressed Arcadius, who granted him the rank of patrician and the ordinary consulship in Constantinople in 399.

In the meantime, Alaric's raiding bore fruit as Arcadius allowed him the title of *magister militum per Illyricum* in 397, granting him access to funds, men, and matériel. 'He who breaks a treaty wins riches, while he who observes one lives in want,' commented Claudian, a partisan of Stilicho and inveterate enemy of Eutropius, 'the ravager of Achaea and recent devastator of defenceless Epirus is lord of Illyria' (*Against Eutropius*, 2.228–31). This sudden turn of events caught Stilicho off-guard: after carrying out an amphibious landing in Greece to address Alaric's raiding, Stilicho found that the eastern court had censured him as a public enemy. Eutropius, too, fell afoul of suspicions in the palace and emerged the worse for wear from the rebellion of a Gothic leader named Tribigild, whose chief demand was the removal of Eutropius. The hated *praepositus* sought refuge in the Church of Holy Wisdom even as John Chrysostom (Greek for 'golden mouth') delivered a sermon that mocked his vanity, and the hapless eunuch was later murdered at Chalcedon. Gainas also fell from grace after making a rash of demands, including the consulate for 400. When Gainas's Arian soldiers and a population with a lingering fear of the Goths clashed in Constantinople's streets, Arcadius called in Fravitta, the Gothic *magister militum per Orientem*, and in the ensuing conflict Gainas fled across the Danube, only to be murdered in Gothia. Despite the fact that Fravitta succeeded to Gainas's position, it is noteworthy that the extremely forthright commentary by Synesius of Cyrene, *On Kingship*, urged Arcadius to abandon alliances with Goths in particular, and to get out of the palace and into the field, to lead Roman (and not Gothic) troops into battle. Arcadius chose to concentrate on domestic matters: his wife, Eudoxia, became Augusta in 400, and their young son, Theodosius, was proclaimed Augustus at the Hebdomon in 402. In 403, Arcadius fell out with John Chrysostom, who had criticised Eudoxia as a latter day Jezebel, and John was exiled to distant Armenia. A mysterious fire in the Church of Holy Wisdom spread to the senate house on the night he left, burning it to the ground.

In the west, Stilicho had strengthened his position at court by betrothing his daughter, Maria, to Honorius in 398. Claudian suggested that Stilicho also organised a naval expedition to Britannia in 399, against the Saxons and Picts (*Against Eutropius*, 1.391–3), but only two years later, he withdrew even more units from Britannia's denuded garrison to fight Alaric (Claudian, *The Gothic War*, 416–18). In 402, the western court moved to Ravenna which, facing the Adriatic, could be supplied by sea and provided better communications with Illyricum and Constantinople; the city's infamous malarial marshes also protected it from a landward attack. At around the same time, Arcadius terminated Alaric's position and Alaric subsequently appeared in northern Italy, where he fought Stilicho in two battles at Verona and Pollentia. In the aftermath Stilicho arranged for Alaric to become the *magister militum per Illyricum*—the same position he had held before, but this time appointed by the western court. This move worsened the infighting between Ravenna and Constantinople. Earlier, Arcadius had accepted the loyalty of Gildo, the *comes Africae* and brother of Firmus, who promised to ship Africa's grain to Constantinople and not to Italy. Honorius's response was to turn Gildo's brother, Mascezel, against him.

In 405, a Gothic warlord named Radagaisus led a force of opportunists through Noricum into northern Italy. Stilicho rushed northwards, patching together a force of Roman troops from the western *comitatus*; he won an important victory, defeating

Radagaisus near Florence, and drafted as many as 12,000 survivors into the Roman army (Olympiodorus = Photius, *Bibliotheca*, 80). At around the same time, in the winter of either 405/06 or 406/07, a massive force of Vandals, Suebi, Alans, and their allies cut through the Franks east of the Rhine and invaded Gaul. Both the invasion of Radagaisus and that over the Rhine were likely linked to the growing power of the Huns, who were migrating to the west of the Carpathian mountains. Stilicho was unable to stop such a large incursion so soon after he had fought Radagaisus, and three imperial usurpations quickly followed amidst the chaos. The third and most serious was that of Flavius Claudius Constantinus, who took the royal name Constantine III. He established a Gallic fiefdom based at Arelate, to where the seat of the Gallic prefecture had been transferred from Augusta Treverorum in 402/03. In 407, Stilicho assembled a Gothic force under Sarus to unseat Constantine, which enjoyed initial success before being forced back by Constantine's lieutenant, Gerontius; Constantine subsequently consolidated his control over the Alpine passes to protect himself against further attempts from Italy (Figure 13.9).

In 408, Constantine's son Constans campaigned in Spain, and Constantine turned his attention northwards in an attempt to re-establish some form of Roman presence on the Rhine, but northern Gaul remained unstable. Indeed, in a letter written in 408, Jerome recorded that northern Gaul was overrun by 'savage tribes', including 'Quadi, Vandals, Sarmatians, Alans, Gepids, Herules, Saxons, Burgundians, Alamanni and—alas! For the commonwealth, even Pannonians' (*Letters*, 123.16). One of the consequences of these continued disturbances was that Stilicho was prevented from maintaining good relations with Alaric. When the money, supplies, and men that Stilicho had promised Alaric failed to materialise, the Goths, exasperated, raided Noricum and demanded that they be paid. Stilicho, who saw an opportunity to use Alaric against Constantine, calmed fears amidst the senate, and persuaded them to surrender their personal fortunes and pay the massive sum of 1,800 kilograms (4,000 pounds) of gold that Alaric had been promised.

In 404/05, Arcadius appointed Anthemius, who had served previously as the *comes sacrarum largitionum* and *magister officiorum*, as praetorian prefect of Oriens. Largely in response to the emerging problem of the Huns (below), but also in light of the destabilising influence of Alaric's Goths, Anthemius began a new set of fortifications west of the fourth-century walls in Constantinople. Known as the Theodosian Walls, this massive defensive barrier consisted of two walls separated by an open space and fronted by a deep moat; large sections of the wall still survive in modern Istanbul. As work on the walls progressed, Arcadius died in a riding accident in 408, and amid passionate arguments about who should go to Constantinople to wrest control over the valuable eastern provinces, Stilicho prevailed. One of his enemies at court, however, the powerful palatine bureaucrat Olympius, claimed that Stilicho intended to install his own son, Eucherius, as eastern emperor. The army gathered at Ticinum to fight Constantine III was incited to mutiny, and in the ensuing violence the senior officers of the west, loyal to Stilicho, were culled: these included two praetorian prefects, the *magister militum* and *magister equitum*, the imperial quaestor, the *magister officiorum*, and the *comes sacrarum largitionum*. It was a stunning purge of the top level of the western government, and while Stilicho initially evaded capture, he was tracked down and put to death at Ravenna at the end of August. A widescale purge of Germanic elements at court and in the army followed, including the wives and children of Gothic troops in Roman service. The traumatised survivors, full of fear and anger, fled to Alaric.

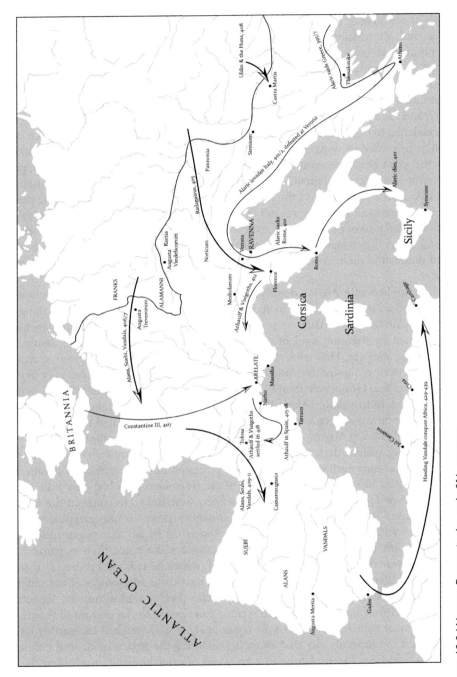

Figure 13.9 Western Europe in the early fifth century.

Source: Illustration by the author.

Olympius became the western *magister officiorum*, and from this position he persuaded Honorius to rebuff Alaric's embassies. In response, the Gothic army marched on Rome and laid siege to the city throughout 408, blockading the Tiber and cutting off supplies; one of the casualties of the siege was Stilicho's widow, Serena, who was murdered within the walls at the urging of Galla Placidia, Honorius's ambitious half-sister, who viewed her as a rival. Eventually, another massive sum of money was paid—2,270 kilograms (5,000 pounds) of gold and 13,600 kilograms (30,000 pounds) of silver—and the siege was lifted with promises from the senators that they would compel Honorius to come to his senses and grant Alaric's requests for food and cash subsidies, the right to settle in Noricum, and the rank of *magister utriusque militiae*. This final request angered Honorius, however, and even though the troublesome Olympius had since been exiled, Honorius felt emboldened to turn Alaric down. Furious and embittered, Alaric returned to Rome in 409, where he cowed the senate into installing the urban prefect of Rome, Priscus Attalus, as emperor: since Honorius would not give Alaric what he wanted, Alaric would appoint his *own* emperor. Alaric's approach reflected an important dynamic of the relationship between Roman authorities and the barbarian warlords of the fifth century—the official source of positions and subsidies was still the imperial court, even in situations where there was a clear imbalance of power. Alaric and the Goths did not seek to destroy the empire in the west; instead, they sought recognition from *the* source of legitimate political authority that had dominated their lives, and those of their ancestors, for as long as anyone could remember.

Attalus complied with Alaric's demands and also bestowed honours on Alaric's brother, Athaulf, who had recently arrived in Italy. Yet Attalus failed to gain control of the grain supply from Africa, which Alaric regarded as crucial to feed his people; he then began to demonstrate an alarming level of political ambition, ignoring Alaric and demanding that Honorius abdicate. Honorius was wavering when a number of legions sent from the eastern court, requested by Stilicho several years previously, unexpectedly arrived at Ravenna by sea. Honorius's stance towards Attalus and Alaric hardened and negoti-ations collapsed. In frustration, Alaric deposed his recalcitrant lackey, and then, after Sarus launched an unprovoked attack on him near Ravenna, Alaric returned to Rome, furious at Roman duplicity. On August 24, 410, Alaric captured Rome and subjected it to a three-day sack, during which Alaric abducted Galla Placidia. Rome may have been politically irrelevant by the early fifth century, but it still possessed immense symbolic significance. For pagan writers like Zosimus, the neglect of the traditional gods had only ever invited catastrophe (*New History*, 2.7), but Christian writers were forced to confront the fact that God had allowed Rome to be captured. The Lusitanian native Orosius grappled with this problem by writing in his apologetic *History Against the Pagans* that pagan history was full of catastrophes, and Christian Rome had brought more peace than its pagan ante-cedent. Augustine delivered his *Sermon 296* in 411, where he ridiculed pagan criticism of Christians and their beliefs, and argued that Rome's sack was an example of the suffering that Christians necessarily endured in order to attain their reward in heaven. Augustine's most famous work, *City of God*, was also written in response to the capture of Rome. Far more intellectual than *History Against the Pagans*, *City of God* weighed the earthly city of Rome against the heavenly city that awaited, pondering the legacy of classical culture in a Christian world. Apologetic Christian expressions of grief, however, overlooked the fact that Alaric was himself a Christian; and they also masked the fact that the Gothic sack of

Rome was a signal failure for Alaric. The Gothic leader's preference all along was to be appointed and recognised by the emperor. After sacking Rome, Alaric had no position, no subsidy, no food, and nowhere to live where he could remain unmolested by a Roman army. Determined to the last to feed his men and their families and better their position, he was in the midst of trying to cross to the grain-rich island of Sicily when he died in the winter of 411.

Arcadius, Theodosius II, Persia, and Attila

Arcadius was succeeded in Constantinople by his six-year-old son, Theodosius II, who remained in the city for almost his entire reign between 408 and 450. Honorius, likewise, mostly stayed behind the walls of Ravenna until his death in 423. Despite the steady political fragmentation in the west, which saw the cleavage of the British provinces from the empire and the coalescence of the first Germanic successor kingdoms, conflicts in the east were brief and intermittent, and the most potent problems, Persia and the emergence of the Huns, were managed principally through diplomacy. The conflicts in the west—far more serious—are addressed in the following section.

Theodosius II and his praetorian prefect, Anthemius, inherited several delicate situations from Arcadius. In 408, Uldin, the first Hunnic leader mentioned in Roman sources, had killed Gainas in Gothia and sent his severed head to Arcadius, with whom he arranged a treaty. When Arcadius died, Uldin abrogated the treaty and seemed disinterested in making a new agreement with Theodosius II. Instead, he raided Moesia and Thrace, capturing the Roman fort at Castra Martis, a *quadriburgium* at Kula (Bulgaria), and rebuffed Roman negotiators by boasting that he could conquer any land on which the sun shone. The response of Theodosius's generals was to suborn key figures in Uldin's entourage with promises of money, and once it became apparent that Uldin's grip on his army was weakening, he was pushed out of Roman territory.

In Persia, Yazdegerd I had come to the throne after his brother, Bahram IV, was murdered in 399. His tenure had opened with the harassment of Christians in Persia, and he had adopted a bellicose attitude towards Arcadius. Claudian wrote of the anxiety produced by the announcement of his accession: 'another sinister messenger flies in' (*Against Eutropius*, 2.474 = *REF2*, p. 31). Tensions were soothed by Anthemius, serving as *comes sacrarum largitionum* before his promotion to praetorian prefect in 404/05, and he arranged for the treaty of 363 to be amended to include Callinicum and Artaxata as centres where Roman and Persian merchants could trade with one another. One member of the embassy was Marutha, the bishop for the Syriac-speaking Christians of Sophanene, who was reported to have cured one of Yazdegerd's sons of an illness. As a result, tensions between the king and the Persian Christians were also eased, and Marutha was given the relics of Persian martyrs, which he installed at Martyropolis (Maypherkat, modern Silvan, east of Amida/Diyarbakir). Marutha and Acacius, the bishop of Amida, urged Yazdegerd to convene the synod that took place at Ctesiphon in 410, which established what has become known as the 'Church of the East', organised under a *catholicos* in the Persian capital who oversaw a network of sees and bishops. With the official recognition of Christianity by Yazdegerd, the influence of the Zoroastrian priesthood was curbed and Christian elites came to play more important roles in government.

Another issue that arose between Rome and Persia was the defence of the Caspian Gates (the Darial Gorge, Chapter 9). According to John Lydus, the loss of territory in northern Mesopotamia that resulted from Julian's defeat in 363 had hampered the empire's ability to defend Armenia and the Caucasus, a problem that affected Persia as well as the Romans (*On the Magistracies*, 3.52). Indeed, this deficit had been laid bare by the Huns, who had carried out such devastating raids between 395 and 398. Yazdegerd took the position that preventing these incursions was a shared responsibility. By the late fourth century, the Persians were asking for funding, and by the end of the century a fortress, Viraparakh, had been built to guard the Caspian Gates. Roman emperors were repeatedly unwilling to commit to any formal, recurring arrangement that might resemble tribute, but frequently made unofficial payments, including in the first years of Theodosius's reign.

Despite the promising start for Theodosius's relationship with Yazdegerd, tensions began to surface that were driven both by Sasanian policy and by developments at the court in Constantinople. In Armenia, Yazdegerd placed his son, Shapur, on the Persamenian throne in 416, which suggested to hawks in Constantinople that a nefarious plan was underway to impose Zoroastrianism on Armenian Christians. Meanwhile, Theodosius's tutor, Antiochus, who had been sent from Ctesiphon at Arcadius's request some years earlier, was removed in 412 and replaced by Pulcheria, the emperor's sister. A Christian hardliner, she was proclaimed Augusta in 414. Pulcheria took over the responsibility of educating her brother, but did so in a sedulous and proselytising fashion that worried contemporaries. Anthemius, who might have restrained Pulcheria, died in 414, and as Theodosius became more intolerant, Jews and pagans both found themselves victimised at the encouragement of the palace and subject to punitive legislation. In Alexandria, the Neoplatonist mathematician Hypatia, the tutor of Synesius of Cyrene, was lynched by a Christian mob in the riots that followed the decision by the city's troublesome patriarch, Cyril, to banish Alexandria's Jewish community in 415. The philosopher Damascius blamed Cyril for her death, but in the aftermath her murderers faced only limited censure (*Life of Isidore*, fr. 102). Theodosius's wife, Eudocia, the daughter of an Athenian sophist whom he married in 421 at Pulcheria's urging, also became a fervent Christian and an important influence on Theodosius. Despite their rivalries that eventually induced Pulcheria to leave the imperial palace for a residence in the Hebdomon, the two royal women had an important impact on the Christian landscape of Constantinople. The relics of St Stephen were installed in a martyrium inside the imperial palace, and when John Chrysostom died, his remains were interred in the Church of the Holy Apostles, the resting place of numerous emperors. This twinning of the imperial infrastructure with Christian relics suffused the city with a profound religiosity. Eudocia also projected her influence beyond the city, principally through visiting and patronising sites in the Holy Land, in which she was encouraged by Melania the Younger; later, after falling prey to a palace conspiracy, she remained in Jerusalem until her death in 460. By now, Christianity extended to almost every facet of Roman life. Christian priests were to be found with Roman military units and the oaths of new recruits were sworn to the Holy Trinity. The influence of Christianity also simplified Roman coin designs. Images of martial triumph were still to be found on the reverse of solidi, but alongside defeated barbarians, the emperor held the Christian battle standard, the *labarum*: his victory was granted through his Christian piety. The diversity of pagan designs featuring the traditional gods of the Graeco-Roman pantheon was slimmed down to just a few that were compatible with the Christian faith, such as the personification of Victory, which now appeared in Christian form.

Religious tensions also flared up once again in Persia, where a Zoroastrian fire altar was demolished by an overly zealous Christian bishop, leading to his execution. Yazdegerd's sudden death in 420 triggered a round of persecution, as his young son Bahram V sought to establish his bona fides with the Zoroastrian priesthood and the Persian nobility. Christian refugees fled Persian territory with harrowing tales of mistreatment, and Roman merchants were harassed and robbed while going about their business. War begun soon afterwards, and for Pulcheria the conflict became a *cause célèbre* as a crusade to save Christian souls in Persia. The *magister militum per Orientem* Anatolius invaded Persarmenia from the fortress that he had established at Karin, renamed Theodosiopolis (Erzurum, north-west of Lake Van), while the *magister militum praesentalis*, an Alan named Ardabur, laid siege to Nisibis. An allied Arab army under the Nasrid Alamoundarus (al-Mundhir) was beaten off by Roman troops and Alamoundarus was drowned in the Euphrates, according to Socrates Scholasticus (*Ecclesiastical History*, 7.18). Neither side made significant progress, and after the Huns began to raid across the Danube into Roman territory, Theodosius called a halt to hostilities and sent his *magister officiorum*, Helion, to arrange a truce in 422. Theodosius and Bahram agreed not to take in allies who might chose to flee from one empire to the other, and they also agreed not to make any significant changes to the defence network along their shared eastern frontier. It also appears that both sides guaranteed freedom of worship, and Theodosius may have made a contribution towards maintaining the fortress at Viraparakh. In the aftermath of this conflict, Acacius raised enough money from his congregation at Amida to free some 7,000 Persian prisoners, an act that seems to have resulted in clemency and freedom for the new *catholicos*, Dadisho, who was languishing in a Persian prison. Dadisho's cellmate, however, who had been set free on the promise that he would not evangelise in the Persian empire, reneged and was executed. This development led to a distinctive change of course in the Church of the East, as Dadisho came to the conclusion that it was necessary to depoliticise Persian Christianity by distancing the Church of the East from the Roman empire. In 424, the Synod of Dadisho established the authority of the Persian *catholicos*, and prohibited appeals to Roman Christian clergy.

Ecclesiastical matters in Constantinople were complicated in 427 when the patriarch Sisinnius died and was replaced by Nestorius. The new patriarch had been a student of Theodore of Mopsuestia, who had himself imbibed the ideas of *his* teacher, Diodore of Tarsus. The position that had developed between these three men was that Christ possessed both a divine nature and a human nature within one person. This idea led Nestorius to reject the traditional name for Mary, Theotokos, 'mother of God', which was the name popularly used by Alexandrian theologians and which was fiercely defended by Cyril, the patriarch of Alexandria. Since Mary could not properly be understood to have given birth to a god, Nestorius reasoned, Mary should instead be called Christotokos, 'Christ-bearer'. His idea did not win great favour, and his position became known pejoratively as Nestorianism. It is also known by the more neutral term, 'dyophysitism', after the Greek words for 'two' and 'nature'. Nestorius's fiercest opponent was Cyril, a strident and aggressive individual who frequently resorted to bribery, and kept a running tab of what was paid and to whom (*Letters*, 51–110). The friction between Cyril and his opponents created faultlines in the eastern church, largely drawn between Alexandria on the one hand, and Antioch and Constantinople on the other. At the Council of Ephesus in 431, Cyril ensured that

Nestorius was deposed, but Nestorius's supporters in Antioch responded by organising their own council, deposing Cyril. Amidst the aftershocks, Nestorius's writings were destroyed, but a surviving Syriac translation of his work *The Bazaar of Heracleides* revealed the deep personal wounds that his condemnation inflicted. The Council of Ephesus also had an important consequence for Syriac-speaking Christians in the east. One of the attendees was the bishop of Edessa, Rabbula (411–35), and his confusion over the subtle distinctions between the teachings of Theodore of Mopsuestia and those of Nestorius resulted in Theodore's condemnation after he died in 428. The result was a cleavage in the Syriac-speaking Christian communities between followers of Cyril, such as Rabbula, and those who continued to follow Theodore. In time, this would lead to pro-Theodore Christians leaving Edessa for Nisibis, where they joined the Church of the East (below).

After the Council of Ephesus in 431, the theological arguments largely remained unsettled. In 433, Cyril attempted a comprise with his rivals in Antioch (the 'Formula of Reunion'), but when he died in 444, he was replaced by a man named Dioscorus, another fierce opponent of Nestorius. A monk named Eutyches, a friend of the *praepositus* of the sacred bed chamber, Chrysaphius, developed Dioscorus's viewpoint, arguing that the two natures of Christ were in fact fused in a single divine nature. This position became known as monophysitism (or miaphysitism), meaning 'one nature'. Cyril had been making murky references to the *mia physis* of the Word before his death, but it was Eutyches and Dioscorus who now butted heads with the patriarchs of both Antioch and Constantinople, along with Ibas of Edessa (who translated the work of Theodore of Mopsuestia into Syriac) and Theodoret, bishop of Cyrrhus; Theodoret, a friend to Nestorius and critic of Cyril, was particularly opposed to this development of Cyril's theology. In 448, Eutyches was condemned by Flavian, the patriarch of Constantinople; yet a year later, in 449, the Second Council of Ephesus was convened by Dioscorus. At the Council, Ibas and Theodoret were condemned in favour of Eutyches and the legacy of Cyril. In the meantime, Leo, the bishop of Rome, had written his famous *Tome* at Flavian's request. The *Tome* rejected Nestorius and Eutyches but advanced a suspiciously dyophysite Christology; the delegates at Ephesus in 449 declined to read it, leading Leo to call the event the 'Robber Council'.

While these Christological controversies taxed the intellectual energies of the empire's bishops, a different academic exercise was underway. This was the *Theodosian Code*, a Latin compendium of Roman law that was started in 429 and completed in 437. The *Code* was a massive undertaking that included more than 2,500 individual legal opinions, and became the standard collection of Roman law until it was superseded by the *Justinianic Code* (Chapter 14). New laws that appeared after each of those compendia were typically referred to as Novels or *Novellae* (sg. *Novella*). The appearance of the *Code* in Latin elevated the status of the language alongside Greek, the common language of the east since the days of the Hellenistic kingdoms, and Theodosius further bolstered Latin's position by making Latin instruction available at state expense. Many of the laws collected in the *Theodosian Code* concerned religious matters: the rights of pagans, Jews, and Samaritans; bans on pagan sacrifice; and laws about the construction of synagogues. For example, while pagans had continued to serve in the army, a law of 416 finally banned them (16.10.21), and the collection openly discriminated against Jews and reified the divisions between Judaism and Christianity. Jews were forbidden from owning Christian slaves (16.9.1 = *RLA* p. 193), were not permitted to marry Christians (3.7.2 = *RLA* p. 193), and Christians were not allowed to convert to Judaism (16.8.7 = *RLA* p. 194). The construction of new synagogues was prohibited (16.8.27) and Jews who 'fled their feral sect' to become Christians, a common feature of some Christian literature (e.g. *Easter Chronicle*, p. 536), were to be protected from punishment (16.8.1 = *RLA* p. 206). At the same time, the *Code* also confusingly supported Judaism, accepting the legality of the faith (16.8.9) and protecting Jewish property and synagogues (e.g. 16.8.20 = *RLA* p. 196). Despite the punitive actions taken against Judaism within an increasingly intolerant Christian empire, which included the abolishment of the Jewish Patriarchate by Theodosius in 425, it was during this period that compilation began on the Jerusalem (or Palestinian) Talmud; this and the survival of individual synagogues, such as the famous example from Apamea discovered in 1934, reflected the ongoing strength of individual Jewish communities and centres of learning. This was especially true for the Persian empire, untouched by the *Theodosian Code*, where the compilation of the Babylonian Talmud was well underway.

In the meantime, the Huns who had raided Thrace in 422 had come under a new leader, named Rua (also known as Rugila or Ruas). His raids in 422 were brought to an end with a treaty scorned by later historians, who viewed Theodosius as weak and ineffectual. The Romans promised to pay 158 kilograms (350 pounds) of gold per year in an extraordinarily lucrative protection racket, but they could afford to do so, having found a new source of gold of exceptional purity in the Caucasus. The treaty also bought years of relative peace, broken only when Rua died in 434 to be succeeded by two brothers, Attila and Bleda. In that year, the Gothic *magister militum praesentalis* and former consul Flavius Plintha managed to persuade Attila and Bleda to accept a new treaty. Far more extortionate than its predecessor, it provided 316 kilograms (700 pounds) of gold per year, created specialised markets for Huns and Romans, and promised the return of Hunnic fugitives—who, the Romans quickly learned, were often impaled. Even those Roman troops who the Huns had captured in battle, if they had managed to escape, had to be returned to a life of slavery unless the Roman court was willing to pay the princely sum of 8 solidi each to purchase their freedom. The bitterest clause of the treaty demanded that the Romans refrain from helping anyone with whom the Huns were at war, the sort of stipulation that was normally the prerogative of the stronger power. Attila and Bleda were not reticent about breaking the treaty, and in 441, as a brief war on the Persian front and a campaign against the Vandals in the west removed troops from the Balkans, Theodosius's court watched helplessly as Viminacium, Singidunum, and Sirmium fell to the Huns, their populations sold into slavery and the Pannonian and Dacian provinces devastated. The capture of Sirmium forced the praetorian prefect of Illyricum to transfer his seat to Thessalonike.

The Huns withdrew in 443, but in 444/45, the Romans stopped paying the annual subsidy, and Attila killed his brother and started a new campaign of extortion against Constantinople. When negotiations broke down, Attila and his army crossed the Danube and passed through Thrace. Capturing the major cities en route, destroying the Roman fortress of Novae and taking thousands of prisoners, Attila crushed an imperial army close to Constantinople. Theodosius hastily sent his former *magister militum* Anatolius to Attila, and peace was once again agreed. Attila insisted that unpaid subsidies worth a staggering 2,721 kilograms (6,000 pounds) of gold be paid to him, along with Roman consent to the same conditions that had been agreed in 434. The annual subsidy was also increased to 950 kilograms (2,100 pounds) of gold and ransom payments for captives to 12 solidi, but in practice they could be much higher: Priscus reported while on an embassy to Attila (below) that 500 solidi were paid for a single female captive (Blockley fr. 14). In 447/48,

Attila started to claim substantial districts in the Balkans, and set the Romans at a distinct disadvantage by demanding that they trade with him only at Naissus, which was to be on the frontier between 'his' territory and that belonging to Theodosius. Priscus derided Theodosius for his cowardice in making this agreement with Attila, saying that it would attract the wrong sort of attention from other barbarians (Blockley fr. 9.3). Attila, further-more, openly used demeaning language when addressing Theodosius, referring to him as his 'slave' and sending an ambassador to Constantinople demanding that the emperor set aside a palace for his 'lord' Attila (Priscus, Blockley fr. 15.2 & *Easter Chronicle*, p. 587). At the same time, however, Priscus was a realist: he knew that Theodosius was constrained by the many demands of the time to assuage at least one enemy, and that this turned out to be Attila (Blockley fr. 10). The heavy defeats suffered by Julian (363) and Valens (378) had also made diplomacy far more preferable to the uncertainties of war. The Romans balanced dip-lomacy with intrigue, infiltrating agents into Hunnic territory to suborn groups that could be turned against Attila (Blockley fr. 11.2 & 14). The most striking example of Roman activity behind the scenes was a botched effort to assassinate Attila in 449, masterminded by Chrysaphius and Martialis, the *magister officiorum*. The plot failed when Edeco, one of the Huns Chrysaphius had bribed to carry out the murder, revealed everything to Attila in the presence of the Roman envoy Maximinus, causing acute embarrassment. Priscus had accompanied Maximinus on this mission, and recorded his impressions of travelling through Hunnic territory and meeting Attila. He was aghast at the devastation at Naissus (which would not be rebuilt for a century) and the mounds of dead littering the land-scape. Priscus noted the wealth of Attila and his entourage, who were waited on by slaves taken from raids into the Roman provinces along the Danube. Priscus also provided an important insight into 'membership' among the Huns. At Viminacium, he encountered a Roman trader who had been enslaved, purchased his freedom, then joined the Huns and had risen to high status among them (Blockley fr. 11.2).

Collapse in the west

After being recognised by Honorius and serving as ordinary consul in 409, the fortunes of Constantine III began to wane. His principal supporter at the imperial court, the *magister equitum* Allobichus, died and was replaced by the more hostile Constantius, who took the position of *magister utriusque militiae* and set about ridding the court of his enemies. These included Olympius, who he arranged to be bludgeoned to death. Constantine's hopes of a deal with Honorius began to crumble, and when Gerontius turned on Constantine and elevated a man named Maximus as Augustus, Constantine was soon bottled up at Arelate while Maximus laid siege to Vienne. By 411, Gerontius, Constantine, and the latter's son Constans were dead, but the chaos between 409 and 411 had allowed the Vandals, Alans, and Suebi—those who had crossed the Rhine between 405 and 407 but who had hith-erto been confined to northern Gaul—to head southwards across the Pyrenees into Spain. The civil war between Constantine and Gerontius also led to the increasing isolation of Britannia and Armorica, which Constantine was unable to defend from Saxon pirates. Zosimus reported that Honorius, in response to a petition, instructed the Britons to look to their own defence (*New History*, 6.10). The separation of Britannia from Roman rule was given a wretched voice by Gildas, who wrote that the British leaders pleaded for Roman help, detailing 'the groans of the British', but they received little aid (*The Ruin of*

Britain, 20). Later, the Saxons settled across much of southern and eastern Britain before suffering a setback at the battle of Badon (precise date and location unknown) at the hands of Ambrosius Aurelianus—a man who Gildas said possessed imperial blood (25). In 429, the bishop of Auxerre, Germanus, was sent to Britain to suppress unwelcome challenges to Augustine's teachings on free will being mounted by a bishop named Pelagius. Germanus found a functioning government of sorts, and an ecclesiastical administration that was in contact with its counterparts in Gaul. The legends that grew up around Germanus's visit claimed that he inspired an unlikely victory over Picts and Saxons by encouraging the browbeaten Britons to yell 'Alleluia!' as they charged. Nevertheless, the *Gallic Chronicle of 452* recorded that Britain came under Saxon control in 441/42, while the sixth-century historian Procopius wrote that after the revolt of Constantine III, 'the Romans never succeeded in recovering Britain, which remained from that time on under the rule of tyrants' (*Wars*, 3.2). Roman coinage in Britannia ended with Constantine III, and several major hoards were buried in the early fifth century, never to be recovered by their original owners. These included the famous Hoxne Hoard (deposited after 408, and now in the British Museum), and it is notable that numerous large hoards were found in East Anglia, the locus of initial Saxon settlement. Much of the history of fifth-century Britain remains opaque: the battle of Badon holds a central place in the myths and legends of king Arthur, and even Magnus Maximus found his way into Welsh legend, where he appears as Macsen Wledig in the famous collection of Welsh folklore, the *Mabinogion*.

In Spain, the Siling and Hasding Vandals, Alans, and Suebi forced the poorly defended mountain passes and crossed the Pyrenees. The Spanish Christian historian Hydatius wrote of a period of unrestrained pillage and disease, accompanied by a famine so dreadful that people resorted to cannibalism and animals ate the human dead (*Chronicle*, 297.16). By 411, the different groups in Spain had divided the peninsula between them, with the Alans, who appear to have been the strongest, receiving the largest portion of land, and by 415 the final, tenuous Roman foothold in Spain under Maximus had all but collapsed. In Gaul, meanwhile, Jovinus had declared himself Augustus at Moguntiacum in 411 with support from Alans, Burgundians, and the Gothic general Sarus. Athaulf was hostile to Sarus, and after killing him he joined the revolt at the urging of Priscus Attalus; he then abruptly changed course and played a key role in suppressing both Jovinus and his brothers in 413. The savage purge of Jovinus's supporters among the Gallic elite that followed, orchestrated by the palatine officials at Ravenna, provided further evidence that the interests of Gallic landowners were best defended not by Honorius and his ineffective leadership, but by others closer to home. A particularly suitable candidate was Athaulf himself, who married Galla Placidia in a glitzy society wedding at Narbo in 414; the couple's union was eulogised by none other than Priscus Attalus. Athaulf was also amenable to the Gallic elites as a leader because, as Orosius wrote, while he had once aimed to 'obliterate the Roman name and to render and name the entire territory of the Romans the empire of the Goths', he had come around to the view that his efforts would best be spent restoring, not destroying, the empire (*History Against the Pagans*, 7.43 = *RLA* p. 303).

The marriage between Galla Placidia and Athaulf signalled a brief period of wary cooperation between Honorius and Athaulf's Goths—subsequently known to history as the Visigoths—but by 415, pressure from Constantius pushed Athaulf into Spain, where he and his successor were murdered later that year. Priscus Attalus, who had been elevated once more as an emperor, was ritually mutilated and then exiled. In 416, Wallia, the new leader of the Visigoths, returned Galla Placidia to Honorius in Ravenna. In exchange for this, Wallia was generously funded and provisioned and then sent into the Spanish peninsula, where he defeated the Alans and killed their king, Addax. The Visigoths also annihilated the Siling Vandals, who disappeared from history after this point, but the Suebi and Hasding Vandals (henceforth, 'Vandals') were left unmolested. Further conflicts in Spain saw Maximus attempt to reassert his authority, and an imperial army under the *comes* Asterius was dispatched to support the Suebi, who were under attack from the Vandals. Asterius's campaign pushed the Vandals into Baetica, where they consolidated their position. Another imperial expeditionary force was sent against the Vandals under the *magister militum* Bonifatius and the *comes domesticorum* Castinus, but after the two generals fell out over Galla Placidia's favour for Bonifatius, and after Bonifatius left for Africa in irritation, Castinus's force was beaten in 422 when the Visigoths abruptly abandoned their alliance with Ravenna. The unexpected victory of the Vandals in this contest left them dominant in Spain, and they followed their triumph by seizing the Balearic Islands and Hispalis (Seville). Securing their hold on the southern Spanish ports, the Vandals also rapidly developed a potent naval capability. Southern Spain provided fertile lands to feed their growing community, but even more attractive pastures beckoned across the Straits of Gibraltar: in the late 420s, the Vandals, under their charismatic king, Gaiseric, who came to power after his brother Gunderic died in 428, crossed to Africa and began to build a position in Mauretania Tingitana.

The *magister militum* Constantius married Galla Placidia in 417; the couple had two children, Honoria and Valentinian (III). Galla despised her new husband, and she had returned from Gaul with a permanent Gothic bodyguard, which helped to underwrite her power at court. Constantius sought to reassert imperial authority in Gaul by creating the Council of the Seven Provinces, a provincial association covering the territories of southern Gaul and northern Spain with an annual meeting at Arelate, and gave a military arm to the Council when he arranged for Wallia and the Visigoths to be settled in Aquitania II. Along the Rhine, isolated pockets of imperial control were maintained at key centres such as Moguntiacum, but the northern provinces of Gaul had, in real terms, been abandoned to the Franks and Alamanni just as Britannia had been abandoned to the Picts and Saxons. In 418 Wallia was succeeded by Theoderic I, who turned what the Romans had likely intended to be a temporary settlement in Aquitania II into a zone of Visigothic control centred around the city of Tolosa (Toulouse). In 421, Honorius and Constantius briefly held power together and Galla Placidia took the title Augusta, but Constantius died in September and a rift immediately emerged between Galla Placidia and Honorius. By 423, their relationship had broken down and Galla fled to her niece, Pulcheria, in Constantinople, and later in the year Honorius died. His reign had seen substantial sections of the tax-paying landowners lose their land to the Visigoths, Vandals, Suebi, and Alans, which resulted in the inability of the court at Ravenna to fund its obligations, recruit and pay effective armies, and maintain control over the western provinces. This process had been underway for some time; however, the invasions of the early fifth century, the disruptions that they caused to people and their land, and the excessive burden they placed on the tax system to support the army all combined to fragment the western empire and, within several generations, caused its final remnants to wither away and collapse.

An important factor that proved fatal to the western court was sustained, bitter, and destructive in-fighting. Honorius was succeeded after a brief interval by the *primicerius*

Figure 13.10 Gold solidus of Licinia Eudoxia, minted in Ravenna before 445. The reverse shows Eudoxia enthroned, with the traditional legend SALVS REI PVBLICAE. The notation 'CONOB' is a royal guarantee of the coin's gold purity.

notariorum, John, who was supported by Castinus but opposed by Bonifatius, who refused to acknowledge him. The rift between the court factions widened when Theodosius II awarded Bonifatius the position of *comes Africae*, and he came to blows with an expedition sent against him by John. The situation worsened yet further when Theodosius recognised Valentinian, the son of Constantius and Galla Placidia, as Caesar at Thessalonike in 424; Valentinian's sister, Honoria, received the title of Augusta. John, meanwhile, sent the *protector* Aëtius to prepare a defence of Italy against the military force that he expected would be sent by Theodosius to bolster the young Valentinian's authority. Aëtius had previously been a political hostage amongst the Huns from 405 to 408, and maintained good relations with Rua; he recruited a substantial force to fight for John's cause, but mysteriously turned up only *after* Theodosius's troops under Aspar captured Ravenna, exiled Castinus, and put John to death. Aëtius then demanded a position within the government, holding the court hostage with the threat of his Hunnic army; he emerged from the rout unscathed and with the position of *magister equitum per Gallias*. Valentinian was crowned as Valentinian III in October 425, and was quickly engaged to Licinia Eudoxia, the daughter of Theodosius II (Figure 13.10).

The court of the six-year-old child-emperor Valentinian III was a hotbed of intrigue and double-dealing. Aëtius, the *magister militum*, the *patricius* Constantius Felix, and the *comes Africae* Bonifatius struggled to control Valentinian and his mother, Galla Placidia, who re-emerged as an important force behind the throne. In 425, Bonifatius was promoted to the position of *comes domesticorum et Africae*, upsetting the balance of power between the three rivals, and as their infighting worsened the Vandals seized the initiative and moved out of their Mauretanian bridgehead to seize the wealth of Africa. Aëtius fought the Visigoths at Arelate in 427 and the Franks in northern Gaul in 428, while Bonifatius, who had fended off two attempts by Felix to remove him before Felix died in opaque circumstances in 430, tried to oppose the expansion of Vandal power in Africa. He was beaten in 429 and fell back on Hippo Regius, the birthplace of Augustine, who died there during the subsequent siege. Terrible reports of massacres of African Christians by the Arian Vandals, magnified by the pens of Nicene Christian writers, spread terror throughout the African communities. Bonifatius held out at Hippo, and in 431 Aspar arrived with a fresh army from the east, but in short order both Bonifatius and Aspar were driven out of Africa amidst another Roman defeat. A year later, Bonifatius was rewarded for his failures with a promotion to *magister militum* and *patricius*, and at the same time open warfare erupted between Aëtius and his enemies, Galla Placidia and Bonifatius. Bonifatius died in the fighting, Aëtius was forced to take refuge with his allies among the Huns, and Bonifatius's vengeful brother Sebastianus was appointed *magister utriusque militiae*; in 433, however, Aëtius returned with another Hunnic army and repeated the demands he had made in 425. He was reinstated, and Sebastianus was forced to flee. All of this internal dissension, which wasted the lives of soldiers and what few funds remained in Roman coffers, continued despite the ongoing collapse of Roman authority in Africa.

In 435, with few other options, Valentinian III agreed to recognise the Vandals' position in the Mauretanian and Numidian provinces, with Hippo handed over to Gaiseric as his principal residence. The treaty was favoured in Rome due to the presence of rich land-owners among the senate, many of whose most precious holdings were in Africa and who preferred peace to devastation. The treaty was couched in the language of the *foedus*, where the districts in which the Vandals settled remained sovereign Roman territory. Between 435 and 439, Gaiseric tested the limits of his power, however, purging his entourage and exiling Nicene bishops. His fleet roamed the Mediterranean, raiding at will along the Sicilian and Italian coast. In 439, Gaiseric moved suddenly on Carthage, catching its Roman garrison off guard. Capturing the city, he continued to promote Arianism and to persecute Nicene Christians. Valentinian was again forced to negotiate with Gaiseric from a position of disadvantage, and this time, by a treaty in 442, land was ceded to the Vandals and passed out of Roman control (Figure 13.11).

Gaiseric's son, Huneric, was sent to Ravenna as surety, and was pledged in marriage to Eudocia (b. 439), the daughter of Valentinian and Licinia Eudoxia. The Vandals had carried off a remarkable coup and were awarded the best lands of Africa: Byzacena and Africa Proconsularis, all of which encompassed the rich and fertile soils that had fed Carthage, and then Rome, since time immemorial. The loss of revenue and prestige were devastating, and the centrality of the African grain shipments to Roman commerce had a tremendous knock-on effect. The grain fleets also carried every other conceivable product, from pottery, to wine, to olive oil, and so on—and while Gaiseric kept the shipments moving,

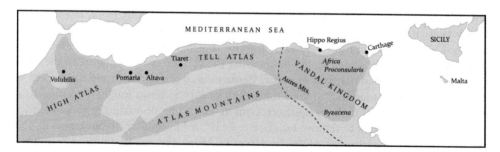

Figure 13.11 Vandal Africa in the mid-fifth century.

Source: Illustration by the author.

they now sailed at a much higher cost to the Roman government, worsening an already difficult financial situation in Ravenna. The tax implications of the loss of the massive imperial estates in Africa in 442 were similarly catastrophic and, combined with the loss of revenues from Gaul and Spain, decisively crippled the empire's ability to fund itself.

In the meantime, Visigothic power had been circumscribed in Gaul by Aëtius in several campaigns between 436 and 448. He continued to employ Huns, who formed an important part of his forces; when the Visigothic siege of Narbo was raised in 439, Hunnic cavalry brought grain into the city to feed its starving residents. Another of Aëtius's targets was the kingdom of the Germanic Burgundians, who had established themselves on the Rhine in collaboration with local landowners—a partnership that some in Ravenna thought could become a threat. After defeating the Burgundians in 437, Aëtius settled them as *foederati* in south-eastern Gaul in 443. Aëtius also fought the Franks, who had sacked Augusta Treverorum in 440. This catastrophe was memorialised by Salvian, a priest living in Massilia, whose doom-laden work interpreted the ongoing invasions as the wrath of God. 'The stench of the dead brought pestilence on the living,' he wrote, 'death breathed out death' (*On the Government of God*, 6.15). A decade later, the Frankish Salii were beaten by Aëtius at Arras, and in the aftermath Aëtius adopted the son of one of the Frankish kings. Aëtius had also engaged his son, Gaudentius, to Placidia (b. c. 439), the second daughter of Valentinian III and Licinia Eudoxia—evidently intending to follow the same approach as Stilicho two generations previously, by creating a dynastic link between himself and the imperial family. In 450, the venerable Galla Placidia died (Figure 13.12). She was buried in Rome, although popular legend has persisted in maintaining that she was interred in the beautifully decorated mausoleum bearing her name that still stands in Ravenna (Figure 13.13).

In 451, Attila abandoned his efforts to extort Constantinople, and he invaded Gaul. Ostensibly, his reason for this move was the fact that Honoria, Valentinian's sister, had attempted to escape the suffocating confines of palace life at Ravenna by offering her hand to Attila. When this was discovered, Honoria was exiled. Whatever the precise cause, Attila's invasion of the west was yet another destructive event for the battered people of northern Gaul. With Attila were Frankish Bructeri, Sciri, Rugi, Heruli, and a group of Goths, known as the Ostrogoths, led by the Amal family under their leaders Valamir, Theodemir, and Vidimir, as well as a group known as the Gepids, led by Ardaric. Attila and his allies burned their way across Gaul, sacking the city of Divodurum (Metz) on the Moselle river. They were able to penetrate the rich lands of the Loire valley before a coalition under Aëtius pushed Attila's army into the country around Durocortorum (Reims). Aëtius brought Attila to battle at the Catalaunian Fields, with an army comprising levies of Frankish Salii, Visigoths, Saxons, Burgundians, and Roman troops, including levies sent from the east (Hydatius, *Chronicle*, s.a. 452). The Visigothic king Theoderic I was killed amidst a terrible slaughter and his son, Thorismund, succeeded him before falling to an assassin in 453; he was succeeded by Theoderic II, whose rulership of what was now a discrete political entity, rather than a temporary settlement of *foederati*, provided a decade of stability in southern Gaul. Attila remained a potent force for a while longer, raiding Italy in 452 as he sought to pressure Valentinian and Aëtius to allow him to marry Honoria. Mediolanum was captured, Aquileia was sacked, and Valentinian took flight to Rome. Priscus wrote that after capturing Mediolanum, and seeing images of trampled barbarians cowering before victorious emperors, Attila ordered a painter to portray *him* with Roman

Figure 13.12 Gold solidus of Galla Placidia, minted in Ravenna 444/45. The reverse shows Victory holding a cross.

Figure 13.13 Mosaic of the Good Shepherd in the Mausoleum of Galla Placidia, Ravenna.

Source: Photograph by Petar Milošević (CC BY-SA 4.0).

emperors cowering and pouring gold before him (Blockley fr. 22.3). Later that year, Attila threatened Theodosius II's successor, Marcian, with a campaign to take Constantinople (Priscus, Blockley fr. 23.1). Yet, in 453, Attila died after a night of excess with the Gothic princess he had married, and the Hunnic empire collapsed (Priscus, Blockley fr. 24).

Attila's death may have brought relief to the courts of Ravenna and Constantinople, but the western court's propensity for in-fighting would yet claim further victims. In 454,

Aëtius was discussing the empire's budget with Valentinian when the emperor, together with his *praepositus* of the sacred bedchamber, the eunuch Heraclius, abruptly murdered him. The purge also took the life of the praetorian prefect of Italy, but only one year later, as Valentinian was engaged in archery practice on the Campus Martius—the Huns' proficiency with the bow had made a considerable impact on the Roman elite—Valentinian was himself murdered by two of Aëtius's former Hunnic comrades. He died at the age of 36, with no heir, and the western empire was set on its last course towards collapse.

After Attila

Theodosius II was succeeded in 450 by Marcian, but without any input from Valentinian III. A Thracian, Marcian was one of Aspar's favourites. In his first year, Marcian cancelled the subsidies due to Attila, while simultaneously offering the Hunnic king gifts if he adopted a peaceful attitude; Marcian may have sensed, perhaps, that Attila's gaze was firmly fixed to the west, on what Priscus called 'the greater war' (Blockley fr. 20.1). After Attila's death in 453, the Gepids under Ardaric wrested control of the disintegrating Hunnic empire in a series of conflicts in Pannonia, while Attila's loyalists and his surviving sons fell back on the Crimea. Marcian was petitioned with requests for permission to settle, which were broadly granted in preference to the costly option of refortifying and maintaining the Danube defences. The Gepids were granted land on the left bank of the Danube; the Amal Ostrogoths of Valamir, Theodemir, and Vidimir were settled in Pannonia I; and another group of Ostrogoths under Triarius (and later Theoderic Strabo) were given land in Thrace. All were granted financial subsidies in return for military service as *foederati* (Jordanes, *Getica*, 263 & 268). There were thus two distinct groups of Ostrogoths negotiating with the Constantinopolitan court: the Pannonians under Valamir and the Thracians under Triarius. The Pannonian Goths were eventually able to build a powerful position amidst the ongoing fallout from the collapse of the Huns.

Persistent concerns over the security of Thrace had tempered Constantinople's stance towards the Persians, to the extent that when Persarmenian Christians appealed to Marcian for help against Zoroastrian evangelists who had recently arrived from Ctesiphon, Marcian left them to their fate. On the other hand, Marcian and his court were keen to keep their grip on Lazica, the name given to the ancient region of Colchis that abutted both the eastern part of the Black Sea and the territory of Iberia. Under Theodosius II, the Romans had used their influence in the region to claim that they alone had the right to nominate the Lazican kings, but when king Gobaz elevated his son without seeking permission from Constantinople, a Roman expeditionary force was dispatched in 456 to restore imperial control. Lazica was important not only for its proximity to Persarmenia, but also because it physically prevented Persia from having access to a Black Sea port, and the kingdoms of the Caucasus would play a crucial role in almost every conflict between Rome and Persia in the fifth, sixth, and seventh centuries (Figure 13.14). Roman armies also campaigned under Ardabur in Syria and responded to raids by the Nobades and Blemmyes against the settlements of Upper Egypt. The main issue was access to the Temple of Isis at Philae, which was being hindered by hardline Christians. While a treaty favourable to the raiders was soon arranged, it quickly fell apart.

After cancelling the detested *collatio globis*, a tax on senatorial wealth, Marcian's principal concern soon became religious reform. Theodoret, the bishop of Cyrrhus, remained

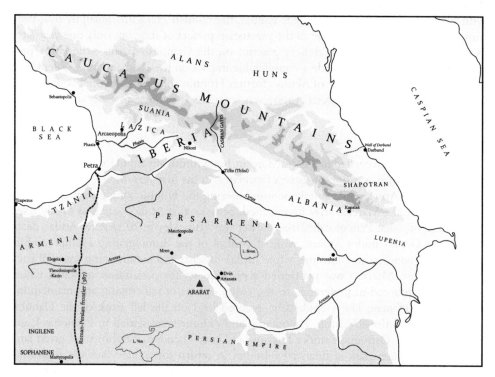

Figure 13.14 The Caucasus in the mid-fifth century.

Source: Illustration by the author.

opposed to the Cyrillian perspective on Christology, and Leo continued to complain about the lack of recognition of his *Tome*. Leo was also sympathetic to the anti-Eutychian views of Flavian, the patriarch of Constantinople, and he was supported by both Pulcheria and Anatolius, Flavian's successor in 449. These competing interests converged at the Council of Chalcedon, held in 451. In short, the council once again rejected Nestorius's views and those of Eutyches; Theodoret and Ibas were absolved; the patriarch of Alexandria, Dioscorus, was deposed; and the authority of the Council of Constantinople and the Nicene-Constantinople Creed (381) were confirmed. Leo's *Tome* finally won recognition and was accepted, leading to the Council's somewhat unhelpful pronouncement on Christology that declared Christ to have two natures within one person; Mary was also reaffirmed as *Theotokos*. Not everyone could accept what eventually became known as the Chalcedonian position. Particularly for the more conservative supporters of Cyril and Eutyches, it looked too much like a dyophysite betrayal. Later, false editions of the *Tome* cropped up in the eastern provinces, painting Leo, and therefore the Chalcedonians, as dyophysites (or 'crypto-Nestorians'). For all its lofty intentions, the Council of Chalcedon just created further division. Chalcedonians often (but not always) had the support of the emperor in Constantinople, while anti-Chalcedonians, who included monophysites, dyophysites, and other sects that appeared and disappeared at irregular intervals, found themselves alternately the targets of persecution or efforts at reconciliation. Notably, and despite the efforts of their opponents to paint them as extremists, not all of the so-called monophysites followed the rigid position of Eutyches, and many Christians believing in a single, fused nature of Christ claimed that they were aligned with the imperial orthodoxy formulated at Ephesus in 431. The modern Syrian Orthodox, Coptic, Ethiopian, and Armenian churches represent the legacy of this pro-Ephesus, anti-Chalcedonian position. Syriac Christians who followed Chalcedonian orthodoxy became known as Melkites, from the Aramaic MLK, meaning 'king'.

After Valentinian III's murder in 455, Petronius Maximus—a *patricius*, former consul, former urban prefect, and praetorian prefect of Italy—was proclaimed Augustus. One of Maximus's first acts was to marry Valentinian's widow, Licinia Eudoxia. This provided instant legitimacy, and his son, who he appointed as Caesar, married Eudoxia's daughter, Eudocia—who had, of course, been promised for some time to Huneric. Gaiseric, who regarded the treaty with Valentinian as void after his death, now decided to annex the remaining Roman provinces in Africa. He then fulfilled the prophecy of Punic vengeance made in the *Aeneid* (Chapter 8) by sailing from Carthage, up the Tiber, and sacking Rome. Maximus and his son were murdered in the mayhem that followed, having lasted a mere 75 days. Gaiseric thoroughly looted Rome, removing the treasure plundered by Titus from the Second Temple, which found its way to Carthage and subsequently on to Constantinople and Jerusalem, after which it vanished in the chaos of the seventh-century Romano-Persian war (Chapter 14). He also spirited off Licinia Eudoxia, and her daughters Eudocia and Placidia (who had recently married a Roman senator named Olybrius), together with the surviving son of Aëtius. The murder of Maximus and the pillage of Rome caused panic, but the Gallo-Roman *magister militum* Avitus was quickly proclaimed at Arelate with the support of the Visigothic king, Theoderic II. Avitus and his half-Visigothic, half-Suebic *comes* Ricimer, a veteran of Aëtius's wars, then struck back against the Vandals at sea, but Ricimer and Majorian, the *comes domesticorum*, rose in revolt and Avitus was executed.

In the east, Marcian died in 457 at the age of 65, and was buried alongside his predecessors in the Church of the Holy Apostles. A brief but anxious period passed without a replacement before the Thracian *comes* Leo, another favourite of Aspar, was proclaimed Augustus at the Hebdomon in February; for the first time, the patriarch of Constantinople was involved in approving the imperial accession. Leo soon acknowledged Majorian as *magister militum* and Ricimer as *patricius*. Majorian was subsequently proclaimed Caesar (April 457) and then Augustus (December 457). Leo's senior officials included Aspar, now a *patricius*, and Marcian's son-in-law, the *magister militum* Anthemius, who was the grandson of Arcadius's praetorian prefect of the same name. In 459, Leo was faced with a revolt by Valamir's Ostrogoths, angry at the cessation of their subsidies and even more irritated by the act that Theoderic Strabo, the son of Triarius, had emerged as a favourite in Constantinople. By 461, the eastern Roman court had accepted peace with Valamir at the cost of 136 kilograms (300 pounds) of gold annually, and Valamir also handed over Theoderic Amal, the son of Valamir's brother, Theodemir, as a political hostage.

Leo was also concerned about affairs in the west. After Huneric married Eudocia in 461/62, Licinia Eudoxia and Placidia were finally released by the Vandals after several of Leo's ambassadors had returned empty handed, and Placidia returned to her husband, Olybrius, in Constantinople. In 467, Leo demanded that Gaiseric leave Africa and Sicily, and when these demands were flatly refused, Leo dispatched a massive naval expedition and a land-based invasion, marching from Egypt, against him. After several quick victories, the Roman force agreed to a Vandal request to a parlay, but as they negotiated, Gaiseric launched a fleet of fireships against the Roman naval armada, inflicting debilitating losses. Various stories abounded to account for the dramatic failure, which cost the eastern empire dearly in ships and men. Leo's meddlesome brother-in-law, Basiliscus, often takes much of the blame, as does Aspar, yet both survived long enough after the disaster to continue their careers. The expedition was not only a military calamity; it was also fantastically expensive, with Procopius writing that it cost 59,000 kilograms (130,000 pounds) of gold (*Wars*, 3.6). In the aftermath of the destruction of the Roman fleet and the retreat by the land-based arm of the expedition, Leo agreed to peace terms with Gaiseric.

The years of 467/68 also witnessed raids by a Turkic-Bulgar people known as the Saraghurs. Crossing the Caucasus, they overwhelmed the Persian defences and raided into Iberia and Persarmenia. The Saraghurs had also menaced the region west of the Black Sea; there, two of the surviving children of Attila became caught up in a series of conflicts against them that resulted in a group of Huns under one of the sons of Attila, Dengizich, being granted the right to settle as *foederati* in Thrace. Their arrival caused turmoil, however, which resulted in Dengizich's death in 469 at the hands of the *magister militum per Thracias* Anagastes; Dengizich's head became a tourist attraction for the people of Constantinople (*Easter Chronicle*, p. 598). Amidst the unrest, Valamir had died fighting the Gepids and Theodemir emerged as the main figure among the Pannonian Ostrogoths. Theodemir cultivated a good relationship with Aspar, and in 469 he crushed a coalition of Sciri, Gepids, and Rugi, further enhancing his position.

As Leo planned the ill-fated Vandal expedition, the situation in Lazica worsened considerably. The Lazican king, Gobaz, travelled to Constantinople in 465/66, where he agreed to convert to Christianity, but only a year later the Suani, who lived between Lazica and the Caucasus mountains, captured several Persian forts. The Lazicans then reneged on their agreement with Rome and pledged their allegiance to the Persians. Peroz, who had succeeded Yazdegerd II in 459, was facing immense pressure from the Kidarites and Saraghurs, and demanded that Leo stop receiving Christians, who were fleeing from Persia in violation of the treaty of 422. Peroz also pointed to the unstable situation in the Caucasus, for which he demanded further subsidies to pay for the defence of the Caspian Gates, and even asked for financial help fighting the Kidarites. Leo remained noncommittal, but sent a former praetorian prefect to the Persian court, although he was sent back after being permitted to visit the Kidarite front and form his own impressions of the fighting there. Subsequent negotiations over the question of subsidies were inconclusive, and the Persians accepted the friendship of the Lazicans, much to Leo's irritation.

In 471, Aspar's son, Ardabur, came under suspicion during a revolt by the *magister militum per Thracias*, Anagastes. Aspar, Ardabur, and Aspar's second son, Patricius, who had recently been named Caesar, were purged, earning Leo the epithet 'the Butcher'. In the aftermath, Zeno, who had been instrumental in 'uncovering' an earlier conspiracy involving Ardabur, became *magister militum praesentalis*. Zeno, whose original name was Tarasicodissa, was from Isauria, a region in southern Anatolia that had formed part of Cilicia, and that had been viewed by officials in the Republic as a den of pirates; 500 years later, Isauria's image had not improved very much, and the Isaurian faction at court was the source of much resentment and volatility. Aspar's murder also caused instability due to his popularity and influence, and in the Balkans a proxy war waged by Roman allies against the Pannonian Ostrogoths ended to the benefit of the latter when Theoderic Amal was returned to his family. The Pannonian faction regarded themselves as favourites, but when they went to war in the region around Singidunum with a group of renegade Sarmatians, they drew approbation from the eastern emperor. By 473, Theoderic Amal was moving eastwards, and Theoderic Strabo, who saw himself as Aspar's legitimate heir through his marriage to Aspar's sister, raised a revolt. Like a latter-day Alaric, Strabo was able to extort the position of *magister militum praesentalis* from the emperor, along with extremely generous terms that included Strabo's recognition as the legitimate king of the Ostrogoths. He and his community were promised 907 kilograms (2,000 pounds) of gold per year. Leo's acquiescence can be explained by his attention to the worsening state of affairs in the west, sending to Ravenna Anthemius (467), Olybrius (472), then Julius Nepos (473), and dealing with the fallout from the failed expedition against the Vandals—indeed, Malchus wrote that in 473/74, 'everything everywhere seemed to be in confusion' (Blockley fr. 1). To the instability in the critical Balkan region was added ferment on the Arabian frontier, as a refugee from Persia, Amorkesos (a Hellenised rendering of the Arabic name Mara al-Qays), defeated a Roman army, captured a Roman customs post, then sent a bishop to treat with Leo. The emperor could do little but accept this fait accompli and appointed Amorkesos as phylarch in Palaestina III. Receiving Amorkesos violated the treaty of 422, but by now Peroz was locked in a life-or-death struggle with the Hephthalite Huns, who had rapidly materialised as the most lethal foe on Persia's eastern frontier; in 476, he was taken prisoner, and was only released when he gave up his son and made a large payment. Leo's health worsened in 473/74, and Zeno's son Leo was advanced to co-Augustus in 473. On Leo's death in 474, he assumed office as Leo II.

In the west, meanwhile, Majorian and his *magister militum per Gallias*, Aegidius—another veteran from the time of Aëtius—together with a *magister epistularum* named Petrus, cowed the Burgundians under their king Gundioc in 458, while Majorian fought the Visigoths under Theoderic II. Gundioc surrendered when he was promised a military appointment at court, although the value of such positions was in rapid decline. These conflicts were accompanied by Aegidius's campaigns against the Franks at Augusta Treverorum and Colonia Agrippinensium, while Majorian took an army into Spain, where he regained the province of Carthaginiensis from the Suebi. A naval failure against the Vandals soon followed, however, which prompted Ricimer to depose Majorian in 461. Majorian was executed, but Ricimer opted to play king-maker, elevating an obscure individual named Libius Severus; the new emperor was accepted neither by Leo nor by Aegidius, who prepared to invade Italy to oust Ricimer. In the manoeuvring that followed, Aegidius's advance was stalled by Libius Severus and the Visigoths, and Gaiseric raided Sicily, Italy, Corsica, Sardinia, and the Balearic Islands.

In 463, Gundioc was rewarded for laying down his arms with the position of *magister militum per Gallias*, and Aegidius allied himself with a Frankish warrior, Childeric. The father of the famous Frankish king, Clovis, Childeric was later buried at Tournai in Belgium. His grave was discovered in 1653, and contained an array of precious Roman and Frankish goods that included a signet ring with the Latin legend CHILDERICI REGIS ('of Childeric the king'), depicting Childeric in Roman military dress; the blend of Roman and barbarian customs that the grave represented, with its Roman brooches, Frankish throwing axes, and the corpses of at least 21 horses, provides a tidy reflection of the shifting political realities of the time. Aegidius was murdered in 464/65, and his army was split between his son Syagrius and Childeric. Numerous other warlords and their warbands dotted the landscape of northern Gaul, including two men who took the title of *comes* and another who materialised from the chaos in Britain. After Childeric's death, the bishop of Durocortorum (Reims) wrote to Clovis, accepting his rule in Belgica II, and at some point in the 480s, Clovis defeated Syagrius and campaigned against his Frankish rivals, establishing a nascent Frankish kingdom in northern Gaul. By the time of Clovis's death in 511, this kingdom had spread to include the Alamanni across the Rhine and almost all of Gaul itself. It is possible that among Clovis's forces were the Roman legions mentioned by Procopius, still serving in Gaul in the sixth century in a remarkable continuity of military tradition. 'Even at the present day,' he wrote, 'they are clearly recognised as belonging to the legions to which they were assigned in ancient times' (*Wars*, 5.12).

Libius Severus died in November 465, and Ricimer once again played kingmaker—but this time, his request went to Constantinople. The Vandals expected that the new emperor in Ravenna would be Olybrius, a 'member' of their broader royal house through his marriage to their former hostage Placidia; the Vandals' ongoing efforts to attach their fortunes to imperial legitimacy were also reflected in their maintenance of the imperial cult, which had otherwise died out across the west despite Gregory of Nazianzus's assertion that a form of ruler cult, subordinated to Christianity, was acceptable (*Orations*, 4.80 = *RLA* pp. 7–8). Leo's choice for the throne in Ravenna was not Olybrius, however, but Marcian's son-in-law, Anthemius, who was proclaimed Augustus in April 467 after he arrived in Italy with an army. Epiphanius, the bishop of Ravenna, arranged a truce between Anthemius and Ricimer, with the latter marrying Anthemius's daughter, Alypia. The Gallo-Roman poet Sidonius Apollinaris travelled to Rome to deliver a fulsome panegyric to Anthemius, for which he was rewarded with the appointment of urban prefect. In the end, Anthemius's reign came to little. He appointed a friend of Majorian, Marcellinus, to lead the western empire's contributions against the Vandals in 468, but had little to offer when Euric, who had murdered Theoderic II in 466, went on to capture Arelate in 471. One of Anthemius's sons was killed in the conflict, and Euric's victory definitively marked the end of Gaul as a Roman possession. Ricimer and Anthemius then fell out, and in 472, with Ricimer's Burgundian nephew Gundobad on the scene, Rome and Anthemius came under siege. At this point, Leo sent Olybrius to try to find a solution to this quarrel, but in a move that surprised everyone, Ricimer declared Olybrius emperor, Rome was captured, and Anthemius murdered. Both Ricimer and Olybrius died soon afterwards, leaving Gundobad to become the kingmaker for the western throne. He chose to elevate Glycerius, the *comes domesticorum*. In April 473 the Roman court issued its final edict—concerning priests—and Euric and the Visigoths invaded Italy. They were beaten off by Gundobad's regime, but by now the western empire existed only as an idea.

Following Leo's death in 474, the young Leo II was joined by his father, Zeno, who ruled as sole Augustus after his son died, aged seven, in 474. With Leo I dead, Gaiseric regarded his treaty as annulled and dispatched Vandal raiding parties to plunder the eastern Mediterranean. Zeno sent him a high-ranking envoy, the *patricius* Severus, and under considerable pressure, and close to the end of his life, Gaiseric agreed to cease his piracy and also to end the persecution of Nicene Christians in the Vandal kingdom. Despite this diplomatic triumph, Zeno faced a revolt by Basiliscus, who was supported by Illus, one of the Isaurians in his *consistorium*. Illus was joined by Theoderic Strabo, the *magister militum per Thracias*, Armatus, and Zeno's mother-in-law (and Basiliscus's sister), Verina. Zeno fled Constantinople with the treasury and his family, and Basiliscus was acclaimed Augustus in the east and won acceptance in the west. He quickly sidelined Verina by appointing his wife, Zenonis, as Augusta, and executed the *magister officiorum*, who may have been having an affair with Verina.

The most innovative event of Basiliscus's brief reign in 475/76 was the anti-Chalcedonian encyclical that he issued in April 475, in collusion with the anti-Chalcedonian patriarch of Alexandria, Timothy 'the Cat'. His encyclical cancelled much of what the Council of Chalcedon had decided, and rejected Leo's *Tome*. The encyclical enjoyed initial success, but was later shunned—most dramatically by the patriarch of Constantinople, Acacius, who covered the Church of Holy Wisdom in black cloth and began a campaign of public mourning. Illus, who had been campaigning against Zeno, now switched sides, and when Zeno returned unopposed to claim his throne, Basiliscus and his family were exiled to Cappadocia. Back on the throne, Zeno filled the court with his fellow Isaurians. The encyclical of Basiliscus was cancelled, and in 482 Zeno issued the so-called *Henotikon*, another attempt to resolve the problems created by the Council of Chalcedon by falling back on the primacy of Nicaea. It was quite moderate in its attempt to bridge the gaps between the various positions: it condemned both Eutyches and Nestorius; it avoided discussing the Council of Chalcedon; and it accepted some of the writings of Cyril. While the Chalcedonian clergy were willing to go along with the *Henotikon*, the arch-Chalcedonian 'Sleepless Monks' (so-called for their 24-hour liturgy) in the capital kept a line of communication open with Felix III, the bishop of Rome. Felix excommunicated Acacius, the *Henotikon*'s author, creating the Acacian Schism between Constantinople and Rome that lasted until 519.

Meanwhile, Zeno had turned his attention to the two Theoderics. In a woeful tale of palace intrigue that rivalled the worst depredations of the western court, Zeno imprisoned his mother-in-law, Verina, turned on Theoderic Amal, pushed the people of Thessalonike to the brink of rebellion, and so thoroughly alienated the Goths that Theoderic Amal and Theoderic Strabo joined forces. In the confusion that followed, Theoderic Amal turned down a lucrative offer from Zeno, in part because it required him to fight Strabo, while Strabo accepted the position of *magister militum praesentalis* and command over two *scholae* of the palatine guard. Theoderic Amal thus became an imperial enemy and retreated to Epirus Nova, but after Zeno fell out with Strabo and a group of Turkic Bulgars was hired to fight him, Strabo made an attempt on Constantinople. When this failed, he was killed in a bizarre accident that, according to the chronicler Marcellinus Comes, involved him being thrown from his horse onto a well-positioned spear (s.a. 481); his son, Recitach, was then murdered, and this brought the Thracian Ostrogoths as a meaningful political force to an end. All of this was to the benefit of Theoderic Amal, who became *magister militum praesentalis* and ordinary consul in 484.

Between 484 and 488, Zeno became preoccupied by the renewed machinations of Illus and Verina. Illus had married Leo I's daughter, Leontia, held the consulship in 478, and served as *magister officiorum*. Together, Illus and Verina raised first Marcian, Verina's son-in-law, and then the *magister militum per Thracias*, Leontius, to the imperial throne. An army that included Gothic levies fighting under Theoderic Amal penned Leontius into the mountain fastness of Papirius, where Verina died. Illus and Leontius were both captured and executed, with Leontius's head used to adorn a javelin on Constantinople's walls. In the final years of Zeno's reign, the revolt of the Samaritan leader Justasas against over-zealous Christian interference was crushed, and the centre of Samaritan worship on Mt Gerezim was transformed into a church. A rebellion in Persarmenia against Zoroastrians in 481 drew in Iberians and Roman Armenians, and in this febrile climate, Peroz took a harsh line against Persian Christians; when the *catholicos* Babowai tried to open negoti-ations with Zeno, he was executed in 484. In the same year, Peroz was killed in action at Herat, fighting the Hephthalites, but Roman-Persian tensions continued, made worse by a drought that caused raiding around Nisibis by Roman and Persian Arabs in 485. A letter written to the new *catholicos* by Barsauma, the bishop of Nisibis, provided vivid testimony of the widespread destruction of farms, livestock, and villages that were caused by 'the mob of tribes from the south' (*Synodicon Orientale*, pp. 526–7). The position of Persian Christians was improved under Peroz's successor, Balash, who accepted the dominance of Christianity in Persarmenia. In 486, a synod at Ctesiphon recognised dyophysite Christianity as its offi-cial doctrine, which caused a further split between Roman and Persian Christians, and in 489, Zeno closed the 'School of the Persians'—the centre for theological training at Edessa that followed Theodore of Mopsuestia—and its members moved to Persian-held Nisibis. Today, the descendants of this tradition are members of the Assyrian Church of the East.

Romulus, Odoacer, and Theoderic

The final act of the western Roman empire got underway with the deposition of Glycerius by Julius Nepos, the *magister militum Dalmatiae* and nephew of Majorian's friend, Marcellinus. Unusually for the time, Glycerius was allowed to survive in exile. Instead of seizing the purple or maintaining his Roman military title, Gundobad retired to the Burgundian court—a sharp reflection of the diminished value of the imperial throne. With the help of Epiphanius, the bishop of Ravenna, Nepos also accepted Visigothic royal power in southern Gaul and the existence of Gaiseric's Vandal kingdom in Africa. In another reflection of western imperial malaise, when he was faced with a revolt in 475, Nepos did not even attempt to contest it, but retired into five years of relative obscurity. The rebellion was led by the *patricius* and *magister militum*, Orestes, who set up his son as Augustus. With marvellous historical irony, Orestes's son—the last recognised Roman emperor in the west—was named Romulus. Orestes and Romulus were soon opposed by Odoacer, a man who was very much a creature of his time: his father was a key member of Attila's court, he had come to prominence fighting both for and against the Romans, he was believed to be either from the Sciri, Rugi, Goths, or some combination thereof, and he was, at the time, serving in some capacity in the Roman military. After gathering a force of Sciri, Odoacer removed Orestes and deposed Romulus on September 4, 476 (*Anonymous Valesianus*, 8). The Roman senate sent an embassy to Zeno, returning the imperial robes and asking him to reunify the empire with Odoacer acting as his *patricius* and deputy. Zeno, taking the position that there was still a legally appointed emperor in the west, opted to maintain his support for Nepos, who still tenuously claimed the title of Augustus from self-imposed exile in Dalmatia. However, Zeno took no definitive action either in Nepos's favour or against Odoacer. Gaiseric died in 477, which eased the threat from Africa, and Huneric, who succeeded his father, agreed to honour the peace with Constantinople. In the same year, Odoacer won a measure of local fame in Rome when he arranged for the Vandals to return Sicily, which benefited the remaining landowners in the senate.

Nepos was murdered in 480, and following a mutual defence treaty with Childeric in 481/2, Odoacer was faced with a fresh problem in 486 as Zeno, recognising the possibility that he might join the rebellion of Illus and Leontius, persuaded the Rugi to raid into Noricum and threaten Italy. In 487, Odoacer responded aggressively, defeating the Rugi and killing their king; the Rugi survivors fled to Theoderic Amal in Moesia. In the same year, Theoderic threatened Constantinople and Zeno's patience with him came to an end. Turning him against Odoacer in 488 with a grant of patrician status, he promised him the right to rule Italy as Zeno's viceroy if he was victorious. Theoderic departed from the old Roman fortress of Novae on the Danube with levies of Goths, Rugi, Romans, and other adventurers. Heading west, he defeated the Gepids at Sirmium and then Odoacer in 489, driving him back to Ravenna. Theoderic sent an embassy led by the *princeps senatus* and *patricius* Festus to Zeno, reporting on his achievements; and despite desperate attempts to shore up his position, which included summoning the Burgundian Gundobad, Odoacer steadily lost ground. Theoderic entered Ravenna on March 5, 493, and Odoacer was murdered. A new chapter in Italy's history had begun.

AD 493

The tale of the end of the western empire is a monotonous litany of intrigue, in-fighting, and corruption, while the reigns of Leo, Zeno, and Basiliscus in the east also fail to inspire confidence. The total dominance of self-interest in the court at Ravenna to the detriment of imperial unity, fiscal responsibility, sound judgement, or any of the qualities that defined Rome's successful emperors—men like Marcus Aurelius or Antoninus Pius—is truly astonishing. By 493, Roman imperial authority had collapsed in western Europe and was tenuous at the extreme in the Balkans. A striking viewpoint of this total breakdown is given by Eugippius, who wrote a hagiography of St Severinus of Noricum (d. c. 482). Soldiers paid by the central government had once secured the frontier communities in Noricum from harm, Eugippius wrote. While most had now fled, he went on, the Batavians remained in their fort until, desperate, they sent a group of soldiers from among themselves to go to Italy to obtain pay and reinforcements; they never returned (*Life of St Severinus*, 20.1 = RLA p. 78). How often this kind of scenario played out along the Rhine and Danube, and in Britannia and northern Gaul, can only be imagined, but it is easy to imagine how isolated detachments, cut off from public funding due to the collapse of the taxation system, succumbed to the inevitable, striking off on their own to support family and friends. The sixth-century Gallic legions mentioned by Procopius illustrate the other option—to gamely carry on, and maintain a semblance of discipline and unit cohesion under new commanders. In the case of the inhabitants of Noricum, there was some form of succor when Onoulph, Odoacer's brother, resettled part of its population in Italy, bringing with him the relics of St Severinus, but such evacuations were an exception—and also of dubious value, as Italy itself was hardly secure.

The processes that led to collapse in the west resulted in the formation of several discrete kingdoms, whose political bases were founded on cooperation between provincial landowning elites, Christian clergy, and a military stratum that was provided by the Vandals, Goths, Burgundians, and Franks. In many cases, these barbarians had become what Peter Brown once called 'alternative Romans': the long history of contact and cooperation between barbarians and Roman landowners, office holders, and bureaucrats had narrowed the differences between Romans and the people who had once been derided by Roman writers as 'the other'. Sidonius Apollinaris, for instance, writing to his brother-in-law, described the Visigothic king Theoderic I in flattering terms that depicted an ascetic aristocrat, fully in control of himself, holding court, dispensing law, and meeting the expectations of the Gallo-Roman clergy (e.g. *Letters*, 2). Older scholarship on the decline of the Roman empire took delight in the image of hordes of Goths swarming through the streets of Rome but, as we have seen, Alaric's goal was recognition from the state, not its destruction. As the successor kingdoms took shape in the former provinces of the empire, provincial elites generally came to terms with their new powerbrokers. Local administration continued to function, coins were minted, magistrates took office, and law codes were adjusted to meet the demands of the different parts of society. The *Lex Gundobada*, for instance, brought together Roman laws and Burgundian legal customs to adjudicate for a mixed population, and introduced a Germanic custom, the payment of *wergild*, as a means of atonement when a Burgundian murdered another Burgundian. The *Lex* also brought a new perspective to law by setting the date of 451—the defeat of Attila—as the earliest date for which retroactive litigation could be considered. The Visigoths approached the legal problem by producing the *Breviarium of Alaric* (the *Lex Romana Visigothorum*), a compendium of Roman law, as well as the *Code of Euric*, a law that appears to have been intended for Goths. The new princes and kings held titles such as *magister militum* and *patricius*; later on, the emperor Anastasius even bestowed an entirely fictional consulate on Clovis, the king of the Franks, because imperial recognition still mattered. Roman officials adapted as well. A letter between Sidonius Apollinaris and Syagrius praised the latter for learning what he called 'the German tongue' in order to advance his career (*Letters*, 5.5). One of the most interesting reflections of the continued stamp of *Romanitas* in the most stable of those regions that came under barbarian control, but once formed the western provinces—Italy, Spain, and parts of southern Gaul—is the continuity in place names. Narbo is Narbonne; Arelate, Arles; Massilia, Marseille; Tolosa, Toulouse, Augusta Merita, Mérida, Carthago Nova, Cartagena. In contrast, the toponyms of northern Gaul and Britannia were considerably altered by dropping out of the Romano-barbarian world. Lutetia (Paris), for instance, reverted to its Celtic name commemorating the tribe of the Parisii, while in Britain, place names ending in -stead, -stow, -ton/tun, -hurst, -barrow, -bury, and so on are all derived from the language brought by Saxon settlement. An indication of just how deeply Britain was thought to have fallen out of the Mediterranean world was provided by Procopius, who related that the souls of the dead were consigned by sea to Britain from Gaul, under cover of night (*Wars*, 8.20).

While the history of the Roman empire in the sixth century is largely that of the eastern empire, the western successor states, the Franks, the Visigoths, the Vandals, and the Ostrogothic kingdom of Theoderic Amal in Italy, were important to the eastern Roman regime in Constantinople. In the sixth century, Arabia and its population also became more important than ever before, and from the Arabian Peninsula a new power emerged that destroyed the Sasanian monarchy and transformed the eastern Roman empire into a rump state centred on the Balkans. To this tumultuous final period of Roman history, which did so much to shape the medieval world, we shall now turn—bringing our journey through the world of ancient Rome to an end.

Chapter 14

The end of antiquity, 491–642

The Greeks have been defeated / In the nearest part of the land.

Quran, 30.2–3, on the fall of Jerusalem (AD 614)

The history of the Roman empire in the sixth century is dominated by the long reign of Justinian (527–65), whose ambitious military campaigns in the Mediterranean temporarily returned Africa and Italy to imperial control. Justinian sought compromise with anti-Chalcedonian Christians, and embarked on a prodigious construction program throughout the Balkans, the eastern provinces, and in Constantinople. Justinian and his predecessors, Anastasius (491–518) and Justin I (518–27), also developed a greater dependence on Arab alliances, installing the phylarch Arethas (c. 500–27), then al-Harith (c. 529–69) and his son, al-Mundhir (569–82), as 'super-phylarchs' on the eastern frontier. Al-Harith and al-Mundhir hailed from the Jafnid clan of Ghassan; achieving high rank among the *illustres* and holding the title of *patrikios*, they proved to be formidable adversaries on the battle-field and also became important patrons for the anti-Chalcedonian communities in Syria and Arabia. Al-Mundhir also served as a church mediator for Tiberius II (578–82) and, like his father, was prominently associated with the international Christian cult of St Sergius, whose powerful patrons included Justinian and his wife, Theodora, as well as the Persian king, Khusrau II, and his Christian wife, Shirin. The type of leadership promoted by the Jafnids was a unique development of the eastern Roman frontier; combining aggressive battlefield success and an association with saints, priests, and bishops, Jafnid leadership prefigured the military-religious leadership of Muslim Arab chiefs in the seventh century.

The sixth century was also marked by an important climate event, triggered by a volcanic eruption in North America in 536. The cooling period that followed lasted until c. 660 and was accompanied by famines and a devastating plague, which emerged in Egypt in 541 and returned in waves until the mid-eighth century. An important result of these recurring disasters was a dramatic intensification of the role of Christian belief in everyday life. Known as liturgification, this intensified religiosity was characterised by the promotion of Christian cults, particularly that of the Virgin Mary; an increased reliance on religious icons as talismans, especially in wartime; and the transformation of the emperor into a near-saintly figure who mediated between God and his people. Liturgification became especially prominent during the reign of Justinian and Justin II (565–78), and was subsequently reimagined by Heraclius (610–41).

Changes in climate were also partly responsible for raiding by groups of Huns and Avars, and the late sixth century witnessed the development of political ties between the imperial court and the western Turks. Italy and Africa became mired in rebellion

DOI: 10.4324/9781003202523-14

and war, and much of Italy fell to the Lombards in the 560s. In South Arabia, a revolt in Himyar resulted in the murder of the Christian population of Najran, an event that sent shockwaves throughout the Middle East; later, Himyar came under the dominance of its final king, the Christian monarch Abraha, before South Arabia was invaded and occupied by the Persians in 570. Conflicts between the Romans and their eastern neighbours were frequent, and in the early seventh century, Khusrau II (590–628) launched an ambitious invasion of the empire that captured almost every major region and city except for Constantinople. Undone through a daring campaign by Heraclius, Khusrau was toppled and the empire recovered its lost territories—only to be invaded shortly afterwards by armies from Arabia, who were embracing a new faith, Islam. The loss of Alexandria in 642 marked the definitive end of the Roman state as a Mediterranean empire, and henceforth the eastern Roman empire would be concentrated on Constantinople, the Balkans, and parts of Anatolia.

The historical sources for the sixth and early seventh centuries vary widely in their coverage and consistency. A coherent narrative for much of Justinian's reign is provided by the Greek works of Procopius (c. 500–60), a native of Caesarea in Palestine. Procopius served with Justinian's *magister militum* Belisarius for much of his career, and he participated in much of what he wrote about in the *Wars*, a classicising narrative of the Persian, Ostrogothic, and Vandal wars. Procopius was also the author of the panegyrical *Buildings*, a paean to Justinian's construction projects, and is believed to have written the vicious *Secret History*, a savage denunciation of Justinian and his powerful wife, Theodora. Procopius's work was continued by Agathias (c. 532–80), Menander Protector (late sixth century), and Theophylact Simocatta (c. 580–641). Theophylact brought to a close the long chain of classicising history that traced its origins all the way back to Thucydides. Secular history of this sort was progressively subsumed by Christian historical writing, and numerous Latin, Greek, and Syriac Christian works were produced during the sixth and early seventh centuries. Christian Greek works include the seventh-century *Easter Chronicle* and the Chalcedonian *Ecclesiastical History* of Evagrius, a lawyer from Epiphania (Hama, b. 535) who worked in the office of the patriarch of Antioch, while the *Chronicle* of the Antiochene writer John Malalas (fl. 6th c.) provides a useful witness to the reign of Justinian. Syriac works became particularly important in the sixth and seventh centuries, a reflection of the growth of Syriac Christianity in the eastern provinces. Much of what survives of the sources does so in fragments or through fortuitous preservation in later texts. The anti-Chalcedonian *Ecclesiastical History* of John of Ephesus (c. 507–88), for instance, is missing its first part and nearly complete in its third part, while much of its second part was preserved in the eight-century Syriac *Chronicle of Zuqnin*. (The latter text is also known as the *Chronicle of Ps.-Dionysius of Tel-Mahre*; Ps., 'pseudo', indicates a false authorial attribution.) The *Chronicle of Zuqnin* also preserved the *Chronicle* of Ps.-Joshua the Stylite, a crucial witness for the Romano-Persian war of the early sixth century. The sixth-century epigraphic record is less helpful than for preceding periods, but it is significant for a clutch of Christian inscriptions in an early form of the Arabic script from Roman Syria, and for texts relating to the foundation of churches and monasteries. The history of Himyar and Axum in this period is almost entirely known from inscriptions. Sources for the seventh century became markedly more problematic; they are addressed at the appropriate point in the narrative that follows.

Anastasius, 491–518

Zeno died on April 9, 491, and his widow, Ariadne, called the people of Constantinople to assemble at the Hippodrome. Standing alongside her in the *kathisma*, the *magister libellorum* announced the succession: the choice fell on Anastasius, a member of a palatine *schola* known as the *silentarii*, ushers who managed meetings of the *consistorium* and other imperial meetings. Two days later, in a mixture of Germanic and Christian customs, Anastasius was raised aloft on a shield as Julian had been more than 130 years earlier, and he then received the crown from Euphemius, the patriarch of Constantinople. Anastasius's subsequent marriage to Ariadne caused anger among the Isaurians at court, and a rebellion began almost immediately, led by Illus's brother, the *comes Isauriae* Lilingis. A purge of Isaurians widened the rebellion, which dragged on until 498. During this protracted conflict, Turkic-Bulgar groups known as the Onoghurs, Utrigurs, and Kutrighurs emerged as a dangerous force in the Balkans. Moving into the eastern steppe after the collapse of the Huns, the Onoghurs had been known to Priscus, who wrote about their conflict with the Sabir Huns in 463 (Blockley fr. 40). The Utrigurs and Kutrighurs fought both one another and the Romans, who suffered a damaging defeat in 499, and in 502 the suburbs of Constantinople were raided. In response, Anastasius ordered the construction of the Anastasian Wall (or 'Long Walls') in 503/04, an advance network of fortifications that provided Constantinople with another layer of defence.

While the Bulgars threatened Thrace and Constantinople, there were also problems on the eastern frontier, where Arab raids at the turn of the sixth century harried Euphratesia and Mesopotamia. One of the sources for these events is the Greek *Chronicle* of Theophanes the Confessor (d. 818), a record of political and ecclesiastical matters dated annalistically according to the number of years since the Creation (*anno mundi*, or 'AM'). Theophanes, as well as Evagrius, both reported that during these disturbances, the customs post that had been poached by Amorkesos in 473 was returned to Roman control. Romanus, the military commander in Palestine, also defeated an Arab named Gabalas and captured another, Ogaros, the son of a certain Arethas (Theophanes, *Chronicle*, AM 5990/p. 141; Evagrius, *Ecclesiastical History*, 3.36 = *AEBI* § 5.2 & 5.3). Theophanes characterised Arethas as 'the son of Thalabene', a reference to an Arab tribe known in Roman sources as the Thalabites. They, in turn, were sometimes to be found in the company of a western Arabian group named Mudar, whose members included Quraysh, the tribe of the Prophet Muhammad. Both the Thalabites and Mudar were clients of the Himyarite kingdom, and appear on a later Himyarite royal inscription dated to 521 recording a raid into southern Persia. The upshot of these disturbances in c. 500 was that Arethas, 'son of Thalabene', and his two sons, Ogaros and Badicharimos, concluded a treaty with Anastasius. The agreement was arranged by Euphrasius, the elder statesman of a multi-generational family firm of envoys specialising in Red Sea diplomacy. The treaty terms are not recorded, but a notice regarding Arethas's death in 527/28 (see below) recorded that he was appointed as phylarch of the province of Palaestina I, and thus he provided military service—most likely in return for subsidies.

Arab-Islamic sources also describe these conflicts, but portray them in a slightly different light. According to the Baghdadi philologist Ibn Habib (d. 860), the primary cause was the migration of Ghassan, a south Arabian tribe. The migration displaced Salih, who Ibn Habib claims were the main Arab allies of the Roman empire in the fifth century (*Kitab al-Muhabbar*, p. 370 = *AEBI* §8.29). Salih do not appear in Roman sources, but they appear again in the text of al-Yaqubi (d. c. 905), who described Salih's defeat by Ghassan in the reign of 'Nushir', a reference to Anastasius (*Tarikh*, 1 = *AEBI* §8.30). The folk memories preserved here are a valuable complement to the Roman sources because al-Harith, who became Rome's principal Arab ally in 527/28, and his son, al-Mundhir, who took over in 569, were thought to be descended from the Gabalas mentioned by Theophanes, a member of the Jafnid dynasty of Ghassan. Separately, a Basran philologist named Al-Asmai (d. 828) related how 'the clan of Mundhir' (i.e. the Nasrids) ruled Iraq, and 'the clan of Jafna' (the Jafnids) ruled Syria (*Tarikh*, 88 = *AEBI* §8.4). The importance of this episode lies in the fact that it marked the beginning of a prolonged period of alliance between Arab leaders and Roman emperors. Amidst a subsequent reorganisation by Justinian, this relationship would accord an unprecedented position to the Arab Jafnid family and encourage the same sort of concentration of power in non-Roman leaders that had taken place on the Rhine–Danube frontier with Goths, Franks, and others, as we saw in Chapters 12 and 13.

The Persian war of Anastasius

In 502, the long-standing peace between Rome and Persia collapsed. Following the death of Peroz in 484, Balash had lasted only four years on the throne before being mutilated and imprisoned by his nephew, Kavadh I. The new king promoted Mazdakism, a Zoroastrian social reform movement that encouraged a form of ascetic living and undermined the traditionally powerful Zoroastrian priesthood together with large segments of the Persian nobility, whose wealth was targeted for redistribution among Persian society. Kavadh was aggressive: in 490/91, a Persian embassy was on its way to Zeno to demand subsidies, but when Zeno died before it could arrive, the Persian ambassador received instructions to make the same demands to Anastasius. The new emperor refused and insisted instead on the return of Nisibis, and in 492, when Kavadh again demanded money, he was met with the insulting offer of a loan with interest. In 496, Kavadh was deposed in favour of his brother, Zamasp, and fled to the Hephthalites. He returned with a Hephthalite army in 499, and after beginning his second reign, he seems to have made another demand for funding from Anastasius. The emperor refused once again, and Kavadh launched an invasion of the Roman empire in 502.

Kavadh's expedition began well. Theodosiopolis-Karin and Martyropolis both surrendered; then, in 503, as Arab raids harried the Edessene countryside, Amida fell once again to the Persians and the population was put to the sword (Ps.-Zachariah, *Chronicle*, 7.4d = *REF2* p. 63). The crisis in Osrhoene was vividly described by the *Chronicle* of Ps.-Joshua the Stylite, written by an anonymous Edessene monk and preserved in the *Chronicle of Zuqnin*. The *Chronicle* recorded the aggressive raids of the Nasrid al-Numan, which netted thousands of prisoners as his army swept the districts of Carrhae and Edessa, taking advantage of the fact that much of the urban population had gone out into the countryside to help bring in the harvest (51–3 = *AEBI* §5.5). As winter approached, Kavadh withdrew to Nisibis, having achieved a great deal for only the loss of Theodosiopolis-Karin, retaken by the Romans in a sharp counter-attack by the *dux Armeniae*. In 503, the *magister militum per Orientem* Flavius Areobindus assembled a large army with Hypatius and Patricius, both of whom served in the field as *magister militum praesentalis*. Areobindus was a relative of Aspar and the husband of Anicia Juliana; the daughter of Olybrius and Placidia, Anicia was the patron of an important church in Constantinople (below). During the campaign, Ps.-Joshua described how an army of Roman-allied *tayyaye* roved in advance of the Roman forces and harried the region around al-Hira in Iraq. This raid angered al-Numan, who boasted to Kavadh that he would capture Edessa in revenge. In his description of the episode, Ps.-Joshua invoked Edessa's special relationship with Christ, stemming from the correspondence between Abgar V and Jesus (Chapter 9) that had granted Edessa divine protection. Despite being warned by a Christian in his entourage to back down, as soon as al-Numan threatened to lay a finger on Edessa, an old injury became inflamed and he died several days later in agony in his tent (*Chronicle*, 57–8 = *AEBI* §5.6). Undeterred, Kavadh appointed a new Nasrid prince and the war continued.

Patricius and Hypatius had a difficult relationship with Areobindus, and the three proved unable to coordinate their efforts. Both Patricius and Hypatius were beaten during the summer offensive of 503, and retired to Samosata. Kavadh threatened Constantia and Sarug (Batnae), then laid siege to Areobindus at Edessa; the cash-strapped Persian king demanded 4,500 kilograms (10,000 pounds) of gold to raise the siege, but the Romans refused. The two forces battled each other to a stalemate, but the new Nasrid leader, known to Roman sources as Alamoundaros (al-Mundhir), was aggressive and highly capable. In 503, he penetrated deep into Palestine and Arabia, raiding and taking prisoners. The Roman defensive system—including the phylarchs established by Anastasius—were unable to stop his incursions. As the winter approached, Kavadh attacked the Roman fortress at Callinicum, where he failed to score a success, and in 503/04, a frustrated Anastasius sent his *magister officiorum*, Celer, to reverse Roman failures in Mesopotamia. Areobindus plundered the Persarmenian countryside; looking to redeem himself, Patricius laid siege to Amida, while Celer gathered the Roman army at Theodosiopolis-Rhesaina. (Like Karin, Rhesaina had also taken the honorific name of Theodosiopolis: to avoid confusion, the cities are referred to here as Theodosiopolis-Karin and Theodosiopolis-Rhesaina.) The *dux* of Callinicum, Timostratus, launched an attack on Kavadh's animal train, then made his way with his cavalry to Amida. Neither side made headway and both agreed to settle their differences at the negotiating table in 505. As talks were held, however, both Persian and Roman Arabs raided the territory of the other, leading to savage reprisals by imperial authorities (Ps.-Joshua, *Chronicle*, 79 & 88 = *AEBI* §5.8 & 5.9). More provocative was the construction of the massive Roman fortress at Dara (Anastasiopolis), which began during the negotiations and was completed by 509. Watered by the Dara river, the city was located at the point where the mountain plateau of the Tur Abdin met the plains of Mesopotamia, and lay fewer than 25 kilometres (15 miles) from Nisibis. John Lydus called Dara a fortress 'placed at the throat of the enemy'; it was designed to compensate for the loss of Nisibis in 363 by serving as both a forward base and a refuge. It was well stocked with water retained in deep cisterns, and flush with stores of food and weapons (*On the Magistracies*, 3.28). Defensive work was also carried out at a range of sites throughout the eastern frontier region, including Palmyra, Dibsi Faraj, Halabiya-Zenobia, Rusafa-Sergiopolis, Edessa, Theodosiopolis-Karin, and Batnae. The construction of Dara clearly violated the treaty agreed in 422 (Chapter 13), which prohibited new building work, but peace was nevertheless agreed late in 506. Amida was returned to the Romans and prisoners were exchanged, and Anastasius apparently agreed to a fixed payment, to be revisited at a later date, to cover the cost of defending the Caspian Gates (Figure 14.1).

The war had generally benefited Anastasius. Many of Kavadh's petitions were successfully deflected, including the demand that work at Dara and Theodosiopolis-Karin should

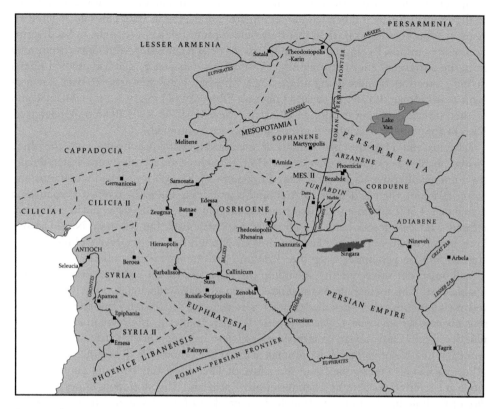

Figure 14.1 Syria, Mesopotamia, and Osrhoene during the war between Anastasius and Kavadh.

Source: Illustration by the author.

cease, and the Roman defensive network received a significant and overdue upgrade. Anastasius even felt sufficiently secure in his position to encourage the charismatic anti-Chalcedonian bishop, Simeon of Beth Arsham, to lobby at the Persian court for the better treatment of Persia's growing anti-Chalcedonian Christian community.

The western kingdoms during the reign of Anastasius

In Italy, Theoderic Amal had become king of a burgeoning Ostrogothic kingdom and set about establishing his position. He married Audofleda, the sister of Clovis, and betrothed his sister, Amalfrida, to Thrasamund (496–523), who had succeeded Huneric as king of the Vandals in Carthage. Theoderic also created dynastic links with the Visigothic king Alaric II, the Burgundian Sigismund, and king Hermanifried of the Thuringi, who had battled the Rugi in Noricum and built a substantial kingdom along the river Elbe. While several embassies from Theoderic to Anastasius seeking formal recognition had been frustrated, in 497 Anastasius returned the imperial robes that had been sent to Constantinople in 476, acknowledging Theoderic's position as his subordinate.

Theoderic's leadership style was two-pronged, with one approach for the Italians and another for the Goths. Like its Visigothic and Vandalic contemporaries, the Ostrogothic kingdom was a political and cultural hybrid that combined aspects of both Roman and Gothic culture. The way barbarian identities developed in the post-Roman west has often been framed in terms of 'ethnogenesis', a loaded term that has caused spirited debate for decades. Ethnogenesis refers to the crystallisation of a specific set of identity markers, often around a dominant clan; it is frequently associated with struggles and challenges, and because of its connection with migrations, which provided fertile ground for the sorts of struggles and challenges that could 'create' a people, ethnogenesis became caught up in the same sorts of ideological minefields that characterised the early history of the Goths (see Chapter 12 and Further Reading section). The processes of ethnogenesis and acculturation, and the peculiarities of frontier politics, ensured that one of the most prominent features of the post-Roman western kingdoms was the sort of political, cultural, and religious hybridity on display in Ostrogothic Italy. Theoderic, for example, very much acted according to what the senate expected of a Roman leader. He provided subsidised grain and patronised building projects, and he also allowed himself to be portrayed as 'victorious and triumphant, the perpetual Augustus', on a Latin inscription recording repairs to the via Appia (*ILS* 827). Theoderic made his *adventus* into Rome in 500 with all the pomp of a bygone Roman emperor, delivering a speech to the senate in the forum and honouring Rome's Nicene bishop, despite his own Homoean faith. For the Goths, however, Theoderic was a *rex* who supported Gothic Homoean Christianity and carefully maintained the militarised persona of a lord who crushed his opponents in battle. Latin panegyrics delivered by the bishop of Mediolanum in the 490s celebrated his rustic manliness: his success, and his manly *virtus*, protected the population of Italy and ensured that he maintained his position at the apex of Gothic society.

Theoderic's rule was given a literary dimension by Cassiodorus, who served the Ostrogothic king as quaestor, consul (in 514), *magister officiorum*, and then the praetorian prefect of Italy. Cassiodorus's *Variae* stressed *civilitas*, the respectful harmony between Goths and Romans in the new state, bound by Roman laws. Another insight into the developing Ostrogothic identity was provided by Jordanes in his *Getica*. Theoderic's father was Theodemir, and his uncle was Valamir—but his lineage beyond this point was distinctly murky. Against this was arrayed the longevity of the Roman empire, its lists of consuls, kings, and emperors, and so Jordanes followed Cassiodorus by conjuring a noble lineage of the Amal dynasty that set Theoderic on an equally ancient level, and made him worthy of brotherhood with the Romans (*Getica*, 14). For his part, Procopius regarded Theoderic as a man who met Roman expectations by being 'exceedingly careful to observe justice' and who 'protected the land and kept it safe from barbarians' (*Wars*, 5.1.24–26). In 504/ 05, Theoderic created a buffer zone protecting the northern approaches to Italy with campaigns against the Gepids in Pannonia II and Illyricum—even though, by straying too far into Moesia, he invited a naval raid from Anastasius that harried the Italian coast in 507. In 510, Theoderic returned some of the Pannonian territory that he had conquered, but relations with Anastasius were often frosty. The emperor recognised one of Theoderic's rivals, the Burgundian Sigismund, while Theoderic supported the rebellion of Vitalian (below).

In Gaul, the Burgundian and Frankish kingdoms presented a very similar picture. Burgundian documents and inscriptions continued to use the consular dating system, and when the Nicene Sigismund pledged his loyalty to Anastasius with the formula *gentis rex sed militum vestrum*, 'king of a people, but your soldier', he was rewarded with the rank of *patricius* (Avitus of Vienne, *Letters*, 46A). The Burgundians were eventually swallowed up between 523 and 534 by the Ostrogoths, and by the Gallic expansion of the Franks. Clovis was the architect of early Frankish power; marrying a Nicene Burgundian noblewoman, Clothilda, who pestered him to convert to Christianity, Clovis eventually did so in the aftermath of an undated and obscure conflict with the Alamanni. Clovis pledged his loyalty to the Christian God if he emerged victorious—a rather formulaic story that found its way into the *History of the Franks* (2.30), the epic work of Gregory, the bishop of Tours (539–94). Like the Amals, Clovis and his family also suffered from a lack of history. Clovis was Childeric's son, and Childeric's father was Merovech (hence, 'Merovingian'), but one of Merovech's parents was a bull-like creature who lived in the sea. Clovis thus closely identified his cause with the bishop of Vienne and portrayed himself as a Christian warrior-king, an image that was bolstered when Anastasius awarded him an honorary consulate. 'In St Martin's church he stood clad in a purple tunic and the military mantle,' wrote Gregory of Tours, and 'he then rode out on his horse, showered gold and silver coins among the people present all the way from St Martin's church to Tours Cathedral; and from that day on he was called consul or Augustus' (*History of the Franks*, 2.38). Imperial recognition helped to address Clovis's lack of regal history, and Gregory recognised him as a 'new Constantine' (2.31). Clovis quickly developed a reputation as a successful and aggressive warrior. His wars involved the destruction of the Thuringians, creating a vacuum that was quickly filled by the Langobardi (Lombards), and in 507 Clovis defeated the Visigothic king Alaric II in single combat, establishing Frankish control over almost all the former Gallic provinces, except for a Visigothic foothold that was maintained in Septimania (Languedoc). Clovis minted gold solidi on Roman standards, imitating eastern imperial coins, while the Visigoths, too, followed this approach, imitating recent western imperial coinage (Figure 14.2). With the exception of Septimania, the Visigoths from this point were confined to Spain, where the kingdom, under its final sovereign, Roderic, fell to Muslim Arab invaders after 711.

Vandal Africa was administered through a partnership between a small Vandal elite and the residents of the cities and farms in the countryside. By the treaty of 442 and

Figure 14.2 Visigothic gold coin of uncertain mint and king, imitating a solidus of Valentinian III.

his subsequent campaigns, Gaiseric had appropriated large estates that had hitherto been imperial property; the income from these lands was substantial, and he could also afford to dole them out to supporters without causing too much disruption to local Roman land-owners. The imperial cult survived throughout much of the fifth century (Chapter 13), perhaps as a result of an attempt by Gaiseric to build a sense of imperial legitimacy. At the fringes of Vandal power in the west were communities of Romano-Berbers with a long acquaintance with Roman authority (for the locations of the places discussed here, see Figure 13.11). At Altava near the Severan-era military road that connected Volubilis with Tlemcen (Pomaria), Altava, and then led eastwards, a Latin inscription dated to 508 was discovered that recorded the construction of a fort. It was dedicated by a prefect and a procurator to Masuna, *rex gentium Maurorum et Romanorum*—'king of the Moorish [Berber] people and the Roman people' (*CIL* 8.9835). Another Latin inscription, found in the Numidian Aurès mountains in 1941, was dedicated to the memory of a certain Masties. Preceded by the pagan formula *dis manibus sacrum*, 'sacred to the spirits of the departed', the text recorded Masties's career: '*dux* for sixty-seven years, *imperator* for ten years, + [cross], I never betrayed, nor broke the faith, neither with the Romans, nor with the Moors [Berbers] and I obeyed [God] in war as in peace'. The position of *dux* was probably an imperial appointment, either by the Vandals or from Ravenna. According to Procopius, there were revolts in the Aurès during the reign of Huneric (477–84), which ejected the Vandals from the region (*Wars*, 3.8), and this might lie behind the use of the title *imperator*, which represented a claim to royal Roman power. With the collapse of imperial control, *imperator* could be used safely, especially if intended for local consumption, and established a veneer of Roman continuity in the context of a difficult relationship with the Vandals in Carthage.

A series of 13 monuments in western Algeria near Tiaret, known as the *djedars*, provide further expressions of the sorts of hybridised cultural and political identities so characteristic of the post-Roman period. The *djedars* are square monuments surmounted by stone pyramids, and they borrow heavily from the architecture of prehistoric Saharan tombs, while at the same time featuring Christian designs; one, for instance, includes what was apparently a painting of Christ as the Good Shepherd. A worn Latin inscription on one refers to a *dux* and an illegible provincial era date, suggesting that its occupant held a Roman (or post-Roman) military appointment. South-west of Leptis Magna at the Bir ed-Dreder cemetery, tombstones recorded men who had Libyan names, but also referred to themselves as Flavius (in homage to Constantine) and held Roman titles; at Ghirza, to the east, mausolea of men with Roman and Libyan names show figures seated on senatorial curule chairs, attended by figures bearing sceptres. The African evidence is intriguing in its blend of Roman iconography and local traditions, and provides a snapshot of a flourishing Romano-Berber community that would, in just several decades, be brought to the edge of ruin by Justinian's ambitious military expedition to bring Africa and Italy back into the empire.

Economy and religion

Before his death in 518, Anastasius conducted a range of important economic reforms. The hated *chrysargyron* was cancelled in 498, and a new range of copper coins intended to facilitate small-scale financial transactions, principally the nummus and the follis (worth

40 nummi), achieved wide circulation. Unlike precious metal coins such as the solidus, the copper coins could not be debased, which gave the lower-level currency an important measure of stability. Two other issues consumed the emperor: the ongoing tussle between anti-Chalcedonian and Chalcedonian Christians, and the stability of the Balkans.

Anastasius was openly sympathetic to the substantial anti-Chalcedonian communities in the empire, and this, together with his support for the *Henotikon*, led to a difficult relationship with the Chalcedonian patriarch of Constantinople, Euphemius. The Alexandrian anti-Chalcedonians saw an opportunity to strike a blow against their enemies, and persuaded the emperor to hold a council in 496 to address their scandalous charge that Euphemius was a 'secret Nestorian'. Assailed from all sides, Euphemius was deposed and exiled. His replacement, Macedonius, took a conciliatory approach despite his Chalcedonian background. His enemies were not as agreeable, however, and Anastasius took no action when the virulently anti-Chalcedonian clergyman Severus demanded that Macedonius sign a document condemning Chalcedonian orthodoxy. The predictable result of Macedonius's refusal was his exile in 511, and in 512, Severus became patriarch of Antioch in the aftermath of a violent riot started by his allies. The violence spread to Constantinople, where a group of outraged Chalcedonians declared the former *magister militum per Orientem* Areobindus emperor and fought running battles against imperial troops. Areobindus kept a low profile while Anastasius offered to resign the throne, but in the end Anastasius was acclaimed by crowds in the Hippodrome; the danger had passed, but the divisions that had been so violently exposed between the different communities would continue to fester.

In the Balkans, the vacuum left by the departure of Theoderic Amal had been filled by *foederati*, principally drawn from the Heruli. A revolt flared up in 514, however, when the imperial court cancelled federate subsidies. The rebellion showed just how tenuous imperial rule was in this difficult area: Vitalian, the *magister militum per Thracias*, threw in his lot with the rebels and suborned the *dux Moesiae*; he could also count on support from Theoderic Amal, who had a difficult relationship with Anastasius, as mentioned earlier, and saw an opportunity to weaken the emperor's position. Vitalian demanded the restoration of Euphemius and Macedonius, but the only response from Constantinople was the dismissal of the ineffectual *magister militum praesentalis*, Hypatius. The situation then degenerated into farce: Hypatius's replacement was murdered at Odessa, while he was replaced by another Hypatius, a relative of the emperor. A man named Alatharius was entrusted with the position of *magister militum per Thracias*, but both he and the second Hypatius were taken captive following an embarrassing military debacle. After negotiations broke down, Vitalian was eventually beaten on the battlefield by the praetorian prefect of Oriens. In a reflection of their growing political clout, the circus factions, known as the 'Blues' and 'Greens' for the teams they supported in the Hippodrome, offered their considerable armed support to the emperor. This crisis also passed, and a few years later Anastasius died, on July 8, 518; he was buried with Ariadne (d. 515) in the Church of the Holy Apostles. Despite the unrest during his reign, his currency and economic reforms delivered a surplus of 145,000 kilograms (320,000 pounds) of gold to the Roman treasury.

Justin I, 518–27

Justin was from the region of Naissus, and he had served in Anastasius's conflict with the Isaurians, in the Persian war of 502–05, and in the war against Vitalian. On his accession, he was serving as the *comes excubitorum*, the commander of an elite palatine guard unit (the 'excubitors'), formed by Leo I. Justin was a Chalcedonian, and, together with his wife Euphemia and John II, the patriarch of Constantinople, he ended the Acacian Schism and closed the door on Anastasius's support for anti-Chalcedonian Christians. He recalled Severus from Antioch, although the patriarch instead chose to banish himself to anti-Chalcedonian Alexandria, where he found a welcome from patriarch Timothy IV, before dying in 538. The anti-Chalcedonian bishop of Hierapolis (Mabbug), Philoxenus, who had prospered under Anastasius, was also removed and died in exile in 523. Vitalian was recalled and appointed *magister militum praesentalis* and ordinary consul for 520. He was a fierce supporter of Justin's policies, but his rehabilitation was brief: Justin's ambitious nephew, Justinian, arranged Vitalian's murder in the same year, then took over his military command. Justinian was consul in 521, and then—in a marriage vehemently opposed by Euphemia before her death in 523/24—he married Theodora. The marriage scandalised Procopius: Theodora's father, he claimed, kept bears for the Green circus faction, and her mother was an actress. In Procopius's sensationalist account, Theodora gained notoriety for her lewd performances on stage and her unquenchable sexual appetite (e.g. *Secret History*, 9.20–6). Theodora's low birth should, theoretically, have barred her from marrying Justinian, but Justin was persuaded to alter the law to his nephew's benefit.

Vitalian's death defused the tense sectarian climate, and the anti-Chalcedonian bishop of Edessa, Paul, who had earlier been deposed, was restored by the emperor with the promise of a more reconciliatory attitude. He used his return to office to consecrate two further anti-Chalcedonian bishops, Jacob of Serug and John of Tella, although each lasted only until 521. Despite this abrupt reversion to tolerance, the repeated use of exile, deposition, and summary judgement contributed to the way anti-Chalcedonian Christians came to understand their relationship with imperial authorities. These repeated struggles influenced anti-Chalcedonian hagiographies of pious figures whose virtuous toil in the face of impossible odds reflected the *true* Christianity. For anti-Chalcedonian Syriac-speaking Christians, it was *their* religion that was the orthodox, and it was Chalcedonian Christianity that was heretical. When the Christians of Najran were massacred in the 520s (see below), the anti-Chalcedonian movement received its first martyrs; from exile in Egypt, Severus would write of the unity of the Egyptian and Syrian churches, bonded by their shared 'orthodox' faith.

The central issue of Justin's reign was the empire's relationship with its neighbours. In 519, the emperor took the ordinary consulship with Flavius Eutharicus, the son-in-law of Theoderic Amal. Justin designated his colleague *filius per arma*, 'son-in-arms', a form of adoption that accepted Ostrogothic autonomy. Hilderic, the son of Eudocia and Huneric, was living in Constantinople and was on good terms with Justinian. Relations with the Persians were also cordial, despite the defection of the Lazican king, Tzath, to the Romans; Tzath, who Malalas reported was expecting to be crowned king by the Persians, sought conversion to Christianity and appointment by Justin instead (*Chronicle*, 17.9). The Iberian king Gourgenes followed his example not long afterwards. Kavadh was able to accept these developments, and even suggested that Justin adopt his son and successor, Khusrau, to protect him from the inevitable palace intrigue that was to come when Kavadh died. Both Justin and Justinian agreed, but the imperial quaestor Proculus firmly opposed the plan, pointing out that Khusrau might find himself in a position to inherit the eastern empire on Justin's death (Procopius, *Wars*, 1.11). Justin proposed instead that Khusrau, like Eutharicus, be adopted as *filius per arma*, but negotiations collapsed.

The region with the greatest instability, however, was southern Arabia. In c. 500, Axum invaded Himyar from across the Red Sea, installing Christian kings who answered to their masters in Ethiopia. Himyar's conqueror, Kaleb Ella Asbeha, commemorated his victory on a monumental inscription written in Geez, the liturgical language of Axum. The expedition was heady with militant Christianity: 'With the power of God and with the grace of Jesus Christ, son of God, the Victor, in whom I believe,' the text begins, 'He who gave me a kingdom with power, with which I subjected my enemies and I trampled the heads of those who despise me.' Kaleb enthroned his client Marthadilan Yanuf and founded 'a sanctuary ... filled with zeal for the name of the Son of God' (*AEBI* §3.13). When Marthadilan died in 515, he was succeeded by a steadfast Christian named Madikarib Yafur, and with Himyar now joined with Constantinople via a Christian axis that passed through Axum, Madikarib launched an ambitious expedition to southern Iraq in 521. According to an inscription from Masal al-Jumh in central Arabia, allied auxiliaries from Mudar and from among the Thalabite Arabs took part (*AEBI* §3.14). The expedition's target was 'Mudhdhir'—Persia's Nasrid client Alamoundaros, who had continued his raiding unchecked and even captured two Roman *duces*, John and Timostratus. Madikarib returned from the expedition in the same year, but died in 521/22 and was replaced by another Axumite appointee, Joseph, but in a violent rebellion, Joseph killed the Axumite garrison in Zafar and burned its church. Afterwards, the Jews of Himyar 'in bitter wrath slew and destroyed all the Christian people there, men, women, young people and little children, poor and rich' (*Chronicle of Zuqnin* 3, p. 56 = *AEBI* §6.45). Joseph ordered a prince of the dhu-Yazan, Sharahil Yaqbul, to besiege Najran, which had communities of monophysite and dyophysite Christians, as well as Jews and pagans; the Christians of Najran were the primary target, and by the summer of 523, Sharahil had surrounded Najran, trapping its population inside. Joseph then arrived on the scene: an inscription set up by Sharahil at Hima in July 523 recorded the blockade of the city and the massacre perpetrated on its population—a toll of '12,500 slain' and '11,000 prisoners, 290,000 camels, cows and sheep' taken as booty (*AEBI* §3.16).

The destruction of the Najrani Christian community was a major event and, like the Roman defeat at Adrianople, produced a near-instantaneous literary impact. The texts that celebrated the Najrani martyrs included the Greek *Martyrdom of Arethas* and the Syriac *Book of the Himyarites*, but one of the most important responses was a letter written by Simeon of Beth Arsham. The so-called 'Letter C', the best-preserved version of which is found in the sixth-century Syriac *Chronicle* of Ps.-Zachariah, was addressed to the bishop of Gabbula in Syria. Simeon was at Ramla when a diplomatic mission sent by Joseph arrived and met with the Nasrid Alamoundaros, and in his letter Simeon provided an eyewitness account of what happened. Through his envoy, Joseph boasted of his success at Najran and of his rededication of the Axumite church in Zafar as a synagogue, and revealed that he had promised the Najrani Christians their lives if they surrendered. When they did, he killed them anyway, and desecrated the body of the city's bishop (Ps.-Zachariah, *Chronicle*, 8.3a–b = *AEBI* §6.46). The envoy did not succeed in recruiting Alamoundaros to his king's cause, however, and Simeon said this was because of the Christians serving within his own army (8.3d = *AEBI* §6.47). Simeon's letter ended with an appeal to the bishop of Gabbula to intercede with Roman authorities on behalf of the Najrani survivors, which appears to have borne fruit: Kaleb and the Axumites invaded Himyar once again in 525, possibly with Roman naval support in the Red Sea, removing Joseph and re-establishing the Christian monarchy. A campaign of unrestrained retribution against Himyar's Jews followed. In the Arab-Islamic tradition, Joseph was given a romanticised death as he rode his horse into the Red Sea, never to return (*Tarikh* 5 p. 210 = *AEBI* §8.9).

Justinian, 527–65

Justinian, the Balkans, and the Persians

Justinian became co-emperor in April 527, and assumed sole rulership when Justin died in August. Defence was Justinian's first priority, and in 528 he created the new position of *magister militum per Armeniam et Pontum Polemoniacum et gentes*, a recognition of the wavering political loyalties of the Iberians and the importance of Lazica and its western neighbour, Tzania, to defending the region. The new *magister militum* was based at Theodosiopolis-Karin, with six *duces* under his control, and his force was raised from Armenians and bolstered by the transfer of several *numeri* from the eastern army (*REF2* pp. 83–84). Defence works were also carried out at Martyropolis, Dara, Amida, Edessa, and Palmyra. At some point during this time, an image of Christ enthroned was painted in the *cella* of the Temple of Bel at Palmyra, due its transformation into a church; just visible in 2007, it was destroyed when the *cella* was blown up by Daesh/ISIS in 2015 (Figure 14.3).

Sittas, Theodora's brother-in-law and *magister utriusque militiae praesentalis*, raided Tzania and garrisoned the mountainous region as a bulwark against Persian inroads; Justinian also sent missionaries to the Tzani in an effort to win them over. The Romans raided around Nisibis and began to fortify Thannuris on the Khabur (Tall Tuneinir) in 527/28, but raids from Persian-held Singara, only 88 kilometres (55 miles) to the east, hampered Roman efforts. A Samaritan revolt was put down in 529, and the Persian Arab Alamoundaros continued to raid, reaching as far as Antioch and Chalcedon in March 529 and easily evading the newly appointed *dux* at Palmyra (Malalas, *Chronicle*, 18.32 = *AEBI* §5.11). Alamoundaros also succeeded in killing Arethas, who Anastasius had appointed phylarch of Palaestina I. A massive manhunt was organised for Alamoundaros, involving several provincial *duces* and three Arab phylarchs. One of these three phylarchs was another Arethas—for the sake of clarity, we shall refer to him by his Arabic name, al-Harith. In the aftermath of these devastating raids, Justinian took the unprecedented step of appointing this same al-Harith as chief phylarch, placing all of the empire's other Arab phylarchs under his control. This new super-phylarcate mimicked the position of the Nasrid Alamoundaros himself, who Procopius wrote 'ruled alone over all the Saracens in Persia'. Procopius also stressed Alamoundaros's ability to raid with near impunity, which provided Justinian with the impetus to find an Arab ally of his own who could match him. Al-Harith's appointment came with 'the dignity of king' (*Wars*, 1.17.40–48 = *AEBI* §5.15), but the nature of this 'dignity' has never been clear. However, a contemporary Arabic graffito from Jabal Says in southern Syria, dated to 528/29, referred to al-Harith as *malik*, 'king' (*AEBI* §7.6), and after his appointment al-Harith and his family were enrolled amongst the senatorial order. Al-Harith was later awarded the honorific position of *stratelatos* (*magister militum*) and the rank of *patrikios* (*patricius*). Al-Harith's primary mission was to control Alamoundaros's raiding and find a way to kill him—a goal he eventually achieved, but not without drawing severe criticism from Procopius along the way.

Figure 14.3 Christian wall painting within the Temple of Bel at Palmyra (July 2007).

Source: Photograph by the author.

Justinian's promotion of al-Harith was part of a coherent southern policy that sought to project Roman power into the desert and the Arabian Peninsula. Procopius explained that during the reigns of Kaleb Ella Asbeha and Sumuyafa Ashwa, Joseph's successor on the Himyarite throne, Justinian sent an ambassador called Julianus to both rulers with the message that 'on account of their community of religion [they] should make common cause with the Romans in the war against the Persians' (*Wars*, 1.20). In addition to assisting the Roman armies, Justinian also hoped his allies would wage a commercial war: this would be achieved by Axumite merchants buying up as much silk as possible to undercut the Persian quasi-monopoly on the silk trade, which they held through their Indian Ocean fleet and their merchants in Sogdia. Justinian also sought to interfere in the Himyarite client networks that spanned the Arabian interior by appointing a phylarch named Caïsus over control of the central Arabian confederation of Maadd, which was historically under

Himyarite patronage via the kings of the south Arabian tribe of Kinda. The most detailed explanation of this ambitious effort was provided by Nonnosus, the grandson of the diplomat Euphrasius, whose work was excerpted by the ninth-century patriarch and bibliophile Photius. Caïsus appeared in Nonnosus's account as Kaisos, a relative of the Arethas who became phylarch of Palaestina I during the reign of Anastasius. Nonnosus's father, Abrames, was on good terms with Kaisos and had returned from a previous diplomatic mission with his son, Mavias, as a hostage. Kaisos was the phylarch of Kinda and Maadd, and in this capacity he was invited to Constantinople for an audience with Justinian. A later mission by Abrames eventually succeeded in bringing Kaisos to the capital, where he was appointed phylarch for one of the Palestinian provinces and his brothers became Roman clients in central Arabia (Photius, *Bibliotheca*, 3 = *AEBI* §5.18). Two other pieces of information round out this picture: according to Malalas, an unnamed Roman ambassador was sent to Kaleb with mountains of gifts, ordering him to launch a war against Kavadh (*Chronicle*, 18.56), while Procopius wrote that Abu Karib, the brother of al-Harith, held a phylarcate in Palestine and maintained control on Justinian's behalf over 'the Palm Groves', a location that is usually associated with the regions around the al-Ula oasis near Hegra/Madain Salih in north-western Arabia (*Wars*, 1.19 = *AEBI* §5.19). These various embassies and appointments all took place within a few years of each other, and, taken together, reflect Justinian's attempt to create a client network that brought the western coast of Arabia, central Arabia, Axum, and Himyar under Roman influence. The rationale for this was straightforward, as the Persians had long claimed a stake in Mazun (Oman) and controlled much of the Arabian coastline of the Persian Gulf. Justinian would have been aware of the possibility of a Himyarite–Persian axis, as this had already been attempted by Joseph's embassy to Alamoundaros. Furthermore, Arabian folklore maintained that there were dynastic links between the Nasrids and Kinda: the wife of Alamoundaros, Hind the Elder, was believed to be a direct descendant of the famous Kinda king Hujr, a stalwart of early Arab histories and the individual usually identified with a laconic graffito found to the north of Najran that recorded 'Hujr b. Amr, king of Kiddat [Kinda]'. Hind later became the patron of a famous monastery at al-Hira (Ibn Habib, *Kitab al-Muhabbar*, pp. 368–70 = *AEBI* §8.6, and see *AEBI* §3.10). Disrupting the links between Himyar, central Arabia, and the southern flank of the Persian empire was thus a pragmatic policy goal for the Romans.

In 530, after Justinian refused Kavadh's demand for gold, the Persians launched a determined assault on Dara. The Persian army was defeated by Justinian's newly minted *magister militum per Orientem*, Belisarius. Kavadh also made an attempt on Lazica, but Sittas held the Persian force at Satala. The following year, a Persian army advanced up the Euphrates and had almost reached Barbalissos when Belisarius, who had been caught wrong-footed, assembled a force from troops withdrawn from Dara and those taken from another force under the *magister officiorum* Hermogenes. The two armies met on Easter Saturday in 531, near the Roman fortress of Callinicum. The Roman troops had been fasting during Holy Week, and suffered a serious defeat. Procopius pinned the blame squarely on al-Harith, accusing him and his troops of betraying Belisarius by pulling out of the Roman battle line (*Wars*, 1.18). Justinian was furious at the debacle and replaced Belisarius following a damning inquest, while Ephrem, the Chalcedonian patriarch of Antioch (527–45), raised money to ransom prisoners who had been taken by Alamoundaros. Kavadh died during a second, failed attempt to threaten Amida in 531, and his successor, Khusrau I 'Anushirvan' ('Immortal Soul') opened peace negotiations with Justinian. The result, arranged by

Hermogenes and the ambassador Rufinus, was the Eternal Peace of 532. Justinian made a generous payment of 450 kilograms (990 pounds) of gold towards the defence of the Caspian Gates, and Khusrau relinquished Persian claims on several districts in Armenia and Lazica. Malalas recorded that the treaty established the brotherhood of the two rulers, and promised that if either needed cash or military assistance, that the other should deliver it (*Chronicle*, 18.76 = *REF2* p. 97). For a time, relations between Rome and Persia were the warmest in decades, and Roman and Persian troops mounted joint patrols of the border area around Singara.

The Justinianic Code, the Nika riot, and the western kingdoms

As Theodosius II had before him, Justinian ordered the compilation of an ambitious and comprehensive law code. By the spring of 529, the first volume of the *Justinianic Code* appeared, covering imperial laws that had been scrutinised carefully for their accuracy. Work then began on a second volume, addressing the work of the jurists who had produced thousands and thousands of pages of juridical exegesis: the result was the *Digest*, which appeared in 533. A textbook of Roman law, the *Institutes*, was published the same year and then a revised version of the *Justinianic Code* made its appearance in 534. The project was wholly Christian in conception and execution, and God and Christ were present throughout: with *Novel* 47, issued in 537, Justinian ordered his praetorian prefect John the Cappadocian to ensure that judicial records commenced by recognising 'God the creator'; with *Novel* 131.1, issued in 545, church law was accepted as civil law. Justinian elected to omit some of the laws from the *Theodosian Code* that benefited Jews, particularly the acceptance of Judaism as a legal faith (16.8.9, Chapter 13); the *Justinianic Code* also gave the emperor the right to interfere in synagogue life and curtailed a range of Jewish rights. In 529, Justinian also ended the right of pagans to teach philosophy in Athens, leading a number of philosophers to decamp to Persia (Agathias, *Histories*, 2.30–31 = *RLA* pp. 273–4). The Christian unity of the empire, under Justinian's rulership, did not leave a great deal of room for other beliefs.

The penchant for reorganisation and standardisation represented by this legal project was reflected by a restructuring that abolished the dioceses of the empire and created numerous new provinces. Military matters were handled by provincial *duces* and their phylarchs, where they existed, under the authority of the regional *magister militum*. In some areas military and civilian powers were combined, such as in the region that lay between the Long Walls and the Theodosian Walls, which came under the control of a new *praetor per Thracias*. A praetor was also established to govern Pisidia under the supervision of the emperor, evoking the memory of the propraetorian legates of the past.

In 532, Justinian faced a serious riot in Constantinople. Street fighting broke out between the Blues and the Greens, and when the nascent riot was suppressed by the urban prefect, the two sides threw in their lot with one another amidst cries of *Nika!* (Victory!), and laid siege to the prefect's residence. Buildings were torched and demands were made in the Hippodrome, while the rioters roamed the city searching for a relative of Anastasius to proclaim as emperor. Justinian turned to Belisarius, who was still in Constantinople after his defeat at Callinicum, and the Gepid nobleman Mundo, who had fought alongside Theoderic Amal, but was now *magister militum per Illyricum*. Both men and their *bucellarii* bodyguards, together with the *excubitores*, were sent to the Hippodrome where as many as 35,000 rioters were butchered in its confined space.

In 530, the Nicene Vandal king, Hilderic, was toppled in a coup by his cousin, Gelimer. Hilderic was popular in Constantinople and enjoyed the support of the church authorities in Italy; his removal was followed by a vicious purge of his relatives. Despite virtually all of the advice to the contrary, particularly from his praetorian prefect, John the Cappadocian, Justinian decided to invade Africa under the pretext of 'recovering' it for the empire. Belisarius would be given the chance to redeem himself and, with his wife Antonina accompanying him, he set out in 533. Procopius took part in the expedition, sent on ahead to Sicily to find out what he could about the disposition of Gelimer's defences. From a friend in Syracuse, he learned that large parts of the Vandal army were absent from Carthage, and that news of the Roman expedition had yet to reach Gelimer's ears (*Wars*, 3.14). As a result, Belisarius easily overcame the remaining defences, capturing Carthage in the autumn of 533. Carthage was renamed Carthago Justiniana, and many of the treasures looted by Gaiseric were recovered, including those from the Second Temple, which made their way back to the east. Roman administrative control was restored under a praetorian prefect, a *magister militum per Africam*, and four individual *duces* to command frontier troops.

Gelimer was given the opportunity to retire to Galatia, while his troops were sent to the eastern frontier where they would bolster Roman levies when the Eternal Peace inevitably failed. Belisarius became the first individual outside the imperial family to celebrate a triumph for more than half a millennium. Despite some disturbances in 536, the African success produced giddiness in Constantinople and a distinct feeling of mission creep set in, turning hungry eyes towards Italy. *Novel* 30 of Justinian, issued in 535, had already expressed hope that God would allow the emperor to regain control of the remaining domains that the 'Romans lost by their negligence', a clear reference to Italy, and perhaps even to Gaul and other places further afield. The timing was auspicious: in Ravenna, growing suspicion between Theoderic and his senatorial allies in the final years of his reign—the product of tensions amongst conservative Goths who were concerned that their culture was overly Romanised—had seen the end of the consulship (in 530) and the unpopular execution of the former consul and *magister officiorum*, Boethius. One of the most influential thinkers of his time, Boethius wrote his famous *Consolation of Philosophy* in prison in 523. The unstable climate also claimed the life of Quintus Aurelius Memmius Symmachus, the great-grandson of the staunch opponent of Ambrose of Mediolanum (Chapter 13). Symmachus had held the ordinary consulship in 485 and served both as urban prefect and an ambassador for Theoderic; he had also undertaken repairs to the Theatre of Pompey and penned a history of Rome. His connections with Boethius, his son-in-law, resulted in treason charges and his execution in 525. When Theoderic died a year later, to be buried in his famous Ravenna mausoleum that is half-nomad tent and half-imitation of the tomb of Augustus, the Ostrogothic kingdom came under the rule of Theoderic's daughter Amalasuntha and her young son Athalaric, with Cassiodorus serving as *magister officiorum*. Athalaric died in 534 and, after a general purge, Amalasuntha elevated her cousin, Theodohad, through whom she intended to rule. As Justinian pondered the wisdom of expanding his conquests, Theodohad had Amalasuntha removed and executed in 534/35. Her violent end, and the conclusion of hostilities in Africa, provided Justinian with the necessary opportunity for invasion.

The Italian campaign opened with an invasion of Dalmatia by Mundo, serving as *magister militum per Illyricum*. Seizing Sirmium, he forced the Ostrogothic troops to fall back on Italy, but was later killed in the fighting. Belisarius launched the second prong of the invasion, which captured Sicily, and from there he crossed the Tyrrhenian Sea and landed on the west coast of Italy. Everything then began to go wrong. The Italo-Gothic population of Italy had no need to be liberated from their Ostrogothic leaders, who had delivered stable rule, efficient government, a well-defended frontier, and a good level of prosperity. The last thing anyone wanted was a war prosecuted in their fields, vineyards, and towns by the 'Greeks', as they called the east Roman army, and Belisarius found to his dismay that his invasion was vigorously contested by Goths and Italians alike. At Naples, the Goths 'promised that they would guard the circuit wall safely', and Procopius noted the prominent role of the Jewish population in the defence of the city; no doubt Naples' Jews harboured well-founded anxieties over what a successful conquest by a strict Christian administration would mean for religious policies and toleration (*Wars*, 5.8.41–43 = *RLA* p. 207). Theodohad, who had provided little leadership, was replaced by Vitigis, whose manly credentials were captured by the stirring prose of Cassiodorus. 'I was not sought among the subtle debates of sycophants,' Cassiodorus wrote for him, 'but as the trumpets blared, so that the Gothic race of Mars, roused by such a din and longing for their native courage, might find themselves a martial king!' (*Variae*, 10.31). Belisarius captured Rome as the Ostrogoths prepared for a new offensive, and when Vitigis laid siege to the city in 537 and the war continued without respite, the backbone of Ostrogothic government—the senatorial administrative class, represented by Cassiodorus—left the city for Constantinople.

In 538, Narses, a eunuch holding the position of *sacellarius*, a palatine official who managed the emperor's personal finances, arrived in Italy and his rivalry considerably complicated Belisarius's mission. The Franks also sent an army to northern Italy in 539, hoping to win territory and plunder at the expense of both the Ostrogoths and the eastern Roman forces. Feuding with Belisarius resulted in a lack of determined resistance when Vitigis marched on Mediolanum, and the terrible slaughter of the city's men and the sale of its women and children into slavery among the Burgundians forced all sides to step back. Vitigis surrendered in 540, and with a truce agreed, both Belisarius and Vitigis travelled to Constantinople. The Ostrogothic leader was awarded the rank of *patricius* and disappeared into a genteel retirement, while Belisarius soon became embroiled in a new war with Persia (see below). Back in Italy, the Ostrogoths flatly rejected the imposition of taxes payable to Constantinople and appointed a new leader; he was soon murdered, as was his successor, but in 541 Totila emerged as king and launched an effective and energetic campaign that won him Naples in 543. Belisarius returned to Italy in 544, and Rome changed hands twice more in 547 and 549. The population of the city 'found themselves reduced to such straits', wrote Procopius, 'that they clothed themselves in the garments of slaves and rustics, and lived by begging' (*Wars*, 7.20–27). Belisarius was recalled once again in 549 and replaced by Germanus, Justinian's cousin, who sought to find peace by marrying Theoderic's granddaughter, Matasuntha. He was dead only one year later, however, and his position was filled by Narses, who had since been promoted to *praepositus* of the sacred bedchamber. Totila invaded Sicily in 550, and it was not until 552 that Narses ran him to ground, killing him. Justinian declared victory in 553, but the final Ostrogothic garrisons held out until 561. The vulnerable regions of northern Italy were divided into four districts, each under a *magister militum*, and royal land was transferred to the imperial fisc. There was once again a praetorian prefect of Italy, and Ravenna was the capital; the Roman mint was reopened and Roman law was restored. The offices of *magister officiorum*, *comes rei privatae*, and quaestor were abolished, however, and the emperor in Constantinople directly appointed his subordinates in Italy. Narses was promoted to the rank of *patricius* for his services, and remained in Italy until his death in c. 574. Italy had become an outlier, a client state of Constantinople, and this change caused lasting damage and deep resentment.

The Ostrogothic war had been a much bloodier and longer affair than Justinian had ever intended; Procopius scorned both this and the African war in a chapter of his *Secret History* entitled 'How Justinian killed a trillion people'. The infrastructure in Rome, including many of its aqueducts, was thoroughly destroyed. The war culled the city's population and signalled the demise of the Roman senate—a body that had met for over 1,000 years. Revolts in Africa from Berbers and Roman troops alike in 534 and 536 also caused instability, and the situation there was worsened when a Berber army defeated the praetorian prefect Solomon in 544 and then won two further consecutive victories in 545 and 546. Only with the arrival of John Troglita as *magister militum per Africam* did the tide turn in favour of the Romans. Despite these ongoing difficulties, an expeditionary force was sent to Visigothic Spain in 552 at the invitation of Athanagild, a contestant for the throne, but when the Roman troops arrived, they once again found a people with no wish to be liberated—and Athanagild subsequently turned against them. But perhaps the most serious consequence of Justinian's wars of conquest was the fallout from removing the Ostrogothic buffer zone that protected Italy and the Balkans. During the war, the Gepids under Cunimund had moved in to Pannonia and occupied Sirmium, cutting the principal land route between Italy and Constantinople. In an effort to address this problem, Justinian allowed the Lombards under their king, Audoin (547–60), to expand their landholdings into Noricum and Pannonia. The Gepids and Lombards fought each other repeatedly, and Cunimund later petitioned Justinian's successor, Justin II, for military assistance, promising to return Sirmium to the eastern court. Justin agreed, but when Cunimund double-crossed the emperor, Justin abandoned him; emerging victorious in the power struggle that followed, Audoin's son and successor, Alboin (560–72), celebrated by drinking beer from Cunimund's hollowed-out skull. With the Gepid kingdom destroyed, Alboin led the Lombards into Italy in 568 where they swiftly crushed the imperial garrisons and established strongholds (dukedoms, led by *duces*) at places such as Beneventum. Alboin was murdered at Verona in 572, and his successor in 574, splitting the Lombards into numerous factions. North of the lower Danube, communities of Slavs had emerged and had begun to raid the Balkans, alone or in the company of Gepids and Huns. In 559, the Kutrighurs under Zabergan raided deep into Greece and the Thracian Chersonesus, reaching as far as the Long Walls of Constantinople. The Walls had been damaged in an earthquake in 557, and the danger to the city brought Belisarius out of retirement to assist Germanus in facing the threat. Then, in 558, the Avars emerged on the scene from central Asia. Their migration was linked with episodes of drought, perhaps brought on by climate change that affected access to pasture (below), as well as to the defeat of the Rouran empire (to which they belonged) by the growing power of the Turks, who thought of the Avars as their slaves (Evagrius, *Ecclesiastical History*, 5.1). The Avars brought with them a revolutionary piece of equestrian equipment—the stirrup. An Avar embassy to Justinian proposing an alliance in 558 was accepted, according to Menander (Blockley fr. 5.2). The Avars systematically plundered and cowed their neighbours—the Sabir Huns, Utrigurs, Kutrighurs, Slavs, and Bulgars, and even managed to beat the Frankish king, Sigibert, on the Elbe. Once the Lombards moved into Italy, the Avars, led by Baian (Bajan), their khagan (king), consolidated their hold on central Europe and became a serious menace.

Making an attempt on Sirmium, which had come into Roman hands after Cunimund's death in 567, they made peace with Justin II in 571.

Axum and South Arabia during the reign of Justinian

In c. 531, Sumuyafa Ashwa was overthrown by a man named Abraha, a slave from Adulis. Abraha was a Christian, but he presented himself as a Himyarite king, erecting inscriptions in Sabaic and taking pains to appeal to the remaining Judeo-Monotheists in the kingdom. Kaleb's son, Wazeb, continued to claim sovereignty over Himyar from across the Red Sea, and Procopius wrote that Abraha paid Kaleb tribute (*Wars*, 1.20). Abraha distanced himself from Axumite Christianity, however, invoking older Himyarite terms for God and using Syriac loan words for terms such as messiah and church, reflecting a reorientation towards Syriac anti-Chalcedonian Christianity. Two attempts by Kaleb to reconquer Himyar failed, and later Kaleb retired to a monastery and sent his crown as a gift to Jerusalem. In 547, Abraha organised a diplomatic conference that involved representatives from Rome, Persia, Axum, and both the Roman and Persian Arabs. The meeting was commemorated on part of an inscription at Marib recording repairs to the Marib Dam, and that also recorded the establishment of a church at Marib and the suppression of a revolt of Himyar's own Kinda Arab allies (*AEBI* §3.21). According to Procopius, Abraha repeatedly promised Justinian that he would launch a military campaign against the Persians, but never did so (*Wars*, 1.20), and his military expeditions concentrated instead on central Arabia. An inscription recording a military foray in 552 from Murayghan, north-west of Najran, states that Amr (the son of the Persian Arab Alamoundaros) gave Abraha a son as a political hostage and was appointed as Abraha's governor over Maadd, suggesting that Justinian's attempt to influence the client networks in central Arabia was being contested (*AEBI* §3.23). The arrangement soured, however; an undated inscription from Murayghan records that Abraha was forced to remove Amr and reassert direct rule in central Arabia, including over Yathrib (Medina) (*AEBI* §3.24). This would have taken place prior to the death of Alamoundaros in 554, at which time Amr replaced him as leader of the Nasrid polity at al-Hira.

Two other elements of Abraha's rule are of interest here. The first is his construction of a church in Sanaa that became famous in the Arab-Islamic tradition as al-Qalis, an Arabicisation of the Greek word *ekklesia*. The last dated Himyarite inscription, in 559/60, records the elaborate construction of a building that may be the famous church (*AEBI* §3.25). Al-Tabari wrote that Abraha had requested help from 'Qaysar', either Justinian or his successor Justin II, and that 'Qaysar accordingly sent back to him skilled artisans, mosaic cubes, and marble'—the result, in al-Tabari's enthusiastic words, was 'a marvellous building, whose like had never been seen before, using gold and remarkable dyestuffs and stains' (*Tarikh* 5, p. 220 = *AEBI* §8.10). The second point is related to the first, for Abraha was widely thought to have launched an assault on Mecca, in order to lessen Mecca's importance and thus divert pilgrims to al-Qalis in Sanaa instead. Sura 105 in the Quran begins exultantly with the phrase 'have you not seen how your Lord dealt with the men with the elephants?', referring to the belief that Abraha's expedition, led by a grumpy elephant named Mahmud, was a signal failure. When Mahmud's handlers pointed him towards Himyar, he 'got up and started off; however, when pointed towards Mecca, he knelt stubbornly in the sand (Ibn Ishaq, *Sira* 35–6 = *AEBI* §8.14). The relationship between the Quranic verse and the folklore surrounding Mecca and the elephant, as well as whether or not this event happened at all, have long been the subject of debate; but discoveries of ancient petroglyphs of elephants near Hima suggest that it may, in fact, have had some basis in reality.

War with Persia—again

Procopius wrote that Khusrau was jealous of Justinian's successes in Europe, and instructed Alamoundaros to find a way to break the Eternal Peace (*Wars*, 2.1). Jealousy may have been a factor, but there was also the incessant requirement for cash and a streak of opportunism, with so many Roman troops absent fighting in Europe. Justinian's actions in the Caucasus may also have been an irritant. In 536, he published a decree that would force Roman Armenians to obey Roman law, and this was followed by the extension of Roman fortifications in Armenia and additional garrisons to man them; Armenia was reorganised into four provinces, with its principal city at Martyropolis. In Lazica, the city of Petra was built on the Black Sea coast to consolidate imperial control and monopolise the main supply routes in and out of the kingdom.

Alamoundaros broke the peace on Khusrau's behalf by complaining that al-Harith had done 'him violence in a matter of boundary lines', and raids into Roman territory followed; as for Alamoundaros, 'he was not breaking the treaty between the Persians and Romans', continued Procopius, 'for neither one of them had included him in it' (*Wars*, 2.1 = *AEBI* §5.21). This oversight in the Eternal Peace led directly to a renewed war, despite Justinian's attempts to stall for time by assigning a *patricius* named Strategius and Summus, the brother of the diplomat Julianus, to listen to Khusrau's demands. In 540, the Persian king rejected these peace overtures and launched an invasion north through the Euphrates flood plain, bypassing Circesium and the fortified bastion at Halabiya-Zenobia, and heading instead for Sura, which was captured. After a Roman force under Bouzes, the *magister militum per Orientem*, failed to hold Khusrau, the king extorted protection money from Hierapolis (Mabbug) and took Beroea, which placed Antioch in an acutely vulnerable position. The Antiochenes rejected a financial demand to spare the city, and when Khusrau ordered his troops to attack, the Roman force and many of the Antiochenes fled, even while the city's circus factions fought the Persians from street to street. Those Antiochenes who were unfortunate enough to be captured were deported to a new city near Ctesiphon called Veh-Antioch-Khusrau ('Khusrau's-Better-than-Antioch'). Emboldened by his success, Khusrau menaced Edessa and Dara, and then withdrew, flush with captives and plunder. 'It was the whole of Syria that he carried off to Persia,' lamented John Lydus. 'There was not a farmer or a tax-payer left to the treasury' (*On the Magistracies*, 3.54 = *REF2* p. 105).

The peace was also broken in the Caucasus in 541 when requests for Persian assistance were sent to Khusrau, first by a delegation of Armenians and then by a diplomatic mission from Lazica's king, Gobazes. Khusrau seized Petra, and its defenders surrendered and joined his army. War in Lazica would continue in one form or another for over two decades. Gobazes and much of local public opinion drifted back towards Constantinople, however, and in 554 he rejoined the alliance with Rome, only to be murdered by the *magister militum* Martinus in 555. Peace was eventually made in 562 (below), but not before the region of Suania, which lay between Lazica and the Caucasus mountains, adopted a pro-Persian stance that caused unresolved tensions throughout the sixth century. Belisarius, meanwhile, had now returned from Italy, and in 541 and 542 the Romans raided past Nisibis into Assyria while al-Harith and his troops plundered the countryside. An ambitious invasion of Persarmenia stalled, and while Khusrau failed to capture Rusafa-Sergiopolis, he did manage to take Callinicum, 43 kilometres (27 miles) to the north-east. The following year, the Persians laid siege to Edessa, constructing a circumvallation that sealed off the city from help and reinforcements. The Edessenes, still faithful to the legends that guaranteed the city's safety, were able to destroy part of the circumvallation and force Khusrau to withdraw. These three years of warfare had thoroughly exhausted both sides, and a truce was called in 545—but this was studiously ignored by both al-Harith and Alamoundaros, who nurtured a deadly hatred towards each other. In 545, Alamoundaros captured one of al-Harith's sons, 'and straightway sacrificed him to Aphrodite' (Procopius, *Wars*, 2.28 = *AEBI* §5.22). The two continued to hunt each other in the Syrian desert even as Justinian and Khusrau extended the truce past 551, and Justinian made a payment towards the defence of the Caspian Gates. In 554, al-Harith finally caught up with his enemy and Alamoundaros was killed in battle. Three Syriac medieval chronicles recorded this event—the *Chronicle* of Michael the Syrian (9.33 = *AEBI* §5.23), the *Chronicle to 1234* (p. 192), and the *Chronicle* of Bar Hebraeus (81). The most detailed account, however, is from the Greek hagiography of Symeon the Stylite the Younger. Symeon entered a trance, the text recorded, and the saint told of how he 'saw in front of me a mass of horsemen who were coming with Alamoundaros the tyrant, as numerous as the stars in the sky, and the grains of sand next to the sea'. The Roman and allied Arab troops were terrified, but Symeon watched as Christ launched a flaming ball of energy at Alamoundaros, killing him. Later, Roman soldiers returning to Antioch from the battle confirmed the saint's vision—'and from that point the whole of the east, having obtained peace, lived in a great tranquillity' (*Life of Symeon the Stylite the Younger* 186–7 = *AEBI* §6.12). The death of Alamoundaros was a serious blow to Khusrau, and after further efforts to foment intrigue in Lazica yielded few results, serious negoti-ations began in 557 that led to a comprehensive 50-year treaty in 562. Differences were settled by Khusrau's renunciation of his claims over Lazica, and Justinian committed to an annual gold payment of 133 kilograms (293 pounds), a practical response to stave off further predatory, cash-driven wars, but one that irritated some of Justinian's critics. The details of the treaty were recorded by Menander, a *protector* in imperial service. With the collapse of the Eternal Peace in mind, the treaty bound both sets of Arab allies to the main provisions of the agreement. Among other matters including mechanisms for dis-pute resolution, the peace also made provisions that:

- business would be carried out at specific posts, according to pre-existing custom
- exiles and defectors who fled in time of war would be able to return
- the Persians accepted Dara, but no other fortifications by either side would be allowed
- the army at Dara should be restricted in size, and the *magister militum per Orientem* was not permitted to base himself there (Menander, Blockley fr. 6.1 = *REF2* pp. 132–3).

A codicil to the treaty established the rights of Christians in Persia to worship free from interference and to bury their dead unhindered (Menander, Blockley fr. 6.1 = *REF2* p. 134). Menander also made detailed notes of the intricate high-level diplomatic negotiations

whom they felt should also be condemned: Theodore of Mopsuestia (associated with Nestorius), Theodoret of Cyrrhus (an opponent of Cyril of Alexandria and friend of Nestorius), and Ibas of Edessa (associated with Theodore of Mopsuestia). Justinian was open to compromise and eventually condemned the Three Chapters by decree in c. 544 and at the Second Council of Constantinople in 553. This position irritated western clergy and particularly the bishop of Rome, Vigilius (537–55), who was recalled from Italy and placed under house arrest until he recanted.

Despite his amenable attitude, Justinian's olive branch to the anti-Chalcedonians in 532 failed. Justinian tried again in the following year, publishing his *Edict on Faith*, which suppressed explicit references to Chalcedon, and in 535, Severus was invited from exile to Constantinople; he won the support of Anthimius, the patriarch of Constantinople, and Timothy IV was replaced in Alexandria by another anti-Chalcedonian, Theodosius. This promising climate of reconciliation was short-lived. Almost immediately, the dogmatically Chalcedonian monks at the Monastery of St Maron in Syria II appealed to Agapetus, the bishop of Rome (535–36), who had been sent by Theodohad to Constantinople as war threatened in the west. The result was the resignation of Anthimius and his replacement by the more pliable Menas. Severus was once again *persona non grata* and retired to the Egyptian wilderness, while Theodosius was forced out of Alexandria in 536/37 and placed under house arrest in Constantinople. Both Severus and John of Tella died in 538. In Egypt, Theodosius continued to claim the patriarchate from exile in Constantinople, even as imperial authorities replaced him with their own Chalcedonian nominee.

The anti-Chalcedonians received an important boost in 542. Anti-Chalcedonian Christianity was popular in the rural districts of Syria and Arabia, where the Jafnid phylarch al-Harith was active. Likely sensing a political opportunity, al-Harith successfully lobbied Justinian and Theodora to provide bishops for these communities. Theodosius, the exiled patriarch of Alexandria, consecrated two new bishops: Jacob Burdaya (better known as Jacob Baradaeus), and Theodore; the former was nominally assigned to Edessa, the latter to Bostra, although in reality the sees of both men were broadly defined as 'northern' and 'southern' respectively. Jacob set about his new task with alacrity, roaming the countryside and ordaining anti-Chalcedonian clergy. Theodora was also instrumental in dispatching the anti-Chalcedonians Longinus and Julian to evangelise the Nobades in Egypt—a mission that resulted in the desecration of the famed Temple of Isis at Philae.

Amongst this flurry of activity, Jacob consecrated a certain John as bishop of Ephesus (also in a non-resident capacity) in 558. John of Ephesus had been in a monastery since his childhood and had served Justinian as an energetic propagator of the Christian faith in Lydia, Phrygia, and other parts of Asia Minor (hence his alternative name, 'John of Asia'). In addition to his ecclesiastical history, John was also the author of a collection of Syriac hagiography known as *The Lives of the Eastern Saints*, which eulogised, among others, his patron Jacob Baradaeus, who had established 27 new bishops by 566. John lauded 'the Christ-loving queen Theodora' for her support of the anti-Chalcedonians, but it is now thought that the empress's position was less dogmatic than John made it seem (see *AEBI* §6.19). In political terms, Theodora could support the anti-Chalcedonians in ways that would otherwise have proven rather difficult for her husband, and by maintaining friendly relationships with leading anti-Chalcedonian figures, she helped Justinian sustain open lines of communication without excessive political risk.

The tacit imperial approval that lay behind the work of Jacob, Theodore, and their allies such as John of Ephesus was an important facet in the continued vitality of Syriac-speaking anti-Chalcedonians in the empire's eastern provinces, and represented a distinct reversal from the period of gloom that had followed the accession of Justin I. That same imperial approval also meant that opposition among Syriac-speaking Christians to the Council of Chalcedon took on an aura of legitimacy as its own form of Christian orthodoxy—and this orthodoxy was accompanied by a burgeoning corpus of Christian literary works in Syriac. Contemporary Syriac texts, Greek works translated into Syriac, the preservation of the works of earlier Syriac writers such as Ephrem the Syrian and Jacob of Serug (d. 521), and works such as the *Teaching of Addai* and the Peshitta, the Syriac editions of the Old Testament (second century) and the New Testament (fifth century) all proved to be important components of this literary corpus. Syriac-speaking anti-Chalcedonians did not necessarily represent a breakaway movement from the empire, nor did they necessarily comprise a homogeneous ethnic or political movement. Nevertheless, the failure of the Second Council of Constantinople in 553 to explicitly support an anti-Chalcedonian formula signalled, to some, the end of any real prospect of compromise between the Chalcedonian and anti-Chalcedonian positions. After the disappointments of the sixth century, imperial authorities could no longer claim to be the only arbiters of Christian orthodoxy. Indeed, Edessa in particular could claim a Christian history that was far older than the Roman Christian empire itself.

Syriac-speaking anti-Chalcedonian monophysite Christians also lived and worshipped in an international space that included large parts of the Persian empire. With representatives such as Simeon of Beth Arsham, known as 'the debater' for his love of animated discussion with his theological opponents within the Church of the East, and Ahudemmeh, the bishop of the Jazira (d. 559), anti-Chalcedonian monophysite Christianity flourished in Persia. Ahudemmeh was consecrated by Jacob Baradaeus, and spent much of his career ministering to Arab populations of the Jazira, founding churches that he named for individual tribes (*AEBI*, §6.38). He also became a patron of the cult of St Sergius in Persia (below), but died in prison during the reign of Khusrau I. When the Arab invasions of the seventh century pushed imperial authorities from Egypt, Syria, and Arabia, and toppled the Persian empire, Syriac Christianity possessed a sufficiently robust identity and episcopal organisation from over two centuries of defining itself against challenges and persecutions as the orthodox faith, to emerge as a distinctive Christian community in the early middle ages.

Art and architecture in Constantinople and beyond

The reign of Justinian witnessed an outpouring of imperial, Christian art that fused Christian symbols and messages, images of imperial might, and the relationship between Christ and the imperial throne. The gold solidi coinage of Justinian's reign typically shows the emperor in military attire, with an angel on the reverse holding a staurogram (the chi-rho) and a globe cruciger—an orb topped by a cross, signifying Christian royal and military authority; in his panegyrical *Buildings*, Procopius described the cruciger as 'the emblem by which alone [Justinian] has obtained both his Empire and his victory in war' (1.2) (Figure 14.4).

The favour of Christ and his support for Justinian's military ventures is the central motif on the famous Barberini Ivory in the Musée du Louvre. The ivory leaf,

Figure 14.4 Gold solidus of Justinian minted in Constantinople. Obverse: bust of Justinian, with globus cruciger and shield; reverse: angel with staurogram (left) and globus cruciger (right).

Figure 14.5 The mosaic panel depicting Theodora at San Vitale.

Source: Photograph by Petar Milošević (CC BY-SA 4.0).

part of a diptych, is an equestrian portrait of Justinian, surmounted by Christ, who is accompanied by angels on either side. The ancient Roman motif of Victory personified accompanies the emperor. The most famous representation of the emperor, however, is from the Church of San Vitale in Ravenna, which was dedicated in 547. Two colossal mosaics depict Theodora (who died in 548) and her attendants (Figure 14.5) and Justinian and his entourage, including Maximian, who became bishop of Ravenna in 546 (Figure 14.6). Justinian is shown in the traditional pose of an emperor offering sacrifice—although here, of course, the context is the performance of Christian ritual.

Figure 14.6 The mosaic panel depicting Justinian at San Vitale.

Source: Photograph by Roger Culos (CC BY-SA 3.0).

The troops of Justinian's bodyguard carry oval shields bearing the chi–rho, and the gold torques around their necks suggest a Germanic background. Theodora is depicted with stunning finery, wearing jewels and pearls, and a purple robe with a hem embroidered with images of the three Magi.

One of the oldest painted images of Christ was created during the sixth century and survives at the Monastery of St Catherine in the Sinai, built between 548 and 565. The image of Christ and his piercing gaze are both powerful and haunting, creating a deeply spiritual impact that recalls the Egyptian funerary portraiture of the second century (Figure 14.7). The Monastery of St Catherine includes another breathtaking image of Christ, portrayed in the apse of the monastery's main church at the moment of his trans-figuration (Matthew 17.1–13). Christ is depicted within a blue mandorla, an oval-shaped aura that signifies his divinity. Five figures look on, identified by Greek inscriptions: Moses, Elijah, and the three apostles, James, John, and Peter.

Procopius credited Justinian with a widespread program of construction, which he eulogised in the *Buildings*. The emperor responded to the devastation wrought by Khusrau at Antioch and upgraded and refortified numerous military installations, especially on the eastern frontier at locations such as Halabiya-Zenobia and Rusafa-Sergiopolis. Procopius also credited Justinian with over 600 fortifications in the Balkans, but Procopius was prone in the panegyrical *Buildings* to attributing pre-existing structures to the emperor. Nevertheless, fortification work was carried out at Thermopylae, and the isthmus of Corinth was defended by a new wall. Fortification walls at key locations such as Serdica were also rebuilt, repaired, or strengthened. Building work frequently mingled fortifications

Figure 14.7 The sixth-century painted panel depicting Christ from the Monastery of St Catherine.

Source: Anonymous photograph in the public domain, via Wikimedia Commons.

and religious structures, reflecting the indivisibility of the political and religious spheres. The emperor also founded a city named Justiniana Prima at his birthplace, near Naissus, and made it the seat of the praetorian prefect of Illyricum. Church patronage was one of the most important aspects of Justinian's building program and was an important way to demonstrate imperial piety. The locations for Justinian's patronage were those of great significance to Christians everywhere: Bethlehem (the Church of the Nativity), Sinai (the Monastery of St Catherine), and Jerusalem (The Church of the Theotokos), as well as at major urban centres such as Antioch and Constantinople. Imperial patronage of the holy land stimulated Palestine's economy and encouraged settlement—the city of Caesarea,

Figure 14.8 Jerusalem (ΗΑΓΙΑ ΠΟΛΙC) on the Madaba Map.

Source: Photograph by the author.

for instance, occupied nearly three times as much space in the sixth century as its first-century ancestor. At Madaba, south of modern Amman, the Church of St George was endowed with a famous mosaic map of the empire, with Jerusalem (Hagia Polis) at its centre (Figure 14.8).

Justinian's Constantinople had developed considerably since the time of Constantine: in addition to the three circuits of walls, a sea–wall was constructed in the fifth century to protect the city from a naval assault. The interior of the city was littered with imperial statues and dozens of churches. Fifth-century constructions included the Church of the Virgin, built under Leo I to house Mary's vestments and refurbished by Justinian; adjacent to the church stood the Blachernae palace complex. Justinian rebuilt the Church of the Holy Apostles and constructed a new imperial mausoleum close by, in which Theodora was buried when she died in 548. The imposing Church of St Polyeuktos had been financed by Anicia Juliana, who was also the owner of the spectacular illuminated medical manuscript preserving the work of the first-century polymath Pedanius Dioscorides, known today as the Juliana Anicia Codex or the Vienna Dioscorides. Prior to the reconstruction of the Church of Holy Wisdom (below), St Polyeuktos was the largest church in the city; plundered in the Crusader sack of Constantinople in 1204, parts of the church ended up in Venice, along with the statues of the Tetrarchs (Chapter 12). Massive cisterns built by Aetius, the urban prefect in 421, as well as Aspar during the reign of Marcian, provided an ample supply of water. Justinian constructed the so–called Basilica Cistern, a huge underground reservoir near Holy Wisdom that stored water carried into the city by the Aqueduct of Valens. Between the Constantinian and Theodosian walls lay open fields, produce from which helped to feed the population of the city, which may have numbered as many as 500,000 in the sixth century. Grain was still brought into the city by ship, and the emperor possessed a private granary with a dedicated bakery; olive oil and wine were likewise imported and, together with grain, formed part of the city *annona*. Previous emperors had constructed a number of fora—there was the Forum of Arcadius, for example, and the Forum of Theodosius I with its triumphal arch, celebrating 'victory' over the Goths in the 380s. The centrepiece of the Forum of Theodosius was a spiral column (which vanished after the fifteenth century), based on Trajan's Column in Rome.

Much of the city had been badly damaged during the Nika riots. The Church of Holy Peace (now in the grounds of the Topkapı Palace) was rebuilt in 548. The Augustaion fronting the Church of Holy Wisdom and its peristyle were also rebuilt, as were the Baths of Zeuxippos, which functioned as the senate house. A famous equestrian statue of Justinian, attired as the hero Achilles, dominated the Augustaion: 'he looks toward the rising sun,' wrote Procopius grandiloquently, 'directing his course, I suppose, against the Persians' (*Buildings*, 1.2). The entrance to the imperial palace was also rebuilt after 532 as the Chalke (Bronze Gate), decorated with elaborate mosaics commemorating Justinian's victories in Italy and Africa (*Buildings*, 1.10). The palace complex itself was massive; little survives today except for some stately remains of the so-called Boukoleon Palace (the 'House of Justinian') facing the Sea of Marmara (Figure 14.9), but excavations in the

Figure 14.9 Remains of the Boukoleon Palace in southern Istanbul, facing Kennedy Caddesi.

Source: Photograph by the author.

Figure 14.10 The Church of Ss Sergius and Bacchus, Istanbul. Interior view showing the Greek dedicatory inscription.

Source: Photograph by the author.

area between the palace and the *kathisma* uncovered mosaics of exceptional quality that
adorned a peristyle hall, oriented at a right-angle to the walls of the Hippodrome, and
thought to date to the late sixth or early seventh centuries.

Further rebuilding took place throughout the sixth century in response to the natural
disasters that periodically afflicted the city. These included dangerous electrical storms,
heavy thunderstorms, numerous fires, and the devastating earthquake of 557, which
generated an annual church service of supplication in the years that followed. There were
also further riots between the restive Blues and Greens, particularly in 547, 562, and 563,
which necessitated repair and reconstruction work.

In the imperial city, two churches of the period stand out above all others, largely
through their survival down to the present day. The first is the Church of Ss Sergius
and Bacchus, soldiers who were martyred in c. 300; Sergius was also the object of a cult
that came to assume greater importance in the second half of the sixth century (below).
Ss Sergius and Bacchus was finished in 536, and consisted of a 16-sided dome with an
eastward-facing apse. A Greek inscription written in hexameter runs around the interior
of the dome's lower entablature, honouring Justinian and Theodora (Figure 14.10). The
church has survived because of its reuse as a mosque, and the same is true for Justinian's
most famous creation, the Church of Holy Wisdom (Hagia Sophia). The earlier structure at the site had been burned during the Nika riots and, in an extraordinary display of
efficiency, the new building was dedicated at the end of December 537. The Church of

Figure 14.11 The interior of Holy Wisdom (Hagia Sophia) in Istanbul.

Source: Photograph by the author.

Holy Wisdom was designed by the mathematicians and scientists Anthemius of Tralles and Isidore of Miletus, who were also probably responsible for Ss Sergius and Bacchus. Holy Wisdom shares some architectural similarities with Ss Sergius and Bacchus, but magnified on a truly breathtaking scale. The main dome of Holy Wisdom is 30 metres (100 feet) wide and 55 metres (180 feet) high, held aloft by 40 individual ribs that soar heavenward from large arched windows. Arcaded galleries support further tiers of windows, all of which light the massive interior (Figure 14.11).

The sixth-century historian Theophanes of Byzantium, whose work was excerpted by Photius, recorded that during Justinian's reign the Romans were finally able to obtain

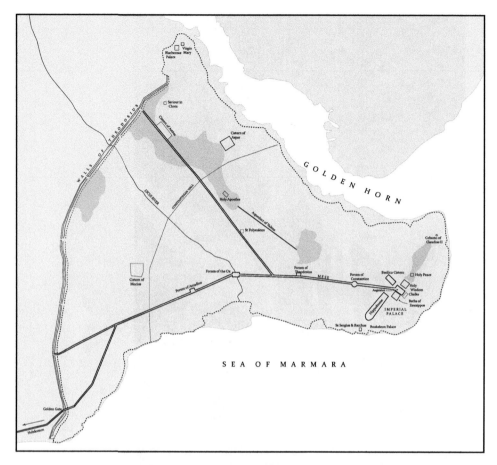

Figure 14.12 Constantinople in the sixth century.

Source: Illustration by the author.

silkworms; eggs of these precious creatures, obtained from the Chinese, were smuggled to Constantinople by a Persian traveller (Photius, *Bibliotheca*, 64). With homegrown silk at his disposal, Justinian was able to provide lavishly decorated silken furnishings for Holy Wisdom, although these have long since disappeared. Nevertheless, even without these objects, the sheer scale of Holy Wisdom is awe inspiring and represented an astonishing display of imperial wealth in the service of Christian piety. In 563, the church received a fitting eulogy, a 1,029-verse effort delivered by Paul, a *silentarius* in the palace, after repairs following the earthquake of 557 (Figure 14.12).

Plague and climate change during the reign of Justinian

In 541, a pandemic spread all across the world from north-western Europe to China. Conventionally called the 'Justinianic Plague', the illness is thought to have originated in either central Asia or central Africa. It reached Pelusium on the Egyptian coast in summer of 541, and between 541 and 543 the disease spread into the Persian empire, to Rome, Alexandria, Constantinople, and Antioch, and as far west as Gaul, Germany, Spain, and the British Isles. This first wave was followed by several more, and the disease was still killing people in Italy in 600, in Constantinople in 747, and in the Middle East in the 750s.

Procopius was in Constantinople when the disease arrived, and he provided a detailed description of its effects. These included swellings in the groin, and 'also inside the armpit, and in some cases also beside the ears, and at different points on the thighs' (*Wars*, 2.22). The disease is attested more through contemporary literature than by epigraphic evidence, although one notable Greek inscription from the Syrian Hauran, dated to 542/43, commemorates a bishop 'on whom God brought the evil death of groin and armpit' (*Wadd.* 2497). Gregory of Tours recorded the plague's arrival in Rome, and the death of Pelagius II, the bishop of Rome, from the disease of the *inguen*—the groin (*History of the Franks*, 10.1). John of Ephesus was another eyewitness, writing about the plague in part of the lost second book of the *Ecclesiastical History* that was fortuitously included in the *Chronicle of Zuqnin*. John, whose description of the bubonic swellings agrees with that provided by Procopius, saw 'desolate and groaning villages and corpses spread out on the earth, with no one to take up (and bury) them'. In the fields, animals were untended and wandered around aimlessly, 'having forgotten (life in) a cultivated land and the human voice which used to lead them'; trees were full of unpicked fruit, and grain stood tall, with nobody to bring in the harvest (*Chronicle of Zuqnin* 3, p. 87). Paul the Deacon provided a similar view of abandoned farmland in Liguria (*History of the Lombards*, 2.4). John of Ephesus also vividly described the climate of terror and the appearance of frightening visions that accompanied the disease, and he also reported seeing rats suffering from the same illness (*Chronicle of Zuqnin* 3, pp. 95–6). Justinian caught the plague and survived, as did the church historian Evagrius, although he lost many members of his family (*Ecclesiastical History*, 4.29).

On the basis of the literary evidence, medical historians have identified the pathogen as *Yersinia pestis*—the bubonic plague—and the later isolation of *Yersinia pestis* from some 45 individuals in Europe from the period provides a certain degree of diagnostic confidence. There is less consensus, however, on the impact of the disease: while estimates have ranged as high as 30–60 per cent mortality within the Roman empire, recent arguments have attacked flaws in the methodologies used to reach those estimates. Nevertheless, the plague had a distinct impact on society and was surely a horrifying event for its victims: the personal experience of Evagrius, whose faith had been shaken by the loss of his children, and who questioned why the children of pagans survived, indicates the social and religious dislocation caused by the pandemic (*Ecclesiastical History*, 6.23). In 541/42, Justinian became sufficiently concerned to appoint a palatine bureaucrat to oversee the burial of plague victims (Procopius, *Wars*, 2.23). *Novel* 122, issued in 544, referred to the plague, and *Novel* 128 (545) addressed the problem of collecting taxes from land that had been abandoned. The financial impact of the plague might be behind Procopius' comment that on the eastern front, soldiers deserted to Khusrau I with the 'grievance that the government owed them their pay for a long time' (*Wars*, 2.7). Financial problems are also suggested by the appearance of a lighter gold solidus throughout the 540s, and a series of famines accompanied the emergence of the plague, in 543, 545/46, 546/47, 556, 560, and 562. Many of these famines were reported in the second book of John of Ephesus. His description of a famine in Amida in 546/47 is particularly noteworthy: it was caused by a lack of seed, suggesting that not enough had been generated from the previous harvest to provide for the new crop. Furthermore, when seed was found and grew, 'it faded and withered', causing people to wander from region to region, looking for food (*Chronicle of Zuqnin* 3, p. 114).

The failure of crops at Amida suggests that conditions during this period were not particularly favourable for agriculture, and it is very probable that the outbreak of the Justinianic Plague was connected to an important shift in climate that began in 536. 'It came about during this year that a most dread portent took place,' wrote Procopius, 'for the sun gave forth its light without brightness, like the moon, during this whole year, and it seemed exceedingly like the sun in eclipse' (*Wars*, 4.14). Dendrochronological evidence from across the northern hemisphere as far apart as North America and Asia has shown that temperatures dropped considerably, leading to snowfall, crop failure, and famine. Poor harvests are indicated in Ireland in 536 (*Annals of Ulster*, s.a. 536), and in Italy, mass starvation took place as the harvest failed and the war with the Ostrogoths took its toll. 'I shall now tell of the appearance which they came to have and in what manner they died,' Procopius began in his apocalyptic description of the victims of a period of famine in Italy, 'for I was an eye witness.' The account recalls the terrible images of the Biafran famine in the late 1960s—dry and leathery skin that lost its healthy hue; eyes sunken within sockets; and 'a sort of insane stare'. Birds flocked around, awaiting the opportunity to eat what little flesh remained on the bone, and cannibalism was rife (*Wars*, 6.20). Recently, an analysis of ice cores has demonstrated that a substantial volcanic eruption in North America in March 536 resulted in large clouds of ash and sulphur being introduced into the atmosphere. Sunlight was dimmed by the spring of 536, and these adverse conditions persisted for 14–18 months, leading to temperature drops as low as 2.5°C (4.5°F) from normal. Further eruptions in 540 and 547 produced additional atmospheric pollution and, combined with expanding areas of sea ice and glacial activity, sustained lower than average temperatures until c. 660—a phenomenon that has been called the 'Late Antique Little Ice Age'.

As noted in Chapter 12, a connection has been drawn between climate change and the emergence of the Plague of Cyprian, and it is possible that the temperature changes initiated by the volcanic eruption of 536 impacted the plague's vectors—rats, together with the tropical rat flea *Xenopsylla cheopis*. Another link between the plague and climate change is inferred from the incidences of famine noted earlier. In addition to the famines that followed the outbreak of the plague, which could be related to a combination of climate and reduced human resources, there were also famines that *preceded* the plague's appearance in 541. The possibility exists that, in addition to enduring the normal stresses such as warfare and disease, the population was under-nourished; a period of famine would also foreshadow the arrival of the most infamous episode of the bubonic plague, the Black Death, in the fourteenth century. Further pain was caused to the exhausted eastern provinces in 551, when a massive tsunami caused severe damage along the Levantine coast. According to Malalas, 'the sea retreated out to the deep for a mile', before surging back again and drowning onlookers (*Chronicle*, 18.118).

An important consequence of the plague was its cultural impact. Christian expectations of the end-time apocalypse, given flesh by the early sixth-century *Oracle of Baalbek*, had pinned the day of judgement to c. 500, a time that came and went (*Oracle of Baalbek*,

136–227 = *RLA* pp. 160–2). When the plague arrived with all its concomitant horrors, and other disasters took place, such as the fallout from the volcanic eruption in 536 and the capture of Antioch in 540, end-time anxieties were dramatically magnified even as the calamities continued, but the world stubbornly refused to end. Evagrius's angst-ridden worries about why God inflicted such tortures on him and his family, but spared his pagan neighbours, reflect the ways in which contemporary expectations of life had become completely upended. Yet, rather than turn away from their Christian faith, the Romans, led by their emperor, deliberately and dramatically intensified their links with it. Most prominently, the cult of the Virgin Mary became explicitly associated with the fortune of Constantinople, to the point where Justinian turned the festival of Hypapante (the Presentation of Christ or Candlemas) into a celebration of Mary. The Theotokos also received an annual festival, held on August 15. Religious images and icons, long shunned by Christians, assumed greater importance as talismans against all manner of evils, ranging from protection from enemy attack to protection from disease. Cults of saints, whose relics were enshrined in purpose-built martyria, also became particularly important. In 542, for instance, Khusrau I laid siege to Rusafa-Sergiopolis in an attempt to seize a bejewelled cross and 'the all-holy relics of the victorious martyr Sergius', but the defenders believed that he was undone through the protection of St Sergius himself, who tapped the supernatural to cause 'myriad shields' to appear on the city's battlements (Evagrius, *Ecclesiastical History*, 4.28). The Edessenes likewise believed that an image of Christ foiled Khusrau in 544 (Evagrius, *Ecclesiastical History*, 4.27). Apamea was 'guarded' by a fragment of the True Cross (Procopius, *Wars*, 2.11), and the later Avar siege of Constantinople was raised in 626 through the intervention of the Virgin Mary (*Easter Chronicle*, p. 724). A number of Roman cities used saintly relics to ward off the plague, including the head of John the Baptist at Emesa (Ps.-Zachariah, *Chronicle*, 10.9.a) and the body of the patriarch Ephrem at Antioch (Evagrius, *Ecclesiastical History*, 4.35). As emperor and a supposed viceroy of God, Justinian's position was particularly precarious, and as he promoted the cult of Mary he also magnified his own piety, taking on a particularly ascetic lifestyle and claiming that he had been healed from serious pain by divine intercession (Procopius, *Buildings*, 1.7). Justinian thus became a divine arbiter for his people, almost saint-like in his behaviour and self-representation.

This surge in religiosity in the city and the empire has come to be known as 'liturgification'. The penetration of Roman society by Christian belief, which had accelerated during and after the reign of Constantine, had already reached a stage by which patriarchs crowned emperors and members of the royal family patronised churches and holy sites in Palestine. By the mid-sixth century, however, Christianity became very much more important as everyone from the emperor downwards fought to make sense of what was happening. In 533, when an earthquake struck Constantinople, the people gathered in the Forum of Constantine and chanted prayers until sunrise (*Easter Chronicle*, p. 629); after the earthquake of 557, an annual church service of supplication was instituted, as noted earlier. In the same year, Justinian returned to Constantinople, and his behaviour during his *adventus* reflects the prominent place accorded to Christian ritual and prayer. His procession, accompanied by troops, senators, clergy, the urban prefect, and the people of the city, led to the Church of the Holy Apostles, where the emperor paused in silent prayer for Theodora. The intensely religious nature of the *adventus* and the ostentatious displays of piety characterised the atmosphere in Constantinople and the empire in the wake of the plague. There is a distinctive difference between the image of the emperor on the Barberini Ivory, with its central presentation of a victorious equestrian emperor, and whose pose would not have been out of place a century or more earlier, and the fervent power of the painted icon of Christ from the Monastery of St Catherine. There were also important historiographical shifts: the classicising tradition that stretched back to Thucydides ended with Theophylact, and Agathias, one of the final classicising authors, found that one of the cornerstones of the classicising approach—to explain events through an appreciation of rational causality—was no longer sufficient. Classicising historical works were replaced by Christian historiography, and it is telling that the last ordinary consul in the eastern empire held office in 541, after which imperial political life turned its back on this age-old tradition. After Justinian's death, the poet Corippus would write of his successor Justin II that the empire was in the hands of God (*In Praise of Justin*, 3.333). Liturgification was to have momentous consequences in the seventh century—as we shall see in the conclusion to this chapter.

Justin II (565–78) and Tiberius II (578–82)

Justinian died in November 565 and was succeeded by his nephew, Justin II, whose wife, Sophia, was Theodora's niece. The succession was somewhat opaque: Justinian died in the presence of his *praepositus*, Callinicus, who apparently interpreted the emperor's final words to Justin's benefit. Closely guarded by the *excubitores* and their commander, Tiberius, Justin was crowned by the patriarch of Constantinople, John Scholasticus, then formally announced to the people in the Hippodrome. His reign began inauspiciously with the execution of a relative and several senators. On the other hand, Justin displayed a conciliatory approach towards anti-Chalcedonians, welcoming Jacob Baradaeus to Constantinople and issuing a statement of faith in 566 that avoided mentioning the Council of Chalcedon. However, Jacob's authority was being challenged by a splinter group known as the Tritheists; they quickly became a major problem for anti-Chalcedonian clergy. This schism was particularly dangerous because it robbed the anti-Chalcedonians of a unified position, essential if negotiations with the emperor were to prove successful. When a council convened at Callinicum in 567 failed to resolve the differences among the anti-Chalcedonians, Justin's patience ran out and a wave of persecution followed; one of its victims was John of Ephesus, who wrote the third part of his *Ecclesiastical History* in prison.

A collection of Syriac documents compiled towards the end of the sixth century shows how Jacob Baradaeus turned to his patron, al-Harith, in an attempt to solve the growing Tritheist problem. Document 39 reveals that 'the glorious and Christ-loving *patrikios*' al-Harith had personally contacted the two most troublesome Tritheists, Conon and Eugenius, to persuade them to change their position, even arranging a conference in the province of Arabia to discuss the issue; both bishops were, however, deposed and imprisoned in 569. Efforts continued, and document 40 in the collection places al-Harith in Constantinople, seeking to forge a consensus between the Tritheists and other anti-Chalcedonians. Document 41, known as 'the Letter of the Archimandrites', is an affirmation of faith addressed to Jacob Baradaeus by 137 anti-Chalcedonian clergy. Subscription no. 119 in the document refers to a monastery named HLYWRM, which has been identified with the site called 'Heliarama' on the Peutinger Table, and with the ruins in the desert on the Damascus–Rusafa–Sergiopolis road west of Palmyra, known as Qasr al-Hayr al-Gharbi. Excavations at Qasr al-Hayr in the 1930s uncovered five panels with several inscriptions referring to al-Harith by his Greek name, Arethas. One refers to a period 'when the *endoxotatos* Arethas the *stratelatos* was phylarch', while another refers to 'Flavius Arethas, *patrikios*' (*IGLS* 5.2553 B, D = *AEBI* §6.23). These Greek inscriptions at an anti-Chalcedonian monastery provide further evidence for the high esteem accorded to al-Harith amongst the anti-Chalcedonian clergy; indeed, John of Ephesus thought highly enough of al-Harith to include him in a list of 'kings who are famous' along with Khusrau I, Justinian, and Abraha of Himyar (*Chronicle of Zuqnin* 3, p. 110). After al-Harith's death, al-Mundhir would continue to lobby for the anti-Chalcedonians. In subscription no. 121 of document 41, he is recorded as the 'Christ-loving *patrikios*'.

On his accession in 569, al-Mundhir faced a series of raids from his Nasrid opponent, Qabus. He responded by raiding around al-Hira, plundering the animal herds and causing havoc in the rear of Qabus's army. John of Ephesus, who was a fierce advocate for al-Mundhir, paints a somewhat over-hyped portrait of a fearless and vigorous warrior. When Qabus taunted al-Mundhir to see whether he was brave enough to face him in open battle, the Jafnid phylarch was more than ready. 'Why do you trouble yourselves?' he replied. 'I am coming' (*Ecclesiastical History*, 3.6.3). Al-Mundhir's directness did not please everyone. After his victory over Qabus, he requested a payment of gold from Justin to hire additional troops and make good the losses he had suffered in the conflict. The emperor was furious, and 'strove to kill him through a secret treachery' (John of Ephesus, *Ecclesiastical History*, 3.6.3). The story of the plot is so ridiculously convoluted that its authenticity has long been questioned. Justin wrote two letters: one to al-Mundhir, requesting that he visit a *patricius* named Marcian, and one to Marcian, instructing him to kill al-Mundhir on arrival. The letters were switched, al-Mundhir discovered the plot, and he retired into the desert, fuming with anger and resentment.

While al-Mundhir stewed in self-imposed exile, the Lombards had destroyed the Gepids and invaded Italy, and war had raged with the Avars in the Balkans. Justin faced continued revolts in Roman-held Africa, losing a praetorian prefect and two *magistri* in consecutive years to Berber revolts, which were only suppressed in 578. The most serious issue of Justin's reign was, however, the failure of the peace with Persia. Justin had given his tacit support to a Persarmenian embassy that declared a willingness to live under Roman rule, and the subsequent revolt took the life of the Persian governor (Evagrius, *Ecclesiastical History*, 5.7 = *REF2* p. 138). When Khusrau attempted to calm regional anxieties by sending a Christian ambassador to Justin, he was met with a declaration that the peace of 562 had lapsed, and the emperor provided further insult by refusing to make the expected annual payment for the Caspian Gates. Justin could feel emboldened because new allies had emerged in the shape of an embassy from the Turks, which arrived in Constantinople in 568/69. After establishing an empire in what is now western Mongolia, part of this empire, led by Istemi (Sizaboulos, in Roman sources; 552–76), had begun a rapid expansion westwards. Fighting initially as Persian allies, the Turks defeated the Hephthalites (557–61), then took control over Sogdia and its pole position in the silk trade, enrolling the Sogdians as silk-brokers. When attempts to sell silk to the Persians were rejected by Khusrau, Istemi sent an embassy to Constantinople led by a Sogdian named Maniakh. Justin responded favourably, and dispatched the *magister militum per Orientem* Zemarchus to Sogdia, where he arranged a treaty with Istemi. This whole process took several years, and Zemarchus did not return until 571/72 (Menander, fr. 10 &13.5; Photius, *Bibliotheca*,

64). While he was away, Zemarchus took part on a Turkish raid into Media, and on the return journey the Persians attempted to poison the Turkish ambassadors, which did little to improve relations between Justin and Khusrau.

In South Arabia, the Himyarite king Abraha had died in 565, and his sons, Masruq and Yaksum, were unable to keep control over the kingdom. A Persian invasion followed, crushing Himyarite resistance and bringing the kingdom under Persian control. The sources are divided over why Khusrau decided on this path: the ninth-century writer Ibn Hisham wrote that Sayf b. dhu-Yazan, one of the princes from the ancient Hadrami clan of the dhu-Yazan, was concerned about an Axumite invasion and requested Persian intervention from the Nasrid leader al-Numan (*Sirat rasul Allah*, pp. 41–3). Al-Tabari wrote that Sayf had initially petitioned Justin for help, but had eventually given up and turned to the Persians (*Tarikh* 5, p. 237). Whatever the precise cause and sequence of events, the contemporary historian Theophanes of Byzantium recorded that the Persian general Miranes captured Masruq and sacked the capital (Photius, *Bibliotheca*, 64). The Persian occupation of Himyar marked the definitive failure of Constantinople's policy in Arabia and the Red Sea, and it is noteworthy that Justin's attempt to remove al-Mundhir in Syria took place at about the same time as Himyar was lost to the Romans as a Christian ally. The relationship between Rome and Persia was becoming more bellicose, and the Arab allies of both states had begun to experience the consequences. For now, Justin cited the Persian invasion of Himyar for his belief that the peace of 562 had lapsed, justifying the hardening Roman attitude over Persarmenia, while Khusrau regarded Justin's friendliness towards the Turks and his support of the Persarmenian rebellion as a suitable pretext for action (John of Epiphania 2 = *REF2*, p. 141).

The war that resulted from these convergent aggravations proved catastrophic for Justin. The *magister militum per Orientem* Marcian, one of Justin's relatives, led troops into northern Mesopotamia, but a siege of Nisibis in 573 failed when Marcian was abruptly relieved of his command and the leaderless Roman army scattered. Al-Mundhir was still in exile, and a Persian army under Adarmahan and accompanied by Persia's Nasrid Arab allies was able to penetrate deep into Syria, sacking Apamea and reaching the Antiochene suburbs. In 574, Khusrau took his army to Dara, having plundered the abandoned Roman siege equipment at Nisibis and helping himself to the numerous catapults and siege towers that Marcian had left behind. Conscripting a large body of Persian farmers to help with the labour, Khusrau cut off Dara's water supply by diverting the feed to the main aqueduct. He then built a circumvallation and prepared several siege mounds against the city's perimeter wall. When the Persians eventually breached the walls, they locked the gates, and either systematically killed its inhabitants (John of Ephesus, *Ecclesiastical History*, 3.6.5) or deported them to Persia (*Chronicle to 724*, AG 884). When news of Dara's capture reached the palace, Justin succumbed to a ferocious depression; the Augusta Sophia took over the day-to-day management of the government, and organised a peace initiative with Khusrau. A year later, recognising his frailty, Justin elevated the *comes excubitorum* Tiberius as Caesar in December 574 with the agreement of both Sophia and the senate. In 574, Tiberius, via his envoys, the imperial quaestor Trajan, and a physician named Zacharias, brought the war with Persia to a temporary end at the price of 200 kilograms (440 pounds) of gold for the first year and 130 kilograms (286 pounds) annually thereafter for five years. The peace deal did not cover the Caucasus, however, and fighting continued there; however, in 576, Khusrau was defeated at Melitene. Retiring in disorder across the Euphrates, thousands of Persian troops drowned, and the following year Roman soldiers captured the king of Suania and his family. These multiple setbacks triggered a new round of negotiations, during which Tiberius almost achieved the return of Dara before an unexpected Persian military victory under Tamkhusrau scuppered the deal. War continued: in 577, the *comes excubitorum* Maurice was promoted to *magister militum per Orientem*, and raided as far as Corduene, to the south of Lake Van. Maurice's campaign was a success, and in 578, as winter approached, he took a measure of revenge for past humiliations by sacking Singara. Roman elation was offset, however, by the collapse of the treaty with the Turks. Istemi's son, Tardu (576–603), broke the peace in anger at Constantinople's friendly treatment of the Avars, and captured the Crimea in 576. "'Your emperor shall pay me due penalty,'" Tardu raged at the Roman envoy Valentinus, "'for he has spoken words of friendship to me while making a treaty with the Uarkhonitai [Avars], our slaves'" (Menander, fr. 19.1 = *RLA*, pp. 331–3). Subsequently, there was a civil war between different Turkish factions, which broke the Turks into western and eastern khaganates, a development that proved to be of crucial importance during the war between Khusrau II and Heraclius (below).

In 575, al-Mundhir had finally returned to Roman service. He was aware of the Persian attack into Syria and of the role played by the Nasrid Arabs, who had plundered the country and taken numerous captives back to Persia. It was for this reason, says John of Ephesus, that he determined to make peace (*Ecclesiastical History*, 3.6.4). The reconciliation took place through a meeting between al-Mundhir and the *magister militum per Orientem*, Justinian (a relative of the former emperor) at the shrine of St Sergius at Rusafa-Sergiopolis. This sacred city lay south of Callinicum in the semi-desert and on the old *Strata Diocletiana*, and was adorned with numerous churches and equipped with massive water cisterns. It had also become a place of great importance to the Jafnid family. The link between the Jafnids and the Sergius cult is apparent in the inscription from Tall al-Umayri East (above), and al-Harith was also honoured with a mosaic inscription from the Church of St Sergius at Nitl, near Madaba (see *AEBI* §6.30). The main centre for the cult was, however, Rusafa-Sergiopolis, and the massive 'Basilica A' at the city contained Sergius's relics. The cult had been patronised by Anastasius, Justinian, and Theodora, and like many other Christian cults, the non-denominational cult of Sergius was an international phenomenon. It was also particularly popular with Arabs. Sergius proved so popular that the bishop Ahudemmeh created a rival cult centre at Qasr Serij, near Mosul, and later Khusrau II and his Christian wife, Shirin, prayed to Sergius when Shirin was trying to conceive.

Outside the imposing defensive walls of Rusafa-Sergiopolis, on or near the supposed site where Sergius had been martyred, al-Mundhir had built a small chapel-like building, in which a Greek inscription proclaimed 'the fortune of al-Mundhir triumphs' (*AEBI* §6.29). The building was detached from the city, but it was located close to its beautifully elaborate northern gateway, where pilgrims travelling on the Callinicum road would enter the city to pray to the saint. Mark Whittow aptly called the building 'the equivalent of a great shaykh's seven-pole tent, but built in stone and in a Roman idiom' (Whittow, 'Rome and the Jafnids', p. 222). It was designed as a place for al-Mundhir to hold audiences when people from all over the ancient world arrived for the feast day of Sergius on October 7, and provided a place for mediation and arbitration, at which the Jafnid leaders excelled (Figure 14.13). The building's hybridity was wholly in keeping with the development of

Figure 14.13 The 'al-Mundhir' building at Rusafa-Sergiopolis.

Source: Photograph by the author.

non-Roman identities at the edges of imperial power, and in the way that non-Romans framed their own authority—in this, it finds parallels in structures such as the *djedars* and the tomb of Theoderic Amal in Ravenna.

Back in Roman service, al-Mundhir attacked al-Hira and gathered a mass of plunder, which he gave to the anti-Chalcedonian monasteries in Arabia (John of Ephesus, *Ecclesiastical History*, 3.6.4). Meanwhile, Tiberius was promoted to Augustus in September 578, and Justin died shortly afterwards; Sophia survived her husband and retired to one of the royal palaces. Al-Mundhir offered his congratulations to Tiberius in person, but took offence when the emperor angrily accused him of bad faith and judgement for sending himself into exile when the empire was under attack; however, when al-Mundhir showed him the incriminating letters, Tiberius apologised. Al-Mundhir also gained the emperor's promise to cease the persecutions of anti-Chalcedonians that had taken place under Justin II, and that had robbed John of Ephesus of his freedom (Michael the Syrian, *Chronicle*, pp. 370–1). Tiberius was amenable to this request because of the numerous problems he had inherited from Justin. In the Balkans, a Roman-allied Avar army clashed with the Slavs, but then attacked Sirmium, laying siege to the city for over four years before it fell in 582. On the Persian front, Khusrau had died in 579, but his son, Hormizd IV, proved bellicose and unwilling to agree to peace. Maurice and his army raided across the Tigris in retaliation, while Hormizd sent his son and eventual successor, Khusrau, to Caucasian Albania where he would try to undo some of Rome's diplomatic advances there. Then, in 581, Maurice and al-Mundhir invaded Persia. The expedition was a failure—and the fallout would have severe consequences for the Jafnid alliance.

The campaign of 581 was preceded by an invitation from Tiberius to al-Mundhir to mediate between rival anti-Chalcedonian factions in Constantinople: like Justinian and Justin before him, Tiberius was trying to establish a credible group of anti-Chalcedonian representatives with whom he could negotiate. The principal issue was a deep-seated conflict between the patriarchates of Antioch and Alexandria, where various clergy had been consecrated, exiled, and deposed. Jacob Baradaeus had taken sides, prompting a sharp response from his enemies, but then he, along with two of the most difficult protagonists, died in 578. However, the patriarch of Alexandria, Damian, refused to let the matter rest, leading to an intractable dispute that John of Ephesus called 'the furnace of the Babylonians' (*Ecclesiastical History*, 3.4.39). John attended the meeting that al-Mundhir chaired in Constantinople, and praised his efforts to bring the different sides together. Tiberius was also fulsome, showering al-Mundhir and his sons with gifts and titles. Aside from a 'royal diadem', John does not describe these blandishments, but an undated inscription from al-Burj in western Syria records the children as *endoxotatoi* and al-Mundhir as 'Flavius Alamoundaros, *paneuphemos*, *patrikios*, phylarch' (*AEBI* §6.32; see also §6.26). It is not known when al-Mundhir was promoted to *paneuphemos*, the highest senatorial grade in the *illustres*, but its tenure reflects al-Mundhir's exceptional authority and the trust that Tiberius had placed in him. On March 2, 580, it seemed that the emperor's confidence was well placed. Al-Mundhir got a result; however, Damian, who disliked both al-Mundhir and the deal, went behind al-Mundhir's back to destroy it.

As the fallout from Damian's betrayal spread, Maurice and al-Mundhir invaded Persia. Departing from Circesium, Maurice's target was Ctesiphon, but he was recalled when Hormizd launched a counter-attack directed at Edessa. A key bridge had also mysteriously been destroyed. An intelligence leak was immediately suspected, and Maurice pointed the finger at al-Mundhir. 'The Saracen tribe is known to be the most unreliable and fickle,' wrote Theophylact, 'their mind is not steadfast, and their judgement is not firmly grounded in prudence' (3.17.7). Prejudice towards 'outsiders' was still freely on display in the capital, and there was no doubt in conservative senatorial circles about who should take the blame. Maurice and al-Mundhir engaged in a war of words and letters, but the Arab phylarch was always going to lose a palatine contest, especially when Tiberius died and Maurice became the new emperor. In short order, al-Mundhir was arrested; 'he felt weak and beaten,' wrote John of Ephesus of his hero, 'like a lion of the desert, which was shut up inside a cage' (*Ecclesiastical History*, 3.3.41). Al-Mundhir was subsequently exiled with his family to Sicily in 582. A brief war followed between his son al-Numan and Roman authorities around Bostra, and al-Numan, after refusing an offer of alliance, eventually joined his father in Sicily. The Roman experiment with the super-phylarcate had come to an abrupt, but perhaps inevitable, end. 'The kingdom of the Tayyaye was broken up amongst fifteen princes,' wrote Michael the Syrian. 'The majority of them joined the Persians, and from then on the empire of the Christian Tayyaye ended' (*Chronicle*, 10.19 = *AEBI* §5.33). Michael's pessimism was not entirely warranted, however, as it is clear from subsequent events that Arab leaders remained in Roman service, facilitating communications between Constantinople and Ctesiphon during one of the most stunning upsets on the eastern front: the Persian civil war, which began in 590.

Maurice (582–602) and Phocas (602–10)

Maurice, a Cappadocian, had a background as a *notarius*, and combined this with his military experience to write a well-received tactical manual, the *Strategikon*, which memorably described the Avars as 'scoundrels, devious, and very experienced in military matters' (11.2 = *RLA* pp. 328–9). Military and financial problems preoccupied Maurice after the free-spending years of Tiberius II, which had left 'the palace swept clean by a broom and the royal treasury emptied' (*Chronicle to 1234*, p. 213). Maurice cut army expenditures, leading to mutinies in 588 and 594. His reign witnessed the creation of exarchates in those parts of Italy (584, Ravenna) and Africa (591, Carthage) still under Roman control; exarchs became the top-ranked individuals, and in Africa the exarch combined the positions of praetorian prefect and *magister militum*. In Italy, Maurice attempted to destabilise the Lombards, hiring the Frankish king Childebert to invade in 584, and fighting between Lombards and the Roman exarch and his Frankish allies continued into the 590s. The Avars temporarily seized Singidunum in 583, and used this leverage to extract a substantial increase in their annual gold subsidy from Maurice, and Avar raids reached Marcianople, Thessalonike, and Adrianople between 584 and 587. In 588, the Avar khagan displayed himself wearing Roman imperial robes, a clear affront to the emperor. Maurice broke with sixth-century tradition when he took to the field at the head of an army, fighting the Avars in 590; by 600/01, Avar power had been dramatically curtailed by a string of successful campaigns. At court, Maurice clashed with Gregory, a former urban prefect whom the bishop of Rome, Pelagius II, had sent as his ambassador. Returning to Italy in 586, Gregory would assume the bishopric when Pelagius II died of the plague, and be remembered as one of the most important popes in the history of the church (590–604).

In the Caucasus and the east, Roman and Persian armies continued to spar over Suania, Nisibis, and Martyropolis, and in 586 the *magister militum per Orientem*, Philippicus, defeated a Persian army at Solachon, east of Lake Van. As the enemy approached, 'Philippicus displayed the image of God incarnate', and walked through the ranks, exhorting his men (Theophylact, 2.3.4). According to Evagrius, he also displayed the head of Symeon the Stylite, which had somehow retained its freshness (*Ecclesiastical History*, 1.13). Theophylact also told the astonishing tale of how a group of Romans who had been captured at Dara and imprisoned within the Fortress of Oblivion managed an unlikely escape and reached Roman territory, evading Persian patrols along the way (Theophylact, 3.5.1).

In the Caucasus, Persarmenia had been returned to Persian control, and Martyropolis had been captured after it was betrayed by its commander. The Persian general Bahram Chobin, who had defeated the eastern Turks, was now transferred to the west and turned his attention to Suania and Lazica. Meeting defeat, however, he was fired by Hormizd IV. The furious general led a revolt in 589/90 that killed Hormizd, and when a new conflict erupted between Bahram and Khusrau (Hormizd's son, who had been crowned as Khusrau II), the latter fled west with his entourage and presented himself at Circesium, asking for asylum. According to the *Chronicle to 1234*, a certain Abu Jafna Numan

b. al-Mundhir, who resided at Rusafa-Sergiopolis, acted as a mediator between Khusrau and Maurice; intriguingly, a graffito from Rusafa-Sergiopolis mentions one 'Nouminos', a Greek rendition of the Arabic al-Numan (*Chronicle to 1234*, p. 215 = *AEBI* §5.34). The super-phylarcate may have collapsed, but Arabs remained in Roman service.

Amidst a frenzy of diplomatic activity, the Romans accepted Khusrau as the legitimate king and Persian negotiators offered to return Dara and Martyropolis. Khusrau would make no demands for cash and he also promised to cede Iberia and large parts of Armenia (Sebeos, *Armenian History*, 76.8–18 = *REF2*, p. 172). Maurice and his *consistorium*, which now included the patriarch of Constantinople, John IV, listened patiently. As he made plain in his *Strategikon*, Maurice respected the Persians, particularly their attention to order and discipline, their skill in battle, and their hardiness, and he took care to come to a reasoned decision (*Strategikon*, 11.1). While there was some debate about the wisdom of acting in support of a Persian king, and while John considered that Khusrau had his father's blood on his hands, and thus did not deserve to be helped, Maurice decided to offer Khusrau his support, furnishing a generous supply of gold and an army for Khusrau's use. Bahram made a counter-proposal that included the tantalising offer of Nisibis, but Maurice was true to his word. In 591, the communities of the east witnessed a rare moment as a combined Romano-Persian force under the command of the *magister militum per Orientem* Narses invaded the Persian empire, defeating Bahram and restoring Khusrau to his throne. The Persian king had prayed ostentatiously to St Sergius on the way, and the combined army was protected by the Virgin Mary, extending her intercession to the Persians fighting with their Roman partners (Theophylact, 5.10).

By the turn of the seventh century, relations with the Persians were better than they had been for decades. A Roman garrison was back at Dara, and Khusrau had dedicated a golden cross to St Sergius and sent it to Rusafa-Sergiopolis, where it was installed with Maurice's permission. Khusrau, many of whose senior courtiers were Christian, began a church-building campaign in Persia. Diplomatic contacts were maintained through bishops, working as envoys, and an uprising in Armenia was suppressed by a joint Romano-Persian army. Peace in the east had allowed Maurice to turn his full attention to the Balkans, where the Avars continued to raid and capture Roman cities, using them as bargaining chips to demand increases in their subsidies. These were generally granted, although Roman offensives across the Danube proved successful; in one campaign in 599, the *magister militum* Comentiolus and Maurice's brother, the *magister militum per Thracias*, Peter, crushed the Avars and their allies in four consecutive engagements, taking thousands of prisoners. In 602, however, everything fell apart.

Following a fruitful campaign against the Slavs that had capitalised on a decade of successful campaigns along the Danube, Peter received orders to winter north of the river. In tandem with orders that Maurice had also issued for cuts to military pay as a cost-saving measure, the prospect of a chilly central European winter moved the troops to mutiny. After the mutineers' demands were rebuffed, the army responded by proclaiming emperor one of their own, Phocas, and marched on Constantinople. A fully fledged coup was now underway—the first for a long time—and it would nearly prove to be the empire's ruin. In Constantinople, riots broke out and Maurice was forced to flee to Chalcedon, even as the Green circus faction welcomed Phocas. He was then accepted by the senate at the Hebdomon and crowned by Cyriacus, the patriarch. Maurice was captured, and on November 27, 602, he was forced to watch as his sons were killed one by one. The purge also took the lives of his close associates, including Peter and Comentiolus, whose 'body was eaten by dogs' (*Easter Chronicle*, p. 693). In the aftermath of Maurice's death, al-Mundhir was released from his Sicilian exile, but with this he abruptly disappeared from the contemporary historical record (*Chronicle to 1234*, p. 219).

The reign of Phocas was brief and miserable. There were circus riots in 603, and executions of palatine officials who were suspected of disloyalty. The purges were unspeakably brutal. The *vir illustris* Elpidius, for instance, 'had his tongue cut out and his four extremities removed; he was paraded on a stretcher and carried down to the sea; when his eyes had been gouged out, he was thrown into a skiff and burnt' (*Easter Chronicle*, p. 696). The purges even took the life of Maurice's wife, Constantina (the daughter of Tiberius II), who was beheaded along with her female children who had survived the initial coup. In 603, the *magister militum per Orientem* Narses raised a revolt against Phocas, barricading himself behind the walls of Edessa and—according to one tradition—asking Khusrau for help. If so, his request fell on fertile ears, for as early as 602, when the envoy Lilius had travelled to Persia to announce the accession of Phocas, Khusrau had apparently taken the decision to use the coup against Maurice as a pretext for invasion. Maurice had assisted him, the legitimate king, against a usurper; a usurper had taken the life of his benefactor, killed his family, and seized his throne. The revolt of Narses in 603 thus gave further impetus to his plans, as did internal unrest amongst the eastern Turks on Persia's eastern frontier, allowing Khusrau to contemplate a sustained effort in the west. According to legend, one of Maurice's sons had also escaped execution and found his way to Khusrau, while the Persian king was also reputed to have married Maria, a daughter of Maurice (*Chronicle to 1234*, p. 217 & *Khuzistan Chronicle*, p. 20 = REF2, p. 232).

By the end of 603, Khusrau had led his army into Mesopotamia. After capturing Dara at the end of an 18-month siege in 604, Khusrau returned to Persia and entrusted the continuation of the war to his general Shahrvaraz. Between c. 602 and 606, Khusrau had also toppled the Nasrid client monarchy at al-Hira. The reasons for this are unclear, but it is thought that following the capture of Himyar, which devolved control of central Arabia to the Persians, and with Khusrau's plans to invade the Roman empire, there was no longer any need to maintain a force whose power had traditionally been directed south and west into the desert. As al-Mundhir's self-imposed exile had done for the Romans, the elimination of the final Nasrid leader, al-Numan, removed an important military buffer. Not long afterwards, an Arab army defeated a Persian force at Dhu Qar, an event that was celebrated in Arabic poetry and prose for centuries to come.

By 604/05, Phocas had transferred reinforcements from the Balkans, made possible by buying an expensive peace with the Avars. In the Balkans, the Avars and their Slav allies had largely filled the power vacuum once occupied by the Ostrogoths, Gepids, and Lombards. Nikopolis ad-Istrum had long been abandoned, and Slavs had displaced the population of Justiniana Prima by the early seventh century; Isidore of Seville also recorded that the Slavs had occupied large swathes of Greece (*Chronicle*, 120). The Balkan reinforcements enabled Phocas to dislodge Narses from Edessa, and Narses was eventually betrayed by Phocas's nephew, Domentziolus, who promised him his life if he surrendered—but arranged for him to be burned alive instead. A pro-Maurice survivor of the purge in 602, Priscus, who had been in Armenia when Phocas seized the throne, had rehabilitated himself through his marriage to Phocas's daughter and managed to be appointed as *comes excubitorum*. The relationship between father- and son-in-law soured, however, and Priscus wrote to Heraclius, a former comrade-in-arms from the regime of Maurice and now exarch of Africa, encouraging him to revolt. In 608, Heraclius sent his son Heraclius to Constantinople with a naval force, and a landward arm of the invasion under the younger Heraclius's cousin, Nicetas, marched across Africa. Meanwhile as the Persian invasion progressed, riots broke out between the circus factions in Antioch, and the patriarch, Anastasius II, was lynched in 609 or 610. Phocas sent his *comes Orientis* Bonosus to Antioch and, after carrying out a purge, Bonosus was sent to repel Nicetas, but was beaten by the end of 609.

From the very beginning, Heraclius's campaign was permeated by an intense form of Christianity. His arrival in Constantinople was heralded by 'fortified ships that had on their masts reliquaries and icons of the Mother of God', appropriating the protection of the Virgin Mary and overtly legitimising his claim to the city and the empire. The *Easter Chronicle* claimed that Phocas was paraded nude through the streets of the city and then taken around the harbour in a boat, so that the men in Heraclius's fleet could see his downfall. His head was impaled and exhibited in a procession along the Mese, and together with those of his *sacellarius* Leontius, Phocas's remains were burned (pp. 700–1). The flag of the Blue circus faction, which had vocally supported Phocas, was also ritualistically burned in the Hippodrome, and the race starter, linked with the Blue faction, was burned alive. Priscus was too much of a liability to allow him his freedom, but neither could Heraclius kill him, given Priscus's friendship with his father. A more practical solution beckoned—and Priscus was consigned to a monastery.

The final struggle: Heraclius (610–41) and Khusrau II (591–628)

The *History* of Theophylact ended in 603, leaving one of the most crucial periods in world history without a continuous narrative. Instead, we are dependent on a broad selection of Christian chronicles written in Greek and Syriac, Greek praise poetry, Armenian chronicles, medieval Syriac chronicles that drew on sources that are now largely lost (such as the work of Dionysius of Tel-Mahre, Syriac Orthodox patriarch from 818–45) and later Arabic and Persian sources written after the Arab conquests. There is also the lost work of Theophilus of Edessa, the head astrologer in Baghdad under the caliph al-Mahdi (775–85). His *Chronicle* has largely been reconstructed through its later witnesses, principally the Syriac *Chronicle* of Michael the Syrian, the Syriac *Chronicle to 1234*, the Arabic *Kitab al-Unwan* of Agapius (the bishop of Hierapolis/Mabbug/Menbij, d. 941), and the Greek *Chronicle* of Theophanes. The intricacies of the historiography for this difficult period are laid out in detail by James Howard-Johnston in *Witnesses to a World Crisis*, and by Robert Hoyland in his critical edition of Theophilus's *Chronicle* (see Further Reading section).

Heraclius was crowned by the patriarch of Constantinople, Sergius, in October 610. He married the African noblewoman Eudocia, and the marriage produced two children: Epiphania (611) and Heraclius Constantinus (612). Eudocia died in 613, and Heraclius was betrothed to his niece, Martina—a marriage that Sergius openly disliked, but that he reluctantly allowed to proceed. Following his coronation, Heraclius sent an embassy to Khusrau to announce his accession, but the Roman envoys were murdered, delivering a stark message about Khusrau's intentions. The problems facing Heraclius were many. 'The Avars had devastated Europe, while the Persians had destroyed all of Asia and had captured the cities and annihilated in battle the Roman army,' wrote Theophanes. 'On seeing these things, he was at a loss at what to do'—but he nevertheless took a pragmatic approach, holding a census to see what troops, if any, were available (Theophanes, *Chronicle*, AM 6103/p. 300). The other problem facing Heraclius was that it was clear from the start that this conflict would be different. The Persian forces showed no inclination to follow the patterns of previous campaigns, where they had extorted financial concessions from cities, or plundered their treasuries and their people, and then retired. This time Persian forces stayed, and in the years between 602 and 610, Persian armies systematically reduced the fortified Roman cities of Mesopotamia and Osrhoene, and a humanitarian crisis unfolded as thousands of desperate people fled westwards. Amida fell in 607 and Theodosiopolis-Rhesaina in 608. A second Persian attack laid siege to Theodosiopolis-Karin and captured Satala by 607; in 608, the Persian general Shahin pushed the Roman army from Armenia, and Theodosiopolis-Karin finally fell in 610 or 611. Khusrau gave orders for anti-Chalcedonian bishops to be restored where possible, stoking the division between the increasingly intolerant Chalcedonian authorities in Constantinople and the anti-Chalcedonian communities scattered across the east (*Chronicle to 1234*, pp. 224–5). Later, Khusrau would forcibly convert Chalcedonian Christians under Persian occupation to the dyophysite Christianity of the Church of the East, and he plundered churches in Syria and Mesopotamia to punish the Melkites (Agapius, *Kitab al-Unwan*, 451). As civil war between Heraclius and Phocas diverted imperial attention and consumed precious resources, Persian forces took Circesium, Callinicum, Carrhae, and Edessa in 609/10. The loss of Edessa was a particularly cruel blow, due to long-standing beliefs about its inviolability. All the Roman strongholds east of the Euphrates had now been captured. Halabiya-Zenobia was taken by Shahrvaraz in the late summer of 610, marking the first Persian conquest on the west bank of the Euphrates (*Chronicle to 724*, AG 921).

Heraclius, leading the army in person, forced the Persian army to retire to Armenia. He had by now appointed his cousin Nicetas as *comes excubitorum*, and Philippicus (the victor at Solachon in 586) as *magister militum per Orientem*. In 613, the Roman counter-offensive drew success in Armenia but failure against a Persian army outside Antioch, which was brutally sacked. Beaten again in Cilicia, Heraclius had no choice but to fall back with Philippicus into Cappadocia. A Persian army under the general Shahrvaraz captured Damascus in 613, then Jerusalem in 614. Much of the population of Jerusalem was put to the sword, nearly all of the holy relics (including the True Cross) were seized, and the survivors with their patriarch, Zacharias, were deported to Persia. The capture of Jerusalem inflamed tensions between Jews and Christians, and it was widely rumoured at the time that the city's Jews had formed a fifth column that had betrayed the city (Theophanes, *Chronicle*, AM 6106/p. 301). Sophronius, the future patriarch of Jerusalem, witnessed the city's end. 'O Christ,' he lamented, 'may you curb by the hands of Christians the ill-fated children of impious Persia!' (*Anacreontic Odes*, p. 107 = *REF2*, p. 191). John Moschus, a monk and friend of Sophronius, was also horrified, particularly by the massacres that ensued (*Spiritual Meadow*, p. 222). Ephesus was also sacked in 614, but worse was to come when Shahin reached Chalcedon in 615. Heraclius desperately opened negotiations, but because Khusrau had not recognised him, it was left to the senate to plead for mercy. The Roman offer was extraordinary: the senate would accept client status and a ruler of Khusrau's choosing, but in the winter of 615/16 this proposal was rejected and the emissaries were thrown into prison and subsequently murdered. Khusrau also demanded that Heraclius renounce his Christian faith (Theophanes, *Chronicle*, AM 6109/p. 301). Why did Khusrau reject an offer that would have granted him a greater victory than any other Persian king in history? As Howard-Johnston has observed, the reasons surely lay in Khusrau's assessment that the Turkish empire to Persia's east constituted the greater enemy (*Witnesses to a World Crisis*, p. 440). Only a decisive victory in the west would do; a more perilous struggle for Persia's existence lay on the horizon.

In the Balkans, Slavic raids repeatedly threatened Thessalonike in 618 and succeeded in capturing Naissus. The exarchate in Ravenna had reached a wary *modus vivendi* with the Lombards and their congenial king, Adaloaldus (616–26), but two successive exarchs rebelled against Heraclius in 616 and 619 and subsequent Lombard kings proved less friendly. The main threat was, however, firmly in the east. In 616 Palestine fell, Persian forces laid waste to Anatolia in 617, and between 619 and 621 the conquest was all but complete as Alexandria fell and the Nile valley came under Persian control. Across the conquered territories, Roman officials continued to manage local administration, but now they did so for new masters. The loss of Egypt caused particular pain as it brought an abrupt end to free and subsidised grain in Constantinople. The imperial mint at Nicomedia ceased operations in 619, and a new silver coin was introduced in Constantinople to pay salaries; known as the hexagram, it bore the Latin motto *Deus adiuta Romanis*, 'God help the Romans!' (Figure 14.14). In 622, the patriarch Sergius gave Heraclius permission to melt down the wealth of the church to finance an increasingly futile resistance. A risky and daring idea took shape in the emperor's mind, and Heraclius recruited and trained a new army deep in Asia Minor, leading exercises spurred on by a large image of Christ. Late in the year, Heraclius scored an important victory over Shahrvaraz in Armenia, lifting Roman morale for the first time in over a decade—but he was then forced to return to Constantinople to address the growing threat of the Avars.

Heraclius was due to meet with the Avar khagan when he got wind of a plot to take him captive. The Avars succeeded in breaking through the Long Walls and plundered homes and churches in the suburbs; they were only dissuaded by a timely payment of gold, 200,000 solidi—approximately 898 kilograms (1,979 pounds)—which Heraclius could ill afford. The emperor remained undeterred, however, even as Rhodes fell, its population deported

Figure 14.14 Silver hexagram minted at Constantinople. The obverse shows Heraclius and his son, Heraclius; the reverse, a prominent cross with the Latin text written as ∂ЄчS A∂IчтA ROmANIS.

to Persia. In March 624, Heraclius set his plan into action, leaving Constantinople in the company of his family on the symbolically important day of the Annunciation of the Virgin Mary (*Easter Chronicle*, pp. 713–14). The emperor bypassed Theodosiopolis-Karin to sack Dvin in Persarmenia, causing Shahrvaraz to break off his operations and head quickly to the north-east. Over the winter of 624/25, Heraclius sent an embassy to the western Turks, and in 625 he campaigned in the Caucasus while Shahrvaraz and his army, along with two other Persian forces, attempted to bring him to battle. As Khusrau deported the population of Edessa (Agapius, *Kitab al-Unwan*, 460), Heraclius wintered in the Caucasus in 625/26. In 626, intermittent sparring continued between Shahrvaraz and the Roman army, and in the same year the Avars, emboldened by Roman failures, swayed by Persian promises, and bolstered by contingents of Slavs, abandoned their tenuous alliance with Heraclius and joined with Shahrvaraz to lay siege to Constantinople. The Theodosian Walls proved resistant, however, and the Avars gave up in the face of Roman naval control of the surrounding waters and the public torture and mutilation, at Roman hands, of several Persian envoys (*Easter Chronicle*, pp. 722–23). Following the Avar retreat, a festival of thanksgiving was held at the Church of the Virgin Mary at Blachernae (Nikephorus, *Short History*, 13 = *RLA* pp. 330–1). The failure at Constantinople resulted in the recall of Shahrvaraz who, when he learned that he was due to be executed, revolted against Khusrau. At around the same time, Shahin was defeated by Heraclius's brother, Theodore, and subsequently died. His corpse was packed in salt and sent to Khusrau, who subjected it 'to many outrages' (Theophanes, *Chronicle*, AM 6117/p. 315).

The western Turks had responded favourably to Heraclius, who had also pledged his daughter Eudocia to their khagan, Jebu Xak'an (Ziebel). The Turks invaded the Caucasus through the Caspian Gates in 626, and placed a substantial force at Heraclius's disposal. In 627, a group of western Turks continued operations in Caucasian Albania, where they inspired terror among the region's inhabitants and later, in 629, conducted a brutal sack of Tiflis (Tblisi) in Iberia. A tenth-century Armenian text recalled the 'ravenous shameless wolves' who killed everyone in their path: 'they did not pass over the crippled or the old, nor did they show pity nor did their heartstrings writhe with compassion for the children' (Movses Daskhurani, *History*, 2.11 = *REF2*, p. 210).

In 627, Heraclius gathered his army for the final contest. In an era where the kingdoms of the Caucasus had assumed a greater importance for Roman emperors than at any other time previously, it is fitting that Heraclius avoided Syria and instead chose to invade Persia from Armenia. According to Sebeos (*Armenian History*, 126), Heraclius passed by Dvin and Lake Urmia and then through the Zagros mountains, emerging into Persian territory near the city of Takht-i Sulayman. On December 1, 627, Heraclius camped at Nineveh and routed the Persian army with his combined force of Romans and Turks. Persian resistance collapsed, and Khusrau was forced on the run. Heraclius captured the Sasanian palace at Dastagerd, replete with its gardens of exotic animals and stores of precious items that included over 300 Roman standards, captured by Persian armies over the preceding five centuries. He also liberated thousands of Edessene and Alexandrian captives taken by the Persians and deported to the east (Theophanes, *Chronicle*, AM 6118/p. 322 = *REF2*, p. 215). In February 628, Khusrau was deposed and murdered by his son Kavadh II (also known as Siroe/Shiroe), who sued for peace before his own death in the same year. In the meantime, Roman forces under the *praepositus* of the sacred bedchamber, Narses, had been campaigning in the west, driving the Persian armies out of Roman territory, and he was also joined by Heraclius's brother, Theodore. Shahrvaraz and Heraclius subsequently met at Arabissus in

Cappadocia and agreed on a peace treaty in 629 (*Chronicle to 724*, AG 940). The remaining elements of the Persian army in the west were evacuated, and Shahrvaraz promised to return the True Cross (later delivered to Heraclius at Hierapolis) and then assumed the Persian throne, deposing Ardashir III, the young son of Kavadh II, with Heraclius's permission; a few months later, however, Shahrvaraz succumbed to an assassin and was replaced by Khusrau's daughter, Boran. At Edessa, the Persian garrison left with some reluctance, and Heraclius attempted to restore a measure of unity by taking communion from the city's bishop, Isaiah. He was met with refusal, however, for his strong Chalcedonian beliefs. Isaiah 'was zealous to a fault', records the notice in the *Chronicle to 1234*, 'or rather, to tell the truth, an uneducated idiot'. Despite all that the empire had endured, and all that Heraclius had achieved, Isaiah demanded the repeal of Chalcedon (*Chronicle to 1234*, p. 236). Through persistence and great daring, Heraclius had managed a near-impossible victory that rivalled Rome's triumph in the Hannibalic War. The latent threat posed by the western Turkish forces in the Caucasus was subsequently neutralised thousands of kilometres away by the Tang Chinese, who had been fighting the eastern Turkish leader Illig Qaghan throughout the 620s and won a decisive victory over the Turks in 630. The western Turks were drawn into this turmoil and their leader, Tung Yabghu, was murdered in the same year, breaking western Turkish power in the Caucasus (Figure 14.15).

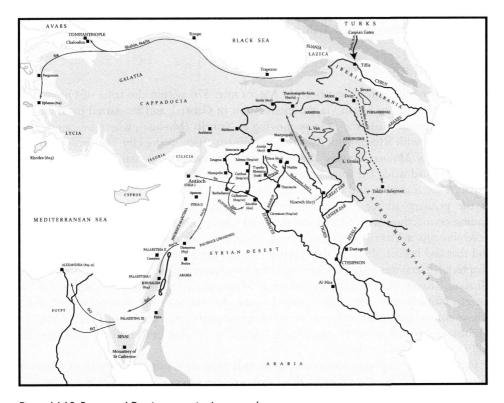

Figure 14.15 Rome and Persia at war in the seventh century.

Source: Illustration by the author.

The Persians had transformed a near-unassailable position into one of total defeat, and Heraclius's triumphant entry to Jerusalem with the True Cross on March 21, 630 confirmed Roman Christian military power. 'God and our Lady the Mother of God collaborated with us and our Christ-loving contingents beyond mortal understanding,' wrote Heraclius in his earlier victory despatch, sent from the field in Persia and read in the Church of Holy Wisdom on May 15, 628. The Romans had triumphed over the 'God-abhorred and execrated Chosroes [Khusrau]' (*Easter Chronicle*, p. 730). It was an auspicious time for vengeance against those who Heraclius deemed to be the enemies of God. The Jewish populations of the east were explicitly targeted for their perceived collaborationism: the surviving population at Jerusalem was massacred, and in 632, Heraclius issued an edict that all Jews and Samaritans must convert to Christianity. Heraclius also sought to reassert control over the empire's Christian communities by resolving the lingering tensions between Chalcedonians and their rivals. The first attempt, monoenergism, was developed in the 620s and promulgated in 633, but received fierce opposition from the incoming patriarch of Jerusalem, Sophronius. A second doctrine, monotheletism, sought to agree with the outcome of the Council of Chalcedon, but proposed that Christ possessed a singular will, a position that Heraclius hoped would also be acceptable to anti-Chalcedonians. Monotheletism was promoted in a document known as the *Ecthesis*, written by the patriarch of Constantinople, Sergius, and published in 638. Opposition to monotheletism arose in Africa, and both it and monoenergism were condemned in Rome in 649. The lack of religious unity in the empire was a contributing factor in the Roman failure to mount a united defence when the first Arab armies arrived in Arabia and Palestine in the late 620s.

The end of antiquity

The Prophet Muhammad was born in Mecca in c. 570 within the tribe of Quraysh. In c. 610, his revelations began via the intercession of Gabriel, and he started to preach. In 622, Muhammad made the *hijra* by moving to Yathrib (Medina), where he came to an arrangement with Khazraj and Aws, two prominent tribes in the city. The agreement, the *Constitution of Medina*, outlined the new *umma*, or community, established the rights of those who had made the *hijra*, known as the *muhajirun*, and determined the relationship between the *muhajirun* and some of Yathrib's Jewish tribes. It also established Muhammad as the primary arbiter between different members of the *umma*. The Romans had trading connections with Mecca and powerful Quraysh, and were also certainly aware of developments in Yathrib, perhaps through Thalaba, a tribe that appears in the *Constitution* and that had historical ties to the Roman empire (the Thalabites, discussed earlier in this chapter). Khazraj was linked with the tribe of Ghassan, and it has even been argued that via Ghassan, Khazraj mediated the acceptance of Muhammad and his followers within Yathribi society. Notably, the *Constitution* worked to the detriment of the Jews of upper Yathrib, whose community could well have come under suspicion after the fall of Jerusalem in 614. Muhammad would go on to capture Mecca in 630; he died in 632 after performing the *hajj*, the pilgrimage to Mecca.

Early Islam was a potent universal religion that demanded submission from its adherents in return for salvation and, freed from bishops and priests, offered a more immersive experience than Christianity. The new faith also had deep ties to the world of late antiquity. It developed at one of the focal points of interstate competition between

Rome, Persia, and Himyar, and it possessed a certain appeal to Jews and Christians, who Muhammad regarded as lapsed monotheists who could earn redemption by converting. There was a tradition in antiquity that Muhammad had often travelled to Palestine, where he encountered Christians; then, returning to Arabia, he began to preach to those who became his followers. The story overlooks the fact that Christianity was no stranger to Arabia (even if it had been largely confined to the south and also in the east, through the expansion of the Church of the East throughout the Persian Gulf), but it nevertheless provides a window into what people thought at the time (e.g. *Chronicle to 1234*, pp. 227–8). Another perspective is illustrated by the ways in which Jewish and Christian writers had long explored the similarities and differences between Arabs and their neighbours in the Roman empire, seeking avenues through which Arabs could be integrated into a Judeo-Christian historiographical framework with a shared history of the Book. This was mainly accomplished by developing a connection between Arabs and Abraham via Ishmael and Sarah, and Josephus had explored this idea as early as the first century AD. The association was occasionally deployed for negative purposes, but it was also used to render Arab converts 'heirs of the promise' and candidates for baptism (Cyril of Scythopolis, *Life of St Euthymius*, 10 = *AEBI* §6.13). Sozomen went further by explicitly connecting Arab practices of circumcision and abstention from pork with a shared Jewish heritage (*Ecclesiastical History*, 6.38 = *AEBI* §6.25). The links with Ishmael led to the term 'Ishmaelite' as a shorthand for Arabs: the seventh-century Syriac *Apocalypse of Pseudo-Methodius* identified the Arab invaders as 'Children of Ishmael' coming out 'from the desert of Yathrib' (11.1 = *RLA* pp. 162–64), and the association was made even later by Dionysius of Tel-Mahre (*Chronicle to 1234*, p. 239). It is also noteworthy that while, for a long time, the only pre-Islamic inscriptions in an early form of the Arabic script were known from Roman Syria, numerous Arabic inscriptions from the fifth century have now been found near Hima in South Arabia. They are written using a script similar to the examples from Syria, and several are explicitly Christian in nature and feature the provincial era dating system used in the province of Arabia. The Arab communities of the pre-Islamic Middle East were very much part of the broader late antique world, dominated by Rome and Persia, and were no less influenced by its political, cultural, and religious eddies than those in distant Suania, Lazica, or Armenia.

Stories of similarity and difference developed within what has been described as a 'sectarian milieu', a heavily politicised set of times and spaces where persecution, martyrdom, religious and secular forms of violence, and imperial support for differing religious positions were commonplace. Different communities, such as Chalcedonians, Homoeans, Mazdakites, anti-Chalcedonians (both monophysites and dyophysites), Jews, pagans, Manichaeans, Zoroastrians, all expended a great deal of effort establishing their own positions vis-à-vis their neighbours—some more loudly and violently than others. Early Islam was responsive to these concerns, rejecting Trinitarian understandings of God in favour of a single God and, via the Quran, delineating Islam's differences against Judaism and Christianity. Within such an environment, and set against the violence and spiritual fervour of the Romano-Persian war, the phenomenon of an emergent monotheistic faith that combined Judeo-Christian end-time anxieties with an expansionist and deeply militant streak was very much in tune with the predominant concerns of the period. Apocalyptic themes frequently appear in the Quran—for example, Sura 82, 'The Rending', which anticipates the end of days: 'Over you are guardians / Generous, recording / Who know what you do. / The pious will be in bliss. / The profligate will be in Hell; / They will roast in it on the Day of Judgement' (Quran, 82.10–15). Sura 81, 'The Enveloping' is even more striking, imagining a time 'When the seas are made to boil' and 'When the sky is stripped' (Quran, 81.6 & 12). Within the context of the ever-expanding debate over Islamic origins and the voluminous literature that the debate continues to produce (see Further Reading), two specific elements can be discussed here that show further how the emergence of Islam can be understood, in part, within the context of late Roman history.

The Jafnids: military-religious Arab leadership at the edge of empire

Roman frontier politics steered the development of Arab leadership in a very particular direction and, as noted earlier, the communities of the southern provinces had become accustomed in the sixth century to a specific type of Arab leader. As interlocutors between holy men, church authorities, and Roman provincial communities, Arab leaders supplied spiritual resources and solved problems. They were not holy men, but they acquired an aura of religious, moral authority through their close links with bishops such as Jacob Baradaeus, through their association with cults of the saints, and through their patronage of churches and monasteries. The Jafnids' link with the cult of St Sergius is of particular interest because the cult was an international and non-denominational phenomenon that cut across sectarian and tribal divides. The Christian dimension of Jafnid leadership was combined with an equally important military role, for the Jafnid phylarchs were Christian warriors who fought for the Christian Roman empire. Even the Nasrid kings were drawn into this potent mix of militancy and piety, with the poet al-Nabigha referring to the early seventh-century Christian Nasrid leader al-Numan as a new Solomon. It is also clear that the prominence of the Jafnids in Christian affairs encouraged others. Two of the three inscriptions in both the Arabic language and script within the Roman empire (with all three found in Syria) were Christian dedications, and one was linked to the cult of St Sergius.

The first inscription is from a martyrion from Zabad in northern Syria, dedicated to St Sergius, with three texts in Greek, Syriac, and Arabic. The Greek and Syriac texts were dated by the Seleucid Era to September 512. The three texts are different from one another, and only the Greek text explicitly mentions the martyrion and the saint; the appearance of Arabic here, commemorating otherwise unknown individuals who were apparently involved in the martyrion's construction, is usually interpreted as a conscious decision and a statement of cultural identity (see *AEBI* § 6.33 & 7.5). The second text is from Harran, south of Damascus, and features Greek and Arabic texts with substantial differences between the two. The Greek text names one Sharahil, a phylarch, and records a martyrion dedicated to St John; the combination of military office (via the office of phylarch) and piety is once again brought to the fore. The Arabic text gives much the same information as its Greek counterpart, but in addition to a provincial era date it is also dated 'one year after the rebellion of Khaybar', an event recorded by Ibn Qutayba (828–89), but about which little else is known (*Kitab al-Maarif*, 642). The use of Arabic was again clearly intentional, and the record of an event that was presumably of relevance to Sharahil and his community underlines the distinctive effort at making a statement about cultural identity (see *AEBI* §6.34 & 7.7).

The careers of the Jafnid phylarchs and the limited evidence for sixth-century Arabic inscriptions show the prominent link between Arabs and Christian cults, and, in particular, the support of Christian activities by men who were also senior members of the Roman military aristocracy. This fusion of militancy and piety—and, through the support of the Sergius cult, a piety that was supra-tribal in nature—anticipated the defining characteristics of the early Islamic caliphs, who derived their authority from success in battle and their proximity to Muhammad and his memory. It is noteworthy that the Jafnid model of leadership was very close to late Roman class-conscious society, with senatorial grades, positions, and titles. Part of Islam's appeal is its egalitarianism, and this may explain why those Arab elites with the closest ties to the Roman empire did not play a major role in the Arab invasions and their aftermath. The success of Muhammad's message was not dependent on membership in the senatorial *illustres*: its victory was instead a result of the divine order that it brought to society, rendering tribal boundaries less important than faith and, at least at the beginning, ensuring that faith was more important than the sorts of doctrinal controversies that consumed Christianity. The success of Muhammad's message was also emboldened through militarised expansion that crushed the enemies of the *umma*, as its members strived for *jihad*, the struggle to follow the path of God, before the imminent day of judgement arrived.

The war in the north, the struggle in the south

The savagery of the war in the north percolated southwards, as did its intensely religious nature and its ostentatious displays of piety. This potent cocktail of monotheistic religious fervour and feats of military daring created an atmosphere in Arabia that was profoundly receptive to the development of a new Abrahamic monotheism.

As we have seen throughout this book, and as noted above, there were numerous lines of communication between the Roman and Persian empires and the communities of the Arabian Peninsula, and both trade and religious and cultural ideas flowed freely back and forth between the different areas. In the sixth and seventh centuries, commercial links between Roman authorities and western Arabia also existed in the form of the leather trade with Mecca. Arab auxiliaries fought for the Roman army in the seventh century and, as noted earlier, had helped to mediate between Maurice and Khusrau II. Heraclius's victory despatch made an explicit reference to the 'Saracens who are subject to our Christ-loving state', indicating their continued participation in imperial affairs (*Easter Chronicle*, p. 730). Quranic commentators later believed that part of the *umma* was sympathetic towards Rome's desperate plight as the war progressed, and this and the recognition of the fall of Jerusalem in the Quran suggest that the outcome of the war was closely followed in Arabia.

From the very beginning of his revolt against Phocas, Heraclius had defined his claims to the imperial throne through displays of piety, arriving in Constantinople with reliquaries of the Virgin Mary. Yet, as Mischa Meier has outlined (see Further Reading section), he also had to address the fact that the sacralisation of the emperor, begun by Justinian, had eventually failed when Justinian caught the plague, Justin II lost his sanity, and Maurice and Phocas met brutal ends. The loss of Jerusalem and its holy relics, 'a calamity that deserves unceasing lamentations', had also undermined claims that the empire possessed a privileged relationship with God (*Easter Chronicle*, p. 704). Heraclius's response to these problems was to undertake what we would now think of as a holy war. In 624, he portrayed the looming showdown with Persia in end-time, messianic terms. "'Let us keep in mind the fear of God,'" Theophanes imagined him saying to his assembled soldiers, "'and fight to avenge the insult done to God. Let us stand bravely against the enemy who have inflicted many terrible things on the Christians'" (*Chronicle*, AM 6114/p. 307). In the same year, the emperor also directly reminded the troops of their heavenly rewards: "May we win the crown of martyrdom, so that we may be praised in the future and receive recompense from God" (*Chronicle*, AM 6115/p. 311). In 624, Muhammad had also assured his own troops of an eternal life in paradise as they fought the Meccans at the battle of Badr. The concept of a just war, fought for God with paradise as its reward, was being developed in both the Roman east and in the western Arabian Peninsula at precisely the same time. In 628, Heraclius further refined his views by portraying the war with Khusrau as a struggle against the enemies of Christians everywhere (*Easter Chronicle*, p. 728).

As the central figure in the crusade against the Persians, Heraclius was transformed by his most effective propagandist, George of Pisidia, a deacon at the Church of Holy Wisdom in Constantinople and a friend of the patriarch Sergius. Heraclius already resembled a reincarnation of Constantine, the empire's greatest Christian warrior-king, but George's writing turned Heraclius into an apocalyptic figure of messianic capabilities and extraordinary piety, tapping the all-pervading end-time anxieties that the war generated. Under George's pen, Heraclius became the *soter*, 'saviour', of the world by defeating the 'world-destroyer' Khusrau (*On Bonus*, 123 & *Heraclius*, 1.77). He was a new David (*On the Restitution of the Holy Cross*, 71–74), and the 'arch-shepherd' of his Roman flock. It was also George, in common with the *Easter Chronicle*, who attributed Constantinople's deliverance from the Avars in 626 to the Virgin Mary (*The Avar War* & *Easter Chronicle*, pp. 716 & 723). Not to be outdone, Theophanes even compared Heraclius directly with God, for the parallel between the six days of creation and a seventh day of rest, and Heraclius's six years of warfare and peace in the seventh (*Chronicle*, AM 6119/pp. 327–8).

The key moment of Heraclius's transformation was his restoration of the True Cross to Jerusalem in 630. George compared his *adventus* to Jerusalem after the war to Christ's own entry into the city on Palm Sunday (*Persian Expedition*, 3.322 & *On the Restitution of the Holy Cross*, 5–8). The Latin *Reversio Sanctae Crucis*, developed from seventh-century ideas about Heraclius's return, similarly described the emperor's humble *adventus* in explicitly Christian terms. The emperor approached the city uncrowned, on foot and through the east gate. A remarkable contemporary viewpoint of this event is provided by the north frieze on the Cathedral of Mren in Armenia (now in the Armenian-Turkish border zone west of Yerevan), whose Armenian dedicatory inscription records its construction by an Armenian client prince serving Heraclius. The cathedral has been dated to 639/40, and the north frieze shows a humble Heraclius, bent in supplication next to a horse in plain clothes and devoid of any imperial finery, returning the True Cross (Figure 14.16).

For George of Pisidia, Heraclius was the saviour of the world who had created a new age—one that would bring about the end of time and lead inexorably to the final day of judgement (*On the Restitution of the Holy Cross*, 109–110). Heraclius's messianic transformation also took place during his entry into a city—Jerusalem—that possessed immense significance for all of the Abrahamic faiths. Jerusalem had also been long

Figure 14.16 The north frieze on the Cathedral of Mren.

Source: Photograph by Dominik Matus (CC BY-SA 4.0).

identified with end-time apocalyptic prophecies and came to assume a high degree of importance for Muslims, due to the belief that it was from Jerusalem that Muhammad ascended after his death in 632. Meier has argued that these factors combined to create a deadly rivalry with Muhammad and the *umma*, resulting in the Arab raids that began in 629; there may even have been an attempt to convert Heraclius to Islam between 632 and 634. Raids into Roman territory increased in frequency after Muhammad's death in 632, and the election of Abu Bakr as his successor, or caliph. Soon the famous general Khalid ibn-Walid began the first raids into Persia, which was still suffering from political intrigue and weak leadership. In Arabia, Aila and Udruh surrendered and Bostra and Damascus fell to the invaders, and a Roman army was lost at Gaza in 634 (*Chronicle to 724*, AG 945). Jerusalem fell in 635, and in 636 the Roman field army, under the Armenian general Vahan and the *sacellarius* Theodore, was defeated by Khalid ibn-Walid and Abu Ubayda ibn al-Jarrah at Yarmuk in the valley of the river Jordan. The staggering defeat, which St Anastasius, writing in the Sinai in c. 700, called 'the first and fearful and incurable fall of the Roman army', proved disastrous (*Sermon against monotheletism*, 3.1). The eastern provinces rapidly capitulated, and Heraclius died in 641. In the east, the Persians under their final king, Yazdegerd III, suffered a decisive defeat at Qadisiyya in 636 and Ctesiphon was captured not long afterwards; the fatal blow against the Persians came in 642, at Nivahand in Media. Egypt was invaded in 640, and when the Trajanic-era fortress of Babylon fell in 641 and Alexandria was evacuated in 642, the Roman empire ceased to exist as a Mediterranean entity.

The speed of the collapse was extraordinary, and numerous factors have been proposed as an explanation. These have traditionally included the general exhaustion of both the Roman and Persian armies; the profound disconnect, principally Chalcedonian/anti-Chalcedonian but also administrative, between Constantinople and the provinces; and the skill, faith, and fervour of the invading Arab armies. The unity of the Arab cause was also remarkable, with divisions having been purged in the *ridda* wars (632–34), and tribal rivalries suppressed by a strong ethos of communal membership in the *umma*. Each military victory proved the power of the Muslim God and the corresponding weakness of the Christian God, an emotive result that led to numerous instances of sudden collapse or spontaneous surrender. Muslim warriors could also draw strength from the belief that their struggle with their Roman enemies was part of the end-time war to end all wars, leading inexorably to the successful assault on Constantinople. In such situations, defeat invited only greater efforts to achieve the end of time. Christians also interpreted the invasions as the harbinger of the end of days: in 636, Sophronius attributed the string of Roman defeats to chronic Christian sinners and the mutterings of prophets who had long foretold this pageant of devastation. It is also distinctly possible that the climate at the time played a role in facilitating the Arab conquests, as the cooling trend that persisted until 660 had increased rainfall in the Arabian Peninsula, enabling larger herds of camels to be raised and fed, and making a greater area of land available for agricultural production. The confluence of these various factors, creating a vigorous, well-fed, well-supplied, and highly motivated army, fighting its impoverished, fractured, and exhausted northern neighbours, is an attractive hypothesis to explain the rapid and conclusive victories that the Arab armies enjoyed in the mid-seventh century.

Eventually, almost all of the lands across the Middle East became part of the Umayyad Caliphate and its successor, the Abbasid Caliphate. As Heraclius withdrew from Syria for the final time, he gazed longingly at the land, and uttered a final epitaph for the eastern Roman empire:

'Peace be upon you, O Syria,' he said. 'This is the farewell after which there will be no return.'

—al-Tabari, *Tarikh* 12, p. 182

Glossary

Roman numerals

I	1	VI	6	Multiples: XX = 20, XXX = 30, XXII = 22, etc.	
II	2	VII	7	L	50
III	3	VIII	8	C	100
IV*	4	IX	9	D	500
V	5	X	10	M	1000

* note that IV is sometimes rendered as IIII, especially in legionary titles

Definitions of terms used in this book

a libellis	palace official managing imperial petitions
ab epistulis	palace official managing Latin (and later, Greek) imperial correspondence
adventus	ceremonial entry of an emperor into a city, principally Rome or Constantinople
aedile (curule)	officials managing public events, drawn from the *patrician class
aedile (plebeian)	officials managing public events, drawn from the *plebeian class
aerarium militare	military pension fund instituted by Augustus
AG	'anno Graecorum' (year of the Greeks': dating system counting from the foundation of the Seleucid empire in 312/11 BC
agentes in rebus	spy/courier service (fourth century AD)
ager publicus	the public land belonging to the Roman state
agnomen	part of the Roman system of personal names denoting a special honour
agoge	Spartan military education system
Agri Decumates	angle created by the Rhine and Danube in western Europe
ala, alae	cavalry troop
alimenta	public welfare scheme instituted either by Nerva or Trajan
AM	'anno Mundi': dating system counting from the Creation
amphora	ceramic container used to store and transport wine, oil, grain, etc.
annona	subsidy or stipend; also the name given to the subsidised supply of grain and other provisions in Rome and, later, Constantinople
antoninianus	silver/billon coin of the third century AD

apotheosis	ritual ceremony through which an emperor was deified
Arabia Deserta	Roman name for central Arabia
archon	chief magistrate in Athens
Arianism	form of Christianity promoted by Arius, granting precedence in the Trinity to the Father
ascetic	follower of a minimalist lifestyle, for philosophical or religious reasons
auctoritas	the concept of authority wielded by Augustus
augurs	priests who interpreted the acts of birds and animals to measure divine favour
Augusta	honorific title of the empress or other royal women
aureus	primary gold coin of the empire before the fourth century AD
aurum tironicum	scheme whereby cash could be paid by landowners to exempt workers from military service
auspices	a ritual that sought to provide divine consent for an intended action, such as starting a war or conducting public business
auxilia palatina	elite infantry in the western *comitatus*
auxiliary	troops normally levied from non-Roman allies
Avesta	Zoroastrian holy text
ballista/-ae	Roman field artillery
barbarian	generic term for non-Roman, especially beyond the Rhine/Danube frontier
Barbaricum	Roman term for the land beyond the Rhine/Danube frontier
basilica	commercial/public building; later, name for a Christian church
Blues	supporters of a circus faction in the late empire; see *Greens
boskoi	extreme followers of an *ascetic lifestyle
boule	Greek term for municipal government, typically of eastern cities
bucellarii	late imperial bodyguards, attending senior officials
caligae	military boots used by Roman soldiers
candidati	unit of elite bodyguards serving with the *scholae palatinae*
caput	human taxation measurement instituted by Diocletian
cardo	north-south street in Roman urban planning
carpentum	type of transport for aristocratic Roman women
Cassian Treaty	alliance between Rome and the *Latin League
cataphract	heavy armoured cavalry
censors	elected officials responsible for the *census
census	periodic registration of people and property, used to determine military service, taxation, and other civic obligations
centuries	divisions in Roman society, classified by wealth; later, units in the army
centurion	officer commanding a century or, later, a cohort
Chalcedonian Christianity	theological position established at the Council of Chalcedon (451)
chi-rho	Christian symbol drawn from the two first letters of Christ's name in Greek
Christotokos	'Christ-bearer', the name proposed by Nestorius to replace *Theotokos
chrysargyron	tax of the fourth century AD imposed on merchants
Church of the East	Persian church, headquartered in Ctesiphon
civilitas	civility or harmony
civitas optimo iure	the legal definition of full Roman citizenship

civitates	Roman urban-based governmental centres in the western provinces
civitates stipendiariae	tax-paying *civitates*
clarissimus	term denoting senatorial status; after the fourth century AD, the lowest senatorial grade; see also *illustris* and *spectabilis*
clementia	the policy of clemency associated with Julius Caesar
clibinarii	heavy armoured cavalry, analogous to *cataphract
clipeus votivus	golden shield awarded to Augustus
cloaca maxima	principal sewer of Rome
cohors praetoria	praetorian cohort, the forerunner of the *Praetorian Guard
cohors speculatorum	picked force associated with Marc Antony
cohort	infantry unit, approximately 500–600-strong (see also *milliary)
collatio globis	tax on senators' wealth
collegia	associations in the city of Rome, such as for tradespeople or religious cults
colony	community of Latins/Romans settled in newly-conquered or restive lands
colonus	peasant of the late empire
comes	companion; later, military title, 'count'
comes domesticorum	commander of the *protectores domestici
comes excubitorum	commander of the *excubitors
comes orientis	senior military official in the *prefecture of *Oriens
comes rei militaris	'count of military things': military position without a specific portfolio
comes rei privatae	official managing the *res privata
comes sacrarum largitionum	official managing the *sacrae largitiones
comitatus	'posse' or 'warband': the entourage of the emperor; later, the mobile field army of the late empire
comitia centuriata	main political assembly of Rome, composed of adult male citizens
comitia curiata	forerunner of the *comitia centuriata
comitia tributa	assembly of the *tribes
comitium	open-air area for political assembly
communes	settled tribes of South Arabia
concilium plebis	assembly of *plebeian Romans; elected the *plebeian tribune
concordia	peace
concordia augustorum	peace between emperors
constantia	Republican virtue of tenacity
consul, consulship	annual and collegial elected chief magistrate in the Republic; later, the 'main' consulship became the ordinary consulship, with additional consuls known as 'suffect' consuls
consular tribune	magistrate ranked lower than the consul, but with a form of *imperium comparable to the consul
conventus	legal assize circuit where a provincial governor travelled the province hearing cases
consistorium	imperial advisory council after the fourth century AD
corona aurea	the golden crown, awarded for courage in battle
corona civica	the civic crown, awarded to a soldier for saving the life of a Roman citizen
corona muralis	the mural crown, awarded to the soldier first over the enemy's walls

corrector	officials appearing during the reign of Trajan, invested with *imperium, intended to address specific problems
corrector orientis	sporadic title indicating a position of high authority in the eastern provinces
corvus	naval boarding ramp
cunei equitum	cavalry 'wedges', appearing in the fourth century AD
curator	officials first appearing in the reign of Trajan, intended to provide quick solutions to municipal problems
curia, curiae	subdivisions of Roman *tribes, providing the basis for military recruitment and political participation; later, a term that referred to the group of municipal officials who managed the day-to-day management of Roman cities
curia Hostilia	early Roman senate house
curia Julia	Roman senate house built by Julius Caesar
curiales	collective term for municipal officials in the empire
cursus honorum	the 'run of offices'—the public office career track
cursus publicus	imperial messaging service, relying on a series of relay stations and fresh horses
cydaris	Persian royal diadem
damnatio memoriae	'damnation of memory'—posthumous erasure from official documents, inscriptions, etc., as punishment for deeds committed when alive
decemviri	name for ten-man board of inquiry
decumanus	east–west street in Roman urban planning
decurion	municipal magistrate
deditio in fidem	a form of surrender by an enemy that placed them in the *fides of the Romans
demoi	subdivisions of Athenian *phulai
denarius	primary silver coin of the empire until the fourth century AD
devotio	a religious ritual of self-sacrifice, usually to save an army from peril
dictator	emergency appointment, superior to the *consul
diocese	group of provinces in the empire of Diocletian
diplomas	military discharge certificates
djedar	pyramidal stone tomb in north Africa
domi militiaeque	the highest form of imperium, 'at home and at war'—that is, within the city and outside of it
dominus	lord
Domus Aurea	the ostentatious palace of the emperor Nero in central Rome
duoviri navales	early Republican naval command
dux	Latin term for warrior, often used to refer to *barbarian kings; later, Roman title for senior provincial military officer, such as *dux Mesopotamiae*
dyophysitism	belief that Christ possessed two natures, human and divine; see *Nestorianism
egregius	lowest rank in the equestrian order in the fourth century, later abolished by Constantine
Eleusinian Mysteries	Athenian mystery cult
eminentissimus	top rank in the equestrian order in the fourth century, later abolished by Constantine

endoxotatos	Latin for the (temporarily) senior grade in the re-graded *illustres* (*★gloriosissimus*)
epitome	abridged version of a longer book
equestrian	member of the Roman middle class, from the ancient financial requirement to provide a horse for the army in times of war
equites	cavalry
equites singulares Augusti	the cavalry wing of the ★Praetorian Guard, instituted by the Flavians
exarch	senior official in late sixth-century Africa and Italy
exarchate	the territory managed by the ★exarch
excubitors	late imperial palatine guard unit in Constantinople
exergue	the space on the 'tails' (reverse) side of a coin, below the main design
fabricae	state-run factories, especially those making weapons for the army
famosissimus	Latin term for the most senior grade in the *illustres*, introduced in 497 (*★paneuphemos*)
fasces	bundle of axes and rods representing authority
fasti consulares	list of consuls elected during the Republic
fasti triumphales	list of victorious Roman magistrates set up in the Roman forum by Augustus
fetiales (fetials)	priests who conducted rituals concerned with declarations of war
fides	Republican virtue of good faith, with a moral/religious dimension
filius per arma	'son-in-arms': form of late imperial adoption between allies or equals
flamines	priests
foederati	non-Roman troops serving under a *★foedus*
foedus	treaty, normally between the emperor and non-Romans enrolled as troops
follis	base metal, low-denomination coin of the late empire
forum	public space in Roman city planning, similar to the Greek agora
frumentarii	officials managing the grain *★annona*; also served as spies
gens, gentes	family clans
gentiles	non-Roman military recruits in the later empire
Ghassanids	see ★Jafnids
gladius	Roman short-sword used by the infantry
gladius Hispaniensis	Spanish sword adopted by the Roman army in the Republican period
globe cruciger	orb surmounted by a cross; symbol of Christian political authority
gloria	political glory or renown, primarily earned on the battlefield and/or through holding elected office
gloriosissimus	Latin for the (temporarily) senior grade in the re-graded *illustres* = (*★endoxotatos*)
Gothia	name given to the lands north of the Danube in the fourth century AD
gravitas	Republican virtue of self-restraint, and Augustan idea of influence
Greens	supporters of a circus faction in the late empire; see ★Blues
haeresis	see ★heresy
hagiography	biography of a saint, martyr, or other Christian individual
hajj	Muslim pilgrimage to Mecca

haruspices	priests who observed the entrails of animals to measure divine favour
hastati	front ranks in the manipular legion (see *manipulus*)
hastatus posterior	*centurion in an infantry *cohort
hastatus prior	*centurion in an infantry *cohort
Hebdomon	district of Constantinople, west of the city's defensive walls
heresy	religious belief opposed to *orthodoxy
hijra	the journey from Mecca to Medina made by the Prophet Muhammad and his companions in AD 622
hippodrome	long sports stadium with curved ends used for chariot races and public assembly
Homoean Creed	a compromise in the mid-fourth century AD between *Arianism and *Nicene Christianity
honestiores	generic term for upper class
humiliores	generic term for lower class
hyperphuestatos	senior grade in the re-graded *illustres*, introduced in AD 489
hypospondoi	Greek term for *foederati*
illustris (illustres)	most senior senatorial rank between the fourth and fifth centuries AD; re-graded in the late empire; see also *clarissimus* and *spectabilis*
Illyriciani	elite cavalry in the western *comitatus*
imperator	battlefield acclamation for a successful warrior; later, title of the emperor
imperial cult	religious cult organised around the veneration of Rome and the emperor
imperium	Roman concept of civic/religious/military authority wielded by magistrates
imperium sine fine	concept from Virgil's *Aeneid* of the 'empire without end'
impluvia	hollow openings in Roman houses, for collecting rainwater
indiction cycle	15-year taxation cycle instituted by Diocletian
interrex	literally 'in-between king', appointed in an emergency to hold new elections for *consul
Iranshahr	geographical space (Iran) as well as cosmological concept in the *Avesta
iugum	land taxation measurement instituted by Diocletian
iuridici	judges
iustitia	Republican/Augustan virtue of justice
Jafnids	principal Arab allies of the Roman empire in the sixth century
jihad	'the struggle'—belief that Muslims should endeavour to follow the path of God
juniores	young men expected to fight in the front ranks of the *legio
Justinianic Code	compendium of Roman law compiled under Justinian
kathisma	royal box at the *hippodrome in Constantinople
khagan	term for Avar or Turkish kings
komes	Greek for *comes*
labarum	cross-shaped military standard
laura	monastic community
laeti	term referring to non-Romans settled in the west, who also rendered military service
Lakhmids	see *Nasrids

lamprotatos	Greek for *clarissimus*
lancea	late Roman infantry javelin used by the *lanciarii*
lanciarii	elite infantry in the late Roman *comitatus*
lares	household gods (see also *penates*)
lares Augusti	the Augustan household gods
Latin League	alliance of city states in *Latium
Latin rights	set of privileges conferred on communities in *Latium and, later, throughout the empire
Latium	the district around Rome, now known as Lazio
legate	provincial governor (see *propraetorian legate) or legionary commander
legio (legion)	legion, the quintessential Roman military force
libellus	receipt or petition
lictor	attendant to an official with *imperium; carried the *fasces
limitanei	garrison army after the fourth century AD
liturgification	the extensive permeation of late Roman society by Christian belief and ritual
lituus	a wand used by Roman *augurs
lorica hamata	armour similar to chain mail
lorica segmentata	armour made of overlapping iron plates
ludi	games
lustrum	ritual purification ceremony, usually held at the end of the *census
magister epistularum	name for the head of the office of *ab epistulis (fourth century AD)
magister equitum	cavalry commander (fourth century AD)
magister libellorum	name for the head of the office of *a libellis (fourth century AD)
magister memoriae	head of the office drafting correspondence (fourth century AD)
magister militum	senior military commander (fourth century AD)
magister militum per Illyricum	regional command for Illyria
per Orientem	regional command for the east
per Thracias	regional command for Thrace
magister officiorum	master of offices: the most senior palatine official (fourth century AD)
magister peditum	infantry commander (fourth century AD)
magister utriusque militiae	commander of both services—infantry and cavalry
magnificentissimus	Latin for the lowest grade of the re-graded *illustres* (*megaloprepestatos)
maiestas	treason
maius imperium	the 'greater' imperium wielded by Augustus
manipulus	maniple: a flexible unit-level military formation
manumission	Roman procedure for granting freedom to slaves
martyrion/a	chapel or church housing relics of a saint or martyr
mastarna	Etruscan office of dictator (temporary supreme leader)
master of cavalry	second-in-command to the *dictator
mater castrorum	'mother of the camps', honorific term amongst the troops, for the *Augusta
meddix	elected Samnite official

megaloprepestatos	Greek for the lowest grade of the re-graded *illustres* (*★magnificentissimus*)
Melkites	★Syriac-speaking Christians who followed ★Chalcedonian Christianity
Mese	the main east–west street in Constantinople
metrocolonia	exceptional honour granted to certain cities, such as Palmyra
miaphysitism	see ★monophysitism
military tribune	staff officers serving the legionary ★legate
militia	term for the late Roman civil service
milliary	a designation for a ★cohort reflecting a paper strength of 1,000
mlk	Aramaic or Arabic term for king; analogous to ★*rex*
monoenergism	seventh-century AD theological policy
monophysitism	position that the two natures of Christ were fused in a single divine nature
monotheletism	seventh-century AD theological policy
mos maiorum	moralising phrase evoking traditional customs
muhajirun	those who made the ★*hijra*
municipium	'municipal' allied status conferring Roman citizenship
municipium sine suffragio	'municipal' allied status conferring Roman citizenship, but without any voting rights
Nahrmalcha	canal linking the Euphrates and Tigris rivers near Ctesiphon
Nasrids	principal Arab allies of the Persian empire, fourth–seventh centuries AD
negotiares	traders or merchants
neokoros	Greek honorific term denoting that a community was a centre for the ★imperial cult
Nestorianism	the position that Christ had two distinct natures, human and divine, in one body
nexum	debt bondage
Nicene Christianity	Christian belief anchored around the Nicene Creed, developed in AD 325
nobiles	ex-office holders among the ★patricians; old, elite families from the Republican era
notarii	officials who managed letters of appointment, maintained register of officials, etc.
Novel, Novella	laws issued after the compilation of the ★*Theodosian Code* & the ★*Justinianic Code*
novus homo	'new man', the first member of a family to hold major political office
numeri	military units in the later empire recruited from non-Romans
nummus	base metal, low-denomination coin of the late empire
nymphaeum	urban architectural feature sacred to water nymphs
odeon	public space for performing arts
oikumene	Greek term referring to the inhabited world, with connotations of 'commonwealth'
optimates	conservative, senatorial faction in late Republican politics
Oriens	'the east'—name for one of the ★prefectures of the late Roman empire
ornamenta triumphalia	imperial-era lesser form of triumph for individuals outside the royal family

orthodoxy	religious belief approved by religious authorities and/or the Roman emperor
ovation	a lesser form of the *triumph
palimpsest	a manuscript in which one text overwrites another, leaving traces of the earlier text beneath
paneuphemos	Greek for the most senior grade in the *illustres*, introduced in AD 497 (*famosissimus)
parens	parent
paterfamilias	male head of a Roman family
pater patriae	'father of the country', an honorific bestowed on a Roman politician or emperor
patres	'fathers', elder men in society
patria	Augustan-era concept of the fatherland
patrician(s)	the institutionalised *patres*, forming a distinct elite social order in the Republic
patricius	rank of *patrician(s) reintroduced by Constantine
patrikios	Greek for *patricius*
patron	wealthy or influential man who protected clients in return for political or military support
pax Romana	'the Roman peace', a period of time between c. 30 BC and AD 180 during which the Mediterranean was (mostly) at peace
penates	household gods (see also *lares*)
peregrini	foreigners/non-Romans
perfectissimus	middle rank in the equestrian order in the fourth century
peribleptos	Greek for *spectabilis*
pilum	Roman throwing javelin
pharmaka	medicinal ingredients
philoromaios	epithet meaning 'friend to the Romans', often appearing on coins of Roman client kings
phulai	Athenian tribes
phylarch	literally 'tribal leader': military command, held predominantly by Arabs
pietas	Republican virtue of pity
plebeian	class of non-*patrician Romans, ranging from very poor to very wealthy; often at odds with the patricians
plebeian tribune	elected official representing *plebeian interests
pomerium	sacred boundary demarcating the limits of the city of Rome
pontifex maximus	chief priest in ancient Rome
populares	populist faction in late Republican politics
praefectus castrorum	camp prefect, the senior quartermaster of a legionary camp
praefectus classis	naval commander
praepositus	palatine official
praesentalis	'in the emperor's presence': epithet used for military commanders campaigning with the emperor
praeses (pl.) *praesides*	term used for provincial governors after the fourth century AD
praesidia	fortified way-stations
praetentura Italiae et Alpium	name for the command instituted by Marcus Aurelius to defend northern Italy
praetor	officials initially concerned with law, later used as provincial governors

Praetorian Guard	imperial bodyguard instituted by Augustus; abolished by Constantine
praetorian prefect	commander of the *Praetorian Guard and later civilian administrator of a *prefecture
praetor maximus	early Republican office
prefecture	group of *dioceses under a *praetorian prefect
primicerius notariorum	senior palatine official managing the *notarii*
primus inter pares	'first among equals': a leader who prides himself on his accessibility
primus pilus	senior *centurion in an infantry *cohort
princeps	'leading man'—the title taken by Augustus
princeps iuventutis	young prince, with the connotation of 'crown prince'—that is, the heir to the throne
princeps posterior	*centurion in an infantry *cohort
princeps prior	*centurion in an infantry *cohort
princeps senatus	the most senior member of the *senate; analogous to the role of the Speaker in some western governments
principes	second ranks in the manipular legion (see *manipulus*)
principate	name given to the early empire, between the reigns of Augustus and Marcus Aurelius
pro-	prefix added to titles of offices, indicating that the holder possessed the *imperium of the office but had not been elected to it—for example, proconsul, propraetor
procurator	official, often managing financial matters, instituted by Augustus
promoti	'promoted', a term denoting elite status of cavalry in the late Roman army
propraetorian legate	governors of imperial provinces in the administration set up by Augustus
proskynesis	eastern form of ritual obeisance before a monarch
protector	term appearing in the third century AD, referring to members of an emergent elite officer corps
protectores domestici	elite bodyguard serving with the *scholae palatinae*
provinciae	provinces—initially regions in which magistrates served, then provinces of the empire
provocatio	the legal right to appeal
prorogation	extension of office past the normal time limit
pseudocomitatenses	military units of the *limitanei* upgraded to the *comitatus*
publicani	contractor/merchant class in the Republic, also associated with tax collection
pudicitia	female parallel of *virtus*
quadriburgium	Roman fort with four towers, usually associated with the later empire
quadrifrons	Latin term for *tetrapylon
quaestor	official who managed Roman finances
quaestor *sacri palatii*	imperial quaestor (fourth century AD)
quattuorviri consulares	board of four ex-consuls instituted by Hadrian to manage Italy
rationales	late Roman financial officials
res publica	'public thing': the Republic
res privata	late Roman office managing private (imperial) money
res summa	late Roman office managing public money

restitutor	restorer, normally in a military sense—for example, 'restorer of the east'
rex, reges	king, such as the king of early Rome or client kings of the empire
rex sacrorum	'king of sacrifices', an early Roman office
ripa Gothica	'Gothic bank', the left bank of the Danube in the fourth century AD
ripenses	border troops analogous to *limitanei
s.a.	*sub anno*, a means of dating in chronicles, 'by year'/'under the year'
sacellarius	late imperial palatine official managing the emperor's finances
sacrae largitiones	name for the *res summa* in the fourth century AD
Sanhedrin	council of Jewish elders
Saracen	name used after the fourth century AD for *scenitae
satrap	name for provincial governor in the Persian empire
satrapy	name for province in the Persian empire
Scala Gemoniae	steps in Rome, onto which executed prisoners were traditionally dumped after their deaths
senate	advisory body of the Republic made up of ex-magistrates and elder statesmen
senator	member of the senate; later, term for aristocrat holding senatorial status
senatus consultum	a senatorial decree, advisory in nature but often with the force of law
senatus consultum ultimum	the 'ultimate decree'—authorisation by the senate to the consuls to do whatever was thought necessary to restore public order
scenitae	generic Latin and Greek term for 'tent-dwellers'—that is, Arabs of the desert
scorpion	Roman field artillery
scholae palatinae	imperial bodyguard founded by Constantine, replacing the *Praetorian Guard
scrinia	name for the bureaucratic offices of the late empire
scrinium epistularum	office managed by the *magister epistularum*
scrinium libellorum	office managed by the *magister libellorum*
scrinium memoriae	office managed by the *magister memoriae*
scutum	military shield
Second Sophistic	cultural movement in the second and third centuries AD that looked back to the high culture of Athens
Seleucid Era	see *AG
seniores	veterans who made up the rear ranks of the *legio
shahanshah	Persian title meaning 'King of Kings'
Sibylline Books	collection of ancient oracles held in Rome (not to be confused with *Sibylline Oracles*)
Sibylline Oracles	a series of prophetic texts, many of which were Jewish or Christian in origin
silentarius/-ii	palace ushers in the late empire
socii	Roman allies, without citizenship or voting rights, but sometimes with the *Latin rights
sodales Flaviales	college of priests linked with the imperial cult, instituted by the Flavians
sodales Titii	ancient Roman cult linked with Romulus
solidus	standardised gold coin introduced by Constantine I
sophist	itinerant teacher

soter	Greek word meaning 'saviour'
spectabilis	middle rank in the senatorial order after the fourth century AD; see also *clarissimus and *illustris
spolia opima	award given to the Roman soldier who killed the enemy leader in combat
staurogram	see *chi-rho
Strata Diocletiana	military road in the eastern provinces constructed under Diocletian
strategos	Greek term for military general
stratelatos	Greek term for *magister militum
suffete	highest elected official at Carthage
synedroi	Carthaginian senators
Syriac	dialect of Aramaic, particularly associated with Christian communities such as Edessa
tabula ansata	decorative border typically used for Roman inscriptions, in the following shape:

talent	Greek measure of weight: an Attic talent was 26 kilograms (57 pounds)
tayyaye	Syriac name for *Saracens
temenos	sacred precinct, often associated with a temple
tetarte	25 per cent import levy for goods brought into the Roman empire
tetradrachm	silver coin in widespread use in the Greek world
tetrapylon	four-sided monumental gateway
Tetrarchy	the late third-/early fourth-century rule of two senior and two junior emperors
Theodosian Code	compendium of Roman law compiled under Theodosius II
Theotokos	'mother of God', the name given to Mary
toga virilis	item of clothing presented to a Roman youth, representing his passage into manhood
traditores	'traitors', Christian clergy who handed over sacred texts during persecutions
triarii	rear ranks in the manipular legion (see *manipulus), similar to *seniores
tribe	artificial political groupings in Rome, based on geographical location; term for groups of people living under chiefs or kings
tribunal	raised platform used for giving speeches
tribune of the plebs	*see* plebeian tribune
tribunician power	power of the *plebeian tribune, without holding the office; used by Augustus and his successors
Tritheism	late sixth-century AD schism amongst some of the opponents of *Chalcedonian Christianity
triumph	military parade in Rome awarded to a successful general
Twelve Tables	early Roman law code
tyche	Greek name for the goddess Fortuna
umma	the name given to the early Muslim community

urban cohort	police force in Rome, instituted by Augustus
urban prefect	senior official tasked with the administration of the city of Rome (and later Constantinople)
velites	skirmishers in the manipular legion (see *manipulus)
Vestal Virgins	all-female priestly college that managed the communal hearth
vexillation	detachment of a *legion or cavalry *ala
vicar	administrator of a *diocese
vici (sg. *vicus*)	civilian settlements associated with military camps and fortresses
vigiles	fire service instituted by Augustus
vigintivirate	a collection of 20 minor offices, the tenure of one or more of which typically began a career in public service
vindicta	rod used for the *manumission of slaves
virtus	the Republican idea of virtue, made up of *constantia, *fides, *gravitas, and *pietas
zilath	Etruscan elected magistrate

Further reading

This section provides a list of suggested further reading, both in print and on the web. The list is not exhaustive, but it is intended as an introduction to accessible works in English that address some of the major themes and events explored in this book. To that end, I have given preference to accessibility, especially for inscriptions and textual sources. Some texts have received newer translations from outlets such as Penguin Classics, Loeb Classics, or Liverpool's Translated Texts for Historians series, and readers are encouraged to visit their websites for further information.

The list below includes: (1) primary sources; (2) selected secondary sources; and (3) a selection of specific themes such as the ancient climate, plague, women in Roman society, warfare, and so on.

Translations of primary sources

Websites

Loeb Classics: www.loebclassics.com
Penguin Classics: www.penguinclassics.com
Translated Texts for Historians: www.liverpooluniversitypress.co.uk/series/series-12316
www.attalus.org—translations of Greek and Roman texts and inscriptions, timelines, indices, and much more.
https://penelope.uchicago.edu/Thayer/E/Roman/home.html—one of the most useful classical-themed sites on the internet, containing an archive of out-of-copyright Loeb classics and much more
https://ccel.org/fathers —Christian texts at the Christian Classics Ethereal Library
www.newadvent.org/fathers—similar coverage to CCEL
www.tertullian.org—the Tertullian Project, containing a vast array of texts. Many old translations of Christian and non-Christian texts are at: www.tertullian.org/fathers
www.livius.org—a website with a database of images, articles, and numerous translated texts
www.poetryintranslation.com—collection of English translations of poems, including much of the poetry of the ancient world

Modern print collections

Austin M.M. *The Hellenistic World from Alexander to the Roman Conquest*, 2nd edn. Cambridge, 2006, doi:10.1017/CBO9780511818080
Campbell B. *The Roman Army, 31 BC–AD 337. A Sourcebook.* New York, 2000, doi:10.4324/9780203137307

Dignas B. & Winter E. *Rome and Persia in Late Antiquity. Neighbours and Rivals.* Cambridge, 2007, doi:10.1017/CBO9780511619182

Dodgeon M.H. & Lieu S.N.C. *The Roman Eastern Frontier and the Persian Wars, AD 226–363. A Documentary History.* New York, 2002, doi:10.4324/9780203425343

Fisher G. (ed) *Arabs and Empires Before Islam.* Oxford, 2015, doi:10.1093/acprof:oso/9780199654 529.001.0001

Greatrex G. & Lieu S.N.C. *The Roman Eastern Frontier and the Persian Wars, Part II: AD 363– 630.* New York, 2008, doi:10.4324/9780203994542

Maas M. *Readings in Late Antiquity. A Sourcebook,* 2nd edn. New York, 2009, doi:10.4324/9780203544013

Mathisen R.W. *Ancient Roman Civilization: History and Sources.* Oxford, 2018

Maxfield V.A. & Dobson B. (eds) *Inscriptions of Roman Britain,* 3rd edn. London, 1995

McLachlan B. *Women in Ancient Rome. A Sourcebook.* London, 2013

Poole A. & Maule J. (eds) *The Oxford Book of Classical Verse.* Oxford, 1995

Sherk R.K. *Rome and the Greek East to the Death of Augustus.* Cambridge, 1984, doi:10.1017/CBO9780511552687

Sherk R.K. *The Roman Empire: Augustus to Hadrian.* Cambridge, 1984, doi:10.1017/CBO97805 11552670

Ancient Inscriptions and Papyri

AE

Cagnat R. & Corbier M. (eds) *Année Épigraphique.* Paris, 1888–

CIL

Corpus Inscriptionum Latinarum. Available online at: https://arachne.uni-koeln.de/drupal/?q=en/node/291

IGLS

Jalabert L., Mouterde R. et al. (eds) *Inscriptions grecques et latines de la Syrie.* Paris, 1929–

ILS

Dessau H. (ed.) *Inscriptiones Latinae Selectae,* 3 vols. Berlin, 1892–1916

IRB

= Maxfield & Dobson, above

P.Dura

Wells C.B., Fink R.O. & Gilliam J.F. (eds) *Excavations at Dura-Europos, Final Report Volume V, Part I The Parchments and Papyri.* New Haven, 1959

RIB

https://romaninscriptionsofbritain.org

SEG

Supplementum epigraphicum graecum. Leiden/Amsterdam, 1923–

SCPP = Senatus Consultum de Cn. Pisone Patre

D.S. Potter & C. Damon, The 'Senatus Consultum de Cn. Pisone Patre'. *American Journal of Philology*, 120/1 (1999): 13–42, doi:10.1353/ajp.1999.0010

SKZ

http://parthiansources.com/texts/skz/

Wadd.

Le Bas P. & Waddington W.H. (eds) *Inscriptions grecques et latines recueillies en Grèce et en Asie Mineure.* Paris, 1853–1870

Jewish sources & Sibylline Oracles

Citations from Talmudic sources and Jewish material relevant to the revolts discussed throughout this book are drawn from the excellent website of the European Research Council-funded project, *Judaism and Rome*:
www.judaism-and-rome.org
For the *Sibylline Oracles* and the *Greek Apocalypse of Baruch*, see further:
Charles R.H. (ed.) *The Apocrypha and Pseudoepigrapha of the Old Testament*, Oxford, 1913. Full text available at www.archive.org
Terry M.S. (ed.) *The Sibylline Oracles*. New York, 1899. Available online at: www.sacred-texts.com/cla/sib/index.htm
A translation of *The Greek Apocalypse of Baruch* is available online at: www.pseudepigrapha.com/pseudepigrapha/3Baruch.html

Hou Hanshu

For the *Hou Hanshu* and its comments on the Roman empire, see: https://depts.washington.edu/silkroad/texts/hhshu/hou_han_shu.html

Latin, Greek, Syriac, and Arabic texts
Achilles Tatius

Leucippe and Clitophon = Reardon B.P. *Collected Ancient Greek Novels*, 2nd edn. Berkeley, CA, 2008

Aelian

On Animals, translated by A.F. Scolfield. Cambridge, MA, 1958–59, doi:10.4159/DLCL.aelian-characteristics_animals.1958
Available online at: www.attalus.org/info/aelian.html

Aelius Aristides

P. Aelius Aristides, *The Complete Works*, translated by C. Behr, vol. 2. Leiden, 1981

Aelius Gellius

Attic Nights, translated by J.C. Rolfe, 3 vols. Cambridge, MA, 1927, doi:10.4159/DLCL.gellius-attic_nights.1927. Available online at: https://penelope.uchicago.edu/Thayer/E/Roman/Texts/Gellius/home.html

Agapius

Kitab al-Unwan, translated by A.A. Vasiliev. Paris, 1910–1912

Agathangelos

History of the Armenians, translated by R.W. Thomson. Albany, NY, 1976

Ammianus Marcellinus

History, translated by J.C. Rolfe, 3 vols. Cambridge MA, 1939–1950, doi:10.4159/DLCL.amminanus_marcellinus-history.1950. Available online at: http://penelope.uchicago.edu/Thayer/E/Roman/Texts/Ammian/home.html

Anonymous Valesianus

Anonymous Valesianus, translated by J.C. Rolfe. Cambridge, MA, 1939, doi:10.4159/DLCL.excerpta_valesiana.1939. Available online at: https://penelope.uchicago.edu/Thayer/E/Roman/Texts/Excerpta_Valesiana/home.html

Apocryphal Acts of Peter

Apocryphal Acts of Peter, translated by M.R. James. Oxford, 1924. Available online at: www.earlychristianwritings.com/text/actspeter.html

Appian

Wars, translated by H. White. Cambridge MA, 1912–13. Available online at: https://penelope.uchicago.edu/Thayer/E/Roman/Texts/Appian/home.html

Arrian

Anabasis of Alexander, translated by P.A. Brunt, 2 vols. Cambridge MA, 1976–83, doi:10.4159/DLCL.arrian-anabasis_alexander.1976

Augustine

City of God, translated by H. Bettenson. London: Penguin, 1984

City of God, translated by M. Dods. Buffalo, NY, 1887. Available online at: www.newadvent.org/
fathers/1201.htm

Augustus

Res Gestae Divi Augusti, translated by A. Cooley. Cambridge, 2009, doi:10.1017/
CBO9780511815966.004. An older translation by T. Bushnell is available online at: http://
classics.mit.edu/Augustus/deeds.html

Aurelius Victor

On the Caesars = De Caesaribus, translated by H.W. Bird. Liverpool, 1994

Bar Hebraeus

The Chronography of Gregory Abu'l Faraj, commonly known as Bar Hebraeus, translated by E.W. Budge.
Oxford, 1932

Basil of Caesarea

On the Holy Spirit, translated by B. Jackson. Buffalo, NY, 1895. Available online at: www.newadvent.
org/fathers/3203.htm

Boethius

Consolation of Philosophy, translated by H.F. Stewart et al. Cambridge, MA, 1973, doi:10.4159/DLCL.
boethius-consolation_philosophy.1973

Cassius Dio

Roman History, translated by E. Cary. Cambridge, MA, 1914–27, doi:10.4159/DLCL.dio_cassius-
roman_history.1914. Available online at: https://penelope.uchicago.edu/Thayer/E/Roman/
Texts/Cassius_Dio/home.html

Cato the Elder

On Agriculture, translated by W.D. Hooper & H.B. Ash. Cambridge, MA, 1934, doi:10.4159/DLCL.
cato-agriculture.1934
Available online at:https://penelope.uchicago.edu/Thayer/E/Roman/Texts/Cato/De_Agricultura/
home.html

Chronicle of Zuqnin

Pseudo-Dionysius of Tel-Mahre. Chronicle (also known as the Chronicle of Zuqnin) Part III, translated by
W. Witakowski. Liverpool, 1996, doi:10.3828/978-0-85323-760-0

Chronicle to 724

The Seventh Century in the West-Syrian Chronicles, translated by A. Palmer. Liverpool, 1993, doi:10.3828/978-0-85323-238-4

Chronicle to 1234

Chronicon anonymum ad annum Christi 1234 pertinens, translated by J.-B. Chabot & A. Abouna, 2 vols. Paris, 1916–1974; see also *The Seventh Century in the West-Syrian Chronicles*, translated by A. Palmer. Liverpool, 1993, pp. 111–221, doi:10.3828/978-0-85323-238-4

Cicero

Against Catiline, translated by C.D. Yonge. London, 1917. Available online at: www.perseus.tufts. edu/hopper/text?doc=Perseus:text:1999.02.0019:text=Catil.:speech=1:chapter=1

Against Piso, translated by C.D. Yonge. London, 1916. Available online at: www.perseus.tufts.edu/hopper/text?doc=Cic.+Pis.+1

Brutus, translated by E. Jones. London, 1776. Available online at: www.attalus.org/old/brutus1.html

On the Reply of the Haruspices, translated by C.D. Yonge. London, 1891. Available online at: www. perseus.tufts.edu/hopper/text?doc=Perseus%3Atext%3A1999.02.0020%3Atext%3DHar

To Atticus, translated by E. Shuckburgh. Perseus Project, Tufts University, Chicago. Available online at: http://perseus.uchicago.edu/perseus-cgi/citequery3.pl?dbname=PerseusLatinTexts&getid=1 &query=Cic.%20Att.

To Friends, translated by D.R. Shackleton-Bailey, 3 vols. Cambridge, MA, 2001, doi:10.4159/DLCL. marcus_tullius_cicero-letters_friends.2001

See also: http://perseus.uchicago.edu/perseus-cgi/citequery3.pl?dbname=PerseusLatinTexts&geti d=1&query=Cic.%20Fam.

Claudian

Against Eutropius, translated by M. Platnauer. Cambridge MA, 1922, doi:10.4159/DLCL.claudian_ claudianus-eutropius.1922. Available online at: http://penelope.uchicago.edu/Thayer/E/ Roman/Texts/Claudian/home.html

Columella

On Agriculture, translated by H.B. Ash. Cambridge, MA, 1941–55, doi:10.4159/DLCL.columella-agriculture.1941

Cornelius Nepos

Lives of Eminent Commanders, translated by J.S. Watson. Cambridge, MA, 1886. Available online at: www.tertullian.org/fathers/nepos_eintro.htm

Cyril of Scythopolis

The Lives of the Monks of Palestine, translated by R.M. Price. Kalamazoo, 1991

Diodorus Siculus

Library of History, translated by C.H. Oldfather et al., Cambridge, MA, 1933–67, doi:10.4159/ DLCL.diodorus_siculus-library_history.1933. Available online at: http://penelope.uchicago.edu/ Thayer/E/Roman/Texts/Diodorus_Siculus/home.html

Dio Chrysostom

Discourses on Royalty, translated by E. Cary. Cambridge, MA, 1932–51. Available online at: http:// penelope.uchicago.edu/Thayer/E/Roman/Texts/Dio_Chrysostom/home.html

Dionysius of Halicarnassus

Roman Antiquities, translated by E. Cary. Cambridge, MA, 1937–50. Available online at: http:// penelope.uchicago.edu/Thayer/e/roman/texts/dionysius_of_halicarnassus/home.html

Easter Chronicle

Chronicon Paschale, 284–628 AD, translated by M. Whitby & M. Whitby. Liverpool, 1989, doi:10.3828/978-0-85323-096-0

Ennius

Remains of Old Latin: Ennius and Caecilius, translated by E.H. Warmington. Cambridge, MA, 1936

Epictetus

Discourses, translated by T.W. Higginson. New York, 1890. Available online at: www.perseus.tufts. edu/hopper/text?doc=Perseus%3Atext%3A1999.01.0237%3Atext%3Ddisc%3Abook%3D1

Epistle of Barnabas

Epistle of Barnabas, translated by A. Roberts & J. Donaldson. Buffalo, NY, 1885. Available online at: www.newadvent.org/fathers/0124.htm

Epitome De Caesaribus

Epitome De Caesaribus, translated by T.M. Banchich. Buffalo, NY, 2018. Available online at: www. roman-emperors.org/epitome.htm

Eunapius

Lives of the Sophists, translated by W.C. Wright. Cambridge MA, 1921
The Fragmentary Classicising Historians of the Later Roman Empire: Eunapius, Olympiodorus, Priscus, and Malchus, translated by R.C. Blockley, 2 vols. Liverpool, 1981–83

Eusebius of Caesarea

Ecclesiastical History, translated by A.C. McGiffert. Buffalo, 1890. Available online at: www.newadvent. org/fathers/2501.htm
Life of Constantine, translated by Av. Cameron & S.G. Hall. Oxford, 1999
Life of Constantine, translated by E.C. Richardson. Buffalo, 1890. Available online at: www.newadvent. org/fathers/25021.htm
Preparation for the Gospel, translated by E.H. Gifford (1903: no publication details available) Available online at: www.tertullian.org/fathers/eusebius_pe_01_book1.htm

Eutropius

Breviarium, translated by J.S. Watson. London,1886. Available online at: www.tertullian.org/fathers/ eutropius_breviarium_2_text.htm

Evagrius

The Ecclesiastical History of Evagrius Scholasticus, translated by M. Whitby. Liverpool, 2000, doi:10.3828/ 978-0-85323-605-4

fasti consulares

https://en.wikipedia.org/wiki/List_of_Roman_consuls; see also: www.attalus.org/docs/ej_fasti. html

fasti triumphales

www.attalus.org/translate/fasti.html

Festus

Breviarium, translated by T.M. Banchich & J.A. Meka. Buffalo, 2001. Available online at: www.attalus. org/translate/festus.html

Frontinus

Stratagems. Aqueducts of Rome, translated by C.E. Bennett et al. Cambridge, MA, 1925

Fronto

Correspondence, Volume I, translated by C.R. Haines. Cambridge MA, 1919
Correspondence, Volume II, translated by C.R. Haines. Cambridge MA, 1920
These texts include *On Eloquence* and the *Principia Historiae*. Certain translations are available online: www.attalus.org/info/fronto.html

Gildas

The Ruin of Britain = *De Excidio Britanniae*, translated by M. Winterbottom. London, 1978

Gregory of Nazianzus

On Faith, translated by H.A. Wilson. Buffalo, NY, 1893 Available online at: www.newadvent.org/fathers/2906.htm
Oration 33, translated by C.G. Browne & J.E. Swallow. Buffalo, 1894 Available online at: www.newadvent.org/fathers/310233.htm

Gregory of Tours

History of the Franks, translated by E. Brehaut (1916; no publication details available) Available online at: https://sourcebooks.fordham.edu/basis/gregory-hist.asp

Heliodorus

Ethiopian Tale = B.P. Reardon, *Collected Ancient Greek Novels*, 2nd edn. Berkeley, CA, 2008

Herodian

History of the Empire, translated by C.R. Whittaker, 2 vols. Cambridge, MA, 1969–70, doi:10.4159/DLCL.herodian-history_empire.1969
Roman History, translated by E.C. Echols. Los Angeles, CA, 1961. Available online at: www.livius.org/sources/content/herodian-s-roman-history

Historia Augusta

Historia Augusta, translated by D. Magie. Cambridge, MA, 1921–32 Available online at: http://penelope.uchicago.edu/Thayer/E/Roman/Texts/Historia_Augusta/home.html

Horace

Odes, translated by A.S. Kline. Available online at: www.poetryintranslation.com/PITBR/Latin/HoraceOdesBkI.php
Odes and Carmen Saeculare of Horace, translated by J. Connington. London, 1872. Available online at: www.perseus.tufts.edu/hopper/text?doc=Perseus%3Atext%3A1999.02.0025

Hydatius

The Chronicle of Hydatius and the Consularia Constantinopolitana: Two Contemporary Accounts of the Final Years of the Roman Empire, translated by R.W. Burgess. Oxford, 1993, doi:10.1093/actrade/9780198147879.book.1

Iamblichus

Babylonian Tale = Reardon B.P. *Collected Ancient Greek Novels*, 2nd edn. Berkeley, CA, 2008

Ignatius of Antioch

See www.newadvent.org/cathen/07644a.htm

In Praise of Piso

In Praise of Piso, translated by J.W. Duff & A.M. Duff. Cambridge, MA, 1934. Available online at: http://penelope.uchicago.edu/Thayer/e/roman/texts/laus_pisonis/text*.html

Isidore of Charax

Parthian Stations, translated by W.H. Schoff. New York, 1912. Available online at: www.parthia.com/doc/parthian_stations.htm

Jerome

Against Rufinus, translated by W.H. Fremantle. Buffalo, NY, 1892. Available online at: www.newadvent.org/fathers/2710.htm
Letter 123, translated by W.H. Fremantle et al. Buffalo, NY, 1893. Available online at: www.newadvent.org/fathers/3001123.htm
Jerome's additional letters available online at: www.newadvent.org/fathers/3001.htm

John of Ephesus

Iohannis Ephesini Historiae ecclesiasticae pars tertia, translated by E.W. Brooks, 2 vols. Paris, 1935–1936. See also: www.tertullian.org/fathers/index.htm#John_of_Ephesus
Lives of the Eastern Saints, translated by E.W. Brooks. Paris, 1923–1925

John Lydus

On the Magistracies, translated by A.C. Bandy. Philadelphia, PA, 1935
On the Months, translated by M. Hooker (2012) Available online at: http://penelope.uchicago.edu/Thayer/E/Roman/Texts/Lydus/de_Mensibus/home.html

John Moschus

The Spiritual Meadow, translated by J. Wortley. Kalamazoo, 1992

Jordanes

Romana and Getica, translated by P. Van Nuffelen & L. Van Hoof. Liverpool, 2020

Josephus

Judaean Antiquities, translated by L.H. Feldman. Boston, 2004
The Jewish War, translated by H. St. J. Thackeray, 3 vols. Cambridge, MA, 1927–1928, doi:10.4159/DLCL.josephus-jewish_war.1927
The Works of Flavius Josephus, translated by W. Whiston. Buffalo, 1895. Available online at: www.perseus.tufts.edu/hopper/text?doc=Perseus%3Atext%3A1999.01.0148

Ps.-Joshua the Stylite

The Chronicle of Pseudo-Joshua the Stylite, translated by F. Trombley & J.W. Watt. Liverpool, 2000, doi:10.3828/978-0-85323-585-9

Julian

Caesares, translated by W.C. Wright. Cambridge MA, 1913. Available online at: www.attalus.org/translate/caesars.html

Letters, translated by W.C. Wright, 4 vols. Cambridge, MA, 1913–23

Misopogon, translated by W.C. Wright. Cambridge, MA, 1913 Available online at: www.attalus.org/translate/misopogon.html

Orations = Julian, Volume 1 & Volume 2, translated by W.C. Wright. Cambridge, MA, 1913

Orations, Letters to Themistius, To the Senate and the People of Athens, To a Priest, The Caesars, Misopogon, translated by W.C. Wright. Cambridge, MA, 1913

Julius Caesar

Civil War, translated by A.G. Peskett. Cambridge, MA, 1914. Available online at: http://penelope.uchicago.edu/Thayer/E/Roman/Texts/Caesar/Civil_Wars/home.html

Commentaries, translated by W.A. McDevitte & W.S. Bohn. New York, 1869. Available online at: http://classics.mit.edu/Caesar/gallic.html

Justin

Epitome of Pompeius Trogus, translated by J.S. Watson. London, 1886. Available online at: www.attalus.org/info/justinus.html

Justinianic Code

Available online at: https://droitromain.univ-grenoble-alpes.fr/Anglica/codjust_Scott.htm

Justin Martyr

Dialogue with Trypho, translated by M. Dods & G. Reith. Buffalo, 1885. Available online at: www.newadvent.org/fathers/0128.htm

First Apology, translated by M. Dods & G. Reith. Buffalo, 1885. Available online at: www.newadvent.org/fathers/0126.htm

Juvenal

Satires, translated by A.S. Kline. Available online at: www.poetryintranslation.com/PITBR/Latin/Juvenalhome.php

Lactantius

On the Deaths of the Persecutors. Available online at: https://people.ucalgary.ca/~vandersp/Courses/texts/lactant/lactperf.html

Latin Panegyrics

In Praise of Later Roman Emperors: The Panegyrici Latini, translated by C.E.V. Nixon & B.S. Rodgers. Berkeley, 2015

Libanius

Letters, translated by A.F. Norman, 2 vols. Cambridge, MA, 1992
Orations, translated by A.F. Norman, 22 vols. Cambridge, MA, 1977–92

Liber Pontificalis

The Book of Pontiffs, translated by R. Davis. Liverpool, 2009

Livius Andronicus

Remains of Old Latin: Livius Andronicus, Naevius, Pacuvius Accius, translated by E.H. Warmington. Cambridge MA, 1936

Livy

Rome and the Mediterranean, translated by Henry Bettenson. London, 1976
The Early History of Rome, translated by Aubrey de Selincourt. London, 2002
The War With Hannibal, translated by Aubrey de Selincourt. London, 2004. See also: www.perseus. tufts.edu/hopper/text?doc=Perseus:text:1999.02.0026

Longus

Daphnis and Chloe = B.P. Reardon, *Collected Ancient Greek Novels*, 2nd edn. Berkeley, CA, 2008

Lucan

The Civil War (Pharsalia), translated by J.D. Duff. Cambridge, MA, 1928

Lucian

A True Story = B.P. Reardon, *Collected Ancient Greek Novels*, 2nd edn. Berkeley, CA, 2008
Alexander = Lucian Volume IV, translated by A.M. Harmon. Cambridge MA, 1925
How to Write History = Lucian Volume VI, translated by K. Kilburn. Cambridge MA, 1959

Lucretius

On the Nature of Things, translated by W.E. Leonard. London, 1921 Available online at: http://classics. mit.edu/Carus/nature_things.html

Machiavelli

The Discourses, translated by L.J. Walker. London, 1984
The Prince, translated by G. Bull. London, 2003

Malalas

The Chronicle of John Malalas, translated by E. Jeffreys et al. Melbourne, 1986

Malchus

The Fragmentary Classicising Historians of the Later Roman Empire: Eunapius, Olympiodorus, Priscus, and Malchus, translated by R.C. Blockley, 2 vols. Liverpool, 1981–1983

Marcellinus Comes

Marcellinus Comes. Chronicon, translated by B. Croke. Sydney, 1995

Marcus Aurelius

Meditations, translated by R. Hard & C. Gill. Oxford, 2011. The older translation by George Long is available online at: http://classics.mit.edu/Antoninus/meditations.html

Martial

Epigrams, translated by A.S. Kline. Available online at: www.poetryintranslation.com/PITBR/Latin/Martial.php

Maurice

Maurice's Strategikon, translated by D.T. Thomas. Philadelphia, PA, 1984

Menander

The History of Menander the Guardsman, translated by R.C. Blockley. Liverpool, 1985

Michael the Syrian

Chronique, translated by J.-B. Chabot, 4 vols. Paris, 1899–1910

Naevius

Remains of Old Latin: Livius Andronicus, Naevius, Pacuvius Accius, translated by E.H. Warmington. Cambridge MA, 1936

Nicolaus of Damascus

Life of Augustus, translated by M. Toher. Cambridge, 2017, doi:10.1017/9781139871839. Note that the older translation of C.M. Hall is available online at: www.attalus.org/translate/nicolaus1.html

Nonnosus

Photius, *Bibliothèque,* translated by R. Henry. 9 vols. Paris, 1959–74. Translation of J.H. Freese available online at www.tertullian.org/fathers/photius_03bibliotheca.htm#3

Notitia Dignitatum

Notitia Dignitatum accedunt Notitia Urbis Constantinopolitanae et Laterculi Provinciarum, ed. O. Seeck. Berlin, 1876. See also: https://sourcebooks.fordham.edu/source/notitiadignitatum.asp and http://lukeuedasarson.com/NotitiaPatterns.html

Olympiodorus

The Fragmentary Classicising Historians of the Later Roman Empire: Eunapius, Olympiodorus, Priscus, and Malchus, translated by R.C. Blockley, 2 vols. Liverpool, 1981–1983

Photius, *Bibliothèque*, translated by R. Henry. 9 vols. Paris, 1959–74 Translation of J.H. Freese available online at www.tertullian.org/fathers/photius_03bibliotheca.htm#80

Orosius

History Against the Pagans, translated by A.T. Fear. Liverpool, 2010. The older translation of I.W. Raymond is available at: http://attalus.org/info/orosius.html

Ovid

Art of Love, translated by A.S. Kline. Available online at: www.poetryintranslation.com/PITBR/Latin/ArtofLoveBkI.php

Fasti, translated by A.S. Kline. Available online at: www.poetryintranslation.com/PITBR/Latin/Fastihome.php

Metamorphoses, translated by S. Garth & J. Dryden. Dublin, 1717. Available online at: http://classics.mit.edu/Ovid/metam.html

Paul the Deacon

History of the Lombards, translated by W.D. Foulke. Philadelphia, PA, 1975

Pausanias

Description of Greece, translated by W.H.S. Jones et al. 5 vols. Cambridge, MA, 1918–35, doi:10.4159/DLCL.pausanias-description_greece.1918

Periplus

Periplus Maris Erythraei, Text with Introduction, Translation, and Commentary, translated by L. Casson. Princeton, NJ, 1989. See also: *Periplus of the Erythrean Sea*, translated by W.H. Schoff. New York, 1912. Available online at: https://depts.washington.edu/silkroad/texts/periplus/periplus.html

Peter the Patrician

The Lost History of Peter the Patrician: An Account of Rome's Imperial Past from the Age of Justinian, translated by T.M. Banchich. London, 2015, doi:10.4324/9781315714585

Petronius

Satyricon, translated by M. Heseltine. London, 1913 Available online at: www.perseus.tufts.edu/hopper/text?doc=Perseus%3Atext%3A2007.01.0027%3Atext%3DSatyricon

Philo

Against Flaccus, translated by C.D. Yonge. London, 1855. Available online at: http://penelope.uchicago.edu/Thayer/E/Roman/Texts/Philo/in_Flaccum*.html
Embassy to Gaius, translated by F.H. Colson. Cambridge, MA, 1962, doi:10.4159/DLCL.philo_judaeus-embassy_gaius_first_part_treatise_virtues.1962

Philostratus

Lives of the Sophists, translated by W.C. Wright. Cambridge, MA, 1921

Pliny the Elder

Natural History, translated by A.C. Andrews et al., 10 vols. Cambridge, MA, 1938–1962, doi:10.4159/DLCL.pliny_elder-natural_history.1938
Natural History, translated by J. Bostock & H.T. Riley. London, 1885 Available online at: www.perseus.tufts.edu/hopper/text?doc=Plin.+Nat.+toc

Pliny the Younger

Panegyric = Letters, Volume II: Boos 8–10, Panegyricus, translated by B. Radice. Cambridge, MA, 1969
The Letters of the Younger Pliny, translated by B. Radice. London, 2003. The older translation of J.B. Firth is available online at: www.attalus.org/info/pliny.html

Plutarch

Parallel Lives, translated by B. Perrin. Cambridge, MA, 1914–26. Available online at: https://penelope.uchicago.edu/Thayer/E/Roman/Texts/Plutarch/Lives/home.html

Polyaenus

Stratagems, translated by R. Shepherd. Chicago, 1974. Available online at: http://attalus.org/info/polyaenus.html

Polybius

The Histories, translated by W.R. Paton. Cambridge, MA, 1922–27. Available online at: https://penelope.uchicago.edu/Thayer/E/Roman/Texts/Polybius/home.html. There is also a newer translation of Polybius, used in Chapters 3 and 4.
The Histories, translated by R. Waterfield & B. McGing. Oxford, 2010

Pontius

Life of Cyprian, translated by R.E. Wallis. Buffalo, NY, 1886. Available online at: www.newadvent. org/fathers/0505.htm

Priscus

The Fragmentary Classicising Historians of the Later Roman Empire: Eunapius, Olympiodorus, Priscus, and Malchus, translated by R.C. Blockley, 2 vols. Liverpool, 1981–83

Procopius

Buildings, translated by H.B. Dewing. Cambridge, MA, 1940, doi:10.4159/DLCL.procopius-buildings.1940. Available online at: http://penelope.uchicago.edu/Thayer/E/Roman/Texts/ Procopius/Buildings/home.html

History of the Wars, translated by H.B. Dewing, 5 vols. Cambridge, MA, 1914–1928, doi:10.4159/ DLCL.procopius-history_wars.1914. Available online at: https://penelope.uchicago.edu/ Thayer/E/Roman/Texts/Procopius/Wars/home.html#BG

Secret History, translated by H.B. Dewing. Cambridge, MA, 1935, doi:10.4159/DLCL.procopius-anecdota_secret_history.1935. Available online at: http://penelope.uchicago.edu/Thayer/E/ Roman/Texts/Procopius/Anecdota/home.html

Propertius

Elegies, translated by A.S. Kline. Available online at: www.poetryintranslation.com/PITBR/Latin/ Prophome.php

Elegies, translated by V. Katz. Los Angeles, 1995 Available online at: www.perseus.tufts.edu/hopper/ text?doc=Perseus%3Atext%3A1999.02.0067

Ptolemy

Ptolemy Geography, Book 6. Middle East, Central and North Asia, China. Part 1, translated by S. Ziegler. Wiesbaden, 1998

The Geography, translated by E.L. Stevenson. Toronto, 1991

Quintilian

Education of the Orator, translated by H.E. Butler. Cambridge, MA, 1920–22. Available online at: http://penelope.uchicago.edu/Thayer/E/Roman/Texts/Quintilian/Institutio_Oratoria/ home.html

Quran

Quran, translated by A. Jones. Cambridge, 2007

Sallust

Catiline Conspiracy, translated by J.C. Rolfe. Cambridge, MA, 1921, doi:10.4159/DLCL.sallust-war_ catiline.2013

Histories, translated by J.C. Rolfe. Cambridge, MA, 1921, doi:10.4159/DLCL.sallust-histories.2015

War with Jugurtha, translated by J.C. Rolfe. Cambridge, MA, 1921, doi:10.4159/DLCL.sallust-war_jugurtha.2013

All three works available online at: https://penelope.uchicago.edu/Thayer/E/Roman/Texts/Sallust/home.html

Salvian

On the Government of God, translated by E. Sanford. New York, 1930. Available online at: www.tertullian.org/fathers/salvian_gov_00_intro.htm

Sebeos

The Armenian History Attributed to Sebeos, translated by R. Thomson. Liverpool, 1999

Seneca

Apocolocyntosis, translated by W.H.D. Rouse. London, 1913. Available online at: www.perseus.tufts.edu/hopper/text?doc=Perseus%3Atext%3A2007.01.0029

Letters, translated by R.M. Gummere. Cambridge, MA, 1917–25

Natural Questions, translated by T.H. Corcoran. Cambridge, MA, 1971–72, doi:10.4159/DLCL.seneca_younger-natural_questions.1971

On Clemency, translated by A. Stewart. London, 1900. Available online at: https://en.wikisource.org/wiki/Of_Clemency/Book_I

On the Happy Life = *Moral Essays, Volume II: De Consolatione ad Marciam. De Vita Beata. De Otio. De Tranquillitate Animi. De Brevitate Vitae. De Consolatione ad Polybium. De Consolatione ad Helviam.* Translated by J.W. Basore. Cambridge, MA, 1932

On the Shortness of Life, translated by J.W. Basore. Cambridge, MA, 1932. Also available online at: https://en.wikisource.org/wiki/On_the_shortness_of_life

Socrates Scholasticus

Ecclesiastical History, translated by A.C. Zenos. Grand Rapids, MI, 1890–1900. Available online at: www.ccel.org/ccel/schaff/npnf202.toc.html

Sozomen

Ecclesiastical History, translated by C.D. Hartranft. Grand Rapids, MI, 1890–1900
Available online at: www.ccel.org/ccel/schaff/npnf202.toc.html

Strabo

Geography, translated by H.L. Jones. Cambridge, MA, 1917–32. Available online at: https://penelope.uchicago.edu/Thayer/E/Roman/Texts/Strabo/home.html

Suetonius

Lives of the Twelve Caesars, translated by J.C. Rolfe. Cambridge, MA, 1913–14. Available online at: https://penelope.uchicago.edu/Thayer/E/Roman/Texts/Suetonius/12Caesars/home.html

Sulpicia

Poems, translated by A.S. Kline. Available online at: www.poetryintranslation.com/PITBR/Latin/
Tibullus.php

Symeon the Stylite

The Lives of Symeon Stylites, translated by R. Doran. Kalamazoo, 1992

Symeon the Stylite the Younger

La vie ancienne de S. Syméon le Jeune, translated by P. van den Ven, 2 vols. Brussels, 1962–1970.

Synodicon Orientale

Synodicon orientale, ed. J.-B. Chabot. Paris, 1902–

al-Tabari

The History of al-Tabari, Volume 5: The Sasanids, the Byzantines, the Lakhmids, and Yemen, translated by
C.W. Bosworth. Albany, NY, 1999

Tacitus

Agricola, Germania. Translated by M. Hutton et al. Cambridge, MA, 1914, doi:10.4159/DLCL.
tacitus-agricola.1914
Agricola, translated by S. Bryant. New York, 1942. Available online at: www.perseus.tufts.edu/
hopper/text?doc=Perseus%3Atext%3A1999.02.0081
Annals, translated by J. Jackson, 3 vols. Cambridge, MA, 1931–1937, doi:10.4159/DLCL.
tacitus-annals.1931
Histories, translated by C.H. Moore, 2 vols. Cambridge MA, 1925–1931, doi:10.4159/DLCL.
tacitus-histories.1925 Available online at: http://penelope.uchicago.edu/Thayer/E/Roman/
Texts/Tacitus/home.html

Teaching of Addai

Teaching of Addai, translated by G. Phillips, 1876. Available online at: www.tertullian.org/fathers/
addai_2_text.htm

Tertullian

Apology, translated by S. Thelwall. Buffalo, NY, 1885. Available online at: www.newadvent.org/
fathers/0301.htm
Against the Jews, translated by S. Thelwall. Buffalo, NY, 1885. Available online at: www.newadvent.
org/fathers/0308.htm

Themistius

Politics, Philosophy and Empire in the Fourth Century: Themistius' Select Orations, translated by P. Heather.
Liverpool, 2001

Theodosian Code

Available online at: https://droitromain.univ-grenoble-alpes.fr/Codex_Theod.htm

Theophanes

The Chronicle of Theophanes Confessor: Byzantine and Near Eastern history, A.D. 284–813, translated by C. Mango & R. Scott. Oxford, 1997

Theophanes of Byzantium

Photius, *Bibliothèque*, translated by R. Henry. 9 vols. Paris, 1959–74. Translation of J.H. Freese available online at www.tertullian.org/fathers/photius_03bibliotheca.htm#64

Theophilus of Edessa

Theophilus of Edessa's Chronicle and the Circulation of Historical Knowledge in Late Antiquity and Early Islam, translated by R. Hoyland. Liverpool, 2011

Theophylact Simocatta

The History of Theophylact Simocatta, translated by M. Whitby & M. Whitby. Oxford, 1986

Tibullus

Poems, translated by A.S. Kline. Available online at: www.poetryintranslation.com/PITBR/Latin/Tibullus.php

Twelve Tables

Remains of Old Latin: Lucilius and the Twelve Tables, translated by E.H. Warmington. Cambridge, MA, 1938

Valerius Maximus

Memorable Deeds and Sayings. One Thousand Tales From Ancient Rome, translated by H.J. Walker. Indianapolis, IN, 2004

Varro (Marcus Terentius)

On Agriculture, translated by W.D. Hooper & H.B. Ash. Cambridge, MA, 1934, doi:10.4159/DLCL.varro-agriculture.1934. Available online at: https://penelope.uchicago.edu/Thayer/E/Roman/Texts/Varro/de_Re_Rustica/home.html

Vegetius

On Roman Military Matters, translated by J. Clarke. St Petersburg, FL, 1767

Velleius Paterculus

Roman History, translated by F.W. Shipley. Cambridge, MA, 1924. Available online at: https://penelope.uchicago.edu/Thayer/E/Roman/Texts/Velleius_Paterculus/home.html

Virgil

Aeneid, translated by D. West. London, 2020

Aeneid, translated by J. Dryden. New York, 1909. Available online at: http://classics.mit.edu/Virgil/aeneid.html

Aeneid, translated by A.S. Kline. Available online at: www.poetryintranslation.com/PITBR/Latin/VirgilAeneidI.php

Eclogues, Georgics, Aeneid. Books 1–6, translated by H.R. Fairclough. Cambridge, MA, 1916

Aeneid, Books 7–12, translated by H.R. Fairclough. Cambridge, MA: Harvard University Press, 1918

Vitruvius

On Architecture, translated by M.H. Morgan. Cambridge, MA, 1914. Available online at: http://penelope.uchicago.edu/Thayer/E/Roman/Texts/Vitruvius/home.html

Ps.-Zachariah

The Chronicle of Pseudo-Zachariah Rhetor. Church and War in Late Antiquity, edited by G. Greatrex, translated by R. Phenix & C. Horn. Liverpool, 2011, doi:10.3828/978-1-84631-493-3

Zonaras

The History of Zonaras From Alexander Severus to the Death of Theodosius the Great, translated by T.M. Banchich & E.N. Lane. New York, 2009, doi:10.4324/9780203882047

Zosimus

New History, translated by R.T. Ridley. Canberra, 1982. See also: www.livius.org/sources/content/zosimus

Selected modern works

van Ackeren M. *A Companion to Marcus Aurelius*. Oxford, 2012, doi:10.1002/9781118219836

Arnason J.P. & Raaflaub K.A. (eds) *The Roman Empire in Context. Historical and Comparative Perspectives*. Oxford, 2011, doi:10.1002/9781444390186

Beard M. *SPQR. A History of Ancient Rome*. London, 2015

de la Bédoyère G. *Roman Britain. A New History*. New York, 2010

Beeley C. *The Unity of Christ. Continuity and Conflict in Patristic Tradition*. New Haven, CT, 2012

Bromwich J. *The Roman Remains of Southern France. A Guidebook*. London, 1996

Bruun C. & Edmondson J. (eds) *The Oxford Handbook of Roman Epigraphy*. Oxford, 2014, doi:10.1093/oxfordhb/9780195336467.001.0001

Buckley E. & Dinter M.T. (eds) *A Companion to the Neronian Age*. Oxford, 2013, doi:10.1002/9781118316771

Burns S. *The Monuments of Syria. A Guide.* London, 2009

Cameron, Av. *The Mediterranean World in Late Antiquity, AD 395–700,* 2nd edn. London, 2012, doi:10.4324/9780203809082

Cotton H. et al. The papyrology of the Roman Near East: a survey. *Journal of Roman Studies* 85 (1995): 214–35, doi:10.2307/301063

Dalby A. & Grainger S. *The Classical Cookbook.* London, 1996

Davenport C. *A History of the Roman Equestrian Order.* Cambridge, 2018, doi:10.1017/9781139506403

Davenport C. & Mallan C. Dexippus and the Gothic invasions: interpreting the new Vienna fragment (*Codex Vindobonensis Hist. gr.* 73, ff. 192^v–193^r). *Journal of Roman Studies* 105 (2015): 203–26, doi:10.1017/S0075435815000970

Elton H. *The Roman Empire in Late Antiquity. A Political and Military History.* Cambridge, 2018, doi:10.1017/9781139030236

Fisher, G. *Hannibal and Scipio.* Cheltenham, 2016

Fowden E.K. *The Barbarian Plain. Saint Sergius Between Rome and Iran.* Berkeley, CA, 1999

Fowden G. *Before and After Muhammad. The First Millennium Refocused.* Princeton, NJ, 2014, doi:10.23943/princeton/9780691158532.001.0001

Frere S. *Britannia. A History of Roman Britain.* London, 1987

Gabriel P. *Scipio Africanus. Rome's Greatest General.* Washington, DC, 2008

Galinsky K (ed.) *The Cambridge Companion to the Age of Augustus.* Cambridge, 2007, doi:10.1017/CCOL0521807964

Goldsworthy A. *Pax Romana. War, Peace, and Conquest in the Roman World.* London, 2017

Green P. *Alexander to Actium. The Historical Evolution of the Hellenistic Age.* Berkeley, CA, 1990

Heather P. *Rome Resurgent. War and Empire in the Age of Justinian.* Oxford, 2018

Hoyos D. (ed) *A Companion to the Punic Wars.* Oxford, 2011, doi:10.1002/9781444393712

Johnson S.F. (ed) *The Oxford Handbook of Late Antiquity.* Oxford, 2012, doi:10.1093/oxfordhb/9780195336931.001.0001

Jones A.H.M. *The Later Roman Empire, 284–602. A Social, Economic, and Administrative Survey,* 3 vols. Oxford, 1964

Kulikowski M. *The Tragedy of Empire. From Constantine to the Destruction of Roman Italy.* Cambridge, MA, 2019

Kulikowski M. *The Triumph of Empire. The Roman World from Hadrian to Constantine.* Cambridge, MA, 2016

Lenski N. *Initium mali Romano imperio*: contemporary reactions to the Battle of Adrianople. *Transactions of the American Philological Association* 127 (1997): 129–68

Lenski M. (ed.) *The Cambridge Companion to the Age of Constantine.* Cambridge, 2010, doi:10.1017/CCOL0521818389

Lomas K. *The Rise of Rome. From the Iron Age to the Punic Wars.* Cambridge, MA, 2018

Maas M. (ed.) *The Cambridge Companion to the Age of Attila.* Cambridge, 2015, doi:10.1017/CCO9781139128964

Maas M. (ed.) *The Cambridge Companion to the Age of Justinian.* Cambridge, 2005, doi:10.1017/CCOL0521817463

Marincola J. *Greek and Roman Historiography.* Oxford, 2001

Martin G. & Grusková J. "Scythica Vindobonensia" by Dexippus (?): New Fragments on Decius' Gothic Wars. *Greek, Roman, and Byzantine Studies* 54 (2014): 728–54

Mattingly D.J. *Tripolitania.* London, 1995

McKeown J.C. *A Cabinet of Roman Curiosities.* Oxford, 2010

McLynn F. *Marcus Aurelius. A Life.* Cambridge MA, 2009

Mitchell S. *A History of the Later Roman Empire, AD 284–641.* Oxford, 2007

Moorhead J. *The Roman Empire Divided, 400–700,* 2nd edn. London, 2013, doi:10.4324/9781315833293

Potter D. *The Origin of Empire. Rome from the Republic to Hadrian*. Cambridge, MA, 2019

Potter D. *The Roman Empire at Bay*, AD *180–395*, 2nd edn. New York, 2013, doi:10.4324/978 1315882567

Potter D. (ed) *A Companion to the Roman Empire*. Oxford, 2010, doi:10.1002/9780470996942

Potts D. (ed) *Oxford Handbook of Ancient Iran*. Oxford, 2013, doi:10.1093/oxfordhb/97801997 33309.001.0001

Rohrbacher D. *The Historians of Late Antiquity*. New York, 2002

Rosenstein N. *Rome and the Mediterranean 290 to 146 BC: The Imperial Republic*. Edinburgh, 2012

Rosenstein N. & Morstein-Marx R. (eds) *A Companion to the Roman Republic*. Oxford, 2006, doi:10.1002/9780470996980

Ross S.K. *Roman Edessa. Politics and Culture on the Eastern Fringes of the Roman Empire, 114–242 CE*. London, 2001, doi:10.4324/9780203991978

Saint-Laurent J.-N. M. *Missionary Stories and the Formation of the Syriac Churches*. Oakland, CA, 2015, doi:10.1525/California/9780520284968.001.0001

Sarris P. *Empires of Faith: The Fall of Rome to the Rise of Islam, 500–700*. Oxford, 2011, doi:10.1093/ acprof:oso/9780199261260.001.0001

Sauer E.W. (ed.) *Sasanian Persia. Between Rome and the Steppes of Eurasia*. Edinburgh, 2017

Segal J.B. *Edessa 'The Blessed City'*. Oxford, 1970

Shipley G. *The Greek World After Alexander*. New York, 2000, doi:10.4324/9780203523087

Southern P. *The Roman Empire from Severus to Constantine*. New York, 2001

Syme R. *The Roman Revolution*. Oxford, 1939

Whittow M. Ruling the late Roman and early Byzantine city: a continuous history. *Past and Present* 129 (1990): 3–29, doi:10.1093/past/129.1.3

Wickham C. *Framing the Early Middle Ages: Europe and the Mediterranean, 400–800*. Oxford, 2005, doi:10.1093/acprof:oso/9780199264490.001.0001

Wickham C. *The Inheritance of Rome. A History of Europe from 400 to 1000*. London, 2010

Wiemer H.-U. & Rebenich S. *A Companion to Julian the Apostate*. Leiden, 2020

Selected books, articles, and websites by topic

Actium memorial

Murray W.M. Augustus' victory monument, 3D modeling, and new directions for warship research. Unpublished. See: www.academia.edu/9946546/Augustus_s_Victory_Monument_3D_ Modeling_and_New_Directions_for_Warship_Research

Murray W.M. & Petsas P.M. Octavian's campsite memorial for the Actian war. *Transactions of the American Philosophical Society* 79/4 (1989): 1–172, doi:10.2307/1006504.

See the computerised reconstruction of the memorial at: www.vizin.org/projects/actium/gallery. html

Zachos K.L. The *tropaeum* of the sea-battle of Actium at Nikopolis: interim report. *Journal of Roman Archaeology* 16 (2003): 64–92, doi:10.1017/S1047759400013003

Arabia, the eastern provinces, and Islam

al-Azmeh A. *The Arabs and Islam in Late Antiquity. A Critique of Approaches to Arabic Sources*. Berlin, 2014

al-Azmeh A. *The Emergence of Islam in Late Antiquity. Allah and His People*. Cambridge, 2014, doi:10.1017/CBO9781139410854

Bakhos C. & Cook M. (eds) *Islam and Its Past. Jahiliyya, Late Antiquity, and the Quran*. Oxford, 2017, doi:10.1093/oso/9780198748496.001.0001

Ball W. *Rome in the East. The Transformation of an Empire*, 2nd edn. New York, 2016, doi:10.4324/9781315646886

Berkey J. *The Formation of Islam. Religion and Society in the Near East, 600–1800.* Cambridge, 2003, doi: 10.1017/CBO9780511817861

Blockley R.C. *East Roman Foreign Policy. Formation and Conduct from Diocletian to Anastasius.* Leeds, 1992

de Blois F. Islam in its Arabian context. In A. Neuwirth, N. Sinai & M. Marx (eds), *The Qur'an in Context: Historical and Literary Investigations into the Quranic Milieu.* Leiden, 2010, doi:10.1163/ej.9789004176881.i-864.169

Bowersock G. *Roman Arabia.* Cambridge, MA, 1983

Bowersock G. *The Crucible of Islam.* Cambridge, MA, 2017

Bowersock G. *The Throne of Adulis. Red Sea Wars on the Eve of Islam.* Oxford, 2013

Butcher K. *Roman Syria and the Near East.* London, 2003

Donner F. *Muhammad and the Believers: At the Origins of Islam.* Cambridge, MA, 2010

Edwell P. *Between Rome and Persia. The Middle Euphrates, Mesopotamia, and Palmyra Under Roman Control.* New York, 2008, doi:10.4324/9780203938331

Fisher, G. *Rome, Persia, and Arabia. Shaping the Middle East from Pompey to Muhammad.* New York, 2020, doi:10.4324/9780429356483

Howard-Johnston J. *Witnesses to a World Crisis. Historians and Histories of the Middle East in the Seventh Century.* Oxford, 2010, doi:10.1093/acprof:oso/9780199208593.001.0001

Hoyland R. *In God's Path. The Arab Conquests and the Creation of an Islamic Empire.* Oxford, 2015, doi:10.14296/RiH/2014/1780

Konrad M. Research on the Roman and early Byzantine frontier in North Syria. *Journal of Roman Archaeology* 12 (1999): 392–410, doi:10.1017/S1047759400018122

Meier M. The Roman context of early Islam. *Millennium* 17/1 (2020): 265–302, doi:10.1515/mill-2020-0009

Millar F. *Religion, Language, and Community in the Roman Near East, Constantine to Muhammad.* London, 2010

Millar F. *The Roman Near East. 31 BC–AD 337.* Cambridge, 1993

Palermo R. *On the Edge of Empires. North Mesopotamia During the Roman Period (2nd–4th c CE).* New York, 2019, doi:10.4324/9781315648255

Payne R.E. *A State of Mixture. Christians, Zoroastrians, and Iranian Political Culture in Late Antiquity.* Berkeley, CA, 2015, doi:10.1525/california/9780520286191.001.0001

Sartre M. *The Middle East Under Rome*, translated by C. Porter & E. Rawlings. Cambridge, MA, 2005

Sinai N. *The Quran. A Historical-Critical Introduction.* Edinburgh, 2017

Wakeley J.M. *The Two Falls of Rome in Late Antiquity. The Arabian Conquests in Comparative Perspective.* London, 2018, doi:10.1007/978-3-319-69796-3

Wansbrough J. *Quranic Studies: Sources and Methods of Scriptural Interpretation.* Oxford, 1977

Whittow M. Rome and the Jafnids: writing the history of a 6th-c. tribal dynasty. in J. Humphrey (ed.), *The Roman and Byzantine Near East: Some Recent Archaeological Research*, 3 vols. Portsmouth, RI, 1995

Arch of Titus Project

www.yu.edu/cis/activities/arch-of-titus

Army

Dando-Collins S. *Legions of Rome.* London, 2010

Davenport C. The building inscription from the fort at Udruh and Aelius Flavianus, tetrarchic *praeses* of *Palaestina*. *Journal of Roman Archaeology* 23 (2010): 349–57, doi:10.1017/S1047759400002440

Dart C.J. & Vervaet F.J. The significance of the naval triumph in Roman history. *Zeitschrift für Papyrologie und Epigraphik* 176 (2011): 267–80

Erdkamp P. (ed) *A Companion to the Roman Army*. Oxford, 2004, doi:10.1002/9780470996577

Goldsworthy A. *The Complete Roman Army*. New York, 2003

Isaac B. *The Limits of Empire. The Roman Army in the East*, rev. edn. Oxford, 2000

James S. *Rome and the Sword. How Warriors and Weapons Shaped Roman History*. New York, 2011

Kennedy D. *The Roman Army in Jordan*. London, 2004

Kennedy D. & Falahat H. *Castra Legionis VI Ferratae*: a building inscription for the legionary fortress of Udruh near Petra. *Journal of Roman Archaeology* 21 (2008): 150–69, doi:10.1017/S1047759400004426

Kennedy D. & Riley D. *Rome's Desert Frontier from the Air*. London, 1990

Keppie, L. *The Making of the Roman Army. From Republic to Empire*. Norman, OK, 1984

Kulikowski M. *Rome's Gothic Wars*. Cambridge, 2007

Lee A.D. *War in Late Antiquity. A Social History*. Oxford, 2007

Southern P. & Dixon K.R. *The Late Roman Army*. New Haven, CT, 1996

Tusa S. & Royal J. The landscape of the naval battle at the Egadi Islands (241 BC). *Journal of Roman Archaeology* 25 (2012): 7–48, doi:10.1017/S1047759400001124

Biographies of individual Roman legions: www.livius.org/articles/misc/legion

VarusandKalkriese:www.kalkriese-varusschlacht.de/en/research/archaeology/excavations-in-kalkriese

See also the incredibly useful website on Roman fortifications: www.legionaryfortresses.info/

Barbarians (including ethnogenesis)

Halsall G. *Barbarian Migrations and the Roman West, 376–568*. Cambridge, 2007

Heather P. *Empires and Barbarians. Migration, Development, and the Birth of Europe*. London, 2009

Heather P. *The Restoration of Rome. Barbarian Popes and Imperial Pretenders*. Oxford, 2013

Parker S.T. Peasants, pastoralists, and the *pax romana*. *Bulletin of the American Schools of Oriental Research* 261 (1986): 25–50, doi:10.2307/1357062

Pohl W. (ed.) *Kingdoms of the Empire. The Integration of Barbarians in Late Antiquity*. Leiden, 1997

Pohl W. & Reimitz H. (eds) *Strategies of Distinction. The Construction of Ethnic Communities, 300–800*. Leiden, 1998

Shaw B.D. 'Eaters of flesh, drinkers of milk': The ancient Mediterranean ideology of the pastoral nomad. *Ancient Society* 13/14 (1982): 5–31.

Ward-Perkins B. *The Fall of Rome and the End of Civilization*. Oxford, 2005

Wood I. Barbarians, historians, and the construction of national identities. *Journal of Late Antiquity* 1/1 (2008): 61–81, doi:10.1353/jla.0.0007

Woolf G. *Tales of the Barbarians. Ethnography and Empire in the Roman West*. Oxford, 2011

Census

Ancient census figures: www.csun.edu/~hcfll004/romancensus.html

Climate change and pollution

Büntgen U. et al. Cooling and societal change during the Late Antique Little Ice Age from 536 to around 660 AD. *Nature GeoScience* 9 (2016): 231–37, doi:10.1038/NGEO2652

Loveluck C. et al. Alpine ice-core evidence for the transformation of the European monetary system, AD 640–670. *Antiquity* 366 (2018): 1571–85, doi:10.15184/aqy.2018.110. Note: despite the date range in the title, this article does contain material relevant for the imperial period.

McCormick M. et al. Climate change during and after the Roman empire: Reconstructing the past from scientific and historical evidence. *The Journal of Interdisciplinary History* 43/2 (2012): 169–220 10.1162/JINH_a_00379

Sigl M. et al. Timing and climate forcing of volcanic eruptions for the past 2,500 years. *Nature* 523 (2015): 543–49, doi:10.1038/nature14565

Lead in Greenland ice cores: https://arstechnica.com/science/2018/05/greenland-ice-cores-track-roman-lead-pollution-in-year-by-year-detail

Coins

Metcalf W.E. *The Oxford Handbook of Greek and Roman Coinage.* Oxford, 2012, doi:10.1093/oxfordhb/9780195305746.001.0001

The website of the Classical Numismatics Group contains an archive of every coin the group has sold at auction, with historical articles, detailed notes on coin legends and types, high-resolution images, and so on. See www.cngcoins.com and www.cngcoins.com/Coins_sold.aspx

Constantinople

Visualisation of the city: www.byzantium1200.com/

Dura-Europos

Baird J. The ruination of Dura-Europos. *Theoretical Roman Archaeology Journal* 3(1): 1–20, doi:10.16995/traj.421

Baird J. *Dura Deserta*: The death and afterlife of Dura-Europos, in A. Augenti and N. Christie (eds), *Vrbes Extinctae. Archaeologies of Abandoned Classical Towns.* London, 2016, doi:10.4324/9781315234465

James S. Of colossal camps and a Roman battlefield: remote sensing, archival archaeology, and the 'conflict landscape' of Dura-Europos, Syria, in D.J. Breeze et al. (eds), *Understanding Roman Frontiers. A Celebration for Professor Bill Hanson.* Edinburgh, 2015, pp. 328–45

James S. Stratagems, combat, and 'chemical warfare' in the siege mines of Dura-Europos. *American Journal of Archaeology* 115/1 (2011): 69–101, doi:10.3764/aja.115.1.0069

James S. *The Roman Military Base at Dura-Europos, Syria. An Archaeological Visualisation.* Oxford, 2019

Welles C.B. The epitaph of Julius Terentius. *The Harvard Theological Review*, 34/2 (1941): 79– 102

See also: https://artgallery.yale.edu/ancient-art

Economy and trade

Ball, W. *Rome in the East. The Transformation of an Empire*, 2nd edn, New York, 2016, doi:10.4324/9781315646886

Cobb M.A. Balancing the trade: Roman cargo shipments to India. *Oxford Journal of Archaeology* 34/2 (2015): 185–203, doi:10.1111/ojoa.12055

Finley M.I. *The Ancient Economy*, 2nd edn. Berkeley, CA, 1985

Fitzpatrick M.P. The Indian Ocean trade network and Roman imperialism. *Journal of World History* 22/1 (2011): 27–54

Pollard E.A. Pliny's *Natural History* and the Flavian Templum Pacis: Botanical imperialism in first-century C.E. Rome. *Journal of World History* 20/3 (2009): 309–38

Seland E.H. Ancient Afghanistan and the Indian Ocean: Maritime links of the Kushan empire ca. 50–200 CE. *Journal of Indian Ocean Archaeology* 9 (2013): 66–74

Sidebotham S.E. *Roman Economic Policy in the Erythra Thalassa, 30 B.C.–A.D. 217.* Leiden, 1986, doi:10.1163/9789004328266

Tomber R. *Indo-Roman Trade. From Pots to Pepper.* London, 2008

Young G.K. *Rome's Eastern Trade. International Commerce and Imperial Policy, 31 BC—AD 305.* London, 2001

See also: The Oxford Roman Economy Project: www.romaneconomy.ox.ac.uk

Frontiers

Breeze D. The value of studying Roman frontiers. *Theoretical Roman Archaeology Journal* 1/1 (2018): 1–17, doi:10.16995/traj.212

Parker, P. *The Empire Stops Here. A Journey Along the Frontiers of the Roman World.* London, 2010

Whittaker C. *Frontiers of the Roman Empire. A Social and Economic Study.* Baltimore, MD, 1994

The German *limes* road: www.limesstrasse.de/deutsche-limes-strasse/about-us/german-limes-road/?L=1

The Danube frontier: http://danubelimesbrand.org

Hadrian and his travels:

Opper T. (ed) *Hadrian: Art, Politics, and Economy.* London, 2013

For a great deal of information on Hadrian and thousands of photographs, visit Carole Raddato's blog, *Following Hadrian:* https://followinghadrian.com

Maps and atlases

Scarre C. *The Penguin Historical Atlas of Ancient Rome.* London, 1995

Talbert J.A. (ed.) *Atlas of Classical History.* London, 2007 10.4324/9780203405352

Talbert J.A. (ed.) *Barrington Atlas of the Greek and Roman World.* Princeton, NJ, 2000

See also the Ancient World Mapping Centre: http://awmc.unc.edu/wordpress/

Marble Plan Online

https://formaurbis.stanford.edu

Mausoleum of Augustus restoration project

www.mausoleodiaugusto.it/en/the-restoration-project

Palmyra

Computerised visualisation of the city and its monuments: https://newpalmyra.org

Plague and illness in antiquity

Benovitz N. The Justinianic plague: evidence from the dated Greek epitaphs of Byzantine Palestine and Arabia. *Journal of Roman Archaeology* 27 (2014): 487–98, doi:10.1017/S1047759414001378

Bruun C. The Antonine plague in Rome and Ostia. *Journal of Roman Archaeology* 16 (2003): 426–34, doi:10.1017/S1047759400013234

Duncan-Jones R. P. The impact of the Antonine plague. *Journal of Roman Archaeology* 9 (1996): 108–36, doi:10.1017/S1047759400016524

Haldon J. et al. Plagues, climate change, and the end of an empire. A response to Kyle Harper's *The Fate of Rome (2)*: Plagues and a crisis of empire. *History Compass* 16/12 (2018): 1–10, doi:10.1111/hic3.12506

Harper K. Another eyewitness to the plague described by Cyprian, with notes on the 'Persecution of Decius'. *Journal of Roman Archaeology* 29 (2016): 473–6, doi:10.1017/S1047759400072263

Harper K. Pandemics and passages to late antiquity: rethinking the plague of c.249–270 described by Cyprian. *Journal of Roman Archaeology* 28 (2015): 223–60, doi:10.1017/S1047759415002470

Harper K. People, plagues, and princes in the Roman world: the evidence from Egypt. *The Journal of Economic History* 76/3 (2016): 803–39, doi:10.1017/S0022050716000826

Keller M. et al. Ancient *Yersinia pestis* genomes from across Western Europe reveal early diversification during the First Pandemic (541–750). *Proceedings of the National Academy of Sciences* 116/25: 12363–12372, doi:10.1073/pnas.1820447116

Meier M. The 'Justinianic Plague': the economic consequences of the pandemic in the eastern Roman empire and its cultural and religious effects. *Early Medieval Europe* 24/3 (2016): 267–92, doi:10.1111/emed.12152

Mordechai L. et al. The Justinianic Plague: An inconsequential pandemic? *Proceedings of the National Academy of Sciences* 116/51: 25546–54, doi:10.1073/pnas.1903797116

Murad A. A neurological mystery from history: The case of Claudius Caesar. *Journal of the History of the Neurosciences* 19/3 (2010): 221–7, doi:10.1080/09647040902872775

Sarris P. The Justinianic Plague: origins and effects. *Continuity and Change* 17/2 (2002): 169–82, doi:10.1017/S0268416002004137

Sidwell B. Gaius Caligula's mental illness. *Classical World* 103/2 (2010): 183–206, doi:10.1353/clw.0.0165

Stathakopoulos, D. C. *Famine and Pestilence in the Late Roman and Early Byzantine Empire: A Systematic Survey of Subsistence Crises and Epidemics*. New York, 2004, doi:10.4324/9781315255439

Prosopography of the Later Roman Empire

Jones A.H.M. et al. (eds), *The Prosopography of the Later Roman Empire*, eds A.H.M. Jones et al., 3 vols. Cambridge, 1971–92

Rome

Claridge A. *Rome. An Oxford Archaeological Guide*, 2nd edn. Oxford, 2010, doi:10.1017/S0003581511000230

Scanned copy of Platner's *Topographical Dictionary of Ancient Rome*: www3.lib.uchicago.edu/cgi-bin/eos/eos_page.pl?DPI=100&callnum=DG16.P72&object=1

Searchable copy of Platner: https://penelope.uchicago.edu/Thayer/E/Gazetteer/Places/Europe/Italy/Lazio/Roma/Rome/_Texts/PLATOP*/home.html

Slavery

There is a vast amount written about ancient slavery, but an excellent place to start is:

Bradley K. & Cartledge P. *The Cambridge World History of Slavery*, vol. 1. *The Ancient Mediterranean World*. Cambridge, 2011, doi:10.1017/CHOL9780521840668

See also:

Harper K. *Slavery in the Late Roman World, AD 275–425*. Cambridge, 2011, doi:10.1017/CBO9780511973451

Vesuvius

Luongo G. et al. Impact of the AD 79 explosive eruption on Pompeii, I. Relations amongst the depositional mechanisms of the pyroclastic products, the framework of the buildings, and the associated destructive effects. *Journal of Volcanology and Geothermal Research* 126 (2003): 201–23, doi:10.1016/S0377-0273(03)00146-X

Martyn R. *et al.* A re-evaluation of manner of death at Roman Herculaneum following the AD 79 eruption of Vesuvius. *Antiquity* 373 (2020): 76–91, doi:10.15184/aqy.2019.215

Mastrolorenzo, G. et al. 'Herculaneum victims of Vesuvius in AD 79.' *Nature* 410 (2001): 769, doi:10.1038/35071167

Mastrolorenzo, G. et al. Lethal thermal impact at periphery of pyroclastic surges: evidences at Pompeii, *PLoS One* 5/6 (2010): 1–12, doi:10.1371/journal.pone.0011127

Sigurdsson, H., Cashdollar, S. & Sparks, S.R.J. The eruption of Vesuvius in AD 79: Reconstruction from historical and volcanological evidence. *American Journal of Archaeology* 86/1 (1982): 39–51, doi:10.2307/504292

Women in ancient Rome

Barrett A. *Agrippina. Mother of Nero*. London, 1996, doi:10.4324/9780203012352

Clack J. To those who fell on Agrippina's pen. *The Classical World* 69 (1975): 45–53, doi:10.2307/4348328

Clark G. *Women in Late Antiquity. Pagan and Christian Lifestyles*. Oxford, 1993

James S.L. & Dillon S. *A Companion to Women in the Ancient World*. Oxford, 2012, doi:10.1002/9781444355024

Dixon S. *Reading Roman Women*. Bristol, 2001

Pomeroy S.B. *Goddesses, Whores, Wives, and Slaves. Women in Classical Antiquity*, 2nd edn. New York, 1995

Schiff S. *Cleopatra. A Life*. New York, 2011

Southern P. *Empress Zenobia. Palmyra's Rebel Queen*. Edinburgh, 2008

Wilkinson K. *Women and Modesty in Late Antiquity*. Cambridge, 2019, doi:10.1017/CBO9781139343343

Index of individuals, deities, and saints

Note to the reader: names are included here in the form in which they are commonly encountered, e.g. Scipio Africanus, under -S, and Julius Caesar under -J. The prefix of al- (Arabic definite article) is ignored; al-Harith is under -H. Where kings appear in sequence, e.g. Ptolemy I, Ptolemy II, the order provided in the index is chronological.

Where helpful or necessary, brief biographical details are provided to differentiate between individuals. For entries on Christianity, Judaism, Islam, Manichaeism, and Zoroastrianism, see the General Index.

General index